For Eric Fisher,

With all best
wishes to one of
my favorite assassins [?]

Marty Liebowitz

S0-BFC-536

3/27/2000

AN INSTITUTIONAL INVESTOR PUBLICATION

INVESTING

THE COLLECTED WORKS OF

MARTIN L. LEIBOWITZ

FRANK J. FABOZZI

EDITOR

FOREWORD BY WILLIAM F. SHARPE

PROBUS PUBLISHING COMPANY
Chicago, Illinois
Cambridge, England

© 1992, Martin L. Leibowitz

ALL RIGHTS RESERVED. No part of this publication may be reproduced, stored in a retrieval system, or transmitted by any means, electronic, mechanical, photocopying, recording, or otherwise, without the prior written permission of the publisher and the copyright holder.

This publication is designed to provide accurate and authoritative information in regard to the subject matter covered. It is sold with the understanding that the publisher is not engaged in rendering legal, accounting or other professional service.

Authorization to photocopy items for internal or personal use, or the internal or personal use of specific clients, is granted by Probus Publishing Company, provided that the US$ 7.00 per page fee is paid directly to Copyright Clearance Center, 27 Congress Street, Salem MA 01970, USA. For those organizations that have been granted a photocopy license by CCC, a separate system of payment has been arranged. The fee code for users of the Transactional Reporting Service is: 1-55738-198-4/92/$0.00 + $7.00

ISBN 1-55738-198-4

Printed in the United States of America

BB

2 3 4 5 6 7 8 9 0

This volume is dedicated to
Sidney Homer,
co-author of my first book,
and
to my family,
co-authors of a larger book.

—Martin L. Leibowitz

Contents

Part II. Stocks, Real Estate and Convertibles

Preface by Frank J. Fabozzi

Investing: The Collected Works of Martin L. Leibowitz

The articles in this volume were selected in order to have the greatest possible continuing interest to a broad base of readers. This criterion has led to a larger concentration of the more recent studies. However, there is also a sampling of earlier articles, especially structural analyses that remain relevant or studies that are representative of the development of a particularly interesting phase of the financial markets.

The articles are organized around three major areas of Dr. Leibowitz's professional interest. Part I is devoted to asset allocation, especially as it applies to the asset/liability structure of pension funds. The work in this area began in 1986, sparked by the prospective introduction of FASB 87 guidelines for the market-driven reporting of changes in the status of corporate pension funds.

Part II addresses equity and equity-related securities. This work began largely as an offshoot of the early asset allocation studies where Leibowitz and his associates, from the vantage point of bond men, explored how interest rate sensitivity linked pension liabilities with *all* asset classes—equity as well as fixed income. This led to studies of equity duration, the dividend discount model, and eventually to the recent concept of the Franchise Factor and its role in equity valuation.

Part III deals with bond portfolio analysis. This is the largest section since the papers cover a span of years that dates from 1970 to the present. These papers range from a retrospective view of the evolution of the U.S. bond market over the past three decades (published in the Fifth Edition of Graham and Dodd's *Security Analysis*) to recent articles suggesting a procedure for incorporating corporate bonds of a given credit quality into a total portfolio framework.

In each of these sections, there is a combination of early papers that reflect interesting milestones in the development of the investment thinking as well as a number of more current studies. The following overview will describe the key papers in each section in terms of their historical background, their primary motivation, and their placement in their respective subject areas.

PART I—ASSET ALLOCATION AND PENSION FUND STRATEGIES

The prospect of FASB 87 sparked a major reassessment of the role of liabilities within the U.S. private pension fund (*Pension Fund Management Under FAS 87*— 1987). While assets had long been marked-to-the-market and viewed on a total return basis, the valuation of liabilities had been left in the hands of the accountants and actuaries. Liabilities were subject to various smoothing and amortization schemes, some of which were rather arcane. With FASB 87, corporate pension funds were confronted with the need to mark discount rates to the current level of interest rates, at least with regard to certain major actuarial yardsticks that had to be publicly reported. This change was highly controversial. Some argued that the more volatile market-related liability value was still highly artificial, too nominal in format, and overly focused on short-term transient effects. However, corporate sponsors took the impending change seriously and began to trace out its implications.

In this new context of rate-sensitive liability values, the interest rate sensitivity of the *total* portfolio became a critical factor in gauging funding status risk. While the concept of duration largely answered the question for the fixed-income component of the portfolio, the issue of equity duration was one that had been inconsistently addressed in the prior literature. On the one hand, earlier studies of equity duration had focused on simple applications to the dividend discount model (DDM) and had arrived at the conclusions that equities, because of their growth prospects, have very long durations—on the order of 25 years or higher. It was not uncommon to hear comments that it was the long duration of equities that justified their use as a counterbalance to the long duration of the fund's ultimate liabilities. While there are some grains of truth in these arguments, there is also much confusion.

In *Total Portfolio Duration* (1986), Leibowitz reasoned that if duration is interpreted as interest rate sensitivity, then the duration of equities could be estimated empirically from historical data. By regressing S&P Index returns against a newly developed bond market index, Leibowitz was able to show that equities had a duration that was very low (on the order of 2-3 years) and very *unstable*. Furthermore, he showed that this empirical duration result was consistent (as it naturally should have been) with the correlation estimates that pension funds typically used in their asset allocation studies. It was subsequently published in

per, *Optimal Cash Flow Matching* (1981), to achieve this marking-to-the-market of their pension liabilities.

The high interest rates of 1980-82 offered funds the opportunity to lock up yields that were well above their required returns. At the same time, there was a reluctance to forgo the prospects of even better returns through active management. In this environment, Leibowitz and Weinberger developed a discipline that would allow for a controlled degree of active management and still "promise" a minimum floor return that was only modestly lower than market rates. The key was a monitoring system that, in the case of adverse performance, would "trigger" the portfolio into immunization at the floor rate. For this reason, this technique was named "contingent immunization." The first paper, *Contingent Immunization* (1981), introduced the basic technique. The next two papers, *Contingent Immunization Procedures—Part I: Risk Control* (1982) and *Contingent Immunization Procedures—Part II: Problem Areas* (1983), discuss various monitoring approaches. This last study includes simulation of the process of active management given varying levels of skill and conviction. It was illuminating to see how many complexities were encountered in trying to develop a model for such a fundamental investment problem as the behavior of active managers. The idea of Contingent Immunization generated significant interest among practitioners, with the General Motors pension fund leading the way by placing half of its fixed-income assets under this discipline in 1981.

By 1983, many pension funds had established cash-matched portfolios against their future liabilities. The stringency (and associated cost) ranged from the strictest dollar-for-dollar match to relatively loose parametric immunization. However, most of dedicated portfolios were designed to the standard of a fairly tight cash match. The idea of *Horizon Matching* (1983) was to blend the best features of both techniques in one integrated portfolio. Under horizon matching, the near-term cash outflows remained fully matched, while the longer-term liabilities (i.e., those beyond the "horizon") were controlled through a duration strategy. This approach fit well with the actuarial realities that had motivated these dedications: Short-term flows were better defined (as well as being more imminent), while the longer-term flows were far more subject to uncertainties in the actuarial projections. The looser structure also allowed for more flexible active management of the overall portfolio. Over the next several years, many funds realized substantial cost savings by converting from the pure cash match model to the horizon match design.

The next paper, *Effects of Yield Curve Behavior on Immunized Portfolios* (1983), is the result of a collaboration between Leibowitz and Professor Larry Fisher of Rutgers University. This study provides academic formalization for using the Rolling Yield and the Horizon Duration in setting achievable target rates for bullet immunizations. In classical immunization, this target was simply taken to be the forward rate for the given horizon. However, as is evident in the paper, the precise targeting is generally a more complex process that depends critically on the prescribed model of yield curve behavior. In general, this issue of target rates is an intriguing one that has received insufficient attention in either the academic or the practitioner literature.

The next paper, *Duration Targeting and the Management of Multiperiod Returns* (1990), addresses the long-term implications of managing to a prescribed duration (or to a duration range). Whether explicitly recognized or not, this technique (or some close variant) is really the basic management discipline for almost all fixed-income funds in the U.S. (whether actively or passively managed). The paper is lead-authored by Terence Langetieg and reflects his insights from a simulation that he personally developed. These efforts were all the more remarkable since they were completed during a period when Terry struggled with the illness that led to his untimely death at the age of 41. The monograph was completed in December 1989, and it was immediately accepted for publication in the *Financial Analysts Journal*. Dr. Langetieg passed away three months later. This is an important paper that has already provided a strong foundation for a number of research efforts. It will surely continue to be widely referenced in future years.

The last paper, *A Shortfall Approach to Duration Management* (1990), introduces the idea of the shortfall constraint as setting a limit to the maximum maturity or duration that can be tolerated while still providing a specified degree of downside protection. This approach has application both at the tactical level and for setting overall strategic policy.

The next section contains papers addressed specifically to the area of corporate bonds. In the first paper, *Sources of Return in Corporate Bond Portfolios* (1978), the component market events that comprise the total return for a corporate bond are set forth and categorized. These include changes in interest rate levels, reshapings of yield curves, and movements of spreads at both the sector and individual bond level.

In the next paper, *Spread Duration* (1988), published exactly 10 years later, the authors look more closely at how changes in yield spread affect the returns from bonds of different qualities and durations. By combining mathematical duration with a statistical estimate of relative spread sensitivity, an effective "spread duration" can be developed for a single bond or for an entire corporate portfolio. The portfolio's spread duration can then be used to help estimate its sensitivity to widening or tightening spreads in the market as a whole.

The following paper, *The Analysis of Credit Barbells* (1988), shows how the spread duration can be used to create different bond portfolios that have equivalent levels of spread sensitivity. With this methodology, one can pursue active management strategies aimed at return enhancements given certain market assumptions.

Leverageability of Corporate Assets (1990) delves more deeply into a firm's capital structure and examines how overall corporate risk is affected by different

and Hutzler. At the time, Sidney Homer was in charge of Salomon Brothers Research Department, which consisted of Henry Kaufman as Chief Economist and a small number of associates. Through these meetings, Leibowitz learned more about Salomon Brothers' role in the bond market. He became particularly fascinated by the intrinsically mathematical nature of the bond contract.

A memorable conversation took place in 1969 when Sidney Homer dragged out the draft of a book that he had started several years before. The subject was the mathematics of bonds. Homer had run into a stumbling block when he discovered that the tables describing bond price behavior failed to support his text describing "what everyone *knew* about how bonds of different coupons and maturities behaved." Finding himself at an impasse in trying to explain this inconsistency between what was "common knowledge" and the stark mathematical facts that he himself had compiled, Homer had relegated this particular project to the file reserved for the indefinite future.

As one might expect, Leibowitz found this puzzle to be a challenge and one that actually could be quickly resolved once the mathematics of the standard yield calculation were clearly set forth. This led to a series of lively discussions, first with Homer, and then with a number of the other Salomon partners and traders such as Morris Offit, Harry Petersen and Charles Simon. Leibowitz soon found himself being offered a position as the first "house mathematician" in a U.S. bond house.

In spite of the significant cut in salary that was entailed, Leibowitz felt compelled to follow his interests and join the firm in its facility at 60 Wall Street. At this point, Salomon Brothers consisted of one very cramped trading floor and very little else. Sidney Homer had the only office of any note. In this environment, Leibowitz found himself sitting in front of the firm's only computer terminal, situated right next to the corporate trading desk in the midst of a crowded, noisy and often frantic trading floor. While this location hardly seemed suitable for doing any sort of mathematical research, it actually proved to be a blessing in disguise.

Leibowitz's work with Homer continued and led to a series of memoranda that essentially completed the book on bond mathematics that Homer had retrieved from his dusty file. The first memorandum in the series was published on October 5, 1970. At this time, bonds were bought and sold on the basis of their "promised yield," with market participants giving little thought to what this yield value really meant. Homer and Leibowitz's first memorandum, "Interest on Interest," made the point that a bond's long-term return could differ significantly from its "promised yield." In particular, the paper presented a table that showed how the realized return depended critically on the rates at which coupon receipts could be reinvested. This attack on the sanctity of the "promised yield" measure was greeted with outrage by many of the crustier members of the bond community. Homer received many indignant calls and letters from valued friends and even more valued customers. In Homer's characteristically grand style, he turned all of these communications over to Leibowitz and charged him with responding to—and convincing—each and every complainant. As Leibowitz chewed through the correspondence that Homer piled on his desk, he found himself coming into contact with the pillars of the bond community.

Most were soothed by Leibowitz's written explanations. Some were not. Homer pressed Leibowitz to visit the offices of the remaining recalcitrants. In the final analysis, since the mathematics was fundamentally straightforward and therefore pretty hard to resist, Leibowitz was eventually able to report back to Homer that his reputation remained intact.

The next two memoranda, on price volatility, received a much more gracious reception, even though they surprised many readers by pointing out that low-coupon bonds could be more volatile than par bonds with much longer maturities.

The subsequent memoranda dealt with a variety of subjects—zero-coupon bonds, (long before zero-coupon bonds were issued), callable bonds, and the total return concept for bonds of different maturities and coupons. These new efforts were readily digested by a growing readership.

In many ways, it was the last memorandum that had the greatest impact on the actual practice of bond portfolio management. At the time, bond managers and traders had a tendency to characterize all secondary market activity as "swaps." This failure to differentiate among different types of swaps led to serious confusion among market participants. Homer and Leibowitz proposed a classification system that identified four distinct categories of "swaps": 1.) yield pick-up swaps; 2.) substitution swaps; 3.) sector swaps; and 4.) rate-anticipation swaps. This terminology proved useful as a way of distinguishing one activity from another and rapidly worked its way into the standard vocabulary of the bond market.

The memoranda were broadly distributed and redistributed both in the U.S. and internationally (they were quickly translated into Japanese and German). They were widely integrated into many financial market training programs, not only at Salomon Brothers but at many other Wall Street firms as well (often in photocopied form). It was not long before the New York Institute of Finance urged Homer and Leibowitz to expand the memoranda into a book form. The resulting volume was first published in 1972 under the title *Inside the Yield Book*. It has subsequently gone through many reprintings and has frequently been described as a "bible" of the bond market.

From today's vantage point, Homer and Leibowitz made a classic mistake in their choice of the book's title. The term "Yield Book" referred to the big volumes of numerical tables used to find the yields associated with a given bond price. At the time, these Yield Books were invaluable tools, with every bond trader treasuring his personal copy with its most thumb-worn pages corresponding to current market levels. However, with the advent of hand-held calculators, Yield Books quickly became extinct. In fact, today's young traders have neither seen nor heard of a Yield Book. Meanwhile, a more complete spectrum of U.S. Government maturities had been issued, with the result that the Treasury "yield curve" became the fundamental benchmark for all sectors of the bond market. With the disappearance of Yield Books from the face of the earth, and with the "yield curve" playing such a central role in the market, the Homer/Leibowitz text is now almost universally referred to as *Inside the Yield "Curve."*

The *Inside the Yield Book* memoranda helped Leibowitz to gain a certain following outside Salomon Brothers. However, inside the Firm, the breakthrough event with the traders on Salomon's "floor" occurred as a result of rising interest rates. In late 1970, corporate yields surged beyond 8%, which was the highest coupon level contained in the traders' cherished Yield Book tables. Since customers required yield values to consummate trades, the frustrated traders were ecstatic when they discovered that their "academic" neighbor could extract accurate yields from his handy computer terminal. Needless to say, Leibowitz soon found many new friends among the corporate bond traders that lined up behind his computer to get a yield value for their next trade.

In the ensuing years, the role of the computer expanded rapidly as a practical technique for evaluating various bond trades, largely in accordance with the methodology set forth by *Inside the Yield Book*. In 1973, growth of this activity led to the formation of the Bond Portfolio Analysis Group within Salomon Brothers. It was the first quantitative analysis group in the area of fixed income in the United States.

The role of quantitative applications grew apace with changes in the fixed-income markets. As book accounting, and the associated "buy and hold" approach, gave way to the introduction of the total return concept and performance measurement, managers needed new ways to analyze bond portfolios and evaluate trading strategies. Leibowitz's group developed a series of computer programs that were widely used to facilitate these analyses. They also published a series of papers that provided the foundation for this methodology.

Leibowitz and his associates were deeply involved in the many innovations that transformed the bond markets throughout the late 1970's and the 1980's. These included numerous applications of the duration measure of volatility, the development of the first performance index for the U.S. bond market, the analysis of floating-rate debt instruments, the issuance of deep-discount and zero-coupon bonds, the stripping of Treasury coupons, the routine analysis of embedded call options, the application of immunization to achieve actuarial benefits, and the analytic foundation associated with the explosive growth of mortgage securities. More and more, bond portfolio management depended upon structured approaches that were based on analytical computer tools.

In 1977, Leibowitz was named a General Partner at Salomon Brothers. In 1981, when the firm merged with Phibro Corporation, this title was changed to

Managing Director. He became a Deputy Director of the Research Department in 1986, reporting to Henry Kaufman. In 1991, he was appointed Directorof the Research Department and became a member of the firm's Executive Committee.

In the mid-1980's, Leibowitz's personal interest turned to the broader issues of asset allocation and asset/liability management. This led to a series of studies that incorporated liabilities into the traditional asset allocation methodology. Leibowitz pursued a non-traditional approach, focusing on *downside* risk and the "shortfall probability" as a better way of characterizing risk. This orientation may have reflected the conservative nature of his fixed-income background. In any case, it led to a number of different insights into the allocation process. Two of the papers in this area, *Total Portfolio Duration* (1986) and *Surplus Management* (1987), were awarded Graham and Dodd Plaques for the best article published that year in the *Financial Analysts Journal*.

The asset allocation problem raised a number of questions regarding the character of long-term returns from asset classes such as equity and real estate. Here again, his fixed-income background, with its emphasis on the rate sensitivity and long-term effects, may have proved fortuitous. Leibowitz's "bond-like approach" uncovered a number of new findings regarding the duration characteristics of equity and real estate, the persistence of equity risk, and the probability of stock underperformance relative to bonds. Further probing into the discounted value of the explicit and implicit cash flows from an equity investment led to studies on the role of the business franchise in determining a stock's price/earnings ratio.

Over the years, many of Leibowitz's papers have been published in the *Financial Analysts Journal* and *The Journal of Portfolio Management*. In addition to the two Plaques cited above, his papers received four "Graham and Dodd Awards" for excellence in financial writing from The Financial Analysts Federation.

In 1988, he was asked to write the section on bond investment for the Fifth Edition of the Graham and Dodd text on *Security Analysis*.

In 1990, he was the recipient of the Outstanding Financial Executive Award from the Financial Management Association (FMA). In the same year, he ws awarded a Professional Achievement citation from the University of Chicago.

Leibowitz serves on the Executive Council of The New York Academy of Sciences. He is the Chairman of the Advisory Council for New York University's Salomon Center at the Graduate School of Business. He is a member of the Board of the Institute for Quantitative Research in Finance and is an Associate Editor of the *Financial Analysts Journal*.

Leibowitz attributes the unusual course of his career to a liberal arts education that led to a deep respect for the written word, to an intellectual curiosity that always found itself in conflict between the analytical and the practical—and most importantly—to the incredible good fortune (and great pleasure) of having had the opportunity to collaborate with a very special group of talented and stimulating associates, colleagues, and coauthors.

these relations, based upon the data used from the earlier numerical example. With a correlation of zero—that is, complete independence between the two asset classes—total duration declines from the bond market duration at a 100% bond allocation down to zero at a 0% bond allocation. With a correlation of +0.34, it moves from 4.27 at the 100% bond allocation down to 2.19 at a 100% stock allocation. With a high positive correlation of +0.70, the duration actually rises with an increasing stock market component, reaching 4.57 for an all-stock portfolio.

EFFECTIVE ASSET ALLOCATION

The analysis suggests that the traditional framework for characterizing the allocation of asset classes may be inappropriate in a surplus function framework. Allocating 40% of a portfolio to bonds and 60% to stocks will have very different implications in terms of total portfolio durations, depending on the correlation assumptions. As Figure O shows, a 40% allocation to bonds when there is a +0.34 correlation provides a total duration of 3.02. This is the same total portfolio duration value that would be achieved under a 70% allocation to bonds in an environment in which bonds were thought to be uncorrelated with stocks. In some sense, then, one can talk of an "effective asset allocation" to interest-rate-sensitive assets that may be far greater than the literal allocation to bonds *per se*.

Generalizing on this concept, it is clear that the key variable is the definition used as the benchmark for measuring the impact of any given asset allocation. If it is defined in terms of achieving bond market index returns apart from any stock market comovement, then the traditional bond allocation percentage may be a sufficient guide. To the extent that the actual bond component has a duration greater than the bond market duration, and to the extent that some positive stock-bond correlation is assumed, then the "effective allocation" to interest-rate-sensitive assets could be markedly higher than the literal bond allocation.

It might be more useful at times, however, to use the duration of the liabilities as the interest-rate-sensitivity benchmark. When the total portfolio duration matches the liability duration, the surplus function is "immunized" with respect to interest rate movements. With this benchmark, such a position would correspond to an effective allocation of 100%. Higher or lower allocations would obviously entail different risk exposures to interest rate changes.

PORTFOLIO OPTIMIZATION

The surplus function approach can be used to develop expected values of returns as well as measures of variability with respect to both interest rates and other market factors. With this quantification, the asset allocation problem can again be formulated as an optimization problem aimed at achieving the desired balance between return and risk as measured through the fund's surplus values. In this context, the difference between total portfolio duration and liability duration should be taken as one risk measure; the effect of the non-interest-rate factors would then constitute a second dimension of risk.

In this surplus/liability framework, asset allocations can be developed through a portfolio optimization process that is similar to existing procedures. The resulting allocations, however, would be more consistent with the fund's liability framework, hence more directed toward the sponsor's real objectives.

Appendix

We first express the comovement of equity market returns, R_E with bond market returns, R_B, through Equation (A1)

$$\tilde{R}_E - R_F = A_1 + B\,(\tilde{R}_B - R_F) + \tilde{e}_1 \tag{A1}$$

where R_F is the risk-free rate and $\tilde{e}_1$ represents all market factors other than the bond market that can affect equity returns. We can place the following requirements upon $\tilde{e}_1$:

$$E(\tilde{e}_1) = 0 \text{ and } E(\tilde{e}_1 \cdot \tilde{R}_B) = 0. \tag{A2}$$

One can then express the regression coefficient, B, as:

$$B = \left(\frac{\sigma_E}{\sigma_B}\right)\rho(E, B), \tag{A3}$$

where σ_E is the standard deviation of R_E, σ_B is the standard deviation of R_B, and $\rho(E, B)$ is the correlation coefficient of R_E and R_B.

The next step is to express bond market returns as a linear function of $\tilde{\delta}$, the change in a benchmark long-term yield:

$$\tilde{R}_B - R_F = A_2 - D_B\tilde{\delta} + \tilde{e}_2. \tag{A4}$$

The coefficient D_B is the "effective duration" of the bond market relative to shifts in the benchmark yield (taken as 10-year Treasuries for the example in the text). The random variable, $\tilde{e}_2$, accounts for all other market effects from yield curve reshapings, spread changes, etc. Once again, we assume that:

$$E(\tilde{e}_2) = 0 \text{ and } E(\tilde{\delta} \cdot \tilde{e}_2) = 0. \tag{A5}$$

We then combine Equations (A1) and (A4) to relate equity market returns to yield changes:

$$\tilde{R}_E - R_F = A_3 - D_E\tilde{\delta} + \tilde{e}_3 \tag{A6}$$

where

$$D_E = D_B B \tag{A7}$$

and

$$\tilde{e}_3 = B\tilde{e}_2 + \tilde{e}_1 . \tag{A8}$$

Here, we make the assumption that nonparallel shift effects are independent of stock market behavior, so that

$$E\left(\tilde{e}_2 \cdot \tilde{e}_1\right) = 0 \tag{A9}$$

and that all parallel shift effects upon the stock market are sufficiently represented through bond market returns, that is:

$$E\left(\tilde{\delta} \cdot \tilde{e}_1\right) = 0. \tag{A10}$$

The latter assumption enables us to conclude that:

$$E\left(\tilde{\delta} \cdot \tilde{e}_3\right) = 0. \tag{A11}$$

(It should be noted that the above assumptions are nontrivial; for example, certain nonparallel yield curve effects such as changing short to long-term rate spreads could have a direct impact on stock market behavior.)

With the result in Equation (A11) one can demonstrate that

$$\rho(E, \delta) = \rho(E, B)\rho(B, \delta) \tag{A12}$$

and that

$$D_E = D_B \left(\frac{\sigma_E}{\sigma_B}\right)(B, E) \tag{A13}$$

has the statistical property of being an "equity market duration."

Moreover, since from Equation (A4) one has:

$$D_B = -\left(\frac{\sigma_B}{\sigma_\delta}\right)\rho(B, \delta), \tag{A14}$$

one can express the equity/yield change correlation Equation (A12) as:

$$\rho(E, \delta) = -\rho(E, B)\left(\frac{\sigma_\delta}{\sigma_B}\right)D_B. \tag{A15}$$

For a portfolio of bonds and stocks, the total return R_T becomes:

$$\tilde{R}_T = W_{BP}\tilde{R}_{BP} + W_{EP}\tilde{R}_{EP} \tag{A16}$$

where W_{BP} and W_{EP} are the fractional allocations to the bond and stock portfolios, and $\tilde{R}_{BP}$ and $\tilde{R}_{EP}$ are the respective component returns.

Suppose the bond portfolio has a duration of D_{BP} and that its returns are related to parallel yield shifts through the following:

$$\tilde{R}_{BP} - R_F = A_4 - D_{BP}\tilde{\delta} + \tilde{e}_4 \tag{A17}$$

where once again

$$E(\tilde{e}_4) = 0 \text{ and } E(\tilde{\delta} \cdot \tilde{e}_4) = 0. \tag{A18}$$

Also suppose that the equity portfolio has a beta value of β_{EP} and that its return is related to the equity market return by:

$$\tilde{R}_{EP} - R_F = A_5 + \beta_{EP}(\tilde{R}_E - R_F) + \tilde{e}_5. \tag{A19}$$

By carrying out the same type of combination of Equations (A18), (A1) and (A4) as in the earlier derivation, one can obtain:

$$\tilde{R}_{EP} - R_F = A_6 - \beta_{EP}D_E\tilde{\delta} + \tilde{e}_6. \tag{A20}$$

Using similar assumptions as before, one can again have $\tilde{e}_6$ independent of δ. (The assumption that $\tilde{e}_5$ is uncorrelated with δ implies that the equity portfolio was constructed to achieve a pure β_{EP} magnification of the volatility of the market as a whole; that is, all "yield tilt" and/or interest rate factors retain the same proportional weight as in the equity market index.) With these assumptions, one obtains:

$$\begin{aligned} D_{EP} &= \beta_{EP}D_E \\ &= \beta_{EP}D_B\left(\frac{\sigma_E}{\sigma_B}\right)\rho(B, E), \end{aligned} \tag{A21}$$

which can serve as a duration measure for the equity portfolio.

The objective is to be able to express the total portfolio return in terms of a parallel rate shift term and an "all other market factors" term:

$$\tilde{R}_{TP} - R_F = A_7 - D_{TP}\tilde{\delta} + \tilde{e}_7. \tag{A22}$$

This follows directly from Equations (A16) and (A19) together with the assumptions that we have made regarding the independence of the $\tilde{e}$ residuals. Moreover, the total portfolio duration D_{TP} can be written as:

$$D_{TP} = W_{BP}D_{BP} + W_{EP}\beta_{EP}D_B \left(\frac{\sigma_E}{\sigma_B}\right)\rho(B, E). \tag{A23}$$

The effective allocation to the fixed income market could now be expressed as the equivalent interest rate sensitivity of the total portfolio. This could be articulated in a number of ways. For example, for a given portfolio allocation where a given correlation $\rho(B,E)$ is assumed, one might ask what the corresponding bond allocations W_B^* would be in a traditional environment (where $\rho = 0$) to achieve the same total rate sensitivity:

$$D_B W_B^* = D_{TP} \cdot 1 \tag{A24}$$

or

$$\begin{aligned} W_B^* &= \frac{D_{TP}}{D_B} \\ &= W_{BP}\frac{D_{BP}}{D_B} + W_{EP}\beta_{EP}\left(\frac{\sigma_E}{\sigma_B}\right)(B, E). \end{aligned} \tag{A25}$$

More generally, one could gauge the allocation against a benchmark bond portfolio having any "target duration," D_{TGT}:

$$W_B^* = \frac{D_{TP}}{D_{TGT}}. \tag{A26}$$

In particular, if one chose the liability duration, D_1, as the target, then the surplus function would be "immunized" (to the first order) when $W_B^{**} = 100\%$, and at risk with higher or lower W_B^{**} values.

The surplus function, S, is simply the difference in the total portfolio value, V_{TP}, and the present value, V_L, of the liabilities:

$$S = V_{TP} - V_L. \tag{A27}$$

If D_L is the duration of the liabilities, then the first-order linear effect of interest changes upon the surplus function becomes:

$$\Delta S = \left[\frac{\partial V_{TP}}{\partial \delta} - \frac{\partial V_L}{\partial \delta}\right]\tilde{\delta} + \tilde{e}_8. \tag{A28}$$

But

$$\frac{\partial V_{TP}}{\partial \delta} = -D_{TP}V_{TP}{}^0 \tag{A29}$$

and

$$\frac{\partial V_L}{\partial \delta} = -D_L V_L^0, \tag{A30}$$

so that

$$\Delta S = -[D_{TB} V_{TP}^0 - D_L V_L^0] \, \tilde{\delta} + \tilde{e}_8$$

$$= -V_L^0 \left[D_{TP} \left(\frac{V_{TP}^0}{V_L^0} \right) - D_L \right] \tilde{\delta} + \tilde{e}_8. \tag{A31}$$

Thus, relative to the initial value of the liabilities as a base, the expression D_S,

$$D_S = D_{TP} \left(\frac{V_{TP}^0}{V_L^0} \right) - D_L, \tag{A32}$$

can serve as a first-order approximation for the parallel rate shift sensitivity of the surplus function.

Chapter I-3

Liability Returns

By any performance standard, the bond and stock markets have provided extraordinary returns recently. Among the ranks of professional investment managers, there may be some mixed feelings as managers compare themselves with the broad market return indexes. Few managers of real-life portfolios with real-life clients have found themselves totally free from the return-dampening influences of portfolio cash, call/refunding effects, prepayments, or the cautionary impulses that naturally arise after a rally that thunders forward for one record-setting week after another. While money managers may have mixed feelings, there is a much more consistent view among their sponsor clients: elation! In particular, pension fund sponsors—virtually regardless of their pattern of asset allocation—have seen their assets surge to giddy levels. With such superb absolute performance, it may seem almost petty to quibble when their managers' relative performance falls somewhat short of the broad market indexes.

The general euphoria among sponsors may be somewhat short-sighted. Assets are not the only component of the pension fund structure that have grown apace during the same time period. Quietly and without the fanfare of broadly cited performance numbers, the cost of pension liabilities has also exploded.

Martin L. Leibowitz, "Liability Returns: A New Perspective on Asset Allocation," *The Journal of Portfolio Management*, Winter 1987. Reprinted with permission.

This extraordinary growth in liability costs—this high level of "liability returns"—has been fueled by the same dramatic decline in interest rates that has driven the historic rally in bonds and stocks.

The net impact varies greatly from one fund to another. However, in many cases, the liability return has far outdistanced the fund's asset growth. The "liability portfolio," after all, is relatively free from the return-dampening factors that restrain the asset portfolio—liabilities are unfettered by those calls/refundings, prepayments, cautionary and/or frictional cash components, etc.

In this article, we will discuss these "liability returns" and how they compare with market performance recently and longer historical periods. This analysis is consistent with the "liability framework" discussed in a study on total portfolio duration.[1] These concepts have major implications for the structure of the asset allocation process for pension funds. In particular, one clear finding is that for many pension funds, interest rate volatility is a key—if not an overriding—risk factor affecting surplus status. Since a fund's total portfolio duration provides a measure of control for this risk, asset allocations would be chosen with at least some consideration of the resulting total duration value. More pointedly, the process of asset allocation should be expressed not in stock/bond ratios, as is the current general practice, but in terms of equity weightings and "total portfolio duration."

RISK AND RETURN IN A LIABILITY FRAMEWORK

The traditional approach to asset allocation within a pension fund focuses on the return/risk characteristics of various market asset classes. There is rarely an explicit orientation to the liability framework that defines the fund's ultimate purpose. Historically, the long-term nature and statistical character of the pension liabilities have often blurred the true importance of the asset/liability approach in this area.

New FASB initiatives and the greater potential for fund terminations have recently provided compelling reasons for a greater sensitivity to the behavior of the liability side of the pension balance sheet. Still, it appears that considerable progress needs to be made in developing asset allocation frameworks that integrate asset return/risk profiles with the "performance" characteristics of liabilities.

In another study, we developed a procedure for computing a comprehensive value for the interest rate sensitivity of a portfolio that included stocks as

---

[1] Martin L. Leibowitz, *Total Portfolio Duration: A New Perspective on Asset Allocation.* New York: Salomon Brothers Inc, February 1986.

well as bonds.[2] We showed how this "total portfolio duration" value could then be related to the interest rate sensitivity of the liabilities. The emphasis was on gauging the net interest rate risk for a given asset allocation. To estimate the duration for the stock market, we explored the volatility and correlation characteristics of the S&P 500 relative to the Salomon Brothers Broad Investment-Grade Bond Index. One of the surprising results from these empirical studies was that the S&P duration value turns out to be far lower than the generally accepted values that have been derived from dividend discount models.

In this article, we turn from the risk dimension to the return dimension. The "returns" from representative pension liabilities (that is, the changes in the present value of future benefits) are compared with returns from the S&P 500 and the Salomon Brothers Broad Investment-Grade Index. Again we encounter some surprising results.

While the asset returns of both classes have done rather well over the 6-1/4 year period beginning January 1, 1980 (and spectacularly well recently), the "return on the liabilities" has also been extremely high.

In fact, the liability returns from the long-duration "active lives" liability schedule far exceed the stellar performance of both the stock and bond markets. In more concrete terms, this means that for significant classes of pension fund situations, there has been an actual shrinkage in the true economic surplus just as asset performance has been forging ahead at a historic pace.

MARKET RETURNS AND ASSET DURATIONS

As a first step, it might be worthwhile to update the historical results from the previous study. Basically, those numbers were based upon monthly returns achieved from January 1, 1980 through November 1, 1985. Exhibit 1 depicts the returns by fixed-income components over this period together with the subsequent five months to March 31, 1986. In Exhibit 2, the total return figures for the Broad Index are compared with the returns from the S&P 500.

Exhibit 3 updates the rolling volatilities over trailing one-year periods for these two markets. The average volatilities over the entire span now come in at 9.40% for the Broad Market Index and 14.34% for the S&P 500.

The rolling one-year correlations show a different story. As shown in Exhibit 4, the correlation for the last 12 months investigated has surged to a high value of 0.78. This is virtually as high a correlation as there has been for any 12-month period over the past 6 1/4 years. This high level is consistent with the intuition of many market participants that lower interest rates have been a particularly direct driving force behind the current stock market rally.

---

[2] *Ibid.*

Exhibit 1: Salomon Brothers Broad Index Returns, January 1980-March 1986

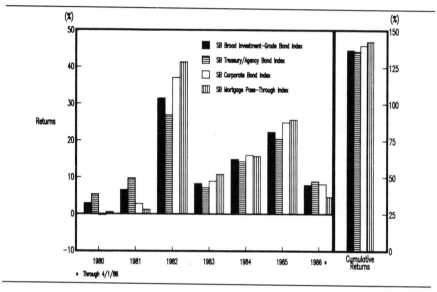

Exhibit 2: Equity and Fixed-Income Returns, January 1980-March 1986

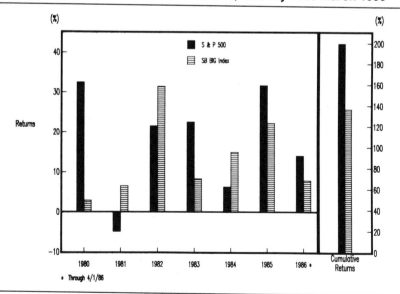

Exhibit 3: Rolling One-Year Volatility, Fixed-Income and Equity Markets, 1981-1986

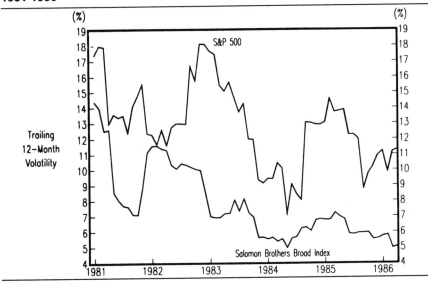

Exhibit 4: Rolling One-Year Correlations, Fixed-Income and Equity Markets, 1981-1986

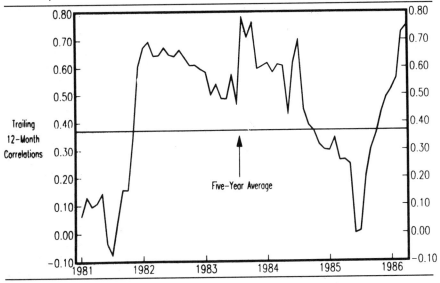

This high correlation level has several implications. For example, Exhibit 5 shows the scatter pattern for S&P returns versus changes in the ten-year Treasury rates. A regression line for the entire period is shown. Because of the high weight assigned to the earlier period, this regression reflects an empirical duration of 2.47, which is close to the 2.41 value found earlier using the January 1980 to November 1, 1985 data. The overall correlation of 0.38 is only marginally different from the earlier value of 0.34.

In Exhibit 6, the scattergram is shown for the trailing 12 months ending April 1, 1986. Although statistical reliability is compromised by using such a small number of data points, the results are nonetheless startling. The correlation, of course, is 0.78, corresponding to the last point plotted on Exhibit 4, and the duration is 6.18, more than twice as great as the duration estimated over the entire 6-1/4 year period. Moreover, the last five months of data reflect an even stronger enhancement of this trend.

There is no reason to believe that the stock market duration should be stable over time; in fact, our intuitions suggest that the duration could be significantly greater during some market periods than others. The current period appears to be one of them.

LIABILITY STRUCTURES FOR PENSION PLANS

Basically, a pension plan can be viewed as having two types of liabilities: active lives and retired lives. These two classes have quite different characteristics.

The retired lives represent employees who are retired and currently receiving benefits as well as terminated pensioners who will receive deferred benefits. A snapshot of the benefit payments that would be actuarially scheduled to be paid out to a fixed pool of retirees would have the general pattern that is exhibited in Exhibit 7. With such a frozen pool of existing retirees, the benefits typically decline over time in accordance with mortality tables. This pattern, therefore, reflects a front-end loading that typically declines on an "exponential basis" with the passing years.

In contrast, the "active lives" component of the pension liability reflects current employees who have vested (or accrued but unvested) interests in future benefits. For members of this class, the receipt of payments is deferred until some actuarially specified retirement time. Consequently, the projected schedule of benefit payments for active lives will begin to build up with those who are about to retire and then grow to a peak that represents the bulk load of future retirement benefits. This flow is backloaded and includes some very long-term flows. A representative schedule of benefits for an active lives liability is shown in Exhibit 8.

The actuarial procedure for determining these patterns is detailed, complex and highly customized to the individual fund's circumstance. Many sources of

Exhibit 5: The S&P Return Versus Change in Ten-Year Treasury Yield, January 1980-March 1986

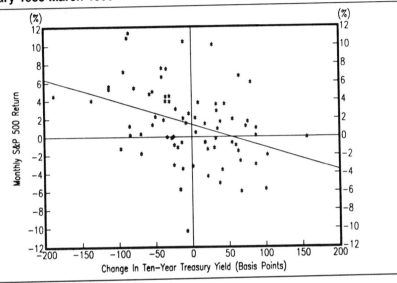

Exhibit 6: The S&P Versus Change in Ten-Year Treasury Yield, April 1985-March 1986

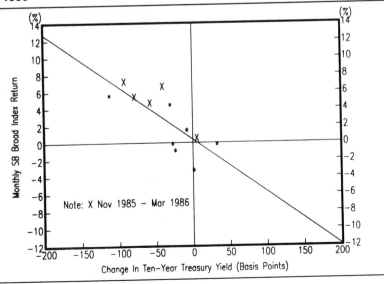

Exhibit 7: Retired Lives Liability Schedule (Dollars in Millions)

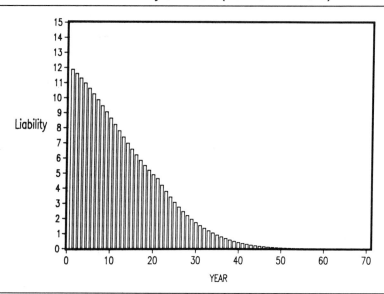

Exhibit 8: Active Lives Liability Schedule (Dollars in Millions)

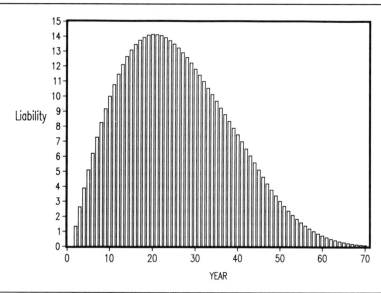

complication arise in practice. In particular, the active lives projections clearly depend upon a whole host of assumptions regarding future benefit/payroll statistics. Different active lives schedules may be used for the same payroll for different actuarial and reporting purposes. Moreover, there are sure to be interactions with the inflation rate, which will then feed back into any more refined duration calculations.

The flow of future contributions can also have a profound effect on interest rate sensitivity. The fixed flow of nominal dollar payout, depicted in Exhibit 8, admittedly captures none of these important effects: It is for illustrative purposes only. Our sole intention is to indicate the typical shape of this pattern without trying to venture too far into areas that we will leave to the true professionals in this field—the actuaries.

LIABILITY RETURNS

It has often been remarked that semantics can alter patterns of thought. In this case, it is common to speak of the return from assets and to contrast it with the cost of liabilities. While the expression "return" has a dynamic connotation (certainly for any market participant), the term "cost" tends to imply a well-defined and relatively unchanging value. This semantic distinction has tended to obscure the structural similarity between assets and liabilities in the asset allocation equation. In particular, we are already accustomed to how changes in the market environment can lead to better or worse returns for different asset classes. This overemphasis on the asset return side of the equation tends to obscure a broader view that would also include concomitant changes in a more comprehensive measure of the fund's status—the surplus function, that is, the difference between the market value of the assets and the present value of the liabilities. To address this imbalance, the impact of market changes on the cost of the liabilities should be investigated. In practice, this can be an intricate process to carry out for a specific fund. However, at least one facet of this effect can be readily explored—the impact of changing interest rates on the present value of a prescribed liability stream.

In fact, to turn this discussion around and to introduce a more comfortable terminology, we suggest that changes in the liabilities' cost be viewed as a kind of negative return. By defining this "liability return" properly, a measure that is directly comparable with asset returns can be obtained. Thus, for a given fund, to the extent that the asset return matches the liability return over a given period, the funding status would remain in balance (at least for the initial set of liabilities). To proceed in this direction, we simply define the liability return as follows:

$$\frac{\left(\begin{array}{c}\text{Discounted Present}\\\text{Value of Liability}\\\text{End of Period}\end{array}\right) - \left(\begin{array}{c}\text{Discounted Present}\\\text{Value of Liability}\\\text{Beginning of Period}\end{array}\right) + \left(\begin{array}{c}\text{Liabilities Discharged}\\\text{During the}\\\text{Period}\end{array}\right)}{\left(\begin{array}{c}\text{Discounted Present}\\\text{Value of Liability}\\\text{Beginning of Period}\end{array}\right)}$$

In this formulation, we refer to the liabilities that existed at the beginning of the period—that is, this return calculation does not incorporate additional liabilities that may accrue during the course of each period.

As an example of this calculation, suppose the retired lives liabilities depicted in Exhibit 7 were subject to a market discount rate of 8% at the beginning of the year, resulting in a present value of $100 million. The first-year benefits of $11.87 million are paid out over the course of the year. At the end of the period, the remaining schedule is then discounted at a new market rate of 7%, resulting in a year-end present value of $102.86 million. The liability return in this case would therefore be equal to the following:

$$\frac{\$102.86 \text{ Million} - \$100 \text{ Million} + \$11.87 \text{ Million}}{100} = 14.73\%^3$$

In the past, actuarial smoothing and the highly lagged process for revision of actuarial valuation rates contributed to the perception that the present value of the liabilities had little immediate bearing on fund management. In such an environment, the liability return calculation would have limited appeal. In the new environment, however, rate-driven changes in the value of liabilities can be of great and immediate significance to the pension plan and the sponsor organization. The new FASB regulations argue clearly in the direction of using a market-sensitive discount rate to value the liabilities. In addition, with the increasingly routine consideration of potential annuity purchases, the fluctuating cost of these liabilities takes on the hard bite of a real dollars-and-cents impact. With these trends, the concept of liability return has become far more relevant today than it has ever been in the past.

LIABILITY PERFORMANCE

This model for liability returns can be applied retrospectively to develop performance results for the changing costs of liabilities over various historical periods. To carry out this analysis, the structure of the flows for each evaluation

---

[3] This result ignores intraperiod compounding.

point, together with a discounting mechanism, must be specified. Consider, for example, the retired lives schedule in Exhibit 7. Suppose that the discounting mechanism corresponded to a uniform interest rate approximated by the ten-year new A Industrial rate.[4]

On January 1, 1980, this interest rate stood at 11.13%. Applied to the retired lives flow of Exhibit 7, it yields a present value of $81.82 million and a modified duration of 5.87 years. During January 1980, approximately $1 million would have been paid out to beneficiaries, and the remaining flow (aged one month) could then be discounted at the ten-year A new Industrial rate on February 1, 1980—12.00%. This results in a February 1, 1980 value of $77.60 million. Using our simplified liability return format, we find that the "return" for this retired lives liability amounts to -3.94%.

It is interesting to compare this number with the Broad Index return for January 1980, which is -3.03%. A large part of this difference is explained by the difference in the duration between the two flows—with its shorter duration, the Broad Index was less vulnerable to the increase in interest rates. Thus, for that month, an asset portfolio corresponding to the Broad Index would have gained some ground relative to this retired lives liability.

Next, a liability stream that begins February 1, 1980 is required. This could be achieved in several ways, including simply aging the original stream from the prior month's calculation. However, for simplicity's sake and to retain a consistent archetype over time, we assume that the retired lives on February 1, 1980 has the exact same (unaged) shape as depicted in Exhibit 7. Given this assumption, the liability return for each succeeding month can be computed, and a comparison with the Salomon Brothers Broad Market Index Returns can be developed. This comparison is shown in Exhibit 9.

In 1980 and 1981, the retired lives component turned in slightly lower returns than the Broad Index. In 1982, the Broad Index returns were an excellent 31%, but were surpassed by the 41% liability return. The returns in 1983 were roughly comparable. In 1984, 1985 and the first three months of 1986, however, the liability returns pulled ahead of the Broad Index. Exhibit 9 also shows the S&P equity returns throughout the same period. Over the full 75-month period, the cumulative liability return exceeded the growth in the Broad Index but fell short of the S&P's growth. A $100-million fund that was in perfect balance in January 1980 would have a surplus of $36 million today if it had been invested totally in stocks, but would have incurred a $26-million deficit if it had been invested totally in the Broad Index. It should be noted, however, that this result is highly period specific.

Moreover, the impact of asset and liability returns upon the surplus clearly depends upon the initial surplus condition. Thus, if a fund is in balance—that is,

---

[4] Lawrence Bader, Managing Director of William M. Mercer-Meidinger, Inc., suggested this rate as a convenient but crude proxy for annuity rates.

Exhibit 9: Retired Lives Liability Returns, January 1980-March 1986

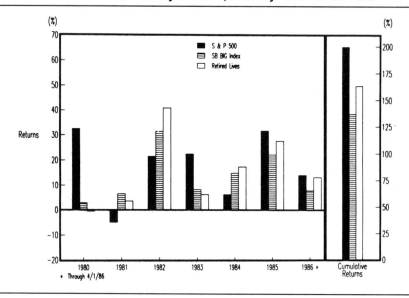

Exhibit 10: Active Lives Liability Returns, January 1980-March 1986

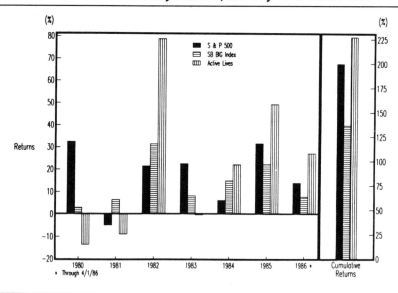

the market value of assets equals the present value of liabilities—market returns over a period can be directly offset against liability returns to determine the net surplus change. However, for a fund with a large starting surplus, the market returns will affect an asset base that is larger than the initial liability value, and appropriate adjustments must be made to find the surplus change.

The same approach can be applied to the active lives, with performance results shown in Exhibit 10. The active lives liability on January 1, 1980 had a theoretical duration of 12.59 years—considerably longer than the retired lives liability or the Broad Market Index. This longer duration could be expected to lead to more volatile liability returns; as Exhibit 10 indicates, this proves to be true. For example, in 1980, the active lives liability return was -13.48%. Thus, an investor in the Broad Market Index with only a +2.90% return over this period would have enjoyed a whopping increase in surplus value to 16.38%, due primarily to the huge decline in the present value of the liabilities.

In contrast, during 1982 the decline in interest rates caused the present value of the active lives schedule to soar by almost 80%. This was a multiple of the returns available in either the S&P 500 or the Broad Market Index. Therefore, it would have been virtually impossible for any fund with a large active lives component to avoid serious erosion in its surplus function in 1982. Some surplus erosion was also likely in 1984, 1985 and for the first three months of 1986. Thus, even despite the great performance of both stocks and bonds in the first three months of 1986, the surplus of virtually every active lives fund would have eroded because of the soaring costs of these liabilities.

INTEGRATED LIABILITY RETURNS

For purposes of clarity, this analysis focused first on pure retired lives liabilities and then on pure active lives liabilities. In practice, a pension fund will have a liability structure that consists of a dynamic combination of both types of liabilities. In fact, the actual schedule can be complex and can change in ways that are unique to an individual fund. To gain insight into a more realistic pattern of liability returns, it can be useful to explore the "performance" of an integrated benefits structure consisting of a well-defined combination of both retired and active lives (see Exhibit 11). The present value of this combined flow comprises 60% retireds and 40% actives, based upon their respective present values under a discount rate of 8%. (Again, any actual fund will have a complex and changing combination of liability structures that usually can be identified only through an intensive actuarial study. Our purpose here is to take a simple archetype liability and compare its liability returns with those of stocks and bonds.) Proceeding with the integrated flow illustrated in Exhibit 11 and again applying the ten-year new A Industrial rates as a discounting proxy, one achieves the performance results shown in Exhibit 12.

Exhibit 11: Integrated Liability Schedule, 60% Retired/40% Active (Dollars in Millions)

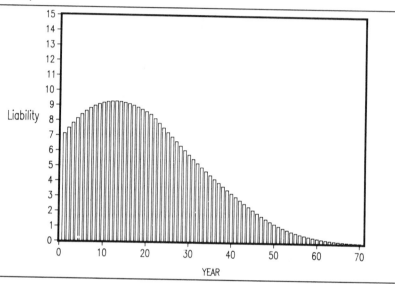

Exhibit 12: Integrated Liability Returns, January 1980-March 1986

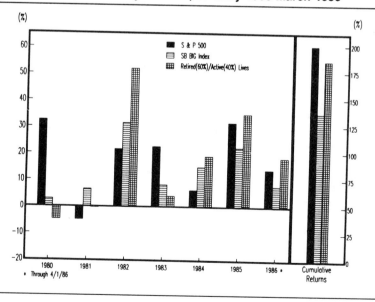

To the extent that this archetype is at all representative, the results are most intriguing. First, over the entire 75-month period, the performance of the bond market would have fallen significantly below the increased costs in this liability structure. S&P returns fared somewhat better than the combined liabilities. In three of the past four calendar years (as well as in the first quarter of 1986), the integrated liability returns actually outdistanced the pure equity returns themselves.

COMPARISON WITH STOCK/BOND PORTFOLIOS

Few portfolios consist totally of all stocks or all bonds. To obtain more representative results, the integrated liability should be compared with a fund allocation that includes both stocks and bonds. For these purposes, we arbitrarily formulated a fund with 60% invested in the S&P 500 and the remaining 40% deployed in the Broad Index. The performance results are depicted in Exhibit 13.

It is discomforting, to say the least, that over the entire period, the fund returns did not pull ahead of the liability performance. This shortfall led to an enlarged deficit of about 11% over the 75-month period. But a closer look at the period-by-period returns suggests even greater cause for concern. In 1982, the liability return far exceeded the fund's asset performance. In 1984 and 1985, the liability performance again ran ahead of the asset performance. Perhaps more seriously, for the first three months of 1986, there was a sizable 6.6% shortfall between the asset performance and that of the combined liability schedule.

THE DURATION OF LIABILITIES

Many of the above results can be traced to the fundamental interest rate sensitivity of the liability streams. The *pro forma* modified duration is quite long for the liabilities: 5.87 years for the retireds, 12.59 years for the actives, and 8.20 years for the integrated flows (all as of January 1, 1980). However, a more meaningful measure of interest rate volatility would be the effective duration relative to a consistent interest rate benchmark. Since we have used the ten-year Treasury rate as a benchmark in computing the effective duration of the Broad Index and the S&P 500, it is natural to adopt it again for the liability side. In Exhibits 14, 15 and 16, the liability returns for each of the 75 months are plotted against corresponding changes in the ten-year Treasury. The regression line provides a measure of the effective duration values—5.71 for retireds, 12.35 for actives, and 7.84 for the integrated schedule.

The effective durations are close to the *pro forma* duration values. This is hardly surprising. While there is a certain quality spread variation between the

Exhibit 13: Portfolio and Integrated Liability Returns, January 1980-March 1986

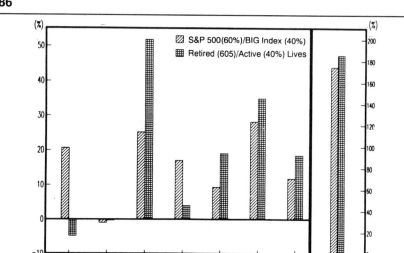

discounting rate (ten-year new A Industrials) and the benchmark rate (ten-year Treasuries), liability streams are free from some of the "adverse convexity problems" that encumber corporate bonds, mortgage securities, agencies, and even certain Treasury issues, especially in times of low interest rates. In this sense, duration value tends to be a better gauge for a liability's volatility than for an actual bond portfolio's volatility.

The point is that the volatility of the integrated flows far exceeds the duration values for the Broad Index. The equity durations are even lower yet. It is possible that with the increased correlation between bonds and stocks in recent periods, the S&P 500 duration may be greater than its historical average value, but a fund with typical allocations in stocks and/or bonds would still have a lower duration than these archetype liabilities. This duration gap would naturally make the fund surplus vulnerable to lower interest rates.

Indeed, past performance results indicate that this is exactly what occurred. When interest rates rose, as they did in 1980 and 1981, the liability returns were low, often leading to increases in the surplus. In contrast, when interest rates fell, the value of the liabilities rose and typically exceeded stock and bond market returns. The pattern shown in Exhibits 9, 10 and 12 is no coincidence, but may reflect a rather fundamental and dangerous "liability trap."

Thus, in terms of surplus growth, the net performance of a pension fund may be most vulnerable precisely when fund sponsors and/or managers en-

Exhibit 14: Effective Duration of Retired Lives Liability

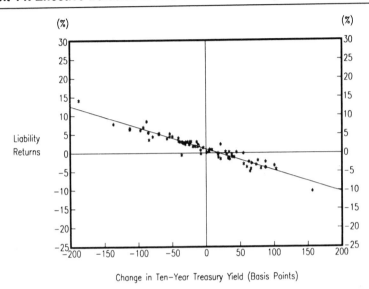

Change in Ten-Year Treasury Yield (Basis Points)

Exhibit 15: Effective Duration of Active Lives Liability

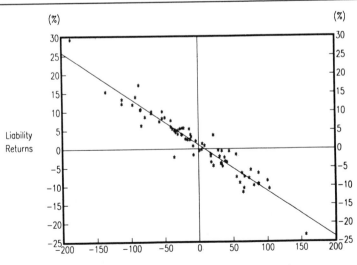

Change in Ten-Year Treasury Yield (Basis Points)

Exhibit 16: Integrated Liability Schedule

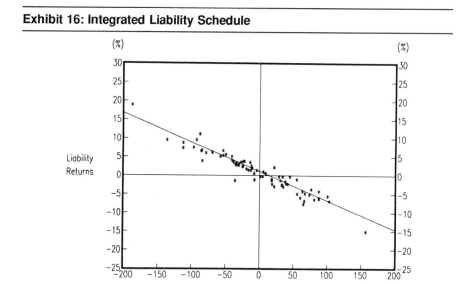

Change in Ten-Year Treasury Yield (Basis Points)

counter the most favorable market returns and are enjoying ample growth in the market value of their portfolios.

ALLOCATIONS USING "TOTAL PORTFOLIO DURATIONS"

These performance results provide striking evidence of the vulnerability of the pension fund surplus in today's markets. The high level of interest rate volatility and the long duration of representative liability schedules create the potential for wide variations in liability returns. While surplus is not the only yardstick that determines pension fund allocations, it is certainly becoming increasingly important in light of recent developments in the accounting/actuarial environment.

Traditional asset allocation procedures generally do not address this question of surplus vulnerability. Stocks are usually ascribed both a higher expected return and a higher volatility than bonds. Over longer horizon periods, this places equities on the "asset of choice" pedestal. However, too high an equity component engenders unacceptably high levels of volatility in portfolio value. The bond component is therefore added as a sort of bland "filler" to cut portfolio variability down to tolerable levels. In many of these approaches, the "fixed-income component" is defined as some benchmark bond or bond market index that is taken to have an essentially constant duration. With this static choice for "fixed income," the bond component is prized primarily as a predictably dull "volatility dilution agent." Thus, in traditional allocation procedures, the sole decision variable is the magnitude of the equity component. The bond component basically becomes a derived residual that follows from the primary equity decision.

This traditional approach fails to address three major facets of today's pension and market environment. First, it focuses solely on asset return, without any explicit treatment of liability return, liability risk or the resultant surplus vulnerability. Second, it fails to recognize the high level of interest rate volatility that now appears endemic. (Even within the traditional framework itself, this rate volatility erodes the role of "bonds" as risk-dampening agents.) Third, it does not recognize a major development in the capital markets over the past decade—the spectrum of new instruments that allows the practical construction of fixed-income portfolios that span an extremely wide range of durations. (While this is true for conventional bonds and zero-coupon instruments, the range obviously expands even further when futures and options can be applied.) In a certain sense, for large funds, the range of (duration) risk levels readily available for the fixed-income component may be much wider than the practical (beta) risk range available for the equity component.

From the viewpoint of the liability/surplus framework, these problems can be addressed only through a revised asset allocation process that explicitly models the interest rate risk characteristics of all fund components—bonds, equity, liabilities, etc. This makes the total portfolio duration an important risk measure for the asset side. This framework would have implications for return enhancement as well as for risk control. Thus, for certain interest rate scenarios within a tactical allocation, the liability return could potentially become a significant positive contributor to surplus.

In any case, the total duration approach would begin to allow for measurement and control of interest rate risk. Together with the wide range of duration vehicles available in the market, this presents the fund with the opportunity to adjust the duration of the bond component to achieve a desired level of overall fund exposure to rate movements. Thus for a given equity weighting, the duration of the bond component can be selected to achieve vastly different target durations for the total portfolio. For example, with 60% in equities, the 40% "fixed-income" portion can be invested in cash equivalents for a total portfolio duration under one year, or in longer instruments to achieve total duration beyond six years. For the same fixed proportion invested in bonds, different bond portfolios can clearly lead to vastly different "total portfolio durations" for the overall fund. (Once the equity weighting is determined, the second decision can be stated in terms of either the bond component duration or the duration target for the total portfolio.)

Thus without transforming the allocation process into a highly modeled form based upon the surplus function, it becomes clear that there are compelling reasons to make some simple changes in the traditional way of even thinking about asset allocation. The range of choices in the bond component is so wide and so important that a simplistic "stock/bond ratio" is no longer appropriate. Rather, the fund sponsor should recognize that there are two semi-independent choices—the equity weighting and the portfolio duration for the total fund. (This is very different from the traditional framework, where the equity weighting basically dictates all facets of the fund allocation.) These two choices are clearly related. The portfolio duration can provide some risk compensation for the equity weighting. In the final analysis, the overall vulnerability of both the portfolio value and the surplus will depend upon equity weight and the duration of the fixed-income component.

A comprehensive liability framework would ultimately form the most desirable basis for a more sophisticated asset allocation model. At the very least, the semantics of the allocation process should be modernized so that decisions are framed in terms of equity weightings and "total portfolio durations."

Chapter I-4

Surplus Management

The level of interest rates will always be a critical factor in the health of a pension plan. The interest rate factor poses a particularly insidious danger because it often operates in a counterintuitive fashion. The highly visible effects of rate movements on the asset side tend to carry more "perceptual" weight than their less frequently noted (but nonetheless significant) impact on the liability side. Lower—not higher—rates represent one of the most serious threats to pension plans.

This may be seen if one looks at a plan's "surplus function"—the excess (deficit) of the plan's asset value over (under) the present value of its liabilities. The present value of liabilities is extremely sensitive to interest rate movements; plan liabilities generally have durations well in excess of eight years. The asset side of the pension equation is less sensitive; bond durations have averaged about 4.16 over the past six years, while the equity durations have averaged only 2.29. When interest rates fall, the present value of pension liabilities will tend to rise, and to rise faster than corresponding movements in stock and bond prices; the plan's surplus position will be vulnerable to significant erosion.

The wider the gap between the duration of a plan's assets and the duration of its liabilities, the more vulnerable the surplus function will be. Given the relatively short durations of equities, increasing a portfolio's commitment to stocks will increase surplus

Martin L. Leibowitz, "Pension Asset Allocation through Surplus Management, *Financial Analysts Journal*, March/April 1987. (Received Graham & Dodd Plaque for 1987.) Reprinted with permission.

volatility. In fact, even the 60% equity, 40% bond allocation of the typical pension plan exposes it to severe surplus risk; such a plan that was fully funded in January 1981 would have seen its funded status decline to 69% by June 1986, i.e., a deficit of 31% relative to the new level of its liability. Fortunately, control of portfolio surplus risk can be improved by using the portfolio's bond component to counterbalance duration shortfalls resulting from substantial equity weightings.

New developments in actuarial and accounting procedures for pension funds, together with changes in the capital markets themselves, have led to a renewed focus on the link between a fund's asset returns and its liability framework. The most direct method for quantifying this link is the surplus function— the excess of the plan's asset value over the present value of its liabilities.[1] A fund with an ample surplus is deemed to be comfortably situated, while a fund with a negative surplus (that is, a deficit) must address the need for "catch-up" funding.

Over most of the 1980s, the surplus posture of a typical fund would have eroded considerably, despite extraordinarily positive equity market returns. The problem has been the radical changes in interest rates over this period. With the new FASB initiatives and the removal of traditional smoothing techniques, interest rate movements are emerging as the central factor linking assets and liabilities. Rate-driven changes in liability values may represent a greater threat to a plan's surplus than any potential variation in portfolio value, and ignoring them can lead to inappropriate asset allocations.

The volatility in the value of liabilities has not received as much attention as the volatility of stocks, bonds and other asset classes used in modern asset allocation. Two earlier studies have identified the interest rate sensitivity of a total portfolio including stocks, bonds and other asset classes, as well as the rate sensitivity of a representative liability structure.[2] This article combines these approaches to explore how interest rate sensitivity can be a dominant consideration in determining the growth or erosion of the surplus level. It shows that traditional allocations between stocks and bonds lead to highly vulnerable surplus functions.

---

[1] A pension plan has many different factors and time frames. Thus a plan's liability and the corresponding surplus can be defined in a number of ways, depending on the context. Although the specific values and procedures must obviously be tailored to individual situations, the analytical approach described in this article is generally applicable to any surplus measure.

[2] See M. L. Leibowitz, "Total Portfolio Duration: A New Perspective on Asset Allocation," *Financial Analysts Journal*, September/October 1986, and Leibowitz, "Liability Returns: A New Perspective on Asset Allocation" (Salomon Brothers Inc, New York, May 1986).

Figure A: Equity and Fixed Income Returns, January 1980-July 1986

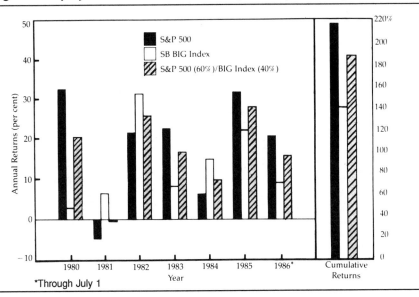

*Through July 1

ASSET RETURNS AND PORTFOLIO DURATION

Figure A shows the total returns from January 1, 1980 through June 30, 1986, for the S&P 500 index and for the Salomon Brothers Broad Investment-Grade Index™ as a proxy for the bond market. In addition, Figure A shows the combined returns from a portfolio invested 60% in the S&P 500 and 40% in the Salomon Brothers Broad Index.

The figure suggests some degree of comovement between bond market and stock market returns. The correlation is typically assumed to fall between 0.30 and 0.40; we found that a correlation of 0.34 represented the average value of monthly bond-stock returns for the January 1980 through November 1985 period.[3] Such a correlation suggests that a similar direct correlation must exist between equities and interest rate movements. This leads to the notion that a duration yardstick for stocks can be derived from any observed (or assumed) level of stock-bond correlation. In fact, for the 1980-85 period, the S&P 500 had an average duration of 2.19 years.

This result is surprising on two counts. First of all, stock market behavior has frequently been viewed as being largely driven by changes in interest rates.

---

[3] See Leibowitz, "Total Portfolio Duration," *op. cit.*

Figure B: Rolling One-Year Empirical Duration for S&P 500

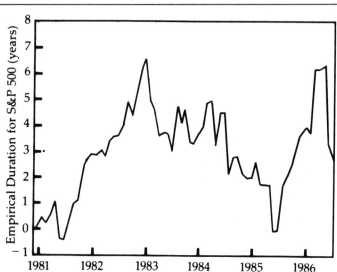

Second, prior work addressing the question of stock durations (based on dividend discount models) had concluded that stocks had very long duration values—20, 30, even 50 years.[4] A duration of 2.19 years for the S&P 500 contradicts these preconceptions.

Subsequent work has shown that a wide range of duration values has existed for various stock sectors over different time periods. For example, in the 12-month period ended March 31, 1986, monthly S&P 500 returns had a very high correlation with interest rate movements—0.78—supporting the general perception of the driving role of interest rates in stock market rallies. This correlation was about as high as any achieved over any 12-month period within the 1980s, and it implied an S&P duration of 6.18 years—about as large a duration as we have witnessed in our empirical investigations.

Figure B shows the S&P 500's duration, based upon trailing 12-month returns for the period January 1980 through June 1986. The extraordinarily high duration of 6.18 reached as of last March was short-lived. The trailing 12-month duration values "regressed" rapidly to a level of 2.90 years at the end of June 1986. Over the entire period, the empirical duration value averaged 2.29 years.

---

[4] The author is himself guilty of having reached an essentially similar conclusion in "Bond Equivalents of Stock Returns" (Salomon Brothers Inc, New York, June 1976).

It takes a rare combination of a high correlation and a high equity-bond volatility ratio to achieve equity durations as high as six years. Indeed, equity duration values of two to five years seem to dominate the *ex post* results shown in Figure B. A similar range of duration values results from computations based on typical *ex ante* market assumptions used in asset allocation studies.

The plain fact is that equity portfolios have low empirical durations in terms of return sensitivity to nominal interest rate movements. All the results from dividend discount models that suggest the contrary are, to put it bluntly, wrong. (It is interesting to speculate about the possible explanations for the excessively high duration numbers derived from dividend discount models.) For our purposes, the key point is that the S&P 500—and equity portfolios in general—have durations that almost always fall below five years.

Figure C provides a corresponding time chart of the empirical durations of the Salomon Brothers Broad Index, measured against yield movements of 10-year Treasuries. As one can see, these are far more stable, generally ranging between 3.5 and 4.7. Taking the mean values of 2.29 for the duration of the S&P 500 and 4.16 for the Broad Index, one finds that a 60/40 traditional stock-bond portfolio would have an asset duration of 3.04. If one were to assume that the correlation of the equity and bond markets was particularly high—say, 0.78—the 60/40 portfolio would still have a total duration of only 5.12. Even this

Figure C: Rolling One-Year Empirical Duration for Salomon Brothers Broad Index

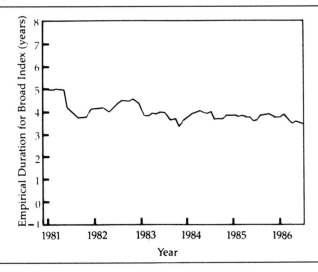

maximum duration value falls far short of the duration needed to match the interest rate sensitivity of pension liabilities.

LIABILITY RETURNS

The liability schedule depicted in Figure D is essentially derived from a mixture of 60% retired lives and 40% active lives for a representative corporate pension fund. Although the ratio of retired to active lives varies over a wide spectrum for plans at different levels of maturity, 60/40 is a higher dose of retirees than one finds in most ongoing plans, hence it represents a conservative choice; a higher percentage of actives would lead to even more striking results.

The present value of this liability stream depends on the interest rate used as a discounting factor. Figure E depicts the present value across a range of interest rates. This present value cost can be interpreted as the dollar amount of assets required to fund the liabilities fully when invested at the specified interest rate. (It should be noted that both the liability schedules and the discount rates have been depicted in nominal terms. This general method can be extended to deal with the effects of inflation, but that discussion lies outside the scope of this article.)

Figure D: Integrated Liability Schedule, 60% Retired/40% Active

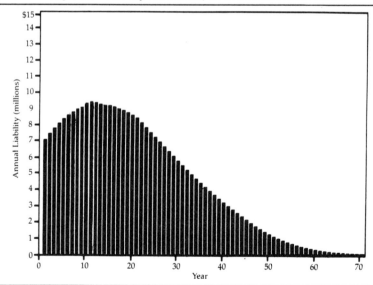

Figure E: Present Value of Liabilities

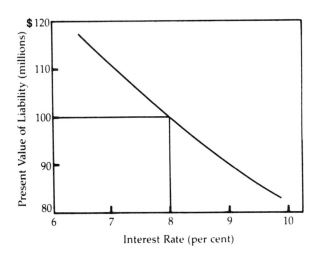

As interest rates change, so will the cost of the liabilities. Thus, as Figure F shows, a drop in interest rates from 8% to 7% would lead to an $11 million increase in the present value cost of these liabilities. This constitutes an 11% growth in liability costs. Employing the terminology usually reserved for the asset side, we could refer to this 11% rate of increase in costs as a "liability return."

The liability return represents a return threshold the assets must match in order to maintain a given surplus level. In particular, if the assets and the liabilities are equal at the outset—that is, if the surplus is zero—then the asset returns must equal this liability return in order for the asset and liability values to remain even. If the surplus is not zero—that is, if there is a positive surplus or a negative deficit—the asset returns must be equal in dollar terms to the liability returns in order to maintain a constant dollar surplus. This implies that, for the surplus condition to be preserved, the asset return times the asset base must equal the liability return times the liability base.

Applying the 10-year single A industrial rate as a discounting proxy for the liability flows on a monthly basis to the integrated liability schedule generates the sequence of "liability returns" given in Figure G. The liability returns are very volatile. One can see that there have been many months in which the liability returns have reached significant positive levels of 5% or more. Moreover, there have been several periods in which there were significant "runs" of such

Figure F: Liability Return

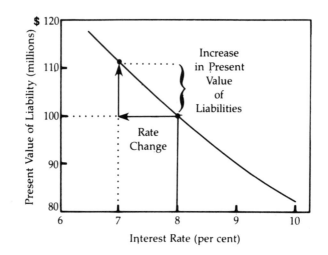

Figure G: Integrated Liability Returns, January 1980-July 1986

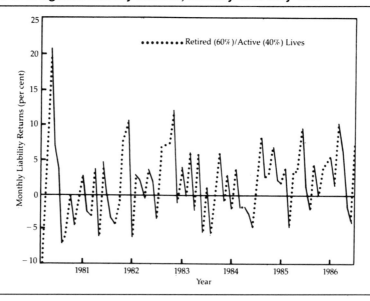

Figure H: Asset Returns and Liability Returns, 60% S&P 500/40% Salomon Brothers Broad Index

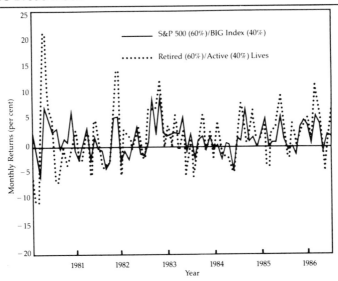

high monthly returns. This is hardly surprising in a period when interest rates declined broadly.

Figure H overlays the liability returns on the asset returns from the 60% S&P 500, 40% Broad Index portfolio. In many instances, the liability returns exceed the asset returns month by month, as well as over a span of several months.

The liability schedule used in these calculations had a duration of approximately eight years. If we had taken a more realistic liability schedule—that is, one with a larger component of active lives—then the resulting liability schedule would have had a significantly longer duration. Given the four to five-year durations associated with traditional asset mixes, one can see why the asset side tends to have a chronic shortfall in duration relative to the liabilities.

HISTORICAL SURPLUS CHANGES

A fund that begins the month in a net even position—that is, with a surplus of zero—will increase its surplus to the extent that asset returns exceed liability returns. The difference between the two series of monthly returns depicted in Figure H could be graphed to show the surplus changes in a fund that started

---

Figure I: Monthly Surplus Changes as a Percentage of Liability Value

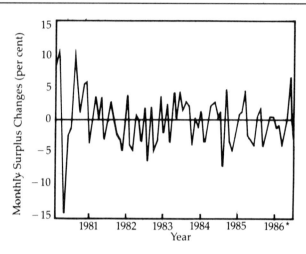

*Through July 1.

---

even at the beginning of each month. This "difference series" is shown in Figure I. The magnitude of these effects is notable: Almost all the monthly surplus changes exceed 3%, either on the negative or positive side, and in several months they fluctuate by more than 5%. Clearly, on a monthly basis, even this conservative surplus function exhibits a high degree of volatility.

To gain more insight into cumulative surplus changes, we must examine periods longer than one month. This is done in Figures J, K and L. Figure J shows the cumulative surplus changes over quarterly periods. There were seven quarters during this period in which the surplus declined (that is, the deficit increased) to -5% or less.

Figure K, showing the surplus changes on an annual basis, gives a somewhat more comforting result. Year by year, with one exception, the surplus changes have been relatively moderate—that is, less than ±10%. However, most of them have been negative—somewhat surprising in an era of extraordinary portfolio returns. The most severe surplus loss occurred in 1982, when the liability return exceeded the asset return by almost 26%. Aside from this dramatic year, the liability returns and asset returns were relatively closely matched.

Figure L shows a less comforting view. Here, the cumulative asset and liability returns have been computed from year-beginning start dates over periods that all end on June 30, 1986. For example, the first set of bars covers the period from January 1, 1980 through June 30, 1986. These results naturally coin-

Figure J: Quarterly Surplus Changes

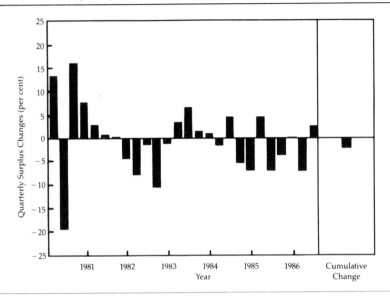

Figure K: Annual Surplus Changes

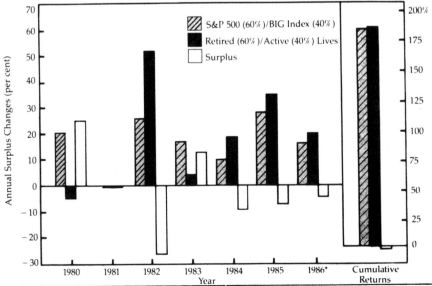

*Through July 1.

Figure L: Cumulative Surplus Changes from Various Starting Dates

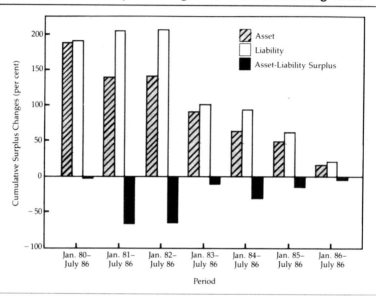

Figure M: Monthly Surplus Changes and Interest Rate Movements

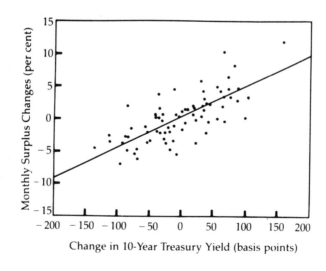

cide with the cumulative return results shown in Figure K. The second set of bars represents the period from January 1, 1981 through June 30, 1986. In this period, the liability returns of 204% exceeded the asset returns of 139%, resulting in a surplus decrease of over 65%. For a fund starting in January 1982, a virtually identical experience ensued, with another surplus loss of 65%. Similarly, for start dates of January 1983, 1984 and 1985, the subsequent years led to surplus losses of various magnitudes. Even for the first half of 1986—a period of truly exceptional asset returns—there was a net surplus loss. Such results are hardly comforting to fund sponsors who would normally feel comfortable with a surplus on the order of 15% or so. (It should be noted that these results are for a closed system that does not take into consideration additional contributions or new structural liabilities.)

DURATION OF SURPLUS CHANGES

Figure M plots the monthly surplus changes from Figure I against the interest rate changes that occurred during the respective months. There is a strong regression here, with a slope of 4.8 years.

This slope represents a kind of "surplus duration." Its value is related to the gap between the total portfolio duration and the liability duration. The total portfolio duration for the 60% S&P 500, 40% Broad Index portfolio was found earlier to be 3.04 years. The liability duration is 7.84 years. Thus the duration gap is approximately -4.80 years. It is hardly surprising to see that these surplus changes exhibit a regression slope of 4.80.

Control of this duration gap is one of the major challenges in surplus management. Figure N depicts the surplus regression lines that would have been achieved with 100% weightings in the S&P 500 and in the Salomon Brothers Broad Investment-Grade Bond Index^{TM}. Allocations that consist of mixtures of these two asset categories would lead to slopes falling within these two extreme positions. Clearly, all such combinations produce surplus functions with considerable interest rate sensitivity. Once again, we see that traditional asset allocations will always result in highly vulnerable surplus positions.

What can be done to reduce this surplus vulnerability? Figure O shows the regression slope that would have been associated with a customized bond index with a total portfolio duration of seven years. As would be expected, with this move toward an immunized portfolio, there is a considerable reduction in the interest rate risk. This risk reduction must be weighed against the loss of the *ex ante* return increment that is the normal motivation behind the higher weighting in the S&P 500.

The surplus risk from lower rates can be reduced by extending the duration of the bond component beyond the four years associated with portfolios that reflect overall bond market characteristics. As the portfolio's equity component

Figure N: Surplus Changes Relative to Stock and Bond Index Portfolios

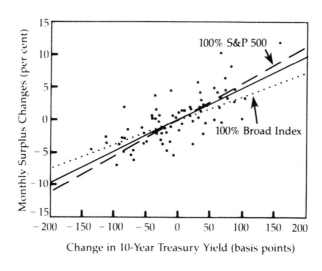

Figure O: Surplus Changes Relative to Customized Index Portfolio

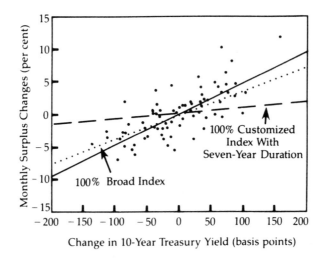

becomes proportionately larger, extensions of the bond component's duration can help to increase total portfolio duration. Without such counterbalancing, increasing equity weights result in far greater risk levels than one might expect from standard volatility studies.

This increase in risk results because equities by themselves contribute to surplus risk in two ways—by the interest rate risk derived from their low durations and through residual volatility from other causes. By using the bond component to counterbalance the duration shortfall that results from significant equity weightings, one can achieve improved control of the portfolio's total surplus risk.

Any such extensions of duration should be evaluated against the potential for future interest rate movements. When only limited declines of interest rates are expected, the sponsor may elect to utilize the "liability component" of his portfolio in an opportunistic fashion. In other words, he may purposely decide to maintain a relatively low asset duration in order to remain poised for significant cost reductions from rising rates.

AN EARNINGS CUSHION

The short-term surplus measure can be interpreted in a long-term context that provides valuable insight into the nature of the funding process. Figure P de-

Figure P: Surplus as an Earnings Rate Cushion

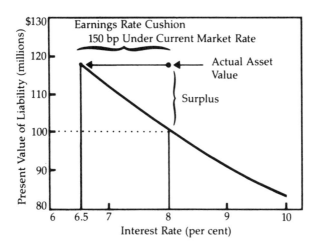

picts a fund with a positive surplus. Current market rates are 8%. If the asset value remained unchanged, the discounting rate could fall to 6 1/2% and, because of the surplus, assets would still be sufficient to fund the liabilities. In other words, the surplus is sufficient to allow the existing fund to fall 150 basis points below the current market rate and still fulfill the liabilities. The surplus acts as a 150-basis-point "earnings cushion." The fund thus has a margin of comfort amounting to 150 basis points below the current market rate to cover contingencies in future returns and the dangers associated with riskier asset classes.

By the same token, a negative surplus (a deficit) may be viewed as a negative earnings rate cushion. It acts as a sort of "hurdle spread" that the fund must earn above market rates in order to fulfill its liabilities without additional cash injections. Consider, for example, a pension fund with a deficit that corresponds to a required earnings rate of 9 1/2%. In an 8% market, the assets in hand would have to earn 150 basis points more than the current market rate in order to provide adequate funding by themselves. Obviously, when the surplus is zero, the assets are by definition just sufficient to fund the liabilities at the presumed market rate. At this point, there is neither cushion nor hurdle.

Surplus changes can be viewed as changes in these cushion/hurdle spreads. Figure Q shows the hurdle/cushion spreads for annual periods beginning in 1980. This figure essentially translates the annual surplus changes from Figure K

Figure Q: Earnings Cushions Developed Over Annual Periods

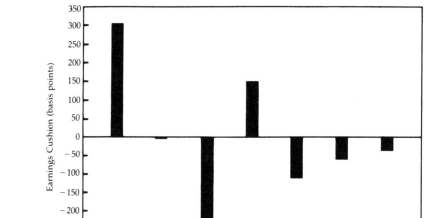

Figure R: Cumulative Earnings Cushions Developed from Various Starting Dates

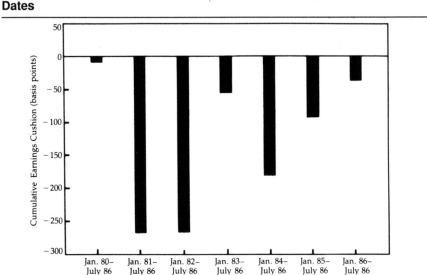

into the terms of an earnings rate cushion. The -26% surplus change over 1982 becomes a 260-basis-point deficit in the long-term earnings rate. Thus, with the A industrial rate at 11.63% at the end of 1982, a fund that started 1982 with a zero surplus would have to earn at a rate of 14.23% (11.63 plus 2.60%) in order to fulfill its liabilities without additional cash injections.

Figure R shows the earnings cushions for periods of different start dates, all ending June 30, 1986. As one can see, significant hurdle spreads are associated with the surplus losses incurred over this period.

A fund with a high hurdle spread above market rates finds itself in a difficult position, assuming it does not plan to contribute further funds. It must achieve earnings rates that exceed market rates by at least the hurdle spread. On the one hand, such a fund might be tempted to undertake risky positions in the hope of achieving returns above those available in a risk-neutral or immunizing portfolio. On the other hand, the fund has no room for return shortfalls that would exacerbate the deficit and hurdle spread situation.

The earnings cushion approach is consistent with the common practice of evaluating various asset classes in terms of their expected return increments over current market rates. This view of the deficit and surplus and their associated changes indicates that the surplus clearly does represent an economically significant long-term variable. Surplus management has relevance not only for pension sponsors concerned with near-term accounting results or potential early terminations, but also for sponsors who seek a well controlled investment procedure for the long-term funding of their liabilities.

IMPLICATIONS

One problem in coming to grips with surplus management is to overcome the traditional view that positive correlation is an evil to be avoided. The traditional efficient portfolio is constructed by seeking asset classes that have the lowest correlation (ideally, even a negative correlation) with each other. In the new surplus framework, on the other hand, where there is a chronic shortage of duration on the asset side, there is a definite value to positive correlations with bond returns. Thus any asset class having a high (negative) correlation with interest rates is far more desirable for a given prospective return (and a given level of residual risk). There is clearly an opportunity for domestic bonds to play a special and distinguished role as a hedging vehicle in helping to moderate this duration shortfall.

Moreover, the wide duration spectrum available within domestic bond markets can act as an important bridge toward a new allocation procedure directed toward surplus management. In traditional allocation, the asset class percentages are set at a "macro" level, and the composition of each class is then determined at the "micro" level by the assigned managers or by the nature of the index selected as a core fund. This process leads to durations for the bond component—and, indeed, for the total portfolio—that have been selected for all sorts of reasons, but probably with little concern for the control of surplus risk.

In the new surplus context, a more efficient portfolio would result through a closer integration of the macro and micro decisions, especially with respect to the bond component. The bond duration could be derived by an interactive process with the macro decisions that set the percentage weightings of all other asset classes. With this interactive approach, the total risk incurred by a greater equity ratio (and the tendency toward an even greater duration gap) could be counterbalanced by setting higher duration targets for the fixed income portfolio.

A deeper problem for effective surplus management is the tendency for sponsors to view the surplus value itself as being of a strictly short-term or *pro forma* nature. In reality, the surplus function truly links long- and short-term considerations. The long-term interpretation of the surplus can be clarified by viewing it as an earnings rate cushion. A fund with zero surplus should be in a position to fulfill its associated liabilities exactly through the purchase of annuities or the construction of an immunizing bond portfolio at current market interest rates. A fund with a positive surplus should have some room to fulfill its liabilities, even if the long-term earnings rate should fall somewhat below current annuity rates. The fund then has a cushion that allows it to take on market risk in the search for excess returns. Thus, the *short-term* measure of surplus status clearly has an important implication in terms of the long-term earnings rate needed to achieve fulfillment of the fund's liabilities.

Chapter I-5

Effective Duration of Pension Liabilities

In this article, we develop a framework for measuring the interest rate sensitivity of pension liabilities under the new reporting requirements of Financial Accounting Standards Board (FASB) Statement 87, which applies to corporate sponsors of defined-benefit pension plans. Before FASB 87, interest sensitivity could be "managed" to a considerable extent because of the latitude permitted in selecting the actuarial discount rate. FASB 87, however, requires plan sponsors to use market interest rates in the actuarial valuation of pension liabilities. In particular, FASB's requirement of "mark-to-market" liability valuation introduces a new volatility, with the possibility of substantial adverse fluctuations on both the income statement and the balance sheet.[1]

Efforts to stabilize reported pension obligations were formerly focused on stabilizing assets. Liabilities, while subject to fluctuations from changes in plan demographics, were not subject to interest rate shocks. In fact, the generally con-

---

[1] Note that the relevant rules for funding pension plans, set forth in the Internal Revenue Code and ERISA regulations, have not changed, and funding patterns therefore need not be subject to the same interest sensitivity as accounting results.

Terence C. Langetieg, Lawrence N. Bader, Martin L. Leibowitz, and Alfred Weinberger, "Measuring the Effective Duration of Pension Liabilities," Salomon Brothers Inc, November 1986.

servative approach to selecting the actuarial interest assumption and the secular upward trend in interest rates often made it possible to offset increases in reported pension liabilities due to plan changes or other factors simply by raising the interest assumption. With liabilities under control, the plan sponsor could turn to the asset side and manage the asset volatility with a combination of actuarial smoothing techniques and investment strategies that were often independent of the liability structure and liability risk.

FASB 87 requires a valuation of pension liabilities based on market interest rates and significantly reduces the ability to smooth changes in assets and liabilities. Furthermore, under the new reporting requirements, volatility in market interest rates will be transmitted, via changes in pension assets and pension liabilities, to the income statement and, for deficit plans, to the balance sheet. In the future, asset management will occur in a setting that recognizes not only the sponsor's long-term risk and return objectives but also the short-term implications for the income statement and the balance sheet.

The key to meeting long- and short-term objectives successfully is to develop a new perspective in which assets and liabilities are jointly managed to control surplus volatility.[2] The integrating link between assets and liabilities is interest rate risk. The most important aspect of surplus management is the control of the effective duration of the pension surplus, which in turn reflects the combined interest rate sensitivities of pension assets and pension liabilities.

MEASUREMENT OF PENSION LIABILITIES UNDER FASB 87

Accurate measurement of the effective duration of pension liabilities is now essential. Without such measurement, it is virtually impossible to gain control of surplus volatility and its consequences for the balance sheet, or expense volatility and its consequences for corporate earnings. The effectiveness of protective asset-allocation strategies, such as immunization or dynamic hedging, depends critically on accurate measurement of the interest rate sensitivities of both pension liabilities and pension assets.

In this article, we examine three types of pension liability, each with different interest sensitivity: the accumulated benefit obligation (ABO); the projected benefit obligation (PBO); and the service cost.

---

[2] For a discussion of the volatility and interest rate sensitivity of the pension surplus in recent years, see Martin L. Leibowitz, *Surplus Management: A New Perspective on Asset Allocation*, Salomon Brothers Inc, October 1986.

The Accumulated Benefit Obligation

The ABO is the actuarial value of all benefits earned to date. It is used in several ways:

- Many plan sponsors and participants consider it the minimum level of benefit security: Plan assets should at least cover all benefits earned to date.

- It is the focus of disclosure under FASB 36, the standard that governed pension reporting before FASB 87, and continues to be disclosed under the new standard.

- It offers a measure of the cost of terminating the plan, although various adjustments may be applicable on an actual termination. Subject to these adjustments, it is useful in estimating the cash available to the firm through a termination/reversion or the deficiency that would have to be made up if an underfunded plan was terminated.

- It becomes the basis of a balance sheet liability under FASB 87. Beginning in 1989, any shortfall of pension assets against the ABO must be recorded on the balance sheet. (There is no corresponding balance sheet asset for overfunding.)

The Projected Benefit Obligation

Like the ABO, the PBO reflects benefits earned to date, but it also reflects the effect of future salary increases on those benefits. This is demonstrated in the following example:

The plan used for illustration provides a benefit of 2% of final salary for each year of service. Consider an employee with ten years of service, currently earning $20,000 but with a projected final salary of $50,000 at age 65. The ABO reflects an annual pension benefit equal to 20% of his $20,000 salary, or $4,000. The calculation of the PBO, however, recognizes that when the employee retires, the 20% benefit already earned will apply to a $50,000, rather than a $20,000 salary, so the employee's annual pension benefit is taken as $10,000, rather than $4,000.

The PBO is also used in several ways:

- FASB 87 continues to require the disclosure of the ABO, but it shifts the focus to the PBO. FASB 87 requires the new disclosure of the PBO as well as the critical assumptions used in its calculation.

- It measures the current value of the firm's pension liability for an *ongoing plan*. (In contrast, the ABO is closer to the termination liability.) Therefore, the PBO can be used by securities analysts to assess the full extent of the firm's pension liability. The impact of this new disclosure requirement on securities prices remains to be seen.

- It is a key figure in determining the annual pension expense under FASB 87. At the date of compliance with FASB 87, the PBO surplus (or deficit) is reflected in future pension expenses on an amortized basis. A PBO surplus will decrease future pension expenses, whereas a PBO deficit will increase future expenses. Subsequent changes in the PBO surplus resulting from plan amendments or actuarial gains or losses are amortized in the calculation of annual expense.

- An acquisition accounted for under the purchase method requires the recording of an asset (or liability) corresponding to the amount of overfunding (or underfunding) of the PBO in the acquired company's plans.

The Service Cost

The service cost is the value of benefits earned during the current year and represents the increment to the PBO resulting from the employee's current service. It is an important component of the annual pension expense.

Each of these three measures of the pension liability has a different interest rate sensitivity. Interest sensitivities, or effective durations,[3] can range from 0 to 20 or more, depending on several factors:

- The benefit formula (flat benefit, final salary and career average salary).

- Benefit indexing for cost-of-living adjustments (COLAs) related to either automatic COLA provisions or recurring ad hoc adjustments.

- The demographics of the work force, including the age distribution, years of service, salary levels, and other factors.

- Actuarial assumptions regarding retirement, turnover and mortality.

---

[3] An effective duration of 20 means that a 1% (100-basis-point) change in the interest rate results in a change of approximately 20% in the value of the liability.

- The level of interest rates.

- The relationships among the salary growth rate, the general inflation rate and interest rates.

THE INTEREST RATE SENSITIVITY OF PENSION LIABILITIES

A change in interest rates can affect pension liabilities in two ways:

- First, there is "discount rate sensitivity"—like the value of stocks, bonds and other cash flow streams, the value of pension liabilities is sensitive to changes in the discount rate. Under FASB 87, the actuarial discount rate is the rate inherent in the price that an insurance company would charge to settle the liability through an annuity purchase. That rate reflects current market yields on high-grade bonds. As market interest rates change, annuity purchase rates and the actuarial discount rate also change. Thus, the actuarial present value of the pension obligation is sensitive to changes in market interest rates, just as any fixed-income security would be.

- Second, there is "pension benefit sensitivity"—the interest sensitivity of the pension benefit itself. Interest rate changes are often associated with changes in inflation expectations. Estimates of future benefit payments are linked to inflation when benefit payments are pay-related or adjusted for changes in the cost of living. To the extent that future inflation, interest rates and pension benefits are positively correlated, there will be a compensatory effect on interest rate sensitivity. Inflation-driven salary increases lead to higher benefit payments, but inflation also reduces present values because of higher discount rates. This counterbalancing effect reduces the overall interest rate sensitivity of pension liabilities.

These interest sensitivities have always existed in an economic sense; FASB 87 has only heightened the awareness and concern about them, by requiring a market-based valuation and by giving balance sheet status to pension liabilities.

To illustrate these two types of interest sensitivity, we will examine the measures of the firm's actuarial pension liability that are reported under FASB 87: the ABO, PBO, and the service cost. Without a COLA provision, the interest rate sensitivity of the ABO is entirely the result of its discount rate sensitivity. Since the ABO measures only accrued benefits and does not reflect future salaries, the benefit stream associated with the ABO is based entirely on the current salary or salary history; therefore, the ABO has no "pension benefit sensitivity" to changes in interest rates.

The PBO and the service cost exhibit both discount rate sensitivity and pension benefit sensitivity. Since their interest rate sensitivities are based on a projection of future salaries, the benefit streams are uncertain. Changes in the inflation rate are likely to affect both future salaries and the associated pension benefits.

Our analysis will include a consideration of variations in plan provisions, including the COLA provision. With a COLA provision, the ABO develops pension benefit sensitivity to interest rate changes, and the pension benefit sensitivities of the PBO and service cost are magnified. But as pension benefit sensitivity increases, the overall interest sensitivity of the liability measures decreases. Lastly, we will also consider alternative employee demographics.

AN ILLUSTRATIVE PENSION PLAN: PLAN PROVISIONS, ACTUARIAL ASSUMPTIONS AND EMPLOYEE DEMOGRAPHICS

A pension plan's interest sensitivity depends on the age/service/pay characteristics of the work force; plan provisions; and assumptions about turnover, mortality, salary increases, retirement, and other events. Simplified provisions and assumptions will be used to illustrate the measurement of interest rate sensitivity; the conclusions, however, are applicable to virtually all defined-benefit plans.

Like many existing defined-benefit plans, the pension plan we will use provides benefits based on final salary. Specifically, the retirement pension is equal to 2% of final salary for each year of service. This benefit is payable annually, beginning at age 65 and continuing for the remainder of the retiree's life, with no survivor benefits. The basic plan does not include adjustments for inflation in retirement years; however, a COLA provision will be examined later.

Pension plans provide varying benefits to employees who terminate service before they reach retirement age, depending on length of service and the reason for terminating. For simplicity, the basic plan is assumed to provide all employees who terminate before age 65 a deferred benefit at age 65 that is equal to 90% of the benefit accrued at the termination date.

Because of the simplified plan provisions, it is not necessary to make detailed assumptions about rates of death, disability, termination, and voluntary change of jobs before age 65. The probability of survival to age 65 is shown in

Exhibit 1: Probability of Remaining in Active Service to Age 65

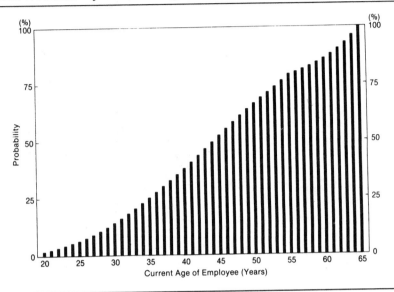

Exhibit 2: Probability of Surviving from Age 65 to Indicated Age

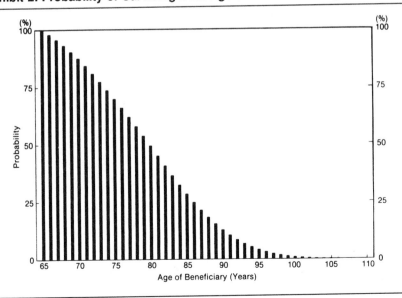

Exhibit 3: Current Salary Scale

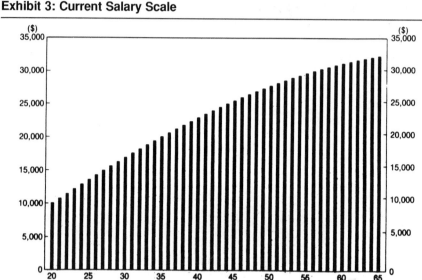

Exhibit 1, and actuarial mortality probabilities for the retirement years are shown in Exhibit 2.[4]

Participants' salaries are assumed to increase in real terms with age. A participant hired at age 20 is assumed to earn a real or inflation-adjusted salary of $10,000 annually, growing to $32,253 at age 65. The nominal growth in salary is equal to the real growth plus an adjustment for inflation. The analysis ignores any salary lags and differences between expected and actual inflation. The effect is that the salary is assumed to increase according to the real scale shown in Exhibit 3, plus an adjustment for expected inflation.

The active employee population used in our illustration is a "normal group, (which) represents a reasonably mature and stable group that is projected to continue to grow. It is typical of many large companies."[5] The age distribution for this normal group is shown in Exhibit 4. A typical retiree group was developed with the age distribution shown in Exhibit 5; at a 10% interest rate, the

---

[4] See Dan M. McGill, *Fundamentals of Private Pensions* (Homewood, IL, Richard D. Irwin, 1984) and Harold R. Greenlee, Jr. and Alfonso D. Keh, "The 1971 Group Annuity Mortality Table," *Transactions of the Society of Actuaries*, 23, 1971, pp. 569-604.

[5] The active employee population is Employee Group A from *Pension Cost Method Analysis*, American Academy of Actuaries, 1985.

Exhibit 4: Age Distribution of Active Participants

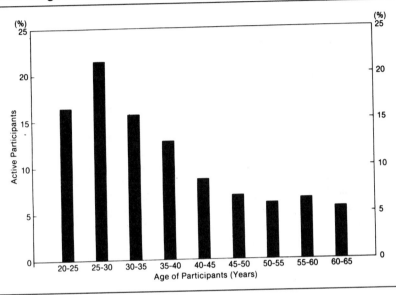

Exhibit 5: Age Distribution of Retired Participants

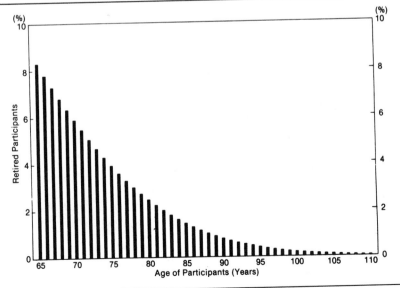

ABO of the retiree group is assumed to be half that of the active employees, or one third of the total ABO.

EFFECTIVE DURATION OF THE ABO

Under FASB 87, the ABO achieves balance sheet status: If the market value of pension assets falls below the ABO, the deficit is reported on the balance sheet. Deficits are measured plan by plan; overfunding in one plan cannot be used to offset underfunding in another. Thus, FASB 87 motivates the firm to keep all plans in a surplus condition. To avoid balance sheet fluctuations caused by volatility in the ABO, the firm must devise new asset-allocation strategies to offset adverse fluctuations in the ABO. A necessary first step in developing an effective asset allocation is to measure the interest sensitivity of the ABO.

Under FASB 87, the ABO represents the actuarial present value of accrued benefits, calculated according to the plan formula. In our example, the benefits for the ABO calculation are based on the current salary and the accumulated years of service:

$$\begin{bmatrix} \text{Benefit} \end{bmatrix} = \begin{bmatrix} \text{Current} \\ \text{Salary} \end{bmatrix} \times \begin{bmatrix} \text{Years of} \\ \text{Service} \end{bmatrix} \times \begin{bmatrix} 2\% \end{bmatrix} \quad (1)$$

The actuarial value of the benefit stream is based on four factors:

- The annual benefit at age 65;

- The value at age 65 of an annuity paid until death, based on a mortality table (see Exhibit 2) and a market-based discount rate;

- An actuarial adjustment for the probability that the employee will not survive to age 65 to receive the benefit (see Exhibit 1); and

- A discount for interest from the employee's current age to age 65.

The actuarial value of the ABO is summarized as follows:

$$\begin{bmatrix} \text{ABO With} \\ \text{Respect to} \\ \text{Benefits} \\ \text{Payable} \\ \text{at Age 65} \end{bmatrix} = \begin{bmatrix} \text{Benefit} \end{bmatrix} \times \begin{bmatrix} \text{Probability} \\ \text{of Survival} \\ \text{to Age 65} \end{bmatrix} \times \begin{bmatrix} \text{Present} \\ \text{Value of} \\ \text{Annuity} \\ \text{Starting} \\ \text{at Age 65} \end{bmatrix} \times \begin{bmatrix} \text{Interest} \\ \text{Discount} \\ \text{From} \\ \text{Current Age} \\ \text{to Age 65} \end{bmatrix} \quad (2)$$

Consider a worker at age 55 with ten years of service and a current salary of $29,703. Using Equation (1) the worker's benefit at age 65 is $5,941 (29,703 × 10 × .02). Suppose the appropriate market interest rate is 10%. Using the mortality probabilities shown in Exhibit 2, the present value at age 65 of a $1 life annuity is $7.7065. The probability that a 55-year-old worker will reach retirement age in active service is 79.1% (see Exhibit 1). Therefore, the ABO for this worker, excluding benefits payable in the event of termination before age 65, is equal to the following:

$$\text{ABO (Active to Age 65)} = \$5{,}941 \times .791 \times 7.7065 \times \frac{1}{1.10^{10}}$$

$$= \$13{,}963 \tag{3}$$

Under the plan, participants terminating before age 65, for any reason, are assumed to receive an average of 90% of the accrued normal retirement benefit based on the appropriate salary. If 79.1% of 55-year-old workers remain in service to age 65, 20.9% will exit early. Therefore, with respect to benefits payable on termination before age 65, the ABO is equal to the following:

$$\text{ABO (Exits before Age 65)} = .90 \times \$5{,}941 \times .209 \times 7.7065 \times \frac{1}{1.10^{10}}$$

$$= \$3{,}320 \tag{4}$$

Exhibit 6: Forecast ABO Cash Flows—Active Participants, Retirees, and All Participants (Dollars in Millions)

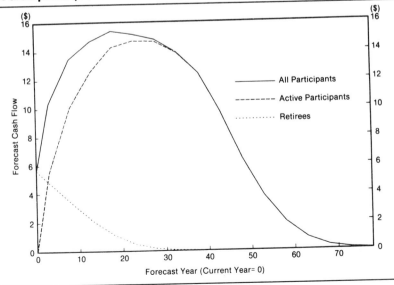

Exhibit 7: ABO for Active Participants, Retirees, and All Participants (Dollars in Millions)

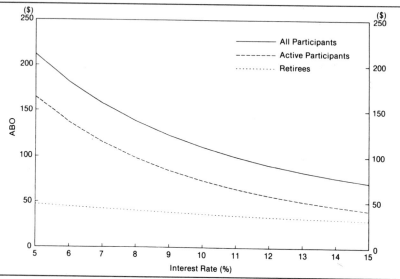

The total of amounts in equations 3 and 4 is equal to the ABO for an employee at age 55 with ten years of service:

$$\text{ABO (Age 55 with 10 Years of Service)} = \$13{,}963 + \$3{,}320 = \$17{,}283 \quad (5)$$

The calculation for workers at other ages is similar, yielding an ABO of $110,176,283 for a work force of 10,000 active participants and retirees. Without a COLA, the projected cash flow stream for the ABO is independent of interest rates, so its calculation at any interest rate is straightforward (see Exhibit 6). The ABO at interest rates from 5% to 15%, for retired and active participants separately and combined, is shown in Exhibit 7. At a 5% interest rate, retirees account for only 22% of the total liability; at a 10% rate, they account for 33%, and at a 15% rate, they account for 42% of the totals.

To determine the ABO's interest sensitivity, suppose the interest rate increases from 10% to 10.01%. At 10.01%, the ABO drops by .1050% to $110,060,580. This represents an interest rate sensitivity comparable to that of a bond with a duration of 10.50. In other words, the current value of this liability stream changes by approximately 10.50% for a 1% change in the level of interest rates. If interest rates increase (or decrease) by 2%, we can expect the current value of the ABO to fall (or rise) by approximately 21% (2 × 10.50%), and so

Exhibit 8: Effective Duration of the ABO for Active Participants, Retirees, and All Participants

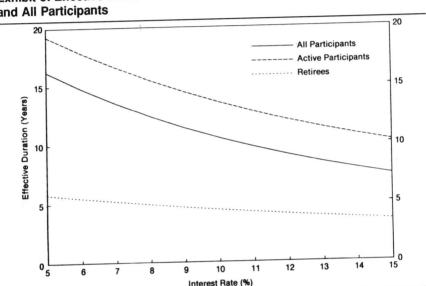

forth. Compared with almost all fixed-income investments, the ABO's interest sensitivity is extremely high.

The ABO's duration for the active and retired components is shown separately at different interest rate levels in Exhibit 8. At a 10% interest rate, the duration for the retired component is 4.42, while the duration for the active component is 13.54. This large difference reflects the fact that the active participants' cash flow is more distant than that of the retirees (see Exhibit 6). The retired component comprises participants currently receiving benefits; its cash flows are weighted heavily over the next ten years. On the other hand, the active component has an average age of 36; therefore, the average active participant has 29 years to retirement, and the duration of the resulting benefit stream is much higher.

FASB 87 requires the use of a market-based interest rate in actuarial calculations. For plans that have an ABO deficit, an ABO sensitivity of the magnitude indicated here raises the potential for large fluctuations on the corporate balance sheet. Many firms may choose to develop an asset-allocation strategy to hedge the current ABO surplus or deficit against adverse changes in interest rates. A fund consisting of a dedicated portfolio for retirees—who have a relatively short duration—and a typical unmatched portfolio for active participants—who have a duration of 13.54 in this example—will be highly vulnerable to surplus impairment during a period of declining interest rates.

EFFECTIVE DURATION OF THE PBO

The ABO represents the firm's current pension liability on a termination basis and has balance sheet significance under FASB 87. For a firm that intends to terminate in the near term, the PBO is of little significance. However, if the firm intends to maintain a defined-benefit retirement plan indefinitely, the PBO is a much better gauge of the current value of the firm's future obligation. If the firm is to make good on its defined-benefit promises, it must fund toward the PBO, rather than the ABO. For the ongoing plan with a long horizon, the "economic surplus" is equal to the market value of pension assets minus the PBO. Therefore, strategies for hedging the economic surplus must focus on the PBO's interest sensitivity.

The actuarial value of the PBO can be obtained in a fashion similar to that used for the ABO. In the PBO calculation, however, a projected benefit[6] is used, and it must reflect projected salary increases based on merit, longevity and inflation.[7] The benefit for the PBO calculation is the following:

$$[\text{Benefit}] = \begin{bmatrix} \text{Projected Salary at Age} \\ \text{65 or at Exit Age} \end{bmatrix} \times \begin{bmatrix} \text{Current Years} \\ \text{of Service} \end{bmatrix} \times [2\%] \qquad (6)$$

Consider a 55-year-old worker who is currently earning $29,703 and who is expected to earn $32,285 at age 65 in current dollars (see Exhibit 3). Suppose the current interest rate is 10%, reflecting an expected inflation rate of 5.75%. The final salary of this worker is projected to be $56,468 ($32,285 × $1.0575^{(65-55)}$). Using the projected salary and the benefit formula in Equation (6), the 55-year-old worker with ten years of service has a PBO benefit at age 65 equal to $11,294, compared with the ABO benefit of only $5,941.

The projected exit salary must also be determined for workers who terminate before age 65. The probabilities of continuing in service (see Exhibit 1) can be used to determine the probability of cost at each age. These probabilities are then applied to the corresponding salaries to determine the benefit amounts and actuarial liabilities. The formula in Equation (6) must be applied to each exit age; thus, the PBO calculation is more complicated than the ABO calculation.

The PBO and ABO for active participants at different ages are compared in Exhibit 9. For retirees, the PBO and ABO are the same. Since the current salary is close to the projected retirement salary for older workers, the ABO is very close to the PBO. For younger workers, however, the difference between the

---

[6] This benefit is projected in terms of salary, but not in terms of additional 2% benefit units, which may be credited for years of future service.

[7] The PBO must also reflect benefit increases based on a COLA clause, if one exists, and must reflect future benefit liberalizations if the firm has a substantial commitment to such increases.

Exhibit 9: ABO and PBO for Active Participants (Dollars in Thousands)

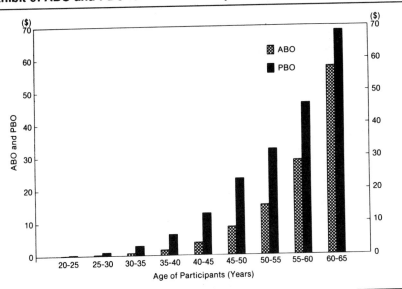

ABO and the PBO is quite dramatic, since the difference between current salary and the projected retirement salary is very large.

The projected cash flows of the PBO and ABO for the current work force of 10,000 plus retirees are shown in Exhibit 10. The PBO's cash flows are larger, since they are based on future salaries. The average maturity of the PBO's cash flow is also more distant than the ABO's. This is because the difference between projected and current salary is greatest for younger workers, and the more distant cash flows are associated with the retirement of the younger workers. In sum, the anticipation of future salary levels both increases the amount of the PBO relative to the ABO and extends its average maturity.

The PBO's Discount Rate Sensitivity

To determine the interest sensitivity of the PBO, we must specify how the projected cash flows will change as interest rates change. First, suppose that the PBO's cash flows are invariant with respect to changes in interest rates. In this case, the PBO's interest sensitivity is due entirely to discount rate sensitivity. For the cash flow stream shown in Exhibit 10, the PBO is $167,323,234 when discounted at 10%. Discounting the same cash flow stream at 10.01%, the PBO is $167,090,800. Thus, a one-basis-point change in the interest rate produces a

Exhibit 10: Forecast Cash Flows—ABO Versus PBO (Dollars in Millions)

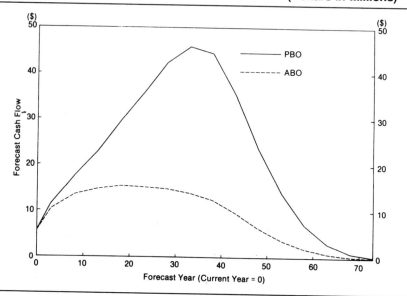

Exhibit 11: Effective Duration of the ABO and the PBO—Constant Pension Benefits

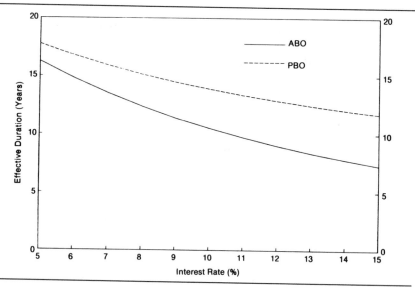

.1389% change in the PBO. Assuming that future salaries are independent of interest rate changes, it follows that the duration of pension liabilities is 13.89. This is substantially higher than the 10.50 duration calculated for the ABO, because of the greater weight the PBO assigns to younger employees through the projection of salaries. When benefits are salary related but invariant to interest rate changes, the PBO's duration is always higher than the ABO's (see Exhibit 11).

The PBO's Pension Benefit Sensitivity

For most salary-based plans, the assumption that future pension payments are independent of interest rates is questionable. Interest rate changes—and, over the long run, salary increases—generally reflect changes in anticipated inflation. While actual changes in inflation rates, interest rates and salary growth rates are not perfectly correlated, a 1% increase in the *anticipated* inflation rate is likely to increase expectations for both salary growth rates and interest rates by 1%, at lease over the long run.

The next PBO duration calculation is based on the assumption that the change in interest rates is matched by an equal change in the rate of salary inflation. The real salary scale in Exhibit 3 remains unchanged. In the short run, it is unlikely that a change in interest rates will be matched by an equal change in salary growth rates. For the long forecasting horizon required in the PBO calculation, however, it is more plausible to assume this than to assume that cash flows are constant.

Again suppose the interest rate increases from 10% to 10.01%. At 10%, the PBO is equal to $167,323,234. If the interest rate rises to 10.01%, the PBO drops to $167,090,800 (a .1389% decrease) *before* pension benefit sensitivity is considered. If there is a corresponding .01% increase in the salary inflation rate, the PBO moves back up to $167,216,880, for a net decline in value of .0636%. The increase in the salary growth rate offsets about half the effect of the increase in the discount rate.[8] Thus, when salary growth rates and interest rates move together, the PBO has the same interest sensitivity as a bond with a fixed cash flow stream and a duration of 6.36. This 6.36 duration is significantly less than the duration of 13.89 obtained when the PBO cash flows are fixed and insensitive to interest rate changes.

---

[8] Changes in the salary growth rate are assumed to be exactly equal to changes in the interest rate, but the PBO is still sensitive to interest rate changes. The residual sensitivity exists because benefits are not adjusted for inflation during the retirement years nor are benefits adjusted during preretirement years for those workers who leave the work force before retirement.

Exhibit 12: Effective Duration of the ABO and PBO—Interest-Sensitive Benefits

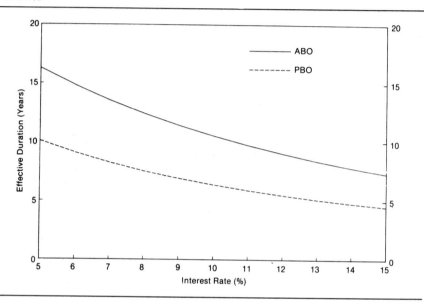

It is interesting that the PBO's inflation-adjusted duration of 6.36 is also substantially less than the ABO's interest sensitivity of 10.50. The cash flow profiles in Exhibit 10 might imply a higher interest sensitivity for the PBO, since it clearly has a longer average maturity. The PBO does have a higher discount rate sensitivity. When the pension benefit sensitivity is considered, however, with expected salary growth rates perfectly correlated with interest rates, the PBO turns out to be less interest sensitive than the ABO. This relationship is shown in Exhibit 12 over a range of interest rates.

THE EFFECTIVE DURATION OF THE SERVICE COST

The service cost—a key element of pension expense—can be thought of as a PBO for benefits newly earned during the year. This new or incremental PBO is clearly of longer duration than the existing PBO. The existing PBO includes retirees, with their short duration, while the service cost does not, since retirees are no longer earning benefits. The existing PBO is also more heavily weighted toward older workers, because of their higher accumulation of service units. In

Exhibit 13: Effective Duration of the Service Cost, ABO, and PBO

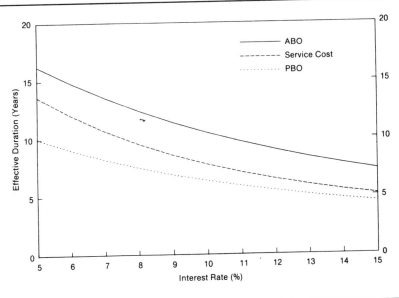

the service cost calculation, each worker is weighted by only one service unit. For example, a 60-year-old worker might have a weighting of 40 years of service in the PBO calculation but only one year of service in the service cost calculation—the same as a new, 20-year-old employee.

The duration of the service cost for the final-pay plan, assuming benefit sensitivity, is shown in Exhibit 13. As noted, the duration of the service cost is somewhat above the PBO's, but not as high as the ABO's. Exhibit 14 shows the effective duration of the service cost at different interest rates for the pay-related plan and a flat benefit plan (that is, a plan without benefit payment sensitivity). When benefits are held constant, the effective duration ranges from about 26 at low interest rates to 12 at high interest rates.

When benefit payment sensitivity is introduced, the effective duration is about halved, ranging from 13 to 5. Since salary growth is not likely to be correlated perfectly with interest rates, many plans will probably have a service cost duration of 10 to 15. With such a high interest sensitivity, a 2% change in rates could produce a 20%-30% change in the service cost. This level of volatility is significantly larger than that of the more manageable pre-FASB 87 pension expense.

THE EFFECTS OF ALTERNATIVE PLAN PROVISIONS

There is a limitless number of benefit formulas, and we believe it useful to consider how variations affect liability duration. We will now examine flat benefit plans, career-average pay plans and COLAs.

Plans with Flat Benefits

Plans for union or other hourly paid employees are typically independent of pay, providing a fixed amount of pension, such as $20 monthly for each year of service. The $20 figure could be adjusted periodically as a result of negotiations or, in a nonunion plan, unilateral changes. Unless the employer has a "substantive commitment" to such changes, however, they are not anticipated in the FASB 87 accounting.

The durations of the ABO are generally slightly longer than those of pay-related plans. In a pay-related plan, younger workers earn benefits at the same rate as older workers, but their longer durations get somewhat less weight because they tend to be lower paid. A duration of 10.79 for the flat benefit plan at

Exhibit 14: Effective Duration of the ABO and PBO—Flat Benefit Versus Pay-Related Benefit

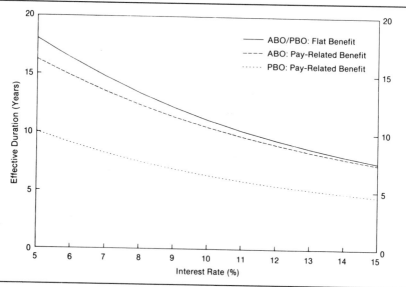

Exhibit 15: Effective Duration of the Service Cost—Flat Benefit Versus Pay-Related Benefit

---

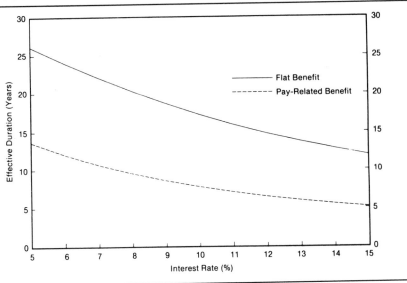

---

a 10% interest rate is shown in Exhibit 14. This is marginally higher than the 10.50 duration of the pay-related plan.

Since flat benefit plans do not involve salary projections, the PBO is the same as the ABO. The PBO has no pension benefit sensitivity unless the plan has a COLA provision; therefore, it has a significantly higher duration than the PBO of a pay-related plan. (A firm might, however, find it desirable to manage an adjusted PBO that reflects expected benefit increases, although FASB 87 does not require current recognition.) At a 10% interest rate, the duration of the flat benefit plan is 10.79—70% higher than the 6.36 duration of the pay-related plan (see Exhibit 14).

The duration of a flat benefit plan's service cost is also significantly higher than that of a pay-related plan because of the absence of benefit payment sensitivity. At a 10% interest rate, the duration is 122% higher for the flat benefit plan (17.23 versus 7.77) (see Exhibit 15).

Plans Based on Career-Average Salary

The benefit formula introduced in Equation (6) is a final-pay formula, relating benefits to the participant's pay at the time of retirement. Most final-pay

Exhibit 16: ABO and PBO for Plans With and Without a COLA Provision (Dollars in Millions)

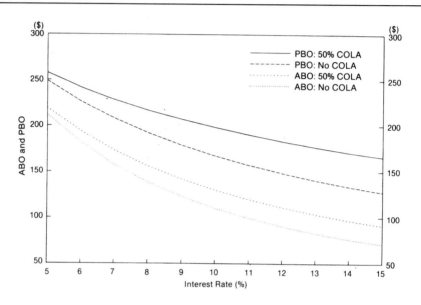

plans relate benefits to pay averaged over a period of three or five years. This lessens the pension benefit sensitivity slightly, since the effect of salary inflation is reduced during the averaging period. With a lower benefit sensitivity, there is a slight increase in the overall interest sensitivity of the PBO and service cost. There is not effect on the ABO's interest sensitivity, since the ABO's cash flows are constant (in the absence of a COLA provision).

The reduction in pension benefit sensitivity is far more significant for career-average pay formulas, which relate benefits to pay averaged over the partici-pant's entire career. These plans have benefit sensitivities that are about half the sensitivities of final-pay plans, so the overall interest sensitivities of the PBO and service cost tend to be about halfway between those of the flat-benefit and final-pay formulas.

Plans with COLA Provisions

The preceding examples assumed that pensions are fixed at retirement, with no automatic COLA provision. FASB 87 requires advance recognition of both auto-

---

Exhibit 17: Service Cost for Plans With and Without a COLA Provision (Dollars in Millions)

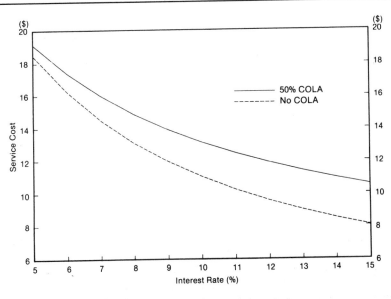

matic indexing and ad hoc increases for which the plan sponsor has a "substantive commitment." When changes in the interest rate are caused by inflation in the cost of living, a COLA provision reduces the effective durations of the ABO, PBO and service cost significantly. The COLA provision introduces pension benefit sensitivity, which partially offsets the actuarial discount sensitivity.

While many firms make it a practice to grant periodic increases to retirees, few grant the full amount implied by the inflation rate, either by automatic indexing or ad hoc increases. Therefore, the following example assumes that each 1% change in interest rate is associated with a .5% increase in anticipated cost-of-living increases, and that salary growth assumptions move in tandem with interest rates. The values of the ABO, PBO and service cost for the final-pay plan with and without a COLA provision are shown in Exhibits 16 and 17. At a 10% interest rate—implying a 5.75% inflation rate in the example—these values are approximately 20% higher with a 50% COLA provision.

Effective durations with and without a COLA provision are shown in Exhibits 18 and 19. At a 10% interest rate, a COLA provision reduces the ABO's duration from 10.50 to 8.39, the PBO's duration from 6.36 to 4.16, and the service cost's duration from 7.77 to 5.50. By tying pension benefits to inflation in the

Exhibit 18: Effective Duration of the ABO and PBO for Plans With and Without a COLA Provision

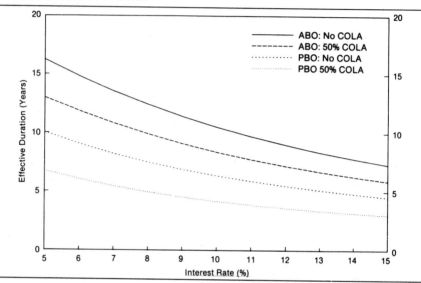

Exhibit 19: Effective Duration of the Service Cost for Plans With and Without a COLA Provision

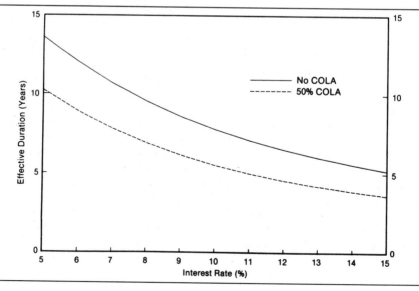

post-retirement years, the COLA increases pension benefit sensitivity and reduces overall interest rate sensitivity by 20%-35%.[9]

THE EFFECTS OF ALTERNATIVE EMPLOYEE DEMOGRAPHICS

Naturally, duration depends on the age distribution of the employees. In Exhibit 19, we compare the group we have used thus far with two other groups.[10] Each group is assigned a retiree population with the same age distribution as in Exhibit 5, but scaled to an appropriate size. The characteristics of the three groups are compared in Exhibit 20.

Exhibit 20: Characteristics of Different Plan Participant Groups

	Average Age (Years)	Average Service (Years)	Retiree ABO as Percentage of Active ABO (10% Discount Rate)
Normal Group	36.3	7.7	50%
Older Group	40.2	13.4	100%
New Group	38.9	4.3	10%

The ABO's duration of the three groups for the pay-related plan without a COLA provision is shown in Exhibit 21. As might be expected, the "Older Group" has a lower duration, while the "New Group" has a higher duration. The ABO's duration for the Normal Group and the Older Group are nearly equal; however, the duration for the New Group is 40% higher (14.6 versus 10.5, at a 10% interest rate).

The effective durations of the PBO and the service cost for the three groups are shown in Exhibits 22 and 23. While the PBO's duration is slightly higher for the New Group, the difference in duration between groups is only one year at a 10% interest rate. The service cost's durations are also very close for all three

---

[9] As a theoretical point, note that if salary inflation, the COLA provision and the discount rate all reflect inflation equally, and if the COLA begins at the date of service termination rather than retirement, then pension benefit sensitivity would exactly offset the discount rate sensitivity, and the effective durations of the PBO and the service cost would be zero.

[10] The other two groups are Group D—"Older Group with Long Service"—and Group H—"New Group (typical of emerging high-technology companies)"—also from *Pension Cost Method Analysis*.

Exhibit 21: Effective Duration of the ABO for Different Age Groups

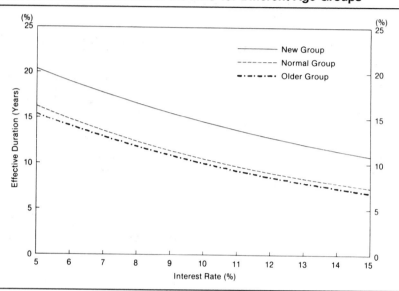

Exhibit 22: Effective Duration of the PBO for Different Age Groups

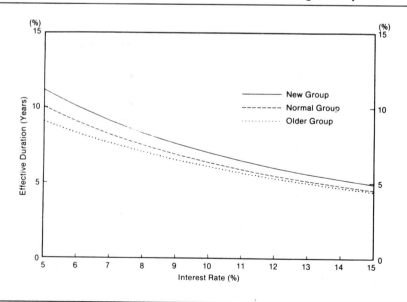

Exhibit 23: Effective Duration of the Service Cost for Different Age Groups

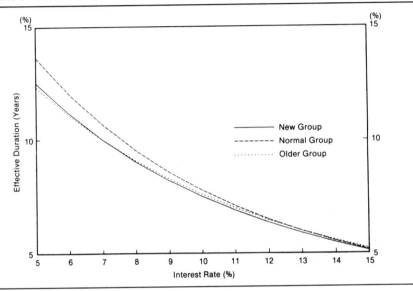

groups, with a maximum difference of one year at very low interest rates. Over-all, the durations of both the PBO and the service cost are relatively insensitive to group demographics, at least for these three groups.[11]

DEVELOPING AN INTEGRATED APPROACH FOR SURPLUS MANAGEMENT

FASB 87 has added several new concerns to the pension plan sponsor's already difficult task. Traditionally, the plan sponsor selected an asset-allocation policy to balance the advantages of a lower average funding cost provided by a high-return strategy against the disadvantages of uncertain investment performance. Typically, the sponsor would take a long-term perspective, since short-term per-formance had little effect on earnings or on the balance sheet, given the use of

---

[11] The demographics of a particular plan may differ significantly from those of the Normal Group, Older Group and new Group. In particular, many mature plans have retiree populations which represent a much larger proportion of the PBO than in the groups illustrated here. Thus, it is possible that a particular plan's interest sensitivity can exhibit unique characteristics not reflected in these examples.

actuarial smoothing techniques. Under FASB 87, an asset allocation policy will have new short-term implications for both the balance sheet and the income statement. In particular, FASB 87's requirement of mark-to-market liability valuation may produce substantial adverse fluctuations in both the pension surplus and pension expense.

To develop an effective asset-allocation policy under FASB 87, the sponsor must adopt an integrated approach in which the assets and liabilities are managed together, rather than separately, with the objective of controlling the interest rate sensitivity of surplus and the resulting balance sheet and expense volatilities. Toward this end, we recently introduced a conceptual framework termed "surplus management," that integrates the asset-allocation decision with a market-valued pension liability.[12] The integrating link between assets and liabilities is interest rate risk. The plan's interest rate risk is best measured by the effective duration of the pension surplus. The pension surplus can be thought of as a portfolio with a "long" position in pension assets and a "short" position in pension liabilities, from which the interest sensitivity of the surplus is readily determined. Of course, successful control of interest rate risk requires accurate measurement of the effective duration of pension assets and pension liabilities. With an integrated approach to surplus management, an asset-allocation strategy can be designed to manage the new balance sheet and expense volatilities introduced by FASB 87, as well as the traditional long-term risk and return objectives.

To apply these concepts in practice, plan sponsors must think through their objectives clearly. For example, the difference between the interest sensitivities of the ABO and PBO makes it impossible to hedge both simultaneously. Therefore, a sponsor concerned about managing its surplus must decide whether it is more important to control near-term balance sheet volatility by managing the interest sensitivity of the ABO, or to control longer-term volatility by managing the interest sensitivity of the PBO. When benefits are nominal and constant, the PBO's effective duration is longer than the ABO's; however, it may be difficult to construct an asset portfolio that has a sufficiently high duration to match the durations of either the ABO or PBO. Of course, a shortfall in duration on the asset side exposes the surplus to a loss (or gain) if interest rates fall (or rise). When benefits are salary related and interest sensitive, the effective duration of the PBO may be shorter than that of the ABO. In this case, the appropriate hedging strategy is to hold very long-term assets if the sponsor's priorities are

---

[12] See Martin L. Leibowitz, *Total Portfolio Duration: A New Perspective on Asset Allocation,* New York: Salomon Brothers Inc, February 1986 and "Liability Returns: A New Perspective on Asset Allocation," a previous article in this book, for an extended discussion of the effective duration of the pension sets, pension liabilities and the pension surplus.

short term, and hold relatively shorter-term assets if the sponsor's priorities are long term.

The objective of managing expense volatility introduces additional complexity. The pension expense under FASB 87 comprises several components, all with different interest sensitivities: service cost, changes in the PBO surplus ("actuarial gains and losses"), and interest on the surplus. Certain smoothing techniques are also permitted. The management of pension expense volatility is an important issue that is worthy of future research.

Chapter I-6

The Surge in Pension Fund Surplus

SUMMARY

The first eight months of 1987 have witnessed a large run-up in the equity markets and a substantial decline in the fixed-income markets. The combination of these two divergent market movements provides an ideal environment for nurturing pension fund surplus.[1] It is, therefore, reasonable to assume that most pension funds have experienced extraordinary growth in their surplus since year-end 1986. More important, this surge in pension fund surplus is occurring in an environment where, for the first time, true market-related measures of the funding ratio must be reported in corporate financial statements under Financial Accounting Standards Board (FASB) Statement 87.[2] For the Fortune 500 compa-

---

[1] See *Portfolio Managers' Weekly Research Summary*, Salomon Brothers Inc, September 7, 1987.

[2] As used in this report, funding ratio means the ratio of pension fund assets, measured at market value, to the accumulated benefit obligation (ABO), discounted at current market interest rates. The ABO is the actuarial present value of all benefits earned to date, approximating the liability on a plan termination basis.

Martin L. Leibowitz, Lawrence N. Bader, and Ardavan Nozari, "The Surge in Pension Fund Surplus: Strategies for the New Market Environment," Salomon Brothers Inc, September 1987.

nies, we estimate that the aggregate funding ratio has risen to 197% as of September 1, 1987. We believe that this visible jump in surpluses that have corporate wide significance is an important event in the evolution of pension fund management. Fund sponsors, who are now in control of unprecedented corporate wealth, will find themselves at a major crossroads in terms of the fund's ongoing objectives. On the one hand, they have gained the freedom to concentrate on the asset management of their funds with minimal near-term concerns about the FASB 87 pension expense and balance sheet hazards. On the other hand, they are responsible for a precious (and very visible) surplus that has become a major corporate asset in its own right. A corporate desire to protect this surplus, rather than to protect only the liabilities defined by FASB 87, will surely entail a major review of the current investment strategy, as well as a potential revision of the entire strategic decision-making process.

RECENT MARKET RETURNS

In an earlier report, we traced the effect of market returns and interest rate changes through the period from January 1, 1980 to December 31, 1986.[3] In this section, we update these results through the first eight months of 1987. Figure 1 shows the market returns in both the stock market, as measured by the S&P 500, and the bond market, as measured by the Salomon Brothers Broad Investment-Grade Bond Index[SM] and the Salomon Brothers Large Pension Fund Baseline Bond Index[SM]. Thus far, 1987 has clearly been an exceptional period, marked by both the remarkable return of the equity market and the significant decline in the fixed-income market.

Behavior in the fixed-income market is driven by interest rates, which have risen from their 1986 year-end lows by approximately 150 basis points, as shown in Figure 2. Figure 2 plots ten-year new A industrial rates as a reasonable proxy for the rates that must be used to discount pension liabilities under FASB 87. In the earlier report, these formed the basis for computing the liability values of a representative pension fund as a result of interest rate changes.

The 1987 upturn in rates has reduced these liability values and, hence, has led to a negative "liability return." In Figure 3, liability returns are shown for the period ranging from 1980 through the first eight months of 1987. As can be seen from Figure 3, this year has provided the lowest (most favorable) liability return of any year in this decade.

Figure 4 plots representative portfolio trends against liability returns for this entire time span. The portfolio is structured with an allocation policy of 60% in

---

[3] See *FASB 87-Equivalent Funding Ratios: Pension Surplus Trends, 1980-86,* Salomon Brothers Inc, March 1987.

Figure 1: Equity and Fixed-Income Returns, 1980-87

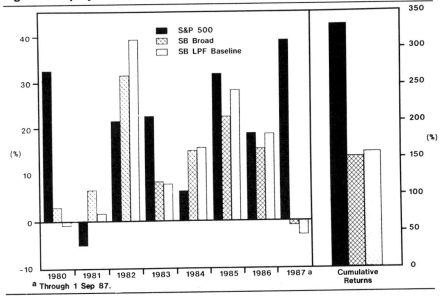

a Through 1 Sep 87.

Figure 2: Ten-Year New A Industrial Rates, 1980-87

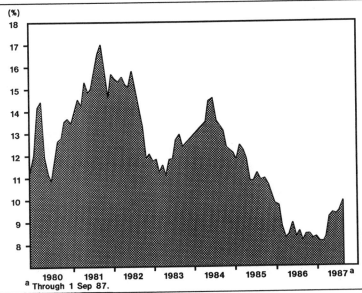

a Through 1 Sep 87.

Figure 3: Liability Returns, 1980-87

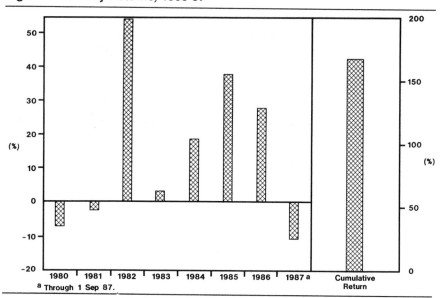

Figure 4: Portfolio and Liability Returns, 1980-87

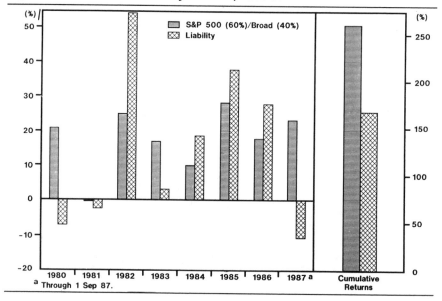

the S&P 500 and 40% in the Broad Index at the beginning of each year. The first eight months of 1987 are unlike all prior periods with the exception of 1980, both in terms of the magnitude of the portfolio and liability returns and the divergence between them.

UPDATING THE FORTUNE 500 FUNDING RATIO

In our prior study, cumulative liability returns and portfolio returns were very close over the seven-year period ending December 31, 1986. The recent eight-month period created a wide separation, however, with the cumulative asset returns now far exceeding the liability returns. To understand the effect of this occurrence on pension fund surplus, we have updated our earlier estimates of the pension funding ratios of the Fortune 500 companies.

In our earlier research, we took the data gathered by a Hewitt Associates study of asset/liability ratios for the Fortune 500 companies over the period 1980 through year-end 1985. We then plotted the aggregate values for the reported funding ratios as shown in Figure 5.

We have accepted the asset values as reported, but we have adjusted the liability values to reflect market-based discount rates, rather than the nonmarket

Figure 5: Funding Ratios 1980-87: Disclosed versus FASB 87-Equivalent

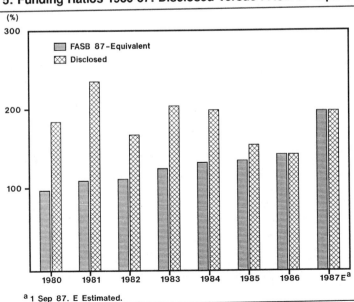

a 1 Sep. 87. E Estimated.

discount rates used under the pre-FASB 87 disclosure rules. The ten-year new A industrial series shown in Figure 2 was used for this purpose. Consequently, we have altered the reported funding ratios as shown in Figure 5. The 99% funding ratio reported in 1980 soared to 186% when restated as a "FASB 87-equivalent" ratio. This is because the liabilities were discounted for reporting purposes at an actuarial rate of 7.3%, while a market rate of 13.4% would have been called for had FASB 87 been in effect in 1980. The basic intent of our earlier report was to illustrate that, during the 1980s, the funding ratios behaved quite differently than had been perceived. The perception from the reported values was that funding ratios had, in aggregate, grown steadily and smoothly from about 100% to 145% by the end of 1986. In terms of FASB 87-equivalent ratios, however, the funding ratios have actually followed a highly erratic path and have deteriorated, although the perceived path and the actual path have converged as market rates declined and FASB 87 was implemented.

In other words, the sense of comfort in the stability and growth of funding ratios is unfounded. Corporate management has reason to be concerned about this unstable measure of pension fund health, which is vulnerable to significant changes under even normal market movements.

Figure 5 includes the estimated aggregate funding ratio for the Fortune 500 based upon market behavior through the first eight months of 1987. The current value of 197% is not the highest value achieved in recent history.[4] However, it is the first time that values of such magnitude have been made clearly *visible* through FASB 87-type reporting to corporate management and shareholders at large. It is this visibility that creates a major change in the pension fund situation.

UPDATING AN INDIVIDUAL CORPORATION'S FUNDING RATIO

The results shown in Figure 5 are for the Fortune 500 companies in total. The impact of market returns on funding ratios is very dependent on the specific characteristics of an individual fund. Therefore, large errors would be produced by extrapolating the implications for individual funds from the results for the aggregate Fortune 500, even in the brief eight-month span from the end of 1986. To help an individual corporation to estimate the value of its current funding ratio, we have developed the updating matrix shown in Figure 6. This matrix covers the range of year-end 1986 funding ratios from 80% through 300% for a wide range of asset allocations. The actual surplus change of an individual fund

---

[4] Like other estimates in this report, the 197% figure is based on the standard plan used in our earlier report, a 60/40 portfolio as used in Figure 4, and the assumption that contributions, benefit payments and accrual of new benefits have no net effect on funding ratios.

Figure 6: Funding Ratio Updating Matrix

Funding Ratio 12/31/86	Asset Allocation				
	60/40	Broad	S&P 500	Large Pension Fund Baseline	Targeted Index Matrix 50% 12 Year
80%	110%	89%	124%	87%	81%
90	124	100	140	98	91
100	138	111	156	109	101
110	152	122	171	120	111
120	165	133	187	130	121
130	179	144	202	141	131
140	193	155	218	152	142
*143	197	159	223	155	145
150	207	167	233	163	152
200	276	222	311	217	202
250	344	278	389	272	253
300	413	333	467	326	303

will depend on many circumstances not captured in this matrix approach, such as cash holdings, specific asset allocations among classes, individual security selections, timing of investment cash flows, and contributions. However, we believe that Figure 6 provides a useful guide to the behavior of funding ratios during 1987.

In our earlier report, the 1986 year-end aggregate funding ratio was estimated to be 143% for the Fortune 500. Using this value as a base, Figure 7 illustrates the computational process for deriving the new funding ratio of 197% for a 60/40 allocation. (This result corresponds to the row in Figure 6 that is denoted by the asterisk.)

Figure 6 also demonstrates that the funding ratio change varies widely with its starting value. The estimated aggregate funding ratio increased from 143% to 197%. A deficit fund, however, would have performed very differently. For example, a fund that started with an 80% funding ratio and was invested in a 60/40 portfolio would now be in surplus, with a funding ratio of roughly 110%, which is an increase of approximately 30 percentage points over the period. At the other extreme, a similarly invested fund that started with a 300% funding ratio would have grown to 413%, an increment of 113 percentage points. In fact, all of the funding ratios have a percentage increase of 38%, a figure related to the excess of the asset return over the liability return.

Figure 6 also shows results for other asset allocations, including 100% S&P, 100% Broad Index, 100% Large Pension Fund Baseline Index, and 100% in a

---

Figure 7: Updating the Funding Ratio, 31 Dec 86-1 Sep 87

---

31 Dec 86		
Assets = 143	Liability = 100 Funding Ratio = 143%	

1 Jan 86 - 1 Sep 87
S&P Return = 38.90%
Broad Return = -0.86%
Liability Return = -10.73%

31 Dec 86 Assets in S&P:	60% × 143 = 85.80
1 Sep 87 Assets in S&P:	85.80 × (1 + 0.3890) = 119.18

31 Dec 86 Assets in Broad Index:	40% × 143 = 57.20
1 Sep 87 Assets in Broad Index:	57.20 × (1 - 0.0086) = 56.71
1 Sep 87 Assets	175.89

1 Sep 87 Liability =	100 × (1 - 0.1073) = 89.27

1 Sep 87 Funding Ratio =	$\dfrac{\text{1 Sep 87 Assets}}{\text{1 Sep 87 Liability}} = \dfrac{175.89}{89.27} = 197\%$

12-Year Duration Bond Index Fund. The latter results are derived from the recently introduced Targeted Index Matrix^{SM}, which allows for selections of various durations and percentages of a corporate/mortgage core portfolio while following the basic structured disciplines of an index tracking approach.[5] In this particular case, the 12-year duration portfolio comprises 50% long-duration Treasury bonds and a 50% core of the corporate and mortgage security sectors of the Broad Index universe.

This 12-year index had a return over the first eight months of 1987 of -9.72%, which is relatively close to the liability return of -10.73% that was computed for 1987 to date. Because the asset return for such a portfolio approximates the liability return, the funding ratios are virtually unchanged. Thus, the 12-year duration index approximates a "matched duration" strategy for "immunizing" the pension liability.

CHANGING RISK TOLERANCE WITH HIGHER FUNDING RATIOS

Both in theory and in practice, a major factor in determining asset allocations is the tolerance for risk that a pension fund sponsor has at a given time. In certain

---

[5] See *Introducing the Salomon Brothers Targeted Index Matrix^{SM}: A Family of Generalized Bond Indexes for Quality/Duration Customization*, Salomon Brothers Inc, August 1987.

Figure 8: Changing Risk Tolerance at Different Funding Ratios

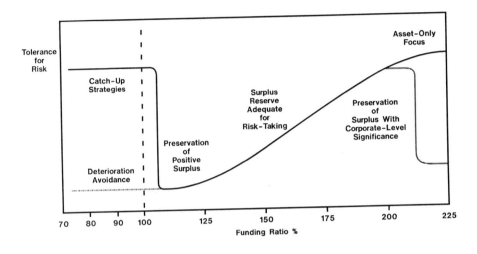

circumstances, risk tolerance is related to the trade-off between shorter- and longer-term considerations. With a high risk tolerance, an investor will be able to seek a maximum long-term return, while being able to accept whatever interim market fluctuations take place. Investors with low risk tolerance may forgo even relatively assured long-term returns if they are accompanied by high doses of interim uncertainty.

Although there are well-developed mathematical theories about how investors should behave in terms of risk tolerance, in practice patterns are very diverse. In particular, for pension funds, we have tried to portray some of these behaviors in the schematic diagram shown in Figure 8. This diagram attempts to plot tolerance for risk as a function of increased funding ratios.

- At funding ratios below 100%, which place the fund in a deficit condition, there are two basic modes of balancing the trade-offs between risk—the danger of having the deficit worsen—and reward—the prospect of moving toward a more fully funded position. One group of plan sponsors, while cognizant of the risk, might be more interested in reaching full funding than in protecting their current position; consequently, they would follow an aggressive strategy characterized by a high risk tolerance. Another group might be more concerned that a worsening deficit would have disastrous balance sheet and investor relations consequences. These sponsors would show very low risk tolerance, subordinating the objective of reaching full funding to the need to protect their current position.

- At funding ratios of 100% or slightly higher, most sponsors would tend to show low risk tolerance, with the fear of falling into a deficit position overshadowing the desire to fatten the cushion. Most sponsors would be highly adverse to reporting a deficit in their financial statements, as FASB 87 requires beginning in 1989.

- As funding ratios increase to 120% and beyond, the margin for risk taking becomes larger and sponsors are freer to seek high returns with less fear of a deficit. Some will wish to concentrate solely on the asset side to maximize the return of the fund, aside from any liability framework. Ratios moving toward 150% offer an environment in which sponsors can gain substantial theoretical and practical freedom to do so.

- Another important level, typically in the 140%-150% range, is reached when the plan is funded well enough so that no contributions are required by the funding standards of the Employee Retirement Income Security Act of 1974. Plan sponsors below this level may aggressively seek to reach it; those who have reached it may aggressively seek to increase the surplus to a level that extends their prospective "contribution holiday" to five years or so.

- Some plan sponsors may maintain a risky stance through higher and higher funding levels, as many models of investor behavior postulate. When the funding ratio has reached a high enough level, however, perhaps 175%-200% for a mature company, the plan sponsor has met all of the basic objectives for funding. At such time, the company has the prospect of not having to contribute to the plan for the indefinite future, even allowing for modest plan improvements, such as cost-of-living increases for retirees. Apart from cashing in on its surplus through a plan termination, the company has little tangible benefit to be gained by further surplus growth. At this point the sponsor may view the rewards of extending the surplus as minimal (or possibly even negative). The sponsor's risk tolerance may, therefore, drop to an extremely low level, as the goal becomes to avoid losing the prize that has already been won.

This position may be viewed as a change in the structure of the liability framework: The floor level of assets to be protected has been raised from the accumulated benefit obligation (ABO) to some level of surplus near the existing one. One can readily see what such an orientation might do to the risk tolerance.

Figure 8 portrays the shift in risk tolerance that may occur if it becomes important to preserve a specific funding ratio as a precious store of value for the corporation. A dramatic fall in the tolerance for risk is depicted as occurring at about a 200% funding ratio. This low risk tolerance could be sustained for quite some time and across a wide range of even higher funding ratios. Such a radical decline in risk tolerance would occasion a complete rethinking of asset allocation procedures.

PROJECTING FUNDING RATIOS FOR INDIVIDUAL CORPORATIONS

In evaluating the current risk tolerance of a plan sponsor, it is useful to examine the variability in funding ratios that might occur during the remainder of 1987. For the single case of a 60/40 allocation, Figure 9 portrays the funding ratios that would appear at year-end 1987 under four different market scenarios.

The first column in Figure 9 enables a fund to fix its position based on its estimated funding ratio as of September 1, 1987. The four arbitrarily chosen sce-

Figure 9: Surplus Projections for Year-End 1987, 60% S&P 500/40% Broad Index

Funding Ratio 1 Sep 87	Market Scenario			
	S&P 500: -15% Interest Rate: - 150 bp	-15% +150 bp	+15% -150 bp	+15% +150 bp
80%	63%	80%	75%	96%
90	71	90	85	107
100	79	99	94	119
110	87	109	103	131
120	95	119	113	143
130	103	129	122	155
140	111	139	132	167
150	119	149	141	179
*197	156	196	185	235
200	158	199	188	239
250	198	249	235	299
300	237	298	282	358

Note: Percentages reflect changes in the S&P 500; basis points reflect changes in the Broad Index.

narios are combinations of ±15% S&P returns and ±150 basis point parallel moves in the fixed-income markets. For each of these scenarios, the returns on the 60/40 asset portfolio and the associated liability returns were determined and the corresponding funding ratio changes were computed. Although the market scenarios selected were limited, it is interesting to observe that two of the scenarios produce very minor changes in the funding ratio. A deterioration of -15% in the S&P 500 is almost *exactly* offset by a 150-basis-point rise in interest rates. Similar stability in the funding ratios is witnessed if a 15% surge in the S&P is accompanied by a 150-basis-point drop in rates. The substantial movements in funding ratios occur when both equity market and interest rates fall or rise in tandem. The former case, with both assets and liabilities moving against the plan, obviously represents the situation of a deteriorating funding ratio and the magnitude of the deteriorations is quite surprising.

As can be seen from the second column in Figure 9, the 197% funding ratio would decline to 156% under the quite reasonable market moves shown. With higher funding ratios, because of the leverage effect, there would be an even greater decline under the scenario represented in the first column. Thus, for example, a 300% level funding ratio would fall by over 60 percentage points to 237%, given a 15% S&P 500 falloff and a 150-basis-point downward rate movement.

CONCLUSION

The mathematics of the situation is not new. What is new, however, is the increased visibility of market-valued liabilities, assets and funding ratios in the corporate world. In addition, the sheer growth in the size of pension funds has made these funding ratios significant in terms of surplus dollars. For many corporations, the pension fund is not merely comparable to an important division in the overall corporate framework; rather, it may be the largest such division, and the pension surplus may even exceed the net worth of the company as a whole. With such surplus magnitudes especially in a much more visible framework, there may be radical departures in the way that corporations view the management of these funds.

Like a major division of the company, a pension fund cannot simply be run in the same fashion year after year, while its surplus (or net worth) moves up and down through an extraordinary range. Risk profiles must be reassessed in the light of what a surplus at various levels means to the plan and the plan sponsor. For many funds, this reassessment will lead to profound changes in the conceptual foundation underlying the asset allocation process.

Chapter I-7

Portfolio Optimization within a Surplus Framework

Portfolio optimization aims to achieve the asset mix that offers the highest expected return at a given level of risk. This process eliminates sources of portfolio risk that do not provide an expected return premium for investors.

Portfolio optimization can also be applied to the asset allocation decision when the investor has both assets and liabilities. The liabilities can be treated as a short position within the overall portfolio. Return and risk are then measured in terms of changes in the surplus of the asset value over the liability value. In this surplus framework, the optimal asset mix may differ drastically from the mix that is optimal when assets only are considered.

One dimension of the riskiness of pension liabilities is their sensitivity to interest rates. This source of risk can be neutralized by creating an "immunized bond fund" that precisely funds the liabilities. This immunized fund takes the place of cash as the riskless asset. Cash, with zero duration, cannot offset changes in liability values resulting from interest rate changes and carries a high surplus risk. The addition of equities to the immunized fund, however, increases portfolio expected return and risk, just as the addition of equities to an all-cash portfolio does in the assets-only framework.

Furthermore, in the surplus framework, bonds with durations longer than the liability duration represent substantial diversification potential when the effective duration of equities is less than that of the liabilities. Their value will tend to rise by more than the

Martin L. Leibowitz and Roy D. Henricksson, "Portfolio Optimization Within a Surplus Framework," *Financial Analysts Journal*, March/April 1988. Reprinted with permission.

liability value when interest rates decline, potentially creating surplus growth; short-du-
ration bonds, cash and most equities will tend to generate surplus losses under this
condition. In effect, such bonds are negatively correlated with equity; they may be used
in conjunction with an equity/immunized fund mix to achieve the highest expected re-
turn at a given risk level.

In practice, the asset allocation decision may be much more complex. It will require
a more detailed and expanded set of potential assets. It may be necessary to incorporate
other dimensions of risk for liabilities. Investors may have multiple objectives. However,
even with these added complications, portfolio optimization can still be a valuable tool in
the asset allocation decision.

An investor's asset allocation decision is typically examined from the perspective of risk/return tradeoff. Achieving a higher expected return usually requires bearing a higher level of risk, where risk is generally measured as the
standard deviation of the portfolio return. The portfolio optimization process
can be thought of as maximizing the expected return of a portfolio, subject to a
risk constraint.

The optimization process traditionally has focused on asset returns. In many
cases, however, an asset portfolio is meant to fund a specified liability schedule.
The appropriate "portfolio" for optimization in this case should comprise both
assets and liabilities, with the focus on the surplus—the difference between the
market value of the assets and the present value of the liabilities. It then becomes necessary to take into account both the asset and liability returns, where
liabilities act as a fixed short position.

Optimization from a surplus perspective can result in a solution that differs
radically from the solution that would emerge from an asset-only perspective.
The inclusion of liabilities, for example, can dramatically change the relevant
risk characteristics of different asset classes. An asset such as cash, which would
typically reduce the riskiness of an all-asset portfolio, may actually increase the
riskiness of a portfolio that includes liabilities. Thus the optimal asset mix
within a surplus framework may differ drastically from the optimal assets-only
mix. With the appropriate adjustments, however, many of the procedures developed in the traditional assets-only framework can be carried over to the surplus
framework.

This article demonstrates that traditional asset allocation tools can be
adapted to a surplus framework. This is demonstrated using a relatively simplistic formulation for purposes of clarity. However, realistic applications require (1)
a more detailed and expanded investment universe, (2) a recognition that the
appropriate modeling of liabilities may involve several risk dimensions and (3) a
realization that investors may have multiple objectives that must be considered
as part of the asset allocation decision.

TRADITIONAL ASSET OPTIMIZATION

Traditional portfolio optimization considers only assets and focuses on the risk/return tradeoff. Generally, it is necessary to bear more risk to achieve a higher expected return. Conversely, one must accept a lower expected return in order to reduce risk. An exception to this stricture is provided, however, by portfolio diversification.

By combining assets in a portfolio, some of the riskiness of an individual asset is counterbalanced by the variability associated with another asset. This occurs because different asset values do not always change in a similar manner; sometimes the return from one asset will be positive when the return from another asset is negative. This counterbalancing means that the variability of a portfolio will be less than the weighted sum of the variabilities of its individual assets. At the same time, however, the counterbalancing will not affect the portfolio's expected return, which will still be the weighted sum of the individual assets' expected returns.

The reduction in risk afforded by a two-asset portfolio depends on the degree of comovement between the two assets. If the asset values always change together in the same manner, they are perfectly (positively) correlated. If they usually move together, they will be positively correlated. If there is no relation between the two value changes, they will have zero correlation. If the value changes tend to be in opposite directions, they will have negative correlation.

With perfect (positive) correlation, it is not possible to achieve risk reduction without also lowering the expected return of the portfolio. The potential benefits from diversification increase as correlation decreases; potential risk reduction is the greatest when correlation is negative.

The optimization process provides a two-stage technique for determining the optimal asset mix. The first stage achieves the maximum risk reduction through diversification for a feasible expected return. The second stage incorporates the investor's attitude toward risk to choose the optimal expected return/standard deviation tradeoff.

The basic principles of asset-only risk/return optimization can be demonstrated by the use of two risky assets—equities and bonds—and a riskless asset—cash. Figure A illustrates a hypothetical tradeoff between expected return and the standard deviation of returns for the three assets. In the example, bonds and cash are assumed to have the same expected return, and equities are assumed to have a higher expected return and a higher standard deviation.

Figure B presents the risk/return tradeoffs available from portfolios comprising different combinations of these assets. The tradeoff between equities and bonds reflects the influence of diversification. In the example, adding equity to a portfolio that is originally 100% bonds will initially increase the expected return of the portfolio and reduce its riskiness. Beyond a certain proportion of equities,

Figure A: The Basic Risk-Return Tradeoff

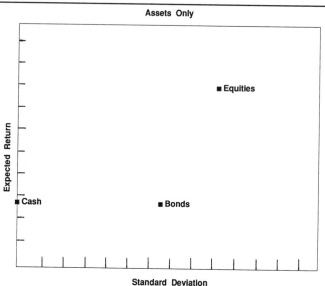

Assets Only

however, the riskiness of the portfolio will begin to rise, as will its expected return.

By adding a small amount of equities to the all-bond portfolio, we introduce a new asset that has a low correlation with the existing portfolio. The potential risk reduction from diversification is high when the correlation is low. As we add more equities, however, the portfolio becomes more of a stock portfolio; its correlation with equities rises. Further increases in the portfolio's equity percentage will have less and less ability to reduce risk and, beyond a certain point, will in fact increase risk.

We must also consider the role of cash. Because cash is assumed to be riskless, it is a powerful risk-reducer in any portfolio mixture. The greater the amount of cash in the portfolio, the lower the risk of the portfolio. Moreover, adding cash to any portfolio mix will reduce its standard deviation in direct proportion to the cash percentage. Thus the sequence of mixtures of cash with any given portfolio will plot as a straight line in the risk/return diagram.

In our example, bonds and cash provide the same expected return, yet cash is the more efficient risk reducer. It is thus hardly surprising that the best trade-off between expected return and risk will be achieved through a portfolio comprising only equities and cash. There will never be any bonds in the optimal solution to the simple example presented in Figure B.

Figure B: The Cash/Equity Line of Optimal Mixes

Assets Only

THE SIMPLISTIC MODEL OF A FLAT YIELD CURVE

The fixed-income market provides an unusually wide spectrum of potential investment opportunities. To examine the full role of bonds across this entire spectrum, it is helpful to start with the ultimate degree of simplification—the "flat yield curve" model.

In Figure C, bond portfolios of increasing duration—2.5, 5.0 and 7.5—are depicted along a flat yield curve. The duration measure is a gauge of price sensitivity to interest rate changes. A bond portfolio with a duration of 5.0 will increase in price by approximately 5% in response to a 1% decline in yield. If we extend our simplified view of the bond market to assume that the flat yield curve moves only in a parallel fashion, then a bond's standard deviation risk will be proportional to its duration (see Figure D). In this case, all bonds are perfectly correlated with one another. Moreover, if we further assume that the expected yield change is zero, then all bonds will have the same *expected* return.

Now consider optimal mixtures when this entire range of duration values is available for the bond component. However, by assumption, these points along the flat yield curve are all perfectly correlated with one another. The key assumption thus becomes the nature of their correlation with equities.

Figure C: The Flat Yield Curve

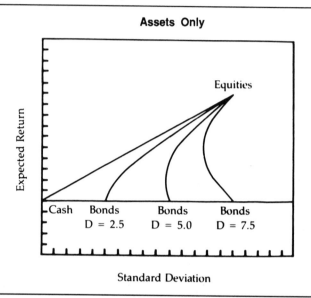

Assets Only

Figure D: Duration and the Riskiness of Bonds

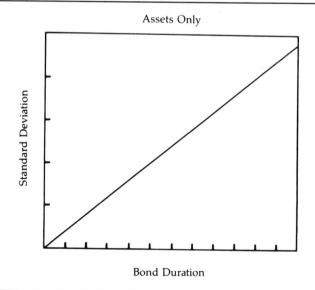

Figure C demonstrates the optimal strategy for combining the risky assets if bond returns and equity returns are assumed to be positively correlated. In this case, an investor can always achieve a lower level of risk for the same expected return by substituting cash for bonds. Cash still provides greater risk reduction than bonds and has the same impact on expected returns (because of the flat yield curve assumptions). This will prove true regardless of the duration of the bond. Thus, even with the entire range of duration values available, bonds will never be part of the optimal portfolio. This multi-asset problem reduces to a two-asset solution as long as stocks and bonds are positively correlated and bonds do not offer a higher expected return than cash.

THE NEGATIVE CORRELATION CASE

Most allocation studies do in fact assume that stocks and bonds have a positive correlation, usually in the range of 0.3 to 0.4. This is tantamount to stating that stocks, like bonds, tend to exhibit positive returns when interest rates decline. This interest-rate sensitivity of equities corresponds to a duration value of 2 to 6, depending on the relative volatility estimates for stocks and bonds. This wide range reflects the statistical nature of the equity duration concept, in contrast to the bond duration value, which is a more analytical, hence a more reliable, gauge of interest-rate sensitivity. Nevertheless, if stocks and bonds are positively correlated, both will have a positive duration and tend to reinforce each other's exposure to interest rate risk. For this reason, cash, which is uncorrelated with equities, will once again provide a more efficient diversification mechanism than any bond portfolios along the flat yield curve.

But what if stocks tend to respond in the opposite direction to bond movement—that is, if stock prices tend to fall with declining interest rates? Despite historical evidence, this theory is not farfetched. In fact, it closely corresponds to an earlier "classical" view of stocks as a levered inflation hedge. Our purpose is not to argue one theory or the other, however, but simply to illustrate the intriguing behavior of two negatively correlated assets.

The influence of correlation on portfolio risk can be seen in Figure E. For the same asset mix, portfolio risk will always be less when the correlation is negative than when it is positive. The two trivial exceptions are when the portfolio is either 100% stocks or 100% bonds. Of course, no benefits can be derived from diversification if only one asset is held.

As discussed, in a world of flat yield curves, it would be desirable to hold bonds in a portfolio only if they offered greater potential for risk reduction than cash. This will be the case only if equities and bonds are negatively correlated. This is demonstrated in Figure F, in which some combination of equities and bonds results in a more favorable tradeoff between portfolio expected return and risk than can be achieved by combining only equities and cash. An investor

Figure E: Diversification Through Negative Correlation

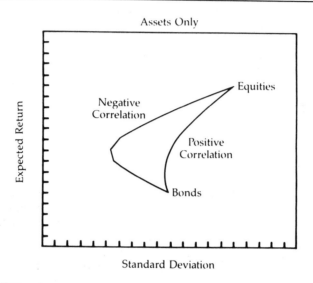

Assets Only

Standard Deviation

Figure F: The New Frontier with Negative Correlation

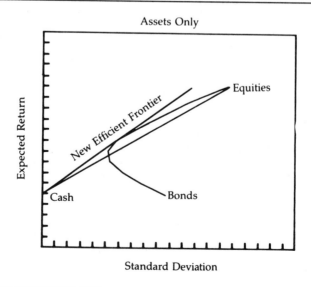

Assets Only

Standard Deviation

is able to realize a lower level of risk for the same expected return, because combining the negatively correlated equities and bonds in a portfolio has allowed the investor to neutralize or reduce overall portfolio risk. This negative correlation creates a particularly valuable opportunity for reaping the benefits of diversification.

THE SURPLUS FRAMEWORK

The same approach can be carried over to the surplus framework, in which asset returns are transformed into their returns (or changes in value) relative to the changes in value of the relevant liabilities. In this framework, the relevant portfolio is expanded to include both assets and liabilities. The liabilities do not really differ from an asset in which the investor is required to have a prespecified short position. The size of the short position (the negative weight) will be the present value of the liabilities.

Liability returns are calculated from value changes, just as they would be for any asset.[1] Returns and riskiness can then be measured with respect to changes in the asset-liability surplus. Figure G shows a hypothetical risk/return tradeoff for individual assets; for simplicity, we have assumed that all of the variation in liability value can be explained by changes in interest rates. In this spirit, it is also assumed that the investor can create an "immunized bond fund" that precisely funds the liabilities.

In this new framework, the immunized fund becomes the riskless asset, while cash may carry a high level of surplus risk—perhaps even greater than that of equities.

These seemingly paradoxical relations between cash, bonds and immunized funds can be clarified as follows: Figure H shows the duration gap—the asset duration minus the liability duration—for bond funds of varying duration values. By our assumption, variation in bond returns and in the liabilities are driven solely by interest rates. Hence the surplus risk of a bond fund is proportional to its duration gap. Figure I plots this surplus risk—the standard deviation of surplus changes—across the range of bond funds.

Cash—with zero duration—does nothing to offset the interest rate risk of the liabilities. If we assume that the liabilities have a duration of 12, an all-cash portfolio entails a significant duration gap of -12 and a correspondingly high level of surplus risk. As one moves toward bonds with larger duration values, however, the (negative) duration gap shrinks and the surplus risk declines. This continues until one obtains a bond fund duration that equals the liability dura-

---

[1] See M.L. Leibowitz, "Liability Returns: A New Perspective on Asset Allocation" (Salomon Brothers Inc, May 1986).

Figure G: Risk-Return Tradeoffs in a Surplus Framework

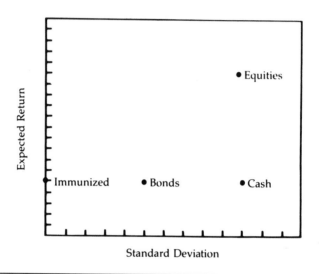

Figure H: Duration Gap with Assets Over Liabilities

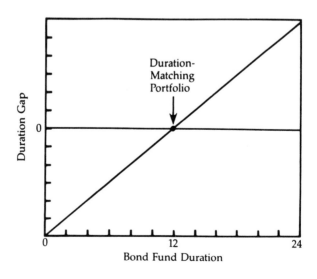

Figure I: Surplus Versus Bond Portfolio Duration

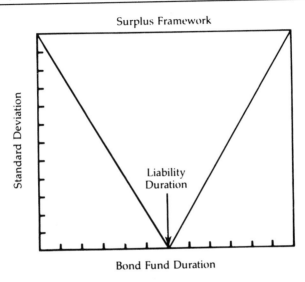

Surplus Framework

Standard Deviation

Liability
Duration

Bond Fund Duration

tion. At this point, the duration gap is zero, the surplus risk vanishes, and the surplus is "immunized." By moving beyond the point of immunization into longer-duration bonds, one encounters larger (but now positive) duration gaps and increasing levels of surplus risk.

Figure J presents the risk/return tradeoffs available from portfolios comprising different combinations of assets. As the immunized fund has now become the riskless asset, there is a linear tradeoff between the expected returns and standard deviations for portfolios comprising some combination of the immunized fund and the risky assets. Thus the immunized fund now fulfills the role that cash had in the asset-only case: The greater the amount of the immunized fund in the portfolio, the lower the risk of the portfolio from a surplus perspective.

The risk/return tradeoffs shown in Figure J assume that the correlations between equities, bonds and cash are positive. This will be the case as long as the effective durations of equities, bonds and cash are all less than or all greater than the effective duration of the liabilities. Figure J demonstrates that there will be no demand for bonds or cash if they are positively correlated with equities and do not offer a higher expected return than the immunized fund. The optimal portfolio in such a surplus framework will be some combination of the immunized fund and equities.

Figure J: Positive Correlation Within the Surplus Framework

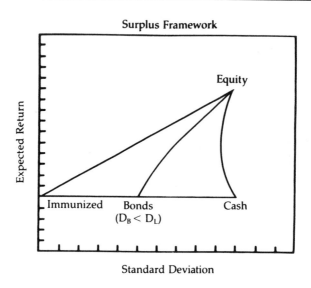

Surplus Framework

(Expected Return vs. Standard Deviation; curve from Immunized through Bonds ($D_B < D_L$) and Cash to Equity)

Standard Deviation

NEGATIVE CORRELATION AND THE EFFICIENT FRONTIER

For a typical pension fund, the effective duration of equities and cash will almost always be less than the duration of the liabilities.[2] It will often be possible, however, to construct a bond portfolio that will have a higher duration than the liabilities. This long-duration portfolio will rise by more than the liability value when rates decline, resulting in surplus growth. This behavior contrasts with that of shorter-duration bonds and cash, which will generate surplus losses under interest rate declines. Because of the low duration of equities, they too will tend to produce losses when interest rates drop. Thus long-duration bond portfolios would affect surplus in a way opposite to that of cash or equities.

In this framework, such long-bond portfolios and equities are *negatively correlated* with respect to their impact on surplus values. Negative correlations provide an excellent opportunity for significant diversification benefits. The potential benefit from the negative correlation between stocks and bonds—

---

[2] See M.L. Leibowitz, "Surplus Management: A New Perspective on Asset Allocation" (Salomon Brothers Inc, September 1986).

Figure K: Negative Correlation Within the Surplus Framework

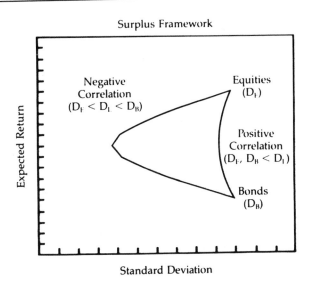

Surplus Framework

(y-axis) Expected Return

Negative
Correlation
($D_E < D_L < D_B$)

Equities
(D_E)

Positive
Correlation
($D_E, D_B < D_L$)

Bonds
(D_B)

Standard Deviation

achievable when the duration of the bonds exceeds the duration of the liabilities—is illustrated in Figure K.

Moreover, it can be demonstrated that negative correlation results in portfolio mixes that lie above the equity/immunized fund line (see Figure L). Such portfolios provide greater return, at the same risk level, than the corresponding equity/immunized fund mix. The equity/immunized fund line served as the "efficient frontier" of optimal portfolios in the case of positively correlated assets. As negatively correlated long-bond/equity mixes lie above this line, however, it clearly no longer defines the efficient frontier.

The immunized fund has zero risk in the surplus framework. Hence varying mixtures of the immunized fund with any given portfolio will trace out a straight line in the surplus risk/return diagram. Figure L shows the immunized line that is tangent to the curve representing mixtures of equity and a (negatively correlated) long-bond portfolio. This tangent line would appear to be a potential candidate for the new efficient frontier.

The portfolio mix at the tangent point can be shown to have an effective duration that just matches the effective duration of the liabilities. This portfolio mix is similar to the immunized fund in that it removes interest rate risk. It differs from the immunized fund, however, in containing a certain proportion of

Figure L: The Duration-Matching Mixture of Equities and Long Bonds

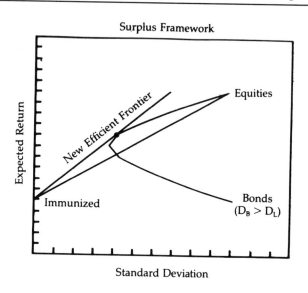

equities. Thus it has a higher expected return, as well as a risk component quite apart from interest rate volatility.

For any given equity percentage, one can theoretically find bonds of sufficiently long durations to match exactly the effective duration of the liabilities.[3] This will result in the elimination of interest rate risk with no loss in expected return. This risk reduction can be achieved as shown in Figure M. In this simplistic case, the optimal risk reduction is accomplished by matching the total portfolio duration of the assets to that of the liabilities.

Figure M shows optimal duration-matching portfolios for three different equity percentages, using long-bond portfolios of increasing duration. From the diagram, it appears as if all three optimal portfolios lie on the same tangent line. One can in fact demonstrate that the envelope of all such duration-matching portfolios does plot along a single line. Moreover, this tangent line turns out to be the new efficient frontier of optimal mixes.

---

[3] See M.L. Leibowitz, "Total Portfolio Duration: A New Perspective on Asset Allocation," *Financial Analysts Journal*, September/October 1986.

Figure M: The New Efficient Frontier of Duration-Matching Portfolios

---

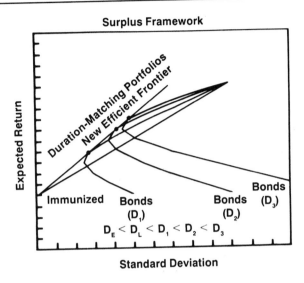

DURATION-MATCHING PORTFOLIOS

The negative correlation between stocks and bonds in the surplus framework leads to a potential three-asset solution. Even in this situation, however, the solution really consists of only two components—the desired amount of equity exposure and the duration matching of assets and liabilities. In our simplified example, investors receive no reward in the form of a higher expected return for bearing interest rate risk. It is, therefore, optimal to hold a portfolio of equities, bonds and the immunized fund that has an effective duration exactly matching that of the liabilities, eliminating the interest rate exposure of the portfolio. Because equities usually have a lower effective duration than the liabilities, the greater the equity proportion of the portfolio, the greater the required duration of the remaining combined position in bonds and the immunized fund (see Table I).

If an investor wants to have 25% of the portfolio's assets in equities, the combined effective duration of the bonds and immunized fund will have to be 15 for the duration of the assets to match the duration of the liabilities. This can be accomplished by holding 18.75% bonds with a duration of 24 and 56.25% immunized fund. Of course, it could also be achieved by holding 75% bonds with a duration of 15, or by many other possible combinations.

**Table I: Duration Matching in a Surplus Framework
(initial asset value = 100; initial liability value = 100)**

	Effective Duration	Portfolio Weights	
		Portfolio 1	Portfolio 2
Liability	12	-100	-100
Equities	3	25%	50%
Long Bonds	24	18.75	37.50
Immunized Fund	12	56.25	12.50
Combined Duration of Long Bonds and Immunized Fund		15	21
Combined Duration of Assets		12	12

If an investor wants to have 50% of the portfolio's assets in equities, the combined duration for bonds and the immunized fund will have to be 21. This can be accomplished by holding 37.50% bonds with a duration of 24 and 12.50% immunized fund. It could also be accomplished by holding 50% bonds with a duration of 21, or by many other possible combinations.

The duration-matching process reduces portfolio risk with no loss in expected return. Many fixed-income combinations can accomplish the duration matching. In practice, an investor would want to choose the cheapest and most liquid combination. This is just another example of seeking the highest expected return for a given level of risk.

Duration matching is the optimal strategy in the example because an investor does not receive a higher expected return for bearing interest rate risk, and investors will always want to eliminate any uncompensated sources of risk from the portfolio. An investor will be willing to bear interest rate risk only if it provides the opportunity to increase the portfolio's expected return. For example, if an investor expects yields to increase, it may be desirable to hold assets with a total portfolio duration less than the duration of liabilities, because this will increase the expected return of the surplus. The optimal portfolio would depend on the desired tradeoff between portfolio expected return and portfolio risk.

In the same spirit, equities offer an opportunity to increase the expected return—and the riskiness—of the portfolio. The duration-matching process counters the portion of equity/liability risk that is caused by interest rate changes. Investors must bear the remaining risk to obtain higher expected returns.

APPLICATION IN PRACTICE

We have adopted a relatively simplistic surplus formulation for illustrative purposes. Realistic applications would require a much more detailed representation of the various asset classes. This would mean going well beyond our simple flat yield curve characterization for the entire fixed-income market. One would also want to consider other available asset classes, such as international equity, international fixed income and real estate. In practice, the typical surplus problem may have several critical liability dimensions that require a far more intricate risk formulation. In addition, there may be a number of other important considerations that must be factored into the solution process—multiple benchmarks, inflation effects, short-term versus long-term horizons. This may call for the use of nonstandard combinations of optimization and simulation to shape a comprehensive allocation policy. The optimal solution in such practical situations may differ considerably from the solutions described above.

For pension funds, the surplus framework permits one to examine the new Financial Accounting Standards Board (FASB) Statement 87 accounting factor in a familiar return/risk context. While much recent work has focused on the implications of FASB 87, the applicability of the surplus approach extends far beyond FASB 87. Indeed, most investment funds are motivated by the need to serve some liability, whether or not it is explicitly defined. In principle, the surplus optimization approach can be extended to institutions such as thrifts, insurance companies, property/casualty companies, and endowment and foundation funds. The surplus framework can also be applied to certain managed funds in which performance is determined relative to a well-defined benchmark index.

Indeed, the surplus framework is a more general formulation than the assets-only framework. It can be viewed as the asset case expanded to allow for short positions. The surplus structure then takes on the character of a general arbitrage framework. From this vantage point, the asset-only situation can be construed as a relatively narrow special case in which the liability is defined as a zero payout. The surplus framework thus leads to a broader and more flexible characterization of the optimal asset allocation problem for a variety of institutional applications.

Chapter I-8

Portfolio Optimization under Shortfall Constraints

The portfolio optimization process determines the set of portfolios that achieve the highest expected returns at given risk levels. In this context, risk is usually measured by the standard deviation of the portfolio's returns. But many problems associated with return dispersion can be expressed in terms of a shortfall constraint—the minimum return that must be exceeded with a given probability. This "confidence limit" approach may provide a more meaningful description of risk for many investment situations.

Consider investors who are judged relative to a benchmark portfolio, such as an index or basket of indexes. The return and risk characteristics of potential investment portfolios and the benchmark portfolio can be used to determine a distribution of deviations from the benchmark. The portfolio optimization process can then be limited to portfolios that have a given probability (e.g., 95%) of not underperforming the benchmark by more than a specified amount (e.g., 5%). Constrained optimization may be especially helpful for investors who are subject to multiple, and potentially conflicting, objectives.

Martin L. Leibowitz and Roy D. Henriksson, "Portfolio Optimization with Shortfall Constraints: A Confidence-Limit Approach to Maintaining Downside Risk," *Financial Analysts Journal*, March/April 1989. Reprinted with permission.

The portfolio optimization process focuses on the tradeoff between expected return and standard deviation. The hypothetical efficient frontier comprises the set of portfolios with the highest achievable expected returns for given standard deviations. Such portfolios thus represent the best possible tradeoffs between expected return and standard deviation; to achieve a higher expected return, an investor would have to accept a higher standard deviation.

The standard deviation is a measure of the dispersion of a distribution—in this case, the distribution of portfolio returns. Figure A illustrates the normal distribution of returns for a portfolio with an expected return of 8% and a standard deviation of 10%. One-half the potential outcomes will be greater than the expected value (8%) and one-half will be less than the expected value.

Approximately 68% of the potential outcomes will be within one standard deviation of the mean value (8%) and approximately 95% of the potential outcomes will be within two standard deviations. The realized return will be between -2% and +18% (plus or minus one standard deviation) approximately 68% of the time and between -12% and +28% (plus or minus two standard deviations) approximately 95% of the time.

AN ALTERNATIVE RISK MEASURE

A normal distribution is completely specified by its mean and standard deviation; a normal distribution is symmetric around the mean, with the probability of any particular outcome being a decreasing function of the deviation from the mean value. A normal distribution can also be completely specified by its expected value and the probability that a specified minimum return level will be exceeded. The distribution shown in Figure A, with an expected return of 8% and a standard deviation of 10%, can also be described as having an expected return of 8% with a 78.81% probability of exceeding a 0% return (see the appendix).

This approach can be extended to a more general "shortfall constraint"—a minimum return that will be exceeded with some specified probability. For example, for the portfolio with an expected return and standard deviation of 8% and 10%, respectively, only 10% of the distribution represents returns that fall below the expected 8% return by more than 1.282 standard deviations, or 12.82%. The -4.82% return (8% minus 12.82%) represents the 90% threshold for this portfolio (see Figure B).

For the same distribution, a return of -8.45% will be exceeded with 95% probability. Only 5% of the distribution is more than 1.645 standard deviations below the expected return. This minimum return can be thought of as a confidence limit—the return that will be exceeded with 95% confidence.

Figure A: Normal Distribution of Returns

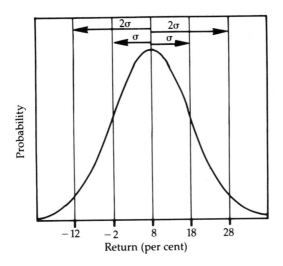

Figure B: A 90% Confidence Limit

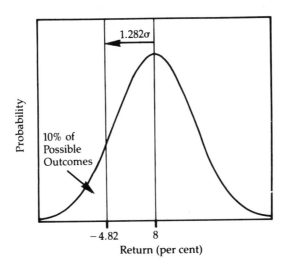

SHORTFALL CONSTRAINTS IN RISK-RETURN DIAGRAMS

How can the concept of a shortfall constraint be carried over to the universe of all possible portfolios, each having its own distinct return distribution? If we continue to assume that portfolio return distributions are normal, then we can use a simple formula for identifying portfolios that satisfy a given confidence limit.

As noted earlier, any normal distribution with expected return, $\overline{R}_P$, and standard deviation, σ_P, has only a 10% probability of an outcome that falls more than 1.282 standard deviations (1.282σ) below $\overline{R}_P$. Therefore, for each ($\overline{R}_P$, σ_P) portfolio, there is a 90% probability that return will exceed the value of R_P – 1.282σ_P. For our (8%, 10%) portfolio, we found a 90% probability of returns exceeding -4.82%.

In general, what are the characteristics of *all* portfolios that will have a 90% probability of beating a -4.82% return? The answer is simply all portfolios with a combination of expected returns and standard deviations such that:

$$\overline{R}_P - 1.282\sigma_P = -4.82\%.$$

In the risk-return diagram, this includes all portfolios lying on the straight line with slope 1.282 and a Y-axis intersect of -4.82% (see Figure C). For all portfolios that lie above this line, return will exceed -4.82% with 90% confidence.

Figure C: The Shortfall Constraint in a Risk-Return Diagram

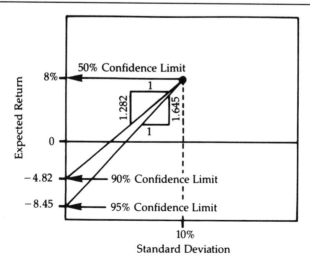

Suppose one wanted a 95% confidence limit, instead of 90%. Figure C shows that the 95% threshold will be -8.45% for the (8%, 10%) portfolio. This minimum value represents the intersection with the vertical axis of a straight line with a slope of 1.645 falling from the (8%, 10%) portfolio.

Although most risk-related confidence limits will have high probabilities, it is instructive to consider the 50% limit. Given symmetry of the return distribution, such portfolios have a 50% probability of exceeding the expected return. This translates into a slope factor of zero, so that the formula for portfolios that provide a 50% confidence of exceeding 8% becomes:

$$\overline{R}_P - 0\sigma_P = 8.00\%.$$

This equation is depicted by the horizontal line running through the 8% expected return level in Figure C. All portfolios lying above this line will have greater than 50% confidence of exceeding a return of 8%.

As one would expect, the minimum return for a given confidence level will increase as the expected return increases (holding the standard deviation constant) and will decrease as the standard deviation increases (holding the expected return constant). Figure D shows that the 95% confidence limit increases by 1 percentage point (from -8.45% to -7.45%) when the portfolio's expected return increases from 8% to 9% and decreases by 1 percentage point (from -8.45% to -9.45%) when the portfolio's expected return decreases to 7% from 8%.

Figure D: Impact of Expected Return on the Confidence Limit

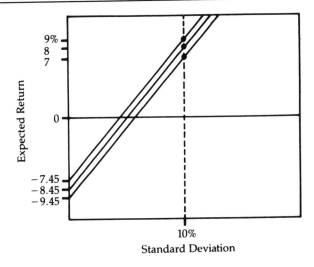

Standard Deviation

Figure E: Impact of Standard Deviation on the Confidence Limit

---

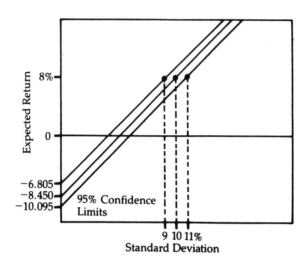

Figure E shows that a 1 percentage point increase in the portfolio's standard deviation (from 10% to 11%) will cause the 95% confidence limit to fall from -8.45% to -10.09% and a 1 percentage point decrease in the portfolio's standard deviation (from 10% to 9%) will cause the 95% confidence limit to increase to -6.805%. The 95% confidence limit changes by 1 percentage point for every 1 percentage point change in the expected return (holding the standard deviation constant) and by 1.645%, in the opposite direction, for every 1 percentage point change in the standard deviation (holding the expected return constant).

USING CONFIDENCE LIMITS TO CONSTRAIN RISK

The concept of a confidence limit is similar to that of a floor in dynamic hedging. The floor—the minimum allowable return—is intended to limit potential loss. In theory, given the assumption of "continuous trading," the floor would correspond to a 100% confidence limit for the specified strategy. In practice, however, the continuous trading assumption may be a very tenuous one, as many have learned in recent times.

A required confidence limit—such as a return of -5% or more, with 95% confidence—can also act as a potential constraint on the investor's expected return. This would limit the portfolio's statistical risk without requiring dynamic hedging. Unlike a floor, a confidence limit implies an acceptable probability of falling below the specified limit, which may be greater than zero. Figure F illustrates the role of such a constraint on the portfolio decision.

Using the example from Figure C of a 95% confidence limit with a minimum return of -8.45%, the shortfall constraint segments the combination of expected returns and risks. Portfolios to the right of the solid line violate the constraint; their realized returns do not exceed -8.45% with 95% confidence. Portfolios to the left of the line actually satisfy a higher 95% confidence limit than -8.45%.

Of course, only portfolio risk-return tradeoffs on or below the efficient frontier are feasible. As Figure F shows, the set of feasible portfolios satisfying a shortfall constraint may be limited. The set of portfolios to be considered in the optimization decision is limited to the small shaded area of portfolios that are feasible and also satisfy the specified shortfall constraint.

With a 95% confidence limit, the highest achievable return from our hypothetical efficient frontier will be -6.89%. This is achieved by the "tangency portfolio," which is derived from a straight line with a slope of 1.645%. The

Figure F: Influence of the Allowable Shortfall

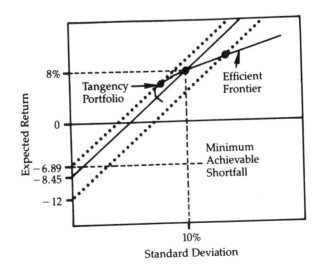

tangency portfolio in Figure F has an expected return of 5.8% and a standard deviation of 7.7%. It is interesting to note that this tangency portfolio is not the portfolio with the lowest standard deviation. (It should also be noted that one cannot achieve, with 95% confidence, a higher minimum return than -6.89%.)

As one would expect, lowering the confidence limit, either by lowering the required return or the required probability, allows portfolios with a higher expected return. If the required return for a 95% confidence limit is lowered to -12%, a portfolio with an expected return of approximately 10.3% is possible, compared with an expected return of only 8% when the required return is -8.45%.

Figure G shows the effects of varying the required probability, while holding the required return constant. With a 95% confidence limit on a return of -8.45%, the maximum expected return is 8% for the hypothetical efficient frontier. If the probability is reduced to 90%, the straight line will have a slope of only 1.282 and a portfolio with an expected return of 11.43% is possible. If the probability is increased to 97.5%, the straight line will have a slope of 1.96, and none of the portfolios on the efficient frontier will be able to achieve a return of -8.45% with 97.5% confidence.

Figure G: Effect of Changing the Required Probability

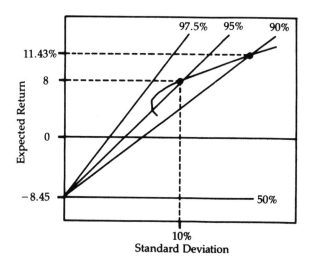

CONSTRAINT RELATIVE TO A BENCHMARK PORTFOLIO

The concept of a confidence limit can be used to examine the returns of candidate investment portfolios relative to a benchmark portfolio. The simplest case would involve a riskless benchmark portfolio. This is equivalent to the cases discussed above, in which the candidate portfolios are those that can provide a given confidence level of exceeding some prescribed minimum return.

The more general case of benchmark constraints compares portfolio returns with an index or a basket of indexes. The confidence limit might be the probability of falling below an allowable shortfall from the index. As the benchmark index return is uncertain, the portfolio return corresponding to an allowable shortfall would be conditional upon the benchmark return. For example, for an allowable shortfall of 5%, a minimum portfolio return of -5% would be required if the actual benchmark return was zero, while a minimum portfolio return of 15% would be required if the benchmark return turned out to be 20%.

The expected return required to achieve the shortfall constraint will depend on the standard deviation of the portfolio and its correlation with the benchmark (see the appendix). If the portfolio is perfectly correlated with the benchmark, then the expected return required to achieve an allowable shortfall will increase linearly with the difference between the standard deviation of the portfolio and that of the benchmark, as the solid line in Figure H shows. As the

Figure H: Role of Correlation in Constraining Deviations

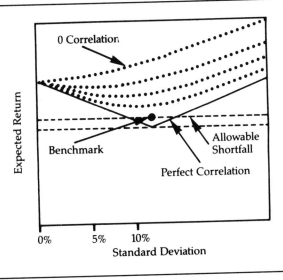

Figure I: Reducing the Volatility of the Benchmark

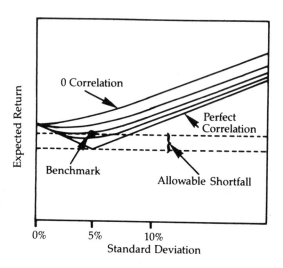

Figure J: Constraint Line for the Riskless Benchmark

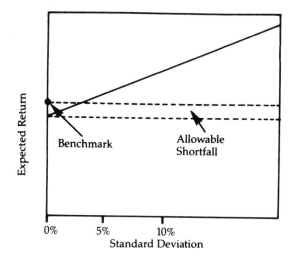

correlation declines, the required expected return for the same standard deviation will increase to compensate for the greater dispersion between the portfolio and the benchmark returns (the dotted lines in Figure H).

The importance of correlation increases with the standard deviation of the benchmark returns. As the benchmark's standard deviation decreases, the "bundle" of curves defining the constraint for different correlations shrinks (see Figure I). For benchmarks whose volatility approaches zero, the bundle of constraints collapses into the same straight line for all correlation values (Figure J). This is exactly what would be expected, because a risk-free benchmark is equivalent to the minimum-return constraints shown in Figure F.

SHORTFALL CONSTRAINTS AND HEDGING

The use of a shortfall constraint is similar to the "arbitrage" strategies followed by many traders trying to exploit the relative mispricing of a particular asset (or portfolio of assets) without having to bear all the risk of the asset. By taking an offsetting position in similar, but fairly priced (or mispriced in the opposite direction) assets, an investor may reduce the risk of the position and still capture the targeted incremental return. The ability of the offsetting asset to hedge or reduce the risk of the investor's position will depend on its correlation with the mispriced asset. The higher the correlation, the better the hedge and the greater the risk reduction.

The dispersion of the differences in return between a portfolio and its benchmark will be a function of their respective standard deviations and the associated correlation. For a given pair of standard deviations, the dispersion of the return deviations will increase as the correlation declines. This means that the probability that a portfolio will underperform the benchmark increases as its correlation with the benchmark decreases. Given portfolios with the same standard deviation and the same shortfall constraint, the portfolio with the lower correlation with the benchmark will require a higher expected return to overcome the greater dispersion of its return differences.

This is the same tradeoff faced in the evaluation of enhanced indexing strategies. The greater the deviation of the portfolio from the structured characteristics of the index, the more uncertainty there will be in the tracking process. A successful enhancement strategy presumably compensates the investor with a higher expected return. This incremental return helps to reduce the probability of a significant shortfall.

A shortfall constraint, relative to a benchmark portfolio, can act as a stochastic constraint on the traditional mean-variance optimization process. Solving for the "optimal" constrained portfolio requires an iterative process that examines simultaneously the optimization objective and the shortfall constraint.

Figure K: Violation of the Benchmark Constraint

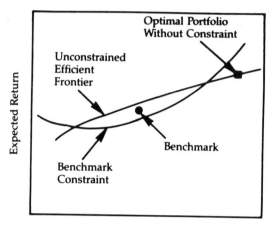

Standard Deviation

Whether or not an "optimal" portfolio will satisfy a particular shortfall constraint will depend on the correlation between the "optimal" portfolio and the benchmark and their relative expected returns and standard deviations. Figure K shows a case where the "optimal" portfolio violates the required shortfall constraint and Figure L highlights an example in which the constraint is satisfied. Because alternative portfolios on the unconstrained efficient frontier will have different correlations with the benchmark, each portfolio will be subject to a different constraint curve. The shortfall-constrained optimal portfolio may in fact lie below the unconstrained efficient frontier.

There are many possible applications of mean-variance optimization in the context of shortfall constraints. It may be used (1) to constrain potential portfolio performance relative to a normal or long-term benchmark, (2) to optimize with respect to an asset-liability surplus while constraining the portfolio relative to some asset-only benchmark (or vice versa), or (3) to constrain the inflation-adjusted performance of the portfolio.[1] The multiple objectives may conflict, in

---

[1] The influence of liabilities in the optimization process is discussed in M.L. Leibowitz and R.D. Henriksson, "Portfolio Optimization Within A Surplus Framework," *Financial Analysts Journal*, March/April 1988.

Figure L: Satisfying the Benchmark Constraint

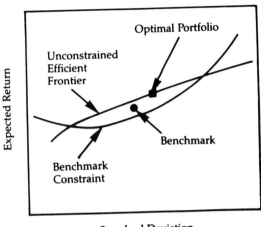

Standard Deviation

which case the choices for the optimized portfolio may be limited unless the shortfall constraint is quite large.

In all cases, the shortfall-constraint approach can play a valuable role in the asset allocation process by allowing for the simultaneous evaluation of multiple tradeoffs between portfolio objectives.

Appendix

The expected return, or mean, of a distribution of returns, R_P, is the probability-weighted average of the range of possible outcomes:

$$E(\tilde{R}_P) = \sum_{R_P=-\infty}^{\infty} p_i R_{P_i} \equiv \overline{R}_P, \tag{A1}$$

where E ( ) is the expectations operator and p_i is the probability of the realized return being R_{Pi}. As the set of possible outcomes becomes large, the discrete probability distribution used in Equation (A1) will approach a continuous distribution and Equation (A1) can be rewritten as:

$$E(\tilde{R}_P) = \int_{-\infty}^{\infty} \tilde{R}_P f(\tilde{R}_P) d\tilde{R}_P, \tag{A2}$$

where the probability p is replaced by the probability element $f(\tilde{R}_P)d\tilde{R}_P$.

The variance of $\tilde{R}_P$ is defined as:

$$\sigma_P^2 \equiv E\,[(\tilde{R}_P - \overline{R}_P)^2] = E\left(\tilde{R}_P^2\right) - \overline{R}_P^2. \tag{A3}$$

The standard deviation of the distribution of returns will simply be the square root of the variance:

$$\sigma_P \equiv \sqrt{\sigma_P^2}. \tag{A4}$$

A normal distribution can be completely described by its mean and standard deviation. The normal density function is defined as:

$$f\left(\tilde{R}_P\right) = \frac{1}{\sqrt{2\pi}\,\sigma_P} \cdot$$

$$\exp\left[-\frac{1}{2}\left(\frac{\tilde{R}_P - \overline{R}_P}{\sigma_P}\right)^2 \right], \tag{A5}$$

and the distribution or cumulative density function is the integral of the density function, specifying the probability of a specified return, R_P^*, not being exceeded:

$$p\left(\tilde{R}_P < R_P^*\right) = \int_{-\infty}^{R_P^*} f\left(\tilde{R}_P\right) d\tilde{R}_p. \tag{A6}$$

The probability of an outcome being within one standard deviation of the mean will be:

$$p\left(\overline{R}_P - \sigma_P < \tilde{R}_P < \overline{R}_P + \sigma_P\right) = \int_{\overline{R}_P - \sigma_P}^{\overline{R}_P + \sigma_P} f\left(\tilde{R}_P\right) d\tilde{R}_P = 68.26\%. \tag{A7}$$

The probability of an outcome being within two standard deviations of the mean will be:

$$p\left(\overline{R}_P - 2\sigma_P < \tilde{R}_P < \overline{R}_P + 2\sigma_P\right) = \int_{\overline{R}_P - 2\sigma_P}^{\overline{R}_P + 2\sigma_P} f\left(\tilde{R}_P\right) d\tilde{R}_P = 95.44\%. \tag{A8}$$

The probability of a return exceeding a specified value, R_P^*, will be:

$$p\left(\tilde{R}_p > R_P^*\right) = \int_{R_P^*}^{\infty} f\left(\tilde{R}_P\right) d\tilde{R}_P. \tag{A9}$$

The return that will be exceeded with 90% probability will be $\overline{R}_P - 1.282\,\sigma_P$, as follows.

$$p\left(\tilde{R}_P > \overline{R}_P - 1.282\,\sigma_p\right) = \int_{\overline{R}_P - 1.282\sigma_P}^{\infty} f\left(\tilde{R}_P\right) d\tilde{R}_P = 90\%. \tag{A10}$$

The return that will be exceeded with 95% probability will be $\bar{R}_P - 1.645 \, \sigma_P$:

$$p\left(\tilde{R}_P > \bar{R}_P - 1.645 \, \sigma_P\right) = \int_{\bar{R}_P - 1.645\sigma_P}^{\infty} f\left(\tilde{R}_P\right) d\tilde{R}_P = 95\%. \tag{A11}$$

It follows that a portfolio will exceed a minimum return R_M with 95% probability if:

$$\bar{R}_P - 1.645 \, \sigma_P = R_M. \tag{A12}$$

Similarly, all $(\bar{R}_P, \sigma_P)$ portfolios for which

$$\bar{R}_P - 1.645 \, \sigma_P \geq R_M \tag{A13}$$

will exceed the minimum return with *at least* 95% confidence.

The distribution of the difference between a portfolio return, $\tilde{R}_p$, and a benchmark return, $\tilde{R}_B$, will be defined by the respective expected returns, $\bar{R}_P$ and $\bar{R}_B$, the respective standard deviations, σ_P and σ_B, and the correlation between the two returns, ρ_{PB}. The expected return of the differences, $\bar{R}_D$, will be:

$$\bar{R}_D = \bar{R}_P - \bar{R}_B. \tag{A14}$$

The variance of the differences, $\sigma_D{}^2$, is:

$$\sigma_D{}^2 = \sigma_P{}^2 + \sigma_B{}^2 - 2\left(\rho_{PB}\sigma_P\sigma_B\right). \tag{A15}$$

The standard deviation, σ_D, will be:

$$\sigma_D = \sqrt{\sigma_D{}^2}. \tag{A16}$$

Because σ_P and σ_B must be positive, it follows from Equations (A14) and (A15) that the standard deviation of the return differences, $\tilde{R}_P - \tilde{R}_B$, will decline as the correlation ρ_{PB} increases.

The distribution of deviations is simply a transformation of the returns distribution and can be constrained to exceed an allowable shortfall, S, with a specified probability. By applying the preceding method to the distribution of deviations, it follows that, for example, a 95% confidence level will be achieved by all $(\bar{R}_P, \sigma_P)$ portfolios satisfying:

$$\bar{R}_D - 1.645 \, \sigma_D \geq S, \tag{A17}$$

or

$$\overline{R}_P \geq \overline{R}_B + 1.645 \, [\sigma_P{}^2 + \sigma_B{}^2 - 2\rho_{PB}\sigma_P\sigma_B]^{1/2} + S.$$

Chapter I-9

Portfolio Optimization Utilizing the Full Yield Curve

SUMMARY

In recent years, mean-variance analysis has become a widely used tool for portfolio optimization. It provides the portfolio manager with a computationally tractable way to deal with the diversification effects of large numbers of securities and furnishes a well-defined criterion for selecting assets with the maximum return for a given amount of risk. The same principles are directly applicable to the surplus management of pension funds, where the relevant portfolio may consist not only of the assets but also of the "total portfolio," including liabilities. In such cases, a key objective may be the maximization of surplus, the difference between the market value of assets and the present value of the liabilities.

Despite the computational ease of mean-variance optimization even with large numbers of securities, most previous applications have greatly restricted the dimensions of the problem by assuming that "bonds" are represented as a

---

Martin L. Leibowitz, Roy D. Henriksson, and William S. Krasker, "Portfolio Optimization Utilizing the Full Yield Curve: An Improved Approach to Fixed Income as an Asset Class," Salomon Brothers Inc, October 1987.

single asset "point." That single asset is usually chosen to be a capitalization-weighted index, such as the Salomon Brothers Broad Investment-Grade Bond Index^{TM} (Broad Index). In this paper, we discuss the implications of this simplification, and then present and analyze a more realistic model of the fixed-income market. Some of our findings corroborate the conclusions of earlier analyses. For example, we demonstrate that bonds are an important component of an efficient portfolio, because their longer durations more closely match the duration of the liabilities and thereby reduce the investor's exposure to interest rate risk. Beyond this, we show how the expected values and standard deviations of the security returns, together with the correlations among those returns, determine the set of bonds to hold. We will see that the risk/return trade-off can be improved by using the empirically observed correlations among bonds of different maturities, rather than relying solely on the portfolio duration and its implicit assumption of parallel yield curve shifts. Our main conclusion, however, is that it is important to model the full range of yields and maturities that are available. Portfolio optimization that incorporates the full set of assets available along the yield curve will produce a much better risk/return trade-off than will the conventional approach, which assumes that bonds are a single asset. This is particularly true when the pension liabilities are taken into account.

COMPONENTS OF A MEAN-VARIANCE OPTIMIZATION

There are three essential inputs to any mean-variance portfolio optimization problem: the expected returns to the securities, the standard deviations of those returns and the correlations among them.

The expected return to stocks consists of the dividend yield, which is relatively certain, plus the expected price appreciation, which is largely subjective. For example, if the dividend yield is 4% and the expected annualized rate of price appreciation is 8%, then the expected return to stocks is 12%.

For bonds, the expected return is directly related to the expected change in yield. If the expected yield change is zero, then the return to a bond is simply its "yield to maturity," as the bond will earn its yield each period. The standard deviations of the security returns and the correlations among those returns can be estimated from historical data.

TRADITIONAL VIEW OF BONDS AS A SINGLE ASSET

Despite the wide range of coupons, maturities and yields in the bond market, previous mean-variance analyses often treated bonds as a single asset. The risk/return trade-off facing the portfolio manager is then as depicted in Figure

1. Stocks have a higher expected return than do "bonds," but also more risk, as represented by the higher standard deviation of return. By varying the percentage of stocks in the portfolio, the portfolio manager can achieve any combination of expected return and standard deviation on the curve connecting bonds and stocks. The curve is not straight because bonds and stocks are not perfectly correlated. The curvature of the risk/return trade-off generated by varying mixtures of stocks and bonds represents the beneficial effect of diversification.

BONDS AS A CONTINUUM OF ASSETS

In reality, the portfolio manager can invest in bonds of all different coupons and maturities. The simplest way to extend the model of Figure 1 is to assume that all bonds have the same expected return (that is, a flat yield curve) and that all shifts of the yield curve are parallel. The risk/return diagram for stocks and bonds is then as shown in Figure 2. The expected return and standard deviation for each bond lies somewhere on the horizontal line in the figure, with higher-duration bonds corresponding to higher standard deviations. The relative locations of bonds with the same duration as the Broad Index and the Salomon Brothers Large Pension Fund Index (LPF) would be as shown.

Figure 1: Risk/Return Trade-Off with Bonds as a Single Asset

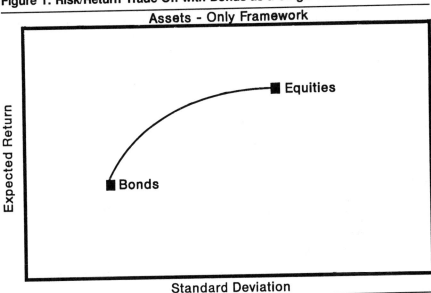

Figure 2: Risk/Return Trade-Off for Flat Yield Curve

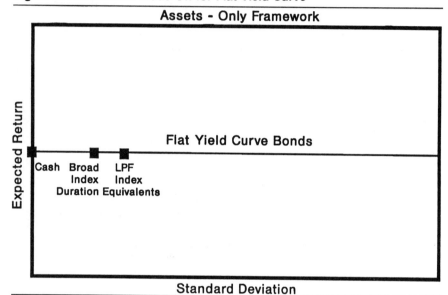

Figure 3: Equity/Bond Mixtures with Flat Yield Curve

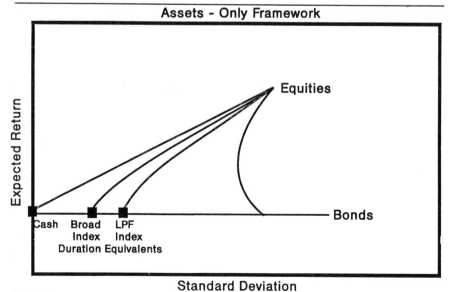

Figure 4: STRIPS Yield Curve

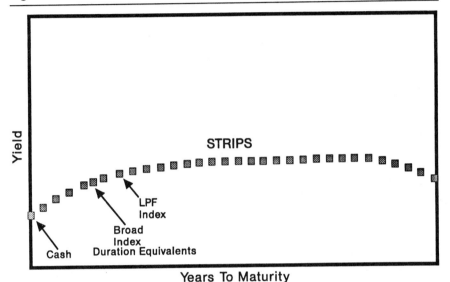

Figure 3 shows a few of the risk/return trade-offs that are obtained by portfolios in which stocks are combined with a single bond. If that bond is the riskless bond with zero duration (that is, cash), then the risk/return trade-off is simply the straight line segment connecting that bond with stocks. As noted earlier, provided that stock returns and interest rates are not perfectly correlated, the risk/return trade-off obtained by mixing stocks with a risky bond will be curved. However, as Figure 3 suggests, cash "dominates"[1] risky bonds under the conditions shown there. No matter what standard deviation is chosen, the highest possible expected return is obtained by a portfolio consisting of stocks and cash. As long as risky bonds are positively correlated with stocks, it can never make sense for a portfolio manager to hold risky bonds unless they offer a higher expected return than cash.

This exclusion of bonds will probably not be appropriate, however, if bonds offer a higher expected return than cash. This can be demonstrated using Treasury STRIPS, single-payment bonds with maturities of one to 30 years. A recent STRIPS yield curve is shown in Figure 4. The two STRIPS with durations that are equivalent to the Broad Index and the LPF Index are identified. If we as-

---

[1] See *Portfolio Optimization Within a Surplus Framework: A New Perspective on Asset Allocation*, Salomon Brothers Inc, April 1987.

Figure 5: Risk/Return Trade-Off for Equities and STRIPS of all Maturities

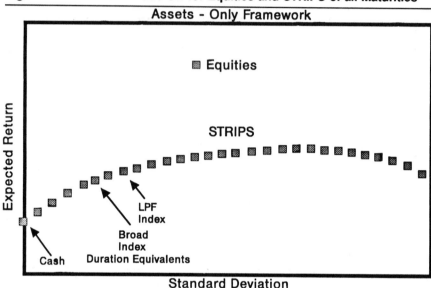

Assets - Only Framework

sume that the expected return of a STRIPS issue equals its yield and that the yield curve shifts are always parallel, then the STRIPS' standard deviations will be nearly proportional to their maturities; the risk/return diagram will be as in Figure 5.

Because cash has a lower expected return than do risky STRIPS, it is possible that a portfolio consisting of stocks and a single STRIPS issue will attain a risk/return trade-off that cannot be achieved with only stocks and cash (see Figure 6). Still better results may be possible by forming portfolios that combine stocks with more than one STRIPS issue (although if all yield curve shifts are parallel, no more than two STRIPS issues will be needed).

If STRIPS of all maturities are available, the full efficient frontier will be a smooth curve, as shown in Figure 7.

THE SURPLUS FRAMEWORK

Although risky bonds are typically a component of an efficient portfolio even in the assets-only case, their role becomes crucial when pension liabilities are taken into account. Intuitively, the pension liability cash flows can be regarded as a fixed short position consisting of a portfolio of single-payment bonds such as

Figure 6: Optimal Mixes of Cash, Equities and Single STRIPS

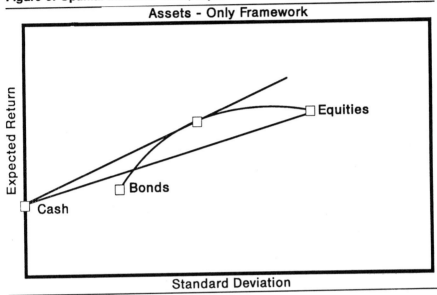

Assets - Only Framework

Figure 7: Efficient Frontier

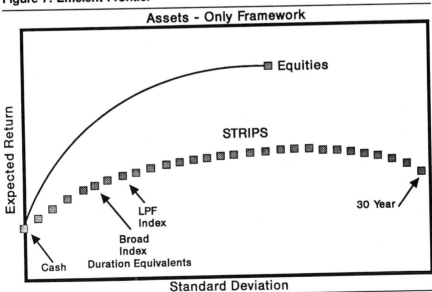

Assets - Only Framework

Figure 8: Risk/Return Trade-Off in a Surplus Framework

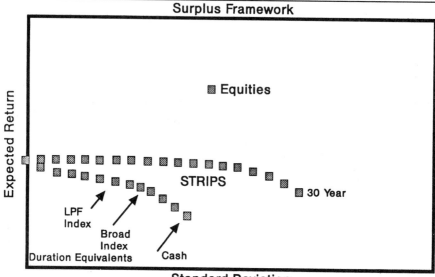

Treasury STRIPS. Generally, this "liability portfolio" will have a long duration. Long-duration bonds in the asset portfolio "cancel" the interest rate exposure of the liabilities, thereby causing substantial risk reduction for the pension surplus.

A convenient way to visualize this effect is through the risk/return diagram shown in Figure 8, where the assets are STRIPS of all maturities and stocks. The expected returns and standard deviations are not those of the assets but rather of the pension surplus. Given the duration of the liabilities, there will be a STRIPS issue of a certain maturity whose interest rate risk equals that of the liabilities. In terms of the surplus, this particular STRIPS issue is "riskless," and hence, it is plotted in Figure 8 with a standard deviation of zero. STRIPS with either longer or shorter durations will be risky. Based on the yields shown in Figure 4, STRIPS with shorter durations are represented by the lower part of the curve in Figure 8, while the longer-duration STRIPS comprise the upper part.

THE EFFICIENT FRONTIER IN A SURPLUS FRAMEWORK

The efficient frontier for the surplus—representing the highest expected surplus that can be attained for each surplus standard deviation—is shown in Figure 9. The efficient frontier represents a significant gain over what could be obtained

Figure 9: Efficient Frontier in a Surplus Framework

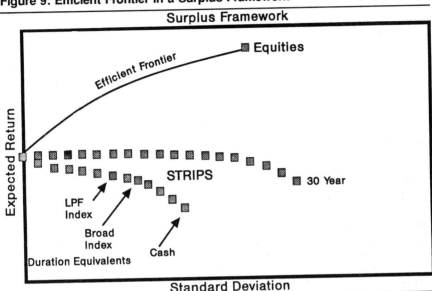

by a portfolio consisting of any single asset. By combining stocks (which have a high expected return but a duration shorter than that of the liabilities) with long-duration bonds, the pension fund manager can achieve a considerable reduction in risk without sacrificing too much return.

In fact, Figure 9 understates the potential for risk reduction as it reflects the limitations of the available STRIPS. Given that the longest existing STRIPS have a duration (and maturity) of 30 years, an investor may be required to bear interest rate risk (through a mismatch in duration) to hold the desired allocation of equities. For example, if equities have an effective duration of three years and the duration of the liabilities is 12 years, an investor could not allocate more than two thirds of his portfolio to equities and still achieve a duration matching of assets and liabilities using equities and STRIPS. (Of course, funds that can use Treasury bond futures will be able to lengthen the duration of their portfolios beyond that available from STRIPS alone.)

IMPROVING THE RISK/RETURN TRADE-OFF WITH STRIPS

Our explicit consideration of STRIPS of all maturities makes clear how the traditional treatment of "bonds" as a single asset leads to inefficient portfolios. Suppose, for example, that bonds are represented by the Broad Index, which has an effective duration that is close to four years. Treating this as the only fixed-income security corresponds, in the current analysis, to constraining the holdings of all STRIPS other than the four-year to zero. This would be a severe restriction. Clearly, if the liabilities had a long duration, then it would be impossible to match their interest rate exposure. Even with very short-duration liabilities, controlling the interest rate risk might necessitate placing *nearly all* the fund's assets in the bond portfolio, leaving little room for stocks. If, on the other hand, STRIPS of all maturities are available, then the fund manager could achieve the same degree of risk reduction with a smaller amount of money in long-duration STRIPS and the rest in stocks, which have a higher expected return.

The potential risk reduction can be demonstrated for the illustrative liabilities shown in Figure 10. Using the STRIPS yield curve, these liabilities have a duration of approximately 12 years and a present value of 111.86. If the pension fund has assets worth 115, then the surplus is 3.14. Figure 11 demonstrates the potential gains from using bonds along the entire yield curve in a surplus framework. If an investor can hold only equities and four-year STRIPS, the efficient portfolio with a standard deviation of 13 will have an expected (surplus) return of only 0.67. However, if the entire set of STRIPS is available, it is possible to achieve an expected return of 3.61, while maintaining the same portfolio standard deviation of 13. This is accomplished by effectively matching the duration of the assets and liabilities, using 24-year STRIPS and increasing the equity

Figure 10: Annual Liability Flows

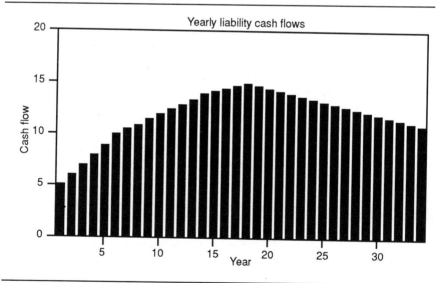

Figure 11: Using the Full Yield Curve in a Surplus Framework

Using Only Four-Year STRIPS

Efficient Portfolio	26.0 Equities
	89.0 Four-Year STRIPS

Portfolio Expected Surplus Gain	0.67
Portfolio Standard Deviation	13.00

Using Full Set of STRIPS

Efficient Portfolio	92.9 Equities
	22.1 24-Year STRIPS

Portfolio Expected Surplus Gain	3.20
Portfolio Standard Deviation	13.00

---

holding from 26.0 to 92.9 (out of 115). The long-maturity STRIPS allow the investor to replace interest rate risk, for which there is little expected return compensation, with equity risk, which offers the higher expected return.

NONPARALLEL YIELD CURVE MOVEMENTS

All of the preceding discussion has been based on the assumption that yield curve shifts are always parallel, so that all STRIPS are perfectly correlated. This implies that all of the uncertainty of bonds can be explained by parallel shifts in the yield curve and that the riskiness of a bond is entirely determined by its duration. If, as is actually the case, STRIPS of different maturities are not perfectly correlated, no portfolio comprising a single STRIPS issue can reduce the surplus risk to zero.

This is because the liabilities can also be thought of as a portfolio of STRIPS, and if the STRIPS are not perfectly correlated, no single STRIPS issue will be able to hedge the risk of the portfolio.

On the other hand, by purchasing a portfolio of STRIPS whose cash flows exactly match those of the liabilities (a "dedicated portfolio"), and placing any excess funds (the surplus) in cash, the surplus risk (in dollar terms)[2] can be eliminated. The efficient frontier, derived using the full set of STRIPS, therefore includes a riskless total portfolio and represents an even better risk/return trade-off than can be achieved by combining stocks with only a single STRIPS

---

[2] But not the risk of the funding ratio.

issue. To summarize, if all yield curve shifts were parallel and STRIPS of all different maturities were perfectly correlated, an efficient portfolio would never have to include more than two different STRIPS. Yet under the actual imperfect correlations among STRIPS, substantial risk reduction in a surplus framework requires holding a large number of different STRIPS. (In practice, when the entire universe of fixed-income securities is available, the risk-reducing portfolio would extend beyond STRIPS to include a variety of Government, corporate and mortgage securities.) This suggests that a portfolio optimization technique that assumes parallel shifts will produce inefficient portfolios. This is demonstrated in the example that follows.

A GENERAL PORTFOLIO PROBLEM

In this example, we examine a general portfolio problem in which the available assets are those used in the previous discussion. We will again regard the pension liabilities, which entail certain payments each year, as a fixed short position of STRIPS (see Figure 10).

A typical portfolio on the efficient frontier is shown in Figure 12; the correlations among STRIPS are calculated from historical data. The portfolio surplus has a standard deviation of 2.85 and an expected increase of 1.44. Note that only about one sixth of the assets is placed in stocks and the rest in intermediate- and long-maturity STRIPS. In practice, this allocation could be achieved exactly by purchasing STRIPS, or it could be approximated by ordinary coupon bonds with appropriate maturities.

PROBLEM WITH PARALLEL SHIFT ASSUMPTION

Figure 13 describes a portfolio that would be efficient if yield curve shifts were always parallel. This portfolio has an expected surplus increase of 1.78. Moreover, under the empirically determined correlation structure, its surplus standard deviation is 5.09.

To find the degree of inefficiency from assuming parallel shifts, we find the true optimal portfolio with the highest expected surplus among those with the same standard deviation of 5.09. This portfolio, shown in Figure 14, has an expected surplus increase of 2.08. Thus, one can see the benefit of more precisely modeling the true correlation structure for STRIPS, rather than simply assuming that they are all perfectly correlated.

In general, portfolios that are optimal under the parallel shift assumption will always be inefficient with realistic correlation assumptions. By introducing

Figure 12: Composition of an Efficient Portfolio Under Nonparallel Yield Curve Movements

Assets	Market Value
Stocks	21.36
STRIPS Maturity (Years)	
8	9.08
9	11.48
10	10.81
11	9.30
12	7.80
13	6.54
14	5.58
15	4.82
16	4.29
17	3.92
18	3.69
19	3.43
20	3.23
21	3.01
22	2.72
23	2.23
24	1.48
25	0.23
Total	115.00
Expected Surplus Gain	1.44
Surplus Standard Deviation	2.85

Figure 13: Efficient Portfolio Under Parallel Shift Assumption

Assets	Market Value
Stocks	29.03
STRIPS Maturity (Years)	
14	10.75
15	75.22
Total	115.00
Expected Surplus Gain	1.78
Surplus Standard Deviation	5.09

Figure 14: Dominating Portfolio

Assets	Market Value
Stocks	39.75
STRIPS Maturity (Years)	
11	7.08
12	9.51
13	9.51
14	8.70
15	7.68
16	6.79
17	6.08
18	5.51
19	4.91
20	4.24
21	3.32
22	1.92
Total	115.00
Expected Surplus Gain	2.08
Surplus Standard Deviation	5.09

those correlations, we can find portfolios with higher expected surplus returns *and* lower risk.

MANAGING INTEREST RATE EXPOSURE

By utilizing the full range of investment opportunities available in the fixed-income markets, a pension manager can improve the available risk/return trade-off, especially in a surplus framework. With the more explicit visibility of surplus fluctuations under the new Financial Accounting Standards Board (FASB) 87 requirements, pension funds must become more sensitive to fluctuations in interest rates.[3] By combining the full yield curve approach with a surplus framework, the asset allocation decision can be analyzed in a way that properly integrates the impact of this interest rate exposure.

---

[3] See *The Surge in Pension Fund Surplus: Strategies for the New Market Environment*, Salomon Brothers Inc, September 1987.

Chapter I-10

Shortfall Risk and the Asset Allocation Decision

Asset allocation is the single most important element of investment policy for pension plans, foundations, endowments, trusts, and a variety of other investment funds. The asset allocation decision is of fundamental importance for both short- and long-term investment performance. Yet perhaps the most difficult aspect of the asset allocation decision is determining how to balance the fund's need for long-term growth against the manager's need to achieve investment results within shorter time frames.

One article of faith in investment mythology is that a steadfast adherence to the asset with the highest average growth rate will, over time, almost surely produce superior performance. Unfortunately, our analysis indicates that risk persists at surprisingly high levels, even over investment horizons as long as twenty years. For those of us with human time frames, investment results must be achieved much sooner, often within three to five years.

In this article, we use Monte Carlo simulation as a tool for investigation of long-run risk and return. This follows on the work of Leibowitz and Krasker (1988), which compares the return potential of stocks and bonds over long in-

Martin L. Leibowitz and Terence C. Langetieg, "Shortfall Risk and the Asset Allocation Decision: A Simulation Analysis of Stock and Bond Risk Profiles," *The Journal of Portfolio Management*, Fall 1989. Reprinted with permission.

vestment horizons. Stocks are often viewed as a superior long-term investment, yet our analysis reveals that their long-run risk is considerable.

Using standard return and volatility assumptions, for example, we found that there is a 36% chance that stocks will underperform bonds over a five-year horizon. Even over a twenty-year horizon, the probability that stocks will underperform remains a surprisingly high 24%. Given the commonly held belief that stocks will outperform bonds in the long run, it is disquieting to find that equity risk appears to be so stubbornly persistent.

Over the past sixty-two years, the average arithmetic return of stocks has exceeded the bond return by 6.8%.[1] Unfortunately, a risk premium of 6.8% is not enough to guarantee superior performance, even over investment horizons as long as twenty years. Stocks turned in their worst twenty-year performance relative to bonds from January 1929 to December 1948, when they produced an average compound return of 3.1%, compared with a bond return of 4.8%. The worst five- and ten-year periods for stocks occurred in the 1930s, when the average compound bond return exceeded the stock return by 18% in 1930-1934 and by 7.8% in 1929-1938. In their best five-, ten-, and twenty-year periods—in the 1940s, 1950s, and 1960s—stocks outperformed bonds by 10% or more per year. In the 1970s, the average compound return for bonds exceeded that of stocks by 0.3%, but stocks produced a 31% return advantage from 1980 to 1987.

Many investors believe that both bond yields and bond returns over much of the past sixty years were artificially low and not representative of future investment performance. In the past decade, for instance, a restructuring of the fixed-income markets has resulted in more volatile and significantly higher interest rates in both nominal and real terms. In the early 1980s, interest rates reached historical highs, as deficit spending stressed capital markets at unprecedented levels, and the Federal Reserve sought to curb the inflationary excesses of the 1970s. Current estimates of the arithmetic average risk premium for stocks range from 2% to 6%. The mean of these estimates, 4%, has been taken as the base case for our study.

Our primary results are as follows:

- Equity risk should be viewed as strongly persistent and capable of producing significant shortfalls over investment horizons as long as twenty years. The relative investment performance of stocks improves when the risk premium for stock is high or when stock volatility is low. Relative performance is not very sensitive to the interest rate process.

---

[1] For a historical record for the S&P 500 and long-term corporate bonds, see Ibbotson (1988), exhibits 25, 30, C-1, and C-3.

- Diversification pays off in both the single- and multi-period framework. A diversified portfolio of 30% stocks and 70% bonds is very attractive relative to a 100% bond portfolio over a five-year investment horizon. As the investment horizon is extended, most investors will choose to allocate an increasing percentage to equities. Over a twenty-year horizon, a 60% stock/40% bond portfolio is very attractive compared to both a 100% bond portfolio and a 30% stock/70% bond portfolio.

- We must sharpen our understanding of what "risk" means in the multi-period framework. Over investment horizons of three to five years or longer, there is increasing asymmetry in investment results, and "volatility" loses some of its intuitive appeal as a complete measure of risk. To assess risk when returns are asymmetrical, we must examine downside outcomes directly.

  The concept of "shortfall risk" provides a simple and intuitive measure of downside risk. For example, a plan sponsor may perceive risk as the loss of a prescribed amount of the pension surplus or as an excessively high pension expense. The "shortfall" probability measures the chances of jeopardizing one of the sponsor's goals. The shortfall magnitude measures the amount by which such a goal could be violated.

- The concept of shortfall risk provides an intuitive and policy-oriented way to present investment prospects, especially to the boards and committees that often are the ultimate arbiters of a given risk exposure. Shortfall risk can be a means for translating investment results into such plan sponsor concerns as preserving the pension surplus or achieving a target rate of return. Finally, assessment of shortfall risk can facilitate the development of an asset allocation policy that better reflects the plan sponsor's overall objectives.

SIMULATION AS A TOOL FOR ASSESSING FUTURE INVESTMENT PERFORMANCE

Leibowitz and Krasker (1988) introduced a model to compare the long-run investment performance of stocks and bonds. It is based on several simplifying assumptions that facilitate the development of an analytical solution. As more general assumptions are introduced, the analytical model becomes increasingly

Table 1: Summary of Assumptions for Stock and Bond Returns

Interest Rates:	Reversion rate of 15% toward a nominal rate of 9%; No trend when the interest rate is 9%; Year-to-year volatility of 150 basis points.
Bond Returns:	Starting yield of 9%; Duration of 4.5 years.
Stock Returns:	Starting expected return of 13%; Risk premium of 4%; Total volatility of 17%; No correlation with interest rates or bond returns.

complex. In this case, simulation provides a tool for studying the most general types of interest rate and return behavior.

The simulation starts with a model for single-period returns based on our best estimate of such parameters as expected returns, risk premiums, volatilities, and correlations (see Table 1). The multi-period return is calculated from a compounded sequence of single-period returns. By simulating a large number of multi-period returns, we can estimate the distribution of long-run returns and can assess the relative investment performance of stocks and bonds.[2] The simulation of multi-period returns for a 60% stock/40% bond portfolio is illustrated in Table 2.

Figure 1 shows one-, five-, ten-, and twenty-year interest rate forecasts for a mean-reverting process with a 15% reversion rate toward a mean or normal rate of 9%. The starting interest rate is assumed to equal the 9% normal rate, so the first-year forecast is a pure random walk. The bars represent the 80% confidence interval for the interest rate at the end of the particular year. Each bar is divided by lines corresponding to the tenth, twenty-fifth, fiftieth, seventy-fifth, and ninetieth percentiles. The average interest rate is indicated by the "handlebar," which coincides with the fiftieth percentile or median in this case.

When interest rates are below (above) 9%, there is a slight upward (downward) trend toward 9%, closing the gap at an average rate of 15% per year. The interest rate forecast converges after about five years to a stable distribution with an 80% probability of being between 5% and 13%. While there is a 20% chance of rates lower than 5% or higher than 13%, the chances of rates as low as 1% or as high as 20% are virtually nil.

To model bond returns, we use a bond portfolio with a duration of 4.5 years and an initial yield to maturity of 9%. A 4.5-year duration is approximately equal to the duration of a typical well-diversified, investment-grade bond port-

---

[2] For further discussion of Monte Carlo simulation, see Ripley (1987).

Table 2: Simulating Returns for a 60% Stock/40% Bond Portfolio

Time 0: Initial Values

Initial Interest Rate = 9%

Initial Portfolio Value = $100 ($60 in Stocks, $40 in Bonds)

Time 1: First-Year Returns

Interest Rate Change = .15 Reversion Rate × (9% Long-Run Normal Rate − 9% Beginning Interest Rate) + (1.5% Interest Rate Volatility × .667 Random Term #1) = +1% => 10% Year-End Interest Rate

Bond Return = 9% Beginning Bond Yield − 4.5 Bond Duration × (1% Interest Rate Change) = 4.5%

Stock Return = 9% Beginning Interest Rate + 4% Stock Risk Premium + (17% Stock Volatility × 1.0 Random Term #2) = 30%

Portfolio Return = (60% Stock Allocation × 30% Stock Return) + (40% Bond Allocation × 4.5% Bond Return) = 19.8% => $119.80 Year-End Portfolio Value

Time 2: Second-Year Returns

Interest Rate Change = .15 Reversion Rate × (9% Long-Run Normal Rate − 10% Beginning Interest Rate) + (1.5% Interest Rate Volatility × −2.0 Random Term #3) = −3.15% => 6.85% Year-End Interest Rate

Bond Return = 10% Beginning Bond Yield − 4.5 Bond Duration × (−3.15% Interest Rate Change) = 24.175%

Stock Return = 10% Beginning Interest Rate + 4% Stock Risk Premium + (17% Stock Volatility × 0.5 Random Term #4) = 22.5%

Portfolio Return = (60% Stock Allocation × 22.5% Stock Return) + (40% Bond Allocation × 24.175% Bond Return) = 23.17% => $147.56 Year-End Portfolio Value

Annualized Compound Return $= \sqrt[2]{\dfrac{\$147.56}{\$100.00}} - 1 = \sqrt[2]{1.198 \times 1.2317} - 1 = .2147$ or 21.47%

Figure 1: Interest Rate Forecast with Mean Reversion Toward 9%

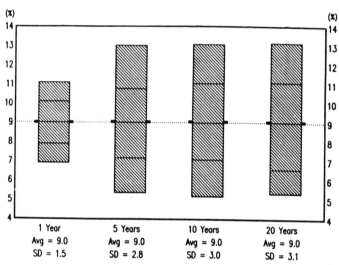

folio such as the Salomon Brothers Broad Investment-Grade (BIG) Index^{TM}. The bond portfolio is rebalanced annually to maintain a constant duration of 4.5 years.

To model stock returns, we employ the lognormal distribution, a widely used characterization of historical stock returns. The base case assumes that stocks have an arithmetic average return premium of 4% over bond yields. Thus, at an initial bond yield of 9%, stocks will have a 13% expected return. As the bond yield rises and falls through the course of time, the expected stock return changes accordingly. The base case assumes that the stock return volatility, or standard deviation, is 17%, which is consistent with actual stock return volatility over much of the past two decades.

The base case also assumes that *single-period* stock returns are uncorrelated with changes in interest rates. Because the stock's expected return is adjusted one-to-one with changes in the interest rate, however, *multi-period* returns will exhibit an increasingly positive correlation with the cumulative change in interest rates as the investment horizon is extended.

Figure 2: Comparison of Stock and Bond Returns

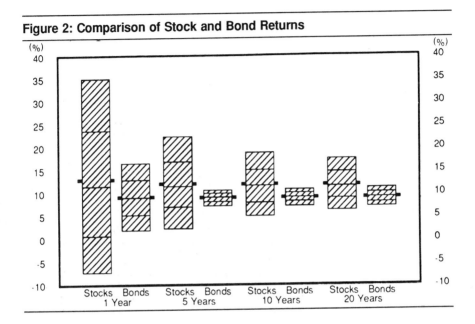

COMPARISON OF STOCK AND BOND INVESTMENT PERFORMANCE

Figure 2 shows annualized compound stock and bond returns over one-, five-, ten-, and twenty-year investment horizons. Both stock and bond returns are very volatile in Year 1, but the range of returns shrinks quite rapidly over time. Note that the greater volatility of stocks in comparison to bonds results in a persistently wider range of stock returns than of bond returns. Note also that the average annualized compound stock return erodes over time from 13% over the first year to the median return value of 11.7%. Most of this erosion takes place within value of 11.7%. Most of this erosion takes place within five years and is a consequence of the volatility of the stock portfolio.[3]

---

[3] One mathematical property of multi-period compounded returns is that the average compound return will erode toward the median return as the number of compounding periods increases. The median return is approximately equal to the single-period average return reduced by one-half the single-period variance. Thus, the greater a security's volatility, the more erosion of the average compound return over time.

Figure 3: Stock/Bond Ratio in 1, 5, 10, and 20 Years

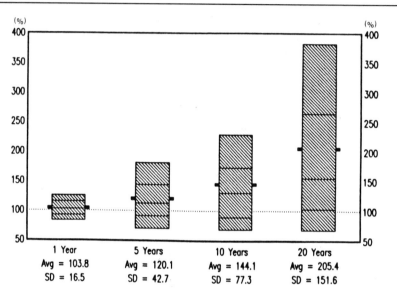

Relative stock/bond performance can be measured more directly by computing the ratio of stock to bond portfolio values. In Figure 3, the portions of the bars below 100 indicate the cases where an all-stock allocation underperforms an all-bond allocation. The probability of inferior stock performance is 44% over one year, 36% over five years, and 24% over twenty years. While stocks provide some extraordinary opportunities to outperform bonds, the worst-case stock return is considerably lower than the worst-case bond return.

Figure 4 shows a sampling of simulated stock and bond returns over five years. The Equal Return Line indicates the break-even point, where the stock return is exactly equal to the bond return. Most of the outcomes are above the Equal Return Line; in fact, the stock return exceeds the bond return 64% of the time—sometimes by as much as 20%. On the other hand, stock performance is inferior to bond performance 36% of the time, and shortfalls of 10% are not uncommon. The randomness of the scatter around the Stock Regression Line reflects a zero to slightly positive correlation between five-year stock and bond returns.

Figure 4: Stock Versus Bond Returns in 5 Years

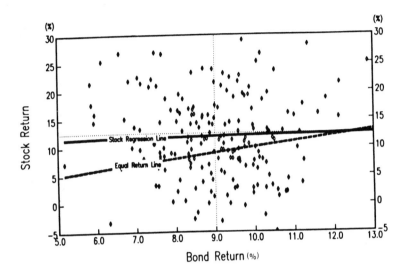

Bond Return (%)

THE EFFECT OF VARYING ASSUMPTIONS FOR THE INTEREST RATE PROCESS

Our simulation model has produced the interesting but perhaps disturbing prediction that equity risk persists at very high levels. For those of us who believe that equities will dominate bonds over the long run, it is disquieting to discover that stocks remain so risky for so long. Before discarding long-held beliefs, we must determine whether these results are valid for a wide range of modeling assumptions or are limited to special cases.

Figure 5 presents the stock/bond ratio under alternative assumptions for the interest rate process. The first case is based on the assumption in Table 1 that interest rates follow a mean-reverting process.

This assumption is dropped in the second case, where we assume that interest rates follow a random walk; they are allowed to drift as low as 0% or to arbitrarily high values in the long run. The random walk produces a much greater range of interest rates, which in turn produces more volatile bond returns. While reversion (or lack of reversion) has a significant effect on individual bond returns, the net effect on the relative performance of stocks and bonds is negligible.

Figure 5: The Effect of Varying Assumptions for the Interest Rate Process on the Stock/Bond Ratio in 5 Years

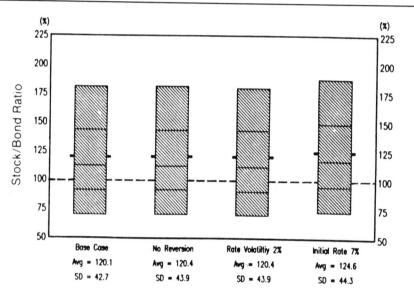

In the third case, rate reversion is retained, but the interest rate volatility is increased to 2%. While this change obviously has a major impact on the range of bond returns, it has virtually no effect on the stock/bond ratio.

The fourth case assumes an initial interest rate of 7%, which reverts to a long-run rate of 9%. A 2% rise in rates reduces the bond return by about 9%; that is, the bond's "price effect" is approximately 4.5 x 2% (the duration times the rate change).

On balance, the interest rate process appears to have little effect on the shortfall risk of stocks relative to bonds. In all four cases, there remains about a 36% chance that stocks will underperform bonds. The magnitude of the potential shortfall, as measured by the tenth percentile stock/bond ratio, is nearly the same for all four interest rate processes. In fact, for every reasonable interest rate process we examined, we found essentially the same results. We conclude that the *relative* performance of stocks and bonds does *not* depend in any significant way on the underlying interest rate process.

Figure 6: Favorable Assumptions for Stocks: 5-Year Investment Horizon

---

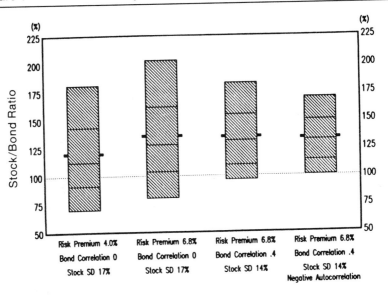

	Risk Premium 4.0%	Risk Premium 6.8%	Risk Premium 6.8%	Risk Premium 6.8%
	Bond Correlation 0	Bond Correlation 0	Bond Correlation .4	Bond Correlation .4
	Stock SD 17%	Stock SD 17%	Stock SD 14%	Stock SD 14%
				Negative Autocorrelation

IDENTIFYING INVESTMENT CONDITIONS FAVORABLE FOR STOCKS

If we limit our choice to stocks and bonds, then under virtually any reasonable set of assumptions, stocks will almost surely outperform bonds as the investment horizon is extended to infinity.[4] Unfortunately, most of us do not have an infinite period of time to work out near-term losses. In order to obtain a better stock/bond ratio over a reasonable investment horizon, it appears that we must seek more favorable assumptions for equity behavior.

In Figure 6, we examine a sequence of assumptions that are favorable for stocks. The first bar again represents the base case. In the second case, the stock risk premium is increased to 6.8%—the sixty-year historical average excess re-

---

[4] Latané's (1959) optimal growth model shows that the allocation with the highest geometric mean return will almost surely outperform any other allocation as the investment horizon extends to infinity. Merton and Samuelson (1974) have observed that while the strategy of maximizing the geometric mean is optimal for investors with a logarithmic utility function, the growth-optimal strategy is suboptimal and undesirable for many important classes of utility functions.

turn of stocks over bonds. The higher risk premium produces a significant increase in the average stock/bond ratio and reduces the chances of underperformance over a five-year horizon from 36% to 23%.

The third case also assumes a 6.8% risk premium, but with a 14% volatility
and a positive correlation of 0.4 between stock and bond returns. A 14% volatility is at the low end of the range of volatilities observed over the past twenty
years. A positive return correlation reduces the likelihood of getting a bad stock
return together with a good bond return. Thus the chances of equity underperformance are reduced. The positive correlation and the lower volatility have little effect on the average stock/bond ratio, but the range of outcomes is reduced,
and the probability of inferior stock performance falls to 15%.

The fourth case introduces a negative autocorrelation in stock returns (that
is, returns over successive periods are negatively correlated).[5] In this case, a
large gain or loss is likely to be followed by a partial correction, and the chances
of extremely good or bad returns are reduced. This final combination of assumptions produces an additional improvement in the stock/bond ratio: The
tenth percentile is raised to 100. In other words, under these highly favorable
conditions, there is a 90% probability that stocks will outperform bonds over
five years.

ASSET ALLOCATION OVER MULTI-PERIOD INVESTMENT HORIZONS

The persistence of equity risk over long horizons does not imply that stocks are
undesirable. After all, a 25% shortfall probability also means that stocks have a
75% chance of beating bonds and sometimes by very large amounts. However,
the fact that stocks can greatly underperform in both the short and long term
may cause many investors to seek a safer route than a 100% stock portfolio. In
this section, we continue to use our base case assumption to explore the long-
run merits of diversification by examining alternative allocations between stocks
and bonds. The desired asset mix is maintained with annual rebalancing.

Over a one-year investment horizon, the choice between stocks and bonds
reflects a standard risk/return trade-off. Over a five-year horizon, the benefits of
diversification start to emerge. Figure 7 shows that an allocation of 30% in
stocks and 70% in bonds outperforms the 100% bond allocation at all percentiles
above the twenty-fifth, with a significantly higher average return and upside
potential. The downside risk of the 30% stock/70% bond allocation at the tenth
percentile is nearly the same as the 100% bond allocation.

---

[5] There is growing evidence that stock returns are not randomly distributed over time.
See Poterba and Summers (1988), for example.

Figure 7: Portfolio Returns Over a 5-Year Investment Horizon

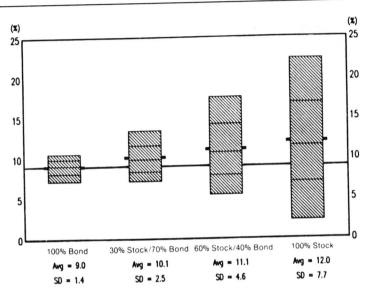

It is important to recognize, however, that higher percentiles at and above the tenth percentile do not imply superior performance 90% of the time. In fact, the 30% stock/70% bond allocation underperforms the 100% bond allocation 32% of the time. Over a twenty-year horizon, the 30% stock/70% bond allocation decisively outperforms the 100% bond allocation at and above the tenth percentile return.

In fact, in a simulation with 50,000 trials, the 30% stock/70% bond allocation has higher returns at all percentiles above one-tenth of 1%. For all practical purposes, the 30% stock/70% bond allocation dominates the 100% bond allocation over a twenty-year investment horizon.

DEVELOPING A NEW PERSPECTIVE ON THE NATURE OF RISK

The mean-variance model of modern portfolio theory provides a rigorous approach for managing risk and return. Modern portfolio theory works best over short investment horizons, however, where security returns are approximately normally distributed, and "risk" can be adequately measured by the return variance. While the mean-variance model works well for managing short-term investment results, it may fail to address some legitimate concerns of pension plans, foundations, and other investors with long-term investment horizons.

As the investment horizon lengthens, the distribution of portfolio values becomes increasingly asymmetric, and the variance loses its intuitive value as a complete measure of risk. To manage investment performance over planning horizons of three to five years or longer, we must sharpen our understanding of risk. To assess risk when returns are asymmetrical, we must examine downside outcomes directly, and the concept of "shortfall risk" provides a simple and intuitive measure to do this.

The "shortfall probability" measures the chances of jeopardizing one or more of the sponsor's goals. The "shortfall magnitude" measures the amount by which such a goal is likely to be violated.[6] These goals can be stated in terms of a minimum return objective or a minimum surplus or even in terms of shareholder wealth.

Shortfall risk can be defined in a way that is directly related to the sponsor's strategic objectives. Thus, it serves as a means of translating investment results into terms that are meaningful from a policy perspective. For example, consider a $1.25 billion pension plan with a current surplus of $250 million and a current funding ratio of 125%. The pension liability has an effective duration of ten and will grow at a 9% rate given a stable interest forecast.[7]

Suppose the sponsor's objective is to achieve a high return on investment while limiting risk exposure. Suppose also that the sponsor has set two thresholds for assessing the risk exposure: 1) achieving a minimum threshold return of at least 9%, the riskless rate; and 2) producing a return that is large enough to avoid a reportable deficit.

Table 3 illustrates how investment results can be translated into two measures of shortfall risk that directly reflect the sponsor's desire to achieve a minimum return of 9% and to avoid a deficit. Again, we see that the 30% stock/70% bond allocation is very attractive compared to the 100% bond allocation. The 30% stock/70% bond allocation provides a higher average return and surplus, while its shortfall risk is less than that of the 100% bond allocation. Stock allocations above 30% provide an even higher average return and surplus but also produce greater shortfall risk measured either in surplus terms or relative to the 9% return threshold. To justify a stock allocation higher than 30%, one must

---

[6] Bawa and Lindenberg (1977) provide a rigorous utility-based justification for "shortfall risk" for the arbitrary, asymmetric return distribution. They show that the zero-order partial moment is equal to the probability of obtaining an outcome below a threshold level—or what we call the "shortfall probability." The first- and second-order partial moments measure the magnitude of the outcome below the threshold or what we term the "shortfall magnitude."

[7] For simplicity, we assume that contributions, benefits, and new service costs are equal. The liability discount rate is assumed to be 9% and to change one-to-one with changes in bond yield.

Table 3: Investment Prospects in Terms of Strategic Risk Limits (Dollars in Millions)

	Results at the End of 5 Years			
	100% Bonds	30% Stocks/ 70% Bonds	60% Stocks/ 40% Bonds	100% Stocks
Investment Results				
Average Return on Investment	9.0%	10.1%	11.1%	12.0%
Standard Deviation of Returns	1.4	2.5	4.6	7.7
10th Percentile Return	7.2	7.1	5.4	2.2
Shortfall Risk Relative to a 9% Minimum Return Threshold				
Probability of a Shortfall	50.0%	33.0%	34.0%	36.0%
Magnitude of Shortfall Below 9% at the 10th Percentile Return	(1.8)%	(1.9)%	(3.6)%	(6.8)%
Shortfall Risk in Surplus Terms[a]				
Average Surplus	$326	$438	$549	$705
Average Funding Ratio	123.0%	130.0%	138.0%	149.0%
Probability of a Deficit	9.0%	8.0%	14.0%	22.0%
Surplus (Deficit) at the 10th Percentile Return	$46	$73	$(62)	$(273)

[a] The initial pension surplus and funding ratio are $250 million and 125%, respectively.

carefully weigh the incremental rewards against the incremental risks of jeopardizing strategic objectives.

The concept of "shortfall risk" provides an intuitive and policy-oriented risk gauge that facilitates more productive decision-making. In a typical pension fund or foundation, a review board or committee has oversight in matters of investment policy. Usually, one or two members at most are investment professionals. As the overall board must ultimately bear responsibility for the fund's investment risk, it is crucial that the long-term risk implications of alternative policies be presented as clearly as possible. The standard risk measure—volatility expressed as a standard deviation—does not meet this criterion of clarity, especially with respect to multiple risk goals or planning horizons of three to five years or longer.

In contrast, the concept of shortfall risk better conforms to most individuals' intuitive sense of what "risk" is really all about. The shortfall approach attempts to quantify the "risk event" directly in terms of a probability of occurrence and a likely magnitude of the shortfall. With more intuitive yardsticks for the risk event that the fund hopes to control, it should be possible to strike a better balance between long-term risk exposure and return potential. Ultimately, this should facilitate the development of an asset allocation policy that is more fully integrated with the sponsor's overall strategic objectives.

References

Bawa, Vijay S., and Eric B. Lindenberg. "Capital Market Equilibrium in a Mean-Lower Partial Moment Framework." *Journal of Financial Economics*, 5, 1977.

Latané, Henry. "Criteria for Choice Among Risky Ventures." *Journal of Political Economics*, April 1959.

Leibowitz, Martin L., and William S. Krasker. "Persistence of Risk: Shortfall Probabilities Over the Long Term." *Financial Analysts Journal*, November/December, 1988.

Merton, Robert C., and Paul A. Samuelson. "Fallacy of the Lognormal Approximation to Optimal Portfolio Decision Making Over Many Periods." *Journal of Financial Economics*, March 1974.

Poterba, James M., and Lawrence H. Summers. "Mean Reversion in Stock Prices, Evidence and Implications." *Journal of Financial Economics*, October 1988.

Ripley, Brian D. *Stochastic Simulation*, New York: John Wiley & Sons, 1987.

Stocks, Bonds, Bills and Inflation: 1988 Yearbook. Chicago: Ibbotson Associates, Inc., 1988.

Chapter I-11

Asset Allocation Under Shortfall Constraints

INTRODUCTION

Over the long term, equity investors have been richly rewarded for the risks that they have endured. For example, during the 1926-87 period, the S&P provided an annual return advantage of 6.8%, compared with long-term corporate bonds. By contrast, over shorter periods, stocks actually underperformed cash on a surprisingly frequent basis. In particular, over the past 15 years, stocks have underperformed Treasury bills in almost 35% of 6- to 18-month time periods.[1] These shorter horizons are comparable to the periods over which the performance of money managers is monitored. Thus, although we may reasonably expect superior equity returns over long investment horizons, few professional investors are able to observe calmly and passively while high volatility buffets their portfolio's value over the short run.

Most fund sponsors control their overall risk by adjusting the extent of their equity position. By adding cash or bonds and, thereby, lowering the equity exposure, fund sponsors reduce the volatility of their portfolio. At the same time,

[1] See *Investment Policy Weekly*, R.S. Salomon, Jr., Caroline H. Davenport, Maria A. Fiore, and Susan G. Brand, Salomon Brothers Inc , February 5, 1990.

Martin L. Leibowitz and Stanley Kogelman, "Asset Allocation Under Shortfall Constraints," Salomon Brothers Inc, June 1990.

however, they give up a portion of the risk premium that equity offers. Thus, decreased exposure to equity leads to a reduction in expected returns.

In this paper, we focus on the balance between risky and risk-free assets. Although we use equity as the proxy for *all* of the risky assets in a portfolio, the methodology of this paper applies equally to any basket of risky assets. We offer a simple model of how risk tolerance can be quantified and then used to determine the maximal equity investment.

We measure downside risk by the "shortfall probability" relative to a minimum return threshold.[2] By specifying both this threshold and a shortfall probability, we can establish a "shortfall constraint" to determine the maximum allocation to risky assets. We also consider the sensitivity of the risky asset allocation to changes in volatility, equity risk premium, return threshold, and shortfall probability. Finally, we show how this methodology can be applied to multiyear investment horizons.

THE EFFICIENT FRONTIER FOR AN EQUITY/CASH PORTFOLIO

A portfolio manager with a well-established horizon always has a continuum of choices between risky and riskless assets. For example, over a one-year investment horizon, the one-year Treasury STRIP provides a riskless return equal to its yield, that is, this "cash" asset has no return volatility. However, modern theory suggests that a holder of risky assets should be compensated for the associated volatility ("risk") by means of a positive increment in expected return—the so-called "risk premium." Current estimates of the equity risk premium for U.S. equities range from a 4% expected return advantage to a 6% expected return advantage. Because "cash" does not have any return volatility, the volatility in an equity/cash portfolio entirely reflects the proportion of equity in that portfolio. Thus, the portfolio manager can control volatility risk by adjusting the equity/cash balance. As the percentage of equity increases, so do both the portfolio risk and expected return. In Figure 1, we illustrate the linear relationship between the expected return and risk for the full spectrum of equity/cash portfolios over a one-year holding period.

In Figure 1, we assume that the riskless asset yields 8%, the equity risk premium is 5%, and the expected return is equal to the nominal yield. The risk measure is the standard deviation of returns, which we assume is 17% for equity. If "equity" is taken to represent the market portfolio of risky assets, the straight line in Figure 1 can be interpreted as the "efficient frontier" that repre-

---

[2] The "shortfall" approach is discussed in detail in *A Shortfall Approach to Duration Management*, Martin L. Leibowitz, Stanley Kogelman and Thomas E. Klaffky, Salomon Brothers Inc, April 1990.

Figure 1: The Efficient Frontier for an Equity/Cash Portfolio (One-Year Horizon)

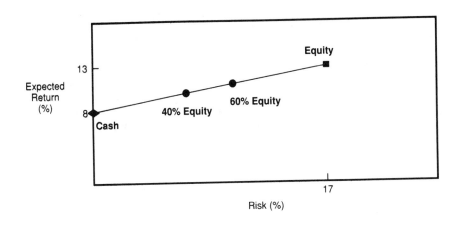

sents portfolios that provide the maximal return for any given level of risk. The left end point of the efficient frontier represents a portfolio with 0% equity, while the right end point represents 100% equity. In addition, we have indicated the location of those portfolios that consist of 40% equity and 60% equity.

THE SHORTFALL LINE

The equity portfolio manager is faced with a critically important strategic decision regarding the appropriate extent of his equity position. The determination of the "right" equity/cash balance ultimately depends on the fund's risk tolerance. In this section, we quantify "risk tolerance" in a simple and intuitive manner by considering first the minimum return that can be tolerated over a given investment horizon. For purposes of exposition, we assume that the plan sponsor believes that it is worth risking a one-year return as low as 3% for the potential gain that can be achieved from equity investment.

Unfortunately, although investment in a one-year 8% Treasury STRIP ensures an 8% return, there can be no minimum return guarantee with an equity investment. However, by adjusting the equity/cash balance, it is possible to lower the probability of failing to meet the 3% minimum return objective. In

Figure 2: Portfolios With a 50% Probability of Exceeding a 3% Return

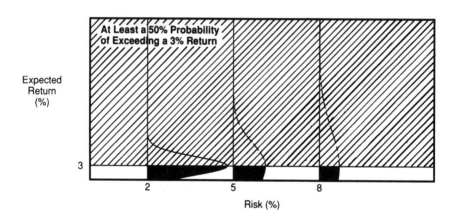

particular, we seek to fulfill the following "shortfall constraint" under the assumption that returns are normally distributed: It is required that there be a probability of 10% or less that returns fall below a 3% threshold over the one-year horizon.[3]

This shortfall constraint will lead to a "shortfall line" in the return/risk diagram that divides the diagram into two regions. All portfolios that have return/risk characteristics that place them in the upper region will meet or exceed the shortfall constraint. Those portfolios that fall in the lower region will fail to satisfy the shortfall constraint. To understand how the shortfall line is constructed, we first consider all of the portfolios that have an expected return of 3%. Such portfolios are represented in Figure 2 by the horizontal line at the 3% return level. Each point on this line represents a different degree of volatility,

---

[3] The shortfall probability is an incomplete measure of risk, because it fails to provide any indication of how bad the shortfall will be in the event that one should occur. For a more fully developed theory of shortfall analysis that incorporates these broader considerations, see "Asset Pricing in a Generalized Mean-Lower Partial Moment Framework; Theory and Evidence," W.V. Harlow and R. Rao, in *Journal of Financial and Quantitative Analysis*, September 1989; and "Capital Market Equilibrium in a Mean, Lower Partial Moment Framework," V. Bawa and E.B. Lindenberg, in *Journal of Financial Economics*, November 1977.

with higher volatilities leading to more "spread out" distributions. Thus, as illustrated, the distribution that corresponds to a standard deviation of 5% has a higher concentration of returns near 3% than the distribution that corresponds to a standard deviation of 8%. In all cases, however, 50% of the returns fall below the expected value of 3%; that is, there is a 50% shortfall probability. The lower tail of the distribution, which is shaded in Figure 2, is called the "shortfall region." The size of the shortfall region corresponds to the shortfall probability.

Now we focus our attention on the portfolio with a standard deviation of 5%. To reduce the size of the shortfall region to 10%, we must "push up" the distribution (that is, raise the expected return to 9.4%) so that only 10% of the returns falls below 3%. In a similar manner, by sufficiently raising the expected return at all risk levels, we create the 10% shortfall line in Figure 3.

It can be shown that, under a wide range of conditions, the shortfall constraint always leads to a straight line in the expected return/risk diagram. Comparing Figure 2 with Figure 3, we can see that both shortfall lines emanate from the threshold point of 3% on the vertical axis. However, the 50% shortfall line of Figure 3 was horizontal (that is, it had a slope of 0), while the 10% shortfall line in Figure 4 had a much more positive slope. The general result is that more stringent shortfall probabilities require more steeply sloped shortfall lines. In Figure 4, we reproduce the "shortfall line" (note that we have changed the scale) and observe that all portfolios above the line have sufficiently large expected

Figure 3: Portfolios With a 90% Probability of Exceeding a 3% Return

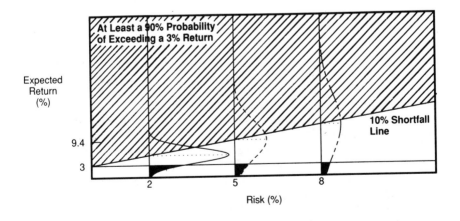

Figure 4: The Shortfall Line

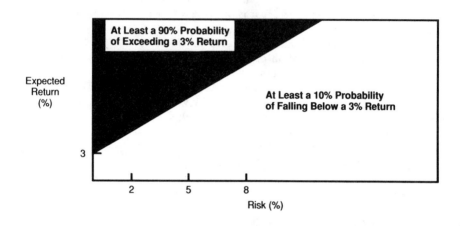

returns so that they offer at least a 90% probability of a 3% or greater return. Similarly, all portfolios below the line have less than a 90% probability of producing returns above 3%.

THE SHORTFALL CONSTRAINT AND THE EFFICIENT FRONTIER

Our goal of locating portfolios that meet or exceed the shortfall constraint in the previous section now can be achieved by superimposing the shortfall line on the efficient frontier in Figure 1. In Figure 5, we note that *all* points on the efficient frontier that lie above the shortfall line will meet or exceed the requirement of at most a 10% probability of returns below the 3% threshold. The maximum equity holding that is consistent with this shortfall constraint is found at the intersection of the shortfall line and the efficient frontier. As indicated in the graph, this intersection point corresponds to a 30%/70% equity/cash portfolio. The expected return of this portfolio is 9.49%, and its standard deviation is 5.06%.

The low percentage of equity in the portfolio at first may seem counterintuitive. However, it actually reflects the powerful impact of the high volatility of equity over a one-year horizon. In a later section of this paper, we will show

Figure 5: The Shortfall Constraint and the Efficient Frontier (One-Year Horizon)

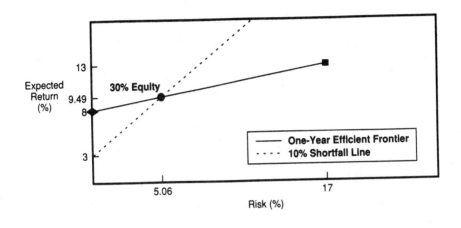

Figure 6: A Shortfall Interpretation of the Efficient Frontier

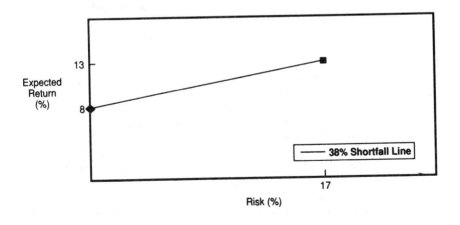

how much larger equity percentages become feasible as we move to longer investment horizons.

Further insight into the equity allocation in Figure 5 may be gained by observing that the efficient frontier is itself a shortfall line that corresponds to an 8% minimum return threshold, because it emanates from the 8% point on the return axis. In fact, we can show that the slope of the efficient frontier corresponds to a 38% probability of shortfall (see Figure 6). Such a shortfall line implies that *all* portfolios with greater than 0% equity have a 38% probability of a one-year return below the risk-free rate of 8%. In this context, it is not surprising that the portfolio manager would want only a limited amount of equity in his portfolio as long as he had a *strictly* one-year horizon (and no market view other than that implied by the expected return estimates).

SENSITIVITY TO ALTERNATIVE VOLATILITY AND RISK PREMIUM ESTIMATES

In our example, we assume that equity volatility is 17% over a one-year period. Because volatility is, in fact, not constant but varies with changing market conditions, we must test the sensitivity of the equity allocation to variations in volatility. The impact of changes in volatility is illustrated in Figure 7, where we observe that the end point of the efficient frontier shifts horizontally as volatility varies. Observe that lower volatilities increase the slope of the efficient frontier. Consequently, with lower volatility, as we should expect, the maximum admissible equity allocation increases. This increase in equity allocation is evident in Figure 8, where we superimpose the shortfall line on the efficient frontiers from Figure 7.

Note that the effect of volatility on the allowable equity holding is asymmetric. A 3% increase in the volatility estimate lowers the equity percentage by 6%, while a 3% decrease in volatility raises the equity percentage by 9%.

Next, we consider the impact of changes in estimates of the risk premium on the equity allocation. In Figure 9, we show both the shortfall line and the efficient frontiers for risk premiums of 3%, 5% and 7%. Changing the risk premium moves the end point of the efficient frontier vertically, but its slope only undergoes a modest change. Consequently, for the one-year horizon, the equity allocation is fairly insensitive to the risk premium. In fact, it only varies from a low of 27% at a 3% risk premium to a high of 34% at a 7% risk premium.

In summary, over one-year horizons, we have found that the equity allocation is moderately sensitive to the volatility estimate and fairly insensitive to the risk premium estimate. This is fortuitous, because market estimates of the volatility tend to be more stable than estimates of the risk premium. Thus, for the

Figure 7: The Efficient Frontier With Alternative Volatility Estimates

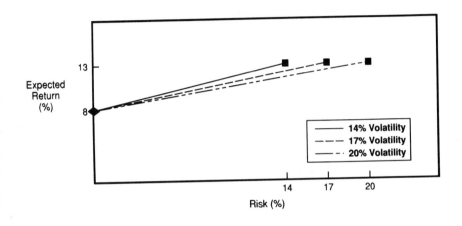

Figure 8: The Impact of Equity Volatility on the Maximum Equity Holding

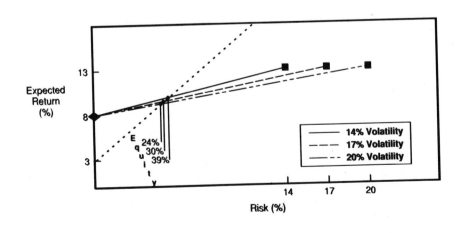

Figure 9: The Impact of Alternative Risk Premium Estimates

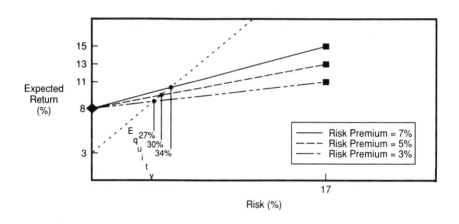

Risk (%)

one-year horizon, the shortfall constraint itself, rather than market estimates, most strongly influences the equity allocation.

SENSITIVITY TO VARIATIONS IN THE SHORTFALL CONSTRAINT

The shortfall constraint consists of both a minimum return threshold and a shortfall probability. In Figure 10, we illustrate the impact of changes in the minimum return threshold on the equity allocation.

Because the shortfall line always emanates from the threshold value on the vertical axis, the changing minimum return threshold simply results in a parallel shift of the shortfall line. Observe that a 2% change in the minimum return threshold results in a 12% change in the equity allocation. For example, a 1% minimum return threshold allows for an increase in the equity allocation from 30% to 42%.

In Figure 11, we illustrate the impact of changes in the shortfall probability. As noted earlier, the more stringent probabilities lead to steeper slopes for the shortfall lines and vice versa for more liberal probabilities. Thus, if we only require a 15% shortfall probability relative to a 3% return threshold, the lower

Figure 10: The Impact of the Minimum Return Threshold on the Maximum Equity Holding

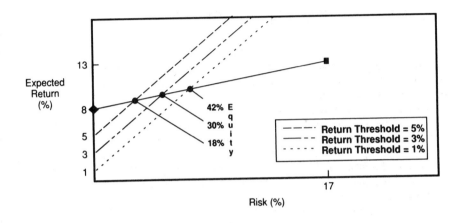

Figure 11: The Impact of Shortfall Probability

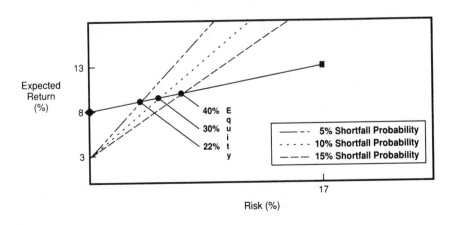

slope leads to an increase in the maximum equity holding to 40%. However, if we demand a more stringent 5% shortfall probability, the slope is steeper and the maximum equity holding falls to 22%.

THE MULTIYEAR INVESTMENT HORIZON

In this section, we consider the impact of an extension in the investment horizon on the equity/cash mix. To this end, we use the expected annualized compound return as our return measure and the standard deviation of annualized returns as the risk measure. These choices of annualized return/risk measures enable us to use the same shortfall line as we did for a one-year horizon.

In Figure 12, we illustrate the efficient frontier for a one-, three- and five-year horizon. Here, we assume that, for any horizon, there is a riskless asset with an 8% expected return, that is, one-year, three-year and five-year STRIPs. Note that the efficient frontier steepens significantly as the horizon increases, because the *annualized* volatility of returns decreases dramatically from 17% to 7.7% as we lengthen the horizon from one year to five years.[4]

Proceeding with our analysis, now we superimpose the shortfall constraint on the efficient frontiers for the three different time periods (see Figure 13). The maximum equity allocation increases dramatically as the horizon increases. In particular, it extends from 30% over a one-year horizon to 60% for a three-year horizon and to 85% for a five-year horizon. For any horizon that is longer than about six years, our shortfall constraint allows a 100% equity allocation.

Of course, over a five-year horizon, the 3% threshold is probably too generous. A more realistic 6% threshold dramatically reduces the maximal equity allocation from 85% to only 34%, as shown in Figure 14.

Longer horizons offer a greater opportunity to capture more fully the benefits of high risk premiums. Thus, we should expect the maximum equity allocation to become sensitive to the risk premium estimate. For a fixed three-year horizon, this sensitivity is illustrated in Figure 15. Here we observe that an increase in the risk premium from 5% to 7% leads to a rise in the maximum equity allocation from 60% to 80%. We also observe that the sensitivity to the risk pre-

---

[4] The decrease in annualized return volatility reflects the standard random walk model. In this model, the volatility of cumulative return increases with the square root of elapsed time. As a result, the volatility of the *annualized* returns over the investment horizon actually declines as the horizon period lengthens. We also can see from Figure 12 that, for the five-year horizon, the expected return on equity decreases from 13% to 12%. This drop is a result of what has been termed "volatility drag." For a detailed discussion of this concept, see *Equity Risk Premiums and the 'Volatility Drag,'* Martin L. Leibowitz, Stanley Kogelman and Terence C. Langetieg, Salomon Brothers Inc, April 1989.

Figure 12: The Efficient Frontier for Multiyear Horizons

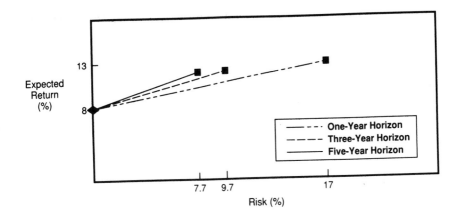

Figure 13: The Multiyear Shortfall Constraint With a 3% Return Threshold

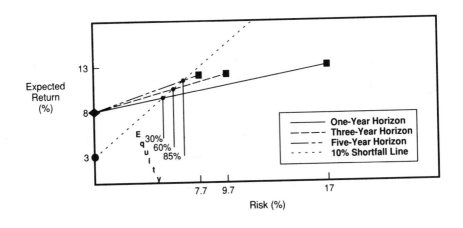

Figure 14: The Multiyear Shortfall Constraint With a 6% Return Threshold

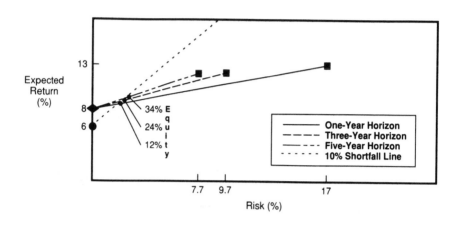

Figure 15: The Three-Year Shortfall Constraint With Alternative Risk Premium Estimates

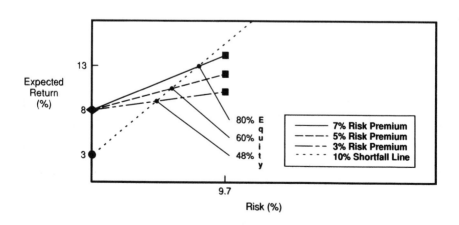

mium is asymmetric. In particular, a 2% decrease in the risk premium only drops the maximum equity allocation from 60% to 48%.

SUMMARY AND CONCLUSION

In this paper, we have utilized a simple shortfall methodology to gain insight into the maximal allocation of risky assets. There are three critical ingredients to this analysis: (1) the investment horizon; (2) the minimum return threshold; and (3) the allowable probability that returns will fall below this threshold. Surprisingly, we found that with a 10% shortfall probability, a 3% return threshold and a one-year horizon, only 30% of the portfolio should be in risky assets. Over the short term, the volatility of risky assets creates a high probability of poor returns. In effect, there is insufficient time to reliably capture the risk premium that these assets offer. As long as we focus on a one-year horizon, this result holds across a wide range of risk premiums.

By contrast, as the horizon increases, there is a marked decrease in annualized return volatility. As a result, the allowable equity allocation increases dramatically. We found, for our example, that over a five-year horizon, the risky asset allocation could be increased to 85% for a minimum return threshold of 3%. Moreover, the multiyear allocations are more sensitive to the risk premium, with higher risk premiums leading to substantially greater equity allocations.

The strength of our shortfall model lies in its ability to capture the allocation impact of a simply stated measure of risk tolerance across one or more investment horizons. Accordingly, this shortfall approach should help fund sponsors address the delicate problem of finding a balance between seeking long-term gains and defending against the risk of adverse performance.

Chapter I-12

Return Enhancement from "Foreign" Assets

INTRODUCTION AND SUMMARY

In recent years, there has been a growing acceptance of asset allocation principles that, if carried to their logical conclusion, would call for fund sponsors to raise their strategic target for foreign assets to significant levels (that is, to 20% or more). Nevertheless, U.S. pension funds still have much less international exposure than those theoretical analyses suggest. The root causes for this apparent resistance to a full international allocation are various and complex. However, one problem is that the standard formulation of allocation arguments tends to systematically *understate* the benefits of international diversification.

The understatement of benefits arises when asset allocation studies compare a current domestic benchmark portfolio with the opportunities presented by an efficient frontier that includes a new asset class. The natural and easiest comparison is to keep volatility constant, while increasing expected return. In a risk/return plot, this is done by moving vertically from the benchmark portfolio point to the efficient frontier. This method of portfolio construction assumes that

Martin L. Leibowitz and Stanley Kogelman, "Return Enhancement from 'Foreign' Assets: A New Approach to the Risk/Return Trade-Off," Salomon Brothers Inc, February 1991.

volatility is symmetric. It fails to distinguish between "good" risk (the upside) and "bad" risk (the downside). Consequently, this "constant-volatility" portfolio may significantly understate the magnitude of improvement that is available when risk is primarily viewed in terms of *downside* protection. The "shortfall approach," which we utilize in this paper, provides one simple way of correcting this understatement.[1]

Among the many methodologies used to address downside risk, the shortfall approach is attractive because of its intuitive appeal and ease of use.[2] When applied to international diversification, this approach leads to a portfolio that includes a greater proportion of global equity than the constant-volatility portfolio. Consequently, compared with the constant-volatility approach, the shortfall approach generates a significantly greater return advantage relative to the domestic benchmark. For a range of fairly standard market assumptions, we find that the incremental return advantage from international diversification can be enhanced by 50% or more. For example, in one case, when the return advantage of the constant-volatility portfolio is 132 basis points, the shortfall approach results in a portfolio that has a 205-basis-point advantage over the domestic benchmark.

Our analysis is general in that it can be applied to the introduction of *any* new asset class that provides diversification and/or return benefits. This level of generality goes beyond our current focus on international diversification. To simplify and focus our discussion, we assume only one domestic asset, U.S. equity, and one nondollar asset, "foreign" equity. In actuality, the foreign investment may be viewed as hedged or unhedged equity or fixed-income denominated in a single currency or in a basket of currencies. The key point is that any asset class that is "foreign" to the existing portfolio can be incorporated using the methodology of this paper.[3]

Although the shortfall approach may provide an improved estimate of the benefits of diversification, many practical constraints on the movement toward higher international allocations remain. In particular, U.S. investors have been

---

[1] See *Asset Allocation Under Shortfall Constraints*, Salomon Brothers Inc, June 1990, for a development of the shortfall technique and its application to equity/cash portfolios.

[2] For a discussion of some rigorous methodologies for addressing downside risk, see "Asset Pricing in a Generalized Mean-Lower Partial Moment Framework; Theory and Evidence," W.V. Harlow and R. Rao, in *Journal of Financial and Quantitative Analysis*, September 1989; and "Capital Market Equilibrium in an Mean, Lower Partial Moment Framework," V. Bawa and E.B. Lindenberg, in *Journal of Financial Economics*, November 1977.

[3] For example, see *Currency Hedging and International Diversification*, Vilas Gadkari, Salomon Brothers Inc, October 1989; *Changing Global Stock Markets: The World is Getting Larger*, Eric H. Sorensen and Joseph J. Mezrich, Salomon Brothers Inc, October 1989; and *International Equity Flows; 1990 Edition*, Michael Howell and Angela Cozzini, Salomon Brothers Inc, August 1990.

most comfortable within the confines of their domestic markets. This preference may be ascribed to an historical U.S. insularity and the happy coincidence of having some of the best capital markets in the world. Even though many foreign markets have matured to a reasonable level of efficiency, the persistent perception of non-U.S. investments as "exotic" prevails. Because of this "exotica" constraint, many funds require special protection against sizable losses directly attributable to foreign equity investment. Fortunately, an array of risk-control procedures and techniques are now available that enable the fund sponsor to approach a more optimal proportion of nondollar equity, while hedging against excessive currency risk or market fluctuations. Although we do not address such techniques explicitly in this paper, we do indicate how a simplified "exotica" constraint can be incorporated into the shortfall approach.

Looking forward, we expect a gradual relaxation of the exotica constraint and, with the help of appropriate risk-control techniques, a steady progression toward foreign allocation levels that can make substantial contributions to overall fund performance.

A FRAMEWORK FOR RISK-REDUCTION ANALYSIS

To gain deeper insight into the trade-offs between expected return, volatility and shortfall risk, this paper focuses on three approaches to risk reduction. First, we consider the effect of decreasing the exposure to risky assets while increasing cash holdings. Because we assume that cash is riskless, an increase in cash holdings always results in lower portfolio volatility.

The second approach to risk reduction is diversification. The volatility of portfolios with appropriately weighted combinations of two risky assets may be less than volatility of either asset alone. For example, because U.S. and foreign equity are less than fully correlated, investors can reduce volatility by adding nondollar equity to their portfolios.

The next step in our analysis is to use the shortfall approach to determine the implicit downside risk associated with a domestic benchmark portfolio. With this implied shortfall constraint as a starting point, we find the maximum return portfolio of cash, U.S. equity and foreign equity that satisfies this same constraint. This global portfolio has a significant return advantage over the traditional constraint-volatility global portfolio.

In the final section of this paper, we show how an exotica constraint limits nondollar equity as a percentage of the total equity in a portfolio. This limitation then is translated into a modification of the efficient frontier. Once this is done, the shortfall approach is utilized to construct a diversified global portfolio that outperforms the domestic benchmark portfolio.

THE RISK PROFILE OF CASH/EQUITY PORTFOLIOS

In the traditional approach to asset allocation, returns are assumed to be normally distributed, and the reward and risk of each asset class is measured by its mean and standard deviation. When we consider only two assets, the "efficient frontier" represents the risk/return plot of all portfolios made up of two assets.

As a first example, we consider cash and U.S. equity as the only two asset classes. The investment horizon is one year, and the "cash" asset is one-year Treasury STRIPS with an 8% yield. Under these assumptions, cash is riskless, because the buyer of one-year STRIPS is assured of receiving the quoted 8% yield. We assume that equity offers a 5% risk premium over cash and that the annual volatility of equity returns is 17%. These assumptions are outlined in Figure 1.

Figure 1: The U.S. Cash/Equity Portfolio

Yield on One-Year Treasury STRIPS	8%
U.S. Equity Risk Premium	5
Expected Return on U.S. Equity	13%
Treasury STRIP Volatility	0%
U.S. Equity Volatility	17

The "efficient frontier" for cash/equity portfolios will be the straight line that joins the all-cash and all-equity portfolios in the risk/return plot (see Figure 2). The efficient frontier is a line, because all of the portfolio volatility is attributable to the equity portion. As the percentage of equity in the portfolio increases, both the expected return and the volatility increase proportionally.

The high volatility of equity leads to a return distribution that is flat and spread out (see Figure 3). Distributions of this type exhibit a high probability of extreme returns. Thus, both the upside potential and the downside risk are sizable. For example, over a one-year horizon, there is a 10% chance that the return on equity will be less than -8.8%.

In contrast to equity, cash has no volatility over the one-year horizon, and in the absence of default risk, it provides an assured 8% return. When cash is mixed with equity, the return and risk of the resulting portfolio lie between that of the high-return/high-risk posture of pure equity and the low-return/zero-risk cash position. For example, consider a portfolio that consists of 48% U.S. equity and 52% cash. In Figure 4, we superimpose the distribution of this portfolio onto the distribution of the all-equity portfolio. The volatility has decreased dramatically (from 17% to 8.1%), while the expected return has declined to 10.4% from 13.0%. In addition, the probability of extreme returns has been severely cur-

Figure 2: The "Efficient Frontier" for Cash/Equity Portfolios

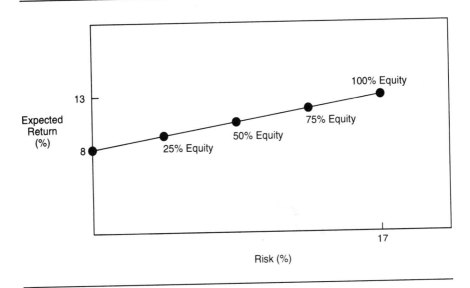

**Figure 3: Return Distribution for U.S. Equity
(Expected Return = 13%; Volatility = 17%)**

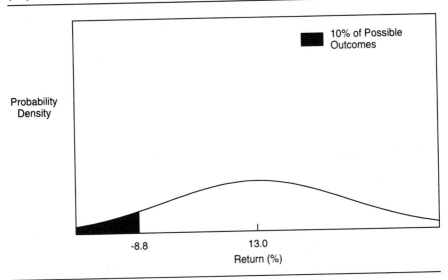

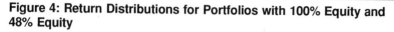

Figure 4: Return Distributions for Portfolios with 100% Equity and 48% Equity

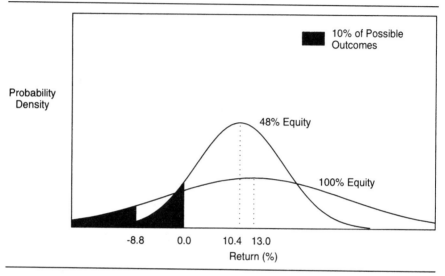

tailed. For example, by reducing the equity holdings to 48%, we have created a portfolio with only 10% probability of a negative return. We can think of the lower expected return as the "cost" of this volatility reduction.

Throughout this paper, we will use the 48% U.S. equity portfolio as the "domestic" benchmark against which the performance of all other portfolios will be measured. Further insight into the gains and costs of volatility reduction can be obtained by comparing the 10th, 50th and 90th percentile returns for the all-cash, all U.S. equity and domestic benchmark portfolios (see Figure 5). The cash portfolio offers absolute downside protection but has no upside potential. The all-equity portfolio offers both the worst 10th percentile and the best 50th and 90th percentile returns. The domestic benchmark portfolio offers a balance between downside risk and upside potential. On the downside, the benchmark has only a 10% probability of negative returns. On the upside, there is a 10% probability that the portfolio returns will exceed 20.8%.

GLOBAL EQUITY PORTFOLIOS

Suppose that a U.S. fund sponsor considers investing a portion of his funds in nondollar equity. For the moment, we assume that foreign equity returns are uncorrelated with U.S. returns and that foreign equity has both a higher volatil-

Figure 5: A Comparison of Percentile Returns for Three Portfolios—100% Cash, 100% U.S. Equity and 48% U.S. Equity Benchmark

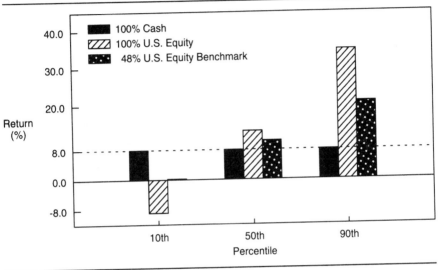

ity (20% versus 17%) and a higher expected return (15% versus 13%). All "global" portfolios that contain a mixture of U.S. and nondollar equity are represented by a curved risk/return plot (see Figure 6). All points on this curve provide higher expected returns than U.S. equity alone. Moreover, the global portfolios on the darkened portion of the curve have less volatility than U.S. equity alone. These portfolios provide the highest return for the given level of risk.

If the risk/return trade-off were the only consideration in portfolio construction, any global portfolio that offered both higher return and less risk than U.S. equity alone clearly would be superior. However, it is possible that all the global portfolios would pose too great a risk for a fund sponsor. To reduce the risk of any global portfolio to an acceptable level, the sponsor can add cash. The net effect of this cash addition is to create a portfolio that would plot along the line between the 100% cash (zero volatility) portfolio point and the global portfolio point on the efficient frontier. When this line is tangent to the global equity efficient frontier, the points on the line represent cash/equity mixtures with the greatest possible return for a given risk level (see Figure 7).[4] We will refer to the

---

[4] This is strictly true for all risk levels only when we assume that the global portfolio at the point of tangency can be leveraged through borrowing at the same 8% cash rate.

Figure 6: The Efficient Frontier for Global Equity Portfolios (With Zero Correlation

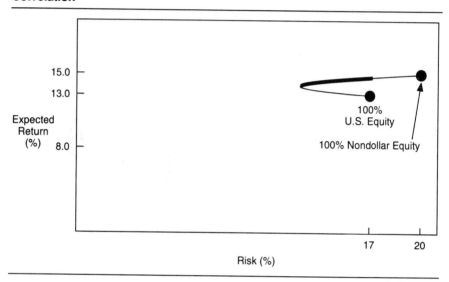

Figure 7: The Optimal Global Portfolio

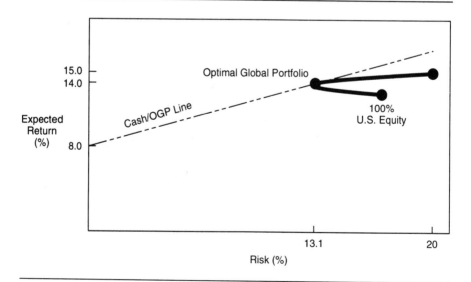

Figure 8: The "Constant-Volatility" Portfolio (62% OGP)

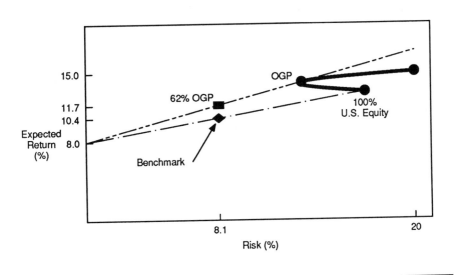

global portfolio at the point of tangency as the Optimal Global Portfolio (OGP). The tangent line is called the cash/OGP line.

In the above example, the OGP consists of about 50% U.S. equity and 50% foreign equity. Its expected return (14.0%) is midway between that of U.S. equity and nondollar equity, while its volatility is only 13.1%—significantly below the volatility of U.S. equity. At a given level of risk, a higher expected return can be achieved with a portfolio on the cash/OGP line than with either a cash/U.S. equity portfolio or a cash/foreign equity portfolio. For example, the portfolio with 38% cash and 62%, OGP has the same volatility as the domestic benchmark portfolio, but its expected return is 132 basis points greater. This 62% OGP portfolio is illustrated in Figure 8, where we also have added the cash/U.S. equity line to Figure 7.

Given our domestic benchmark portfolio, the usual approach to international diversification would be for the fund sponsor to restructure the portfolio and create the 62% OGP portfolio. In doing so, the sponsor would maintain the volatility of the benchmark and have a new portfolio that would dominate the benchmark at all percentiles of the return distribution. Although this approach to portfolio diversification clearly results in superior performance relative to the benchmark, it fails to consider one of the fund's true concerns—the level of downside risk.

THE SHORTFALL LINE

As we have seen in the previous section, the cash/OGP line dominates the cash/U.S. equity line. Although this dominance illustrates the general advantages of adding foreign equity, the extent of the benefit that can be realized depends on the risk/return trade-off selected for comparison. One way to articulate this trade-off is through the "shortfall approach."[5] For example, suppose that an investor wishes to construct a portfolio with a 90% probability that the one-year return will be greater than zero. The "0%" return is called the minimum threshold return. This constraint implies that there is only a 10% probability of "shortfall" below the minimum threshold. That is, there is only a 10% chance that returns will be negative.

Portfolios that meet the shortfall constraint must provide sufficient expected return to compensate for the portfolio risk. Such portfolios can be located in the risk/return diagram by constructing a "shortfall line" (see Figure 9). This line

Figure 9: The Shortfall Line

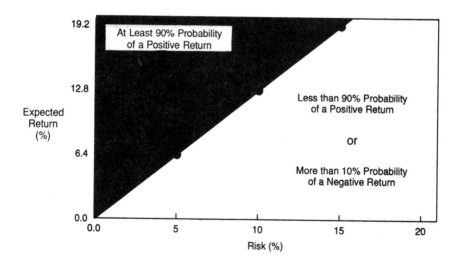

---

[5] See *Asset Allocation Under Shortfall Constraints.*

extends from the 0% point to the expected return axis. Its slope is determined from the shortfall probability.[6] The shortfall line divides the risk/return diagram into two regions. All portfolios that fulfill the shortfall constraint have a risk/return balance that places them on or above the shortfall line. Portfolios below that line will fail to meet the shortfall constraint.

THE IMPLICIT SHORTFALL CONSTRAINT

The shortfall constraint can be viewed from a somewhat different perspective. Under adverse conditions, any portfolio that includes risky assets also bears some risk of poor performance. Consequently, every such portfolio *implicitly* includes a shortfall constraint. If the volatility and expected return of the portfolio are known, it is possible to back into the shortfall constraint.[7] For example, suppose we want to determine the 10th percentile return for the domestic benchmark portfolio. To do so, we construct a shortfall line through the benchmark risk/return point with a slope appropriate to a 10% shortfall probability.[8] The point at which the shortfall line intersects the return axis is the implicit minimum return threshold (see Figure 10). The intersection point is at a 0% return. In other words, there is a 10% probability that the benchmark portfolio return will be negative over a one-year horizon. This is not coincidental. We intentionally constructed a benchmark portfolio that would have this convenient implicit shortfall constraint.

Now suppose that our criterion for constructing a cash/OGP portfolio is to preserve the implied shortfall constraint. That is, we want the cash/OGP portfolio, like the domestic benchmark, to have only a 10% probability of negative returns. All portfolios that fulfill this shortfall condition have a risk/return point that falls on the shortfall line. Consequently, the cash/OGP portfolio that meets the shortfall condition can be found by superimposing the shortfall line on the graph that includes the efficient frontier and the cash/OGP line (see Figure 7). We find that the two lines intersect at a portfolio with 74% invested in the OGP and the balance in cash assets (see Figure 11 and the blowup in Figure 12).

The 74% OGP "shortfall portfolio" provides a higher expected return and greater upside potential than either the domestic benchmark portfolio or the 62% OGP "constant-volatility" portfolio. The expected return advantage of the

---

[6] For a 10% shortfall probability, the shortfall line is given by the following relationship:
Expected Return = Minimum Threshold + 1.282 × Volatility.

[7] Although we assume that the portfolio return distribution is normal, we can generalize the shortfall approach to other return distributions.

[8] In this case, the slope can be shown to be 1.282. See *A Shortfall Approach to Duration Management*, Salomon Brothers Inc, April 1990.

Figure 10: The Implicit Shortfall Constraint for the Benchmark Portfolio

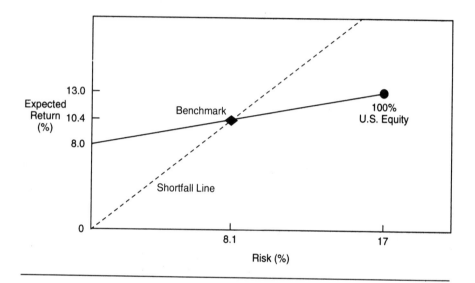

Figure 11: The Shortfall Constraint for the Optimal Global Portfolio

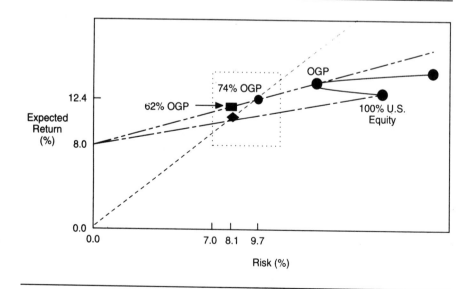

Figure 12: The Return Advantage of the Optimal Global Portfolio

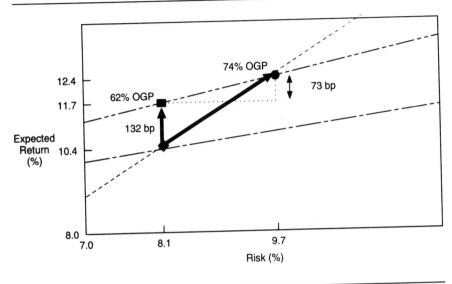

OGP shortfall portfolio is 205 basis points relative to the benchmark portfolio and 73 basis points relative to the constant-volatility portfolio. Thus, the return increment attributable to the OGP shortfall portfolio is about 55% greater than the 132-basis-point return increment of the constant-volatility portfolio. In addition, the 90th percentile return of the OGP shortfall portfolio is more than 400 basis points greater than that of the benchmark and about 280 basis points greater than that of the constant-volatility portfolio (see Figure 13).

At low percentiles, the OGP shortfall portfolio will underperform the constant-volatility portfolio. For example, at the 10th percentile, the constant-volatility portfolio has a return of about 1.3%—considerably higher than the 0% threshold return of shortfall portfolio. However, if the fund sponsor is willing to

Figure 13: A Comparison of the Return Characteristics of Three Portfolios—Optimal Global Portfolio, 50% U.S. Equity and 50% Nondollar Equity

Portfolio	Cash	U.S. Equity	OGP	Standard Deviation	Percentile Return 10th	Percentile Return 50th[a]	Percentile Return 90th
Benchmark	52.4%	47.6%	—	8.1%	0.0%	10.4%	20.8%
Constant Volatiltiy	38.4	—	61.6%	8.1	1.3	11.7	22.1
Shortfall OGP	26.2	—	73.8	9.7	0.0	12.4	24.9

[a] Mean. OGP Optimal Global Portfolio.

accept the same shortfall risk as the domestic benchmark implies, the OGP shortfall portfolio remains attractive because of its superior upside potential.

THE LIMITING SHORTFALL PORTFOLIO

In the previous section, an implicit shortfall constraint for the domestic benchmark portfolio was derived based on the arbitrary choice of the 10th percentile as the point at which downside risk was controlled. Now, we consider the effects of changes in the shortfall probability.

In Figure 14, we have constructed three shortfall lines through the domestic benchmark with slopes appropriate to a 20%, 10% and 1% shortfall probability. As the shortfall probability decreases, the slope of the shortfall line increases. As a result of this increased slope, the point of intersection of the shortfall line and the cash/OGP line moves closer to the constant-volatility portfolio. Thus, the constant-volatility portfolio can be viewed as a limiting shortfall portfolio.

Every portfolio on the cash/OGP line that lies above the constant-volatility portfolio will have some shortfall constraint in common with the domestic benchmark portfolio. For example, both the benchmark portfolio and an 88% OGP portfolio will have a 20% probability that the return over a one-year hori-

Figure 14: The Effect of Changes in the Shortfall Probability

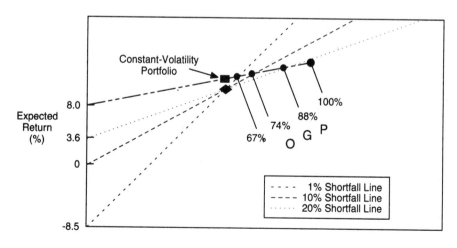

zon will be less than 3.6%. However, the 88% OGP portfolio has considerably greater upside potential than the benchmark, and it also has a 160-basis-point expected return advantage relative to the constant-volatility portfolio.

As we approach the constant-volatility portfolio, the shortfall constraint becomes extraordinarily stringent. The 67% OGP portfolio has the same 1% shortfall constraint as the benchmark, but it still has a 34-basis-point expected return advantage over the constant-volatility portfolio. In effect, the constant-volatility portfolio offers too much shortfall protection. The price of this unnecessary protection can be substantial give-up in expected return.

The shortfall approach always will lead to a portfolio that has a higher expected return and greater upside potential than the constant-volatility portfolio, regardless of the stringency of the shortfall constraint.

DIVERSIFIED PORTFOLIOS OF ASSETS WITH EQUAL EXPECTED RETURNS

In the previous section, we saw that there were significant benefits to diversification when uncorrelated foreign equity had both a higher expected return and a higher volatility than U.S. equity. In this section, we consider the potential impact of foreign equity on portfolio performance under the assumption that all equity markets have the same expected return. For the moment, we continue to assume that foreign equity has a higher volatility (20%) than U.S. equity (17%) and that the correlation between these asset classes is zero.

In practice, estimates of volatilities and correlations usually are based on historical data. Although these statistics vary over time, the past five to ten years of data usually are taken as reasonable estimates of current relationships. However, expected returns are difficult to forecast, and historical data rarely provide accurate estimates of future performance. Many analysts assume that over time, unhedged nondollar equity returns will tend to provide the same risk premium as U.S. equity. Fortunately, the benefits of diversification do not depend solely on the existence of an expected return advantage.

Because of the equality of expected returns, the efficient frontier in Figure 6 flattens out so that all portfolios provide the same expected return in dollar terms. However, it is still possible to reduce risk significantly by adding foreign equity. Portfolios with up to 85% nondollar equity have lower risk than an all-U.S. equity portfolio. These portfolios comprise the darkened portion of the "curve" in Figure 15. For this simplistic case, in which all portfolios have the same expected return, the OGP clearly will be the portfolio with the least risk. Thus, the OGP is located at the left-most point on the efficient frontier. This OGP contains 58% U.S. equity and 42% foreign equity. It has an expected return

Figure 15: Diversification with Equal Expected Returns

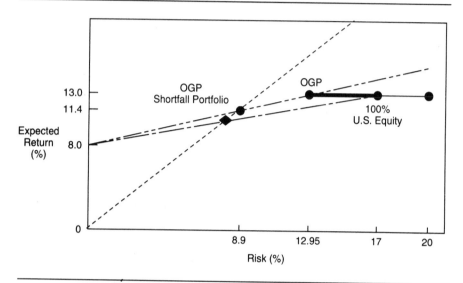

of 13% and a 12.95% volatility. In Figure 15, the cash/U.S. equity line, the cash/OGP line and the 10% shortfall line are illustrated.

From Figure 15, we again can see the significant improvement in expected return associated with the global portfolio. The benefits of international diversification clearly do not depend on the presumption of an expected return advantage for foreign equity. In fact, the power of including foreign assets is so great that shortfall portfolios with nondollar equity will exhibit superior return profiles even in cases where the nondollar equity has a lower return than U.S. equity. Moreover, in the preceding examples, we assumed that foreign equity was more volatile than U.S. equity. If the volatilities had been the same, the benefits of nondollar assets would have been even greater.

SENSITIVITY ANALYSIS

In this section, we test the sensitivity of our analysis to variations in the value of the foreign equity's return, volatility and correlation coefficient. The results of our analysis are summarized in Figure 16. Our base case, in which foreign equity returns are uncorrelated with U.S. equity returns, appears in the second row of the table. In this base case, foreign equity is more volatile than U.S. equity and has a 200-basis-point return advantage.

Figure 16: Summary Characteristics of the OGP Shortfall Portfolios

Foreign/U.S. Correlation	Foreign Equity Standard Deviation	Foreign Equity Return Spread	Total Pct. Equity	Standard Deviation	Advantage Relative to Benchmark Portfolio	Advantage Relative to Constant-Volatility Portfolio
Benchmark	—	—	47.7%	8.1%	0bp	—
0.0	20.0%	400bp	79.6%	10.8%	340bp	142bp
0.0[a]	20.0	200	73.8	9.7	205	73
0.0	20.0	0	68.9	8.9	106	31
0.0	20.0	-200	63.1	8.4	39	10
0.0	17.0%	400bp	94.6%	11.8%	478bp	226bp
0.0	17.0	200	84.6	10.3	284	112
0.0	17.0	0	76.8	9.2	146	47
0.0	17.0	-200	68.8	8.5	54	14
0.3	17.0%	200bp	68.3%	9.6%	193bp	68bp
0.5	17.0%	200bp	60.9%	9.3%	157bp	52bp
1.0	17.0%	200bp	54.1%	9.2%	140bp	45bp
1.0	17.0	100	50.7	8.6	66	18
1.0	17.0	0	47.7	8.1	0	0

[a] Base case. bp Basis points.

When the foreign equity return advantage is increased to 400 basis points, the OGP shortfall portfolio advantage relative to the domestic benchmark increases from 205 basis points to 340 basis points. In addition, the advantage relative to the constant-volatility portfolio increases from 73 basis points to 142 basis points. The OGP shortfall portfolio still has a 39-basis-point return advantage relative to the benchmark, even if the expected return of foreign equity is 200 basis points *below* that of U.S. equity.

In the second section of the summary table, we assume that foreign equity has the same volatility as U.S. equity. In this case, the return advantage of the OGP shortfall portfolio increases dramatically. For the base case of a 200-basis-point foreign equity return spread, the OGP shortfall portfolio advantage relative to the domestic benchmark grows to 284 basis points. The pure impact of diversification is observed when the returns and volatilities of foreign and U.S. equity are identical. In this case, the return advantage relative to the benchmark is an impressive 146 basis points.

To this point, we have assumed that foreign equity and U.S. equity are uncorrelated. As the correlation between asset classes increases, diversification benefits erode. A fairly typical assumption for the correlation between U.S. and nondollar equity is 0.3. Suppose that nondollar equity has a 200-basis-point expected return advantage and the same 17% volatility as U.S. equity. In that case, the OGP shortfall portfolio return advantage relative to the benchmark is still a substantial 193 basis points, although that is considerably less than the 284-basis-point advantage realized with a zero correlation.

The return advantage of the OGP shortfall portfolio declines as the correlation increases. At the limit, when the correlation is 1.0, the OGP shortfall portfolio return advantage entirely reflects the higher expected return of nondollar equity. If there is no foreign return spread, there will not be any benefit to diversification. There is no advantage to including a highly correlated asset in a portfolio unless it provides a greater return.

THE EXOTICA CONSTRAINT

Fund sponsors may be reluctant to invest too large a portion of their equity allocation in foreign equity. Although the expected returns and diversification benefits of nondollar equity may be attractive, the repercussions of a substantial loss may more than outweigh the potential gains. In essence, the sponsor may consider the asset class that consists of nondollar equity to be "exotica." Conse-

Figure 17: The Shortfall Portfolio with an Exotica Constraint

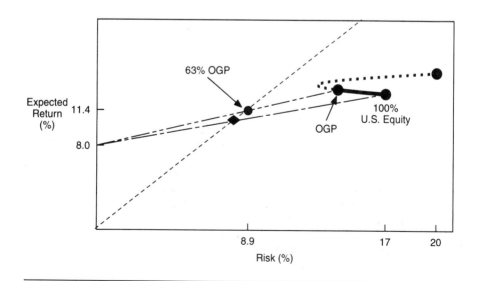

quently, it might be necessary to impose an additional loss constraint that reduces the likelihood of significant underperformance attributable to foreign investment. The effect of such a constraint will be to place an upper limit on the holdings of nondollar equity. For example, suppose that the "exotica constraint" limits nondollar equity investment to a maximum of 20% of the total equity investment. In Figure 17, the points along the solid portion of the efficient frontier represent portfolios with 0%-20% in nondollar equity. Under this exotica constraint, the OGP would have 20% nondollar equity, an expected return of 13.4% and a 14.2% volatility.

The optimal portfolio that meets the shortfall constraint can again be found by superimposing the 10% shortfall line on a cash/OGP line that extends from the 8% risk-free rate to the constrained OGP (see Figure 17). The expected return of this shortfall portfolio is still 100 basis points greater than that of the domestic benchmark portfolio. At the 90th percentile, the exotica shortfall portfolio has a 200-basis-point return advantage over the benchmark.

As the exotica constraint becomes more stringent, the location of the maximal exotica portfolio on the efficient frontier moves closer to the 100% U.S. equity portfolio. Consequently, the advantage of the exotica shortfall portfolio will erode as the maximal exposure to nondollar equity declines.

SUMMARY AND CONCLUSION

Ten years ago, the primary asset classes considered by U.S. fund sponsors were cash, stocks and bonds. Since then, there has been a dramatic globalization of the financial markets, and fund sponsors have become increasingly aware of the gains that can be achieved through investment in international assets.

The methodology of this paper helps to address one misconception that arises when asset allocation studies suggest including a new asset class. The problem is that the standard formulation of the allocation argument tends to understate the magnitude of improvement available from diversification. In part, this understatement can be attributed to the criteria used to choose new portfolios. Traditionally, fund sponsors have sought to construct global portfolios that have a higher expected return but the same volatility as their domestic benchmark. This approach neglects what in fact may be a greater concern—the implicit downside risk in their benchmark.

In this paper, we have used the shortfall approach to create global portfolios with the same downside risk constraint as the domestic benchmark. As an example, we showed that a 52% U.S. cash/48% U.S. equity benchmark portfolio has an implicit 10% probability of negative returns. We then constructed a global portfolio with this same shortfall probability. This global portfolio has a return advantage over the benchmark that was 55% greater than the return advantage of the constant-volatility portfolio.

In addition, we tested the sensitivity of our analysis to variations in the expected return and the volatility of foreign equity and to variations in the correlation between U.S. and foreign equity. Over a wide range of fairly realistic assumptions, we found that compared with the constant-volatility approach, the shortfall approach continued to produce portfolios with significant performance advantages.

Chapter I-13

Asset Performance and Surplus Control

INTRODUCTION

This paper presents an asset allocation methodology for constructing portfolios that strike a balance between asset performance and maintenance of acceptable levels of downside risk in *both* asset and surplus contexts. In the real world, pension fund sponsors do not have the luxury of being able to pursue a single well-defined goal. Rather, they must contend with a complex set of multiple objectives. These include achieving market-related returns on assets when the market does well and attaining at least some minimum return when the market does poorly. At the same time, sponsors are expected to maintain or improve their funding status relative to a variety of liability measures.

Even when the plan's funding status is not considered, the strategic asset allocation decision is not easy. The fundamental issue is how to capture the risk premium of equity while avoiding excessively high levels of volatility. Through a combination of mean-variance analysis and tradition, most funds have settled

The authors wish to express their appreciation for the helpful comments and suggestions from Keith Ambachtsheer, Allan Emkin, Michael Granito, and William Sharpe.

Martin L. Leibowitz, Stanley Kogelman, and Lawrence N. Bader, "Asset Performance and Surplus Control: A Dual-Shortfall Approach," Salomon Brothers Inc, July 1991.

243

on a long-term strategic allocation target of a 50%-60% investment in equity-like assets, with the balance primarily in fixed-income securities. The fixed-income component tends to be regarded as a single asset class whose characteristics reflect the bond market as a whole. This characterization leads to a duration that is representative of the investment-grade bond market—currently about 4.64 years.[1] In essence, when stripped of the (usually token) investments in other asset classes, many allocation studies really lead to a single decision: the percentage to be allocated to equity.

Unfortunately, the resulting 60% stock/40% bond portfolio has far less interest rate sensitivity than a pension plan's accumulated benefit obligation (ABO), which typically has a duration of about 10 years. Thus, the standard allocation leads to significant surplus volatility, because the pension fund is vulnerable both to poor equity returns when the stock market weakens, and to high-liability returns when the bond market rallies. In recent years, particularly with the advent of the Financial Accounting Standards Board Statement 87 (FASB 87), there has been a growing interest in models that set the allocation problem in a liability framework.[2] However, these new asset/liability models generally have problems of their own.

At one extreme, an "immunized" portfolio minimizes surplus risk by matching the duration of a 100% bond portfolio to the duration of the liability. While "immunization" may be useful in the short-term management of the ABO under unusual circumstances, a dynamic ongoing fund has a far more complex liability structure than can be represented by the ABO alone. Thus, immunizing against the ABO (or indeed, against any single liability measure) tends to foreclose the growth opportunities and inflation protection needed for the long-term benefit of plan sponsors and participants alike.

However, there are more general surplus-based models that treat bonds as a "variable asset class" with duration/volatility values that range from Treasury bills up to risk levels that far exceed that of domestic equities. In contrast to asset-only models that essentially prescribe only an equity percentage, these generalized surplus-based models tend to characterize allocations in terms of an equity percentage *and* a duration target for the bond component. These models move beyond immunization and can accommodate significant equity holdings. However, surplus optimizations almost invariably push the duration to extremes by forcing the dollar-duration of the bond component to match the dollar-duration of the liabilities. The resulting bond durations of 15 years or longer

---

[1] Over the past seven years, the effective duration of the Salomon Brothers Broad Investment-Grade (BIG) Bond Index has ranged from a low of 3.87 years to a high of 4.69 years. On April 1, 1991, the duration was 4.64 years.

[2] For example, see *A New Perspective on Asset Allocation*, The Research Foundation of The Institute of Chartered Financial Analysts, December 1987.

may make sense from a narrowly defined surplus-only vantage point, but they entail extraordinary levels of asset volatility.[3]

For these reasons, surplus optimization models have not proven productive in generating allocations that most funds would find viable. To achieve a reasonable balance between asset and surplus risks, this paper presents a methodology for applying simultaneous shortfall constraints on both the asset performance *and* the fund surplus. As an example of this methodology, we construct a new portfolio with the same asset-only shortfall risk as the 60/40 benchmark portfolio but with a more stringent limit on the surplus shortfall. One surprising finding is that modest adjustments to the bond duration and equity percentage are often sufficient to satisfy both constraints. This finding contrasts with surplus optimization approaches that tend to suggest unpalatably long durations. Thus, our dual-shortfall approach avoids the problem of extreme portfolios to which single-objective optimizations are notoriously prone. By design, this approach can develop allocations that are better crafted for the more realistic situation where the fund faces conflicting goals.

THE ASSET-ONLY FRAMEWORK

To analyze the risk/return characteristics of stock/bond portfolios with bonds of varying durations, we must make assumptions regarding expected returns, volatilities and the stock/bond correlation (see Figure 1). We assume that the one-year expected return for the BIG Index is 8.0%, and that U.S. equity provides a 5% risk premium over bonds. The one-year volatility of U.S. equity is taken as 17%, interest rate volatility is 1.5%, and the stock/bond correlation is 0.35. Under these assumptions, the bond asset class will have a volatility of approximately 7.0%.[4] For later reference, Figure 1 also shows the expected return and standard deviation of the benchmark portfolio.

The volatilities and expected returns of portfolios consisting of varying proportions of stocks and the BIG Index plot along a curve in a risk/return diagram, as illustrated in Figure 2. As equity is added to the bond portfolio, the portfolio return increases proportionately. The volatility of the portfolio returns also changes with the additional equity. However, because the correlation is

---

[3] For one approach that avoids many of these problems, see "Liabilities—A New Approach," William F. Sharpe and Lawrence G. Tint, *Journal of Portfolio Management*, Winter 1990.

[4] Because the duration of the BIG Index is fairly stable, we estimate the return volatility by multiplying the 4.64-year duration by the 1.5% interest rate volatility. In this paper, we make the simplifying assumption that the interest rate volatility is the same at all points along the yield curve.

Figure 1: Assumptions on Stock and Bond Returns (Stock/Bond Correlation = 0.35)

Asset	Expected Return	Standard Deviation
Equity	13.0%	17.0%
BIG Index	8.0	7.0
60% Stock/40% BIG Index (Benchmark)	11.0	11.5

fairly low, diversification may initially lead to a decrease (or very gradual increase) in volatility.

We now broaden our discussion of asset allocation by varying the duration of the fixed-income component of the portfolio. To clarify the impact of duration, we use an artificial "flat yield curve" model that makes two assumptions: (1) Bonds of all maturities provide the same 8% yield; and (2) the *expected return* is equal to the yield. The "cash" asset is taken to be 1-year Treasury STRIPS that have an initial duration of 1 year and a zero volatility at the end of the 1-year holding period. As the duration of bonds increases, so does the return volatility. This is shown in Figure 3, where we have indicated a range of fixed-income portfolio durations along a horizontal line at an 8% expected return.

Figure 2: The Risk/Return Trade-Off for Stock/Bond Portfolios (Duration = 4.64 Years)

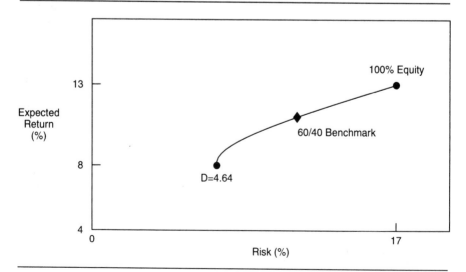

Figure 3: The Flat Yield Curve

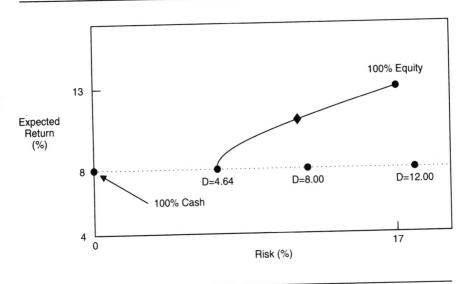

In Figure 4 we have drawn a diagonal line from the cash point to the 100%-equity point. This line represents the risk/return characteristics of the full range of cash/equity portfolios. These portfolios plot on a straight line because all of the portfolio risk is due to the proportion of equity. At any given level of risk, by moving vertically in the risk/return diagram, we see that the cash/equity portfolio provides a higher return than a portfolio of stocks and 4.64-year duration bonds. This results from the zero volatility of cash, which permits a higher proportion of equity for a given portfolio volatility.

In Figure 4, we have also added the risk/return curve for portfolios containing 12-year duration bonds. The "efficient" portfolios are located on the upper portion of this curve. The deep "bubble" to the left reflects the fact that the benefits of diversification are more pronounced for these long-duration, high-volatility bonds.

More generally, every point in the risk/return diagram represents a unique stock/bond portfolio that is characterized by the equity percentage and the duration of the fixed-income component. With our simplistic assumption of a flat yield curve and a positive stock/bond correlation, the portfolio that provides the highest return for a given level of risk will always be a cash/equity portfolio. In this sense, cash/equity portfolios dominate all other stock/bond portfolios.

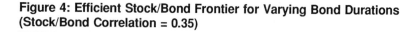

**Figure 4: Efficient Stock/Bond Frontier for Varying Bond Durations
(Stock/Bond Correlation = 0.35)**

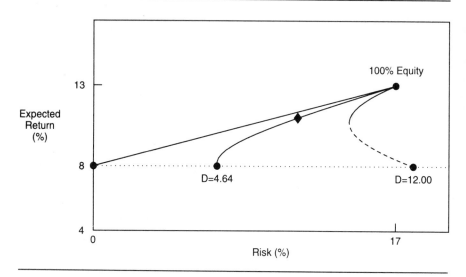

If the yield curve is not flat, there may be mixes of cash, bonds and equities that dominate the cash/equity portfolios. In addition, it should be noted that although the stock/bond correlation tends to be positive over long time periods, there are occasional periods when the correlation is negative. During such periods, longer-duration bonds may provide significant diversification benefits even if the yield curve is flat.[5]

THE RETURN DISTRIBUTION FOR THE BENCHMARK PORTFOLIO

To gain some perspective on the expected performance of the benchmark portfolio, we assume that both stock and bond returns over a one-year horizon are normally distributed. In Figure 5, we illustrate the 60/40 benchmark portfolio return distribution. It can be shown that this 60% stock/40% bond portfolio has an expected return of 11% and a standard deviation of 11.5%. For any normal

[5] See *Portfolio Optimization Utilizing the Full Yield Curve: An Improved Approach to Fixed Income as an Asset Class*, Salomon Brothers Inc, October 1987.

Figure 5: The Return Distribution for the Benchmark Portfolio

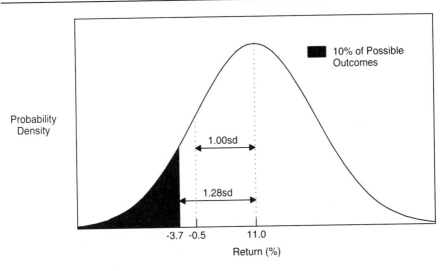

10% of Possible Outcomes

Probability Density

1.00sd

1.28sd

-3.7 -0.5 11.0

Return (%)

sd Standard deviation.

distribution, there is a 16% probability that returns will fall more than one standard deviation below the mean (that is, below -0.5% = 11.0% - 11.5%), and there is a 10% probability that returns will be more than 1.28 standard deviations below the mean (that is, below -3.7% = 11.0% - 1.28 × 11.5%). The region to the left of -3.7% is shaded and will be referred to as the 10% shortfall region. A return of -3.7% will be referred to as the threshold return.

The -3.7% threshold return represents the implicit shortfall risk inherent in the benchmark portfolio. We will assume that the plan sponsor is comfortable with this level of asset-only risk. Consequently, any new allocation that offers a higher expected return but the same shortfall risk as the benchmark portfolio will be viewed as a portfolio improvement.[6]

---

[6] We utilize the indicated measure of shortfall risk because it is intuitively appealing and easy to apply. However, the shortfall probability we have defined is an incomplete measure of risk. It fails to provide any indication of how bad the shortfall will be in the event that one should occur. For a more fully developed theory of shortfall analysis that incorporates these "higher" considerations, see "Asset Pricing in a Generalized Mean-Lower Partial Moment Framework: Theory and Evidence," W.V. Harlow and R. Rao, in *Journal of Financial and Quantitative Analysis*, September 1989; and "Capital Market Equilibruim in a Mean, Lower Partial Moment Framework," V. Bawa and E.B. Lindenberg, in *Journal of Financial Economics*, November 1977.

Figure 6: The Implicit Shortfall Constraint for the Benchmark Portfolio

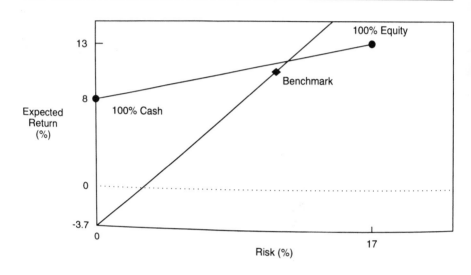

In previous papers, we have shown that all portfolios with equivalent short-fall risk plot along a straight line in a risk/return diagram.[7] In Figure 6, we have constructed a 10% shortfall line through the benchmark portfolio point. Note that this line intersects the (vertical) expected return axis at -3.7%—the threshold return point. All points along the shortfall line represent portfolios for which the expected return offsets the portfolio volatility sufficiently to insure a 90% prob-ability that the one-year return will exceed -3.7% (that is, there is only a 10% chance that returns will fall below the -3.7% threshold). Portfolios above the shortfall line have a higher expected return for a given shortfall risk than portfo-lios on the line. Consequently, all portfolios above the line have a *greater* than 90% probability that the one-year return will exceed -3.7%. Conversely, portfo-lios below the shortfall line have inferior shortfall performance.

The shortfall line in Figure 6 can be shown to intersect the cash/equity line at a point representing a portfolio with 70% stocks and 30% bonds. This portfo-lio has the same shortfall risk as the benchmark portfolio, but it has an expected return of 11.5%. Thus, by moving to the 70/30 portfolio, the fund manager can

[7] See, for example, Martin L. Leibowitz, Stanley Kogelman, and Thomas E. Klaffky, "A Shortfall Approach to Duration Management," Salomon Brothers Inc, April 1990, and Martin L. Leibowitz and Stanley Kogelman, "Asset Allocation Under Shortfall Constraints," Salomon Brothers Inc, June 1990.

pick up 50 basis points in expected return while maintaining the same level of asset shortfall risk.

MODELING THE LIABILITY

Our analysis focuses on the relatively well-defined ABO. The ABO is the value of benefits earned to date by retirees, former employees with vested rights and current employees. It approximates the termination liability of the plan. Thus, a comparison of the ABO with the current value of plan assets indicates the deficit or surplus that would exist if the plan were terminated.

The ABO is also the basis for a balance sheet liability under FASB 87, and a proxy for the "current liability" used under ERISA to determine whether plan contributions are currently required from the employer. Because the future events reflected in the ABO are primarily demographic (mortality, age at retirement), rather than economic (salary increases), the ABO benefit stream may be regarded as essentially fixed for investment purposes. Consequently, the ABO can be modeled as if it were a fixed-income security. The benefit payments associated with more comprehensive measures of liability, such as the projected benefit obligation (PBO), reflect future economic events and have a more complex structure.

The ABO duration is plan-specific, depending on the mix of active and retired plan participants, their ages, the assumed retirement ages of active employees, and the benefit formula. Most plans have ABO durations in the range of 9-12 years.

In computing the ABO, FASB 87 directs the use of a discount rate equivalent to that at which plan benefits could be "settled," for example by an annuity purchase. The yield on high-quality fixed-income investments (8% in our examples) is suggested as a suitable guide for this settlement rate. This rate may also be interpreted as the expected "liability return." In other words, the ABO is expected to grow at 8%, apart from benefit payments and adjustments for the additional benefits that employees earn each year (that is, the "service cost").

In Figure 7, we illustrate the position of the ABO in the risk/return diagram of Figure 4. Note that the benchmark portfolio point and the liability point are quite far apart; that is, the risk/return characteristics of the benchmark portfolio differ markedly from those of the ABO liability. We should therefore expect considerable variations in the pension fund surplus over time.[8]

---

[8] Our approach can easily be extended so that a performance benchmark is viewed as a "liability" against which "surplus" returns are measured. Thus, the dual-shortfall approach can be viewed as simultaneously controlling both the absolute asset risk and the risk relative to a designated performance benchmark.

Figure 7: A Ten-Year-Duration ABO Liability

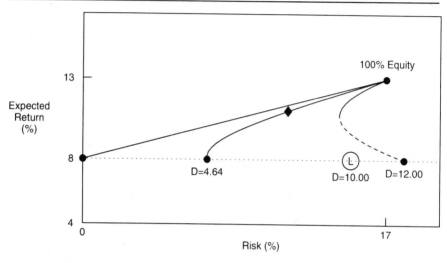

ABO Accumulated Benefit Obligation. L Liability.

THE SURPLUS RETURN

The pension fund surplus is the difference between the current value of the assets and the present value of the liability.[9] Over time, as the value of assets and liabilities changes, so will the surplus. There are a number of ways to define a "surplus return" measure. Since the surplus itself is commonly expressed as a percentage of the liability, we define our surplus return as follows:[10]

$$\text{Surplus Return} = \frac{\text{Change in Surplus}}{\text{Initial Value of Liabilities}}$$

---

[9] For a discussion of the application of the shortfall approach to managing an insurance company's surplus, see *Asset Allocation for Property/Casualty Insurance Companies: A Going-Concern Approach*, Alfred Weinberger and Vincent Kaminski, Salomon Brothers Inc, July 1991.

[10] The surplus could just as easily have been measured against the current value of assets. For example, see "Asset Allocation," William F. Sharpe, in *Managing Investment Portfolios*, Second Edition, Edited by John L. Maginn and Donald L. Tuttle, Warren, Gorham & Lamont, 1990. Our results can be converted to surplus returns relative to the current asset value by dividing by the funding ratio. Also, our results can be converted to dollar surplus changes by multiplying by the initial liability value.

Figure 8: A Liability-Based Surplus Return Example (Dollars in Millions)

Funding Ratio		Initial Value	Final Value	Liability or Asset Return	Surplus Return
	Liability	$100.0	$108.0	8.0%	
140%	Assets	140.0	155.4	11.0	
	Surplus	40.0	47.4		7.4%
100	Assets	100.0	111.0	11.0	
	Surplus	0.0	3.0		3.0
60	Assets	60.0	66.6	11.0	
	Surplus	(40.0)	(41.4)		(1.4)

For example (see Figure 8), suppose that the initial liability is $100 million and the initial assets are $140 million. Then the funding ratio is 140% ($140 million/$100 million) and the surplus is $40 million. If the liability increases by 8% to $108 million, and the assets increase by 11% to $155.4 million, the surplus will have increased by $7.4 million to $47.4 million ($155.4 million - $108.0 million). This surplus increase is 7.4% of the initial liability.

Figure 8 also shows how the value of the surplus return depends on the initial funding ratio. In general, if two pension plans have the same asset and liability returns, the plan with the greater funding ratio will have the greater surplus return. For example, if the funding ratio is 100%, the assets and liabilities are equal and the surplus is zero. In this case, 11% asset growth leads to a surplus return of 3%. If the funding ratio is less than 100%, the assets will be less than the liability and the surplus may decrease even though the asset return is greater than the liability return. For a 60% funding ratio, for example, the surplus return is -1.4%, despite the 11% asset growth.

We will now focus on the distribution of surplus returns when the funding ratio is 140% and the assets are represented by our benchmark portfolio. Because both the asset and liability returns are assumed to be normally distributed, the surplus returns are normally distributed as well. Under our assumptions, the expected surplus return is 7.4% and the standard deviation of surplus returns is 14.7% (see Appendix for details). For any normal return distribution, there is a 10% probability that the return will be 1.28 or more standard deviations below the 7.4% mean. Thus, there is a 10% probability of a surplus decline of at least 11.5% (-11.5% = 7.4% - 1.28 x 14.7%). In Figure 9, we summarize the return and shortfall characteristics from both asset and surplus perspectives. The last column in the figure shows target 10th percentile returns that will be discussed in subsequent sections.

Figure 9: Performance Summary for the Benchmark Portfolio

	Current Expected Return	Current Standard Deviation	Current 10th Percentile Return	Target 10th Percentile Return
Asset-Only Performance	11.0%	11.5%	(3.7)%	(3.7)%
Surplus Performance	7.4	14.7	(11.5)	(7.0)

THE SHORTFALL CURVE FOR THE SURPLUS RETURN

Pension fund sponsors who wish to achieve stability in the plan's surplus can do so with a bond portfolio that matches the liability in present value, duration and other volatility characteristics. Such an "immunized portfolio" will preserve the surplus within some reasonable range of interest rate changes. Most sponsors, however, do not require this degree of safety. Typically, a sponsor with a 140% funding ratio might be willing to sustain some surplus risk provided that the portfolio had substantial upside potential. However, there usually will be some limit to the surplus loss that a sponsor can comfortably sustain. This loss limit will depend on a variety of factors, including the current funding ratio, the fund's performance over prior years, and the level of funding needed to avoid a balance sheet liability or sustain a contribution holiday. To quantify surplus return risk, we focus on the 10th percentile surplus return and somewhat arbitrarily impose the following **surplus shortfall condition:**

There should be no more than a 10% probability that the surplus return will be less than -7%. That is, we require 90% assurance of a surplus return in excess of -7%.

In an earlier section of this paper, we showed that an asset shortfall constraint that was similar to the above surplus constraint could be represented by a straight line in a risk/return diagram. The surplus constraint pattern is far more complicated, and it is represented by an "egg-shaped" convex curve (see Appendix for a theoretical discussion).

In Figure 10, we illustrate the surplus shortfall curve for a pension fund with a 140% funding ratio and a 10-year duration liability. Each point within the "egg" represents an asset portfolio that fulfills the surplus shortfall condition. We have also included the benchmark portfolio and the immunizing portfolio points for reference. The immunizing portfolio is an all-bond portfolio that has the same dollar sensitivity to interest rate changes as the liability. The duration of the immunizing portfolio is 7.1 years (that is, the 10-year liability duration divided by the 140% funding ratio). To see why this is so, we first observe that if the liability is $100 million, the assets are $140 million. If interest rates decline by 1%, the liability, with its 10-year duration, will grow by approximately 10% or

Figure 10: The Surplus Shortfall Curve (Funding Ratio = 140%)

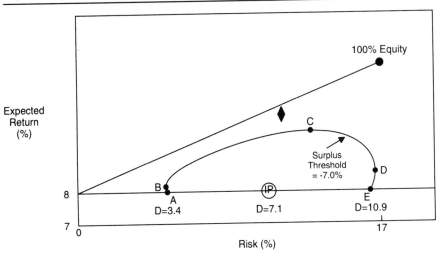

IP Immunizing portfolio.

$10 million (10% of $100 million). At the same time, the assets will increase by 7.1% (the 7.1-year duration multiplied by 1%). In dollar terms, this also represents a $10-million increase (7.1% of $140 million).

To develop an intuitive understanding of the shortfall curve, we first observe that point A in Figure 10 represents a 100% bond portfolio with a 3.4-year duration. This is the shortest duration all-bond portfolio for which there is at most a 10% probability that the surplus return will be -7% or less. For any all-bond portfolios with shorter duration, the gap between the bond duration and the immunizing portfolio is too large, and the shortfall probability will exceed 10%.

As we move to the right of portfolio A, we encounter all-bond portfolios with durations that are closer to the 7.1-year immunizing duration. Consequently, such portfolios will have better shortfall performance than portfolio A. Ultimately, we reach portfolio E, which has a 10.9-year duration. Because the durations of portfolios A and E are equidistant from the 7.1-year immunizing duration, both of these portfolios have the same duration gap and therefore the same -7% surplus shortfall threshold. Portfolios to the right of portfolio E have longer durations than E and will not meet the shortfall constraint.

We now consider the impact of adding equity to portfolio A. Since equity provides a 5% expected return premium over fixed income, the portfolio return will increase as the equity percentage increases. In addition, the low correlation between equity and the liability at first causes the surplus volatility to increase more slowly than the surplus return. Consequently, the initial additions of equity actually *reduce* the surplus shortfall probability, and the shortfall curve bubbles slightly to the left as we move upward from A. However, a point (B) is reached where further equity additions cause the surplus volatility to increase very rapidly. To compensate for this equity-related volatility, the bond duration must be increased so as to bring the asset portfolio duration closer to the immunizing duration.

Under the assumptions of our example, each point along the shortfall curve represents a unique portfolio characterized by the percentage of equity in the portfolio and the duration of the fixed-income component. Portfolio C is the maximum equity portfolio that fulfills the shortfall constraint. It consists of 47% stocks and 53% bonds. From a surplus perspective, portfolio C looks very attractive because of its high expected return. However, the long duration (close to 10 years) of the fixed-income portion of the portfolio leads to high volatility from an asset-only perspective.

Portfolios that lie on the portion of the shortfall curve from C to E can be understood by applying logic similar to that used for portfolios from A to C. It suffices to note that these points correspond to very long duration portfolios consisting of a decreasing percentage of equity.

All portfolios that fall on or within the shortfall "egg" will meet or exceed the surplus shortfall condition. Because the benchmark portfolio "diamond" falls outside the shortfall curve, it fails to meet the surplus shortfall condition. The portion of the "egg" between portfolios B and C can be thought of as a "shortfall efficient frontier" because, among all portfolios meeting the surplus constraint, these portfolios offer the most favorable risk/return trade-off. However, from an *asset-only* perspective, some of these portfolios will have greater shortfall risk than the benchmark portfolio. In the next section, we show how the asset and surplus shortfall constraints can be jointly managed.

BALANCING ASSET AND SURPLUS SHORTFALL REQUIREMENTS

We have observed that the benchmark portfolio lies outside of the surplus shortfall curve corresponding to a minimum surplus return of -7%. This is consistent with the earlier observation that the 10th percentile surplus return for the benchmark portfolio was -11.5%. Thus, meeting the surplus constraint will require restructuring the asset portfolio so that the new portfolio lies on or within the surplus shortfall curve. In choosing this new portfolio, we must be careful that the asset-only constraints are also maintained.

Under the assumption that the plan sponsor finds the asset-only risk of the benchmark portfolio to be acceptable (that is, a -3.7% asset-return threshold), we

Figure 11: A Portfolio that Meets Both Asset-Only and Surplus Shortfall Constraints

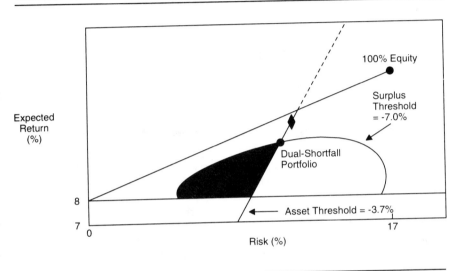

now construct a portfolio that maintains that level of asset-only shortfall *and* meets the surplus constraint. Earlier in this paper, we observed that all portfolios that met the asset constraint were located on or above the shortfall line drawn through the benchmark portfolio (see Figure 6). In Figure 11, we superimpose this line on the surplus shortfall curve of Figure 10. The region above the line but inside the "egg" consists of all portfolios that meet both the asset and surplus shortfall requirements. The indicated point of intersection between the asset-only line and the surplus "egg" corresponds to the portfolio with the highest expected return that meets both shortfall requirements. This "dual-shortfall" portfolio consists of 44% stocks and 56% bonds with a 6.6-year duration.

In comparison to the benchmark portfolio, the reduced equity allocation in the dual-shortfall portfolio leads to an 82-basis-point reduction in expected return, from 11.00% to 10.18%. This reduction can be interpreted as the "cost" of bringing the surplus shortfall risk to an acceptable level. On the other hand, the dual-shortfall portfolio has a significantly higher expected return and about the same volatility as the immunizing portfolio.[11] Thus, even in this simple case, the

---

[11] See *Shortfall Risks and the Asset Allocation Decision: A Simulation Analysis of Stock and Bond Risk Profiles*, Salomon Brothers Inc, January 1989; and *Asset Allocation Under Shortfall Constraints*, Salomon Brothers Inc, June 1990.

dual-shortfall solution provides for more acceptable return/risk characteristics than either the original 60/40 benchmark portfolio (which has too great a surplus risk) or the immunizing portfolio (which guarantees low asset return *and* high asset volatility).

It should be noted that these results strongly depend on the one-year investment horizon assumed in our analysis. The one-year time frame allows a relatively short period in which to reliably capture the equity risk premium. Over longer horizons, reasonable surplus shortfall constraints can be achieved with substantially higher equity allocations and with more moderate duration shifts.

THE IMPACT OF CHANGES IN THE SHORTFALL THRESHOLDS

In the previous sections, we arbitrarily imposed a -7% threshold on the surplus return and assumed that the -3.7% asset-only threshold should be maintained. More often, however, the problem is determining the appropriate balance between asset-only and surplus risks. After assessing the implicit shortfall risks in the portfolio, the plan sponsor may decide that the current portfolio structure is satisfactory. If that is not the case, the sponsor must decide whether the current risk posture should be modified in either an asset-only context, a surplus con-

Figure 12: Implicit Shortfall Constraints in Asset-Only and Surplus Contexts

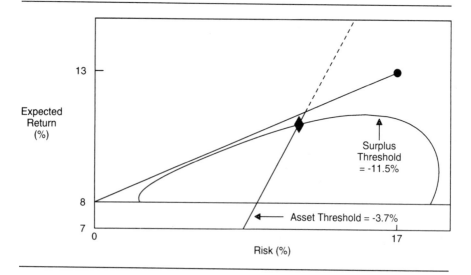

text, or both. In contrast to our earlier example, this assessment might lead to a tightening of the asset constraint, while allowing for greater surplus variability.

In order to better understand the available options for portfolio restructuring, we first review the shortfall characteristics of our benchmark portfolio with 140% funding ratio and 10-year duration liability. Recall that in Figure 6, we constructed an implicit shortfall constraint for the benchmark portfolio. To that figure, we now add the surplus shortfall curve corresponding to the benchmark portfolio's *implicit* -11.5% surplus return threshold. The benchmark portfolio with the shortfall line and "-11.5% egg" are shown in Figure 12. Note that a -11.5% threshold, the surplus shortfall requirement is so weak that it is met by almost all stock/bond portfolios. If we had set -14% as the surplus threshold, the "egg" would have been still larger and would have begun to merge with the cash/equity line.

Every portfolio on the "egg" in Figure 12 will have a 10% probability of a surplus decline of 11.5% or more. In addition, every portfolio on the asset shortfall line will have a 10% probability of an asset decline of 3.7% or more. Both of these conditions are fulfilled at the point of intersection of the shortfall line and shortfall curve (the benchmark in this case).[12]

Changes in the asset threshold return requirement can be viewed as parallel shifts of the shortfall line. In Figure 13, we illustrate the effect of moving the asset threshold return to a less stringent -6% and to a more stringent -1%. As we increase the threshold return requirement, we move to the left along the "egg" and must accept a lower expected return in order to meet the same surplus shortfall condition. By contrast, as we lower the threshold return, we move to the right along the "egg" and can achieve higher expected returns with the same -11.5% surplus shortfall threshold.

Raising the surplus return threshold will shrink the "egg" and significantly reduce the range of acceptable asset portfolios. As an example, in Figure 14, we show the surplus "eggs" corresponding to 10th percentile surplus returns of -7% (our example from the last section) and -3%.

In effect, we can think of the entire risk/return diagram as being covered by a grid of shortfall lines and shortfall curves (see Figure 15). Within this grid, the portfolio manager must select an appropriate surplus shortfall curve and a suitable asset shortfall line. The highest intersection point of the line and the curve represents a balanced portfolio that meets the dual-shortfall condition. For example, the most stringent surplus threshold (-3%) would require a portfolio with only 26% stocks, with the balance invested in 6.9-year duration bonds to meet the surplus requirement and still have the same asset shortfall characteristics as

---

[12] For simplicity, we are treating the two shortfall conditions separately. We require that *each* shortfall probability is 10%; that is, we require a 90% assurance of satisfying the asset shortfall and a 90% probability of meeting the surplus requirement. Note that this is *not* equivalent to a 90% probability that all shortfall requirements are satisfied.

Figure 13: Changing the Asset Return Threshold

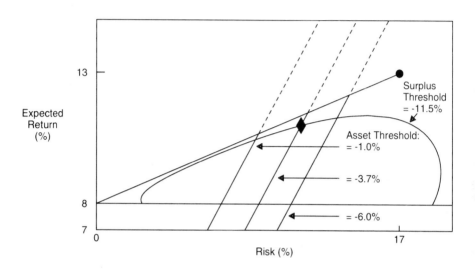

Figure 14: Changing the Surplus Return Threshold

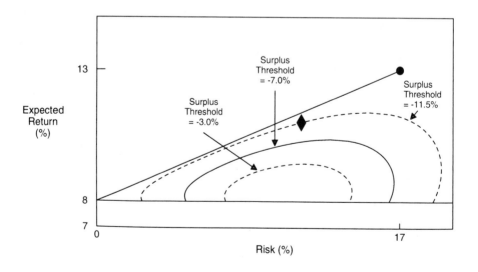

Figure 15: The Shortfall Grid

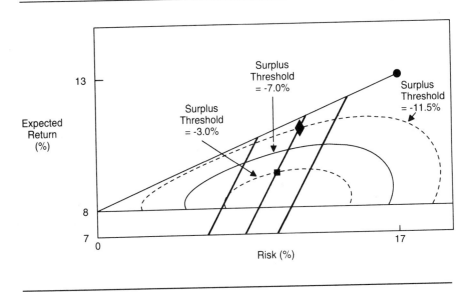

---

the benchmark (see the "square" in Figure 15). When no intersection point exists, either the asset or the surplus shortfall requirement (or both) must be relaxed before a suitable portfolio can be found.

THE IMPACT OF THE FUNDING RATIO

To this point, our examples have focused on pension funds for which the funding ratio is 140%. In actuality, individual funds may have very different goals in terms of surplus preservation. For example, even two funds having the same high funding ratio may set very different courses. One fund may desire to lock in the surplus and therefore adopt a more conservative surplus threshold. In contrast, a second fund may feel that its ample surplus allows room to sustain additional surplus risk in order to reach for higher returns.

Thus, funds with the same funding ratios may use different surplus constraints. If the funding ratios are different, we should not be surprised to encounter an even greater range of allocation choices. In fact, it turns out that the allocation trade-offs are radically altered at different funding ratios, even when the surplus constraints are kept the same.

Figure 16: Changing Funding Ratios (Surplus Threshold = -7%)

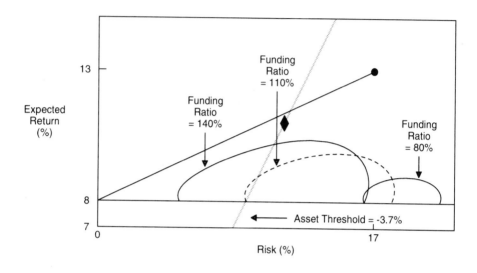

To better understand this "funding ratio effect," we will maintain a -7% surplus threshold while varying the funding ratio.[13] In Figure 16, we compare the shortfall "eggs" for funding ratios of 140%, 110% and 80%. At a 140% funding ratio, the shortfall "egg" covers a wide swath of portfolios having reasonable performance characteristics and also satisfying the asset-only shortfall constraint. As the funding ratio declines, the "eggs" get smaller and move to the right. This means that as the funding ratio declines, the choice of asset portfolios becomes increasingly limited, and the duration of the fixed-income portfolio is forced to more closely approximate an even longer immunizing duration. At a funding ratio of 110%, the 9.1-year immunizing duration (10 years divided by 1.1) is almost the same as the 10-year liability duration. The "egg" is now considerably smaller and has a less desirable location in terms of asset volatility. The asset-only shortfall line passes through the "egg," but the set of relatively low-return portfolios that satisfies both constraints is very restricted.

At a funding ratio of 80%, no portfolios meet the dual-shortfall conditions. In the case of such low funding ratios, there is no easy solution. An immunizing portfolio will simply lock in a negative surplus return by eliminating surplus

---

[13] The degree to which a plan is vulnerable to surplus shortfall risk can also be analyzed in terms of changes in the funding ratio rather than surplus returns.

volatility. Moreover, immunization would create a very volatile portfolio (duration = 12.5 years) from an asset-only perspective. As duration is decreased, asset risk decreases, but the surplus risk increases and the expected surplus return remains negative. Our methodology does not provide a solution to the underfunding problem, but it does offer a convenient process for assessing the trade-offs in this very difficult environment.

More generally, this analysis shows that a fund's initial funding ratio and its tolerance for surplus risk will significantly affect the optimal target duration. Consequently, one would expect the plan sponsor to find that a more customized fixed-income benchmark is better suited to the plan's goals than any broad market benchmark such as the BIG Index. Fortunately, the diversity of the fixed-income markets naturally allows for the construction of a wide range of such customized indexes.[14]

SUMMARY AND CONCLUSION

This paper represents a blend of three themes presented in earlier works: (1) surplus management; (2) shortfall constraints; and (3) the expansion of fixed income from a single asset class to a full continuum of available duration points. With our simple flat "return curve" assumption, cash/equity portfolios dominate all other bond/equity portfolios in terms of asset-only performance. In a surplus context, however, the picture changes dramatically. Cash/equity portfolios have considerable surplus volatility and will be inferior to portfolios where the bond component has a reasonable duration.

In a standard risk/return diagram, the asset-only shortfall constraint is represented by a simple diagonal line. In contrast, the surplus shortfall constraint requires a far more complex "egg-shaped" curve that is roughly centered on top of the immunizing portfolio point. By overlaying these two constraint patterns, it becomes clear how a relatively modest adjustment to the duration and equity percentage can bring the surplus shortfall to within reasonable limits. The trick is to do this without violating restrictions on the asset shortfall.

By extending the process, an asset and surplus shortfall grid can be created that enables the plan sponsor to quickly assess the trade-offs that must be made between asset-only performance and surplus control. The nature of this grid pattern is highly dependent on the initial funding ratio. Moreover, for two funds with the same funding ratio, the choice of an acceptable allocation will depend critically on the plan sponsor's risk tolerance, both in absolute and in relative terms. Consequently, one would expect the optimal portfolio duration target to vary markedly from plan to plan. It would be a rare plan that would find, by

---

[14] See *Salomon Brothers Fixed-Income Indexes*, Salomon Brothers Inc, July 1989.

happenstance, that its duration target coincided with the duration of a broad market index. Thus, this dual-shortfall approach offers a promising technique for sponsors who are willing to break away from the traditional benchmarks and pursue allocations that are truly based on their own fund's needs and objectives.

Appendix

THE SURPLUS RETURN DISTRIBUTION

For any pension fund, the surplus is defined to be the excess of the market value of the assets over the present value of the liability. We will assume that the liability discount rate is the yield on high-quality fixed-income instruments.

Because the values of the assets and the liabilities change with changing market conditions, so will the value of the surplus. To model the surplus distribution, we assume that the values of the assets and liabilities are normally distributed. Symbols for the relevant variables are introduced in Figure A1.

Figure A1: Definition of Asset, Liability and Surplus Variables

Variable	Initial Value	Random Value	One-Year Return	Mean Return	Standard Deviation of Returns	Correlation of Returns with Asset Return
Assets	A_0	$\tilde{A}$	$\tilde{r}_A$	μ_A	σ_A	1.0
Liabilities	L_0	$\tilde{L}$	$\tilde{r}_L$	μ_L	σ_L	ρ_{AL}
Surplus	S_0	$\tilde{S}$	$\tilde{r}_S$	μ_S	σ_S	—

The initial values of the surplus and funding ratio are

$$S_0 = A_0 - L_0 \qquad (1)$$

$$F_0 = A_0/L_0 \qquad (2)$$

After one year the values of the assets, liabilities and surplus will have changed to $\tilde{A}, \tilde{L}$ and $\tilde{S}$ according to the following:

$$\tilde{A} = (1 + \tilde{r}_A)A_0$$
$$\tilde{L} = (1 + \tilde{r}_L)L_0$$

$$\tilde{S} = \tilde{A} - \tilde{L}$$
$$\tilde{S} = (1 + \tilde{r}_A)A_0 - (1 + \tilde{r}_L)L_0$$
$$\tilde{S} = (A_0 - L_0) + \tilde{r}_A A_0 - \tilde{r}_L L_0 .$$

In the above equation, the first term on the right is S_0. Hence,

$$\tilde{S} - S_0 = L_0[\tilde{r}_A(A_0/L_0) - \tilde{r}_L] . \tag{3}$$

Because S_0 may be zero, it is necessary to define a convenient base against which surplus changes can be measured. The natural choice for this base is either A_0 or L_0. We find it convenient to choose L_0, because it is the base against which the surplus usually is measured. After dividing both sides of equation (3) by L_0 and replacing A_0/L_0 by F_0 (see equation [2]), the surplus return can be expressed as follows:

$$\tilde{r}_S \equiv \frac{\tilde{S} - S_0}{L_0}$$
$$\tilde{r}_S = F_0\tilde{r}_A - \tilde{r}_L . \tag{4}$$

If we think of $F_0\,\tilde{r}_A$ as an "adjusted-asset return," equation (4) states that the surplus return is the difference between the adjusted-asset return and the liability return.

The mean of the surplus return distribution can be found by calculating the expected value of both sides of (4).

$$\mu_S = E[\tilde{r}_S] = E[F_0\tilde{r}_A - \tilde{r}_L]$$
$$\mu_S = F_0\mu_A - \mu_L . \tag{5}$$

By definition, the variance of the surplus return distribution is

$$\sigma_S^2 = E[(\tilde{r}_S - \mu_S)^2] .$$

By using equations (4) and (5), we derive the following formula for the surplus variance:

$$\sigma_S^2 = E[\{F_0(\tilde{r}_A - \mu_A) - (\tilde{r}_L - \mu_L)\}^2]$$
$$= (F_0\sigma_A)^2 + (\sigma_L)^2 - 2(F_0\sigma_A)\sigma_L\rho_{AL} .$$

The standard deviation of the surplus return distributions is

$$\sigma_S = \sqrt{(F_0\sigma_A)^2 + \sigma_L^2 - 2(F_0\sigma_A)\sigma_L\rho_{AL}} . \tag{6}$$

ALLOCATION VARIABLES

In the previous section, we showed that the volatility of surplus returns depends on both the volatility of the portfolio and the asset/liability correlation. Both these variables depend on the composition of the asset portfolio. Thus, we must derive a formula for σ_A and ρ_{AL} in terms of the relevant asset variables and their respective allocation weights. A summary of symbols for the asset variables is provided in Figure A2.

Figure A2: Definition of Asset Variables

Asset	Percent of Portfolio	One-Year Return	Mean Return	Standard Deviation of Returns	Correlation of Returns with Equity Return	Correlation of Returns with Liability Return
Equity	w	$\tilde{r}_E$	μ_E	σ_E	1.0	ρ_{EL}
Bonds	$1 - w$	$\tilde{r}_B$	μ_B	σ_B	ρ_{EB}	ρ_{BL}

Because the asset portfolio consists of only stocks and bonds, its return is the weighted average of the stock and bond returns. That is,

$$\tilde{r}_A = w\tilde{r}_E + (1-w)\tilde{r}_B . \tag{7}$$

Likewise,

$$\mu_A = w\mu_E + (1-w)\mu_B . \tag{8}$$

Also, from the definition of the standard deviation and the correlation coefficient, it follows that

$$\sigma_A = \sqrt{[w\sigma_E]^2 + [(1-w)\sigma_B]^2 + 2w(1-w)\sigma_E \sigma_B \rho_{EB}} . \tag{9}$$

To find ρ_{AL}, we must first find the asset/liability covariance, σ_{AL}. By definition,

$$\sigma_{AL} = E[(\tilde{r}_A - \mu_A)(\tilde{r}_L - \mu_L)] . \tag{10}$$

After utilizing (7) and (8) in (10), we find that

$$\sigma_{AL} = wE[(\tilde{r}_E - \mu_E)(\tilde{r}_L - \mu_L)] + (1-w)E[(\tilde{r}_B - \mu_B)(\tilde{r}_L - \mu_L)] . \tag{11}$$

The first expectation in (11) is the equity/liability covariance, σ_{EL}, and the second expectation is the bond/liability covariance, σ_{BL}. Thus, σ_{AL} is the weighted-average covariance,

$$\sigma_{AL} = w\sigma_{EL} + (1-w)\sigma_{BL} \ . \tag{12}$$

In general, the covariance between two random variables is the product of the correlation coefficient and the two standard deviations. Thus, (12) can be rewritten as follows:

$$\sigma_A\,\sigma_L\,\rho_{AL} = w\sigma_E\,\sigma_L\,\rho_{EL} + (1-w)\sigma_B\,\sigma_L\,\rho_{BL}$$

or,

$$\rho_{AL} = [w\sigma_E\,\rho_{EL} + (1-w)\sigma_B\,\rho_{BL}\,]/\sigma_A \ .$$

If we assume that $\rho_{BL} = 1$, and the return distributions are normal, then $\rho_{EL} = \rho_{EB}$ and

$$\rho_{AL} = [w\sigma_E\,\rho_{EB} + (1-w)\sigma_B\,]/\sigma_A \ . \tag{13}$$

As an example of the use of the formulas we have developed, we consider the assets and liabilities given in Figure A3.

Figure A3: A Pension Fund Example (Dollars in Millions)

Asset or Liability	Initial Value	Expected Return	Standard Deviation of Returns	Correlation with Bonds
Equity	$84.0	13.0%	17.00%	0.35
Bonds	56.0	8.0	6.96	1.00
Liability	100.0	8.0	15.00	1.00

We observe that the asset portfolio is 60% stocks/40% bonds and use equations (8) and (9) to find μ_A and σ_A.

$$\mu_A = 0.6 \times 13.0\% + 0.4 \times 8.0\% = 11.0\%$$

$$\sigma_A = \sqrt{(0.6 \times 0.17)^2 + (0.4 \times 0.0696)^2 + 2 \times (0.6 \times 0.4) \times (0.17 \times 0.0696) \times 0.35}$$

$$= 11.5\% \ .$$

Turning our attention to the pension fund surplus, we first observe that the funding ratio is 140% ([84 + 56]/100). Then, according to equation (5)

$$\mu_S = (1.4 \times 11.0\%) - 8.0\% = 7.4\% \ .$$

We now use equation (13) to find ρ_{AL}, and equation (6) to compute σ_S.

$$\rho_{AL} = [(0.60 \times 0.17 \times 0.35) + (0.4 \times .0696)]/0.115 = 0.554$$

and

$$\sigma_S = \sqrt{(1.4 \times 0.115)^2 + (0.15)^2 - 2 \times (1.4 \times 0.115) \times 0.554}$$

$$= 14.7\% \ .$$

THE SURPLUS SHORTFALL CONSTRAINT

We wish to locate all stock/bond portfolios whose risk/return characteristics are such that there is a probability k that the surplus return $\tilde{r}_S$ will exceed some minimum threshold S_{MIN}. This requirement can be expressed as follows:

$$P[\tilde{r}_S \geq S_{MIN}] = k \ . \tag{14}$$

The above requirement is equivalent to

$$P(\tilde{r}_S - \mu_S)/\sigma_S \geq (S_{MIN} - \mu_S)/\sigma_S] = k \ . \tag{15}$$

Because the quantity to the left of the inequality in (15) is a standard normal variate, there is a positive value z_k (assuming $k > 0.5$), such that the shortfall constraint (14) is satisfied when

$$(S_{MIN} - \mu_S)/\sigma_S = -z_k$$

or, equivalently, when

$$\mu_S = S_{MIN} + z_k \sigma_S \ . \tag{16}$$

As an example, we note that $z_k = 1.282$ when $k = 0.90$, because there is a 90% probability that a standard normal variable will exceed -1.282.

Equation (16) looks deceptively simple, because it is expressed in surplus terms. To locate the asset portfolios that fulfill equation (16), we must express μ_S and σ_S in terms of asset variables by making use of the various equations in this Appendix.

Although the resulting mathematical relationship between μ_A and σ_A is complicated, the portfolios that fulfill that relationship can readily be graphed in a risk/return diagram. The "shape" of the relationship between μ_A and σ_A for portfolios that satisfy the surplus shortfall condition can best be described as "egg-like." Examples of these surplus shortfall "eggs" are provided in the body of this paper.

Chapter I-14

Risk-Adjusted Surplus

INTRODUCTION

When describing a pension plan's status, one generally speaks in terms of a surplus measure defined by the excess of the market value of assets over the measured liability cost.[1] A pension plan with an asset-to-liability ratio of 140% usually is considered to reflect an ample funded status with the happy prospect of several years of reduced contributions. This statement of "raw" surplus does not leave any room for a capital cushion or for any reserve that compensates for the riskiness embodied in the plan's portfolio. Thus, the plan will continue to be regarded as 140% funded, even when the portfolio is based on a relatively con-

---

[1] The methodology of this paper is applicable to a broad range of liability structures; however, for purposes of illustration, we have chosen to deal with a simple liability that behaves like a bond and confine our analysis to the effect of investment risk on surplus measurement. Other authors have addressed different elements of surplus management. For example, see "Asset Allocation by Surplus Optimization," D. Don Ezra, *Financial Analysts Journal*, January/February 1991; "Liabilities—A New Approach," William F. Sharpe and Lawrence G. Tint, *Journal of Portfolio Management*, Winter 1990; and *Pension Funds and the Bottom Line*, Keith P. Ambachtsheer, Dow Jones-Irwin, 1986.

Martin L. Leibowitz, Stanley Kogelman and Lawrence N. Bader, "Risk-Adjusted Surplus—A New Measure of Pension Fund Risk," Salomon Brothers Inc, August 1991.

sistent long-term strategic asset allocation that intentionally embraces a high level of volatility.

In most asset/liability contexts—for example, banks, insurance companies and broker/dealers—there is a clear concept of the capital reserve that is *required* to "back up" a given book of business. This required reserve naturally depends on the risk levels of the assets and the liabilities. For example, a block of Treasury bills would require less capital than a comparable amount of long Baa corporate bonds. Different regulators use different terminology—such as risk-weighting, "haircutting" or security valuation reserves—to describe formalized procedures for computing the required reserve needed for a given risk category of assets. An institution is deemed to have "excess capital" only to the extent that its nominal surplus exceeds the required level.

The trend toward increasingly explicit reserve requirements is exemplified by the banking industry, where capital requirements have been made more stringent through the promulgation of the Bank for International Settlements (BIS) risk-weighting rules. In contrast, corporate pension funds and public retirement systems do not use any such risk-reserving procedures. Although asset (and liability) risk is reflected in sophisticated allocation and actuarial models, there appears to be no standard method for risk-adjusting either the funding ratio or the surplus—the key "front line" numbers used to gauge the health of a pension fund.

At a time when pension funds and their sponsors are hard-pressed to minimize the strain of contributions, it becomes all the more important that any assessment of funding status incorporate some sense of risk. In this report, we define a "risk-adjusted surplus" based on the notion that some type of insurance cushion is needed to compensate for the downside risk in a volatile portfolio. With this approach, the funding ratio is reduced from its "raw" value to a "zero-risk" equivalent.[2] While such reductions are not a common practice in a pension fund context, the risk-adjustment procedure does provide some indication of the reserve that is appropriate for a given strategic allocation. In the final analysis, there *always* is an implicit reserve, and that reserve takes the form of a call on the resources of the sponsoring organization.

---

[2] Although we limit our discussion to pension funds, we believe that this technique can be customized to encompass current BIS risk-weighting rules for banks and rules that currently are under discussion for insurance companies. For a more general discussion of the management of asset and surplus shortfall risk, see *Asset Performance and Surplus Control*, Salomon Brothers Inc, July 1991.

A SHORTFALL DEFINITION OF RISK-ADJUSTED ASSETS

We begin our study of asset reserves by considering a hypothetical pension fund for which the liability is $108 million due in one year. At an 8% discount rate, the present value of the liabilities is $100 million. If assets of $100 million are invested in "cash" at an 8% risk-free rate, the plan is certain to be fully funded. However, if the plan invests in risky assets in the expectation of achieving higher returns, its fully funded status will be at risk. To keep the probability of a shortfall within tolerable limits, we must augment the initial asset value so that the excess capital can absorb the fluctuations that accompany risky investments.

In Figure 1, we schematically illustrate the asset levels needed for risky portfolios to provide equal levels of protection relative to the liability. If the asset portfolio is made up of "cash" assets, a funding ratio of 100% will ensure that the liability can be met. As the percentage of equity in the portfolio increases, the assets become more risky, and additional reserves are required.

To make the above intuitive discussion of capital reserves more concrete, we must formulate a measure of *risk-equivalence*. Although there are many ways to quantify a required reserve level, we define a risk-adjustment or "haircut" in terms of the shortfall measures that have been introduced in earlier publications.[3] In those publications, we measured a portfolio's "shortfall risk" by its tenth percentile return. This measure is equivalent to taking the conservative position of gauging a fund's downside risk by the minimum level that can be promised with 90% assurance. Two portfolios will be regarded as risk-equivalent if they have equal tenth percentile returns.

To illustrate this equivalence, we consider the distribution of year-end values for a $118-million portfolio that is 100% invested in equities (see the lower graph in Figure 2). We assume that the expected return from equities is 13% (that is, a return premium of 5% above the 8% risk-free rate) and that the volatility is 17%. These assumptions lead to a 10% probability that the year-end value of a $118-million portfolio could fall below $108 million.[4] This same year-end value could have been attained without risk by investing $100 million at 8% (see the upper graph in Figure 2). In essence, an all-equity portfolio with an $18-million capital cushion has a distribution that is shifted so far to the right that it provides a 90% probability of surpassing the $108-million year-end value of a

---

[3] The shortfall approach (and its limitations as a risk measure) are discussed in *A Shortfall Approach to Duration Management*, Salomon Brothers Inc, April 1990; *Asset Allocation Under Shortfall Constraints*, Salomon Brothers Inc, June 1990; and *Return Enhancement from "Foreign" Assets*, Salomon Brothers Inc, February 1991.

[4] For simplicity, we assume that portfolio returns are normally distributed. For equities, the tenth percentile return is -8.8% (=13% - 1.282 × 17%). The tenth percentile fund value is therefore (1 - 0.088) × 118 = 108. We assume static asset allocations in this paper; a dynamic policy would require alterations to our model.

Figure 1: Asset Portfolios with Equivalent Funding Protection (Dollars in Millions)

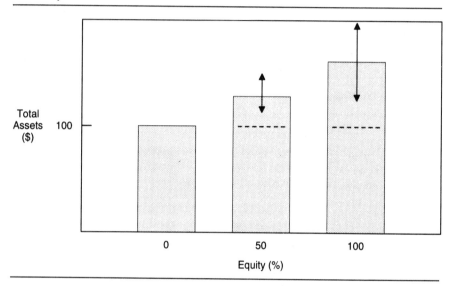

Figure 2: The Year-End Value Distribution for Two Portfolios (Dollars in Millions)

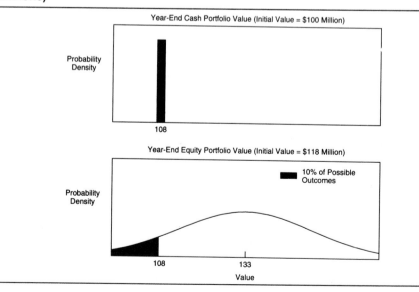

$100-million cash portfolio. Thus, we can view the all-equity fund, with its $18-million surplus, as risk-equivalent to an all-cash portfolio with a surplus of zero (that is, a 100% funding ratio).

RISK-ADJUSTED SURPLUS

The portfolio examples of the previous section illustrated the concept of a risk-adjustment. According to this concept, an all-equity portfolio with a nominal funding ratio of 118% may have a risk-adjusted funding ratio of only 100%. In other words, if a $100-million liability is funded by a 100% equity portfolio, an incremental $18 million may be *required* as a reserve to cushion the volatility of equity.

To gain a broader view of how the funding ratio risk-adjustment is related to volatility, we must have some concept of how risk is rewarded in an investment context. In Figure 3, we present a traditional risk/return diagram for asset allocations consisting of varying proportions of equity and cash. All such portfolios plot along a diagonal line between these two asset classes. The horizontal axis displays the portfolio volatility. The vertical axis represents the expected return over a one-year investment horizon. As the equity allocation increases,

Figure 3: The "Efficient Frontier" for Cash/Equity Portfolios

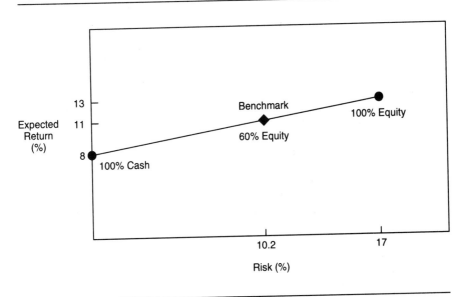

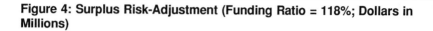

Figure 4: Surplus Risk-Adjustment (Funding Ratio = 118%; Dollars in Millions)

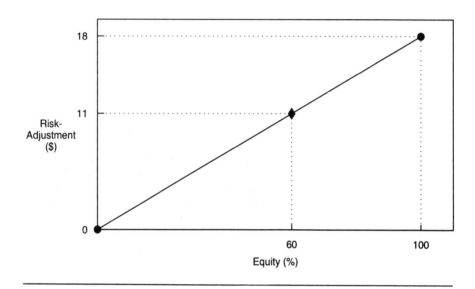

the portfolio takes on greater levels of both expected return and volatility. The risk/return characteristics of a benchmark 60% equity portfolio are indicated by a "diamond." This portfolio has an 11% expected return and 10.2% volatility.[5]

The risk/return relationship shown in Figure 3 enables us to trace out how the required risk-adjustment for a $118-million portfolio changes as the equity proportion increases (see Figure 4). At a 0% equity allocation, there is no volatility, and no risk-adjustment is required. As the equity allocation grows, so does the volatility. The risk-adjustment increases linearly until it reaches $18 million at a 100% equity allocation.

The methodology for computing the risk-adjustment at intermediate equity allocations will be illustrated for a 60/40 portfolio. First, we compute the tenth percentile portfolio value. For the 60/40 portfolio, the tenth percentile return is -2.1% (the 11% expected return, less 1.282 times the standard deviation of 10.2%). Thus, the tenth percentile value of a $118-million portfolio is $116 million (97.9% of $118). Next, we find that the present value of $116 million at year-end is $107 million ($116 divided by 1.08). This means that the same $116-

[5] The return premium for the 60/40 portfolio is 60% of the 5% equity risk premium, or 3%. The portfolio volatility is 60% of the 17% volatility of equities, or 10.2%.

million value could have been achieved by investing $107 million in risk-free assets. Consequently, for a 60/40 portfolio, a nominal 118% funding ratio requires an 11% risk-adjustment. This adjustment leads to a risk-adjusted funding ratio of 107%.

RISK-ADJUSTED SURPLUS WITH INTEREST-SENSITIVE LIABILITIES

In this section, we extend our methodology to liabilities that are sensitive to changes in interest rates. We introduce this generalization through an example in which the liability has a 10-year duration, all fixed-income investments have the same 8% expected return, and the initial funding ration is 140%.[6]

In this new context, the riskless investment is an all-bond portfolio with the same interest rate sensitivity as the liability; that is, an immunized portfolio. The immunized portfolio is structured so that the dollar durations of the assets and liabilities are equal. In our example, the immunizing duration is 7.1 years (the liability duration of 10 years divided by the 140% funding ratio). All nonimmunizing portfolios are susceptible to surplus risk.

We introduce the following measure of *risk-adjusted surplus:*

The risk-adjusted surplus is the tenth percentile year-end surplus value, discounted at the risk-free rate.

For example, if the pension fund's liability is $100 million, and $140 million is invested in 3.1-year duration bonds, the tenth percentile year-end surplus value is $32.4 million.[7] This is the same year-end surplus that can be obtained from a risk-free immunized portfolio with an 8% return and an initial value of $130 million, because the $30 million surplus will grow to $32.4 million with a year's interest. Thus, one needs a risk-adjustment reserve of $10 million, or a 10% "haircut" in terms of the funding ratios. The 10% funding ratio "haircut" is attributable to the 4-year mismatch between the portfolio duration and the immunizing duration. Because a $140-million bond portfolio with a duration that is 4 years longer than the immunizing duration (11.1 years) has the same mismatch, it requires the same risk-adjustment as the 3.1-year duration portfolio. In

---

[6] This "flat yield curve" expected return assumption is made to simplify the exposition. Our results easily can be extended to encompass a positive risk/return trade-off for fixed-income securities.

[7] If annual interest rate volatility is 1.5%, the return volatilities for a 3.1-year duration bond and a 10-year liability are 4.7% (3.1 × 1.5%) and 15% (10 × 1.5%), respectively. If liability and bond returns are perfectly correlated, the surplus volatility is $8.4 million (the absolute difference between $140 × 4.7% and $100 × 15%). The expected surplus value is $43.2 million (1.08 × $40). If all distributions are normal, the tenth percentile surplus value is $32.4 million ($43.2 - 1.282 × $8.4).

Figure 5: Funding Ratio Risk-Adjustment for All-Bond Portfolios (Liability Duration = 10 Years; Funding Ratio = 140%)

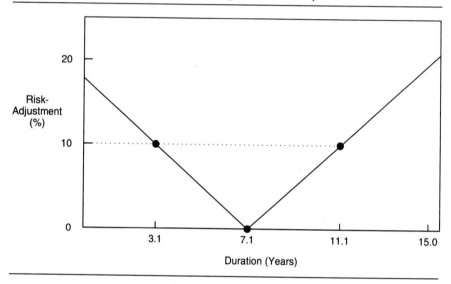

Figure 6: Risk-Adjustment for Varying Equity Allocation

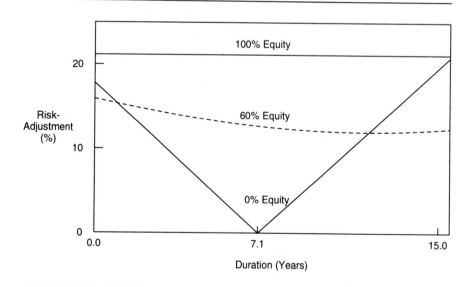

general, the risk-adjustment for all-bond portfolios increases linearly as the duration mismatch increases (see Figure 5).

We now shift our attention from an all-bond portfolio to a $140-million all-equity portfolio. In this case, the funding ratio risk-adjustment can be shown to be 21.1% (see Figure 6). This risk-adjustment is significantly greater than it would be for all but the longest-duration bond portfolios.[8]

In Figure 6, we also show the risk-adjustment for portfolios with a more typical allocation of 60% stocks and 40% bonds. Observe that the risk-adjustment for the 60/40 portfolio is 16% when the 40% fixed-income component has a 0-year duration. The risk-adjustment decreases gradually to a floor of 12% at a bond duration of 11.9 years and then increases slowly.[9] The "flatness" of the risk-adjustment curve near the 11.9-year duration point indicates a low sensitivity to the choice of bond duration. This insensitivity reflects the fact that, at a 60% equity allocation, almost all of the surplus volatility arises from the volatility of equities. The "flatness" also illustrates an inherent problem in traditional surplus optimizations. While an "optimal" solution may always be found, there is a wide range of suboptimal portfolios offering virtually equivalent surplus protection. These "suboptimal" portfolios may be more attractive from other vantage points, for example, in the context of asset-only performance.

IMPACT OF THE EQUITY ALLOCATION AND FUNDING RATIO

In this section, we show how the funding ratio and the equity allocation affect the risk-adjustment. As a first example, we plot the funding ratio risk-adjustment against the equity percentage for two different durations when the nominal funding ratio is 140% (see Figure 7).

An all-bond portfolio with a 4.64-year duration (the current duration of the Salomon Brothers Broad Investment-Grade Bond Index[SM]) will have surplus risk because of the 2.5-year mismatch relative to the 7.1-year immunizing duration. An all-bond portfolio with a 0-year duration will have even more surplus risk because of the greater duration gap. Consequently, the risk adjustment is greater for the 0-year duration portfolio.

---

[8] The surplus risk in the equity portfolio is derived from the riskiness of equity and the volatility of the liability. This risk will decrease as the correlation between equity returns and the liability returns increases. We assume that the correlation between equities and the liability is 0.35. With this correlation and our volatility assumptions for bonds and equity, it can be shown that equity has an implicit duration of 4.0 years. See *Total Portfolio Duration: A New Perspective on Asset Allocation*, Salomon Brothers Inc, February 1986.

[9] At a bond duration of 11.9 years, the interest rate sensitivity for the total 60/40 portfolio equals that of the liability. See *Total Portfolio Duration: A New Perspective on Asset Allocation*.

Figure 7: Funding Ratio Risk-Adjustment versus Equity Allocation (Funding Ratio = 140%)

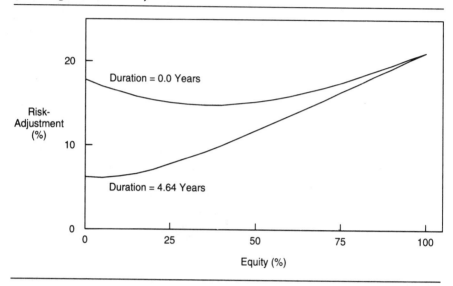

Figure 8: Risk-Adjustments at Different Funding Ratios (Duration = 4.64 Years)

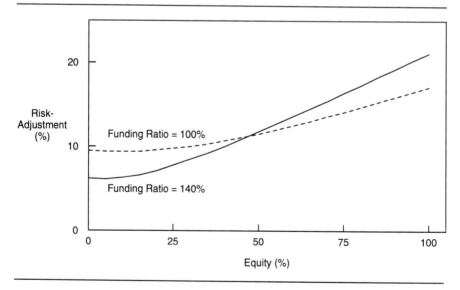

The addition of equity affects the risk-adjustment in rather different ways, depending on the magnitude of the duration gap. For 4.64-year duration bonds, equity additions lead to ever larger risk-adjustments. However, at a 0-year duration, the portfolio already has equity-like volatility because of the greater gap relative to the 7.1-year immunizing duration. Small equity additions lead to a decline in surplus volatility because of the positive correlation between equity returns and interest rates. This volatility decrease is reflected in a lower risk-adjustment. At larger equity percentages, equity becomes the dominant component of surplus risk, and the required funding ratio risk-adjustment rises toward the 21.1% level of an all-equity portfolio.

To see the effect of the funding ratio, we compare the risk-adjustment for a plan with a 100% funding ratio to a 140% funded plan (see Figure 8). Although the bond duration is 4.64 years in both cases, the duration mismatch is greater for the 100% funding ratio because of its longer immunizing duration (10 years versus 7.1 years). Consequently, the all-bond portfolio with a 100% funding ratio requires a greater adjustment for surplus risk.

High funding ratios reflect a greater proportion of assets to liabilities. Consequently, at higher funding ratios, the riskiness of the assets has a more pronounced impact on the risk-adjustment. As the equity allocation increases, the risk-adjustment tends to grow more rapidly for plans with higher funding ratios.[10]

IMPACT OF RISK TOLERANCE

To this point, our risk-adjustment calculations have been arbitrarily based on the tenth percentile surplus return. More risk-averse plan sponsors may decide to focus on a lower percentile return (for example 5%, or a 95% assurance level) and accept the resulting greater risk-adjustment. However, more risk-tolerant sponsors may focus on higher percentile returns and take a smaller "haircut."

Insight into the effect of a sponsor's risk-tolerance can be gained by comparing the funding ratio risk-adjustment for a range of shortfall probabilities and funding ratios (see Figure 9). These cases are based on a constant benchmark allocation of 60% equity and 40% bonds with a 4.64-year duration.

In Figure 9, at all funding ratios, we observe a substantial sensitivity to changes in the shortfall probability. For example, with a 100% funding ratio, the risk-adjustment increases by 4.3% (from 12.5% to 16.8%) when the shortfall probability decreases from 10% to 5%. However, the risk-adjusted surplus is less

---

[10] A different perspective on the impact of the equity allocation on a fund's shortfall risk is provided in "Shortfall Risk and Pension Fund Asset Management," Zvi Bodie, *Financial Analysts Journal*, May/June 1991.

Figure 9: Funding Ratio Risk-Adjustment (60% Equity/40% Bond Portfolio)

	Risk-Adjustment			
	Shortfall Probability			
Funding Ratio	5%	10%	15%	38%
100%	16.8%	12.5%	9.6%	0.7%
120	17.4	12.8	9.7	0.4
140	18.5	13.6	10.2	0.1
160	20.0	14.6	10.9	(0.1)

---

sensitive to the funding ratio than it is to the sponsor's risk tolerance. For example, at a 10% shortfall probability, there is only a 2.1% difference between the risk-adjustment for a 100% funding ratio and a 160% funding ratio.

At higher shortfall probabilities, we can see the effects of greatly relaxed risk tolerance. For example, a 38% shortfall probability approximates the asset-only risk/return trade-off that is imbedded in the market, given our assumption of a 5% equity premium. Because the added return roughly provides the required compensation, there is no need for a risk-adjustment at this shortfall probability. This is the risk tolerance that is implied by the conventional practice of viewing a portfolio as providing a fixed funding assurance, regardless of its asset allocation.

CONCLUSION

In this paper, we have defined the risk-adjusted surplus of a pension fund based on a one-year horizon. Many would argue that a one-year test, although appropriate in certain narrow circumstances, is irrelevant and indeed inimical to developing sound pension funding and investment policies.

To frame this view persuasively, we can use the example of a large public employee retirement system—one of the longest-term undertakings in the realm of finance. One can argue that such a system should adopt an investment policy that maximizes long-term return and should establish a contribution policy that is consistent with long-term return expectations. The system's investment and actuarial status should be reviewed periodically, not to respond to or anticipate each flutter in the markets, but to see whether the long-term outlook has changed fundamentally to an extent that demands restructuring. A temporary dip in the funding ratio below 100% is virtually a nonevent, unlike the catastrophic impact that a comparable event would have on a bank or an insurance company. Short-term pension fund volatility therefore should be tamed by the passage of time, not by compromising the pursuit of long-term return.

This appealing stance reflects a large part—but not all—of the plan sponsor's responsibilities. It fails to reflect the need for prudent contingency planning and the fact that volatility is not evanescent but persistent. Consider the case of a plan sponsor who seeks to justify a lower contribution level by proposing a high-return 100% equity portfolio for a fully funded public plan with $100 million in assets and liabilities. It is easy for the sponsor to dismiss a one-year calculation that shows that the new risk-adjusted surplus is in fact a deficit of $17.1 million. It would be more difficult to dismiss an analogous calculation that produced a similar deficit over 20 years. Although we have not formulated a 20-year definition of risk-adjusted surplus in this paper, simulations indicate significant potential deficits even over a period of decades.[11]

We would not argue that the risk-adjustment that takes the plan from fully funded status with an immunization strategy to a deficit when equity is introduced necessarily makes equity exposure imprudent. No single point on the continuum from full immunization to 100% equity is right for all sponsors, but risk-adjusted surplus offers a means of comparing various points on the continuum in the light of a particular sponsor's risk tolerance.

In practice, many plan sponsors might be tempted to use the higher expected return from equities to justify an increased discount rate, without considering the downside possibilities. They would thereby lower their stated liability and *increase* the reported surplus. In our view, tying a higher surplus and therefore a lower contribution stream to a riskier investment strategy is a step that should be taken only with due consideration for potentially disappointing results. The risk-adjusted surplus can be useful as an approximate measure of the potential disappointment.

---

[11] Insight into the relationship between short- and long-term risk can be found in *Shortfall Risks and the Asset Allocation Decision*, Salomon Brothers Inc, January 1989.

PART II

Stocks, Real Estate and Convertibles

Chapter II-1

Inside the P/E Ratio: The Franchise Factor

This article looks "inside" the DDM-based price/earnings ratio and provides a surprisingly simple model of the future investment opportunities required to support an above-market P/E. The analysis is done under the idealized assumptions of certain returns, no taxes and no leverage. Further, all stocks are taken to be priced according to the dividend discount model. Under these conditions, the ingredients of P/E expansion can be separated into two factors—(1) a Franchise Factor that represents the P/E impact of new investments at a specified return and (2) a growth measure that reflects the magnitude of these new investment opportunities.

The Franchise Factor depends on the return available on new investments. For at-market-rate returns, the Franchise Factor is zero. Consequently, investments that provide such returns do not add to the P/E. Only investments that provide above-market returns lead to a positive Franchise Factor and an above-market P/E. Two surprising results of the analysis are the small size of the Franchise Factor and the extraordinary magnitude of growth required to raise P/E significantly. For example, a firm with an ROE 300 basis points above the market rate must have franchise investment opportunities equivalent, in present-value terms, to five times its current book value to support a P/E that is twice the market rate.

The decomposition of the P/E suggested in this article allows the analyst to cut through the confusion that can arise from the standard DDM formulation, which intertwines assumptions regarding a constant-growth process, implicit return levels and dividend-payout policies. As a result, the Franchise Factor approach can provide a

Martin L. Leibowitz and Stanley Kogelman, "Inside the P/E Ratio: The Franchise Factor," *Financial Analysts Journal*, November-December 1990. Reprinted with permission.

sharper understanding of the real ingredients that lead to higher equity values and better P/E multiples.

SUMMARY

Equity analysts use a combination of judgment, understanding of an industry, detailed knowledge of individual companies, and an arsenal of analytical models and measures to help them assess value. The measures include cash flow, return on equity (ROE), dividend yield, and financial ratios such as price/earnings, price/book, earnings per share and sales per share. Among the ratios, the price/earnings ratio (P/E) stands out as one of the most scrutinized, modeled and studied measures in use today.

The classical model used to estimate a theoretical P/E ratio is the dividend discount model (DDM). This model was originally proposed by J.B. Williams and then modified and extended by M. Gordon, M.H. Miller and F. Modigliani, and others.[1] DDM-based models can yield significant insights into how various factors influence P/E.

We have found that investors generally fail to appreciate the magnitude and type of growth required to support a high P/E multiple. The problem stems in large part from our tendency to view growth in an overly simplistic manner— i.e., as a smooth pattern of constant growth, self-funded by retained earnings, generating added earnings with each growth increment.

This is a convenient and appealing concept. It forms the basis for most standard forms of the DDM, which are built on the assumption that dividends, earnings and/or book values grow at the same constant rate. Typically, growth is assumed either to continue at the same rate forever or to be composed of two or three different growth rates covering various consecutive time periods. Most DDMs further assume that growth in dividends is solely the result of retained earnings. Beyond its role in DDM models, the smooth-growth concept has had an even greater impact as the basis for many of our intuitions regarding the value of equity.

Despite its appeal, this simple concept of growth can be misleading on several counts. First, not all growth produces incremental value. Consider, as a simple illustration, the "growth" in the amortized value of a discount bond. This

---

[1] See, for example, J.B. Williams, *The Theory of Investment Value* (Cambridge, MA: Harvard University Press, 1938); M.J. Gordon, *The Investment Financing and Valuation of the Corporation* (Homewood, IL: Richard D. Irwin, 1962); M.H. Miller and F. Modigliani, "Dividend Policy, Growth, and the Valuation of Shares," *Journal of Business*, October 1961. For a current update on dividend discount models, see the November-December 1985 issue of *Financial Analysts Journal*.

growth does not add to the bond's promised yield to maturity; it is simply one means of *delivering* on that original promise.

Similarly, for equities, *growth alone is not enough.* The routine investments that a firm makes at the market rate do not add net value, even though they may contribute to nominal earnings growth. (Investments at below-market returns actually subtract from value.) Incremental value is generated only through investment in *exceptional* opportunities that promise above-market ROEs. Only this exceptional "high-octane" growth fuels the engine for higher P/E multiples.

Another point of confusion inherent in our usual assumptions about growth is the notion that growth should be self-funded out of retained earnings. This concept is also appealing: A smoothly growing flow of new investments would appear to be the just reward for a thrifty corporation and its investors. The key issue, however, is *not* whether the company has retained sufficient earnings to self-fund a new investment opportunity, but rather whether that opportunity offers an above-market return. Such exceptional opportunities, by definition, only come in fits and starts. They tend to result from some monopolistic event that may or may not be sustainable.

When a corporation is presented with such an exceptional "franchise" opportunity, the investment should be pursued regardless of whether the funds are available within the corporate coffers.[2] In today's financial markets, the ability to self-fund should not be a constraint. Theoretically, the market should always be willing, through the purchase of new securities, to supply funds to facilitate participation in an above-market return. The pursuit of exceptional returns should be limited only by the infrequency of their occurrence.

This article looks "inside" the DDM-based P/E and beyond the restrictions of smooth growth through retained earnings. The result is a surprisingly simple model of the exceptional future investment opportunities implicit in any given P/E. By representing all future investments by their present values, we can capture the impact of embedded opportunities on the P/E in a single number, which we call the "Franchise Factor."

A BRIEF DESCRIPTION

Our focus is narrow. We consider only a no-tax world, and we always assume a stable market in which all stocks are unleveraged and priced according to the DDM. We do not account for the uncertainty and volatility endemic to the eq-

---

[2] We thank R. Merton for his many insightful comments regarding the "franchise" concept. For a discussion of the duration of franchise opportunities and the driving forces behind them, see J.L. Treynor, "The Elements of Investment Value" (Paper presented at Brigham Young University, October 13, 1983).

uity markets. We also assume that all earnings are properly reported and that each firm's ROE remains unchanged over time.

In fact, our discussion of P/E treats equity investments as if their earnings, growth and dividends were all certain. We thus tackle the complex and uncertain cash flows associated with equities in much the same manner as one analyzes the price/yield characteristics of risk-free bonds.

To explore the interactions between P/E, ROE, growth and the Franchise Factor, we consider the cash flows and reinvestment income of four illustrative firms (A, B, C and D). Firm A's ROE precisely equals the market capitalization rate. The firm retains two-thirds of its earnings and reinvests them at the market rate. By contrast, Firm B has the same ROE as Firm A, but it maintains a 100% dividend-payout policy. We show that Firm A's growth is deceptive in that it does not add to current value or to P/E. In fact, according to the DDM, Firms A and B have exactly the same stock price and the same P/E.

Firm C has a higher ROE than Firm B based on its historical book value, but like Firm B, it maintains a 100% dividend-payout policy. Despite its high ROE and premium price, Firm C has no growth. We might think of this firm as offering a very specialized service within a limited but saturated market: There is no opportunity for business expansion, but the firm's products command a premium price. Although the return on initial investment may be quite high, the market value of the firm is such that it only offers the same P/E as Firms A and B. Neither growth alone nor above-market ROE alone is sufficient to command a premium P/E.

Firm D illustrates the importance of combining growth *and* above-market returns on the new investments comprising that growth. This firm has an ROE 300 basis points above the market rate and a P/E twice that of the other three firms. The DDM leads to the rather surprising implication that Firm D requires exceptional investment opportunities that, in present-value terms, amount to a 500% "jump" in the firm's current book value.

P/E INGREDIENTS

The results for these four firms can be explained in terms of the Franchise Factor concept. For a specified return on new investments, the Franchise Factor is the P/E increase that results from one unit of present-value "growth." In other words, if we were to make new investments in magnitude equivalent to the current size of the firm, then the P/E multiple would rise by an amount equal to the Franchise Factor.

The Franchise Factor depends on the return available on new investments. For at-market-rate returns, the Franchise Factor is zero. At higher-than-market returns, the FF increases—quickly at first, but ultimately approaching a maximum level. At the return level for Firm D, the Franchise Factor is 1.67—a reasonably high value. By combining Firm D's five units of "growth" (500% of original book value) with its Franchise Factor of 1.67, we arrive at a new and more penetrating view of why its P/E ratio is twice the P/E of the other three firms.

We can separate the ingredients of P/E expansion into two factors—(1) a Franchise Factor that represents the P/E impact of new investments at a specified return and (2) a growth measure that reflects the magnitude of these new investment opportunities.[3] This simple decomposition allows the analyst to cut through the confusion that arises because of the way the DDM intertwines assumptions regarding a constant-growth process, implicit return levels and dividend-payout policies. As a result, we believe that the Franchise Factor approach can provide a sharper picture of the real components of enhanced equity value and P/E multiple.

STABLE GROWTH IN EARNINGS AND DIVIDENDS

Firm A maintains a constant dividend-payout policy (i.e., the dividend-payout ratio is maintained at 33 1/3% of earnings) and expects earnings to grow at a steady 8% per year far into the future (see Table I). The market capitalization rate is constant at 12%; the firm's ROE is also 12%. The initial book equity is

Table I: Firm A, with a Constant 8% Growth Rate and a 12% ROE

Book Equity	$100.00
ROE	12.00%
Earnings	$12.00
Payout Ratio	33 1/3%
Dividend	$4.00
Market Rate	12.00%
Price	$100.00
Dividend Yield	4.00%
Growth Rate	8.00%
P/E Ratio	8.33

---

[3] The Franchise Factor and Growth Equivalent are consistent with the net present value concept. For a detailed discussion of the latter, see R.A. Brealey and S.C. Myers, *Principles of Corporate Finance* (New York: McGraw-Hill, 1988).

Figure A: Dividend Growth Over Time for Firm A

ROE = 12%; payout ratio = 1/3; growth rate = 8%.

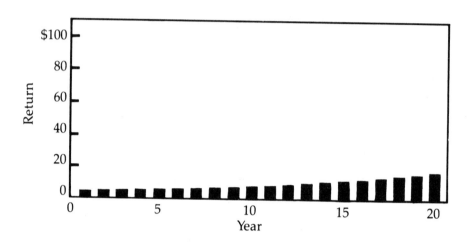

$100, so a 12% ROE leads to earnings of $12, dividends of $4 and retained earnings of $8. The price of the stock is $100, according to the standard DDM.

What are the cash flows to an investor in Firm A, under the simplifying assumptions that the investment is subject to neither risk nor taxes? The investor's return will have three components—dividend return, price return and reinvestment return.[4] Because, by assumption, the firm's earnings grow at 8% and dividend policy remains unchanged, dividends will also grow at the same 8% rate. Figure A illustrates this.

Price appreciation is a consequence of our assumptions regarding the firm and our use of the DDM for pricing the stock. In particular, the DDM implies that, in a static market, price growth will keep pace with dividend growth. Thus, if dividends grow at 8%, stock price will also grow at 8%.

A new investor who buys Firm A's stock will realize a 4% return from dividends and an 8% return from price appreciation. In total, over the course of one year, the investor will experience a return on the stock purchase price that is equal to the market rate of 12%. In Figure B, the year-to-year dollar price appreciation is added to the dividend flow at each point in time. Observe that, in

---

[4] For fixed income securities, the realized compound yield or total return incorporates all of the components of return. This concept is discussed in S. Homer and M.L. Leibowitz, *Inside the Yield Book* (Englewood Cliffs, NJ: Prentice-Hall, 1972).

Figure B: Growth in Dividends and Price Over Time for Firm A

ROE = 12%; growth rate = 8%.

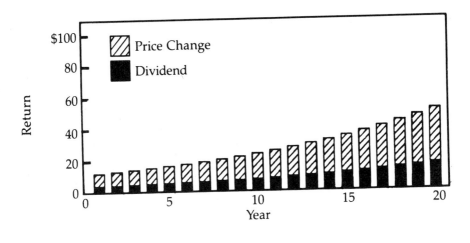

dollar terms, the combination of price appreciation and dividends increases dramatically.

In the absence of risk, the stock of Firm A is equivalent to a perpetual bond that has a constant 4% coupon based on a principal balance that appreciates at 8% per year. If the perpetual's principal is initially $100, the first coupon payment is $4. This $4 payment is the same as the first dividend for Firm A.

At the end of the first year, the perpetual's principal is assumed to increase by 8% to $108. As a result, the second coupon will be $4.32 (4% of $108). This agrees with the second dividend payment of Firm A, because the dividend grows at 8%. Over time, the perpetual bond provides coupon payments that are the same as the dividends for Firm A.

Figure B provides an incomplete picture of growth in asset value for a long-term, tax-free investor, because it does not account for the third component of investor return—the gains from reinvesting all dividends. We assume that the investor has the opportunity to continue to invest in the equity market and earn the 12% market rate.[5] Thus, if all dividend payments are invested, and those

---

[5] With fixed income securities, reinvestment is generally assumed to be in riskless assets, which may offer a lower return than the original investment. Here dividends are reinvested in equity assets that offer the same expected return as the original investment.

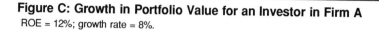

Figure C: Growth in Portfolio Value for an Investor in Firm A
ROE = 12%; growth rate = 8%.

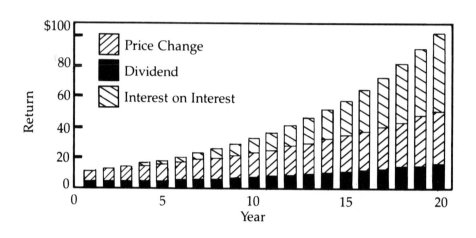

investments compound at a 12% rate, the investor will build a growing "side pool" of wealth. This pool will consist of all accumulated dividends, "interest" on those dividends, and the further compounding of this additional "interest on interest" (or, more accurately, "dividends on dividends").

Figure C adds the incremental year-by-year return from this compound interest on interest to the combination of price appreciation and dividends. It thus gives us the full picture of the growth in portfolio value for an investor in Firm A. At first glance, the overall pattern of total investment return seems to correspond to what would be characterized as a "growth" investment. In the early years, price growth is the dominant component of return. Over time, however, interest on interest begins to dominate. The increasing importance of interest on interest is consistent with the return patterns of fixed-income securities.

STABLE GROWTH VS. ZERO GROWTH

Firm B appears, at least on the surface, to be quite different from Firm A. As Table II indicates, Firm B has the same earnings as Firm A, but it has a 100% payout ratio; that is, all earnings are paid out as dividends on a year-by-year

Table II: Firm B with No Growth

Book Equity	$100.00
ROE	12.00%
Earnings	$12.00
Payout Ratio	100.00%
Dividend	$12.00
Market Rate	12.00%
Price	$100.00
Dividend Yield	12.00%
Growth Rate	0.00%
P/E Ratio	8.33

basis. Thus Firm B is just the opposite of a growth stock; it has no growth in earnings, dividends or price.

Figure D illustrates the (rather dull) stream of direct payments from Firm B. Dividends remain constant and, in the absence of a change in the discount rate, there is no price appreciation. The payment stream for Firm B is identical to the

Figure D: Dividends Over Time for Firm B

ROE = 12%; payout ratio = 1; growth rate = 8%.

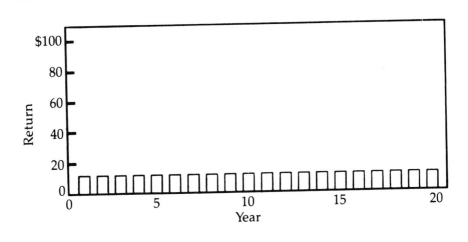

Figure E: The Dividend Streams of Firm A and Firm B

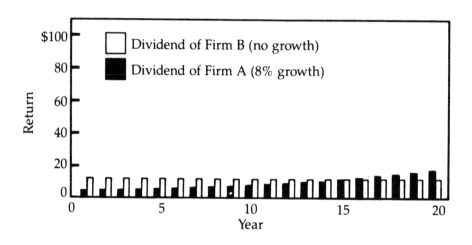

payment stream for a perpetual bond with a 12% coupon and a principal of $100.

Figure E compares the period-by-period dividends of Firms A and B. The dividend stream of Firm B clearly dominates in the early years. By year 15, however, Firm A's earnings have grown enough that its dividends surpass those of Firm B.

Figure F illustrates the total of price appreciation and dividends for Firm B and for Firm A. For Firm B, the price never changes; the firm's 100% dividend-payout policy means no growth. For Firm A, the first year's 4% dividend yield plus 8% price gain matches the 12% dividend payment of Firm B. As time passes, however, both the dividend and the price gain from Firm A grow in dollar terms. The combined gain pulls increasingly ahead of the fixed $12 payment from Firm B.

DIRECT VS. INDIRECT INVESTMENT

The comparison in Figure F seems to suggest that the growth properties of Firm A enable it to outrun the stable 12% return from Firm B. Firm B does have one advantage over Firm A, however. Because Firm B pays out all earnings as divi-

Figure F: Total of Dividends and Price Appreciation for Firm A and Firm B

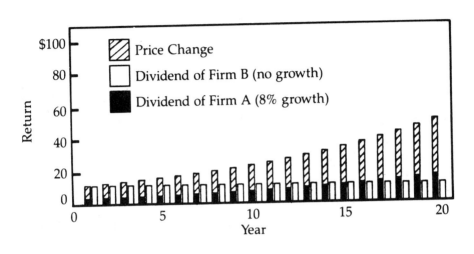

dends, an investor in this firm has the option either to spend or to reinvest his dividend proceeds. By contrast, Firm A's price appreciation cannot be "spent" by the investor. By retaining earnings and adding to book value, Firm A in essence takes charge of a major component of the reinvestment process.

According to the assumptions of the DDM, 66 2/3% of Firm A's earnings are retained (100% less than 33 1/3% payout). These retained earnings are reinvested to produce additional income at the same rate as the firm's initial ROE. For Firm A, this implies that retained earnings earn the 12% market rate, because that was the initial ROE.

The same investment opportunity is *directly* available to an investor in Firm B. This investor can invest all dividend receipts into the general equity market and earn the 12% rate. All the earnings of both firms will thus be put to work at 12%, either by Firm A's investment of retained earnings or by Firm B's investors' reinvestment of dividends received.

On the basis of returns alone, an investor should be indifferent between Firm A and Firm B. As Figure G illustrates, when the incremental year-by-year return from interest on interest is layered on top of dividends and price gains, Firm B offers precisely the same year-by-year increments in portfolio value as Firm A. Thus, under stable market conditions, both firms produce compound returns equal to the 12% market rate.

Figure G: Total Annual Growth in Portfoliio Value for an Investor in Firm B vs. Investor in Firm A

Assuming equal initial investment.

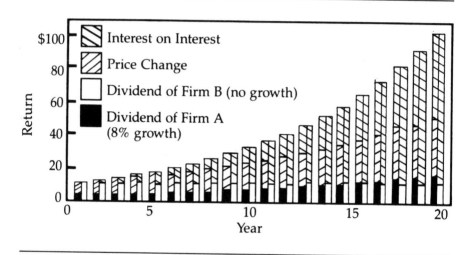

It should be noted that the stocks of the two firms will exhibit different sensitivities to changes in market assumptions. Because the growth stock of Firm A "compounds internally" at 12%, it may have a longer duration, hence a greater sensitivity to declining market discount rates, than the stock of Firm B.[6] The stocks are thus not identical under dynamic market conditions. Our focus, however, is total portfolio returns under *stable* conditions.

In summary, from the point of view of the fully compounding, tax-free investor, Firms A and B are equivalent in terms of total return. They are also equivalent in terms of price, because the dividend streams from both firms have the same present value of $100. Moreover, because the earnings are the same, both stocks have the same P/E ratio—8.33. Figure H highlights the differences between the dividend yields, payout ratios and growth rates of the two firms and the similarity in the firms' P/E ratios.

---

[6] A detailed comparison of the total return on a stock and the total return on a bond is provided in M.L. Leibowitz, "Bond Equivalents of Stock Returns," *Journal of Portfolio Management*, Spring 1978. For an in-depth discussion of equity duration, see M.L. Leibowitz, "Total Portfolio Duration: A New Perspective on Asset Allocation," *Financial Analysts Journal*, September-October 1986 and "A Total Differential Approach to Equity Duration," *Financial Analysts Journal*, September-October 1989.

Figure H: A Comparison of the Characteristics of Firms A and B

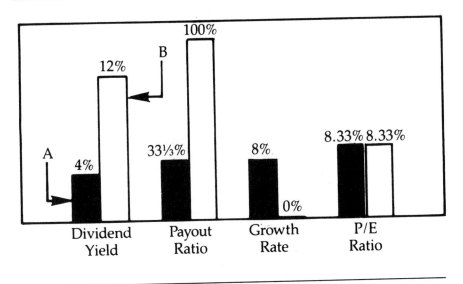

INTERNAL GROWTH VS. EXTERNAL GROWTH

To gain more insight into the P/E ratios of the two firms, we now turn to an analysis of their earnings streams. Both firms start with a book value of $100 and first-year earnings of $12 (12% of $100). Firm B continually pays out all its earnings as dividends, and its book value remains constant at $100. In contrast, Firm A retains 66 2/3% of each year's earnings and adds this amount to its book value.

In the first year, Firm A retains $8 (two-thirds of 12% of $100), thereby bringing its book value up to $108 (1.08 × $100) by the end of that year. As book value increases, total dollar earnings rise, because the same 12% ROE applies to an ever-larger base. The firm's earnings will be $12.96 in year 2 (that is, the ROE of 12% applied to a book value of $108), $14.00 in year 3, and so on. Firm A thus has a pattern of continual earnings growth similar to the return pattern illustrated in Figure B.

We can now compare the year-by-year P/Es of the two firms. At the outset, both stocks are priced at $100 and have earnings of $12. Hence both stocks have identical P/Es of 8.33. For Firm B, however, neither price nor earnings ever grow beyond their initial value, because all earnings are paid out as dividends.

Hence the P/E for Firm B always remains at 8.33. We refer to this figure as the "base P/E."

Some insight into this base P/E of 8.33 can be gained by comparing Firm B's stock with a perpetual bond with a 12% coupon. The price of such a bond is found by dividing the earnings (that is, the coupon payment of $12) by the yield (that is, the 12% market rate). This is equivalent to the requirement that the P/E ratio be the same as the reciprocal of the yield. Thus our P/E ratio of 8.33 is the same as 1/0.12.

For Firm A, we just observed that dollar earnings build year by year in direct proportion to the 8% growth in book value. Under the assumed stable market conditions, the price of Firm A's stock also appreciates by 8% per year, in accordance with the growth in dividends and earnings. The price will be $100.00 in year 1, $108.00 in year 2, $116.64 in year 3 and so on. Accordingly, in year 2, the P/E for Firm A will equal:

$$P/E = (\$100 \times 1.08)/(\$12 \times 1.08)$$

$$= \$100/\$12 = 8.33.$$

In year 3, the P/E will be:

$$P/E = (\$100 \times 1.08^2)/(\$12 \times 1.08^2)$$

$$= \$100/\$12 = 8.33.$$

In other words, the P/E for Firm A remains at its initial value of 8.33. Thus Firm A has exactly the same P/E as Firm B, in every period.

One might have intuitively expected a higher P/E ratio for Firm A because it appears to be a growth firm. As we saw earlier, however, any firm that reinvests only at the market rate is not providing any special service to its investors; they could themselves reinvest dividend receipts at this same rate. Reinvestment at the market rate is thus tantamount to paying out all earnings to the investors: The reinvestment rates are the same; only the labels are different.

Firm A, although a growing enterprise, is fundamentally generating the same value for the investor as the full-payout Firm B. All full-payout firms and full-payout equivalents, such as Firm A, have the same price as a perpetual bond with an annual coupon payment equal to its (current) earnings. Moreover, while the prices of full-payout-equivalent stocks will depend on their respective firms' earnings, they will all have the same base P/E ratio of 8.33.

In particular, under our scenario, any firm with a 12% ROE is equivalent in P/E value to Firm B, regardless of the firm's dividend payout policy. Furthermore, as we shall demonstrate below, any full-payout firm is also equivalent in P/E value to Firm B, regardless of its ROE.

A key conclusion emerging from this comparison of Firms A and B is that investors will not "pay up" in price or in P/E ratio for a firm that reinvests at just the market rate. A firm must achieve a return in *excess* of the market rate on *new* investments to command a P/E in excess of the base P/E.

ABOVE-MARKET ROEs

Firm C has a 15% ROE but, like Firm B, a 100% dividend-payout policy. It thus has no expectation of future growth (see Table III).

Table III: Firm C, with a 15% ROE and No Growth

Book Equity	$100.00
ROE	15.00%
Earnings	$15.00
Payout Ratio	100.00%
Dividend	$15.00
Market Rate	12.00%
Price	$125.00
Dividend Yield	12.00%
Growth Rate	0.00%
P/E Ratio	8.33

Based on an initial book value of $100, Firm C earns $15 annually in perpetuity. Consequently, the price of its stock must be at a premium to book (that is, the stock is priced at $125) to bring its return down to the market rate of 12% (= [15/125] × 100%).[7] Because all earnings are paid out as dividends, the dividend yield for this firm is also 12%.

As in the case of Firm B, Firm C's stock is equivalent to a perpetual bond. The difference between the two perpetuals is that Firm C's stock is equivalent to a sort of premium bond with a 15% coupon, while Firm B's stock is equivalent to a par bond with a 12% coupon. From an investor's viewpoint, Firm C offers no advantage over Firm B. Both firms provide the same dividend yield and no price appreciation. The only difference between them is their stock price. The fundamental similarity between Firms B and C is reflected in their P/E ratios:

---

[7] For a study that relates the DDM approach to the price-to-book ratio, see T. Estep, "A New Model for Valuing Common Stocks," *Financial Analysts Journal*, November-December 1985.

Firm C has the same 8.33 ($125/$15) base P/E as Firm B. Thus Firms A, B and C are all full-payout-equivalent firms.

A REINVESTING FIRM WITH AN ABOVE-MARKET ROE

Firm D is significantly different from the full-payout-equivalent Firms A, B and C. Firm D has the same 15% ROE as Firm C, but a 33 1/3% payout ratio. It differs from all the preceding firms in that it can apply its above-market ROE of 15% to any new investment based on retained earnings.

As a result of its above-market investment opportunities and 10% growth rate, Firm D will be worth more than the $125 price of Firm C. In fact, Firm D's initial price is $250 (see the next section and the appendix for details). Table IV gives the basic characteristics of Firm D.

Table IV: Firm D, with a Constant 10% Growth Rate

Book Equity	$100.00
ROE	15.00%
Earnings	$15.00
Payout Ratio	33 1/3%
Dividend	$5.00
Market Rate	12.00%
Price	$250.00
Dividend Yield	2.00%
Growth Rate	10.00%
P/E Ratio	16.67

Our investigation of Firm D begins with an analysis of the three components of return for fully compounding, tax-free investors. Because the initial stock price is no longer $100, a comparison with our earlier results for Firms A and B is facilitated by expressing the three components of return as a percentage of the original price of $250. Thus, while Firm D's dividend of $5 is higher than the dollar value of Firm A's dividend, it represents a lower dividend yield—2%, compared with 4% for Firm A.

Figure I compares the yearly dividends of Firm A and Firm D (as a percentage of the original price). Despite the rapid 10% growth of Firm D, the dividends of Firm A continue to dominate for many years. An investor in Firm D, however, should expect yearly price increments to keep pace with the 10%

Figure I: A Comparison of the Dividends of Firm D and Firm A
As percentage of original price.

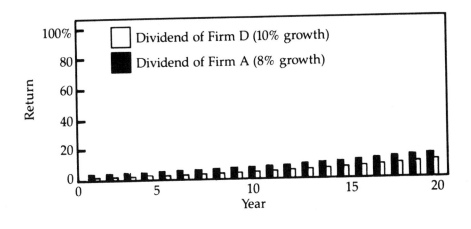

Figure J: Annual Dividends and Price Appreciation for Firm D and Firm A
As percentage of original price.

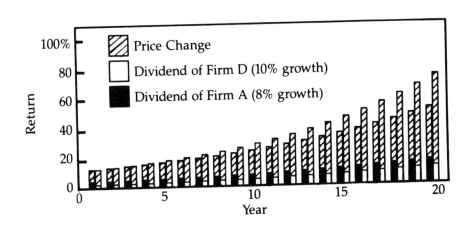

growth in book value and earnings that Firm D experiences. Thus, over the course of one year, Firm D's 2% dividend yield combined with a 10% price gain will provide a new investor with the 12% market return.

Figure J compares the dividend and price increments for Firms A and D. The 10% annual price return of Firm D is sufficient to bring the combination of its dividends and price increments (expressed as a percentage of Firm D's initial $250 price) to a level that completely dominates the dividends and price increments for Firm A.

We can compare Firm D's stock to a perpetual bond. In the absence of risk, Firm D's stock—like that of Firm A—is equivalent to a perpetual bond with increasing principal. The only difference is that the coupon is now 2% and the principal increases by 10% per year.

TOTAL GROWTH

We complete our comparison of the two firms by considering the *total* portfolio growth that an investor in Firm D can be expected to receive. A fully compounding investor in Firm D will create a side pool of wealth that compounds at the assumed 12% market rate.

Because dividends for Firm D represent a relatively small percentage of the initial investment, this side pool will grow more slowly than it would for an investment in the other firms. In fact, the side pool for Firm D grows just enough, in comparison with that of Firm A, that when all the components of return are considered, the period-by-period returns for the two firms are identical (see Figure K).

In the context of our narrow model, the positive impact of the combination of growth and high ROE is not on return, but on the P/E ratio. It is this ratio that reflects both current earnings and embedded future franchise opportunities. To understand better how this works, we will now look "inside" the P/E ratios of the sample firms.

A CLOSER LOOK AT THE INVESTMENT PROCESS

We observed that Firm D's stock is priced at $250, compared with an initial price of $100 for Firm A. This price reflects *both* Firm D's high current earnings and the expectation of future above-market investment opportunities. By virtue of its business franchise, Firm D has the special opportunity to reinvest a portion of its earnings at the above-market, 15% rate. This opportunity is not directly available to investors because, in our equilibrium model, investors are able to achieve only the 12% market return.

Figure K: A Comparison of Year-by-Year Returns for Firm D and Firm A
As percentage of original price.

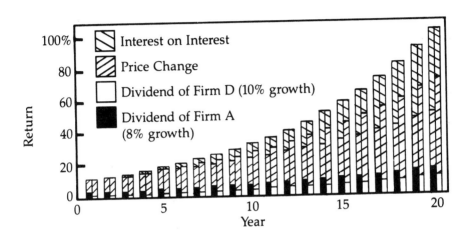

In contrast to Firm A, Firm D is able to achieve a 3% return advantage on a prescribed stream of future investments. This excess 3% return produces a pool of incremental value beyond what the investor could achieve with his external side pool. This compounding stream of excess returns will have real value to the investor, and he will naturally "pay up" to access it.

The value of the excess returns is reflected in the P/E ratio for Firm D. Because this firm earns $15 the first year, its P/E is 16.67 ($250/$15). This is twice the P/E ratio of the other firms. In effect, Firm D is priced at a premium of 8.34 above and beyond the base P/E of 8.33. This P/E increment can be interpreted as a premium for franchise opportunities.

Figure L compares the P/E ratios of Firms A, B, C and D. As we have already observed, when the ROE is the same as the market rate (Firms A and B), the P/E always remains at its base level, regardless of the firm's payout policy or growth rate. When a firm has an above-market ROE but no growth (Firm C), it too offers only the base P/E. A growth firm with an *above-market* ROE (Firm D), however, will have a P/E that is *higher* than the base P/E of 8.33. (It should also be noted that a growth firm with a *below-market* ROE will have a P/E ratio *below* 8.33.)

Figure L: The P/E Ratios for A, B, C and D

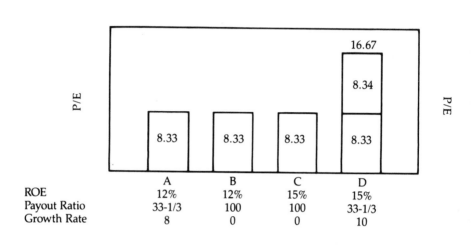

	A	B	C	D
ROE	12%	12%	15%	15%
Payout Ratio	33-1/3	100	100	33-1/3
Growth Rate	8	0	0	10

SOURCE OF PREMIUM

To see how this premium value is created, we must focus more closely on the reinvestment process. After one year, Firm D pays out $5 of its $15 in earnings as dividends and retains and reinvests the remaining $10. As a result, the firm's book value grows to $110. The new book value may be viewed as consisting of the original $100 (the base source of earnings at the outset) and a $10 new investment (a source of "new earnings"). This new $10 per share investment will, by assumption, produce returns at the 15% ROE level in perpetuity.

The year-end reinvestment of $10 can itself be viewed as achieving a 3% premium return over the 12% market rate because of some special franchise situation enjoyed by Firm D. As we saw in the comparison of Firms A and B, reinvestment at the 12% market rate provides no added value to the investor: It will not lead to any increment in the P/E multiple. The real added value from Firm D is derived totally from the 3% excess return that it can earn on its new investments.

Because, by assumption, all new investments provide 3% in excess earnings in perpetuity, Firm D provides a compounding stream of incremental earnings. In the second year, the retained earnings available for new investment will grow to $11 (that is, 1.10 × $10). In the third year, Firm D has $12.10 (that is, $10 ×

1.10^2) to invest. Over time, this sequence of opportunities produces a growing aggregate stream of excess earnings.

If we were to calculate the present value of this compounding stream of excess earnings, we would find that it amounts to $125 per share—that is, 50% of Firm D's price according to the DDM. The other 50% of Firm D's value is simply derived from its full-payout equivalence to Firm C. (Recall that the price of Firm C's stock is precisely $125.) In summary, Firm D can be viewed as a combination of the following—(1) a full-payout-equivalent firm, such as Firms A, B and C, and (2) a stream of opportunities for investment at 3% above the market rate.

We've seen that all full-payout equivalents have the same P/E ratio in a given market—8.33 at the assumed 12% market rate. Firm D's P/E ratio of 16.67 can now be viewed as consisting of this base value of 8.33 plus an incremental P/E multiple of 8.34 for its stream of excess earnings on new investments.

THE PRESENT-VALUE GROWTH EQUIVALENT

A firm's opportunities to earn returns in excess of the equilibrium market rate can be thought of as "franchise growth opportunities." The traditional DDM implicitly assumes that a firm always has the opportunity to make investments that offer a return equal to the firm's initial ROE. The DDM also implicitly assumes that such investments are made along a smooth growth pattern determined by the firm's sequence of retained earnings.

It is clearly more realistic to assume that franchise opportunities arise on a less-than-regular schedule. Furthermore, there is no guarantee that the extent of the franchise opportunity will equal available cash. A firm will nevertheless want to take full advantage of *any* opportunities to earn above-market returns— whether or not the opportunities happen to coincide with the timing or magnitude of the firm's retained earnings. In today's capital markets, a firm should always be able to raise the capital needed to fund projects that offer exceptional returns. We thus assume that the firm will fully utilize all franchise opportunities, and that the cost of capital will be the assumed market rate.[8]

As we have shown, the value of new investments is derived solely from the return they offer in excess of the market rate. The firm can always raise new funds through the issuance of additional equity, paying the market rate for such funds. It therefore does not matter whether new investments are funded by retained earnings or by additional equity issuance. (In this analysis, we deal with

---

[8] It is more realistic to assume that franchise opportunities will offer a range of returns. For ease of exposition, we consider only the case where the return is equal to initial ROE.

the unleveraged firm. For this reason, we do not address the obviously realistic alternative of debt financing for new investment opportunities.)

The stream of all future franchise opportunities implied by the DDM can be encapsulated in a single number—G, the present-value *Growth Equivalent* of these investments. The present value of the Growth Equivalent can be derived by discounting all future franchise opportunities at the market rate and then expressing the result as a percentage of the original book value of the firm.[9] The Growth Equivalent enables us to view the stream of future opportunities as equivalent to a single, immediate opportunity to invest and then earn the ROE in perpetuity. In other words, we are reducing all growth patterns to the simple model of a single, immediate jump in book value. The Growth Equivalent is quite general; it can represent *any* sequence of opportunities.

The Growth Equivalent approach can help to penetrate the facade of smooth growth that often obscures the real implications of many DDM models. The Growth Equivalent thus provides insight into the magnitude of the investment implicit in any given constant-growth assumption.

IMMEDIATE INVESTMENT VS. SERIAL INVESTMENT

As an example, consider Firm D. Recall that its P/E is at an 8.34 premium to the base P/E of 8.33. Basically, this incremental multiple is the value attached to the growing sequence of opportunities to invest at 3% above the market rate. As we observed, this sequence coincides with Firm D's pattern of retained earnings.

By computing the Growth Equivalent of this series of investments, we find the magnitude of the single, immediate opportunity that provides the same present value as the smooth growth pattern associated with Firm D's retained earnings. It turns out that this equivalent investment, G, corresponds to 500% of Firm D's current book value.[10] In present-value terms, Firm D must immediately invest an amount equal to five times its current book value and earn 15% on that investment in perpetuity.

Figure M illustrates how Firm D's book value increases by larger and larger increments by virtue of actual growth at the 10% annual rate. It also shows the hypothetical book value of the corresponding Growth Equivalent. Both cases start with an original book value of $100. For the Growth Equivalent firm, however, book value immediately jumps by $500, to $600, and remains constant at this level.

---

[9] For a constant growth rate, g, and market rate, k, $G = g/(k - g)$. See the appendix for a derivation of this formula.

[10] Because $G = g/(k - g)$ and $g = 10\%$ for Firm D, it follows that $G = 0.10/(0.12 - 0.10) = 500\%$.

Figure M: The Present-Value Growth Equivalent for a 10% Growth Firm

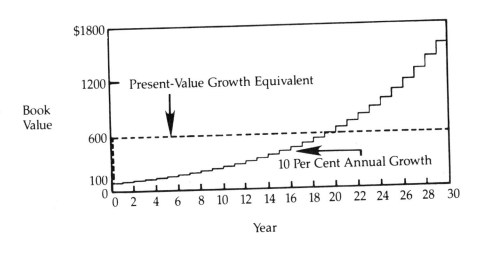

The Growth Equivalent approach creates a hypothetical "alter ego" for any growth firm. After the immediate jump in book value, the alter ego has no further growth. Because it does not have further growth, it retains none of its earnings, and all net flows are paid out immediately as dividends. Consequently, the alter ego can be viewed as an "augmented" full-payout equivalent of a growth firm. This can be seen more clearly in Figure N, which compares the dividend flows from the growing Firm D with the constant dividend payments of its full-payout alter ego.

The payouts for Firm D begin with the initial dividend of $5 (2% of $250) and grow at a constant rate of 10% forever. In contrast, the Growth Equivalent provides an annual payout consisting of (1) the original $15 of earnings (that is, the full-payout equivalent), augmented by (2) an additional $15 from the 3% excess return (= 15% - 12%) on the $500 Growth Equivalent investment. This hypothetical Growth Equivalent thus provides a constant annual payout of $30 in perpetuity. When discounted at the market rate, both cash flows have the same present value of $250.

The expected level of above-market-rate investments implicit in a P/E of 16.67 is startling. For a start-up firm with a new product and an incontestable franchise, it is probably not too difficult to imagine several years of spectacular investment opportunities. But it must be difficult for a mature, large company in

Figure N: A Comparison of the Cash Flows of a 10% Growth Firm with a Growth-Equivalent Firm

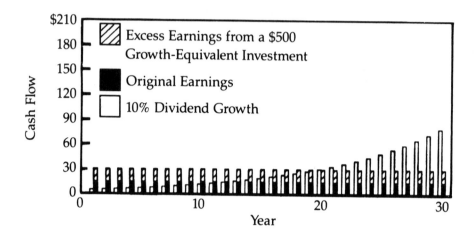

a highly competitive market to find an opportunity to invest five times its current book value and earn a return significantly higher than the market's.

THE FRANCHISE FACTOR

As we have seen, firms that offer both growth and above-market ROEs are valued at a premium to the base P/E. To measure the impact of above-market investments on P/E ratio, we introduce a new measure, called the Franchise Factor (FF). The FF is the increase in P/E that results from one unit of present-value Growth Equivalent.

In a stable market, the FF depends only on the firm's ROE. Computationally, the FF is the return premium offered by the firm divided by the product of the ROE and the market rate (see the appendix for the derivation of the FF):

$$FF = \frac{r - k}{rk},$$

where r is the firm's ROE, k is the market rate, and all values are expressed as decimals.

To understand how the FF works, consider Firm D. Because the ROE is 15% and the market rate is 12%, the FF for this firm is:

$$FF = \frac{0.15 - 0.12}{(0.15)(0.12)} = \frac{0.03}{0.018} = 1.67.$$

Firm D's P/E will increase 1.67 units for each unit gain in book value (in present-value terms). We have already seen that the present-value Growth Equivalent for Firm D is 500% of book. As a consequence of the FF, Firm D's P/E ratio is lifted 8.34 (= 1.67 × 5) units above the base P/E ratio, to a total level of 16.67.

We can express P/E ratio in terms of the market rate, the Growth Equivalent (G) and the Franchise Factor (FF), as follows:

$$P/E = \frac{1}{k} + FF \cdot G, \text{ or}$$

$$P/E = (\text{Base } P/E) + FF \cdot G.$$

The first term is the base P/E. The second term is the product of the Franchise Factor and the Growth Equivalent. This term captures the increase in the P/E ratio that results from the combination of growth and above-market ROE. We have already observed that, in a stable market, the FF depends only on the ROE. G depends only on the assumed growth rate. Thus the FF and G fully—but separately—capture the impact of ROE and growth on P/E ratio.

ROE, GROWTH AND P/E

Figure O illustrates the FF for a wide range of ROEs. When the ROE is the same as the market rate, the FF is zero. As a result, growth makes no contribution to the P/E ratio. Recall that Firm A had 8% growth but an ROE only equal to the market's. The FF for Firm A is thus zero. As we observed earlier, growth without incremental ROE makes no contribution to P/E.

Now consider a firm with an FF of one (that is, reading from Figure O, a firm with an ROE of 13.64%). For such a firm, an immediate investment equal to 100% of current book value lifts the P/E ratio by only a single unit (that is, from 8.33 to 9.33). The magnitude of this immediate investment illustrates the growth required to raise the P/E ratio. With an FF of four (that is, an ROE of 23.08%), an investment equal to 100% of book raises the P/E ratio by only four units. This analysis underscores the difficulty inherent in creating a high P/E ratio.

As ROE increases, so does the FF. As we would expect, the higher the ROE, the greater the impact of new investments on P/E. However, as Figure O shows, this impact eventually levels off. In particular, as ROE approaches infinity, the FF approaches the inverse of the market rate. With our assumed 12% market

---

Figure O: The Franchise Factor

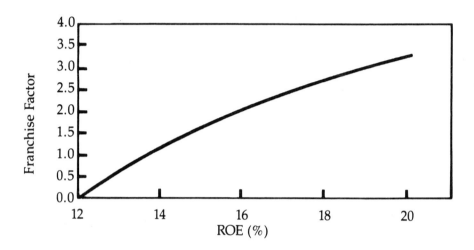

---

rate, this implies that a 100% (one unit) increase in book can never increase P/E by more than 8.33.

Table V summarizes our findings. Because Firms B and C have no growth, their Growth Equivalent is zero. By contrast, Firm A has a 200% Growth Equivalent, and Firm D has a 500% Growth Equivalent. However, Firm A's growth fails to add value, because its FF is zero (its ROE being the 12% market rate). In addition, observe that Firm C may have untapped potential: It has the same FF as Firm D, as it has the same 15% ROE. Yet, because of a lack of new investment, Firm C's potential is not utilized, and it commands only a base P/E. Only

---

Table V: The P/E Ratios and Franchise Factors for Firms A, B, C and D

Firm	ROE	Growth Rate	Growth Equivalent	Franchise Factor	P/E Increment	P/E
A	12%	8%	200%	0	0.00	8.33
B	12	0	0	0	0.00	8.33
C	15	0	0	1.67	0.00	8.33
D	15	10	500	1.67	8.34	16.67

Figure P: Interpreting the P/E Ratio through the Franchise Factor

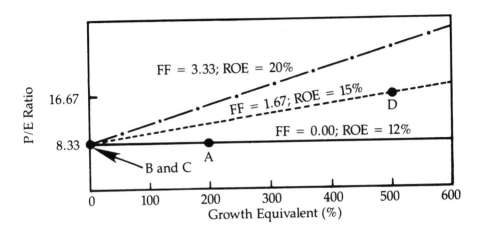

Firm D, with its combination of positive growth and positive FF, is able to command a premium P/E.

Figure P presents a more graphic view of how the FF and Growth Equivalent explain the P/E levels of our four firms. When the P/E is plotted against the Growth Equivalent, all firms that have the same ROE plot along a straight line. This line always starts at the base P/E ratio (8.33 in our example). The slope of the line is just the FF for that ROE. Thus firms with a 12% ROE have an FF of zero and plot as a horizontal line. Firms with a 15% ROE plot along the line with a slope of 1.67.

In this diagram, Firm A has 200% growth, but it is on the horizontal (FF = 0) line. It thus commands only the base P/E of 8.33. Firms B and C have no growth, hence they too can obtain only the 8.33 base P/E (regardless of their ROE or FF values). Only Firm D has the right combination of growth (a 500% Growth Equivalent) and an above-market ROE (15%). It lies on the line with a slope (FF value) of 1.67, hence enjoys a high P/E ratio.

Figure P also shows how firms with a 20% ROE plot. As we can see, a high ROE certainly makes growth more valuable. At the same time, to obtain a high P/E ratio, even with an ROE significantly above the market, a firm must possess rather sizable growth prospects.

CONCLUSION

We have represented all above-market investment opportunities implicitly embedded in the DDM by their present value. In so doing, we are able to look beyond a pattern of either smooth constant growth or multiphase growth. The analysis can thus readily be extended to incorporate an entire portfolio of investment opportunities. Each investment can have its own (possibly irregular) capital schedule, return pattern and life cycle.

In reality, taxes, leverage and uncertainty do exist, and prices do not coincide with theoretical values. Market rates, investment opportunities and year-to-year ROEs change constantly. Thus our results, derived under highly simplistic assumptions, must be interpreted with appropriately large caveats. They nonetheless appear to provide valuable insights into the structural relations inside the P/E ratio.

Appendix

According to the standard dividend discount model (DDM), a theoretical stock price is computed by discounting the stream of all future dividends at the market rate, k. Thus:

$$P = \frac{D_1}{1+k} + \frac{D_2}{(1+k)^2} + \ldots + \frac{D_N}{(1+k)^N} + \ldots,$$

where

D_i = dividend at time i.

If we assume that dividends grow annually at a constant rate g, then P can be shown to be:

$$P = \frac{D_1}{k-g}. \tag{A1}$$

This is the standard Gordon formula. Note that this was derived without regard to the source of dividend growth.

Dividend growth is related to a firm's return on equity (ROE) and to the growth in book value that results from retained earnings. To see this, note that the dollar dividend payout at time i depends on the firm's earnings over the period from time (i - 1) to time i. These earnings are symbolized by E_i. The dividend payout is expressed as a fraction of earnings, called the dividend payout ratio. Here we assume that the dividend payout ratio is a constant b over time. Thus:

$D_i = bE_i.$

The earnings E_i are the product of the firm's ROE and the book value B_{i-1} at the beginning of the period. We assume that the ROE is a constant r, so that:

$$E_i = rB_{i-1}; \; i = 1, 2, \ldots, N. \tag{A2}$$

Because earnings are a constant multiple of book value, they will grow at the same rate as book value. All earnings not paid out as dividends (that is, retained

315

earnings) add to book value. (For the moment, we assume there are no other sources of additions to book, e.g., no new equity issuance.) The earnings retention rate q is:

q = (1 - b).

If B_0 is the initial book value, book value at the end of the first year, B_1, is:

$B_1 = B_0 + qE_1$.

Because $E_1 = rB_0$, we have:

$B_1 = B_0 + qrB_0$

$= (1 + qr)B_0$.

Thus book value grows at the rate qr. Because both earnings and dividend streams grow with book value, qr is the sustainable growth rate. That is:

g = qr = (1 - Payout Ratio) • ROE.

Note that the Gordon formula, Equation (A1), can be rewritten in terms of initial earnings and dividend payout ratio, as follows:

$$P = \frac{bE_1}{k-g}.$$ (A3)

The theoretical P/E ratio is thus:

$$P/E = \frac{b}{k-g}.$$ (A4)

Table AI provides four examples—the four firms discussed in the text—illustrating the pricing and P/E ratio formulas given above. In all cases, we assume that the market rate k is 12%.

By algebraic manipulation, formula (A4) can be transformed into the Miller and Modigliani (MM) formula. We first write:

$$P/E = \frac{b}{k-g} = \frac{1-q}{k-rq}.$$

Factoring out 1/k, we have:

$$P/E = \frac{1}{k} \bullet \left[\frac{k(1-q)}{k-rq}\right] = \frac{1}{k} \bullet \left[\frac{k-kq}{k-rq}\right].$$

Subtracting and adding rq to the numerator of the term in brackets, we have:

Table AI: Theoretical Stock Prices and P/E Ratios for Four Firms (12% market rate)

	Specifications			Resulting Values				P/E Ratio
Firm	Payout Ratio (b)	ROE (r)	Initial Book Value (B₀)	Retention Rate (q)	Growth Rate (rq)	Initial Earnings (rB₀)	Price [brB₀/(k-g)]	[b/(k-g)]
A	1/3	12%	100	2/3	8%	12	100	8.33
B	1	12	100	0	0	12	100	8.33
C	1	15	100	0	0	15	125	8.33
D	1/3	15	100	2/3	10	15	250	16.67

$$P/E = \frac{1}{k} \cdot \left[\frac{k-rq+rq-kq}{k-rq} \right].$$

Carrying out the indicated division results in the following MM formula:

$$P/E = \frac{1}{k} \cdot \left[1 + \frac{q(r-k)}{k-rq} \right]. \tag{A5}$$

If there is no growth (q = 0), the second term in brackets vanishes, and the P/E ratio is simply the inverse of the market rate, regardless of the value of r. Thus, for example, if q = 0 and k = 12%, P/E = 1/(0.12) = 8.33. Thus both Firms B and C in Table AI have a P/E ratio of 8.33 (the base P/E).

If q is greater than 0, but the return on equity r is the same as the market rate k, the second term above still vanishes. Again, P/E = 1/k. Thus, because r = 12% for Firm A, it also has a base P/E of 8.33.

For the P/E to rise above the base P/E, we must have both growth and reinvestment at an above-market ROE. Growth alone is not enough. For Firm D, where q = 2/3 and r = 15%, the P/E ratio is 16.67.

Additional insight into the nature of growth can be gained by rewriting Equation (A5) in terms of price and initial book value, rather than P/E. We thus multiply both sides of Equation (A5) by E and replace E by rB_0 in the second term:

$$P = \frac{E}{k} + \frac{qrB_0(r-k)}{k(k-rq)},$$

or

$$P = \frac{E}{k} + \frac{r-k}{k} \cdot \frac{g}{(k-g)} \cdot B_0. \tag{A6}$$

The first term in Equation (A6) represents the present value of a perpetual stream of unchanging earnings of magnitude E. In other words, this term corresponds to a firm's full-payout equivalent. The second term can be shown to represent the earnings impact of a series of new investments. The magnitude of these new investments is $B_0 \bullet g/(k - g)$. The factor $g/(k - g)$ can be interpreted as an immediate percentage increase in book value. Thus we set

$$G = \frac{g}{(k - g)} \tag{A7}$$

and regard G as the present-value Growth Equivalent of all book increases. (See below for a more detailed discussion of G.) The new investments, $G \bullet B_0$, provide perpetual incremental above-market earnings of $(r - k)$. The present value of this perpetual stream is obtained by dividing $(r - k) \bullet G \bullet B_0$ by k.

Equation (A6) can be rewritten in terms of G as follows:

$$P = \frac{E}{k} + \frac{r - k}{k} \bullet G \bullet B_0 . \tag{A8}$$

We now show that G is, in fact, the present value of *all* future investments implied by the DDM model, expressed as a percentage of B_0.

The firm's book value at time i, B_i, is:

$$B_i = (1 + g)^i B_0.$$

The increment to book at time i is symbolized by b_i and is equal to $B_i - B_{i-1}$. Thus:

$$b_i = B_i - B_{i-1} = (1 + g)^i B_0 - (1 + g)^{i-1} B_0,$$

or

$$b_i = (1 + g)^{i-1} g B_0.$$

The present value of all such book increments is as follows:

$$PV \ [b_1, b_2, b_3, \ldots] = \frac{g B_0}{1 + k} + \frac{g B_0 (1 + g)}{(1 + k)^2} + \frac{g B_0 (1 + g)^2}{(1 + k)^3} + \ldots$$

$$= \frac{g B_0}{1 + k} \bullet \left[1 + \frac{1 + g}{1 + k} + \frac{(1 + g)^2}{(1 + k)^2} + \ldots \right]$$

$$= \frac{g B_0}{k - g} .$$

Thus,

$$\frac{\text{PV } [b_1, b_2, b_3, \ldots]}{B_0} = \frac{g}{k-g}.$$

This is precisely G as defined above. Note that G is independent of the funding of the book value increments. That is, the assumption that only retained earnings are used to fund new investments is artificial. If an opportunity to invest b_i and earn r exists at time i, this investment could be funded through the issuance of equity at a cost k. The earnings on this new investment, net of financing costs, would then be precisely (r - k).

We further note that it is the magnitude of G—not the specific timing of investment opportunities—that matters. That is, a different sequence of book increments b_1^*, b_2^*, b_3^*, . . . for which PV[b_1^*, b_2^*, b_3^*, . . .]/B_0 is equal to G, would have precisely the same impact on the theoretical price as the sequence of book increments implied by our constant-growth model.

As an example of the magnitude of growth G implicit in the DDM, consider Firm D. Since g = 10% and k = 12%, G is (0.10)/(0.02), or 500%! For this firm to sustain a P/E ratio of 16.67 (Table AI), there must be some sequence of investments that, in present-value terms, is equal to 500% of the current book value of the firm. Furthermore, each of these investments must earn 15%. These extraordinary opportunities are reflected in the firm's price through the present value of the excess returns on those investments, as illustrated in the Equation (A8).

For Firm D, because r = 15%, B_0 = $100 and E = $15, we have the following:

$$P = \frac{15}{0.12} + \frac{0.15 - 0.12}{0.12} \bullet 500\% \bullet 100$$

$$= 125 + 125 = 250.$$

Thus the value of the present earnings of $15 in perpetuity is $125, and the value of all future excess earnings is also $125.

To understand better the impact of G, we turn our attention to the P/E ratio. By dividing both sides of Equation (A8) by E (that is, by rB_0, we obtain

$$P/E = \frac{1}{k} + \frac{r-k}{rk} \bullet G. \tag{A9}$$

The first term, 1/k, is the "base P/E" (that is, P/E = 8.33 when k = 12%). If the second term is positive, the P/E will be above this base level. If that term is negative, the P/E will be below the base P/E ratio.

The factor (r - k)/rk measures the impact of opportunities to make new investments that provide a return equal to the firm's ROE. We call this the Franchise Factor, or FF. Thus

$$FF = (r - k)/rk \qquad (A10)$$

and

$$P/E = \frac{1}{k} + FF \bullet G. \qquad (A11)$$

Because G is measured in units of initial book value (that is, G is expressed as a percentage of B_0), FF is the increase in P/E ratio per "book unit" of investment. Note that, when r = k, FF = 0. This is consistent with our earlier observation

---

Table AII: Franchise Factors for Varying ROEs (with a 12% market rate)

ROE (r)	12%	13%	14%	15%	16%	17%	18%	19%	20%	50%
FF	0.00	0.64	1.19	1.67	2.08	2.45	2.78	3.07	3.33	6.33

---

that growth alone is not enough to affect the P/E ratio. However, as r increases, the impact of growth on P/E increases. These results are illustrated in Table AII.

Consider, for example, the case of Firm D. Because r = 15%, FF = 1.67. An investment equal to 100% of this firm's initial book value (that is, $100) will lift the P/E ratio by 1.67 units. An investment of five times book will lift the P/E ratio by 8.34 units—just enough to bring it from the base P/E ratio of 8.33 to its actual P/E ratio of 16.67.

Finally, we observe that, as r approaches infinity, FF levels off at the inverse of the market rate k. That is, no matter how large the ROE, with a 12% market rate, FF can never rise above 8.33. In particular, at least a 100% increase in book is required to raise the P/E ratio from 8.33 to 16.67, no matter how large the reinvestment rate.

Chapter II-2

Inside the P/E Ratio (Part II): The Franchise Portfolio

INTRODUCTION AND SUMMARY

In an earlier paper, we introduced the Franchise Factor (FF) as a measure of the price/earnings (P/E) impact of new investments.[1] Investments with above-market returns have positive Franchise Factors and, consequently, add to a firm's P/E. In contrast, investments with below-market returns have negative Franchise Factors. Thus, such investments constitute an "anti-franchise," which reduces the P/E ratio. In the absence of investment opportunities, a firm with a steady earnings stream will have a zero Franchise Factor and its P/E will simply be the inverse of the market capitalization rate.[2] Thus, all such firms have exactly the same P/E, regardless of their dividend payout policy. This result follows from the well-known fact that retained earnings invested at the market rate provide no added value to investors.

---

[1] See *Inside the P/E Ratio: The Franchise Factor*, Salomon Brothers Inc, July 1990.

[2] See "Dividend Policy, Growth, and the Valuation of Shares," *The Journal of Business*, Merton H. Miller and Franco Modigliani, October 1961.

Martin L. Leibowitz and Stanley Kogelman, "Inside the P/E Ratio (Part II): The Franchise Portfolio," Salomon Brothers Inc, January 1991.

In this paper, we develop a methodology for estimating the theoretical P/E impact of the portfolio of investment opportunities available to a firm. Our analysis makes the highly restrictive assumptions of a world without taxes, leverage or uncertainty.

There are two components to a franchise opportunity: the magnitude of investments; and the pattern of payments that evolves over time. Naturally, one would prefer to make investments in projects that have outstanding returns. However, there probably will be only limited opportunities for such investments. We measure the "magnitude" of a given investment opportunity by the present value of the total amount of funds that can be invested in it. Since the accumulation of these investments comprises the growth in the firm's book value, we refer to this measure as the Growth Equivalent (G), the first component of the franchise opportunity.

The second component of the franchise opportunity is the "return phase," which is the pattern of payments generated by the investment. These return patterns may exhibit a wide variety of shapes. For example, annual returns may increase rapidly at first and then level off at an above-market rate. Ultimately, there may be a period of deteriorating returns as a result of the declining value of the franchise. The P/E-producing "power" of a given return pattern is captured in its Franchise Factor. For example, if an investment opportunity has a Franchise Factor of two, each unit of Growth Equivalent investment will add two units to the firm's P/E. Thus, the incremental P/E value of a specific investment opportunity is given by the product of its Franchise Factor and the size of the investment as measured by its Growth Equivalent. There are infinitely many combinations of Franchise Factors and Growth Equivalents that can give rise to the same P/E increment.

In the first section of this paper, we briefly review the application of the Franchise Factor approach to investments that provide constant annual returns in perpetuity. Then, we turn to more general return patterns and develop a duration-based formula that can be used to approximate the Franchise Factor. The approximation formula involves both the Internal Rate of Return (IRR) of an investment and the duration of its payment stream. The structure of this formula also provides insight into the well-known deficiencies of the IRR as a measure of relative investment value.[3]

One approach to finding the exact Franchise Factor that corresponds to any pattern of investment returns is to compute its perpetual equivalent return. This perpetual equivalent is simply a constant annual payment that has the same present value as the payment pattern. In contrast to the IRR, the perpetual equivalent, like the Net Present Value, uniquely determines an investment's P/E impact. Two projects with that same perpetual equivalent will have the same

---

[3] Our observations are consistent with the usual capital budgeting considerations. See, for example, *Financial Management*, Ramesh K.S. Rao, Macmillan, 1987.

Franchise Factor and will provide the same addition to P/E (per unit of Growth Equivalent).

After developing the tools of analysis, we apply our methodology to a portfolio of franchise investment opportunities. Each such opportunity will have its own Franchise Factor and Growth Equivalent. The combined P/E impact of these franchise opportunities then can be determined by using "vector" addition. This approach easily encompasses multiphase growth models. Our analysis also provides simple decision rules for the financing of new investments and the sale of nonproductive businesses.

THE FRANCHISE FACTOR MODEL

In this section, we review the Franchise Factor method of theoretical P/E estimation (see the *Appendix* for the derivation of this model). According to this method, the three ingredients in estimating P/E are as follows: (1) the Base Market P/E; (2) the Growth Equivalent; and (3) the Franchise Factor.

- The **Base Market P/E** is the P/E of a firm with constant earnings over time. The P/E of such a firm is the inverse of the market capitalization rate. For example, if the market rate is 12%, the Base P/E is 8.33 $(1 \div 0.12)$.

- The **Growth Equivalent** (G) is the sum of the present values of all future investments (discounted at the market rate) expressed as a percentage of the original book value of a firm.

- The **Franchise Factor** (FF) is the P/E increase that results from one unit of Growth Equivalent investment in a specific pattern of returns. In other words, if the present value of new investments is equivalent to the current book value of the firm, the P/E multiple will increase by the value of the Franchise Factor.

According to the FF model, the theoretical P/E can be computed from the following equation:

$$P/E = \left[\begin{array}{c} \text{Base Market} \\ \text{No–Growth} \end{array} P/E \right] + \left[\begin{array}{c} \text{Franchise} \\ \text{Factor} \end{array} \right] \bullet \left[\begin{array}{c} \text{Growth} \\ \text{Equivalent} \end{array} \right].$$

When the FF is positive, investments (as measured by G) lead to an above-market P/E. The graph of the relationship between P/E and G is a straight line (see Figure 1). This P/E line always starts at the Base P/E (8.33 in our example), and its slope is the FF.

Figure 1: Interpreting the P/E Ratio Through the Franchise Factor

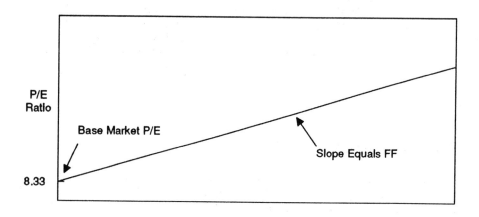

Growth Equivalent (%)

For example, consider a firm that currently has a return on equity (ROE) of 15% (3% above the market rate of 12%). Assume that the firm's business franchise enables it to make new investments at the end of each year equal to 10% of the firm's book value at the beginning of the year. Each investment is assumed to earn 15% in perpetuity. The FF for each investment can be computed according to the following formula:

$$FF = \frac{R - k}{rk}.$$

The variables in the above formula are defined as follows:

R = Perpetual Return (Annual Payment Rate) on new investment;

r = Return on initial book equity; and

k = Market capitalization rate.

In our example, both the return on new investment and the return on initial book equity are 15%. We assume that k is 12%. Substituting these values into the FF formula, we find the following:

$$FF = \frac{0.15 - 0.12}{0.15 \times 0.12} = 1.67.$$

Under the constant growth assumption, G is computed by the following formula:

$$G = \frac{g}{k - g}.$$

In the example, g = 10%; thus,

$$G = \frac{0.10}{0.12 - 0.10} = 5.00,$$

or in percentage terms, G = 500%. The product of FF and G is 8.34; thus, the P/E ratio is 16.67 (that is, the base P/E of 8.33 plus 8.34). As illustrated in Figure 2, there is an infinite number of combinations of FFs and Gs that give rise to the same P/E of 16.67%. For high growth equivalents, there is a leveling off of the required FF. However, for Gs below 200%, the FF becomes very large. For example, if G is 100%, investments must have an FF of 8.34 to bring the P/E up to 16.67%. Such a high FF is unrealizable in practice, because it requires an investment that has annual returns of 27% per year in perpetuity.

Figure 2: The Building Blocks of an Above-Market P/E

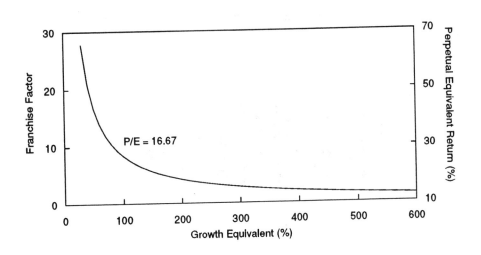

At first, the assumption of a perpetual return on new investments may seem artificial. Normally, the return on a new investment will change over time. For example, there might be a period of rising returns, followed by a period of high steady returns. However, high returns probably cannot be sustained forever. Ultimately, returns will start to decline.

In subsequent sections of this paper, we will show how FF can be determined for any pattern of the timing of returns. We also show how G can be computed for any pattern of new investment over time.

A DURATION-BASED APPROXIMATION TO THE FRANCHISE FACTOR

Before developing a formula that can be used to compute an exact FF for any return pattern, we first provide a formula for approximating FF. To do so, we consider a choice between two different investment opportunities (see Figure 3). Investment A provides annual earnings equal to 20% of the investment for 10 years. At the end of 10 years, both the returns and the salvage value of the

Figure 3: The Returns from a 10- and 20-Year Investment—Investments A and B

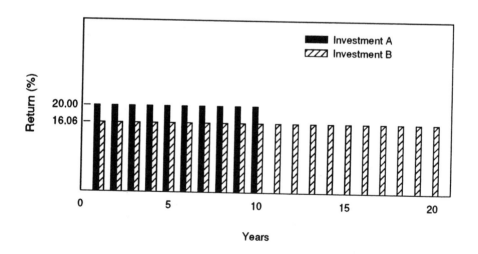

investment drop to zero. Investment B offers a lower return (16.06%) than Investment A, but this return is sustained for 20 years. Since the returns for both investments are constant over a fixed interval, the earnings flows from these investments are level payment annuities.

The evaluation of the two investments begins with the computation of their Net Present Values (NPVs) per $100 of investment. This is done by discounting the returns back to the time that the investment is made, subtracting the original $100 investment and dividing by 100. The results of these calculations for a range of discount of rates are illustrated in Figure 4. Observe that the 20-year investment has a higher NPV than the 10-year investment when discount rates are low. When the discount rate reaches 15.1%, the NPV for each investment is equal to zero. For discount rates above 15.1%, the NPV of the 10-year investment is higher than that for the 20-year investment.

By definition, the internal rate of return (IRR) is the discount rate at which the NPV of an investment is zero. Thus, both A and B have a 15.1% IRR. If the only measure of the relative worthiness of investments were the IRR, we would conclude that Investments A and B were of equal value to investors. The problem with the IRR is that it fails to account either for the timing of returns or for the sensitivity of returns to changes in the discount rate. For example, at the 12% market rate, the NPVs of the 10- and 20-year investments are $13.00 and $19.98,

---

Figure 4: Net Present Value Per $100 Investment for a 10- and 20-Year Investment

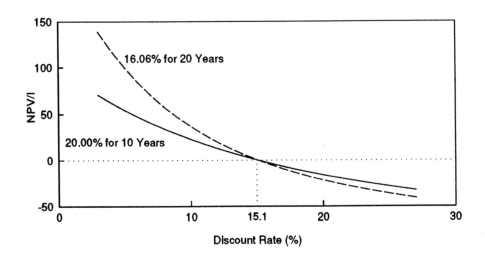

respectively. Clearly, at this rate, the 20-year 16.06% annuity adds significantly more "present value" than the 10-year 20% annuity.

Referring back to Figure 4, the greater slope of the NPV curve for the 20-year annuity compared with that of the 10-year annuity indicates that the value of the longer annuity is more sensitive to changes in the discount rate. This variation in sensitivity is consistent with the well-known duration concept for bonds. All other things being equal, bonds (investments) with longer maturities have longer durations than bonds with shorter maturities. As a result, the price (present value) of a long-maturity bond will be more sensitive to changes in interest rates than the price of the shorter-maturity bond.

The importance of both investment duration (D) and IRR in providing additional P/E is captured in the approximation formula for FF, which is given below. The formula is derived in the Appendix for **any** payment pattern. Thus, this formula has general application in that it applies to any pattern of investment payoffs, not only to annuities.[4]

$$FF \approx \frac{D \bullet (IRR - k)}{r} \ .$$

Observe that when the IRR is the same as the market rate, k, the FF will be zero. In that case, the investment will not add value, regardless of its duration. However, when the IRR is greater than k, duration is critically important, because the FF is computed by multiplying the difference between the IRR and the market rate by the duration. In the case of both of our example annuities, the IRR is 15.1%. Thus, both investments offer the same 3.1% IRR "advantage" over the 12% market rate. Yet, the investments bear different durations. The duration of the 10-year annuity is 4.09 years, while the duration of the 20-year annuity is 6.27 years. Assuming that the firm has a 15% ROE on its initial book, we find that the FFs for the 10- and 20-year investments are approximately 0.85 and 1.29, respectively. Thus, each unit of investment in the 20-year annuity contributes 1.29 units to the P/E, compared with only 0.85 unit of investment in the 10-year annuity. The greater duration of the 20-year investment makes its IRR advantage count more in terms of P/E expansion.

The duration of an annuity increases with the term of the annuity but is independent of the magnitude of the cash flow (assuming a constant discount rate). In addition, as the term increases, the annuity approaches a perpetuity. Thus, the duration of the annuity approaches the duration of a perpetuity, whose duration is just the inverse of the discount rate. Since we evaluate the duration at the market rate, the perpetuity duration in our examples is 8.33 (1 ÷ 0.12). The relationship between duration and the years of return is illustrated in

---

[4] In the approximation formula, D is the modified duration of the investment computed at a discount rate equal to k.

Figure 5: Duration versus Years of Annuity Returns (At a 12% Discount Rate)

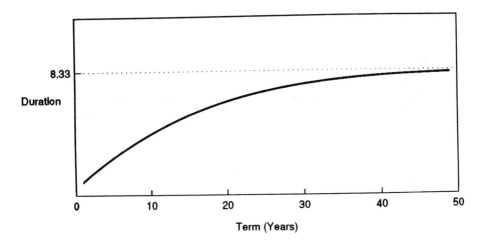

Figure 5. The duration initially increases rapidly as the number of years of earnings increases. Eventually, the rate of increase slows as the duration approaches 8.33.

We now turn to the other component of FF estimation—the IRR advantage. As we indicated earlier, the IRR is an incomplete measure of value. There is an infinite number of combinations of annual payment rates and payment periods that will result in the same IRR. The combinations of payment rate and payment period required to maintain a constant IRR are illustrated in Figure 6 for IRRs of 15% and 20%.

Our observations regarding the IRR and the duration of annuities can lead to a deeper appreciation of what it takes to achieve high FFs. For a given IRR, it follows from the approximation formula that the FF increases with duration. Because the duration of an annuity lengthens with its term, the FF increases as well and eventually reaches a maximum value for a perpetual annuity, that is, for a duration of 8.33. In addition, at a given duration, the FF increases with the IRR. These results are illustrated in Figure 7. Again, observe that the FF is zero when the IRR is 12%, and the FF will be negative if the IRR is less than 12%.

A further insight into our approximation formula can be gained by noting that as the number of years of returns increases, the duration approaches $1/k$,

Figure 6: Annual Payment Rate versus Years of Returns

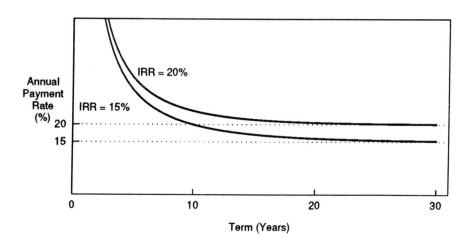

Figure 7: Approximate Franchise Factor versus Annuity Duration
(ROE = 15%)

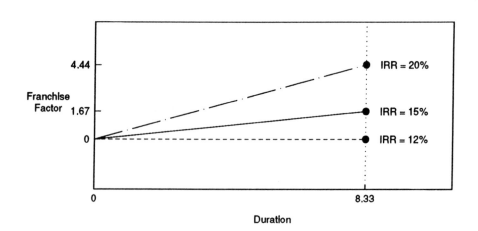

Figure 8: Approximate versus Actual Franchise Factors (For 20-Year Level Payment Annuities)

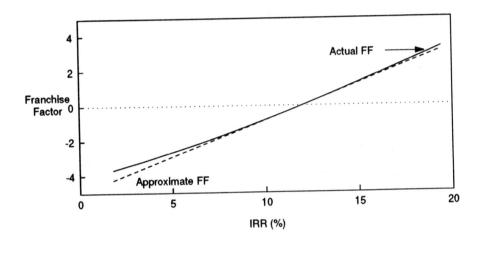

while the annual return approaches the IRR. Thus, as the term of the annuity increases, the approximation formula,

$$FF \approx \frac{D \bullet (IRR - k)}{r}.$$

approaches the exact FF formula,[5]

$$FF = \frac{1}{k} \bullet \frac{R - k}{r}.$$

To illustrate the accuracy of the FF approximation formula, Figure 8 plots the actual and approximate FF for 20-year annuities with a range of IRRs.[6] In Figure 8, we see that the FF approximation is quite accurate for IRRs that are within about 400 basis points of the 12% market rate. For example, if the IRR is 17%, the error in this approximation is slightly more than 4% of the FF value.

---

[5] The methodology for computing the actual FF for annual investment returns that vary year to year is introduced in a subsequent section of this paper.

[6] For investments whose payoffs are in the form of 20-year level payment annuities, higher annual returns lead to higher IRRs.

DURATION AND THE P/E RATIO

In the previous section, we saw the close relationship between the duration of the payment annuity and the FF. Furthermore, in the Appendix, we show that the approximation formula holds for arbitrary payment patterns. This observation prompts us to delve more deeply into the relationship between the P/E and duration. When all investments generate the same pattern of payments, the theoretical P/E is given by the following formula:

$$P/E = \frac{1}{k} + FF \bullet G.$$

In this formula, the base market P/E, $1/k$, can be interpreted as the duration of the perpetuity that corresponds to the level earnings on the firm's initial book. Turning to the second term in the P/E formula, we found that the FF is approximately equal to the duration of the new investment payment multiplied by the investment's IRR advantage. Consequently, the P/E can be written as

$$P/E = \frac{1}{r} \bullet \left[\left[\begin{array}{c} \text{Duration of} \\ \text{Base Earnings} \end{array} \right] \bullet r + \left[\begin{array}{c} \text{Duration of} \\ \text{New Investment} \end{array} \right] \bullet (IRR - k) \bullet G \right].$$

The above formula for the P/E shows that the P/E builds from duration-weighted net earnings (expressed as a fraction of base earnings, r). In the first term in brackets, the net earnings are the same as the base earnings r (per $100 book value), because we do not assume any financing costs associated with the firm's basic book of business. The duration is interpreted as the present-value weighted average time at which earnings occur.[7] In the second term in brackets, net earnings on new investment are measured by the investment's IRR advantage over the market rate, multiplied by the magnitude of the investment as measured by G.

THE PERPETUAL EQUIVALENT RETURN

In the standard Dividend Discount Model (DDM), all new investments are assumed to provide the same return in perpetuity. By using this perpetual return

---

[7] It is actually the Macaulay duration, rather than the modified duration, that precisely measures the weighted-average time of payments. However, the two are sufficiently close so that the intuitive interpretation of the modified duration as a weighted-average time is still valid. The relation between the two durations is $(1 + k)$ $D_{MOD} = D_{MAC}$.

Figure 9: Returns of 20% Per Year for 10 Years and the Perpetual Equivalent Return

---

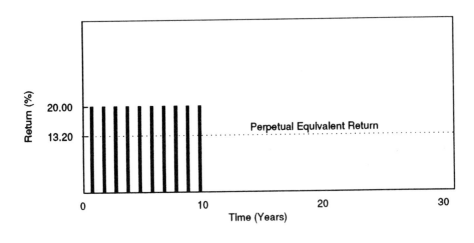

---

model, we were able to develop a particularly simple formula for the exact FF.[8] In a certain sense, the perpetual return model turns out to be general, because any pattern of payments can be converted to an equivalent perpetual return (see Appendix). An exact FF can be computed for any return pattern by using the perpetual equivalent return in the original FF formula. We define the **Perpetual Equivalent Return** as the return on a perpetual investment that provides the same present value (at the market capitalization rate) as a given return pattern.

For example, an investment that provides an annual return of 20% for 10 years (Investment A) is equivalent in present value to an equal investment that provides a 13.56% annual return in perpetuity.[9] The actual and perpetual equivalent returns are illustrated in Figure 9.

Figure 10 shows the behavior of the perpetual equivalent return as the years of constant annual returns extend over longer time periods. At first, the perpetual equivalent increases rapidly. After 15 or 20 years, however, the perpetual equivalent begins to level off, slowly approaching the constant annual return as the period extends to infinity. For example, an investment that returns 20% an-

---

[8] See *Inside the P/E Ratio: The Franchise Factor.*

[9] The present value of $20 per year for 10 years at a 12% discount rate is $113.00. The present value of the perpetual equivalent is $R_p/0.12$. Thus, $R_p = 0.12 \times 113 = 13.56$.

Figure 10: Perpetual Equivalent Returns for 20% and 15% Annuities with a Range of Terms

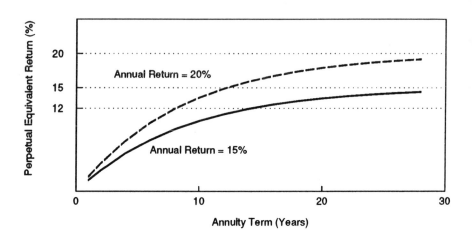

Figure 11: A Rising and Falling Pattern of Returns

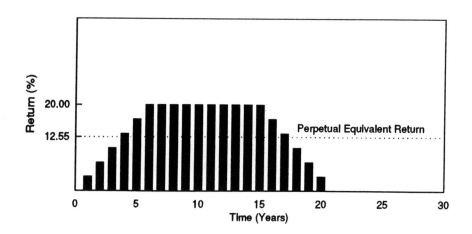

nually for 20 years has a perpetual equivalent of 17.93%. Since investments that provide 20% returns for 20 years are not easy to find, we can assume that perpetual equivalents above 18% are difficult to attain. Furthermore, with more normal patterns of rising and declining returns, the perpetual equivalents will be lower still.

In Figure 11, we turn to a somewhat more "normal" return pattern. The annual investment returns increase steadily for five years until they reach the 20% level. These superior returns continue for ten years, after which the payments decline to zero. The IRR for this investment is 12.62%, and the perpetual equivalent is 12.55%. This perpetual equivalent represents only a 55-basis-point advantage over the market rate. Because such an investment has an FF of only 0.31, it contributes little to the firm's P/E.

The exact FF can be computed from the perpetual return, R_p, according to the formula provided in the previous section of this paper:

$$FF = \frac{R_p - k}{rk}.$$

In Figure 12, we illustrate the linear relationship between FF and R_p for a firm with a 15% return on its initial book equity. The FF is zero when the return on investment is the same as the market rate, and FF increases by 0.56 unit for

Figure 12: Franchise Factor versus Perpetual Equivalent Return

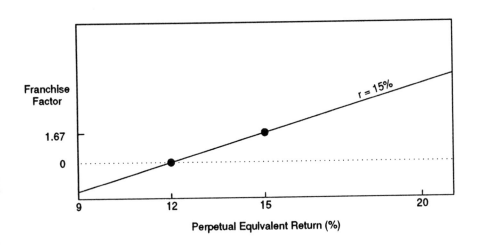

Perpetual Equivalent Return (%)

each 100-basis-point rise in R_p.[10] Thus, when R_p is 15% (that is, 300 basis points above the market rate), FF increases to 1.67 (3 × 0.56). In addition, FF is negative if R_p is less than the market rate.

Perpetual equivalent returns can be used to evaluate investment opportunities. If a firm has a fixed amount of capital to invest and must choose between several different potential projects, the project with the highest perpetual equivalent will make the greatest P/E contribution. This result is both intuitively reasonable and consistent with the FF approach. It also is consistent with the NPV approach to project valuation. That is, the ranking of projects by the magnitude of their NPVs will be the same as the ranking of projects by the magnitude of their perpetual equivalent returns.

THE GROWTH EQUIVALENT

In the formula for the P/E ratio, the P/E gain from new investment is the product of FF and G. If two investments have the same G, the one with the higher FF will have the greater P/E impact. Similarly, the magnitude of investment required to raise the P/E by one unit will decrease as FF increases (see Figure 13). For perpetual equivalent returns above 16%, G levels off. However, even at high perpetual returns, a substantial investment is required to raise the P/E. For example, at a return of 18%, an investment equal to 30% of book is required to raise the P/E by one unit. Observe that when the perpetual equivalent return drops below about 16%, the growth required to raise the P/E increases dramatically. If the perpetual equivalent return is 14% (200 basis points above the market rate), an investment equal to 90% of the current book value is needed to raise the P/E by just one unit.

We now turn to the factors that influence G. Suppose that, by virtue of its business franchise, a firm expects to have a 9% annual growth rate for the next ten years. This means that at the end of each year, the firm can make a new investment equal to 9% of its book value at the beginning of the year (see Figure 14). We also assume that on each new investment, the firm will achieve a perpetual equivalent return equal to the firm's current ROE. As discussed in a previous section, if the ROE is 15%, the FF for each such investment will be 1.67.

For example, if the firm has an initial book value of $100, it is assumed to have a $9 investment opportunity (9% of $100) at the end of the first year, and the book value will increase to $109. At the end of the second year, the investment opportunity is $9.81 (9% of $109). This pattern of growth continues for ten years. The G is found by computing the present value of all future investments

---

[10]The slope of the FF line is $1/rk$. Since $r = 15\%$ and $k = 12\%$, $1/rk = 55.56$. If the change in R_p is 100 basis points (= 0.01), the change in the FF will be $0.01 \times 55.56 = 0.56$.

Figure 13: Required Growth Equivalent Per Unit P/E

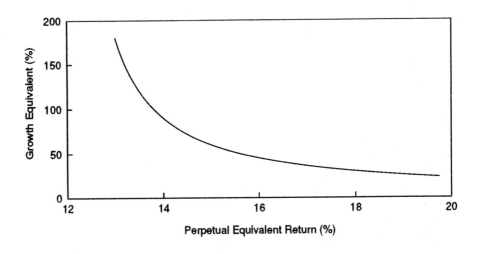

---

and expressing that present value as a percentage of the current book value. By doing this computation, we find that G is $71.33.

As an alternative to the above-mentioned series of investments, suppose that the firm could invest $71.33 immediately and earn 15% per year in perpetuity. Under these conditions, the immediate investment and the series of investments are of the same value to current stockholders. For this reason, we call G the Growth Equivalent.

Figure 14: A Firm with a 15% ROE that Grows at a 9% Annual Rate

Year	Book Value at Beginning of Year	Amount of New Investment at Year-End	Present Value of New Investments at 12% Discount Rate
1	$100.00	$9.00	$ 8.04
2	109.00	9.81	7.82
. . .	. . .	. . .	. . .
10	217.19	19.55	6.29
Total			**$71.33**

Figure 15: Growth Equivalents at a 12% Discount Rate

Years of Investment	Amount Invested Annually as a Percentage of Book Value		
	8%	9%	10%
5	33.25%	38.08%	43.08%
10	60.98	71.33	82.44
20	103.36	125.70	151.29
50	167.54	222.81	296.90
∞	200.00	300.00	500.00

In Figure 15, we exhibit values of G for three different growth rates. We assume that growth continues for a fixed number of years and then stops. For a given number of years of growth, the higher the growth rate, the greater the value of G. As the number years of growth increases, so does the value of G. However, if the growth rate is less than the market capitalization rate, the value of G levels off as the number of years of growth approaches infinity. This result is illustrated in Figure 16 for a firm with 9% annual growth. Observe that although a 9% growth rate may sound modest, it represents a significant 300% of book value in present value terms.

If the growth rate is the same as the market rate, G increases linearly with the years of growth. If the growth rate is greater than the market rate, G will increase exponentially with time (see Figure 17). Clearly, growth rates at or above the market rate can be sustained for only a limited number of years.

MULTIPHASE GROWTH

The FF method for P/E estimation can be extended to accommodate two or more periods during which a firm experiences different types of growth and return opportunities (see Appendix). In general, opportunities to invest at a given FF will vary in both magnitude and time of occurrence. Because G incorporates both of these factors, any pattern of investment opportunities and returns is accommodated by computing the sum of the products of FFs and corresponding Gs to obtain the total above-market P/E increment. This general result is derived in the Appendix and is summarized in the following formula:

$$P/E = \frac{1}{k} + FF_1 \bullet G_1 + FF_2 \bullet G_2 + \ldots$$

In our model, investments may be financed through either retained earnings or borrowing at the market rate. With the broad range of financing alterna-

Figure 16: Growth Equivalent versus Years of New Investment (At an Annual Rate of 9%)

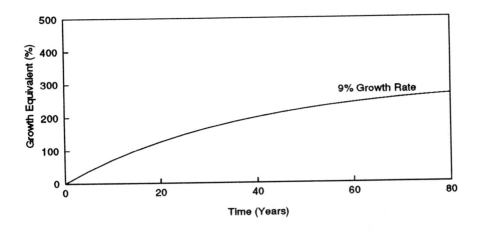

Figure 17: Growth Equivalents for Various Growth Rates

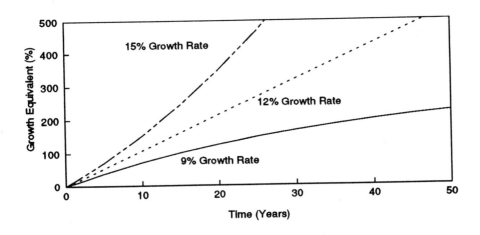

tives available in today's capital markets, growth more likely will be limited by the availability of franchise opportunities than by the lack of financing for those opportunities.

As an example of our general methodology, consider the two-phase growth example illustrated in Figure 18. During years one through ten, the firm invests 10% of book value each year and earns 18% in perpetuity on each investment.

Figure 18: Two-Phase Growth Example

Phase	Years	Growth Rate	Perpetual Return	Franchise Factor	Growth Equivalent
I	1 - 10	10%	18%	3.33	82.44%
II	11 - ∞	5	15	1.67	59.65

The FF for these investments is 3.33, and the G is 82.44%. During the final investment phase, the firm grows at a 5% annual rate and earns 15% on each investment. In this case, the FF and the G are 1.67 and 59.65%, respectively.

Phase I growth contributes 2.75 units to the P/E (FF × G = 3.33 × 0.8244), while Phase II growth contributes just one unit to the P/E (1.67 × 0.5965). Thus, the P/E of our two-phase growth firm is 12.08 (8.33 + 2.75 + 1.00).

The accumulation of the additional P/E provided by the firm's growth can be illustrated in a "vector" diagram. In Figure 19, our first vector corresponding to Phase I growth brings us from a P/E of 8.33 (the base P/E) to a P/E of 11.08. The slope of this vector is 3.33, the FF for Phase I, and the vector extends over 82.44 "units" of Phase I growth. The slope of the second vector, 1.67, is the FF for Phase II, and this vector extends over an additional 59.65 units of growth, bringing the P/E up to 12.08. The timing of investments matters only to the extent that it affects the value of G. Thus, although Phase II follows Phase I in our example, once the phases are reduced to their G and FF values, the sequence becomes irrelevant.

THE FRANCHISE PORTFOLIO

At any point in time, a firm with a unique business franchise will have a range of current and expected investment opportunities. If the company's sole objective is to maximize P/E, the FF method can be a guide in choosing between investments. In Figure 20, we consider a firm's franchise opportunities to be fully described by their FF and G. The firm has an initial book value of $100 and can invest $50 (in present value terms) and achieve an extraordinary 20% return

Figure 19: A Vector Diagram of Two-Phase Growth

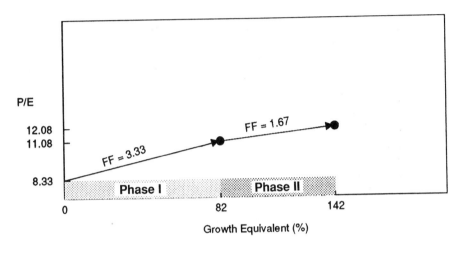

in perpetuity. Other investments provide successively lower returns and, hence, have lower FFs.

The P/E increment from each investment is computed by multiplying the FF by the G. The third investment is three times as large as the first (G = $150). Nevertheless, this investment contributes less to P/E than the first because of its low FF. The fourth investment has a zero FF, because it only provides the market return. As a result, this investment does not provide added value for inves-

Figure 20: The Franchise Portfolio—An Example for a Firm with $100 Book Value

Investment	Perpetual Return	Franchise Factor	Growth Equivalent	P/E Increment
1	20%	4.44	$50	2.22
2	15	1.67	100	1.67
3	13	0.56	150	0.83
4	12	0.00	200	0.00
Total			$500	4.72

Figure 21: A Vector Diagram of P/E Growth

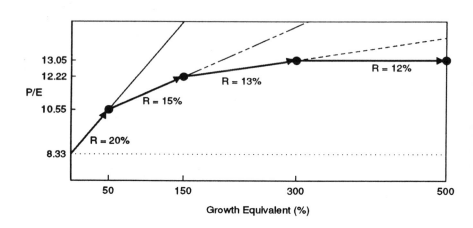

Figure 22: A Schematic Diagram of Investments and Payments

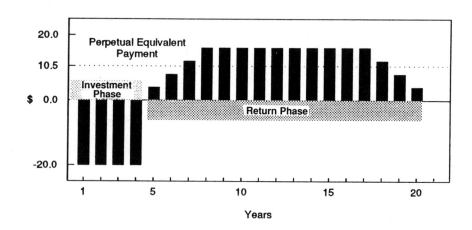

tors. Only the first three investments, with their combined G of $300, will add value. The accumulation of P/E value can be represented by a "vector diagram" (see Figure 21).

Suppose that the firm in our example expects to build up its cash holdings by retaining a portion of its earnings year after year. This cash then becomes available as a source of financing for franchise opportunities. The present value of all such future cash generation is the G available from retained earnings. If the firm expects to have less than $300 available, it should borrow up to that level to fully achieve its P/E potential. However, funds beyond $300 will not add to P/E and thus should be returned to investors in the form of either increased dividend payments or stock buybacks. These idealized conclusions neglect the fact that in the "real" world, the firm must consider other factors beyond P/E gain. For example, they must take into account the signaling effect that increases in dividends have on stock prices.

Finally, we note that the FF method can accommodate the more general situation in which there is an investment phase and an earnings phase. For example, suppose that a firm needs four years to build a new plant. Consequently, the firm must continue to add to its investment during each of these years. These investments are illustrated schematically by the inflows and outflows in Figure 22. The payoff on the investments begins in year five and grows to a maximum level that is sustained for ten years before it begins to decline. Determination of the P/E impact of such a pattern of investments and payments can be accomplished as before by simply computing appropriate FFs for the annual payments and Gs for the investments.

SUMMARY AND CONCLUSION

A firm with an exceptional business franchise should have a variety of opportunities to make investments that provide above-market returns. However, both the timing of investments and the pattern of payments on those investments is variable. In this paper, we have introduced a general methodology to assess the P/E impact of a portfolio of variable franchise opportunities. Our procedure involves three steps. The first step is to calculate a perpetual return that has the same present value as the actual flow of returns on investment. Although this step is not crucial, the perpetual equivalent return does simplify the computation of the Franchise Factor and provides a convenient measure for comparing investment returns. Next, we compute the Franchise Factor that measures the P/E impact per unit growth in new investment. Finally, the magnitude of investment is represented by its Growth Equivalent. The P/E impact of new investment is the product of the Franchise Factor and the Growth Equivalent.

The analysis takes place in an idealized world in which there is no volatility, leverage or taxes. Despite these restrictive assumptions, our theoretical model provides insight into the inherent difficulty firms have in raising their P/Es. Furthermore, if a firm's only goal is to maximize its P/E, our model adds an additional dimension to considerations regarding dividend increases and/or stock repurchases.

By translating fairly realistic patterns of investment payoffs into their perpetual equivalent returns, we realize that perpetual returns above 18% are extremely difficult to achieve. For example, an investment that provides a 20% return for 20 years has a perpetual equivalent of 17.9%. Since the Franchise Factor for this investment is 3.3, an investment equal to 30% of current book (in present value terms) would be necessary to raise the P/E by just one unit. A high Franchise Factor alone cannot elevate the P/E. Both a high Franchise Factor and a Growth Equivalent that represents a substantial percentage of current book are needed to significantly raise the P/E.

Since the Franchise Factor emerges as a fundamental measure of the P/E impact of new investments, we provide a simple formula for its estimation. This formula involves the IRR of a new investment and the duration of its payments. The IRR is shown to be an incomplete measure of value, because it fails to take the timing of payments into account. As with fixed-income instruments, the duration is a measure of the average time at which those payments are received. The Franchise Factor is essentially the product of the excess annual return that the investment generates (compared with the market rate) and the duration of its payments.

In general, franchise situations tend to erode over time unless there is a process not only of maintenance, but of renewal. Only in extraordinary situations do we expect franchises to sustain themselves forever. Rather, the lucky firm that has a franchise will consume its prospective opportunity in the normal course of time and embed the resulting earnings into its basic flow of business. However, certain business enterprises appear to be able to continuously capitalize on their basic strengths. Thus, they seem to "compound" their franchise positions. It is as if these firms have a franchise on the generation of new franchise opportunities. In the terminology of this paper, these firms have what it takes to justify exceptionally high P/Es: a superior Franchise Factor on large Growth Equivalent investments.

Appendix

AN INVESTMENT OPPORTUNITY APPROACH TO FIRM VALUATION

The value of a stock depends on both the firm's current earnings and new investment opportunities, which by virtue of the firm's unique business franchise, enable it to earn above-market returns. To develop a theoretical formula[11] for valuing a firm's stock, we will make use of the following variables:

k = Market capitalization rate;

B = Inital book value;

r = ROE = Return on initial book value;

NPV_j = Net present value at time j of a new investment made at time j; and

I_j = Magnitude of investment opportunity at time j.

We assume that the earnings on initial book remains rB in perpetuity. Thus, this earnings stream contributes rB/k to the current value of the firm. The contribution of all new investments to firm value is the sum of the discounted NPVs of these investments. Thus, the present value of the firm can be expressed as follows:

$$P = \frac{rB}{k} + \sum_{j=1}^{\infty} \frac{NPV_j}{(1+k)^j}.$$ (1)

We now assume that *the investment I_j provides payments P_{j1}, P_{j2}, . . . at times $j + 1, j + 2, ...* Then,

$$NPV_j = PV_j - I_j,$$ (2)

---

[11] Our approach to valuation is based on "Dividend Policy, Growth, and the Valuation of Shares," Merton H. Miller and Franco Modigliani, *The Journal of Business*, October 1961, pp. 411-433.

where PV_j is the sum of the present values (at time j) of the payments $P_{j1}, P_{j2} \ldots$. That is,

$$PV_j = \sum_{i=1}^{\infty} \frac{P_{ji}}{(1+k)^i} .$$

The payment stream provided by investment I_j always can be represented by a perpetual equivalent return, R_{pj}, on investment I_j. To do this, we require that the present value of the perpetual payments be the same as PV_j. Since the present value of the perpetual is found by dividing by the discount rate, we have the following:

$$PV_j = \frac{R_{pj} \bullet I_j}{k} ,$$

or,

$$R_{pj} = k \bullet \frac{PV_j}{I_j} . \tag{3}$$

By combining equations (1) and (3), we can express NPV_j in terms of the perpetual equivalent:

$$NPV_j = \frac{R_{pj} I_j}{k} - I_j = \left(\frac{R_{pj} - k}{k} \right) \bullet I_j . \tag{4}$$

By substituting (4) in (1) and rearranging terms, P can be rewritten as:

$$P = \frac{rB}{k} + \sum_{j=1}^{\infty} \left(\frac{R_{pj} - k}{k} \right) \bullet \left(\frac{I_j}{(1+k)^j} \right) \tag{5}$$

Observe that in this general model, no assumption has to be made regarding the source of financing for new investments.[12] This financing could be internal, external or a combination of the two.

THE FRANCHISE FACTOR AND PRESENT VALUE GROWTH EQUIVALENT

In the special case in which all new investments provide the same perpetual return, R_p, equation (5) becomes

---

[12] This result is precisely the formula derived by Miller and Modigliani.

$$P = \frac{rB}{k} + \left(\frac{R_p - k}{k}\right) \bullet \sum_{j=1}^{\infty} \frac{I_j}{(1+k)^j} \cdot \tag{6}$$

The P/E ratio can be found by dividing both sides of (6) by the initial earnings rB. That is,

$$P/E = \frac{1}{k} + \left(\frac{R_p - k}{rk}\right) \bullet \left[\left(\sum_{j=1}^{\infty} \frac{I_j}{(1+k)^j}\right) \div B\right]. \tag{7}$$

The last term in brackets is the present value of all future investment opportunities expressed as a percentage of the initial book value. The factor $(R_p-k)/rk$ gives the P/E impact of each unit increase in book value. That is, if the book value increases by 100%, the P/E increases by $(R_p-k)/rk$. We call this expression the Franchise Factor,

$$FF = \frac{R_p - k}{rk} \tag{8}$$

Furthermore, we define

$$G = \left(\sum_{j=1}^{\infty} \frac{I_j}{(1+k)^j}\right) \div B \tag{9}$$

and interpret G as the present value growth equivalent of all future investments that return R_p in perpetuity. This definition is motivated by the observation that an immediate investment of magnitude G that earned R_p in perpetuity would have precisely the same price impact as our more complex stream of investment opportunities.

The P/E formula (7) can now be rewritten as follows:

$$P/E = \frac{1}{k} + FF \bullet G. \tag{10}$$

In general, different new investments will have different perpetual equivalent returns and distinct Franchise Factors. We symbolize the Franchise Factor corresponding to perpetual equivalent return R_{pi} by FF_i where

$$FF_i = \frac{R_{pi} - k}{rk}. $$

The present value of all future investments with Franchise Factor FF_i is symbolized by the Growth Equivalent, G_i. Under the above assumptions, the P/E formula (10) can be generalized to encompass n distinct Franchise Factors as follows:

$$P/E = \frac{1}{k} + \sum_{i=1}^{n} FF_i \bullet G_i .$$ (11)

An example of the development of equation (11) is provided in a subsequent section of the Appendix, in which we consider multiphase growth.

A DURATION-BASED APPROXIMATION TO THE FRANCHISE FACTOR

In the previous section, the magnitude of FF was shown to depend on the size of R_p. By substituting the formula for R_p—equation (3)—into the formula for FF—equation (8)—we obtain the following formula for FF in terms of the present value of the payments on investment I:

$$FF = \frac{PV - I}{rI} .$$ (12)

In the above formula, we assume that PV is computed at the market discount rate, k. That is,

$$PV = PV(k).$$

Since the IRR is the discount rate at which the present value equals the value of investment, we have the following:

$$I = PV(IRR).$$

Thus, the numerator in equation (12) is PV(k) - PV(IRR). The difference between these present values can be approximated by a Taylor series:

$$PV(k) - PV(IRR) = PV'(IRR)(k - IRR) + \ldots$$

Since, by definition, the modified duration is - PV'/PV, the above equation can be rewritten as follows:

$$PV(k) - PV(IRR) = PV(IRR) \bullet D(IRR) \bullet (IRR - k) + \ldots$$

An approximate formula for FF is obtained by substituting the above formula in equation (12), approximating D(IRR) by D(k) and dropping higher order terms.

$$FF \approx \frac{D \bullet (IRR - k)}{r} .$$ (13)

MULTIPHASE GROWTH

To better understand multiphase growth, we first consider the case in which the investment opportunity at time j is always the same fixed percentage, g, of the firm's book value at time $j - 1$. For example, if $g = 10\%$ and $B = \$100$, we assume that the firm has an investment opportunity at time 1 equal to $\$10$ (that is, 10% of the initial book value of $\$100$). After taking advantage of this investment opportunity, the firm's book value increases by $\$10$ to $\$110$ (110% of $\$100$). The following year, another investment opportunity arises whose magnitude is $\$11$ (10% of $\$110$). This leads to a new book value of $\$121$ (110% of $\$100$). This pattern of investment opportunities and book enhancements is illustrated in Figure A1.

Figure A1: Investment Opportunities and Book Value When Firm Grows at 10% Per Year

Time	Investment Opportunity	New Book Value
0	—	$100.00
1	$10.00	110.00
2	11.00	121.00
3	12.10	133.10

More generally, we can write

$$I_1 = gB$$

$$I_2 = g(1 + g)B$$

$$I_3 = g(1 + g)^2 B, \text{ etc.}$$

If this pattern of constant growth continues forever,[13]

$$G = \frac{g}{k - g}. \tag{14}$$

We now turn to multiphase growth. For simplicity, we restrict ourselves to the case in which the investments $I_1, I_2, \ldots I_n$ earn in R_{p1} in perpetuity and all subsequent investments, $I_{n+1}, I_{n+2}, \ldots$, earn R_{p2} in perpetuity. Then, from (5),

---

[13] See *Inside the P/E Ratio: The Franchise Factor.*

$$P = \frac{rB}{k} + \left(\frac{R_{p1} - k}{k}\right) \cdot \sum_{j=1}^{n} \frac{I_j}{(1+k)^j} + \left(\frac{R_{p2} - k}{k}\right) \cdot \sum_{j=1}^{\infty} \frac{I_{n+j}}{(1+k)^{n+j}} \, . \tag{15}$$

Dividing both sides of (15) by the initial earnings rB, we obtain

$$P/E = \frac{1}{k} + FF_1G_1 + FF_2G_2 \, .$$

Observe that the above equation is the same as equation (11) with n = 2. The Growth Equivalents G_1 and G_2 are given by the following:

$$G_1 = \left(\sum_{j=1}^{n} \frac{I_j}{(1+k)^j}\right) \div B \tag{16}$$

$$G_2 = \left(\sum_{j=1}^{n} \frac{I_{n+j}}{(1+k)^{n+j}}\right) \div B \, . \tag{17}$$

We now make the additional assumption that I_j, $j = 1, \ldots ,n$ is a constant percentage, g_1, of the book value at time j-1. Furthermore, I_j, $j = n+1, n+2, \ldots$ is taken to be a different constant percentage, g_2, of the prior year's book value.

Thus,

$$I_1 = g_1 B$$

$$I_2 = g_1(1 + g_1)B$$

$$I_3 = g_1(1 + g_1)^2 B$$

$$\ldots \ldots \ldots$$

$$I_n = g_1(1 + g_1)^{n-1}B$$

$$I_{n+1} = g_2(1 + g_1)^n B$$

$$I_{n+2} = g_2(1 + g_2)(1 + g_1)^n B$$

$$\ldots \ldots \ldots$$

Using the above in (16) and (17) and summing the resulting geometric progression provides the following:

$$G_1 = \left\{ \begin{array}{ll} \left(\dfrac{g_1}{k-g_1}\right) \bullet \left[1 - \left(\dfrac{1+g_1}{1+k}\right)^n \right] & \text{if } g_1 \neq k \\[2em] \dfrac{ng_1}{1+k} & \text{if } g_1 = k \end{array} \right\} \tag{18}$$

$$G_2 = \left(\dfrac{g_2}{k-g_2}\right) \bullet \left(\dfrac{1+g_1}{1+k}\right)^n \qquad \text{if } g_2 < k \ . \tag{19}$$

Because the series for G_1 was finite, no restriction had to be made on g_1. By contrast, the infinite geometric progression involving g_2 only converges when $g_2 < k$. Furthermore, n approaches infinity, G_2 approaches zero, while G_1 approaches G as given in (14). When $g_1 = g_2$, G_1 and G_2 combined give the G of equation (14).

As an example of the use of formulas (18) and (19), consider the case of ten years of growth at 10% and growth at 5% for each succeeding year. If k=12%, then (18) and (19) give the following:

$$G_1 = \left(\frac{0.10}{0.12-0.10}\right) \bullet \left[1 - \left(\frac{1+0.10}{1++0.12}\right)^{10} \right] = 0.8244 = 82.44\%$$

$$G_2 = \left(\frac{0.05}{0.12-0.05}\right) \bullet \left(\frac{1+0.10}{1+0.12}\right)^{10} = 0.5965 = 59.65\% \ .$$

Chapter II-3

A Franchise Factor Model for Spread Banking [1991]

INTRODUCTION AND SUMMARY

Spread banking firms borrow money at one rate and lend it out at a higher rate, thereby profiting from the "spread" between the two. Although the term "spread banking" is most commonly associated with commercial banks and thrift institutions, many other financial firms, such as insurance companies, also engage in spread banking activities. In addition, many nonfinancial firms have important facets that essentially can be viewed as spread banking.

This paper offers a theoretical model for relating a spread banking firm's price/earnings (P/E) ratio to the "Franchise Factors" that characterize returns on its *prospective* new books of business.[1] The value of a new investment's Franchise Factor is determined by the allowable leverage, the anticipated net spread on borrowed funds and the "duration" of that net spread. We find the incremental P/E value of an investment by multiplying the Franchise Factor by a measure of the investment's size, called the Growth Equivalent. In theory, a firm

---

[1] See *Inside the P/E Ratio: The Franchise Factor, Financial Analysts Journal,* November-December 1990 (reprinted with permission); and *Inside the P/E Ratio (Part II): The Franchise Portfolio,* Salomon Brothers Inc, January 1991.

Martin L. Leibowitz and Stanley Kogelman, "A Franchise Factor Model for Spread Banking," Salomon Brothers Inc, April 1991.

353

should try to expand its footings to include all opportunities that provide a positive Franchise Factor (even if doing so means reducing the overall return on book equity). At this point, the firm will have reached its optimal size and should resist the temptation to expand further.

The scope of our analysis is limited to the development of generic relationships. We do not attempt to address, in any depth, the specific business characteristics of commercial banks, insurance companies, or other "spread banking" sectors. Our methodology is based on several simplifying assumptions. In particular, we assume an equilibrium market in which there is no uncertainty regarding prospective returns. In addition, our P/E analysis is based on a firm's sustainable economic earnings (which may depart significantly from the firm's reported accounting earnings in any given year).

To some extent, the profitability of spread banking firms depends on their ability to seize opportunities by shifting resources quickly from businesses with tightening spreads to fast-growing new businesses with ample returns. However, such opportunities cannot always be fully and rigorously pursued because of explicit regulatory constraints. In addition, *implicit* regulatory constraints may limit the magnitude and sustainability of large spread opportunities. By contrast, industrial concerns can conceivably have virtually unlimited growth prospects as a result of the creation of entirely new markets through, for example, discoveries and patents. For these (and other) reasons, the equity of spread banking concerns is usually not placed in the category of growth stocks.

However, the subject of growth is never simple. In the area of asset size, or "footings," U.S. commercial banks certainly have demonstrated an ability to sustain substantial growth over the years. Because commercial banks are geared to the transactional flows of the economy at large, it is reasonable to expect bank assets to grow in tandem with growth in nominal gross national product (GNP). In a gross sense (although certainly not in every year), this correspondence has held remarkably true over the past 41 years. From December 31, 1949, until December 31, 1990, the assets of commercial banks insured by the Federal Deposit Insurance Corporation (FDIC) grew at an annualized compound rate of 7.8%. Over that same time frame, nominal GNP grew at an average rate of 7.7% per year. While a correspondence between these growth rates was to be expected, their closeness is surprising, especially when we consider the structural shifts that have occurred in the business lines that comprise commercial bank assets.

However, in spread banking, as in all businesses, asset growth *alone* does not guarantee either earnings or price performance. In fact, despite an almost sixfold increase in bank assets over the past two decades, bank P/Es chronically have remained significantly below average market levels. The theoretical model of this paper provides some insight into why such low P/Es have persisted.

spread structure. Even a small decline in spreads may be so magnified by leverage that the Franchise Factor changes from a strongly positive value to a significantly negative value. In that case, a prospective business that was expected to boost the P/E may actually lower it. Changes in the leverage multiple also have a pronounced impact on the Franchise Factor. For example, consider a potential investment that provides a 50-basis-point spread. When the leverage multiple is 20, this investment will have a positive Franchise Factor and lift the P/E. However, if changing conditions should force a reduction in the maximum leverage multiple to 10, this same 50-basis-point net spread will result in a negative Franchise Factor and a decrease in the firm's P/E.

Another problem is the high level of inertia inherent in the theoretical P/E ratio. To achieve a significant upward move in the P/E, a firm must find a new business opportunity with *both* a significantly positive sustainable spread *and* a substantial market depth. For example, a new project with a highly attractive 20% return on equity will provide a Franchise Factor of 3.33 (assuming a 12% market rate). However, the size of this investment must loom large relative to the current business to have a noticeable impact on the firm's P/E. Even if the 20% return could be obtained on an investment that amounted to a whopping 25% of the firm's current book value, the P/E impact would be only 0.83 unit. Moreover, even once achieved, a high P/E has an intrinsically fragile character. To maintain a high P/E, a growing firm must be able to *continually* uncover new franchise opportunities of ever greater magnitude than those currently embedded in today's P/E valuation.

Unfortunately, most spread banking lines of business look best at the outset. The initial spreads are booked into the earnings stream immediately, while the prospect of negative surprises lurks in the future. The effective spread between borrowing costs and lending income can narrow quickly in response to events such as a sudden rise in market interest rates, a change in credit quality, or increased competition. Thus, there may be considerable vulnerability in the net spread structure of both current and prospective businesses. Such questions about the reliability and/or sustainability of spread businesses lead to lower Franchise Factors, and this may partly explain the banking industry's below-market P/E.

In summary, this paper utilizes a simple model to clarify the relationship between market forces and the P/E valuation of spread banking firms. The model does not pretend to address fully the spectrum of issues, complexities and interrelationships that must be considered when analyzing specific firms or sectors. However, even in this simple form, the Franchise Factor model can prove helpful in illustrating and sharpening the insights derived from more traditional analyses of spread banking problems and opportunities.

BUILDING RETURN ON EQUITY THROUGH LEVERAGE

In this paper, we assume that a bank always earns a risk-free rate on its equity capital. With this equity capital as a base, the bank then can borrow up to some maximum multiple, L, of the equity capital and make loans or investments with those borrowed funds. If the net spread earned on leveraged funds is positive, leverage enables the bank to add to its return on equity (ROE). For the purpose of this paper, we define the net spread (NS) as the after-tax difference between the marginal cost of borrowed funds and the net return on those funds (that is, the net return after expenses). The formula for the ROE is as follows:

ROE = Risk-Free Rate + (Leveraged Multiple × Net Spread)

$$= R_f + L \times NS$$

For example, consider a bank that has $100 in equity capital and an after-tax rate borrowing cost of 5%.[2] If the bank is allowed to borrow up to 20 times capital, it will be able to borrow an additional $2,000 by paying 5% interest. We further assume that the lending rate that can be earned on these borrowed funds is 5.75% after taxes and expenses.[3] This combination of lending and borrowing rates is illustrated in the region to the left of the dotted line in Figure 1. This region represents current borrowings.

In terms of potential avenues for expansion, the bank believes that it will have the opportunity to extend another $1,500 in loans at 5.75% (above and beyond the initial $2,000 in loans). To take advantage of this opportunity, the bank would have to raise an additional $75 in equity capital (at the assumed 20:1 leverage ratio), thereby bringing the total equity capital to $175. Beyond this level, $500 in lending opportunities exists at a lower 5.50% rate. This final opportunity would require another $25 addition to the capital base.

The cost of borrowed funds follows a different path than the lending rate (see Figure 1): 5% for the first $2,500 in borrowings; and 5.25% for the next $1,500 in borrowings. By calculating the difference between the lending rate and the cost of funds, we see that a 75-basis-point NS is earned on the $2,000 in current borrowings (see Region A in Figure 2). This same 75-basis-point NS also is expected to be attained on the first $500 in new borrowings (Region B). The next $1,000 in new borrowings (Region C) produces an NS of 50 basis point, and the final $500 in new borrowings (Region D) yields an NS of only 25 basis points. At this point, we make the simplifying assumption that each NS can be

---

[2] If the borrowing rate is 7.58% and the bank's marginal tax rate is 34%, the after-tax borrowing rate is 66% of 7.58%, or 5%.

[3] If the bank earns 9.71% on borrowed funds and it estimates expenses at 100 basis points, earnings after expenses and taxes equal 66% of (9.71%-1.00%), or 5.75%.

Figure 1: The Lending Rate and the Cost of Funds

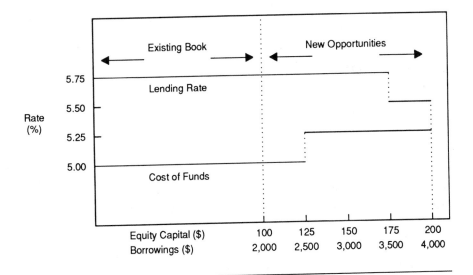

Figure 2: The Net Spread on Borrowed Funds

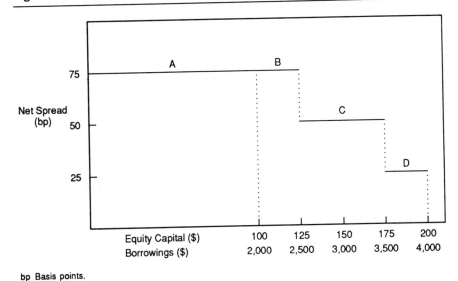

bp Basis points.

earned in perpetuity. As indicated in Figure 2, the borrowings of $500, $1,000 and $500 will require $25, $50 and $25 in new equity capital, respectively.

We now turn our attention to the ROE for the current book of business and the prospective ROE for the investments related to new businesses B, C and D. In general, we distinguish between earnings on equity capital and earnings on borrowings. We assume that equity capital is invested in risk-free instruments that earn 5% after taxes. The ROE for both the current $100 in equity capital (Region A) and the first $25 in new equity capital (Region B) is computed as follows:

$$ROE = R_f + L \times NS$$

$$= 5\% + 20 \times 0.75\%$$

$$= 20\%.$$

In Figure 3, we illustrate the relationship between ROE and NS. Point A corresponds to the 20% ROE on the current book. Because the first incremental expansion of the equity capital base also generates an NS of 75 basis points, the new capital provides the same 20% ROE (point B in Figure 3). Further expansion leads to lower spreads of 50 basis points (point C) and 25 basis points (point D), with ROEs of 15 % and 10%, respectively. At the limit, if the NS were zero, there would be nothing to gain from leveraging, and the ROE would be the same as the 5% risk-free rate.

A PERSPECTIVE ON ASSET GROWTH

Although we focus on the generic structure of spread banking entities in this paper, it is illuminating to look at the rate at which commercial bank assets have grown over the past 41 years. Because these assets are geared to the transactional flows of the economy at large, it is reasonable to expect a correspondence between the growth in nominal GNP and the growth in bank assets. In Figure 4, we compare the compound annual growth rates of nominal GNP bank assets over three-year periods from December 31, 1949, to December 31, 1988, and over the final two-year period ended December 31, 1990. During the 1949-52 period, GNP grew almost twice as fast as bank assets. However, that time frame represents the last three-year period of such extreme dominance. In most nonoverlapping three-year periods until the early 1980s, bank assets grew somewhat faster than GNP. By contrast, since the beginning of the 1980s, nominal growth in both GNP and bank assets has slowed, with GNP growth dominating bank asset growth.

In Figure 5, we compare the cumulative growth in GNP and bank assets. To do so, we assume that the value of GNP and the value of commercial bank assets were both $100 on December 31, 1949. The rapid rise in GNP during the

Figure 3: Return on Equity versus Net Spread (Leverage = 20)

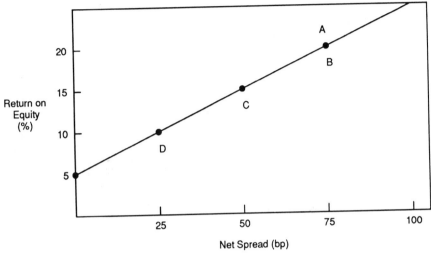

bp Basis points.

Figure 4: Growth in Nominal GNP and Bank Assets, 1949-90 (Compound Growth Rate Over Three-Year Periods)

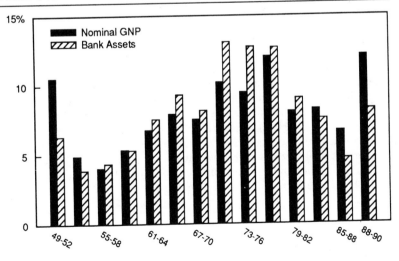

GNP Gross national product.

**Figure 5: Cumulative Growth in Nominal GNP and Bank Assets, 1949-90
(Relative to a Base of $100 on December 31, 1949)**

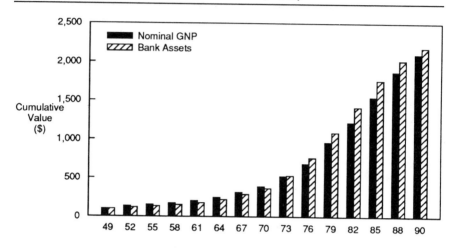

GNP Gross national product.

early 1950s enabled it to stay ahead of commercial bank assets until the 1970s. By this time, the steady dominance of bank asset growth through most of the 1960s allowed cumulative bank asset growth to overtake cumulative GNP growth by 1973. Over the entire 41-year period ended December 31, 1990, the compound annual growth rate of bank assets was 7.8%, compared with 7.7% for GNP.

While a correspondence between the growth in bank assets and GNP was expected, the closeness of that correspondence over the past 41 years is rather surprising, given the dramatic changes in the financial markets during that time period. If asset growth alone was enough to ensure high P/E ratios, we would expect the shares of banks to sell at rather ample P/E multiples. However, bank P/Es consistently have been below average market P/Es for many years prior to the current well-advertised troubles in the banking sector.[4] Insight into some of the causes of this underperformance can be gained by looking at the sensitivity of the Franchise Factor for spread investments.

_____

[4] See *A Review of Bank Performance: 1990 Edition,* Thomas H. Hanley et al., Salomon Brothers Inc, 1990.

THE FRANCHISE FACTOR

In this section, we turn our attention to the P/E impact of new investment opportunities. When comparing the P/E ratio, the base earnings, E, represents the (sustainable) earnings from the firm's current book of business. If the firm does not experience growth or contraction and current earnings are maintained in perpetuity, the investor's sole source of return consists of his annual earnings, E. In equilibrium, this perpetual stream of earnings would be capitalized at the general market rate k. This earnings capitalization results in a theoretical price P, which is equal to E/k. This price/earnings relationship implies a "base P/E" of 1/k for all firms, apart from any consideration of new opportunities' capitalization for future growth. For example, when the equity market is priced to yield 12%, k is 0.12 and the base P/E is 8.33 (1.0/0.12).

If current earnings are fully and properly reflected in the base P/E, an above-market P/E can be realized only if, by virtue of a firm's business franchise, the market foresees future opportunities for the firm to invest in new projects with above-market returns.[5] In earlier papers, we provided a formula for computing the theoretical P/E ratio that explicitly incorporates the impact of future earnings expectations.[6] The formula is as follows:

P/E = Base P/E + [Franchise Factor × Growth Equivalent].

The Franchise Factor (FF) is a measure of the P/E-producing power of a prospective investment opportunity. The Growth Equivalent (G) is the *present value* measure of the *size* of that opportunity, expressed as a percentage of the existing book value of the firm. In general, each new investment opportunity will have its own FF and G. In the case of multiple investment opportunities, the P/E is computed by adding in the FF×G term for each new investment. The above formula underscores the fact that, without any new investment opportunities, all firms would sell at a P/E multiple of 8.33.

The FF for an investment is computed according to the following formula:

FF = (R - k)/(rk).

---

[5] If current earnings are believed to be understated as reported, a corrected earnings estimate may be used in place of the current earnings.

[6] See *Inside the P/E Ratio: The Franchise Factor* and *Inside the P/E Ratio (Part II): The Franchise Factor Portfolio*. The development in these papers is based on an extensive foundation of literature relating to dividend discount models. We cite several of the key papers by J.B. Williams, Miller and Modigliani, and others in our previous papers. Another work that provides a similar structure for tracing out the relationship between firm value and future investment opportunities is *Financial Strategy: Studies in the Creation, Transfer, and Destruction of Shareholder Value*, William E. Fruhan, Richard D. Irwin, Inc., 1979.

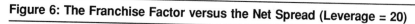

Figure 6: The Franchise Factor versus the Net Spread (Leverage = 20)

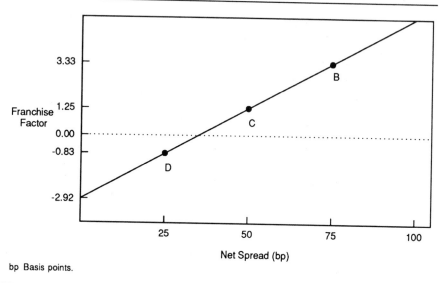

bp Basis points.

In the current context, r is the ROE that applies to the existing book of business (20% in our example), and R is the ROE on the new investment opportunity (20% for B, 15% for C and 10% for D). For example, we compute the FF for investment C as follows:

$$FF = (0.15 - 0.12)/(0.20 \times 0.12) = 1.25.$$

Because the total equity investment in C was $50 (that is, 50% of the $100 existing book), C adds 0.625 units to the P/E (FF × G = 1.25 × 0.50).

In the previous section (Figure 3), we observed that if the degree of leverage was fixed, ROE increased with NS. Consequently, FF also will increase with NS. Assuming that the market capitalization rate is 12%, the relationship between FF and NS is illustrated in Figure 6. In this Figure, we have indicated the FFs for the incremental new investments B, C and D.

We see that investment D has an NS of only 25 basis points (and a 10% ROE) and its FF is -0.83. Prospective investments with negative FFs will reduce the P/E and, consequently, reduce the firm's value to shareholders. A negative FF results whenever the ROE of an investment falls below the 12% market capitalization rate. This makes intuitive sense, because shareholders can achieve the 12% market return by investing for themselves. To better understand how investment D and the other investments affect the P/E, we turn to the relationship between the size of the prospective investments and the magnitude of the P/E increment.

THE IMPACT OF FUTURE FRANCHISE OPPORTUNITIES

To see the dynamics of the P/E impact of prospective projects more clearly, consider a firm that has only one future investment opportunity. When the time comes to implement this final *anticipated* project, the firm will access the needed equity capital (possibly through the issuance of new shares), fund the requisite investment with borrowed funds and begin to reap the project's promised returns. However, once these returns are fully implemented, the firm's overall earnings stabilize at a higher level. At this point of equilibrium, the firm can be viewed as providing this new earnings stream on an ongoing basis, with no further prospect of change. When these conditions are realized, the P/E again must return to the base P/E level of 8.33. Thus, although the *anticipation* of additional earnings from new projects will lead to higher P/E values, the complete *realization* of the project will bring the P/E (relative to the expanded earnings) back to the base level.

If a firm is to maintain an above-market P/E while "consuming" its previously known franchise opportunities, it must be able to replenish expectations continually by generating new future franchise opportunities that are of the same magnitude as those that have been consumed (quite a tall order!). If the potential for new projects gradually is exhausted, the P/E will erode to the base level.

The Franchise Factor method of theoretical P/E estimation explicitly shows how the ROE and the size of *future* investments lift the P/E above the base level. In particular, because the P/E increment attributable to a prospective investment is simply the product of the investor's FF and G, the P/E gain increases in proportion to the size of investment.

In Figure 7, we illustrate the P/E gains (or losses) that result from expectations that our bank will pursue new business opportunities. The horizontal axis is the G available for a given investment opportunity. The slope of each of the three lines in the figure corresponds to the FF for a new business activity. Each line represents the relationship between the expected P/E increment attributable to a new business and the size of that business. For example, the P/E impact of B can be read as 0.83 unit, corresponding to a size limit of $25 (that is, 25% of the $100 current equity capital) and an FF of 3.33. Although business C has a lower FF than business B, it provides almost as much P/E enhancement because of the greater magnitude of C's opportunity. C can accommodate an equity investment that is twice that of B. However, D's negative FF results in a reduction in the P/E.

Figure 7: P/E Gain versus Size of Investment
(With Varying Franchise Factors)

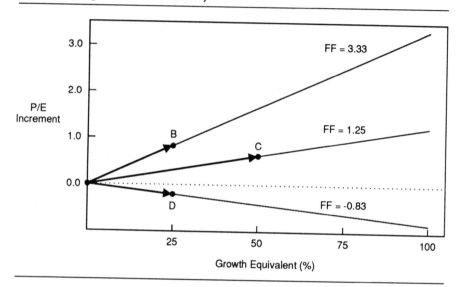

Growth Equivalent (%)

Figure 8: A Vector Diagram of P/E Value

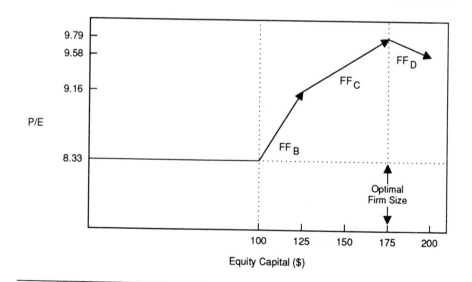

Equity Capital ($)

The P/E of our bank is illustrated in Figure 8. Here, we use a "vector diagram" to add the P/E increments due to businesses B, C and D to the base P/E of 8.33. If all of these businesses are expected to be undertaken, the P/E ratio would equal 9.58. However, if the firm's goal is to maximize value to shareholders, it will not undertake business D. Without business D, the P/E becomes 9.79.

At this point, it is worth observing how difficult it is to achieve significant improvements in the theoretical P/E value. In our example, we have almost doubled the footings of the bank (from $100 to $175), and the P/E has only improved from 8.33 to 9.79. Even if we could find additional opportunities at the 20% ROE level, a full doubling of the bank's size still would result in a P/E below 12.

In Figure 9, we compare the relationship between the P/E and the ROE at various levels of expansion of the bank's capital base. At the outset, it may seem curious that the above-mentioned 20% ROE on the current book of business does not provide P/E enhancement. Although the 20% ROE does produce an enhanced level of earnings, the share price should already have adjusted upward to drive the base P/E to its equilibrium value of 8.33. By contrast, the prospect of undertaking new opportunity B is attractive to current shareholders, because it holds out the promise of *incremental* gain above and beyond the current level of earnings. B's 20% ROE represents an 8% return advantage over the

Figure 9: A Comparison of Return on Equity and P/E

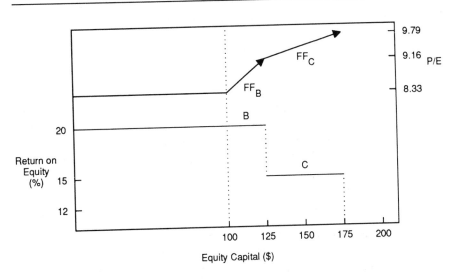

cost of new equity capital (which we have assumed to be 12%). This incremental value is reflected in the price, and the P/E is pushed up by 0.83 unit to 9.16.

Since B's ROE is the same as the 20% ROE on the current book, the firm's overall ROE will remain at 20% as earnings from B are realized. Because C provides a 3% return advantage over the cost of equity capital, anticipated expansion into C will raise the P/E. However, as earnings from C are realized, C's 15% ROE will reduce the *average* return on total equity capital to 18.6%. This expected future ROE reduction should not deter the bank from moving into C. By expanding into C, the bank achieves its optimal size in terms of shareholder value. In general, any new investment that has an ROE greater than 12% will have a positive FF and, consequently, will enhance the P/E value of the bank. By contrast, an ROE that is positive but below 12% would be viewed negatively by shareholders.

THE IMPACT OF CHANGES IN INVESTMENT DURATION AND LEVERAGE

To this point, we have made the simplifying assumption that the net spread for each business unit could be sustained in perpetuity. In addition, we have assumed that a leverage ratio of 20 always is attainable. In this section, we show that a relaxation of these assumptions influences the FF and, consequently, the P/E.

In Figure 10, we illustrate the relationship between FF and NS when NS is constant for five years.[7] For comparative purposes, Figure 10 also includes the FF line for perpetuities (see Figure 6). For spreads above 35 basis points, the line for perpetuals appears above the five-year line. This dominance is to be expected, because one surely would prefer good spreads forever to good spreads for only five years. At spreads below 35 basis points, the ROEs are below 12%, and the FFs are negative. Hence, the shorter five-year period would be "preferred," at least on a relative basis.

As an example of the relationship between FF and the magnitude and duration of NS, consider an investment, C*, that offers a 70-basis-point NS for five years. Although C* initially has a 20-basis-point higher NS than C, the FFs for C* and C are equal. Consequently, equal investments in C* and C would have the same P/E impact. This equality reflects the fact that the net spreads for C*

---

[7] To compute FF when NS varies over time, we find a perpetual equivalent NS by equating the present value of the varying spread pattern to the present value of the perpetual equivalent NS. In the examples of this section for which spreads are sustained for five years, we assume that beyond the initial five-year period, equity capital earns the 12% market rate. For details of the computation of perpetual equivalent returns, see *Inside the P/E Ratio (Part II): The Franchise Portfolio*.

Figure 10: The Franchise Factor versus Net Spread when the Net Spread Changes After Five Years

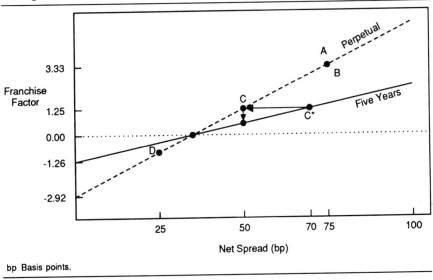

bp Basis points.

and C have the same present value. In effect, C*'s higher NS during the first five years is just enough to counterbalance its lower NS in later years.

Figure 10 also enables us to see the impact of a change in *expectations* regarding a given NS. Suppose that as a result of increased competition in spread banking, C's NS of 50 basis points is now expected to only last for five more years. The revised FF can be found in Figure 10 by moving vertically downward from point C to the five-year spread line, where the FF is only 0.54. This 57% decrease in the FF (from 1.25) means that the P/E gain from a $50 investment in C is 57% lower than expected.

Changes in the leverage ratio can also dramatically affect the P/E. For any positive NS, the ROE decreases as the leverage multiple falls. Consequently, lowering the leverage results in a lower FF and a decrease in the P/E impact of a new investment opportunity (see Figure 11). The upper line in Figure 11, as in Figure 6, represents the relationship between FF and NS when the leverage multiple is at our assumed level of 20. The lower line represents FF when the leverage is lowered to 10. As indicated earlier, investment C provides an FF of 1.25 when the leverage is 20, but FF becomes negative when the leverage is reduced to 10. Thus, although C adds to the P/E when the leverage is 20, the investment should not be made if the leverage is 10.

Figure 12 illustrates how leverage and NS produce a given ROE. As the leverage multiple decreases, it becomes extremely difficult to achieve good re-

Figure 11: The Franchise Factor versus Net Spread with Varying Leverage

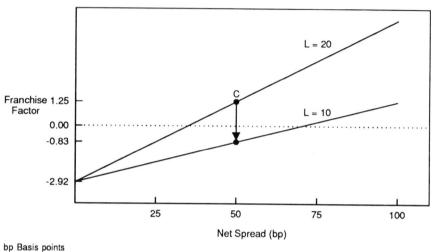

bp Basis points

Figure 12: Leverage Required to Achieve a Given Return on Equity versus Net Spread

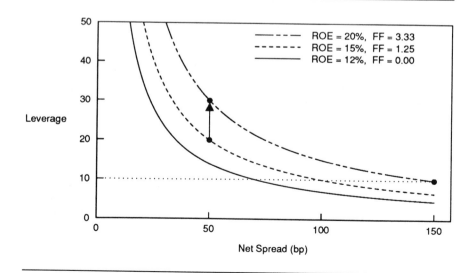

turns through spread banking, because an ever-increasing NS is necessary to achieve a desired ROE. For example, at a leverage multiple of 10, an NS of 150 basis points is required to match the 20% ROE on the existing book of business.

By the same token, if NS becomes too tight, an unacceptably high leverage multiple may be necessary to achieve a target ROE. For example, if NS is 50 basis points, a leverage multiple of 30 is required to achieve a 20% ROE.

RESTRUCTURING THE EXISTING BOOK OF BUSINESS

The concept of a base P/E derives from the implicit assumption that earnings on the current book of business (that is, the current ROE, r) can be sustained in perpetuity.[8] However, if it is possible to restructure the current book and obtain a higher ROE, we would expect current shareholders to benefit. We now show how our FF methodology can provide insight into the benefits of such restructurings.

Our analysis begins with the observation that the "base P/E" can be expressed in a formula that is similar to the overall P/E formula.[9] In the earlier formula for P/E, incremental P/E value was shown to depend on the FFs of *future* investments. For the base P/E, a similar type of incremental P/E value can be ascribed to the FFs of the subunits of the *current* book of business.

In the bank example, we assumed that a leverage multiple of 20 applied to the current book and that the corresponding average NS on leveraged assets was 75 basis points. These assumptions resulted in a 20% average ROE. Now, we make the additional assumption that the current book of business is comprised of three subunits—B_1, B_2 and B_3—each of which represents $33.33 in equity capital. The NSs for these subunits are 133 basis points, 75 basis points and 17 basis points, respectively. In Figure 13, we summarize these assumptions and include the ROEs and FFs of the subunits. The "incremental P/E" attributable to each subunit is computed by multiplying its FF by its size measure (33 1/3% of the total $100 in current book equity). The total incremental P/E value provided by the subunits is equal to an overall "current book" FF of 3.33.

To arrive at the base P/E of 8.33, we add the incremental P/E value of 3.33 to 1/r (1.0/0.2 = 5.0).[10] This result is illustrated by a vector diagram in Figure 14. Observe that the first vector emanates from the 5.00 point on the P/E axis.

---

[8] In actuality, earnings will obviously fluctuate with changing market conditions and changes in the firm structure. In the context of this model, the value of the earnings E and the ROE r should be interpreted as long-term sustainable values.

[9] The development of this FF formulation for the base P/E is provided in the Appendix.

[10] In the formula for the full P/E, the incremental P/E is added to 1/k. In the Appendix, we show that when computing the base P/E, the incremental P/E must be added to the book equity capital to earnings ratio, 1/r.

Figure 13: The P/E Value of Subunits of the Current Book Equity

Business Subunit	Dollar Value	Net Spread	Return on Equity	Franchise Factor	Incremental P/E Value
B₁	$33.33	133 bp	31.6%	8.17	2.72
B₂	33.33	75	20.0	3.33	1.11
B₃	33.33	17	8.4	-1.50	-0.50
Overall	**$100.00**	**75 bp**	**20%**	**3.33**	**3.33**

bp Basis points.

The slope of this vector, 8.17, is the FF for subunit B₁. The vector extends over the first $33.33 of equity capital, thereby boosting the P/E by 2.72 units to 7.72. Similarly, the second vector extends over the next $33.33 in equity capital and raises the P/E by an additional 1.11 units to 8.83.

The final vector corresponds to a negative FF and therefore slopes downward. The P/E is reduced by 0.50 units, which brings it down to the 8.33 base level. Clearly, B₃ reduces value. Shareholders would be better off if this last business could be unwound and the book equity released for a more effective deployment.

Figure 14: A Vector Diagram of P/E Value for the Current Book of Business

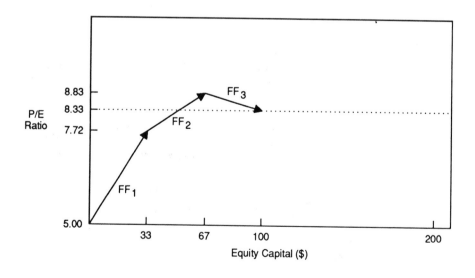

Figure 15: Restructuring the Current Book of Business

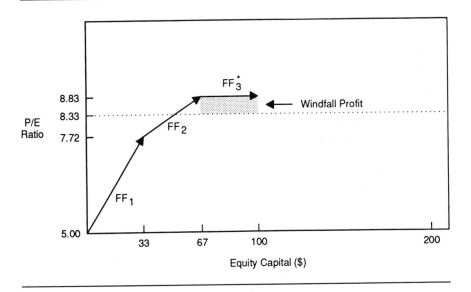

For example, if the full $33.33 book value of B_3 could be redirected to earn the 12% market rate, FF_3 would increase from -1.50 to 0.0, reflecting a 6% increase in earnings from $20.00 to $21.20 (see FF_3^* in Figure 15).[11] As an interim step, FF^* could be viewed as increasing the base P/E to 8.83. However, the new level of earnings quickly would be capitalized into a 6% increase in market price, as the process of market equilibrium drives the P/E back to 8.33. The net effect would be to provide an immediate windfall profit to current investors (as indicated by the height of the shaded area in Figure 15).

CONCLUSION

Spread banking is particularly well suited to Franchise Factor analysis for several reasons. In spread banking, the return on equity capital for a given book of business is determined by the spread between borrowing and lending rates and

---

[11] The new weighted-average return on book equity is computed as follows:
  $(0.33 \times 31.6\%) + (0.33 \times 20\%) + (0.33 \times 12\%) = 21.20\%$.
  Note that the 6% earnings (and the 6% price) increase also could be computed by dividing the instantaneous 0.50 unit P/E change by the base P/E of 8.33.

the degree of leverage. For many spread banking activities, the allowable leverage (or, equivalently, the equity capital requirement) is specified through regulation of one form or another. This specification results in well-defined values for the return on equity, and hence, the Franchise Factor can be readily computed. In addition, the financial nature of spread banking generally leads to a relatively simple time pattern of returns. This simple pattern contrasts with the more complex investment and payback flows generated by a typical manufacturing project. Moreover, spread banking lines of business tend to be both more homogeneous and better delineated in scope than manufacturing businesses. At the conceptual level at least, the relative simplicity of spread banking makes it easier to characterize the Franchise Factors for a spread banking firm than for a general industrial concern.

At first, we assumed that the same degree of leverage could be achieved for a firm's entire equity base. In addition, we assumed that the net spread on borrowed funds was earned in perpetuity. Later, we relaxed both of these unrealistic assumptions and showed the sensitivity of the P/E-producing power of an investment to changes in the assumed leverage or the duration of a given net spread. For example, if the leverage multiple were 20 and borrowed funds could earn a net spread of 50 basis points (or more) for only five years, the P/E producing power of an equity investment would be 57% lower than it would have been if that same net spread could be earned in perpetuity.

In our study of prospective new businesses, we showed how any anticipated opportunity with a positive Franchise Factor raises the P/E. By the same token, a new investment with a negative Franchise Factor will lower the P/E. By accepting all P/E-enhancing business and rejecting businesses that fail to add to the firm's P/E, a spread banking firm is able to set a long-term growth target that will maximize its P/E.

We also examined a bank's existing book to see how it might be improved. For example, if one of the subunits has a negative Franchise Factor, the shareholders will benefit from exiting that line of business. If a merger or restructuring achieves cost efficiencies that result in a net spread increase, the Franchise Factor for that subunit also will increase. Any action that raises the Franchise Factor of a component of the existing book of business should be attractive to existing shareholders, because it provides them with an immediate windfall profit.

Appendix

In an earlier paper,[12] we showed that, for a firm with a n future investment opportunities, Franchise Factors FF_i, and Growth Equivalents G_i, the theoretical P/E could be expressed as follows:

$$P/E = \frac{1}{k} + \sum_{i=1}^{n} FF_i \bullet G_i \,, \tag{1}$$

where $1/k$ is the base P/E.

In the above formula, k is the market capitalization rate. If a new investment of magnitude I_i is made n years from today, FF_i and G_i can be computed from the following formulas:

$$FF_i = \frac{R_i - k}{rk}\,, \tag{2}$$

$$G_i = \frac{I_i}{(1+k)^n} \div B,$$

where

R_i = Perpetual equivalent return on investment I_i,

r = ROE = perpetual return on initial book value, and

B = Initial book value.

In spread banking, R_i can be expressed in terms of NS_i (the net spread on borrowed funds), L_i (the leverage multiple) and R_i (the risk-free rate),

$$R_i = R_f + L_i \bullet NS_i.$$

Now, FF_i can be expressed in terms of the above variables as follows:

---

[12] See *Inside the P/E Ratio (Part II): The Franchise Portfolio.*

$$FF_i = \frac{R_f + L_i \bullet NS_i - k}{rk}.$$

We will now show how the P/E formula (1) can be extended to include Franchise Factors for a firm's current book of business, B. To develop this more general P/E formula, we assume that the current book comprises m subunits. The size of each subunit, b_i, is expressed as a percentage of the current book so that

$$\sum_{i=1}^{m} b_i \bullet B = B$$

and

$$\sum_{i=1}^{m} b_i = 1. \tag{3}$$

We further define r_i to be the ROE for subunit b_i. Thus, the current earnings, E, can be written as follows:

$$E = rB = \sum_{i=1}^{m} r_i \, b_i \, B.$$

Consequently,

$$r = \sum_{i=1}^{m} r_i \, b_i. \tag{4}$$

That is, r is the weighted-average return on book equity, and the weights are the sizes of the subunits.

There are three components to the value (P) of a firm. If a firm has no growth opportunities and book equity capital earns k in perpetuity (that is, $r=k$), the capitalized value of current earnings is $kB/k=B$. Thus, in this case, the firm's value would be the same as its book value. However, if the current business provides a return that exceeds the market rate k, there will be an incremental value consisting of P_0.

P_0 = The capitalized value of the excess earnings on the current book equity (assuming that those earnings continue year after year).

Thus, P_0 can be viewed as a franchise value associated with the *current* book of business.

Finally, if there are *future* opportunities that the firm can pursue that have above-market returns, there is a third component of value, P_1.

P_1 = The net present value of all anticipated future earnings from new investments.

That is, P_1 is the franchise value associated with future investment opportunities.

Thus,

$$P = B + P_0 + P_1,$$

and the P/E ratio is

$$P/E = \frac{B + P_0 + P_1}{E} = B/E + P_0/E + P_1/E. \tag{5}$$

Note that by multiplying both sides of equation (5) by E/B, we derive a formula for the price-to-book ratio in terms of the incremental values P_0 and P_1. The P/B formula is

$$P/B = 1 + P_0/B + P_1/B. \tag{6}$$

The above formula also shows that the premium to book is the sum of P_0/B and P_1/B,

$$\frac{P - B}{B} = P_0/B + P_1/B. \tag{7}$$

Returning to the P/E, we note that since $E=rB$,

$$B/E = \frac{B}{rB} = \frac{1}{r}. \tag{8}$$

From the above definition of P_0,

$$P_0 = \frac{rB - kB}{k} = \frac{(r-k) \bullet B}{k}$$

and

$$P_0/E = \frac{(r-k) \bullet B}{k} \bullet \frac{1}{rB},$$

$$P_0/E = \frac{r-k}{rk}. \tag{9}$$

Using (8) and (9), we see from the following that the first two terms in the P/E formula (5) combine to produce the base P/E, $1/k$:

$$B/E + P_0/E = \frac{1}{r} + \frac{(r-k)}{rk}$$

$$= \frac{1}{r} \bullet \left[1 + \frac{r-k}{k} \right]$$

$$= \frac{1}{k} \, .$$

The last term in formula (5), P_1/E, corresponds to the last term in formula (1). That is,

$$P_1/E = \sum_{i=1}^{n} FF_i \bullet G_i \, .$$

We also can express P_0/E in Franchise Factor format by utilizing equations (3) and (4) in equation (9) and rearranging terms:

$$P_0/E = \frac{\sum r_i b_i - k \sum b_i}{rk}$$

$$= \sum \frac{(r_i - k)}{rk} \bullet b_i \, . \quad 3$$

Using equation (2) as a guide, we define the Franchise Factor for the current book of business as follows:

$$FF_i^{(b)} = \frac{r_i - k}{rk} \, .$$

Thus, the base P/E can be expressed as follows:

$$Base\ P/E = B/E + P_0/E = \frac{1}{r} + \sum_{i=1}^{j} FF_i^{(b)} \bullet b_i \, . \tag{10}$$

The primary difference between the above formula and the general P/E formula (1) is that in the general formula, the term $1/k$ (the base P/E) has been replaced by the B/E ratio ($1/r$). By using (5), we can now write a more general form of the P/E formula.

$$P/E = \frac{1}{r} + \sum_{i=1}^{j} FF_i^{(b)} \bullet b_i + \sum_{I=1}^{n} FF_i \bullet G_i \,. \tag{11}$$

Chapter II-4

Inside the P/E Ratio (Part III): The Franchise Factor for Leveraged Firms

INTRODUCTION AND SUMMARY

In earlier papers, we introduced the Franchise Factor (FF) as a theoretical measure of the price/earnings ratio (P/E) impact of new investments assuming no taxes, leverage or uncertainty.[1] Under these restrictions, we developed a model that provided new insights into the driving mechanisms behind P/E ratios. A key component of a high P/E is a firm's opportunity for franchise investments at above-market rates of return. One striking result from the earlier studies was the high level of future "franchise investment" required for even moderately high P/E ratios. For example, a P/E of 15.0 implies that such franchise investments must have a magnitude of 2.5 to 5.0 times the current book value of eq-

---

[1] See *Inside the P/E Ratio: The Franchise Factor*, Salomon Brothers Inc, July 1990; *Inside the P/E Ratio (Part II): The Franchise Portfolio*, Salomon Brothers Inc, January 1991; and *A Franchise Factor Model for Spread Banking*, Salomon Brothers Inc, April 1991.

The authors wish to express their appreciation for the helpful comments and suggestions from Edward Altman, James Farrell and Robert Ferguson. They also wish to thank Carmela Nardi for her special help in the preparation of this report.

Martin L. Leibowitz and Stanley Kogelman, "Inside the P/E Ratio (Part III): The Franchise Factor for Leveraged Firms," Salomon Brothers Inc, October 1991.

379

uity, even when the available return on new investment is fairly high—in the 15% to 18% range. In this paper, we address the question of whether debt financing might moderate these unusual findings and lead to more reasonable levels for the required franchise investment.

The general topic of the effect of leverage on the P/E ratio has received little attention in either academic or practitioner literature. Because leveraging the current book shrinks both shareholder equity and firm earnings, it is difficult to develop a good intuition regarding the net impact of leverage on the P/E ratio. For this reason alone, it is interesting to see whether leverage leads to increasing, decreasing or even stable P/E ratios.

Our initial debt model assumes a tax-free environment in which (1) the total firm value is unaffected by the financial structure; and (2) the cost of debt is fixed and remains constant at all levels of leverage.[2] These assumptions do not attempt to capture the increasing debt cost and default risk associated with higher leverage ratios; bankruptcy costs also remain outside of this simple model. However, the above assumptions are consistent with a standard "first-cut" approach and should provide a reasonable approximation to the P/E impact for modest levels of leverage.

This debt model reveals P/E effects that may be surprising: *Leverage changes the P/E ratio in different directions, depending on the firm's starting P/E ratio.* For firms with low P/E ratios, leverage reduces the P/E further. In contrast, for firms with high P/Es, the introduction of leverage results in even higher P/Es.

While these divergent P/E effects do not depend on our Franchise Factor model, this model does provide some interesting insights that help to explain the P/E divergence. The magnitude of a firm's "Franchise value" can be viewed as the key to direction of the P/E response to leverage. In fact, there is a threshold franchise value that separates the two response patterns. Firms with franchise values above this threshold will exhibit an increasing P/E response to leverage, while the opposite occurs for firms with franchise values below the threshold.

Although the divergence of the P/E response is interesting, the overriding result is that its magnitude is modest for the parameter values that characterize most of Corporate America. For example, we show that an unleveraged firm with a P/E of 16.7 will raise its P/E to only 17.8 at 40% leverage (that is, at a 40% debt-to-book value ratio). When taxation is introduced, the basic results generally remain the same, except that they are even more subdued in magnitude. Using a 30% tax rate, a P/E of 16.7 grows to only 17.4 at 40% leverage. Thus, changes to the financial structure alone are insufficient to explain high P/Es. We find that our expanded model preserves the earlier theoretical finding

---

[2] See "The Cost of Capital, Corporation Finance, and the Theory of Investment," Franco Modigliani and Merton H. Miller, *The American Economic Review*, June 1958.

that high levels of franchise investment are needed to support even moderately high P/Es.

THE IMPACT OF LEVERAGE ON CURRENT EARNINGS

The value of a firm derives from two fundamental sources: (1) the *tangible value* of the current book of business; and (2) the *franchise value* based on future opportunities that enable the firm to experience productive growth. The total market value is simply the sum of these two terms, or

$$\text{Market Value} = \text{Tangible Value} + \text{Franchise Value}$$

In this section, we focus primarily on the *tangible value*; we consider the *franchise value* in later sections. We use the term *tangible value* to describe the total of (1) the *book value* of assets; and (2) the additional *premium over book* value for firms that are able to generate above-market returns on *existing* book assets. Thus,

$$\text{Tangible Value} = \text{Book Value} + \text{Premium Over Book.}$$

It should be noted that the above definition of "tangible" is *not* the usual accounting definition.

As an illustration, we consider a tax-free firm that has a book value of $100 million (MM), a 15% return on book equity and no franchise opportunities (see Figure 1). Although we can expect the $15 million in earnings (15% of $100 million) generated by today's book to fluctuate from year to year, we use a simplified deterministic model in which the firm generates a perpetual earnings stream of $15 million annually.[3] We take the market capitalization rate for the unleveraged firm to be 12% and assume that the cost of debt is 8%, regardless of the extent of leverage or the likelihood of bankruptcy. For this example of a firm without productive growth prospects, the tangible value (and its total market value) is $125 million. This theoretical value results from capitalizing the prospective $15 million in earnings at the 12% market rate. The $25-million premium over book value is a direct consequence of the fact that the return on equity is 3% greater than the market capitalization rate.

We can determine the P/E ratio by dividing the market value by the total earnings,

$$P/E = \$125 \text{ MM}/\$15 \text{ MM} = 8.33.$$

---

[3] The more general case of risky cash flows can be accommodated by replacing the constant return values by expected values. In addition, we only consider firms for which operating earnings are unaffected by leverage.

Figure 1: Basic Assumptions

			Per-Share Values[a]
Book Value (B)	$100 Million	Book Value	$100
Return on Equity[b] (r)	15%		
Earnings (E)	$15 Million	Premium Over Book for	25
Market Capitalization Rate (k)	12%	Current Earnings	
Total Market Value	$125 Million	Share Price	125

[a] One million share. [b] Unleveraged.

We now turn to the impact of leverage. We assume an equilibrium model where debt is used to repurchase shares so that the firm's total value remains unchanged. Thus, leverage alters the financial structure of the *existing* firm, but it does not expand the capital base. This equilibrium model assumes that the firm is fairly priced and that all transfers take place at fair market value. There are no windfalls to any shareholders—be they the original shareholders who sold out during the repurchase process, or the remaining shareholders in the leveraged firm.[4]

If the firm is free of debt, all of the earnings belong to the equityholders. As debt is used to repurchase shares, there are two immediate effects: (1) The earnings available to shareholders are reduced by interest payments; and (2) the aggregate shareholder claim to some percentage of the firm's (unchanged) total value is reduced by the total value of the debt. For example, if the firm is leveraged 50%,[5] we have the following:

Debt	=	50% of Book Value	=	$50 MM;
Annual Interst	=	8% of $50 MM	=	$4 MM; and
Earnings	=	$15 MM - $4 MM	=	$11 MM.

If the firm is leveraged to 100% of book value, the interest payments will be $8 million, and the earnings will drop to $7 million (see Figure 2). Our assump-

---

[4] Even in this equilibrium world where the firm's *total value* remains constant, different financial structures will lead to different P/E ratios.

[5] The degree of leverage can be characterized in many different ways. In general, academic studies reflect the debt load as a percentage of the total market value of all of the firm's securities (both debt and equity). However, among equity market participants and credit analysts, the common practice is to express the leverage percentage relative to the total capitalization, that is, as a percentage of the firm's initial book value prior to any leveraging. We accept this latter convention, because it is somewhat more intuitive. The general methodology of this study is not affected by this choice of leverage numeraire.

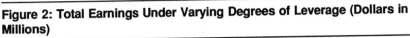

Figure 2: Total Earnings Under Varying Degrees of Leverage (Dollars in Millions)

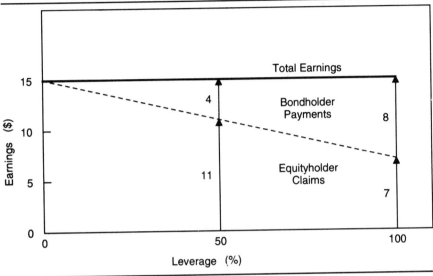

tion of a constant 8% debt rate ignores the fact that both the probability of bankruptcy and the agency costs increase with leverage.

LEVERAGE AND THE "TANGIBLE VALUE" FIRM

In the previous section, we focused on the effect of leverage on the distribution of earnings claims between bondholders and equityholders. The second effect of leverage is the reduction in shareholder equity. For the firm in our example, we assume that the unleveraged market value of $125 million is constant under increasing leverage. If $50 million in loan proceeds is used to repurchase shares and the price per share does not change, the *total* value of the firm will remain at $125 million, but the equity value will drop to $75 million. At a leverage ratio of 100% of book (an impractical but theoretically illuminating level), there is still $25 million in residual shareholder value (see Figure 3), because our leverage is defined relative to the book value, rather than to the market value.

We now combine our findings on earnings and shareholder equity to determine how leverage affects the P/E. For example of 50% leverage, a P/E ratio of 6.82 is obtained by dividing the revised $75-million equity value by the $11 million in earnings,

Figure 3: Equity Value versus Leverage (Dollars in Millions)

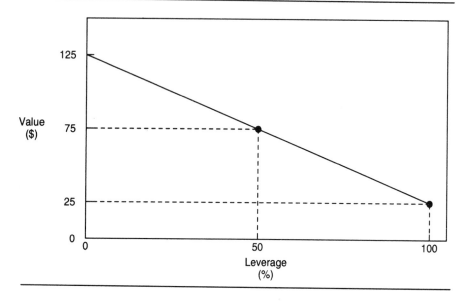

$$P/E = \$75 \text{ MM}/\$11 \text{ MM} = 6.82.$$

Similarly, at 100% leverage, the P/E ratio drops to 3.57. Over the full range of leverage ratios, we have a declining P/E curve (see Figure 4).[6]

From the preceding examples, we conclude that leverage leads to a declining P/E ratio for any firm that derives all of its value from the current book of business. As long as the debt cost is less than the market rate, the P/E will start at 8.33 (the reciprocal of the 12% market capitalization rate) and follow a pattern of decline similar to that exhibited in Figure 4.

From the preceding examples, we conclude that leverage leads to a declining P/E ratio for any firm that derives all of its value from the current book of business. As long as the debt cost is less than the market rate, the P/E will start at 8.33 (the reciprocal of the 12% market capitalization rate) and follow a pattern of decline similar to that exhibited in Figure 4.

---

[6] These same P/E ratios could have been obtained by examining the earnings per share resulting from leverage-induced declines in both total earnings and the number of shares outstanding.

Figure 4: P/E versus Leverage for the "Tangible Value" Firm

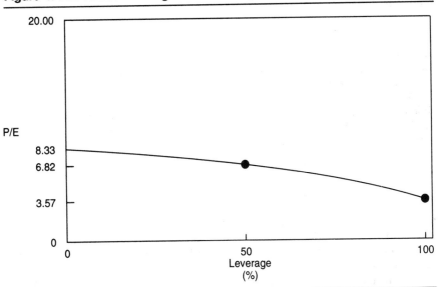

GROWTH OPPORTUNITIES AND THE FRANCHISE VALUE FIRM

In the preceding sections, the firm generated $15 million in earnings per year but had no prospects for productive growth. We now turn to the more representative situation in which the firm has opportunities for future growth through investment at above-market returns. We assume that firms are able to take advantage of all franchise investment opportunities, because the market always should be willing, theoretically, to supply sufficient funds for such purposes.

Now we suppose that the firm has the opportunity to make a series of investments in productive new business areas. This special opportunity in itself represents a franchise value, even though it does not contribute to current book value. We assume that this franchise amounts to $80 million of net present value above and beyond the cost of financing the requisite future investments. The addition of this $80-million *franchise value* brings the total market value of the firm to $205 million, or

$$
\begin{aligned}
\text{Market Value} \quad &= \quad \text{Tangible Value} + \text{Franchise Value} \\
&= \quad \$125 \text{ MM} + \$80 \text{ MM} \\
&= \quad \$205 \text{ MM}.
\end{aligned}
$$

Without leverage, the P/E of this *franchise firm* is this $205 million divided by the $15 million in current earnings, or

$$P/E = \$205 \text{ MM}/\$15 \text{ MM} = 13.67.$$

The above P/E is 5.33 units higher than the 8.33-unit P/E of the unleveraged tangible value firm. We regard 8.33 as a "base P/E," because it is the P/E of a no-growth firm with constant earnings over time.

We now look at the effect of leverage on the equity value and the P/E multiple of this franchise value firm. At 50% leverage, the equity value falls by $50 million from $205 million to $155 million, and the earnings drop to $11 million. Consequently, the P/E *increases* as follows:

$$P/E = \$155 \text{ MM}/\$11 \text{ MM} = 14.09.$$

At 100% leverage, the equity value drops by $100 million, leaving only $105 million. Because the earnings decline to $7 million, the P/E grows to 15.0. Intermediate values for the P/E are plotted in Figure 5, where the P/E curve is seen to *rise* with increasing leverage.

In general, any firm with a positive franchise value will have an initial (unleveraged) P/E that is greater than the 8.33-unit base P/E. If the unleveraged P/E is greater than a certain "threshold" value, the P/E will follow a pattern of increase similar to that in Figure 5. To see how such a threshold P/E responds to leverage, we consider a firm with $15 million in current earnings and a franchise value of $62.5 million. The total market value will be $187.5 million, and the initial P/E will be 12.5,

$$P/E = \$187.5 \text{ MM}/\$15 \text{ MM} = 12.5.$$

At 50% leverage, the P/E also is 12.5,

$$P/E = \$137.5 \text{ MM}/\$11 \text{ MM} = 12.5.$$

In fact, when the franchise value is $62.5 million, the P/E remains *unchanged* at 12.5 across all leverage ratios.

In Figure 6, we combine the results from all previous examples. This figure graphically illustrates a finding that might surprise many market participants. The directional effect of leverage on P/E depends on the "value structure" of the existing firm. For a no-growth firm in which the equity value is derived solely from *current* earnings, the P/E always starts at 8.33 (if the capitalization rate is 12%), and higher debt ratios lead to lower P/Es. The same declining P/E pattern is observed for all firms with P/Es below a threshold value (12.5 in our example). In contrast, for firms with future franchise opportunities that place the initial P/E above the threshold level, leverage results in *higher* P/Es.

Figure 5: P/E versus Leverage for a Franchise Firm

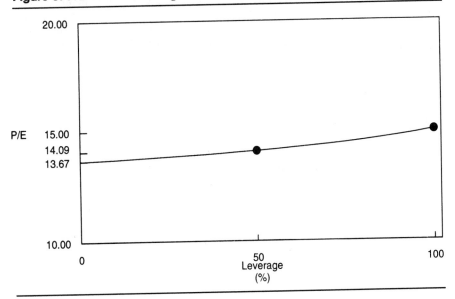

Figure 6: P/E versus Leverage for Three Firms

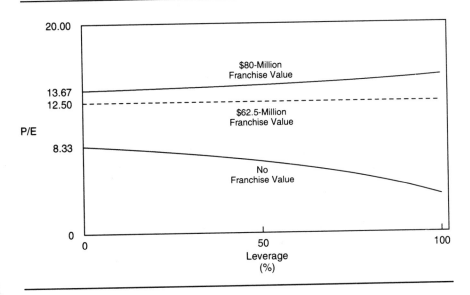

Figure 6 could have been obtained without reference to either the base P/E or the franchise value. The results of our analysis are totally general, because they require only our basic assumptions of a fixed debt cost and a constant firm value. The critical determinant of the direction of the leverage effect is the initial P/E. The base P/E and the franchise value simply provide a convenient means of explaining the mechanisms that lead to differential leverage effects.

THE FRANCHISE FACTOR MODEL

In this section, we briefly review the Franchise Factor (FF) model that we developed in earlier papers for unleveraged firms (see *Appendix* for a more detailed development). Then, we show how this model can be extended and used to explain the relationship between leverage and the P/E.

The Unleveraged Firm

The basic FF model expresses an unleveraged firm's P/E as follows:

P/E = Base P/E + (Franchise Factor) x (Growth Equivalent).

The base P/E represents the contribution of the tangible value to the total P/E. This quantity is calculated by dividing the tangible value by the current earnings. It turns out that,

$$\text{Base P/E} = \frac{\text{Tangible Value}}{\text{Earnings}} = \frac{1}{\text{Capitalization Rate}} \text{,}$$

or for our example,

$$\text{Base P/E} = 1.0/0.12 = 8.33.$$

The second term in the P/E formula represents the extent to which the franchise value adds to the P/E. This term could have been computed by dividing the franchise value by current earnings. However, additional insight is gained by expressing the incremental P/E as the product of two factors: (1) a Franchise Factor (FF) that characterizes the P/E impact provided by the level of above-market return embedded in the franchise; and (2) a Growth Equivalent (G) that reflects the present-value magnitude of the franchise opportunity, expressed as a percentage of the initial book value.

The Franchise Factor

The FF is computed from the following formula:

$$FF = \frac{R-k}{rk},$$

where

r = Return on current book equity;

R = Return on future franchise investments; and

k = Market capitalization rate.

As an illustration, consider the earlier example in which a franchise value of $80 million led to an initial P/E of 13.67, that is, 5.33 units above the base P/E. To show how this franchise value might be generated, assume that R = 18%, r = 15% and K= 12%. Then,

$$FF = \frac{0.18-0.12}{0.15 \times 0.12} = 3.33.$$

This level of FF implies that the P/E increases by 3.33 units for each unit of franchise investment, G. To achieve this 5.33-unit P/E increment, the magnitude of the firm's franchise opportunities would have to be equivalent to a present-value investment of $160 million, or 160% of the original book value (that is, a G of 1.60). Using these values for FF and G, the P/E is computed as follows:

$$P/E = \text{Base P/E} + FF \bullet G$$

$$= 8.33 + 3.33 \times 1.60$$

$$= 8.33 + 5.33$$

$$= 13.67.$$

Because FF is fixed for a given return on new investments, the P/E is a linear function of G, with FF as the slope. Figure 7 shows the magnitude of G needed to generate the P/Es for our earlier three examples. The threshold P/E of 12.5 corresponds to a G of 125%.

The Leveraged Firm

The basic FF model can be applied to leveraged firms by extending our earlier definitions. First, we revise the base P/E by reducing the tangible value of the unleveraged firm by the size of the debt incurred. This adjusted tangible value corresponds to the capitalized value of the current earnings stream, given the

Figure 7: P/E versus Growth Equivalent

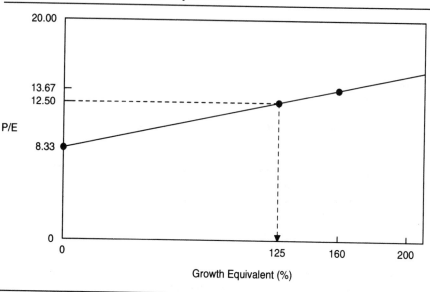

new debt load. Now, we can calculate the leveraged base P/E by dividing the adjusted tangible value by the annual earnings, net of interest payments,

Base P/E (Leveraged) = (Tangible Value - Debt Value)/Net Earnings,

where

Net Earnings = Annual Earnings - Annual Interest Payments.

For example, if the tangible value is $125 million and the firm is 50% leveraged against a $100-million book value, then the debt value is $50 million, and the adjusted tangible value is $75 million. The graph of this revised base P/E (versus leverage) is exactly the same as in Figure 4 for any firm that has a 15% return on unleveraged equity.

Because the debt-induced decrement to shareholder value is embedded into the adjusted tangible value, the franchise value can be viewed as remaining constant in the face of leverage. This invariance can be interpreted in the following way: (1) The current shareholders are entitled to the full value of the franchise; (2) the franchise value reflects the excess of the return on new investment *above* the cost of future capital; and (3) the weighted-average cost of future capital theoretically will be equal to the market capitalization rate, *regardless* of the extent of leverage used in future financings.

The Franchise Factor (Leveraged)

As in the unleveraged case, we can find the P/E increment from the franchise value by dividing this value by the net earnings. Because the net earnings *decrease* as leverage increases, the P/E increment from a given franchise always will be *greater* than in the unleveraged case. In our FF model, the P/E increment from franchise value is captured in the product of FF and G. It is logical to presume that G, the present-value equivalent of future growth prospects, will not be affected by leverage. Because G does not change, the entire impact of leverage effectively is "loaded" into a higher FF (see *Appendix* for details):

$$\text{FF (Leveraged)} = \frac{R-k}{(r-ih)k} \text{ ,}$$

where

i = Interest rate on debt; and

h = Leverage as a percentage of book value.

As in our earlier examples, R = 18%, r = 15% and k = 12%, so that FF is 3.33 for the unleveraged firm. At first, FF grows slowly with leverage, reaching 4.55 at 50% leverage (see Figure 8),

$$\text{FF (50\% Leveraged)} = \frac{0.18 - 0.12}{(0.15 - 0.08 \times 0.50) \times 0.12} = 4.55 \text{ .}$$

Figure 8: Franchise Factor versus Leverage

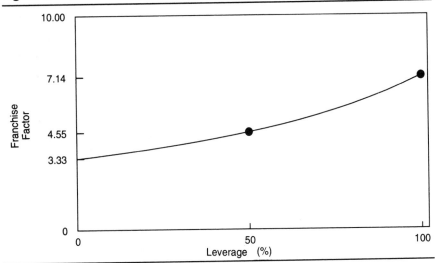

At higher leverage percentages, FF increases more rapidly, reaching 7.14 for the 100% leveraged firm. The increasing FF suggests that the P/E gain from a given franchise situation increases when the current firm includes a higher proportion of debt funding.

The Total P/E

In Figure 9, we plot the two P/E components to show their response to leverage. The base P/E reflects the firm's tangible value, and its value always declines with added debt. By contrast, for a G of 160%, the incremental P/E from the franchise value exhibits an ascending pattern. The sum of these two terms is the firm's P/E, and it increases with leverage. If the G value were lowered, the P/E increment from the franchise value would rise more slowly, and consequently, so would the overall P/E. At a G of 125%, the incremental P/E will just offset the declining base P/E. The net result will be an overall P/E that is constant in the face of leverage.

The combined effects of the level of franchise opportunities and the degree of leverage are shown in Figure 10. At 0% leverage, the P/E starts at an unleveraged base value of 8.33 and rises by 3.33 units (the unleveraged FF) for each unit

---

Figure 9: P/E versus Leverage (Growth Equivalent = 160%)

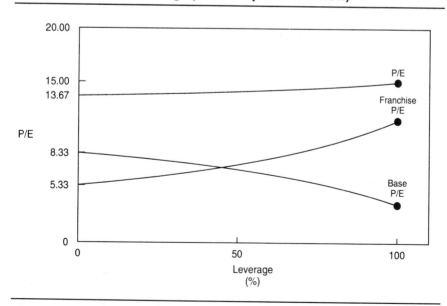

increase in G (as in Figure 7). At 50% leverage, the base P/E drops to 6.82, but the P/E grows faster because of the greater FF slope of 4.55. For the 100% leverage case, the base P/E drops further to 3.57, but the P/E line has an even greater slope that corresponds to the leveraged FF value of 7.14.

In Figure 10, all of the lines cross at a G of 125%, thereby giving a common P/E of 12.5. For firms with this P/E multiple, the earnings yield (that is, the reciprocal of the P/E) is equal to the 8% debt rate. Consequently, the addition of debt blends in with the original structure and leaves the earnings yield unchanged. From another vantage point, one can see that substantial franchise investments—125% of current book value—are needed just to sustain this relatively modest P/E of 12.5. When G is less than 125%, the decline in the base P/E with leverage overpowers any gain from franchise value; thus, at low G values, the P/E is greatest when the firm is unleveraged. If G is greater than 125%, there is a positive P/E response to leverage, which means that with leverage, a somewhat lower G value is needed to sustain a given P/E. However, the G reduction is not sufficiently dramatic to alter our earlier finding that substantial investments are required to sustain even moderately high P/Es. Thus, regardless of the financial structure, the key ingredient for high P/Es remains the access to substantial franchise opportunities.

Figure 10: P/E versus Growth Equivalent at Varying Degrees of Leverage

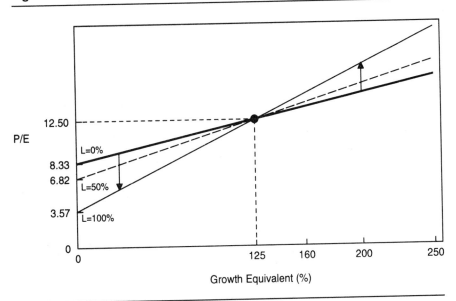

Growth Equivalent (%)

SENSITIVITY ANALYSIS

In previous sections, we observed that the P/E may rise or fall with leverage. We found that both the direction and magnitude of the P/E change depend on the extent of the firm's franchise opportunities. We now look more closely at the *magnitude* of P/E variation for "reasonable" levels of leverage and initial P/E.

In Figure 11, we show the variation of P/E with leverage for initial P/Es ranging from 8.33 to 16.67. Regardless of the initial P/E, the leverage effect is modest for firms that are as much as 40% leveraged.

The muted leverage effect stems from the counterbalancing behavior of the base P/E and the franchise P/E. Another factor is the "numeraire" that we have chosen to measure the degree of leverage. By expressing the debt as a percentage of book value, rather than market value, we are in effect understating the firm's theoretical leverageability. For firms with high P/Es, the book value may be only a small percentage of market value. Consequently, a high leverage ratio relative to the book value actually may be a modest ratio relative to a larger market value. In Figure 12, we show how the leverage as a percentage of market value compares with the same amount of debt expressed as a percentage of book value.

Figure 11: P/E versus Leverage at Varying Initial P/Es.

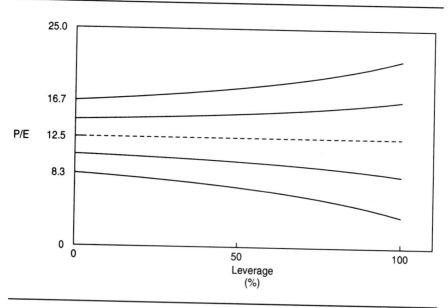

Figure 12: Market Percentage of Debt versus Book Percentage of Debt

---

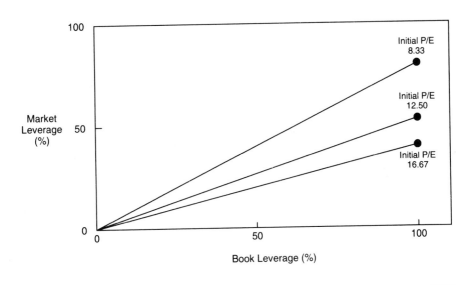

THE IMPACT OF TAXES

To this point, our analysis has proceeded under a no-tax assumption. In the real world, the differential taxation of debt and equity creates several problems and opportunities. In terms of adjustments to the FF model, two tax effects are relevant: (1) Earnings are reduced by the after-tax (rather than pretax) interest payments; and (2) the total value of the firm is augmented by the introduction of debt.[7] The value enhancement can be modeled by assuming that the additional value is just the magnitude of the "tax wedge" (that is, the tax rate times the debt amount).

It can be shown that the two tax effects can be incorporated into the base and franchise components of the P/E by replacing the literal leverage with the "after-tax" leverage (see the *Appendix* for a derivation of this result). For example, if the firm's marginal tax rate is 30%, we can determine the P/E at 50% leverage by using the base P/E and FF for a nontaxable firm with a leverage of 35% (that is, 70% of 50%).

---

[7] We assume a taxable corporation and tax-exempt investors. Thus, we do not consider the effect of investor tax rates.

Figure 13: The P/E Effect of Taxes

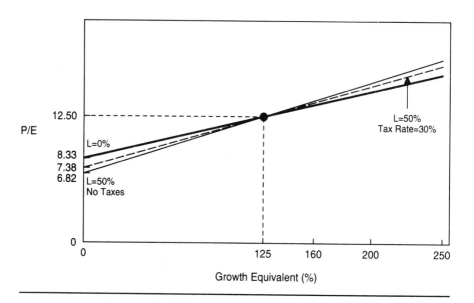

In Figure 13, we illustrate how the P/E impact of leverage is moderated for taxable firms. The P/E lines still intersect when G is 125%. However, at all other values of G, the P/E line for 50% leverage (and a 30% tax rate) is closer to the P/E line for the unleveraged firm than it was in the tax-free environment of Figure 10.[8]

CONCLUSION

The key to understanding the P/E ratio can be found in what we have called the franchise value. Firms with a high franchise value have high P/Es, and a large component of their stock price is based on future earnings. For such firms, the theoretical response to leverage—no matter what the taxation environment—is to place an even higher P/E on the existing earnings. At the other end of the

---

[8] Figure 13 represents a comparison between a taxable and a tax-exempt entity and assumes that, in the absence of leverage, both firms provide the same return on equity on an *after-tax* basis.

scale, low P/E stocks should experience the opposite effect — a decline in P/E with greater leverage.

However, over a relevant range of leverage ratios — 0% to 40% — the P/E changes are relatively modest. Thus, even with an expanded FF model that incorporates taxes and leverage, the key finding of our earlier studies remains intact: Regardless of the firm's financial structure, the fundamental basis for high P/E ratios is access to substantial franchise investments. For typical rates of return, these new investments must reach levels that can be measured in terms of multiples of the firm's current book value.

Appendix

In previous work, we showed that the P/E ratio for an unleveraged tax-free firm could be expressed in terms of a base P/E, a Franchise Factor (FF) and a Growth Equivalent (G).[9] The more general (and realistic) use of a leveraged, fully taxable entity requires an extension of our former results.

The Unleveraged Firm

We begin our analysis with the unleveraged firm assuming that all returns are perpetual and net of taxes. For reference, a summary of all variables is provided in Figure A1. The value of the unleveraged firm, V^u, is the sum of the firm's tangible value and its franchise value. The *tangible value* is the capitalized value of earnings generated by the current book of business (rB), that is,

$$\text{Tangible Value} = \frac{rB}{k}.$$

The franchise value is the net present value (NPV) of anticipated new businesses. If the earnings rate on new assets is R and the present value of all funds invested in franchise businesses is G•B, the present value of new earnings is R•G•B/k, and

$$\text{Franchise Value} = \frac{R•G•B}{k} - G•B$$

$$= \frac{R-k}{k} •G•B$$

and

[9] See *Inside the P/E Ratio: the Franchise Factor*, Salomon Brothers Inc, July 1990; and *Inside the P/E Ratio (Part II): The Franchise Portfolio*, Salomon Brothers Inc, January 1991. For an early discussion of the relationship between growth, above-market returns and firm value, see *The Theory of Financial Management*, Ezra Solomon, Columbia University Press, 1963.

399

Figure A1: Definition of Variables

Assets	
Total Current Assets (Unleveraged Book Value)	B
Present-Value Magnitude of Anticipated Funds to Be Invested in Franchise Businesses (As a Percentage of Book Value)	G
Present Value of Franchise Investments	G•B
Returns and Rates	
After-Tax (Perpetual) Return on Current Assets, ROE	r
After-Tax (Perpetual) Return on Franchise Investment	R
Pretax Interest Rate on Debt	i
Marginal Tax Rate	t
Capitalization Rate for Unleveraged Firm	k
Capitalization Rate for Equity	k_E
Firm Values	
Market Value of Unleveraged Firm	V^U
Market Value of Leveraged Firm	V^L
Market Value of Equity (For Leveraged Firm)	V_E^L
Face Value of Debt	D
Debt Value as a Fraction of Book Value	h

$$V^U = \text{Tangible Value} + \text{Franchise Value}$$

$$= \frac{rB}{k} + \frac{R-k}{k} \cdot G \cdot B . \tag{1}$$

The P/E ratio is obtained by dividing the value of the firm, V^u, by the earnings, rB.

$$P/E \text{ (Unleveraged)} = \frac{V^U}{rB}$$

$$= \frac{1}{k} + \frac{R-k}{rk} \cdot G .$$

As in our earlier papers, we define the base P/E and FF as follows:

$$\text{Base P/E (Unleveraged)} = \frac{1}{k}$$

$$\text{FF (Unleveraged)} = \frac{R-k}{rk} .$$

Thus,

$$P/E \text{ (Unleveraged)} = \text{Base-P/E} + \text{FF} \cdot G . \tag{2}$$

The Leveraged, Tax-Free Firm

We now turn our attention to a leveraged firm with a perpetual debt, D, that is priced at par. In the absence of taxes, we assume that leverage does not change the firm's value.[10] Thus,

$$V^L = V^U$$

The value of the leveraged firm's equity, V_E^L, is the difference between the total firm value and the value of debt,

$$V_E^L = V^L - D.$$

We will express the firm's debt as a percentage, h, of the current book value of assets,

$$D = hB.$$

Thus,

$$V_E^L = V^U - hB. \tag{3}$$

The earnings are reduced by the debt payments, ihB, so that

$$\text{Net Earnings} = rB - ihB$$
$$= (r - ih)B \tag{4}$$

We require that the firm's earnings be greater than the debt payments. Thus,

$$r - ih > 0.$$

The P/E ratio now is obtained by dividing the value of the firm's equity by the net earnings.

$$\text{P/E (Leveraged)} = \frac{V_E^L}{(r - ih)B}. \tag{5}$$

To express the P/E in terms of a leverage-adjusted based P/E and Franchise Factor we first must express V_E^L in an appropriate algebraic format. In equation (3), we replace V^U by the expression given in equation (1) and obtain the following relationship:

---

[10]See "The Cost of Capital, Corporation Finance, and the Theory of Investment," Franco Modigliani and Merton H. Miller, *The American Economic Review*, June 1958.

$$V_E^L = \frac{rB}{k} + \frac{R-k}{k} \bullet G \bullet B - hB .$$

Then, we interchange the last two terms in the above expression,

$$V_E^L = \frac{rB}{k} - hB + \frac{R-k}{k} \bullet G \bullet B$$

$$= \frac{(r-kh)B}{k} + \frac{R-k}{k} \bullet G \bullet B . \tag{6}$$

The first term in the equation (6) is the difference between the firm's tangible value and the value of the debt. If that difference is positive,

$$r - kh > 0.$$

A P/E ratio formula is again found by dividing the equity value [equation (6)] by the net earnings [equation (4)],

$$P/E \text{ (Leveraged)} = \frac{r-kh}{k(r-ih)} + \frac{R-k}{k(r-ih)} \bullet G . \tag{7}$$

We now define an equity capitalization rate, k_E, as follows (we discuss the relationship between k_E and the weighted-average cost of capital later in the *Appendix*):

$$k_E \equiv \frac{k(r-ih)}{r-kh} . \tag{8}$$

If the debt rate, i is less than the cost of capital, k, then r - ih > r - kh. Thus, $k_E > k$. In addition, k_E increases with leverage. With the above definition of k_E, the P/E for the leveraged firm is as follows:

$$P/E \text{ (Leveraged)} = \frac{1}{k_E} + \frac{R-k}{(r-ih)k} \bullet G .$$

After comparing the above P/E formulation with the P/E for the unleveraged firm [see equation (2)], we see that the base P/E and FF for the leveraged firm can be defined as follows:

$$\text{Base P/E} = \frac{1}{k_E} . \tag{9}$$

$$FF = \frac{R-k}{(r-ih)k} . \tag{10}$$

With the above definitions, the P/E always can be expressed as the sum of a base P/E and franchise P/E. The franchise P/E is the product of FF and G, where G is unaffected by leverage.

The Weighted-Average Cost of Capital

We now turn our attention to the interpretation of k_E. From the defining equation for k_E [equation (8)], it follows that

$$(r - kh)k_E = (r - ih)k.$$

Thus,

$$(r - kh)k_E + ihk = rk$$

and

$$[1 - (k/r)h]k_E + [(k/r)h]\,i = k.$$

If k is assumed to be constant, the above equation appears to indicate that k_E is determined from the weighted-average cost of capital. The weight, $(k/r)h$, will now be shown to be the percentage of total debt relative to the tangible value of the unleveraged firm.

$$\frac{kh}{r} = \frac{khB}{rB}$$

$$= \frac{hB}{rB/k}$$

$$= \frac{D}{\text{Tangible Value}}.$$

We can interpret k_E as the cost of equity for a leveraged tangible value firm (that is, a firm without franchise value). If we assume a constant debt rate, the required return on equity, k_E will increase with leverage so that k remains constant. This increasing equity capitalization rate can be viewed (in accordance with Modigliani and Miller) as a consequence of the fact that, as leverage increases, so does the riskiness of the remaining equity cash flows.

At first, it may seem surprising that regardless of the extent of the franchise value, k_E is based only on the tangible component of the firm's full market value. In fact, it can be shown that our results are mathematically equivalent to computing a risk-adjusted discount rate, k^*, for the entire equity component of the firm's market value. This more general approach would have led to precisely the same value of leveraged equity as we obtained in equation (6). Our definition of k_E generally will be larger than k*. The advantage to our decomposition is found in the simplicity and parallelism with the base P/E and FF for the unleveraged firm.

The Leveraged, Fully Taxable Firm

We now turn to the effect of taxes. In contrast to tax-free firms, taxable firms will gain from leverage. For simplicity, we assume that the full benefits of the tax shield pass directly to the corporate entity. If the annual debt payments are iD, the Tax gain is tiD, and because the debt is assumed to be priced at par, the *tax wedge* is

$$\frac{tiD}{i} = tD.$$

The value of the leveraged firm is simply the value of the unleveraged firm plus the tax wedge.

$$V^L = V^U + tD.$$

As before, the value of the leveraged firm's equity is the difference between the total value and the value of debt,

$$V_E^L = V^L - D$$

$$= V^U + tD - D$$

$$= V^U - (1 - t)\, D.$$

Thus,

$$V_E^L = V^U - (1 - t)\, h\, B. \tag{11}$$

We compute the net earnings for the taxable firm by reducing the earnings (which are assumed to be "after taxes") by the *after-tax* debt payments,

$$\text{Net Earnings} = rB - (1 - t)\, i\, h\, B$$

$$= [r - i(1 - t)h]B. \tag{12}$$

When comparing the above formulas for the equity value and net earnings with similar formulas for the tax-free firm [equations (3) and (4)], we observe that the only difference is that "h" always appears in combination with (1 - t). Consequently, the base P/E and FF for the taxable firm will be the same as in equations (9) and (10), with h replaced by (1 - t)h. That is, the taxable firm can be treated as if it were a tax-free firm with an "adjusted" leverage of (1 - t)h.

Chapter II-5

A Total Differential Approach to Equity Duration

Most of the risk associated with fixed income price movements is accounted for by their duration—that is, their sensitivity to changes in the discount rate. Thus, for bonds, duration and interest rate sensitivity are virtually synonymous. For equities, however, duration is only one of several factors describing risk.

A major source of confusion in evaluating equity duration is the definition of "duration" itself. Measured as a function of the sensitivity of stock price to the discount rate—ignoring all links between the discount rate and the growth rate—the traditional dividend discount model (DDM) duration is long—20 years or more. But this measure of duration fails to take into account the offsetting effects of inflation-induced rate increases on corporate profits.

A measure of the total sensitivity of stock prices to interest rate movements recognizes that the two components of nominal interest rates—inflation and the real rate—affect both the equity discount rate and the equity earnings growth rate, but not necessarily in the same direction. The stock market as a whole is less sensitive to changes in inflation expectations than to changes in real rates, because most companies can raise prices, hence nominal growth rates, in times of inflation. Thus a measure of stock price total sensitivity to interest rates will generally be substantially shorter than the duration measure derived from the traditional DDM.

Martin L. Leibowitz, Eric H. Sorensen, Robert D. Arnott, and H. Nicholas Hanson, "A Total Differential Approach to Equity Duration," *Financial Analysts Journal*, September/October 1989. (Received Graham & Dodd Scroll for 1989.) Reprinted with permission.

The duration of an equity portfolio—its sensitivity to the discount rate—has a meaningful impact on its relative performance. Perhaps more importantly, the duration of a portfolio has a profound effect on the match (or mismatch) between the assets in a portfolio and the interest rate sensitivity of the liabilities covered by that portfolio. Financial Accounting Standards Board Statement No. 87 will increase the importance of this correlation between assets and liabilities for plan sponsors. Any mismatch between assets and liabilities will affect the bottom line by increasing the volatility in earnings and pension surplus. There is thus a need for a more precise measure of the contribution of equities to the duration of a total portfolio.

For fixed income securities, duration accounts for the majority of the risk associated with price movements. Thus duration and interest rate sensitivity are virtually identical properties in the context of bond price behavior. For equities, duration is only one of several important factors that describe risk. An understanding of equity duration is nevertheless necessary for managing assets effectively in a liability context.

Considerable confusion has arisen regarding the "proper" measure for equity duration. The early work on equity duration was derived from valuation techniques based on some form of the dividend discount model (DDM). Equity duration was taken as the elasticity of a stock's theoretical DDM value with respect to changes in the discount rate, or "internal rate of return."

The early DDM duration calculations typically led to values ranging from 20 to 50 years, with growth companies exhibiting the longest duration values. An alternative form of analysis using straightforward regression techniques has been used to estimate empirically actual stock price sensitivity to interest rate changes. This has led to "empirical duration" values that range between two and six years—significantly less than the duration estimates derived from the DDM approach.[1]

This apparent "paradox" has important implications for the DDM model, both in terms of its theoretical underpinnings and its practical applications. This article differentiates between a stock's duration, using the DDM discount rate, and its interest rate sensitivity. We begin with the basic valuation model and then show how certain relationships can help reconcile the concepts of stock duration and interest rate sensitivity.

---

[1] See M.L. Leibowitz, "Total Portfolio Duration: A New Perspective on Asset Allocation," *Financial Analysts Journal*, September/October 1986.

EARLY DEVELOPMENT OF DURATION

Duration measures the time horizon of an asset, based on the present-value-weighted average time to receipt of income or principal. As a direct result of this formulation, Hicks and Macaulay, in the late 1930s, demonstrated that duration is the elasticity of the value of a capital asset with respect to changes in the discount factor.[2]

Much of the original duration work focused on fixed income instruments. Strategies such as dedication and bond portfolio immunization were based explicitly on the use of duration to control the risk exposure of a bond portfolio.[3] It was discovered that the structure of a bond portfolio could be adjusted so that the duration of the assets precisely matched that of the contractual liabilities, thereby leading to a nearly risk-free fit between a bond portfolio and contractual liabilities.

This structure defines interest rate sensitivity only for bonds. Enlarging the asset framework by introducing equities into the portfolio alters the potential for immunization. More generally, the way in which we view equity duration affects the degree to which we can model total portfolio duration and, thereby, control interest rate risk.

STOCK DURATION: THE DDM FORMULATION

Stock valuation, like bond valuation, provides a framework for assessing duration. Most approaches rely on a valuation equation such as the following:

$$P = \sum_{t=1}^{\infty} \frac{D_t}{(1+k)^t} , \tag{1}$$

where

P = the theoretical value of the stock,

D_t = the dividend at end of period t and

---

[2] J.R. Hicks, *Value and Capital* (Cambridge: Oxford University Press, 1939) and F.R. Macaulay, *Some Theoretical Problems Suggested by the Movement of Interest Rates, Bond Yields, and Stock Prices Since 1856* (New York: National Bureau of Economic Research, 1938).

[3] See L. Fisher and R. Weil, "Coping with the Risk of Interest Rate Fluctuations: Returns to Bondholders from Naive and Optimal Strategies," *Journal of Business*, October 1972. See also M. Hopewell and G. Kaufman, "Bond Price Volatility and Term to Maturity: A Generalized Perspective," *American Economic Review*, September 1973.

k = the discount rate.

This generalized valuation formula, which uses the dividend discount model, can be used to derive the duration of a dividend stream through iterative calculations. However, the mathematics of this formulation is complex.

The derivation of duration and calculation of sources of duration are much easier if we shift to a Gordon-Shapiro formulation for the dividend discount model. This simplification assumes that future dividends are determined by a constant growth rate. Equation (1) then becomes:

$$P = \sum_{t=1}^{\infty} \frac{D_0(1+g)^t}{(1+k)^t} , \tag{2}$$

where g is the dividend growth rate.

The Gordon-Shapiro formulation for the DDM simplifies the derivation of and implications for equity duration, without straying too far afield from the more generalized DDM structure. Equation (2) can be modified in a number of ways to model the elasticity of value with respect to changes in the discount rate.[4] Equation (2) reduces to the well known growth formula:

$$P = \frac{D_0(1+g)}{k-g}. \tag{3}$$

DDM duration, D_{DDM}, is evaluated by taking the derivative of the natural logarithm of P with respect to the discount rate. This results in:

$$D_{DDM} = -\frac{\partial \ln P}{\partial k} = \frac{1}{k-g}. \tag{4}$$

A stock with a long-term growth forecast of 10% and a discount rate of 14% would in this case have a DDM duration of 1.0/0.04, or 25 years.

MISUSE OF DDM DURATION

This formulation of DDM duration is overly simplistic because it lacks the dynamic elements of cause and effect. It assumes that the estimate of future growth in dividends (or earnings), g, is unrelated to changes in the discount rate, k.

---

[4] See E.H. Sorensen and S.B. Kreichman, "Valuation Factors: Introducing the E-MODEL" (Salomon Brothers Inc, May 12, 1987).

In reality, factors affecting the dividend growth rate will also affect the discount rate. A change in inflation, for example, may cause k to rise through the transmission mechanism of equilibrium interest rates; that is, as inflation changes, so do interest rates and capital market rates in general. But dividend growth may also respond to inflation, and this would tend to dampen the duration effect. In this case, Equation (4) would overstate true duration.

The total interest rate sensitivity of an asset relates to the impact of interest rate changes on the growth of future earnings, as well as their impact on the discount rate. Moreover, changes in the discount rate come not only from periodic shifts in interest rates, but also from changes in the overall equity market risk premium.

The duration estimates produced from Equation (4) assume that a stock's future dividend growth rate is constant. In the long run, with substantial smoothing, this may be a reasonable assumption. Over shorter intervals, however, constant growth is a poor assumption. Figure A provides a graphic representation of the 27-year history of growth in the S&P 500 dividend, as well as the history of inflation as measured by the Consumer Price Index (CPI).

It is apparent that dividends for the broad market do not grow at a constant rate, year to year. The long-term average growth in dividends is approximately 5.75%, but there is a great deal of variability of growth. Over short and intermediate investment horizons, stock prices react to the expectation of variable future

Figure A: Dividend Growth and Inflation

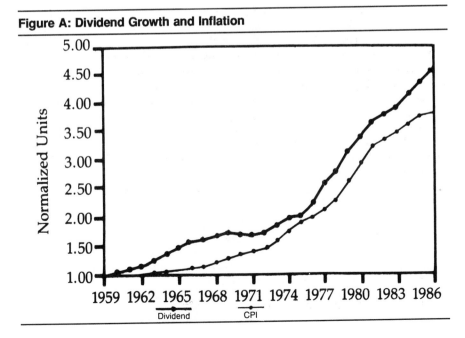

growth, rather than constant growth. The propensity for the growth rate to fluctuate implies that Equation (4) is not a realistic reflection of stock price response to interest rate change.

TOTAL INTEREST RATE SENSITIVITY

We approached equity duration from a different perspective from conventional DDM duration calculations. Our approach emphasizes the importance of covariance between changes in stock prices and changes in interest rates.[5] An important aspect of this work is the attempt to capture the statistical significance of a most important variable—actual price change. The analysis of total portfolio duration improves our ability to assess the link between stock market returns and bond market returns in targeting pension surplus.

A MODEL

A comprehensive model of equity duration requires a framework that encompasses the dynamics of both earnings growth and the equity market risk premium. Our initial assumption is that fluctuating real interest rates and the inflation component of interest rates are the underlying variables that relate changes in the interest rate and the equity risk premium to equity duration.

It is impossible to model all the possible factors that may affect discount rates, dividend growth rates and equity risk premiums.[6] We can, however, clearly identify inflation and real interest rates. These two factors alone can have a profound impact on equity duration.

To simplify the calculations, we assume that all rates are continuously compounded and all cash flows are received continuously (see the appendix). In this case, the links between the discount rate, k, the nominal interest rate, i, inflation, I, and the growth rate, g, can be expressed as:

$$k = i + h(I, r, \ldots), \tag{5}$$

$$i = r + I, \tag{6}$$

$$g = g_0 = +\gamma r + \lambda I, \tag{7}$$

---

[5] See Leibowitz, "Total Portfolio Duration," *op. cit.*

[6] See T. Estep, N. Hanson and C. Johnson, "Sources of Value and Risk in Common Stocks," *Journal of Portfolio Management*, Summer 1983.

where

    i = the nominal interest rate,

    h = the equity market risk premium,

    r = a real component of nominal rates,

    I = an inflation component of nominal rates,

    g_0 = a constant-growth parameter,

    γ = the growth rate sensitivity to real interest rates and

    λ = an inflation flow-through parameter.

The discount rate for equities, k, comprises a real return, r, an inflation rate, I, and an equity market risk premium, h. The first two factors relate directly to nominal yields in the bond market, and the third factor is the incremental discount rate in the equity market.

The growth function, g, is a modification of the constant-growth model. Variability in growth has two components. The parameter λ captures the inflation flow-through, which is the effect of inflation on the growth in corporate profits. The parameter γ measures the sensitivity of corporate profit growth rates to changes in real interest rates.

We have made the assumption that interest rates are driven by inflation and real interest rates. In addition, we have assumed that the equity discount rate and earnings growth rate are also influenced by these same two factors. It is now necessary to determine the total impact of changes in both the real rate of interest and the rate of inflation on the theoretical price. This is accomplished by computing the total differential of the price function.

Formally, the total differential for stock price is:

$$\frac{dP}{P} = -D_{DDM}\left(1 - \gamma + \frac{\partial h}{\partial r}\right)dr - D_{DDM}\left(1 - \lambda + \frac{\partial h}{\partial I}\right)dI. \tag{8}$$

This formula may look a little forbidding! Fortunately, there is considerable intuition behind the formulation. (The appendix provides the mathematical details of how to determine the total differential of the price function.)

First, Equation (8) states that price sensitivity is directly related to the DDM model, in that the higher the DDM duration, the higher the sensitivity of the stock to interest rate change. Second, an investor should think of stock duration not only as it relates to *nominal* changes in interest rates, but also as it relates to *real* changes in interest rates.

The formula has two terms. The right-hand term says that, irrespective of a stock's DDM duration, companies with high levels of inflation flow-through (say, λ approaching one), may have very low interest rate sensitivities. The left-hand term says that, notwithstanding a stock's DDM duration, companies that are adversely affected by increases in real interest rates, because of financial or business-related reasons, will have accentuated interest rate sensitivity.

THE REAL RATE VS. INFLATION

The dichotomy between the sensitivity of stock prices to inflation and their sensitivity to the real interest rate is best illustrated by an example. Suppose that (k - g) is 4%, so the D_{DDM} is 25 years. Assume that interest rates rise by 100 basis points, solely in response to investor expectations of rising inflation. In addition, assume that the equity risk premium does not change with changing inflation expectations ($\partial h / \partial I = 0$).

For the S&P 500, λ is, empirically, about 0.80.[7] In other words, 80% of any change in inflation rates tends to "flow through" equities in the form of earnings growth. A 1% inflation-induced rise in interest rates would thus cause the price of the S&P 500 to change as follows:

$$\frac{\Delta P}{P} \approx - D_{DDM} (1 - \lambda) \Delta I$$

$$= - 25(1 - 0.8)(1\%),$$

$$= - 5\%.$$

Suppose, alternatively, that nominal rates of interest rise by 100 basis points as a result of a 100-basis-point increase in real interest rates. This produces very different results. Higher real rates may increase the cost of doing business. Furthermore, a rise in real interest rates should, all else equal, increase savings relative to consumption, thereby making it difficult for firms to recover the higher costs through product pricing. In such a scenario, the sensitivity of earnings growth to a change in real interest rates may be negative, so that $(1 - \gamma)$ would exceed unity.[8]

---

[7] We have estimated the flow-through of inflation for various industries. The range of estimates is wide, but the average across all industries from 1980 to 1987 was estimated to be 0.8. In addition, the estimates depend upon how the lead-lag structure is modeled.

[8] Such a scenario is consistent with a real rate resulting from an unanticipated change in monetary policy. If, however, the rise in real rates is due to other exogenous forces, such as real economic expansion, then earnings growth sensitivity may not be negative.

Suppose that a 100-basis-point increase in real interest rates reduces dividend growth rates by 20 basis points. (And assume that $\partial h/\partial r = 0$.) This would mean that a 100-basis-point increase in real interest rates would result in a drop in stock prices of:

$$\frac{\Delta P}{P} \approx -D_{DDM}\,(1 - \lambda)\,\Delta I$$

$$= -25(1 + 0.2)(1\%),$$

$$= -30\%.$$

Figures B and C illustrate the effects of λ and γ. We can see that the stock market is much less sensitive to changes in inflation expectations than to changes in the real rate of interest. This is because most companies can raise prices and, consequently, nominal growth rates of dividends in time of inflation.

Firms with low flow-throughs, such as electric utilities, exhibit large price swings when interest rates change. By contrast, firms that are perfectly indexed to inflation ($\lambda = 1$) exhibit little, if any, price sensitivity to changes in inflation expectations. These companies could, however, demonstrate great sensitivity to interest rate changes resulting from changes in the real rate of interest.

Figure B: Price Sensitivity vs. DDM Duration for Different Flow-Throughs

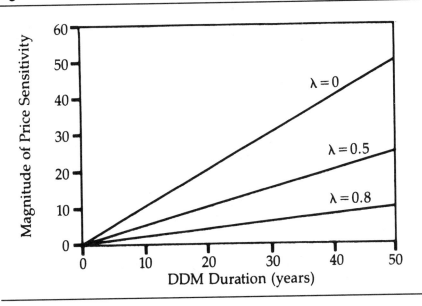

Figure C: Price Sensitivity vs. DDM Duration for Different Real Rate Sensitivities

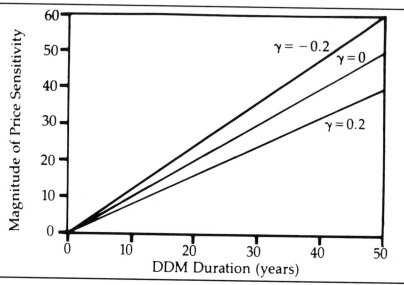

DYNAMICS OF THE RISK PREMIUM

The equity market risk premium varies over time. The risk premium is typically measured by solving the dividend discount model for the discount rate, k.[9] Risk premiums change with shifts in investors' perceptions of risk and their tolerance of it. As stock prices rise or fall, the resulting expected return, when measured against other available returns such as those for cash or bonds, reflects changes in the risk premium.

The risk premium has an important role in our duration model. DDM duration assumes that a change in the discount rate, k, is precipitated by either a change in interest rates or a change in the risk premium. The traditional DDM approach does not address the potential interaction between changing interest rate levels and changing equity risk premiums.

In Equation (8), ∂h represents the dynamic element of the risk premium. If the risk premium rises with an increase in inflation or real interest rates, then ∂h might be considered "duration-augmenting." If the risk premium falls as inflation or real rates rise, then ∂h might be considered "duration-dampening."

---

[9] See E.H. Sorensen and R.D. Arnott, "The Equity Risk Premium and Stock Market Performance," *Journal of Portfolio Management*, Summer 1988.

An analysis of the sources of returns leads us to focus on the equity risk premium and its response to changing conditions. Even if we equate risk premium changes with inflation changes, we are confronted with some surprising subtleties in the nature of ∂h.

The heart of the issue lies in the manner in which inflation shifts occur and the manner in which investors react to inflation. Consider a "burst" in inflation. On the one hand, a burst of inflation may be disruptive to investor expectations. This will undoubtedly increase economic uncertainty and, consequently, should cause the risk premium to rise. On the other hand, a burst in inflation may enhance investors' appetite for inflation protection. Because the income stream of stocks offers significant inflation protection, an inflation shock may actually reduce the risk premium for stocks.

It thus seems necessary to differentiate between two aspects of inflation. Consider a two-factor mechanism in which an external shock affects ∂I in the manner illustrated in Figure D. The first factor, ∂I_e, represents the interest rate change resulting from a change in perception about expected future inflation. The second factor, ∂I_σ, is unexpected inflation, or variability around the level of expected inflation. The impact of higher or lower inflation can be attributed jointly to changes in expected inflation and changes in uncertainty about future inflation.

Figure D: The Nature of the Inflation Shock

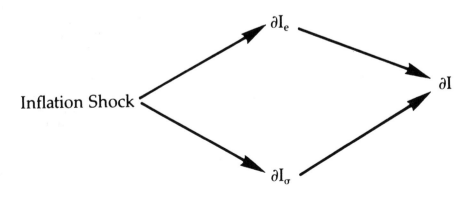

CONCLUSIONS

One of the sources of confusion in evaluating equity duration stems from the definition of the word "duration" itself. If we measure duration as a function of the sensitivity of stock price to the discount rate, k, and ignore all links between the discount rate and the growth rate or other shared factors, the result is the traditional DDM duration—typically 20 years. If we measure the sensitivity of stock prices to interest rate movements, we get a very different result. The disparity is not a result of one formulation being incorrect, but stems from the use of different definitions for duration. Our analysis resolves the apparent paradox by demonstrating the sensitivity of stock prices to a variety of factors.

We have assumed that inflation and the real rate of interest are the media linking interest rate change with discount rate change, hence with total equity duration. Whereas DDM duration may be 20 years or more, corporate profits will be largely hedged against rises in inflation. As inflation rises, pressure on equity valuations through the discount rate will be offset to some extent by increases in the expected growth of nominal profitability. Thus the sensitivity of equity prices to inflation movements will tend to be far lower than the DDM duration.

The sensitivity of stock prices to shifts in real interest rates can, theoretically, be quite significant. Because real interest rates must be defined as long-term interest rates less the expected long-term rate of inflation, the level of real interest rates is impossible to measure accurately. We can, however, demonstrate that movements in real interest rates, so defined, have a profound effect on equity valuation—of a magnitude consistent with traditional DDM duration.

In the absence of inflation flow-through or any link between the equity risk premium and inflation, interest rate sensitivity and stock duration would be synonymous and very long. In reality, flow-through is a positive number. In the long term, it can approach 1.0 for the market as a whole. This inflation flow-through largely explains why the empirical duration of equities, as measured by interest rates, is so much shorter than the calculated DDM duration as measured by the discount rate. This also suggests an important subtlety in the difference between inflation sensitivity and real interest rate sensitivity: Although interest rate changes that stem from shifts in inflation have only a modest effect on the stock market as a whole, changes in real interest rates can have a much more profound impact on equity pricing.

Appendix

Macaulay's duration is defined to be the present-value-weighted average time to receipt of a payment. Using our convention of continuous compounding and cash flows, duration is given by:

$$D = \frac{1}{P} \int_0^T td(t)e^{-kt}dt,$$

where

$$P = \int_0^T d(t)e^{-kt}dt \text{ and}$$

$d(t)$ = the dividend in period t.

We note that

$$\frac{\partial \ln P}{\partial k} = \frac{1}{P}\frac{\partial P}{\partial k} = -\frac{1}{P}\int_0^T td(t)e^{-kt} = -D.$$

This leads to the familiar interpretation of duration as a measure of the sensitivity of asset price to discount rate:

$$\frac{\Delta P}{P} \approx -D\Delta k.$$

For a stock with constant dividend growth rate,

$$d(t) = D_0e^{gt}$$

and

$$P = \int_0^\infty D_0e^{(g-k)t}\,dt = \frac{D_0}{k-g}.$$

The duration is given by:

$$D_{DDM} = -\frac{\partial \ln P}{\partial k} = \frac{1}{k-g}.$$

Because

$$k - g = \frac{D_0}{P},$$

we recognize the duration as the reciprocal of the yield.

A helpful interpretation of the duration is obtained by computing the amount of the present value that is obtained from the first t years of the payment stream. This is given by:

$$P(t) = \int_0^t D_0 e^{(g-k)t} dt$$

$$= \frac{D_0}{k-g}(1 - e^{(g-k)t}) = P(1 - e^{-t/D_{DDM}}).$$

It follows that:

$$P(D_{DDM}) = P\left(1 - \frac{1}{e}\right) = 0.63P.$$

That is, 63% of the present value of the payment stream comes from the dividends received over a time equal to the duration. Half the present value comes from:

$$P(T_{1/2}) = \frac{P}{2} = P(1 - e^{-(T_{1/2})/D_{DDM}}), \text{ or}$$

$$e^{-(T_{1/2})/D_{DDM}} = \frac{1}{2}.$$

Taking the natural logarithm of both sides, we obtain:

$$T_{1/2} = D_{DDM}\ln 2 \approx 0.7\, D_{DDM}.$$

Thus, for a constant-growth stock, 50% of the present value of the payment stream comes from dividends received over a time equal to approximately 70% of the duration. This is depicted in Figure AA for a stock that yields 10% and, therefore, has a duration equal to 10 years. As the figure illustrates, half the present value comes from the first seven years of dividends. Each successive seven-year period accounts for half the remaining present value.

Figure AA: Present Value of Dividends over Time

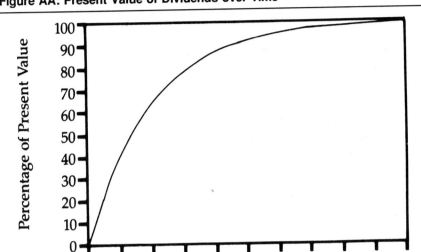

EQUITY DURATION WITH INFLATION

From Equation (3) in the text, with continuous compounding and cash flows, we get:

$$P = \frac{D_0}{k - g},$$

$$\ln P = \ln D_0 - \ln (k - g),$$

$$\frac{dP}{P} = d \ln P = \frac{\partial \ln P}{\partial k} dk + \frac{\partial \ln P}{\partial g} dg$$

$$= -\frac{1}{k - g}(dk - dg) = -D_{DDM}(dk - dg).$$

From Equations (5), (6) and (7) in the text we get:

$$dk = dr + dI + \frac{\partial h}{\partial I} dI + \frac{\partial h}{\partial r} dr,$$

$$dg = \gamma\, dr + \lambda\, dI.$$

We thus arrive at Equation (8):

$$\frac{dP}{P} = -D_{DDM}\left(1 - \gamma + \frac{\partial h}{\partial r}\right)dr - D_{DDM}\left(1 - \lambda + \frac{\partial h}{\partial I}\right)dI.$$

Equation (8) provides a convenient framework for understanding the sensitivity of stock prices to changes in interest rates. The sensitivity to changes in the real rate of interest is:

$$-D_{DDM}\left(1 - \gamma + \frac{\partial h}{\partial r}\right).$$

The sensitivity to changes in interest rates resulting from changes in inflation expectations is:

$$-D_{DDM}\left(1 - \lambda + \frac{\partial h}{\partial I}\right).$$

Chapter II-6

The Persistence of Risk: Stocks versus Bonds over the Long Term

One of the most common tenets of investing holds that the asset with the highest expected return over the long run is virtually certain to provide superior performance. Thus investors are willing to bear the greater short-term risks associated with equities as compared with bonds, say, because they know the equities will eventually outperform the bonds. But risk doesn't disappear over time. According to standard analytical models, an equity portfolio is virtually certain to outperform a fixed income portfolio over a long enough period. But 10, or even 30, years may not be "long enough."

A simple model using standard assumptions about asset volatilities and risk premiums, for example, shows that a stock portfolio has a 32% chance of underperforming a bond portfolio over a 10-year horizon. Even after 30 years, there remains a substantial 21% probability that stocks will fall short of bonds.

Investment decisions are often framed in terms of the appropriate tradeoff between risk and expected return. A further dimension arises when the investor must balance long-term goals with short-term concerns. Greater short-term risk is viewed as the price of better "long-term" returns. Long-term returns seem to be naturally associated with better "expected returns" and with the hope that

Martin L. Leibowitz and William S. Krasker, "The Persistence of Risk: Stocks Versus Bonds Over the Long Term," *Financial Analysts Journal*, November/December 1988. (Received Graham & Dodd Scroll for 1988.) Reprinted with permission.

short-term risks will fade when compared with the return growth over the long run.

Such long-term return/short-term risk rationales underlie many investment situations, including stock/bond allocations, yield curve maturity selections, yield pickup bond swaps, and high-yield/low-yield currency preferences. In all these situations, a key question is whether the greater expected returns will eventually overwhelm the impact of the associated risks. For most investors, intuition implies that they will. However, given the standard analytical models, we can show that there are many cases in which this intuition has theoretical justification only for the very long "long run." Over the more relevant intermediate term, the standard model gives rise to a more complex pattern that includes some strikingly counterintuitive results.

If we extrapolate the standard input assumptions, an equity portfolio is virtually certain to outperform any fixed income investment over a long enough period. The question is what constitutes "long enough." Most investors would be surprised to learn that these assumptions imply that, after 10 years, there is a 32% probability that a stock portfolio will underperform a bond benchmark. After 20 years, the shortfall probability is still slightly above 25%. Even more striking, after 30 years the probability that bonds will outrun stocks remains a hefty 21%. These results follow directly from the evolution over time of the theoretical probability distribution for relative returns.

In general, the standard models focus on the variance of the short-term return as a measure of risk. Because our analysis is based on such models, the only long-term risk discussed below is the accumulated impact of this variability. It should be pointed out, however, that these standard models are patently simplistic. There are more facets to return than a constant, nominal-dollar expected return, and there are surely more dimensions to long-term risk than the accumulation of short-term variability (for example, credit risks, disaster scenarios, major secular reversals). Nevertheless, despite their limitations, these standard models have a widespread impact in practice, where they are both applied explicitly and form an implicit basis for intuitive decisions. It is therefore important to trace more fully their implications for the persistence of shortfall risks over the two to 30-year intermediate term that forms the relevant period for most of us mortals and our institutions.

DISTRIBUTION OF RETURNS OVER TIME

We base our analysis on a theoretical model of asset returns, in which successive returns are independent and have lognormal probability distributions. Specifically, the logarithmic return—the logarithm of one plus the ordinary return—has the familiar bell-shaped normal distribution. Figure A depicts the resulting lognormal distribution for the value of an equity portfolio in one year, assuming

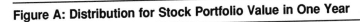

Figure A: Distribution for Stock Portfolio Value in One Year

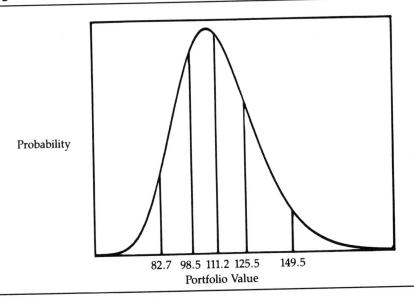

Probability

82.7 98.5 111.2 125.5   149.5

Portfolio Value

that its initial value is 100, the expected return is 13% and the logarithmic volatility—the standard deviation of the logarithmic return—is 18%.[1]

At the end of the one-year period, the expected value (or mean) of the portfolio is 113. As shown, there is a 0.25 probability that the portfolio value will be above 125.5 and a 0.25 probability that the portfolio value will be below 98.5. In addition, there is a 0.05 probability that the portfolio value will exceed 149.5, but also a 0.05 probability that it will fall below 82.7. Moreover, the 50th percentile (the median) occurs at 111.2. This value differs slightly from the mean of 113, reflecting a modest skewness in the distribution.

Figure B introduces an alternative graphic representation of the percentiles to illustrate how the probability distribution for the value of the equity portfolio changes as the number of years in the fund horizon increases. The boxes represent the distributions at one, two and three-year horizons and show explicitly the expected value as "handlebars," as well as the fifth, 25th, 50th, 75th and 95th percentiles of the distribution. (The percentiles in the first-year box correspond with those in Figure A.)

---

[1] The ordinary expected return, R, the expected logarithmic return, μ, and the volatility, σ, are related by the following formula: $\log (1 + R) = \mu + 1/20^2$.

Figure B: Distribution for Stock Portfolio Value at Different Horizons

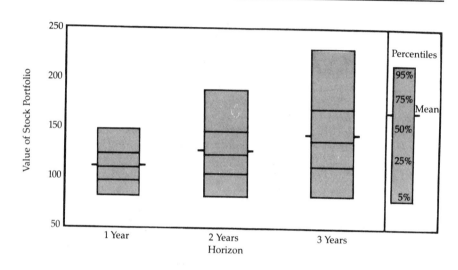

Although the expected portfolio value increases steadily as the horizon is lengthened, the variability also rises; the net effect on the downside risk thus depends on the particular percentile selected. For example, if we measure the risk by the 25th percentile—the level below which the portfolio has only a 0.25 probability of falling—this return threshold rises from one year to the next. If we focus instead on the fifth percentile—the bottom of the boxes—the return threshold value remains nearly the same.

THE STOCK/BOND RATIO

Figures A and B depict the absolute returns from all-equity portfolios. Figure C compares the probability distributions for the value of the equity portfolio at different horizons with the value of a bond portfolio having the same starting value of 100. The bond portfolio has an expected return of 9% and a logarithmic volatility of 10%, roughly corresponding to a portfolio with a six-year effective duration (or a par bond maturity of approximately 10 years at the outset).

Figure C shows that although the expected portfolio value is smaller for bonds, the risk is also substantially lower. At a three-year horizon, the bond value exceeds 95.9 with a 0.95 probability (that is, the bottom of the box). For

Figure C: Stock and Bond Distributions

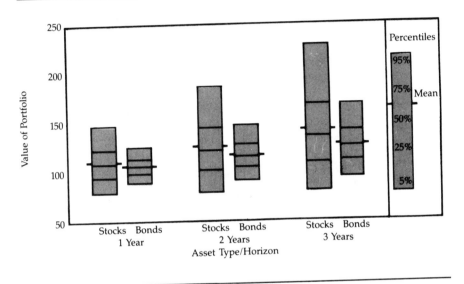

this same probability, the wider stock distribution can provide a threshold of only 82.3.

With constant absolute levels of expected returns, these results cannot be extended beyond short horizons. Indeed, the very existence of uncertainty about bond returns implies changes in yields, which presumably imply changes in expected returns. Therefore, for the remainder of this article we shall assume that it is the *relative* risk premium that remains constant. More precisely, for technical reasons we will keep the difference between the expected stock logarithmic return and the expected bond logarithmic return at a constant level that closely approximates a 4% ordinary one-year risk premium. In addition, we will assume the same asset volatilities used earlier and make a more or less standard correlation assumption of 0.4 between the stock and bond logarithmic returns.

Now consider the ratio of the cumulative value of a 100% stock portfolio to the cumulative value of a 100% bond portfolio. Figure D shows the probability boxes for the stock/bond ratio for horizons of up to three years. A ratio of 100% means that the stock and bond portfolios are equal, while ratios greater than 100% imply that the stock value exceeds the bond value. Clearly, on average, a pension fund would achieve a better performance from stocks over a three-year period: The expected value of the ratio of stocks to bonds grows to 112.4% by the third year. However, the figure also shows that there is substantial risk at

Figure D: Ratio of Stock Portfolio Value to Bond Portfolio Value

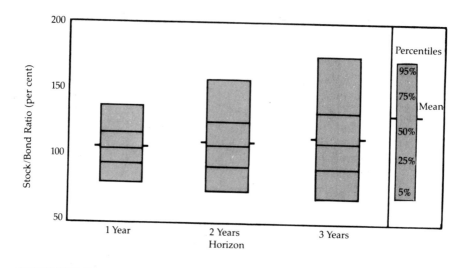

the three-year horizon. At that date, there is a 25% probability that the ratio of stock value to bond value will be less than 88.6%.

The probability that the stock value will fall below the bond value remains high even for what would normally be regarded as the long run. Figure E shows this shortfall probability as a function of the number of years in the horizon. At a 20-year horizon, there is still a 25% probability that the bond value will exceed the stock value. At the same time, the expected value of the stock/bond ratio grows to an attractive 217% over 20 years. Clearly, for these long horizons, the prospect of exciting (and even stellar) relative performance appears to coexist with the significant probability of shortfalls. Although these precise numerical results depend on the selected volatilities, correlation and expected change in the stock/bond ratio, the qualitative conclusions about the persistence of risk hold for any reasonable range of these parameters.

The presence of a high expected value for the stock/bond ratio, despite a substantial probability that the ratio will be less than 100%, is a manifestation of the pronounced skewness that develops as time passes. As Figure F shows, the distribution at the 20-year horizon simply does not have the symmetry that most people tend to visualize. The stock/bond ratio is considerably more likely to be below its expected value of 217% than above, and, in fact, the median of the distribution is only 164%. Offsetting this, however, is the fact that the distri-

Figure E: Probability that Bond Portfolio Value Exceeds Stock Portfolio Value

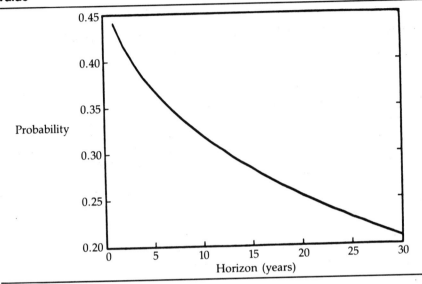

Figure F: Distribution for Stock/Bond Ratio in 20 Years

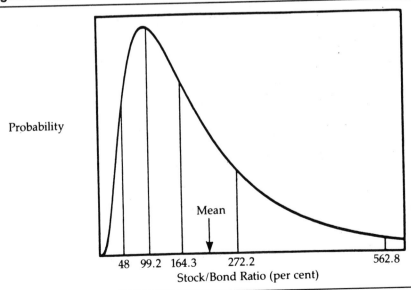

bution has a very "long tail" on the upside. For example, there is a 5% chance that the ratio will exceed 563%.

SHORTFALL PROBABILITIES FOR SPECIFIED STOCK/BOND RATIOS

One way to evaluate the riskiness of stocks relative to bonds—or to pension liabilities, which have roughly similar risk characteristics in a nominal-dollar framework—is to choose a particular shortfall level and determine the probability that the ratio of stock value to bond value will fall below that level. Figure G shows this shortfall probability as a function of the years in the horizon for several specified stock bond ratios. (The case in which the ratio equals 1.0 is the same as that in Figure F.)

The curves slope downward when the number of years to the horizon becomes very large. This is a consequence of the intuitive notion that, in the long run, the higher expected return of equities must dominate its larger standard deviation. However, Figure G contains two surprises. First, for certain outcomes, such as a ratio of 90% or 80%, the probability actually increases at the beginning. (This can be interpreted in terms of the minimum time span required for bad

Figure G: Shortfall Probabilities for Specified Stock/Bond Ratios

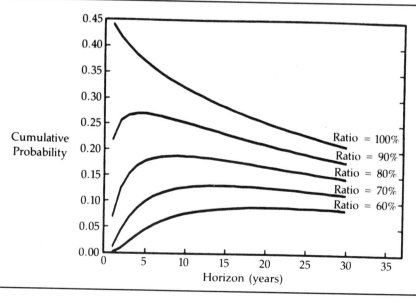

shortfalls to develop.) This growth in risk continues for several years: The risk of falling below a 60% shortfall level is substantially higher at a 10-year, or even a 15-year, horizon than at a one-year horizon. The second surprising finding, which emerges most clearly in the graph corresponding to the 90% shortfall level, is that even when the curve becomes downward sloping, it takes a very long time to reach a low probability level.

Suppose, for example, that a pension fund manager views a funding ratio of 80% of its current level as an unacceptable shortfall and would like to know the probability that the level will be penetrated. According to Figure G, the probability of such a shortfall is only 7% if the horizon is one year, but it rises to 19% if the horizon is 10 years. The probability remains at a high 17% even with a 20-year horizon.

STOCK/BOND PERCENTILES OVER TIME

Another way to measure the shortfall risk is by percentiles of the probability distribution for the stock/bond ratio. Specifically, we choose a particular probability of a shortfall and then compute the stock/bond ratio to which it corresponds.

Figure H shows these percentile ratios as a function of the number of years in the horizon for several different shortfall probabilities. Once again, intuition would at first suggest that these shortfall percentiles should improve with longer time horizons. Specifically, for a given probability of shortfall, we might expect the shortfall level to be an increasing function of the time to the horizon.

This turns out to be consistently true only after a transition period, which can be surprisingly long. Over relevant horizons, such as 10 or 20 years, the relationship can be just the opposite. For example, the 10th percentile of the stock/bond ratio does not reach its minimum—63%—until the horizon is 19 years.

EFFECTS OF DIFFERENT RISK PREMIUMS AND CORRELATIONS

The preceding analysis has been based on our assumption that the logarithmic risk premium is constant at a level that implies an ordinary risk premium of approximately 4%. Not surprisingly, the results are sensitive to the value that is assumed for this risk premium.

Figure I graphs the 10th-percentile shortfall level as a function of the number of years in the horizon for several different logarithmic risk premiums. The curves are labeled by the ordinary risk premiums to which they correspond

Figure H: Percentiles of Stock/Bond Ratio

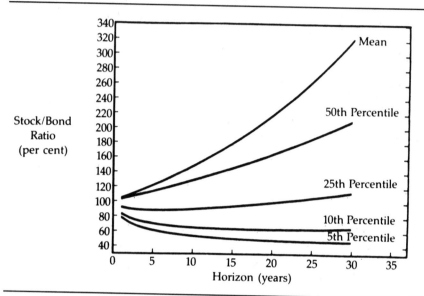

Figure I: Shortfall Levels for Different Risk Premiums

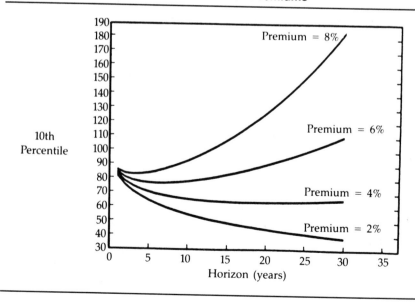

Figure J: Shortfall Levels for Different Correlations

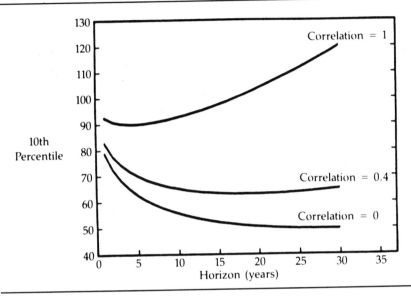

when the bond expected return is 9%. (The curve for the risk premium of 4% matches the 10th-percentile curve in Figure H.)

In effect, the larger the risk premium, the shorter the time period necessary for the "long-run" effects to take hold. For example, with the original risk premium of 4%, the 10th percentile of the stock/bond ratio does not reach its minimum until the horizon reaches 19 years. However, with an 8% risk premium, the 10th percentile achieves its smallest value at a three-year horizon.

In the standard asset allocation problem, lower correlations represent a desirable opportunity for diversification. However, when one is dealing with relative returns—either relative to a benchmark index or to a liability framework—it turns out that higher correlations are desirable.[2] These results are illustrated in Figure J, which shows the acceleration of the "long-run" benefits for the hypothetical case of perfect correlation (as well as the deceleration for the case of zero correlation). These correlation effects become significant in various bond-to-bond comparisons, or when a bond portfolio is compared with an interest-rate-related benchmark.

---

[2] See "Portfolio Optimization Under Shortfall Constraints: A Confidence Limit Approach to Managing Downside Risk" (Salomon Brothers Inc, New York, August 1987).

CONCLUSION

These results are based on a highly simplistic model, in which the probability distribution for percentage changes in the stock/bond ratio is constant over time. There is no explicit treatment for inflation, macroeconomic cycles or profit growth. We assume a rigid long-term adherence to the asset class, with all incremental returns implicitly reinvested in the original asset structure. There is no provision for active management or portfolio-rebalancing strategies which could reduce the likelihood of the most adverse outcomes.

In other words, these results could be nothing more than a mathematical curiosity spawned by pushing short-term models too far into the future. Consequently, considerable caution should be exercised when taking the extrapolations of such models as a literal characterization of long-term return prospects for any asset class.

Nevertheless, our core finding sheds important light on certain perceptions that have become embedded in our investment mythology. One such article of faith is that a steadfast adherence to the "asset of choice" with the highest expected return will, over time, virtually ensure a superior performance. However, over long time periods, even while return expectations grow ever more favorable, risks refuse to fade. Risk persists—and at surprisingly high levels of significance. Even the most determinedly long-run investor—one who has steeled himself to persevere relentlessly through repeated bouts of short-term turmoil—will find that he must still come to grips with long-term risk and its continuing uncertainty.

Chapter II-7

Equity Risk Premiums and the "Volatility Drag"

INTRODUCTION

Equity investors are naturally disappointed when the performance of their stock portfolio falls below the level of bond returns. In two recent studies, this "shortfall risk" was shown to be surprisingly high and to remain high over long periods of time.[1] Under standard return volatility assumptions, the shortfall probability of stocks relative to bonds was found to be 44% after one year, 39% after three years, 36% after five years, and 24% after 20 years.

These results were based upon an assumed 4% equity "risk premium"—the expected year-to-year return increment for stocks over bonds. This 4% value, while well below the historical arithmetic average risk premium of 6.8% for the 1926-87 period, was used because it is representative of estimates currently being used in long-term asset allocation studies. At *higher* risk premiums (more than 4%), the shortfall risk was shown to be lower, but still remained at troubling levels over long time horizons. In this paper, we examine the impact of *low* risk premiums—for example, 0% and 2%. The theoretical case of a 0% risk pre-

---

[1] See *The Persistence of Risk*, Salomon Brothers Inc, May 1988; and *Shortfall Risks and the Asset Allocation Decision*, Salomon Brothers Inc, January 1989.

Martin L. Leibowitz, Stanley Kogelman, and Terence C. Langetieg, "Equity Risk Premiums and the 'Volatility Drag,'" Salomon Brothers Inc, April 1989.

mium provides a clear illustration of an important investment phenomenon that we call the "volatility drag." Through some simple examples, we will show how this "drag" reduces the compound return of any volatile investment.

Recently, several market observers have suggested that risk premiums of 2%-2 1/2% might be embedded in the equity markets, both in the United States and abroad. If these risk premiums are interpreted as an expected annual increment over bond yields, the volatility drag will be especially important. We will show that such low risk premiums lead to a drastically higher probability that equity will underperform bonds over virtually all relevant investment horizons. For example, with a 2% risk premium, the equity investor is subject to a 46% probability of underperformance over a five-year horizon. Consequently, risk premiums as low as 2% may be inconsistent with the notion of a positive risk/return trade-off and, hence, may be inherently unstable. Investors who anticipate such low arithmetic risk premiums should realize that this forecast may have major (and rather immediate) implications for their asset allocation.

ANNUALIZED COMPOUND RETURN

The performance of a portfolio over time is measured generally by its annualized compound return. While historical returns often are reported as the *arithmetic* average of annual returns over the period in question, this average likely will overstate the portfolio's compound growth rate.

We illustrate this property by considering several interest rate scenarios over a three-year horizon. For example, if the portfolio return is 5%, 10% and 12% in years 1, 2 and 3, respectively, the average value of these annual returns is 9%. Over a three-year period, a $1.00 investment would grow to:

$$1.05 \times 1.10 \times 1.12 = 1.2936$$

The annualized compound return, 8.96%, then satisfies the relationship:

$$(1 + 0.0896)^3 = 1.2936$$

Thus, if $1.00 grew at the rate of 8.96% compounded annually, its value at the end of three years would be $1.2936; this same final value would be attained if $1.00 grew by 5% in year 1, by an additional 10% in year 2, and finally by 12% in year 3. Thus, the annualized compound return, 8.96%, is a single number that represents the average year-to-year growth of a portfolio.

In Figure 1, we illustrate several return sequences that have an arithmetic average of 9.00% per year. However, the portfolio performance at the end of three years, as measured by the annualized compound return, can be extremely sensitive to the actual sequence of year-by-year returns.

Figure 1: Arithmetic Average versus Annualized Compound Return

Year	Path of Annual Return					
	A	**B**	**C**	**D**	**E**	**F**
1	9%	5%	0%	0%	-1%	-5%
2	9	10	7	0	-1	-8
3	9	12	20	27	29	40
Average Return	9.00%	9.00%	9.00%	9.00%	9.00%	9.00%
Compound Return	9.00	8.96	8.69	8.29	8.13	6.96
Volatility (Std. Deviation)	0.00	2.94	8.29	12.73	14.14	21.95

Note that the highest three-year portfolio value is 1.2950 (1.09 × 1.09 × 1.09) as achieved in Case A. The lowest, 1.2236, is a result of the return sequence in Case F (0.95 × 0.92 × 1.40). In all cases, higher volatility leads to lower portfolio growth and to a lower annualized compound return.

THE COST OF VOLATILITY

The preceding examples illustrate the effect of "volatility drag" in a simple historical context. The same drag effect is encountered when estimating prospective portfolio growth, but it acts in a more complex fashion. This drag becomes particularly important when comparing high-volatility asset classes such as equities with lower-volatility classes such as short- or intermediate-term bond portfolios.

Another simple way to see this effect is to consider a hypothetical asset that, through a series of alternating better and worse years, provides an arithmetic average return, r, over time. Let x represent the variability from r. In good years, the realized return is (r + x), while in bad years, the return is (r - x). The *compound* growth over any two-year period, therefore, will be:

$$[(1 + r) + x] [(1 + r) - x] = (1 + r)^2 - x^2$$

The greater the deviation, x, from the average return, the greater the reduction in the compound growth.

Our simplistic example is intended only to provide an intuitive feel for how an increasing proportion of outcomes falls below the compounded value of the expected one-year return. Over long time horizons, volatility drag leads to a skewed distribution of portfolio values with a small number of truly spectacular outcomes being offset by a very high concentration of relatively mediocre results. For example, suppose that both stocks and bonds have an average year-to-year return of 9% (that is, the equity risk premium is 0%), but stock returns are

Figure 2: Distribution of 20-Year Equity Values (0% Risk Premium, 17% Volatility)

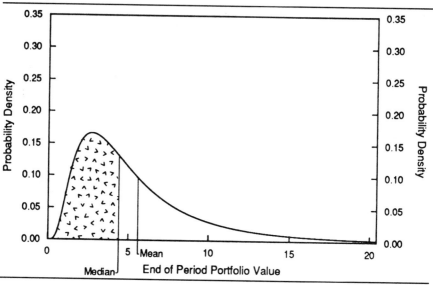

Figure 3: Distribution of 20-Year Bond Values (9% Year-to-Year Return)

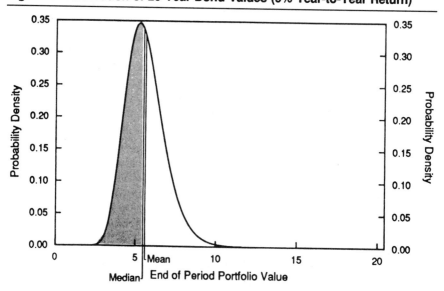

considerably more volatile than bond returns. Then, the distribution of equity returns will be quite skewed, as illustrated in Figure 2. Here, we show the distribution of values of a $1 equity portfolio after 20 years. We assume that the returns are lognormally distributed with a 17% volatility. Observe that the median of the distribution, $4.41, is considerably to the left of the mean portfolio value, which is $5.60.[2]

In Figure 3, we show the distribution of a $1 bond portfolio after 20 years. The expected one-year bond return also is assumed to be 90%, with a volatility that approximates that of the Salomon Brothers Broad Investment-Grade Bond Index[SM]. Note that the low volatility of bond returns in comparison to equity returns leads to a distribution of values that is only slightly skewed. In particular, the median bond portfolio value falls only slightly to the left of the mean, which is $5.60.

To facilitate comparison, we combine Figures 2 and 3 in Figure 4. Here, it is evident that the variance of the equity portfolio value is far greater than that of the bond portfolio. However, the primary point to observe is the striking difference in the shape of the two distributions.

Note that the distribution of equity values is both flatter and more highly skewed. This asymmetry is further evidenced by the equity median of 4.41, which lies far to the left of the bond median (5.48) and the common mean of 5.60.

The effect of volatility on the annualized compound return and on the distribution of portfolio values over time has many complex facets and has been the subject of numerous articles in the financial literature over the past 20 years.[3] Although a full discussion of the underlying mathematics is beyond the scope of this publication, we demonstrate below that the impact of volatility drag becomes particularly evident when stated in terms of shortfall probabilities.

SHORTFALL RISK

In an earlier paper, we presented the results of a simulation study on the relative growth in stock and bond portfolios over various horizons.[4] One measure of comparison was the shortfall risk—the probability that an all-stock portfolio would underperform an all-bond portfolio. The base case parameters used were

---

[2] The mean, 5.60, can be shown to be the one-year expected portfolio value compounded for 20 years, that is, $5.60 = (1 + 0.09)^{20}$.

[3] For the benefit of the interested reader, we include an abbreviated bibliography at the end of this chapter.

[4] See *Shortfall Risks and the Asset Allocation Decision*.

Figure 4: Distribution of 20-Year Portfolio Values (0% Risk Premium, 17% Stock Volatility)

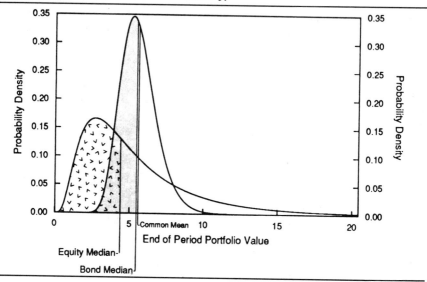

Figure 5: Probability that Stocks Will Underperform Bonds: 4% Risk Premium

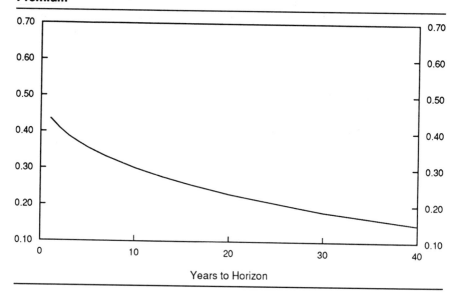

an initial bond yield of 9%, an equity risk premium of 4% and, thus, an expected equity return of 13% at the outset. The shortfall probability resulting from these simulations is plotted for various time horizons in Figure 5: The shortfall risk declines from 44% after one year to 36% after five years and to 24% after 20 years.

In Figure 6, we show the results for new simulations conducted with a 0% premium. In this case, the initial return expectation for both bonds and stocks is 9%. As bond yields varied over time, the expected stock return always coincided with the new yield value; that is, the risk premium remained constant at 0%. Because the volatility of stocks was maintained at 17%, the results of the simulation entirely reflect "volatility drag." The contrast between the two shortfall probability curves is dramatic. For the 0% premium, the shortfall risk rises with time—from 53% after one year to 61% after 20 years.

In other words, even if bonds and stocks have exactly the same expected return over each one-year period, the greater volatility of stocks leads to a 61% probability that they will underperform bonds after 20 years.

There is an even more fundamental difference between the 0% and the 4% risk premium cases. If we were to carry out the 4% premium simulation for a long enough period (as if 20 years were too short), the shortfall risk would approach 0%. This corresponds to most investors' intuitions: Over a sufficiently long time, the incremental return of stocks dominates their greater relative vola-

Figure 6: Probability that Stocks Will Underperform Bonds: 0% versus 4% Risk Premiums

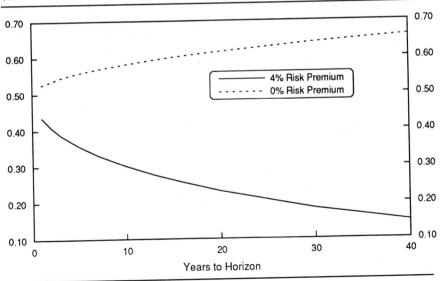

Years to Horizon

tility, and the equity investor ultimately will be assured of achieving returns superior to bonds. However, for a 0% stock risk premium, just the opposite holds true. Over a long enough time period, the shortfall risk approaches 100%. A stock investment ultimately will underperform a less volatile bond investment. These results can be explained readily in terms of our earlier discussion of the volatility drag.

RISK PREMIUMS AND THE COMPOUND RETURN

Our simulations were based upon a constant risk premium for each annual period. For example, the earlier paper used a one-year risk premium value of 4% as a base case. In each year, the expected return from stocks was then determined by adding this 4% value to the simulated bond yield at the beginning of that year. Thus, for example, if the bond yield were 7% at the start of the sixth year, the expected stock return would be 11% for that year. Even though the return advantage was kept constant in each individual year, the greater volatility of stocks erodes this advantage *over a period of years*. This erosion is caused by the volatility drag.

The magnitude of this volatility drag is illustrated in Figure 7, which is reproduced from our earlier report. Here, the compound return declines from 13.0% for the first year to 11.8% over the 20-year period. In this figure, each bar represents the 80% confidence interval for the annualized compound stock return at the end of the indicated year. The bars are divided by lines corresponding to the 10th, 25th, 50th, 75th, and 90th percentiles. Note that, over time, the mean return (as indicated by the "handlebars") moves toward the median (50th percentile return). For very long time periods (longer than 20 years), our simulation shows that the expected compound return for stocks will decline to 13.0% - 1.3% = 11.7%. (This assumes a 17% annual volatility and a lognormal return distribution.)[5]

It should be noted that this "volatility drag" acts directly upon the return dimension. It is above and beyond the role of volatility as a major component of the risk dimension. In other words, although volatility often is viewed as a primary gauge of *risk*, it also has a significant effect in reducing *probable return* over longer time horizons.

---

[5] For the mathematically curious, we note that the relationship between the expected compound return and the expected one-year return over long time periods can be approximated by:

$$\text{Expected Compound Return} \approx \sqrt{(1 + \text{Expected One–Year Return})^2 - (\text{Volatility})^2} - 1$$

This formula can be found in the references provided at the end of this chapter.

Figure 7: Annualized Compound Returns for Stocks: 4% Risk Premium

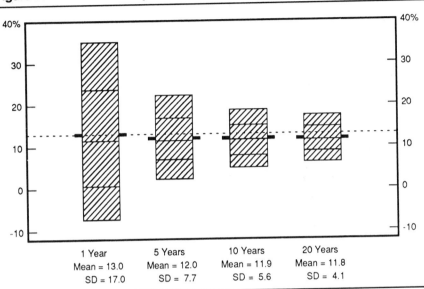

	1 Year	5 Years	10 Years	20 Years
Mean =	13.0	12.0	11.9	11.8
SD =	17.0	7.7	5.6	4.1

Because the bond returns have low volatility, there will be little drag effect, and the expected compound return for bonds will remain close to the initial 9% level. Thus, the incremental return for equity can be viewed as eroding from 4.0% over one year down to 2.7% over a very long period. The risk premium's impact on the compound return erodes with time, even when the premium itself remains at a constant 4% in any given year.

We can now explain the shortfall risk results for the 0% risk premium. Figure 8 shows the annualized compound return for stocks given a risk premium of 0%. In this case, stocks and bonds have the same expected return over any one-year period, but because of equity's greater volatility, its incremental return over a long horizon actually will be a *negative* 1.3%; that is, stocks will have a *lower* expected annualized compound return than bonds. Observe that the shortfall risk worsens with longer time horizons. Eventually, the stocks' annualized compound return clusters around 9.0% - 1.3% = 7.7% and is dominated by the bond's 9.0% expected return. After a long period of time, the return differences overwhelm the volatility effects, and the shortfall risk approaches 100%.

The 1.3% decrement (at a volatility level of 17%) may be viewed as a "break-even" risk premium. For risk premiums above 1.3%, the shortfall probability will decrease with time; risk premiums below 1.3% lead to a shortfall probability that increases with time. However, as we see later in this paper, risk premiums

Figure 8: Annualized Compound Returns for Stocks: 0% Risk Premium

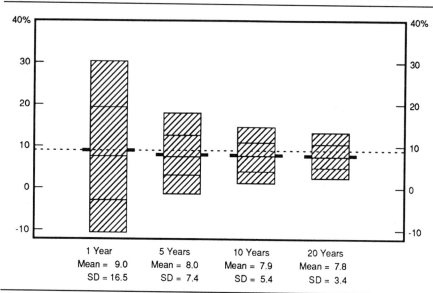

	1 Year	5 Years	10 Years	20 Years
Mean =	9.0	8.0	7.9	7.8
SD =	16.5	7.4	5.4	3.4

that are not substantially greater than 1.3% may fail to provide adequate compensation for the shortfall risk that must be endured.

SPECIFICATION OF RISK PREMIUMS

Because risk premiums are relatively small, with estimates ranging from an arithmetic average of 2% to 6%, the long-term decrement of -1.3% will have a severe impact on long-term returns as measured by the annualized compound return. Therefore, it is critically important that risk premium estimates be clearly identified as being either one-year expected values or long-term annualized compound return increments. In our preceding paper, we defined the risk premium to be the one-year expected value. This seems to be the most natural choice, and it appears to be the interpretation applied in most asset allocation studies. In addition, it is consistent with standard empirical volatility estimates, which are based on the distribution of year-to-year returns. Nevertheless, because one could use either definition, it is important to be clear in the meaning intended.

Figure 9: Probability that Stocks Will Underperform Bonds: 0%, 2% and 4% Risk Premiums

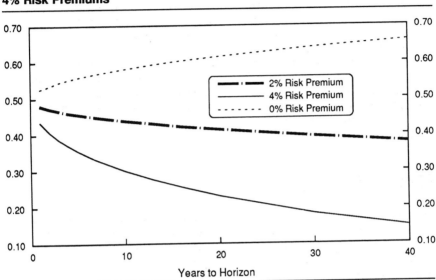

Years to Horizon

THE 2% RISK PREMIUM

The need for clarity in risk premium specification becomes particularly important when performing analysis using risk premiums as low as 2%. Recently, several analysts have put forth 2%-2 1/2% as an estimate of the equity risk premium embedded in the recent market structure. If we interpret this 2% value as a one-year expected return increment, we can draw several quite dramatic conclusions.

Figure 9 shows the shortfall probability as a function of time for the 2% premium case. The results generally fall between the curves for the 4% premium and the 0% premium. However, the 2% case presents one distinctive result: In the two preceding cases, the shortfall risk fell or rose significantly over time. For the 2% case, the shortfall risk varies very little (from 48% to 41%) over time horizons ranging from one year to 20 years. Indeed, over a 40-year horizon (which is far beyond that of even the most patient investor), the shortfall risk still remains at a high 38%. By contrast, with a 4% risk premium, the shortfall risk drops to 15% over 40 years, while it rises to 68% with a 0% risk premium.

The striking aspect of this finding is not just the stability of shortfall risk associated with a 2% risk premium, but the sustained high level of risk. Somehow, it is difficult to believe that many equity investors would feel comfortable in a market that exposed them to over a 40% probability of underperforming bonds over *any relevant investment horizon*. Thus, if the 2% risk premium were to become the widespread estimate, one would expect fairly significant realloca- tions away from equities. As a result, a long-term 2% risk premium *as a one-year expected return increment* does not appear to provide sufficient compensation for the high risk level of equities.

If the 2% risk premium is unsustainable as a long-run consensus estimate, the stock market will have to adjust to levels that reflect a higher reward for bearing risk. Such realignments in the equity risk premium can be achieved only through quite dramatic market moves. For example, to increase the risk pre- mium by 1% through equity price action alone, the equity market would have to decline from 20% to 30%. [6]

CONCLUSION

The concept of risk premium plays a central role in equity valuation and in the assessment of risk/return trade-offs. Because market analysts have generally come to believe that the historical risk premiums provide only a hazy guide to the future, this places a greater importance on the process of estimating for- ward-looking risk premiums. In turn, this argues for a far deeper appreciation of the many implications of such forecasts for the equity investor, as well as for the asset allocation decision.

---

[6] See *A Total Differential Approach to Equity Duration*, Salomon Brothers Inc, September 1987.

Bibliography

Nils H. Hakansson, "Multi-Period Mean-Variance Analysis: Toward a General Theory of Portfolio Choice," *Journal of Finance*, Vol. 26, July 1971.

Henry A. Latané, "Criteria for Choice Among Risky Ventures," *Journal of Political Economy* 62, April 1969.

Richard W. McEnally, "Latané's Bequest: The Best of Portfolio Strategies," *The Journal of Portfolio Management*, Winter 1986.

Richard O. Michaud, "Risk Policy and Long-Term Investment," *Journal of Financial and Quantitative Analysis*, Vol. 16, June 1981.

Paul A. Samuelson and Robert C. Merton, "Generalized Mean-Variance Tradeoffs for Best Perturbation Corrections to Approximate Portfolio Decisions," *Journal of Finance*, Vol. 39, March 1974.

Chapter II-8

Bond Equivalents of Stock Returns

The dividend growth model reveals stocks as very deep discount bonds—with surprising insights as to their comparative values.

Any bond portfolio manager considering diverting a portion of his long-term bond money into high yielding common stocks should recognize that he is undertaking a very complex evaluation. Vast differences exist between the bondholder and the stockholder. The bondholder is a creditor. The stockholder is an owner, and must accept all the special risks and uncertainties of corporate ownership. As investment vehicles, there are fundamental differences between bonds and stocks. Each specific bond-to-stock situation requires a probing analysis of these differences.

If a bond portfolio manager makes a deliberate decision to accept the *added risk that is clearly associated with common stock*, then there arises the calculational problem of insuring that any comparisons of stock-to-bond returns are based upon a mathematically consistent procedure. These comparisons often take the form of viewing the stock's estimated rate of return in terms of an interest rate spread over the bond's conventional yield-to-maturity. Even when there is a full recognition of all the risks and uncertainties involved in any given estimate of a stock's rate of return, any such spread comparison will still suffer from a rather substantial problem of computational technique. Such stock-to-bond comparisons are analogous to looking solely at conventional yields when evaluating a

Martin L. Leibowitz, "Bond Equivalents of Stock Returns," *The Journal of Portfolio Management*, Spring 1978. Reprinted with permission.

447

straight bond-to-bond swap over a long-term horizon. For a compounding bond portfolio, this conventional yield comparison can be misleading, because it neglects the effect of coupon reinvestment. When this reinvestment effect is properly taken into account, low coupon discount bonds display a structural advantage over par bonds that is not reflected in the conventional yield spread.

For stocks that might be considered as potential bond substitutes, estimates of the long-term rate of return are often based upon some form of the dividend growth model. The use of such a highly simplified model in itself represents a major investment decision, especially in light of the model's tacit assumptions that the stock's dividend producing capability will remain in a continual uptrend and that the company's credit worthiness will remain essentially unimpaired.

Once a decision has been made to use this model with any given dividend growth value (or range of values), the stock's estimated cash flow will have many of the characteristics of a very deep discount bond. In particular, it will provide considerable structural protection against the usual degradation in effective return associated with the lower reinvestment rates assumed by most bond portfolio managers. Consequently, any given estimate of the stock's conventional rate of return will tend to significantly *understate* the stock's relative value as a bond substitute.

This memorandum suggests a technique for dealing with this reinvestment effect so as to provide for more accurate bond-to-stock comparisons.

THE DIVIDEND GROWTH MODEL

The returns from common stocks—especially the "income stocks" of utility companies—are often analyzed in terms of a simple dividend growth model. In its most basic form, the stock is assumed to produce a stream of dividends that grows at *some* uniform, compound rate over time. At the investment horizon, the stock price is then determined in terms of an assumed future dividend yield. Over the time to a specified investment horizon, this model implies a cash flow consisting of the initial dividend yield, the (hopefully positive) growth in dividends, and the capital gain (or loss) determined by the dividend growth and future dividend yield assumptions. The stock's attraction to potential investors will be based upon the totality of these various components of return.

At the outset, the simplest case is to assume that the future dividend yield coincides with the initial dividend yield. When the horizon price is based on a constant dividend yield, the stock's rate of return will be very close to the sum of the dividend yield plus the dividend growth rate. As a basic example, with an 8% dividend yield both today and at the end of a twenty-year investment horizon, a stock with a 4% dividend growth rate would provide a rate of return of 12.26%. (Variations in the assumed future dividend yields and stock price at

Figure 1: A Stock's Cash Flow and Total Return Schedule

Initial Annual Dividend Yield = $8 Per Share
Price Per Share = $100
Assumed Dividend Growth = 4%
Investment Horizon = 20 Years
Terminal Price Based on Dividend Yield = 8%
Conventional Rate-of-Return = 12.26%
Reinvestment Rate = 8%

Quarter Beginning	Dividends Per Share			Interest on Interest	Total Return	Cumulative Total Return
	Initial Rate	Incremental Growth	Total			
0 Years	2.000	.020	2.020	0	2.020	2.020
.25	2.000	.040	2.040	.040	2.080	4.100
.50	2.000	.061	2.061	.081	2.142	6.242
.75	2.000	.081	2.081	.124	2.205	8.447
1.00	2.000	.102	2.102	.167	2.269	10.716
.	.	.	.	.	.	.
.	.	.	.	.	.	.
.	.	.	.	.	.	.
19.25	2.000	2.346	4.346	9.692	14.038	503.424
19.50	2.000	2.390	4.390	9.970	14.359	517.783
19.75	2.000	2.433	4.433	10.254	14.688	532.471
Totals	160.000	85.766	245.776	286.695	532.471	532.471

Capital Gain	121.672
Total Return	654.143
Realized Compound Yield	10.36%
Effective Par Rate	13.77%

the horizon have surprisingly small impact on an income stock's rate of return over the twenty-year period. This phenomenon will be explored at a later point.)

The cash flow from this dividend growth model is shown in Figure 1.

The conventional rate of return figure of 12.26% has the same computational basis as the yield-to-maturity on a bond. If *Yield Books* existed for bonds with growing quarterly coupons, this figure of 12.26% would be found there. (For clarity of exposition, all yields and rates of return are expressed in terms of the semiannually compounded figures that are standard in the bond market.)

From Figure 1, we see that the $8.00 dividend per share grows to an annual rate of $17.73 per share by the 20th year. Since the current price per share is $100, the initial dividend yield is 8%. If the stock is assumed to be selling at this same 8% dividend yield in the 20th year, then the terminal price of the stock will be 221.672. In bond terminology, this "horizon value" would be analogous to the bond's redemption value. Pursuing this view of the stock in the context of bond terminology, all the characteristics of the stock's cash flow can be expressed as a percentage of its "horizon value." Thus, the stock's Dollar Price becomes

$$100\% \left(\frac{100}{221.672} \right) = 45.11$$

when restated as a percentage of its assumed "horizon value." The initial "coupon" rate can be expressed as

$$100\% \left(\frac{8}{221.672} \right) = 3.61\%,$$

growing to an ultimate coupon rate of

$$100\% \left(\frac{17.73}{221.672} \right) = 8.00\%$$

at the maturity of this twenty-year horizon.

When viewed in these terms, the stock corresponds to a very deep-discount bond (with a growing stream of quarterly coupon payments).

A BOND-TO-STOCK SWAP

Now suppose a bond portfolio manager is considering swapping out of some bond holdings into this income stock.

For the purpose of clarity, suppose the current holdings consist of 9% 20-year bonds issued by the same company. The portfolio manager's intent is to enhance his long-term total return over the 20-year horizon. His interest in the swap is motivated by long-term considerations; i.e., he is not rendering a judgment based on beliefs about the relative price action of the stock or bond over the next few months. While the move may represent a fairly permanent commitment, he is not considering the swap as part of any strategic shift in the equity-to-fixed-income structure of his portfolio. In making an investment judgment, he is simply looking at the fixed-income return from the bond in comparison with the greater, but obviously riskier, cash flow from the stock. The intent of any actual swap would be to achieve an improvement in long-term return.

INTEREST-ON-INTEREST

In this context, the stock is being viewed as a bond substitute, and the swap essentially corresponds to a Yield Pick-Up bond swap.

For a portfolio that reinvests and compounds all coupon receipts, there is an additional component of a bond's total return—interest-on-interest. This is the return derived from the compounded reinvestment of the bond's direct interest payments.

In evaluating a Yield Pick-Up bond swap over a long-term horizon, consistent estimates must be made of the interest-on-interest contributions from both bonds. This is usually achieved by assuming that all coupon flows are reinvested and compounded at some specified rate.

Figure 2: Cash Flow and Total Return Schedule of a 20-Year 9.00% Par Bond

Conventional Rate-of-Return = 9.00%
(Yield-to-Maturity)
Reinvestment Rate = 8%

Semiannual Period Beginning	Coupons Per $100 Investment Initial Rate	Incremental Growth	on Total	Interest on Interest	Total Return	Cumulative Total Return
0 Years	4.500	0	4.500	0	4.500	4.500
.50	4.500	0	4.500	.180	4.680	9.180
1.00	4.500	0	4.500	.367	4.867	14.047
1.50	4.500	0	4.500	.562	5.062	19.109
.	.	.	.	.	.	.
.	.	.	.	.	.	.
.	.	.	.	.	.	.
18.50	4.500	0	4.500	14.706	19.206	386.867
19.00	4.500	0	4.500	15.475	19.975	406.841
19.50	4.500	0	4.500	16.274	20.774	427.615
Totals	180.000	0	180.000	247.615	427.615	427.615

Capital Gain	0
Total Return	427.615
Realized Compound Yield	8.49%
Effective Par Rate	9.00%

Returning to our example of the bond-to-stock swap, suppose that the portfolio manager expects to be able to reinvest all coupon or dividend receipts at a compound rate of 8%. Figures 1 and 2 show how the interest-on-interest from the stock and the bond would accumulate under these conditions.

As expected, the total return from the stock far exceeds that from the bond. It is also worth looking at the distribution of the sources of return. The interest-on-interest on the bond amounts to $247.615, or 58% of the total of $427.615 return. The direct coupon payments account for the remaining 42% of the total return. There is, of course, no capital gain component from a par bond.

For the stock, on the other hand, the initial rate of dividends contributes $160.00, or only about 24% of the total return of $654.143. The capital gain of $121.672 amounts to nearly 19% of the total return. The dividend growth contributes $85.766, or 13% of the total return. The interest-on-interest amounts to $286.695. This is a larger dollar amount of interest-on-interest than that from the bond. However, this interest-on-interest component constitutes only 44% of the stock's overall return, far less than the 58% figure for the bond.

The stock's low interest-on-interest component results from two factors. First the 19% capital gain component is insulated from reinvestment throughout the investment horizon. The second component is the incremental dividend growth. As Figure 1 illustrates, the bulk of these added dividends are paid out in the later years of the investment period. This "back-ending" of this cash flow component renders it less sensitive to the cumulative effects of reinvestment.

These two factors combine to provide the stock—under the dividend growth model—with a high level of structural protection against adverse reinvestment conditions.

NEW MEASURES OF BOND RETURN

In *Inside the Yield Book*,[1] the realized compound yield was suggested as a method for comparing two bonds whose cash flows would be reinvested at some given rate. The realized compound yield simply describes the effective annual growth rate in total return over the investment horizon. At the 8% reinvestment rate, the realized compound yields are 10.36% for the stock and 8.49% for the bond.

In a later supplement to *Inside the Yield Book* for portfolios subject to taxation,[2] we suggested another technique for comparing cash flows under common reinvestment rate (and tax) conditions. This method—the "effective par rate"—

---

[1] *Inside the Yield Book*, Sidney Homer and Martin L. Leibowitz, Ph.D., 1972, Prentice-Hall, Inc. and New York Institute of Finance.

[2] *Total After-Tax Bond Performance and Yield Measures*, Martin L. Leibowitz, 1974, Salomon Brothers.

can provide some interesting insights into the present situation. The effective par rate of an investment is simply the coupon rate required on a (non-callable) par bond in order to generate the same overall return as the given investment under the specified reinvestment (and tax) conditions. Using this concept, any complex cash flow pattern can be related to the familiar yield scale of the par bond.

Figure 3 shows that a 20-year non-callable par bond would have to carry a coupon rate of 13.77% to match the $654.13 return from the stock. This high effective par rate, 151 basis points above the conventional rate of return, is a measure of the stock's structural advantage in the face of reinvestment rates below its 12.26% conventional rate of return. The effective par rate of the 9% bond remains, of course, at 9.00%. Under the assumed conditions, a swap into the stock would, therefore, provide an increase in long-term return equivalent to a 477 basis point increase in coupon rate.

Figure 3: Cash Flow and Total Return Schedule of a 20-Year 13.77% Par Bond

---

Conventional Rate-of-Return = 13.77%
(Yield-to-Maturity)
Reinvestment Rate = 8%

Semiannual Period Beginning	Coupons Per $100 Investment			Interest on Interest	Total Return	Cumulative Total Return
	Initial Rate	Incremental Growth	Total			
0 Years	6.884	0	6.884	0	6.884	6.884
.50	6.884	0	6.884	.275	7.159	14.043
1.00	6.884	0	6.884	.562	7.446	21.489
1.50	6.884	0	6.884	.860	7.744	29.233
.	.	.	.	.	.	.
.	.	.	.	.	.	.
18.50	6.884	0	6.884	22.498	29.382	591.808
19.00	6.884	0	6.884	23.672	30.556	622.364
19.50	6.884	0	6.884	24.895	31.779	654.143
Totals	275.360	0	275.360	378.783	654.143	654.143

Capital Gain	0
Total Return	654.143
Realized Compound Yield	10.36%
Effective Par Rate	13.77%

Figure 4: Realized Compound Yields and Effective Par Rates Under Various Reinvestment Assumptions

Stock and Bond as Described in Figures 1 and 2

Reinvestment Rate	Realized Compound Yield		Effective Par Rate	
	Bond	Stock	Bond	Stock
0%	5.21%	7.86%	9.00%	18.37%
6	7.54	9.61	9.00	14.68
7	8.00	9.97	9.00	14.21
8	8.49	10.36	9.00	13.77
9	9.00	10.77	9.00	13.36
10	9.53	11.20	9.00	12.99
12	10.65	12.13	9.00	12.34
12.26*	10.80	12.26*	9.00	12.26
14	11.84	13.15	9.00	11.80
16	13.10	14.25	9.00	11.35
18	14.42	15.43	9.00	10.98
20	15.80	16.68	9.00	10.67

* Stock's conventional rate of return.

One must take care to be sure that this effective par rate of 13.77% is interpreted correctly. It is *not* a realized compound yield or a rate of return. Under the 8% reinvestment rate, the stock's realized compound yield is 10.36%. In other words, a $100 stock investment produces the same dollar return at the end of the 20-year horizon as would result from semiannually compounding the $100 at a fixed 10.36% rate. The stock's realized compound yield is actually reduced well below its 12.26% rate of return because its dividends are assumed to be reinvested at the much lower 8.00% rate. (As a bond substitute, the stock's dividends would flow back into the bond portfolio, and so would be subject to the bond portfolio's reinvestment assumptions.) But when compared with a par bond, the stock suffers relatively less degradation in realized compound yield as a result of lower reinvestment rates. Consequently, for a par bond to achieve the same 10.36% level of realized compound yield and the same associated dollar return, it would have to carry the very high coupon rate of 13.77%.

In this sense, the 13.77% effective par rate is the "bond equivalent" of the stock's return.

THE REINVESTMENT GAP

The stock's high effective par rate is an exaggeration of a phenomenon we have noted previously in dealing with discount bonds. When present yield levels far exceed the rate levels assumed for long-term reinvestment, there develops a "reinvestment gap" that can become quite favorable to discount bonds.[3] In the present case, the reinvestment gap is extraordinarily large, reaching from conservative bond portfolio estimates up to expected equity returns.

Figure 4 illustrates how the stock's return and effective par rate depend on the reinvestment rate assumption. At a 6% reinvestment rate, the stock's effective par rate rises to 242 basis points above the rate of return. Even at a 10% reinvestment rate, the effective par rate remains at an enhanced level of 12.99%. At a reinvestment rate of 12.26%, i.e., just equal to the stock's rate of return under its assumed cash flow, the realized compound yield and the effective par rate all become equal to this rate of return value. At even higher reinvestment rates, the discount character becomes a handicap, and the effective par rate drops below the level of the stock's rate of return.

In the final analysis, each portfolio manager must make his own judgments regarding appropriate reinvestment rate assumptions. Consequently, even if two managers have identical estimates for a stock's cash flow, their respective effective par rates may be quite different because of a difference in their reinvestment assumptions. The effective par rate is a highly customized investment measure.

In the event of a significant decrease in interest rates, the stock may have a further advantage over bonds. The bonds could be called and refunded, resulting in an even more pronounced deterioration of the bondholder's long-term return. Common stocks cannot be refunded in the usual sense of the word. However, it should be remembered that the corporation's option to reduce dividend payments constitutes a theoretical kind of refunding capability.

THE EFFECTS OF VARYING DIVIDEND YIELD AND GROWTH ASSUMPTIONS

Figures 5 and 6 show the realized compound yields and the effective par rates associated with different combinations of dividend yields and dividend growth rates.

The special role of the dividend growth is evident in Figure 6. A stock with an initial dividend yield of 6% and a growth rate of 6% would have a rate of

---

[3] *Discount Bonds and the Reinvestment Gap*, Martin L. Leibowitz, October 16, 1974, Salomon Brothers.

Assumed Growth Rate of Dividends	Initial Dividend Yield					
	5%	6%	7%	8%	9%	10%
8%	11.70	12.20	12.66	13.09	13.48	13.85
7	10.93	11.45	11.93	12.37	12.78	13.15
6	10.18	10.72	11.22	11.67	12.09	12.48
5	9.45	10.02	10.54	11.01	11.44	11.84
4	8.75	9.34	9.88	10.36	10.81	11.22
3	8.08	8.69	9.24	9.74	10.20	10.62
2	7.43	8.07	8.64	9.15	9.62	10.05
0	6.21	6.89	7.50	8.04	8.53	8.98
-2	5.11	5.83	6.47	7.03	7.55	8.01

Figure 5: Realized Compound Yields of Common Stocks with Various Initial Dividend Yields and Growth Rates

20-Year Horizon
Terminal Price Based on Initial Dividend Yield
Reinvestment Rate = 8%

return of 12.27%, i.e., essentially the same value as for the earlier example of an 8% dividend yield with a 4% growth rate. Yet Figure 6 shows that its effective par rate is 14.90%, 113 basis points more than the earlier example's effective par rate of 13.77%.

More generally, Figure 6 shows a number of interesting patterns. At relatively low growth rates, the effective par rate increases in step with increases in the growth rate itself. For example, in moving from a growth rate of 2% to 3%, the effective par rate increases from 121 to 171 basis points, depending on the initial dividend yield. However, at higher growth rates, the relative move in effective par rates becomes greater. In moving from a 7% to an 8% growth assumption, the effective par rates jump from 278 to 373 basis points.

This suggests that a real growth stock might have an extremely high effective par rate. This is true, but there then arise questions with respect to the long-term applicability of the dividend growth model itself, as well as questions regarding the suitability of a growth stock as a bond substitute.

Figure 6: Effective Par Rates of Common Stocks with Various Initial Dividend Yields and Growth Rates

20-Year Horizon
Terminal Price Based on Initial Dividend Yield
Reinvestment Rate = 8%

Assumed Growth Rate of Dividends	Initial Dividend Yield					
	5%	6%	7%	8%	9%	10%
8%	18.34	20.38	22.41	24.45	26.49	28.52
7	15.56	17.41	19.25	21.10	22.95	24.79
6	13.22	14.90	16.57	18.25	19.93	21.61
5	11.24	12.77	14.30	15.83	17.36	18.90
4	9.56	10.97	12.37	13.77	15.17	16.57
3	8.15	9.43	10.72	12.00	13.29	14.57
2	6.94	8.13	9.31	10.49	11.68	12.86
0	5.05	6.06	7.07	8.08	9.09	10.10
-2	3.66	4.54	5.41	6.28	7.15	8.02

Figure 6 also illustrates an interesting effect with respect to the dividend yield. At low growth rates, the effective par rate changes approximately basis point for basis point with changes in the dividend yield. However, at the higher growth rates, the effective par rate increases twice as fast as the dividend yield.

Figure 6 can also be used to gain insight into the variability of the effective par rate across a given range of uncertainty in the dividend and growth assumptions. For example, suppose a stock has an initial dividend yield of 8%, and the estimates of the long-term dividend growth rate range from a low of 3% to a high of 7%. Figure 6 then shows that the corresponding range in the stock's effective par rate is from a low of 12.00% to a high of 21.10%. Moreover, for the stock to break even against an alternative 9% par bond, Figure 6 indicates that the dividend growth rate would have to fall well below 2%.

Of course, it should be remembered that Figures 5 and 6 are based upon an 8% reinvestment assumption. The effective par rates are quite sensitive to even small changes in the reinvestment assumption. A truly comprehensive analysis should jointly explore the uncertainties in both the reinvestment and growth rate estimates. Computer analysis can be a very valuable aid in performing such evaluations.

VARYING CAPITAL GAIN ASSUMPTIONS

The assumption of a long-term dividend growth rate, combined with a constant dividend yield, implies a sizable capital gain over the 20-year horizon. In our basic example of an 8% dividend yield with a 4% growth rate, the capital gain amounts to 122%. However, even if the assumed dividend growth is achieved, the actual capital gain will still depend on future interest rates and stock market conditions. Consequently, it is natural to question how our results would be affected by different dividend yields at the horizon.

Figure 7 shows the conventional rate of return, realized compound yields, and effective par rates for a wide range of dividend yields. Over the historically reasonable range of dividend yields, the stock retains a strong return advantage relative to the bond. In fact, it is rather surprising how little the stock's return depends on its horizon price. Thus, even with a horizon price of 0, the stock provides an effective par rate of 9.10%, i.e., a slightly superior return to the 9% par bond alternative.

This suggests that for income stocks with a relatively high initial dividend yield, the dividend growth rate is by far the most crucial variable in any evaluation of the stock's prospective long-term return.

TAXED PORTFOLIOS

The preceding discussion has all been based on the assumption of a bond portfolio completely free from any forms of taxation. The effective par rate was actually developed to assist in interpreting bond cash flows made complex as a result of the interaction of various tax and reinvestment effects. Consequently, it can be readily adapted to evaluating a stock's contribution to a bond portfolio subject to taxation.

It is difficult to cite general figures in this area because of the critical dependence on the individual tax characteristics of the portfolio with respect to the marginal income rate, dividend exclusion, capital gains treatment, carryforward gain/loss status, asset tax applicability, etc. (In dealing with the more complex tax situations, the capability to develop computer analyses can obviously prove extraordinarily valuable.)

As one might suspect, there are certain situations in this area of taxed portfolios where the effective par rate approach can be most illuminating.

Figure 7: Conventional Rates-of-Return and Realized Compound Yields and Effective Par Rates Under Various Capital Gain Assumptions

Stock as Described in Figure 1
Reinvestment Rate = 8%

At 20-Year Horizon		Conventional Rate-of-Return	Realized Compound Yield	Effective Par Rate
Dividend Yield	Stock Price			
6%	295.56	12.93%	10.85%	15.32%
7	253.34	12.56	10.58	14.43
8*	221.67	12.26	10.36	13.77
9	197.04	12.02	10.19	13.25
10	177.34	11.81	10.04	12.83
12	147.781	11.48	9.82	12.21
15	118.22	11.12	9.59	11.59
17.73	100.00	10.88	9.44	11.21
20	88.67	10.73	9.34	10.97
—	0	9.25	8.54	9.10

* Initial dividend yield.

THE ULTIMATE MEANING

In any analysis of a common stock, it should be remembered that the dividend growth model is a simplified representation of highly complex and uncertain phenomena. The most critical questions in any bond/stock analysis are concerned with the very applicability of the dividend growth model, even when used with a wide range of growth assumptions. However, once a decision has been made to use this growth model in the context of a fully compounding bond portfolio, then the effective par rate can provide an important new insight into the stock's value as a long-term bond substitute.

Chapter II-9

A Look at Real Estate Duration

The analysis of duration, or the sensitivity of an asset's value to changes in interest rates, has followed an interesting path since the development of duration concepts for investments outside the fixed-income area. The duration concept has been extended to common equities, liability structures, and the management of the pension surplus. In this article, we use the effective duration concept to analyze real estate, with a look toward consolidating the contractual differences between real estate holdings and the equity duration model.[1] This topic is particularly relevant in the measurement of total portfolio duration for portfolios with a significant real estate content.

Real estate duration can be determined using methods similar to those for common stocks, such as the dividend discount model (DDM). As with common equity, however, empirical estimates of duration vary considerably between the traditional dividend discount model and newer techniques. We analyze these differences, using examples that differ in their ability to pass through inflation to net income. In particular, we model the speed of adjustment to inflation in lease contracts. This factor determines how quickly total returns adjust to infla-

---

[1] See *A Total Differential Approach to Equity Duration*, Salomon Brothers Inc, September 1987.

David J. Hartzell, David G. Shulman, Terence C. Langetieg, and Martin L. Leibowitz, "A Look at Real estate Duration," *The Journal of Portfolio Management*, Fall 1988. Reprinted with permission.

tion-induced changes in interest rates and, hence, the effective duration of the asset class.

We analyze duration under a number of scenarios, which differ by inflation adjustment assumptions. First, we define real estate as an investment vehicle, with a particular focus on the microfactors affecting real estate performance. Second, we describe the different rental adjustment processes used as inputs to duration calculations. The results show that different lease rollover assumptions result in different durations. Third, we discuss the impacts of a change in real interest rates. Finally, we present our conclusions and implications of the analysis.

REAL ESTATE DEFINED

Equity real estate has the same attributes as common stock and can be viewed as an industry segment within a broad securities index. As a result, the equity duration model is applicable. An investor receives a stream of payments called net rents and holds a claim on the residual value of the asset.

Real estate is also characterized by three factors that differentiate it from common stock. Real estate represents an unusually large segment of the economy, which is subject to its own cycle and is a major factor of production in all industries. Hence, investors can diversify within real estate with relative ease, which is not possible for other given industry groups. For example, it is easier to diversify away unsystematic risk in real estate than in almost any of the S&P industry groupings. Even though there is a general real estate "cycle," the heterogeneity of local markets, as well as the different lease and economic characteristics of the various property types, creates the potential for risk reduction through diversification within the real estate portfolio (Hartzell et al., 1986).

Second, the contractual nature of the cash flows, which are determined by the property's leasing structure, means that equity real estate embodies some debt aspects. We can generate differing maturities and bond-like cash flows by altering the terms of the portfolio of leases.

Finally, real estate rents and values are determined by replacement costs that approximate inflation. This offers investors the long-term potential to receive rates of return indexed to inflation.

Three factors affect the indexation of returns and, therefore, the duration of real estate: the lease structure, the supply and demand cycle for real estate, and product deterioration or enhancement over time. The two polar extremes for lease structure are fully-indexed leases and non-indexed leases. The former allow the full pass-through of inflation into rents on a periodic basis. The pass-through can be accomplished contractually by indexation clauses in leases or by rolling over short-term leases in markets where real estate supply and demand conditions remain unchanged. From this perspective, hotel leases provide the ultimate inflation sensitivity, because they can be adjusted overnight; such leases also create vacancy risk, because these short-term contracts are typically not renewed.

At the other extreme are financing leases, where lease rates remain unchanged for a decade or more. The only way to pass inflation through to the investor with this type of lease structure is to release the space at the expiration of the lease, at which time the capital value of the asset would adjust to reflect the new level of rents. The trade-off here is between a non-indexed rent stream and a guaranteed occupancy level for the term of the contract. Reality in the real estate marketplace is somewhere between the two extremes; even with indexed leases, there is sufficient friction to prevent a full pass-through of inflation.

Superimposed on the lease structure are market risks generated by real estate supply and demand conditions that historically have been more of a national, rather than local, phenomenon. These market risks require a fully-diversified real estate portfolio to have a time diversification dimension, as well as product and geographic diversification dimensions. Real rents fluctuate in response to local supply and demand conditions, which are influenced by national economic conditions.[2] Consequently, rents may increase at rates higher or lower than the underlying rate of inflation in the short run. This obviously influences the ability of real estate to pass through inflation-based returns to its owners. In the long run, however, competition erodes abnormal returns, as long-term supply adjusts to long-run demand. As a result of recent overbuilding, "long-term" in real estate could be very long indeed.

The third aspect of real estate risk lies in the notion of product obsolescence and enhancement. Although many financial models of real estate transactions make assumptions concerning these risks, obsolescence and enhancement exist and ultimately affect the residual value of the asset. If the product maintains its attractiveness over time, then its value in equilibrium will be its replacement cost. If there is obsolescence or deterioration, however, its value would be lower than its replacement cost, preventing the residual value from fully passing through the inflation increases. Conversely, if the product improves over time because its site value is enhanced, its replacement cost would increase at a rate faster than that of inflation (Corcoran, 1987).

---

[2] See *Rent Projections in the Context of a Rent Cycle*, Salomon Brothers Inc, October 22, 1986, and *Adjustment Mechanisms in Real Estate Markets*, Lawrence B. Smith, Salomon Brothers Inc, June 1987.

RELATION TO PREVIOUS RESEARCH

The adjustment in real estate returns as a result of changing inflation rates has been discussed in prior studies (Hartzell et al., 1987; Brueggeman et al., 1984). A fundamental problem with these studies concerns the quality of data that they employ, and, in a more general sense, the unavailability of real estate return data with which to analyze theoretical finance issues.

The ability of real estate to provide hedges against inflation can be determined by testing for the empirical reaction of real estate returns to changes in the expected and unexpected components of inflation. In general, studies have found that real estate provides a strong hedge against expected inflation. On the other hand, only the Hartzell, Hekman, and Miles study (1987) found a strong hedge against unexpected inflation. This study categorizes the data sample by different property characteristics, which leads to similar conclusions for various property types (office, retail, and industrial) and property sizes. Most studies do not shed light on the way changes in inflation affect real estate returns, beyond a discussion of methodology and empirical results.

One problem in previous studies is the use of appraisals to calculate the holding-period returns. The typical appraisal process that commingled real estate funds—the source of data—follow includes at least annual external appraisals, with in-house employees updating these values in the quarters between reappraisal. It is likely that the in-house appraisers merely adjust for inflation in the values of the properties, which would lead to an obvious inflation hedge finding. Such a problem is inherent in the use of any data series that uses appraised values as proxies of transaction values to calculate holding-period returns. In tests of duration, with real estate returns measured by appraisals, we find duration levels of zero.

Returns exhibited by equity real estate investment trusts (REITs) have been suggested as proxies for measuring the performance of real estate portfolios. Given the possibility of induced stock-like price volatility and the use of financial leverage for this type of security, though, most observers believe that these returns are not an accurate reflection of the nature of the underlying properties. Estimates of duration using equity REIT returns over the 1980s range from two to four years, about two-thirds of the duration of the S&P 500 over the same time period.

Given the limitations of existing real estate data sources, we propose an analytical approach to measuring effective duration. Using a realistic valuation model of market rents and lease contracts, we analyze the impact of changing inflation rates on duration and real interest rates for several different contracting regimes.

THE VALUATION OF REAL ESTATE

We begin with the premise that the rate of increase in real estate income is a function of the inflation rate modified by lease structure, real supply and demand conditions, and the degree of product enhancement or deterioration that occurs over time. *In this form, real estate can be viewed as a bond whose principal is inflation-indexed and whose coupons range from zero to full indexation.* Thus, the price of real estate can be reduced to the following equation:[3]

$$
\begin{pmatrix} \text{Current} \\ \text{Property} \\ \text{Value} \end{pmatrix} = \begin{pmatrix} \text{Present Value of} & \text{Present Value of} \\ \text{Net Rents Over} & + \text{Expected Market Price} \\ \text{Next T Years} & \text{in T Years} \end{pmatrix}
$$

$$
P_0 = \sum_{t=1}^{T} \left(\frac{\overline{NR}}{(1 + k_0)^t} \right) + \tag{1}
$$

$$
\frac{E\,[NR_0(1 + g_0 + \tilde{u}_1)(1 + g_0 + \tilde{u}_2)\dots(1 + g_0 + \tilde{u}_T) \times \tilde{M}_T]}{(1 + k_0)^T}
$$

where:

P_0 = present value of future cash flows generated by the property;

T = term of lease;

$\overline{NR}$ = net rental income on lease (fixed over T years);

NR_0 = current level of market rents;

g_0 = current expected growth rate in property value, which reflects the expected economywide inflation rate;

$\tilde{u}_t$ = unexpected growth rate in rents in year t that reflects unexpected inflation, local supply and demand imbalances, as well as obsolescence and enhancements, which are interrelated with local market conditions;

$\tilde{M}_t$ = price-to-rent multiple in year T;

---

[3] We discuss the valuation model in detail in the Appendix to *A Look at Real Estate Duration*, Salomon Brothers Inc, December 1987.

k_0 = current required rate of return; and

$E[\bullet]$ = expected property value in T years.

The net rent variable in the equation is determined by the interaction of the structure of the contracts underlying the real property, the supply and demand conditions within local markets, and inflation. For the former, net rents will rise or fall depending on the ability of the landlord/property-owner to roll over leases, thereby adjusting for inflation. In our annual model, for example, the interval for which lease payments are fixed can range from one year to more than twenty years. At the short end, rents adjust as announcements of inflation are made. Over the long term, rents do not adjust at all to inflation and are held constant for the entire lease term. At lease renewal, rents adjust to "catch up" for all previous inflation during the fixed contract period. Thus, the interaction of inflation rates and speed of adjustment determines the effective duration of the asset class.

With this valuation equation, we can calculate the effective duration of real estate by measuring asset price changes in response to changes in interest rates under varying types of lease contracts. In this context, an asset with an effective duration of five years would experience a 5% decrease in value in response to a 1% increase in interest rates. We assume that there is direct and instantaneous transmittal of changes in the expected inflation rate to the discount rate. Initially, we assume that the expected real rate of return is constant and that there is no unanticipated rent growth. Later, we allow changes in the underlying real rate or real estate risk premium to cause changes in the nominal interest rate.

ALTERNATIVE LEASE STRUCTURES: PERFECT MARKETS VERSUS MARKET FRICTIONS

The limited availability of appropriate data to use in empirical tests of duration requires us to use an analytical valuation model. Our duration calculations are based on Equation (1), with five alternative contract terms:

- Continuous rent adjustment to the prevailing market rent;

- Rent adjustments every two years;

- Rent adjustments every five years;

- Rent adjustments every ten years; and

- Rent adjustments every twenty years.

In all five cases, we assume a ten-year holding period, which is typical for most real estate investment managers. In the case of a twenty-year lease, we have assumed a sale at the end of the tenth year, by discounting the net rents from years 11-20 and the residual value at the end of the period.

Our analysis assumes a 6% real rate of return for real estate, a rate real estate investment managers use frequently for quality assets. The real return consists of a general economic real interest rate plus a risk premium appropriate for real estate.[4] An initial 5% expected inflation rate is also assumed for the base case. This translates into an initial discount rate (k) of 11.3%. The expected growth rate of the rental stream at the beginning of the holding period is equal to the expected inflation rate.

With continuous rent adjustment, inflation over the next year is fully embedded into next year's rents and in every subsequent year's rents during the holding period, as well as in the terminal value of the property. For fixed-rent contracts, the adjustment to the new rate of inflation takes place at the end of the contract term. With a contract term of ten years, for example, there is no rent adjustment to inflation during the next ten years. Nevertheless, inflation is embedded in the growth of the property value, as represented by the second term in Equation (1). This case is similar to a ten-year bond with a fixed coupon and an indexed principal.

We analyze two generic types of leasing contracts. Both types assume that the contracting term is held constant throughout the holding period. That is, at the end of an initial lease term, a new lease is put into effect with the same term as the initial one. From that point forward, the contract rolls over every T years until the end of the holding period. Further, the property, after the assumed ten-year holding period, is sold under the condition that leases have been contractually set so that their maturities will equal T in the future.

The first contract regime, which we call the "market frictions regime," assumes an equal rent for all lease terms. Contracts with different terms are not present value equivalents unless the expected inflation rate is equal to zero, but the market frictions regime is typical of existing rent contracts in major markets where there is often little difference between rents on contracts with different terms. One explanation for this is the possible presence of substantial periods of vacancy, leasing commissions, and other contracting costs. The potential cost of those market frictions is much greater with short-term leases than with long-term contracts. Consequently, benefits arising from inflation may be reduced

---

[4] We initially assume the expected real return is invariant to the lease structure, which may not necessarily be the case; however, we examine the effects of changes in the expected real return later in this article.

with a long-term fixed-rent contract, but substantial costs resulting from market frictions are avoided.

The second contract type, which we call the "perfect markets regime," sets the fixed rent such that the present value of the rent payments until the leases roll over is equal to the present value of the expected inflation-indexed rent payments over the same time period. At the end of the investment horizon, the property value is equal to the market value of a fully-indexed cash flow stream, which is also the value of a perpetual floating-rent contract. The assumption is that the two contracts have equivalent present values. Given information asymmetries and market frictions related to local market supply and demand conditions, as well as inflexibility in setting lease terms, this case is more theoretical than real.

A graphic example serves to clarify this cash flow generation process. Figure 1 shows the cash flows earned by the property for a floating-rent contract and a five-year fixed-rent contract in the perfect markets regime. Assuming the base case, where expected inflation is 5% throughout the holding period, the present value of the five-year fixed-rent contract is $114.84, which is equal to the present value of a five-year rental stream starting at $105 that increases annually at the 5% expected inflation rate. After the initial five-year contracting period, the fixed rent is increased to $146.56. The present value of this second five-year annuity is equal to the present value of the floating-rent contract, which starts at $134.01 in year six ($105 \times 1.05^5 = $134.01), and is again indexed to the 5% expected inflation rate. A similar process is employed for leases with terms not equal to five years.

Figure 2 shows the rents for the fixed-rent and floating-rent leases in the market frictions regime. The fixed-rental stream is equal initially to the initial year's indexed-rent flow of $105. For the sixth year, the indexed rent rises to $134.01, and the fixed rent is set equal to this amount for the remaining five years of the holding period.

To illustrate the effect of a change in expected inflation, suppose that the rent contract is determined on the basis of a 5% inflation rate, and a shock occurs causing inflation expectations to increase to 6%. The effect of this change on the rental stream depends on the lease term, which determines how long it takes until rents can adjust to the inflation rate.

Figure 3 shows the rental stream for the market frictions regime before and after the instantaneous increase in inflation expectation from 5% to 6%. As the five-year contract is put into place prior to the shock, the base rent remains at $105 for the first five years. In year six, the new fixed rent—given that inflation has been rising at 6%—is $141.85. This is obviously higher than the fixed rent of $134.01, because the new contract adjusts to catch up to 6% versus 5% inflation. A similar adjustment takes place in the perfect market regime to preserve the "present value equivalence" in years 6-10.

Figure 1: Cash Flows for a Five-Year Lease—Perfect Markets Regime

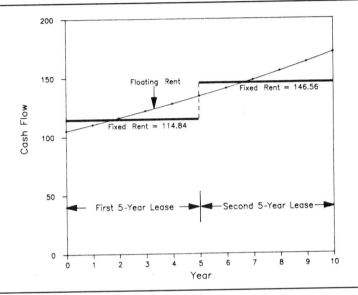

Figure 2: Cash Flows for Five-Year Lease—Market Frictions Regime

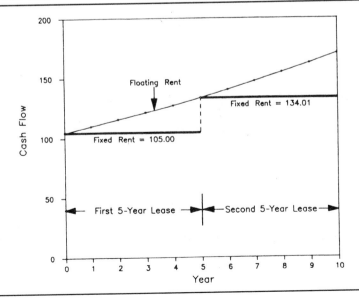

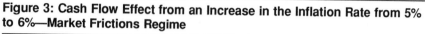

Figure 3: Cash Flow Effect from an Increase in the Inflation Rate from 5% to 6%—Market Frictions Regime

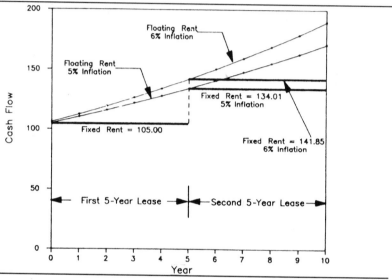

PRICE SENSITIVITY TO CHANGES IN THE EXPECTED INFLATION RATE

A floating-rent or fully-indexed contract has a base payment in year zero of $100. With an expected inflation rate of 5%, the first-year payment is expected to be $105, the second-year payment $110.25, and so forth. The property value with a perpetual floating-rent contract is $1,667 for our example, with a 5% expected inflation rate and 11.3% discount rate.[5] This translates into a capitalization rate—equivalent to a dividend yield—of 6.3% on income in year one.

An instantaneous increase in the expected inflation rate to 6% after the lease contract is entered into would have no effect on value, because the lease is assumed to be fully and immediately indexed to inflation. This automatically increases income in year one to $106 and the discount rate to 12.36%. Consequently, there is no effect on asset value from a 100 basis point change in

---

[5] For a floating-rent contract, the price can be calculated from the familiar Gordon-Shapiro model

$$P_0 = \frac{NR_0(1+g)}{k-g} = \frac{105}{0.113 - 0.05} = \$1,667$$

inflation, and the value of the property remains at $1,667. Thus, the effective duration in the fully-indexed case is zero in both simulations.

A ten-year fixed-rent lease obviously leads to a different conclusion. In this case, the lease income remains unchanged at $105 during the life of the lease, but the residual value at expiration increases at the rate of inflation. This implies an initial value of the asset of $1,383 and a residual value of $2,253. The loss of coupon indexation results in a 17% diminution in value. We derive these values by assuming the capitalization rate in year ten is the same as in year zero.

If the expected inflation rate increases to 6%, the lease contract rents remain unchanged, but the discount rate increases by 106 basis points, and the resulting value falls to $1,324. This represents a 4.26% drop in value and an effective duration of approximately 4.02 years for the market frictions case.[6] By contrast, the change in value for a ten-year lease contracting period in the perfect markets case is 1.8%.

DEVELOPING AN EQUIVALENT MEASURE OF INFLATION PASS-THROUGH

The inflation sensitivities that we find in these calculations can also provide some insights regarding the flow-through of inflation for real estate with different leasing structures. Given the indicated inflation sensitivities and the extension of the DDM incorporating inflation sensitivity, we can estimate an implied pass-through parameter. The price sensitivity of a floating-rent contract to a change in the expected inflation rate is equal to:[7]

$$\begin{pmatrix} \text{Price Sensitivity} \\ \text{to a Change} \\ \text{in the Expected} \\ \text{Inflation Rate} \end{pmatrix} = -D_{DDM}(1 - \lambda)\Delta I \qquad (2)$$

---

[6] The effective duration is equal to:
$$\frac{-\delta P/\delta k}{P} = \frac{-\Delta P/\Delta k}{P} = -\frac{(1324 - 1383)/0.0106}{1383} = 4.02 .$$

[7] Equation (2) shows the price sensitivity for a floating-rate contract with continuous, rather than discrete, rent payments. In this context D_{DDM} is equal to $1/(k^c - g^c)$, where k^c and g^c are interpreted as continuous rates. We set $k^c = 0.11$ and $g^c = 0.05$, which produces a property value of $1,667 and a D_{DDM} of 16.67 for the continuous floating-rent case. We focus on the continuous case so that our estimate of inflation pass-through is consistent with the concept of inflation pass-through developed for common stocks in *A Total Differential Approach to Equity Duration*, Salomon Brothers Inc, September 1987. For more detail, see the Appendix to *A Look at Real Estate Duration*, Salomon Brothers Inc, December 1987.

where:

D_{DDM} $= \dfrac{1}{k-g} =$ duration of the dividend discount model;

ΔI = change in the expected inflation rate; and

λ = inflation flow-through parameter.

D_{DDM} represents the duration in the traditional sense. It measures the price sensitivity to a change in the discount rate, holding the cash flow stream constant. A change in interest rates caused by a change in the expected inflation rate will also increase rents. For the floating-rent lease, we have assumed complete pass-through of inflation, hence λ is equal to one, and the price sensitivity to a change in the expected inflation rate is zero.

For the fixed-rent lease, we determine the price sensitivity to a change in the expected inflation rate as discussed above. Having determined the left-hand side of Equation (2), we then solve for λ to obtain a measure of the imputed inflation pass-through. Thus, we can determine an equivalent measure of inflation pass-through, which we then can use to compare contracts with level payments for fixed terms with contracts in which rents continuously adjust to reflect all or part of inflation.

Estimates of Inflation Sensitivity and Effective Duration

Given the methodology and assumptions underlying the valuation equation, the percentage change in value resulting from a 1% inflation-induced change in interest rates can be obtained for both the market friction and perfect markets cases. As mentioned above, estimates of the inflation flow-through measure are implied in these effective durations.[8]

The results, presented in Table 1 and Figure 4, are intuitively appealing. They show that effective duration, or the price change arising from a 1% increase in inflation rates, increases with the lease term. In what we consider our typical leasing arrangement, with a five-year term, the duration of real estate is 2.1 years in the more realistic market frictions case. By contrast, under the assumption of perfect markets, the duration of real estate is only 0.6 year. This number is higher than what was found for appraisal-based returns, but at the low end of the range when REIT data were used to measure returns.

---

[8] The implied λ^* is not an instantaneous pass-through parameter. Rather, it is a pass-through equivalent parameter implied under the varying lease terms used in the simulations. The actual pass-through comes at the rollover of the leases.

Table 1: Changes to Value and Duration When a Discount Rate Increase Results From 1% Increase in the Expected Inflation Rate

	Market Frictions Regime			Perfect Markets Regime		
Inflation Rate	5%	6%		5%	6%	
Discount Rate	11.3%	12.4%		11.3%	12.4%	
Term	Value		Effective Duration[a]	Value		Effective Duration[a]
1 Year	$1,667	$1,667	0	$1,667	$1,667	0
2 Years	1,628	1,617	0.6	1,667	1,664	0.1
5 Years	1,524	1,490	2.1	1,667	1,656	0.6
10 Years	1,383	1,324	4.0	1,667	1,635	1.8
20 Years	1,191	1,114	6.1	1,667	1,592	4.2

[a] See Footnote 6 for the calculation of effective duration.

Figure 4: Effects of a Changing Lease Term on Duration

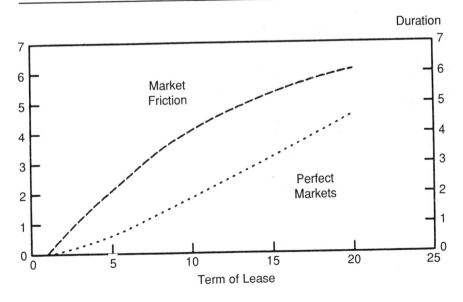

Next we look at the equivalent inflation pass-through, λ^*, of a fixed-rent lease, which is defined as follows:

$$\begin{pmatrix} \text{Equivalent} \\ \text{Inflation} \\ \text{Pass–Through } (\lambda*) \end{pmatrix} = 1 + \begin{pmatrix} \text{Price Sensitivity} \\ \text{to a Change in the} \\ \text{Expected Inflation Rate} \end{pmatrix} / D_{DDM}$$

As an example, in the market frictions regime the current property value for the five-year lease is \$1,524. If the expected inflation rate increases from 5% to 6%, the price drops to \$1,490, a drop of 2.23%. Using Equation (2), this results in an equivalent inflation pass-through of:

$$\lambda^* = 1 - (2.23/16.67) = 0.87.$$

In other words, a five-year fixed-rate lease has an inflation pass-through that is equivalent to a floating-rent lease that passes through 87% of inflation.

Figure 5 illustrates the inflation pass-through for leases of different terms. Obviously, the amount of implicit pass-through decreases as the length of the adjustment period, or lease term, increases. Furthermore, the decrease occurs at a declining rate. The pass-through is also higher under the perfect markets assumption, because fixed-rent leases are assumed to compensate investors partially for expected inflation at the beginning of the lease term.

Price Sensitivity to Changes in the Real Rate of Return

In theory, the discount rate for real estate has three components: the expected inflation rate (I), the expected real interest rate (R), and the real estate risk premium (H). Up to now we have been concerned only with inflation sensitivity. The underlying real interest rate and real estate risk premium, however, can change as well, and these effects can be far more powerful than changes in the inflation premium. For the floating-rent contract, the price sensitivity to changes in the expected real interest rate is equal to:

$$\begin{pmatrix} \text{Price Sensitivity} \\ \text{to a Change in the} \\ \text{Expected Real Rate} \end{pmatrix} = -D_{DDM}(1 - \gamma)\,\Delta R \qquad (3)$$

where:

ΔR = change in the expected real interest rate, and

γ = sensitivity of rents of changes in real interest rates.

Figure 5: Estimates of Equivalent Inflation Pass-Through

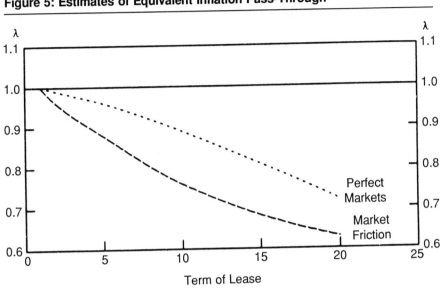

In a similar way, we can determine the price sensitivity to changes in the risk premium, H:

$$\begin{pmatrix}\text{Price Sensitivity} \\ \text{to a Change in the} \\ \text{Risk Premium}\end{pmatrix} = -D_{DDM}\Delta H \qquad (4)$$

where:

ΔH = change in the risk premium.

The real interest rate directly affects the discount rate and also may affect the level of rents as represented in the sensitivity parameter. On the other hand, a change in the risk premium affects only the discount rate. Together, the real interest rate plus the risk premium represent the expected real rate of return on real estate. Combining Equations (4) and (5), the price sensitivity to a change in the expected real rate of return is equal to:

$$\begin{pmatrix}\text{Price Sensitivity} \\ \text{to a Change} \\ \text{in the Expected} \\ \text{Real Rate of Return}\end{pmatrix} = -D_{DDM}[(1-\gamma)\Delta R + \Delta H] \qquad (5)$$

Table 2: Estimates of the Equivalent Inflation Pass-Through with Varying Real Rates and Lease Contract Terms

Term	Market Frictions Regime Expected Real ROR[a]			Perfect Markets Regime Expected Real ROR[a]		
	4%	6%	8%	4%	6%	8%
1 Year	1.00	1.00	1.00	1.00	1.00	1.00
2 Years	0.97	0.96	0.95	0.99	0.99	0.98
5 Years	0.92	0.87	0.83	0.98	0.96	0.94
10 Years	0.84	0.76	0.68	0.94	0.89	0.83
20 Years	0.76	0.63	0.51	0.85	0.74	0.63

[a] The expected real rate of return (ROR) consists of the real interest rate plus the risk premium.

where:

$$R + H = \text{expected real rate of return.}$$

In our calculations, the expected real rate of return is 6%. If a change in either the real interest rate or the risk premium caused the expected real return to increase from 6% to 7%, the value of our hypothetical real estate asset would

Figure 6: Estimates of Equivalent Inflation Pass-Through—Market Frictions Regime

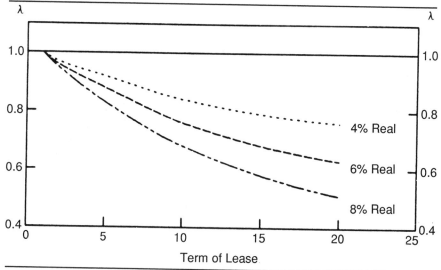

fall from \$1,667 to \$1,429, a drop of 14.3%. As a result, changes in the discount rate caused by changes in the real rate introduce the potential for very high interest rate sensitivity or duration.

Furthermore, both floating-rent and fixed-rent contracts in either market regime have very high price sensitivities when the interest rate change is due to a change in the real interest rate or the risk premium. By comparison, a duration of 14.3 years is far higher than durations in the one-to-six range reported in Table 1 for interest rate changes caused by changes in expected inflation. In either case, however, real estate has a positive duration.

In addition, the level of real interest rates and the risk premium have implications for inflation pass-through. Table 2 and Figure 6 illustrate the impact of an inflation pass-through at 4%, 6%, and 8% real rates in the market frictions case. The higher the real expected rate of return, the lower the inflation pass-through for a given lease term, because the real rate has an inverse relation to D_{DDM}. A lower inflation pass-through is a result of discounting a given inflation-indexed residual value at a higher discount rate. Thus, a higher real rate per se diminishes the attractiveness of real estate as an inflation hedge.

CAN REAL ESTATE DURATION BE NEGATIVE?

Our analysis has shown that an increase in interest rates caused by an increase in the expected inflation rate or the real interest rate leads to a decline in real estate prices. Although this result is characteristic of a positive duration investment, it appears to be counterintuitive because real estate seemed to increase in value in the face of rising interest rates during the late 1970s and early 1980s. Two factors can explain this apparent contradiction.

First, although the economywide real interest rate increased during that time, the risk premium for real estate actually declined as investors switched from financial assets to other assets, such as real estate, that offered the potential for a high inflation flow-through. High and uncertain inflation increases the importance of assets that have a high inflation pass-through. The effects of rising real interest rates and declining risk premiums tend to offset one another to some degree. The net effect could even be a reduction in the expected real rate of return. This decreased return would cause investors to bid up the price of real estate as a result of their willingness to accept a lower real return. There can be a very significant price increase associated with declines in expected real rates of return.

Second, these events occurred during the period when net rents were increasing faster than the inflation rate because of very tight real estate markets. Thus, in the short run, real estate offered a pass-through factor in excess of one, which empirically gives the appearance of a negative duration. Consequently, two factors were at work that resulted in a price increase in the face of rising interest rates.

Rising real rents, rising real estate prices, and the willingness of investors to accept lower real returns became a clear signal to create more real estate. In the late 1970s and early 1980s, the development community responded with the greatest commercial real estate building boom in history. Within our framework, this reduces the growth rate of rents below expectations, thereby lowering the value of real estate and limiting the ability of the asset to permit the flow-through inflation. The negative duration aspects of real estate during the late 1970s and early 1980s were eroded by increased supply, which lowered both net rents and residual value. To protect themselves, both renters and owners also moved toward longer lease contracts, effectively lengthening the duration of real estate.

IMPLICATIONS AND CONCLUSIONS

This analysis has two implications. First, given market conditions, real estate investors have some control over the duration of the asset through the lease contracting process. Second, the duration of real estate is not always as low as investors implicitly assume it to be. Duration is a function of lease contracts and market conditions. The longer the lease contract (excluding indexed leases), the longer the duration of the asset. Real estate investors who hold assets with long leases in reality own annuities with a claim on an inflation-indexed residual.

Market conditions influence the duration of real estate in two ways: The length of the lease term contract is market-determined to some extent, and the residual value of the asset, which affects inflation sensitivity, is determined not only by the cumulative inflation over the lease term but also by market conditions at the end of the lease. To the extent that the real estate investor can control the term of the lease, the investor has some control over the duration of the position. The management of real estate duration is further augmented by the ability to structure real estate financing in conjunction with the underlying lease contract.

References

Brueggeman, W., A. Chen, and T. Thibodeau, "Real Estate Investment Funds: Performance and Portfolio Considerations." *AREUEA Journal*, Fall 1984.

Corcoran, Patrick. "Explaining the Commercial Real Estate Market." *Journal of Portfolio Management*, Spring 1987.

Hartzell, D., J.S. Hekman, and M. Miles. "Diversification Categories in Investment Real Estate." *AREUEA Journal*, Fall 1986.

"Returns and Inflation." *AREUEA Journal*, Spring 1987.

Hartzell, D., D.G. Shulman, T.C. Langetieg, and M.L. Leibowitz. *A Look at Real Estate Duration*. Salomon Brothers Inc, December 1987.

Rent Projections in the Context of a Rent Cycle. Salomon Brothers Inc, October 22, 1986.

Smith, Lawrence B. *Adjustment Mechanisms in Real Estate Markets*. Salomon Brothers Inc, June 1987.

A Total Differential Approach to Equity Duration. Salomon Brothers Inc, September 1987.

Chapter II-10

Relative Return Analysis of Convertible Securities

Convertible bonds and convertible preferreds have many common features, and we shall compress much of our discussion by referring to both bonds and preferreds under the general heading of "convertible securities."

A convertible bond or preferred stock is simply a bond or a preferred stock, often of junior grade, with a conversion feature. The conversion feature is usually formulated as an option granting the investor the right to exchange, at any time of his choosing, each of his convertible securities for a fixed number of the company's common shares.

There are many possible variations on this simple scheme. The exchange ratio (or "conversion ratio" as it is sometimes called) can change over time, either stepping up or stepping down according to some prescribed schedule. The exchange ratio may depend on the price movement of the common.

The exchange option need not be continuous throughout time. For example, the right to convert may be restricted to certain dates within the calendar year (a constraint frequently found among British convertibles). The conversion right may end at a certain time prior to the security's maturity. Or the right to convert may be deferred for a certain period. The exchange can require a further pay up

Martin L. Leibowitz, "Relative Return Analysis of Convertible Securities," *Financial Analysts Journal*, November-December 1974. Reprinted with permission.

of either cash or fixed-interest securities. One could go on and on citing actual and theoretical variations upon the basic conversion concept.

As a bond or a preferred stock, the convertible has the character of a fixed-interest security. It will provide scheduled fixed payments of interest or dividends. The company is liable for the full amount of these payments whether or not they are earned. Consequently, as long as the company maintains its financial ability to discharge its debt obligations, the convertible will retain a certain investment value as a fixed-interest instrument. This investment value can be viewed as the hypothetical price that the convertible would command if it lost its conversion feature. The convertible's investment value is popularly regarded as a sort of rigid "floor" under the price of the convertible—i.e., as setting a level that the convertible's price will always remain above, regardless of the price action of the underlying common stock.

THE CONVERTIBLE'S RESPONSE PATTERN

Figure 1 illustrates how the market price of a convertible bond might be expected to respond to changing price levels in the underlying common stock. (To keep it simple, the remaining discussion will be framed in terms of convertible bonds. The translation of these discussions and formulas to the case of convertible preferreds is straightforward.)

As Figure 1 shows, when the common price is sufficiently depressed, the value of the conversion feature will be dwarfed by the convertible's debt value, and the convertible will sell very near to the floor price set by its investment value. As the common price rises, the conversion feature becomes increasingly valuable, because the prospect of a conversion value in excess of investment value becomes more likely.

At higher common price levels, the convertible approaches the value of the common stock into which it is convertible and little extra value is accorded its fixed-interest characteristics, which become somewhat diluted at these higher levels. The convertible's current yield and yield to maturity are now much lower than that available on straight bonds or preferreds. It is now a long way down to the investment value floors. And the threat of call may loom, which would essentially force the investor to exercise the conversion at current price levels, and thereby lose any premium in excess of conversion value.

Although Figure 1 is reasonably descriptive, in practice, such diagrams can easily prove a little too pat and possibly even lead the analyst into a trap. An investment value is a somewhat intangible concept at the best of times, yet its estimate becomes significant only under the worst of times. Thus an estimate of investment value is often made when the company and its stock appear to be reasonably attractive—at least attractive enough for the company and its convertible to be considered viable investment candidates. Suppose that the analyst

Figure 1: The Price Response Curve of a Convertible Bond

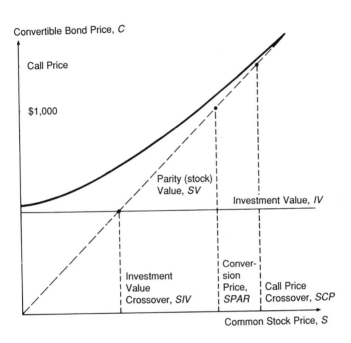

constructed a response curve based on such an estimate of the investment value as a floor. If the common stock price should then plunge, either through a dimming of the company's prospects or the effects of very high interest rates, then these combined adverse circumstances might invalidate the original estimate of the investment value at the very time when a rigid floor would be most needed.

THE CONVERTIBLE AS A STOCK SUBSTITUTE

The dual structure of the convertible allows many different approaches to evaluating its investment merits. However, the viewpoint of this article will be that of the equity investor considering an alternative to the stock, as opposed to that of the arbitrageur or the bond portfolio manager seeking an equity "kicker." Most institutional portfolio managers approach convertible securities as a relatively defensive alternative vehicle for taking a commitment in the underlying common stock.

One often hears portfolio managers say that they cannot (or would not) consider an investment in a given convertible security unless they or their institution were favorably inclined toward the company itself and the underlying common stock. For such investors, who view a convertible purchase as a direct alternative to a pure equity position, it is natural to compare the convertible's return relative to the equity alternative.

THE CONVERSION PREMIUM

The convertible has attraction as a stock substitute for three basic reasons: (1) generally higher current yield than the underlying common, (2) higher "quality" of yield and (3) greater resistance to price declines, as exemplified in Figure 1.

In order to obtain these incremental benefits, the investor must generally pay a premium above and beyond the market value of the underlying common stock. This "conversion premium" is usually defined as a percentage value, and it is one of the key measures used in the convertible market. Its value at a given time, the relationship of this value to past values, and its estimated response to common stock movements all enter critically into the convertible's investment equation.

To characterize these concepts more precisely, let us define the following symbols:

N = the exchange ratio, i.e., the number of shares of common stock received upon conversion.

S = common stock price per share.

$SV = N \times S =$ parity value (sometimes called the "stock value" or "conversion value"), i.e., the market value of the common stock that would be obtained if the conversion were to be immediately exercised.

C = the convertible security's cost *per unit*, i.e., the price per share for convertible preferreds or the price of a bond of $1,000 par amount. Note that the conventionally quoted "dollar price" of a bond would then be given by $(C/10)$.

The "dollar premium" PD can then be defined as the amount by which the convertible's price exceeds its parity value, i.e.,

$$PD = C - SV.$$

The "percentage conversion premium" P is then defined as this dollar premium as a percentage of parity,

$$P = 100\% \times (PD/SV).$$

Alternately, one can express the premium as

$$P = 100\% \left[\frac{(C - SV)}{SV} \right]$$

$$= 100\% [(C/SV) - 1]$$
$$= 100\% [1/N (C/S) - 1].$$

This last expression shows how the premium depends critically on the ratio of the convertible price to the common price.

THE RESPONSE PATTERN OF THE CONVERSION PREMIUM

If the convertible price responds to stock movements in accordance with Figure 1, then the premium would respond as shown in Figure 2. As the stock price rises, at some point the parity value will exceed the bond's call price. At this point, if the corporation were to call the issue, the investor would have to exercise his conversion option quickly to obtain the parity value instead of the lower call price. Thus, whenever the parity value exceeds the call price, the corporation can force the issue's conversion. Under the threat of call, the investor faces the sudden loss of any premium paid for the convertible. Consequently, at such high price levels, the conversion premiums will be very small, zero or sometimes even slightly negative.

At the other extreme, when a plunging stock price causes the convertible's parity value to fall below its investment value, the percentage premium can grow rapidly to astronomical values, reflecting the fact that the convertible is then primarily a debt, rather than equity, investment.

As the stock price rises, the premium falls, and the increasing parity value pushes the convertible's price toward the point where the threat of call puts any premium at risk. The decreasing premium also reflects the convertible's changing risk character. At higher prices, it is a longer way down to the investment value floor, and so the convertible's risk level more nearly approaches that of the common stock itself.

Figure 2: The Response Curve of the Percentage Conversion Premium

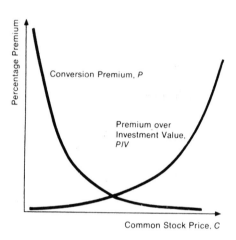

THE PREMIUM OVER INVESTMENT VALUE

The convertible's changing risk characteristics can also further be quantified in terms of a "percentage premium over investment value." If the symbol IV denotes the investment value, then the percentage premium over investment value, PIV, can be defined as

$$PIV = 100\% \times \left(\frac{C - IV}{IV}\right).$$

Figure 2 shows how this premium over investment value responds to changes in the common stock price. The conversion premium and premium over investment value clearly stand in a trade-off relationship to one another. Some analysts make this relationship explicit by constructing diagrams such as Figure 3 where the two premiums are plotted along different axes.

While the "trade-off diagram" is illuminating and represents a valid mathematical relationship, the author has some reservations about the extent to which the conversion premium can usefully be regarded as the "opposite" of the premium over investment value. In particular, whereas the premium over investment value can be rescaled to reflect the percentage downside risk (provided the

---

Figure 3: The Trade-Off Between the Premium Over Investment Value and the Conversion Premium

---

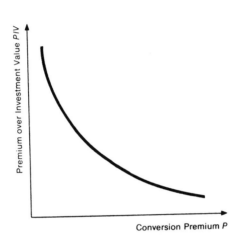

---

investment value has been correctly estimated), the conversion premium is not a measure of upside potential.

KEY CONVERTIBLE LEVELS IN TERMS OF THE STOCK PRICE

Figures 1 and 2 illustrate how the key equity and debt characteristics of the convertible depend upon the underlying common stock price. One might therefore think that investors would want to see the convertible's "extreme points," i.e., the investment value and the call price, expressed in terms of the corresponding common stock prices. Curiously, this is rarely done, although these price levels can be defined quite simply. For example, we may define the "investment value crossover" to be that stock price, SIV, where the convertible's parity value equals its investment value,

$$SIV = (IV/N).$$

Because of the implicit assumption that the bond is valued at $1,000, the conversion price may be a misnomer except when the bond is indeed priced at par, e.g., at issue or at maturity price. Similarly, the "call price crossover" could be defined to be that stock price, SCP, where the convertible's parity value just equals the call price CP,

$$SCP = (CP/N).$$

The one figure that is commonly quoted in terms of the stock price is the "conversion price." For a convertible bond, this is the stock price at which the bond's nominal $1,000 par value can be converted into equity. In other words, if SPAR is the conversion price, then

$$SPAR = (1,000/N).$$

THE CURRENT YIELD ADVANTAGE

As noted earlier, the convertible's generally greater and more assured current yield is one of the important considerations that determine the conversion premium. Assuming that the common stock pays a constant annual dividend of D dollars per share, its current yield will be

$$100\% \ (D/S).$$

If the bond's annual coupon payment amounts to R dollars (i.e., a percentage coupon rate of $(R/10)$), then its current yield will be

$$100\% \ (R/C),$$

and the convertible's "current yield advantage" CYA will be

$$CYA = 100\% \ [(R/C) - (D/S)].$$

On a purely mathematical basis, the current yield advantage may actually be greatest in the "middle" range of stock prices. At very high stock prices, the current yields of both the common and the convertible may become too small for their differences to have much significance. On the other hand, at lower stock prices, the convertible's current yield will begin to stabilize while the common's current yield will continue to rise rapidly. This latter situation is often somewhat hypothetical since, when the stock price plunges into the depths, the assumption that the dividend will remain constant may be dubious at best.

The current yield advantage bears quite directly upon the magnitude of the conversion premium. To see this, consider a dollar-for-dollar swap from the common into the convertible. For each share of common sold, S dollars are received which can be used to purchase

$$(S/C)$$

units of the convertible. Each convertible unit has a dollar premium over conversion value of

$$PD = (C - N \times S),$$

so that the total premium "cost" per share of common sold is

$$(S/C) \times PD = (S/C) \times (C - N \times S).$$

In terms of current income, each share of common sold means forgoing an annual dividend D in return for R dollars of coupon payments from each of the (S/C) bonds purchased. The dollar-for-dollar swap, therefore, increases the current income by the annual amount,

$$R \times (S/C) - D = S \times [R/C - D/S]$$
$$= S \times (CYA/100)$$

which is just the dollar price of the common shares sold times the current yield advantage.

BREAKEVEN TIMES FOR A DOLLAR-FOR-DOLLAR SWAP

The concept of Breakeven Times is so fundamental and apparently so simple that it seems to have been deemed unworthy of discussion in the literature. The objective is to try to determine how long it takes for the convertible's current yield advantage to recoup the "disadvantage" of the conversion premium. A low Breakeven Time is considered an inducement for the investor to swap from the common into the convertible. Actually, there are at least three different Breakeven formulas in use, each of which may give quite significantly different results.

The first Breakeven Time formula arises from the straightforward dollar-for-dollar swap. For each share of common, the total dollar premium purchased was shown to be

$$(S/C) \times PD.$$

This premium amount would be recouped by the current yield advantage after a period of B years where,

$$B = \frac{(S/C) \times PD}{S \times (CYA/100)}$$

$$= \frac{(PD/C)}{(CYA/100)}.$$

The numerator in this ratio is the dollar premium divided by the convertible's price, and may therefore be viewed as the number of pennies of "premium component" per dollar invested in the convertible. This turns out to be a most useful alternative measure of the conversion premium, so let us formally define the "percentage premium component" PC to be

$$PC = 100\% \times (PD/C).$$

The first Breakeven Time can then be expressed very simply as

$$B = (PC/CYA).$$

If the premium paid is viewed as being at risk, then after B years, the convertible's current yield advantage will have recouped the amount at risk—covering, for example, the premium loss resulting from forced conversion. Another way of looking at the first Breakeven Time concept is that the investor can take the accumulated incremental income and purchase a dollar amount of equity equal to the equity he gave up in exchanging shares for bonds. If the common stock price remains unchanged over this period, then this purchase would put the investor back into his original common stock position in terms of number of shares held directly and/or indirectly through the convertible while, at the same time, permitting him to continue to enjoy the convertible's defensive and higher yielding characteristics. The basic problem with this model is, of course, the presumption that the stock price will stand still for the duration of the Breakeven period.

BREAKEVEN TIMES FOR AN EQUITY MAINTENANCE (PAY-UP) SWAP

An alternative approach is a pay-up swap that maintains the original equity interest from the outset. Here the investor adds an amount of cash equal to the dollar premium and uses it to purchase additional common stock. For each share of stock originally sold, the investor would then have a holding consisting of

$$(S/C)$$

convertible units and

$$\frac{[(S/C) \times PD]}{S} = \frac{PD}{C}$$

shares of common stock. His total equity interest would then consist of the number of shares represented by the parity value of his convertible holding,

$$(S/C) \times N$$

plus his outright stock purchases for a total of

$$(S/C) \times N + (PD/C) = (S/C) \times N + \frac{[C - (N \times S)]}{C}$$
$$= 1/C \, [S \times N + C - N \times S]$$
$$= 1/C \, [C]$$
$$= 1.$$

The investor has thus received a net one share equity interest for every share originally sold. In other words, his equity interest has been maintained. At this point, the incremental income from the swap is typically computed to be the convertible income,

$$(S/C) \times R$$

less the income from the parity portion of the common,

$$(S/C) \times (SV/S) \times D = (S/C) \times (N \times S/S) \times D$$
$$= (S/C) \times (N \times D),$$

for a net increase in annual income of

$$(S/C) \times [R - (N \times D)].$$

With this formula for the incremental income, the premium pay up would be recovered in BPE years, where

$$BPE = \frac{(S/C \times PD)}{(S/C) \times [R - (N \times D)]}$$
$$= \frac{PD}{R - N \times D}.$$

This is an appealingly simple computation and this may be the reason for its fairly common use. It has one rather serious problem, however, in that it fails to accord any alternative opportunity value to the cash pay up. After all, the cash used to effect the pay up could have alternatively been invested in some fixed-interest instrument having a percentage yield of I per year. The incremental income from the swap would then consist of the convertible coupons,

$$(S/C) \, R$$

plus the dividends from the additional stock purchase,

$$(S/C) \times (PD/S) \times D$$

less the sum of the original stock dividend D and the alternative interest from the cash pay up,

$$(S/C) \times PD \times (I/100),$$

for a net incremental income of

$(S/C) \times R + (S/C) \times (PD/S) \times D - D - (S/C) \times PD \times (I/100)$

$= (S/C) \times [R + (PD/S) \times D - PD \times (I/100)] - D$

$= (S/C) \times [R + PD(D/S - I/100)] - D$

$= S/C [R + (C - NS) \times (D/S - I/100)] - D$

$= S/C [R - ND - (C - NS) \times (I/100)].$

Consequently, a more reasonable appraisal of the Breakeven Time under a "pay-up" or "equity-maintenance" swap model would be

$$BP = \frac{(S/C) \times PD}{(S/C) [R - ND - PD \times (I/100)]}$$

$$= \frac{PD}{R - ND - PD(I/100)}.$$

This formula gives the same answer as the "erroneous" pay-up Breakeven Time formula BPE when $I = 0$. It can also be shown to give the same answer as the dollar-for-dollar Breakeven Time formula (i.e., the first formula) when the interest rate I is set equal to the stock's current yield.

The above expression for BP shows that the higher the opportunity rate I, the longer will be the Breakeven Time for a given premium. Turning it around, one may say that in order to keep the Breakeven Time reasonably constant, premiums must shrink when interest rates rise. (The appropriate interest rate for assessing the opportunity cost of the cash pay up is not necessarily the longer-term yield level that determines the bond's investment value.)

For more complete accuracy, both Breakeven Time models should really incorporate the effects of compounded reinvestment of the incremental income. However, these models are generally used only when the convertible is selling fairly high in its price range, i.e., well above the investment floor. Under such conditions, the Breakeven Time will be fairly short and hence reinvestment effects are rarely significant.

Although Breakeven Time is a popular concept, and useful as a measure of the premium "per unit of current yield advantage," it is essentially static, and fails to reflect many of the key dynamic factors involved in using the convertible as a stock substitute.

TOTAL RETURN OVER TIME

A convertible security's total return can be viewed in terms of three primary factors: 1) coupon income, 2) gain in parity value and 3) changes in the conversion premium. (This is not a complete list. There are a number of second-order factors to be considered, such as the direct effects of changing interest rates on the investment value, coupon reinvestment, amortization of the investment value and possible sinking fund activity.)

If we let CRPD denote the convertible's gain per dollar of original investment over a holding period of T years, then

$$CRPD = \frac{T \times R + (C' - C)}{C}$$

$$= T(R/C) + (C'/C) - 1$$

where C' represents the convertible's price at the end of the holding period. Now let S' symbolize the stock price at this point. Next, at the time T, let $P_T(S')$ be the expected response curve for the percentage premium as a function of the stock price S'. Then by the definition of the percentage premium,

$$P_T(S') = \frac{100\% (C' - N \times S')}{NS'}$$

and we can write

$$C' = (P_T(S')/100) \times N \times S' + N \times S'.$$

However, the current premium level may be aberrantly high or low relative to today's "normal" premium curve. If $P_0(S)$ represents today's normal curve, then one can express the actual premium in terms of this curve value plus an aberration from that curve value,

$$P = P_0(S) + [P - P_0(S)]$$

and today's convertible price then becomes

$$C = (P/100) \times N \times S + NS$$

$$= (1/100) \{P_0(S) + [P - P_0(S)]\} \times NS + NS.$$

Over the period T, the convertible's price change then becomes

$$C' - C = P_T(S') \times N \times S' + N + N \times S'$$
$$- \{P_0(S) + [P - P_0(S)]\} \times N \times S$$
$$- N \times S$$

$$= [P_T(S') \times N \times S' - P_0(S) \times N \times S]$$
$$+ [P_0(S) - P] \times N \times S$$
$$+ N[S' - S].$$

In the above equation, the first term represents the change in the *normal* (dollar) premium due to stock price move and/or a change in the normal premium curve over time. The second term is the return from the presumed unwinding of the current aberrant premium. Finally, the third term reflects the direct change in parity value.

This situation is shown in Figure 4, where the convertible's return per dollar is plotted against the stock price for holding periods of T = 1 year, T = 2 years, etc. The first element of return is the aberrant premium which is shown here as being recouped in fairly short order. Then the return follows a rescaled version of the convertible price response curve depicted in Figure 1. With the passage of time, the curve shifts upward with accumulation of the convertible current yield.

The common stock return has only two primary sources of return: principal appreciation and dividends. Consequently, the equity's return per invested dollar is just

$$SRPD = \frac{T \times D + (S' - S)}{S}$$
$$= T \times (D/S) + (S'/S) - 1.$$

Plotted graphically, the equity's return is just a series of 45 degree straight lines, shifting upward by the magnitude of the annual dividend yield. With proper rescaling, these parallel return lines can be superimposed on the convertible's pattern of return over time (Figure 4), as shown in Figure 5. The convertible and stock returns for a given holding period, i.e., for the same T value, are directly comparable in this graph. The shaded portion indicates the stock price region where the convertible provides the greater relative return.

This graphic presentation also affords some insights into the limitations of the dollar-for-dollar Breakeven Time. Suppose the convertible premium collapsed to nothing at the outset. Then the convertible's return per dollar invested would become

$$CRPD = 0 \times (R/C) + (NS/C) - 1$$
$$= \frac{(NS - C)}{C}$$
$$= \frac{-(C - NS)}{C}$$
$$= -(PC/100),$$

i.e., just the negative of the "premium component" PC. The dollar-for-dollar Breakeven Time B was earlier shown to be

$$B = \frac{(PC)}{(CYA)}$$

or

Figure 4: The Convertible's "Orbits" of Total Return Per Dollar Invested

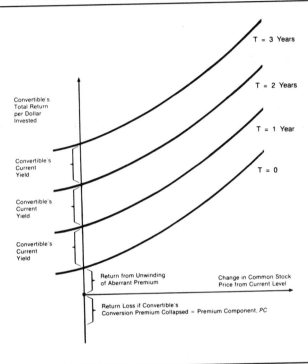

$$B \times [(R/C) - (D/S)] = PC.$$

But now when the common price and the convertible premium remain unchanged, the convertible's relative return advantage over time becomes

$$\begin{aligned}
CRPD - SRPD &= [T \times (R/C) + C'/C - 1] \\
&\quad - [T \times (D/S) + S'/S - 1] \\
&= T \times [(R/C) - (D/S)].
\end{aligned}$$

Under these highly restricted circumstances, when the current yield advantage accumulating over time T reaches the level PC, then

$$\begin{aligned}
PC &= CRPD - SRPD \\
&= T [(R/C) - (D/S)]
\end{aligned}$$

and so this time T must be the Breakeven Time B.

In this context of the dynamics of total return as shown in Figure 5, the Breakeven Time is seen to be a rather limited view of the overall investment problem.

THE THRESHOLD COMMON LEVEL

As Figure 5 illustrates, for each holding period T, there is always one common price at which the equity's return begins to exceed the return from the convertible. As the stock's future price falls below this Threshold Common Level, the convertible's return becomes increasingly attractive relative to the return on the common. Thus, for a given investment horizon, the critical question is the magnitude of the expected stock price move relative to the Threshold Common Level.

Figure 5: Comparison of Relative Returns

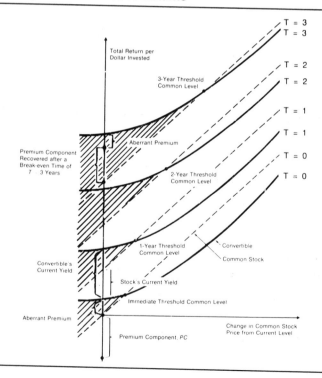

If the stock price moves adversely, both the declining sensitivity of the convertible and its accumulating current yield advantage work to reduce the investor's downside risk. In an actual investment situation, uncertainties regarding future premium curves as well as stock prices must be factored into the decision framework.

Figure 5 illustrates the key importance of the interrelationships among the factors of accumulating current yield over time, changing premiums and stock price movements. Any dollar-for-dollar swap from an equity position into the convertible with a positive premium leads to a certain "delevering"; an instantaneous upward movement in stock price will almost always induce a lower percentage move in the convertible. However, with the passage of time, the convertible with a current yield advantage builds up a cushion of accumulated return that may be supplemented or reduced by the unwinding of any aberrant premium. The resulting cushion compensates for this de-levering effect, and the stock price must undergo an increasingly large upward move before reaching the Threshold Common Level. For this reason, the longer the investor's horizon

Figure 6: The Threshold Common Level Over Time

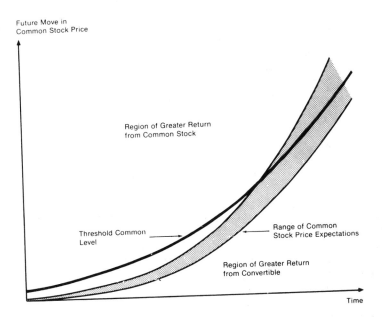

and the more modest his expectations for the growth rate of the common stock price, the stronger becomes the case for using the convertible rather than the equity shares.

As Figure 5 shows, the Threshold Common Level will tend to grow over time, provided that the convertible enjoys a positive current yield advantage at the outset. In fact, over longer investment horizons, this growth may become quite rapid. A typical time pattern for the Threshold Common Level is shown in Figure 6. The range of expectations regarding the behavior of the stock price over time can then be superimposed upon this time plot, also shown. From such analyses, one can see that the same premium curve assumption might lead one investor to stay fully levered in an equity position while a second investor, with a somewhat longer-term or more conservative view, would be led to de-lever his position into the convertible.

SHORT-TERM OPPORTUNITIES

The actual price action of the common stock as well as that of the convertible can provide many short-term opportunities even for the basically long-term equity investor. For the same assumptions regarding future premium curves, changes in the present common stock price will lead to radical shifts in the Threshold Common Levels, signaling a corresponding shift from the convertibles to the common, or vice versa. On the other hand, changes in the convertible price may lead to aberrant conversion premiums whose effects can either be avoided or used to advantage. By astute tracking of such short-term price movements, there may be a whole series of profitable interim convertible-to-common-stock moves and reversals, even for an intrinsically long-term investor operating within the framework of a basically stable equity outlook.

OTHER APPROACHES

There are a number of other ways of analyzing convertible securities. For example, if a convertible is decomposed into a bond with attached implicit warrants, the theory of option pricing can be brought to bear.

Quite a different tactic is taken in the London market. There, the conversion premium is commonly analyzed in terms of the convertible's cash flow advantage to the point in time where the common stock, with an assumed growth in dividends, begins to provide the greater current yield. The cash flow advantage over this period is then discounted to determine a present value which is viewed as a kind of conversion premium. This approach, while quite sophisticated, represents a rather long-term point of view which may overlook some of the shorter-term opportunities generated by the dynamics of the marketplace.

PART III

Bond Portfolio Management

PART III A

General Trends in
Bond Portfolio Management

Chapter III A-1

The Bond Investing Environment

The U.S. fixed-income markets have undergone a remarkable transformation in both structure and style. In the years before the 1970s, the maturity of the instrument dictated its application. A traditionalistic buy-and-hold philosophy prevailed, and the yield to maturity was the reigning gauge of investment value. The very certainty of the cash flows laid the foundation for a certain type of highly structured approach to investment. Long-term bonds were held for long-term investment periods. Bonds were predictable, even somewhat dull.

The current market, in contrast, places enormous emphasis on liquidity and flexibility. Investment goals vary much more widely from one institutional investor to another, and the portfolio objectives of any one fund can change quite radically from one day to the next. The financial activities of market participants are more attuned to the competitive pressures of the day. With the long-term prospect so volatile and uncertain, naturally a greater emphasis is placed on adapting to short-term needs. At the investment level, this emphasis has led to increasing focus on short-term rate of returns and to a sizable premium for portfolio flexibility.

However, even in today's hectic marketplace, the investor still looks to a portfolio's fixed-income component for the reliable achievement of certain specific objectives, although these objectives are now more likely to be characterized in terms of short-term requirements for both adequacy of return as well

"The Bond Investing Environment," Martin L. Leibowitz, *Graham & Dodd's Security Analysis*, Fifth Edition, McGraw-Hill, Inc., by Sidney Cottle, Roger F. Murray, and Frank E. Block, 1988, pages 403-437.

as flexibility for revision. The trend in bond investment is toward new forms of structured management that can reliably provide more targeted results, at least in relative terms. This search for closely targeted outcomes, even in the short term, can derive only from the promised long-term cash flows that are the distinguishing hallmarks of the fixed-income market.

This paper traces some of the key historical developments that led to the new management styles, the new structured strategies, the enormously increased range of new vehicles that form today's bond market, and the resulting analytical judgments required of the security analyst.

BUY-AND-HOLD MANAGEMENT

In the United States prior to 1970, the fixed-income market functioned largely as a primary market. The issuance of bills, bonds, notes, and "placements" raised funds for government and corporate entities and simultaneously served to help fund the future liabilities of financial institutions and individuals. In these early days, the *intention* of most bond investors was to keep the bonds, clip the coupons, and ultimately reap the redemption payment at maturity. Although statistics are scanty, bonds were mostly held to maturity, and interim sales occurred only in extraordinary circumstances.

The accounting techniques at most financial institutions certainly encouraged this buy-and-hold approach. Bond investments were kept on the books at amortized purchase cost. If the current market rate was higher than the purchase yield, a sale would generate an immediate book loss. However, if the current rates were lower than the purchase rate, then the sale would create a capital gain tax liability as well as lead to a decline in the overall book yield. All these outcomes were generally viewed as undesirable. Clearly, these attitudes led to only one course of "action"—continued holding.

YIELD MAXIMIZATION

In such a buy-and-hold world, bond investors measured their success by how high a yield they could obtain—in terms of overall portfolio yields, yield on annual investments, or the yield they could obtain in an "acceptable" bond purchase. Naturally, this led to stretching for yields within certain "acceptability bounds." The security analyst's assignment was to define those bounds, to avoid downgradings of credits, and to aid the search for additional fractions of 1% in yield as a reward for making less conventional or more complicated bond investments.

Investing solely by yield maximization risked certain pitfalls, for example, acceptance of lower credits; uncertain liquidity; and less desirable characteristics in terms of call features, sinking funds, covenants, etc. These potential problems were controlled to some extent by the high degree of market segmentation that prevailed in these times.

SEGMENTED INVESTING

Long-Term Corporate Securities

Prior to 1970, by far the highest yielding bonds were corporate securities (see Figure 1). High-grade industrial and utility issuers were primarily interested in selling 25-year and 30-year bonds that matched the lifetime of the capital project that they funded. Consequently, the preponderance of high-grade corporate bonds were long-term maturities (see Figure 2). Thus, as they reached for higher yielding but still acceptably high-grade bonds, pension funds and insurance companies found themselves largely focused on long-term corporate securities. These long-term purchases seemed to fit into the nature of these institutions' liabilities in a general sort of way. There were often very specific limitations on the credit-rating structure of the overall portfolio, for instance, no more than

Figure 1: Time Chart of Yield Levels: Long U.S. Treasuries Versus New Long AA Utilities

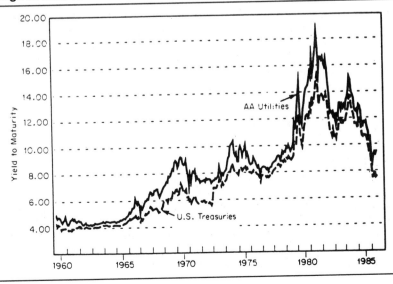

Figure 2: Changing Maturity Structure

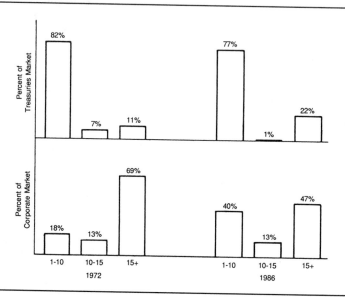

10% A or no more than 60% AA. In the "old days," a bond's credit rating was more stable than in these days of "event risk," so this quality structuring by rating probably had greater validity and relevance.

Given the limited choice of market sector, the yield maximization styles of our predecessors made some sense. This style certainly had a more reasonable basis than one might believe from a current vantage point. This may be yet another example where modern people's scorn of their ancestors' practices is itself rooted in ignorance: The old-timers were acting in a perfectly rational fashion within the framework of what was relevant in their time.

Treasury Securities

There were other market segments. The short-term market existed primarily in the form of Treasury securities (T-bills). Certificates of deposit (CDs) and commercial paper started to become a major market in the 1970s. The U.S. Treasury and various departmental agencies were, of course, issuing short- and intermediate-term notes as well as long bonds. However, notes were fewer than 7 years in maturity, whereas long Treasury bonds had maturities of 25 or 30 years. Thus, even the Treasury yield curve was spotty and had large gaps. Moreover, a law prohibited the U.S. Treasury from issuing "bonds" with a coupon rate exceeding 4.25%. (This quaint law is *still* on the books, but a sequence of special exemptions was passed by Congress starting in 1973.) As rates rose beyond this level in the mid-1960s and stayed there, all long Treasury bonds became deep discounts. In itself, this turned the long Treasury market into a relatively moribund secondary market. However, the "moribund" turned into the "morbid" as these long 3.5% and 4.25% Treasury bonds began trading on their special value for payment of estate taxes. Simply put, these long Treasuries could be used to pay estate taxes at their full *par* values. Since the higher market rates meant that these bonds could be purchased at a substantial discount, the about-to-become-deceased investor could pay off $1 of estate taxes by purchasing 70 cents of these so-called flower bonds. This rather specialized application soon dominated the market for long Treasuries, causing them to sell at higher prices (and hence lower yields) than their coupon rates would justify.

Taken together, this relatively low-yielding, purely secondary market in long Treasuries was properly deemed unacceptable by healthy long-term investors of both the individual and the institutional variety (see Table 1). This market segmentation and the buy-and-hold approach characterized the bond market prior to 1970. This fairly rigid structure led to managers focusing solely on yield improvements through the purchase of new corporate issues from the flow of new funds that they *had* to invest.

Table 1: Changing Portfolio Structures (In Billions of Dollars)

	1970		1985	
	Treasuries	Corporates*	Treasuries	Corporates*
Private pension funds	2.1	29.4	134.1	97.1
State and local retirement systems	5.1	35.1	78.5	114.9

*Includes privates and convertibles.

FORCES OF CHANGE

In the years after 1970, these bond market traditions were stretched and shattered by the impact of many new forces:

- The onslaught of inflation and the associated rise in interest rates

- The renewed issuance of long-term U.S. Treasury bonds as a result of the lifting of the 4.25% maximum coupon restriction in 1973

- The unbelievable growth of the U.S. deficit and the concomitant explosion in the U.S. Treasury securities market (see Figure 3)

Figure 3: Change in Debt Market Structure: Public Issues—Amount Outstanding

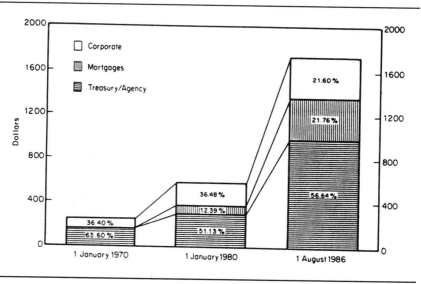

- The deregulation of interest rates within the financial system

- Internationalization of the credit markets and of all the capital markets

- The delinking (in the corporate area, at least) of capital project lifetimes with the maturity of the debt instruments used to fund these projects

- The changing attitude toward financial leverage by corporate and governmental issuers

- The explosion of liability management (a battle that was so thoroughly won that most people today have forgotten there ever was any controversy about the need to manage the liability side of a financial institution)

- The development of new interest-rate-sensitive products in the insurance, banking, and thrift areas

- The increased volatility of liability costs within financial institutions

- The transformation of many financial institutions from primary investors to wholesalers and repackagers

- The explosion of private and public pension funds

- The transformation of the investment and management business from a "relationship" business to a largely stand-alone competitive business based on short-term rate-of-return performance (first in the equity markets and then transformed investment practices in the debt markets as well).

These basic changes in the financial system were mirrored over the years by changes in investment styles, by the development of new investment techniques, and of course by the emergence of a whole new array of fixed-income vehicles.

Fundamentally, all these changes can be summed up in one word—*flexibility.* The environment changed from a traditional segmented market characterized by a crusty buy-and-hold mentality to one with an enormous appetite for flexibility by both investors and suppliers of credit instruments. All participants in these changed markets have found themselves vulnerable to eroding margins, to more volatile liabilities, to a changing business environment, and to a far more competitive market for their products (both domestically and internationally). Capital market participants now require an unbelievably flexible range of vehicles, instruments, and styles to keep step with the competitive pressures that they face on a daily basis.

EMERGENCE OF ACTIVE BOND MANAGEMENT

The evolution of bond investment strategy must be viewed from the framework of the changes in interest rates that accompanied this process. Figure 1 traces the yields of new long AA utility bonds from 1960 to 1986. In this rather hidebound environment, the range of management activities was relatively limited. The traditional market segmentation was so strong that managers would typically have few strategic considerations. Funds were put into a well-defined market sector; managers did not hoard cash, at least not for very long, nor did they go back and forth between long-term and short-term areas of the maturity spectrum. Nevertheless, on some occasions bonds would be traded, usually in response to some developing credit consideration or concern or to pick up yield. For the most part these trading decisions were based on assessments of factors related to a specific issuer or a rather narrow sector. The analyst would identify candidates for downgrades and upgrades in agency ratings or other measures of creditworthiness before the market realized the changes. Indeed, for many years, active management was considered equivalent to carrying out "bond swaps."

The very term *bond swap* reveals the highly tactical nature of this early activity in the fixed-income area.

THE PURE YIELD PICK-UP SWAP

The granddaddy of all bond swaps is the pure yield pick-up swap. The ideal form of this swap would be a 1-for-1 exchange of a portfolio holding for a bond that matches the held security in all important characteristics and yet, for some reason, has a higher yield to maturity in the marketplace. The purpose here is to increase the total contractual yield over the bond's life.

The pure yield pick-up swap seems so obvious and irresistible that one wonders how such opportunities could arise in an efficient and competitive marketplace. The answer to this question provides a highly revealing insight into how traditionalistic rigidities can create market inefficiencies. With the passage of time and with market movements, these inefficiencies can lead to sizable and clear-cut opportunities. In turn, the very obvious character and magnitude of the trading opportunity then stimulates a powerful drive toward greater flexibility. Ultimately, this struggle to realize the obvious benefits from enhanced flexibility overcomes traditionalism, arbitrages out most of the market inefficiency, and then feeds on itself to generate a far greater appetite for flexible active management.

A major source of opportunities for yield pick-up swaps was the combination of the secular rise in interest rates that began in the mid-1960s with the various accounting restraints that limited funds' ability to realize book losses. These constraints forced many funds to carry positions of low-yield bonds far beyond the point where they represented appropriate holdings for their portfolio. However, to the extent that such issues did become available for trading, their very discount nature often had a special appeal for certain types of fresh investors. For example, the older long-term U.S. Treasury bonds were priced at the lower-than-market yields (and hence higher prices) because of the specialized demand from flower bond buyers who were looking to estate tax value as an overriding inducement. In other cases, corporate bonds with sinking funds that required periodic mandatory retirements often sold at higher prices than comparable current coupon issues. Deep discount bonds, because of the favorable capital gains tax treatment at this time, had special appeal for certain classes of taxable institutions, especially if a large reservoir of losses could be used to offset any capital gains liability.

In each of these cases, the original purchasers found that their portfolios now contained bonds that were of far more use to someone else than to them. In concrete terms, the market was willing to pay a higher price, that is, a lower yield, for the security. In turn, the investors could sell these particular bond holdings at their lower yields and take the proceeds and invest them in a higher coupon issue of comparable credit or maturity and achieve a significant increase in yield.

As rates moved even higher, the incentives for such pure yield pick-up activity became ever more compelling. Of course, taking advantage of this seemingly irresistible opportunity required some weakening of the absolute prohibition against book losses. This weakening started in the late 1960s and continued apace during the early 1970s. Various types of special accounting offsets were developed for dealing with the book loss problems. Many state legislatures actually enacted special rules that allowed their retirement systems to incur book losses provided that they could be "made up" by the additional yield generated from the bond swap within a specified number of years.

A number of other doors were opened to enable large funds to take advantage of these yield pick-up opportunities. A veritable garden of accounting fictions sprang up reflecting various formulas for determining loss recovery times and/or for amortizing realized losses as a charge against the portfolio's future income stream. Ingenuity bordered on the bizarre. Many of the formulas were inconsistent or flawed from a true investment point of view. For example, they often failed to deal correctly with the coupon reinvestment and compounding process. Nevertheless, virtually all these loss recovery formulas could be satisfied with a sufficiently large improvement in yield to maturity. The preceding years of total loss constraint ensured that many portfolios contained ample opportunities for the needed sizable yield improvements. This led to increasing levels of pure yield pick-up swapping. Some older pension funds spent years moving out of their massive accumulated holdings of low-yield Treasury and corporate bonds.

From an economic point of view, the key point is that the funds began actively to seek out trading opportunities—especially the irresistible ones. As a corollary, managers began to realize that the very actions of the market could take what had been a perfectly legitimate set of portfolio holdings and transform them so that they no longer fit the needs of the fund. In other words, the passage of time and the market movement itself could render a portfolio in need of management activity just to keep it freshly attuned to sponsor's goals.

MANAGEMENT FOR SHORT-TERM RETURNS

The movement toward recognition of the need continually to freshen a bond portfolio contributed to an atmosphere in which active management could take some beginning steps. This trend was further enhanced by changes in the stable traditional relationships that had long characterized the professional investment management community. Such changes had long been under way in the equity markets, and the equity markets had also led the race toward total return performance measurement as a hallmark of the modern management process. For competitive equity managers, total return held a particular appeal as a natural measure of management activity.

The bond market was much slower to accept the total return yardstick. Undoubtedly, the natural traditionalism of the bond market was reinforced by bonds' other measure—long-term yield—that had seemed to suffice for many years. However, as the new breed of bond managers sought to establish their credentials, they embraced the short-term total return measures. The combination of these trends in portfolio management and in the investment management community opened up a new dimension in the world of tactical bond activity—the substitution swap.

THE SUBSTITUTION SWAP

In the early 1970s, interest rates were relatively stable. The new breed of bond managers was eager to take advantage of the highly liquid marketable bonds that formed the fixed-income component of pension portfolios. The new managers recognized that the cost of this liquidity was generally lower yields, and they were determined to make this liquidity pay for itself on an ongoing basis. The managers focused on short-term trading activity and on the substitution swap in particular.

In substitution swaps, the portfolio manager tracked the yield spread (or price spread) relationship among groups of substitutable bonds. When the spread between any two bonds within the same group reached some extreme limit, a swap was executed in the hope of obtaining a prompt, profitable reversal as the spread later returned to more normal levels. In essence, the substitution swap amounted to selling overpriced bonds and buying underpriced bonds. Because the bonds were so similar, a substitution swap usually involved little or no change in maturity, credit, or sector exposure.

Portfolio managers hoped that the under- or overpriced condition was a temporary aberration and that the swap would profit from a relatively quick return to a more normal relationship. Because of the institutional dominance of the bond market, such temporary market imbalances were not unusual for a host of reasons.

The rewards from any single substitution swap would naturally be fairly limited. However, a reversal could be a very clear-cut demonstration of management success. Thus, swaps from A into B and then from B back to A could be quite dramatic when the portfolio reestablished its original holding, having accumulated extra funds in the process. For many managers, a cleanly executed string of substitution swaps paved the way for even greater investment flexibility. Of course, the security analyst had to be able to certify to no loss of investment quality. If the spread opened because someone else had recognized a deterioration in creditworthiness, profitable completion of the round trip was in jeopardy.

SECTOR MANAGEMENT

Sector Swaps

By 1972, this drive for flexibility and performance had begun to manifest itself in the rise of sector swapping. Basically, this bolder form of active bond management focused on rearrangements of the sector distributions within a portfolio. Thus, the manager in a sector swap would try to capitalize on changing value relationships between distinguishable market sectors. For example, the manager might swap from utilities into industrials or from Canadians to U.S. agencies. Sectors could be defined in many ways—by type of issuer, as in the preceding example; by coupon, for example, from discounts to current coupon bonds; by credit rating, to upgrade from single A's to double A's or vice-versa, for example.

Sector swapping was greatly facilitated by the broader trends in the fixed-income marketplace. The upsurge in yields over the preceding few years had clearly distinguished the current coupon bonds from the older discount bonds. Increased issuance of nonutility corporate debt (straight industrials and finance paper) provided a wider choice of sectors. The beginning of the mortgage security market with the introduction of the Government National Mortgage Association (GNMA) pass-throughs represented a major opportunity for sector swapping—a veritable magnet for such activity, which has continued for a number of years.

In fact, the GNMA pass-through provides several classic illustrations of a sector swap. For example, in the fall of 1973, the yield on GNMA pass-throughs rose to unprecedented levels relative to both corporates and other agency issues. The underlying cause was clear—the natural initial purchaser of these instruments, the thrift institutions, had basically run out of investable funds. (The GNMA pass-throughs were intended to tap the pension fund market. However, this goal had not yet been reached because pension fund managers were put off by the GNMA's apparent complexity and the associated accounting problems.) As the GNMA yields continued to rise to ever-higher levels over corporates, a certain number of alert corporate bond investors began to take notice. The pension fund managers who undertook these sizable sector swaps into the pass-throughs reaped considerable rewards, as the spreads did narrow relative to corporates in the course of the next several months.

By their very nature, sector swaps involved major percentages of the portfolio. Consequently, they had a larger impact on the structure and performance of a bond portfolio than did 1-for-1 substitution swaps.

Rate-of-Return Performance Measurement

This narrowing of yield spreads was particularly important in light of the increased application of rate-of-return performance measurement. The first rate-of-return index for the bond market was introduced in 1972 by Salomon Brothers—the High-Grade Long-Term Corporate Bond Rate-of-Return Index. At the time, it served as a benchmark for the natural baseline investment of most bond managers in the pension fund area. In later years, as the view of the natural hunting ground for bond managers expanded across the maturity spectrum and moved toward a capital market orientation, more broadly based rate-of-return indexes became popular, for example, the Shearson Lehman Government/Corporate Index, the Merrill Lynch Bond Index, and the Salomon Brothers Broad Index (see Figure 4). The combination of sector swaps and rate-of-return measurement led more bond portfolio managers to turn from a focus on yield to a focus on "value." The best rate of return over short-term periods would not be achieved by continuing the ancient policy of reaching for the highest-yield security. Rather, it was the bond and/or bond sector that appreciated most in relative price that mattered over the short term. These swings in relative price would swamp the short-term effects of greater yield. Managers sought the current best value, and they would pursue this "cheap sector" even if it meant giving up (that is, moving down in) yield. Thus, yield maximization ceased to be the sacred cow of the bond market and gave way to short-term performance.

Figure 4: Historical Returns Over Calendar Years (through August 1, 1986)

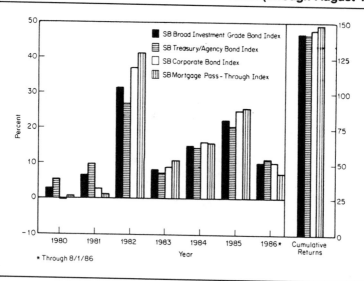

RATE ANTICIPATION: MATURITY MANAGEMENT

By and large, the sector swap tended to preserve the maturity structure of the original portfolio: The long portfolio remained a long portfolio; the intermediate portfolio remained an intermediate portfolio. Sector swaps could be pursued independently of the direction of interest rates. Bond portfolio managers of a pension fund or insurance company still felt that their natural investment habitat was the long market, and that was where they put their funds. Apart from the temporary accumulation of new investable funds for slightly longer periods, these managers did not really try to base major investment decisions on their forecast of the direction of interest rates.

All this began to change in 1973. By this time, performance measurement was quite entrenched. Starting in early 1973, interest rates began a rise that continued through most of 1974 and led to a devastating erosion in the value of the typical bond portfolio. This erosion was often as large as 25%, and the devastation afflicted all bond managers: the substitution swappers, the sector swappers, the passive managers, the insightful managers, and so on.

There were a few exceptions. Certain managers who by insight or great luck were able to foresee the continuing rise in rates took bold action and put substantial portions of their portfolios into short-term securities. These few managers preserved the market value of their portfolios and enjoyed huge performance advantages. Needless to say, the results of this maturity strategy attracted great attention within the swapping focused on relative values that existed (to a large extent) in the bond community, especially as the successful managers were (understandably) not shy about marketing their spectacular results.

This 1973-1974 debacle was hardly the first adverse cycle for bond prices, but it was the first time that such horrendous results were *fully visible* because of the widespread tracking of portfolio performance. This visibility led to a dramatic change in the style of bond portfolio management. First, it demonstrated that a fortuitous maturity structure could lead to returns that far exceeded any benefits from even the most successful substitution or sector swaps. Second, it helped to foster the impression that bond managers could anticipate broad movements in interest rates. This powerful combination led many investment managers to the widespread adoption of rate anticipation strategies. Rate anticipation managers focused primarily on forecasting the direction of interest rates and then making corresponding changes in their portfolios' maturity structure. The resulting portfolio restructurings were often quite dramatic, with changes from one maturity extreme to the other.

The stature of rate anticipation was further enhanced by two rounds of back-to-back successes: A number of the new anticipators correctly anticipated the rate rise during 1973 and 1974 and then correctly called the turn when rates plunged during 1975 and 1976. This second round of successes naturally heaped fuel on an already strongly burning fire. Active bond management soon became equated with rate anticipation. The gifted active managers widely believed that interest rates could be predicted and that the only useful role for bonds was to seek the maximum return through such maturity strategies. It is interesting that these beliefs were widely held even by fund sponsors who fully embraced the efficient market theory as it applied to their equity portfolios. Timing was generally thought to be impossible in terms of choosing direction of the equity market, but the pejorative word *timing* was virtually never applied to the growing ranks of rate anticipators within the bond market.

The bloom came off this rose relatively slowly. As interest rates proceeded on one roller coaster ride after another throughout the 1970s and into the early 1980s, the markets themselves may have changed. With the increasing deregulation and the huge buildup of the credit flows from many different sources (see Figure 3), reasonable estimates of the factors affecting bond market movements became more difficult to obtain. In addition, the very growth of ever more anticipatory investment funds seeking to capitalize on any prospective change in the direction of rates helped to create a much more volatile and more unpredictable market. A fully anticipatory market is obviously the most difficult one for anticipators.

Whatever the reasons, it seemed to become harder and harder to maintain an unblemished record of rate anticipation for one cycle after another. One by one, the heroes of the rate anticipation movement seemed to stumble. These missteps proved costly. The rate anticipators' portfolio shifts were extremely radical, and hence their returns suffered all the more when they proved wrong. With clearly more difficult markets and consistency problems among the well-known rate anticipators, sponsors' faith in rate anticipation began to erode.

DURATION: THE SEARCH FOR MORE DELIBERATE RISK CONTROL

By the early 1980s, sponsors were clearly seeking ways to exercise greater control over the interest rate sensitivity of their bond component. Rather than leave such key decisions to the discretion of an anticipatory manager, sponsors began to seek ways for the management of their bond portfolio to serve the larger purposes of the fund. This trend took place in an environment of historically high interest rates, which spawned a spectrum of new tools and new vehicles. These new tools proved to be well-suited to the sponsor's emerging needs for better control of rate sensitivity. The most basic of these tools was the *duration* measure.

The concept of duration began to be broadly used as a gauge of price sensitivity during the late 1970s. In the new world of rate-of-return measurement, changes in the market value of portfolios dominated all other considerations. For bond portfolios, the key became the price sensitivity of individual securities to changes in a common interest rate. In earlier days, the maturity of individual bonds or a portfolio's average maturity would have sufficed as rough sensitivity gauges, but the new investment environment required a more refined level of control. A manager's short-term performance might be carefully scrutinized quarter by quarter or even month by month. A given manager's returns would be compared with other managers' results as well as with the returns from bond market indexes. Bond portfolio managers now needed to know how their interest rate sensitivity compared with that of their peers and the major indexes.

For these purposes, a bond's maturity was far too crude a tool. The price sensitivity of a bond is derived from its *total* cash flow—coupon payments, sinking fund payments, as well as the maturity redemption. All these components of the cash flow enter into the equation that determines the present value (its price) of a bond for a given discounting rate (its yield). The maturity reflects only one component of this total cash flow. Indeed, for longer instruments, the maturity payment may be a relatively minor part of the bond's present value. Clearly, a more reliable guide would apply the present value formula to all cash flows and then mathematically derive an expression for the percentage price change associated with small changes in the discount rate. This expression is termed the bond's *duration*.

The duration concept was particularly intriguing because it could be interpreted in two seemingly different ways. On the one hand, it was indeed a better measure of average life. On the other hand, it provided a useful measure of "tangential" price sensitivity (Figure 5). At first glance, price sensitivity and average life would appear to be quite different concepts. Upon reflection (or simple mathematical manipulation), one can see that these two characteristics are virtually identical for fixed-income instruments.

As a measure of price sensitivity, duration had a number of advantages: It could be easily computed for individual bonds; by using market value weighting, a bond's duration could be combined with other bonds in a portfolio to arrive at an overall portfolio duration value; the differences in duration between two portfolios provided a useful gauge of the subsequent differences in their price behavior.

However, duration was still far from a perfect measure for these purposes. It was accurate in a strict sense only for infinitesimal interest rate movements—the kind that never happen! For large interest rate movements, duration would lead to only approximate answers whose accuracy would erode with the size of the yield move. More seriously, these duration errors would depend on the direction of interest rate movements. In general, the errors became much more severe as interest rates declined. In a portfolio context, the duration approach depended on a common interest rate affecting all bonds. This assumption was

Figure 5: Duration of a Bond

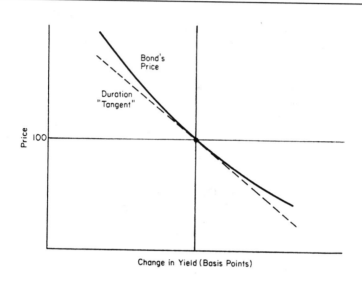

Change in Yield (Basis Points)

clearly compromised by changing sector spreads and market movements that reshaped the yield curves across maturities.

These problems with the duration concept were further aggravated by the optional features embedded in many bond portfolios. These optional characteristics create a so-called convexity problem that severely limits the effectiveness of duration as a guide to price response. For example, most corporate bonds (as well as many agency and long-term Treasury bonds) are subject to refunding calls as of some specified future date. In essence, this is an option that the issuer retains to "call in" the bond should the outstanding interest rate drop sufficiently below its coupon rate. Consequently, as interest rates decline below a bond's coupon rate, the bond's price response is increasingly dampened by the threat of such refunding calls. A similar but far more complex phenomenon affects mortgage securities where the cash flow can be accelerated through prepayments of refunding-oriented mortgagors.

These effects lead to a radical curtailment in the price sensitivity of fixed-income portfolios in lower-interest environments. The *pro forma* duration of such portfolios based on maturity dates cannot capture this "adverse convexity effect." However, in the high-interest markets of the late 1970s and the early 1980s, these low interest rate problems had a low priority in the bond manager's consciousness; this helped the simple duration tools to find widespread applications as a measure of portfolio price sensitivity.

IMMUNIZATION OF RETURNS

Duration had another source of appeal in this environment. Just as maturity was an unacceptably crude gauge for price sensitivity, the bond's yield to maturity was an inadequate guide to the return that could be captured over a span of time. Thus, in a time of high interest rates, certain bond portfolio managers sought to lock up high yields for a prescribed period of time. Traditional coupon-bearing instruments could not be used for these purposes in the normal buy-and-hold mode because of the problem of coupon reinvestment: Future coupon payments had to be reinvested at whatever interest rates then prevailed. Since this future reinvestment rate could conceivably be far lower than the initial yield level at which the bonds were purchased, it followed that no satisfactory yield lockup could be achieved by simply buying and holding coupon-bearing bonds.

A new technique based on the duration concept, *bond immunization*, allowed for this lockup (within certain limits). For example, suppose that in a 14% interest rate environment a manager wished to provide a fully compounded return of 14% over a five-year period. The problem is how to overcome the reinvestment problem, that is, having to reinvest coupon payments at a rate below 14% should the general level of interest rates decline. Clearly, five-year 14% coupon bonds will not do. However, if a zero-coupon five-year bond at an interest rate of 14% were available, the problem would be immediately solved. Unfortunately at the time, a wide range of zero-coupon bonds had not yet become available. (Even now, the full maturity spectrum of zero coupons is available only at the lower rates embedded in the U.S. Treasury yield curve.) To achieve this high degree of return lockup with coupon-paying bonds, the reinvestment of those coupons must be "immunized" against changes in future interest rates. In 1952, the British actuary F.M. Redington developed a very clever scheme for achieving this immunization.[1]

The central idea was to create a portfolio of assets whose value coincided with the present value of the scheduled liabilities and whose interest rate sensitivity exhibited the dominance pattern illustrated in Figure 6. In other words, under a prescribed set of interest rate changes, the market value of the assets would always remain greater than the present value of the liabilities. This dominance pattern would ensure that as interest rates changed, the changes in reinvestment income and capital gains would always compensate. Thus, under lower rates, the reduced reinvestment income would be offset by increased capital gains.

The basic mechanism for immunization relies on several measures based on present value. First, an asset's present value (usually taken as the market value)

---

[1] F.M. Redington, "Review of the Principles of Life-Office Valuations," *Journal of the Institute of Actuaries*, vol. 78, no. 3, 1952.

Figure 6: The Immunization Concept

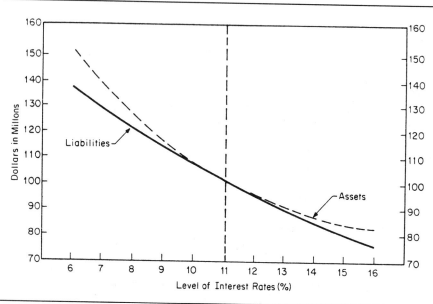

must match the present value of the liabilities. Second, the assets and the liabilities must have the same average life when weighted by the present value of their respective flows—this is just the duration measure of average life. Thus, the duration model is the first key to the immunization procedure. (However, additional second-order conditions are required to ensure the dominance pattern of Figure 6—even under relatively simple changes in interest rates.)

Immunization inherently requires portfolio changes over time. This need for continuing changes in immunized portfolios is derived from the need to preserve the dominance pattern over time. However, each cash inflow or outflow disrupts this pattern and requires some rebalancing of the immunized portfolio. These forced rebalancings are an intrinsic part of the immunization process.

Immunization of returns was an intriguing idea and quickly caught the attention of the bond community, although it seemed to be discussed more than applied. The problem was that some limited purposes truly demanded an exact lockup of a prespecified return. Immunization and related techniques did not really take off until they were embedded in the framework of the pension fund's liability schedule, which began with the rise of corporate interest in dedicated bond portfolios.

DEDICATED BOND PORTFOLIOS

The early 1980s saw explosive growth in the development of specialized bond portfolios *dedicated* to funding a prescribed set of corporate pension payouts over time. The techniques used in constructing these specialized portfolios were referred to in various ways—dedication, immunization, cash matching, horizon matching, combination matching, and so on. The fundamental objective of all these techniques was to reduce the uncertainty of long-term investment results as they related to the fulfillment of specific liabilities. Such reductions of uncertainty, in turn, led to a number of direct and indirect benefits at the corporate and institutional level.

These benefits were particularly large with market interest rates at levels materially higher than the *pro forma* or actuarial discount rate used to value the liabilities. At this time, many corporations found their profit and cash flow levels under considerable pressure, and their pension contributions had risen to a particularly onerous level. Concurrently, interest rates had risen to such historically high levels that many corporate sponsors felt that bonds represented a unique investment opportunity—at least for the long term, if not for the short term as well. This confluence of events led corporate sponsors to (1) a strong desire to reduce pension costs and (2) a willingness to allocate larger portions of their overall assets into the fixed-income area.

The dedicated portfolio fitted these needs like a glove. The basic motivation is depicted in Figure 7. Suppose a pension fund had a class of liabilities on its books at an actuarial return rate of 7%. When discounted at this rate, these liabilities had an actuarial present value of around $128 million. Suppose further that they could be fulfilled, almost dollar for dollar, in a relatively assumption-free way with a cash-matched dedicated portfolio that cost $88 million at the 14% market yields that were available in the early days of dedication. Moreover, suppose this procedure was so assumption-free that the firm's actuary would have no problem accepting it.

The $40 million gap between these two figures translated into a 31% reduction in the fund's *pro forma* liability costs. This reduction would be realized on an amortized basis over time. The appeal of such a technique is clear—it was, in effect, a rather significant funding deferment.

This was the original motivation behind the dedication trend. In subsequent years, the role of dedication in pension funding has expanded considerably, both in terms of the purposes and in the financial situations of the corporations that have embraced its use. Dedication is no longer the sole province of the cash- or earnings-stretched company. Many leading actuaries have accepted dedication (in at least some forms), and it has become a fairly standard tool in the corporate pension planners' kit bag. Many of the recent applications have been by a variety of corporations with the highest possible financial standing. In

Figure 7: Present Value of Retired-Lives Liability

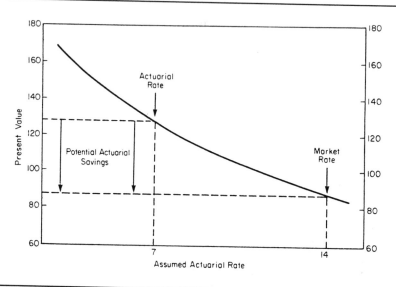

fact, it is becoming increasingly used by corporations with *overfunded* pension funds.

From a bond investment viewpoint, the problem is again one of yield lockup. However, the objective target has moved from a compounded return target to the fulfillment of a prescribed schedule of pension fund payouts that can stretch over many years. Obviously, bond credit losses are not acceptable in this kind of a program, and the security analyst must be satisfied as to the quality of individual issues.

The terms *dedication* and *immunization* are often used interchangeably. However, it is more fruitful to distinguish the individual techniques by such specific terms as *cash matching, immunization,* and *horizon matching.* This reserves *dedication* for a more encompassing description of all these formalized techniques for bond portfolios *dedicated* to servicing a prescribed set of liabilities.

CASH MATCHING

The simplest dedicated approach is cash matching. The typical cash-matching problem begins with a liability schedule such as that depicted in Figure 8. The

---

Figure 8: A Prescribed Schedule of Liabilities

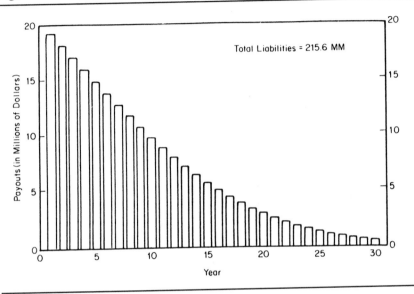

declining series of liability payouts represents the retired-lives component of a pension system.

The objective of cash matching is to develop a fixed-income portfolio that will provide a stream of payments from coupons, sinking funds, and maturing principal payments that will "match" the prescribed liability schedule. More precisely, the problem is to receive sufficient funds in advance of each scheduled payout so as to have full assurance that the payouts will be met from the dedicated portfolio alone.

The portfolio in Figure 9 represents the theoretical case of an exact match. With the exact match, each dollar of coupon and principal receipts on a given date is immediately used to support the required payout on that same date. This would seem to be the ideal fit for a cash flow matched portfolio. However, it turns out that such an exact match portfolio—even when possible—would usually not be optimal!

In practice, there will be a much larger universe of acceptable bonds that have coupon and principal payments on dates other than the exact payout dates of the liability schedule. In general, this larger universe will contain acceptable bonds with higher yields than their exact maturity counterparts. The inclusion of such higher-yielding securities naturally results in lower portfolio costs. When such bonds are used in a cash flow matching portfolio, the coupon and/or principal receipts must be accumulated for a period prior to their use on

Figure 9: An Exact-Match Portfolio

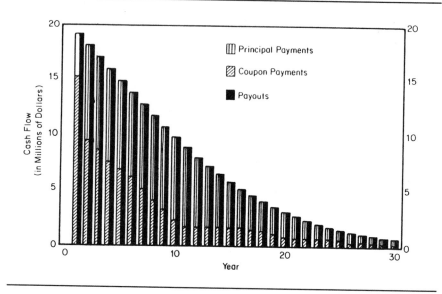

the payout date. Under such circumstances, these prior receipts must be reinvested at some rate until they are needed.

In practice, cash-matching portfolios are subjected to a variety of constraints imposed by both the logic of the problem and the degree of conservatism sought by the fund's sponsor. These constraints relate to call vulnerability, quality, type of issuer, diversification across type and individual issuer, the utilization of holdings from preexisting portfolios, and so on.

Considerable incremental savings could be extracted through energetic management of a cash-matched portfolio. At the same time, cash matching was a relatively stringent and tightly constrained period-by-period approach to the problem.

IMMUNIZATION OF LIABILITY SCHEDULES

To achieve greater flexibility and perhaps somewhat lower costs, portfolio managers need a procedure for funding scheduled liabilities without being constrained at the outset to match each individual payout, especially the relatively uncertain ones in later years. It turns out that the concept of immunization has a natural extension for dealing with this problem of scheduled liabilities.

In this application, immunization requires that the stream of liabilities be expressed in terms of their present value and their duration. Once again, by maintaining a match between the present values and durations of assets and liabilities, immunization can be achieved. The key difference here is that the asset flows and asset sales must be used to meet the cash outflows required by the liability schedule. This somewhat complicates the immunization process, as shown in Figure 10.

With the immunization concept, the portfolio structure can take on many forms as long as the interest rate sensitivity meets the several conditions required to achieve the dominance pattern of the asset curve over liability curve. This provides a high level of flexibility in choosing an immunized portfolio, but

Figure 10: The Immunization Process

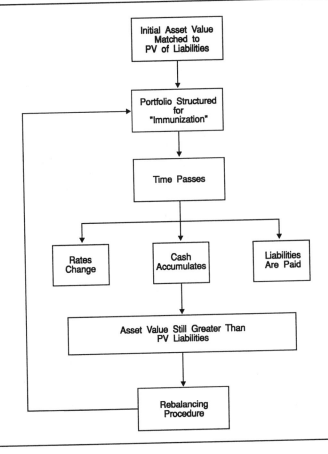

it also means that the ultimate fulfillment of the liabilities depends far more upon the specific assumptions that underlie immunization theory. Unfortunately, the actual behavior of the fixed-income markets has sometimes violated these assumptions, parallel movements in the yield curve, constant sector spreads, etc.

For instance, Redington's initial proposal required that interest rates be restricted to a flat yield curve subject only to parallel movements. Although modern techniques have enabled immunization to address a wider range of yield curve behaviors, immunization procedures still remain vulnerable to certain sequences of market movements.

HORIZON MATCHING

The preceding discussion of cash matching and immunization revealed that a properly balanced combination of these two tools could lead to a very desirable new technique. A number of such combinations were explored. In 1983, the concept of horizon matching was introduced. Horizon matching provides just such a valuable blend—one that incorporates the best features of both techniques.

The central concept of horizon matching is illustrated in Figure 11. Essentially, the liability stream is divided into two segments by the selection of an appropriate horizon. Then, a single integrated portfolio is created that simultaneously fulfills the two liability segments in different ways. In the first segment, the portfolio must provide a full cash matching of the liabilities that occur up to and including the specified horizon date. This cash-matched portion will be subject to the same stringent constraints that would apply to any cash-matched portfolio.

For purposes of illustration, the horizon is assumed to be five years. For these first five years, the sponsor will have full assurance that the horizon-matched portfolio will provide cash flows adequate to meet the specified payouts. The liabilities beyond the fifth year will be covered through a duration-matching discipline that is based on immunization principles.

Figure 11 illustrates the types of cash flows generated by a horizon-matched portfolio with a five-year horizon. In this case, the first five years are shown to be almost perfectly matched on a year-by-year basis. However, in the duration-matched period from the fifth year on, the asset flows can depart—even radically—from the pattern of the liability schedule. However, these asset flows are structured so that the overall system satisfies the interest rate sensitivity requirements (that is, the duration match of asset and liabilities) as well as a number of second-order conditions.

This structure should allow more room for elective management, and the portfolio will serve its function even if it remains passive for the first five years. Thus, theoretically, the sponsor can simply pay out the liabilities as needed dur-

Figure 11: Horizon-Matched Portfolio

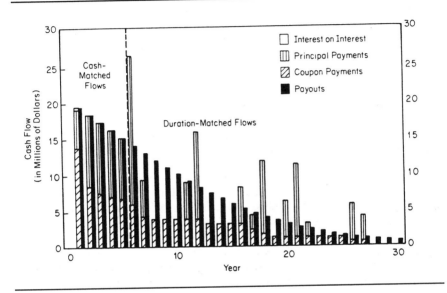

ing the first five years and not worry about the passage of time. Even with such a passive stance, the dominance condition will be maintained throughout the course of the initial horizon period as long as interest rate movements fall within the broadly prescribed range.

One problem with the practical application of immunization had to do with nonparallel movements of the yield curve. This vulnerability to yield curve re-shaping is largely eliminated in a horizon-matched portfolio with horizons of three to five years or more for the simple reason that the most severe yield curve reshapings occur in the shortest maturities.

The benefits of horizon matching do entail the acceptance of some degree of additional risk. The horizon-matched portfolio, by definition, will have a lower asset value than the fully cash-matched portfolio with its far tighter constraints. Consequently, there can be no assurance that the horizon-matched portfolio can be transformed into a fully cash-matched portfolio at any given time. Moreover, although the portfolio will retain its cash-matched characteristics through the horizon period without any further rebalancing, certain types of market movements could lead to shortfalls in the duration-matched portion once the horizon period has passed. Thus, horizon matching would fall somewhere between optimal cash matching and pure immunization in terms of both cost and the risk of potential shortfalls.

An additional advantage of horizon matching lies in the fact that the outer years of the liability schedule are often conservatively stated at the outset. Hence, the demands are likely to be relaxed with the passage of time. Horizon matching enables the portfolio to obtain cost efficiency by fully matching the more definite near-term liabilities without being hostage to specific *pro forma* liabilities that are likely to change in amount and time over the years.

CONTINGENT IMMUNIZATION

It has long been recognized that immunization procedures that stretch for the highest possible portfolio yields in a given market environment also incur the greatest risk of future shortfall. By the same token, economists have also observed that a "cushion" below this maximum rate provides additional comfort as well as flexibility to any immunization procedure. This concept of cushion flexibility can be extended to allow a significant degree of active management within a conservatively structured portfolio framework.

As interest rates rose to unprecedentedly high levels in 1981, minimum returns that were *well below* the maximum possible market rate became acceptable. Thus, when the market rate was 15%, a minimum return of 14% seemed to be a highly satisfactory level of return. For this 100-basis-point *cushion spread* (from 15% to 14%), a certain degree of portfolio flexibility could be obtained. In fact, cushion spreads of 100 to 200 basis points create a surprisingly large latitude for the pursuit of active management. With these cushion spreads, there could be a series of repeated adverse movements—the traditional "whipsaw" nightmare of every portfolio manager—and the portfolio would still retain some residual cushion above the promised minimum rate. It was this realization of the degree of flexibility afforded by reasonable cushion spreads that motivated the concept of contingent immunization.

The key idea is that managers can pursue active strategies as long as they retain a positive safety cushion. Should the market erode this safety cushion, the move is triggered to an immunized portfolio and the originally promised minimum floor return will still be achieved.

Suppose, for example, that a portfolio manager was strongly optimistic and wished to hold a portfolio of 30-year, 15% par bonds. The duration would then be seven years—far longer than the five-year horizon. This portfolio would clearly not be immunized. In fact, the least adverse movement (i.e., upward move in rates) would immediately violate the required assets line for the 15% target rate. However, if the fund is willing to accept the lower 14% floor rate as a minimum return, a wide range is tolerated in the subsequent price behavior of 30-year bonds.

If yields declined, the active strategy would have proved successful, and the safety margin of excess assets would rise with the superior performance of the 30-year bond portfolio. This successful move would enable the portfolio to generate five-year returns well in excess of the original 15% market rate. However, should interest rates rise, the safety margin would decrease, and the portfolio's assets would approach the minimum required asset level. In fact, the value of 30-year bonds would decline to the required asset level after an upward rate move of about 350 basis points. At this point, the safety margin would have been totally eroded, and the portfolio would have to be immunized to ensure fulfillment of the 14% floor rate. In this example, the portfolio can tolerate adverse market movements of more than 350 basis points even after having adopted the longest possible maturity stance in the par bond market.

How does contingent immunization compare with classical immunization? Classical immunization carries a high opportunity cost: the forgone potential profits of successful active management. Contingent immunization restores this profit potential in exchange for the spread between the immunized rate and the floor return. More generally, in the dedication context, contingent immunization incurs a somewhat higher initial portfolio cost to gain the flexibility for potential takeouts. With successful active management, these takeouts could significantly reduce the effective cost of funding the entire liability schedule.

NEW FIXED-INCOME VEHICLES

The drive for flexibility on the part of both the investor and the issuer of debt securities led to an entirely new spectrum of investment vehicles in the late 1970s and the 1980s. Together with the new portfolio strategies described above, these new instruments enabled market participants more precisely to fulfill their objectives in the increasingly volatile and competitive environment.

THE TREASURY YIELD CURVE

With the special exemptions to the rule prohibiting long Treasuries above 4.25%, the U.S. government began in 1973 to issue bonds along the entire yield curve. This was accompanied by increasing budget deficits that fueled huge increases in the net issuance of Treasury securities of all maturities. The Treasury market came to realize, in *practice*, its natural *theoretical* role as a benchmark for virtually every area of the fixed-income market. All bond spreads in every sector came to be measured relative to the Treasury yield curve level for that maturity.

FLOATING-RATE INSTRUMENTS

The late 1970s witnessed the successful introduction of a whole new class of fixed-income securities that represented a hybrid between ensured long-term financing and an economic sensitivity to short-term interest rates. *Basically,* the floating-rate bond has a coupon payment rate that is determined as a specified function of the value of some interest rate index when the coupon payment becomes due. Thus, the coupon payment "floats" with the level of interest rates. Floating-rate notes first became popular with international banks as a way of obtaining long-term financing with interest rate costs geared to the floating-rate character of their loan portfolios. With the onslaught of high interest rates and high volatility in the debt market, floating-rate notes soon found a far wider audience among issuers who wished to ensure long-term financing at current market rates without locking into the high rates that prevailed at the time of issue. Since typical floating-rate notes offered a significant yield spread advantage to actual short-term instruments (at least in the U.S. markets), they quickly found a strong appetite among investors who wished to remain in the short-term end of the maturity spectrum.

FUTURES AND OPTIONS

In 1975, the first interest rate future—based on the GNMA pass-through—was introduced on the Chicago Board of Trade. This was soon followed (January 1976) by a Treasury bill futures contract on the Chicago Mercantile Exchange. The T-bill contract quickly became a highly successful and intensively traded futures contract. It was followed in 1977 by the Treasury bond future on the Chicago Board of Trade, which has become the most successful contract in the history of exchange-traded futures. Other futures contracts in the United States include CDs, Eurodollar CDs, Treasury notes, and municipals. Futures exchanges in other countries have introduced interest rate contracts based on U.K. gilts, Japanese government yen bonds, and Eurodollar CDs.

The initial appetite for the U.S. futures contracts was provided by many of the speculators (or "locals") that traded commodity futures. However, traditional bond market participants soon learned how to use futures as effective hedging vehicles, and they began to spread to an ever-widening circle of applications. Dealers and commercial banks were among the first to use them to hedge their inventory positions. Recently, pension funds and, to a certain extent, insurance companies have utilized futures contracts to shape their interest rate sensitivity or to help in achieving transitions between changing asset allocations. In the latter applications, futures serve as a sort of highly liquid bridge that enables the fund to lock in its desired allocations until the actual cash security transactions can be more comfortably implemented. Recently, the role of futures has expanded to include the new dynamic hedging procedures that have recently become popular among corporate pension funds.

Options on Treasury bond futures were introduced on the Chicago Board of Trade in 1982. These options became popular and found a number of applications among institutional investors. Options can serve as protection for issuers who wish to lock in current interest rates for a span of time and are willing to pay the associated insurance "premium." On the asset side, options can protect the value of an investment portfolio over a limited time. They have been integrated into certain forms of dynamic hedging. The exchange-traded options contracts are often supplemented with a series of over-the-counter forward contracts on interest rates, sometimes in the form of *caps* or *floors*.

Many conventional fixed-income securities have embedded options that the investor implicitly grants to the issuer. For example, corporate bonds usually carry an explicit schedule of prices where the bond can be "called in" and redeemed prior to maturity. These call features are really a complex series of options that convey a definite economic benefit to the issuer under a sufficient decline in rates. Similarly, in mortgage securities, the ultimate mortgagor retains an option to pay off the loan under a wide variety of circumstances. Exchange-traded options can often be combined with conventional securities having embedded options to produce a package with a more desirable payoff pattern. For example, in the lower rate environment of 1985 to 1986, many such "synthetic" packages were constructed that used exchange-traded call options to offset the prepayment risks associated with high-coupon mortgage pass-throughs.

ORIGINAL ISSUED DISCOUNT BONDS

Moderate original issue discount bonds (OIDs) had long been in various markets, as the prices of new bond issues were adjusted slightly away from par in order to bring them into alignment with the current market. Actually, the tax-exempt market had seen some issuance of *nickel bonds* carrying the near-zero coupon rate of 0.05%. (These nickels were small tail components in a package of serial maturities that comprised a single municipal underwriting.) However, in 1980, a new wave of taxable OIDs surfaced. These issues carried coupon rates that were significantly lower than market yields and hence were issued at prices ranging from 35 to 85. They were harbingers of a whole new family of first low-coupon and then zero-coupon securities that have had a profound impact on the bond market as a whole.

The initial motivation for the early OIDs sprang from certain tax advantages that became attractive in a higher interest rate environment. The issuers of such securities obtained a significant benefit from the then available tax regulations which enabled them to deduct computed interest on a straight-line basis (this rule has been subsequently changed). Investors were attracted to such securities because, at high interest rates, the OIDs afforded extraordinary call protection and a high duration with the associated protection from lower reinvestment rates over the bond life. This combination of motivations led to its ultimate realization in the form of a zero-coupon security where the only interest payment consisted of a lump-sum payment at maturity. Many corporate and international issuers came forth with such securities and they were quite popular in the marketplace for a period of time. Security analysts must include the accrual of discount as an interest item in their measurement of debt service coverage. Cash outflows will, of course, be concentrated in the maturity year.

ZERO-COUPON BONDS

Since the zero-coupon bond provided no interim payments until maturity, the credit of the issuing entity was emphasized. This naturally led to a strong interest in obtaining zero-coupon instruments based on U.S. Treasury securities. By "stripping" the coupons from a U.S. Treasury bond, one could obtain individual coupon payments (and of course one maturity payment) that would act as such single-payment instruments. These so called "stripped Treasuries" were available from time to time, but the supply was limited because U.S. Treasury regulations discouraged their formation.

In 1982, in conjunction with changes in tax rules that rationalized their tax treatment, the U.S. Treasury lifted these restrictions. Investment dealers immediately began to create various forms of single-payment instruments derived from stripped Treasury bonds. These instruments were immensely popular, and large proportions of certain Treasury issues were transformed into these specialized securities. These instruments were given an amusing set of acronyms, all depicting different species of the feline family: *TIGERS* (Treasury Investment New Growth Receipts), *CATS* (Certificates of Accrual for Treasury Securities), etc. These new securities developed into a relatively liquid market with pure single-payment instruments that spanned the entire yield curve. At long last, the academic's dream of having market-determined discount rates for virtually every point in the future was now at hand (subject to a few mild distortions that always seem inevitable in any real capital market). Any fixed-income security could—in theory—be decomposed into its individual cash flows, and then these flows could be valued relative to the corresponding maturity point on the "spot rate" yield curve.

In practice, these single-payment vehicles were used in a host of applications in the new high interest rate environment. For the investor who wished to lock up yield over a specified period, they provided the ideal vehicle. For the rate-of-return investor who wished to obtain a precise duration instrument, these single-payment bonds provided the answer. For the dedicated portfolio that needed to fit additional dollar flows into precise periods in the future, the single-payment bond was the perfect "plug."

The various packagers of such securities waged a considerable battle until the U.S. Treasury decided to get directly into the act in 1985. At this point, the U.S. Treasury announced that it would henceforth allow for strips to be created out of Treasury bonds at the instigation of the holder. In essence, the U.S. government would perform the role of stripping dealer by dismembering a Treasury security into its component cash flows and registering each of the components separately. This "strips" market continued to flourish on this new basis until the appetite for single-payment instruments abated during the lower interest rate periods that followed the great rallies of 1984 and 1985 to 1986.

INTEREST RATE SWAPS

Another phenomenon of the 1980s has been the quiet marketplace explosion of interest rate swaps. An interest rate swap is basically a contract in which one party agrees to pay a series of fixed-rate coupon payments in exchange for the receipt of floating-rate coupon payments from a second party. There is no exchange of principal payments. Thus, in an interest rate swap, an investor who holds a fixed-rate instrument can agree to swap its coupon flows for the flows that would be received from a floating-rate instrument.

Interest rate swaps can be used either for investors such as thrifts and insurance companies (asset-based swaps) or for issuers (liability-based swaps). Interest rate swaps can be struck across many maturities and with a wide range of counterparties. They are powerful weapons in the battle for greater flexibility for both investors and issuers, and they have a very wide range of applications: The swap market grew from a standing start in 1982 to over $200 billion by 1986!

Issuers can use interest rate swaps to achieve important savings in financing costs. For example, suppose a given issuer wishes to obtain floating-rate financing, but the issuer represents a more attractive credit to investors as a long-term issuer in certain markets. The issuer can proceed to issue long-term debt at the preferential rates, then execute an interest rate swap with a counterparty into a more attractive floating-rate exposure than could have been obtained by going directly to the floating-rate market. As another example of a liability-based application, suppose an issuer of outstanding long-term debt feels that rates may be heading lower. Participation in that decline can be achieved by swapping the currently outstanding long-term payments for floating-rate payments.

On the investment side, interest rate swaps can be used to transform the cash flow of a fixed-payment portfolio to that of a floating-rate portfolio or vice-versa. Moreover, since the floating-rate component acts as a proxy for future short-term rates, the floating-rate side can be used as a hedge against arbitrage financing costs or against the costs of future cash borrowings. By entering into an interest rate swap that substitutes floating-rate payments for a series of fixed payments, investors also significantly lower the duration of an existing component of their portfolios. Note that interest rate swaps can often have accounting advantages. For example, by acting as a counterhedge to an existing investment position, swaps can reduce the interest rate exposure of existing bond holdings. The use of swaps can materially alter the interest rate sensitivity and cash flow characteristics of a portfolio without incurring the adverse tax and accounting consequences of an outright sale.

In today's world, the drive for flexibility has become paramount, and the interest rate swap is indeed a powerful tool. From this brief sampling of its many applications, one can see why the interest rate swap market has so quickly grown to its current size.

The corporate borrower who issues floating-rate obligations or engages in interest rate swaps makes life difficult for the security analyst seeking to project borrowing costs. There is no practical alternative to selecting some arbitrary but reasonable average rate.

THE MOVE TOWARD STRUCTURED MANAGEMENT

The 1980s have seen a vast change in the goals and styles of bond portfolio management. In some ways, it has been a disappointing period of lowered expectations. In other ways, it has laid the foundation for a better-defined and more realistic appraisal of the entire role of the bonds component within various institutional funds.

Investors have become considerably disenchanted, perhaps predictably, with the ability of bond managers to consistently "time" the swings in the bond market and to reap excess returns through rate anticipation. The return statistics from the early 1980s indicated that the majority of active managers failed to outperform the broad market rate-of-return indexes. Bond managers found themselves in need of a credible new approach that could ensure more reliable performance results.

Bond dedication appeared to be *the* solution for a while. As one fund after another elected to construct a dedicated portfolio, a massive transition seemed under way from fully active management to this highly structured form of bond management. Bond dedication did indeed eliminate many of the problems associated with the recent adverse experience with unfettered active management. However, dedication derived much of its appeal from the high interest rates and the wide actuarial spreads that prevailed in the early 1980s. Bond dedication could not serve as bond strategy for *all* times and for *all* purposes.

With the decline in rates from the highs of 1981, a clear need developed for structural approaches other than dedication to bond management.

The key element of any structured approach was the disciplined control of rate risk. By controlling the portfolio's interest rate sensitivity relative to some benchmark index, professional bond managers could pursue a series of active strategies based on relative value, and their results would no longer depend totally on an explicit (or implicit) bet on the direction of interest rates. Two major benefits resulted: (1) Managers could focus on professional insights in pursuit of *incremental* relative returns, and (2) sponsors could begin to expect *total* returns that had a certain degree of consistency relative to the bond market as a whole.

As more bond managers began to measure their performances against the broad market indexes as well as against each other, and as they sought to avoid the timing problems of the past, the range of returns achieved by managers began to close in around broad market index returns. Managers began to use a series of structural techniques to bring themselves within specified proximity to these index returns. These techniques included various forms of closet indexing and duration control relative to the index. Finally, as fund sponsors began to seek basic market returns with minimum management costs (especially those sponsors with very large funds), money began to flow into *explicit* bond index funds, first in 1985 and then much more significantly in 1986.

At this point many fund sponsors basically want to achieve returns from their bond component that coincide with the broad market indexes. Pension fund money continues to be directed toward bond index funds that simply mimic this broad structure of the fixed-income market. The fixed-income area is following an evolutionary trend in management styles that is similar to that which occurred several years earlier in the equity area. A considerable degree of commitment to some form of active bond management remains, but such active management is increasingly subject to various explicit forms of structured risk control.

The structure of risk control may take various forms. For example, the portfolio may be required to have returns that must approximate those of an explicit index. There may be carefully controlled departures gauged so that the portfolio returns cannot fall more than a certain tolerance limit below the index returns. Or the control structure may take the related form of a duration target which is set jointly with the sponsor. This target may differ from index control if the chosen duration is significantly shorter or longer than the index duration. Recently, the techniques of *dynamic hedging* have been applied to risk control in the bond market. Dynamic hedging is a procedure that changes the portfolio duration in accordance with a well-defined discipline to achieve an option-like return over a specified period. Thus, the first response to the disenchantment with all-out timing forms of active management has been to cluster around a broad index of the fixed-income markets or to enter into some highly specialized structured portfolio such as dedication. Peering into the future, one might expect that the greater concern with liabilities would lead to bond management styles that more directly address the asset and liability problem.

To a certain extent, the liabilities certainly did thrust themselves on the bond managers' consciousness during the heyday of bond dedications. However, a much more generalized approach can be envisioned in terms of a spectrum of active strategies structured around baseline indexes that are directly related to liabilities. A continuum of departures from the pure matched-funding strategy, entailing various degrees of risk, could minimize the risk of fulfilling the specified liabilities. The key ingredient would be a baseline index that captures the interest rate sensitivity and other risk characteristics of the liabilities and establishes a customized target for each fund. In such a context, active managers would be able to pursue their professional insights in search of improved returns relative to this baseline target, thus retaining active management within a structure that is directed toward the ultimate goals of the fund.

The ability to readily define such a baseline index is certainly more characteristic of the fixed-income markets than of the equity markets. (In fact, this may be an important distinguishing feature of bonds as an asset class.) Managers and fund sponsors alike should take advantage of this natural opportunity that the fixed-income markets afford.

PART III B

Basic Analytical Tools

Chapter III B-1

Conventional Measures of Bond Value

PRICING OF CORPORATE BONDS

At the time when an agreement is reached to trade a given block of bonds, it is highly likely that neither side will know the exact trading price. This remarkable statement is not an indictment. Rather, it is a tribute to the bond market's standardized price and yield measures which allow traders to focus more on the value of a trade instead of a potentially misleading market price.

To understand this somewhat paradoxical statement, let us take a 30-year, 7% bond as a concrete example. Assume that this bond has just been issued at a dollar price of 100% and that the first coupon will be made in exactly six months. Under these circumstances, the dollar price of 100% means that these bonds could be purchased at a cost equal to 100% of the bond's face amount, i.e., each $1,000 bond would cost $1,000. Now suppose that the level of interest rates remains absolutely stable for a period of three months. What price would we expect to pay for these same bonds? One might reason that since interest rates had not changed, there would be no market forces leading to a price change, and therefore we can expect to still pay $1,000 for each bond.

"An Analytic Approach to the Bond Market," Martin L. Leibowitz, *Financial Analyst's Handbook I, Methods, Theory, & Portfolio Management*, Dow Jones-Irwin, Inc., 1975, Chapter 9, Pages 234-246.

This answer would be wrong! The correct answer is that this bond would have a market price of about 101.75%, i.e., $1,017.50 per bond. The additional $17.50 arises because the purchaser at this point in time is not only buying a long-term 7% instrument in a 7% market, he is also buying the right to receive the next $35 coupon payment due in three months' time. By the same token, the seller of the bond is forgoing all rights to any part of this coupon payment. However, the seller has invested for three months in a 7% interest-bearing instrument, and he would naturally expect to receive some appropriate interest payment. This incremental payment of $17.50 of accrued interest is a mechanism for settling all these claims.

Under our assumption of absolutely stable interest rates, the actual market price would grow over time as shown in Figure 1. The slight curvature in this curve represents the effect of implicit compounding at that daily rate which provides a 3.5% growth every six months. After three months, the exact market price would be $1,017.35. Because of the compounding effect, this value is slightly under the figure of $1,017.50 used above. The market price continues to grow until six months have elapsed. At this point, the market would be exactly equal to $1,035. However, the bond's owner on the beginning of this day is entitled to receive a $35 coupon payment. If the owner were to sell his bond at this six-month point, this coupon payment would fully reimburse him for all interest due. Consequently, the seller would not need to seek additional interest-due compensation from the bond's buyer, i.e., the sale would take place at a market price of $1,000. On the following day, the bondholder would have earned one day's interest, and this would again have to be reflected by an increment in the bond's market price. Over the subsequent six months, we would again see the interest amount being impounded in the bond's market price. This interest cycle is repeated every six months as shown in Figure 1.

This interest cycle effect means that the market price of a par bond changes every day even when there is absolutely no change in interest rate levels. Most market participants would be interested in this bond in terms of its *promised* interest rates and the relationship of this bond to other bonds with similar promised interest rates. They would view this interest cycle effect as essentially irrelevant to these judgments. They would feel that the daily variation in market price was undesirable, confusing the basic value of the bond as a 7% instrument in a 7% market.

For these reasons, the bond market has developed the convention of trading on a price figure which excludes this interest build-up cycle. This is done in the following manner. First, the coupon payment is divided by the number of days in the six-month cycle. This gives a value for the amount of interest accrued each day. Whenever the bond is sold, this accrual would have developed over the period from the last coupon payment to the date of sale, i.e., the delivery date. By multiplying the number of days since the last coupon payment by interest accrued per day, we obtain a figure called the accrued interest for that

Figure 1: Market Value Over Time at the Same Market Level (30-Year, 7% Bond Priced at Par to Yield 7%)

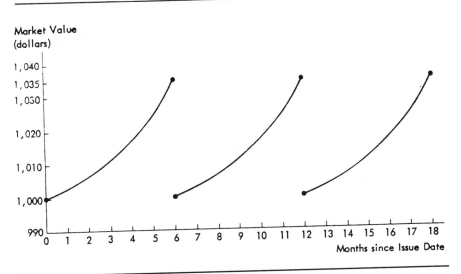

specific trading date. This accrued interest figure is taken as a measure of the holder's fractional interest in the next coupon payment.

The magnitude of the accrued interest grows day by day as shown in Figure 2, until the six-month point is reached. Then the next coupon payment is made. Consequently, on that payment day, there are zero days since the last coupon payment, and the accrued interest amount drops to zero. The accrued interest then starts to grow once more day by day until the subsequent coupon payment.

Comparing Figure 2 with Figure 1, we see (not unexpectedly) that the pattern of accrued interest over time closely matches the interest cycle in the bond's market price. This is the basis for the market trading price convention. When the accrued interest for a given day is subtracted from the market price for that day, we obtain a number called the bond's *principal value*. This term indicates that it represents the cost of buying the bond's intrinsic principal as opposed to its incidental interest accrual. As seen from Figure 3, the principal value figure is removed from most of the effects of the interest cycle. The principal value is an essentially constant price in a constant market. This is precisely what the marketplace wants. The market can focus on this principal value figure even though it knows that the accrued interest must be added to determine the final trade price. The accrued interest is just a straightforward mechanical computation.

Figure 2: Growth of Accrued Interest Over Time (30-Year, 7% Bond)

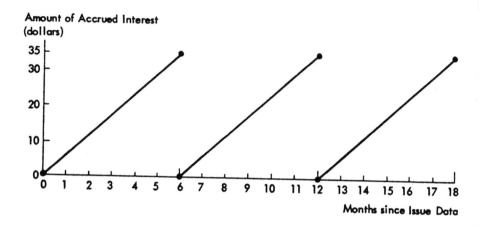

Amount of Accrued Interest
(dollars)

Months since Issue Data

Figure 3: Principal Value Over Time at the Same Market Level (30-Year, 7% Bond Priced at Par to Yield 7%)

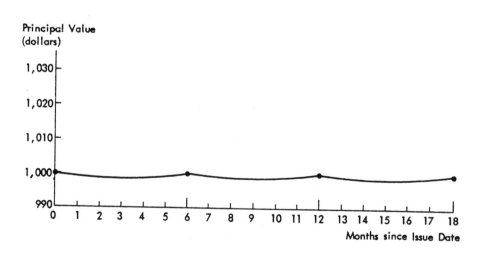

Principal Value
(dollars)

Months since Issue Date

Consequently, all the forces of market fluctuation can be viewed as expressed in the principal value figure.

The market has one further convention: the principal value is stated as a percentage of the bond's face value. This percentage figure is referred to as the "dollar price" (a curiously inappropriate choice of terms). Thus, for a 7% bond with the usual face value of $1,000 at a time three months past its last coupon payment, a dollar price of 100 would imply a principal value of $1,000 and a market cost of $1,000 plus accrued interest of $17.50, i.e., a market cost of $1,017.50. Similarly, a dollar price of 80 would correspond to a principal value of $800.00 and a market cost of $817.50.

Looking closely at Figure 3, we see that there still remains some slight coupon cycle effect. This arises because the bond's market price has a slight curvature associated with the increasing growth rate achieved through compounding. However, to keep trade computations simple, the accrued interest grows along the straight-line curve characteristic of simple interest. This slight inconsistency explains the market paradox of why 7% bonds in a 7% market do not always have a dollar price of exactly 100.

In the above, we have avoided any discussion of many detailed conventions and standards used in trade computations for different fixed interest securities. For example, there is one method for counting the elapsed time from the last coupon date for corporates, and quite another method for Treasury bonds. As another example, Figures 1 and 3 show the market price and principal value as a smooth curve over time. The exact curve depends on the interpolation techniques used in the pricing process. Here again, these interpolation standards vary from corporates to treasuries to agencies.[1]

THE YIELD BOOK

Bonds are evaluated and traded in terms of their yield-to-maturity values. For a given coupon, maturity, and dollar price, these yield values can be quickly determined from a set of tables called a *yield book*. A sample page from a yield book is shown in Figure 4. The yield book is sometimes referred to as the "basis book" or as the "bond value book."

Yield books are usually organized first by coupon section, starting with the lowest and proceeding in steps of one eighth of 1% to the highest coupons covered. Within each coupon section, each column corresponds to a different remaining life, usually incrementing from one-month steps under five years to

---

[1] For a comprehensive, detailed discussion of the various standard price computation methods, see Bruce Spence, Jacob Y. Graudenz, and John J. Lynch, Jr., *Standard Securities Calculation Methods* (Security Industry Association, 1973).

Figure 4: Sample Page from a Yield Book

7% YEARS and MONTHS

Yield	26-6	27-0	27-6	28-0	28-6	29-0	29-6	30-0
4.00	148.74	149.26	149.76	150.26	150.74	151.22	151.68	152.14
4.20	144.51	144.96	145.41	145.85	146.28	146.69	147.11	147.51
4.40	140.44	140.84	141.24	141.62	142.00	142.37	142.73	143.08
4.60	136.54	136.89	137.24	137.57	137.90	138.22	138.53	138.84
4.80	132.79	133.10	133.40	133.69	133.97	134.25	134.52	134.79
5.00	129.19	129.46	129.71	129.96	130.21	130.45	130.68	130.91
5.20	125.73	125.96	126.18	126.39	126.60	126.80	127.00	127.19
5.40	122.41	122.60	122.78	122.96	123.14	123.31	123.48	123.64
5.60	119.21	119.37	119.53	119.67	119.82	119.96	120.10	120.23
5.80	116.14	116.27	116.40	116.52	116.63	116.75	116.86	116.97
6.00	113.19	113.29	113.39	113.48	113.58	113.67	113.75	113.84
6.10	111.75	111.84	111.93	112.01	112.09	112.17	112.25	112.32
6.20	110.34	110.42	110.50	110.57	110.64	110.71	110.77	110.84
6.30	108.96	109.03	109.09	109.15	109.21	109.27	109.33	109.38
6.40	107.61	107.66	107.72	107.77	107.82	107.87	107.91	107.96
6.50	106.28	106.32	106.37	106.41	106.45	106.49	106.53	106.56
6.60	104.98	105.01	105.04	105.08	105.11	105.14	105.17	105.20
6.70	103.70	103.72	103.75	103.77	103.79	103.82	103.84	103.86
6.80	102.44	102.46	102.47	102.49	102.50	102.52	102.53	102.55
6.90	101.21	101.22	101.22	101.23	101.24	101.25	101.25	101.26
7.00	100.00	100.00	100.00	100.00	100.00	100.00	100.00	100.00
7.10	98.81	98.81	98.80	98.79	98.78	98.78	98.77	98.77
7.20	97.65	97.63	97.62	97.61	97.59	97.58	97.57	97.55
7.30	96.51	96.48	96.46	96.44	96.42	96.40	96.39	96.37
7.40	95.38	95.35	95.33	95.30	95.28	95.25	95.23	95.21
7.50	94.28	94.25	94.21	94.18	94.15	94.12	94.09	94.07
7.60	93.20	93.16	93.12	93.08	93.05	93.01	92.98	92.95
7.70	92.14	92.09	92.05	92.01	91.96	91.93	91.89	91.85
7.80	91.09	91.04	90.99	90.90	90.90	90.86	90.82	90.78
7.90	90.07	90.01	89.96	89.91	89.86	89.81	89.77	89.72
8.00	89.06	89.00	88.95	88.89	88.84	88.79	88.74	88.69
8.10	88.08	88.01	87.95	87.95	87.83	87.78	87.72	87.67
8.20	87.11	87.04	86.97	86.91	86.85	86.79	86.73	86.68
8.30	86.15	86.08	86.01	85.94	85.88	85.82	85.76	85.70
8.40	85.22	85.14	85.07	85.00	84.93	84.87	84.80	84.75
8.50	84.30	84.22	84.14	84.07	84.00	83.93	83.87	83.81
8.60	83.39	83.31	83.23	83.16	83.08	83.01	82.95	82.88
8.70	82.51	82.42	82.34	82.26	82.19	82.11	82.04	81.98
8.80	81.63	81.55	81.46	81.38	81.30	81.23	81.16	81.09
8.90	80.78	80.69	80.60	80.52	80.44	80.36	80.29	80.22
9.00	79.93	79.84	79.75	79.67	79.59	79.51	79.43	79.36
9.10	79.11	79.01	78.92	78.83	78.75	78.67	78.59	78.52
9.20	78.29	78.20	78.10	78.01	77.93	77.85	77.77	77.70
9.30	77.49	77.39	77.30	77.21	77.12	77.04	76.96	76.89
9.40	76.71	76.61	76.51	76.42	76.33	76.25	76.17	76.09
9.50	75.93	75.83	75.73	75.64	75.55	75.47	75.39	75.31
9.60	75.17	75.07	74.97	74.88	74.79	74.70	74.62	74.54
9.70	74.43	74.32	74.22	74.13	74.04	73.95	73.87	73.79
9.80	73.69	73.59	73.49	73.39	73.30	73.21	73.13	73.05
9.90	72.97	72.86	72.76	72.66	72.57	72.48	72.40	72.32
10.00	72.26	72.15	72.05	71.95	71.86	71.77	71.69	71.61
10.20	70.87	70.77	70.66	70.56	70.47	70.38	70.29	70.21
10.40	69.53	69.42	69.32	69.22	69.13	69.04	68.95	68.87
10.60	68.24	68.13	68.02	67.92	67.83	67.74	67.65	67.57
10.80	66.98	66.87	66.77	66.67	66.57	66.48	66.40	66.31
11.00	65.77	65.65	65.55	65.45	65.36	65.27	65.18	65.10
11.20	64.59	64.48	64.37	64.27	64.18	64.09	64.01	63.93
11.40	63.45	63.34	63.23	63.13	63.04	62.95	62.87	62.79
11.60	62.34	62.23	62.13	62.03	61.94	61.85	61.77	61.69
11.80	61.27	61.16	61.06	60.96	60.87	60.79	60.70	60.63
12.00	60.23	60.13	60.02	59.93	59.84	59.75	59.67	59.60

Source: Reproduced from Expanded Bond Value Tables, desk edition, p. 738, copyright 1970, Financial Publishing Company, Boston, Mass.

six-month steps for longer lives. (As we shall see, the reason for this higher resolution at the shorter life is that the price/yield relationships are more critically dependent here on the passage of time.) The rows designate different yield values, usually at increments of 0.10% within the practically important range of values. The body of the yield table contains dollar prices. For each specific yield value, i.e., a given row, and each specific remaining life, i.e., a given column, there is a corresponding dollar price shown where the row and column intersect.

As an example of how a yield book is used in practice, suppose we have a bond with a 7% coupon and a remaining life of 30 years. First we assume that the bond has a yield of 7.5%. We then want to find the bond's dollar price. We would first turn to the 7% coupon section of the yield book. Then we would find that page in that section containing a column heading of 30 years. Figure 4 represents one such page. We would then find the row (shown in the left-most column) associated with our desired yield value of 7.5%.

At the intersection of the 30-year column and the 7.5% row, we find our answer—a dollar price of 94.07. This says that a 30-year, 7% bond selling to yield 7.50% to maturity would have a dollar price of 94.07.

By the same token, we could also turn the above statement around and say that a 30-year, 7% bond selling at a dollar price of 94.07 provides a yield to maturity of 7.50%. The yield book can also be used in this reverse fashion to find the yield value corresponding to a given dollar price. For example, if we had only known that our 30-year, 7% bond was selling at a dollar price of 94.07, then we would have searched down the 30-year column until we found the dollar price of 94.07. By tracing across this row to the left, we would find that this corresponds to the yield value of 7.50%. As another example of finding the yield value associated from a given price, suppose that our 30-year, 7% bond now has a dollar price of 100. Searching down the 30-year column, we find the figure 100 in a certain row. Tracing across that row to the left, we see that this dollar price of 100 corresponds to a yield of exactly 7.00%.

Even the thickest yield books only contain a limited representation of different values for lifetimes, coupons, yields, and dollar prices. Fortunately, bonds do trade more often than at six-month intervals and they do move in yield increments of less than 0.10%. As with any tabular presentation, the gaps in the yield book are filled by a process of interpolation. Using this interpolation process, one can find the dollar price corresponding to any yield value for any given bond. The process can also be reversed to find the yield value corresponding to any bond's dollar price.[2]

---

[2] For a more theoretical explanation of interpolation methodology, the reader is referred to Sidney Homer and Martin L. Leibowitz, *Inside the Yield Book* (New York Institute of Finance and Prentice-Hall, Inc., 1972); or Spence, Graudenz, and Lynch, *Standard Securities Calculation Methods*.

A skilled practitioner with the yield book can perform the table lookup and interpolation process in an amazingly brief span of time. In fact, most professional traders can immediately provide a good estimate of a bond's yield—without any reference at all to a yield book.

In recent years, several compact computer calculators have been developed which have the capability of computing yields from prices or prices from yields. These calculators perform all interpolations and produce exact results. These are rapidly becoming invaluable tools on many trading desks.

THE MANY FACETS OF YIELD TO MATURITY

It is relatively easy to learn how to calculate a yield-to-maturity value for a given bond. However, it is quite another matter to understand what this yield value really means.

Most people think of the yield to maturity as an average percentage rate at which coupon income plus principal gain accumulates over the bond's life. This corresponds closely with the main connotation of the word *yield* as a rate of return. It is certainly this interpretation which underlies most yield-related investment decisions.

However, there are a surprising number of different ways of interpreting the conventional yield to maturity. These interpretations may seem, at first glance, very different from one another. Yet every one of them is consistent with the basic mathematics for computing yield to maturity. Consequently, all of these interpretations are mathematically equivalent with one another.

First of all, one can interpret the yield to maturity as a special discount rate. The cash flow of a bond consists of its coupon payments together with its redemption payment at maturity. The present value of this cash flow depends on the assumed discount rate. As the discount rate increases, the bond's fixed cash flow is discounted more severely, and so its present value *decreases*. If the discount rate is increased, step by step, from a sufficiently low starting level, then the present value will gradually decrease until it just equals the bond's market price. The yield to maturity is that specific discount rate which produces this equality of present value and market price.

Thus, when future cash flows are discounted at the yield rate, then the bond's cost corresponds precisely to its investment worth as measured by its present value.

This interpretation coincides with the definition of the fundamental analytic concept of an internal rate of return (IRR). It is quite proper to say that a yield to maturity is just the internal rate of return over the bond's remaining life. However, it should be recognized that yield to maturity is an internal rate of return expressed in terms of certain special bond market conventions. For example, the yield figure is based upon semiannual compounding and is actually quoted as twice the semiannual rate.

The equality of the bond's market cost with its present value at the yield rate provides the key to a related interpretation. The bond's present value can be expressed as the sum of the present value of its stream of coupon payments and the present value of its redemption payment. But the present value of the redemption payment less the bond's market cost is just the bond's principal appreciation in terms of present value. Actually, this appreciation is invariably negative, i.e., the investor always incurs a loss of principal value in terms of present value. However, this principal loss in present value is exactly compensated by the present value of the coupon stream. This compensation follows directly from the starting equality of the present value of all future payments with the bond's cost. This "break-even situation" when discounting at the yield rate means that the investor cannot increase his present worth by purchasing the bond: He gets precisely what he pays for and no more. Thus, when he gives up the cost value of the bond, he accepts a future principal repayment having a smaller present value. In return for this principal loss, he receives compensation through the coupon stream. Because of the break-even situation, the principal loss must exactly match the worth of the coupon stream in present value terms.

For example, consider a 30-year, 7% bond with a market cost of $940.65. The yield to maturity is 7.50%. Using this value of 7.50% as a discount rate, the $1,000 redemption payment due 30 years from now would have a present value today of $109.83. Since the principal value of the bond today is $940.65, the investor would experience a net principal loss of:

$$\$109.83 - \$940.65 = -\$830.82$$

in terms of present value. Again using the 7.50% yield value as a discount rate, a stream of 60 semiannual payments of $35 has a total present value of:

$$23.74 \times \$35.00 = \$830.82.$$

So we see that the buyer of this bond accepts a principal loss worth $830.82 today and in return receives a future coupon stream having this same present value of $830.82.

The present value break-even situation provides yet another interesting and somewhat surprising interpretation. Consider a par bond with a coupon rate equal to the yield rate of the given bond and having the same maturity date. This par bond will, by definition, have the same yield to maturity as the given bond. The break-even situation for the par bond will consist of equality between the par cost of $1,000 and the sum of the present value of the yield-level coupon stream and the present value of the future redemption payment. If we take the difference between the equalities for these two bonds, then the present value of the redemption payment drops out. This says that the difference between par and the given bond's market cost must be equal to the difference between the present values of the two coupon streams. This difference, in turn, is just equal to the present value of the incremental coupon stream of the yield-level par bond over the given bond. Assuming that the investor could theoretically purchase such a yield-level par bond, then by forgoing this par bond in favor of, say, a lower coupon discount bond, he is, in a sense, forgoing this incremental coupon stream. In return, the investor of course pays a reduced price for his discount bond. In fact, he saves the discount and this savings just equals the present value lost through his giving up the incremental coupon stream.

Thus, a bond's discount (or premium) can be viewed as exact compensation in present value terms for the greater (or lesser) coupon flow that would be theoretically available from a par bond having the same yield.

As a numerical illustration, take our earlier example of a 30-year, 7% bond priced at 94.065 for a yield to maturity of 7.50%. As we saw earlier, the market cost of $940.65 per bond can be equated to the present value of the semiannual $35.00 coupons, $830.82, plus the $109.83 present value of the final $1,000.00 redemption payment ($940.65 = $830.82 + $109.83). The corresponding yield-level bond would be a 30-year, 7.50% bond selling at 100 for a yield to maturity of 7.50%. This bond would provide 60 semiannual coupon payments of $37.50 each. This is $2.50 more per coupon payment than we would get from the 7% bond. These 60 semiannual increments of $2.50 each have a combined present value of $59.35. The investor who chooses the 7.00% bond over the theoretically available 7.50% bond gives up this incremental present value of $59.35. In return, he only pays $940.65 for the 7% bond. This is exactly $59.35 ($1,000.00 − $940.65 = $59.35) less than he would have paid for the 7.50% par bond. This discount of $59.35 precisely matches the $59.35 present value of the incremental coupon flow forgone.

In the interpretations of yield to maturity discussed above, only the original cost price of the bonds has been mentioned. There has been no reference to any interim price values for the bond between the purchase date and maturity. The mathematical calculation of yield to maturity is indeed based upon a bond purchased today at a given price and then held to its maturity date. Consequently, for the computation of yield to maturity, it is not necessary to make any assumptions regarding interim prices.

However, there is one important interpretation of yield which leads to a normative statement about interim prices. The key idea here is that a bond provides a constant uniform yield over every six-month period. To the extent that the coupon payment falls short, the yield deficit is made up by an assumed amortization of the bond's principal value. One can actually define the yield to maturity as that uniform rate which just amortizes the bond to its $1,000 maturity value over its remaining life.

To see how this works, again take the example of our 30-year, 7.00% bond priced at 94.065 for a yield to maturity of 7.50%. Over the first six-month period, this interpretation would require a return of:

$$7.50\% \div 2 = 3.75\%$$

or

$$0.0375 \times \$940.65 = \$35.27.$$

The first coupon payment would only provide $35.00, so that the additional

$$\$35.27 - \$35.00 = \$.27$$

would have to be achieved through principal amortization. Adding this $.27 to the original $940.65 cost value, the bond's amortized value after six months becomes $940.92. Over the next six months, the return must now be

$$0.0375 \times \$940.92 = \$35.28.$$

The second coupon payment will handle $35.00 of the requirement, leaving $.28 to be obtained through amortization. Consequently, at the end of one year, the bond will have an amortized value of $941.20, or an amortized dollar price of $94.12. If we continued in this fashion for each of the next 58 semiannual periods, we would find that the bond's amortized value just reached $1,000, or a dollar price of 100, at the end of the last period.

This method of price amortization is often referred to as *scientific amortization.*

As mentioned earlier, one can actually define yield to maturity as that constant yield rate which produces a scientific amortization to 100 at maturity. Consequently, the scientifically amortized price value at any given interim point in time must result in the same yield to maturity. For example, we saw that a 30-year, 7% bond costing 94.065 would have a scientifically amortized value after the first six months of 94.092, corresponding to the yield rate of 7.50%. Now suppose one could purchase a 29.5-year, 7% bond for 94.092. Since this bond lies along the same scientific amortization path, we would expect both bonds to have same yield to maturity, i.e., 7.50%. Similarly, after one year, our 30-year, 7% bond would have scientifically amortized to a value of 94.12, which corresponds to a 7.50% yield to maturity for a 29-year, 7% bond.

Thus, scientific amortization can be viewed in terms of the sequence of dollar prices that would result if the bond maintained a constant yield to maturity over time. In other words, scientific amortization corresponds to the sequence of prices lying in the same row of the yield book (Figure 4).

This observation leads to another closely related interpretation of yield to maturity. The yield to maturity can be defined as the total return rate over the next six-month period when the bond is then assumed to be priced at the same yield to maturity. While this definition seems somewhat circular, it is worth stressing the assumptions required to turn the yield-to-maturity figure into a rate of return value, even over the first six months.

As a side point, it might be noted that under conditions of generally stable interest rates, the price of a discount bond will move upwards towards par with the passage of time. Of course, the particular orbit of prices which it will follow over time cannot be known precisely, even under the dullest and most stable of real-life markets. However, it is very convenient, both for purposes of accounting as well as for investment analysis, to have some normative method of describing price amortization over time. For such purposes, a bond is often treated as maintaining an absolutely constant book yield to maturity over its entire life. Scientific amortization then becomes the most natural and consistent price amortization technique for use with this constant yield convention. The only other amortization scheme in common usage, the straight-line method, has the utmost in simplicity as being its only rationale. Whatever amortization scheme may be used, the investor is well advised to keep constantly in mind that it is a highly artificial projection of prices, that amortized price figures need not reflect any market or opportunity value, and that amortization schemes have been designed for convenience and do not represent even the most elementary factors (e.g., yield curves) which are sure to affect future price levels in reality.

The yield to maturity can also be interpreted as a growth rate of total compounded return, but only under some rather restrictive assumptions. First of all, the bond must be held to maturity. Second, all coupon payments must be reinvested and compounded at the yield rate itself. Third, the yield must be accepted as an *equivalent* growth rate over the bond's entire life, with no implication about rates of return over interim periods. If the growth at the yield rate is assumed to be *uniform* over interim periods, then this implies that scientific price amortization is assumed to be occurring in the marketplace. These rather restrictive conditions cause problems.

All the above interpretations are perfectly valid, and each would equally well serve as the definition of yield to maturity. However, there is little doubt that most practitioners subjectively interpret yield to maturity as a rate of growth from the combined dollar value of interest and principal. This growth rate of total net return is the measure that indeed should be most important to bond investment decisions. Consequently it is reasonable to suspect that most practitioners conveniently presume that the yield-to-maturity value is equivalent to this fully compounded growth rate measure. This presumption can be misleading when yields to maturity, interpreted as growth rates, are used to compare two different bonds with their different maturity dates in the long run, and their different price actions in the short run.

To summarize, all of these interpretations of yield to maturity show a number of important features. They are all measures of *total* cash flow in the sense that they incorporate both income and principal appreciation to maturity. Moreover, the yield to maturity does not distinguish between coupon income and principal repayments as elements of this cash flow, except, of course, in terms of their timing.

Time value means that a dollar received in the future will be measurably less valuable than a dollar available today for use or investment. In all the interpretations of yield to maturity, the entire cash flow is assumed to be time-valued (or reinvestable) at a constant, uniform discount rate throughout the bond's life, and this time-valuing rate is just the yield to maturity itself. This time-value rate may be interpreted as either a discount rate, an opportunity rate, a consumption value rate, or a reinvestment rate. In any case, this time valuing is crucial, and the time-valuing link between different future points is through *full compounding* at the yield rate. Thus, compounded time-valuation is an intrinsic and inescapable ingredient of the yield-to-maturity concept.

THE YIELD TO CALL

One can extend the principles used to compute yields to maturity to evaluate a bond where the coupon payments are terminated by an assumed call. When the date of the call and the call premium are specified, then this leads to a *yield-to-call* figure. If there is no definite specification, the yield to call generally represents a computation to the first date of possible refunding.

There are a number of problems in the conventional use of the yield to call (see *Inside the Yield Book* for a discussion of some of these problems). However, a discussion of this important subject would constitute too great a digression for the scope of this chapter.

Chapter III B-2

New Tools in Bond Portfolio Management

Because of the recent historically high levels and wide fluctuations of long term interest rates, corporate bonds are now being considered by more and more investors as an investment medium needing "and deserving" active management. To accurately and consistently deal with the multitude of opportunities and risks inherent in active bond management, the portfolio manager needs tools for measuring the prospective return of alternative bond investments under a variety of assumed market conditions. The conventional yardstick for measuring a bond's return—"yield-to-maturity"—was not designed for the active manager facing the range of uncertainties characterizing today's bond market.

Over the past two years, Sidney Homer and I have undertaken a series of studies at Salomon Brothers aimed at trying to devise mathematical tools that would provide true measures of value and thus serve the purposes of the active bond manager. These studies culminated in a series of memoranda circulated privately to Salomon Brothers' customers under the title, *Inside The Yield Book*.[1]

My purpose in this article is to briefly describe some of our findings and to provide some examples of their application in certain important investment situations.

---

[1] A hardcover volume with the same title, based on these memoranda together with considerable additional material, was published jointly by Prentice-Hall, Inc. and the New York Institute of Finance.

"New Tools in Bond Portfolio Management," Martin L. Leibowitz, *Trusts & Estates*, Communication Channels, Inc., 1973.

Our first step was to identify and quantify the three basic components of a bond's total return over a given investment period. The first two sources are well-known: Capital gain and coupon income. However, the importance of the third source of return, interest-on-interest, is often forgotten.

INTEREST-ON-INTEREST

Interest-on-interest is the term used to describe the return earned through the compounded reinvestment of coupon payments. A tax-free portfolio which retains and reinvests all coupon payments will often accrue an amount of interest-on-interest over the life of a long term bond which *far exceeds* the direct coupon income! This is illustrated in Table 1 for the case of a 20-year 8% par bond.

Table 1: An 8% Non-Callable 20-Year Bond Bought at 100 to Yield 8%

Interest-on-Interest						Total
Reinvest-ment Rate	% of Total Return	Amount	Coupon Income	Discount	Total Return	Realized Compound Yield
0%	0%	$ 0	$1,600	0	$1,600	4.84%
5	41	1,096	1,600	0	2,696	6.64
6	47	1,416	1,600	0	3,016	7.07
7	53	1,782	1,600	0	3,382	7.53
8*	58*	2,201*	1,600*	0	3,801*	8.00*
9	63	2,681	1,600	0	4,281	8.50
10	67	3,232	1,600	0	4,832	9.00

*Yield from Yield Book.

The amount of interest-on-interest depends on the assumed rate at which coupons are reinvested and compounded over the bond's life. Table 1 shows the dollars of interest-on-interest accumulated from compounding at fixed rates over the bond's life, e.g., at a 6% fixed reinvestment rate, the interest-on-interest would accumulate to $1,416, or 47% of the bond's total return. At an 8% reinvestment rate, the accumulated interest-on-interest becomes $2,201, or 58% of the total dollar return.

Many investors are surprised by the magnitude of these interest-on-interest figures. Since every bond forces a certain cash flow schedule upon the investor which he must either reinvest or use in some time-valued fashion, this interest-on-interest must be considered in comparing alternative bond investments.

Without an assumption on the reinvestment of the coupons, a dollar and cents analysis of a bond swap over time will give inconsistent results. This is because coupon income, received periodically, becomes truly comparable with a capital discount realized at maturity, only when the evaluation is performed at some common point in time. When the evaluation is performed at maturity, then the estimated interest-on-interest reflects the added value of the coupon income obtainable through reinvestment. On the other hand, when the present is taken as the evaluation point, then the discounting needed to find the Present Value also reflects the added value of earlier payments. In both cases, the same important principle is at work: the time value of money derived from its potential reinvestability.

Reinvestment Rates

In developing estimates of interest-on-interest, the key question is, of course, what reinvestment rate (or rates) should be used. In addition to expected market conditions over the bond's life, the choice of reinvestment rate depends on many factors intrinsic to the portfolio structure, the long term investment strategy, and the magnitude of retained coupon payments. Clearly, a portfolio which maintains its retained coupons in highly liquid short-term assets would have a different reinvestment rate estimate from a portfolio undergoing a strategic long term shift of all cash inflows into the equity market. Similarly, a mutual fund or trust which pays out all its current income would attach a different (but positive) time value to coupon flows than would a growing pension fund. Even after consideration of all such factors, any chosen reinvestment rate is at best only a starting assumption, and higher and lower alternative rates should be used to check the sensitivity of the analysis.

Consistent Comparison Possible

Once an explicit reinvestment rate (or a spectrum of rates) has been selected, one can readily compute the interest-on-interest amounts accumulated by different bonds. The investor then has a quantitative value for this third component of the bond's total return. Upon adding in the other two components—capital gains and coupon income—he has a numerical estimate of the total dollar return of a given bond within the context of his own market expectations and reinvestment strategy. This provides a method for consistent comparison of the prospective total dollars of return from alternative bond investments. A key to this consistency is that all alternatives can be evaluated in the same framework of a *common* explicit reinvestment rate (or rates) over a given time period.

REALIZED COMPOUND YIELD

A fully compounding investor will want to base his investment judgments on the total estimated dollars of return accumulated by a given bond over an investment period of his own choosing. This will incorporate the investor's assumptions regarding both interest rate moves and average reinvestment rates. To evaluate the risks associated with these estimates, the investor should also look at the effect of alternative reinvestment rate assumptions on the total dollars of return.

However, the investor will probably feel more comfortable when these total dollars of return figures are translated into the more familiar terms of an average annual growth rate. By performing this annualization, using several technical conventions which are common to the bond market, we obtain a rate of return measure which we call the *realized compound yield* (or the effective yield). Essentially, the realized compound yield is the equivalent savings bank rate that would take an original investment, equal to the bond's current market value, and through full compounding on a semiannual basis would accumulate, over the investment period, an amount of interest equal to the bond's total dollars of return.

Table 2: Use of Compound Interest Tables to Compute the Future Value and Realized Compound Yield for a 30-Year 4% Bond Purchased at a Cost of $671.82 (YTM = 6.50%) with Reinvestment at an Assumed 6% Rate and Sold Two Years Later at a Market Value of $730.34 (YTM = 6.00%)

Coupon Payment	$20
× 2-Year Future Value of $1 Per Period for 4 Periods (2 Years) at 3% Per Period	× 4.184
= 2-Year Future Value of Coupons and Interest-on-Interest	83.68
+ 2-Year Future Value of Principal (Market Value 2 Years Hence)	+ 730.34
= 2-Year Future Value	814.02
÷ Today's Market Cost	÷ 671.82
= 2-Year Future Value Per Dollar	= 1.212
Realized Compound Yield (Interest Rate Providing above Future Value Per Dollar in 2 Years)	= 9.833%

Table 3: Effect of Various Review Periods on the Realized Compound Yield of a 30-Year 4% Bond Purchased at $671.82 (YTM = 6.50%) With Reinvestment at 6% and Various End-of-Review-Period Market Values

Yield-to-Maturity at End of Review Period	Realized Compound Yield Over Review Period Number of Years in Review Period					
	1-Year	2-Years	5-Years	10 Years	20 Years	30 Years
8.00%	-12.26	-2.47	3.51	5.37	6.10	6.25
7.50	-6.46	.34	4.44	5.69	6.17	6.25
7.00	-.23	3.32	5.41	6.03	6.24	6.25
6.80	2.40	4.56	5.82	6.17	6.27	6.25
6.60	5.11	5.83	6.23	6.31	6.29	6.25
6.50*	6.49*	6.48*	6.44*	6.39*	6.31*	6.25*
6.40	7.90	7.13	6.65	6.46	6.32	6.25
6.20	10.78	8.47	7.08	6.61	6.35	6.25
6.00	13.74	9.83	7.53	6.76	6.38	6.25
5.50	21.55	13.39	8.67	7.15	6.46	6.25
5.00	29.98	17.16	9.87	7.57	6.53	6.25

*Corresponds to scientific amortization.

Table 2 illustrates this computation for the case of a 30 year 4% bond purchased at 67.18 (yield-to-maturity = 6.50%) and sold 2 years later at a 6.00% yield-to-maturity.

The realized compound yield provides an interesting view of the effects of price volatility over time. This is illustrated in Table 3, where we see that a 10 basis point change in yield-to-maturity can lead to a gain in realized compound yield of from 141 basis points over a one year workout time to 7 basis points if the gain occurs over a 10 year period.

Different coupon rates make available different cash flows, even at the same yield-to-maturity, and often lead to accumulation of markedly different amounts of interest-on-interest. This is illustrated in Table 4. At one extreme, a 0% coupon bond (i.e., a pure discount instrument like Series E Savings Bonds) provides its entire return through gain in Principal Value and it therefore generates neither coupon income nor interest-on-interest. This 0% coupon bond is completely insensitive to the reinvestment rate assumption. At the other extreme, a high coupon premium bond provides a very high early cash flow and a large amount of interest-on-interest. This premium bond is of course very sensitive to the assumed reinvestment rate.

As Table 1 and Table 4 illustrate, the yield-to-maturity coincides with the realized compound yield over the bond's life only when the coupons are reinvested at the yield rate itself.

Table 4: Effect of Various Reinvestment Rates and Coupon Rates on the Realized Compound Yield for 30-Year Bonds. All Priced to Have a 6.50% Yield-to-Maturity Realized Compound Yield Over Bond's Life

Coupon Rate	Reinvestment Rate							
	3%	4%	5%	6%	6.5%	7%	8%	9%
0.00%	6.50	6.50	6.50	6.50	6.50	6.50	6.50	6.50
1.00	5.65	5.86	6.09	6.35	6.50	6.66	7.00	7.38
2.00	5.29	5.59	5.93	6.30	6.50	6.71	7.16	7.65
3.00	5.09	5.45	5.84	6.27	6.50	6.74	7.24	7.78
4.00	4.96	5.36	5.79	6.25	6.50	6.76	7.29	7.86
5.00	4.87	5.29	5.75	6.24	6.50	6.77	7.32	7.91
6.00	4.81	5.25	5.72	6.23	6.50	6.77	7.35	7.95
6.50	4.78	5.23	5.71	6.23	6.50	6.78	7.36	7.96
7.00	4.76	5.21	5.70	6.23	6.50	6.78	7.36	7.98
8.00	4.72	5.19	5.69	6.22	6.50	6.79	7.38	8.00
9.00	4.69	5.16	5.68	6.22	6.50	6.79	7.39	8.01

Coupon Comparisons

The interaction of coupon rate, price moves, and reinvestment rates can be viewed in another way which permits immediate comparison with the levels of the corresponding new issue market. Suppose the investor is considering a 30 year 4% bond priced today at 67.18 (6.50% yield-to-maturity). As we saw from Table 4, at a 5% reinvestment rate, this bond produces a realized compound yield of 5.79% over its life (as opposed to the yield-to-maturity of 6.50%). To obtain the same realized compound yield from a 30 year par bond, it would have to carry a coupon rate of 6.67%. From the viewpoint of return over the 30 year period, the investor would rule out the 30 year 4% bond at 6.50% if the 30-year new issue market offered higher coupon rates than 6.67% (with adequate call protection). However, suppose the investor is bullish and believes that over a 5-year workout period, the 30 year 4's will move to a price of 72.23, equal to a 6.20% yield-to-maturity. Retaining the estimated 5% reinvestment rate, these assumptions would lead to a realized compound yield of 6.97%. Now because the investment horizon is 5 years, the new issue market for 5 year instruments of comparable quality represents at least a theoretical alternative investment. Consequently, the investor might find it useful to know what coupon rate would be required for a new 5 year par bond to provide this same realized compound yield of 6.97%. The answer is 7.30%. In other words, if a 5 year par bond could be purchased at a yield greater than this "break-even par bond yield" of 7.30%, then this par bond would provide a better 5-year realized compound yield than the 6.97% provided by the original 30 year 4% bond under the assumed conditions. In general, for a common assumed reinvestment rate over a specified workout period, any bond's anticipated price behavior can be quickly compared in this fashion against the effective yields available in the usually more familiar and more certain market for par bonds with maturities spanning the workout period.

The realized compound yield approach has also proven to be a useful and practical analytic method for exploring the more complicated cash flows arising from bonds facing probable calls, pro rata sinking funds, "early" sinkers, etc. It is, we feel, a superior tool for comparing a bond's prospective return in the context of an actively managed portfolio with that of any other bond. It captures all three components of total return. It can readily be adapted to investment horizons other than the bond's maturity date. It can incorporate the effects of anticipated price moves over the investment period. It is based on an explicit reinvestment rate assumption, and it permits several alternative bond investments to be evaluated within the consistent framework of this *common* reinvestment rate. In contrast, yield-to-maturity comparisons start with *different* reinvestment rate assumptions and hence must be inaccurate or misleading.

EVALUATION OF BOND PORTFOLIO SWAPS

Four important types of swaps can be identified which depend for their validity on correct mathematical comparisons: (1) Substitution Swaps; (2) Intermarket Spread Swaps; (3) Rate Anticipation Swaps; and (4) Pure Yield Pickup Swaps.

Substitution Swap

The Substitution Swap is the simplest of all. In its ideal form, the investor swaps a portfolio bond for its perfect substitute at a price advantage which exists because of some temporary market aberration. This swap can be evaluated in the context of the anticipated restoration of normal values over an estimated workout period.

For example, suppose the investor holds a 30-year 7% bond which is currently priced at par (on a bid basis). He is offered, on swap, another 30-year 7% bond, priced at 98.77 for a yield-to-maturity of 7.10%. Except for this price advantage, the offered bond is substantially identical to the investor's bond on all counts, including its normal trading level. The investor believes that the market aberration should work itself out by the end of a year and that the bonds should then be trading at an equal price level (on a bid basis). For purposes of illustration, assume that both the market level and the reinvestment rate are 7%. Then by executing the swap, the investor would achieve a realized compound yield of 8.29% for one year only. This 8.29% can be compared with the 7% figure obtained through continued holding of the original bond. Thus, from a 10 basis point opportunity in yield-to-maturity, the investor has achieved a 129 basis point improvement in realized compound yield over the one year.

There are large classes of bonds which are sufficiently similar in coupon, maturity, quality, industry, sinking fund, etc., so that they have generally stable, normal trading relationships under a spectrum of market conditions. Between any two such bonds, this normal trading relationship is often characterized in terms of a yield-to-maturity "spread." From time to time, market aberrations will occur which distort this normal yield spread relationship. This creates a swap opportunity through the potential realignment of the spreads to their normal relationship. As illustrated above, the ability to take advantage of this "spread potential" can prove very profitable indeed. Moreover, to the extent that the swap is a true substitution, there is minimal risk from adverse fluctuations in overall interest rates.

Since by their very nature, a substitution swap represents a temporary aberration, the investor who wishes to avail himself of these opportunities must maintain an active, flexible posture. He must be able to quickly evaluate a proposed swap both in terms of the degree of substitutability as well as the "spread potential" available through a return to normal trading relationships. And to take advantage of the full range of opportunities, he must be able to initiate swaps at a give-up in yield-to-maturity. Since many bond portfolio managers are either proscribed from or are reluctant to give up yield-to-maturity on a swap, it stands to reason that the flexible investor can profit here from the opportunities created by the inflexibility of others.

Intermarket Spread Swap

The second category of swaps is the Intermarket Spread Swap—for example, a swap from premium bonds to discount bonds or the reverse. Here, the investor believes that the yield spread between two components of the bond market is temporarily out-of-line, and swaps are done out of the "overpriced" component into the "underpriced" component. The two market components might be differentiated by many possible features, e.g., quality, coupon, industry type, maturity, etc. As in the case of Substitution Swaps, the primary intention is to profit from realignment of trading relationships, rather than to forecast overall interest rate behavior. Because of the wider fluctuations in spreads between market components, the potential improvement in realized compound yield may be far more dramatic from Intermarket Spread Swaps than from substitution swapping. They can also involve a greater segment of the investor's portfolio at a single point in time, thus leading to greater overall levels of return.

However, the Intermarket Spread Swap also entails much greater risks. A general market move can drastically alter normal spread relationships. Even in stable overall markets, the spread may not realign itself within the anticipated workout period. And when the swap has been initiated in a yield give-up direction, an extended workout time works against the investor.

Rate Anticipation Swap

The most potentially profitable and the riskiest swap of all is the Rate Anticipation Swap. Here, the investor acts to either reduce or increase the volatility of his portfolio to take advantage of an anticipated move in long term interest rates. For the investor who is free to change the portfolio's maturity structure, this is usually done by shortening maturities in anticipation of rising long term rates and lengthening when lower rates are expected. The yield and volatility effects of such actions can combine to lead to very dramatic improvements in the realized compound yield over the workout period—if the investor is right! If the investor is wrong, then the actual or opportunity loss can often be equally dramatic.

In evaluating proposed Rate Anticipation Swaps, there are two threshold values that are often helpful in clarifying the numerical aspects of the problem. Suppose the investor has swapped from 30-year 7's at 100 into one year 5% bills in anticipation of an upward move in rates. Over a one year period, the realized compound yield of the bills will of course be just 5.00%, while that for the 7's will depend on their price at the end of the year. However, at a price of 97.94, the 7's will just match the bills' 5% realized compound yield. This price of 97.94 corresponds to a "break-even yield-to-maturity" of 7.17% for the 7's. In other words, for the swap to be profitable over a one year workout period, there would have to be an upward move exceeding 17 basis points in the yield-to-maturity of the 7's. Over longer workout periods, the initial yield give-up in the swap works increasingly against the investor, and the "break-even yield-to-maturity" becomes greater and greater. This is illustrated in Table 5.

When the portfolio is primarily oriented towards holding long-term bonds, then a second threshold value may be useful in evaluating Rate Anticipation Swaps. For the example given above, suppose the investor's primary objective is to maximize his realized compound yield over the 30-year period. Assuming a 7% reinvestment rate, he knows that the 7's will provide a realized compound yield of 7%. One way for the swap to be profitable in terms of the overall 30 year period is for the maturing one year 5% bills to be rolled over into a 29-year par bond with a sufficiently high coupon rate so as to match the 7.00% realized compound yield of the 7's. This required "roll-over" coupon rate is 7.17%. For a

Table 5: Break-Even Prices and Yields of a Maturity Reduction Swap 30-Year 7's @ 100 into 5% Bills Rolled at 5%

Time Period	Break-Even Price Decline of 7's	Future Equating Price of 7's	Future Yield to Maturity of 7's
1 Year Hence	2.06 Points	97.94	7.17%
2 Years Hence	4.36 Points	95.64	7.37
3 Years Hence	7.00 Points	93.00	7.61
4 Years Hence	9.87 Points	90.13	7.90
5 Years Hence	13.10 Points	86.90	8.25

five year workout period with bills rolled at 5%, the break-even coupon rate for the 25-year inter-maturity period would be 7.87%. These two threshold values—the longer bond's yield-to-maturity and the inter-maturity coupon rate required for break-even—have proven practically useful not only in Rate Anticipation Swaps, but in many swap situations where there is a significant extension or contraction of maturity.

Pure Yield Pickup Swap

The fourth category is the Pure Yield Pickup Swap. Historically, this has been the most common type of bond swap. It is often executed, as the name implies, purely for a pickup in yield-to-maturity and/or current yield. These swaps are often done with little or no consideration given to yield spreads, interest rate trends, or overvaluation or undervaluation of the issues involved.

The evaluation of the benefits of such seemingly simple swaps is not as simple as it looks. One frequently encounters three types of erroneous computations. The first error arises because the pickup in yield-to-maturity tends to overstate the value of the swap. When both alternative bonds are evaluated at a common reinvestment rate through use of realized compound yields, a more conservative assessment of the swap usually results. For example, a Pure Yield Pickup Swap out of 30-year 4's at a 6.50% yield-to-maturity into 30-year 7's at par appears to provide a 50 basis point pickup in yield-to-maturity. However, when both cash flows are reinvested at some common rate, any common rate, the pickup in realized compound yield shrinks to a more conservative, but still very worthwhile figure. At a 7% rate, the yield gain will be 24 basis points.

A second type of mathematical error arises with portfolios where Pure Yield Pickup Swaps must be justified in terms of the time to recover a book loss. This entire book loss approach unfortunately substitutes accounting fictions for investment facts. However, many portfolio managers are essentially forced to operate under this recovery criterion, and it is important that their recovery time calculations be accurate and consistent. One frequently sees computations here which, by ignoring interest-on-interest, understate the value of the swap in this context.

Consider the above example of a swap out of 30-year 4's at 6.50% yield-to-maturity into 30-year 7's at par. If the 30-year 4's were purchased at par, then this swap would incur an immediate book loss of $328.18 per bond. On a dollar-for-dollar swap, the incremental annual coupon flow would amount to $7.03 per bond. Without including interest-on-interest, this increment coupon would take 47 years to recover the book loss! This is a totally unacceptable figure and would of course lead to rejection of the swap. However, by including interest-on-interest at a 7% rate, the swap recovers in 21 1/2 years—well within the maturity period of the bonds.

A third problem often encountered in Pure Yield Pickup Swaps is that of evaluating the effect of an extension of maturity. For example, suppose the investor holds a 25-year 3 1/2% bond priced at 65.45 to have a yield-to-maturity of 6.25%. On swap, he is offered a 30-year 4% bond at a 6.50 yield-to-maturity. The 25 basis point pickup in yield-to-maturity appears attractive, but the investor recognizes that he is extending his original commitment by 5 years.

There are two ways to view this situation. The first method is to stick with the original 25-year investment horizon, and then view the 30-year 4's as riskier alternative investment over this period. Suppose the investor has selected a 5% reinvestment rate. Then the currently held 25-year 3 1/2's will provide an assured realized compound yield of 5.76% over the 25 years. On the other hand, the realized compound yield from the 30-year 4's will depend critically upon its price at the 25-year point. At a constant yield-to-maturity of 6.50%, the then 5-year bond would be priced at 89.47 and would provide a realized compound yield of 5.86%, or 10 basis points above that from the 3 1/2's. At lower estimated prices for the 4's, the realized compound yield from the 4's will of course become less and less, and at some point will just match the assured 5.76% realized compound yield from the 3 1/2's. This break-even is reached at a price of 82.81 for the 4's, which will then have a maturity of 5 years. This corresponds to a yield-to-maturity of 8.27% for the 5-year 4's. The investor can then use this figure for the "longer bond's break-even yield-to-maturity" to evaluate the probability that the swap will be profitable over the original 25-year commitment period. In other words, if the investor feels that 5-year 4's are unlikely to sell at yields-to-maturity exceeding 8.27%, then he could feel comfortable as to the swap's probable profitability.

A second approach to this same swap situation is to focus on the longer 30-year period. From this viewpoint, the investor is willing and indeed wants to extend his commitment to the 30-year point. In this case, if he executes the swap, it is the 30-year 4's which will provide an assured return over the investment period, i.e., a realized compound yield of 5.79%. The 30-year return from continued holding of the 3 1/2's depends critically on the rate at which their matured Principal Value can be rolled over for the remaining 5 years. While this 5-year inter-maturity period might, in actuality, involve a variety of possible instruments, it is useful to standardize on a rollover into a 5-year par bond for purposes of evaluation. The 30-year realized compound yield obtained from holding the 3 1/2's and then rolling them into this assumed 5-year par bond can then be determined as a function of the estimated coupon rate on the 5-year par bond. At a 5% coupon rate, this results in a realized compound yield of 5.63%, or 16 basis points below the 5.79% obtainable from the 30-year 4's.

At higher coupon rates for the 5-year par bond, the alternative of holding and then rolling the 3 1/2's will look more and more attractive. At some 5-year coupon rate, the realized compound yield will just match the 5.79% obtained from the 4's. For this example, this "inter-maturity coupon rate for break-even" has a value of 7.85%. Thus if the investor feels that 5-year par bonds are likely to be selling at rates below 7.85%, then by implication, he would evaluate the swap into the 4's as being relatively more profitable over the 30-year investment horizon.

The preceding discussion has tacitly focused on the evaluation of a proposed swap relative to the sole alternative of continued holding of the portfolio bond. While this narrow focus serves the purpose of clarity, it should be recognized that the general problem facing the portfolio manager is of course much broader: Ideally, he is seeking the best matching of the values represented by his portfolio and his new money against all the opportunities presented in the marketplace.

Application to Taxable Portfolios[2]

All of the preceding comments were oriented towards tax-free portfolios. While many factors can be simply transformed to deal with the after-tax cash flows, there are several fundamentally new concepts that must be considered for taxable portfolios.

As a concrete example, consider the swap discussed above, but now suppose that the investor pays a 48% tax on marginal coupon income and 30% tax on capital gain.[3] Before computing any after-tax realized compound yields, we must also specify the tax rate on money earned through interest-on-interest. In many accounts, post-tax coupon dollars may be reinvested into a general pool of assets consisting of both taxable and tax-free securities. In such cases, while the

---

[2] Ed. Note: For a further discussion, see the article entitled, "Total After-Tax Bond Performance and Yield Measures."

[3] Ed. Note: At the time this article was written, these were the applicable tax rates. There was a preferential tax rate on qualified capital gains.

pretax reinvestment rate may be rather low (5% is assumed for this example), the tax rate on this reinvestment income may also be lower than the tax rate on marginal coupon income. For this example, we shall take the tax rate on reinvestment income to be 40%.

To determine the prospective return from the 30-year 4's over the original 25-year commitment period, an estimate must be made for their price at the end of 25 years. Assume that these 5-year 4's at that point are priced at 91.47 for a yield-to-maturity of 6.00%. This would represent a 24.29-point capital gain which would be subject to the 30% tax rate. Having now specified all the components of return as well as their respective tax rates, the after-tax realized compound yield from the 4's can now be calculated, and it turns out to be 3.52%.

To obtain a more intuitive yardstick, we can take the approach used earlier and find the yield-to-maturity required on a 25-year taxable par bond to provide the same after-tax realized compound yield figure of 3.52%. This "break-even par bond yield" turns out to be 7.27%. In other words, under the identical tax and reinvestment rate assumptions, a 25-year 7.27% par bond would provide the exact same after-tax realized compound yield as the 30-year 4's purchased at 6.50% and priced 25 years later on a 6.00% yield-to-maturity basis.

Turning now to the 25-year 3 1/2's which the investor currently holds, suppose that the original cost basis for these bonds was 100. Then at the bid price of 65.45, each bond would carry a capital loss of 34.55 points. This has two important implications. First, when the 3 1/2's mature in 25 years, there will be no capital gains tax liability on the gain of 34.55 points. Second, if the swap were to be executed, the 3 1/2's would incur a capital loss which the investor might be able to offset against prior capital gains. If this could be done, then the overall portfolio tax liability would be reduced by the 30% tax on these 34.55 points, i.e., by 10.37 points. This savings of 10.37 points is an additional value realized from selling the 3 1/2's with their imbedded tax loss. Adding this tax savings of 10.37 points to the 65.45 points obtained from the market price, sale of the 3 1/2's can be viewed as making available the sum of 75.82 points, or $758.20 per bond, for exchange with alternative opportunities in the marketplace. By the same token, if the investor continued to hold the 3 1/2's, he would be giving up the opportunity to buy $758.20 of alternative securities.

Consequently, this $758.20 in "opportunity dollars" forms the cost basis against which the after-tax cash flow from the 3 1/2's must be measured. Based on this "opportunity" value, the 3 1/2's provide an after-tax realized compound yield of 3.19%, or 33 basis points less than the 4's. To clearly designate that the "opportunity dollar" base has been used in these realized compound yield calculations, we refer to these figures as "opportunity yields."

Translating this result for the 3 1/2's into the terms of a "break-even par bond yield," we can say that continued holding of the 3 1/2's provides an "opportunity yield" equivalent to that from a taxable 25-year par bond with a 6.28% coupon rate. Since the "break-even par bond yield" from the 4's was 7.27%, this means that under the assumed conditions, this swap corresponds to a 99 basis point improvement in the coupon rate of the respective equivalent 25-year par bonds. However, quite apart from this particular swap, if the comparable 25-year taxable new issue market were offered above the 6.28% "break-even par bond yield" of the 3 1/2's, the investor would immediately be alerted to the availability of improved returns for a swap out of the 3 1/2's. If the investor is free to consider swaps from taxable into tax-exempt securities, then he should also compare this 6.28% figure with the corresponding taxable equivalent yield available in the 25-year tax-exempt market.

This "opportunity dollar" approach is a powerful and facile technique for identifying and measuring swap opportunities in taxable portfolios, including some opportunities which are far from intuitively evident.

ROLE OF THE COMPUTER

In essence, these analytic concepts are all aimed at providing a more comprehensive approach to dealing with the measurable, quantifiable aspects of high grade bonds. In any practical investment situation, such quantifiable factors will constitute only part of the relevant considerations. They will never represent the whole story. They may not even be among the primary considerations. But they will be one of the many tangible factors, along with the many intangible and judgmental factors, that a professional investment manager should incorporate into his decision process.

The preceding analytic techniques were designed to capture these important quantifiable factors and their system of relationships. This often rather complex system reduces to a small number of measures such as realized compound yield, break-even yield-to-maturity, etc. The intention was to design these measures to be as natural, as intuitive, and as simple *as possible*. All of these concepts are really derived from the principle of the time value of money. Consequently, all of these new yield figures can "theoretically" be found, given sufficient time, by running back and forth through the Compound Interest Tables. However, time and the markets wait for no man, and the time allowed for reaching decisions in the bond market is usually all too brief. This is where the computer can play an important role.

The computer can perform all of these computations speedily and accurately. If the computer output formats are designed with great care, then the computer can provide an added value in presenting the results in a form which immediately communicates and highlights their significance. The computer can also serve as a powerful storehouse of information regarding specific securities, holdings, market information, and historical data. On the spot, it can select and retrieve the appropriate data, perform the desired calculations, and then provide an integrated presentation in a form suitable for quick and facile market judgments. Utilization of the computer along these lines would help to truly serve the needs of the investment manager (rather than to just overburden him with numbers). However, this is an ideal description of a goal—not a reality. While there have been significant successes and achievements in this direction, there is a long way to go and much to be learned before the computer can begin to realize its full potential in the bond market.

Chapter III B-3

Horizon Analysis for Managed Bond Portfolios

The fundamental variables of the bond market are interest rate levels, yield curves, and yield spread relationships. The changing structure of values among these variables forms the sources of investment return. However, as shown in *Inside the Yield Book*,[1] the conventional yields, which the market quotes, observes, and tracks on an everyday basis, are very different from the usual portfolio objective of total return.

This article presents a simple analytic framework for relating the portfolio objective of total return over a given investment horizon to the sources of that return—the basic market variables of interest rate levels, yield curves, and yield spread relationships.

This new framework for "Horizon Analysis" turns out to have an interesting interpretation in terms of the swap classification system described in *Inside the Yield Book*. Using this framework, a given bond swap can be viewed, at each point in time, as a well-defined mixture of components from idealized swap categories. A given swap may thus have different quantifiable components re-

---

[1] *Inside the Yield Book* by Sidney Homer and Martin L. Leibowitz, published jointly by New York Institute of Finance and Prentice-Hall, Inc., 1972.

Martin L. Leibowitz, "Horizon Analysis for Managed Bond Portfolios," Salomon Brothers Inc, January 1975. Later appeared in *The Journal of Portfolio Management*, Spring 1975. Reprinted with permission.

flecting the effects of Pure Yield Pickup, Rate Anticipation, changing sector spreads, quality spreads, yield curve effects, and Substitution relationships.

This enables the bond portfolio manager to associate a proposed portfolio action with the primary sources of its expected return. He can then explore the vulnerabilities of this expected return over a range of feasible market conditions. By pursuing this route in a more formal fashion, he can begin to define and quantify the various dimensions of risk.

Horizon Analysis simplifies the computation of certain risk measures such as break-even points for yield levels and yield spreads. It also suggests a role for "sensitivity ratios" to quantify the risk associated with each market force conflicting with the "target" factor motivating the swap.

Horizon Analysis also clarifies how the very passage of time leads to dramatic changes in risk structure.

THE MIDDLE GROUND OF BOND INVESTMENT

The full impact of the passage of time upon bond investment decisions is often overlooked.

Basically, two vantage points are common among bond market participants: the long-term view based on some measure of yield-to-maturity and the very short-term view with a primary focus on day-to-day price movements. Surprisingly few investors consistently explore investment horizons extending beyond the current calendar year but earlier than the shortest maturity bond under consideration. At the same time, the most comfortable projections of bond market relationships often imply workout periods extending beyond the immediate months ahead, but rarely further than a few years into the future. This middle ground "between tomorrow and maturity" offers a relatively unscrutinized arena for uncovering new relationships, new values, and, consequently, fresh opportunities.

However, there are few convenient analytic tools to aid the investor who wishes to explore this middle ground. The conventional Yield Book really indicates the levels of return for holders to maturity, and even there, it has its limitations. On the other hand, most studies of price volatility have really dealt with price and yield moves concentrated at a single instant in time. Relatively little has been done to explore the problem of a bond's volatility and return *over time*.

THE THREE BASIC SOURCES OF RETURN

A bond investment provides value from three basic sources—coupon income, interest-on-interest, and capital gains.

Coupon income is here taken to include coupon payments and any Accrued Interest received should the bond be sold prior to maturity.

Interest-on-interest is the return earned through reinvestment and compounding of this coupon income. Since neither the vehicle nor the rates for this reinvestment process can be specified in advance, the level of accumulation of interest-on-interest is necessarily uncertain. However, interest-on-interest can account for over 70% of the total return for a long-term bond and should, therefore, be included in every comprehensive evaluation of a bond investment. One convenient, although admittedly simplistic, approach is to assume the availability of a reinvestment rate which is constant over time. The impact of the uncertainty associated with reinvestment can then be explored by varying this rate assumption across some range of feasible values.

The capital gains component of return relates to the increase in the bond's market value. For tax-free portfolios, $1 of capital gains enters into the total return in as direct and as valuable fashion as $1 of coupon income or $1 of interest-on-interest.

These three components of total return apply to any investment medium. As a long-term investment vehicle, bonds are characterized by deriving a significant proportion of their *long-term* return from relatively predictable coupon and redemption flows together with the reinvestment of these flows. On the other hand, over short- and intermediate-term time periods, the more uncertain elements of the capital gain or loss can represent a much more significant proportion of the bond's total return. Consequently, these relatively predictable and relatively uncertain factors must be differentiated in order to develop a good handle on the bond's return over short- to intermediate-term investment horizons. As we shall see, this differentiation leads to an important refinement in the capital gains component.

THE GROWTH OF RETURN OVER TIME

As an example, consider a ten-year 4.00% bond purchased at a price of 67.48 for a conventional yield-to-maturity of 9.00%. One such bond would generate coupon income of $40 over the first year, $80 over a two-year period, etc. Upon dividing these figures by the original purchase price of $674.80, the cumulative percentage return becomes,

$$100\% \times (\$40 / \$674.80) = 5.93\%,$$

(i.e., just the bond's current yield) over the first year, 11.86% over a two-year period, and so forth, as shown in Table 1.

Interest-on-interest results from the reinvestment and compounding of the $20 semiannual coupon payments at the assumed semiannual rate of 3.75% (i.e.,

---

Table 1: Growth of Cumulative Percentage Return with Constant Yield Amortization

---

10-Year 4.00% Bond Purchased at 67.48
for a Yield-to-Maturity of 9.00%
Accumulation Capital Gains Based on
Constant-Yield ("Scientific") Amortization at 9.00%
Assumed Reinvestment Rate = 7.50%

	Cumulative Percentage Return			
Investment Horizon	Coupon Income	Interest-on-Interest (at 7.50%)	Accumulation Capital Gain	Total Yield Accumulation Return
0 Years	0%	0%	0%	0%
1.0	5.93	.11	3.14	9.18
2.0	11.86	.68	6.57	19.11
3.0	17.78	1.75	10.32	29.85
4.0	23.71	3.36	14.41	41.48
5.0	29.64	5.54	18.88	54.06
6.0	35.57	8.34	23.76	67.67
7.0	41.49	11.80	29.08	82.37
8.0	47.42	15.98	34.90	98.30
9.0	53.35	20.94	41.25	115.54
10.0	59.28	26.73	48.19	134.20

7.50% annually). For an investment horizon consisting of ten semiannual compounding periods (i.e. five years), the Compound Interest Tables show that each $1 of periodic payment would grow to a total Future Value of $11.868. This Future Value consists of the ten payments plus the resulting interest-on-interest. Since the bond's semiannual payment is $20, the total Future Value for this example would be

$$\$20 \times 11.868 = \$237.36.$$

The pure interest-on-interest here is this Future Value less the ten coupon payments totaling $200,

$$\$237.36 - \$200 = \$37.36.$$

This is the interest-on-interest earned over the five-year investment horizon from each bond. To find the percentage figure shown in Table 1, the previous dollar amount must be divided by the cost per bond,

$$100\% \times (\$37.36/\$674.80) = 5.54\%.$$

The third component of the bond's return, capital gains, cannot really be viewed solely in terms of some continuous process of growth. The capital gain component has two very different facets, and all bond market participants would be well-advised to distinguish between them.

THE ACCUMULATION PORTION OF A BOND'S CAPITAL GAIN

A high-grade discount bond provides a specified capital gain over its life (presuming there is no danger of default). However, this capital gain does not materialize in a flash at the bond's maturity. Rather, it accrues in some fashion on a year-by-year basis throughout the bond's life. Consequently, at each point, prior to a discount bond's maturity, some portion of its capital gain must be attributed to an accretion process which will ultimately bring the bond's price up to par at maturity. The nature of this "Accumulation Capital Gain" makes it fundamentally different from the "Market Capital Gain" derived through interest rate movements.

Any formal scheme for distinguishing between these two facets of capital gain must necessarily contain some arbitrary features. Nevertheless, as a practical method of analysis, one can make a useful distinction based upon the bond's conventional yield-to-maturity. The "Accumulation Capital Gain" would then be defined as the price appreciation that would take place if the bond's yield-to-maturity remained constant throughout the investment period. Any deviation from this amortized price level can then be ascribed to the "Market" changes affecting the bond's yield value.

Return now to the example of the ten-year 4.00% bond purchased at a 9.00% yield-to-maturity. At the end of a five-year horizon, the bond's remaining life would be five years. From the Yield Book, a five-year 4.00% bond at the "amortizing" yield of 9.00% would be priced at 80.218, i.e., an Accumulation Capital Gain of

$$\$802.18 - \$674.80 = \$127.38$$

per bond or a cumulative percentage return of

$$100\% \times (\$127.38/\$674.80) = 18.88\%.$$

Table 1 shows how this Accumulation Capital Gain grows over time.

This constant-yield amortization might at first appear to be related to the so-called "scientific amortization" technique used for writing up the book value of a bond purchased at a discount. However, the resemblance is superficial on many counts. Basically, our intent here is to analyze projected market prices at future horizons, while the purpose of scientific amortization is to provide a consistent accounting treatment over portfolio holding periods presumed to cover the bond's remaining life. Thus, scientific amortization is always based upon the bond's yield at the time of its original purchase. On the other hand, our Accumulation Capital Gain is based upon the bond's yield at the point of investment decision—which is always *TODAY*.

THE YIELD ACCUMULATION RETURN

By adding this Accumulation Capital Gain component to the coupon income and interest-on-interest, one obtains an approximate measure of the bond's accumulating return which is *relatively* free from the uncertainties of day-to-day movements in market rates. Consequently, this sum may be called the "Yield Accumulation Return."

Table 1 shows how the Yield Accumulation Return and its components grow over longer and longer investment horizons. In the early years, the coupon income provides almost twice as much return as the Accumulation Capital Gain, while the interest-on-interest component is virtually negligible at the outset. As the investment horizon lengthens, the coupon income maintains its constant pace, the interest-on-interest grows in the expected fashion, and the capital gain provides an ever increasing contribution.

Table 2 provides a clearer view of these growth patterns. Each column represents the increment to the cumulative percentage return resulting from extending the investment horizon by one additional year. In particular, it is interesting to note how the Accumulation Capital Gain grows to the point of becoming the largest source of incremental return in the last two years of the bond's life.

It should be noted that the key yardstick is the *cumulative* percentage return, i.e., the net gain in Future Value represented as a percentage of the current investment base. For various reasons, we have decided to use the cumulative total return figures throughout, rather than to translate them into the corresponding annualized rates of return.

THE "MARKET" PORTION OF A BOND'S CAPITAL GAIN

The Yield Accumulation Return captures a bond's total return as long as there are no changes in the conventional yield-to-maturity. However, as we know,

Table 2: Annual Increments to Cumulative Percentage Return with Constant-Yield Amortization

10-Year 4.00% Bond
Purchased at 67.48 for a Yield-to-Maturity of 9.00%
Accumulation Capital Gains Based on
Constant-Yield ("Scientific") Amortization at 9.00%
Assumed Reinvestment Rate = 7.50%

| For Annual Period Ending After | Annual Increment to Cumulative Percentage Return | | | |
	Coupon Income	Interest-on-Interest (at 7.50%)	Accumulation Capital Gain	Total "Yield Accumulation" Return
1st Year	5.93%	.11%	3.14%	9.18%
2nd	5.93	.57	3.43	9.93
3rd	5.93	1.07	3.75	10.74
4th	5.93	1.61	4.09	11.63
5th	5.93	2.18	4.47	12.58
6th	5.93	2.80	4.88	13.61
7th	5.93	3.46	5.32	14.70
8th	5.93	4.18	5.82	15.93
9th	5.93	4.96	6.35	17.24
10th	5.93	5.79	6.94	18.66
Total	59.28%	26.73%	48.19%	134.20%

there are *constant changes* in interest rates, in the relationship between different market sectors, and in the precise relative value attached to individual securities. Apart from all these factors, a specific bond's character and its role in the general fixed-interest market change with just the simple passage of time. For all these reasons, the investor must carefully study the effects of bond price and yield movements and their contribution to total return.

As it is buffeted by all the dynamics of the marketplace, a bond's actual price may weave many strange patterns indeed over time. However, once a given investment horizon has been selected, there are only two prices which matter for purposes of computing the bond's capital gain over that period—the starting price and the ending price.

Returning to the earlier example of a ten-year 4.00% bond, Table 3 illustrates a possible price pattern across the page of an abbreviated Yield Book. Starting at its purchase price of 67.48 when the bond has a life of ten years, Table 3 shows the price varying over time and finally winding up five years later at 83.78, resulting in a total capital gain of

Table 3: An Abbreviated Yield Book for 4% Bonds

Showing How a Bond's Price Movement Can be Represented
As
A Constant-Yield Accumulation Over Time
Plus
An Instantaneous Future Yield Move

Yield to maturity	10 Yrs	9 Yrs	...	5 Yrs	...	1 Yr	0 Yrs
7.00%	78.68	80.22		87.53		97.15	100.00
7.50	75.68	77.39	...	85.63	...	96.69	100.00
8.00	72.82	74.68		83.78		76.23	100.00
8.50	70.09	72.09		81.98		95.77	100.00
9.00	67.48	69.60		80.22		95.32	100.00
9.50	64.99	67.22		78.51		94.87	100.00
10.00	62.61	64.92	...	76.83	...	94.42	100.00
10.50	60.34	62.74		75.21		93.98	100.00
11.00	58.17	60.64		73.62		93.54	100.00

"Market" Capital Gain

Actual Price Pattern Over Time

"Accumulation" Capital Gain

$$83.78 - 67.48 = 16.30$$

points, or a cumulative percentage capital gain of

$$100\% \times (16.30/67.48) = 24.16\%.$$

Now in determining this bond's Yield Accumulation Return of 54.06% over these five years, a process of constant-yield amortization was assumed. As shown in Table 3, this amortization process is tantamount to the hypothetical lateral movement across the "9.00% row" in the Yield Book. Over the five-year investment horizon, this hypothetical amortization process would, by itself, carry the bond's price to 80.22. There, of course, remains the price gap of 3.56 points between this amortized price and the bond's actual price of 83.78. This gap could be theoretically ascribed to a sudden (in fact, a hypothetically instantaneous) jump in yields carrying the bond's price from 80.22 *up* the five-year column to its actual price level of 83.78.

This example can, of course, be generalized. Any price movement over a specified horizon can be theoretically represented as the result of a simple two-step process: 1) a constant-yield amortization over the horizon period (i.e., a lateral movement across one row in the Yield Book); and 2) an instantaneous yield change taking place *at the end of the* investment horizon period (i.e., a vertical movement up or down one column in the Yield Book).

Obviously, this two-step representation will *not* provide an accurate description of how the price movement actually took place over time. However, it will provide a mathematically correct result for the total capital gains contribution resulting from any given actual price movement.

The big advantage of this two-step model is that it clearly differentiates the two facets of a bond's capital gain. The first step corresponds to the Accumulation Capital Gain accruing as a result of the passage of time and the bond's consequent march towards its maturity date. The second step corresponds to the effects of any change in the bond's yield. Since most market participants associate such yield changes with market actions, this portion of the capital gain component may be referred to as the "Market Capital Gain."

In terms of cumulative percentage return, the Market Capital Gain is simply added to the Yield Accumulation Return to find the total return. For the example illustrated by price movement in Table 3, the Market Capital Gain of

$$100\% \times (3.56/67.48) = 5.28\%$$

can be added to the five-year Yield Accumulation Return of 54.06% shown in Table 1 to obtain the total cumulative return of 59.34%.

With this approach, the total returns can easily be computed over a range of possible yield moves. Table 4 provides such a presentation for yield moves of -100, 0, and +100 basis points by the end of each investment horizon.

MEASURES OF VOLATILITY

Over short-term investment horizons, price changes can often overwhelm all other sources of return. Table 4 illustrates this effect. Every bond market participant needs some sort of handy guide for linking the market yield movements (which he follows) to the resulting bond price changes (which he feels).

Many practitioners use various simple rules of thumb, e.g., "a 10 basis point move in a 30-year bond corresponds to a 1 3/8 point change." (One of the problems with such rules of thumb is that they tend to become dangerously inaccu-

Table 4: Growth of Cumulative Percentage Return with Market Yield Moves

10-Year 4.00% Bond Purchased at 67.48 for a Yield-to-Maturity of 9.00%
Total Yield Accumulation Return Based on 7.50% Reinvestment Rate
and Constant-Yield Amortization at 9.00%

Investment Horizon (Years)	Total "Yield Accumulation" Return 0%	Percentage Return from "Market" Capital Gain Given Yield Move of			Total Cumulative Percentage Return Given Yield Move of		
		-100 B.P. 7.91%	0 B.P. 0%	+100 B.P. -7.21%	-100 B.P. 7.91%	0 B.P. 0%	+100 B.P. -7.21%
0							
1	9.18	7.53	0	-6.92	16.71	9.18	2.26
2	19.11	7.09	0	-6.56	26.20	19.11	12.55
3	29.85	6.57	0	-6.13	36.42	29.85	23.72
4	41.48	5.97	0	-5.62	47.45	41.48	35.86
5	54.06	5.27	0	-5.02	59.33	54.06	49.04
6	67.67	4.48	0	-4.3C	72.15	67.67	63.37
7	82.37	3.57	0	-3.46	85.94	82.37	78.91
8	98.30	2.53	0	-2.47	100.83	98.30	95.83
9	115.54	1.34	0	-1.33	116.88	115.54	114.21
10	134.20	0	0	0	134.20	134.20	134.20

rate in today's dynamic marketplace. The rule just cited, for example, is really correct only at a 6.00% yield level.)

In *Inside the Yield Book*, a series of tabulations were developed to illustrate how the percentage price volatility increased with: 1) increasing maturity, 2) higher yield levels, and 3) lower coupon rates. A given bond's volatility was also shown to depend upon the direction and magnitude of the yield move.

Many key aspects of these volatility relationships can be read directly from the pages of the Yield Book itself. For example, Table 3 shows that a five-year 4.00% bond with a 9.00% yield carries a price of 80.22. As previously observed, a yield decline to 8.00% would result in a price rise of

$$83.78 - 80.22 = 3.56$$

points, or

$$100\% \times (3.56/80.22) = 4.44\%$$

relative to the starting price of 80.22. On the other hand, an increase in yield to the 10.00% level results in a price decline of

$$80.22 - 76.83 = 3.39$$

points, or a percentage drop of

$$100\% \times (3.39/80.22) = 4.23\%.$$

In other words, an upward yield move leads to a somewhat smaller percentage price change than a downward yield move of the same magnitude.

Table 3 illustrates another aspect of price volatility. Suppose the yield of the five-year 4.00% bond dropped to 8.50%. This would lead to a percentage price change of

$$100\% \times \left(\frac{81.98 - 80.22}{80.22} \right) = 2.19\% \ .$$

Dividing this figure by the 50 basis points of yield move, one gets a value of

$$\frac{2.19\%}{50 \text{ B.P.}} = .0439\%/\text{B.P.}$$

as the percentage price change per basis point move. Upon comparing this value with the .0444 %/B.P. obtained with a move of -100 basis points, we further see that it is not possible to *precisely* determine percentage price changes by multiplying the yield move by some constant volatility factor, i.e., each yield move would correspond to a different value for this "volatility factor."

At the same time, this volatility factor approach can provide a fairly close approximation to percentage price changes across a range of different yield moves. For example, averaging the percentage price changes for yield moves of -100 basis points and +100 basis points leads to a figure of

$$1/2 \times (4.44)\% + 1/2 \times (4.23)\% = 4.33\%$$

or an average volatility factor of .0433% per basis point move. By applying this average factor to the yield move from 9.00% to 8.50%, the approximate percentage price change is found to be

$$-.0433 \%/B.P. \times (-50 \text{ B.P.}) \cong +2.17\%,$$

i.e., fairly close to the exact value of 2.19% found previously.

Now there are a number of more sophisticated techniques for finding volatility factors. One such technique is based on the concept of "Duration" introduced by Macaulay in 1938. A bond's Duration is the weighted average life of all its coupon and principal payments, where the weighting factors consist of Present Values of each payment. As a measure of average life, Duration has many advantages over conventional techniques which only consider principal repayments and even then ignore the time value of different repayment dates. It turns out that, with a simple adjustment, a bond's Duration provides a very useful indication of the bond's price volatility. In fact, for small yield moves, the (adjusted) Duration provides a mathematically *exact* volatility factor.

However, for most investors, Duration is not the easiest thing to compute. For our expository purposes here, the simple average of up and down moves of 100 basis points provides adequate volatility factors. As we shall see, even these approximate volatility factors can fulfill a valuable function in relating projected market movements to the total return expected from different sectors of the bond market. When fine tuning is needed in these computations, there are various computer programs available which can refine the results by incorporating the exact percentage price change associated with each projected yield move.

THE HORIZON VOLATILITY FACTOR

As with most discussions of price volatility, the preceding section focused on *instantaneous* price changes. However, when one wants to determine a bond's total return over an extended investment horizon, then the concept of price volatility must itself be extended beyond the immediate movement. We must proceed from instantaneous volatility to the idea of a volatility *over time*.

This idea of a "volatility over time" can actually be incorporated quite simply into our two-step representation of capital gains. In this model, all price movements derived from yield changes are relegated to the Market Capital Gain component. Recalling Table 3, all such "market" price changes are treated *as if* they occurred at the end of the investment horizon. Moreover, they are treated *as if* they began from a future price level obtained through a constant-yield amortization process.

For example, we just found an instantaneous percentage price change of 4.44% for a five-year 4.00% bond moving from 9.00% to 8.00%. However, this percentage price change was measured relative to an investment base of 80.22, i.e., the price corresponding to a 9.00% yield level for the five-year bond. For the investment problem analyzed in Table 4, the original investment base is the ten-year bond's starting price of 67.48. Over a five-year investment horizon, the constant-yield amortization would carry the bond to a price of 80.22. At this point five years hence, a *future* yield move from the 9.00% to the 8.00% level would then produce the price move of

$$83.78 - 80.22 = 3.56$$

points. In terms of points of price, this move is identical to that generated by the same *instantaneous* yield move in a five-year bond. However, as we noted, the investment base is different in these two cases. Suppose we wished to make use of the five-year bond's instantaneous percentage price change of 4.44% to help determine the Market Capital Gain return for the ten-year bond over a five-year horizon. Then, the investment base must be shifted from the amortized price of 80.22 "backwards" to the original price of 67.48. Multiplying the instantaneous percentage price change by the ratio of the two prices will achieve this backwards translation, i.e.,

$$100\% \times \left(\frac{3.56}{67.48}\right) = 100\% \times \left(\frac{3.56}{80.22}\right) \times \left(\frac{80.22}{67.48}\right)$$

$$= 4.44\% \times \left(\frac{80.22}{67.48}\right)$$

$$= 4.44\% \times (1.1888)$$

$$= 5.28\% .$$

This figure coincides with the Market Capital Gain return shown in Table 4 for a -100 basis point yield move over a five-year horizon.

The price ratio used in this translation, 1.1888, can also be expressed as

$$\frac{100\% + 18.88\%}{100\%},$$

where 18.88% is the Accumulation Capital Gain return shown in Table 1 for the five-year horizon. This result can be generalized. The Accumulation Capital

Gain return over any horizon period can be used to translate an instantaneous percentage price change at the horizon "backwards" into a figure for the Market Capital Gain return.

Moreover, any measure of instantaneous price *volatility* can be translated "backwards" over an investment horizon in exactly the same manner to obtain a volatility factor for the Market Capital Gain. To differentiate it from the instantaneous volatilities, this figure will be referred to as the "Horizon Volatility." As a numerical example, the simple average instantaneous volatility figure of .0433% per basis point move, computed previously for the five-year bond, translates into a Horizon Volatility of

$$\left(\frac{100\% + 18.88\%}{100\%}\right) \times .0433\%/\text{B.P.} = (1.1888) \times .0433\%/\text{B.P.}$$

$$= .0515\%/\text{B.P.}$$

Referring to the five-year horizon in Table 4, this Horizon Volatility of .0515 %/B.P. would approximate Market Capital Gain resulting from a - or +100 basis point yield move by + or -5.15%, compared with the actual figures of 5.27% and -5.02%.

The Accumulation Capital Gain is thus seen to act as a magnifier of the instantaneous volatility at the end of the horizon period. Generally speaking, for discount bonds, this effect will boost the Horizon Volatility above the instantaneous volatility value. Consequently, the longer the horizon period and the larger the Accumulation Capital Gain, the greater will be this magnification effect. On the other hand, for premium bonds, the Accumulation Capital Gain will, of course, be negative, and the Horizon Volatility will be smaller than the instantaneous volatility, whose own value shrinks with the increasing horizon and the consequent shorter maturity.

These volatility factors can also be expressed in terms of the more dramatic scale of "basis points of price move per basis point of yield move." For example, the preceding volatility factor of

.0515%/B.P.

could be restated as

5.15 B.P./B.P.,

meaning that each basis point of yield move produces approximately 5.15 basis points of incremental return.

The great advantage of the Horizon Volatility is that it enables a bond's return over a given horizon to be characterized by two readily computed numbers: 1) a Yield Accumulation Return which depends only upon the selected reinvestment rate, and 2) a Horizon Volatility factor from which Market Capital

Gain figures can be quickly approximated across any range or combination of projected yield moves.

The analytic power of this characterization becomes evident in the context of evaluating a basic dollar-for-dollar bond swap.

A NEW VIEW OF A BOND SWAP

Suppose a portfolio manager now holds the ten-year 4.00% bond used in the preceding example. On a dollar-for-dollar swap basis, he is offered a 20-year 8.00% bond priced at 86.677 for a yield of 9.50%. For ease of reference in the following discussion, the bond now held will be called the H-bond and the bond proposed for purchase will be called the P-bond.

Suppose the portfolio manager wishes to analyze this proposed swap over a five-year investment horizon. Table 1 provides the Yield Accumulation figure for the H-bond. For the P-bond, the comparable figures can be readily computed. For example, the Coupon Income return is just the five years times the P-bond's current yield,

$$5 \times 100\% \times (\$80/\$866.77) = 5 \times 9.23\%$$

$$= 46.15\%.$$

The interest-on-interest component is found by applying the same Future Value factor of 11.868 as before to the P-bond's semiannual coupon of $40,

$$\$40 \times 11.868 = \$474.72$$

and then subtracting the $400 of coupon payments and representing the result as a percentage,

$$(\$474.72 - \$400.00) \times (100\%/\$866.77) = (\$74.72) \times (100\%/\$866.77)$$
$$= 8.62\%.$$

Finally, the Yield Book gives the P-bond's amortized price level at the end of the 5-year horizon as 88.134, i.e., the price of a 15-year 8.00% bond corresponding to a 9.50% yield. The Accumulation Capital Gain as a percentage return is then simply computed as

$$100\% \times \left(\frac{\$881.34 - \$866.77}{\$866.77} \right) = 100\% \times (\$14.57/\$866.77)$$

$$= 1.68\%.$$

The total Yield Accumulation Return for the five-year horizon thus becomes the sum of these three percentage figures,

$$46.15\% + 8.62\% + 1.68\% = 56.45\%.$$

Referring to Table 1, we can determine the net incremental effect that the proposed swap would have on each of the components of return. The net Coupon Income return would be boosted substantially from 29.64% to 46.15% for a net increase of

$$46.15\% - 29.64\% = 16.51\%.$$

The interest-on-interest component would undergo an increase of

$$8.62\% - 5.54\% = 3.08\%.$$

The P-bond's Accumulation Capital Gain return would be much lower than the H-bond's because of its lesser discount and longer maturity, so that net change from this return component would be

$$1.68\% - 18.88\% = -17.20\%.$$

The sum of the changes from these three components gives the Net Yield Accumulation Return added by the proposed swap,

$$16.51\% + 3.08\% - 17.20\% = 2.39\%.$$

For this swap example, Table 5 shows the net changes in the Yield Accumulation Return and its components over investment horizons ranging up to the H-bond's maturity in ten years.

THE "RELATIVELY PREDICTABLE" NET YIELD ACCUMULATION RETURNS

The Net Yield Accumulation Returns shown in Table 5 would project the precise incremental impact of the swap subject only to the two conditions that coupons are indeed reinvested at the assumed 7.50% rate and that there are no changes whatsoever in the yields of either the H-bond or the P-bond.

The results shown in Table 5 are not really that sensitive to the precise reinvestment rates that actually become available over the investment horizon. For example, over the five-year horizon, the net interest-on-interest return would range between 2.42% and 3.78% for reinvestment rates lying anywhere between 6.00% and 9.00%. This amounts to a deviation of less than .70% from the net interest-on-interest return based on the assumed reinvestment rate of 7.50%. For this reason, the Net Yield Accumulation Return can be viewed as a relatively predictable portion of the incremental return produced by the swap, at least over the time horizon in question. More accurately, it can be said to incorporate

Table 5: Growth of a Swap's Net Yield Accumulation Return and Net Horizon Volatility

H-Bond: 10-Year 4.00% Bond Priced at 67.48 to Yield 9.00%
P-Bond: 20-Year 8.00% Bond Priced at 86.677 to Yield 9.50%
Assumed Reinvestment Rate = 7.50%

	Net Swap Improvement in Cumulative Percentage Return				Horizon Volatilities B.P. of Price Per B.P. of Yield Move		
Investment Horizon	Coupon Income	Interest-on-Interest (at 7.50%)	Accumulation Capital Gain	Yield Accumulation Return	H-Bond	P-Bond	Net (P-H)
	0%	0%	0%	0%	7.57 B.P./B.P.	9.21 B.P./B.P.	+1.64 B.P./B.P.
0 Years							
1.0	+ 3.30	+ .06	- 2.86	+ .50	7.22	9.08	+1.86
2.0	+ 6.60	+ .38	- 5.99	+ .99	6.82	8.92	+2.10
3.0	+ 9.91	+ .98	- 9.40	+1.48	6.35	8.76	+2.41
4.0	+13.21	+ 1.87	-13.13	+1.95	5.79	8.57	+2.78
5.0	+16.51	+ 3.08	-17.20	+2.39	5.15	8.36	+3.21
6.0	+19.81	+ 4.64	-21.63	+2.82	4.39	8.12	+3.73
7.0	+23.11	+ 6.57	-26.48	+3.21	3.52	7.86	+4.34
8.0	+26.42	+ 8.90	-31.77	+3.55	2.50	7.57	+5.07
9.0	+29.72	+11.66	-37.54	+3.84	1.34	7.24	+5.90
10.0	+33.02	+14.89	-43.84	+4.07	0	6.90	+6.90

all facets of the incremental return other than the effects of yield changes in either bond.

THE PRIMARY SOURCE OF UNCERTAINTY: DIFFERENT YIELD LEVEL AND YIELD SPREAD SCENARIOS

Yield levels and yield spreads can weave some very curious and unexpected patterns over time. Yet, for any specified investment horizon, it is the structure of yields at that horizon date which determines the Market Capital Gain return from a given bond or bond swap. It is perhaps, therefore, a fortunate coincidence that projections by bond market participants often take the form (or can be stretched into the form) of future horizon scenarios concerning interest rate levels, yield curve patterns, and yield spread relationships. In fact, it may be a somewhat unique characteristic of the bond market that one can frequently capture the range of any participant's expectations in terms of a small number of horizon scenarios consisting of relatively well-defined future yield structures.

Clearly, the impact of such scenarios should be incorporated into the evaluation of a proposed bond swap. The Horizon Analysis framework often provides quick (and sometimes surprising) insights into the role of yield changes in the evaluation of a bond swap.

For a concrete illustration, consider the swap example used in Table 5 for the case of the five-year investment horizon.

Table 6 shows the effect of several different scenarios for the yields of the H-bond and the P-bond at the fifth-year point. The first scenario is the simplest one: Both yields remain unchanged. There is no yield move in either bond, no return from Market Capital Gains, and the swap's net return is just the incremental Yield Accumulation Return of +2.39%.

The second scenario is based upon a general 50 basis point rise in interest rate levels, with the yield curve preserving the same 50 basis point spread of the P-bond over the shorter H-bond. At this point, in order to relate these yield changes to the swap's net return, it becomes convenient to introduce the notion of the "Net Horizon Volatility."

THE NET HORIZON VOLATILITY

In general, the yields of the H-bond and the P-bond will each change over time. If both bonds "shared" the exact same yield change, then the yield spread between them would also remain unchanged. Their yields would have then moved in exact "lockstep." However, even in this case of a completely shared yield move, the resulting price actions might be very different. The bond with a

Table 6: The Net Swap Effect Upon Total Cumulative Return Under Different Yield Level and Yield Spread Scenarios

H-Bond: 10-Year 4.00% Bond Priced at 67.48 to Yield 9.00%
P-Bond: 20-Year 8.00% Bond Priced at 86.677 to Yield 9.50%
Assumed Reinvestment Rate = 7.50%
5-Year Investment Horizon

Scenario	Yield Level		Yield Moves			Approximate Net Market Capital Gain Attributable to		Combined Net Market Capital Gain		Exact Total Net Return From Swap
	H-Bond	P-Bond	H-Bond	P-Bond	Net (P-H)	H-Bond Yield Move x Net Horizon Vol. -.0321%/B.P.	P-Horizon Vol. x Net Yield Move -.0836%/B.P.	Approx. Value	Exact Value	
1. All Yields Unchanged	9.00%	9.50%	0 BP	0 BP	0 BP	0%	0%	0%	0%	+2.39%
2. All Yields Rise by 50 B.P.	9.50	10.00	+50	+50	0	-1.60	0	-1.60	-1.51	.88
3. Yields Curve Flattens	9.00	9.00	0	-50	-.50	0	+4.18	+4.18	+4.29	+6.68
4. All Yields Decline and Yield Curve Flattens	8.50	8.50	-50	-100	-50	+1.60	+4.18	+5.78	+6.25	+8.64
5. Break-Even Spread With H-Bond at 9.00%	9.00	9.79	0	+29	+29	0	-2.39	-2.39	-2.39	0

greater price volatility will undergo a larger price change for the given yield move. The Horizon Volatility can be used to gauge these different responses from the two bonds. By defining the "Net Horizon Volatility" to be the difference between the two Horizon Volatilities, the resulting value can be used to approximate the swap's incremental return resulting from such shared yield moves.

For the sample swap with the five-year horizon, Table 5 shows that the Net Horizon Volatility of .0321%/B.P. is just the H-bond's Horizon Volatility of .0515%/B.P. subtracted from the P-bond's value of .0836%/B.P. Then in Table 6, for the second scenario, the approximate Net Market Gain is found by multiplying this 50 basis points shared yield move by the Net Horizon Volatility

$$(+50 \text{ B.P.}) \times (-.0321\%/\text{B.P.}) = -1.60\%.$$

Thus, relative to continued holding of the H-bond, an executed swap would have lost approximately (-1.60%) of the original investment from the yield movements in this scenario. As we noted earlier, all Volatility factors necessarily represent approximations. This is particularly true for simplistically averaged Volatility factors used in Tables 5 and 6. Nevertheless, these approximations are valuable, both as a quick guide and as a way of looking at the price dynamics in a swap situation. The exact price responses can always be subsequently calculated to refine the results of the initial study. Using exact calculations, the actual Net Market Gain in the second scenario turns out to be a loss of -1.51%. Subtracting this loss from the Net Yield Accumulation Return of 2.39%, the swap turns out to be ahead by +.88%.

This swap began with a pickup of 50 basis points in yield-to-maturity. However, the swap led to an increased volatility as was clearly indicated by the Net Horizon Volatility figure. Under this scenario of yields rising in lockstep, this increased volatility resulted in a significant reduction of the swap's net return.

THE NET YIELD MOVE

In the third scenario in Table 6, the H-bond's yield remains fixed at 9.00%, but the yield curve becomes flat as the P-bond's yield declines by 50 basis points to 9.00%. Here, there is no shared yield move at all, but the yield spread of the P-bond over the H-bond moves from its initial +50 basis points down to 0 basis points at the horizon. In general, we will use the term "Net Yield Move" to describe the yield move of the P-bond *beyond* the common yield move it shares with the H-bond. In this example, the Net Yield Move is -50 basis points beyond the shared yield move of 0 basis points.

As just shown, the product of the H-bond's yield move times the Net Horizon Volatility factor reflects the impact of the shared portion of a yield move on the swap's return. On the other hand, the Net Yield Move is, by definition, just the P-bond's yield move beyond this portion shared with the H-bond. Consequently, it leads to a price response in the P-bond above and beyond that resulting from the shared yield move. This additional P-bond price response can be approximated by multiplying the P-bond's own Horizon Volatility factor by the magnitude of the Net Yield Move. The resulting increment of Market Capital Gain can then be viewed as representing the impact of changes in the yield spread relationship.

This interpretation of the Net Yield Move is particularly simple in the third scenario. Here, multiplying the P-bond's yield move of -50 basis points by the P-bond's Horizon Volatility of -.0836%/B.P., one obtains an approximate Market Capital Gain of

$$(-50 \text{ B.P.}) \times (-.0836\%/\text{B.P.}) = +4.18\%.$$

Computed exactly, this figure would be +4.29%, leading to a net total return from the swap of

$$+4.29\% + 2.39\% = +6.68\%.$$

In this case, the swap becomes far more successful because of a favorable change in the yield spread relationship. Here, the P-bond's sizable Horizon Volatility provides a clear indication of the swap's sensitivity to such favorable moves in the yield spread.

COMBINED CHANGES IN YIELD LEVELS AND YIELD SPREADS

The incremental return provided by any swap over any horizon can be represented by the sum of: 1) the Net Market Capital Gains resulting from the shared yield move, plus 2) the Net Market Capital Gain resulting from the Net Yield Move, plus 3) the Yield Accumulation Return.

These three components are all present in the fourth scenario—interest rate levels fall to 8.50%, the yield curve becomes flat, and both bonds are priced to yield 8.50%. This implies a -50 basis point yield move shared by both bonds with the P-bond yield declining an additional 50 basis points. The swap's Net Market Capital Gain is approximately +5.78%, comprised of the +1.60% resulting from the swap's increased volatility under the shared yield move plus an additional +4.18% resulting from the favorable Net Yield Move of 50 basis points. The exact Market Capital Gain is +6.25%. This combines with the Yield Accumulation Return for a total swap effect of +8.64%. (In this instance, the discrepancy from the "volatility" approximation is particularly large because of the magnitude and common direction of the yield moves. This deviation could be greatly reduced by using "directional" volatility factors.)

CONGRUENCE WITH SWAP CLASSIFICATION SYSTEM

The analysis of any bond swap must be reflective of the motivations and market judgments underlying that swap. Since these underlying intentions range across radically different types of investment decisions, it is most critical that the primary purpose of a swap be clearly defined. It is, in a sense, most unfortunate that the one term "swap" can be conveniently stretched to cover such a wide spectrum of different tactical and strategic actions. This lack of refinement in the language of investment has often led to many unnecessary problems, both in communication and in thinking.

In an attempt to introduce some organization into this area, we defined four idealized swap categories in *Inside the Yield Book*. In spite of its simplicity and limited refinement, this classification scheme has proven most useful. The four categories in this classification scheme are:

I. Substitution Swaps

II. Intermarket Spread Swaps

III. Rate Anticipation Swaps

IV. Pure Yield Pickup Swaps

The Substitution Swap is ideally an exchange of a bond for a perfect substitute or "twin" bond. The motivation here is a temporary price advantage, presumably resulting from a momentary imbalance in the relative supply/demand conditions in the marketplace.

The Intermarket Spread Swap is a more general movement out of one market component and into another with the intention of exploiting a currently advantageous yield relationship. The idea here is to trade off of these changing relationships between the two market components. Short-term Workout Periods are usually anticipated. While such swaps will almost always have some sensitivity to the direction of the overall market, the idealized focus of this type of swap is the spread relationship itself.

On the other hand, the Rate Anticipation Swap is frankly geared towards profiting from an anticipated movement in overall market rates.

The Pure Yield Pickup Swap is oriented towards yield improvement over the long term with little heed being paid to interim price movements in either the respective market components or the market as a whole.

It should be recognized that this categorization implies much sharper demarcations than are encountered in practice. A real life swap may incorporate elements of all four swap categories as well as some considerations well beyond the limits of this simple classification system.

The Horizon Analysis of the sources of a swap's return has an interpretation in terms of this swap classification system. Any given swap can be viewed as containing some elements of a Pure Yield Pickup Swap, some elements of a Rate Anticipation Swap, etc. The analytic framework which has been developed now enables the potential sources of return to be associated with each facet of the swap classification system:

1) The Yield Accumulation Return reflects the Pure Yield Pickup elements of the swap.

2) The Market Gain from the shared yield move represents the effects of changes in the portfolio's incremental volatility, and consequently this can be taken as the swap's Rate Anticipation component.

3) The Market Gain from Net Yield Moves measures the impact of changes in the yield spread relationship which are characteristic of both Substitution and Intermarket Spread Swaps.

For example, under the fourth scenario in Table 6, the sample swap generates a Yield Accumulation Return of +2.39%, a shared yield move Market Gain of +1.60%, and a Net Yield Move return of +4.19%. Thus, the swap's approximated total net return adds to 8.17%, and 29% of this return could then be ascribed to Pure Yield Pickup, 20% to Rate Anticipation, and 51% to an Intermarket Spread component.

Actually, the Net Yield Move component can itself be further refined by examining the different elements comprising each bond's yield, e.g., the general market level, the position along the yield curve, the coupon, quality, and sector spreads, and the bond's individual yield placement within its market sector. When yield spread changes are associated with each of these yield components, then the return from Spread Swaps becomes identifiable as Substitution Swaps, literal Inter-Market Spread Swaps, Sector Swaps, Quality Swaps, Yield Curve Changes, and Yield Curve "Rolls." However, a detailed discussion along these lines would carry us beyond the scope of this article.

RISK MEASURES

This scope limitation precludes anything more than a cursory discussion of how risk can be treated within this analytic framework. However, we can briefly note two examples of the applications of this approach to risk assessment.

First, if the sample swap of Table 6 was intended to provide a Pure Yield Pickup, then a Break-Even figure can be computed to gauge its vulnerability to adverse changes in the yield spread. For example, at the five-year horizon, the swap's Yield Accumulation Return is +2.39%. Using the P-bond's Horizon Volatility figure of -.0836%/B.P., this +2.39% "cushion" could cover an adverse Net Yield Move of up to

$$\frac{-2.39\%}{-.0836\%/\text{B.P.}} = 29 \text{ B.P.}$$

Thus, with the H-bond staying at its original 9.00% yield level, the yield spread could widen from the initial 50 B.P. to as much as 79 B.P. before the swap would cease to be profitable. This is illustrated by the fifth scenario in Table 6.

This Break-Even approach can be generalized to provide a useful picture of the swap's various risk limits.

The second application to risk or sensitivity analysis consists of the "offset ratio" of the P-bond's Horizon Volatility over the Net Horizon Volatility. For the swap in Table 6, this ratio has the value

$$\frac{.0836\%/\text{B.P.}}{.0321\%/\text{B.P.}} = 2.60 \text{ B.P./B.P.}$$

This ratio can be interpreted as a running measure of the approximate shared yield move required to offset each basis point of Net Yield Move. A high value for this offset ratio would imply that the swap is far more sensitive to changes in the yield spread than to shared changes in the general level of rates. On the other hand, a low ratio would imply that the swap is more sensitive to general Rate Anticipation effects.

This offset ratio is often quite dependent upon the particular time horizon, and such a dependence may highlight the changing character of a given swap over different time frames.

THE IMPACT OF THE INVESTMENT HORIZON

This time effect can be illustrated by the swap presented in Tables 5 and 6. All the results shown in Table 6 are for the case of the five-year horizon. As we just noted, for this horizon, the Breakeven Net Yield Move is 29 B.P. and the offset ratio is 2.60 B.P./B.P.

By returning to Table 5, the character of this swap can be explored for other investment horizons. For example, at one year, the Break-Even Net Yield Move is only

$$\frac{+.50\%}{.0908\%/\text{B.P.}} = 5.5 \text{ B.P.}$$

while the offset ratio is

$$\frac{.0908\%/\text{B.P.}}{.0186\%/\text{B.P.}} = 4.88 \text{ B.P./B.P.}$$

In other words, the swap at this point is so spread-sensitive that a 6 B.P. widening of the spread would create a loss, and almost 5 basis points of a favorable shared yield movement would be needed to counteract each 1 B.P. of widening spread.

On the other hand, by the ninth-year horizon, the Break-Even Net Yield Move has risen to a respectable

$$\frac{+3.84\%}{.0590\%/\text{B.P.}} = 65 \text{ B.P.}$$

while the offset ratio has dropped to

$$\frac{.0724\%/\text{B.P.}}{.0590\%/\text{B.P.}} = 1.23 \text{ B.P./B.P.}$$

As would logically be expected for this longer horizon, the swap has a much stronger Pure Yield Pickup footing and far less relative sensitivity to any changes in the yield spread relationship.

A BALANCED APPROACH TO THE SOURCES OF RETURN

One of the virtues of this approach is that a broad constellation of return and risk patterns can be discerned from just two basic calculations for each bond: 1) the Yield Accumulation Return customized to reflect the manager's reinvestment assumptions, and 2) the Horizon Volatility. Once these two values have been computed for lists of candidate H-bonds and P-bonds, then this framework can greatly facilitate the evaluation of multiple swap combinations and portfolio restructurings over a range of projected market scenarios.

The portfolio manager's art should mix well with this Horizon Analysis approach to the sources of bond market return, and the resulting blend should constitute a more balanced technique for integrating both tactical and strategic factors in the decision-making process.

Chapter III B-4

Horizon Annuity

Many institutional portfolios, including most pension funds, have a two-phase life cycle: a long period of growth, followed by a payout phase in which disbursements draw down the funds accumulated in the first phase. The payout level during the second phase can be surprisingly sensitive to the fund's reinvestment rate. A simplified model of a two-phase fund enables the author to analyze a fund's ability to sustain a given payout level.

Many institutions, including pension funds, have a two-phase life cycle. During the first phase, the fund grows and compounds. Sooner or later, however, the fund converts from the compounding phase into the second, payout phase.

The dollars accumulated in the compounding phase depend on the rate at which income can be reinvested. Once a fund has passed the conversion horizon, however, it is not so much the dollars accumulated in the compounding phase that count, but their power to generate income. The latter depends critically on the level of interest rates prevailing beyond the horizon. When reinvestment rates during the compounding phase and beyond the conversion horizon

Martin L. Leibowitz, "Horizon Annuity—Linking the Growth and Payout Phases of Long-Term Bond Portfolios," *Financial Analysts Journal*, May/June 1979. (Received Graham & Dodd Scroll for 1979.) Reprinted with permission.

595

are linked, the level of payout the fund can sustain (the so-called "horizon annuity") becomes very sensitive to the joint rate.

The author develops a simplified model of a two-phase investment fund that permits him to examine the implications of this sensitivity. The model shows that the best passive defense against a secular downtrend in reinvestment rates is a truly long-term portfolio protected against excessive exposure to call. Unfortunately, the best long-term portfolio will often have an extremely volatile short-term performance. The growing popularity of short-term performance measurement has made it difficult for many managers to gear their portfolio structure entirely to long-term objectives.

The very expression "fixed income security" conveys a warm feeling of stability. A high-grade bond may not be exciting, but at least it should provide the promised level of nominal dollar payments.

Unfortunately, this is an uncertain world. For many long-term investment purposes, the fixed income portfolio can only offer relative, not absolute, comfort, even in nominal dollar terms. This is especially true for funds whose "life cycles" take the form of a growth phase followed by a long-term payout phase.

Consider an example at the personal level. Suppose a 45-year-old investor has accumulated $50,000, which he puts into a fixed income portfolio with the hope that it will provide a supplemental source of retirement income. On the basis of an 8.5% interest rate, the investor estimates that his $50,000 investment, with interest compounded, will grow to $264,000 by the time he retires at age 65. With this money, he plans to buy an annuity that will provide annual payments of almost $27,700 over the next 20 years.

Rather impressive, even if we have neglected taxes! Can the calculation really be correct? Aside from the neglect of taxes, it is.

Of course, there is the tacit assumption that interest rates will remain constant at 8.5%. What happens if interest rates drop to 5%? In that case, our investor's retirement income would decline to $10,700 per year, less than 39% of his original estimate.

In principle, of course, he can "lock in" some of today's 8.5% rate by buying a portfolio of long-term bonds. But if he buys a $50,000 portfolio of 40-year, 8.5% par bonds, and rates then drop to 5% (i.e., if all coupon payments and annuity purchases take place at 5%), his annual retirement income level will drop to $17,000—well below his original estimate of $27,700. Moreover, if his 40-year bonds contain the typical call feature, they will almost surely be refunded in the fifth year. In that case, even with full reinvestment of the call premium, his future income level will fall to $12,900.

Obviously, our investor faces surprisingly large variations in his retirement income, and virtually all of the variation can be traced to changes in the reinvestment rate. He can minimize his risk, however, by focusing on achieving a long-term maturity structure that is carefully balanced against excessive call vulnerability.

TWO-PHASE FUNDS

The above example provides a very simple illustration of a two-phase fund. During the first phase, annual contributions to the portfolio exceed disbursements, and all investment income is reinvested. The fund grows and compounds. This growth continues until some point at which the portfolio "converts" into a second phase characterized by disbursements exceeding contributions. During this second, "payout," phase, the portfolio is no longer a full compounder. Some or all of its investment income is being paid out.

Many institutional portfolios, including pension funds, have a similar two-phase life cycle. Initially, they enjoy a long period of growth through retention and reinvestment of investment income, as well as through the flow of net new contributions to the fund. Since this growth phase usually continues for many years, it has become conventional to view these funds as essentially perpetually growing entities. However, in most cases, planned annual payouts eventually increase to the point where they surpass the fund's income and contribution flows. At this point, the fund shifts into a payout phase.

The transition from growth to payout phase represents a fundamental change in the fund's investment character. The value of the fund during the compounding phase depends on the yields to maturity of the fund's current holdings and on the reinvestment rate during the compounding phase. It is natural for the portfolio manager to focus on rate of return during the long-term horizon that coincides with the fund's compounding phase. The reinvestment rate over this horizon will be critical in determining the fund's value at the point at which it converts into a payout phase. But, once the fund has passed into the payout phase, it is not so much the magnitude of the accumulated dollars that counts, but their power to generate income. The level of annuity income they can support during the payout phase depends entirely on the level of interest rates prevailing at the fund's conversion horizon.

On the other hand, it is not unreasonable to assume some linkage between the reinvestment conditions of the compounding phase and the interest rate structure at the fund's point of conversion. For example, when a portfolio manager assumes a 6% average reinvestment rate over the next 20 years, he clearly envisions a major secular downtrend in rates. Thus his assumption for reinvestment rates during the horizon period has strong implications for his expectations for the interest rate that will prevail at the horizon. The investor who assumes a 6% reinvestment rate will also probably expect interest rates to be around 6% (or lower) in the 20th year. An investor exploring a 10% reinvestment rate over the next 20 years presumably thinks in terms of a 10% interest rate prevailing in the 20th year.

Any such linkage will greatly reinforce the impact of the reinvestment assumption on a given investment strategy. For example, a full coupon bond maturing at the conversion horizon will produce considerably fewer accumulated dollars of return under a 6% reinvestment assumption than under a 10% reinvestment assumption. Moreover, these dollars could then presumably generate only a 6% yield rate during the payout phase. Under these linked 6% assumptions, the fund's total projected payout would be far less than the payout expected under a 10% rate assumption. Thus the fund's ability to fulfill its ultimate promise—to provide a certain level of absolute income during the payout period—will depend heavily on the investor's reinvestment rate assumption and long-term investment strategy.

THE HORIZON ANNUITY MODEL

To examine the implications of the investment strategy and reinvestment rate assumption of the compounding period for the ability of the fund to fulfill its promises during the payout period, we developed a highly simplified model of a two-phase investment fund. Our fund consists of one specified fixed-income investment, such as a 20-year, 8.5% bond. All relevant interest rates move suddenly to the level of the specified reinvestment rate and the resultant flat yield curve persists throughout both the compounding and payout phases.

During the compounding phase, all coupon payments and maturing principal of the fund are reinvested at the specified rate level. At the end of the compounding phase (i.e., at the conversion horizon), all the dollars accumulated in the fund are used to purchase a level annuity that will span the fund's payout phase. The cost of the annuity is based upon an interest rate that is the same as the initial reinvestment rate, and the annual annuity payments are designed to exhaust the fund's resources completely by the end of the payout phase.[1]

To determine whether the fund is fulfilling its payout obligations, we use as a convenient yardstick of its productivity during this phase the magnitude of the annual annuity payments. Dividing this amount by the fund's beginning market value provides the number of dollars that can be paid out annually during the payout phase for each dollar initially invested. We refer to this measure, expressed as a percentage, as the fund's "horizon annuity."

Table 1 illustrates the life cycle of one such two-phase fund. Here we assume that $100 million is completely invested in 20-year, 8.5% par bonds, and that the reinvestment rate is 6%. During the first 20 years—the compounding phase—the fund has no payouts, and all coupon receipts are reinvested at the assumed rate. The compounded income derived from this reinvestment process is shown in the "Interest on Interest" column.

---

[1] For clarity, returns and investment measures are expressed solely in terms of nominal dollars, even though inflation effects are clearly a critical factor in any comprehensive evaluation.

Table 1: The Horizon Annuity Concept.
Cash Flow Schedule of $100 Million Portfolio Consisting of 20-Year, 8.5% Par Bonds

20-Year Compounding Phase with Reinvestment at 6%

Semiannual Period Ending After	Principal	Interest on Principal	Interest on Interest	Total Fund Value Before Payouts	Payouts	Total Fund Value After Payouts
0.5 Years	$100.00 MM	$ 4.25 MM	$ 0 MM	$104.25 MM	0	$104.25 MM
1.0	100.00	4.25	0.13	108.63	0	108.63
1.5	100.00	4.25	0.26	113.14	0	113.14
2.0	100.00	4.25	0.39	117.78	0	117.78
:	:	:	:		:	:
19.0	100.00	4.25	8.44	393.92	0	393.92
19.5	100.00	4.25	8.82	406.99	0	406.99
20.0	100.00	4.25	9.21	420.45	0	420.45

Conversion into 20-Year Full Payout Phase Through Purchase of a 6%, 20-Year Annuity Paying $36.38 Million Annually

Semiannual Period Ending After	Principal	Interest on Principal	Interest on Interest	Total Fund Value Before Payouts	Payouts	Total Fund Value After Payouts
20.5 Years	$420.45 MM	$12.61 MM	0	$433.06 MM	$18.19 MM	$414.87 MM
21.0	414.87	12.45	0	427.32	18.19	409.13
21.5	409.13	12.27	0	421.41	18.19	403.22
22.0	403.22	12.10	0	415.31	18.19	397.12
:	:	:	:	:	:	:
39.0	51.46	1.54	0	53.00	18.19	34.81
39.5	34.81	1.04	0	35.85	18.19	17.66
40.0	17.66	0.53	0	18.19	18.19	0

At the end of the compounding phase, the total accumulated value in the fund—$420.45 million—is used to purchase a 20-year, 6% annuity. At this rate, the annuity will provide for 40 semiannual payments of $18.19 million. As with any annuity, this payout level exceeds the interest receipts, so the fund's principal erodes. By our definition, this erosion is scheduled so that the principal is completely exhausted at the end of the 20th year of the payout phase.

In this example, the *annual* payment during the payout phase is $36.38 million (twice the semiannual payment of $18.19). Since the fund's initial investment was $100 million, the annual payout per initial dollar invested is $0.3638 ($36.38 million divided by $100 million). Expressed as a percentage of each initial dollar invested, the fund's horizon annuity is 36.38%.

Table 2 demonstrates what happens to the same fund's future value (its value at the conversion horizon) and horizon annuity when we assume different reinvestment rates. Obviously, the reinvestment assumption will have a strong effect upon the fund's future value. Moving from a reinvestment rate of 5% to one of 10% increases the fund's future value by 58%—from $386.46 million to $613.38 million. The reinvestment rate's effect can also be seen in the fund's realized compound yield—the growth rate of the fund's total value through compounded reinvestment—over the compounding phase. This increases from 6.88% to 9.28% as we move from a reinvestment rate of 5% to one of 10%.

But a change in the reinvestment rate assumption will have an even more profound effect on the fund's horizon annuity. With a change in the rate assumption from 5% to 10%, the horizon annuity increases by over 132%—from

Table 2: Sensitivity of Future Value and Horizon Annuity to Reinvestment Rate—$100 Million Portfolio Consisting of 20-Year, 8.5% Par Bonds

	20-Year Compounding Phase with Fund then Converting into a 20-Year Payout Phase		
Reinvestment Rate	Total Future Value of Fund at 20-Year Conversion Horizon	Realized Compound Yield Over First 20 Years	Horizon Annuity Over Next 20 Years of Payout Phase
5%	$386.46 MM	6.88%	30.79%
6	420.45	7.31	36.38
7	459.33	7.77	43.02
8	503.86	8.25	50.91
9	554.86	8.75	60.31
10	613.38	9.28	71.49

30.79% to 71.49%! The horizon annuity's sensitivity to the reinvestment rate is a result of the direct linkage between the reinvestment rate and the annuity purchase rate.

THE SAVINGS ACCOUNT ANALOGY

The first column of Table 3, labeled "cash," shows the horizon annuity values provided by savings accounts with various guaranteed interest rates. For example, suppose $100 were placed in a savings account that guaranteed 5% interest (semiannual payments). If all interest payments were allowed to remain in the account and compounded for the next 20 years, then exactly $21.39 could be withdrawn every year (in two semiannual installments) over the subsequent 20 years, leaving the account totally empty by the end of the 40th year. This corresponds to the horizon annuity of 21.39% for a "cash" portfolio under a 5% reinvestment assumption. By using Table 3 to explore a range of "savings account" reinvestment rates, one can assess the impact of uncertainty regarding reinvestment rates on the value of the horizon annuity.

The savings account approach can also be enlarged to explain the horizon annuity concept for bond portfolios of various maturities. The last four columns of the table show what horizon annuities the investor can expect if, instead of placing his money in the savings account initially, he purchases 8.5% par bonds of various maturity and, at the end of 20 years, reinvests the accumulated cou-

Table 3: Horizon Annuities of 8.5% Par Bonds with Different Maturities

	20-Year Compounding Phase with Fund then Converting into a 20-Year Payout Phase				
	1	2	3	4	5
Reinvest-ment Rate	Cash	Five-Year Maturity	10-Year Maturity	20-Year Maturity	40-Year Maturity*
5%	21.39%	24.67%	27.23%	30.79%	34.29%
6	28.22	31.23	33.47	36.38	38.88
7	37.08	39.39	41.03	43.02	44.52
8	48.51	49.50	50.16	50.91	51.42
8.5	55.41	55.41	55.41	55.41	55.41
9	63.22	61.96	61.16	60.31	59.81
10	82.06	77.30	74.39	71.49	69.99

* At 20-year conversion horizon, all bonds are assumed priced to yield the reinvestment rate.

pon payments and principal in a savings account that offers a guaranteed interest rate equal to the given reinvestment rate.

Suppose the investor had the one-time opportunity to buy a 20-year, 8.5% bond at par. If he puts his $100 into this bond, instead of into the savings account, he will receive a higher level of interest payments over the bond's life. Now assume he places all these coupon payments, along with the $100 principal repayment, in a 5% savings account. As a result of the first 20 years of higher return, the portfolio's horizon annuity is boosted to 30.79%, as Table 3 shows.

For bond investments with maturities of less than 20 years, of course, we must make some determination regarding the reinvestment of the principal payments for the remainder of the 20-year compounding phase. For purposes of simplicity, it is convenient to treat all maturing principal payments as being rolled over at the given reinvestment rate. This treatment is consistent with our basic assumption of a sudden and permanent move to a flat yield curve.

Table 3 shows a range of horizon annuities dependent, not only upon the assumed reinvestment rate, but upon bond maturities. For a 20-year maturity, the various reinvestment rates yield the same horizon annuities depicted in Table 2; these range from 30.79%, assuming a 5% reinvestment rate, to 71.49%, assuming a 10% rate. But the same selection of reinvestment rates yields a broader range of horizon annuities for a portfolio invested in 10-year maturities; in this case the bottom end of the scale is down to 27.23% and the top up to 74.39%. And the range for a cash portfolio (Column 1) widens considerably more—from 21.39% to 82.06%. Thus, as the initial maturity of the invested portfolio becomes shorter, future reinvestment rates play an increasing role in determining the fund's asset and annuity values.

It is apparent from Table 3 that longer maturity portfolios provide some protection against lower reinvestment rate assumptions. At a 5% reinvestment rate, a cash portfolio would compound like a 5% savings account, providing a horizon annuity of only 21.39%. On the other hand, a 10-year, 8.5% bond would provide a higher interest rate on the original principal for the first 10 years, and this would eventually lead to an improved horizon annuity of 27.23%. The longer one can hold on to the higher return through longer maturity, the higher will be the annuity over the payout phase. If the investor purchases a 20-year, 8.5% bond, the horizon annuity grows to 30.79%, assuming a 5% reinvestment rate.

On the other hand, the effect of portfolio maturity is surprisingly small in comparison to the impact of the reinvestment rate assumption. A guaranteed, 6% savings account provides a horizon annuity of 28.22%—almost as much as a 20-year, 8.5% bond subject to reinvestment and annuity purchase at 5%. Furthermore, the advantage in holding a longer maturity portfolio decreases as assumed reinvestment rates rise. When the reinvestment rate equals the purchase yield of the par bonds, all monies end up being compounded at the same rate—

8.5%. Consequently, it makes no difference whether the initial portfolio consists of cash or of five, 10 or 20-year bonds; the horizon annuity will be 55.41% for all.

As the reinvestment rate rises above this point, the advantage shifts to shorter maturity portfolios. At a 10% reinvestment rate, a cash portfolio will generate a horizon annuity of 82.06%. An 8.5% bond of any maturity would naturally lead to a lower horizon annuity. Table 3 shows that an initial purchase of a 20-year, 8.5% par bond would produce a horizon annuity of only 71.49%.

Maturities beyond the conversion horizon—40-year bonds, in Table 3—form a special case. So far, our basic model has assumed that all fund assets are liquidated at the conversion horizon (20 years) and the proceeds used to purchase an annuity covering the payout phase. To accommodate longer maturity bonds, we have to specify a technique for determining their market value at the end of 20 years. We have used the simplest solution—equating the yield to maturity of outstanding bonds with the assumed reinvestment rate. This is again in keeping with our assumption of a flat yield curve.

Table 3 shows that the extension to 40-year maturities provides a relatively modest shift in the horizon annuity. In most cases, extending the maturity from 10 to 20 years has a greater impact on the horizon annuity than extending it from 20 to 40 years.

DISCOUNT BONDS AND PREMIUM BONDS

Up to this point, the discussion has centered on par bonds. However, a bond's coupon rate is an important determinant of its sensitivity to changing reinvestment rates. As shown in *Inside the Yield Book*, the future value of a zero-coupon pure discount is totally insensitive to reinvestment rates.[2] However, since our model links the annuity purchase rate to the reinvestment assumption, the horizon annuity of even zero-coupon bonds will exhibit some sensitivity to reinvestment rates. The future values, hence horizon annuities, of higher coupon bonds become more and more dependent upon the reinvestment rate, the higher their coupon rate.

Table 4 shows for various reinvestment rate assumptions the horizon annuity values corresponding to the various coupon rates of 20-year bonds priced to a conventional yield to maturity of 8.5%. The zero-coupon, pure discount bond has the smallest range of horizon annuity values—from 42.11% to 61.61%. By contrast, the horizon annuities of a premium bond with a 10% coupon range from 30.46% to 71.78%, depending on the reinvestment rate. For purposes of comparison, the table also shows the corresponding values for a cash portfolio.

---

[2] Sidney Homer and Martin L. Leibowitz, *Inside the Yield Book* (Englewood Cliffs, NJ: Prentice-Hall, 1972).

Table 4: Horizon Annuities of Discount and Premium Bonds

Reinvest- ment Rate	20-Year Compounding Phase with Fund then Converting into a 20-Year Payout Phase					
	1	2	3	4	5	6
	Coupon Rate on 20-Year Bonds Priced to Yield 8.5%					
	Cash	0%	4%	7%	8.5%	10%
5%	21.39%	42.11	32.77	31.23	30.79	30.46
6	28.22	45.73	38.02	36.75	36.38	36.11
7	37.08	49.50	44.15	43.27	43.02	42.83
8	48.51	53.41	51.35	51.01	50.91	50.84
8.5	55.41	55.41	55.41	55.41	55.41	55.41
9	63.22	57.45	59.80	60.20	60.31	60.39
10	82.06	61.61	69.75	71.11	71.49	71.78

Because discount bonds are relatively less sensitive than par bonds, they are better able to preserve a promised higher return in the face of lower reinvestment conditions. Thus, even at a 5% reinvestment rate, the zero-coupon bond provides a horizon annuity of 42.11%; this exceeds the horizon annuity of a savings account with a guaranteed interest rate of 7.5%. Unfortunately, as one moves toward bonds with more realistic coupon levels, this advantage deteriorates rapidly.

FUND PLANNING AND HORIZON ANNUITY

Managers developing an overall fund plan often select a relatively low rate of return value—one which they believe to have a high probability of being exceeded by the portfolio's actual long-term return—to serve as a measure of the minimum long-term investment return. This rate of return assumption becomes the yardstick by which they match asset requirements against expected future liabilities and, as such, plays a critical role in determining the funding procedure for the portfolio. It becomes deeply embedded in virtually all the fund's long-term planning and investment strategy.

There is a connection between our horizon annuity concept and this target rate of return. Suppose, for example, that a $100 million fund is established with a single lump sum contribution—i.e., there will be no future contributions. For the first 20 years, the fund has no liability requirements. Over the second 20 years, it must pay out $37.08 million each year. After 40 years, it has no residual liabilities and can be extinguished. The fund manager has targeted a reinvestment return of 7%.

This case corresponds to our two-phase, $100 million portfolio with a 20-year compounding phase and a 20-year payout phase. By consulting Table 3, we see that a constant 7% compounding and annuity purchase rate will produce exactly the required $37.08 million annuity during the payout phase. If the 7% rate can be assured, then the fund's initial $100 million of assets will just meet its scheduled liabilities.

If interest rates were at the 8.5% level, one might expect the fund to realize the minimum 7% level of return easily. However, it is really the fund's horizon annuity that matters. As Table 3 illustrates, any secular downtrend in interest rates could prevent the fund from achieving the required horizon annuity of 37.08%. For example, if reinvestment rates declined to 6%, then the portfolio would have to be invested in bonds with maturities exceeding 20 years in order to provide the needed horizon annuity.

Given a clear-cut minimum target, it can be useful to express the various outcomes as percentages of this target level. For example, under a reinvestment assumption of 6%, a 20-year portfolio of 8.5% par bonds would achieve only 98% of the fund's minimum target. Table 5 translates the horizon annuity values of Table 3 into "fulfillment percentages."

Since the fixed income portion of a fund is often viewed as playing a special risk-avoidance role, serving as an "anchor to windward," fulfilling minimum objectives is far more important to the bond portfolio than generating returns above any expected levels. Table 5 shows that a secular downtrend in rates can threaten the fulfillment of minimum horizon annuity objectives.

Ironically, higher interest rates pose no such threat. Of course, our model assumes that the portfolio manager does not attempt to anticipate rate movements. The only sale of bonds occurs at the conversion horizon; consequently, price changes become important only if bonds have maturities longer than the conversion horizon. For example, the 40-year, 8.5% bonds in Table 3 would have a remaining life of 20 years at the conversion horizon. At this point, under a 10% reinvestment assumption, these bonds would be sold at a price of $87.13, corresponding to a 10% yield to maturity. In this case, the higher level of reinvestment and annuity purchase would more than compensate for the principal loss.

For our simple two-phase fund, lower interest rates pose a far greater long-term problem than higher interest rates. This threat is further exacerbated by the problem of call vulnerability. In a declining interest rate environment, there is a growing probability of refunding calls.[3]

---

[3] See Martin L. Leibowitz, *Call Vulnerability: A New Fact in the Bond Market* (New York, NY: Salomon Brothers, September 23, 1976).

Table 5: Fulfillment Percentages—Horizon Annuities of 8.5% Par Bonds with Different Maturities as a Percentage of Fund's Minimum Target (Based on a 7% Return Objective)

| Reinvest-ment Rate | 20-Year Compounding Phase with Fund then Converting into a 20-Year Payout Phase | | | | |
| | 1 | 2 | 3 | 4 | 5 |
	Cash	Five-Year Maturity	10-Year Maturity	20-Year Maturity	40-Year Maturity*
5%	58%	66%	73%	83%	92%
6	76	84	90	98	105
7	100	106	111	116	120
8	131	133	135	137	139
8.5	149	149	149	149	149
9	171	167	165	163	161
10	221	208	201	193	189

* At 20-year conversion horizon, all bonds are assumed priced to yield the reinvestment rate.

Table 6 shows the potential impact of call vulnerability for two different cases of call protection—(1) the bond becomes refundable in the fifth year at a call price of 107 and (2) the bond becomes refundable in the 10th year at a call price of 104.

A call is assumed to take place only if it would lead to lower horizon annuity values. For the rate levels depicted in Table 6, this means that refunding calls would occur only in the case of reinvestment assumptions below 8%. The full proceeds from the call—the par value plus the call premium—would be rolled over at the specified reinvestment rate. Thus, under a 6% rate assumption, a call in the fifth year at 107 would lower the horizon annuity from 36.38% to 32.71%. If the fund's minimum return objective were 7%, then the call would mean a decline in the portfolio's fulfillment percentage from 98% to 88%.

Unfortunately, call vulnerability hurts most just when every increment of return is needed to cover the fund's minimum objectives.

INVESTMENT IMPLICATIONS

Our examples have used a series of highly simplifying assumptions—e.g., lump sum funding, no future contributions, nominal dollar liabilities falling into an annuity pattern, a future of flat yield curves, a passive portfolio process, a linkage making the annuity purchase rate exactly equal to the reinvestment rate.

Table 6: Horizon Annuity Values Under Different Degrees of Call Vulnerability—$100 Million Portfolio Consisting of 20-Year 8.5% Par Bonds (Fund's Minimum Target Based on a 7% Return Objective)

20-Year Compounding Phase with Fund then Converting into a 20-Year Payout Phase

Reinvestment Rate	Without Call		Callable in Five Years at 107		Callable in 10 Years at 104	
	Horizon Annuity	Fulfillment Percentage	Horizon Annuity	Fulfillment Percentage	Horizon Annuity	Fulfillment Percentage
5%	30.79%	83%	25.84%	70%	27.75%	75%
6	36.38	98	32.71	88	34.10	92
7	43.02	116	41.23	111	41.78	113
8*	50.91	137	50.91	137	50.91	137
8.5*	55.41	149	55.41	149	55.41	149
9*	60.31	163	60.31	163	60.31	163
10*	71.49	193	71.49	193	71.49	193

* Call not exercised at these levels.

Obviously further development is needed before the horizon annuity concept can become a reasonably good representation of actual pension funds. However, even the simplistic analysis presented here shows that two-phase funds have a special vulnerability to interest rate movements. A secular decline in rates can pose a significant problem for such a fund's payout phase, even when current market rates appear to exceed comfortably the fund's planning rate.

The best passive defense against these problems lies in a truly long-term portfolio balanced against excessive exposure to call. Of course, an actively managed fund will depart from this long-term defensive "baseline" in order to take advantage of various market opportunities. The incremental return anticipated from such activity should perhaps be gauged relative to the risk it introduces.

Aside from the pursuit of market opportunities, there are a variety of reasons why a portfolio manager may find it necessary or desirable to depart from a portfolio structure patterned solely upon long-term objectives. For one thing, even long-term portfolios tend to have a high level of short-term price volatility. (In fact, it can be demonstrated that the most volatile bond over short horizons will theoretically provide the best protection against declining rates over long horizons.) A long-term maturity structure with an implied high degree of volatility may not fit the practical considerations and constraints of actual fund management.

In particular, the growing popularity of performance measurement has tended to focus managers' attention toward increasingly short-term results. If carried to extremes, performance pressures could lead to dangerous overemphasis of the short term. Evaluation would be more balanced if measurement of the fund's short-term performance were expressed in terms of its contribution to long-term goals.

PART III C

Total Returns and
the Yield Curve

Chapter III C-1

Goal-Oriented Bond Portfolio Management

THE YARDSTICK OF TOTAL RETURN

Managers of fixed income portfolios have recently found themselves coming under increasing pressure from various forms of performance monitoring. Primarily, this monitoring has taken the form of total return measurement of portfolio results over relatively short-term measurement periods—i.e., quarters or years. The manager's results are then compared with the returns achieved by general market indices, by short-term investments, or by other portfolios believed to be part of a "peer group." These comparisons increasingly play a major role in the evaluation of the portfolio manager's skills and services.

It is clear that performance monitoring can be helpful in many areas of investment management, especially when the monitoring is based upon objective, concrete measurements. However, the sole reliance upon total return comparisons over short-term periods is subject to a number of criticisms. Total return measurements do provide a useful yardstick of the extent to which the portfolio manager took advantage of general market opportunities during the measurement period. But this is only one factor in the complex process of portfolio man-

Martin L. Leibowitz, "Goal-Oriented Bond Portfolio Management," Salomon Brothers Inc, May 1979. This paper was subsequently included in *Total Return Management*, Salomon Brothers Inc, 1979.

agement. A fundamental problem seems to arise when a *single* yardstick—total return measurement over short-term periods—is taken as *the sole* yardstick for all management activity.

This concentration on the single yardstick of total return can force dangerously simplistic comparisons among portfolios that may actually differ widely in function and purpose. In fact, the same level of achieved return may represent a very satisfactory result for one portfolio while having quite dismal implications for another portfolio with a different set of goals.

Moreover, even within a given portfolio, an overemphasis on short-term return can lead to conflicts with the long-term goals of the fund. For example, it could lead the portfolio manager into concentrating his activity on catching short-term swings in interest rates. In turn, this could lead to a frequent series of major portfolio shifts, thereby introducing considerable timing risk into the overall management process. The resulting volatility risk might be in direct contradiction to the original purpose of placing the funds into a fixed-income portfolio in the first place. This is just one instance of how an exclusive focus on maximization of total return over short periods can violate a fund's policy constraints and cause deviations from the fund's true long-term objectives.

These problems are particularly acute for fixed-income portfolios because of certain distinctive characteristics of the bond market. Much of the institutional investment in bonds is motivated by long-term, risk-avoidance purposes. These long-term purposes typically overshadow any specific requirement for total return over short-term periods. Another important characteristic of the bond market is the structural clarity of its asset classes. This clarity enables the return/risk relationships among the different market sectors to be relatively well defined, especially over longer-term horizons. The longer-term motivation of investors and the market's structural clarity obviously fit hand-in-glove, allowing for the identification of market sectors that are particularly well suited for serving the specific goals of a given fund.

By taking advantage of these special characteristics of the bond market, we believe that a *practical* technique can be developed for relating performance measurements over short-term periods to the fund's long-term goals.

THE BASELINE PORTFOLIO

In theory, the portfolio management process can be viewed as consisting of the four major steps shown in Figure 1. The first step is to identify the long-term objectives of the fund. The second step commences with the manager's judgments regarding market prospects. At this point, the manager must make the broad decisions that relate to portfolio strategy, i.e., to determining the portfolio's maturity structure. Once this has been done, the third step consists of deciding upon the detailed portfolio tactics to be employed. These consist of

---

Figure 1: Overview of the Portfolio Management Process

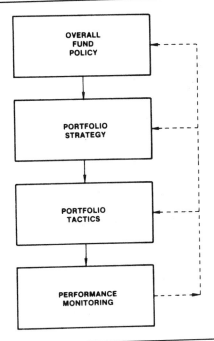

---

selecting specific sectors to take advantage of perceived market opportunities. The fourth step then consists of a continuing performance monitoring (in the most general sense) to ensure that the portfolio objectives are being fulfilled.

The first step is far more difficult than generally believed. It is no simple matter to identify a full set of portfolio objectives and then to define these objectives in a *useful way*. Such efforts tend to lead to either a frustratingly vague description of the objectives or to lead to an impossibly long collection of goals which mix the minor considerations in with the major ones.

For example, Figure 2 illustrates only a partial list of the many objectives that could be ascribed to fixed-income portfolios. Moreover, any set of objectives is closely intertwined with an associated set of risk factors. (In this connection, risk is being defined in a far broader sense than the single volatility measure which has become traditional in many modern analyses. In the sense used here, risk entails all those potential events that could interfere with the portfolio being able to fulfill its long-term objectives.) When there are a large number of potential objectives and associated risk factors, it is no easy task to generate concrete guidelines for portfolio managers.

Figure 2: Portfolio Objectives

MAXIMUM LONG TERM NOMINAL RETURN

MAXIMUM LONG TERM REAL RETURN

MATCH PRESCRIBED LIABILITY SCHEDULE

RESERVE AGAINST UNCERTAIN LIABILITIES

EARNINGS CONTRIBUTION

EARNINGS MANAGEMENT

TAX LIABILITY MANAGEMENT

LIQUIDITY WAREHOUSE

STABILITY OF PRINCIPAL

STABILITY OF INCOME OVER TIME

FACILITATE CORPORATE FLEXIBILITY

CORPORATE COMPLIANCE

AURA OF BALANCE AND PRUDENCE

The purpose of the "Baseline Portfolio" is to provide a practical procedure for articulating the fund's long-term objectives in a concrete and useful fashion. The underlying idea is to take advantage of the relatively well-defined sector structure of the bond market. By selecting market sectors to match the fund's objectives and associated risk factors, one should be able to develop a portfolio structure which best suits the fund's long-term goals (Figure 3). This is called the fund's "Baseline Portfolio."

Since the Baseline Portfolio structure should be determined primarily by the long-range considerations, it should be relatively independent of the active manager's day-to-day market judgments. Thus, the Baseline Portfolio could be defined as the most balanced possible fulfillment of all of the fund's complex objectives and goals in the absence of an active market-related management activity.

Figure 3: The Theoretical Baseline Portfolio

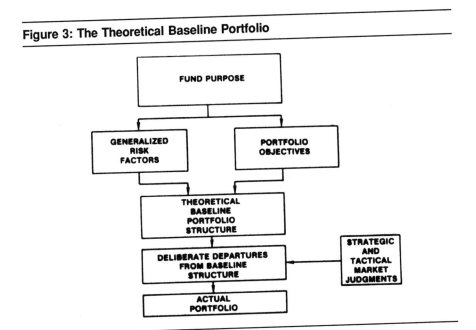

AN EXAMPLE OF A BASELINE PORTFOLIO

Development of a Baseline Portfolio for an actual fund is certainly not a simple task. However, in order to provide a concrete illustration of the baseline approach, we shall show how one might try to develop a highly simplified Baseline Portfolio for a growing pension fund.

For this example, assume that the fixed-income portion of a pension fund is intended to provide a source of long-term nominal-dollar income which can be counted upon under virtually any economic conditions. The pension fund is a growing one, and is expected to experience a positive cash flow for the next 20 years. The fixed-income portion of the fund is envisioned as a nominal-dollar "anchor to the wind"—hopefully to be relatively free from the volatility and economic risks entailed in the sizable equity portions of the fund. Because of the highly risk-averse nature of this fixed-income portion, the fund might be invested in a diversified portfolio of high-grade securities. This risk aversion would also apply to the maturity structure of the fund. However, we shall presume that the primary concern here is the risk related to maintaining a long-term income stream with some assurance, rather than the risk associated with volatility of market value. Consequently, it would seem that the Baseline Portfolio should consist primarily of long-term bonds. Moreover, the insistence upon assured long-term income flows would suggest that a high level of call protection be provided to the Baseline Portfolio. There are a number of ways to achieve this call protection. We shall assume that in this case it is to be achieved by excluding the "higher-coupon" cushion bonds. The resulting Baseline Portfolio might therefore consist largely of long-term high-grade corporate bonds, all with market prices below some modest premium above par.

As illustrated schematically in Figure 4, such a portfolio would behave very differently than a general market index, e.g., the Salomon Brothers Composite Rate-of-Return Index. This Baseline Portfolio would exhibit far more price volatility than the Index. Because of the sacrifice of the higher coupon bond component of the marketplace, it would have a lower overall yield rate. The price departure from the general market would be most evident under major moves in either direction. Under a major market deterioration, this Baseline Portfolio would fall off considerably more in market value than the general long-term market. In contrast, under a major market improvement, there would be a far greater price appreciation of the Baseline Portfolio than of the call-vulnerable general market. These performance characteristics of the Baseline Portfolio are intrinsically related to the fund's stated objectives of trying to assure long-term nominal income.

Figure 4: Return Profiles Over Short-Term Horizons

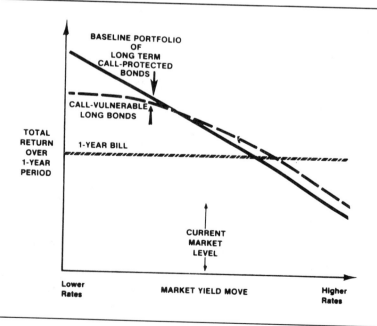

SHORT- VERSUS LONG-TERM RETURN/RISK PROFILES

Figure 5 illustrates how the return/risk profiles over a short-term period can be almost completely reversed over the long-term. Figure 5 is based upon the (admittedly artificial) assumption that the market moves to a flat yield curve at the indicated level and remains there for the next 20 years. The curves in Figure 5 then depict the resulting total return resulting over this 20-year period, incorporating the sizable effects from reinvesting coupons, maturity redemptions, and the proceeds from refunding calls. Over this 20-year period, the greatest variability in returns would be derived from a policy of rolling one-year Bills. The Baseline Portfolio of call-protected bonds would provide the greatest stability, while long-term call-vulnerable bonds would fall somewhere in between.

Figure 5 demonstrates that a higher level of volatility risk as measured by most modern analyses would actually have been necessary in order to provide the most assured approach to long-term return, free from the vagaries of intervening interest rates.

Figure 5: Return Profiles Over Long-Term Horizons

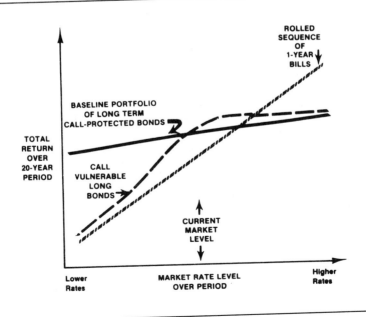

Indeed, for the stated objectives of this portfolio, investment in totally short-term cash instruments would represent the greatest level of true risk—risk here being defined in terms of threats to achieving the fund's long-term objectives.

For many long-term funds, total return analyses such as Figure 5 actually tend to *understate* the problem. By their very nature, total returns only reflect the growth of the dollar value. However, for many fund purposes, a dollar may have different *values* under different interest rate conditions. For example, the ability of a given dollar-size portfolio to provide an annuity of consumable dollars varies widely with future interest rate levels. When interest rates are low, the annuity-producing value of each future $1 is clearly lower than when rates are high. Thus, each unit of long-term return achieved under low interest rate conditions may be far less valuable than the same unit of return achieved at higher rates.[1]

MANAGEMENT ACTIVITY RELATIVE TO THE BASELINE PORTFOLIO

From the vantage point of the Baseline Portfolio, one purpose of investment management is to take advantage of market opportunities. Active management can then be viewed as a series of strategic and tactical judgments such as those shown in Figure 6. These judgments would lead to market-motivated departures from the Baseline Portfolio in an effort to achieve improved portfolio results. The resulting portfolio improvements—as well as the incremental risks incurred in achieving them—should theoretically be measured against the yardstick of the Baseline Portfolio itself.

To see how this measurement can be accomplished, suppose that the actual portfolio's market value could always be converted into immediate cash proceeds. (This concept of equating a fund's nominal market value with a literal cash opportunity value lies at the heart of the conventional rate-of-return measurement process.) Then, at any point in time, the actual portfolio could be translated into cash and these proceeds used to purchase a Baseline Portfolio. Suppose, as shown in Figure 7, that this would lead to a purchase of 100 units of the Baseline Portfolio. If this were done, the manager would have reverted to the best possible passive portfolio structure. In other words, he would have converted all his funds into the "currency" of the fund's long-term objectives, i.e., the Baseline Portfolio itself.

---

[1] For a more detailed discussion of this effect, see *The Horizon Annuity: An Investment Measure for Linking the Growth and Payout Phases of Long Term Bond Portfolios*, Martin L. Leibowitz, Salomon Brothers, 1976. (Ed. Note: This article is published in this book.)

Figure 6: Active Bond Portfolio Management

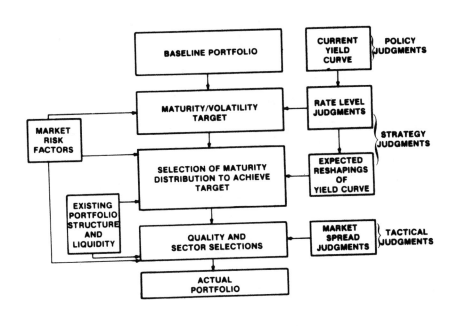

However, in general, the portfolio manager will retain some portfolio structure other than that of the Baseline. During the course of the subsequent measurement period, this actual portfolio will provide a certain total return consisting of both income and principal appreciation: perhaps with a certain amount of reinvestment return as well. This total return may look very acceptable compared to either investment in a general market index, in short-term investments, or to the relative performance of peer portfolios. However, at the end of the measurement period, the actual portfolio could again be subjected to the test of a theoretical repurchase of the Baseline Portfolio. No matter how well the actual portfolio may have done in terms of the traditional comparisons, if it converts back into fewer units of the Baseline Portfolio than before (as is the case in the example of Figure 7), then the fund has lost ground relative to its long-term objectives.

Figure 7: Relating Short-Term Performance to Long-Term Goals

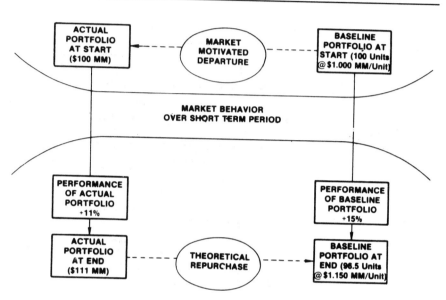

The gain or loss from this hypothetical repurchase of the Baseline is, of course, directly related to the incremental return achieved by the actual portfolio relative to the Baseline.

Figure 7 illustrates this procedure. At the outset, the fund has a market value of $100 MM. Theoretically, this could be used to purchase 100 units of the Baseline Portfolio, where the units have been (arbitrarily) scaled to have a market value of $1 MM. However, based upon various market judgments, the manager has departed from this Baseline and has structured his actual portfolio along somewhat different lines. During the course of the ensuing measurement period, the actual portfolio achieves a total return performance of +11%, resulting in the fund having a total market value of $111 MM. However, over this same period, the Baseline Portfolio has done better, turning in a return of +15%. One unit of the Baseline has thus appreciated in cost from $1.00 MM to $1.15 MM. Consequently, on a hypothetical repurchase of the Baseline, the fund's actual value of $111 MM would only allow purchase of:

$$\frac{\$111\,MM}{\$1.15\,MM/Unit} = 96.5 \text{ Baseline Units}$$

If the fund had remained invested in the Baseline, it would, of course, have maintained the original 100 units, and appreciated by +15% to $115 MM. In this case, the manager's departure from the Baseline proved to be counterproductive.

The portfolio manager, in selecting his actual portfolio, clearly took an incremental risk in departing from the Baseline Portfolio. By so doing, his intentions had to be to seek an incremental return above and beyond what could be achieved with the Baseline Portfolio. Therefore, it becomes clear that the benchmark for measuring the portfolio's return is the return that could have been achieved by simply holding the Baseline Portfolio. To the extent that the achieved return exceeded the Baseline return, to that extent did the portfolio manager add to the achievement of the portfolio results as denominated in the currency of the Baseline Portfolio itself.

The Baseline Portfolio also provides an interesting mechanism for relating short-term incremental returns to long-term measures of value. For example, an extra total return of 400 basis points realized over a one-year period might correspond to an additional 40 basis points of long-term yield over the maturity span of the Baseline Portfolio. In other words, the extra market value achieved over the year could buy an incremental cash flow equivalent to putting the funds to work at a long-term yield 40 basis points higher than the actual market yield. (The appropriate factor here is the Horizon Volatility of the Baseline Portfolio. For most long-term bond portfolios, this factor will generally lie between 9 and 12.)

EVALUATING PROPOSED DEPARTURES FROM THE BASELINE

The Baseline Portfolio can serve both prospective and retrospective functions. After a given investment period has been completed, the Baseline can help the manager to evaluate, retrospectively, the return achieved in terms of his contribution to the fund's long-term goals. However, at the beginning of each investment period, the Baseline can help the portfolio manager to gauge—in a quantitative, objective fashion—the incremental risk incurred *relative to these same goals*. This prospective application of the Baseline Portfolio may be the most important one of all.

Figure 8 illustrates a manager's *prospective* evaluation of the tradeoff between expected return (over a short-term horizon) and some measure of "interest rate risk." For example, if the manager was neutral on the market so that the expected case could be represented as "no change in the yield curve," then the expected return would be the Rolling Yield.[2] On the other hand, if the man-

---

[2] See *The Rolling Yield: A New Approach to Yield Curve Analysis*, Martin L. Leibowitz, Salomon Brothers, April 21, 1977. (Ed. Note: This article is published in this book.)

Figure 8: Market-Motivated Departures from the Baseline Portfolio

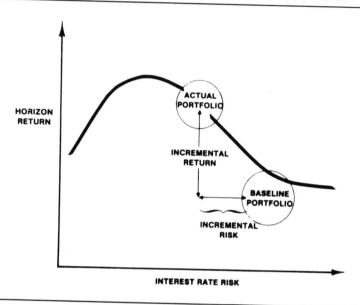

ager's interest rate projections were more optimistic or pessimistic than the neutral case, then these judgments would be reflected in projected returns such as those plotted in Figure 8.

The horizontal axis in Figure 8 represents some measure of "interest rate risk" over the short-term investment period.

As noted earlier, the maturity structure is the most important decision made by an active portfolio manager. By varying the maturity structure, he can control the amount of "interest rate risk" contained in his portfolio. Various proxies for the "interest rate risk" of a portfolio have been proposed—average maturity, historical variability, percentage price volatility, Macaulay's duration, Horizon Volatility, Proportional Volatility.[3] However, for any of these measures, the Baseline can be viewed as the reference point. To the extent that the active manager departs from this Baseline level of interest rate risk, to that extent, he risks falling below the Baseline's performance.

---

[3] For a more complete discussion, see *The Risk Dimension: A New Approach to Yield Curve Analysis*, Martin L. Leibowitz, Salomon Brothers, October 5, 1977. (Ed. Note: This article is published in this book.)

This holds true for departures in *both directions*. As noted earlier, a defensive departure, while risk-reducing in terms of short-term volatility, runs the risk of an insufficient price appreciation to compensate for the lower income-productivity per dollar of market value under a move to lower yield levels.

Figure 8 illustrates the case of a manager undertaking just such a "defensive departure" from the Baseline's risk level. His motivation is clearly to obtain a sizable improvement in incremental returns. However, he is exposing his portfolio to a considerable shortfall in return relative to the Baseline in the event that interest rates move further downward than the level embedded in his projected return curve.

One should take note of the apparent paradox in the situation portrayed in Figure 8. The greatest risk here is the prospect of a stronger-than-expected *downward* move in interest rates. This action would normally be viewed as "improving market." However, in this case, such a "market improvement" would lead to under-performance relative to the Baseline Portfolio, and hence would constitute the gravest threat to the fund's progress towards its long-term goals.

Figure 8 thus shows how a manager can gauge his incremental interest rate risk relative to the Baseline and, by implication, measure his more generalized risk relative to long-term goals. There may be some controversy regarding what constitutes a satisfactory measure of interest rate risk. However, there is no disagreement that a greater level of risk consciousness needs to be introduced into the management process. Once any such volatility measure has been selected, the procedure implied in Figure 8 can be quantified, thereby providing the manager (and the sponsor) with a concrete, numerical indication of the incremental risk associated with a prospective portfolio strategy.

CUSTOMIZED RETURN INDICES

The prospective use of the Baseline requires a manager to periodically specify a range of market expectations sufficiently encompassing to determine expected returns for the Baseline Portfolio as well as for his actual portfolio. In addition, he must determine the corresponding interest rate risks associated with both portfolios. For some managers, these estimations would be natural by-products of their existing market analyses. For others, these estimations would entail considerable special effort and inconvenience.

The retrospective analysis is much simpler to carry out in practice. As indicated in the discussion relating to Figure 7, the primary ingredient is a sufficiently well-defined Baseline Portfolio that can itself be subject to total return performance measurement. The Baseline's period-by-period return then becomes the natural "bogey" for the actual portfolio returns.

In practice, construction of this rate-of-return Baseline can be facilitated through use of a customized total return index. This index could theoretically be comprised of all issues that might actually form the Baseline Portfolio. A far more convenient approach is to utilize the appropriate sector components of existing total return indices. For example, the Salomon Brothers Composite Rate-of-Return Index consists of 88 sectors spanning long-term corporates with ratings from A to AAA. The returns for these 88 sectors are computed on a monthly basis. A satisfactory representation of a fund's Baseline can usually be constructed out of these 88 sectors, together with selected market sectors covering intermediate and shorter maturities as well as the Government/Agency areas. Blending the returns from these sectors in accordance with their assigned weight in the Baseline Portfolio could provide a customized total return index for virtually any fund.

Retrospective analyses of a manager's returns can then be compared against this customized return index, in order to determine both the consistency of incremental returns as well as the variability risk undertaken in the process. More detailed studies could be directed towards identifying the sources of incremental returns beyond the "Baseline Index."

COMMUNICATION BETWEEN SPONSOR AND MANAGER

The Baseline Portfolio approach can facilitate the communication process between sponsor and manager.

At the outset, the Baseline Portfolio should itself be the result of discussions between the fund's sponsor and the manager. In these initial discussions, the sponsor must try to convey his sense of the fund's purpose, to define his overall objectives and their relative priorities, and to identify and delimit the risk factors that concern him. On the other hand, the manager contributes his knowledge of the behavioral characteristics of the various asset classes, along with his belief as to how they will function in the context of different portfolio structures. (At this point, the manager should try to put aside his perceptions of immediate market value, and concentrate on the general long-term characteristics of the various market sectors.)

In all too many instances, this interchange tends to remain at a rather fuzzy level of generality, with both parties espousing the obviously desirable "Nirvana points," e.g., maximum return with minimum risk, highest yield without sacrifice of quality, minimum volatility with greatest stability of income, etc. If the discussion of goals ends at this point, then neither party has communicated his sense of the appropriate tradeoffs. In a rather fundamental sense, no real understanding has been achieved.

However, a joint determination to specify a Baseline Portfolio can drive these discussions down to the concrete level. It will force the difficult choices to be made—and made *jointly* by both sponsor and manager. The sponsor must articulate the subtle priorities that can organize his many objectives, and he must develop a clear-cut structure by relating these priorities—with the manager's help—to choices between specific market sectors. The manager must rise above his active orientation to define the most balanced, passive portfolio structure matching his client needs. In this fashion, both parties are able to merge and consolidate their different points of view. In essence, by specifying a Baseline Portfolio, they have come to agree on a practical, passive alternative to active management.

As with any real process of communication, these interactions may prove painful and arduous at the outset. However, once defined, the Baseline can prove a mutual vantage point for interpreting the actual returns achieved over time. The all-too-common ongoing confusion between conflicting short-term results and long-term goals will be reduced. Because of the sponsor's role in defining the Baseline, the manager will no longer find himself quite so vulnerable to criticism for the many portfolio effects that are (in reality) mandated by the nature of the fund. In particular, having the Baseline as a "baseline" may considerably reduce artificial pressures on a manager with regard to high volatility, yield give-ups, particularly high- or low-quality postures, having the portfolio balanced away from the general market structure, or for deviations from the performance returns achieved by general market indices or theoretical peer groups.

Moreover, by concentrating the objective-setting in an initial phase shared with the sponsor, the Baseline approach should allow the investment manager to focus more clearly on his day-by-day market activities in the fund's behalf.

Chapter III C-2

The Rolling Yield

THE YIELD CURVE

The traditional "yield curve" plots the yields of fixed-income securities against their respective maturities. When the securities plotted are comparable in quality and structure, then the resulting yield curve depicts the available tradeoff between yield and maturity. Figure 1 illustrates the yield curve for Treasury securities as of March 29, 1977.

The yield curve has many different applications as an investment tool. Some market participants study the yield curve for clues to the market forces acting in the different maturity arenas. Some search for historical analogues by comparing the curve's current shape with similar patterns obtained in the past. Some view the yield curve as reflecting the consensus expectations of the marketplace, and they use mathematical techniques to extract these implicit forecasts. Some gauge the relative value of individual securities by comparing their yield/maturity position relative to current and past yield curves. Many investment managers try to forecast the changing shape of the yield curve so that they can then position their portfolio for maximum performance. Other participants try to find "elbows" in the yield curve, i.e., maturity areas which they consider to represent the most attractive short term investment.

Martin L. Leibowitz, "The Rolling Yield," Salomon Brothers Inc, April 1977. This paper was subsequently included in *Total Return Management*, Salomon Brothers Inc, 1979.

Figure 1: The U.S. Treasury Yield Curve

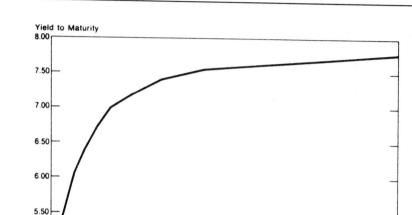

THE YIELD CURVE AS A RETURN/RISK TRADEOFF

The most widespread use of the yield curve is probably the one mentioned at the outset—a portrayal of the available tradeoff between yield and maturity. In other words, the yield curve indicates how much additional yield can be obtained in exchange for each extension in maturity.

The basic investment problem in any market always comes down to an evaluation of the tradeoff between return and risk. Since yield is a measure of total return, and since maturity is closely associated with price volatility, there is a natural temptation to accept the yield curve as depicting this return/risk tradeoff. Unfortunately, this interpretation is seriously faulty on several counts.

First of all, there are a number of problems in equating maturity with risk. Maturity is not the only variable determining mathematical price volatility. Price volatility is not the sole determinant of the volatility of return. And volatility of return over short term periods is not the only (or perhaps even the primary) risk element for many bond portfolios.

With regard to equating yield with return, there is an even more fundamental problem. The concept of total return must refer to a specific investment horizon. Apart from the questions regarding coupon reinvestment, a bond's conventional yield-to-maturity can be used to represent its total return—but only over an investment period coincident with the bond's remaining life. The yield curve, by its very nature, consists of yields over different maturities. Since they do not refer to a common investment horizon, these yield values are not directly comparable as total returns.

As an example, consider a 1-year note with a yield of 6% and a 2-year note with a yield of 7%. Over a 1-year investment horizon, the 1-year 6% note will indeed provide a total return of approximately 6%. However, over this same 1-year period, the total return provided by the 2-year note will depend greatly on its price at year's end. At that point, it will be a 1-year security and its price will then be set by the level of 1-year yields. As these yields range from 5% to 10%, the note's total return will range anywhere from 4.29% to 8.85%. One can see that these total return values can depart widely from the original 7% yield level. In fact, the 2-year note will provide a 7% total return over a 1-year period only if 1-year rates are 7% one year hence. In turn, this would require 1-year rates to rise by 100 basis points over the course of the year.

Extrapolating from this example, the total return provided by any security on the yield curve can thus be seen to depend on the yield curve that will prevail at the end of the investment horizon.

HORIZON ANALYSIS APPLIED TO THE YIELD CURVE

Since no one can predict future yield curves with certainty, there is a corresponding uncertainty in the total returns from any security on the yield curve. However, portfolio managers must come to grips with this uncertainty in one way or another. At the very least, they must be able to translate their market judgment(s) into the corresponding total return implications for the various maturity sectors along the yield curve. The technique of "Horizon Analysis" can prove helpful in this translation process.

Essentially, Horizon Analysis distinguishes the return achieved under "nominal market conditions" from the return achieved by departures from these nominal conditions. In earlier articles,[1] the nominal condition was defined to be that of "constant-yield over time." Recalling the example of a 2-year note with a yield of 7%, this "constant-yield" condition would imply a total return of 7% over a 1-year horizon. If 1-year rates actually fell to 6%, i.e., 1% below the nominal 7% level, then the total return would become 7.92%. In fact, for every basis point that 1-year rates at the horizon fell below the nominal 7% level, the total return will be boosted by approximately .92 basis points. This volatility factor of .92 is called the "Horizon Volatility."

---

[1] See *Horizon Analysis: A New Analytic Framework for Managed Bond Portfolios.* (Ed. Note: This article appears in this book.)

There are several advantages in being able to break down prospective return into a "nominal-condition" return plus a return component derived through a "departure-from-the-nominal-condition." First of all, one can distinguish the returns derived through the passage of time from the return achieved through market movements. In fact, by using the Horizon Volatility factor, changes in market yields can be immediately translated into changes in total return. In the context of a bond or sector swap, Horizon Analysis allows the swap's incremental return to be decomposed into three basic components:

1) A Pure Yield Pick-Up component, resulting from the accumulation of the original yields over time, independent of any market changes.

2) A Rate Anticipation component dependent on the change in overall market levels as magnified by an increase in the Horizon Volatilities of the two bonds (or sectors).

3) A Spread component, determined solely by the changing yield spread relationships between the two bonds or sectors.

In other words, Horizon Analysis facilitates the manager's ability to relate his judgment regarding conventional market variables—yields, yield spreads, and the changes in yields and yield spreads over time—to total return performance. This structuring also enables the manager to clearly see the effect of departures from his primary expectations, and this can assist in evaluating the nature and magnitude of the risks associated with a contemplated course of action.

It would be most helpful if a simple structuring, along the lines of Horizon Analysis, could be made applicable to the yield curve.

However, at the outset, the preceding method runs into a problem with its use of the "constant-yield" as a nominal market condition. The very nature of yield curve implies some change in a bond's yield with the passage of time. Consequently, the "constant-yield" approach must be revised before Horizon Analysis can even begin to be usefully applied to the yield curve.

The problem is to find a reasonable, convenient, and well-defined yield structure that can serve as a benchmark for nominal market conditions at the end of the investment horizon. There are a number of candidates for this nominal yield structure—the existing yield curve, the implied "forward" yield curve, the individual manager's expected yield curve, etc. However, the simplest approach is to work with the existing yield curve itself.

When the *existing* yield curve is used to define the nominal market conditions at *future* horizons, then each bond's nominal future yield is simply determined by the passage of time along the yield curve. This process is often described as "rolling down the yield curve." For that reason, we refer to this nominal total return as the bond's "Rolling Yield."

THE ROLLING YIELD

A security's Rolling Yield can be determined by a relatively simple calculation, at least in theory. Figure 2 provides an illustration.

Suppose the prevailing yield curve has yield levels of 6.50% for 3-year maturities and 6.30% for 2.50-year maturities. A 3-year 6.50% bond lying on the yield curve would then be priced at par to yield 6.50%. We wish to compute this bond's Rolling Yield over a 6-month investment horizon.

The total return consists of three components—market appreciation, coupon income, and reinvestment income (or more generally, the time value of coupon payments). In this particular example, reinvestment income—usually only a negligible factor over short term horizons—is completely eliminated.

Coupon income consists of one semiannual coupon payment of 3.25%.

The market appreciation is derived from the yield changes associated with rolling down the yield curve for the 6-month period. At the end of this period, under the assumed nominal condition of a "constant yield curve," the bond will be priced at the curve's 2.50-year value, i.e., at 6.30%. At this yield, the original par bond will be priced at 100.456. (To maintain the simplicity of this example, we have purposely neglected a number of practically important problems: determining the exact shape of the yield curve, finding the location over time of individual securities relative to the curve itself, the whole question of transaction costs, etc.)

Figure 2: Calculation of a Rolling Yield

A 3-Year 6.50% Par Bond
Rolling Down to a 2.50-Year Yield Curve Value of 6.30%
Over a Six-Month Horizon

Coupon Income (As % of Par)		3.25%
Reinvestment Income (As % of Par)		0
Market Appreciation		
Nominal Price 6 Months Hence Based on Yield Curve Value of 6.30%	100.456	
Price Today	(100.000)	
Price Appreciation	.456	.456
Total Return As % Par		3.706%
Total Return As % Initial Market Value		3.706%
Annualized Total Return (Rolling Yield)		7.41%

The total points of return (as a percentage of par) thus sum up to 3.706%. Since we are dealing with a bond originally priced at par, this 3.706% figure also represents the total return as a percentage of initial market value.

Finally, by annualizing this return figure, we obtain the bond's Rolling Yield of 7.41%.

It is interesting to note that this Rolling Yield of 7.41% exceeds the original 6.50% conventional yield-to-maturity by 91 basis points!

THE ROLLING YIELD CURVE

The basic yield curve consists of a plot of conventional yield against maturity for a set of comparable securities (e.g., the U.S. Treasury market). When the conventional yield for each security is replaced by the corresponding Rolling Yield, the resulting plot may be called a "Rolling Yield curve."

Figure 3 shows the Rolling Yield curve, based on a 6-month investment horizon, corresponding to the basic yield curve depicted in Figure 1.

It is instructive to compare Figures 1 and 3.

The most striking characteristic of the Rolling Yield curve is that essentially all the Rolling Yield values exceed the basic yield curve values for the same

Figure 3: The Rolling Yield Curve

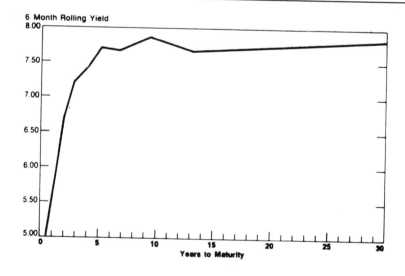

maturity. This "boost" in the Rolling Yield is derived from the process of rolling down to lower yield values over time (see Figure 2). This effect will always be seen with positively sloped—i.e., ascending—yield curves. (An opposite effect will occur in the case of inverted—i.e., descending—yield curves.)

The magnitude of this "boost" of the Rolling Yield above the basic yield varies widely across the maturity scale. The basic yield curve of Figure 1 has the property that the slope is greatest for the shorter maturities. For such yield curves, the roll-down in yield—when measured in basis points—will naturally also be greatest at the shorter maturities. However, the boost in return depends on price volatility as well as the basis point size of the roll-down. As maturity shortens, the roll-down in basis points may increase, but its effect on return will be partially offset by the decline in price volatility. For example, with a 6-month security, there will be no price volatility at all at the 6-month horizon. Consequently, there will of course be no boost in return regardless of the steepness of the underlying yield curve at that point.

This conflict between increasing roll-down and decreasing price volatility will often lead to the boost in return reaching its maximum value at some point among the intermediate maturities. Moreover, when this boost effect is overlaid on a typical positively sloped yield curve, one will often see a peak in the Rolling Yield curve itself. In Figure 3, we see that this peak is reached at the ninth year.

INTERPRETING ROLLING YIELD CURVES

By definition, the Rolling Yield curve shows the total return that will be realized by each security on the yield curve provided that the yield curve remains exactly constant over the investment horizon.

In contrast to the conventional yields, Rolling Yields represent total returns over a common investment horizon. Consequently, Rolling Yields are directly comparable with one another. This comparability of individual Rolling Yields makes it possible to interpret the Rolling Yield curve in a number of interesting ways.

The Rolling Yield curve can be viewed as a plot of nominal returns against maturity. For example, consider the Rolling Yield curve shown in Figure 3. Apart from any changes in the underlying yield curve, Figure 3 tells us that an investment in a 1-year security will provide a total return of 5.62%, a 2-year security will provide a return of 6.70%, etc. Thus, the Rolling Yield curve depicts the tradeoff between comparable *nominal* returns and maturity.

Pursuing this tack one step further, the Rolling Yield curve also shows the compensation in (nominal) return for a given extension in maturity. Thus, Figure 3 shows that a 1-year extension from 1 year to 2 years increases the Rolling Yield from 5.62% to 6.70%, a jump of 108 basis points. However, a 1-year extension from 4 years to 5 years achieves an improvement in Rolling Yield from 7.42% to 7.71%, or 29 basis points.

Similarly, the slope of the Rolling Yield curve indicates the rate of nominal compensation for every month of extension. (However, as noted earlier, each month of maturity extension incurs different degrees of maturity risk.)

If the Rolling Yield curve reaches a maximum, then there is no compensation in *nominal* return for further extension of maturity. Any manager extending his maturity beyond this point would presumably have expectations of favorable changes in the yield curve, i.e., lower overall rates and/or a flattening of the curve in the longer maturities.

Peaks in the Rolling Yield curve are often associated with the so-called "elbow points" in the underlying yield curve. In fact, one could argue that the common market practice of searching for elbows has value precisely because of this association with maximum or near-maximum Rolling Yields. By making these relationships explicit, the Rolling Yield curve can assist in determining the relative risks and rewards of moderate departures from a given elbow point.

The Rolling Yield curve can also be interpreted as the sequence of short term returns provided by a security at various points in its life. For example, the 13-year value of 7.67% in Figure 3 says that a 13-year bond would provide a return of 7.67% over the first 6-month period—as long as the yield curve remains unchanged. Over the next 6 months, this same security will generate—again assuming an unchanged yield curve—a return of 7.70%, i.e., the Rolling Yield curve value associated with the 12.50-year maturity, and so on for each succeeding 6-month period. This leads to the observation that the security will produce its greatest return over the 6-month period that begins when its remaining life has declined to 9 years. After this point, the return falls period by period until it reaches the minimum return of 5.00% in the last 6-month period. Of course, all of this transpires only under the rather strong assumption that the yield curve remains unchanged over the entire 13 years.

Nevertheless, this interpretation is rather intriguing because it quantifies the concept that there is an optimal time to sell every bond as it rolls down the yield curve.

The Rolling Yield curve can also be useful in constructing "bridge swaps." By combining two bonds with different maturities, one can create a "bond package" having an average maturity somewhere between the two original bonds. Similarly, this "bond package" will have an average Rolling Yield lying somewhere between the Rolling Yields of the two bonds. In fact, by adjusting the mixture ratio, one can obtain a bond package falling anywhere on a straight line drawn between the Rolling Yield curve plots of the original two bonds. Suppose this straight line (i.e., the "bridge" across two maturity points) passes significantly below the plot of a third bond on the Rolling Yield curve. Then, as illustrated in Figure 4, a swap out of the appropriately mixed bond package into this

Figure 4: A Bridge Swap

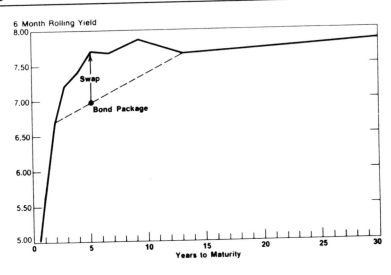

third bond can result in an increase in Rolling Yield while maintaining the same average maturity.

Once again, we must caution that such a swap—like the Rolling Yield itself—depends upon a constant yield curve. In addition, bond packages with the same average maturity can differ widely in their volatility characteristics. (This fundamental problem can be partially overcome by substituting Horizon Volatility for maturity as a measure of price volatility.)

ROLLING YIELDS AND CHANGING YIELD CURVES

Of course, yield curves do change—and sometimes change rather violently. Any comprehensive approach to yield curve analysis must deal with the prospect of both expected and unexpected changes in the yield curve.

Any such change will produce realized returns for a given bond that will be higher or lower than its Rolling Yield. The more adverse the change in the yield curve, the more the realized return will drop below its Rolling Yield. The more favorable the change in the yield curve, the greater the extent by which the realized return will exceed the Rolling Yield.

The Rolling Yield thus serves as benchmark, fully capturing the total return implications of the existing yield curve. One can then focus on potential changes from the existing curve—shifts in overall level as well as sharpenings and/or flattenings at various maturity points. For each maturity, the sum of these changes will result in a given yield move away from the existing curve. Such changes in yield can readily be translated into their approximate value as increments (or decrements) of total return. (The Horizon Volatility for each maturity point provides a handy scaling factor for this translation.) But the point is that each of these increments (or decrements) of total return must be added to (or subtracted from) the Rolling Yield.

By serving this role as a total return benchmark for the existing yield curve, Rolling Yields can help clarify the impact of prospective market changes that may move the yield curve away from its present level and shape.

Chapter III C-3

The Rolling Yield and Changing Markets

For investors concerned with total returns over relatively short horizons, the traditional yield curve can prove deceptive on several counts. As pointed out in the preceding study, *The Rolling Yield*, the yield curve does not represent returns over common horizon periods. In order to estimate such returns, judgments must be made regarding the nature of the yield curve that will prevail at the horizon. If the yield curve is assumed to remain unchanged, each security will "roll down" the curve with the passage of time. This roll-down in yield will generate a certain price appreciation. This appreciation, together with the basic accumulation of yield over time, constitutes the bond's total return over the horizon period. After annualization, the resulting total return figure is called the "Rolling Yield."

When Rolling Yields are plotted against maturity, the resulting "Rolling Yield curve" can be viewed as a transformation of the traditional yield curve into a rate-of-return framework. The Rolling Yield curve has a number of interpretations:

- a plot of the tradeoff between total return and maturity

- the incentive for incremental extensions of maturity

Martin L. Leibowitz, "The Rolling Yield and Changing Markets," Salomon Brothers Inc, June 1977. This paper was subsequently included in *Total Return Management*, Salomon Brothers Inc, 1979.

Figure 1: Yield Curves Under a Parallel Shift of +50 Basis Points

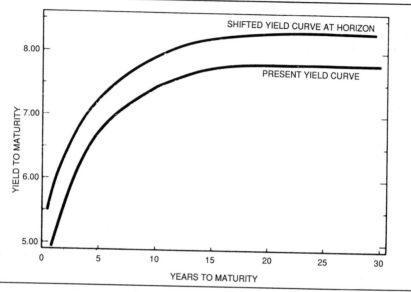

- the return available from repeated "riding the yield curve" starting at a given maturity point

- the lifetime series of horizon returns available as a security "ages."[1]

These interpretations are all based upon the assumption of a constant yield curve. However, in practice, change is at the very heart of all markets. Even in the special case where constant conditions are expected, one must consider the risk of unexpected changes. Any comprehensive analysis must consider how changes in the underlying yield curve will affect the pattern of horizon returns.

PARALLEL SHIFTS

The simplest form of yield curve change is the "parallel shift," where all yields undergo exactly the same basis point move. Figure 1 illustrates a parallel shift of

---

[1] A quite different interpretation of the Rolling Yield relates to the "forward rate" concept used in the expectations theory of interest rates. However, a discussion of this intriguing mathematical equivalence would lead away from the main focus of the present study.

+50 basis points in the U.S. Treasury yield curve of March 29, 1977. (It is interesting to note that parallel shifts almost never really look "parallel" to the eye.)

For any given security, a yield move leads to a corresponding change in price. In turn, this will affect the security's total return over the investment horizon. For the Rolling Yield, this change is based upon a roll-down of the *existing* yield curve. When the yield curve itself changes, then the additional yield and price move must be incorporated into the total return calculation. This computational process is illustrated in Figure 2.

The horizon returns for all securities along the yield curve can be computed in a similar fashion. When these returns are plotted against the original maturity of each security, one obtains a graphic illustration of the effect of changing yield curves.

Figure 3 shows the horizon returns for the +50 basis point parallel shift applied to the yield curve shown in Figure 1. Figure 3 also shows the Rolling Yield

---

Figure 2: Calculation of Horizon Return

A 3-Year 6.50% Par Bond
Rolling Down to a 2.50-Year Yield Curve Value of 6.30%
Over a Six-Month Horizon
Followed by a +50 Basis Point Parallel Shift

Coupon Income (As % of Par)			3.25%
Reinvestment Income (As % of Par)			0
Market Appreciation			
Present Yield Curve Value at 2.50 Years	6.30%		
Magnitude of Parallel Shift	+.50		
Yield Curve Value 6 Months Hence at 2.50 Years	6.80%		
Price 6 Months Hence Based on Yield Curve Value of 6.80%	99.32	99.32	
Price Today @ 6.50%		(100.00)	
Price Appreciation		-.68	-.68%
Total Return As % Par			2.57%
Total Return As % Initial Market Value			2.57%
Annualized Total Return (Rolling Yield)			5.14%

NOTE: For simplicity, this example is based on rounded values and hence does not exactly correspond to Figure 1.

Figure 3: Horizon Returns from Parallel Shift

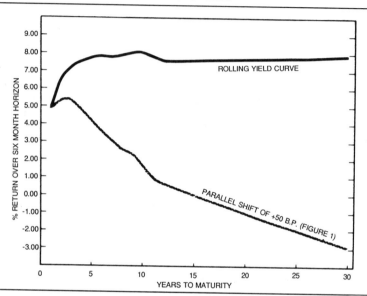

curve as a benchmark for what the horizon returns would have been without any market changes.

The pattern exhibited in Figure 3 can be readily explained in terms of price volatilities. The price impact of a given yield move is determined by the bond's maturity, coupon rate, and its starting yield level. Among these factors, the bond's maturity usually dominates. In particular, for the "current coupon" bonds that comprise the Treasury yield curve, increasing maturity leads to increasing price volatility. In turn, this means that the parallel shift in the yield curve will have increasing price impact at the longer maturities. Consequently, the effect of any parallel shift on returns will always be greatest at the longer end of the curve.

By the same token, at the short end of the yield curve, the effect of a parallel shift will become smaller with decreasing maturity. In fact, for the security whose maturity coincides with the investment horizon, there will be no change whatsoever. In this study, a 6-month horizon is used for all examples. The security at this point on the yield curve is the 6-month Treasury Bill. The Rolling Yield of the 6-month Bill over a 6-month horizon is just its original yield (on a Bond Equivalent basis). Moreover, the 6-month Bill will obviously provide this same return over a 6-month horizon no matter what changes take place in the yield curve. Consequently, this 6-month maturity acts like a fixed point under all yield curve changes.

These volatility responses are clearly evident in Figure 3. One has the fixed point at the 6-month maturity, where the Rolling Yield curve and the horizon return curve meet. As the maturity increases, the horizon returns depart further and further from the Rolling Yield, reflecting the increasing volatility of longer bonds. In fact, the *upward* parallel shift in the yield curve has the overall effect of a *downward* angular rotation of the Rolling Yield curve around the fixed point at the 6-month maturity.

For an investor anticipating the parallel shifts shown in Figure 3, it is immediately evident that the longer maturities are to be avoided. In general, because of its simple response pattern, the investment implications of any parallel shift are usually quite obvious. There is only one problem. Actual changes in the yield curve rarely take the form of a simple parallel shift across all maturities. When the market moves, the yield curve almost always undergoes some change in shape as well as a shift in level.

CHANGING SHAPES

The reshaping that accompanies a shift movement can often have a surprisingly strong impact on the horizon returns. This is illustrated in Figures 4 and 5. Figure 4 depicts a market move where the yields in the shorter and intermediate

Figure 4: Yield Curves Under a Change in Both Shape and Level

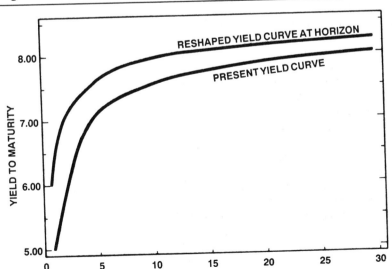

Figure 5: Horizon Returns from Changing Shape and Level

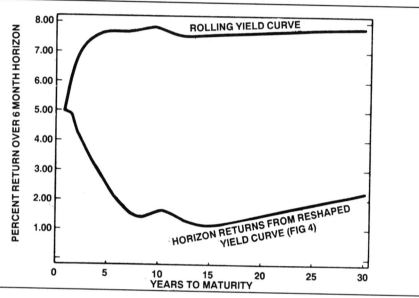

maturities undergo a greater deterioration than yields in the longer maturities. As many investors have learned to their sorrow, such market movements are not uncommon.

Figure 5 shows the horizon returns resulting from this reshaping of the yield curve. One can see that in this case, the simple maxim to avoid long maturities could have led the investor astray. In Figure 5, the intermediate maturities are hit the hardest in terms of total return. In fact, under this market move, the very worst return is recorded at the thirteenth year, where a relatively high Rolling Yield value would have been obtained (i.e., if the yield curve had remained unchanged).

It is useful to contrast the effects of the shape changes shown in Figure 4 with the earlier examples of parallel shift. This comparison is facilitated by Figure 6, which depicts the respective changes in yields at each maturity. For the parallel shift, the yield change is by definition constant at +50 basis points across all maturities. On the other hand, the shape changes of Figure 4 result from a strong yield move of +100 basis points at the short end of the curve, with a pattern of decreasing yield changes as maturity increases. By the ninth year, this yield change declines to +50 basis points, and then decreases thereafter at a somewhat slower pace.

Figure 7 compares the corresponding horizon returns. One can see that there are two points of coincidence. The first of these is the 6-month "fixed

Figure 6: Yield Changes Across Maturity

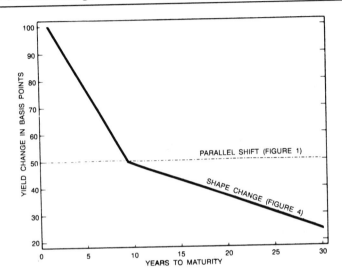

Figure 7: Comparison of Horizon Returns

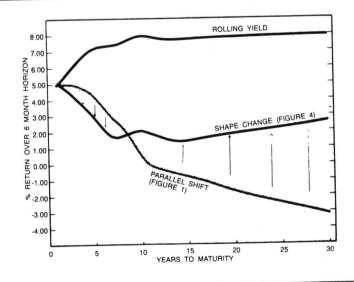

point," where the 6-month horizon return is unaffected by any change in yields. The second point of coincidence is at the ninth year, where the +50 basis point yield change occurs in both cases, and naturally results in the same horizon return of +1.70%.

Between these two intersection points, the flattening shape change provides a significantly worse horizon return than the parallel shift. This is exactly what we would expect given the respective pattern of yield changes shown in Figure 6. At the 1-year maturity, the shape change results in a +97 basis point yield move, over 48 basis points more than the parallel shift. However, because of the limited horizon volatility of the 1-year maturity, this leads only to a small difference in horizon returns. On the other hand, at the 2-year maturity, the horizon volatility is sufficient to generate a −110 basis point difference in return for the +40 basis point difference in the yield changes. The horizon return difference grows to about 150 basis points at the third year. It remains roughly stable around this level until the seventh year. This stability is derived from the compensating effects of increasing volatility against the decreasing difference in the yield change.

At the ninth year, the horizon return curves intersect. After the ninth year, the two factors of less adverse yield changes and increasing horizon volatility work in concert. As a result, the shape change produces an increasingly better return than the parallel shift. By the 30th year, the improvement in horizon return has grown by over 5.00%, from -3.00% for the parallel shift to +2.40% for the shape change.

Thus, it is clear that changing yield curve shapes can have a powerful impact on horizon returns. Consequently, there is a need for techniques to help the portfolio manager in evaluating the effect of potential shape changes. However, in trying to develop such techniques, one immediately encounters a problem in the bewildering profusion of yield curve shapes that can and do arise in the marketplace. One way to come to grips with this problem is to find a simple way for classifying yield curve movements. The first step in this direction is to break down yield curve changes into a parallel shift followed by a series of sharpenings and flattenings.

CLASSIFICATION OF YIELD CURVE CHANGES

In Figure 4, the intermediate 9-year maturity undergoes a +50 basis point change. Suppose this 9-year point is selected as a "benchmark maturity" to define the parallel shift component. Then this parallel shift of +50 basis points can be viewed as the first component in the yield curve's total process of change. The remaining changes will then consist of relative "twists" that act to sharpen or flatten the slopes along the curve.

To help visualize this process as it applies to the shape change in Figure 4, consider the yield changes plotted in Figure 6. In this particular situation, we clearly have the parallel shift of +50 basis points at the ninth year, plus two flattening twists. From the 6-month point to the ninth-year benchmark, the yield change declines from +100 basis points to +50 basis points. At the 6-month point, this represents a "short-end up-twist" of 50 basis points above and beyond the parallel shift of +50 basis points. Similarly, from the ninth year to the 30th year, the changes decline from +50 basis points to +25 basis points. This 25 basis point flattening could be viewed as the result of a uniform "long-end down-twist" having a magnitude of 25 basis points when measured in the 30th year.

As Figure 6 illustrates, this combination of a parallel shift plus the two twists completely describes the yield curve change. This rather pat fit is, of course, a result of the particular situation chosen for Figure 4.

Whenever the yield curve change can be defined in this simple form, the resulting horizon return curve can be visualized as developing from a parallel shift followed by up-twists or down-twists on either side of the benchmark maturity. The parallel shift first leads to a horizon return curve that approximates the angular rotation of the Rolling Yield. If the shape change consists of a short-end up-twist affecting the maturities preceding the benchmark, then the horizon returns will be depressed below the return levels of parallel shift. The difference in the returns, relative to the parallel shift, will start at zero at the 6-month maturity, plummet to some trough value, and then rise to zero again at the benchmark maturity. If a long-end down-twist occurs beyond the benchmark maturity, then the horizon returns will be boosted above the level of the rotated Rolling Yield Curve. The magnitude of this boost will grow with increasing maturity.

On a relative basis, we would see these same effects from up-twists and down-twists regardless of whether the parallel shift was in a positive or negative direction. This has a number of important practical implications. For example, the return from a "bridge swap" tends to be relatively independent from the effects of parallel shifts in either direction. However, up-twists and down-twists can have a severe impact on the profitability of such swaps. Thus, in a short-end up-twist, in the maturities preceding the benchmark, the shorter securities in the bridge will undergo a greater relative upward yield move. In such situations, the horizon return from a bond package can differ significantly from the return provided by the corresponding maturity point on the yield curve.

In the many instances where yield curve changes can be approximated in terms of up-twists or down-twists on either side of an appropriately chosen benchmark security, the horizon returns can be visualized as consisting of three components:

1) The Rolling Yield curve

2) An angular rotation of the Rolling Yield curve to match the shift at the benchmark maturity

3) The different relative return effects of up-twists or down-twists in the maturities preceding and following the benchmark. These effects can be summarized as follows:

   a) *Short-end up-twist* (i.e., increased rates in maturities preceding the benchmark). This will create a "bulge" depression in relative return, growing in magnitude to a maximum trough level at some maturity between the relative fixed points at 6 months and the benchmark maturity.

   b) *Short-end down-twist* (i.e., lower relative rates in maturities preceding the benchmark). This will create an upward bulge in relative return, peaking at some interim point between 6 months and the benchmark.

   c) *Long-end down-twist* (i.e., decreased relative rates in longer maturities beyond the benchmark). The relative return becomes increasingly favorable with the longer maturities.

   d) *Long-end up-twist* (i.e., increased relative rates in the longer maturities beyond the benchmark). The relative return becomes increasingly negative with the longer maturities.

As illustrated in Figure 7, these relative return effects from up-twists and/or down-twists can override the shift changes in the overall level of rates. With this classification system for yield curve changes, we can quickly isolate the key components of return that would affect any contemplated portfolio action.

There are certain patterns of change that cannot be adequately described by a parallel shift followed by only two simple segment twist effects such as in Figure 6. However, even complex patterns of change can be approximated (as closely as desired) by a series of up-twists and down-twists over a sufficient number of consecutive maturity segments.

PROPORTIONAL CHANGES IN YIELDS

Up to this point, a yield curve change has been treated as a movement from the present curve to a single well-defined future curve. In practice, there will always be a certain range of uncertainty surrounding any anticipated future yield curve. It is usually wise to consider how this range of uncertainty can affect the pattern of horizon returns. Once again, this effort can quickly become bogged down in the bewildering range of possible shapes and patterns of change that the market might thrust upon us. However, there is a way to extend the preceding classification system so that it can easily depict the evolution of a wide range of possible future yield curves.

The key assumption is that of "proportional changes" across maturities for each basis point of parallel shift in the benchmark maturity. As an example, consider the pattern of change illustrated in Figure 6. When the benchmark 9-year maturity shifts by +50 basis points, the 6-month maturity undergoes a change of +100 basis points. Now suppose that the 6-month maturity maintained the same change ratio of 2:1 over a range of shifts in the 9-year benchmark. For example, if the 9-year benchmark shifted by only 25 basis points, then the proportional change in the 6-month maturity would be 50 basis points. More generally, whatever the benchmark shift, there would be exactly twice that move in the 6-month maturity. Similarly, the 30-year maturity would also maintain the same change ratio and would move only 50 basis points for every 100 basis point shift in the benchmark. In essence, this technique provides a way to define a relative yield response pattern. In this case, the response pattern was based on beliefs that the yield curve will flatten and sharpen in a particular way. This pattern of change could also be made to reflect beliefs regarding the differential volatilities of rates at various maturities. Thus, one could interpret this response pattern as a statement that 6-month maturities are twice as volatile in yield as 9-year maturities, etc.

With proportional changes relative to the benchmark defined in this fashion, a whole spectrum of yield curves can be constructed. Figure 8 shows the spectrum of yield curves that would be associated with shifts of 0, +10, +20, +30, +40, and +50 basis points in the 9-year benchmark. Each benchmark shift creates a pattern of change for all maturities in accordance with the proportional changes defined in Figure 6.

Different patterns of proportional yield responses might be anticipated if the shift in the yield curve were downward rather than upward. To accommodate this dual pattern, two expected yield curves could be defined—one based on a pessimistic scenario (e.g., Figure 4) and the other based on an optimistic scenario. Each curve then determines a pattern of change across maturities (e.g., Figure 6). (In fact, the revised yield curve itself can be determined by a small number of estimated changes. For example, the pessimistic yield curve in Figure 4 could be defined by three yield changes: +100 basis points at 6 months, +50 basis points at 9 years and +25 basis points at 30 years.) This pessimistic scenario can then be used to define a pattern of proportional yield change relative to any given benchmark shift in a pessimistic direction. By applying this technique to a sequence of incremental shifts, one can obtain a spectrum of yield curves that move toward and finally coincide with the originally defined pessimistic yield curve (e.g., Figure 8).

An identical procedure could then be taken with respect to changes in the optimistic direction.

Figure 8: A Spectrum of Yield Curves

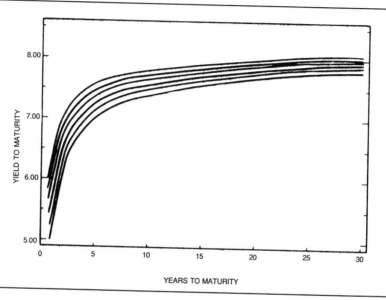

YEARS TO MATURITY

A SPECTRUM OF HORIZON RETURNS

Each curve in the spectrum shown in Figure 8 corresponds to a certain change from the present yield curve. Consequently, each curve will generate a characteristic pattern of horizon returns. This corresponding spectrum of horizon returns is shown in Figure 9.

The yield curves of Figure 8 are related in an inverse sequence to the horizon returns of Figure 9. Thus, the present yield curve (i.e., the one reflecting a scenario of no market movement) lies at the *bottom* of the spectrum in Figure 8. The corresponding horizon return graph is the Rolling Yield curve lying at the *top* of the spectrum in Figure 9. By the same token, the most pessimistic yield curve lies at the top in Figure 8, while its corresponding horizon return curve is naturally the lowest one in Figure 9.

Each of these horizon return curves corresponds to the rotation from a parallel shift followed by the two twist effects. In the 2- to 9-year range, the up-twist acts to first straighten out and then to reverse the strong upward slope of the Rolling Yield curve. In the longer maturities, the different horizon return curves are almost parallel. This is due to the down-twist almost offsetting the volatility increases at the longer maturities. For the 20 basis point shift, these effects combine to produce a virtually flat return curve.

Figure 9: A Spectrum of Horizon Returns

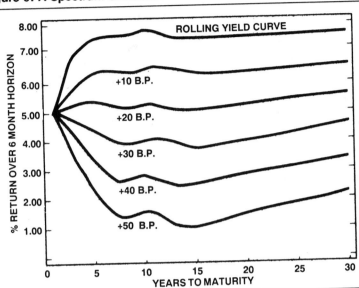

These spectrums must be recognized as highly simplified approximations of a very complex process. However, they do permit an investor to explore the impact of different kinds of yield curve movements on horizon returns. This exploration can often result in some surprising findings. For example, if Figure 9 represented an investor's beliefs, he would see that the longest maturities are not necessarily the most volatile. He would also see that the maturity where the Rolling Yield reaches its peak, the 9-year maturity, may actually represent quite a high risk sector.

Under the most pessimistic assumption, i.e., the bottom curve, the investor would be reluctant to extend beyond the 6-month Bill. However, if his expectations were distributed more equally across all six curves, the investor would clearly extend at least to the 1-year Bill and possibly to the third or fourth year. By the same token, unless he had considerable faith in the most optimistic of the six curves, he would probably be reluctant to extend beyond the fifth year. It should be remembered that this example is restricted to the essentially pessimistic spectrum represented in Figure 9.

In general, by selecting one or more patterns of proportional yield changes, the investor can explore a wide spectrum of horizon return curves that would result from changing yield curves. The effects of both optimistic and pessimistic changes can then be examined. The impact of various types of shape changes can be studied through alternative patterns of proportional yield changes. By associating different horizons with different degrees of shift in the benchmark maturity, one can visualize the evolution of various return curves over time.

In the final analysis, all investment decisions come down to a tradeoff between risk and return. This tradeoff is clearly present in decisions relating to the maturity structure of a fixed-income portfolio. The current shape of the yield curve and prospective changes in its shape constitute critical factors in this tradeoff. With this extension of the Rolling Yield technique, the investor can examine explicit representations of the risk/return tradeoff over a wide range of assumed yield curve conditions.

Chapter III C-4

The Risk Dimension

In the final analysis, most investment decisions require the acceptance of a certain degree of risk in exchange for the prospect of a compensatory level of return. Consequently, there is a natural temptation for a bond portfolio manager to want to view the yield curve as a representation of a return/risk tradeoff. In the first article of this series, *The Rolling Yield*, it was shown that the traditional yield dimension of the yield curve cannot really be interpreted as a consistent set of returns over a common investment horizon. However, by transforming the yield dimension from the traditional yield-to-maturity to a Rolling Yield, one can obtain at least a nominal measure of return across maturities. In the second article, *The Rolling Yield and Changing Markets*, it was shown how a spectrum of horizon returns can be developed that reflects potential patterns of change in the yield curve. With the techniques outlined in these two articles, the return dimension of the yield curve can be calculated across a range of market scenarios.

Up to this point, the primary focus has been on the dimension of return—all graphical illustrations have related returns (on the vertical axis) against maturity (on the horizontal axis). This helps to overcome the problem of confusing conventional yields with returns, but it does little to help replace maturity with a more accurate measure of risk.

The present study is addressed to this problem of the risk dimension in yield curve analysis.

Martin L. Leibowitz, "The Risk Dimension," Salomon Brothers Inc, October 1977. This paper was subsequently included in *Total Return Management*, Salomon Brothers Inc, 1979.

As in the preceding work on the return dimension, our objective will be a limited one. There will be no attempt to try to define risk in any sort of absolute or general sense (probably an impossible task). Rather, we will try to develop techniques for quantifying the vulnerability of investment returns to changing markets. In this way, we hope to clarify the sensitivity of returns at various maturities along the yield curve.

THE YIELD VALUE OF A 32nd

The most widely circulated volatility-related number is the "yield value of a 32nd." Most daily offering sheets for U.S. Treasury securities show this value for every coupon bond. Its primary application is to help in estimating the yield value associated with a new market price.

As an example, consider a 2.50-year 6.50% bond priced at 100 + 14/32. The corresponding yield-to-maturity is 6.308%. If the bond now increases in price by 1/32nd of a point (i.e., .03125 of a point in decimal notation), then the new price will be:

$$100 + 14/32 + 1/32 = 100.43750 + .03125$$
$$= 100.46875.$$

The yield at this new price will then be 6.294, i.e., a yield decrease of:

$$6.308 - 6.294 = .014\%.$$

This yield change of 1.4 basis points is called the "yield value of a 32nd."

Now suppose the price increased by 3/32 to 100 + 17/32. Its yield would then decline by a certain amount. An approximate value for this decrement in yield can be found by multiplying the number of 32nds in this price move, i.e., 3, by the "yield value of a 32nd,"

$$3 \times 1.4 = 4.2 \text{ B.P.}$$

The revised yield estimate would then be:

$$6.308\% - .042\% = 6.266\%[1]$$

This estimate provides a close approximation to the exact yield of 6.267%. Because of the special shape of the price/yield curve, no single factor can fully

---

[1] The general formula is as follows: (yield change) = (price move in 32nds) × (yield value of a 32nd).

Figure 1: Price Volatility and Yield Value of 1/32nd

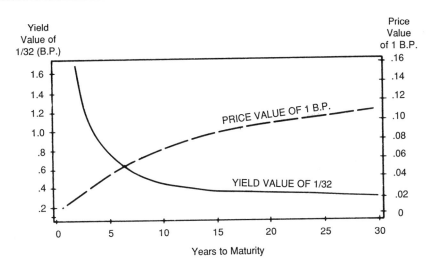

capture the relationship between price and yield. However, this approximation technique is sufficiently accurate so as to prove very useful in practice.

The "yield value of a 32nd" changes dramatically with changes in maturity. For short maturities, a 1/32nd price change must be amortized over a small number of years, resulting in a sizable impact on the yield value. However, as shown in Figure 1, these "yield values of a 32nd" decline dramatically with increasing maturity. At the longer end, a price change of 1/32nd has a relatively small impact on yield. By the same token, this means that a relatively small change in yield is needed to generate a 1/32nd price change in the longer maturities.

The "yield value of a 32nd" can also be used to find the (approximate) incremental price change associated with a given basis point change in yield. In the preceding example of the 2.50-year 6.50% bond priced at 100 + 14/32 to yield 6.308%, a + .03125 price change resulted in a -1.4 B.P. yield move. Reversing this sequence, we could also say that a -1.4 B.P. yield move led to the +.03125 price change. Alternatively, we could say that

$$\frac{+.03125}{1.4} = +.0223$$

is the price change that would follow (approximately) from a -1 B.P. yield change. This value of .0223 might then be called the "price value of 1 basis point." The "price value of 1 B.P." reflects a bond's price volatility to changing interest rates. In our example, a 15 basis point decrease in yield would be accompanied by a price jump of approximately

$$15 \times .0223 = +.3345.$$

The "price value of a basis point" is just the reciprocal of the "yield value of a 32nd." Therefore, at the shorter maturities, when the "yield value of a 32nd" reaches its highest level, the "price value of a basis point" will be at its lowest level. And just as the "yield value of a 32nd" decreases with maturity, so the "price value of a basis point" will increase with maturity. This reciprocal pattern can be seen in Figure 1.

PERCENTAGE PRICE VOLATILITY

For most market-oriented purposes, one wants a measure of *percentage* price volatility. This can be simply attained by dividing the bond's initial price into the "price value of 1 B.P." Thus, in the preceding example, the percentage price volatility becomes

$$100\% \times \frac{.0223}{(100 + 14/32)} = .0222$$

i.e., only slightly different than the .0223 value obtained as the "price value of 1 basis point." However, for bonds priced at levels further from par, this percentage price change can differ significantly from the unadjusted "price value."

The top curve in Figure 2 represents the percentage price volatility plotted against maturities along the yield curve. One can clearly see the expected general pattern of increasing volatility with increasing maturity. However, it is also important to observe that this pattern is not uniform across all maturities. In the early years, price volatility increases almost directly with maturity, i.e., a 1-year Bill has twice the percentage price volatility of a 6-month Bill, a 2-year bond has nearly twice the volatility of a 1-year Bill, etc. However, with increasing maturities, the incremental increase in volatility becomes less and less. For example, a 10-year bond is only about 80% more volatile than a 5-year bond. The 20-year bond is about 60% more volatile than a 10-year bond. Beyond the 15th year, the incremental increase in price volatility becomes very modest—the 30-year bond is only 25% more volatile than the 15-year bond.

Actually, the volatility curve of Figure 2 reflects considerations in addition to maturity. The percentage price volatility of a bond depends on its maturity, coupon rate, and starting yield level. Since the issues comprising the yield curve are all close to par, the coupon rate has a minimal impact in terms of discount or premium effects. There still remains the dependence on the starting yield level. A 100 basis point change in yield creates a greater price change starting

Figure 2: Percentage Price Volatility and Horizon Volatility

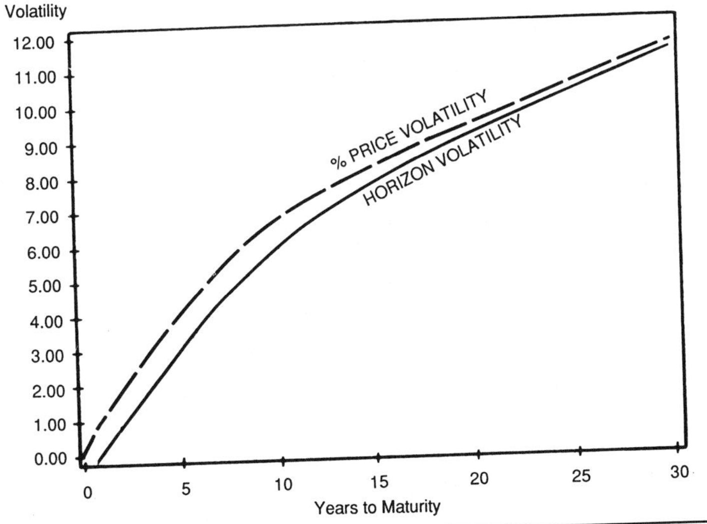

from a low yield level than it will for the same security starting at a higher yield level.[2] Consequently, the plot of percentage price volatility across maturity will depend on the underlying yield curve. At higher overall yield levels, the percentage price volatility will be somewhat lower across all maturities. For flatter yield curves, the price volatility curve will grow more quickly in the early years. However, these yield level effects remain minor considerations compared with the dominating influence of maturity.

The theoretical concept of Duration, first proposed by Macaulay in 1938, can provide insights into the interaction between a bond's volatility and its maturity, coupon and yield level. Duration has proven to be a particularly valuable tool in dealing with the intriguing mathematical problems that relate to "matching" the total long term cash flow from a bond portfolio to a prescribed pattern of liabilities. As a practical tool when dealing with short term investment horizons, Duration can be used as an alternative (and somewhat fancier) technique for computing a bond's price volatility. However, for our purposes in this study, the more fundamental concept is price volatility.

Rather than delve more deeply into Duration or other computational techniques for approximating price volatility, it is more important to move forward

---

[2] These interactions are discussed more fully in *Inside the Yield Book*, Sidney Homer and Martin L. Leibowitz, Prentice-Hall, Inc. and New York Institute of Finance, 1972.

and explore how market changes can impact a bond's total return over a specified investment horizon.

VOLATILITY OF HORIZON RETURNS

The total return formula incorporates price action in terms of the percentage increase in price (or market value) over the horizon period. For any bond, this price action can be divided into two components: (1) the price change derived from amortization of accretion at a constant yield, and (2) the price change derived from changes in the bond's yield. In dealing with "current coupon" securities that comprise the Treasury yield curve, we can narrow our focus and only consider price changes resulting from yield changes.

A bond's price level may fluctuate considerably during the horizon period. However, in computing total return *over* the horizon period, the only price that matters is that reached *at* the horizon itself. Consequently, it is the percentage price volatility at the *horizon* which is important. This leads to a certain reduction in the relevant volatility value. For example, at the end of a 6-month horizon, a 6-month Bill will have matured—its horizon price volatility will be zero. Similarly, at the end of a 6-month horizon, a 2-year bond will have aged into a 1.50-year bond. For this bond, the volatility of its horizon return will, therefore, depend on the percentage price volatility of a 1.50-year bond.

This "horizon effect" reduces the percentage price volatility that applies to the security's horizon return. As shown in Figure 2, this reduction is relatively unimportant for the longer maturities where a 6-month maturity reduction has minor impact on volatility. However, in the shorter maturities, this effect can be quite significant. Consider the relative volatilities of a 2-year and a 1-year security. In terms of instantaneous price volatility, Figure 2 shows that the 2-year security is essentially twice as volatile as the 1-year. However, over a 6-month horizon, the 2-year security becomes *three* times as volatile as a 1-year security.

Although horizon returns are usually presented in an annualized form, it is generally more convenient to express price volatilities in non-annualized form. The percentage volatility of the horizon price can then be interpreted as the sensitivity of the nonannualized horizon *return* per basis point change in yield. For conciseness, we shall refer to this figure as the "Horizon Volatility."[3]

Figure 3 summarizes these computations for the example of the 3-year 6.50% bond. The Horizon Volatility of 2.23 is the (approximate) basis point change in the horizon returns for each basis point change in yield. Equivalently,

---

[3] For a more detailed description of the Horizon Volatility concept, see *Horizon Analysis: A New Analytic Framework for Managed Bond Portfolios*. (Ed. Note: This article appears in this book.)

Figure 3: Calculation of Horizon Volatility

**A 3-Year 6.50% Par Bond
Rolling Down to a 2.50-Year Curve Value of 6.30%
Over a Six-Month Horizon**

For 2.50-Year 6.50% Bond Priced at 100.4375 to Yield 6.30%
Decimal Value of 1/32   .03125
Yield Value of 1/32   ÷ 1.4
Price Value of 1 B.P. (Price Change Per
  1 B.P. Change in Yield)   .0223

Price Value of 1 B.P.   .0223
"Horizon Price"   ÷ 100.4375
Percentage Price Change (Per 1 B.P. Change in Yield)   .0222

For 3-Year 6.50% Par Bond Rolling Down to 6.30% Over a 6-Month Horizon

Percentage Price Change at Horizon   .0222
Ratio of Current Price to "Horizon Price"   ÷ (100/100.4375)

Percentage Price Change at Horizon   .0223
  Expressed as % Market Price Today

Translation Factor for Percentage Price Change   × 100
  to be Expressed as B.P. of Horizon Return

HORIZON VOLATILITY   2.23
(B.P. Change in Horizon Return
  Per 1 B.P. Change in Yield)

---

one can also say that a 100 B.P. change in yield will produce a 2.23% change in horizon returns.

HORIZON VOLATILITY AS THE RISK DIMENSION

The traditional yield curve plots yield-to-maturity against maturity. In the first study in this series, *The Rolling Yield*, we showed that the Rolling Yield was a better measure of nominal horizon return. Therefore, we claimed that an improved view of the return/risk tradeoff could be obtained by replacing the conventional yield by the Rolling Yield. In the preceding analysis, a bond's maturity has been shown to be only a crude measure of volatility risk over short term

Figure 4: Horizon Volatility as the Risk Dimension

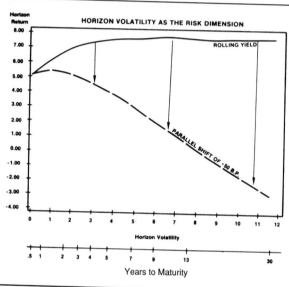

horizons. Therefore, we now suggest that a further step towards an improved return/risk diagram can be achieved by replacing the bond's maturity by its Horizon Volatility.

Figure 4 illustrates this concept. Rolling Yield is plotted on the vertical axis against the Horizon Volatility on the horizontal axis.

In its overall shape, Figure 4 is roughly similar to the Rolling Yield curve plotted against maturity. There are two major differences. First, there is a shift of the entire curve to the left (e.g., the 6-month maturity corresponds to Horizon Volatility of 0). Second, there is a "compression" of the long end of the curve. This compression results from the decreasing impact of maturity on the Horizon Volatility. Thus, the entire maturity range from 15 to 30 years, comprising one-half of the maturity axis, maps into the 8 to 11.5 Horizon Volatility range, i.e., into only 30% of the volatility axis. This compression can have a much greater visual impact when the underlying yield curve exhibits more curvature in the longer maturities.

This substitution of Horizon Volatility for maturity provides Figure 4 with a number of valuable features.

First of all, there is a better ability to visualize the effect of market moves. In the second study in this series, *The Rolling Yield and Changing Markets*, we showed how a parallel shift (i.e., a constant yield move across all maturities) led to a horizon return curve which closely resembled a rotation of the Rolling Yield curve. When the Horizon Volatility is used as the horizontal axis, this resemblance is materially strengthened. Figure 4 shows this "rotation effect" using a parallel shift of + 50 basis points.

If the vulnerability of horizon return to market movements is considered to be a primary component of risk, then this rotation effect is a desirable feature of any return/risk diagram.

In performing bridge swaps, one of the key objectives is to create a package of 2 bonds that will respond to market movements in the same manner as a third bond. In practice, the two bonds are often mixed so that the package's average maturity matches that of the third bond. However, as Figure 2 shows, Horizon Volatility does not increase proportionately with maturity. Consequently, a "matched" average maturity will always leave the package with somewhat less volatility than the third bond. This bias error can be corrected by using the Horizon Volatility to create a matching package. And the search for bridge swap opportunities can be facilitated by a graph of Rolling Yields against Horizon Volatility.

THE MARKET RESPONSE CURVE

In *The Rolling Yield and Changing Markets*, a series of horizon return curves was plotted for specific market changes. There is another way of displaying this same information which can provide valuable insights into the risk dimension.

Figure 5 is a market response curve. For each security displayed, it shows the horizon returns on the vertical axis that would result from a given yield movement along the horizontal axis.

The response curve for the 6-month Bill is a horizontal line—no matter what yield movement occurs, the 6-month Bill will always provide its promised yield as a horizon return.

For the 9-year bond, the response curve is a downward sloping line. Its point of intersection with the vertical axis is the 9-year Rolling Yield since the yield curve remains unchanged at this point. For every basis point change in the yield curve, the annualized horizon return drops by about -12 B.P., or -6 B.P. in terms of nonannualized return. This ratio of -6 basis points for every basis point of parallel shift is just the 9-year bond's Horizon Volatility.

Similarly, for the 30-year bond, the response curve intersects the vertical axis at the Rolling Yield and has a slope corresponding to its Horizon Volatility of 11.5.

Figure 5 represents the response curve for a pure parallel shift—where the movement in yields is the same across all maturities. However, the investor may have expectations of a somewhat more complex pattern of yield curve movements. This pattern would include parallel shifts at some benchmark maturity accompanied by various sorts of "twists" on either side. In *The Rolling Yield and*

Figure 5: Market Response Curves

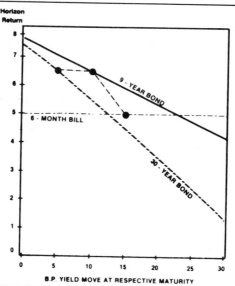

Changing Markets, a pattern of yield curve change is described in terms of changes relative to a 9-year benchmark. For illustrative purposes at this point, we shall retain this general pattern of change, but with somewhat different parameters. For every basis point increase at the benchmark, we shall assume that the 6-month yield increases by 1.5 basis points while the 30-year yield increases by only .5 basis point. For all maturities between the benchmark and the two extremes, the yield increase will be determined on an interpolated basis across these specified maturity points.

With such a pattern of yield curve change, the horizon returns could no longer be described in terms of a simple parallel shift. For any given parallel shift in the benchmark maturity, there would be different prescribed yield changes associated with each of the other maturities. For example, the dots in Figure 5 show the horizon returns that would accompany a +10 basis point move in the 9-year benchmark.

A more convenient approach is to revise the response curve so that the horizon return incorporates the specified pattern of change. This is done in Figure 6. The horizontal axis in Figure 6 represents the yield change at the 9-year benchmark. The response curve for the 30-year bond then reflects its horizon return based on the assumption that the 30-year bond experiences a .5 basis point yield move for every basis point change along the horizontal axis. The response

Figure 6: Proportional Market Response Curves

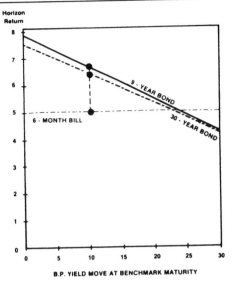

curves for the 9-year benchmark and the 6-month bill remain the same as in Figure 5.

In Figure 6, the response curves intersect the vertical axis at the respective Rolling Yield values, just as in Figure 5. However, in contrast to Figure 5, the slopes of the response curves in Figure 6 reflect the sensitivity of horizon returns to yield movements at the benchmark maturity. Thus, for the 30-year bond response curve in Figure 6, the slope no longer corresponds to its Horizon Volatility as we defined it earlier. The slope here represents the change in the *30-year's* horizon return for each basis point increase at the *9-year benchmark* maturity. In other words, the slope combines the 30-year Horizon Volatility with the assumed pattern of change in 30-year yields.

This immediately suggests a more comprehensive concept of volatility risk.

PROPORTIONAL VOLATILITY

The Horizon Volatility measures the sensitivity of a bond's horizon return to a given change in yield. As such, it is a purely mathematical measure. When used to compare two securities, the difference in their Horizon Volatilities gauges the vulnerability of their respective returns to a common change in yields. In the context of the yield curve, the Horizon Volatility describes the response to a parallel shift, i.e., a constant yield move across all maturities. For example, consider the Horizon Volatility curve in Figure 2. If the vertical axis is scaled in basis points, then this curve describes the basis point change in (nonannualized) horizon return at each maturity for a 1 basis point parallel shift.

However, market movements rarely take the form of parallel shifts. Suppose that one believes that changes in the yield curve are likely to follow the proportional change pattern depicted in Figure 6. To obtain a consistent measure of volatility risk along the yield curve, these judgmental factors regarding proportional yield moves must be integrated with the purely mathematical Horizon Volatility.

This integration process can be easily achieved. In Figure 7, the proportional yield move curve depicts the basis point change at each maturity for a one basis point move in the benchmark. Thus, the 30-year security will undergo a +.5 basis point change for every basis point change on the benchmark. At the 30-year point, the Horizon Volatility is 11.5, indicating an -11.5 basis point move in horizon return for every +1 basis point yield move. By simply multiplying these two factors, we obtain

$$.5 \times (-11.5) = -5.8.$$

Figure 7: The Proportional Volatility

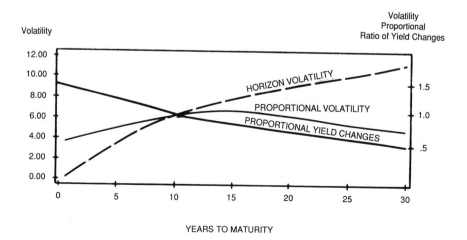

YEARS TO MATURITY

This value of -5.8 corresponds to the B.P. change in (non-annualized) horizon return at the 30th year per +1 B.P. move at the 9-year benchmark. (It is also the slope of the 30-year market response curve in Figure 6.) Thus, by utilizing the assumed proportional patterns of yield change, the sensitivity of the horizon return at every maturity can be related to a yield shift at the benchmark maturity.

We shall refer to this sensitivity measure as the "Proportional Volatility" in order to clearly identify its reliance on the assumed proportional pattern of change.

In Figure 7, the value of the Horizon Volatility curve and the proportional change curve have been multiplied together to obtain a Proportional Volatility curve across maturities. This third curve always coincides with the Horizon Volatility curve at two points—the horizon (i.e., 6 months) and the benchmark maturity. Apart from these two points of coincidence, the Proportional Volatility could be higher or lower than the Horizon Volatility depending on the particular pattern of up-twists and down-twists that are assumed.

If one remains fully aware and appropriately cautious of the judgmental factors involved, then the Proportional Volatility can prove useful as a comprehensive measure of volatility risk.

Figure 8 is a plot of the Rolling Yield Curve against the Proportional Volatility. This diagram is very revealing. First of all, it shows very graphically that the

Figure 8: Horizon Return Versus Proportional Volatility

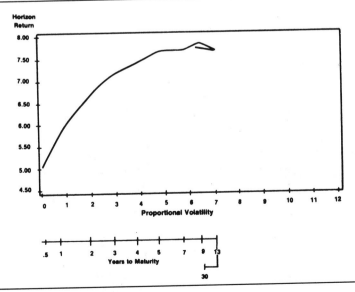

volatility risk may not continue to increase with increasing maturity. With the assumed pattern of yield change, the Proportional Volatility at 30 years is actually less than that at 13 years. The net result is that the Rolling Yield curve doubles back upon itself. Thus, with nearly the same volatility as the 9-year maturity, the 30-year maturity provides a lower horizon return than the 9-year. This suggests that the 9-year horizon returns will dominate those from the 30-year maturity across a range of market moves, as long as the yield curve change corresponds to the assumed proportional pattern.

Figure 8 is also immediately suggestive of certain bridge swaps. For example, the 7-year bond could be swapped into a package of 5-year and 9-year bonds that would provide an improved horizon return. If the mixture of 5- and 9-year bonds in the swap package is based on matched Proportional Volatility, then changes in the package's return will track the changes in the 7-year's return, including the effect of *expected* twists in the yield curve.

SCENARIO ANALYSIS

Figure 9 depicts the horizon return curves associated with -20 B.P., 0 B.P., and +20 B.P. movements at the benchmark maturity. Suppose these three curves rep-

Figure 9: Horizon Return Versus Proportional Volatility

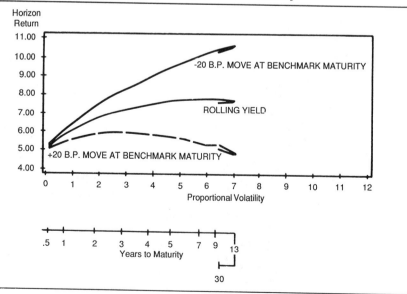

resent a portfolio manager's optimistic, most likely, and pessimistic scenarios. Then, even in the pessimistic case, the risk-free return from 6-month Bill would be exceeded by every maturity except those lying between 11 and 25 years. In the most likely scenario, the best horizon return is achieved at the 9th year. Consequently, the 9-year point might be adopted as the maturity target for a manager willing to accept these risk/return tradeoffs.

On the other hand, in any such scenario analysis, there are two important risk factors that could compromise this simple formulation of the investment problem:

1) the scenario level risk

2) the pattern risk.

The scenario level risk refers to the danger that the benchmark yield moves associated with each scenario could be in error, i.e., the pessimistic case in Figure 9 should perhaps be represented by a +40 basis point move at the benchmark. The pattern risk, of course, refers to the problem of potential deviation from the assumed proportional pattern of yield moves. This risk factor is exacerbated by the problem that such pattern errors do not have the same impact across all maturities. For example, there will be a much greater effect from pattern deviations at the 30th year than from those in the 2nd year.

A plot of horizon returns against Proportional Volatility can help in evaluating the potential impact of level risk, at least on an incremental basis. For example, in Figure 9, the 7th- and 9th-year maturities would provide essentially the same horizon returns under the pessimistic scenario. However, the 9-year maturity has greater Proportional Volatility. If the actual situation turned out worse than the assumed +20 basis point benchmark move, then the 9-year return would deteriorate further than the 7-year return. In light of the possibility of level errors, the risk-averse manager might choose the 7th year as a maturity target even though the 9th year provides a better or equal return in each of the three specified scenarios.

Thus, in scenario analysis, the Proportional Volatility can be viewed as a yardstick for the impact of level errors. In this context, the Proportional Volatility should be based upon a yield response pattern reflecting market movements in the pessimistic direction. (Uncertainties in a favorable direction are indeed a factor in the investment problem, but they do not constitute risk in the usual sense. Few practitioners are really averse to the prospect of pleasant surprises!)

Moreover, it should be recognized that adverse volatility is only one facet of risk. Risk could be defined broadly to consist of all potential events that might somehow interfere with the fulfillment of the portfolio's objectives. Under this broad definition, adverse volatility is clearly only one component of risk. However, it is clearly a critical risk factor for portfolios concerned with maximizing total returns over relatively short term horizon periods.

The Proportional Volatility helps integrate many of the facets of volatility risk—the percentage price volatility, the horizon effect, and the expected pattern of yield curve change. It should be clearly noted that any such expected pattern of change, whether based on historical data or upon anticipated movements in the yield curve, represents a subjective judgment. Consequently, one should remain aware that any given Proportional Volatility is subject to the uncertainty of *unexpected* patterns of change. To the extent possible, of course, one should explore the potential impact of alternative patterns of change.

By their very nature, most fixed-income funds are highly risk-averse. The determination of an appropriate risk/reward tradeoff is often the most crucial of all strategic decisions. In most cases, this determination must incorporate—either explicitly or implicitly—an evaluation of the risk of adverse volatility. By providing a structured technique for this evaluation, the concepts of Horizon Volatility and Proportional Volatility can help the bond portfolio manager in confronting this facet of the risk dimension.

Chapter III C-5

Portfolio Returns and Scenario Analysis

An increasing number of fixed-income portfolios are being directed toward total return management. There are many questions as to whether total return is indeed appropriate as a primary objective for such portfolios. However, the fact is that many portfolio managers find themselves seeking total return over relatively short-term measurement periods. These managers quickly discover that, of all their many investment and trading decisions, the most critical by far are those relating to their portfolio's maturity structure.

This study develops a procedure for translating a manager's interest rate judgments into a return/risk framework for evaluating alternative maturity structures.

The first step is to develop yield curve projections consistent with each interest rate scenario. While any number of scenarios can theoretically be used, a minimum of three is usually needed to capture the basic rate prospects together with the pattern of uncertainties surrounding the most likely projection. For each scenario, the projected total return is computed for an investment into a given maturity area. The resulting "horizon return curves" can then be used to estimate the total return from a portfolio having a given maturity structure.

In discussing the behavior of the fixed-income market, it is often useful to select a specific maturity point on the yield curve to serve as a benchmark. Movements in market levels leading from one interest rate scenario to the next

Martin L. Leibowitz, "Portfolio Returns and Scenario Analysis," Salomon Brothers Inc, January 1978. This paper was subsequently included in *Total Return Management*, Salomon Brothers Inc, 1979.

can then be conveniently defined in terms of changes in yield at this benchmark maturity. By combining this approach with the preceding scenario analysis, the projected returns from a given portfolio can be related to a scale of "market outcomes" described by changes along this benchmark maturity. These graphical presentations, called "portfolio return vectors," greatly facilitate the comparison of alternative maturity structures.

In many forms of portfolio analysis that are popular today, the complex nature of risk is compressed into a single volatility yardstick, with values often based on historical patterns of market volatility. However, volatility is only one facet of risk, and even volatility has a bi-directional character—there is the risk of deviation in an *adverse* direction and the risk of deviation in a more *optimistic* direction. These two risk factors—adverse volatility and optimistic volatility— may be fundamentally different—both in their magnitude and in their impact upon the portfolio decision. In the scenario analysis described in this study, this bi-directional nature of risk is addressed explicitly.

In delineating scenarios on the pessimistic and optimistic sides of the most likely case, the manager may be making an important statement regarding his perception of market risks. By extracting the yield volatilities implied in these scenario specifications, bi-directional volatility factors can be estimated. Moreover, these bi-directional volatility factors will be consistent with the manager's own perceptions of market risk, and may therefore become a much more valuable component of the decision process.

The determination of maturity structure always entails striking some balance among the potential return and risk factors associated with each maturity area. Regardless of what mathematical aids may be employed, it must ultimately be the manager's judgment that determines the risk/return tradeoffs that are appropriate given his market perceptions and portfolio objectives. The purpose of the scenario approach described in this study is to provide a clear, consistent framework for evaluating these tradeoffs.

YIELD CURVE SCENARIOS

Many institutional investors find the scenario approach to be a useful technique for articulating both their beliefs and their uncertainties regarding future interest rate movements. By specifying interest rate levels that they believe to be most probable at each of several maturities, they are—in essence—tracing out a crude view of the yield curve they expect to prevail at the horizon. However, any rational investor will season this view with a good deal of skepticism as to the imponderables and the uncertainties regarding the realization of precisely this particular yield curve. One way of articulating these uncertainties is to define a series of one or more additional scenarios that reflect potential yield curves that might eventuate in the face of more adverse or more favorable market conditions. Theoretically, one could trace out a large number of different yield curve scenarios. In practice, one is well advised to deal with a small number of alternative scenarios on either side of a "most likely" case. For illustrative purposes, we shall restrict this study to consideration of three scenarios—a most likely case, an optimistic case, and a pessimistic case. The techniques described can be readily extended to a more refined structure of multiple scenarios.

In Figure 1, the striped line describes the starting yield curve (actually, it is the curve from March 29, 1977). The three yield curve scenarios at the horizon are described by solid lines. As we can see, each of these scenarios involves a certain amount of shifting and reshaping of the yield curve.

In actual practice, it is most unusual to have any projected yield curve defined across all maturitites. Most portfolio managers will specify a given scenario in terms of the projected rate levels for short and long maturities. In some instances, where there is a more refined belief regarding the yield curve's general shape, the manager will be able to provide additional estimates for the yield values of one or more intermediate maturity points. In any case, one must confront the problem of developing a continuous yield curve given only a small number of specified points. This requires some form of mathematical interpolation. While there are many approaches to this interpolation problem, care must be exercised to ensure that the resulting yield curves provide a reasonable representation of the intended scenarios.

Figure 1: Yield Curve Scenarios

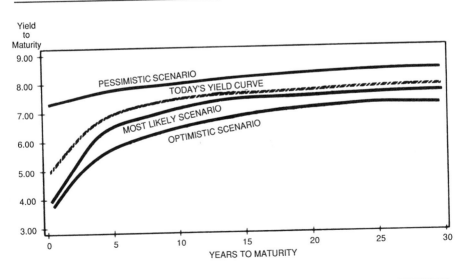

HORIZON RETURN CURVES

Once a market scenario has been projected in terms of a yield curve at the end of the planning horizon, one can proceed to compute the total returns that would be realized under this scenario. There are three components in a bond's total return over any horizon shorter than its maturity—coupon income, price fluctuation and the reinvestment of coupon income. Over relatively short horizons, the reinvestment effect will be minor. Consequently, the realized total return for any maturity point on today's yield curve can be approximated by combining its initial yield rate (as a par bond) with its price appreciation. The price appreciation will be determined by the corresponding "aged" maturity point on the projected yield curve. (Strictly speaking, the yield curve discussed in this study applies to par bonds. Bonds selling at premiums or discounts will generally be priced at some spread relative to this par bond yield curve. However, this effect tends to be of secondary importance relative to the main movements in the overall yield curve.)

For each projected scenario, the resulting "horizon return curve" depicts the total return that would result from an investment at each maturity point on today's yield curve.

For the three yield curve scenarios of Figure 1, the corresponding horizon return curves are shown in Figure 2. It should be noted the sequence of the

Figure 2: Horizon Return Curves

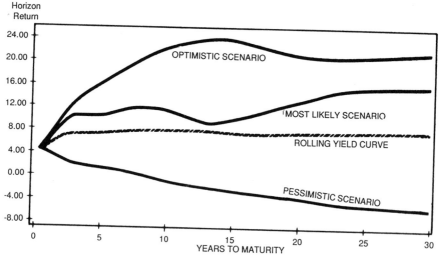

scenarios is inverted as one moves from Figure 1 to Figure 2. For example, the pessimistic scenario is represented by the highest projected yield values, i.e., the *top* curve in Figure 1. However, in Figure 2, these high yield values naturally lead to the greatest price deterioration, and hence to the lowest returns, i.e., to the *lowest* horizon return curve in Figure 2.

The "Rolling Yield" curve in Figure 2 corresponds to the unstated scenario of an unchanged yield curve. It is shown only as a point of reference.

CHARACTERIZING PORTFOLIOS

In dealing with the general fixed-income portfolio, one must speak in terms of sectors that reflect coupon, quality, type and other characteristics in addition to maturity. However, determination of the structure of any general portfolio can be usefully viewed in two stages. The first stage is that of reaching a strategic decision as to the maturity structure. The second stage then consists of the more tactical decisions of determining the best sectors to represent each maturity area. In this study, we focus on the first stage, i.e., that of determining the maturity structure for the portfolio.

As a point of departure, we may focus on a marketplace consisting solely of current coupon Treasury issues. Within this limited marketplace, the maturity structure completely defines the portfolio. This structure is simply the total amount of market dollars invested at each maturity. It can be conveniently displayed through a histogram of the percentage of the portfolio's assets allocated to each maturity area. Three such portfolio distributions are shown in Figure 3.

A portfolio distribution can then be superimposed upon the horizon return curve. In Figure 4 we have taken the horizon return curve for the most likely case and superimposed the portfolio distribution P1 from Figure 3. The portfolio's overall return for this scenario will then be the average of the returns realized at each maturity, weighted by the market value of the portfolio at that maturity.

In Figure 4, the point P1 is plotted so as to correspond to the portfolio's return on the vertical axis and its average maturity on the horizontal axis. The location of the point P1 immediately suggests that an improved portfolio distribution is possible, even without any changes in average maturity. For example, the combination of ten- and thirty-year securities that matched the average maturity of P1 would provide some improvement in the portfolio return for this case.

However, Figure 4 only focuses on one scenario—the most likely case. By repeating this averaging process, the portfolio returns can be determined under each scenario. Having done this, it is useful to compare these returns with those available from other possible portfolio structures as well from the market as a whole. This is done in Figure 5.

Figure 3: Portfolio Distributions

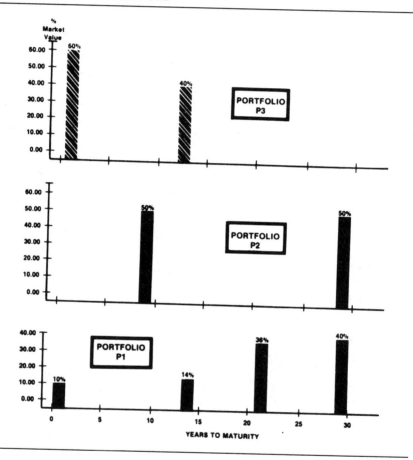

In Figure 5, the portfolio P2—with a reduction in average maturity—appears to provide a better return than P1 in each of the three scenarios, i.e., the portfolio P2 "dominates" portfolio P1. The portfolio P3 represents a considerable reduction in average maturity and is the most conservative of the three portfolios. As might be expected, when compared with P2 (or P1), portfolio P3 provides an improved return under the pessimistic case, but at the cost of reduced return under the two more favorable scenarios.

Figure 4: Horizon Return for a Portfolio

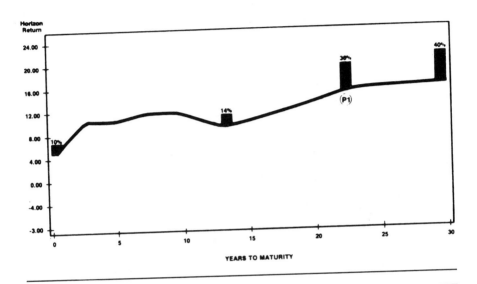

Figure 5: Portfolio Returns Under Different Scenarios

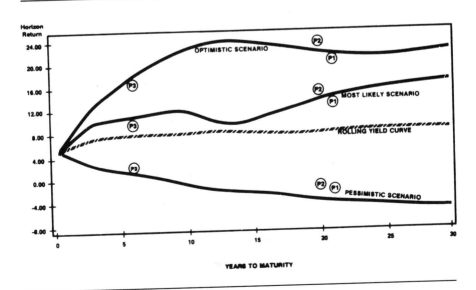

PORTFOLIO RETURN VECTORS

While Figure 5 provides a useful presentation of the relevant factors, it does suffer from a number of deficiencies. First of all, it can quickly become rather cluttered with increases in the number of portfolios and/or scenarios under consideration. A second, more fundamental problem, is the tacit acceptance of the portfolio's average maturity as a measure of risk. Third, there is the related problem that Figure 5 completely neglects the question of "incremental risk," i.e., what happens if the market's action falls somewhat short of the most likely case, but not as far short as the pessimistic case? The latter two problems are closely interrelated and rather complex in nature. It is impossible to hope for any complete solutions solely within the structure of a simple three-scenario analysis. However, all these problems can be clarified by using the technique of "portfolio return vectors."

For a given portfolio, the set of three return values associated with the three scenarios may be called the "return vector" for that portfolio. In order to assess the tradeoff between portfolio P2 and P3, the manager must really compare the return vectors of the two portfolios. These comparisons can be facilitated by developing a numerical dimension for "tagging" the different scenarios. In most situations, this can be achieved by appropriate selection of benchmark maturity. In Figure 6, the nine-year maturity has been chosen for the benchmark. Each

Figure 6: Portfolio Return Vectors

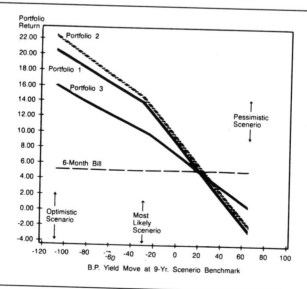

scenario can be uniquely tagged through association with the market movement at this benchmark maturity. Thus, the most likely scenario represents a 30-basis point improvement at the nine-year benchmark maturity, while the pessimistic scenario corresponds to a 70-basis point deterioration in this benchmark maturity. Using the movement along this benchmark maturity as a horizontal axis, we can plot the portfolio return vectors as shown in Figure 6. For example, the left-hand point in Figure 6 corresponds to a 110 b.p. improvement at the benchmark maturity, and the three plotted points correspond to returns from the portfolios P1, P2, and P3 under the most optimistic scenario.

For clarity of comparison, it is tempting to connect the points representing the returns achieved by a given portfolio under the three scenarios. This is done in Figure 6 by using the simple device of drawing straight connecting lines. As we shall see, these connecting straight lines actually correspond to a series of assumptions regarding market behavior "between" scenarios. The nature of these assumptions will be discussed in detail in later sections. For the moment, we shall just view these connecting straight lines as a convenience in describing a portfolio's returns across scenarios.

From Figure 6, we can see that portfolio P2 dominates P1 in all cases. If Figure 6 depicted the totality of the situation, then we would be justified in dismissing the portfolio P1 from further consideration.

Similarly, the conservative nature of portfolio P3 is clarified by Figure 6. We can see that P3 provides better return than P2 under markets approaching the pessimistic case. However, as the scenario benchmark moves toward the most likely case and beyond, the return increasingly falls below P3. Indeed, accepting the straight-line technique employed in Figure 6, we can identify a scenario benchmark move of +20 basis points as the break-even point for P3 versus P2. In other words, if the nine-year benchmark maturity undergoes an adverse yield move of +20 basis points or more, then the conservative portfolio P3 would outperform the portfolio P1.

Over a six-month horizon, the risk-free return is provided by the six-month Bill. For comparative purposes, the return from the six-month Bill is also shown in Figure 6. Since this return is completely unaffected by market movements, it plots as a horizontal line across all scenarios. As described above, the crossover point of these lines could also be used to determine break-even values of specific portfolios against this risk-free rate.

PORTFOLIO COMPARISONS

These diagrams of portfolio return vectors provide a coherent risk/return framework for comparing two or more candidate portfolios. In essence, Figure 6 only relates returns on the vertical axis to a convenient measure of market action on the horizontal axis. In cases of actual dominance such as the choice between P1 and P2, the decision is quite clear—one chooses the dominating portfolio. However, most situations will eventually come to the point where the manager must make a choice between portfolios with "crossing" patterns of return, i.e., where one portfolio provides the better return under some scenarios but a worse return under other scenarios. In such cases, these vector diagrams can only provide the raw input for a decision.

The selection of any portfolio over another will obviously depend upon how the manager assesses the likelihood associated with each scenario *and* on how highly he values incremental return under different market conditions. For example, suppose a portfolio manager felt that the pessimistic case in Figure 6 carried a low probability. If he also felt that incremental return (or lack thereof) had the same value across all scenarios, then he would choose the portfolio P2 over the more conservative P3. On the other hand, suppose this manager believed that a primary emphasis should be assigned to minimizing the loss in return under adverse scenarios. He would then value a unit of "saved return" under the pessimistic case more highly than a unit of "improved return" under more favorable market scenarios. With such a valuation scheme, he might choose the more conservative portfolio P3.

In theory, this decision process could be formalized by using probability distributions and valuation factors. In practice, however, many managers feel uncomfortable in trying to assign precise probability values to various market scenarios, not to mention the problem of trying to define the relative value of incremental return across scenarios. These probability and valuation factors are real considerations and do enter into the manager's decision. However, many managers may be more comfortable in taking return diagrams such as Figure 6, and then intuitively superimposing these factors as part of their decision process. This intuitive analysis is facilitated by relating the horizontal axis to a benchmark maturity that comfortably fits the manager's own way of describing possible market behavior.

In any case, whether formalized or not, return vector diagrams such as Figure 6 provide a simple presentation of the risk/return tradeoff in a way that is consistent with the underlying scenario analysis.

RETURN DECREMENTS

Given that the manager would like to adopt a portfolio that provides a certain type of return vector, the next question is how to go about constructing such portfolios. Within the limits of this study, this becomes a question of how one can select a package of maturities that will provide the desired return patterns. In essence, this brings us to the problem of balancing the "risks" of the more favorable scenarios against the "risks" of the more adverse scenarios.

To consider this problem, we must start with the pattern of horizon return displayed in Figure 2.

In the most likely scenario, the horizon return reaches its highest value at the 30th year. If the portfolio manager was absolutely certain that this scenario would be realized, then he would simply concentrate his funds at the 30th year. However, there is always uncertainty, and any projected scenario should be viewed as only one potential eventuality out of many surrounding possibilities. Apart from any specific statement regarding the "pattern of uncertainty," the risk-averse portfolio manager would probably have some reservations about selecting the longest maturity.

However, by specifying the two alternate scenarios, the portfolio manager *has* made a statement regarding this "pattern of uncertainty."

In tracing out the returns under each scenario, one cannot help but convey something of how the returns might deviate from the most likely case. Specifically, the decline in returns from the most likely scenario to the pessimistic scenario has implications for the relative vulnerability of returns across different maturities. This perceived pattern of return vulnerability as one proceeds to more adverse scenarios would clearly have a major impact upon the selection of an appropriate maturity structure for a portfolio.

It is important to recognize that the very delineation of specific yield curve scenarios has led us to this definition of risk. Portfolio managers may wish to incorporate historical evidence and patterns in describing these scenarios. However, once the yield curve scenarios have been specified, they themselves define the vulnerability of returns as one proceeds from one scenario to the next.

By the very nature of how they are specified, these patterns are generally *asymmetric*, i.e., there is a different pattern associated with adverse movements than with favorable movements. Such asymmetry reflects the deliberate judgment of the portfolio manager when he sets down the scenarios. It should be an important requirement of any decision process that it take cognizance of these *intended* asymmetries.

RISK BALANCING

To this point, we have focused on risk in the sense of a movement from a most likely scenario towards the next-most-adverse scenario. This is usually the primary risk that concerns portfolio managers. But it is not the only risk. It is not even the only volatility risk. There is also the risk of opportunity loss. This is the prospect that returns may be even better than expected under the more likely case. These optimistic returns are not always "favorable" to the rate-of-return investor. If ignored, they can represent a sizable opportunity loss. For example, a manager with a defensive short-maturity portfolio may experience a most unfavorable reaction from a "favorable" market move towards the optimistic scenario. In such an eventuality, the opportunity loss may cut as deep (or deeper) as a real principal loss under adverse market movements.

Ideally, one would like to find a maturity point that maximized the most likely return, provided the best possible improvement under the optimistic conditions, and then fell off the least in the event of the pessimistic scenario. Such an ideal choice is rarely available, and the manager must reach a decision through a process of "risk balancing," i.e., compromise among conflicting objectives.

Figure 7 provides a clearer picture of the choices available. The solid curve in Figure 7 is the return decrement that would follow a move from the most likely case to the pessimistic case. The striped curve shows the increment in return in moving from the most likely to the optimistic case. The third curve is, once again, the horizon returns under the most likely case.

The information content of Figure 7 can be improved by noting that the maturity itself does not really enter into the decision process. Maturity is usually taken as a proxy for adverse risk, but we have a better proxy in the return decrement associated with moving from the most likely to the pessimistic case. In Figure 8, the information content of the three curves in Figure 7 is reduced to two curves by using this return decrement as the horizontal axis. (While maturity *per se* may not enter into the decision framework, one obviously needs a way

Figure 7: Inter-Scenario Returns

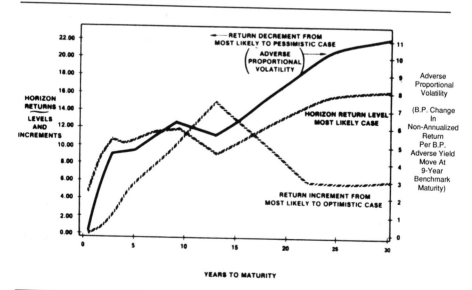

Figure 8: Risk Balancing Across Maturity

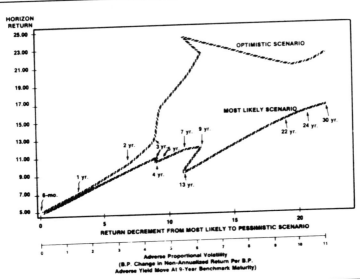

of going back and finding out which maturity goes with which return decrement.)

Specifically, the two curves in Figure 8 display the horizon returns associated with each maturity in the most likely and optimistic cases as a function of the return decrement from the most likely to the pessimistic case.

In general, the risk-averse manager will try to stay as far to the left in Figure 8 as possible. As he ventures further to the right along the horizontal axis, he will incur increasing levels of risk under the pessimistic market scenario. He will move to the right only to achieve sufficiently greater prospects of return under the most likely and optimistic scenarios.

Once one learns how to read the (occasionally curious) meanderings of Figure 8, it can become a powerful tool for balancing asymmetric patterns of risks.

INTER-SCENARIO BEHAVIOR

One of the problems with both Figures 7 and 8 is the tacit assumption that the market can only move to one of the three specified scenarios. In fact, with any scenario analysis, the specified scenarios are only intended to capture limited points across the manager's range of market expectations. Thus, the optimistic and pessimistic scenarios may really represent relatively remote prospects. By definition, the manager's greatest expectations for the market are concentrated on *and around* the most likely scenario. Consequently, it is important to concentrate on the effects of incremental deviations from this scenario. Consideration must, of course, be given to deviations in both the optimistic and the pessimistic directions.

The basic problem is that the usual scenario analysis rarely makes any *explicit* statement about the market behavior "between scenarios." We shall now describe one approach to dealing with inter-scenario behavior which we feel is consistent with the usual intent of scenario analysis. This approach is based upon a "proportionality assumption" regarding the patterns of change of yields and returns as one deviates incrementally from a specified scenario.

When a manager specifies a pessimistic scenario relative to the most likely case, we suggest that he is also conveying some information regarding the way returns may deteriorate should market action fall short of the most likely scenario. For example, in Figure 7, the 30th year maturity undergoes the largest return decrement from the most likely to the pessimistic scenario. This can also be interpreted as a suggestion that the 30th year returns are generally most vulnerable to incremental adverse movements. Figure 7 also shows that the 30th year decrement is two times as large as the 13th year decrement. One could surmise that the scenario analyst meant to convey something about the relative vulnerability of returns at these two maturities, i.e., that incremental adverse movements away from the most likely case would impact 30-year returns considerably more than 13-year returns.

In the "proportionality approach," we assume that the 30-year returns will deteriorate *incrementally* at two times the rate as 13th year returns. More generally, this approach makes the major assumption that each maturity experiences the same patterns of deterioration in returns under incremental adverse deviations as it would experience under a total leap from the most likely to the pessimistic case.

IMPLIED YIELD VOLATILITIES

The proportionality approach can also be applied directly to volatility of yield movements.

In Figure 1, the basic scenarios are defined in terms of three yield curves that may prevail at the horizon. Under a proportionality assumption, the yield differences between the most likely and the pessimistic yield curve can be taken as a measure of the adverse "yield volatility" across maturities. These yield volatility values can then be combined with a factor describing the price sensitivity at each maturity. The procedure is discussed in C4 of this section, *The Risk Dimension*. The result is a measure of the volatility of total return to *market* movements (as defined by yield changes in the specified benchmark maturity). In *The Risk Dimension*, this measure was termed the Proportionality Volatility to emphasize its dependence upon a (necessarily subjective) estimate of proportional yield volatilities relative to the benchmark maturity.

In practice, it matters little whether the proportionality assumption is applied to the return decrements or to the original yield curve scenarios. Both approaches lead to essentially the same pattern of Proportional Volatility across maturity.

BI-DIRECTIONAL VOLATILITY

With the proportionality assumption, Figures 7 and 8 take on an additional interpretation. In Figure 7, the return decrements and increments curves can be viewed (after rescaling) as the Proportional Volatilities for market movements in the pessimistic and optimistic direction, respectively. These two Proportional Volatility values provide a bi-directional risk measure for each maturity.

In Figure 8, the horizontal axis can be then interpreted (again with rescaling) as the Proportional Volatility of returns under adverse movements. This volatility figure would correspond to many managers' concept of incremental risk, i.e., adverse volatility risk. The most likely case return curve in Figure 8 could then be interpreted as a basic return-versus-risk diagram. The optimistic return curve in Figure 8 illustrates the need to balance the reward from *optimistic* deviations against the vulnerability to *adverse* deviations. In turn, this is tantamount to a risk balancing process dealing not just with *jump* movement between discrete scenarios, but with asymmetric, bi-directional patterns of *incremental* volatility around the most likely scenario.

The Proportional Volatility for a given portfolio can be computed as the weighted average of the Proportional Volatilities of its component securities.

With this proportionality assumption, the inter-scenario behavior of individual securities and, more generally, of whole portfolios, can be modeled in a fashion which is consistent with the original scenario projections. In particular, for two adjacent scenarios, this approach implies that increases in a portfolio's return will follow a prescribed ratio to the changes in the yield level at the benchmark security. This prescribed ratio is the Proportionality Volatility.

Recall now our earlier discussion of the portfolio return vectors in Figure 6. At that point in the development, we inserted the return points at each specified scenario, and then "arbitrarily" connected these points by straight lines. It was indicated that a theoretical justification would follow.

The proportionality approach provides this justification. These straight lines—with their constant slope—constitute a graphical statement that equal changes in the benchmark yield levels lead to equal changes in the portfolio return. In fact, the slope of each line corresponds to the portfolio's Proportional Volatility.

The formalism described in this study is intended to help explore the implications of a given set of yield curve scenarios for a portfolio's maturity structure. This approach begins with the specification of multiple yield curve scenarios (Figure 1). Horizon return curves are then computed for each scenario (Figure 2). From these return curves, projected returns can be developed for portfolios defined in terms of maturity distributions (Figures 3, 4, and 5). The return profiles of several portfolios can then be compared and evaluated with the aid of return vector diagrams (Figure 6). A "risk balancing" procedure is required to construct a portfolio having a desired return vector. To help in this "risk balancing," the return levels and decrements can be displayed so as to highlight the various tradeoffs across maturity (Figures 7 and 8). This approach preserves any intended bi-directional asymmetries in the projected market scenarios. By adopting the proportionality assumption, these same techniques can be used to model the market behavior for bi-directional incremental deviations around the most likely case.

Chapter III C-6

The Maturity Decision

In recent years, the growth of a viable intermediate market has presented the corporate officer with a real choice of maturities for an impending debt issue. In order to provide a framework for evaluating this option, we undertook a series of studies in 1974 which were later published under the title, *The Analysis of Intermediate Term Bond Financing.*[1]

It is no coincidence that the corporate officer once again finds himself confronting a similar need to decide between long and intermediate maturities. The purpose of this article is to review some of the earlier findings and to describe a new graphical approach that can substantially clarify the decision-making process. In particular, this graphical approach can help demonstrate that the temptation to pursue lower interest rates at the outset can lead, under certain circumstances, to significantly greater total borrowing costs over the longer term. In addition, this graphical technique shows how the standard break-even calculation can prove sorely inadequate as a guide to maturity selection.

---

[1] *The Analysis of Intermediate Term Bond Financing,* Martin L. Leibowitz, Salomon Brothers, 1975.

Martin L. Leibowitz, "The Maturity Decision," Salomon Brothers Inc, June 1980. Based on a talk by Leibowitz before the Salomon Brothers "Public Utilities Financial Executives Seminar," New York, New York, May 7, 1980.

As an example in a positive yield curve environment, suppose that a traditional 30-year bond would carry a 12% rate while a 7-year intermediate could be floated at an 11% rate. Thus, the intermediate provides a savings of 100 basis points in nominal coupon rate. This savings is significant over the first 7 years, but it leaves open the question of how the intermediate will be refinanced at its maturity. In this analysis, it is assumed that the corporate officer intends to finance over a long-term 30-year planning horizon. In this context, the long-term bond has the innate suitability of precisely spanning the planning period. The long-term bond, with its assured continuity over the planning period, represents the least-risk financing alternative. The intermediate bond, on the other hand, must be viewed as a bridge vehicle—the first step in a series of financings needed to span the planning horizon. From this point of view, the intermediate bond introduces a certain financial risk. Presumably, the motivation for accepting this risk is the prospect of lower total borrowing costs over the planning period. The corporate finance officer must try to gauge the true magnitude of this rate opportunity and balance it against the associated financial risks.[2]

The key uncertainty associated with an intermediate-term issue is the rate at which it can be refinanced at maturity. This uncertainty is modeled by assuming a range of refinancing rates that apply from the intermediate's maturity through the remainder of the planning period. In other words, the intermediate is assumed to be refinanced at some specific rate via an instrument (or a series of instruments) that spans the remaining 23 years. For example, if this refinancing rate is taken to be 14%, the issuer saves 100 basis points per year over the first 7 years, while incurring a 200 basis point additional cost for the subsequent 23 years.

If viewed as one integrated vehicle, the intermediate—together with its assumed refinancing issue—corresponds to a "blended cash flow" spanning the 30-year planning period. The traditional method for evaluating the costs associated with various cash flows is the present value technique. In this approach, every payment of principal and interest is discounted back into "present dollar" terms. To achieve comparability, a present value analysis of alternative cash flows must be based upon a common discount rate assumption. The choice of an appropriate discount rate may vary from one circumstance to another. However, for simplicity in the following discussion, we shall take the long bond yield as the discount rate for all cash flows.

For a $100MM long-term 12% bond, the use of a 12% discount rate applied to the cash flow of borrowing costs (i.e., both interest and principal payments) will naturally lead to a present value of precisely $100MM. Applying this same

---

[2] It should be noted that this approach differs dramatically from any attempt to address the question of the overall maturity distribution of the firm's debt structure. In this article, the focus is the selection between various intermediate maturities and the traditional long-term instruments at a specific point in time.

Figure 1: Pattern of Savings

$100 MM Issue of 30-Year Long at 12%
versus 7-Year Intermediate at 11%

Refinancing Rate	Present Value of Borrowing Costs ($MM)		
	Refinanced Intermediate	Long Bond	Savings From Intermediate
8.00%	$ 82	$100	$18
9.00	85	100	15
10.00	88	100	12
11.00	92	100	8
12.00	95	100	5
13.00	99	100	1
13.35*	100	100	0
14.00	102	100	-2
15.00	106	100	-6
16.00	109	100	-9

* Break-even value.

12% discount rate to the blended cash flow for the 11% intermediate refinanced at 14%, one finds that the borrowing costs would rise to $102MM in present value terms. For refinancing rates above 14%, the blended cash flow associated with the intermediate route will be greater and will naturally lead to even higher borrowing costs. Figure 1 tabulates these borrowing costs for a range of refinancing rates. (It should be noted that we have ignored all issuance costs on both the intermediate and the long issues, as well as on the refinancing issue.) As shown from this tabulation, the intermediate route provides a savings in borrowing costs as long as financing can be effected at rates below 13.35%. This break-even value of 13.35% represents the point where the present value of this savings cushion accumulated over the first 7 years is just offset by the higher refinancing costs over the subsequent 23-year period.

This analysis can be seen from a different perspective in terms of the graph provided in Figure 2. The vertical axis shows the borrowing costs expressed in terms of millions of dollars of present value. The horizontal axis shows the assumed refinancing rate. For this case, the long-term bond is assumed to remain outstanding throughout the 30-year period, no matter what refinancing rate exists. Consequently, the borrowing costs of the long-term bond remain constant at $100MM. This cost is represented by the horizontal line shown in Figure 2. On the other hand, the blended 30-year cash flow associated with the intermediate issue is greatly dependent upon the refinancing rate that applies upon its

Figure 2: Pattern of Savings

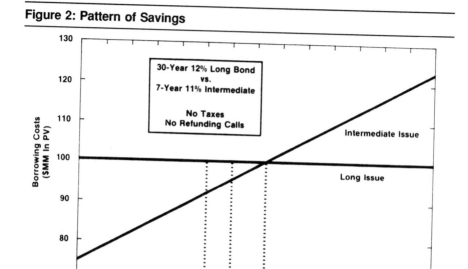

30-Year 12% Long Bond
vs.
7-Year 11% Intermediate

No Taxes
No Refunding Calls

maturity in the 7th year. This dependency is evidenced by the sloped line representing the borrowing costs for the intermediate issue. Lower refinancing rates lead to lower total borrowing costs (over the full 30-year period), while higher refinancing rates lead to higher borrowing costs. In this graphical presentation, the concept of the break-even refinancing rate becomes evident at the point where the sloped line for the intermediate issue intersects the horizontal cost line for the long issue. In addition, this graphical analysis provides a clearer view of the pattern of savings achieved across a range of interest rate conditions. (As will be seen in the following development, this ability to graphically view the entire pattern of savings becomes much more important in the complex— and more realistic—cases involving refunding, taxes, etc.).

REFUNDABILITY OF THE LONG BOND

The preceding analysis bypassed several critical factors relating to the maturity decision. First, it ignored the refunding feature associated with virtually all corporate borrowing. To rectify the situation, suppose we assume that the long bond becomes refundable in the 5th year with a call premium of 110. In order to keep our development at a simple level, assume for the moment that the same refinancing rate applies both to the refunding of the long-term bond and to the refinancing of the intermediate. Let us further assume that the refunding option will be exercised whenever a savings in borrowing costs can be effected. (The criteria for triggering a refunding option are actually quite complex. Various refunding criteria have been the subject of considerable study at both academic and practical levels.[3] However, for the broad purposes of this article, it will suffice to assume that any savings in the present value of borrowing costs will initiate a refunding.)

Under these assumptions, a sufficiently low refinancing rate, e.g., 9%, will result in the refunding of the long-term bond. This will lead to a new blended cash flow consisting of the original 12% coupon rate for the first 5 years, payment of the call premium of 110 in the 5th year, interest payments at the refinanced 9% rate for the remainder of the planning period, and an ultimate repayment of the principal at the end of the planning period. The present value of this blended cash flow can be computed and described as borrowing costs associated with the refunded long bond. By repeating this procedure across the range of rates, one obtains the revised pattern of borrowing costs shown in Figure 3. The refunding of the long bond starts to lower the borrowing costs for refinancing rates below 10.7%. While this does not affect the break-even rate between the long and intermediate issue, it clearly changes the *pattern of savings* that can be obtained through the intermediate vehicle. The intermediate no longer offers the sole route to reducing borrowing costs in a low interest rate environment, i.e., the long bond's refunding capability enables it to participate in these savings. Consequently, the long bond's refunding option reduces the net advantage of the intermediate under lower rate conditions. The graphical analysis helps to clarify these tradeoffs.

IMPACT OF TAXATION

Up to this point, the analysis has neglected the important factor of taxation. Since the coupon payments represent a deductible charge against tax liabilities, their net costs become the actual dollars paid, less the value of the offset to the corporation's overall tax liability. These tax considerations play a particularly important role in dealing with the refunding feature of the long bond. The call premium can often be taken as an interest expense in the year incurred and thus deducted in full from that year's tax liability. The cash flows associated with each financing plan can be transformed into after-tax cash flows in a direct fash-

---

[3] "The Timing of Corporate Refundings," *The Cost of Money for Corporate Finance*, Martin L. Leibowitz, Salomon Brothers, 1975.

Figure 3: Refundability of the Long Bond

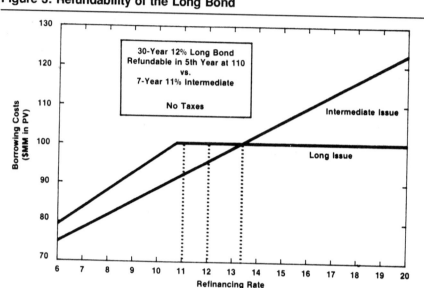

By contrasting the pretax results in Figure 3 with the after-tax results in Figure 4, one can readily see the main effects of the tax considerations. First of all, the break-even rate has been lowered from 13.35% (pretax case) to about 12.73% (after-tax case). Next, the point at which it becomes profitable to refund the long issue has been raised to 11.2%. In addition, the inclusion of tax considerations reduces the magnitude of the savings achieved by the intermediate issue under lower interest rate conditions. Overall, the general pattern of savings in Figure 4 reflects the enormous structural advantage of a long-term issue with a refunding option in the 5th year. This structural advantage is evident even in the face of a positive yield curve where the long bond requires a higher nominal coupon rate than the intermediate.

ion. These tax considerations should also be applied to the discount rate used to translate these cash flows into present value numbers. Thus, at a 46% tax rate, the 12% discount rate becomes an after-tax discount rate of 6.48%. When the after-tax cash flow associated with the unrefunded 12% long bond is discounted at this after-tax 6.48% rate, the present value of the borrowing costs again turns out to be $100MM. When the long issue is refunded, however, the present value of the borrowing costs is changed in a somewhat more involved fashion. The net result of transforming these cash flows into after-tax borrowing costs is shown in Figure 4.

Figure 4: The Impact of Taxation

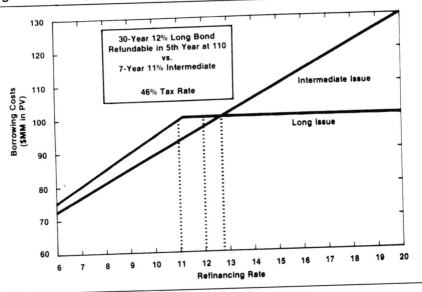

THE INTERMEDIATE'S CALL "WINDOW"

There is another refunding option that must be taken into account in any comprehensive evaluation—the intermediate's call "window." Intermediate issues are almost always callable, at the issuer's option, at some point prior to maturity. In Figure 5, the 7-year intermediate is assumed to become callable in the 5th year at par. Thus, at refinancing rates below the intermediate's original 11% coupon, the issue may be profitably called using the proceeds from a new 25-year issue. Essentially, this corresponds to an "accelerated refinancing." In any case, it enables the intermediate route to take advantage of the lower rates in much the same way as the long bond with its 5-year refundability. This serves to somewhat increase the magnitude of savings that can be achieved at refinancing rates lower than 11%.

INVERTED YIELD CURVES

Under positive yield curves, there are immediate opportunistic savings in coupon rate that can be achieved with intermediate issues. With flat or inverted yield curves, this *immediate* coupon rate savings disappears and the issuer must

Figure 5: The Intermediate's Call "Window"

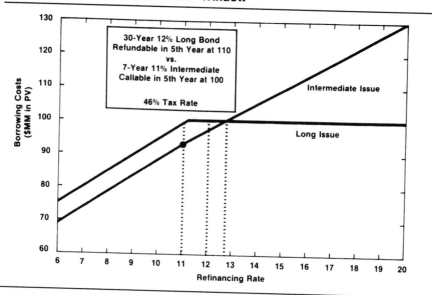

Figure 6: An Inverted Yield Curve Case

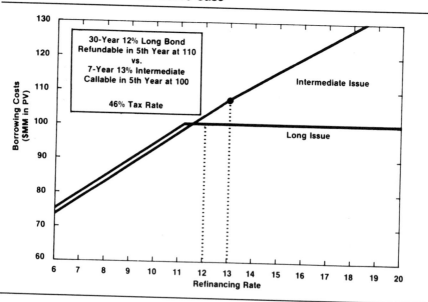

look to the *potential future* rate advantages in order to justify pursuing the intermediate route. Figure 6 illustrates an extreme case. Here the market reflects a sizable yield curve inversion so that the 7-year intermediate would have to be floated at a rate of 13%, i.e., 100 basis points above the 12% long rate. As shown in Figure 6, with this initial 100 basis point disadvantage, it is quite difficult for the intermediate issue to generate any significant reduction in borrowing costs relative to the long bond alternative.

LENGTH OF CALL PROTECTION

The results obtained in the preceding figures are obviously highly dependent upon the assumed structure of the respective debt issues. In particular, the situation changes dramatically as one looks at long issues having a 10-year period of call protection. Figure 7 illustrates one such case. Here the savings obtained by the intermediate can be considerable, especially at the lower refinancing rates.

There are many further facets to the overall question of matu-rity selection. More complex refunding criteria could be studied. One could explore more intricate patterns of interest rate movements over time. An approach could be

Figure 7: 10-Year Call Protection

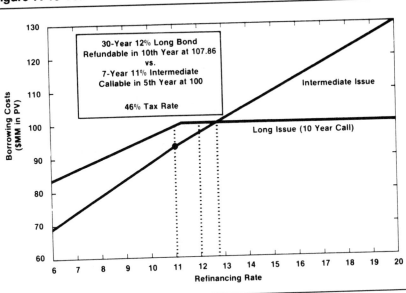

developed for using contingent discount rates that are linked to the interest rate scenarios. The special timing advantage associated with the long-term bond issue could be more fully analyzed. The impact of a sequence of intermediate refinancing vehicles could be studied, i.e., viewing the intermediate route as consisting of a series of multiple financings rather than a simple two-step bridge over the long-term planning period. The effect of various sinking fund provisions could be studied. One could also explore the somewhat more involved question of the impact of prospective open market purchases on the reduction of net borrowing costs. The cost of issuance of the various financing vehicles could be subjected to more intensive analyses.

In any specific financing situation, a comprehensive analysis will involve consideration of many of these factors. However, the main point of this article is to illustrate how a computer-aided graphical analysis can translate highly complex relationships into basically simple visual presentations. We have found this computer-aided graphical approach to be of substantial assistance to the corporate officer and his associates who must ultimately make these maturity decisions.

PART III D

Duration, Immunization
and Dedication

Chapter III D-1

The Dedicated Bond Portfolio in Pension Funds—Part I: Motivations and Basics

Dedicated bond portfolios allow a corporate pension fund to take advantage of favorable fixed income markets and of the actuarial system's willingness to provide special benefits for a minimum-risk investment approach. Purely as an investment approach, a dedicated portfolio serves as a least-risk asset, minimizing the risks involved in fulfilling a large class of nominal-dollar liabilities. Because the process is largely assumption-free, it provides the sponsoring corporation with an actuarially acceptable way to take advantage of available market interest rates to improve funding status.

Cash-matching, the simplest form of dedication, produces a fixed income portfolio that provides a stream of payments from coupons, sinking funds and maturing principal payments that matches a given liability schedule. In many cases the objective will be to assure fulfillment even under totally passive management—that is, no reinvestment. Reinvestment at positive interest rates, however, can lower pension fund costs without substantially increasing risk or complexity. Active management of cash-matched portfolios, within the constraints of the portfolio's conservative purpose, can be employed to take advantage of changes in the market structure.

Over the past few years, there has been explosive growth in the development of specialized bond portfolios dedicated to funding a prescribed set of

Martin L. Leibowitz, "The Dedicated Bond Portfolio in Pension Funds—Part I: Motivations and Basics," *Financial Analysts Journal*, January/February 1986. Reprinted with permission.

payouts over time. The techniques used to construct these portfolios have been variously referred to as dedication, immunization, matching and contingent immunization. The general term "matched funding" characterizes the fundamental objective of all these techniques.

Matched-funding techniques reduce the uncertainty of long-term investment results as they relate to the fulfillment of specific liabilities. Reductions in uncertainty can lead to a number of direct and indirect benefits at the corporate or institutional level. These are magnified when market interest rates are materially higher than the actuarial discount rate used to value the liabilities. This two-part article describes matched-funding techniques in nontechnical terms and provides a context for understanding their increasing popularity.

MOTIVATIONS FOR DEDICATING

In 1980, U.S. corporations faced a general squeeze on operating profits. At the same time, their corporate pension costs had increased substantially, coming to represent a major corporate cost factor. The "retired lives" component was becoming an ever larger proportion of many corporations' overall fund costs. Many companies, too, were facing a realignment of corporate operating divisions, in the form of terminations and sell-offs, that required a better characterization of the associated pension liabilities.

Because of the conservative nature of the actuarial process, pension funds continued to use relatively low actuarial rates and to recognize incremental portfolio returns only gradually. While this conservative treatment had led to greatly improved funding postures for many pension funds, some corporate managers began to feel that it was perpetuating an excessively large pension drain in both cash and accounting terms.

On the economic front, the threat of inflation appeared to be easing. More importantly, interest rates had risen to historically high levels. To many corporate sponsors, bonds began to look like a uniquely attractive investment opportunity for the long term, if not for the short term as well.

This confluence of events aroused in corporate pension sponsors a strong desire to reduce pension costs and a willingness to allocate larger portions of their overall assets to the fixed-income area. The dedicated portfolio fitted these needs like a glove. Figure A shows why.

Here, a hypothetical pension fund has a class of liabilities on its books at an actuarial return rate of 7%. When discounted at this rate, the liabilities have an actuarial present value of around $128 million. Suppose they could be fulfilled, almost dollar for dollar, with a cash-matched dedicated portfolio that cost $88 million at the 14% market yields available in the early days of dedication. Sup-

Figure A: Present Value of Retired-Lives Liability

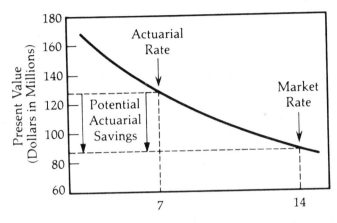

Assumed Actuarial Rate (per cent)

pose, moreover, that the dedication procedure was so assumption-free that the actuary would have no problem accepting it.

The $40 million gap between these two figures translates into a 31% reduction in the fund's *pro forma* liability costs, which would be realized on an amortized basis over time. The appeal of the technique is clear—it is, in effect, a significant funding deferment.[1]

This was the original motivation behind the dedication trend. But dedication is no longer the sole province of the cash or earnings-stretched company. It has become widely accepted (in at least some forms) by many leading actuaries and is now a fairly standard tool in the corporate pension planner's kit bag. A variety of corporations with the highest possible financial standing—and, increasingly, corporations with *over*funded pension funds—uses dedication.

---

[1] See M.L. Leibowitz and A. Weinberger, "Optimal Cash Flow Matching: Minimum Risk Bond Portfolios for Fulfilling Prescribed Schedules of Liabilities" (Salomon Brothers Inc, August 1981).

DEDICATION TODAY

The demonstrably improved funding status it allows remains a strong motivation for dedication. But the reasons go beyond a simple desire to reduce near-term contribution levels or to lower annual pension expense. The very reduction in unfunded status is taken as a value in itself by many of the parties in the pension process.

Pension liabilities are subject to increasing scrutiny by many sectors of the financial community—the Financial Accounting Standards Board, credit rating services and financial analysts—and many corporations are understandably eager to achieve better definition and control of their liabilities. Clarification of the true nature of the pension liability has become an increasingly important goal in itself, both for those within the corporate framework and for the various outside parties involved in the valuation of the firm as a whole.

The clarification function can be as valuable for overfunded plans as it is for underfunded plans. The dedication process offers overfunded plans a more precise identification of the magnitude of the surplus. This can help not only in achieving better control over future costs, but in identifying more appropriate investment functions for the nondedicated components of the fund's assets. With the better definition of nominal-dollar liabilities provided by a dedicated portfolio, surplus can be allocated more aggressively toward other goals— higher returns, wider diversification (including foreign assets) and enhanced inflation protection, for example. Indeed, some financial theorists have claimed that rational allocation of a fund's investments can be made only when the assets and liabilities are partitioned by risk characteristics.[2]

The role of dedication can extend beyond the specialized function of "marking" the actuarial rate to market rates within the framework of a conservative actuarial system. Even when actuarial valuation rates are chosen to coincide with long-term interest rates, dedication (or, more generally, some form of matched funding) is the only way a fund can protect itself against the possibility of the present value of its liabilities ballooning while interest rates decline substantially. From a pure investment point of view, matched funding here serves as the least-risk asset, in the sense of minimizing the risk of fulfillment of a large class of nominal-dollar liabilities.

Apart from any *pro forma* considerations, it can be argued that a large sustained decline in interest rates represents one of the most severe threats to the structure of private pension funds and public retirement systems. Such a decline would affect the investment rate of all further investable flows—whether derived from reinvestment or new contributions—and would also reduce the in-

---

[2] E.A. Mennis, J.L. Valentine and D.L. Mennis, "New Perspectives on Pension Fund Management," *Journal of Portfolio Management*, Spring 1981.

come-producing power of each dollar of the fund's asset value. Some dedications have been undertaken out of just such concerns. In at least a few cases, the corporations have established the dedication solely as an investment decision, without regard to actuarial recognition of relief. (In such "shadow dedications," of course, the actuarial benefits could presumably be applied for in the future, should they become needed.)

In most of the situations discussed above, however, the act of dedication represents both an investment and a corporate/actuarial decision. Without the market conditions that render matched funding with fixed income portfolios attractive and acceptable as an investment decision, there would have been few dedicated portfolios put into place over the past five years. At the same time, the wide range of corporate/actuarial benefits associated with dedication has been a significant reason for the extraordinary activity in this area.

MATCHED VERSUS PROJECTIVE FUNDING

Fixed income securities can serve a number of vastly different functions in a modern portfolio context. A bond portfolio can generate a well-defined cash flow that may be used to fund a schedule of planned expenditures. This is the basic approach we term "matched funding."

"Projective funding" represents a distinctly different viewpoint. Here, the fixed income sector is seen as an asset category that has a lower variability than equities and is useful as a "variability damper" to bring the short-term risk level of an overall portfolio down to tolerable limits. Bonds may also be used in a projective funding framework as an opportunity area for active management. This may involve the use of rather dramatic maturity changes in an effort to anticipate and capitalize on major interest rate movements. (Needless to say, this activity creates a variability of its own as an overlay.)

The matched-funding and the projective-funding functions are often confused. Although there may clearly be overlaps in terms of intent and purpose, it is useful to distinguish the purposes and weight accorded to each function in any given situation. Unfortunately, it is not uncommon for a fixed income component to be justified in terms of one function while actually being implemented in pursuit of the other.

Matched funding is a basically simple (and relatively ancient) concept. Given an obligation to cover a certain schedule of payouts, the simplest possible approach is to try to purchase an instrument that will provide a series of payments that exactly "match" the payout liabilities over time. Such an investment represents the ultimate in uncertainty reduction—the fulfillment of the scheduled liabilities is essentially assured.

PROJECTIVE FUNDING

A much more theoretical approach to asset allocation became the order of the day in the 1960s and 1970s. This approach was based on extrapolation of projected return distributions for various asset classes—equity, fixed income, real estate, foreign securities—to determine the mixture that would provide the most comfortable balance of risk and return.

Return was usually taken to be the expected return over the long term, whereas risk was usually associated with short-term variability. (This melding of long- and short-term characteristics was often justified in terms of short-term variability serving as a proxy for long-term risk.) The asset allocation was then chosen to provide the best possible expected return subject to tolerable variability.

This (admittedly crude) description is intended to cover a number of theoretical models that share one basic feature—the projection of assumed return relations. Although they all attempt to control risk through models of variability and covariability, they are all vulnerable to the underlying model risk—that is, the risk that the assumptions regarding the return behaviors may not prove adequate descriptions of reality.

These projective funding techniques have the important advantage of encompassing any asset class whose return process and associated variability and covariability can be condensed into a well-defined probability distribution. (Of course, one of the nagging concerns with such approaches is that they tend to neglect the special characteristics of individual assets; only the return distributions really matter.) Thus projective funding can be viewed as a sophisticated, theoretically based approach that is capable of incorporating virtually any range of potential assets.

Projective funding is thus a broad-based approach applicable to a wide range of complex investment problems. Matched funding, by contrast, is the ultimate in simplicity. But it can only be used in conjunction with fixed income vehicles applied to nominal-dollar liability schedules. Although it is a narrow approach, it is largely free of assumptions. Within its intended scope, it represents the ultimate in uncertainty reduction.

EARLY MATCHED-FUNDING TECHNIQUES

Matched funding has a long and respected history. Many of its early applications tended to be informal: Long-term liabilities were funded with a portfolio consisting of long-term maturities; intermediate liabilities called for an intermediate-maturity portfolio. This informal maturity structuring has always been a natural procedure for bond market participants. But recent years have seen the

Table I: Matched-Funding Techniques

Informal Maturity Structuring
Baseline Target
Contractual Arrangements
Formalized Management Procedures
- Dedication (Cash Matching)
- Immunization
- Horizon Matching
Contingent Procedures for Structured Active Management
- Contingent Immunization
- Contingent Dedication
- Contingent Horizon Matching
- Dynamic Hedging

development of a variety of procedures for constructing matched-funding portfolios; these are outlined in Table I.

With the development of rate-of-return performance measurement for bond portfolios, there arose a need for a more clearly defined portfolio target to serve as the performance benchmark. This target could be construed as a hypothetical portfolio representing the "optimal" blend of maturities, qualities and other sector characteristics for a given application. One suggested approach was the "baseline" portfolio and the related concepts of a "normal" or a "policy" portfolio.[3] The baseline portfolio may be quite well defined in terms of its component fixed income sectors, but it usually bears only a judgmental or intuitive relation to the funding of specific liabilities.

Recent applications of matched funding in the pension area have, as noted, been motivated by a combination of investment and corporate/actuarial considerations. In essence, these considerations derive largely from the willingness of the actuarial system to provide special benefits for a minimum-risk investment approach. However, the actuary typically requires that the bond portfolio be subject to some formalized procedure for assuring the continued fulfillment of the liability schedule.

One way to provide this formal assurance is through some type of insurance contract—e.g., GICs and annuity contracts. Many pension funds simply purchase an annuity contract for each retiring employee. Such contractual arrangements represent a form of matched funding.

More recently, however, many corporate sponsors have elected to retain control of their pension assets and to establish matched-funding portfolios consisting largely of marketable fixed income securities. This route provides the

---

[3] M.L. Leibowitz, "Total Return Management" (Salomon Brothers Inc, 1979).

corporation with greater flexibility, including the ability to review and revise overall asset allocation and to seek the opportunistic rewards of active management within the formalized matched-funding structure.

Below, and in Part II of this article, we examine the advantages and disadvantages of various formalized management procedures for creating matched-funding bond portfolios. Although "dedication" and "immunization" are often used interchangeably to cover all these techniques, we find it helpful to distinguish the individual techniques by such specific terms as "cash matching," "immunization" and "horizon matching." This reserves "dedication" for a more encompassing description of all the formalized techniques for bond portfolios dedicated to servicing a prescribed set of liabilities.

THE CONCEPT OF CASH-MATCHING

The typical cash-matching problem begins with a liability schedule such as the one depicted in Figure B. The declining series of liability payouts represents the retired-lives component of a pension system.

The objective of cash-matching is to develop a fixed income portfolio that provides a stream of payments from coupons, sinking funds and maturing principal payments that will match this liability schedule. More precisely, the prob-

Figure B: A Prescribed Schedule of Liabilities

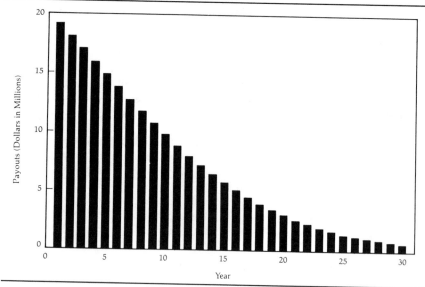

lem is to receive sufficient funds in advance of each scheduled payout to ensure that the payout will be met from the dedicated portfolio alone.

The prescribed payout schedule can theoretically take any one of many forms. In practice, however, certain general forms are more frequent. One common liability schedule is the "exponential decay" of Figure B. The payouts over this 30-year schedule start at $19.2 million and decline to $0.6 million in the last year. Payouts over the entire 30-year span total $215.60 million.

Suppose the market contains a sufficient quantity of acceptable bonds with maturities coinciding with each of the payout dates. Given the availability of a full maturity range of Treasury bonds, CATs and other zero-coupon instruments, an "exact-match" portfolio could theoretically be constructed. Figure C shows the maturity structure of this portfolio and its consequent cash flow. The combination of coupons and maturities at each payout date provides an exact match for the prescribed payout schedule.

THE GENERAL MATCHING PROBLEM

With an exact match, each dollar of coupon and principal receipts on a given date is immediately used to support the required payout on that same date; Figure C diagrams the process. This would seem to be an ideal fit for a cash-

Figure C: An Exact-Match Portfolio

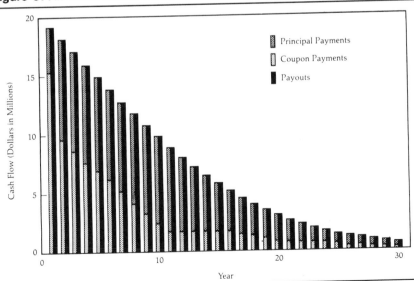

Cash Flow (Dollars in Millions)

Principal Payments
Coupon Payments
Payouts

Year

flow-matched portfolio. However, even when possible, such a portfolio is not usually optimal!

In practice, there will be a much larger universe of acceptable bonds that have coupon and principal payments on dates other than the exact payout dates of the liability schedule. This larger universe will generally contain acceptable bonds with yields higher than their exact-match counterparts. The inclusion of such securities naturally results in lower portfolio costs.

When such bonds are used in a cash-flow-matching portfolio, the coupon and/or principal receipts must be accumulated for their use on the payout date. These "prior receipts" must thus be reinvested at some rate until they are needed.

The fundamental appeal of cash-flow matching, however, lies in its simplicity. The appeal is thus reinforced when the matching portfolio can fulfill the prescribed liabilities even if no further investment action is ever taken. The assurance of fulfillment even under totally passive management is a natural and clear objective in many cases (even in situations where some form of risk-controlled active management is, in fact, pursued). The ultimate in a "total passive assumption" would require a matching portfolio to be designed so that any prior receipts would not be reinvested; in other words, the matching portfolio would be designed to fulfill its mission even when all reinvestment takes place at a 0% rate.

Figure D: General Matching Portfolio with Reinvestment at a 7% Rate

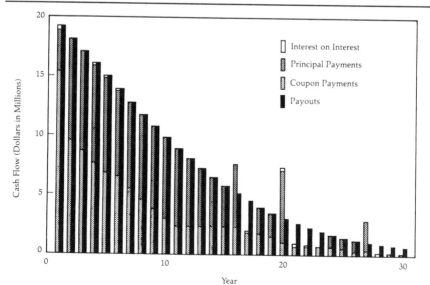

This assumption of a 0% reinvestment rate (or, equivalently, of no reinvestment whatsoever) represents an extremely conservative viewpoint. It may also be extremely expensive. Use of a more reasonable (but still conservative) reinvestment rate assumption opens the door to a wider range of potentially acceptable matching portfolios and to selection of a lower-cost portfolio.

The reduction in immediate costs from planning on the basis of a positive reinvestment rate can be significant. In these cases, the reinvestment rate—even over very short periods of reinvestment—becomes a critical parameter.

Figure D shows a matching portfolio based on the assumption that a reinvestment rate of 7% will be available throughout the entire liability schedule. The 7% reinvestment provides additional dollars both within each period and between successive periods. These increments of interest-on-interest prove just sufficient to enable the cash flow to meet all required payouts. The precise magnitude of the savings realized from a positive reinvestment rate will vary with market conditions and the permissible range of securities.

PORTFOLIO CONSTRAINTS

In practice, cash-flow-matching portfolios are subject to a variety of constraints imposed by both the logic of the problem and the degree of conservatism sought by the fund sponsor. These constraints relate to call vulnerability, quality, type of issuer, diversification across type and individual issuer, and the utilization of holdings from preexisting portfolios, among other things.

The call/prepayment vulnerability of specific bonds or mortgage-backed securities—whether for refunding, sinking fund or other purposes—is an important concern for any portfolio designed to provide a prescribed cash flow. The problem can be avoided by purchasing only noncallable securities. Such a prohibition would rule out many higher-yielding securities, however. A more practical approach is to accept fixed income securities that have coupons low enough that the prospect of a refunding call or mortgage prepayment is either improbable or so productive in terms of windfall gain as to assure adequate reinvestment income.

Similarly, the ultimate in credit quality would be a portfolio consisting of all U.S. Treasury securities. Again, this would prove to be expensive. In most cases, corporate securities of different qualities are acceptable, provided the mixture is appropriately diversified across industries and issuers.

Determining the appropriate overall credit level for the portfolio is aided by a tradeoff diagram such as the one in Figure E. The overall quality level of the portfolio will bear a rough relation to the relative overall yields of the portfolio holdings. Figure E shows how the cost of an optimal portfolio decreases with the increasing yield spread associated with relaxation of the quality constraint.

Figure E: The Effects of Quality on Portfolio Cost

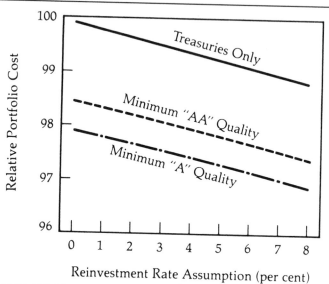

Actual savings will, of course, vary considerably, depending upon market conditions.

Another important constraint relates to preexisting bond portfolios. In many cases, a fund sponsor may wish to construct cash-flow-matching portfolios using as many existing holdings as possible. This may reduce the new cash required to establish the matching portfolio, reduce transaction costs, and avoid problems associated with the recognition of realized gains or losses in the existing portfolio.

The specific structure, aberrations and peculiarities of the marketplace at a given time will have a huge impact on the optimal cash-matched portfolio. The key is to apply the most modern computer optimization techniques to the broadest possible universe of truly available bonds identified with their truly available prices.

ACTIVE MANAGEMENT

Under certain market conditions, certain forms of active management may appear appropriate for even the most risk-averse sponsor of a cash-matched portfolio. The integrity of the portfolio's conservative purpose must be maintained, however, and this may limit the nature of acceptable management activity.

The active management of cash-matched portfolios has developed into a fine art. Many managers have been able to create significant cash takeouts and portfolio improvements by taking advantage of changing market environments. Although changes in the level of the market *per se* tend to have relatively little effect on a cash-matched portfolio, changes in the structure of the market can create sizable opportunities for active management.

Structural changes include reshapings of the yield curve, new issues with different maturities and coupons, and changing spread relations across various sectors. Revisions in the portfolio's cash balance and/or liability schedule over time may also lead to significant, clear-cut savings.

Although energetic management of a cash-matched portfolio can extract considerable incremental savings, it must be recognized that cash matching is a relatively stringent and tightly constrained period-by-period approach to the problem at hand. In the interests of greater flexibility and, perhaps, somewhat lower costs, it would clearly be desirable to have a procedure for funding scheduled liabilities that is not constrained at the outset by the necessity of meeting each individual payout. "Immunization" provides one approach to this goal. It and other dedication techniques—both passive and active—are discussed in Part II of this article.

Chapter III D-2

The Dedicated Bond Portfolio in Pension Funds—Part II: Immunization, Horizon Matching and Contingent Procedures

Immunization, horizon matching and various "contingent" schemes offer pension plan sponsors and managers an opportunity to minimize risk while retaining some degree of management discretion to pursue lower costs or higher returns.

Immunization calls for the creation of a portfolio of bonds whose value coincides with the present value of a given schedule of liabilities and whose duration, or interest rate sensitivity, is the same as that of the liabilities. Because changes in the portfolio's reinvestment income and capital gains will always compensate for interest rate changes, the value of the assets will always meet or exceed the value of the liabilities. Immunization offers greater flexibility than simpler forms of dedication, such as cash matching, but it requires portfolio changes over time and is susceptible to certain sequences of market movements.

Horizon matching combines desirable features of both cash matching and immunization. Essentially, horizon matching requires the division of the liability stream into two segments by selection of an appropriate horizon. The portfolio provides full cash matching of the liabilities that occur up to and including the horizon date; beyond that date, the liabilities are covered through a duration-matching discipline based on immuni-

Martin L. Leibowitz, "The Dedicated Bond Portfolio in Pension Funds—Part II: Immunization, Horizon Matching and Contingent Procedures," *Financial Analysts Journal*, March-April 1986. Reprinted with permission.

zation principles. This allows room for elective management while ensuring fulfillment of the specified payouts over the initial horizon.

By specifying a minimum portfolio return somewhat below the available market rate, the manager can create a "cushion spread" that provides the basis for several contingent schemes. As long as the portfolio retains assets sufficient to meet this target return, it may be actively managed. When adverse market moves threaten this return, the portfolio must be converted into a dedicated mode that will assure the target return. In exchange for accepting a target return below available rates, the manager receives the opportunity to capture profits through active management.

Part I of this article, in the January/February 1986 issue, discussed the motivations that lead corporate pension fund sponsors to adopt dedicated bond portfolios and described one of the simpler forms of dedication—cash matching.

Basically, a dedicated portfolio minimizes the risk involved in fulfilling a large class of nominal dollar liabilities. Furthermore, because the dedication process is largely assumption-free, it provides the sponsor with an actuarially acceptable way to take advantage of available market interest rates to improve funding status.

Cash matching produces a fixed income portfolio that provides a stream of payments from coupons and maturing principal that matches a given liability schedule. Cash matching is appealing because of its simplicity; it can meet prospective liabilities even if no reinvestment takes place. But it is a relatively stringent and constrained approach to the problem. The dedication techniques discussed below provide investment managers with greater flexibility and may also reduce the costs of dedication below those incurred by cash matching.

IMMUNIZATION

In 1952, British actuary F.M. Redington showed how to construct a portfolio that would "immunize" a schedule of liabilities against a certain range of interest rate movements.[1] The essence of this approach is a portfolio of assets whose value coincides with the present value of the scheduled liabilities and whose interest rate sensitivity exhibits the dominance pattern illustrated in Figure A.

This dominance pattern ensures that changes in reinvestment income and capital gains always compensate for interest rate changes. If interest rates decline, reduced reinvestment income is offset by increased capital gains. Thus,

---

[1] F.M. Redington, "Review of the Principles of Life-Office Valuations," *Journal of the Institute of Actuaries*, 1952.

Figure A: The Immunization Concept

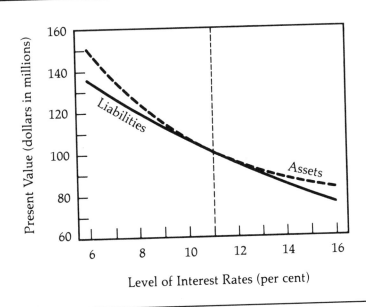

under a prescribed set of interest rate changes, the value of the assets will always meet or exceed the present value of the liabilities.

Immunization depends heavily on the present value concept. Regardless of when the cash flows arrive relative to the payouts, immunization should theoretically hold as long as the present value of the assets can be kept greater than or equal to the present value of the liabilities. In essence, immunization implies that the current interest rate can be "locked in" over the entire liability schedule.

The Basic Mechanism

The basic mechanism of immunization relies on several present value measures. First, the present value (usually taken as the market value) of the assets must match the present value of the liabilities (see Figure A). Second, the assets and the liabilities must have the same average life when weighted by the present value of their respective flows. This is the "duration" measure of average life.

Figure B, showing a series of four annual flows, illustrates this concept. The simplest average life is the midpoint in the diagram—2.5 years. In a present value context, however, this simple notion provides an incorrect sense of the

Figure B: Average Life of a Payment Stream

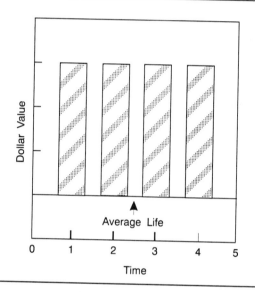

Figure C: Duration of a Payment Stream

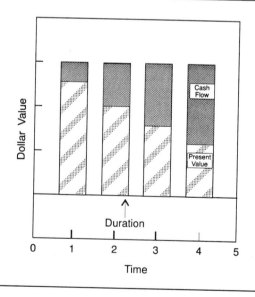

effective life of the flow. Figure C shows the "flow of present values" that results if we replace each actual dollar flow by its present value. The average life of this revised present value flow is the "Macaulay duration."[2] This is a more effective gauge of a cash flow's average life. It also provides a useful measure of a portfolio's sensitivity to interest rate changes.

Immunization requires maintaining the dominance pattern of present value shown in Figure A. Consequently, the asset and liability flows must be matched at the outset in terms of both initial present value and interest rate sensitivity. The latter is achieved by matching the durations of the asset and liability flows. The "duration model" is thus the key to the immunization procedure. More complex "second-order" conditions are required, however, to assure the dominance pattern of Figure A, even under relatively simple changes in interest rates.[3]

Unlike cash matching, immunization requires portfolio changes over time. Whereas cash matching fulfills liabilities through the originally promised flows from coupons and principal maturities, immunization generally requires that portfolio securities be sold at their theoretical values in order to preserve the dominance pattern of Figure A over time. Thus forced rebalancings, as Figure D illustrates, are an intrinsic part of the immunization process.

Pros and Cons

The structure of an immunized portfolio can take on many forms, as long as the portfolio's interest rate sensitivity meets the several conditions required to achieve the dominance pattern of Figure A. In particular, the schedule of cash flows from the immunized portfolio need not correspond exactly to the period-by-period payouts of the liability stream. This allows for a high level of flexibility in choosing an immunized portfolio, but it also means that the ultimate fulfillment of the liabilities depends far more heavily upon the specific assumptions underlying immunization theory. Unfortunately, the actual behavior of fixed income markets has frequently violated these assumptions (often radically), and this has raised questions about the practical reliability of immunization.[4]

Redington's initial proposal required that interest rates be restricted to a flat yield curve subject only to parallel movements. Modern techniques have en-

---

[2] See "Pros & Cons of Immunization: Proceedings of a Seminar on the Roles and Limits of Bond Immunization" (Salomon Brothers Inc, January 17, 1980).

[3] M.R. Granito, *Bond Portfolio Immunization* (New York: Lexington Books, 1984).

[4] M.L. Leibowitz, "How Financial Theory Evolves into the Real World—Or Not: The Case of Duration and Immunization," *Financial Review*, November 1983.

Figure D: The Immunization Process

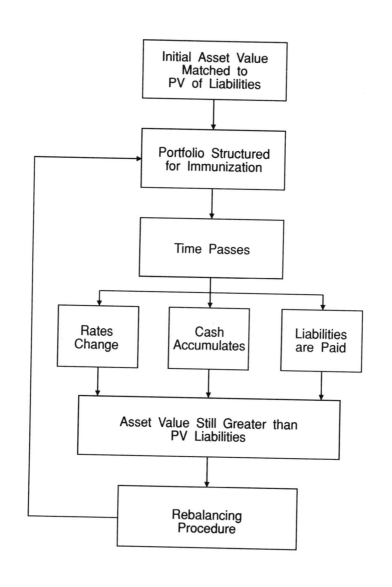

Figure E: Pure Immunization, Relative Costs and Risks

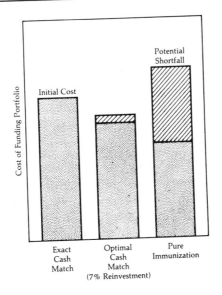

abled immunization to address a wider range of yield curve behavior, but immunization still remains vulnerable to certain sequences of market movements.[5]

A number of other factors also complicate the development of immunized portfolios, including the determination of target returns, changing yield-spread relations and changing bond universes over time.[6] Even with these problems, immunization offers the theoretical promise of a lower cost solution to the matching problem—as long as all the assumptions are met. As Figure E shows, this lower initial cost carries with it the risk of potential future pay-ups if market conditions depart sufficiently from the idealized immunization conditions.

The practical application of immunization has been limited by its greater complexity, its requirement for frequent rebalancing (which must be distinguished from the positive option of active management) and its vulnerability to certain market movements.

---

[5] See various studies in G.G. Kaufman, G.O. Bierwag and A. Toevs, eds., *Innovations in Bond Portfolio Management: Duration Analysis and Immunization* (Greenwich, Conn.: JAI Press, 1983).

[6] L. Fisher and M.L. Leibowitz, "Effects of Alternative Anticipations of Yield-Curve Behavior on the Composition of Immunized Portfolios and on Their Target Returns" (Salomon Brothers Inc, 1983).

HORIZON MATCHING

A properly balanced combination of cash matching and immunization could lead to a very desirable new technique. A number of such combinations have been explored; the concept of horizon matching was introduced in 1983.[7] Horizon matching incorporates the best features of both techniques.

Combining Two Techniques

Figure F illustrates the central concept of horizon matching. Essentially, the liability stream is divided into two segments by the selection of an appropriate "horizon." Then one creates a single integrated portfolio that fulfills the two liability segments in different ways.

In the first segment, the portfolio must provide a full cash matching of the liabilities that occur up to and including the specified horizon date. This cash-matched portion will be subject to the same stringent constraints that would apply to any cash-matched portfolio. In particular, any excess flows available for reinvestment are presumed to be reinvested at the specified (conservative) reinvestment rate prior to the horizon.

Suppose the horizon is five years. For the first five years, then, the sponsor will have full assurance that the horizon-matched portfolio will provide cash flows adequate to meet the specified payouts. The liabilities beyond the fifth year will be covered through a duration-matching discipline based on immunization principles.

Figure F illustrates the type of cash flows generated by a horizon-matched portfolio with a five-year horizon. In this case, the first five years are almost perfectly matched on a year-by-year basis. From the fifth year on, however, the asset flows are concentrated into a series of specific maturities. These are structured so that the overall system satisfies the interest rate sensitivity requirements as well as a number of second-order conditions.

This structure allows more room for elective management, while ensuring that the portfolio serves its function even if it remains passive for the first five years. The sponsor can simply pay out the liabilities as needed during the first five years and not be concerned about the passage of time. Even such a passive stance will maintain the dominance condition of Figure A throughout the course of the initial horizon period, as long as interest rate movements fall within the broadly prescribed range. (A properly constructed horizon-matched portfolio

---

[7] M.L. Leibowitz, T.E. Klaffky, S. Mandel and A. Weinberger, "Horizon Matching: A New Generalized Approach for Developing Minimum-Cost Dedicated Portfolios" (Salomon Brothers Inc, September 1983).

Figure F: Horizon-Matched Portfolio

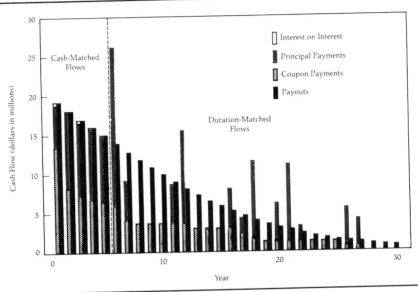

will enable the initial five-year horizon to be "rolled out" year by year under a wide range of market conditions, so that the portfolio remains cash matched for the first five years and duration matched for the rest.)

Costs and Risks

As noted, immunization suffers from its vulnerability to nonparallel movements in the yield curve. This vulnerability to yield curve reshapings is largely eliminated with a horizon-matched portfolio with horizons of three to five years or more for the simple reason that the most severe yield curve reshapings occur in the shortest maturities.

The benefits of horizon matching do entail some degree of additional risk, however. The horizon-matched portfolio, by definition, will have a lower asset value than the fully cash-matched portfolio. Consequently, there can be no assurance that the horizon-matched portfolio can be transformed into a fully cash-matched portfolio at any given time. Moreover, while the portfolio will retain its cash-matched characteristics through the horizon period without any further rebalancing, it is conceivable that certain types of market movements could lead to shortfalls in the duration-matched portion once the horizon period has passed.

Figure G: Horizon Matching, Relative Costs and Risks

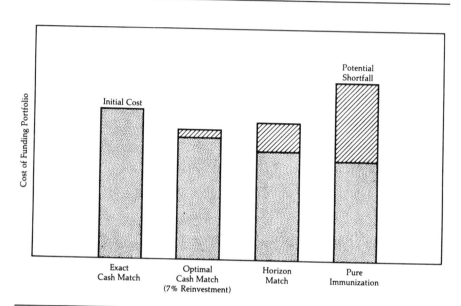

Thus, as Figure G shows, horizon matching may be viewed as falling somewhere between optimal cash matching and pure immunization in terms of both cost and risk of potential shortfall.

An additional advantage of horizon matching stems from the fact that the outer years of the liability schedule are often conservatively stated at the outset, hence are likely to change with the passage of time. Horizon matching offers cost efficiency because it fully matches the more definite near-term liabilities without being hostage to specific *pro forma* liabilities that are likely to change in amount and timing over the years. Moreover, by using the rollout procedure, the comfort of a definitive match of these near-term liabilities can continue to be maintained on a year-by-year basis.

CONTINGENT IMMUNIZATION

It has long been recognized that immunization procedures that stretch for the highest possible portfolio yields in a given market environment also incur the greatest risk of future shortfall. A "cushion" below this maximum rate provides additional comfort as well as flexibility to any immunization procedure. The concept of cushion flexibility can be extended to allow a significant degree of active management within a conservatively structured portfolio framework.

The Cushion Concept

As interest rates rose to unprecedented levels in 1981, acceptable minimum returns fell well below the maximum possible market rate. At a maximum market rate of 15%, a minimum return of 14% seems highly satisfactory. This 100 basis point "cushion spread" (from 15 to 14%) affords a degree of portfolio flexibility.

In fact, cushion spreads of 100 to 200 basis points create a surprisingly large latitude for the pursuit of active management. With these cushion spreads, a portfolio could retain some residual cushion above a promised minimum rate even if subjected to a series of repeated adverse movements—the traditional "whipsaw" nightmare of every portfolio manager. The realization of the degree of flexibility afforded by reasonable cushion spreads motivated the concept of contingent immunization.[8]

Figures H and I illustrate the effect of a 100 basis point cushion on an active strategy. Figure H shows the assets required at different interest rate levels to provide a 15% market return and a 14% "floor" return over a five-year period. At a 15% compounding rate, a $100-million portfolio would grow to $206 million in five years. To achieve this target value in a 15% rate environment, the entire $100-million portfolio would obviously have to be immunized at the 15% market rate. The assets required for the 15% promised return in a 15% market would thus be $100 million (point A in Figure H).

If, in this same 15% market environment, the five-year promised return is lowered to 14%, the five-year target value declines to $197 million. This 14% target could be achieved by investing somewhat less than the entire $100 million—$95.45 million, to be precise—in a 15% compounding vehicle. That is, the assets required to achieve a 14% return in a 15% market would drop to $95.45 million (point B in Figure H). The manager could literally lose $4.55 million and still achieve the 14% promised return on the original $100 million portfolio by immunizing the remaining $95.45 million asset value at the 15% market rate. The $4.55 million acts as a safety cushion, creating a significant opportunity for active management and "maturity tilts."

---

[8] M.L. Leibowitz and A. Weinberger, "Contingent Immunization: A New Procedure for Structured Active Management" (Salomon Brothers Inc, January 28, 1981).

Figure H: Required Assets to Achieve Five-Year Promised Returns in Different Market Environments

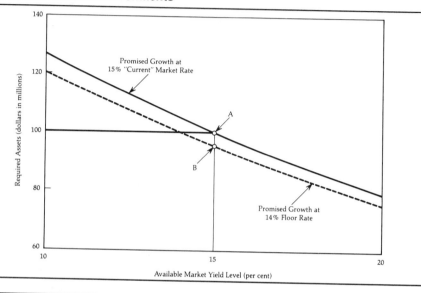

Figure I: Safety Margin for a Portfolio of 30-Year Bonds

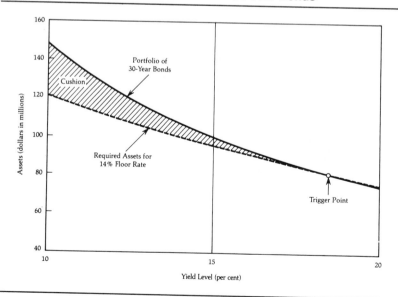

Active Management

The key idea is that the manager can pursue active strategies as long as he retains a positive safety cushion. Should the market turn against him and erode this safety cushion, he can immunize the portfolio and still achieve the promised minimum floor return.

Suppose, for example, that a strongly optimistic portfolio manager wishes to hold a portfolio of 30-year, 15% par bonds. He would have a duration of seven years—far longer than the five-year horizon. This portfolio would clearly not be immunized. In fact, the least adverse movement (i.e., upward move in rates) would immediately violate the required assets line for the 15% target rate. If the fund sponsor were willing to accept a lower, 14% floor rate as the minimum return, however, the price behavior of 30-year bonds could be superimposed on the 14% required asset curve, as Figure I shows.

If yields declined, the active strategy would prove successful and the safety margin of excess assets would rise with the superior performance of the 30-year bond portfolio. This successful move would enable the portfolio to generate five-year returns well in excess of the original 15% market rate. If, on the other hand, interest rates rose, the safety margin would decline and the portfolio's assets would approach the minimum required asset level.

Figure I shows that the active portfolio of 30-year bonds will decline to the required asset level after an upward rate move of about 350 basis points. At this point, the safety margin will have been totally eroded, and the portfolio will have to be immunized in order to ensure fulfillment of the 14% floor rate. In this example, the portfolio can tolerate adverse market movements of more than 350 basis points, even after having adopted the longest possible maturity stance in the par bond market.

It is this latitude for active management that enables the portfolio manager to implement a contingent immunization program—to accept the possibility of adverse movements, to tailor his posture in the face of such movements, and to have ample time to restructure his portfolio into an immunized mode, should that become necessary.

How does contingent immunization compare with classical immunization? Classical immunization carries a high opportunity cost—the forgone profits of successful active management. Contingent immunization restores this profit potential in exchange for the spread between the immunized rate and the floor return (see Figure J). More generally, in the context of matched funding, contingent immunization incurs a somewhat higher initial portfolio cost to gain flexibility for potential takeouts. With successful active management, these takeouts could significantly reduce the effective cost of funding the entire liability schedule.

Figure J: Contingent Immunization and Potential Takeouts

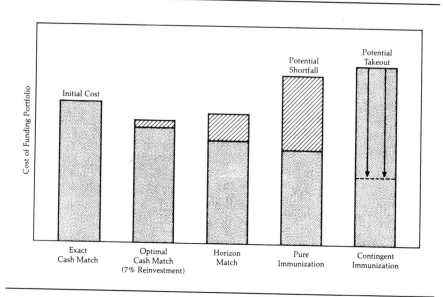

CONTINGENT DEDICATION

The concept behind contingent immunization can be generalized to include a range of fixed income objectives beyond that of a floor return over a fixed investment horizon. For example, a contingent dedication system would blend a cushion allowing for active management with a discipline that would assure—at the very worst—the fulfillment of a specified schedule of liabilities. In this case, the "floor" would be a cash-matched portfolio; the contingent portfolio would have to be managed to ensure that even under adverse performance, there would be sufficient assets to put the cash-matched "floor portfolio" into place.

A contingent system can be extended readily to other "floor objectives," such as various forms of horizon-matched portfolios. A relatively conservative contingent horizon match might consist, for example, of a portfolio that remains continually cash matched prior to the horizon and uses its safety margin to achieve controlled departures from the pure duration match of the post-horizon liabilities. A more aggressive contingent horizon match might consist of an active portfolio constrained only by the requirement that it maintain sufficient asset value to trigger into a horizon-matched floor portfolio under a worst-case yield curve movement.

Contingent systems can also vary in terms of the decision rules employed to achieve the minimum return conditions. These can range from relatively pure mathematical or mechanical procedures, such as those used in so-called "dynamic hedging" systems, to a general process that establishes "bet limits" for a given active risk posture.

Another source of variation is the character of the objective itself. Rather than some prescribed series of liabilities, the "floor" could be a specified performance index. The contingent portfolio in that case would be designed to pursue incremental return relative to this index.

The main idea is that contingent systems allow for active pursuit of return while ensuring some matched-funding objective.

THE CONTINUUM OF FIXED INCOME STRATEGIES

Figure K illustrates the interplay between matched and projective funding. The upper curve in the figure represents the classical risk-return relation. As one moves to the right, accepting greater risk, expected return should increase. This is the basic tradeoff involved in any analysis of projective funding procedures.

The lower curve in the figure corresponds to the minimum return associated with assurance of matched-funding objectives. With more strategy risk, the

---

Figure K: The Continuum of Fixed Income Strategies

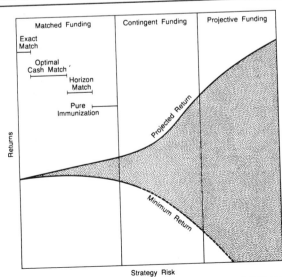

matched-funding component drops further and further away from the highest expected (or "projected" or "hoped for") return. Thus, with exact cash matching based solely on noncallable Treasury bonds, the level of projected return may be relatively low, but the structure of the return is fully coincident to the matched-funding objective. There is essentially no risk that the specified liabilities will not be met.

As we move toward more general forms of cash matching, returns increase, but the risks associated with achieving the minimum return required for the matched-funding objective increase also. Similarly, as one moves to the right, into horizon matching and then pure immunization, projected returns increase, portfolio costs decrease, but shortfall risk increases.

Contingent portfolios lie even farther to the right. "Conservative" contingent systems work with very moderate safety margins, but can take only moderate risk "tilts" away from the matched-funding objective. (In fact, such contingent systems might be "backed into" via successful reoptimization from some form of dedicated portfolio.) Highly aggressive contingent systems might be limited to quite minimal matched-funding "floors"—e.g., assuring fulfillment of only the first seven years of scheduled payments.

Finally, one enters the higher altitudes of expected return—virtually free-form active management with relatively little concern for the fulfillment of any minimum return or cash-flow objective. When applied to a pension context, this is pure projective funding. It places relatively few constraints on the investment manager and seeks the highest possible return from the asset class itself, as well as from unfettered management activity.

The Sponsor's Choice

The continuum of fixed income strategies provides the corporate sponsor with a considerable range of choices. In asset allocation, the sponsor can seek maximum projected return—which, if realized, is its own reward. Or the sponsor can pursue a relatively low-risk matched-funding strategy. These two strategy poles can differ so widely that they comprise two virtually distinct asset classes. It would not be at all inconsistent for the corporate sponsor to have one fixed income portfolio component in full active management while maintaining a dedicated portfolio.

As noted, a decision to dedicate is usually based on the interplay of corporate factors as well as pure investment considerations. In addition to risk reduction itself, dedication usually allows the corporate sponsor to reap significant actuarial benefits. These benefits derive from the fact that an actuarial evaluation, because of the conservative nature of the actuary's mandate, generally focuses on minimum return prospects. In a sense, then, the actuarial system (at least in the near term) often rewards the sponsor in accordance with his demonstrable minimum return, rather than for any notion (no matter how legitimate) of projected return.

The continuum illustrated in Figure K provides some insight into the circumstances that may motivate a corporate sponsor to opt for bond dedication. When the projected return is perceived as relatively flat, with little incremental return for fully flexible management (or for reallocation into other asset classes), then matched funding will have a natural appeal. Higher levels of available minimum return will augment this appeal, because of both pure investment considerations and the greater actuarial benefits associated with higher market spreads over the *pro forma* actuarial discount rate.

The Optimal Strategy

A corporate pension fund may pursue projective funding with virtually any asset class. Matched funding, however, can only be achieved with an appropriately structured fixed income portfolio. The wide range of techniques for implementing matched-funding objectives varies in their initial costs, opportunity costs, shortfall risks, portfolio and management flexibility, and projected returns. Each technique has its advantages and disadvantages.

At the same time, of course, the individual fund sponsor will have its own special needs and unique perception of the tradeoffs between the various forms of matched-funding and/or projective-funding strategies. No one procedure is best for all funds or all times. It is the interplay between their tradeoffs and individual sponsor needs that determines the optimal technique for a given fund at a given time.

Chapter III D-3

How Financial Theory Evolves Into the Real World—Or Not: The Case of Duration and Immunization

Finance is fundamentally a practical subject—a concept derived from man-made economic organizations. Finance does not seek to understand the underlying nature of the physical or the biological world—areas where the understanding is a sufficient goal unto itself. (I suppose that one could dispute this by claiming that every ecological system has its economic and financial facets. For example, even the squirrel that hoards his nuts in the fall in anticipation of a long winter has some sense of the trade-off between present and future value.) Basically, financial theory pursues a subject that is deeply rooted in the doing of practical things. Without the touchstone of potential application in the real world, financial theory would be ethereal indeed.

Therefore, I think it is most interesting—and important—to explore the interaction between financial theory and financial practice by asking the following questions: Does theory precede practice, with theoretical ideas trickling down—after some lag—into the real world? Does the practical world adopt the theory

This paper is based on a speech at the Eastern Finance Association Meeting on April 22, 1983, New York, New York.

Martin L. Leibowitz, "How Financial Theory Evolves Into the Real World—Or Not: The Case of Duration and Immunization," *The Financial Review*, Volume 18, Number 4, November 1983. Reprinted with permission.

only when, and as, needed? And when that theory is lacking, does the real world quickly need to stimulate the development of the required theoretical structure?

Rather than address these questions in the abstract, I would like to explore them in the context of a specific example: the development of the "duration" and "immunization" concepts and their recent integration into the real world of U.S. pension portfolios.

I take this tack for the simple reason that I happen to know something about the recent applications of these techniques. (This last comment should leave no doubt as to where my own axe rests. While I may occasionally make modest forays across the bridge into the world of theory, my association correctly tags me as a practitioner.)

THE ALGEBRA OF CASH FLOWS

By the very nature of finance, one should expect the study of cash flows to play a keystone role, and the algebra and calculus of cash flows to be a widely and intensively studied area. Thus, one might expect to find a well-developed body of knowledge dealing with all aspects of general cash flows:

- valuation;

- reinvestment and accumulation;

- characterization;

- equivalency classes;

- taxation;

- rollover/refunding;

- accountancy; and

- aggregation.

In particular, there are three aspects of cash flows that relate to the subject at hand: (1) How can the effective average life of a cash flow be characterized? (2) How can the relation of the volatility of a cash flow's present value (or market cost) to changes in interest rates be analyzed? (3) How can a portfolio of fixed-income instruments be constructed such that it will accumulate to a prescribed target value at some specified future date? Or, more generally, how can a fixed-income portfolio be constructed that will fulfill a specified stream of liabilities across a wide class of changing interest rates? This last question poses the immunization problem: How can you "immunize" a portfolio process against the "disease" of changing interest rates?

In the old days, if you asked a bond market participant to identify the remaining life of a bondholding, he would undoubtedly give you the time remaining to maturity, i.e., the time to the final principal payment. However, this final maturity date is an obviously unsatisfactory measure of average life for a self-amortizing private placement with periodic principal payments. A more appropriate market response would be to use the "principal average life," i.e., the time to each principal payment weighted by the relative magnitude of that payment. However, after a little more thought, you might begin to wonder whether one should not include the interest payments in computing the average life of the overall flow. This would result in the average time to each payment, weighted by the size of each respective interest and/or principal payment.

The next logical step would be to question whether a $100 payment one year from now should carry the same weight as a $100 payment twenty years hence. The answer is obviously no, and one might therefore search for a different way of weighting the impact of each payment on the total cash flow. It would not be very long before even a beginning student of finance would suggest using the present value of each payment as the weighting system. This method would result in a measure of average life that would be the average time to each payment weighted by the present value of that payment.

This is the reasoning—albeit in a far more elegant fashion—that Frederick Macaulay pursued when he developed his present value weighted measure of average life in 1938. Macaulay called this measure the duration of the cash flow. We now call it "Macaulay's duration."

Macaulay's derivation of the duration concept was only a small component of a monumental study entitled *Some Theoretical Problems Suggested by the Movements of Interest Rates, Bond Yields and Stock Prices in the U.S. Since 1856* [6]. Several aspects of Macaulay's work are relevant. (1) It was a classic, well-recognized document published by the National Bureau of Economic Research (NBER) and was broadly distributed among both academicians and market participants. (2) The entire study was motivated by an investigation of real world problems. (3) As mentioned earlier, the duration finding was treated simply as one small step in the overall study, i.e., Macaulay did not make a big deal out of it in his book.

The first question that we posed related to characterizing the average life of cash flows. The second question—seemingly different—related to the volatility of cash flows, i.e., the sensitivity of present value to interest rate changes. Or, equivalently, we can ask: How does the price of a bond change with fluctuations in its market yield? One would think that this problem need only be stated to be solved.

One naturally would expect the volatility to be somehow related to the cash flow's average life. Generally, longer bonds should be more volatile, so it is worth asking just how volatility is related to Macaulay's duration. It turns out that the relationship is a virtual identity. *The duration value is a direct measure of a bond's volatility.* Bonds with the same duration have the same volatility; a bond with twice the duration of another bond has twice the volatility. (Like all strong statements, this one is strictly correct only under certain conditions.)

Thus, Macaulay's duration plays a central role in the solution to both the first question—characterizing the average life—and the second question—identifying the volatility of cash flows. As we shall see, the duration concept is also fundamental in addressing the third question, which relates to immunization in its simplest form. This is the problem of managing a bond portfolio so as to achieve a target value at some horizon, regardless of intervening interest rate movements. Thus, for example, in a 15% interest rate environment, $1,000 invested at 15% compounded annually will grow to $2,000 in five years. Suppose one wants to put together a portfolio of bonds that will accumulate to $2,000 by the fifth year. Now, if an investor could buy five-year zero-coupon bonds at 15%, the problem would be immediately solved. However, the real world may not provide zero-coupon bonds of the right maturity or yield. So, failing the trivial solution of zero-coupon bonds, how can one construct a $1,000 portfolio of coupon bonds having a 15% yield, but with various coupon rates and maturities, that will grow in value to this 15% compounded target of $2,000 at the end of five years?

It turns out that Macaulay's duration also provides the key to this simple immunization problem. The initial portfolio should be constructed so that its Macaulay's duration equals five years. If the portfolio is then managed so that its duration always coincides with the remaining time to the target horizon, then the target will be achieved. In essence, this simple immunization procedure works by balancing reduced reinvestment income with just the right amount of capital gain at lower rates, and vice versa at higher rates.

All of this ignores many fine points—term structures, differential yield curve volatility, etc. Still, it is clear that duration plays an important role in the algebra of cash flows. One should, therefore, expect that the duration concept would have been accorded a respected position in both financial theory and financial practice. Let us now look at how these concepts were treated in fact, in academia and in practice over the years.

HISTORY IN ACADEMIA

I am indebted to Larry Fisher for his recollections and interpretation. I will try not to misquote him. I am indebted also to a fascinating little note by Roman Weil—"Macaulay's Duration: An Appreciation" [10]. In 1938, as we already discussed, Macaulay published his work in an NBER volume that received wide distribution and recognition by both practitioners and academics. In defining the duration concept, Macaulay focused on characterizing the average life of a generalized cash flow. He did not explicitly make the full formal connection with the volatility of present value.

In 1939, J.R. Hicks published an important volume, *Value & Capital* [3]. In this work, he was searching for a volatility measure as an elasticity. He developed a formulation for this volatility measure and recognized its time characteristics. In fact, he used the expression "average period" for his result. However, he did not seem to emphasize the applicability to all forms of generalized cash flows. Nor was Hicks aware of Macaulay's work, which had just been published the year before.

In 1945, Paul Samuelson published an article in the *American Economic Review* entitled "The Effect of Interest Rate Changes in the Banking System" [8]. As part of this development, he described a measure which he called the "weighted-average time period." Samuelson recognized the connection of the measure to interest rate sensitivity, and, in fact, also noted that his measure could be used to gauge a bank's asset/liability balance with respect to interest rate movements. Specifically, Samuelson observed that an institution with assets that had a longer average-weighted time period than that of its average liabilities would benefit from interest rate declines, and that the opposite was true for an institution with liabilities that were "longer" than its assets. Samuelson did not cite the works of either Macaulay or Hicks in his study.

Backing up for a moment, in 1942, T.C. Koopmans produced a private study for the Penn Mutual Insurance Company entitled "The Risk of Interest Rate Fluctuations in Life Insurance Companies" [4]. In this study, he pointed out that by matching the interest rate sensitivities of the assets and of the liabilities, one could theoretically achieve "immunization," i.e., one would be able to ensure fulfillment of the liability stream under "any" interest rate movement. Again, I do not believe that Koopmans cited Hicks or Macaulay.

Thus, within a period of six years, three economists—all of whom subsequently won Nobel prizes—addressed and solved roughly the same problem, pretty much independently. None of them was fully aware of the preceding work—even the published work.

This central problem and the excellent work done in this field by well-respected and well-known scholars somehow failed to achieve the "critical mass" of academic recognition. In 1952, F.M. Redington—an English actuary who worked for one of the major British insurance companies and ultimately became its president—delivered a beautiful paper that solved the immunization problem in two lines [7]. He showed, in effect, that when the durations of the assets and of the liabilities are equal, and when certain second-order conditions are met, the liabilities could be (at least) fulfilled under a whole class of interest rate movements.

Apart from a rather specialized paper by D. Durand in 1957 [1], little attention was paid to this body of work in the U.S. until 1969, when Fisher and Weil prepared a Center for Research in Security Prices report entitled "Coping with the Risk of Interest-Rate Fluctuations." A subsequent version was published in the *Journal of Business* [2]. The Fisher and Weil article explicitly addressed all preceding work except Hicks. They presented an analytic framework and also were the first to use actual bond data in a simulation analysis of immunization.

In 1972, I.T. Vanderhoof brought the whole subject to the U.S. actuarial profession in a superb article [9].

One common thread wove through all of these earlier works: They were masterful examples of theoretical research produced by remarkable theorists—often at a relatively early point in their careers. Most of these papers are worthy of study quite apart from their direct discussion of duration and immunization concepts. Most were directly stimulated by real world problems. Except for Fisher and Weil, the duration-immunization feature was only one small aspect of a bigger story.

The Fisher and Weil work acted like a seed in the groves of academe. There began a trickle of papers on duration and immunization, which became a flood by the mid-1970s. There were a number of valuable and insightful papers by such authors as Bierwag, Carleton, Cox, Fong, Hopewell, Ingersoll, Kaufman, Marshall, McEnally, Reilly, Ross, Tilley, Vasicek, Yawitz, and others. It became a hot topic for MBA and even Ph.D. theses. Careers were launched. At meetings, there were sometimes multiple sessions on duration and immunization. Duration and immunization continued to be the subject of papers, talks, sessions, whole meetings, seminars, and even several books!

This brief sketch of the academic evolution of duration and immunization raises a number of questions: Why such a fitful history of foundation-laying papers which lay unbuilt upon for so many years? Was it that the algebra of cash flows was considered too simplistic for serious discussion? Was it the focus on single-period returns, which became fashionable, that blocked the interest in duration with its multiperiod implications? Was it the lack of demand from the real world that failed to stimulate theorists to view this as a relevant topic? Was it part of the general academic neglect of fixed-income topics throughout this period? Or, is there some problem in achieving the "critical mass" for a topic to be deemed of academic relevance?

I pose this problem without knowing the answer, although I suspect that all of the above factors may have played some role.

THE HISTORY IN PRACTICE

While academia was taking its time developing these neat concepts, what was happening in the real world?

Prior to the late 1970s, the basic measure of a bond's life was the average maturity. This simplistic measure served in the early days for a number of reasons. First, in a low interest rate environment, the coupon flows were so small relative to the principal payments that the maturity effects dominated the total cash flow. Second, and perhaps even more important, is the fact that the institutional portfolios were far more homogeneous with respect to maturity. For example, corporate bond portfolios were primarily long term. Portfolios of Treasury issues were either short or intermediate term. One rarely found a broad mixture of maturities within a single portfolio. Hence, the average maturity tended to be a fair description of the portfolio's average life. Finally, the available coupons spanned a much smaller range. Thus, it was not necessary in the "old days" to contrast the "length" of zero-coupon bonds with that of 16% par bonds.

With respect to measuring volatility in the world of practice, the average maturity also served as a reasonable, although crude, yardstick. Where more refined volatility measures were needed—the U.K. Gilt market and the U.S. Treasury market, for example—simple surrogates for volatility were used. In the United States the surrogate was "yield value of 1/32." This works well for bonds priced near par and can be extended to discount and premium issues. In Britain, simple numerical calculations of percentage price volatility were performed using the omnipresent bond yield tables.

In Britain, this calculated volatility served even during the development of fairly sophisticated swapping activity based upon maintaining the invariance of the portfolio's volatility. The U.K. Gilt market was populated by many gifted actuaries, who were well aware of the connection between duration and volatility and even referred to the volatility measure as the "mean term." Yet, they found that the direct ±1 basis point calculation—totally devoid of theory—worked fine as a practical market tool.

In the third area, immunization, there was virtually no practical application in the U.S. until the late 1970s. This is in contrast to the U.K. where, according to Vanderhoof, from the time of Redington's paper, immunization has routinely been applied by British insurance companies.

In the practical world, this situation turned around starting in the late 1970s. The first light of the new era came when the bond portfolio management community began to use Macaulay's duration extensively. This was due to several new factors: (1) higher rates and broader coupon ranges, which made average maturity a far less satisfactory measure of average life; (2) greater volatility in rates; (3) development of intermediate-maturity corporate markets; (4) focus on short-term rate-of-return and performance measures; (5) greater maturity flexibility in bond portfolio management, i.e., portfolio managers no longer felt constrained to be chronic long bond buyers, and more managers would make interest rate bets, radically shifting their portfolio's maturity; (6) greater introduction of computer tools in bond portfolio management; and (7) perhaps, cynically, the embracing of Macaulay's duration by some bond practitioners in order to have modern tools akin to the modern portfolio techniques that were wreaking havoc in the equity area.

Practitioners' interest in immunization began toward the end of the 1970s. In 1978, an energetic young man named Len Wissner, who had learned about immunization from Vanderhoof at Equitable Life, decided that this was a message that should be brought to U.S. pension funds. There is no question that many practitioners first heard about immunization from Wissner and his associate, Jim Ward.

A number of computer software vendors began marketing packages that could provide various forms of immunization. Great curiosity started to well up in the bond portfolio management community during this period. In January 1980, Salomon Brothers sponsored a seminar on the "Pros and Cons of Immunization" and more than 400 bond portfolio managers attended.

Over the next several years, an increasing number of pension funds placed a portion of their funds under some form of immunization or cash matching. There were two basic motivations: (1) a desire to lock up the historically high rates, i.e., to circumvent the reinvestment risk; and (2) more importantly, a desire to capitalize on the actuarial benefits that could be reaped when immunization rates of 14% and 15% soared far above the actuarial rate assumptions of 6% to 8%. This meant that the corporate sponsor of a pension fund could achieve a significant immediate savings in the level of pension contributions through immunization.

Several billion dollars were placed under various forms of immunization during this period. Now that the market was "hot" on immunization, new ideas were gobbled up with very little lag. I had a personal experience to attest to this phenomenon.

In January 1981, Fred Weinberger and I published a report describing a procedure for blending active management with an immunization "floor" [5]. This concept—which we dubbed "contingent immunization"—offered the benefits of active management with the comfort of an assured minimum return, i.e., an option-like pattern of return created through a management discipline. Interest in the application of contingent immunization developed rapidly. Within eight months of the paper's publication, a major U.S. industrial concern placed almost $2 billion of its assets under contingent immunization with a group of managers. Another effect of this "hot" market for immunization products was that it contributed to the development of new fixed-income vehicles, such as original issue discounts, zero-coupon bonds, and stripped Treasury certificates such as CATS and TIGRS.[1]

---

[1] CATS: Certificates of Accrual on Treasury Securities. TIGRS: Treasury Investment Growth Receipts.

QUESTIONS POSED BY THE PRACTITIONERS' EXPERIENCE

This thumbnail history shows that the world of practice clearly lagged the world of financial theory in the application of these concepts. The lag is hardly surprising. One is tempted to view it simply as the natural course of events—the usual lag between theory and application. However, I believe that this natural explanation is not correct. I believe that practice would have continued to *lag* and these exciting tools would have continued to be ignored except for one big factor that made their use compelling. That factor is the extraordinary high rate levels that prevailed after October 1979. It was these high rates and the actuarial benefits that could be captured that led to a sudden acceptance and application of these "modern" tools.

QUESTIONS REGARDING THE THEORY-PRACTICE INTERACTION

If it was indeed the market events and not any "natural lag" that led to the market application of duration and immunization, then this raises another most interesting set of questions: Suppose that Macaulay had never published his 1938 work? Suppose the subsequent studies by Hicks, Samuelson, Koopmans, et al. had never seen the light of day? Suppose the entire body of theoretical literature in this area had been lost? Would the same market events have unfolded? Would the high rates of 1979-1982 ultimately have led to the development of an immunization concept, perhaps under another name? (And on a far more modest scale, would there have been a contingent immunization—alas, under some other, surely less elegant, name?)

The sober (and sobering) answer to all these questions is a very definite Yes! The market events would have focused sufficient attention on these problems that the theoretical solutions would have been created—and in fairly short order! I have little doubt that the market would have invented at least the *basic tools* for which it had a current, pressing need.

But the story does not end here; we must ask two further questions.

THE ENRICHED CONTEXT FROM THEORY

It may be that in this instance of duration-immunization the market did not appear to *need* the theoretical work. However, as King Lear pointed out so elegantly, raw *need* is a narrow definition of value. A broader question is, did the practical applications in the U.S. benefit from the prior theoretical work? The answer to this question—I am pleased to say—is "absolutely." The framework of understanding is far more complete and enriched than it would have been from a quick solution mothered solely by necessity. While necessity may indeed be the mother of invention, she is a hard-pressed working parent with two jobs, and she has little time or patience for "nurturing." The works of Macaulay, Weil, Hicks, Koopmans, Redington, Fisher, Vanderhoof, and others have provided a wealth of understanding that would have taken years to develop, no matter how strong the pressure from the "real world."

To anyone immersed in the field, the theoretical problems are far from solved, but now we are clearly dealing with an enriched theoretical framework that has surpassed the critical-mass thresholds for both practical relevance and for real theoretical interest.

WHAT MIGHT HAVE BEEN

In conclusion, I leave you with one last thought. Suppose—just suppose—that the theoretical exploration of duration and immunization had taken hold earlier in this country, say in the early 1950s, and suppose further that it had been communicated more aggressively to the entire world of financial practice.

Clearly, no refined theory is needed to identify the potential vulnerability in borrowing short and lending long. However, the principles of duration and immunization do have a clarity and a force derived from their precision and their coherent theoretical framework.

Is it just possible that they might have served to better crystalize the interest rate vulnerability of many financial institutions? Is it just possible that the financial managements of some of these institutions could have been moved to a somewhat more definite view of their duration mismatch? And is it possible that this more definite view could have been translated into a more positive control of their asset/liability mismatch? If that had transpired in just a few cases, might it not have avoided some of the more disastrous effects that accompanied the rise in interest rates throughout the 1960s and 1970s?

Obviously, no one knows the answer. But it is an interesting scenario to muse about. The question itself has implications—it seems to me—not just for the narrow topic of duration and immunization—but for much of financial history.

I leave you with that thought.

References

[1] Durand, D. "Growth Stocks and the Petersburg Paradox." *Journal of Finance* (September 1957): 348-63.

[2] Fisher, Lawrence, and Weil, Roman L. "Coping with the Risk of Interest-Rate Fluctuations: Returns to Bondholders from Naive and Optimal Strategies." *Journal of Business* 44, No. 4 (October 1971): 408-31.

[3] Hicks, J.R. *Value and Capital*. Oxford: Clarendon Press, 1939.

[4] Koopmans, T.C. "The Risk of Interest Fluctuations in Life Insurance Companies." Philadelphia: Penn Mutual Life Insurance Co., 1942.

[5] Leibowitz, Martin L., and Weinberger, Alfred. *Contingent Immunization*. Salomon Brothers Inc, January 1981.

[6] Macaulay, F.R. *Some Theoretical Problems Suggested by the Movements of Interest Rates, Bond Yields and Stock Prices in the United States Since 1856*. New York: National Bureau of Economic Research, 1938: 44-53.

[7] Redington, F.M. "Review of the Principles of Life-Office Valuations." *Journal of the Institute of Actuaries* 78, No. 3 (1952): 286-340.

[8] Samuelson, P.A. "The Effects of Interest Rate Increases on the Banking System." *American Economic Review* 35 (March 1945): 16-27.

[9] Vanderhoof, I.T. "The Interest Rate Assumption and the Maturity Structure of the Assets of a Life Insurance Company." *Transactions of the Society of Actuaries* Volume XXIV, Meetings No. 69A and 69B, May and June 1972: 157-92.

[10] Weil, R.L. "Macaulay's Duration: An Appreciation." *Journal of Business* Vol. 46 (October 1973): 589-92.

Chapter III D-4

An Introduction to Bond Immunization

IMMUNIZATION AND REINVESTMENT RISK

Immunization is a specialized technique for constructing and rebalancing a bond portfolio in order to achieve a specified return target. The idea is to closely approach or exceed the return target in the face of changes in interest rates, even radical changes in interest rates. In other words, one is trying to "immunize" the portfolio against the "disease" of changing rates.

Bonds, of course, have the nice property that they do mature eventually. As such, they tend to provide a certain natural immunity to changing rates, at least over planning periods ending with the bond's maturity. However, there still remains the uncertainty associated with the future rates at which the bond's coupon payments can be reinvested. It is this reinvestment risk that the Immunizer is trying to squeeze down to even closer tolerances. It should be noted that Immunization in the narrow sense is only one way of achieving the objective of Immunization in this broader risk-reduction sense. There are other ways—Guaranteed Investment Contracts, "matchings" of cash flows against liabilities, what has been called "R-cubed techniques," and so forth.

The following series of diagrams illustrates the basic idea of how Immunization works. If one wanted to immunize over a 5-year period, the first question is

Martin L. Leibowitz, "An Introduction to Bond Immunization," from *Pros & Cons of Immunization: Proceedings of a Seminar on Immunization*, Salomon Brothers Inc, January 17, 1980.

Figure 1: Realized Return from 5-Year 9% Par Bond Over a 5-Year Horizon

Reinvest. Rate	Coupon Income	Capital Gain	Interest On Interest	Total $ Return	Realized Compound Yield
0%	$450	$0	$0	$450	7.57%
7	450	0	78	528	8.66
8	450	0	90	540	8.83
9	450	0	103	553	9.00
10	450	0	116	566	9.17
11	450	0	129	579	9.35

---

why not buy a 5-year bond? Indeed, if one did that, the only risk would be the coupon reinvestment risk. If interest rates moved 200 basis points in a single leap, that reinvestment risk would make the realized return vary from the target return by about 35 basis points over the 5-year period (Figure 1). It is this 35 basis point risk that the immunizer seeks to reduce.

MACAULAY DURATION

One way to achieve this risk reduction is to buy a somewhat longer bond having a maturity of between six and seven years. At the end of the 5th year, this bond will have a capital gain or loss (Figure 2). If interest rates have declined and the interest-on-interest from reinvestment is correspondingly low, then the bond will have a capital gain which will just offset the reinvestment loss. By the

---

Figure 2: Realized Return Over a 5-Year Horizon from a 9% Par Bond Having a 5-Year Duration

Reinvest. Rate & Yield-to-Maturity At Horizon	Coupon Income	Capital Gain	Interest On Interest	Total $ Return*	Realized Compound Yield
7%	$450	$25	$ 78	$553	9.00%
8	450	13	90	553	9.00
9	450	0	103	553	9.00
10	450	-13	116	553	9.00
11	450	-26	129	553	9.00

* For illustrative purposes, this table is based upon the somewhat artificial case of a bond that can be purchased free of accrued interest.

---

same token, higher interest rates will lead to a capital loss which will be offset by the increased reinvestment income. The precise maturity that gives you this "magical" Immunization over the 5-year period is determined by seeking a bond whose "Duration" is 5 years.

Duration is a concept that was first proposed by Frederick Macaulay way back in 1938. He was searching for a way to characterize the average life of a bond in a way that would reflect the Present Value of its total cash flow. Figure 3 illustrates the dollar value of a level payment stream. The average life of this stream would fall at the simple fulcrum point indicated in the diagram. Figure 4 shows a similar level stream, but also illustrates the present value of each of the payments. Macaulay argued that a more appropriate measure of the life of any cash flow would be the average time point of the flow of *present values* (i.e., as opposed to simply the flow of raw dollar amounts). Since the earlier payments have a higher present value than later payments, this would lead to a fulcrum point that is shorter than the conventionally calculated average life (Figure 5).

This measure of the time to each payment, weighted by the present value of that payment, was given the term "Duration" by Macaulay.

Thus, a 1-year Bill has a Duration of one. A 2-year Bill, if you could buy one, has a Duration of two. Coupon securities, however, have Durations which are always less than their maturity. Figure 6 shows how the Duration of 9% par bonds grows with increasing maturity. Because of the way this curve bends at the longer maturities, it turns out that Durations of 10 or 11 are about the longest values that can be obtained in the market. (At higher rate levels, there is an even further shrinkage in the maximum Duration values.) Macaulay defined Duration in this way because he felt that it represented a much more logical measure of a bond's life. At the time, he failed to recognize that the Duration also had another, perhaps even more valuable, property—a gauge of the percentage price change associated with an incremental move in the bond's yield.

DURATION-EQUIVALENTS OF 0-COUPON BONDS

The combination of these properties enables one to use Duration to relate complex cash flows to simple cash flows. In particular, one can use the Duration concept to find real bonds that behave like 0-coupon bonds. For the theoretical case of a pure discount 0-coupon bond, the Duration will coincide with its maturity. Since 0-coupon bonds have no cash flows prior to maturity, they are free from the problem of coupon reinvestment. A 5-year 0-coupon bond priced to yield 9% would always provide the target 9% return over its maturity period— no matter what interest rates may occur over its life. Hence, the 0-coupon bond would be the ideal vehicle for an Immunization strategy. However, there is one minor obstacle: beyond the 1-year maturity range of Treasury Bills, such instruments do not exist!

It would obviously be desirable if we could somehow use real coupon bonds to obtain some of the characteristics of 0-coupon bonds. Fortunately, it turns out that this can be done and that the bond's Duration is the key link. A coupon bond with a given Duration is similar mathematically to a 0-coupon bond having a maturity equal to that Duration. For example, as shown in Figure 6, a 9% target return over a 5-year period could be achieved by either a 5-year maturity 0-coupon discount bond at a 9% yield rate or a 6.7-year 9% par bond. Both these bonds have the same Duration—5 years. Thus, the first step in a simple Immunization procedure is to construct a portfolio having a Duration corresponding to the length of the planning horizon.

THE NEED FOR REBALANCING

By setting the portfolio's Duration to the planning period, Immunization can be achieved for the case of a *single*, immediate jump move in interest rates. These are very stringent conditions compared with the actual behavior of the bond market. In particular, one must refine the Immunization concept to cope with repeated changes in rates throughout the planning period. The key to remaining immunized under multiple rate changes is to *maintain* a Duration that matches the time remaining in the planning period. For example, at the end of the first year, one would need a Duration of 4 to maintain Immunization for the remaining 4 years in the planning period. Unfortunately, that does not happen automatically as the portfolio ages. As can be seen from Figure 6, Duration does not march in lockstep with the passage of time. Thus, the next major conceptual step in an Immunization procedure is to *rebalance* the bond portfolio periodically, say semiannually or annually, so as to maintain the needed Duration value.

AN EXAMPLE WITH DECLINING RATES

Assume that this rebalancing can be accomplished on an annual basis. The initial portfolio consists of a 6.7-year 9% par bond appropriate to the 5-year planning period. Suppose interest rates move down 100 basis points a year each of those 5 years. After the first year, the portfolio will show a nice capital gain, providing a total return over that 1-year period of 13.07% (Figure 7). The portfolio will have a greater dollar value than would have been expected at a constant rate of 9%. That is the good news. The bad news is that this greater asset value can only be invested at the lower rate of 8%. For an immunized portfolio, the good news and the bad news offset each other—they combine into "no news." The increased asset value is just sufficient, when invested at the new lower 8%

rate, to keep the portfolio "on target" towards its original goal of 9% over the full 5-year period. As depicted schematically in Figure 7, the portfolio's return is like a string pinned down at the 0-year and 5-year points. The change in rates at year-end acts to pluck the string away from the horizontal, but it still provides the same 9% cumulative return over the full 5-year period.

At the end of the first year, the portfolio is rebalanced by swapping all assets into a new 8% par bond having the required Duration value of 4. Over the second year, interest rates decline by another 100 basis points to the 7% level. This results in a further capital gain, and a total cumulative return of 12.05% (Figure 8). The portfolio must once again be rebalanced into a 7% par bond having a Duration of 3. This process continues year by year, with 100 basis point declines followed by a total rebalancing (Figure 9). At the end of the fourth year (Figure 10), the cumulative return of 10.02% is just sufficient so that, when blended with the 5% rate available over the last year, the 5-year target of 9% will be realized.

AN EXAMPLE WITH RISING RATES

The preceding scenario moved in the happy direction of lower interest rates and nice capital gains. Suppose the market moves in the opposite direction—higher interest rates and big capital losses. Assume that interest rates increase 100 basis points a year. To gain a somewhat different viewpoint, a new schematic will be used to represent the growth of the portfolio's asset value over time (Figure 11). At the outset, let the asset value be $1,000. It would have to grow to $1,552.97 over the 5-year period in order to achieve the 9% target rate. The scenario now is that, after the first year, interest rates increase to 10%. This results in a capital loss, for a total return of 5%. This reduced asset value is still sufficient, given the higher 10% rate at which it can now be invested, to achieve the original 9% target. After rebalancing, this process continues with +100 basis point increases in the second year (Figure 12), the third year (Figure 13), and the fourth year (Figure 14). Finally, in the fifth year (Figure 15), there is just enough dollar value in the portfolio to reach the original $1,552.97 target after investment for the last year at the 13% rate. In this sequence of rate moves, the portfolio realized a capital loss every single year, but was able to exactly compensate for this loss through its increased earning power at the higher rates.

GENERAL SEQUENCES OF PARALLEL SHIFTS

In these two extreme interest rate scenarios, rates moved either consistently up or consistently down in successive years. The same results with varying interest rate moves could be achieved as long as the correct rebalancing procedure is followed. For example, rates could move up 100 basis points the first year, down 100 basis points the next year, and so on. Any such sequence of steps, as long as the Duration is maintained, will lead to the original target return (Figure 16).

The above examples were developed under the assumptions of a flat yield curve, having investment vehicles at every maturity, and moving in parallel jumps at the end of each year. Even under these ideal conditions, the Immunization process cannot assure an *absolute* matching of the target return, but the approximation will be very close over a very wide range of scenarios.

There are many technical questions that must be resolved for Immunization to be made into a practical market tool. This has been the focus of our research at Salomon Brothers. Some of the results of this research are described in the later section of this volume.

Figure 3: Average Life of Payment Stream

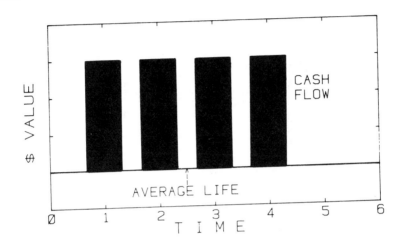

Figure 4: Present Value of Payment Stream

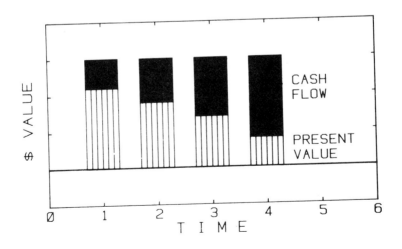

Figure 5: Duration of Payment Stream

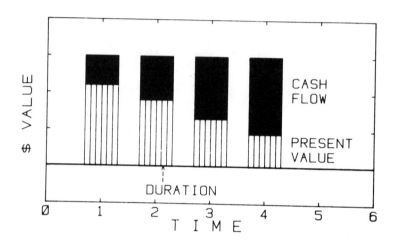

Figure 6: Duration versus Maturity

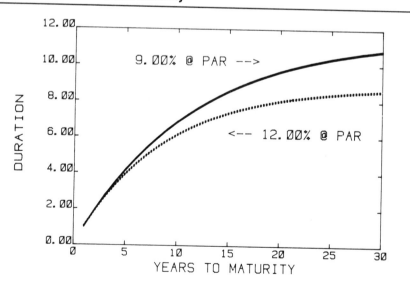

Figure 7: Immunization Through Matching of Realized and Forward Returns: 9.00% Target Rate—Flat Yield Curve with Annual Shifts of -100 Basis Points

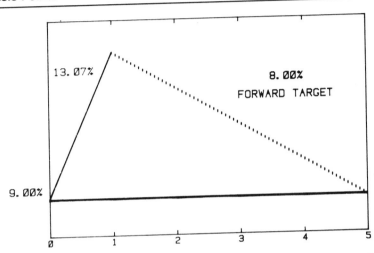

Figure 8: Immunization Through Matching of Realized and Forward Returns: 9.00% Target Rate—Flat Yield Curve with Annual Shifts of -100 Basis Points

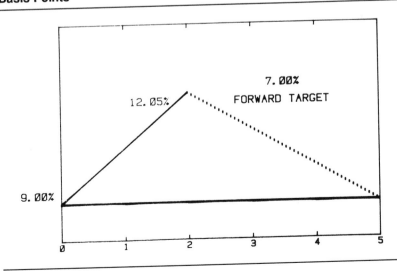

Figure 9: Immunization Through Matching of Realized and Forward
Returns: 9.00% Target Rate—Flat Yield Curve with Annual Shifts of -100
Basis Points

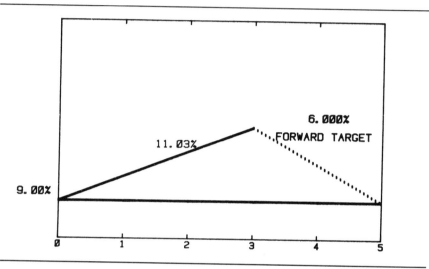

Figure 10: Immunization Through Matching of Realized and Forward
Returns: 9.00% Target Rate—Flat Yield Curve with Annual Shifts of
-100 Basis Points

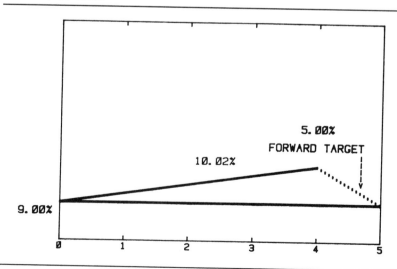

Figure 11: Portfolio Growth Through Immunization: 9.00% Target Rate—
Flat Yield Curve with Annual Shifts of +100 Basis Points

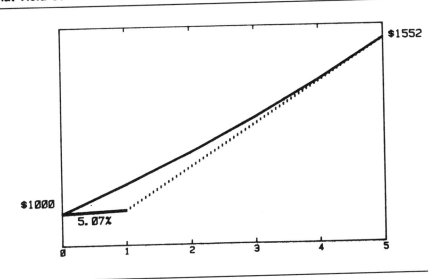

Figure 12: Portfolio Growth Through Immunization: 9.00% Target Rate—
Flat Yield Curve with Annual Shifts of +100 Basis Points

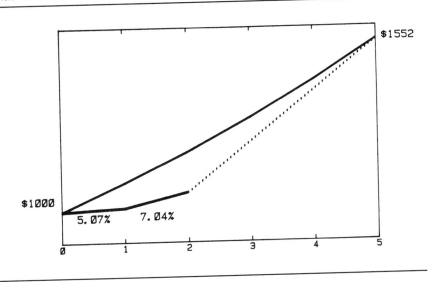

**Figure 13: Portfolio Growth Through Immunization: 9.00% Target Rate—
Flat Yield Curve with Annual Shifts of +100 Basis Points**

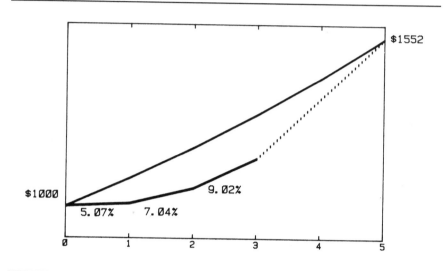

**Figure 14: Portfolio Growth Through Immunization: 9.00% Target Rate—
Flat Yield Curve with Annual Shifts of +100 Basis Points**

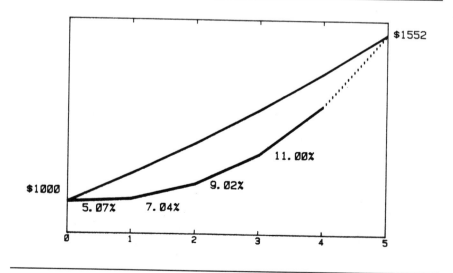

Figure 15: Portfolio Growth Through Immunization: 9.00% Target Rate—Flat Yield Curve with Annual Shifts of +100 Basis Points

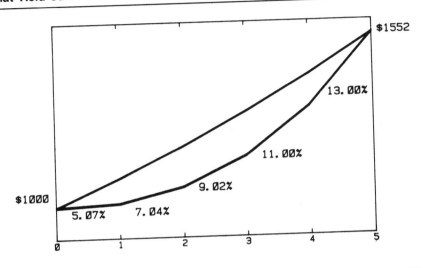

Figure 16: Immunization Returns Under Different Interest Rate Scenarios

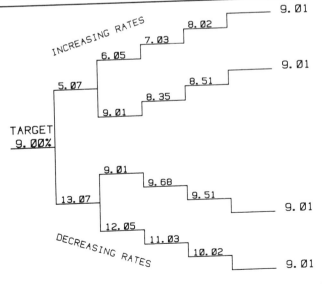

Chapter III D-5

Bond Immunization: A Procedure for Realizing Target Levels of Return

PART I: A PROCEDURE FOR REALIZING TARGET LEVELS OF RETURN

"Immunization" is the term coined to describe the design of bond portfolios that can achieve a target level of return in the face of changing reinvestment rates and price levels. Immunization techniques are relevant for many fixed income funds that must address the need to achieve a well-defined level of realized return over a specified investment period.

This need may arise from a variety of motivations. For example, one fund might have a lump-sum liability payment coming due at the end of the period. Another fund may need a relatively assured return for actuarial or accounting purposes. Another may have a simple desire to lock up what is thought to be a sufficiently high level of rates. Or, in yet another instance, the fund sponsor may simply wish to reduce the uncertainty in his overall portfolio by devoting a portion of his assets to achieving a specified return over a given period. Evidence of the growth in interest in this general form of investment can be seen in the proliferating role of the Guaranteed Investment Contract.

When asked to secure such a target return over a given period such as 5 years, a bond portfolio manager might at first respond by selecting a portfolio of bonds having a maturity of 5 years. If these bonds were of sufficiently high

---

Martin L. Leibowitz, "Bond Immunization (Parts I, II & III)," Salomon Brothers Inc, Part I -October 1979; Part II-November 1979; Part III-December 1979.

Table 1: Realized Return from 5-Year 9% Par Bond Over a 5-Year Horizon

Reinvestment Rate	Coupon Income	Capital Gain	Interest On Interest	Total $ Return	Realized Compound Yield
0%	$450	$0	$0	$450	7.57%
7	450	0	78	528	8.66
8	450	0	90	540	8.83
9	450	0	103	553	9.00
10	450	0	116	566	9.17
11	450	0	129	579	9.35

grade, then the portfolio would indeed be assured of receiving all the coupon income due during the 5 years and of then receiving the redemption payments in the fifth year. However, coupon income and principal payments only constitute two of the three sources of return from a bond portfolio. The third source of return is the "interest-on-interest" derived from the reinvestment of coupon income (and/or the rollover of the maturing principal). Since this reinvestment will take place in the interest rate environments that exist at the time of the coupon receipts, there is no way to insure that one will obtain the amount of interest-on-interest required to achieve the target return.

Table 1 illustrates this point. A 5-year 9% par bond will provide $450 of coupon income and $1,000 of maturing principal over its 5-year life. This would amount to an added return of $450 beyond the original $1,000 investment. However, in order to achieve a 9% compound growth rate in asset value over the 5-year period, the original $1,000 would have to reach a cumulative value of $1,553, i.e., an incremental dollar return of $553. This $103 gap in return has to be overcome through the accumulation of interest-on-interest. As Table 1 shows, this amount of interest-on-interest will be achieved when coupon reinvestment occurs at the same 9% rate as the bond's original yield-to-maturity. At lower reinvestment rates, the interest-on-interest will be less than the amount required and the growth in asset value will fall somewhat short of the required target value of $1,553.

This reinvestment problem becomes even more severe over longer investment periods. Table 2 shows the total dollar amount and the percentage of the target return that must be achieved through interest-on-interest for various investment periods ranging from 1 to 30 years.

This "reinvestment risk" constitutes a major problem in closely achieving any assured level of target return. However, there are ways of limiting this reinvestment risk. For example, Table 3 shows the total return and cumulative asset value for a 5-year bond over investment horizons ranging from 1 to 5 years. For the periods shorter than 5 years, the bond's price in Table 3 has been deter-

Table 2: Magnitude of Interest-On-Interest to Achieve 9% Realized Compound Yield from 9% Par Bonds of Various Maturities

Maturity In Years	Total Dollar Return	Interest-On-Interest At 9% Reinvestment Rate	Interest-On-Interest As Percentage Of Total Return
1	$ 92	$2	2.2%
2	193	13	6.5
3	302	32	10.7
4	422	62	14.7
5	553	103	18.6
7	852	222	26.1
10	1,412	512	36.2
20	4,816	3,016	62.6
30	13,027	10,327	79.3

Table 3: Realized Return from a 5-Year 9% Par Bond Over Various Horizon Periods

Reinvestment Rate and Yield-to-Maturity At Horizon		Horizon Period			
		1 Year	3 Years	4.13 Years	5 Years
	Coupon Income	$90	$270	$372	$450
7%	Capital Gain	$68	$37	$16	$0
	Interest-On-Interest	$2	$25	$51	$78
	Total Dollar Return	$160	$331	$439	$528
	Realized Compound Yield	15.43%	9.77%	9.00%	8.66%
9%	Capital Gain	$0	$0	$0	$0
	Interest-On-Interest	$2	$32	$67	$103
	Total Dollar Return	$92	$302	$439	$553
	Realized Compound Yield	9.00%	9.00%	9.00%	9.00%
11%	Capital Gain	-$63	-$35	-$16	$0
	Interest-On-Interest	$2	$40	$83	$129
	Total Dollar Return	$29	$275	$439	$579
	Realized Compound Yield	2.89%	8.26%	9.00%	9.36%

mined by the simplistic assumption that the yield-to-maturity coincides with the indicated reinvestment rate. This set of assumptions corresponds to a scenario where interest rates immediately move to a flat yield curve at the level of the indicated reinvestment rate and then remain there throughout the entire investment period.

Table 3 illustrates a striking compensation effect for investment periods of less than 5 years. For the 3-year period, at the 7% reinvestment rate assumption, the interest-on-interest naturally falls short of the amount required to support a target return of 9%. However, if the bond could be sold at the price corresponding to the assumed 7% yield-to-maturity rate, then a capital gain would be realized which would more than compensate for the lower value of interest-on-interest. Table 3 illustrates the well-known facts that over the short term, lower interest rates lead to increased returns through price appreciation while, over the longer term, lower interest rates lead to reduced returns through reduced interest-on-interest. For periods lying between the short term and the longer term, it is not surprising to find these two effects providing some compensation for each other.

This leads to the intriguing question as to whether there might be some intermediate point during a bond's life when these compensating effects precisely offset one another. Again, from Table 3, we can see that for a 7% reinvestment rate this offset does exist and occurs at 4.13 years. That such an offset point should exist is not, of course, surprising in a situation where there are two conflicting forces—reinvestment and capital gains—with one force growing stronger and the other force growing weaker with time. What may be somewhat more surprising is that when we look at reinvestment rates of 7%, 9% and 11%, we find that this offset point occurs at the same 4.13 years! (This is not perhaps intuitively obvious, although it can be readily demonstrated through mathematical analysis.)

In the context of the fund seeking an assured level of return, this finding has great significance. If we were seeking to achieve the guaranteed 9% return over 4.13 years, Table 3 tells us that we would have no problem doing so with the 5-year bond, no matter what reinvestment rates existed (as long as they followed the simplistic "flat yield curve pattern" assumed in the construction of Table 3).

This offset effect occurs because the *"Duration"* of a 5-year 9% par bond is 4.13 years. The *Duration* of a bond is a concept first introduced by Frederick Macaulay in 1938.[1] Essentially, it is an average life calculation based upon the *Present Value* of each of the bond's cash flow payments, including coupons as well as principal. For the theoretical case of a pure discount 0-coupon bond, the

---

[1] *Some Theoretical Problems Suggested by the Movements of Interest Rates, Bond Yields and Stock Prices in the United States Since 1856,* Frederick R. Macaulay, National Bureau of Economic Research, 1938.

Duration will coincide with its maturity. Since 0-coupon bonds have no cash flows prior to maturity, they are free from the problem of coupon reinvestment. A 4.13-year 0-coupon bond priced to yield 9% would always provide the target 9% return over its maturity period—no matter what interest rates may occur over its life. Hence, the 0-coupon bond would be the ideal vehicle for the problem of achieving a target return except for one minor obstacle: beyond the 1-year maturity range of Treasury Bills, such instruments do not exist!

It would obviously be desirable if we could somehow use real coupon bonds to obtain some of the characteristics of 0-coupon bonds. Fortunately, it turns out that this can be done and that the bond's *Duration* is the key link. A coupon bond with a given *Duration* is similar mathematically to a 0-coupon bond having a maturity equal to that *Duration*. For example, as shown in Table 3, a 9% target return over a 4.13-year period could be achieved by either a 4.13-year maturity 0-coupon discount bond at a 9% yield rate or a 5-year 9% par bond. Both these bonds have the same *Duration*: 4.13 years. In fact, for the assumptions underlying Table 3, any other bond yielding 9% and having a *Duration* of 4.13 years will achieve the 9% target return. Although far from obvious, this fact can be demonstrated using the mathematical analysis underlying Table 3.

Another feature of the *Duration* concept is that bonds having the same *Duration* will undergo the same percentage price change for small movements in yield-to-maturity. It is this characteristic of *Duration* that enables us to relate a bond's *Duration* directly to its Horizon Volatility.[2]

Table 4 shows the *Duration* of various bonds. Returning to the original objective of providing an assured 9% target return over a 5-year period, we can see that one should choose a bond having a *Duration* of 5 years (as opposed to a maturity of 5 years!)

To obtain a *Duration* of 5-years in a 9% par bond, it turns out that one would need a maturity of around 6.3 years. Table 5 shows how such a bond will indeed achieve the required growth in asset value to provide the 9% guaranteed return compounded semiannually.

This would solve the problem of achieving assured returns over specified periods except for one small point: movements in the interest rate structure are not so accommodating as to provide us with permanent shifts to a flat yield curve, as assumed in Tables 1, 2 and 3. Different patterns of rate movement can completely unwind these carefully contrived results. For example, in Table 5, suppose the reinvestment rate indeed moved to 7% and stayed there for most of the 5-year period, but then jumped up to 11% just before the fifth year when we had to sell the bond. This scenario would mean that we would achieve the reduced level of interest-on-interest associated with the 7% rate together with the

---

[2] For a more complete description of the Horizon Volatility concept, see *The Risk Dimension*, Martin L. Leibowitz, Salomon Brothers, October 5, 1978.

Table 4: Duration of Various Bonds All Priced to Yield 9%

Maturity in Years	Coupon			
	0%	7.5%	9.0%	10.50%
1	1.00	0.98	0.98	0.98
2	2.00	1.89	1.87	1.86
3	3.00	2.74	2.70	2.66
4	4.00	3.51	3.45	3.38
5	5.00	4.23	4.13	4.05
7	7.00	5.50	5.34	5.20
10	10.00	7.04	6.80	6.59
20	20.00	9.96	9.61	9.35
30	30.00	11.05	10.78	10.59
100	100.00	11.61	11.61	11.61

capital *loss* associated with the 11% rate. This combination would provide a total accumulated return of only $502, i.e., far less than the $553 required to achieve the target 9% return.

This immediately raises the following question: Is there any way for the portfolio manager to go about achieving the assured return in a way that will succeed in the face of the far wilder interest rate movements that occur in the real world? One can never achieve this growth in an absolute and precise sense. However, there are techniques for periodic "rebalancing" of the portfolio that will minimize the vulnerability of the achieved return across a wide range of interest rate movements. These techniques are generally referred to as "immunization strategies" since they attempt to "immunize" the portfolio's return against the "disease" of fluctuating reinvestment rates and changing pricing yields.

Table 5: Realized Return from 6-Year, 4-Month 9% Par Bond Over a 5-Year Horizon

Reinvestment Rate and Yield-to-Maturity At Horizon	Coupon Income	Capital Gain	Interest On Interest	Total $ Return*	Realized Compound Yield
7%	$450	$25	$78	$553	9.00%
8	450	13	90	553	9.00
9	450	0	103	553	9.00
10	450	-13	116	553	9.00
11	450	-26	129	553	9.00

*This computation has been based upon a bond purchased free of accrued interest in order to obtain a categorization of the sources of return that is consistent with the preceding tables.

There is an extensive theoretical literature in this field of "immunization strategies." Most of this research work has focused on the more academically convenient case of portfolios consisting of investments along an idealized Treasury yield curve. These portfolios are then periodically rebalanced so as to keep the portfolio's *Duration* equal to the remaining length of the investment period.

In exploring practical applications of an immunization strategy using actual securities from U.S. Treasury, Agency, and/or corporate markets, we have found that it is better to develop initial and rebalanced portfolios based upon criteria involving the Rolling Yield/Horizon Volatility approach. These procedures can also enable the portfolio manager to integrate his market judgments with an immunization strategy in an effort to achieve incremental improvements even beyond the target level of return. This technique could even be used to attune the portfolio risk to levels deemed appropriate for different funds. On the one hand, with stringently specified targets, the manager would follow a rather basic immunization strategy using his market insights primarily to provide additional insurance that the return target will indeed be met. On the other hand, a fund with a greater risk tolerance might establish a more relaxed target for minimum return, thereby allowing the manager to aggressively seek incremental return in the short term while still maintaining a risk-controlled portfolio posture relative to the longer-term horizon.

PART II: PORTFOLIO REBALANCING

In an earlier memorandum,[3] we described "immunization" as a way of designing (and revising) bond portfolios that can achieve a target level of return in the face of changing reinvestment rates and prices. Immunization is a highly specialized technique that obviously may not serve the purposes of all bond portfolios. However, it should be considered by those funds that have a particular need to achieve—with high assurance—a pre-specified level of return on some portion of their assets.

Multiple Changes in Rates

In the earlier report, we showed that it was possible to overcome the reinvestment problem and match the promised yield to maturity—*if* certain rather stringent conditions were satisfied. The key assumption was that interest rates immediately moved from their current level to some given level and remained

---

[3] *Bond Immunization: A Procedure for Realizing Target Levels of Return*, Martin L. Leibowitz, Salomon Brothers, October 10, 1979.

there for the entire planning period. Under this assumption of "a single move to a flat yield curve," the new level determines the reinvestment rate for coupon income as well as the final price of the portfolio. For an initial bond investment whose "Macaulay Duration" corresponded to the length of the planning period, these conditions would result in a realized compound yield that closely matched the promised yield-to-maturity. As noted in the earlier memorandum, this finding would be of only theoretical interest unless one could find ways to deal with more general and more believable assumptions. In particular, before the immunization procedure can really be put into practice, one must come to grips with the assured fact that there will be *multiple* changes in rates during the course of the planning period. In this study, we will explore how rebalancing procedures can be used to accommodate such multiple changes in rates.

It is easy to demonstrate the problems that arise when one drops the "single move" assumption and allows for "multiple movements." In the earlier memorandum, we set out to achieve a 9% target return over a five-year planning period. To obtain a 9% par bond having this Duration, we would need a maturity of 6.7 years.[4] If rates remained at 9% throughout the five-year period, a $1,000 investment in this bond would compound to $1,552.97 i.e., thereby providing the 9% return that one would expect in the "no move" case (Figure 1A). To illustrate the effects of a "single move" in rates, suppose that rates immediately jumped to 12% and then stayed there for the remaining five-year period. This bond would then generate a coupon income of $436.67, interest-on-interest of $162.49 and a capital loss of $42.91. As shown in Figure 1B, this amounts to a total Future Value of $1,556.25, i.e., slightly better than the 9% target level of return.

There is another way of viewing the events in Figure 1B. The sudden rate move generates an immediate capital loss of $131.00. In order for the remaining asset value of $869.00 to grow to the target level, a compound growth rate of 12% must be achieved throughout the next five years, e.g.:

$$\$869.00 \times (1.06)^{10} = \$1,556.25.$$

In this sense, the five-year return of 12% is needed to compensate for the immediate price loss incurred as rates jumped from 9% to 12%.

In any case, the example in Figure 1B illustrates that, under the "single move" assumption, even when the move is as large as 400 basis points, we still manage to realize the required target return.

However, let us see what happens under a simple case involving a "multiple move" in rates. Suppose, as before, that the first move in rates happens

---

[4] This is based on a normal bond structure with accrued interest attached to the bond at the outset. It is in contrast to the bond purchased free of accrued interest that constituted the model for the calculations in Table 5 of the earlier memorandum.

Figure 1: Portfolio Values Developed Under Various Interest Rate Patterns

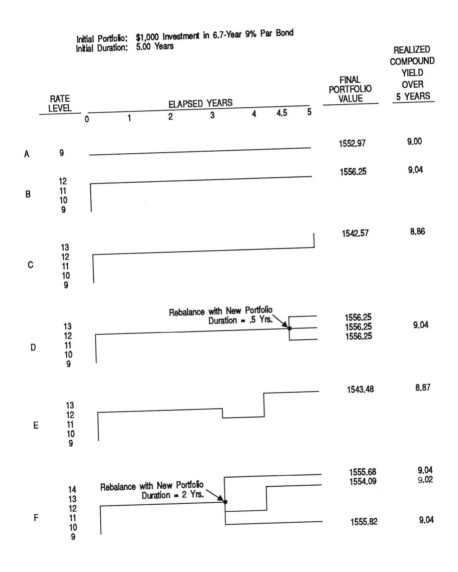

immediately after purchase and changes the yield curve to 12%. This rate persists for the next five years. But then, just before the bond is sold at the fifth year, there is a second jump in interest rates to 13% (Figure 1C). All numbers are then the same as in the earlier example, with the exception of the capital loss which now amounts to $56.58. This greater capital loss brings the total Future Value down to $1,542.57, for a total realized compound yield of 8.86%. Thus, under this simple two-move assumption, the portfolio falls short of its target by more than 14 basis points.

If immunization procedures could not deal with such simple "multiple movements" in rates, there would clearly be a problem in achieving any sort of application in real life. Fortunately, techniques exist involving portfolio rebalancing that can overcome this difficulty.

Rebalancing Using Duration

The problem arising from multiple rate movements can be traced to the way that a bond ages over time. Table 6 illustrates how our theoretical bond, having a starting Duration of 5 years, ages on a year-by-year basis. With each passing year, the maturity obviously gets shorter by one year, but the Duration becomes shorter by less than a year. For example, over the first year, the bond's Duration "ages" from 5.0 to 4.4, a drop of only 0.6 for the year. At the end of the fifth year, when we would clearly like to have a Duration of zero, the original bond has a Duration of 1.5 years. (Even when combined with the cash flow generated by coupon reinvestment, the blended Duration of the portfolio becomes seriously mismatched with the passage of time.)

This "Duration drift" can be overcome by periodic rebalancing of the portfolio. For example, suppose that at the end of 4.5 years, the portfolio had been "rebalanced" in the following fashion. The bond was sold at a yield-to-maturity of 12%, leading to a capital loss of $54.22 and a total Future Value of $1,468.16 (Figure 1D). The entire proceeds were then invested in a 12% par bond, having a

Table 6: Changes in a Bond's Duration with the Passage of Time—9% 6.7-Year Par Bond

Elapsed Time	Maturity	Bond's Duration	Target Duration	Mismatch
0 Yrs.	6.66 Yrs.	5.00 Yrs.	5.00 Yrs.	0 Yrs.
1	5.66	4.42	4.00	.42
2	4.66	3.79	3.00	.79
3	3.66	3.11	2.00	1.11
4	2.66	2.35	1.00	1.35
5	1.66	1.53	0.00	1.53

Duration of precisely 0.5. Clearly, this instrument would assure us of achieving a 12% rate of return over the final 0.5-year period. In turn, this would provide a 12% return over the entire five years and therefore bring the total value of the portfolio up to $1,556.25. In other words, by rebalancing prior to the second movement in interest rates, we would have immunized ourselves to the effects of that movement.

As a further example, suppose that a second move to 11% occurred at the end of the third year and was followed by a third move to 13%. Coupons from the original 9% bond would have been reinvested for three years at 12%, for one year at 11%, and for the remaining year at 13%. At the end of the fifth year, the bond would have been sold on 13% yield-to-maturity, engendering a sizable capital loss. This would lead to a total Future Value of $1,543.48, well below our target level (Figure 1E). However, suppose the portfolio had been rebalanced at the end of the third year, just before the interest rate jump, so as to have a Duration of exactly 2.0 years. This reset in Duration will help ensure that the final two years realize a 12% return. This lockup of the 12% rate over the final two years is just what is needed, together with the return achieved over the first three years, to ensure realizing the original target return of 9% (Figure 1F).

The preceding example illustrates the key idea underlying the immunization process. By rebalancing so as to continually maintain a Duration matching the remaining life of the planning period, the bond portfolio is kept in an immunized state throughout the period. This guarantees that the portfolio will achieve the target return promised at the outset of every sub-period. By working backwards, this implies that the original target return of 9% can be met in the face of multiple movements in interest rates. (The actual proof of this statement entails somewhat involved mathematics, which we do not intend to discuss at this point.)

This rebalancing procedure has a dramatic immunizing power even in the face of radical changes in interest rates. This is illustrated in Table 7 where interest rates increase by 100 basis points at the end of each year. Through annual rebalancing (based upon Duration), the total portfolio value grows to within four basis points of the original 9% target.

Rebalancing as Proxy for a Zero-Coupon Bond Over Time

At first glance, the success of this rebalancing procedure in keeping the portfolio on target may seem to be somewhat magical. An insight into the rebalancing principle can be provided by thinking in terms of our old friend, the zero-coupon bond. For any change in yield level, the zero-coupon bond automatically retains sufficient asset value to provide the original return over its life. For example, in Figure 1B, when interest rates jump from 9% to 12%, a $1,000 investment in a five-year zero-coupon bond would decline from $1,000 to $867.17.

Suppose one were to sell the zero-coupon bond immediately after this jump in rates, realize the $867.17 proceeds, and then hypothetically invest these funds into another five-year zero-coupon bond at its market yield of 12%. Over the remaining five years, the assured 12% compounding would enable the original $867.17 to grow to $1,552.97, i.e., thereby satisfying the original 9% return goal.

The "rebalancing" process just described is, of course, equivalent to continued holding of the zero-coupon bond. The five-year zero-coupon bond purchased at 9% has truly locked in the target 9% return over the five-year planning period. Regardless of the magnitude or frequency of subsequent rate movements, the zero-coupon bond always remains "on target." Moreover, the zero-coupon bond obviously remains *continually* "on target" even with the passage of time. In other words, it always retains the precise amount of asset value needed to realize the original target when compounded at the then yield rate for the remainder of the period.

The key idea here is that the price of the zero-coupon bond moves in lock-step with the change in the required dollar investment at the new interest rate level. Another way of saying this is that, with respect to interest rate movements, the volatility of the zero-coupon bond coincides with the volatility of the assets required to provide the promised payment in the fifth year. Thus, for a bond portfolio to retain the assets needed to stay "on target," it must have the same volatility as the five-year zero-coupon bond. Moreover, it must maintain this volatility equivalence as time passes. As shown in the preceding study, a bond's volatility is related to its Duration. In particular, the Duration of a zero-coupon bond coincides with its remaining life. Thus, in order to stay "on target" with time—as the zero-coupon bond does automatically—an "immunizing bond portfolio" must maintain the same Duration as the zero-coupon bond. An "immunizing" bond portfolio can maintain this equivalence through Duration-based rebalancing. Thus, Duration-based rebalancing can provide a bond portfolio that mimics the automatic "immunizing" behavior of the zero-coupon bond in the face of multiple interest rate movements over time.

Improved Rebalancing Using Horizon Volatility

In a theoretical sense, one should rebalance continually so as to maintain a Duration equal to the remaining life of the planning period. However, in practice, rebalancings are more likely to be scheduled for specific points in time, e.g., annually. In departing from the concept of a continual rebalancing, we can assume a well-defined rebalancing horizon, with the impact of yield movements concentrated at the horizon. Under these assumptions, the volatility of the portfolio is affected by a certain "horizon effect." The classical definition of Duration, while serving well in the case of continual rebalancings, fails to readily accommodate this "horizon effect." For annual rebalancings, such as those used in Table 7, this "horizon effect" accounts for a good portion of the portfolio's four basis point shortfall below the target return.

The concept of Horizon Volatility was specifically developed to accommodate this "horizon effect." It was first discussed in 1975 in a chapter by this author in the *Financial Analyst's Handbook*, and then refined in subsequent articles.[5] The Horizon Volatility does provide a better surrogate for the volatility of the ending portfolio than the Duration, even over one-year horizons. This raises the prospect of using Horizon Volatility as the rebalancing yardstick in an immunization procedure. Table 8 illustrates the results of applying such a procedure to the scenario entailing 100 basis point annual increases in rates. The resulting immunization procedure brings the realized return to 9.01%, i.e., one basis point better than the promised target, and five basis points better than the return achieved by the Duration-based rebalancing shown in Table 7. Of course, Table 8 illustrates only one specific scenario. In Figure 2, we show the results of Horizon Volatility-based rebalancing as applied to 16 different interest rate scenarios involving ±100 basis point annual jumps in interest rates. The results are quite startling in that all sequences lead to final portfolio values that differ by less than $0.11. In addition, all 16 scenarios produced realized returns greater than the targeted 9% level!

These results provide an empirical illustration of the improvement that can be obtained through the use of Horizon Volatility (rather than the classical Duration) as the basis for rebalancing in an immunization procedure. There are mathematical arguments as well, which will be presented in a forthcoming technical paper.

Further Techniques for Practical Immunization

The results achieved through rebalancing, especially those based upon Horizon Volatility, show how the immunization concept can be extended to deal with the prospect of multiple movements in interest rates. However, the discussion has still been in a context of a highly artificial set of assumptions, e.g., flat yield curve, parallel yield movements, no transaction costs, single bond portfolios, etc. Many further techniques are needed to develop bond portfolios in real-life situations which can effectively match target levels of return. Through a series of recent studies, we have made considerable progress in the development of such techniques.

---

[5] "An Analytic Approach to the Bond Market", Martin L. Leibowitz, in *Financial Analyst's Handbook I*, Portfolio Management, Edited by Sumner N. Levine, Dow Jones-Irwin, Inc., Illinois, 1975. "Horizon Analysis for Managed Bond Portfolios," Martin L. Leibowitz, in *The Journal of Portfolio Management*, Spring, 1975. *The Risk Dimension*, Martin L. Leibowitz, Salomon Brothers, October 5, 1978.

Table 7: Portfolio Growth with Duration-Based Rebalancing (Initial Investment = $1,000)

Period Ending Date	Rebalanced Portfolio at Start of Period			Results Over Year			Realized Coupon Yield		
	New Rate Level	Duration	Maturity	Coupon Flow and Interest On-Interest	Capital Gain	Total Proceeds	Over Year	Cumulative	Blended*
1 Year	9%	5.00	6.66 Yrs.	$92.02	$41.18	$1,050.84	5.02%	5.02%	8.99%
2	10	4.00	5.14	107.72	-33.03	1,125.52	6.98	6.00	8.99
3	11	3.00	3.66	127.22	-24.12	1,228.61	8.96	6.98	8.97
4	12	2.00	2.27	151.86	-13.61	1,366.87	10.95	7.97	8.97
5	13	1.00	1.00	183.47	0	1,550.34	13.00	8.96	8.96

* The 5-year return that would result if the portfolio value at that date were to be compounded at the existing new rate level for all remaining periods.

Table 8: Portfolio Growth with Horizon Volatility-Based Rebalancing (Initial Investment = $1,000)

Period Ending Date	Rebalanced Portfolio at Start of Period			Results Over Year			Realized Coupon Yield		
	New Rate Level	Duration	Maturity	Coupon Flow and Interest On-Interest	Capital Gain	Total Proceeds	Over Year	Cumulative	Blended
1 Year	9%	4.97	6.41 Yrs.	$92.03	$-40.71	$1,051.32	5.07%	5.07%	9.00%
2	10	3.97	4.91	107.76	-32.48	1,126.60	7.04	6.05	9.01
3	11	2.97	3.47	127.33	-23.44	1,230.49	9.02	7.03	9.00
4	12	1.94	2.21	152.08	-12.94	1,369.63	11.00	8.02	9.01
5	13	0.97	1.00	183.83	0	1,553.46	13.00	9.01	9.01

Figure 2: Portfolio Growth Across 16 Different Interest Rate Scenarios—Rebalancing Based on Horizon Volatility

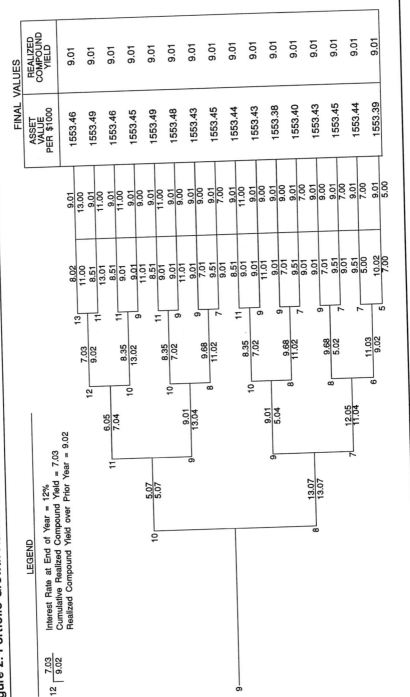

LEGEND

12 | 7.03
   | 9.02

Interest Rate at End of Year = 12%
Cumulative Realized Compound Yield = 7.03
Realized Compound Yield over Prior Year = 9.02

FINAL VALUES

ASSET VALUE PER $1000	REALIZED COMPOUND YIELD
1553.46	9.01
1553.49	9.01
1553.46	9.01
1553.45	9.01
1553.49	9.01
1553.48	9.01
1553.43	9.01
1553.45	9.01
1553.44	9.01
1553.43	9.01
1553.38	9.01
1553.40	9.01
1553.43	9.01
1553.45	9.01
1553.44	9.01
1553.39	9.01

PART III: THE YIELD CURVE CASE

In the previous two memoranda[6], we showed how a bond portfolio could be structured so as to achieve a target level of return in the face of changing reinvestment rates and price levels. We further showed how one could develop a rebalancing procedure that would maintain this "immunization" for the entire planning period. All of the preceding discussion took place in the context of a rather restrictive set of assumptions. In particular, the model focused on parallel movements of a flat yield curve.

In this study, we now take up consideration of yield curves which are truly curves, i.e., not flat. With this modification, one immediately runs into one rather surprising problem: finding an appropriate return target. In the flat yield curve case, it was clear that the initial yield-to-maturity constituted the appropriate target. However, with a more generally shaped yield curve, the necessary rebalancings force the portfolio into a sequence of yields and returns that may bear very little relation to the yield-to-maturity of the initial portfolio. This situation complicates the immunization process and reduces the extent to which the yield-to-maturity can function as a satisfactory return target. In this study, we show how this "targeting" problem can be solved through the use of the "Rolling Yield."

Portfolio Rebalancing Along the Yield Curve

Most of the academic literature on immunization has focused on yield curves consisting of hypothetical forward rates or zero coupon bonds. Under such circumstances, the return target is readily defined. However, when market participants speak of the "yield curve," they are generally referring to a maturity plot of the yields-to-maturity of Treasury par bonds. We shall adopt this market view of a par bond yield curve for the following discussion.

Figure 3 illustrates a particularly simple par bond yield curve. This yield "curve" is a straight line with a positive slope of 50 basis points per year. In the preceding memoranda, we made repeated use of an example where the initial portfolio had a yield level of 9.00% and a maturity of 6.41 years. In order to provide comparability with the earlier results, we have situated our yield curve in Figure 3 so that the initial portfolio would have this same maturity and yield.

In Part II, it was shown that a rebalancing procedure based on the Horizon Volatility provides the required portfolio volatility for the flat yield curve. This technique works equally well for the general yield curve case.

---

[6] *Bond Immunization: A Procedure for Realizing Target Levels of Return*, Martin L. Leibowitz, Salomon Brothers, October 10, 1979. *Bond Immunization—Part II: Portfolio Rebalancing*, Martin L. Leibowitz, Salomon Brothers, November 27, 1979.

Figure 3: A Simple Par Bond Yield Curve

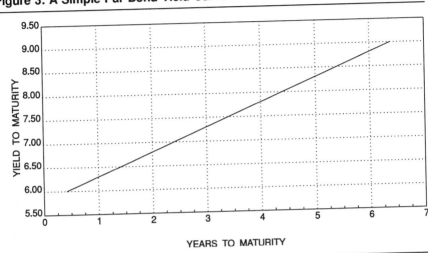

Figure 4 shows the Horizon Volatility associated with each maturity point along our simple yield curve. At the outset, a Horizon Volatility of 4 is needed and this can be achieved by a 6.41-year 9.00% par bond. At the end of the first year, however, a Horizon Volatility of 3 must be solved, and this is achieved with a maturity of 4.8 years.

Using the sequence of rebalancing maturities shown in Figure 4, we can proceed to determine the total returns achieved under the scenario of "no change in the market," i.e., the yield curve remains constant. This sequence of calculations is shown in Figure 5. The resulting total return is 8.56%, well below the initial yield-to-maturity of 9.00%. Clearly, the yield-to-maturity of an initial portfolio cannot function as an immunization target, even for this simple yield curve case. It remains for us to show that the 8.56% figure can constitute a target return that is indeed realized by the immunization procedure, and to then try to understand the nature of this new "targeting process."

The Rolling Yield

In a series of memoranda published beginning in 1977,[7] we tried to formalize the total return associated with the age-old investment concept of "rolling down

---

[7] *The Rolling Yield*, Martin L. Leibowitz, Salomon Brothers, April 21, 1977. *The Rolling Yield and Changing Markets*, Martin L. Leibowitz, Salomon Brothers, June 13, 1977. *The Risk Dimension*, Martin L. Leibowitz, Salomon Brothers, October 5, 1978.

Figure 4: Horizon Volatility

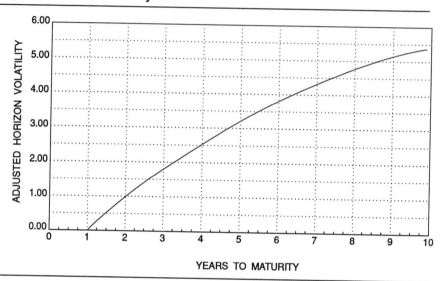

the yield curve." The term "Rolling Yield" was defined to be the total return associated with an investment at a maturity point along the yield curve under the assumption that the yield curve remained constant. From this assumption, it follows that the investment could be priced at the end of the horizon on the basis of its "aged" position on the curve. For example, for the curve shown in Figure 3, the 1-year Rolling Yield associated with an investment into the 6.41-year 9.00% par bond would correspond to the results of subsequently pricing that investment one year later at the 5.41-year point on the yield curve, i.e., at a yield of 8.50%. For any common horizon, one can compute Rolling Yields for investments at every maturity point. The resulting curve is referred to as the Rolling Yield curve.

In Figure 6, we have superimposed the Rolling Yield curve upon the par bond yield curve from Figure 3. For positively sloped yield curves such as this one, the Rolling Yield characteristically will lie above the yield curve itself. This results from the incremental return associated with the implied ability to sell out the investment at a "roll-down" yield that is lower than the initial purchase yield.

We have also highlighted in Figure 6 the specific Rolling Yield values associated with the sequence of maturities needed to achieve the rebalancing procedure shown in Figure 5. As one compares both the Rolling Yield numbers and the concept with the immunization procedure, it becomes apparent that realized compound yields achieved year by year in Figure 5 are nothing more than the

Figure 5: Immunization Procedure Applied to a Yield Curve Situation

Static Scenario: No Change in Curve Over Time
Initial Investment = $1,000

Period Ending	Rebalanced Portfolio at Start of Period			Results Over Year			Realized Coupon Yield			
	Parallel Shift	Initial Yield Level	Maturity	Coupon Flow and Interest On-Interest	Capital Gain	Total Proceeds	Over Year	Cumulative	Forward Target*	Blended**
1 Year	+ 0 b.p.	9.00%	6.41 Yrs.	$92.03	$21.18	$1,113.21	11.02%	11.02%	7.94%	8.56%
2	+ 0	8.17	4.76	92.81	17.56	1,223.58	9.69	10.35	7.37	8.56
3	+ 0	7.46	3.33	92.98	12.81	1,329.37	8.46	9.72	6.82	8.56
4	+ 0	6.85	2.12	92.62	6.91	1,428.90	7.35	9.12	6.29	8.56
5	+ 0	6.29	1.00	91.29	0	1,520.23	6.29	8.56	0	8.56

* The return realized from the immunization procedure for the remainder of the planning period, assuming that the then existing yield curve remains unchanged.

** The 5-year return that would result if the portfolio value at that date could be compounded at the "Forward Target Rate" for all the remaining periods.

Figure 6: The Rolling Yield Curve

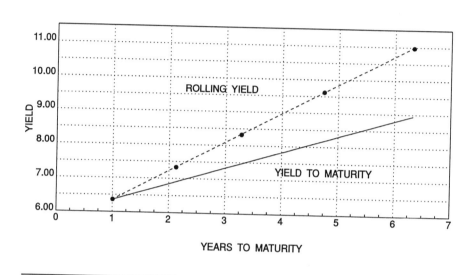

sequence of Rolling Yields as indicated in Figure 6. This result suggests that return targets for the yield curve case may be found by stringing together the appropriate sequence of Rolling Yield values.

Parallel Shifts of the Yield Curve

We have yet to demonstrate that this procedure maintains the target level of return in the face of changing yield curves. We retain the assumption that the yield curve changes through parallel movements. By a +100-basis-point parallel move in the yield curve, we simply mean that the yields associated with every maturity are increased by +100 basis points. As in Part II of this series, we allow for multiple movements concentrated at the end of each year. Figure 7 illustrates a scenario consisting of annual jumps of -100 basis points each. Rebalancing is carried out in accordance with the Horizon Volatility technique. The year-by-year returns are obviously different from those achieved under the static case of Figure 5. However, the total return comes in at 8.54%, only 2 basis points under the target level determined by the sequence of Rolling Yields.

The results of Figure 7 provide encouraging support for the Rolling Yield as a "targeting" process. However, it only represents a single interest rate scenario. In Figure 8, we show the results of 15 other interest rate scenarios, all charac-

Figure 7: Immunization Procedure Applied to a Yield Curve Situation

Annual Rate Movements: -100 B.P. Parallel Shift Per Year
Initial Investment = $1,000

Period Ending	Rebalanced Portfolio at Start of Period			Results Over Year			Realized Coupon Yield			
	Parallel Shift	Initial Yield Level	Maturity	Coupon Flow and Interest On-Interest	Capital Gain	Total Proceeds	Over Year	Cumulative	Forward Target*	Blended**
1 Year	-100 b.p.	9.00%	6.41 Yrs.	$92.03	$65.24	$1,157.27	15.16%	15.16%	6.93%	8.55%
2	-100	7.13	4.67	83.98	55.55	1,296.80	11.71	13.43	5.35	8.54
3	-100	5.41	3.24	71.10	40.78	1,408.69	8.45	11.75	3.81	8.54
4	-100	3.83	2.07	54.44	21.84	1,485.00	5.34	10.13	2.30	8.54
5	-100	2.29	1.00	34.20	0	1,519.20	2.30	8.54	0	8.54

* The return realized from the immunization procedure for the remainder of the planning period, assuming that the then existing yield curve remains unchanged.

** The 5-year return that would result if the portfolio value at that date could be compounded at the "Forward Target Rate" for all the remaining periods.

Figure 8: Portfolio Growth Across 16 Different Scenarios with Parallel Shifts of the Yield Curve
The Case of a Positively Sloped Yield Curve

LEGEND

| +100 | 7.75 |
| | 8.50 |

Parallel Shift of Yield Curve at End of Year = +100 b.p.
Cumulative Realized Compound Yield = 7.75
Realized Compound Yield over Prior Period = 8.50

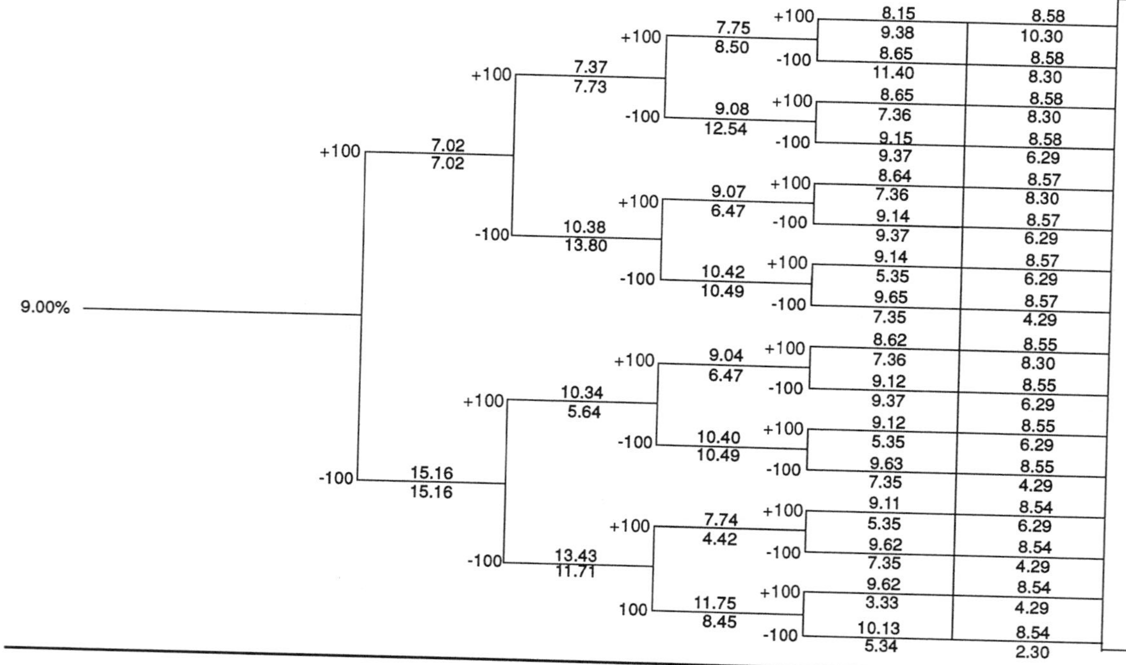

| FINAL VALUES | |
ASSET VALUE PER $1000	REALIZED COMPOUND YIELD
1552.12	8.58
1552.12	8.58
1521.90	8.58
1521.97	8.58
1521.39	8.57
1521.39	8.57
1521.17	8.57
1521.17	8.57
1520.15	8.55
1520.15	8.55
1519.93	8.55
1519.93	8.55
1519.34	8.54
1519.34	8.54
1519.13	8.54
1519.13	8.54

terized by ±100 basis points parallel movements in the yield curve at the end of each year. The results all fall within ±2 basis points of the "Rolling Yield target."

Other Yield Curve Shapes

The foregoing examples are all based upon one extremely simple, positively sloped yield curve. The question immediately arises as to whether this technique applies to more general yield curve shapes. In particular, one might ask how the Rolling Yield curve technique will adapt itself to the case of an inverted yield curve.

Figure 9 illustrates a yield curve having the same magnitude of slope and the same starting maturity/yield combination as in Figure 3, but sloped in an inverted direction. The associated Rolling Yield curve is indicated together with the maturity points, corresponding to annual rebalancing based upon Horizon Volatility. While we will not belabor the calculations, the Rolling Yield target turns out to be 9.40% for this yield curve case. In tracing out the same 16 different sequences of 100 basis point movements, the returns all fall within ±4 basis points of this target level.

Figure 9: An Inverted Yield Curve Case

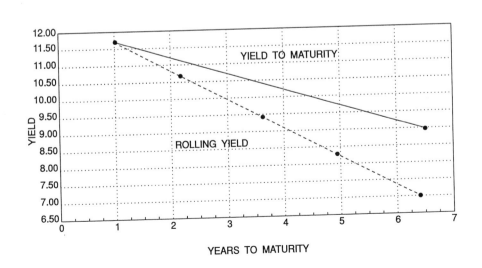

Numerous tests have been carried out on a wide range of both theoretical and historical yield curve shapes. The results are uniform. As long as one restricts the nature of market changes to parallel shifts—even of very large magnitudes—the realized returns from an immunization procedure closely track the target return determined by this Rolling Yield process. These empirical results can be validated through mathematical analysis. This mathematical analysis also indicates that, with a slight modification in the Rolling Yield technique as described here, one can achieve an even tighter tracking of the target return. (For actual historical yield curve movements, the tracking remains reasonably close to target, but the distinction between the Rolling Yield and the yield-to-maturity as a targeting basis becomes less clear-cut.)

In this memorandum, we have extended our discussion from the purely hypothetical flat yield curve case to the more general situation of sloped yield curves. However, it should still be recognized that we have retained a highly theoretical context for our discussion and our examples. Only parallel movements have been allowed. All such movements were concentrated at the end of the year. Only single bond portfolios were discussed. Transaction costs involved in rebalancing have been ignored. The continuous existence of all securities along the yield curve has been assumed. These and other implicit assumptions remain to be addressed before one can set forth to construct reliably immunized portfolios in the real marketplace.

Chapter III D-6

Bond Immunization: Theory and Practice

It is one thing to explore the theory of Immunization within the actuarial and financial research journals. It is quite another matter to face and overcome all the problems involved in putting this technique into practice. This section will describe a series of research studies addressed to the development of guidelines and tools for applying Immunization procedures in real bond markets.

There are four broad areas that will be discussed. Many of the discussions of Immunization take place within the highly theoretical framework based on parallel movements of a flat yield curve. The first set of results is based on work, not with a flat yield curve, but with real starting yield curves that have occurred over the past 22 years. In order to isolate the specific effects of departures from this theoretical model, the first part of the paper assumes that these initial real curves are subject to a series of parallel movements. The second part explores the results of again starting with real historical yield curves, but then using the actual historical sequence of yield curves. The third part deals with the effect of different types of portfolio structures on the Immunization process. The fourth part describes techniques for constructing and monitoring Immunized portfolios using specific securities from the corporate, agency and Treasury markets.

Martin L. Leibowitz, "Theory and Practice," from *Pros & Cons of Immunization: Proceedings of a Seminar on Immunization*, Salomon Brothers Inc, January 17, 1980.

PARALLEL MOVEMENTS OF ACTUAL YIELD CURVES

In the initial studies, the basic research tool was a computer simulation of 5-year Immunization plans using simple point portfolios. These portfolios consisted of a single "maturity point" along the yield curve. The simulations utilized a data base consisting of U.S. Treasury yield curves for the beginning of each month starting with January 1958 and ending in December 1979.

Figure 1 illustrates the procedure followed in the first series of studies. The analysis began with the actual yield curve shape on a given date. Then, at the end of each year, the curve was moved in a parallel fashion by a specified yield increment. Figure 1 illustrates the case of an annual 50 basis point downward move. Rebalancing takes place on an annual basis. By evaluating the Immunization strategy in this context, one can determine the effect of the historical starting yield curve shape. In other words, this will expose and isolate problems arising from the flat yield curve assumption.

SIMULATION TESTS OF THE YTM TARGET

Figure 2 shows the results. Each point along the horizontal axis represents a different starting yield curve. For example, the first Immunization plan began in January 1958. An initial point portfolio was constructed that had a Duration of 5 years in the context of that yield curve. This initial portfolio had a yield-to-maturity (YTM) of 2.78%. In accordance with the usual procedure, this value of 2.78% was then taken as the return target for the 5-year Immunization plan. At the end of each year, the market was assumed to have undergone a 50 basis point downward move across all maturities. The simulation was then carried out with the portfolio being rebalanced every year into a portfolio having the needed Duration.

The cumulative return realized by this Immunization process turned out to be 2.76%. This represented an error of -2 basis points relative to the original YTM-based target of 2.78%. The vertical axis in Figure 2 indicates the magnitude of this "tracking error." This "miss" of -2 basis points for the January 1958 curve is the leftmost point in Figure 2. The next point corresponds to the miss relative to the initial YTM target for the 5-year Immunization plan beginning with the yield curve for February 1958. The plot thus depicts the tracking errors for different Immunization plans starting on successive months from January 1958 through December 1974.

The worst variation occurred in March 1971—a tracking error of -21 basis points. At first, that doesn't sound so bad. In fact, Figure 2 would seem to provide evidence that Immunization strategies have done very well. The problem is these results are based on parallel moves. These are the idealized conditions

Figure 1: Parallel Yield Curves

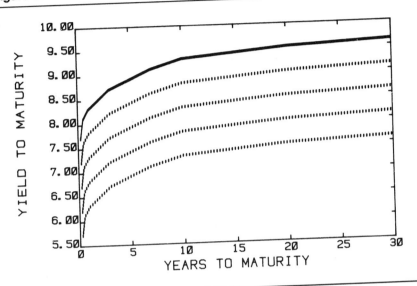

Figure 2: Simulated Immunization Returns Over YTM Target
Annual Parallel Shifts of -50 Basis Points

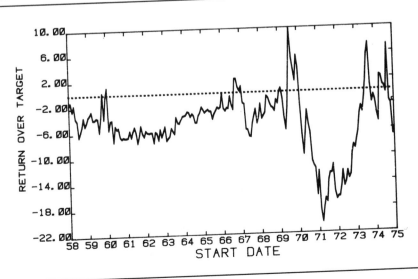

under which Immunization is supposed to function perfectly. Under such idealized circumstances, it is rather disappointing to see the sequence of misses shown in Figure 2.

THE ROLLING YIELD TARGET

Is the Immunization concept at fault? Not really. It turns out that the problem actually has to do with taking the yield-to-maturity as a target for the Immunization process. Appealing as the yield-to-maturity might be for a flat yield curve, it simply does not work for the case of a shaped yield curve. For this general case of a real *curve*, it can be shown that the appropriate target value must be derived from the sequence of returns that would result from rebalancing along the initial yield curve. It turns out that this finding was closely related to earlier research that attempted to characterize returns from rolling down constant yield curves.

This new targeting process is illustrated in Figure 3. Assume that the sloped yield curve remains stable for the entire 5-year period. For a 9% par bond, a Duration of 5 years is obtained with a maturity of 6.7 years. Suppose now that an investment is made at the 6.7-year point and held it for a 1-year period. At the end of the year, the investment would have a remaining maturity of 5.7 years. Because of the downward slope of the yield curve, this holding could be sold at a lower yield, resulting in a capital gain. This capital gain would provide a return that would be higher than the original yield. This return is called the "Rolling Yield" associated with the 6.7-year maturity point. For a positively sloped yield curve, the Rolling Yield will always provide a higher return than the bond's yield-to-maturity. Similarly, for a negatively sloped yield curve, the Rolling Yield will generally provide a lower return value than the yield-to-maturity.

For a point portfolio and a stable yield curve, the Immunization process generates a sequence of these Rolling Yields. Thus, the first year's investment consists of the 6.7-year yield curve point. This provides the required initial Duration of 5 years. At the end of the first year, this investment is sold, thereby realizing the Rolling Yield. The entire proceeds are then rebalanced into the 4.8-year maturity point, i.e., the 4-year Duration point along the yield curve. This new investment is held for 1 year, thereby realizing the Rolling Yield associated with the 4.8-year maturity. At the end of the second year, another rebalancing is carried out, with the accumulated dollar value being invested in the 3.4-year maturity that provides the needed Duration value of 3.0. In this fashion, the Immunization process provides the sequence of Rolling Yields illustrated in Figure 3. Since the static yield curve forms the benchmark case in any Immunization procedure, it is reasonable to expect this sequence of Rolling Yields to function as a return target.

Figure 3: The Rolling Yield Curve

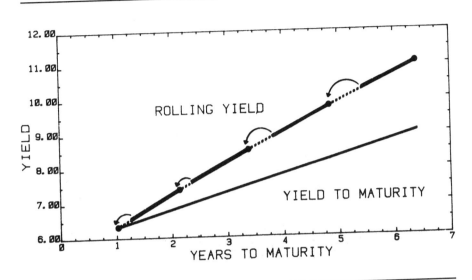

Figure 4: Simulated Immunization Returns Over Rolling Yield Target
Annual Parallel Shifts of -50 Basis Points

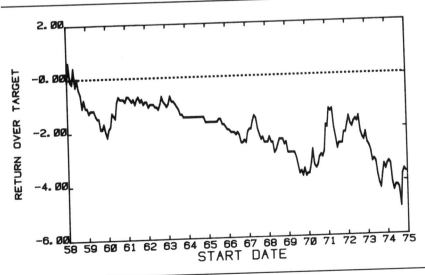

SIMULATION TEST OF THE ROLLING YIELD TARGET

The concept of a Rolling Yield-based target was tested using the simulation procedure described earlier. The results are shown in Figure 4. (Please note that the vertical scale is different from that used in Figure 2.) The worst miss is -5 basis points, compared with a -21 basis point miss for the YTM target. To facilitate comparison of the targeting techniques, Figure 5 shows both sets of simulation results on a single graph. The Rolling Yield target is clearly superior. The result can be proven mathematically: the Rolling Yield provides the correct return target for the case of parallel movements of par bond yield curves.

Do parallel movements ever occur? Well, they do on occasion. For example, as one can see from Figure 6, interest rate movements over calendar year 1979 came close to an upward parallel shift. Figure 7 shows the returns realized in 1979 from an investment at each maturity. This return pattern is characteristic of upward parallel shifts.

However, much as the Immunizer might wish to see parallel movements, the real world often deals out a sequence of rate movements that are anything but parallel. For example, consider just one segment of the yield curve—the spread of 5-year maturities over 1-year Bills. Under parallel shifts, this spread would remain constant over time. As can be seen in Figure 8, there have actually been wide, and often wild, variations in this spread.

This brings us to the second part of this study—the problem of nonparallel shifts.

CHANGING YIELD CURVE SHAPES

In order to appreciate the problems caused by nonparallel shifts, consider the situation of an initially inverted yield curve which snaps down to a positive shape in subsequent years. Figure 8 shows that this situation was not uncommon—it happened in 1969, 1973 and 1974. Figure 9 provides a more detailed view of the snap-down that occurred over the year following September 1974.

When faced with a yield curve shape such as that of September 1974, the Rolling Yield targeting process will count on rolling "up" the curve and capturing the higher yields. Parallel downward shifts would, of course, reduce these yields, but it would also generate sufficient capital gains for an Immunized portfolio to remain "on target." However, when the yield curve snaps down as shown in Figure 9, the yield loss in the short maturities may far exceed the yield move in the intermediate-term maturities. In the early years of an Immunization plan, the portfolio will probably be concentrated in this intermediate range. Consequently, the smaller yield move in these intermediate maturities may not

Figure 5: Comparison of YTM and Rolling Yields as Targets
Annual Parallel Shifts of -50 Basis Points

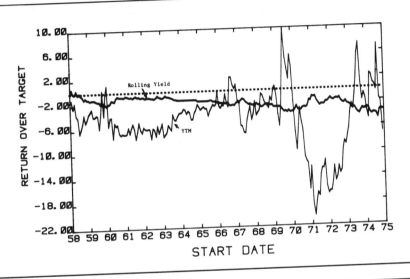

Figure 6: Historical Yield Curves

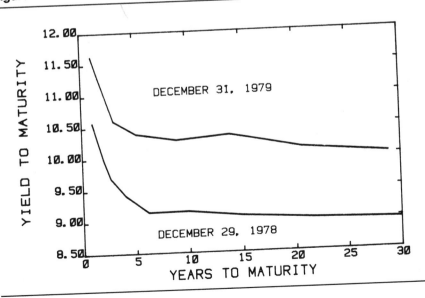

Figure 7: Realized Historical Performance—1979

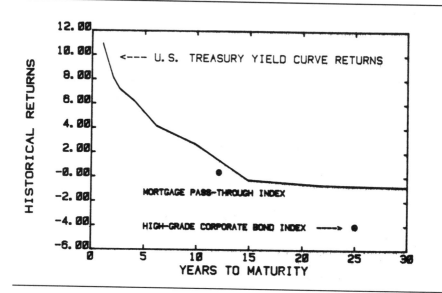

Figure 8: 5 Year/1 Year Treasury Curve Spread

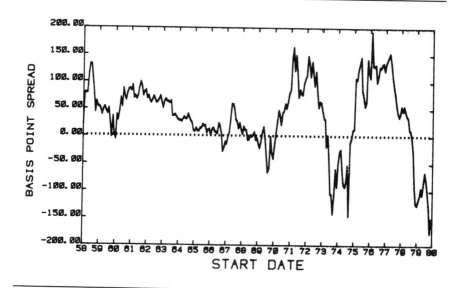

Figure 9: Historical Yield Curves

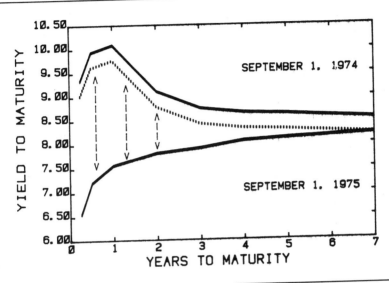

generate sufficient capital gains to provide the needed offset to the much lower yields that will be encountered in the plan's later years.

Thus, one should anticipate that Immunization would run into problems in the face of the snap-downs that followed the inverted yield curves that occurred in 1969, 1973 and 1974.

SIMULATION OF ACTUAL YIELD CURVE SEQUENCES

The computer simulation utilized the same data base of monthly U.S. Treasury yield curves stretching from January 1958 to December 1979. However, the Immunization plan now had to deal with market movements defined by the actual sequence of historical curves.

In general, the typical Immunization plan did track the starting yield levels reasonably well. Figure 10 shows the realized returns from one such plan against the yield level of the initial portfolio. At first blush, this looks like an extraordinary degree of correlation. However, one must remember that in an Immunization context, the idea is not just to track closely, but to track *very* closely. The error tolerance has to be measured in basis points. To see this visu-

Figure 10: Historical Yield Levels and Simulated Immunization Returns

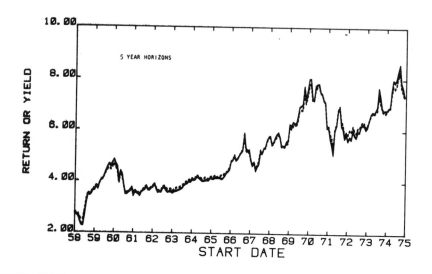

Figure 11: Historical Immunization Returns Over Rolling Yield Target
Actual Sequence of Yield Curves

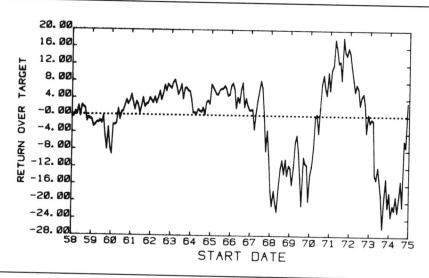

ally, one must plot the basis point spread of realized return over the original targeted return.

The first case to be examined at this detailed level is a 5-year Immunization strategy using a point portfolio with annual rebalancing. This sequence of tracking errors is shown in Figure 11. The results are quite satisfactory for plans begun in 1958-66. Over this period, the Immunization plans usually did better than the target. Then, in 1967, 1968 and 1969, there developed a series of instances where the Immunization strategy underperformed the target by 20 to 24 basis points. Over the next 3 years, from mid-1970 through the end of 1972, the Immunization plans always met their target and, in some cases, outperformed by as much as 18 basis points. The results turned sour once again in 1973, reaching the worst miss of -26 basis points in September 1973. By the end of 1975, the results had begun to improve.

In comparing Figure 11 with the 5- to 1-year spread graph shown in Figure 8, one can roughly identify the most difficult times for Immunization plans. An inverted yield curve followed by a snap-down to a positive curve causes trouble in the standard Immunization strategy. If this situation occurs within the first 2-3 years of the plan's life, it can create distortions that may lead to underperformance. It is not surprising that this situation would place a particular strain upon targets based upon the Rolling Yield.

In order to assess the role of the targeting procedure in these underperformance situations, this series of simulations was repeated using return targets based upon the yield-to-maturity of the original portfolio. As pointed out earlier, this YTM target is theoretically incorrect for the hypothetical situation of parallel yield moves. However, one might expect the YTM to provide a more conservative and hence somewhat better target estimate in just those inverted yield curve situations where the Rolling Yield gets into trouble. From the simulation results presented in Figure 12, it is evident that the YTM target actually does perform somewhat better in those troublesome times. In contrast with the early results shown in Figure 11, there are fewer starting months shown in Figure 12, where the Immunization plan underperformed by more than 16 basis points. Figure 13 provides a more direct comparison of the results using the two different targeting methods.

Another approach to dealing with this problem of yield curve reshaping is to find portfolio structures that may prove more resilient to actual market movements.

In the preceding discussion, all analyses and all simulation results have been based upon a point portfolio. This is a hypothetical portfolio consisting of the par bond having the right maturity to produce the desired Duration value. There are actually many other portfolio structures that can generate the needed sequence of Duration values. It is reasonable to expect that some of these portfolio structures can perform much better than others over time. This brings us to the third topic in this presentation.

**Figure 12: Historical Immunization Returns Over YTM Target Actual
Sequence of Yield Curves**

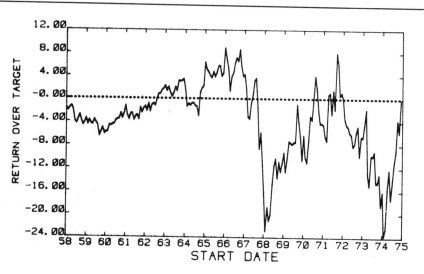

**Figure 13: Comparison of YTM and Rolling Yield as Targets
Actual Sequence of Yield Curves**

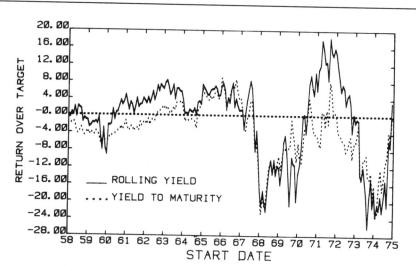

VARIATIONS IN PORTFOLIO STRUCTURE

The dynamics of the point portfolio are schematically illustrated in Figure 14. In this diagram, the yield curve at the outset is represented by the dark line. The dotted lines depict the yield curves in each subsequent year. Thus, the lowest dotted line corresponds to the yield curve at the beginning of the plan's last year. The asterisks represent the movement of the portfolio on a year-by-year basis. Thus, for the point portfolio in Figure 14, the portfolio's total market value is always concentrated at a single maturity point. At the outset, this maturity is determined so as to provide the needed Duration value of 5 years. This portfolio is held throughout the first year with appropriate coupon reinvestment. At the end of the first year, it is sold and all proceeds are invested into that maturity point on the new yield curve which provides the needed Duration value of 4 years. This process continues on a year-by-year basis throughout the plan's life.

Another fundamental portfolio structure is the "barbell." One version of the barbell consists of a combination of 1-year and a long-term maturity. At the outset, the respective proportions of each security would, of course, be determined so as to provide the needed 5-year Duration value. As illustrated in Figure 15, one version of a barbell strategy would then simply "age" the longer maturity, with some rebalancing into the 1-year instrument as needed. Thus, at the end of the first year, the 30-year security would have aged into a 29-year maturity, while the 1-year instrument would have matured into cash. This cash

Figure 14: Immunized Point Portfolio Over Time

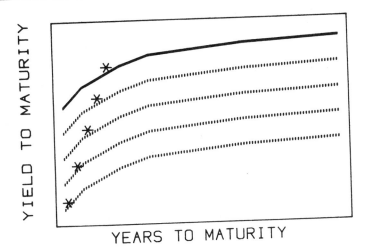

YEARS TO MATURITY

Figure 15: Immunized Barbell Portfolio Over Time

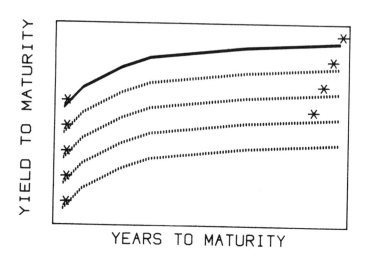

would then be rolled back into a new 1-year security. In addition, it might be necessary to sell some portion of the 29-year security and reinvest into the 1-year area in order to obtain the needed 4-year Duration value. This process is then continued on a year-by-year basis. In the last year, the remaining amount in the longer maturity is sold, since the entire portfolio must now be concentrated at the 1-year point.

Another version of the "barbell" concept, illustrated in Figure 16, involves combining an intermediate maturity with a long maturity. In this case, both securities age over time. The shortening of the Duration value is achieved by selling portions of the longer maturity, as needed, and reinvesting them into the intermediate maturity point. In these "double-aging" barbells, the intermediate maturity must obviously have a short enough Duration value to provide an effective counterbalance throughout the plan's life.

Another class of portfolios is the "ladder." The general idea behind the ladder is to have a series of equal market weights implanted at specific maturity intervals. For example, one might have a ladder starting in the first year with equal weights in the second year, the third year, etc., and proceeding as far out in maturity as needed to obtain the proper Duration value. As illustrated in Figure 17, with each passing year, the "rungs" of the ladder age. The Duration value is maintained by redistributing the cash from redemptions and from the sales out of the longer maturity rungs.

Figure 16: Immunized Barbell Portfolio Over Time

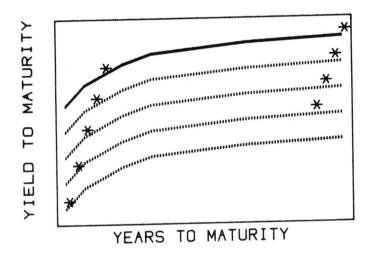

Figure 17: Immunized Laddered Portfolio Over Time

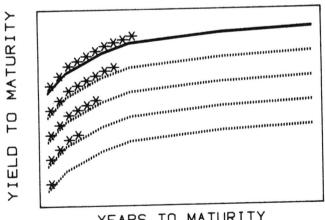

Figure 18: Immunized Laddered Portfolio Over Time

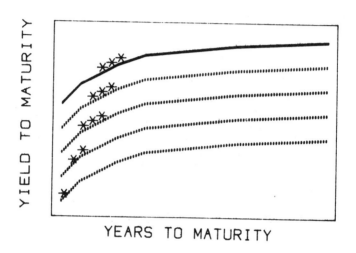

A more general version of the ladder portfolio is shown in Figure 18 where the earliest maturity is designed to be something other than the 1-year point. For example, a 5-year Immunization plan could be developed using a laddered portfolio beginning in the fifth year.

As one delves into this question of characterizing the various dynamic structures, one finds a virtually limitless variety of potential portfolio forms and rebalancing procedures. Our research has encompassed a large number of different portfolio structures, many more than can be described within the context of this presentation. However, the basic thrust of our findings can be summarized in terms of the four structures described in Figures 14-18.

At this point, before proceeding to the simulation results, some discussion is required about the surprisingly intricate subject of different rebalancing procedures.

THE INTRICACIES OF REBALANCING

It turns out that there is much more flexibility and many more questions in the area of rebalancing than is generally realized. Our research into many of these variables has shown that there are numerous surprises which can have a fairly substantial impact upon tracking accuracy. For example, while most of the work presented here is based upon annual rebalancing, we have performed other studies into the effects of using different rebalancing frequencies. The theory suggests that more frequent rebalancing should, apart from the practical considerations involved, prove superior. Curiously, the historical simulations tend to suggest that too frequent rebalancing may introduce more problems than it solves. In fact, these results raised the question as to whether rebalancing should be specified in terms of the time dimension alone. Thus, it appears that improved Duration matching may be obtained by having more adaptive scheduling of the rebalancing action, e.g., triggered by certain thresholds of rate moves, cash inflows, etc.

Another important facet of this problem has to do with the rebalancing criteria itself. To this point, this presentation has been cast in the context of the traditional Macaulay Duration. In actuality, Macaulay's specification of Duration should probably be viewed as one special case of a class of volatility measures. Each volatility measure turns out to be appropriate for a particular set of assumptions regarding the rebalancing horizon, the nature of the market movement and the procedure for reinvesting inter-period cash flows. In fact, for most of the situations analyzed, the Macaulay Duration has turned out *not* to be the best choice from within this class of volatility measures. A full discussion of this subject would lead too far astray for the purposes of this paper, but an example of these considerations is contained in an earlier research paper (Bond Immunization II—Portfolio Rebalancing).[1]

Another aspect of the rebalancing question has to do with the range of choices involved when using specific securities. There are a host of such questions, ranging from the most efficient application of coupon flows, to the selection of the optimal security for liquidation, to the broader issue of constructing initial portfolios using a combination of highly liquid and relatively illiquid securities. Once again, a full discussion of this subject is beyond the scope of this presentation. However, it is important to note that the choice of a rebalancing procedure, even in a prescribed portfolio structure, is a weighty problem in its own right.

TRACKING ACCURACY OF DIFFERENT PORTFOLIO STRUCTURES

The primary purpose in exploring alternative portfolio structures is to see if they can provide more stable tracking over the simulation period. Thus, a simple

---

[1] Martin L. Leibowitz, "Bond Immunization II—Portfolio Rebalancing," Salomon Brothers Inc, November 27, 1979.

way of reporting these results is to show the improvement in return provided by each portfolio structure relative to that which could be obtained with the simple point portfolio.

The first simulation results are shown in Figure 19. The portfolio structure is that of a 1/30 year barbell. It should be pointed out that the vertical scale in Figure 19 is very wide. In fact, for the 5-year plan beginning in January, 1958, the 1/30 year barbell underperformed the point portfolio by over 40 basis points. This was a pretty sorry performance, which subsequently deteriorated even further, reaching a nadir of 130 basis points underperformance in late 1959. The overall pattern of Figure 19 suggests that the 1/30 year barbell does not function well in an Immunization strategy. Indeed, in this context, it could be more appropriately termed a "dumbbell" strategy.

The next set of simulation results are for the case of 5/30 year barbell with both securities "aging" over time. The performance is shown in Figure 20. Note the dramatic compression in scale from the preceding diagram. Here the first underperformance is less than 7 basis points, and there are very few instances of underperformances exceeding 4 basis points. Moreover, the overall pattern of Figure 20 suggests that a fairly consistent improvement in the total return is achieved through the use of this particular barbell pattern.

The results in Figure 20 justify the motivation behind the examination of alternative portfolio structures—it does indeed begin to appear that certain port-

Figure 19: Historical Immunization Returns 1/30 Year Barbell versus Point Portfolio

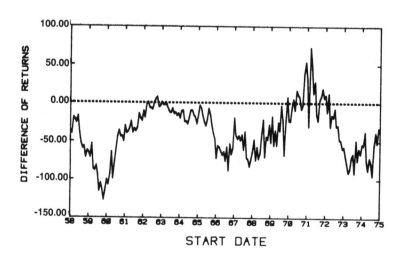

Figure 20: Historical Immunization Returns 5/30 Year Barbell versus Point Portfolio

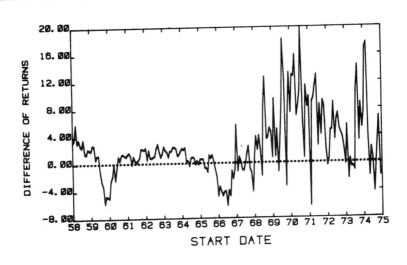

folio structures can provide more consistent tracking than the simple point portfolio.

Figure 21 shows the results for a third type of portfolio structure—the equally weighted ladder beginning in the first year. These results show an overall positive pattern, but with some serious underperformances in 1959-60 and 1974.

A far more consistently positive result is shown in Figure 22 for the case of a laddered portfolio starting in the fifth year. These results look very promising. From 1958 through 1967, there is very close tracking of the point portfolio with some slight improvement in return most of the time. From 1968 through 1973, there is a very sizable and consistent improvement almost on a month-by-month basis. In 1974, this laddered portfolio turns in its worst relative performance, but the most extreme miss only amounts to 4 basis points.

CURVE-DEPENDENT TARGETS

While Figure 22 indicates a very encouraging improvement over the point portfolio results, it must be remembered that this is not a comparison against the original target return. For a true comparison against the original targets, one

Figure 21: Historical Immunization Returns Ladder Starting in 1st Year versus Point Portfolio

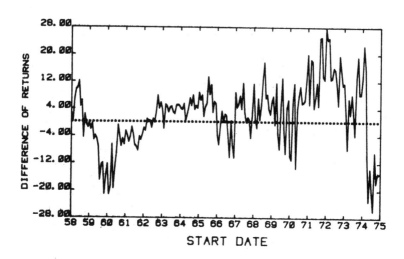

Figure 22: Historical Immunization Returns Ladder Starting in 5th Year versus Point Portfolio

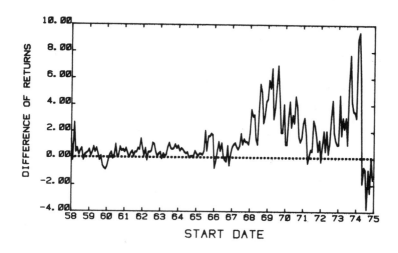

must combine the results in Figure 22 with either Figure 11, which shows the point portfolio returns relative to the Rolling Yield target, or Figure 12, which shows the returns relative to the YTM target.

A simple visual comparison of these three figures suggests a somewhat different approach to the problem of constructing a yield target.

First of all, as noted earlier, the yield-to-maturity provides an improved target over periods when the Immunization plan encompasses an inverted yield curve followed by a subsequent snap-down. Using the YTM target, as shown in Figure 12, troublesome periods still occur in 1968-69 and 1973-74. These are just the time periods when the laddered portfolio in Figure 22 provides an important increment of return beyond that obtained from the point portfolio. These results suggest a "curve-dependent" approach to the portfolio structuring and targeting problems:

> In periods when the yield curve exhibits a flat or positive shape, the target would be designed in terms of the Rolling Yield—(the theoretically correct measure for the case of parallel movements in rates). However, in periods beginning with a yield curve inversion, the target would be based upon the YTM of the point portfolio.

This "curve-dependent" technique leads to a more conservative targeting procedure. This procedure was then combined with the use of an Immunized laddered portfolio starting in the fifth year. The simulation results for this combination approach are shown in Figure 23. These results clearly represent a considerable improvement in tracking accuracy over any of the preceding simulations based upon the actual sequence of yield curves. The worst miss is -16 basis points, and that only occurs once in August 1974. If one were to rule out the 4 worst misses, the remaining data points would all have tracked within -10 basis points or better. In fact, if one excluded the 7 worst cases, then all the other simulations—96% of the 204 Immunization plans—would have come within -8 basis points or better of the original target.

A more graphic illustration of these results is shown in the histogram in Figure 24. The results represented by this histogram are most impressive. If Immunization could reliably provide this level of tracking accuracy on an ongoing basis, then this technique would indeed have to be taken seriously as a route to uncertainty reduction in an uncertain world.

VULNERABILITY OF ANY IMMUNIZATION PLAN

However, it should immediately be pointed out that these results clearly run the danger of being specific to the historical sample that was used for this simulation. While the development of portfolio structures and the concept of a curve-

Figure 23: Historical Immunization Returns Over Curve-Dependent Target Ladder Starting in 5th Year

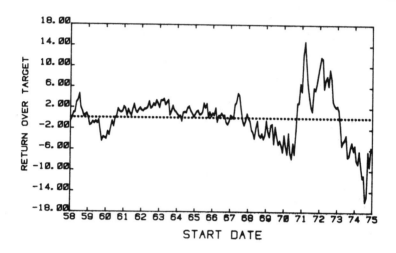

Figure 24: Historical Immunization Returns Over Curve-Dependent Target Ladder Starting in 5th Year

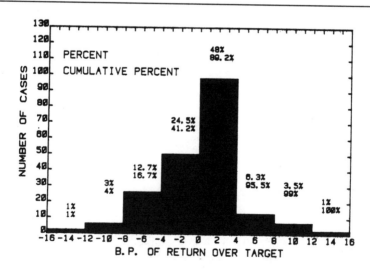

dependent target seems to have a reasonable conceptual justification, one must always be skeptical of such extraordinary tracking accuracy. Moreover, any portfolio structuring and/or targeting procedure will have its own particular set of vulnerabilities. These vulnerabilities may have not fully surfaced even under the range of yield movements and yield curve reshapings that have occurred during the 22-year period used in this simulation.

Indeed, with a little insight, a pathological sequence of yield curve movements can *always* be found that will defeat *any* Immunization strategy. Thus, if one develops a rebalancing procedure for defending against snap-downs and/or snap-ups, it will create portfolios that are vulnerable to other types of yield curve movements. This is a very important point. The theoretical models of Immunization all place some limits on the nature of yield curve movements. Without such limits, or some statistical approach specifying the probability of various pathologies, it is impossible to define an Immunization scheme that will *always* work, i.e., *always* provide tracking within some specified (reasonable) tolerance of the target.

DIFFERENT PLANNING PERIODS

The preceding discussion has been in the context of Immunization plans over 5-year periods. Figure 25 shows the simulation results for a 10-year plan based upon a point portfolio having a Rolling Yield target. In point of fact, it can be argued that Immunization strategies can be more meaningful for longer plans than for shorter plans. The overall pattern for the 10-year plans in Figure 25 indicates a generally similar tracking accuracy to that found for comparable 5-year plans (Figure 11). This provides a sense of comfort that Immunization plans over longer periods will conform to the same general level of tracking accuracy as found earlier for the 5-year plans. Of course, one can only develop Immunization plans for periods as long as the Duration values that are available in the market at any given time. While over the past 22 years, one could find long-term bonds with Durations of 10-11 years, that is no longer the case in the 1980 markets. A bond's Duration decreases with rising interest rates so that the longest Duration value that can be obtained in a 12% rate market is about 8 years.

CONSTRUCTION OF SPECIFIC PORTFOLIOS

To this point, Immunization plans have been examined in terms of either hypothetical or historical yield curves. In turning to the market of specific Trea-

Figure 25: 10 Year Plan—Immunization Returns Over Rolling Yield Target Actual Sequence of Yield Curves

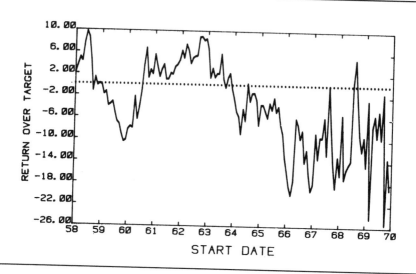

Figure 26: Immunization Planning System Portfolio Construction

```
            1/15/80 POSITION          5.00 YR TARGET DURATION
            ---------------------------------------------------
ISSUE  PAR    TKR   COUPON MATURITY   YTM    PRICE  ACCR   DUR    %MV     $MV

  1   408.3   US  12.125 11/30/81  11.32  101.30  1.52   1.71    42.0    419.7
  2   300.0   US   8.000  8/15/86  10.54   88.14  3.33   4.96    27.4    274.4
  3   297.9   US  10.375 11/15/ 9  10.27  100.94  1.73   9.55    30.6    305.8

     1006.1        10.458 11.7 YR  10.78% 97.58          5.00   100.0%  1000.0
```

sury/Agency, corporate and mortgage[2] securities, one encounters a whole new set of problems and opportunities. First of all, the opportunity exists to take advantage of bonds offering higher yields or better "spread-value." At the same time, one encounters problems such as credit quality, adverse yield spread movements, relative marketability, the occasionally peculiar effects of accrued interest, the potential unavailability of issues filling a desired "coupon/maturity box," etc. The historical analyses can provide valuable guidelines. However, special techniques must be developed to deal with the many practical problems involved in constructing forward-looking Immunization plans in the real world. The fourth part of the presentation will address this subject.

Before proceeding with an Immunization strategy, the portfolio manager would be well advised to have access to a computerized planning system that would allow a specific plan to be designed, pretested, and then monitored over time. The following set of figures represents one version of such an Immunization planning system. For example, suppose that on January 15, 1980, it is desired to construct a 5-year plan with annual rebalancing. Since the yield curve is inverted, a curve-dependent targeting approach would suggest using the yield-to-maturity as a target. Figure 26 illustrates a portfolio of three Treasury bonds having the desired 5-year Duration and an average yield of 10.78%. The analysis carried out in Figure 26 is based on an initial expenditure of $1 million, but the indicated par amounts could be scaled up to reflect the total magnitude of the desired portfolio.

Now suppose one wanted to improve the target return by introducing certain corporate securities into this simple Immunization plan. By selecting among the universe of such securities, one might construct a portfolio such as the one shown in Figure 27, again geared to the 5-year plan with annual rebalancing. The greater yields available in the corporate sector allow for the portfolio's yield to be increased to 11.32%. The question remains as to the extent to which these higher yields provide sufficient compensation for the reduced marketability, yield spread risk and quality levels associated with the corporates. To a certain extent, these problems must be analyzed in the context of the dynamics of the Immunization plan over time. Figure 28 represents a simple first step in the exploration of this dynamic process. Over a 1-year period, the initial scenario in Figure 28 treats the basic static case of "no change in yields." All interim cash flows have been reinvested at a 10% rate, resulting in a total accumulated cash flow of $110,600 available for reinvestment on January 15, 1981. As shown in Figure 29, this cash flow is employed in the rebalancing process to obtain the needed Duration value of 4 years. The holdings of the Treasury 12 1/8's of 11/30/81 are increased to a total market value of $475,000. This is achieved by

---

[2] For a discussion of the potential role of mortgage securities in an Immunization context, see *Cash Flow Characteristics of Mortgage Securities*, Martin L. Leibowitz, Salomon Brothers, March 1980.

Figure 27: Immunization Planning System Portfolio Construction

```
          1/15/80 POSITION        5.00 YR TARGET DURATION
      -------------------------------------------------
ISSUE  PAR   TKR  COUPON MATURITY  YTM   PRICE ACCR  DUR    %MV    $MV

  1   342.3   US  12.125 11/30/81 11.32 101.30 1.52  1.71   35.2   351.9
  2   214.7 CORP   8.000  1/ 1/82 12.20  92.86  .31  1.84   20.0   200.0
  3   220.5 CORP  10.125  3/ 1/ 5 11.75  86.93 3.77  8.30   20.0   200.0
  4   241.6   US  10.375 11/15/ 9 10.27 100.94 1.73  9.55   24.8   248.1

     1019.1         10.466 13.5 YR 11.32% 96.65        5.00  100.0% 1000.0
```

Figure 28: Immunization Planning System Performance Review for No Change in Yields

```
          1.00 YEAR REVIEW PERIOD    1/15/80 TO  1/15/81    10.00% REINV
      -------------------------------------------------------------
                            STARTING    CHANGE              PERFORMANCE
                           ----------  ----------  $CPN+   -----------
ISSUE TKR COUPON MATURITY   YTM  PX+ACR  YTM  PX+ACR REINV  %RTN  %RCY   PAR

  1    US  12.125 11/30/81 11.32 102.81 +.00  -.67  12.58 11.58 11.26  342.3
  2  CORP   8.000  1/ 1/82 12.20  93.17 +.00 +3.43   8.23 12.52 12.15  214.7
  3  CORP  10.125  3/ 1/ 5 11.75  90.70 +.00  +.09  10.76 11.97 11.63  220.5
  4    US  10.375 11/15/ 9 10.27 102.67 +.00  -.01  10.81 10.52 10.26  241.6

PORTFOLIO    $MV 1115.8  =   1000.0  +   5.3  +  110.6       11.27% 1019.1
```

Figure 29: Immunization Planning System Re-Targeting for No Change in Yields

```
         1/15/81 REBALANCING AND REINVESTMENT TRANSACTIONS
         ----------------------------------------------------

 ISSUE   PAR   TKR  COUPON MATURITY  YTM   PRICE ACCR   $MV

   1   +122.8   US  12.125 11/30/81 11.32 100.62 1.52   125.4
   4    -14.5   US  10.375 11/15/ 9 10.27 100.94 1.73   -14.9
                                                        -----
               NET CASH FLOW                           +110.6
```

```
         1/15/81 POSITION        4.00 YR TARGET DURATION
         -------------------------------------------------

 ISSUE   PAR    TKR  COUPON MATURITY  YTM    PRICE ACCR   DUR    %MV    $MV

   1    455.1    US  12.125 11/30/81 11.32 100.62 1.52    .85   42.6   475.0
   2    214.7  CORP   8.000  1/ 1/82 12.20  96.29  .31    .94   18.6   207.4
   3    220.5  CORP  10.125  3/ 1/ 5 11.75  87.02 3.77   8.24   17.9   200.2
   4    227.2    US  10.375 11/15/ 9 10.27 100.94 1.73   9.50   20.9   233.2

       1127.4         10.634 10.9 YR  11.34% 97.44       4.00  100.0% 1115.8
```

Figure 30: Immunization Planning System Performance Review for +100 Basis Point Yield Change

```
       1.00 YEAR REVIEW PERIOD    1/15/80 TO  1/15/81    10.00% REINV
       ------------------------------------------------------------------

                             STARTING       CHANGE             PERFORMANCE
                            -----------   -----------  $CPN+  -----------
 ISSUE TKR COUPON MATURITY  YTM  PX+ACR   YTM  PX+ACR  REINV  %RTN  %RCY    PAR

   1    US 12.125 11/30/81 11.32 102.81 +1.00  -1.49  12.58 10.79 10.51   342.3
   2  CORP  8.000  1/ 1/82 12.20  93.17 +1.00  +2.58   8.23 11.60 11.29   214.7
   3  CORP 10.125  3/ 1/ 5 11.75  90.70 +1.00  -6.50  10.76  4.70  4.64   220.5
   4    US 10.375 11/15/ 9 10.27 102.67 +1.00  -8.58  10.81  2.17  2.16   241.6

 PORTFOLIO     $MV 1076.0  =  1000.0  +  -34.6  +  110.6          7.46% 1019.1
```

first utilizing the accumulated $110,600 of cash flow and then by an incremental sale of $14,500 par amount of Treasury 10 3/8's of '09.

Now consider a scenario in which all yields move upward by 100 basis points as shown in Figure 30. As a result of the capital losses incurred, the portfolio's return declines to 7.46%. Proceeding to the rebalancing shown in Figure 31, it is interesting to note that the target Duration of 4 years can now be obtained in a much different fashion. First of all, there is no need to sell any of the existing holdings. The necessary rebalancing can be completely accomplished using the $110,600 of accumulated cash flow. This is largely due to the fact that as a result of the rise in yield levels, the Duration values of all securities will have decreased. In fact, the rebalancing now requires that $32,300 of the cash flow be applied to the longer Duration Treasury bond in order to achieve the needed Duration length. This illustrates graphically how rebalancing plans may alter depending on the nature of the market movement that has taken place.

On the other hand, should all yields decline by 100 basis points, one would see just the opposite effect—the Duration values of the portfolio holdings would increase. Therefore, a more radical rebalancing procedure would be needed in order to shorten the Duration to the requisite 4 years. One such rebalancing is illustrated in Figure 32.

PRETESTING AND MONITORING

In developing a monitoring scheme, one wants to ensure that the portfolio can indeed remain "on target" across a wide range of interest rate scenarios. Thus, it can be helpful to carry out in advance, a "pretest" simulation procedure. At each rebalancing point, the simulation should display the summary results for all scenarios. For example, as shown in Figure 33, this summary should at least include the cumulative return, the forward target rate, the blended rate combining the cumulative and forward values, and, of course, the comparison with the initial target yield. This tracking process should, of course, be extended to a much wider and more stressful range of interest rate scenarios, and then continued throughout each year of the 5-year plan. On a before-the-fact basis, such a procedure can help to identify the vulnerability points of a given Immunization plan in terms of both yield level changes, yield curve reshapings, and yield spread problems. A similar procedure can then be carried forward with an ongoing plan to serve as a monitor of the plan's progress towards its target return.

After overcoming the initial unfamiliarity, the key ideas behind Immunization actually prove to be rather simple. However, the practical application of this technique does require that the portfolio manager come to grips with a number of knotty and complex questions. Since the whole purpose of Immunization is to track a prescribed target return within very close tolerances, any

Figure 31: Immunization Planning System Re-Targeting for +100 Basis Point Yield Change

```
          1/15/81 REBALANCING AND REINVESTMENT TRANSACTIONS
          -----------------------------------------------------
```

ISSUE	PAR	TKR	COUPON	MATURITY	YTM	PRICE	ACCR	$MV
1	+77.3	US	12.125	11/30/81	12.32	99.81	1.52	78.3
4	+34.3	US	10.375	11/15/ 9	11.27	92.36	1.73	32.3

	NET CASH FLOW							+110.6

```
          1/15/81 POSITION        4.00 YR TARGET DURATION
          -----------------------------------------------------
```

ISSUE	PAR	TKR	COUPON	MATURITY	YTM	PRICE	ACCR	DUR	%MV	$MV
1	419.6	US	12.125	11/30/81	12.32	99.81	1.52	.85	39.5	425.1
2	214.7	CORP	8.000	1/ 1/82	13.20	95.44	.31	.94	19.1	205.6
3	220.5	CORP	10.125	3/ 1/ 5	12.75	80.43	3.77	7.77	17.3	185.6
4	275.9	US	10.375	11/15/ 9	11.27	92.36	1.73	8.89	24.1	259.6
	1130.7		10.570	11.6 YR	12.31%	93.83		4.00	100.0%	1076.0

Figure 32: Immunization Planning System Performance Review for -100 Basis Point Yield Change

```
          1/15/81 REBALANCING AND REINVESTMENT TRANSACTIONS
          -----------------------------------------------------
```

ISSUE	PAR	TKR	COUPON	MATURITY	YTM	PRICE	ACCR	$MV
1	+170.9	US	12.125	11/30/81	10.32	101.45	1.52	176.0
4	-58.0	US	10.375	11/15/ 9	9.27	111.02	1.73	-65.4

	NET CASH FLOW							+110.6

```
          1/15/81 POSITION        4.00 YR TARGET DURATION
          -----------------------------------------------------
```

ISSUE	PAR	TKR	COUPON	MATURITY	YTM	PRICE	ACCR	DUR	%MV	$MV
1	513.2	US	12.125	11/30/81	10.32	101.45	1.52	.85	45.5	528.4
2	214.7	CORP	8.000	1/ 1/82	11.20	97.15	.31	.94	18.0	209.3
3	220.5	CORP	10.125	3/ 1/ 5	10.75	94.63	3.77	8.75	18.7	217.0
4	183.6	US	10.375	11/15/ 9	9.27	111.02	1.73	10.16	17.8	207.0
	1132.0		10.697	10.2 YR	10.37%	101.10		4.00	100.0%	1161.6

Figure 33: Immunization Planning System Portfolio Construction

```
            1/15/80 POSITION          5.00 YR TARGET DURATION
     ------------------------------------------------------------
ISSUE  PAR   TKR   COUPON MATURITY   YTM    PRICE  ACCR   DUR     %MV    $MV

  1   342.3   US  12.125 11/30/81  11.32  101.30  1.52   1.71   35.2   351.9
  2   214.7  CORP  8.000   1/ 1/82  12.20   92.86   .31   1.84   20.0   200.0
  3   220.5  CORP 10.125   3/ 1/ 5  11.75   86.93  3.77   8.30   20.0   200.0
  4   241.6   US  10.375 11/15/ 9  10.27  100.94  1.73   9.55   24.8   248.1

     1019.1        10.466 13.5 YR  11.32%  96.65          5.00  100.0% 1000.0
```

```
                    IMMUNIZATION PERFORMANCE TRACKING

                      REALIZED COMPOUND YIELD
                      -----------------------
```

SCENARIO	1.00 YEAR PERIOD	1.00 YEAR CUMULATIVE	4.00 YEAR FORWARD YTM	5.00 YEAR BLENDED	5.00 YEAR INITIAL YTM
I: NO CHANGE	11.27	11.27	11.34	11.33	11.32
II: +100 B.P.	7.46	7.46	12.31	11.33	11.32
III: -100 B.P.	15.56	15.56	10.37	11.40	11.32

manager embarking upon an Immunization plan is strongly advised to address these problems, as thoroughly as possible, in advance.

Chapter III D-7

Optimal Cash Flow Matching

The need to fulfill a prescribed schedule of payouts over time is a classic investment problem. This problem arises in many different forms and in many different contexts—annuities, retirement benefits, trust payouts, insurance liabilities, debt service management, etc. A portfolio of fixed-income vehicles is a natural solution to this type of problem. Over the years, bonds have been used directly or indirectly to support such liability schedules in many different institutional frameworks. The ability of intermediate and long-term bonds to generate a variety of cash flow schedules make them a natural "match" for a prescribed schedule of liabilities and the consequent payouts.

However, the new debt market environment has created the need for a more precise procedure for constructing matched bond portfolios (or "dedicated portfolios" as they are sometimes called). With the high level of interest rates, the strongly inverted yield curve and the wide spread between bonds of differing qualities and sectors, there exists a far greater number of combinations of different debt instruments that can be put into place to support any prescribed schedule. Moreover, the range of costs between different possible portfolios has

Martin L. Leibowitz and Alfred Weinberger, "Optimal Cash Flow Matching: Minimum Risk Bond Portfolios for Fulfilling Prescribed Schedules of Liabilities," Salomon Brothers Inc, August 1981.

increased to a point where it becomes important to define more precisely the concept of an optimal cash flow matched portfolio.

In some ways, the cash flow matching concept relates to the more recent theory of immunization. In fact, the early work on immunization was directed toward developing a minimum-risk procedure for supporting a prescribed liability schedule. In a broad sense, cash flow matching can be viewed as a specialized form of immunization.[1]

However, cash flow matching is a much simpler concept than immunization. A matched portfolio is based upon direct application of coupon and principal cash flows to support the prescribed payouts. Unlike immunization in a strict sense, there is no requirement for the selling of any securities in the portfolio, for any sort of rebalancing procedure or for any type of subsequent monitoring process once the portfolio is put into place.

It is this very simplicity and assurance of being able to fulfill the cash payout that gives the cash flow matching concept its appeal in these highly uncertain times. In some instances, the matched portfolio acts as an "anchor point" for funds that consist of a mixture of some well-defined nominal-dollar liabilities as well as other highly uncertain and potentially inflation-dependent liabilities. Moreover, under current debt market conditions, this "anchor point" can be established at often strikingly low levels of cost.

In this memorandum, we describe the results of a series of research studies into techniques for constructing optimal cash flow matching bond portfolios. While the concept of such portfolios is a simple one, it turns out that the search for optimal—i.e., least cost—portfolios leads one into a number of interesting but not so simple areas. Indeed, most practical situations of any magnitude require a rather complex series of large-scale computational procedures. For such situations, it has proven necessary to develop a specialized and sophisticated computer system to efficiently implement optimal cash flow matching with the timeliness required by today's fast moving debt market.

THE EXACT MATCH

The basic problem involving cash flow matching is easily described. Figure 1 illustrates the familiar cash flow pattern of a typical bond. A bond portfolio will provide an overall cash flow that represents the aggregate of the cash flows of

---

[1] For a more detailed explanation of immunization techniques and their modern application in the U.S. debt markets, see *Pros and Cons of Immunization*. Proceedings of a Seminar on the Roles and Limits of Bond Immunization, Salomon Brothers, 1980. A general list of other reference documents in this area is contained in a chapter by Martin L. Leibowitz, "Specialized Fixed Income Strategies," in *Financial Handbook*, John Wiley & Sons, Inc., 1981.

Figure 1: Cash Flow Pattern of a Single Bond

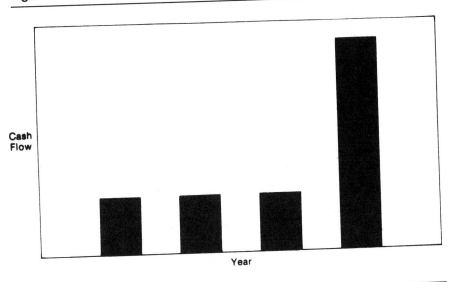

Figure 2: Aggregate Cash Flow from a 4-Bond Portfolio

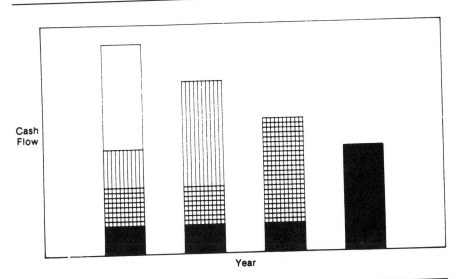

Figure 3: A Prescribed Schedule of Liabilities

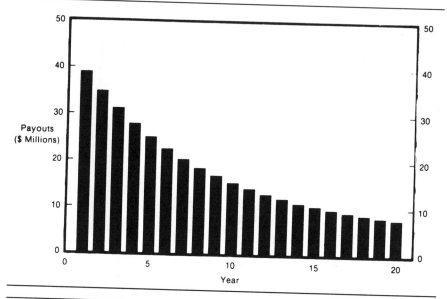

Figure 4: An Exact-Match Portfolio

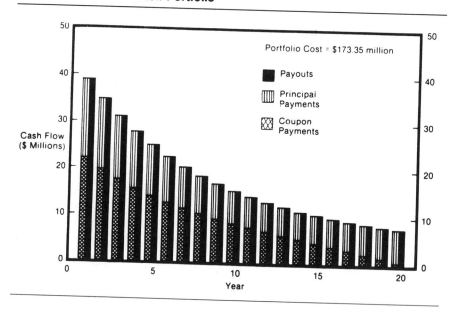

each holding. Thus, with a portfolio of four bonds, one could achieve the overall cash flow schedule shown in Figure 2. The problem of cash flow matching is to take a prescribed schedule of payouts and then construct a bond portfolio that will provide coupon and principal payments to fulfill this schedule.

Theoretically, the prescribed payout schedule may have any one of many possible forms. However, in practice, certain types of general forms are repeatedly encountered. One such common liability schedule is that of the "exponential decay" shown in Figure 3. In this 20-year schedule, the payouts start at $38.9 million in the first year and decline over time, falling to $7.7 million in the 20th year. The sum total of all payouts over the 20-year span amounts to $354.50 million.

For purposes of illustration, suppose the marketplace contains a sufficient quantity of acceptable bonds with maturities coinciding with each of the payout dates shown in Figure 3. Under these conditions, an exact-match portfolio can be constructed. The maturity structure of this portfolio and its consequent cash flow are shown in Figure 4. It can be seen that the combination of coupons and maturities at each semiannual payout date provides an exact match for the prescribed payout schedule.

The cost of this portfolio obviously depends on the price and yield levels of the various bonds involved. For the case of bonds lying along an inverted yield curve that starts at 15% for 6-month securities and declines to the 12% level at 30-year maturities, the cost of this exact-match portfolio turns out to be $173.35 million.

DEPENDENCE ON MARKET ENVIRONMENT

It is interesting to explore how the cost of the exact-match portfolio changes with different levels of interest rates and various shapes of the yield curve. Since the nominal payouts are presumed to remain fixed, it is clearly advantageous to purchase the matching portfolio at times when interest rates are high. This is illustrated in Figure 5. The bottom curve in Figure 5 represents the costs associated with the same yield curve shape as before but at different levels of interest rates. The horizontal axis corresponds to the level of rates as benchmarked by the yield on the 30-year maturity. One can readily see that higher interest rates lead to lower cost portfolios, and vice versa.

The shape of the yield curve can also have a strong effect on the cost of the matching portfolio. The middle plot in Figure 5 corresponds to a flat yield curve. This plot is significantly higher in cost at all yield levels than the "inverted yield curve" plot. The magnitude of this effect is due in part to the shape of the liability schedule, which requires a significant number of shorter maturity securities. The inverted curve naturally leads to higher yields in this maturity area and, consequently, to lower purchase costs for many of the needed securi-

Figure 5: Costs of Matching Portfolios Across a Range of Market Environments

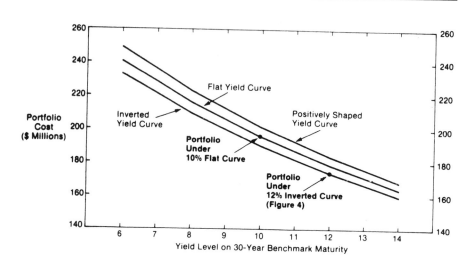

ties. This effect is further illustrated by the top plot in Figure 5, which corresponds to a positive yield curve. This yield curve shape leads to shorter maturities being particularly low in yield and hence high in price. The net result is that a positive yield curve environment is the most costly environment in which to construct a matching portfolio for a liability schedule of the form shown in Figure 3.

Diagrams such as Figure 5 can be helpful in presenting the opportunity cost associated with constructing a matching portfolio in one market environment as opposed to another. For example, with 30-year rates at 12%, the matching portfolio was seen to cost $173.35 million. However, if the same portfolio had to be put together at a time when the yield curve was at a flat 10% level, then the cost would rise to $195.20 million. In other words, there would be an almost $22 million increase in the cost to construct an exact-match portfolio to fulfill the same liability schedule.

Finally, Figure 5 can be interpreted in quite another fashion as the changing market value of an already-constructed portfolio. Thus, using the preceding example, the $173.35 million exact-match portfolio constructed under the inverted yield curve would enjoy an increase of $22 million in its market value should the interest rate structure change to a 10% flat yield curve.

The portfolio in Figure 5 represents the case of an exact-match. With the exact-match, each dollar of coupon and principal receipts on a given date are immediately used to support the required payout on that same date. This would seem to be the ideal fit for a cash flow matched portfolio. However, it turns out that such an exact-match portfolio may not be optimal!

THE GENERAL MATCHING PROBLEM

In practice, there will be a much larger universe of acceptable bonds that have coupon and principal payments on dates other than the exact payout dates of the liability schedule. This larger universe may also contain acceptable bonds with higher yields than their "exact maturity" counterpart. When such bonds are used in a cash flow matching portfolio, the coupon and/or principal receipts must be accumulated for a period of time *prior* to their use on the payout date. Under such circumstances, the normal investment practice would be to reinvest these "prior receipts" for the period of time until they are needed. However, the fundamental appeal of cash flow matching lies in its simplicity. This appeal is reinforced when the matching portfolio can fulfill the prescribed liabilities even if no further investment action is ever taken. The assurance of fulfillment even under *totally passive* management is a natural and clear objective in many cases. (This goal may be sought even in situations where some form of risk-controlled active management will, in fact, be pursued.) This ideal of total passivity may require a matching portfolio to be designed on the assumption that any "prior receipts" would not be reinvested (even though they surely would be). In other words, the matching portfolio would be designed to fulfill its mission even in the case where all reinvestment would take place at a 0% rate.

This assumption of a 0% reinvestment rate obviously provides a strong incentive to achieve as close a degree of matching as possible. For this 0% reinvestment case, one might expect that the exact-match portfolio shown in Figure 4 would prove to have the least cost and hence be the optimal portfolio. In fact, this is not the case. For the liability schedule of Figure 3, one can construct a portfolio with "prior receipts" where some bonds mature before the payment dates. The coupon flows and maturity payments of this portfolio occasionally exceed the payout requirements within a given period and hence "spill over" to the subsequent payout date. This float of prior receipts—both within periods and between periods—is presumed to be carried forward without any reinvestment whatsoever. Nevertheless, the loss of investment income would be more than compensated by the bonds' higher yields. The cost of this 0% reinvestment rate portfolio is $171.04 million—$2.31 million less than the exact-match portfolio shown in Figure 4.

From this example, one can see how the structure of payout dates can be vitally important in determining the optimal matching portfolio. The payout dates are usually prescribed in terms of annual, semiannual, quarterly, or monthly periods. Occasionally, one will have a payout schedule consisting of an irregular series of dates that have no periodic pattern. Whatever the real life characteristics of the prescribed liabilities, the cash flow matching process must be designed to fit the most precise possible definition of these payout dates. In fact, one often finds that the payout dates in the near future are more clearly specified and more frequent than the (potentially less certain) payout dates in the distant future. The ability to accommodate variable payout periods within the overall schedule is an important feature of the problem and should be properly reflected in the construction of a truly optimally matched portfolio.

THE CRITERIA OF PORTFOLIO YIELDS

To this point, the matching portfolio has been described only in terms of its market cost. It is tempting to characterize a bond portfolio in terms of its average yield. At first glance, it would seem to be possible to define the matching problem equally well as one of "yield maximization" as opposed to "cost minimization." However, for a number of reasons, it turns out that "yield maximization" can be a seriously misleading criterion for cash flow matching.

One of the problems has to do with the ambiguity of the concept of a "portfolio yield." At the outset, there too often arises a totally unnecessary confusion regarding the quotation basis of different yield values, i.e., semiannual-based yields being compared with annual-based yield computations, etc. However, the fundamental problem goes beyond questions of the quotation basis.

In many instances, the "portfolio yield" is computed as the market-weighted average of the yields of the individual bond holdings comprising the portfolio. This averaging process is inadequate on several counts. For example, the maturity of the respective holdings is not taken into consideration in a simple market-weighted average. Moreover, because of this problem, one can easily construct portfolios with high average yield values that cost far more than the optimal portfolio.

A more theoretically precise and consistent approach in dealing with general cash flows is the "internal rate of return." This generalization of the yield-to-maturity concept can be applied to any form of cash flow, including the complex aggregate flows from any portfolio of fixed-income securities. The internal rate of return is sometimes referred to as the "cash flow yield" or the "true yield."

The cash flow yield approach can be immediately applied to the prescribed liability schedule. All exact-match portfolios will generate an aggregate cash flow that is by definition coincident with the prescribed liability schedule. Consequently, all such portfolios having the same market cost will have the identical value for their cash flow yield—regardless of the different structures of portfolio holdings that they may contain! This observation has a number of implications.

First of all, it suggests that the costs of exact-match portfolios can be directly plotted against the corresponding "true yield." This is done in Figure 6 for a range of different portfolio costs. In essence, this diagram represents a kind of cost/yield tradeoff for the prescribed liability schedule itself.

Another interesting implication is to compare the conventional "average yield" of different exact-match portfolios with their respective "true yields." From the example cited above, one can see that the average yield for the optimal exact-match portfolio is 13.08% under the inverted yield curve. This portfolio has a market cost of $173.35 million. However, from Figure 6, we can now see that this portfolio's true yield is only 12.61%. Moreover, under a positive yield curve environment, one can see from Figure 5 that the optimal exact-match portfolio with the same market cost would occur when the benchmark 30-year yield is at 13.30%. This portfolio would naturally have the same true yield value of 12.61%, but its average yield turns out to be a very different 12.15%. This example illustrates some of the problems of the average yield technique in the context of cash flow matching.

The portfolio yield approach encounters further difficulties as one proceeds from the case of exact-match portfolios to more general matching problems. For example, one can readily show that, even in terms of the "true yield," the opti-

Figure 6: Yield/Cost Relationship for Exact-Match Portfolios

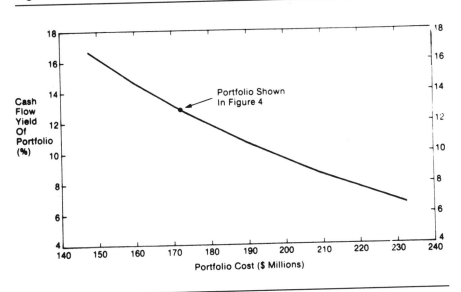

mal least-cost portfolio may not have the highest yield value among all accept-able portfolios. While certain mathematical adjustments can be made to the con-cept of true yield in order to make it more useful in the matching context, it has generally proven advisable in practice to focus on minimizing the cost of the matching portfolio.

POSITIVE REINVESTMENT RATES

The assumption of a 0% reinvestment rate (or equivalently, of no reinvestment whatsoever) is obviously an extremely conservative viewpoint. It can also prove to be an extremely expensive assumption. Portfolios fulfilling the cash flow re-quirements on a 0% assumption will also meet the requirements (or exceed them) on the basis of any higher reinvestment rate. Moreover, by adopting a more reasonable (but still conservative) reinvestment rate assumption, a wider range of potentially acceptable matching portfolios becomes available. In turn, this expansion opens the way to the selection of a lower cost portfolio.

The reduction in immediate costs from planning on the basis of a positive reinvestment rate can be significant. This is particularly true when the market of available and acceptable securities does not provide a complete spectrum of ma-turity dates coinciding with every payout date. In these cases, the reinvestment rate—even for short periods of reinvestment—will become a critical parameter.

An example of this effect is shown in Figure 7. Here, the prescribed payout schedule and the level and shape of the yield curve are the same as in the prior examples. But now, certain gaps are assumed to be present in the available ma-turities along the yield curve. With this new universe of acceptable securities, one obviously *cannot* find an exact-match portfolio. However, there will be a set of matching portfolios based upon a planning assumption of a 0% reinvestment rate. It turns out that the least expensive of these portfolios has a cost of $174.58 million.

Figure 7 depicts a new matching portfolio based on the more reasonable presumption that a reinvestment rate of at least 8% would be available through-out the entire liability schedule. The 8% reinvestment provides additional dol-lars both within each period as well as between successive semiannual periods. These increments of interest-on-interest prove just sufficient to enable the cash flow to meet the required payouts. It is also worth noting that, in this particular case (as is typical in practical applications using a positive reinvestment rate), there is a limited time for each of the compounding processes, i.e., the interest-on-interest builds up only for a short period of time before it is used to meet a payout.

Using the reinvestment rate of 8% as a planning assumption, the portfolio in Figure 7 can be constructed at a purchase cost of $168.78 million. This is $5.80 million cheaper than the best portfolio that could be obtained using the 0% rein-

Figure 7: A General Matching Portfolio with Reinvestment at an 8% Rate

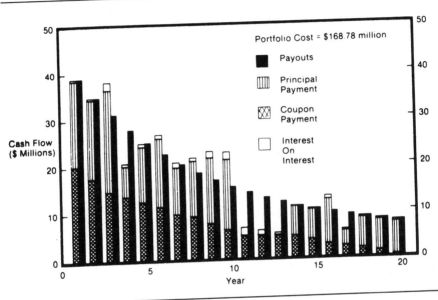

vestment assumption. It is this significant savings in cost that makes the use of a positive (but still conservative) reinvestment planning assumption so crucial in the construction of efficient cash flow matched portfolios.

THE OPTIMAL PORTFOLIO CURVE

The search for an optimal portfolio thus depends on the minimum reinvestment rate assumption. Since higher reinvestment rate assumptions would increase the class of available (and hence potentially cheaper) portfolios, the cost of matching the prescribed liabilities will decrease with higher reinvestment rate assumptions.

This situation is illustrated in Figure 8. The horizontal axis corresponds to the minimum reinvestment rate assumption. The vertical axis is the purchase cost of acceptable portfolios under each reinvestment assumption. Thus, for the case of the 0% reinvestment assumption, the points aligned vertically are intended to (schematically) depict portfolios that meet the payout requirements under the 0% case. The least costly of these portfolios was seen to have a market cost of $174.58 million.

Using a higher nominal reinvestment rate of 4%, the wider vertical spread of points indicates that all of the earlier "0% portfolios" remain acceptable, and there are additional portfolios which have just become acceptable because of the higher assumed reinvestment rate. Some of these new portfolios have lower costs than the earlier "0% portfolios." The cheapest of all acceptable "4% portfolios"—i.e., the lowest cost portfolio for the 4% planning assumption—has a market cost of $171.74 million.

For the case of an 8% planning assumption, there is a still broader range of acceptable portfolios, leading to an even lower net cost. In fact, the least costly portfolio for this 8% case is the one with a market value of $168.78 million that was already depicted in Figure 7.

Thus, for each minimum reinvestment assumption, there exists both a different class of acceptable matching portfolios and a new minimum cost portfolio. To this point, all the portfolios have been presumed to be fully and equally acceptable. Hence, the least costly for each reinvestment case becomes the optimal matching portfolio. The curve forming the lower boundary of the points in Figure 8 then represents the purchase costs of the optimal portfolio for each reinvestment assumption. For the reasons described above, this curve will always decline with increasingly positive reinvestment rates. Moreover, for any given problem, the slope of this curve can help identify the cost savings that can be obtained by proceeding to higher reinvestment rate assumptions.

Figure 8: The Optimal Portfolio Curve

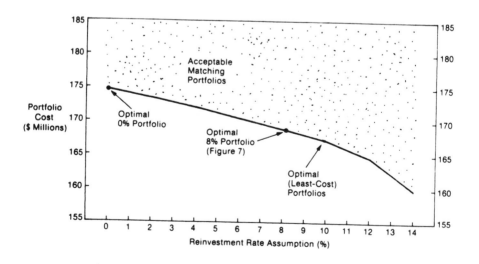

It is important to distinguish between the minimum reinvestment rate assumed for *planning purposes* at the outset and the ultimate reinvestment rates *realized* over time. It is the reinvestment *planning* assumption that will determine the cost of the initial portfolio and it is these rates which are depicted in Figure 8. However, it is the *realized* reinvestment rates that will ultimately determine the magnitude of the excess funds generated by the portfolio. For example, suppose the reinvestment rate in fact turns out to always be above 10%, then the optimal portfolios constructed for the 0% case as well as for the 8% case will both produce levels of interest-on-interest beyond that needed to simply meet the prescribed payout schedule. These excess funds could lead to a series of net takeouts over time. This distinction between the planning assumption and the realized reinvestment rate is important both in theory and practice. It will be discussed in more detail in a later section.

PORTFOLIO CONSTRAINTS

In practice, cash flow matching portfolios will be subject to a variety of constraints imposed by the logic of the problem, as well as by the degree of conservatism sought by the fund's sponsor. These constraints will relate to call vulnerability, quality, type of issuer, diversification across type and individual issuer, the utilization of holdings from preexisting portfolios, etc.

The call vulnerability of specific bonds—whether for refunding, sinking fund, or other purposes—is naturally an important concern in any portfolio designed to provide a prescribed cash flow. The problem of potential calls or refundings can be totally avoided by only purchasing fully non-callable securities. Such a total prohibition would rule out many higher-yielding bonds. It would therefore prove to be a very expensive constraint. A more practical approach is to accept callable bonds that have sufficiently low coupons so as to make the prospect of a refunding call extremely improbable. To achieve further savings, some portfolios might accept a certain limited proportion of bonds where there is a realistic risk of a future call. However, the main point is that, in any particular case, the acceptable limits of overall call vulnerability should be specified and only portfolios satisfying this constraint should be considered.

Another important constraint relates to the credit quality of the securities comprising the portfolio. Of course, the ultimate in credit quality would be a portfolio consisting of all U.S. Treasury securities. This would remove the need for any credit surveillance or concerns. However, once again, such an extreme stance would prove to be quite expensive. In most cases, corporate securities of different qualities are acceptable provided that their overall proportions fall within certain limits and provided that the mixture is appropriately diversified across different industries and issuers.

In trying to determine the appropriate overall credit level for the portfolio, it can be helpful to develop another tradeoff diagram similar to Figure 8. The overall quality level of the portfolio will bear an (admittedly rough) relationship to the relative overall yields of the portfolio holdings. More precisely, the yield spread of the portfolio over the corresponding pure Treasury portfolio will provide a crude gauge for the portfolio's overall quality level. Figure 9 shows how the cost of an optimal portfolio decreases with the increasing yield spread associated with this relaxation of the quality constraint.

Another important constraint often encountered in practice relates to preexisting bond portfolios. In many cases, the fund sponsor may wish to construct cash flow matching portfolios using as many of the existing holdings as possible. There can be numerous motivations. First of all, it can reduce the net new cash required to establish the matching portfolio. Second, it will reduce transaction costs. Third, it may avoid problems associated with the recognition of realized gains or (more likely) realized losses in the existing portfolio.

In theory, this constraint should be a fairly simple one to accommodate. However, in practice, the need to make the most efficient use of preexisting holdings turns out to greatly complicate the cash flow matching procedure. It has proven necessary to develop considerably more sophisticated computer techniques in order to fully implement optimal matching utilizing "preexisting holdings."

Figure 9: The Quality Spread and Matching Portfolio Costs

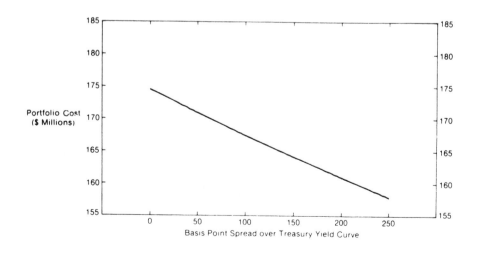

Portfolio Cost ($ Millions)

Basis Point Spread over Treasury Yield Curve

TAKEOUTS OF EXCESS FUNDS

As observed earlier, it is important to distinguish between the experience ultimately realized and the planning assumptions employed in constructing the
original portfolio.

While the realized experience may include a range of different events, it is
useful to focus on the reinvestment rate for purposes of illustration. When the
realized reinvestment rate exceeds the planning reinvestment rate used in constructing the portfolio, excess funds will be generated in terms of interest-on-interest at the higher rate. Theoretically, the excess funds generated within each
period could be "taken out" of the portfolio and returned to the fund sponsor
for other applications. At each point in time, this takeout would have no adverse impact on the ability of the portfolio to fulfill its future cash flow requirements as long as the minimum *planning* reinvestment rate is realized or
exceeded.

The prospect of these takeouts can have important significance in itself. For
example, consider the optimal portfolio for the case of a 0% reinvestment rate.
In the discussion relating to Figure 7, it was noted that this portfolio has an
original market cost of $174.58 million. However, should a reinvestment rate of
10% actually be realized throughout the period, this portfolio would generate a
series of excess funds within different periods. The present value of these potential takeouts (discounted at a standard 8%) would amount to the tidy sum of
$3.80 million. On the other hand, lower realized reinvestment rates would lead
to lower present values of potential takeouts.

This situation is depicted in Figure 10. The horizontal axis in this figure
corresponds to the reinvestment rate realized over the entire span of the matching program. The vertical axis depicts the present value of the potential takeouts
of the excess funds generated by the reinvestment process. The top curve in
Figure 10 represents the optimal portfolio designed for a 0% reinvestment planning assumption. At a 0% *realized* reinvestment rate, the portfolio would just
meet the prescribed payout schedule. Consequently, no excess funds would be
generated and the net takeouts would be zero. With increasing values for the
reinvestment rate, the "0% portfolio" would generate more and more interest-
on-interest. This would lead to a growing level of excess funds and hence to
larger present values for the takeouts.

In the context of Figure 10, an exact-match portfolio (if one existed) would
of course generate no excess funds regardless of the realized reinvestment rates.
Hence, the plot of the exact-match portfolio in Figure 10 would simply be the
horizontal line with a zero present value.

These two curves in Figure 10 illustrate an important point. In principle, one
might expect that a primary goal of the cash flow matching procedure is to
minimize the portfolio's *dependence* on realized reinvestment rates. However, it

Figure 10: Takeouts under Favorable Reinvestment Experience

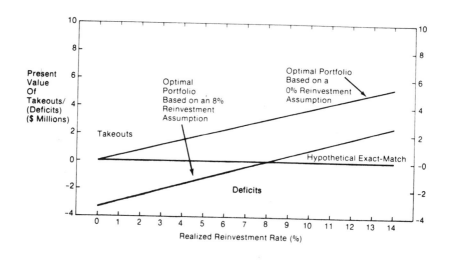

is important to distinguish between a reinvestment *sensitivity* and a *dependence* on reinvestment rates in order to fulfill the prescribed cash flow schedule.

Thus, in Figure 10, the exact-match portfolio has *no sensitivity* to the realized level of reinvestment rates. In contrast, the optimal portfolio for the 0% reinvestment planning assumption does have a *sensitivity* to realized rates. However, this reinvestment sensitivity will never lead to the portfolio having insufficient funds to fulfill the prescribed requirements—by design, the portfolio's cash flow will provide a match even at a 0% reinvestment rate. This top curve, therefore, demonstrates a *positive sensitivity* to reinvestment but *no dependence* on a specific reinvestment rate in order to meet the prescribed schedule.

The bottom curve in Figure 10 corresponds to a portfolio based upon an 8% minimum reinvestment assumption. This portfolio does not begin to generate excess funds until the realized rate exceeds the 8% planning level. For realized rates below this level, the portfolio does not provide sufficient funds in each period to fulfill the prescribed payouts. This series of deficiencies leads to a negative present value for the "takeouts." In particular, for the worst case—a realized rate of 0%—this deficiency would have a present value of -$3.32 million.

This leads into the intriguing concept of a special reserve fund for reinvestment and other contingencies.

THE RESERVE FUND

As stressed at the outset, cash flow matching procedures are usually established in a highly conservative environment. The whole intent of the matching procedure is to be as riskless as possible in terms of the fulfillment of the scheduled payouts. Consequently, it is important to set planning criteria that provide a high degree of assurance (sometimes to second and third parties) that the payout schedule will be met—*regardless* of future investment and/or reinvestment experience. On the one hand, this extreme orientation toward the avoidance of risk tends to lead to a stringent and highly conservative set of planning assumptions—all Government bonds, no call vulnerability, 0% reinvestment rate assumption, etc. On the other hand, the objective still remains to match the target cash flow with a bond portfolio having the least possible cost. In practice, tradeoffs are always made between these two conflicting goals.

The planning guidelines essentially determine the design and hence the cost of the initial portfolio. As with all structures designed for maximum reliability, the initial portfolio is likely to be overdesigned and hence somewhat more costly than necessary at the outset. To a certain extent, this overdesign and its concomitant cost may be reduced by developing an associated reserve fund to provide a level of assurance that will be comfortable for the fund sponsor(s).

Figure 11 provides a schematic outline of the interactions over time between a matching portfolio and its associated reserve fund.

The main role of the reserve fund is to cover the payouts should any deficiencies arise as a result of unfavorable experience with respect to reinvestment or other contingencies. While the reserve fund would represent "an additional cost" in a certain sense, the *realized* experience would be the ultimate determinant of the need to tap the reserve fund. With good experience in terms of reinvestment rates, credit events, refunding calls, liability experience, etc., the matching portfolio will itself generate excess funds, and there would never be a need to tap the reserve fund.

Thus, good experience over time should lead to a net buildup of excess funds within the matching portfolio as well as within the reserve fund itself. At appropriate times, these funds could be drawn down as net takeouts from the matching portfolio system and directed toward other asset applications.

The reserve fund can also provide the flexibility needed to seek structural improvements in the matching portfolio through certain forms of active management.

Figure 11: Net Takeouts from a Matched Portfolio with a Reserve Fund

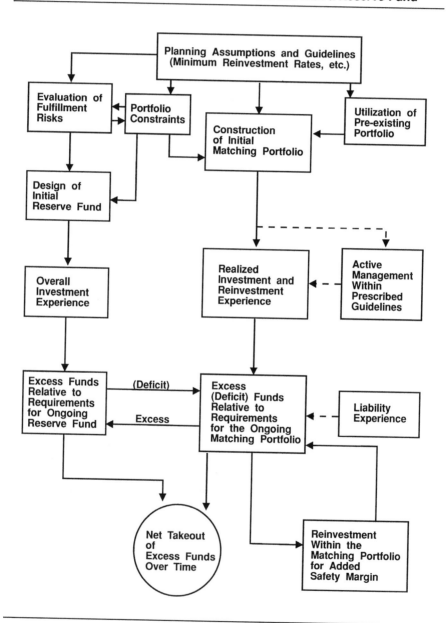

ACTIVE MANAGEMENT WITHIN THE MATCHING PORTFOLIO

As noted earlier, the matched portfolio is theoretically designed so as to fulfill its function even under a totally passive buy-and-hold posture, i.e., the simple mechanical collection of coupon and principal receipts. However, the changing character of the marketplace is likely to create opportunities where certain forms of active management would appear appropriate for even the most risk-averse sponsor of a matched portfolio system. Clearly, the integrity of the portfolio's conservative purpose must be maintained, and this will limit the nature of acceptable management activity. Nevertheless, certain types of activities can reasonably be expected to enhance the prospective takeouts within conservative portfolios, and other forms of activity may be advised in order to further control the residual portfolio risks. The extent and aggressiveness of these activities will, of course, depend upon the limits imposed by the fund sponsor.

The simplest example of a (virtually irresistible) management activity would be true substitution swaps of a yield pickup nature. In a highly institutional and issue-specific bond market, the opportunity arises from time to time for yield pickup swaps with bonds having substantially identical characteristics. Since the portfolio's goal is to provide a prescribed cash flow, any yield pickup swap that enables the cash flow to be maintained and that respects the prescribed portfolio constraints will necessarily lead to a reduced cost for the portfolio, and hence to the possibility of net takeouts.

Sectoral shifts within the marketplace can also provide the opportunity for a more broadly based yield pickup restructuring and hence for larger takeouts. However, in the course of moving in the direction of yield pickup restructurings, one must be careful that the portfolio is not being gradually led down a one-way street toward a subtle deterioration in effective credit quality, call vulnerability, or an *unintentional* loss of marketability and liquidity.

(In point of fact, a more aggressive form of active management might include the opportunity to give up yield on an issue-to-issue basis, in order to achieve advantages in terms of "spread value," credit quality, call vulnerability, marketability, etc. While such swaps would lead to a pay-up within the narrow context of the matched portfolio, they could be readily accommodated on a controlled basis within a system consisting of a matched portfolio together with an associated reserve fund.)

Another important form of active management could be derived from the changing character of the optimal matching portfolio under changing yield curve shapes and levels. As noted earlier, both the cost *and the structure* of the optimal portfolio can vary dramatically under such market movement. In some instances, there may be a compelling and significant incentive to change from the existing (once-optimal) portfolio into a lower cost (newly optimal) portfolio. If the magnitude of the savings is sufficient in light of the transaction effort involved, this could lead to significant additional takeouts. Clearly, it is well worthwhile to monitor both the existing portfolio and the hypothetical newly optimal portfolio on an ongoing basis. The value of an effective computer system to assist in this monitoring process is self-evident.

Finally, one of the major advantages of a matching portfolio of marketable securities is that it enables the fund sponsor to totally redirect his assets should there arise a compelling reason to do so. Such redirection might consist of the substitution of another "matching vehicle" or the actual unwinding of the matching process itself. Clearly, any such unwinding would lead to a concurrent loss of some of the benefits achieved and would presumably not be undertaken lightly or casually. However, in these uncertain times, when unexpected opportunities, problems or totally new organizational events seem to occur with a discomforting frequency, a marketable matching portfolio can provide the fund sponsor with an important dimension of flexibility.

SUMMARY

While cash flow matching is a venerable investment problem, recent events have endowed it with a new importance for the fund sponsor as well as for the investment manager. The high level of bond yields, the extreme shapes of the yield curve, and the wide sectoral spreads provide an historically unique opportunity for constructing relatively low cost portfolios that can safely match different types of prescribed liability schedules. Moreover, the development of new analytical techniques—and the computer systems to implement them—have made optimal portfolio matching into a feasible and practical tool for a much broader range of investment situations.

Chapter III D-8

Contingent Immunization

The traditional motivation for bond investment was to secure a fixed cash flow over some appropriate time frame. The typical bond investor was highly risk averse. He was more than willing to sacrifice the excitement of potentially spectacular results in order to achieve a reliable pattern of return. Over time, a series of active management techniques evolved to take advantage of what were perceived to be market opportunities and/or to avoid the full impact of identifiable market problems. In the early years, active management was simply viewed as a way to enhance the basic return pattern available within the traditional fixed-income framework.

In recent years, however, the traditional role of bonds as an asset category has been buffeted by a series of dramatic changes in the marketplace. Surging interest rates and an explosion in volatility have characterized recent markets. At the same time, total return measurement has become an almost universally applied performance yardstick for bond managers. These measurements have highlighted the disastrous, and often negative, returns in many bond portfolios. When these short-term results are coupled with the unprecedented volatility and uncertainty that now seem to be a hallmark of the debt markets, it is little

Martin L. Leibowitz and Alfred Weinberger, "The Uses of Contingent Immunization: A New Procedure for Structured Active Management," *The Journal of Portfolio Management*, Fall 1981. Reprinted with permission.

wonder that the traditional function of the fixed-income portfolio is being widely reexamined.

This environment imposes a harsh dilemma on the bond portfolio manager: How to pursue prudent active strategies and still provide his client with the comfort level that probably served as the primary basis for allocating funds to the fixed-income market in the first place?

THE ATTRACTIONS OF CONTINGENT IMMUNIZATION

It is this fundamental dilemma that motivated our development of the *contingent immunization* procedure. With this technique, the traditional purpose is served by specifying a minimum return target over an appropriate time frame. This minimum return target acts as the safety net—it provides a well-defined dimension of risk control. In essence, this safety net is woven out of the new developments that comprise the technique of bond immunization. This safety net is not binding, at least not at the outset, but it does place certain risk-control limits upon the management process. As long as the combination of portfolio structures and market circumstances remains within these risk-control limits, the manager can freely pursue enhanced return through active management.

Should a situation develop that threatens the fund's ability to reliably achieve its minimum return target, the portfolio is triggered into an "immunization" mode. In this eventuality, the portfolio is then restructured as an immunized fund designed to provide the minimum return target specified at the outset. Essentially, the portfolio will then have "fallen" into the safety net. Hence, our choice of the term contingent immunization.

A key ingredient in the contingent immunization approach is the development of an objective procedure for continually monitoring the portfolio over time so as to ensure that the safety net remains well placed. Furthermore, in addition to the analytic constraints, the portfolio must remain sufficiently liquid and the manager sufficiently alert so that any actions required to keep the program on track can be implemented on a timely basis. In particular, this presumes that the nature of market movements is consistent with the portfolio restructuring required should the immunization mode become necessary.

With this assurance, contingent immunization can provide a structural solution to the dilemma of the modern bond portfolio manager. On the one hand, the traditional comfort level sought by the fixed-income investor can be restored through an objective procedure with a reliable minimum return target. On the other hand, the manager remains free—usually surprisingly free—to exercise judgment in pursuit of the enhanced return that he and his client both desire.

THE TWO CHARACTERISTIC PARAMETERS

There are two parameters characterizing a given contingent immunization program that serve to define where on the risk/return spectrum the program will be positioned, as well as the degree of flexibility of the active management process. The two parameters are: 1) the minimum return target, or more specifically, the difference between the minimum return target and the immunization return then available in the market, and 2) the acceptable range for the terminal horizon date of the program. In other words, a limited horizon range is used to replace the rigidly fixed horizon date employed in conventional immunization programs. Thus, contingent immunization requires that the manager meet the minimum return target (which will be somewhat lower than the maximum rate currently available) over some investment period that falls within the specified horizon range.

As will become evident, it is the loosening up of the two characteristic parameters—minimum return and a fixed horizon date—that are the key sources of flexibility in a contingent immunization procedure. In the subsequent discussion, we develop examples using the following values for the relevant variables:

immunization return	= 12%,
minimum return target	= 11%,
nominal horizon	= 5 Years,
acceptable horizon range	= 4-6 Years, and
initial portfolio value	= $100.

POTENTIAL RETURN PATTERNS

Figure 1 illustrates the potential rewards, and the risks involved, in contingent immunization relative to classical immunization. In the example, the portfolio manager is positive on the market and purchases a relatively long 30-year portfolio. Now, suppose an immediate favorable yield change occurs. The portfolio will jump in asset value. If the portfolio were liquidated and placed into a 5-year classical immunization mode, the resulting potential return would then reflect the increased return achieved over the entire 5-year period.

For example, suppose there was an immediate yield change of -3%, or a move from 12% to 9%. Then the portfolio would have a sufficiently large capital gain so that, if it were then immunized at the 9% level, the annualized compound return for the full 5 years would be about 14.7%. This type of result would be a positive consequence of the leeway afforded the portfolio manager in constructing the portfolio.

The risk side of the story in this example occurs if yields rise. Thus, an immediate market yield move of about +1.6%, from 12% to 13.6%, would make

Figure 1: 30-Year Portfolio Under Contingent Immunization (Immunization Return = 12%; Minimum Return Target = 11%; Horizon = 5 Years)

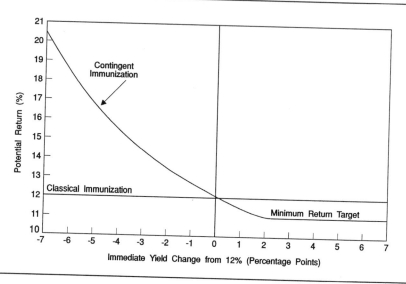

the potential return fall to the minimum target return of 11%. Under the contingent immunization program, this drop would result in the immunization of the portfolio in order to secure the 11% minimum return. In fact, this is precisely the type of contingency that leads to immunization under contingent immunization. Any additional yield increase beyond 13.6% would leave the potential return unchanged because the portfolio will have been immunized. (A reader familiar with the basic profit diagrams for options will immediately recognize their structural similarity to Figure 1.)

PORTFOLIO GROWTH OVER TIME

Figure 1 has demonstrated the nature of the rewards and risks in a contingent immunization plan for a single point in time. Figures 2, 3, and 4 use simulation results to illustrate these risk and reward patterns as they might unfold dynamically through time. By tracing these orbits of portfolio assets over the investment period, one can identify the critical events and the different patterns of realization that can occur with a contingent immunization program.

Figure 2: Unsuccessful Active Management Under Contingent Immunization (Immunization Return = 12%; Minimum Return Target = 11%)

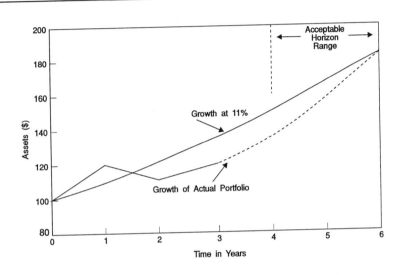

Figure 2 shows the results of a simulation where the efforts at active management have been unsuccessful. At the end of year 3, the portfolio had to be immunized in order to assure the minimum target return of 11% (to the outer limit of the horizon range). The short vertical lines descending from the portfolio growth curve at years 1 and 2 are a measure of how close the portfolio is to requiring immunization in order to assure the target return. In a sense, these lines represent the current latitude available to the portfolio manager. At year 3, this latitude is completely used up.

In contrast, Figure 3 shows the results of a simulation of successful active management. The portfolio has grown considerably faster than would have been the case under strict immunization.

Figure 4 is another way of looking at the preceding simulations of successful and unsuccessful active management. For each year of the simulations, the level of potential return is plotted. This is the return that would have been "locked in" if the portfolio had been immunized at that point. Years in which active management is successful (relative to an immunization mode) increase the potential return. Years in which active management is unsuccessful reduce potential return. Finally, years where the portfolio is immunized for the remaining horizon leave the potential return unchanged.

Figure 3: Successful Active Management Under Contingent Immunization (Immunization Return = 12%; Minimum Return Target = 11%)

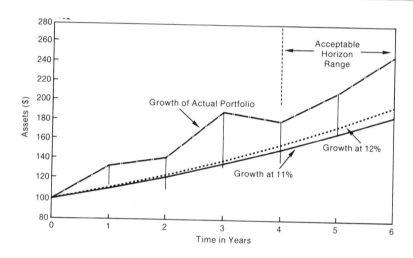

Figure 4: Potential Returns if Immunized over Remaining Time to Horizon (Minimum Return Target = 11%)

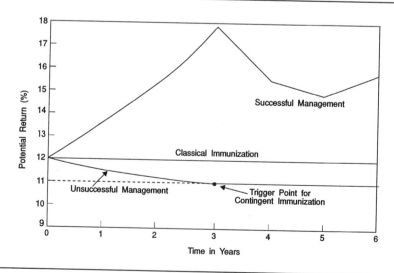

CLASSICAL IMMUNIZATION

Let us now take a closer look at exactly why and how contingent immunization affords the portfolio manager greater flexibility than a classical immunization approach.

We begin with a quick review of some fundamental concepts of immunization. If we start with $100 and wish to realize a target return of 12% a year for 5 years, we would need to generate $176 at the end of 5 years. If the available investment yield level were other than 12%, we would need more or less than $100 to achieve $176 in 5 years. Figure 5 shows how much we would need today at various yield levels. The distinguishing feature of an immunized investment is that, as yield levels change, we are always left with sufficient asset value to achieve, at the then-prevailing interest rates, the target amount at the horizon. Thus, if rates decline, the immunized portfolio must provide a capital gain sufficient to compensate for the reduced growth rate over time. For example, in a 10% interest rate environment, a portfolio value of at least $109 would be required. In other words, a value of $109 compounded at 10% for 5 years would grow to the $176 target value.

Figure 5: Required Assets to Achieve Target (Target = 12%; Horizon = 5 Years)

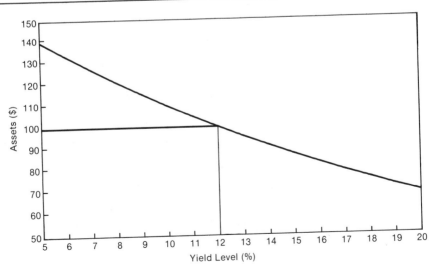

Figure 6: Price Response and Assets Required (Target = 12%; Horizon = 5 Years)

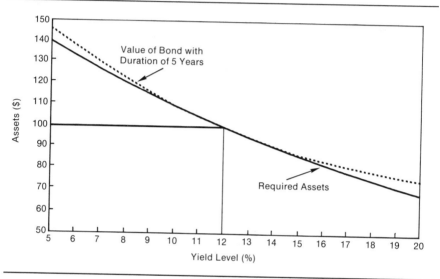

Value of Bond with Duration of 5 Years

Required Assets

Assets ($)

Yield Level (%)

Figure 6 illustrates this point. Superimposed on the curve of Figure 5 is the price response of an asset for different yield levels. The price response does exactly what we would like. In fact, it does even slightly better. This asset is a bond with a *Macaulay Duration*[1] of 5 years at an initial yield level of 12%. If we purchase $100 of this bond, we see that any immediate shift in yields will always leave us with at least sufficient value to achieve the $176 at the end of 5 years. This would assure a realized return equal to the starting yield of 12%. If we choose an asset with a duration other than exactly 5 years, we would find ourselves with insufficient value to achieve the target under some yield moves. In particular, if the asset has a duration greater than 5 years, moves to higher yield levels would be troublesome. The opposite would hold for assets with duration less than 5 years.

---

[1] For general discussion of classical immunization and the role of Macaulay Duration, see *Bond Immunization: A Procedure for Realizing Target Levels of Return*, Martin L. Leibowitz, Salomon Brothers, October 10, 1979. This article was reproduced in *Pros and Cons of Immunization*, Proceedings of a Seminar on the Roles and Limits of Bond Immunization, January 17, 1980.

BUILDING FLEXIBILITY INTO IMMUNIZATION

Now let us see what happens when we start to loosen some of the rigid conditions of strict classical immunization. First, consider a reduction in the target
return. Figure 7 shows the required assets at various yield levels for both the
original immunization target of 12% and for the reduced target of 11%. Clearly,
the reduced target requires a significantly lower asset value at all yield levels.

Figure 8 now shows the increased flexibility available to a portfolio manager
in asset selection. Along with the required asset curve at an 11% target return,
we have the price responses of a 2-year bond (having a 1.8-year duration) and a
30-year bond (with an 8.6-year duration). Both these bonds have durations that
differ widely from the 5-year horizon. Hence, neither one would fulfill the criteria for a strict immunization vehicle over the 5-year horizon. Yet both bonds
have a degree of latitude such that their yields can change in either direction
and there will still be sufficient assets to assure the 11% minimum return.

More specifically, if the portfolio manager were expecting a decline in yield
levels, he would want to position his portfolio in longer maturities, e.g., the
30-year instrument. If yields change in the expected downward direction, then
the portfolio would have a value far in excess of that required to achieve the
original target. Hence, the potential return of the portfolio will have increased.

**Figure 7: Elements of Flexibility: Reduced Minimum Return Target
(Horizon = 5 Years)**

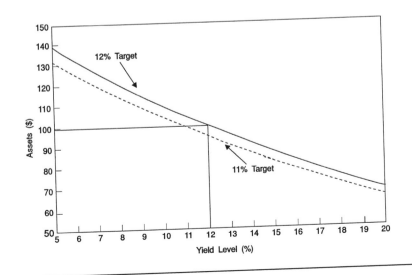

Figure 8: Elements of Flexibility: Asset Maturity Selection (Horizon = 5 Years)

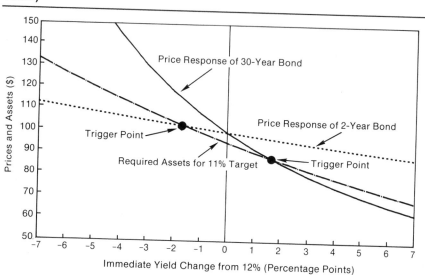

On the other hand, if yields rise, there would still be sufficient assets to continue active management up to the point where the bond value fell below the curve depicting the asset level required to meet the 11% target. This corresponds to the yield level indicated by the trigger point at a yield move of +1.6%. At this level of yields, the manager would have to go into the immunization mode to assure the 11% target.

An active manager expecting higher yield levels could purchase the 2-year instrument. This would prove highly productive if yields rose as anticipated. If yields declined, the 2-year bond would continue to provide an adequate asset value up to the indicated trigger point at a -1.6% yield move.

TRIGGER YIELD CONTOURS

Figure 9 expands this concept of trigger yield moves to include the full range of available maturities. For all portfolio maturities between 0 and 30 years, it shows the yield level that would necessitate a shift into the immunization mode in order to assure the minimum target return. In other words, these are the trigger point yield levels of Figure 8, but for all maturities.

**Figure 9: Degree of Flexibility Achieved through Lower Target Return
(Horizon = 5 Years; Minimum Return Target = 11%)**

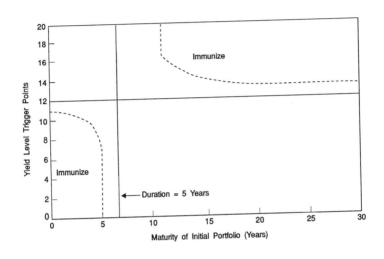

For portfolios where durations are longer than the 5-year horizon, the problems occur in a rising interest rate environment. Thus, the longer the duration, the smaller the adverse yield move that can be tolerated. For portfolios with durations shorter than 5 years, the shorter the duration, the smaller the yield decline to trigger immunization.

For portfolios with maturities between 5 and 11 years, there is *no immediate market move* that could force the portfolio into the "safety net."[2] In other words, within this range of maturities, there is *no way* to blow it in a *single* market event! On the other hand, there always exists some sequence of portfolio restructurings that, accompanied by repeated market fiascoes, would eat up the flexibility cushion and ultimately force the portfolio into the immunization safety net.

---

[2] This effect is related to the minimum return concept for a fixed horizon date that was set forth by W. Marshall and J. Yawitz in "Lower Bounds on Portfolio Performance: A Generalized Immunization Strategy," Working Paper, Institute for Banking and Capital Markets, Washington University, January 1979.

HORIZON RANGES

The discussion to this point has focused on the flexibility in portfolio management introduced by setting a minimum return target below the prevailing level of immunized returns. We now examine the effects of a second relaxation from the discipline of strict immunization. Figure 10 illustrates the effect of setting a horizon range in place of a fixed single-point horizon. In this figure, the minimum return target remains at 11%, but this return is promised for some point between 4 and 6 years in the future, rather than for exactly 5 years. The effect on management flexibility is dramatic:

1. The trigger point for a 30-year portfolio has moved from the 13.6% of Figure 9 to almost 16%.

2. The range of maturities for which there is no trigger point at all for immediate yield moves has expanded to 4.5-20 years.

It is also noteworthy that the expansion in flexibility is most pronounced at the longer end of the maturity scale.

What happens when we change the target return? Figure 11 demonstrates the effects of increases in the minimum return target from 11% to 11.5% and then to 11.75%. Not surprisingly, the range of management maneuverability be-

Figure 10: Added Flexibility through Horizon Range (Horizon Range = 4-6 Years; Minimum Return Target = 11%

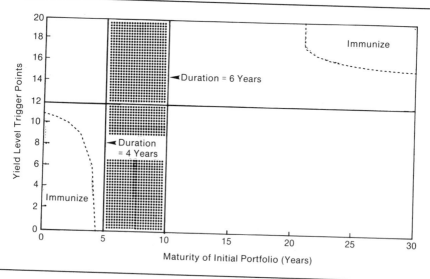

Figure 11: Trigger Point Contours for Various Minimum Return Targets (Horizon Range = 4-6 Years)

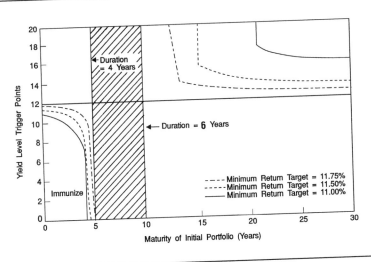

gins to shrink as the minimum return target approaches our assumed immunization return of 12%.

MONITORING PROCEDURE

As was discussed earlier, the contingent immunization process has definite elements of risk control as an integral feature. This risk control must be exercised through close monitoring of the portfolio over time. The control procedures must ensure that the portfolio structure, in the context of prevailing market conditions, remains able to achieve at least the minimum return target. There exists a clear-cut mathematical procedure for establishing these control criteria.

Many facets of contingent immunization deserve further discussion, both in terms of the mathematical theory as well as the practical considerations involved in market applications. Our purpose here has been, in a general way, to offer for consideration an idea that blends different techniques into a new structured approach to the management process. The resulting synthesis of risk control and flexibility would appear to have special appeal to both portfolio managers and their clients—particularly in the volatile and uncertain markets of today.

Chapter III D-9

Contingent Immunization Procedures—
Part I: Risk Control

Contingent Immunization is a procedure for the pursuit of active bond management within a framework that provides a minimum return even under adverse experience. This is achieved through a procedural "safety net" based upon the modern techniques of bond immunization. The portfolio remains in an active management mode as long as the portfolio's asset value places it above this safety net. The portfolio enters the immunization mode only when absolutely necessary to assure a promised minimum return.

Central to the implementation of Contingent Immunization is an effective system for monitoring and risk control. This article details a number of the ideas and the potential problems involved in the development of risk control programs for Contingent Immunization. Part I, in this issue, reviews the basic concept of Contingent Immunization, showing how it fits within a framework encompassing both active management and immunization techniques, and outlines the main ingredients of a risk control process. Part II, to appear in the January/February issue, will identify a series of potential problems that can occur under Contingent Immunization and will point out various ways of mitigating their effects; it will also describe empirical studies that shed light on some of the key assumptions involved in the Contingent Immunization process and examine the rather distinctive character of the risk control process.

Martin L. Leibowitz and Alfred Weinberger, "Contingent Immunization—Part I: Risk Control Procedures," *Financial Analysts Journal*, November/December 1982. Received "Q" Award in 1982. Reprinted with permission.

THE CONCEPT OF CONTINGENT IMMUNIZATION

Contingent Immunization is a form of active management.[1] Active management can encompass a very broad range of fixed-income portfolio activity.[2] In recent years, the nature of the markets has led to rate anticipation becoming one of the primary forms of active management. In essence, rate anticipation constitutes adopting maturity postures that reflect the manager's judgment regarding the future direction of interest rates.

For example, if a portfolio manager believes strongly that interest rates are about to decline, then he may place a substantial portion of his portfolio's assets into long-term bonds. He would then enjoy or suffer, depending upon subsequent movements in interest rates, the price movements depicted in Figure A. If the yield on 30-year bonds decreases by 500 basis points to 10%, an original investment of $100 million will increase in asset value to $147 million. Under this happy circumstance, the active manager will then be free to make a whole range of new choices depending on his market expectations from that point forward.

As one might suspect, rate anticipation is a high-risk technique. Over the course of time, the sequence of rate anticipation decisions, successful as well as unsuccessful, will determine the portfolio's asset value and the corresponding rate of return. This return will essentially constitute the cumulative result of the manager's active management process. Because of the risks associated with rate anticipation, the manager's intent is to achieve a level of return in excess of those available under less risky approaches.

CLASSICAL IMMUNIZATION

Classical immunization seeks a defined return over a specified time horizon. In fact, it can be characterized as a procedure for trying to achieve the maximum return that can be assured with almost full certainty. Immunization thus represents an effort to "lock up" over the chosen horizon the currently available market yield. Placing a major portfolio component under immunization implies a decision to accept currently available market rates. (In this sense, immunization

---

[1] The term Contingent Immunization was first coined in "Contingent Immunization: A New Procedure for Structured Active Management" by Martin L. Leibowitz and Alfred Weinberger (Salomon Brothers Inc, January 28, 1981). A modified version of this original study was published as "The Uses of Contingent Immunization" by Leibowitz and Weinberger in *The Journal of Portfolio Management*, Fall 1981.

[2] For a description of some of the techniques and developments of active management in recent markets, see "Trends in Bond Portfolio Management," in *The Investment Manager's Handbook* (Homewood, IL: Dow Jones-Irwin, Inc., 1979).

Figure A: Price Behavior of a 30-Year Bond

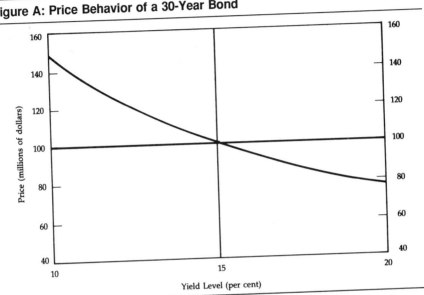

is itself a kind of rate anticipation decision!) Over a well-defined investment horizon, the initial return compounded will translate into an equivalent target future asset value.

For our purposes, immunization can be viewed as a technique of achieving a target return through the construction of portfolios that have the "right" level of price sensitivity at each point in time. Broadly speaking, the right level of price sensitivity is that which provides an asset value that, when compounded at each new prevailing level of rates, will grow to at least the targeted horizon value.

The concept may be clarified by a simple example. Suppose that a portfolio manager has an investment horizon of five years and that the prevailing level of rates is 15%. He would use immunization to insure that this 15% market rate will be effectively compounded throughout the five-year period, so that an initial portfolio of $100 million will grow to $206 million at the end of the fifth year.

As long as interest rates remain constant at the 15% level, this compounding can obviously take place without any problems. Should interest rates decline to 10%, however, the manager will be faced with having to reinvest flows from the portfolio at this new, lower market rate.

The immunization procedure is designed to protect the portfolio against this risk of reinvestment at lower rates. If the portfolio is immunized, its value will rise sufficiently under lower rates so as still to achieve the original dollar target. For the assumed movement from 15% to 10%, suppose that the initial $100 million portfolio rises to an asset value in excess of $127 million; if the manager then sells the entire portfolio and reinvests at 10%, the $127 million compounded at 10% for five years will grow to $206 million. The original target dollar return will still be achieved. (This concept is formalized in the appendix.)

The key to immunization is to maintain a certain pattern of minimum asset values under a range of interest rate movements. Figure B illustrates the pattern of minimum asset values for the case described above. It turns out that, by constructing bond portfolios that have certain price sensitivity characteristics, one can achieve portfolio price patterns that lie above the required asset value line. For example, the dotted line in Figure B plots the asset value of a portfolio consisting of $100 million, 15% par bonds with a maturity of approximately 8 1/2 years. This portfolio will always have sufficient assets to achieve at least the original target and thereby insure the original 15% return. (This portfolio works because it has a "duration" of five years; duration is an analytical gauge of a bond's price sensitivity under certain types of yield curve movements.)

At the same time, it is also apparent from Figure B that the immunization procedure clashes with active management based upon rate anticipation. Consider, for example, an active manager with the 30-year portfolio shown in Figure A. By mentally superimposing the price response in Figure A on the minimum

Figure B: Classical Immunization

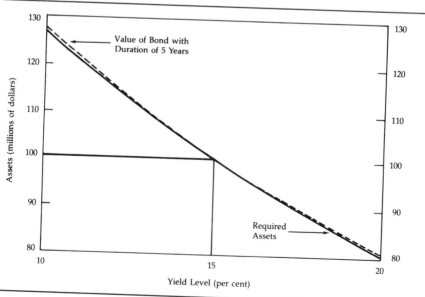

asset values in Figure B, one can see that the active portfolio will violate the immunization criterion with the least upward movement in rates.[3]

ACCEPTING A CUSHION SPREAD

It has long been recognized that attempts to use immunization procedures to insure the highest possible yields are subject to enormously stringent conditions and uncertain results. By the same token, it has also been observed that allowing for a "cushion" below this maximum rate adds a degree of flexibility to even a classically immunized portfolio procedure.[4] And, as interest rates rose to unprecedented levels in 1981, it became possible for portfolio managers to consider very acceptable minimum returns that were well below a maximum possible target rate. In other words, when the maximum market rate is 15%, a minimum return of 14% seems like a very satisfactory level of return.

For this 100 basis point "cushion spread" (from 15% to 14%), one obtains a certain degree of portfolio flexibility. In fact, cushion spreads of 100 to 200 basis points create a surprisingly large latitude for the pursuit of active management. A series of repeated adverse movements—the traditional "whipsaw" nightmare of every portfolio manager—could occur without the portfolio falling below the required asset value for the minimum target return.

Figure C shows the assets required under different interest rate levels to provide a 15% market return and a 14% "floor" return over a five-year period. The curve for the 15% rate is, of course, identical to the one in Figure B; the curve for the 14% floor illustrates the minimum asset value required to be able to generate a 14%, five-year compounded return on a $100 million portfolio when interest rates are at the level indicated.

---

[3] In this example, and for most of Part I, we deal with the simplest model of immunization—parallel movements along a flat yield curve. The literature of bond immunization has grown large in scope and contains many refinements that go far beyond this simple model. See for a partial bibliography of articles relating to immunization theory, *Financial Handbook*, fifth edition (New York: John Wiley & Sons, 1981), Section 19, p. 37.

[4] For example, "Bond Immunization: A Procedure for Realizing Target Levels of Return," by Martin L. Leibowitz (Salomon Brothers Inc, 1979), states:

"On the one hand, with stringently specified targets, the manager would follow a rather basic immunization strategy using his market insights primarily to provide additional insurance that the return target will indeed be met. On the other hand, a fund with a greater risk tolerance might establish a more relaxed target for minimum return, thereby allowing the manager to aggressively seek incremental return in the short term, while still maintaining a risk-controlled portfolio posture relative to the longer-term horizon."

Figure C: Price Behavior Required for Floor Return

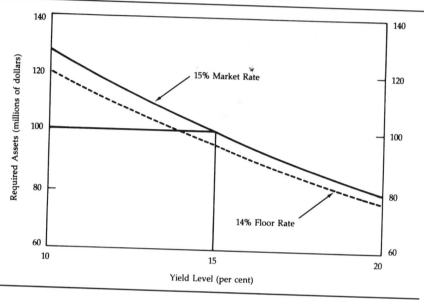

Figure D: Safety Margin for a Portfolio of 30-Year Bonds

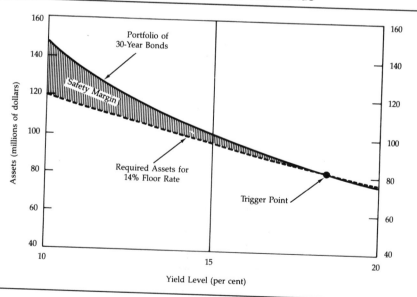

As we noted earlier, an actively managed portfolio of 30-year, 15% par bonds would be vulnerable to violating the required asset line for the 15% target rate—the least upward movement in yields would lead to asset values lower than the required amount. However, superimposing the price behavior of 30-year bonds on the 14% required asset curve yields the configuration shown in Figure D. This shows that, if interest rates remain at the initial 15% level, the $100 million portfolio will clearly have more value than is needed to assure fulfillment of the 14% floor return.

The assets above and beyond the required level are referred to as the "safety margin." Thus one can see that the $100 million portfolio has at the outset a safety margin of about five million dollars. If yields decline, the active strategy proves successful, and the safety margin increases with the superior performance of the 30-year bond portfolio. If interest rates rise, the safety margin decreases, and the portfolio's assets approach the required asset level. In fact, Figure D shows that the active portfolio of 30-year bonds will decline to the required asset level after an upward rate move of about 350 basis points. At this point, the safety margin will have been totally eroded, and the portfolio will have to be immunized in order to assure fulfillment of the 14% floor rate. (A more analytical definition of the safety margin is provided in the appendix.)

Figure D thus illustrates the key idea behind Contingent Immunization. The portfolio manager can take an active stance, even a very high-risk active stance. If market movements prove beneficial to his posture, then he will reap the rewards of his active stance. Even in the face of adverse market movements, however, the manager can still pursue active policies up until a certain point. In this example, the portfolio can tolerate adverse market movements of over 350 basis points—even though the manager has adopted the longest possible maturity stance in the par bond market!

Because of the latitude of movement allowed, a Contingent Immunization program enables the portfolio manager to accept the possibility of adverse movements, to tailor his posture in the face of such movements, and to have ample time to restructure his portfolio into an immunized mode should that become necessary.

POTENTIAL RETURN

The yardstick of "potential return" turns out to be quite helpful in both understanding Contingent Immunization and developing monitoring systems. The potential return is the return the portfolio would achieve over the entire investment horizon if, at any point, the assets in hand were immunized at the then-current market rate. This measurement can be applied at any time during the course of the investment period, but it always relates to the return over the entire period from beginning to end.

Figure E: The Potential Return Concept

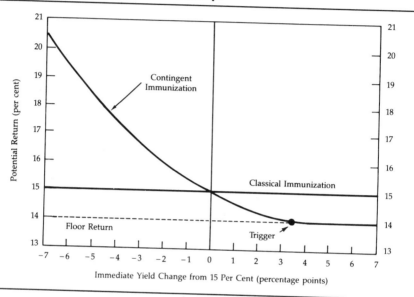

Immediate Yield Change from 15 Per Cent (percentage points)

For example, Figure E shows how the price performance of the portfolio depicted in Figure D translates into a pattern of potential returns. If the portfolio were immediately immunized at the outset—i.e., before any market movement away from the 15% level—it would naturally earn the 15% market rate, and the potential return would therefore be exactly 15%. On the other hand, if yields declined instantaneously to 10%, the portfolio's asset value would increase to $147 million, as shown in Figure D. If this $147 million portfolio were then liquidated, and the proceeds restructured so as to achieve the market rate of 10% over the five-year period, the resulting portfolio would grow to a total value of $239 million. This represents an 18.25% rate of return on the original $100 million portfolio. Consequently, as shown in Figure E, the portfolio's potential return would be 18.25%.

Of course, if interest rates rose, the asset value would decline at a rate faster than the minimum asset value curves in Figure D, and the potential return would decrease in value. For example, at a yield level of 17%, the asset value of the 30-year par bond portfolio would decline to $88 million. If this amount were then restructured into an immunized portfolio at the 17% rate, the resulting compounding would lead to a total value of $199 million at the investment horizon; this corresponds to a potential return of 14.32%.

As Figure D shows, at the 18.50% interest rate level the 30-year bonds would decline to a value of $81 million; the portfolio would have to be restructured into the immunized mode, and its potential return at this point would be exactly 14%. Although yield levels may rise higher than the 18.50% trigger level, the portfolio will already have been immunized to maintain the 14% floor rate. The Contingent Immunization system will, therefore, always maintain a minimum potential return. (A mathematical definition of potential return is contained in the appendix.)

Movements in asset value such as depicted in Figure D can be translated into a potential return diagram. The potential return concept helps to show the effects of short-term movements on longer-term goals. While it is most useful in understanding and developing monitoring systems for Contingent Immunization systems, the potential return concept stands on its own. In particular, potential return can serve as an alternative measure in an era when rates of return over short-term periods are the only hard numbers otherwise available for the assessment of bond portfolio performance.

RISK CONTROL PROCEDURES

The development of any Contingent Immunization system requires the ability to control and monitor the progress of the portfolio over time. Clearly, the control procedures must be dynamic and responsive to changes in portfolio risk characteristics that result from the passage of time and the consequent shortening of the investment horizon.

From the preceding section, it can be immediately appreciated that the safety margin can function as the key control variable. As long as the safety margin remains greater than zero, the portfolio can continue to operate in an active mode. Should the safety margin ever fall to zero, the immunization mode must be triggered.

This was evident in the example shown in Figure D. The active mode persists as long as the portfolio value exceeds the minimum asset level needed to achieve the promised 14% floor. This safety margin criterion can be stated more generally in terms of a hypothetical "floor portfolio." The 14% floor rate will compound to a total dollar value of $196 million by the fifth year; at any point during the investment horizon, and under any interest rate condition, there will always be a theoretical immunized portfolio that can fulfill the $196 million horizon value. This hypothetical portfolio is called the "floor portfolio."[5]

---

[5] This definition can be immediately extended to include all the other market factors (e.g., spreads, yield curve shape) as well as the implications of the more recent developments in immunization theory. The floor portfolio can be further refined in terms of establishing other criteria, such as minimizing the transaction costs entailed in moving from the active portfolio to the immunized mode.

Figure F: Contingent Immunization Over Time

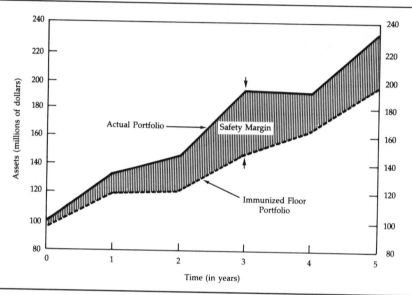

One of the advantages of control procedures based on the safety margin/floor portfolio approach is that such procedures are largely time-independent—i.e., the same control process developed for one point in time can be generalized to any future point in time. For example, Figure F shows that the actual portfolio enjoys a certain safety margin over the floor portfolio at the outset; this initial safety margin represents the dollar value of the starting cushion spread. As time progresses, both the active and the floor portfolio will respond to the natural compounding process, as well as to changes in the interest rate environment, with the active portfolio's asset value being determined largely by the manager's posture. This combination of factors will lead to either decreases or increases in the safety margin.

Over time, the floor portfolio will grow—perhaps in an erratic fashion—from the original $95 million amount at the outset to the $196 million asset value promised by the 14% floor rate of return. As long as the actively managed portfolio retains at each point in time an asset value in excess of the floor portfolio, there will be no need to enter the immunized state. Hence the key problem at any point in time is the same as the problem at the outset: The safety margin must be kept greater than zero. This simplifies the discussion of the control process so that one can focus on the control problem at the outset and know that the same techniques can, by and large, be generalized to any given point in time.

TRIGGER YIELD CONTOURS

The Contingent Immunization approach weaves together active management, which often does not have a well-defined time horizon, and an immunization system, which has an almost rigidly defined time limit. As might be expected, the passage of time leads to increasing constraints on the active management mode in the later years. However, the magnitude of these constraints depends critically on the extent to which the active management mode has been successful. With successful active management in the early years, the constraints in the later years become surprisingly modest.

The limits on active flexibility in a Contingent Immunization system can be viewed in several different ways. One may focus on the cushion spread between the market return available (i.e., through classical immunization) and the promised floor rate. In the earlier example, this cushion spread consisted of the 100-basis-point spread between the 15% market rate and the 14% floor rate. As the portfolio progresses through time, this cushion spread can be generalized as the spread of the potential return over the floor rate. This cushion may also be expressed as a safety margin—i.e., the asset value difference between the actual portfolio and the floor portfolio. In the above example, the actual portfolio consisted at the very outset of the $100 million initial investment, while the floor portfolio had an asset value of $95 million; the resulting safety margin was thus five million dollars.

Both the cushion spread and the safety margin depend solely on the asset value of the active portfolio. They have no reference to the portfolio's composition. However, once the active portfolio is structured in a particular way, additional market insights become apparent. For example, Figures D and E show that an active portfolio consisting of 30-year, 15% par bonds can sustain an approximately 350-basis-point adverse movement in yield before immunization becomes necessary. The yield level at which triggering becomes necessary can be referred to as the "trigger yield." In essence, the trigger yield concept enables one to translate a safety margin into a very informative measure of the tolerable market movement.

When establishing a Contingent Immunization system, the active portfolio manager would want to know the implications of various portfolio postures. For example, the manager would certainly want to know how much tolerance a given posture has for adverse market movements. The trigger yields for different active postures provide a measure of such tolerance. One of the most useful planning diagrams in Contingent Immunization is the one showing trigger yield contours, as in Figure G.

Figure G illustrates a trigger yield contour diagram for the simplest possible situation. The horizontal axis corresponds to the maturity of the portfolio, while the vertical axis indicates the trigger yield values. The yield curve is assumed to be flat at 15%. All portfolios are considered to consist of 15% par bonds having the specified maturities. Thus the right-most point in Figure G corresponds to a portfolio consisting of 30-year, 15% par bonds. Figure G indicates that there will be no need for triggering should yields move down, and that yields could move up to the 18.50% level before immunization is required. This is, of course, the same result observed in different forms in Figures D and E.

As the maturity of the portfolio is shortened to 20 years, the trigger yield rises to 19.25%, allowing for a 425-basis-point adverse movement. Further shortening of the portfolio to the 10-year point leads to a trigger yield that is off the diagram. In other words, the portfolio cannot be forced to immunize with yield movements of +500 basis points. (In point of fact, there is no trigger yield—on, or off, the diagram!)

If we shorten still further to the 8 1/2-year maturity, the portfolio will have a duration of five years. Since this duration is equivalent to the investment horizon, the portfolio will be in a temporary state of implicit immunization, in the sense that general yield movements will have a neutral effect upon the portfolio's potential return—i.e., such movement will leave the safety margin essentially unchanged. The manager may adopt this stance whenever he wishes to express a totally neutral, risk-averse view on the direction of interest rates. In essence, the manager has a well-defined baseline position, in contrast to the more common situation in active management where there is often a lack of understanding between the sponsor and manager as to what constitutes a neutral stance.

The existence of such a clear-cut, risk-free neutral posture has great advantages. On the one hand, it becomes very clear when a risk-seeking active posture is being taken, and the exact magnitude of that risk is known. At the same time, the manager enjoys the availability of a comfortable "safe harbor" during times of uncertainty. This means that he need not feel required to be a hero every day of every year.

Further shortening of the maturity to, say, two years creates an active posture that is "aggressively defensive." Here, increases in interest rates will enable the actual portfolio to pull ahead of the floor portfolio on a relative basis. The risk here lies in falling rates: The trigger yield occurs at the 13.44% level. As one can see, the ultimate defensive stance—very short maturities measured in days—becomes highly risky in that the trigger yields are just 100 basis points away. Consequently, a manager who wishes to be strongly defensive will probably not have as short a maturity under a Contingent Immunization program as he would have under pure active management. This is one example of how a Contingent Immunization program can limit the full flexibility of an active management procedure.

TRIGGER YIELD CONTOURS AS A FUNCTION OF PORTFOLIO DURATION

Strictly speaking, Figure G assumes that all bonds in the portfolio have the exact same maturity. However, it can be shown that the portfolio duration is more effective than the average maturity for describing the performance characteristics of an overall portfolio. The main reason is that the average duration represents a reasonable approximation of the price sensitivity of the overall portfolio to parallel movements in the yield curve.

This suggests that the horizontal axis in the trigger contour diagram should be expressed in terms of duration, rather than maturity. This can be accomplished simply by replacing the maturity of the 15% par bond with its corresponding Macaulay duration. Figure H shows the results. One can see that the right-most point has a duration of seven years, corresponding to a 30-year maturity. As before, the trigger yield level is approximately 18.50%.

The trigger yield contours relative to duration also clarify the role of the neutral baseline point. The five-year duration can be seen to act as a kind of "balance point." The symmetry of the contours around this neutral point provides a certain insight as to the real nature of Contingent Immunization. As the plan progresses through time, various changes in the shape of the contour dia-

Figure G: Trigger Yield Contours

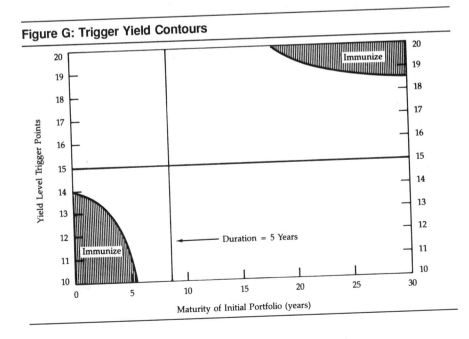

Figure H: Duration-Based Trigger Yield Contours

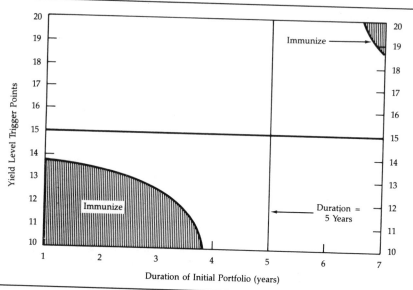

Duration of Initial Portfolio (years)

gram will take place. In particular, this centering neutral point will age from five to four to three years with the passage of calendar time.

While bond portfolios having the same duration tend to move in a more similar fashion than portfolios having the same average maturity, this relationship is strictly true only for small parallel yield movements. For large movements, and also for yield curve reshapings, there can be significant differences between portfolios having the same average duration value. This suggests that trigger yield values should be calculated for particular portfolio compositions. However, this is only one of many fine points that must be addressed in translating these theoretical control techniques into a practical monitoring procedure.

ACTION TIMES

The trigger yield has been defined as the level at which immunization *must* occur. In any practical situation, it takes a certain period of time to restructure a portfolio, especially in the face of what may be a rapidly changing market situation. The portfolio manager would be well advised to establish an early alert point at which to begin initiating the triggering action so that it can be completed by the time rates reach the trigger yield.

The magnitude of this "action time" will depend upon the liquidity structure of the active portfolio. More precisely, it will depend upon the nature of the restructuring required to enter an immunized mode in the event of a sudden market movement. This does not imply that the entire portfolio must be readily marketable. As long as the restructuring into an immunized mode can be done using only the highly marketable components, the action time could be relatively short. (Needless to say, the transaction costs under all circumstances should be incorporated in determining the effective magnitude of the safety margin.)

Another factor that affects estimation of a reasonable action time is the frequency and intensity of portfolio review and monitoring. A portfolio that is reviewed monthly obviously would require less action time than one that is reviewed only once every quarter. In practice, the problem of review frequency can be ameliorated by establishing in addition to the periodic monitoring process certain criteria for initiating a special review.

For any given review or monitoring procedure, there will of course still remain the possibility of market "gaps"—i.e., periods of major market movements that happen with such speed that the necessary transactions cannot be accomplished. This is obviously a critical variable in any Contingent Immunization process. Indeed, it is a critical variable in any portfolio management process whatsoever.

These and other factors can be blended together in terms of what might be called a trigger-alert yield spread. For a given portfolio posture, this would represent the number of basis points prior to the final trigger yield levels that the portfolio manager should begin to initiate triggering action. Thus, for a portfolio of 30-year bonds, the manager may feel that an alert distance of 100 basis points would prove more than adequate, given the expected intensity of his review process and the liquidity of his holdings. This would then imply that he should begin to initiate trigger action at 100 basis points prior to the trigger yield level of 18.50%—i.e., at a yield level of 17.50%. If this same 100-basis-point action distance held across all maturities, then the trigger yield contours in Figure H would be transformed into the trigger-alert contours shown in Figure I.[6]

Figure I shows how the trigger-alert yield spread divides the latitude for market movements into two components. The first component is the "strategy ride" that the manager can tolerate in terms of adverse movements before he must begin to take action. The second component is the allowance for the triggering process itself. One would expect that a manager would only contemplate investment postures that enable a reasonable strategy ride given the uncertainties in the market. For example, even a very defensive manager would be taking

---

[6] Because of different liquidity and volatility considerations affecting different areas of the yield curve, it may be desirable to have action times that vary significantly with the maturity of each portfolio component.

Figure I: Trigger Alert Contours

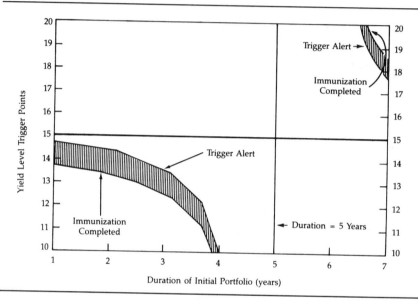

a very severe risk by adopting a posture of six-month maturities (a six-month duration), since that would allow for only 12 basis points of adverse strategy ride. In contrast, an aggressive manager could still feel fairly comfortable adopting a maximum duration of seven years, with its consequent strategy ride of up to 250 basis points.

BRAKING

A manager may choose not to base his entire strategy ride on a single investment decision. Should the market move against him, at some point he may wish to take precautionary action by moderating his posture. For example, suppose a manager has a strong conviction that interest rates will decline and therefore adopts an aggressive stance—a seven-year duration portfolio. Should the market move 75 basis points upward in yield, the manager may rethink his fundamental beliefs or simply decide that he should limit the magnitude of his potential loss. He can do this by restructuring his portfolio's duration closer to the five-year neutral point. In fact, a sequence of braking actions, as shown in Figure J, would probably take place in the event of a sustained yield movement contrary to the manager's initial posture.

Figure J: The Braking Process

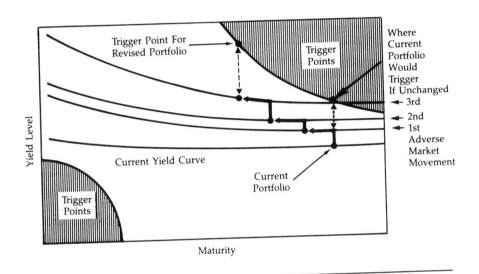

More generally, there are a number of ways for the manager to limit his stake in any one investment decision. For example, his "stake" may be expressed as some fraction of the safety margin or the strategy ride. Once the predetermined stake has been eroded, the manager may return to the neutral stance, make a new investment decision, or shave his stance through some type of braking process. While one can develop various types of models for such processes, they depend in the final analysis upon the manager's judgment.

REALISTIC YIELD CURVE BEHAVIOR

The preceding examples have assumed parallel movements of a flat yield curve consisting only of par bonds. The flat yield curve is a hypothetical beast that has rarely been spotted for long in the actual marketplace. Under the generally shaped yield curve, the situation for Contingent Immunization changes in a number of ways. Figure K depicts the trigger yield contours for a positively sloped yield curve with a 15% yield at the five-year duration point.

The trigger yield contours here tend to be more distant for the longer maturities than they were in Figure G, depicting the flat yield curve case. This is in part the result of the decreased interest rate sensitivity associated with higher

Figure K: Trigger Yield Contours for Positively Sloped Yield Curve

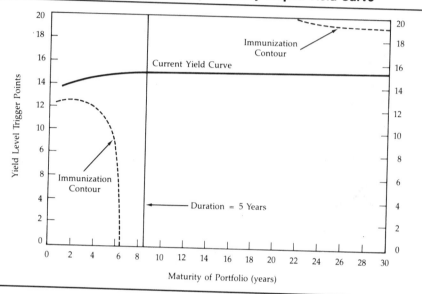

Maturity of Portfolio (years)

Figure L: Trigger Alert Contours for Positively Sloped Yield Curve

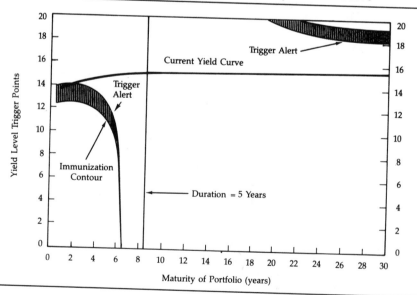

Maturity of Portfolio (years)

yield levels at the longer maturities. At the shorter maturities there is little difference in the magnitudes of the triggering yield moves. The contours can thus be seen to bend with the shape of the yield curve.

When the yield volatility characteristics for different areas of the yield curve are incorporated into the action times, the altered shape of trigger contours becomes very important in the selection of the active strategy. This is true even when the portfolio position offers an ample safety margin. Figure L illustrates the case where short rates are viewed as being subject to more rapid market gapping than the long area of the curve.

There are a host of special considerations that should be built into the control procedure. Some of these can be done in a relatively clear and well-defined fashion. Others must be addressed through an envelope of forward-looking simulations. While the basic concepts underlying Contingent Immunization and its control procedures are fairly well defined and fairly clear-cut, there is no question that market savvy, intensive monitoring and prudent judgment are required both in the active mode and in the rational implementation of any control procedure. Although Contingent Immunization is built on the same scientific principles as modern immunization, both areas still retain many of their "artistic aspects." Part II of this article will address a series of factors that could create problems for Contingent Immunization.

Appendix

Let $A_t(\vec{y_t})$ represent the value, at time t and with a yield curve $\vec{y_t}$, of an actively managed portfolio. If there is an instantaneous shift in the yield curve of $\Delta\vec{y_t}$, then the new value of the portfolio becomes $A_t(\vec{y_t} + \Delta\vec{y_t})$.

Figure A in the text illustrates this variation in portfolio value with changing yield curves for the special case of a portfolio entirely invested in a single asset—30-year, 15% par bonds. Obviously only changes in the 30-year yield are relevant here.

If we have as an objective the achievement of some minimum value at a horizon point, say H years (from the starting date, t = 0), then we can compute for any prevailing yield curve, $\vec{y_t}$, the asset value needed at time t to achieve this objective under the assumption of no future changes in interest rates. Let $R_t(\vec{y_t}, FV)$ represent this asset value, where FV is the future value required. Then we have:

$$R_t(\vec{y_t}, FV) = \frac{FV}{(1 + i_t(\vec{y_t}, H - t))^{H-t}},$$

where $i_t(\vec{y_t}, H - t)$ is the "market return" at time t for money invested for H - t years. We will represent $i_t(\vec{y_t}, H - t)$ as simply i_t in the remaining discussion.

CLASSICAL IMMUNIZATION

Classical immunization is a portfolio procedure for realizing a compounded return equal to the initial "market return" over a horizon of H years, even with subsequent changes in interest rates. We thus have the following:

$$FV = A_0 \times (1 + i_0)^H,$$

where A_0 equals initial asset value. The target dollar amount in H years equals our initial asset value times the market return at time zero compounded for the H years in our horizon. Thus, initially, the required asset value is:

$$R_0(\overrightarrow{y_0},FV) = R'_0\,(\overrightarrow{y_0},i_0) = A_0 \times \frac{(1+i_0)^H}{(1+i_0)^H} = A_0.$$

At any future time t:

$$R'_t(\overrightarrow{y_t},\,i_0) = A_0\,\frac{(1+i_0)^H}{(1+i_t)^{H-t}}\,.$$

Then, one way of expressing the necessary conditions for a portfolio to be immunized at time t is:

$$A_t(\overrightarrow{y_t}) = R'_t(\overrightarrow{y_t},i_0)\,, \qquad\qquad (1)$$

and

$$A_t(\overrightarrow{y_t} + \Delta\overrightarrow{y_t}) \geq R'_t(\overrightarrow{y_t} + \Delta\overrightarrow{y_t},i_0) \qquad\qquad (2)$$

for the relevant class of yield curve movements $\{\Delta\overrightarrow{y_t}\}$.

Thus we need at all times a portfolio value equal to the required asset value assuming no further interest rate changes, and, for any interest rate changes that do occur, our portfolio value must once again be at least equal to the new required asset value after the change. Figure B in the text illustrates such a situation for the simplifying assumption of a flat yield curve, for t equals 0 and i_0 equals 15%. The required value line $R'_t(\overrightarrow{y_t} + \Delta\overrightarrow{y_t},i_0)$ is the solid line. The dotted line represents the $A_t(\overrightarrow{y_t} + \Delta\overrightarrow{y_t})$ for a portfolio of 15% bonds with slightly less than 8 1/2 years to maturity (for which the duration is five years, corresponding to the horizon of five years).

CONTINGENT IMMUNIZATION

With Contingent Immunization, we introduce the cushion spread, c. The floor return, f, is computed as:

$$f = i_0 - c.$$

The concept of a floor portfolio can now be developed from the required asset function $R_t(\overrightarrow{y_t},FV)$ calculated so as to assure the floor return. Thus:

$$FV = A_0 \times (1+f)^H$$

and

$$R'_t(\overrightarrow{y_t},\,f) = A_0 \times \frac{(1+f)^H}{(1+i_t)^{H-t}}\,.$$

We shall call an immunizing portfolio for this required asset function the "floor portfolio," $F_t(\vec{y_t}, f)$. Thus $F_t(\vec{y_t}, f)$ would satisfy the earlier immunization conditions with respect to $R'_t(\vec{y_t}, f)$.

Figure C in the text compares the required asset functions for immunization, $R'_t(\vec{y_t} + \Delta\vec{y_t}, i_0)$, and for Contingent Immunization, $R'_t(\vec{y_t} + \Delta\vec{y_t}, f)$.

By setting a floor return, f, below the initial market return, i_0, we introduce the initial safety margin:

$$S_0 = A_0(\vec{y_0}) - F_0(\vec{y_0}, f) ,$$

the difference between the starting asset value and an initial floor portfolio. In general, the safety margin is a function of time:

$$S = S_t = A_t(\vec{y_t}) - F_t(\vec{y_t}, f) .$$

Thus, as time passes, the manager's cumulative performance results in a changing asset value $A_t(\vec{y_t})$. As well, the floor portfolio has a changing value, $F_t(\vec{y_t}, f)$, a function of the prevailing yield curve. The safety margin is simply the difference between these two time-varying values. Figure F in the text illustrates the changing value of the safety margin over time.

Given the active portfolio value, $A_t(\vec{y_t})$, and the floor portfolio, $F_t(\vec{y_t}, f)$, we can define a trigger point (not necessarily unique) as the shift in the yield curve, $\Delta\vec{y_t}^*$, such that:

$$A_t(\vec{y_t} + \Delta\vec{y_t}^*) = F_t(\vec{y_t} + \Delta\vec{y_t}^*, f) .$$

By the previous definition, this is, of course, the point at which S_t equals zero, or where the entire safety margin has been eroded. Figure D illustrates the trigger point.

THE CONCEPT OF POTENTIAL RETURN

The potential return, r_t, can be expressed as follows:

$$r_t = [(1 + i_t)^{H-t} \times A_t(\vec{y_t})/A_0]^{1/H} - 1 .$$

In words, we compound forward the existing asset value, $A_t(\vec{y_t})$, at the current market rate, to the end of the horizon, and then simply evaluate the resulting average return over the full horizon, H.

We can show that when triggering occurs, the potential return, r_t, equals the floor rate, f. At the trigger point we have:

$$A_t(\vec{y_t}) = F_t(\vec{y_t}, f) ,$$

where

$$F_t(\overrightarrow{y_t}, f) = A_0(1 + f)^H/(1 + i_t)^{H-t}.$$

Substituting F_t for A_t in the earlier expression for r_t, we have:

$$r_t = \left\{ (1 + i_t)^{H-t} \frac{A_0(1 + f)^H}{A_0(1 + i_t)^{H-t}} \right\}^{1/H} - 1 = f.$$

Figure E illustrates the potential return behavior for a portfolio invested in 30-year, 15% bonds under the assumptions of a flat yield curve with level shifts.

TRIGGER YIELD CONTOUR

The trigger yield contour is simply an extension of the trigger point idea to a defined set of portfolio positions that we might adopt. Thus the trigger yield contour may be described as the set of $\Delta \overrightarrow{y}^*$ such that, for each portfolio structure, the corresponding $\Delta \overrightarrow{y}^*$ (if it exists) will make:

$$A_t(\overrightarrow{y_t} + \Delta \overrightarrow{y}^*) = F_t(\overrightarrow{y_t} + \Delta \overrightarrow{y}^*, f).$$

Figure G illustrates the trigger yield contours for the portfolio set consisting of 15% par bonds with maturities from one to thirty years. A flat yield curve and $\Delta \overrightarrow{y}^*$s constrained to level shifts are also assumed. Figure H displays the same contours in terms of these portfolios' durations.

Chapter III D-10

Contingent Immunization Procedures— Part II: Problem Areas

Part I of this article, in the November/December 1982 issue of Financial Analysts Journal, *explained the concept of Contingent Immunization and gave the procedures used to monitor a Contingent Immunization program over time so as to control the risks associated with movements in the yield curve. In essence, Contingent Immunization allows a bond portfolio manager to pursue the highest yields available through active strategies while relying on the techniques of bond immunization to assure that the portfolio will achieve a given minimal return over the investment horizon.*

The difference between this minimal, or floor, rate of return and the maximum possible market rate is termed the cushion spread. Yield movements favorable to the manager's active strategies will enlarge the cushion spread, increasing portfolio return. Adverse yield movements will erode the cushion spread. For any given portfolio, investment horizon and yield curve shape there will be a set of "trigger yield contours" that will determine at what yield levels the portfolio manager must begin to immunize the portfolio if he wishes to insure the floor return.

Contingent Immunization seems to offer the best of both worlds—the pursuit of maximum returns through active management and the limitation of downside risk through immunization. Yet Contingent Immunization is a complex and relatively new

Martin L. Leibowitz and Alfred Weinberger, "Contingent Immunization—Part II: Problem Areas," *Financial Analysts Journal*, January/February 1983. Reprinted with permission.

procedure. Part II of the article examines some of the factors that may create problems for Contingent Immunization, assesses their potential magnitude and offers some methods for ameliorating their effects. Finally, it provides an overall view of Contingent Immunization in terms of its position in the continuum from pure immunization to purely active bond management.

While Contingent Immunization can limit the risks in active bond management, there are risks inherent in the Contingent Immunization procedure itself. In an overall sense, the fundamental risk relates to the ability of the portfolio manager and the control procedure to assure that the floor return is always fulfilled—i.e., that the portfolio's total return over the investment horizon is never less than the promised floor rate.

Constant monitoring by a good manager using good risk control procedures can do much to ameliorate this risk. But achievement of the minimum return may still be threatened by factors outside the control of either manager or sponsor. For instance, there is no guarantee that an immunized portfolio will track the market exactly under certain conditions. Even if immunization worked perfectly, problems could still arise in the translation from the active to the immunized mode; in particular, market yields could move so broadly and suddenly that the manager would be unable to immunize fast enough to insure the floor return. Finally, it is important to recognize that insuring the minimum return may mean forgoing excess returns from purely active management.

It would obviously be desirable to examine these potential problems in light of the actual experiences of Contingent Immunization programs. Because the concept was first introduced in January of 1981, however, the bulk of assets under Contingent Immunization are in plans that have been under way for only a brief period of time; the market evidence to date is simply not enough to give a fair assessment of the effectiveness of Contingent Immunization. On the other hand, evidence provided by historical market behavior and by simulations can help to define the magnitude of the problems identified above and the threat they pose to well-designed Contingent Immunization programs.

PROBLEMS WITH CLASSICAL IMMUNIZATION

One problem with Contingent Immunization is the imprecision surrounding classical immunization itself. Since the concept of classical immunization was first proposed in 1952, it has been the subject of an enormous amount of academic research. While significant controversy still surrounds many facets of immunization theory, there are certain points of agreement that can be stated with reasonable confidence.

First, most empirical studies suggest that immunization—even using the simple Macaulay duration—works reasonably well as long as the portfolio is "reasonably structured."[1] A "reasonably structured" portfolio is one in which the cash flows are clustered around the investment horizon; thus a barbell portfolio would not be considered reasonably structured.

Second, real-life market events create sufficient departures from the classical immunization model that a certain magnitude of variation around the target return should be expected. In real life, portfolio returns are subject to reshapings in yield curves, to changes in sector spreads, to liquidity and availability differences between market sectors.

Third, several refinements of the classical immunization model, proposed and tested through various forms of forward and retrospective simulations, have tried to address one or more of these real-life considerations. So far, none of the more refined models appears to lead to results that are materially superior to those available from the simple duration model.

Fourth, all the immunization models developed to date are based upon certain assumed patterns of market behavior. While some assumed patterns may be more realistic than the simple parallel movement of a flat yield curve, they are still artificial relative to actual market movements. One can always envision a pathological sequence of market movements that would defeat even the most refined immunization models.

Thus immunization is an imprecise art. Clearly, to the extent that this imprecision exists, there exists a risk of underperforming the promised return in any immunization program. Contingent Immunization must share in this imprecision. The magnitude of this risk as indicated by empirical evidence is discussed below.

EMPIRICAL EVIDENCE

We undertook a series of historical simulations based upon monthly U.S. Treasury yield curves stretching from January 1958 to December 1979. The baseline

---

[1] Recent empirical studies on immunization include: Lawrence Fisher and Roman L. Weil, "Coping with the Risk of Interest-Rate Fluctuations: Returns to Bondholders from Naive and Optimal Strategies," *Journal of Business*, October 1971; Martin L. Leibowitz, "Pros and Cons of Immunization: Proceedings of a Seminar on the Roles and Limits of Bond Immunization" (Salomon Brothers Inc, January 1980); G.O. Bierwag, George Kaufman, Robert Schweitzer and Alden Toevs, "Risk and Return for Active and Passive Bond Portfolio Management: Theory and Evidence" (Working paper No. 117, University of Oregon, January 1980); Gifford Fong and Oldrich Vasicek, "A Risk Minimizing Strategy for Multiple Liability Immunization" (Working paper, September 15, 1980); Jonathan E. Ingersoll, Jr., "Is Immunization Feasible? Evidence in CRSP Data" (Working paper 58, Graduate School of Business, University of Chicago, revised July 1981); and Jeffrey Nelson and Stephen Schaefer, "The Dynamics of the Term Structure and Alternative Portfolio Immunization Strategies" (Presented at IQRF Seminar, October 1981).

situation consisted of a five-year plan with annual rebalancings using a "point portfolio" of par bonds whose maturities provided the needed duration. The yield to maturity of the original "duration-matched" portfolio was taken as the return target.[2] The return achieved by the immunization procedure was then simulated from the movements in the yield curve from one rebalancing point to the next. This was replicated for a series of five-year plans starting with each month from January 1958 through January 1975.

Figure M illustrates the general pattern of results. The solid line here is the target return, while the dotted line represents the actual results. As one would expect, the tracking of actual returns to target returns is generally close. However, the purpose of immunization is not just to track closely, but to track *very* closely.

Figure N plots the excess of the realized return over the target return. There is obviously significant variability in the immunization process. Moreover, an examination of the market movements that coincided with the sizable misses indicates that there are certain identifiable types of pathological yield curve movements that have particularly harsh effects on the immunization procedure. For example, one can see that classical immunization could never work if an upward movement in the yield of long maturities were often accompanied by a downward movement in short maturities.[3]

The results displayed in Figure N demonstrate that classical immunization does not work perfectly in the real world. On the other hand, the worst misses are limited in magnitude and in no case exceed 25 basis points. While this maximum miss would have to be revised upward given the higher level and greater volatility of market yields within recent years, it nevertheless suggests that immunization is likely to come reasonably close to its intended target. Moreover, to the extent that a Contingent Immunization program does not require immunization until relatively late in the investment horizon, the immunization will take place over a shorter horizon than the five-year span studied here, hence the range of tracking errors should be smaller.

We examined during the course of these simulations a number of alternative portfolio structures and targeting procedures. One such structure was a laddered portfolio beginning in the horizon year and extending year by year to longer maturities as needed to achieve the required duration. This portfolio exhibited considerably better tracking than the point par bond portfolio. Such a portfolio seemed to provide a certain degree of protection against the more se-

---

[2] It should be noted that, in general, this yield-to-maturity value is not the best estimate for the immunization target return. See Martin L. Leibowitz, "Bond Immunization—Part III: The Yield Curve Case" (Salomon Brothers Inc, December 12, 1979).

[3] See Martin L. Leibowitz, "Pros and Cons of Immunization" for a more detailed description of these simulation results and their implications.

Figure M: Historical Yield Levels and Simulated Immunization Returns

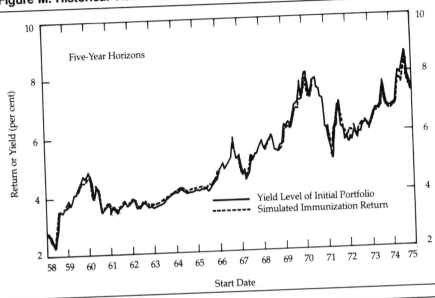

Five-Year Horizons

Return or Yield (per cent)

Start Date

Yield Level of Initial Portfolio
Simulated Immunization Return

Figure N: Historical Immunization Returns over Yield-to-Maturity Target—Actual Sequence of Yield Curves

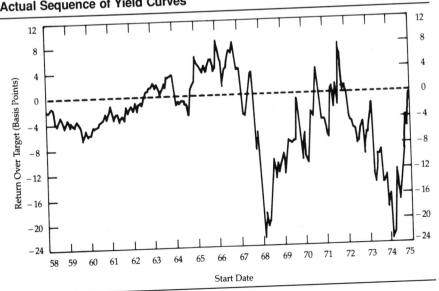

Return Over Target (Basis Points)

Start Date

Figure O: Historical Immunization Returns
(Ladder Starting in Fifth Year Versus Point Portfolio)

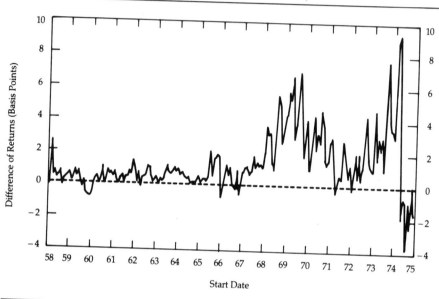

vere yield curve movements, at least for the particular historical period studied. Figure O shows the difference between returns from the laddered portfolio and the point portfolio.

All in all, it is clear that the choice of the cushion spread in a Contingent Immunization program should take into account the variability of the underlying immunization procedure. In part, this choice will depend upon the interpretation of the floor rate. If the manager and the sponsor understand that the floor rate can be taken as the mean value of an immunization process, then the cushion spread can be interpreted as fairly reflecting the latitude allowed for the active strategy. On the other hand, if the floor rate is intended to function as an absolute minimum rate that must be achieved or exceeded with very high probability, then the cushion spread must be widened so as to accommodate the variability of the immunization process itself. In either case, both sponsor and manager should clearly recognize the risks and variability associated with the immunization process and the way this is to be interpreted in terms of the floor rate.

TRANSLATION PROBLEMS

Even if classical immunization in some form worked perfectly, Contingent Immunization would still suffer from problems that arise in the translation from the active to the immunized mode. The liquidity and marketability of various components of the active portfolio and the transaction costs necessitated by triggering can have significant impact on returns to a Contingent Immunization program. Fortunately, their potential effects can be assessed and, to some degree, controlled through use of forward-looking simulation procedures.

The portfolio manager must keep in mind that the key to restructuring the portfolio from the active to the immunized mode is the ability to effect needed transactions within the span of a given market move. Effective control can exist as long as certain, often relatively minor, components of the portfolio can be restructured in time. For example, as long as certain transactions involving the most liquid portion of the portfolio can be carried out prior to the market's moving, say, another 100 basis points, the system will prove workable.

Of course, a critical assumption here is that the market maintain some reasonable degree of continuity. In this sense, perhaps the most obvious threat to a Contingent Immunization system is the possible occurrence of an outsized market movement of such speed and intensity that it constitutes a true "gap" in the marketplace—i.e., a market movement of a magnitude that does not allow sufficient time or resiliency for transactions to be effected. If such a market move is adverse to the manager's posture, the outer limits of the trigger yield contours could be penetrated.

Contingent Immunization will not work if the market is subject to frequent gaps of several hundred basis points or more. Some evidence on the frequency and size of actual market movements is presented below.

EMPIRICAL EVIDENCE

In order to determine the potential magnitude of market discontinuities, we examined the weekly movements of various maturity sectors for the past several years.[4] The weekly time period was chosen because it was felt that a portfolio manager poised to take action should be able to accomplish significant restructuring in a liquid portion of his portfolio within this time span.

---

[4] While such historical studies do indeed provide some insight into actual market movements, they obviously cannot assure that future gaps will not exceed those experienced in the past.

Figure P: Histogram of Weekly Yield Movements—30-Year Treasuries (January 1979-November 1981)

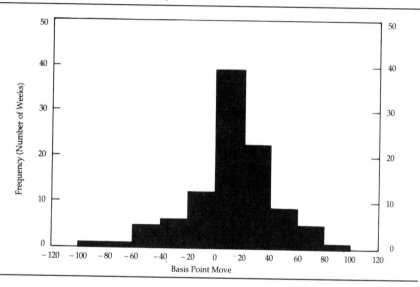

Figure Q: Cumulative Distribution of Weekly Yield Moves—30-Year Treasuries (January 1979-November 1981)

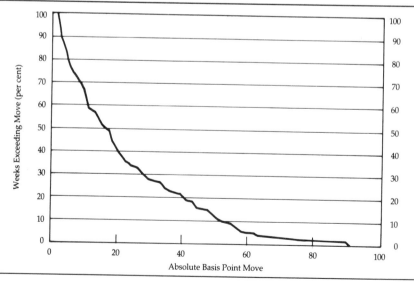

Figure P is a histogram showing the weekly yield changes of 30-year Treasury par bonds from January 1979 to November 1981. Note that this period includes the change in Federal Reserve Board targeting requirements, which took place in October 1979. While this was hardly a stable time for bond markets, it is interesting to note that very large moves were fairly rare. In fact, the weekly move over this interval never exceeded plus or minus 100 basis points.

For our purposes, it is useful to translate the results of Figure P into the form of Figure Q, which shows the cumulative distribution of the absolute magnitude of the weekly yield movements, regardless of their direction. This shows that weekly movements in excess of plus or minus 20 basis points occurred with a frequency of 40% over the period studied. Movements in excess of plus or minus 80 basis points, however, occurred less than 3% of the time. At the 80th percentile level, movements were plus or minus 40 basis points or less.

Of course, it is well known that yield movements tend to be larger in the shorter maturities. Figures R and S provide some comparable statistics on the intermediate and shorter maturity sectors, showing cumulative distributions for the seven-year and one-year areas of the Treasury yield curve, respectively, for the same period of time. The maximum range of movements increases to 107 basis points for the seven-year maturity and to 204 basis points for the one-year maturity. At the 80th percentile level, the cutoffs are 40 basis points for the seven-year maturity and 60 basis points for the one-year maturity.

The intermediate results appear roughly comparable to those for the long maturities. It is clear, however, that problems could arise with a very short maturity portfolio at the outset of a Contingent Immunization program. If one compares the wide range of market movements in Figure S with the limited latitude dictated by the trigger contours in Figure G (Part I), one can see how a very short maturity portfolio may be vulnerable to being plunged through the safety net. This suggests that the prudent manager under Contingent Immunization may be well advised to limit the extremity of any defensive posture he adopts. At the beginning of a five-year immunization, for example, he might go no shorter than a one-and-one-half or two-year average maturity. Of course, this situation changes with the passage of time; as time passes, the trigger yields decline, increasing the latitude for very short maturity portfolios and decreasing the latitude for longer-term portfolios.

Apart from the special problem of very short maturity portfolios (i.e., those under one-and-one-half years), the historical evidence is fairly encouraging. History suggests that there is a limit to the maximum discontinuity of the markets. Moreover, this limit is one that can be readily accommodated within the control procedures described in Part I of this article. Cushion spreads of 100 to 150 basis points will provide ample room for the manager to adopt an active strategy of his choice and to ride with it for several hundred basis points of adverse market movement while retaining sufficient latitude to engage a braking process should immunization become necessary.

Figure R: Cumulative Distribution of Weekly Yield Moves—Seven-Year Treasuries (January 1979-November 1981)

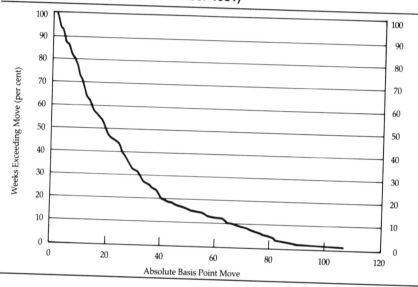

Figure S: Cumulative Distribution of Weekly Yield Moves—One-Year Treasuries (January 1979-November 1981)

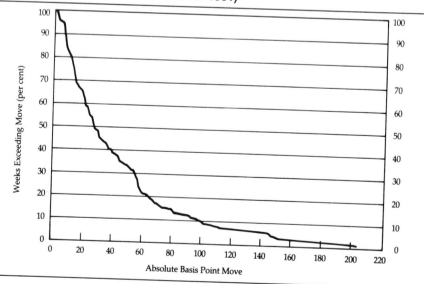

TIME DEPENDENCE

Another problem area with Contingent-Immunization is its significant time dependence. As time progresses and the investment horizon shortens, trigger yield contours change, affecting management flexibility. In particular, in the third, fourth and final years of a five-year program, the portfolio manager will usually find that he faces significant limits in terms of how aggressive a stance he can adopt; i.e., his maximum duration will be significantly below the maximum possible durations available in the market. The extent of this limitation will depend on the characteristics of the specific Contingent Immunization program and the level of performance success that has been enjoyed up to that point. Nevertheless, every Contingent Immunization program will encounter some degree of limitation in the later years. Both manager and sponsor should recognize this at the outset.

The limitations imposed by the shortening of the investment horizon can be ameliorated should the sponsor elect to terminate the existing program prematurely, possibly rolling it into a new Contingent Immunization program for a new five- or six-year span. Such a rollout into a new plan may be requested by the active manager who finds the trigger contours placing onerous restrictions on his ability to pursue particularly attractive market opportunities. The essence of the Contingent Immunization program is, however, that the option to concur (hence to forgo the floor return characteristic of the existing plan) clearly rests with the sponsor.

The same holds true in the case where adverse market movements lead to triggering into an immunized state at a relatively early point. While the floor return may still remain assured, neither the manager nor the sponsor may be particularly happy with the prospect of a straight immunized portfolio for the remainder of the investment horizon. In such a case, the sponsor may consider restructuring the Contingent Immunization program by either lowering the promised floor rate or rolling out the investment horizon.

In essence Contingent Immunization shares with any immunization program an intrinsic dependence on a fixed investment horizon, and any fixed investment horizon is to some extent an artificial device. In certain investment contexts, for example, the true long-term horizon may be either not definable or far greater than any duration available in the market. The key point is that the choice—of the initial horizon, of rolling out the existing horizon or of lowering the acceptable floor rate—rests with the sponsor. (The fact that Contingent Immunization places important options in the hands of the sponsor has interesting implications for the multimanager situation.)

OPPORTUNITY COSTS

Contingent Immunization offers an important structural advantage over pure active management in terms of its pattern of returns over the investment horizon. In exchange for its structural benefits, however, Contingent Immunization will often place a constraining hand on the active manager. Thus, even if the manager follows exactly the same form of active management he would have pursued in a purely active framework, the rewards from Contingent Immunization will exhibit a somewhat different pattern. This results from the fact that certain strategies that result under Contingent Immunization in triggering into an immunized state might, if they were played out, lead to extraordinarily productive returns.

More generally, it can be argued that the active manager will naturally moderate certain (although not all) of his active strategies because of the Contingent Immunization context. This means that there will be some reduction in the boldness of his active behavior. The cost of such a moderated stance will be dictated in part by the magnitude of the cushion spread he is allowed. Hence selection of a floor rate that strikes a comfortable balance between allowing the manager sufficient latitude to reap the benefits of the active mode while still retaining the advantages of a well-defined minimum return is a particularly important factor. Given the objective constraints of a particular Contingent Immunization program, however, the opportunity costs will depend largely on the level of luck and skill of the manager.

Obviously, there is no definitive measure of the opportunity costs of Contingent Immunization. We may be able to shed some light on the problem, however, by posing the question in this fashion: Given an active manager's particular blend of boldness and skill, how will his pattern of return be altered by placing him within a Contingent Immunization framework? A simulation model of an active manager's performance, both in a purely active mode as well as in a Contingent Immunization framework, provides some idea of the answer to this question.

EMPIRICAL EVIDENCE

The problem of the opportunity costs of constrained active management is probably best discussed in terms of the distribution of returns. One might expect the theoretical distributions to take the form shown in Figure T. Classical immunization should theoretically always produce the initial market return (a more realistic treatment would, of course, incorporate some of the expected variability in immunization returns described above). The broader distribution in Figure T represents the pattern of returns one might expect from a good active manager.

Figure T: Comparison of Return Distributions

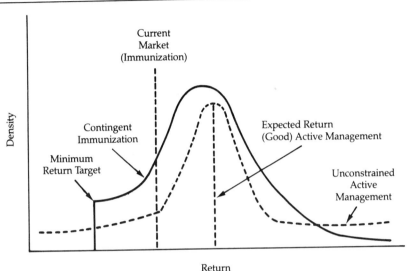

Return

The expected return should exceed the immunized rate by a margin that reflects the manager's "goodness." In addition, there will be a wide spread of possible returns around this mean value—some extremely favorable outcomes as well as some extremely disappointing outcomes.

In the theoretical model of Contingent Immunization, this same active manager would never have returns lower than the specified floor rate. This would lead to a distinct truncated distribution of the form shown in Figure T. Note that there will be certain extraordinarily favorable returns from active management that will not occur under the constraints of Contingent Immunization. These outcomes have been "constrained out" either by the more moderate posture that had to be adopted or because premature triggering interrupted what would have ultimately proved to be an extremely successful strategy. Thus the far right-hand tail of the distribution should be higher for active management than for Contingent Immunization.

In general, this pattern should lead to Contingent Immunization having an expected return that lies between the return from classical immunization and the higher mean value for full active management. As the manager's "goodness" is reduced, the mean return from active management should shift to ever lower levels, eventually dropping below the immunized level for managers who start to be classified as "bad." At some point during the transition from good to bad active management, the mean return from active management will drop below that expected from Contingent Immunization.[5]

In order to gain more insight into the complex interaction between different measures of manager "goodness" and the relative merits of Contingent Immunization, we contructed a multiperiod simulation that would in essence generate return distributions such as those depicted in Figure T. Figure U shows the overall outline of this simulation. At the beginning of each period, the manager estimates the prospective market movements. This estimate is combined with the manager's level of uncertainty in order to form a composite risk-reward measure. This composite measure may, for example, be the same for a small move that is estimated with a high degree of certainty and for a larger move that is associated with a high degree of uncertainty. Thus the manager's increasing conviction with respect to a given market movement will be reflected in increases in the absolute value of the composite risk-reward measure.

The active manager's behavior is described in terms of a "portfolio response function." This function relates the manager's departure from the baseline portfolio duration to the magnitude of the composite risk-reward measure. The baseline duration is the neutral stance the manager would adopt given an absence of conviction regarding future market moves.

Some managers may take no action until the risk-reward measure rises above a certain threshold value. Beyond that point, they may either ease into an increasingly aggressive position or leap to their maximum long position in one fell swoop. Other managers may move smoothly toward a more aggressive (or defensive) position with each increment of the risk-reward measure. In any case, given the manager's composite risk-reward measure for the coming period, the manager's portfolio response function will determine his new portfolio duration. In turn, this leads to a revised portfolio structure that will generate a specific realized return given the actual (i.e., sampled) market movement over that period.

Under Contingent Immunization, the manager's behavior is modeled through certain transformations of his basic active portfolio response function. First of all, the baseline posture for the portfolio duration corresponds to the remaining investment horizon defined by the Contingent Immunization plan. Second, departures from this neutral position are limited by (1) the safety margin that the portfolio has achieved; (2) the maximum market discontinuity that

---

[5] This discussion of return distributions has focused on the single manager situation. As noted earlier in the text, there are certain advantages to Contingent Immunization for a sponsor in a multimanager situation. These advantages would naturally be reflected in the return distribution for the sponsor's total fund.

Figure U: Portfolio Strategy Simulation

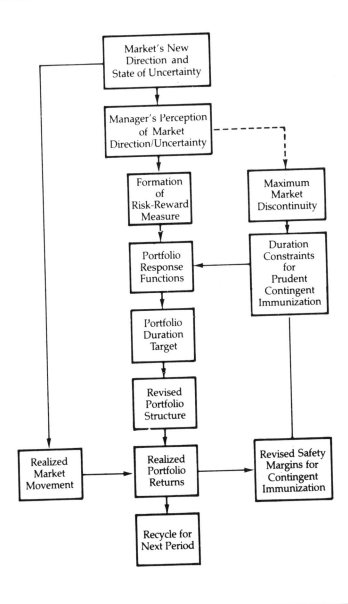

one wishes to assume possible; and (3) the magnitude of the safety margin that the manager is allowed to stake on any one investment decision.[6]

Let us first take the case of a "good" active manager who is an unbiased estimator of market movements, but with a variance matching the uncertainty in the market itself.[7] Assume each investment decision spans a six-month period and that the uncertainty in yield changes over this period has a standard deviation of 100 basis points. The manager's baseline portfolio has a duration of 3.5 years—roughly halfway between the most aggressive and the most defensive posture along the yield curve. His portfolio response function is such that he will maintain the baseline stance until the estimated market move exceeds 20 basis points in either direction. He will then gradually increase (or decrease) the portfolio's duration until a maximum (or minimum) value is reached for an expected market move of plus (or minus) 50 basis points.

Figure V reports the simulated results from this manager's strategy, given a sequence of yield change distributions. The manager's average return over the five-year period was 19.7%—an improvement of 470 basis points over the immunized target return of 15%. His highest return was 28.5%, his lowest 11.9%; the distribution is reasonably symmetrical, given the limited sample size, and has a standard deviation of 3.3%. Out of the 50 runs, two provided returns less than the 14% value taken as the floor rate. It should be noted that, for the parameters used in this simulation, the manager had a 75% chance of correctly forecasting the direction of yield moves; this suggests that we were dealing not just with a "good" active manager, but with a very good active manager.

What returns would this manager have achieved under a Contingent Immunization program? Assume that the floor rate is, again, 14%; that the maximum market gap is plus or minus 100 basis points; and that the manager is allowed to stake only a portion of the portfolio's safety margin in any given six-month period. Aside from these constraints, the manager's forecasting ability and portfolio response functions are identical to what they were under purely active management.

Figure W shows the results for Contingent Immunization. Because of the theoretical treatment of the triggering and immunization process, the minimum return coincides with the floor rate of 14%. On six occasions (12% of the runs), the portfolio fell into the safety net and the immunization mode was triggered. Of these, the average time to triggering was 2.5 years, leaving an average immu-

---

[6] For the case of classical immunization, the portfolio response function becomes a trivial one. Regardless of the manager's perceptions or risk-reward measures, the portfolio is adjusted so that the duration always matches the remaining horizon.

[7] The simulation results reported below constitute only preliminary findings. They are based on only a few designs and a relatively small sample size (50 runs) for a simulation of this complexity. We are in the process of pursuing a greatly expanded experimental design using more satisfactory sizes.

Figure V: Return Distribution for a "Good" Active Manager

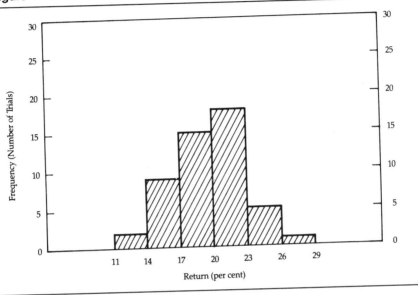

Figure W: Return Distribution for a "Good" Active Manager Under Contingent Immunization

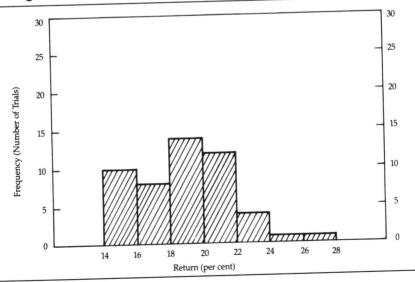

nization period of only 2.5 years. The mean return was 19.0% and the standard deviation was 3.2% (to the extent that a standard deviation means anything for this pattern of return). The range of returns for this simulation was 14.0 to 28.0%.

A comparison of Figures V and W shows that the simulations generally support the *ex ante* relationships depicted in Figure T. The mean return under Contingent Immunization was 70 basis points lower than the return for fully flexible active management, whereas the standard deviation was a bit smaller. This suggests that the tradeoff in undertaking the Contingent Immunization discipline is ceding 70 basis points on average of the substantial 19.7% return in exchange for the assurance of never experiencing a return below the floor of 14%. One should remember, however, that these results were achieved with a high level of management proficiency; returns to active management can be better or worse than returns from Contingent Immunization.

To shed some light on the results achievable with "less than good" active management, we changed the preceding simulation in the following fashion. The manager was assumed to have a forecasting distribution that centered around zero, regardless of actual market movements. (This translates into a 50% chance of being correct on direction.) All the operating characteristics, including the portfolio response function, were kept the same. The results for fully active

Figure X: Return Distribution for an Active Manager with Zero-Centered Forecasting Distribution

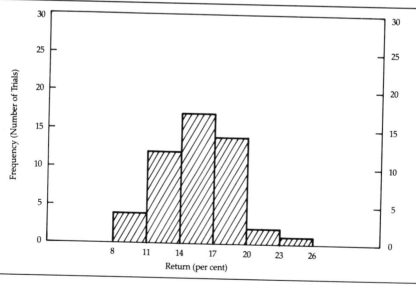

Figure Y: Return Distribution for an Active Manager with Zero-Centered Forecasting Distribution Under Contingent Immunization

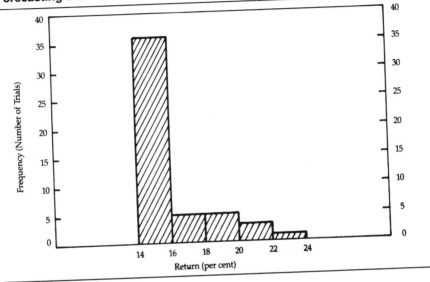

management and for Contingent Immunization are shown in Figures X and Y, respectively. For this manager with no predictive ability, active management turns out (not surprisingly) to have a wide distribution of results. The returns ranged from a low of 8.1% to a high of 25.2%. The mean return turned out to be a "lucky" 15.50% (i.e., presumably as a result of the relatively small sample size). However, in 16 cases, or 32% of the runs, the returns fell below the 14% floor rate! In contrast, Contingent Immunization had returns ranging from the 14% floor rate to a high of 24%. The mean return, which was 15.64%, was essentially comparable to that for active management. This same mean return, however, was achieved with a discipline that never resulted in returns below the floor of 14%.

These results confirm that the relative performance of Contingent Immunization should improve as the quality of the active management deteriorates. One might be tempted to conclude that Contingent Immunization is best suited for poor active management. This would be an incorrect conclusion. When known in advance, inferior active management should obviously be curtailed. Contingent Immunization, like any other form of active management, is worth pursuing only when there is thought to be a fair prospect for better-than-market returns.

IS CONTINGENT IMMUNIZATION A "MIXTURE STRATEGY"?

Can desirable return distributions be achieved by mixing pure active management with pure immunization—by, for example, putting 60% of a fund's assets under classical immunization and the remaining 40% under active management? Could such a "mixture strategy" replicate the results of Contingent Immunization?

Since Contingent Immunization does combine the techniques of active management with the techniques of modern immunization, it is indeed tempting to view it as some form of mixture strategy. However, Contingent Immunization differs from a mixture strategy both in its process and its results.

Contingent Immunization must be woven into the day-to-day process of management. In this sense, it differs from many models that simply adopt a portfolio stance at the beginning of the period and then evaluate the results achieved at the end of the period. Contingent Immunization requires a degree of monitoring that is far more intense and more technically oriented than that required by either pure active management or classical immunization. This may imply that Contingent Immunization could prove to be a relatively costly form of bond management.

On the other hand, with Contingent Immunization, bold positions can be adopted with all the assets under management, at least for some period of time. Thus the full benefits of a highly aggressive stance may be reaped if the market moves in the forecast direction. Moderation of this aggressive stance need occur only in the face of significant adverse market movements. This statement is not true of mixture strategies.

The difference can be immediately seen by the following example. Suppose the manager believes that rates are headed downward and wishes to adopt a maximum maturity position. At a 15% rate level using par bonds, this amounts to a portfolio having a duration of seven. Under Contingent Immunization, such a posture is feasible (as Figures D and E in Part I show). On the other hand, in a mixture strategy some portion of the funds will have been immunized. At any point in time, these immunized portfolios must have a duration equal to the remaining horizon period. Thus, for a five-year plan, the immunized component will have a duration of five at the outset. Since the active component cannot achieve a duration greater than seven, there is no possible way that the overall combined portfolio duration can achieve the maximum level of seven years.

The simulation results in Figures V, W, X and Y also illustrate the difference between mixture strategies and Contingent Immunization. Using the active management distribution from Figure V—the "good" manager—it would take a mixture of 68% immunized and 32% active mode to have all returns exceed the floor rate of 14%. With such a mixture, the mean portfolio return would decline to 16.5%—far below the 19.0% achieved through Contingent Immunization.

GENERALIZATIONS

In some ways, the confusion between mixture strategies and Contingent Immunization stems from the analytical tradition of viewing active strategies in terms of two parameters—expected return and risk. In essence, Contingent Immunization inserts a third parameter that may arise uniquely out of the particular characteristics of fixed-income investment. This third parameter is the floor return.

It is important to distinguish the floor return in Contingent Immunization from the "minimum return goals" often set forth as part of a fund's overall policy statement. In terms of subsequent management practice, these minimum return goals have the character of "soft" objectives—i.e., there is no clear-cut discipline for assuring their realization. For example, such minimum return goals are often incorporated into the scenario analysis approach to active management. A range of market scenarios is envisioned, and the portfolio posture is adjusted so that the minimum return goal is achieved across each scenario. As many market participants discovered the hard way in recent years, actual market behavior is not bound by anyone's preconceived set of scenarios. Bond market actions in 1980-81 repeatedly pierced many "worst-case" scenarios. The floor return in Contingent Immunization is different from such minimum return goals in that it is not scenario-dependent. No matter to what levels the market moves in a given period (as long as the market process remains "reasonable"), the day-to-day control framework under Contingent Immunization should be able to maintain the floor return as a legitimate "hard" objective.

As we have taken great pains to make clear, the floor return cannot be guaranteed in an absolute sense. However, the risks associated with achieving the floor rate as a minimum return tend, by and large, to be different from the risks of active management. Moreover, the evidence suggests that, with a sufficient cushion spread, the floor rate will serve as the realized minimum with sufficiently high probability as to make most sponsors comfortable. Consequently, the floor rate can be taken as a significant and largely independent parameter distinct from the strategy risks associated with the expected return.

This situation can perhaps be best explained in terms of the schematic diagram presented in Figure Z. To the far right, one has the expected returns associated with active strategies. In accordance with theory, these expected returns should increase monotonically with the strategy risks accepted. On the other hand, at the far left we have the classical immunization strategy. In theory, the expected return should be achieved with minimum variation risk, hence the expected return coincides with the floor return.

As one moves from pure immunization to the right, one can envision a spectrum of duration-matched immunization strategies that incur higher levels of yield curve risk, quality risk and spread risks in the hopes of achieving higher expected returns. With the progression in this direction, the minimum return naturally falls somewhat away from the expected return.

Figure Z: The Continuum of Bond Strategies

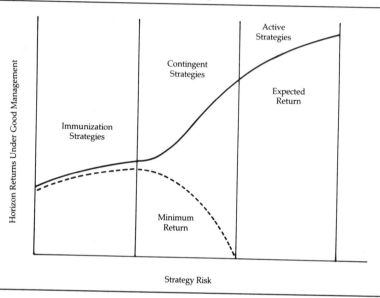

At some point, however, there may be an effort to achieve more duration flexibility, hence higher (albeit riskier) expected returns, through purposeful relaxation of the minimum return requirement. With minimum returns that are lower than the market immunization return, the manager has room for some constrained form of active management. As the acceptable minimum return falls further and further away from the expected return, constraints placed upon the active strategy become less and less, until ultimately it becomes indistinguishable from pure active strategies. Thus Figure Z shows how Contingent Immunization can be viewed as a three-parameter strategy falling between classical immunization and fully active management.

The basic concept of Contingent Immunization can be further generalized to deal with minimal fixed-income objectives other than that of a floor return over a fixed investment horizon. The cash-matching fulfillment of a prescribed liability schedule, the development of an immunization plan for scheduled liabilities, the ability to reenter a prescribed baseline portfolio at the horizon, the ability to purchase a given annuity over a subsequent period of time, and the ability to mimic the results of a simple maturity strategy may all be enhanced by the construction of an analytical safety net.

As long as one can take a specified minimal objective and transform it into this third control parameter, one can achieve the basic concept of Contingent Immunization—the pursuit of active management within a disciplined framework that will achieve the specified minimal objective under virtually all circumstances.

Chapter III D-11

Horizon Matching

SUMMARY

In recent years, the applications of various forms of cash matching have grown and become an important new force in the fixed-income markets. The cash-matching procedure has been used to fulfill prescribed schedules of payouts in a number of different contexts including retirement benefits, annuities, insurance liabilities, and debt service management. The value in cash matching is that it can greatly reduce the uncertainty of fulfillment of a liability schedule and thereby significantly reduce the pro forma or, in many cases, the actual reserves that must be set aside for this purpose. The savings that can be realized can be particularly large when market interest rates are materially higher than the pro forma or actuarial discount rate used to value the liabilities. However, even aside from such pro forma or actuarial savings, there are a number of instances where the cash-matching technique has been implemented simply to pin down

Martin L. Leibowitz, Thomas E. Klaffky, Steven Mandel, Alfred Weinberger, "Horizon Matching: A New Generalized Approach for Developing Minimum-Cost Dedicated Port-folios," SalomonBrothers Inc, September 1983.

the fulfillment of liabilities in a way that is essentially independent of future interest rates.

The considerations involved in cash-matched portfolios (also known as dedicated portfolios) are described in an earlier paper entitled *Optimal Cash Flow Matching*.[1] While the theoretical concept is the ultimate in simplicity, a number of complexities arise in practice as one tries to implement this procedure in an optimal fashion in a changing market environment.

One of the several tradeoffs that the sponsor must evaluate relates to the degree of conservatism in setting the initial design criteria. With highly conservative criteria (for example, low reinvestment rate assumptions), additional savings are likely over time as the actual operating conditions exceed the minimum design assumptions. On the other hand, less conservative design criteria will result in a lower initial portfolio cost but will reduce the prospective savings to be realized over time. In addition, it has become clear through the experience of the past few years that while dedicated portfolios will, by definition, fulfill their purpose in a totally passive fashion, there are large incremental benefits that can be extracted through active management.

In practice, the active management of cash-matched portfolios has developed into a fine art. Many portfolio managers have been able to create significant cash takeouts and portfolio improvements by taking advantage of the changing market environment. While changes in the *level* of the market, per se, tend to have relatively little effect on the cash-matched portfolio, changes in the structure of the market can create sizable opportunities for active management. These structural changes include reshaping of the yield curve, the availability of new issues with different maturities and coupons, and the changing spread relationships among the various sectors. In addition, revisions in the portfolio's cash balances and/or liability schedule over time can lead to significant, clear-cut savings.

It is impressive to see how much incremental savings can be extracted through energetic management of a dedicated portfolio using the latest computer-based optimization techniques, especially considering that the cash-matching concept is intrinsically a highly stringent and tightly constrained approach to the problem at hand. The great virtue of cash matching is that it can assure a virtually assumption-free fulfillment of the scheduled liabilities. However, there may be considerable costs associated with reaching this high level of assurance, both in terms of the initial costs to construct the portfolio and the limited flexibility imposed on its subsequent management. In this study, we introduce a new and more generalized concept that blends cash matching with the principles derived from modern immunization theory into a new procedure called "Horizon Matching."

---

[1] See *Optimal Cash Flow Matching: Minimum Risk Bond Portfolios for Fulfilling Prescribed Schedules of Liabilities*, Salomon Brothers Inc, August 1981.

We believe that Horizon Matching incorporates the best features of both approaches. On the one hand, it provides the same assurance as cash matching of fulfilling the liability flows that will be incurred over the span of time from the present to a prescribed horizon of, say, five years. On the other hand, it capitalizes upon the greater flexibility of the interest rate-sensitivity matching features of immunization to reduce costs while assuring that the liabilities beyond that five-year horizon can be met in the face of a wide range of interest rate movements. Moreover, by restricting the immunization approach to liability flows beyond the prescribed five-year horizon, Horizon Matching reduces the portfolio's vulnerability to the types of market moves that can cause problems for the more traditional immunization procedures. At the same time, Horizon Matching introduces an important new level of flexiblity in the selection of the overall portfolio. It is this flexibility that can lead to major savings in the relative cost of an initial portfolio and, perhaps more importantly, can provide a greater scope for incremental savings from astute active management.

THE CONCEPT OF CASH MATCHING

The typical cash-matching problem begins with a liability schedule such as that depicted in Figure 1. The declining series of liability payouts shown here are representative of a retired-lives component of a pension system.

Of course, virtually any structure of liability payouts can be made amenable to some form of cash matching.

The objective of cash matching is to develop a fixed-income portfolio that will provide a stream of payments from coupons, sinking funds, and maturing principal payments that will "match" this liability schedule. More precisely, the problem is to receive sufficient funds in advance of each scheduled payout so as to have full assurance that the payouts will be met from the dedicated portfolio alone. As shown in *Optimal Cash Flow Matching*, the theoretical ideal of an exact-matched portfolio often turns out *not* to provide the least-cost portfolio in practice. The specific structure, aberrations, and peculiarities of the marketplace at a given point in time will have a huge impact on the optimal cash-matched portfolio. The key to developing an optimal cash-matched portfolio is to apply the most modern computer optimization techniques to the broadest possible universe of truly available bonds identified with their truly available prices.

The cash-matched portfolio will generate a flow of funds, as shown in Figure 2, that will provide a sufficient cash balance at the beginning of each period so as to provide for the payouts due in that period. As shown in the figure, while such portfolios are often very closely matched over certain periods, there may be some degree of anticipatory cash flow and reinvestment in other areas of the time spectrum.

Figure 1: Prescribed Schedule of Liabilities

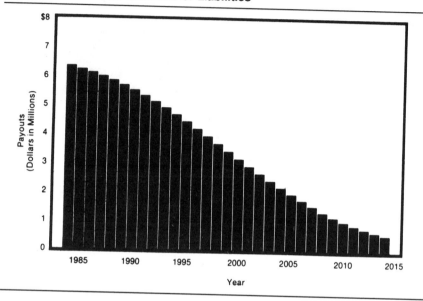

Figure 2: Cash-Matched Portfolio

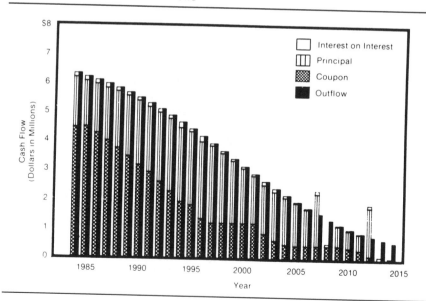

One of the central virtues of cash matching is that it serves its original purpose regardless of changes in the market environment. As long as the bonds involved in the construction of the portfolios pay their coupons and maturity payments as promised, the monies will be available as planned. The problems of credit risk, reinvestment risk, and call risk are usually reduced to comfortable levels by setting various constraint levels as specified by the fund sponsor. With the movement in market yields, the market value of the portfolio will obviously change; however, as long as the conservative design assumptions have been met, these movements will not affect the fulfillment of the original liability schedule.

Figure 3 shows schematically how the market value represented by a portfolio will grow under declining interest rates and decrease under rising rates. Interest rate movements will also affect the liabilities. While the required nominal payout will generally remain unchanged, the present value of the liability schedule, when discounted at an appropriate market rate, will follow a pattern similar to that of the asset value of the dedicated portfolio. It is the comovement of asset and liability values depicted in Figure 3 that forms the basis for the immunization approach.

Figure 3: Interest Rate Sensitivity of Assets and Liabilities

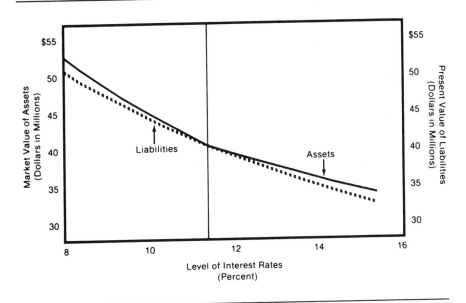

THE CONCEPT OF IMMUNIZATION

In 1952, a British actuary named F.M. Redington showed how a portfolio could be constructed that would "immunize" a schedule of liabilities across a certain range of interest rate movements.[2] The central idea was to create a portfolio of assets whose market value coincided with the present value of the scheduled liabilities and whose interest rate sensitivity exhibited the dominance pattern illustrated in Figure 3. In other words, under a prescribed set of interest rate changes, the value of the assets would always remain greater than the present value of the liabilities. In order to maintain this relationship, a rebalancing procedure would be needed to keep the immunized portfolio attuned to the changes in the interest rate sensitivity of the liabilities with the passage of time.

With the immunization concept, the portfolio structure can take on many forms as long as the needed interest rate sensitivity meets the several conditions required to achieve the dominance pattern of Figure 3. In particular, the schedule of cash flows from the immunized portfolio need not exactly correspond to the period-by-period payouts of the liability stream. While this provides a high level of flexibility in choosing an immunized portfolio, it also means that the ultimate fulfillment of the liabilities is far more dependent upon the specific assumptions that underlie immunization theory. Unfortunately, the actual behavior of the fixed-income markets has frequently violated these assumptions (often quite radically), and this has led to many questions being raised about the practical reliability of immunization.

Redington's initial proposal required that interest rates be restricted to a flat yield curve that was subject only to parallel movements. While modern techniques have enabled immunization to address a wider range of yield curve behaviors,[3] immunization still remains vulnerable to certain sequences of market movements.

In practice, the application of immunization has been limited because of its greater complexity, its requirement for frequent rebalancing (which must be distinguished from the positive *option* of active management) and its vulnerability in certain types of market movements.

---

[2] F.M. Redington, "Review of the Principles of Life-Office Valuations," *Journal of the Institute of Actuaries*, 78, no. 3 (1952): 286-340.

[3] See G.O. Bierwag, George G. Kaufman and Alden Toevs, "Immunization Strategies for Funding Multiple Liabilities," *Journal of Financial and Quantitative Analysis*, Vol. 18, No. 1 (1983): 113-123, and *Pros and Cons of Immunization: Proceedings of a Seminar on the Roles and Limits of Bond Immunization*, Salomon Brothers Inc, January 1980.

THE CONCEPT OF HORIZON MATCHING

From the preceding discussion of cash matching and immunization, it should be evident that a properly balanced combination of these two tools could lead to a very desirable new technique. We believe that Horizon Matching provides just such a valuable blend—one that incorporates the best features of both techniques.

The central concept of Horizon Matching is shown in Figure 4. Essentially, the liability stream is divided into two segments. In the first segment, the portfolio must provide a full cash matching of the liabilities that occur up to and including the specified horizon date. This cash-matched portion will be subject to the same stringent constraints that would apply to any cash-matched portfolio. In particular, any excess flows that are available for reinvestment are presumed to be reinvested at the specified (i.e., conservative) reinvestment rate prior to the horizon. For purposes of illustration, we have assumed that the horizon is five years. For the first five years, the sponsor will have full assurance that the Horizon-Matched portfolio will provide cash flows adequate to meet the specified payouts. The liabilities beyond the fifth year will be covered through a duration-matching discipline that is based on immunization princi-

Figure 4: The Concept of Horizon Matching

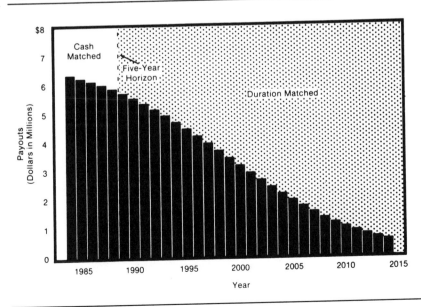

ples. As we shall see, a properly constructed Horizon-Matched portfolio will enable the initial five-year horizon to be "rolled out" year by year, so that the portfolio remains cash matched for the first five years and duration matched for the rest.

This blended approach retains the solid reliability of cash matching for the important early span of years, gains the flexibility to achieve a significantly lower cost initial portfolio, provides ongoing flexibility for productive active management, and has far less vulnerability to market conditions that would defeat more traditional immunization plans.

Figure 5 illustrates the type of cash flows that will be generated by a Horizon-Matched portfolio with a five-year horizon. In this particular case, the first five years are shown to be almost perfectly matched on a year-by-year basis. However, in the duration-matched period from the fifth year on, the asset flows are more concentrated into a series of specific maturities. These are structured so that the overall system satisfies the interest rate sensitivity requirements, as well as a number of second-order conditions.

With this structure, while one should have more room for elective management, the portfolio will serve its function even if it remains passive for the first five years. Thus, the sponsor can simply pay out the liabilities as needed during the first five years and not be concerned about the passage of time. Even with such a passive stance, the dominance condition shown in Figure 3 will be main-

Figure 5: Horizon-Matched Portfolio

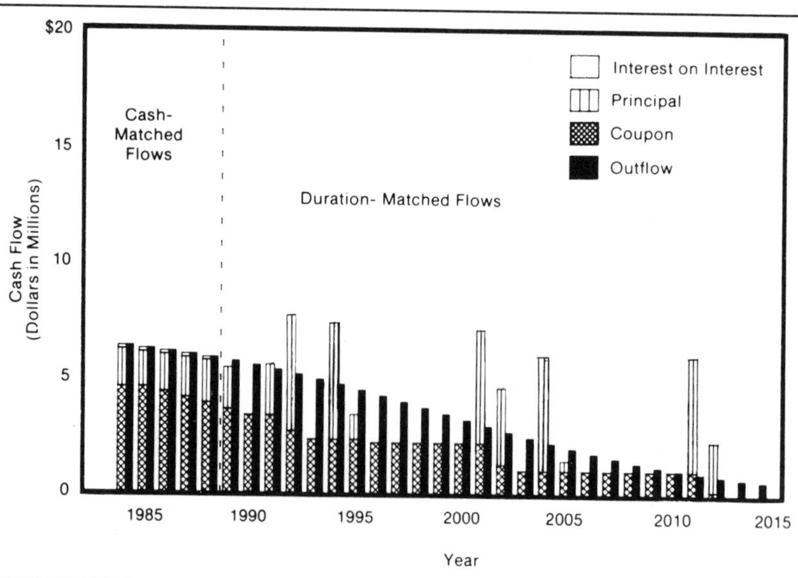

tained throughout the course of the initial horizon period as long as interest rate movements fall within the broadly prescribed range.

One of the most severe problems in practical applications of immunization has to do with nonparallel movements of the yield curve. Various approaches have been proposed to adapt immunization techniques to certain categories of yield curve reshapings. However, the actual yield curve over the past several years has clearly followed a course of its own that is not comfortably described by any tractable mathematical formulation. This vulnerability to yield curve reshaping is largely eliminated in a Horizon-Matched portfolio with horizons of three to five years or more for the simple reason that the most severe yield curve reshapings occur in the shortest maturities. This means that such Horizon-Matched portfolios are far less vulnerable to the most severe pitfalls of traditional immunization procedures. This advantage depends on the length of the design horizon. The five-year horizon offers considerable reshaping protection, while the ten-year horizon provides a huge degree of protection. With a one-year horizon, however, a considerable degree of vulnerability to adverse yield curve movements will still be present in the Horizon-Matched portfolio.

This vulnerability to yield curve reshapings must be balanced against the cost savings that can be achieved with shorter design horizons. As shown in Figure 6, there are theoretical savings available by reducing the horizon period below three years. However, these savings must be compared with the far

Figure 6: Savings from Horizon Matching

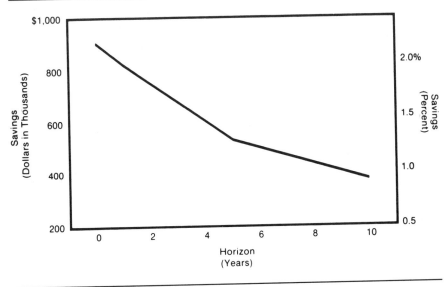

greater vulnerability to the traditional problems of immunization in the shorter maturities. For horizon periods of five or ten years, considerable savings can be achieved in conjunction with a large degree of "reshaping protection." For example, even with a design horizon of ten years, where the overwhelming bulk of the liabilities would be cash matched, the added flexibility beyond ten years from Horizon Matching allows for an incremental savings of more than 0.9% relative to an optimal cash-matched portfolio!

It should be pointed out that the benefits of Horizon Matching do entail the acceptance of some degree of additional risk. The Horizon-Matched portfolio, by definition, will have a lower asset value than the fully cash-matched portfolio. Consequently, there can be no assurance that the Horizon-Matched portfolio can be transformed into a fully cash-matched portfolio at any given point in time. Moreover, while the portfolio will retain its cash-matched characteristic through the horizon period without any further rebalancing, it is conceivable that certain types of market movements could lead to shortfalls in the duration-matched portion once the horizon period has passed. (As we shall see, however, such shortfalls are highly unlikely.)

THE ROLL-OUT PROCEDURE

As noted earlier, the Horizon-Matched portfolio has a valuable feature in common with the cash-matched portfolio: there is no need for portfolio action to be taken during the horizon period. However, with the passage of time, the horizon will get ever closer and the ratio of cash-matched segments to duration-matched segments will decrease. Ideally, one would want the Horizon-Matching procedure to be able to maintain the comfort of the cash-matching period as the years pass. Under a broad range of interest rate movements, this can be achieved through what we call a "roll-out procedure."

Figure 7 illustrates the roll-out for the earlier example of a five-year horizon. The basic concept is very simple. After one year has passed, the original portfolio now consists of four future years of cash matching followed by the duration-matched period. By restructuring the portfolio, the span of the cash matching can be rolled out to capture an additional year and thereby create a new five-year horizon. The key question is: Can this roll-out procedure be achieved without incurring additional costs? In theory, the answer to this question is yes. Indeed, under parallel movements of the yield curve, this roll-out should not only be possible, it should be accomplished with a cash takeout that will increase with the magnitude of the yield change, regardless of the direction in which yields move!

This result is evident in the simulations of the roll-out procedure illustrated in Figure 8. Further simulations have indicated that this roll-out procedure is feasible even under a broad range of yield curve reshapings.

Figure 7: The Roll-Out Procedure for the Horizon-Matched Portfolio

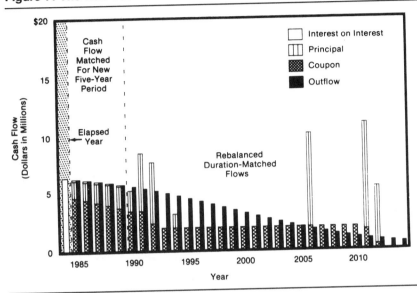

Figure 8: Simulations of the Roll-Out Procedure—Actual versus Required Assets

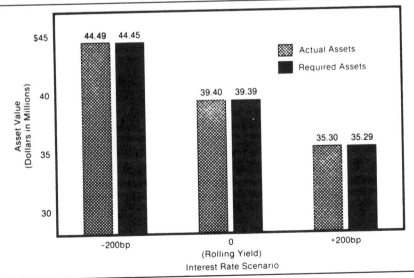

An additional advantage can be derived since the outer years of the liability schedule are often conservatively stated at the outset and, hence, are likely to become further refined with the passage of time. Horizon Matching enables the portfolio to obtain cost efficiency by fully matching the more definite near-term liabilities without being hostage to specific pro forma liabilities that are likely to shift in amount and time over the years. Moreover, by using the roll-out procedure, the comfort of a definitive match of these near-term liabilities can continue to be maintained on a year-by-year basis.

CONCLUSION

Horizon Matching is a more general approach to the overall problem of fulfilling prescribed liability schedules. Moreover, it offers the prospect of greater cost savings at the outset than cash matching and can provide for greater reliability than traditional immunization procedures.

Horizon Matching also greatly enhances the flexibility of the portfolio, which should lead to continuing rewards from active management. In today's rapidly changing marketplace for fixed-income securities, the benefits from this ongoing flexibility should prove increasingly valuable.

Chapter III D-12

Effects of Yield Curve Behavior on Immunized Portfolios

I. INTRODUCTION

The term structure of interest rates at any particular date and the interactions among term structures at various dates have long been of interest to students of money and capital markets—both academicians and market participants. Many authors have suggested that particular relationships of the current term structure and expected future term structures apply. Others have gone further by attempting to describe how the process by which interest rates change might affect the form of the term structure. Such analysis is likely to require rather special assumptions about what the investor in fixed income securities is attempting to do.

The task of paying out a known lump sum at some particular future date is a well-known problem. If the investor must buy a portfolio of coupon bonds, i.e., bonds that pay interest periodically (typically every six months, but once a

---

Lawrence Fisher, Ph.D., Professor of Finance, Rutgers University, and Martin L. Leibowitz, "Effects of Alternative Anticipations of Yield Curve Behavior on the Composition of Immunized Portfolios and on Their Target Returns," Salomon Brothers Inc, 1983.

year for nearly all of the illustrative discussion in this paper), the problem becomes an interesting one. If the investor bought a bond that matured on the same date as the liability (followed a "maturity strategy"), he or she would have to reinvest the interest income at rates that were uncertain at the time of the initial investment. If future interest rates were equal to or greater than expected, the investor would be successful. But if future rates were lower than expected, the maturity strategy would fail. Such a strategy is risky.

Suppose, however, that the investor bought a bond that matured after the liability was due. Then, if interest rates rose or fell unexpectedly, the price of the bond would fall or rise by an amount that might offset the difference between actual and anticipated income from reinvestment of interest. If the hedge were perfect for changes in interest rates that were "small" (in the mathematical sense of the term), the investor's portfolio would be said to be *immune* to changes in interest rates. The investor who attempts to make his or her portfolio immune to interest rate changes is said to be following an *immunization strategy*. However, as interest rates change and as time passes, the relative sensitivities to further fluctuations in interest rates of both reinvestment income and bond prices change. To offset the change in relative sensitivity, the composition of the portfolio must be changed at intervals over its life if it is to remain immunized.

Under some assumptions about the behavior of interest rates, a portfolio is immunized if *Macaulay's duration* of its assets is kept equal to the time until the liability is due. Macaulay's duration is a weighted average of the *number of years until payment* of the rents (principal and interest) due on an asset or portfolio of assets (or a liability or portfolio of liabilities). Each "number of years" receives a weight that is proportional to the present value of its associated rent. Keeping the duration of the assets equal to the duration of the liability (or liabilities) defines a *duration strategy*.

It is fairly well known that whether a duration strategy is, in fact, also an immunization strategy depends on the process by which interest rates change. For example, if the term structure of interest rates were always flat, immunization would be achieved by the duration strategy. However, if short-term interest rates tended to fluctuate more than long-term interest rates, the average duration of the assets might have to be increased.[1]

Much empirical work is concerned with testing the performance of a particular immunization strategy in the face of a series of real or hypothetical changes in the term structure of interest rates. This is a three-step process:

1. For each period to be analyzed, use the then-current term structure to find the holding-period return that would be achieved if the term struc-

---

[1] Ayres, Herbert F., and John Y. Barry, 1979, "Dynamics of the Government Yield Curve" or "The Equilibrium Yield Curve for Government Securities," *Financial Analysts Journal* (May-June), 31-39.

ture behaved as anticipated throughout the holding period. In other words, find the target return.

2. Find the actual holding period return associated with the strategy and the realized prices and interest rates during the holding period.

3. Compare the actual and target returns.

What does not seem to have been given adequate consideration in the past is that both the target or achievable holding-period return and the characteristics of the portfolio to be held depend on the definition of "anticipated" as well as on the initial term structure. This paper investigates those problems.

To provide example cases, we consider some of the implications of three alternative definitions of the *anticipated term structure of interest rates*. Their brief forms are

1. *Lutzian.* If the anticipated structures come to be, the forward rates implicit in the initial term structure of interest rates will prove to be perfect forecasters of all later spot and forward interest rates during the holding period.

2. *Rolling yield curve.* The anticipated situation is one in which each year's relationship between term to maturity and yield to maturity for newly issued bonds selling at par is the same as the initial relationship, i.e., the yield curve as a function of *number of years to maturity* remains unchanged.

3. *Fixed yield.* In the anticipated situation, the yield to maturity of each bond remains the same as it was at the beginning of the holding period, i.e., yields to each *date of maturity* remain unchanged.

Differences among these three definitions of *anticipated* may be illustrated by examining anticipated par-bond yield curves, anticipated implicit forward rate curves, and anticipated single-year returns implied by the observed yield curve of August 17, 1981. The yields used to construct the curve were those for U.S. Treasury bonds and notes that were due in a little less than one year or were quoted at or above par. They were found from the mean of bid and ask quotations certified to the Treasury Department by the Federal Reserve Bank of New York as reported the next day in *The Wall Street Journal*. The nominal yields, which are compounded semiannually, have been restated as effective rates (rates compounded annually). The implications of this yield curve were found using the formulas given in Section III.

Figure 1 shows the current par bond yield curve and the anticipated curves for 1, 3, and 6 years after the quotation date. It is easy to see that the yield curves implied by the rolling yield curve and by the fixed-yield anticipations follow directly from their definitions. Since yields declined as maturity in-

Figure 1: Anticipated Par Bond Yield Curves from August 17, 1981 Prices

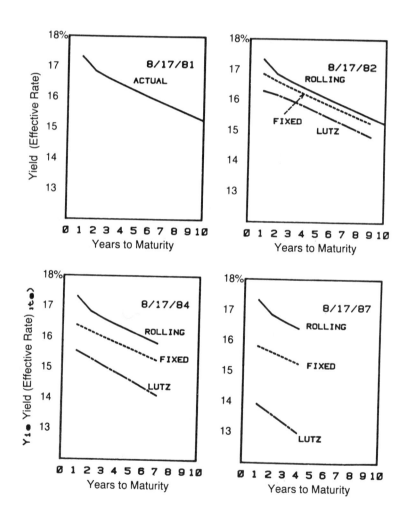

Figure 2: Anticipated Forward Rate Curves from August 17, 1981 Prices

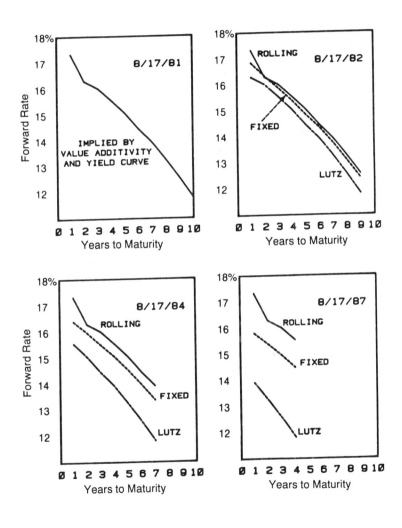

creased, the latter's curves fall more and more below the former's as time passes.

The observed yield curve and the principle of value additivity imply a set of forward rates which decline even more rapidly than the yield curve as the applicable date increases. If Lutzian anticipations are correct, these forward rates will be stationary; and, as time passes, each will become the short-term spot rate of interest. Since a bond yield is a weighted average of the implicit forward rates, an initially declining forward-rate curve and Lutzian anticipations imply lower and lower future par bond yield curves.

Figure 2 shows the initial forward rate curve and the forward rate curves that will be implied if the anticipated yield curves shown in Figure 1 should actually be observed. Again, the curves that are implied by rolling-yield-curve anticipations are all the same. In this case, the position of the forward rate curves implied by fixed-yield anticipations rises with respect to maturity date but falls with respect to years to maturity as time passes. The Lutzian anticipated forward rates are stationary with respect to dates and therefore, in this case, their position, when plotted against number of years to maturity, declines rapidly.

For the investor, perhaps the most important question is how much the portfolio will actually earn each year. Even if anticipations are met, the answer will usually depend on what securities are actually held. Figure 3 shows the anticipated year-to-year returns for individual securities for years beginning in 1981, 1982, 1984, and 1987. The anticipated return depends on how much the price of a par bond must rise or fall during the year if the subsequent year's anticipated yield curve is to be correct. Again, the rolling-yield-curve definition of *anticipated* implies the same schedule of single-year returns year after year. The fixed-yield definition implies that prices are not expected to change. Hence, the fixed-yield anticipated annual-return curves are the same as the fixed-yield anticipated yield curves. The Lutzian definition implies that, in any year in which anticipations are met, all securities will have equal returns. In this case, the Lutzian anticipated returns are highest of all in the first year but fall rapidly thereafter. Under fixed-yield anticipations, the shorter-term anticipated returns tend to be "eaten up" by the passage of time. Hence, in the case at hand, the schedule falls, but the fall is less rapid than that of the Lutzian schedule.

From this example, it should be no surprise that, particularly in recent years, the three definitions of *anticipated* sometimes imply substantially different future values of the portfolio. Moreover, except for the Lutzian definition, the anticipated future value may also depend on the investor's intended strategy. Therefore, both *definition* and *strategy* must be taken into account in the estimation of target values. In most cases, this process requires examination of the intended composition of the portfolio for each year from now until the liability is due.

The *Lutzian* definition is natural under the simplest cases analyzed by Friedrich Lutz [8], which assumed either certainty or that each year's forward inter-

Figure 3: Anticipated Returns for Single Years from August 17, 1981 Prices

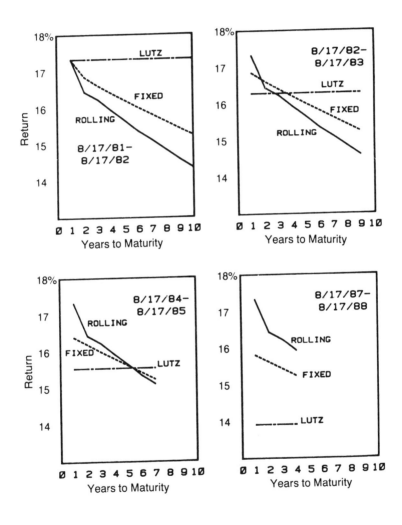

est rate is an unbiased estimator of the future spot rate for that year, negligible transaction costs, and indifference to risk. It is also the easiest to analyze because, as we just noted, during any interval in which anticipations are met under this definition, securities of all maturities have equal realized returns. Hence, under the Lutzian definition, the target holding-period return may be found without considering the particular assets in the immunized portfolio. The Lutzian definition provides a simple definition of market equilibrium.

The *rolling-yield-curve* definition of *anticipated* is natural for many practitioners in the money and bond markets. They tend to describe the state of the market in terms of promised yields of bonds selling at par. Some of its implications have been discussed for many years. It forms a natural point of departure for analyzing scenarios about the course of the bond market as in, e.g., a series of pamphlets by M. L. Leibowitz [7a, 7b]. Moreover, if the simplest Lutzian assumptions are modified to allow for the bias that would result because of the effect of some form of liquidity premium on the quoted spot rate, a rolling yield curve may be consistent with market equilibrium.

The *fixed-yield* definition of *anticipated* has intuitive appeal for several reasons. During an interval in which anticipations are met, each security's realized rate of return is exactly the same as its promised yield. Hence, each bond's anticipated future price may be calculated without reference to any other bond. Because of the latter property, the fixed-yield definition is particularly convenient for analyzing holding-period returns for bonds whose promised yields (yields to maturity or to call) differ for reasons other than maturity or duration, e.g., risk of default, callability, or marketability. In recent years, the fixed-yield definition has been used in Fisher and Lorie's study of returns on stocks and bonds [3], in the associated *CRSP Government Bond File* [2], and by Ayres and Barry [1]. The fixed-yield definition is also implicit whenever one assumes that the quoted yields on bonds of the same maturity but differing coupons are directly comparable, as in most analysis of "yield spreads."

All of these definitions are probably oversimplifications of what most serious students and investors actually anticipate. For example, Lutz's article [8] went on to the analysis of the effects of transaction costs and of various types of uncertainty. Ayres and Barry [1] suggested that empirical study of *ex-post* returns could not disprove the fixed-yield hypothesis. That may well be the case because unanticipated fluctuations may swamp the differences in anticipated returns that are associated with different definitions of *anticipated*.

Particular analytical models of the processes that generate the term structure of interest rates might well imply other definitions of *anticipated*.

While *anticipated* is definitional, one's preference is likely to depend on which definition corresponds to a set of unbiased forecasts of future interest rates or bond prices. Given the present state of empirical evaluation, it is difficult to reject conclusively any of these or a number of more complex hypotheses. The primary reason for the difficulty is that many empirical studies—and not just the early ones—have made crucial assumptions that were invalid. Too many have assumed that a series of yields on actual bonds, which pay interest periodically, could be applied to hypothetical zero coupon notes of the same maturities in order to estimate forward interest rates. That is an invalid procedure for *all but* short-term bonds. Too many have simply assumed that transaction costs could be neglected, which is always troublesome. Hence most such studies are of doubtful validity.

The valid studies contradict the Lutzian assumption that forward interest rates provide unbiased estimates of future spot rates. There appears to be a liquidity premium [5,6,10]. When long-term rates are higher than short-term rates, the existence of liquidity premiums provides the rolling-yield-curve definition of *anticipated* with at least qualitative justification as an equilibrium theory. As we shall see below, if forward rates are equal to one another and the expected spot rate is equal to the current spot rate after deducting the liquidity premium from the "full" forward rate, fulfillment of expectations is also consistent with the rolling-yield-curve definition of *anticipated*. Moreover, in such a case, forward rates tend to level off rapidly; and fulfillment of anticipations also implies nearly equal returns during the coming year for all bonds that mature at least two years from now, which is also an implication of the Lutzian definition.[2] In addition, a theoretical analysis of the stochastic processes that generate future forward and spot rates by Charles Nelson [11] suggests that if errors in the forecasts implied by forward rates are positively correlated, a positive liquidity premium does not imply that the expected holding-period return from long-term bonds held to maturity need be higher than the expected return from a portfolio that always consisted of short-term securities. In other words, Nelson showed that a liquidity premium need not imply liquidity preference. Unfortunately, Nelson's accompanying empirical study is not valid.[3]

Nelson's and later theoretical work also suggest that under uncertainty, yield curves that are always flat are not compatible with competitive equilibrium in bond prices. But that was obvious from Rich's discussion [13] of the paper in which Redington introduced the concept of immunization of portfolios [12]. For example, an investor might want to meet a liability due t years from now. If he knew that yield curves were always flat, he could be certain of meeting his obligation with a portfolio whose initial market value was the same as the present value of the liability, initially by investing one half in a note due in one year and the other half in zero coupon bonds due 2t - 1 years from now. If

[2] Bierwag, G.O., George Kaufman, and Alden Toevs, 1981, "Single Factor Duration Models in a Discrete General Equilibrium Framework," *Journal of Finance*, Vol. 37, No. 2 (May), 325-338.

[3] Fisher, Lawrence (compiler), 1981, *CRSP Monthly File for U.S. Treasury Securities since December 1925*, 1981 edition. Chicago: Center for Research in Security Prices, University of Chicago (magnetic tape).

interest rates did not change, the obligation would be met exactly. If interest rates either rose or fell, the present values of both the obligation and the portfolio would change by nearly the same amounts. However, there is a second-order effect. If yields fell, the rise in the present value of the portfolio would be somewhat greater than that of the obligation. If yields rose, the present value of the portfolio would fall by less than that of the obligation. If immunization were maintained, each change in interest rates would bring further profit. But that would not be an equilibrium situation. Arbitragers would sell additional t-year notes and buy one-year and (2t - 1)-year notes in such large quantities that the yield curve would soon have an appropriate hump.

Empirical study of immunization suggests strongly that, for achieving a given future value, following a duration strategy to immunize a portfolio is substantially less risky than holding a single issue of coupon bonds to maturity at the time horizon. However, returns tend to be slightly less than those suggested by the Lutzian definition of *anticipated* (cf. Fisher and Weil [4]).

Organization

It should be apparent by now that we assume that the reader is familiar with the general idea of portfolio immunization. In Section II, we outline briefly the mechanics of selecting an immunized portfolio and keeping it immunized throughout a planned holding period of several years.

For Section III, we develop some formulas that point out the relationship between par-bond yield curves and forward-rate curves. We present computational formulas for finding Macaulay's duration that are simpler than, but logically equivalent to, his original formulas ([9], pp. 48-50) and a new formula that is valid for transactions taking place between interest-payment dates. Finally, we find the set of returns in the current period that is implied by the current yield curve and the rolling-yield-curve definition of *anticipated*.

In Section IV, we conduct the actual analysis of the effects of anticipations on target holding period returns. Unless the yield curve is flat, each definition of *anticipated* implies

1. A unique set of returns during each year (including the current year) for par bonds with each maturity date

2. Unique sets of sensitivities of later interest rates, yearly returns, and bond prices to unanticipated changes in interest rates.

From the first implication, we deduce that, even with a portfolio chosen without regard for anticipations, e.g., by following either a maturity strategy or a duration strategy, alternative anticipations will imply different target returns.

Analyses of actual and hypothetical yield curves show that these differences may be substantial.

From the second implication, one may infer further that *immunization* as usually stated is not a precise concept. Both the anticipated future interest rates and the hazard or hazards being immunized against must be stated in order to define the criteria for portfolio choice. For each of the three definitions of *anticipated* discussed here, a duration strategy *is* also an immunization strategy. But, in each case, a different hazard is being immunized against. Altering either the choice of hazard or form of anticipations (but not both in an offsetting manner) substantially complicates the finding of both the composition of the immunized portfolios and the target holding-period return.[4]

II. THE IMMUNIZATION PROCESS

Suppose that at time 0 you had a liability of L dollars due at time t, where t is an integral number of years after time 0. At 0, bonds of all integral maturity dates are available. They are coupon bonds that pay interest only once a "year" and sell at par.

Initially, suppose further that the term structure of interest rates were always "flat," i.e., that par bonds of all maturities bore the same interest rate. Let the spot rate at 0 on a single-payment note due at t be s(t). Then the present value at 0 of the liability, under any definition of *anticipated* of this paper, is

$$V_t = L \, v(t) = L \, [1 + s(t)]^{-t} \tag{1}$$

where v(t) is the present value at 0 of \$1 due at t.[5]

Obviously, if you could be sure that interest rates would remain at s(t) at all times between 0 and t, you could meet your obligation in a variety of ways, e.g., by investing in any bonds that were handy at time 0, reinvesting each year's interest payment and principal from maturing bonds as they were received, and finally liquidating the portfolio for L dollars at time t.

However, if interest rates were subject to fluctuation, the value of your assets would almost certainly depend on the particular strategy that you had used to select bonds and on the actual course of interest rates. With most strategies, you might either gain or lose: sometimes by time t your asset would be worth more than L, but other times it would be worth less. All such strategies are risky by definition.

4 _____, 1966, "An Algorithm for Finding Exact Rates of Return," *Journal of Business*, Vol. 39, No. 1, Part II (January), 111-118.

5 _____, 1981, "Discussion of 'Single Factor Duration Models in a Discrete General Equilibrium Framework' by Bierwag, Kaufman, and Toevs," *Journal of Finance*, Vol. 37, No. 2 (May) 325-338.

Nevertheless, there may be some strategies such that a portfolio which is worth V_t at time 0 will be worth at least L at time t, with probability 1.0. Those strategies, if followed, make the portfolio "immune" to fluctuations in interest rates. A portfolio chosen by applying such a strategy is said to be *immunized*. Under the restrictive assumptions of this section, immunization will almost always be feasible.[6] However, when the assumption of flat yield curves is dropped, we will introduce a more precise definition of immunization.

If t = 1 year, the immunization strategy is fairly obvious: buy one-year bonds. Then the appropriate lump sum will be received at time t.

If t = 2 years, the appropriate strategy is neither obvious nor unique. Immunization requires that the average duration of the assets be exactly two years initially. A simple and adequate strategy (so long as yields are less than 61% per annum) is the following "laddered" one: Divide the investment V_t between two-year and three-year bonds so that the weighted average duration of the portfolio is exactly two years. Their durations, and thus the actual division, depend on the interest rate. If interest rates are near zero, almost all of the investment should be in the two-year bonds. As the rate rises, part of the portfolio must be shifted into three-year bonds. For example, at a yield of y = s = 10%, two- and three-year bonds have durations of 1.909 and 2.736 years, respectively. Hence a portfolio of $0.89V_t$ two-year bonds and $0.11V_t$ three-year bonds has a duration of exactly two years. However, at y = s = 20%, the respective durations are 1.833 and 2.528 years; and the appropriate fraction of three-year bonds rises to 0.24. If s were greater than 61%, three-year par bonds would have a duration of less than 2.000 years, and longer term bonds would be needed.

After a year has passed, interest will be received. If interest rates are still the same, the duration of the entire portfolio, *including cash*, will now be one year. However, the cash must be reinvested, forcing an increase in the portfolio's duration. Hence, further changes must be made.[7] The appropriate adjustment is to hold only one-year bonds.

If t = 3 years and y = s = 10%, the initial portfolio worth, V_t, might consist of $0.648V_t$ in three-year bonds and $0.352V_t$ in four-year bonds since the duration of a four-year par bond would be 3.487 years. If at time 1, y = s = 10%, the portfolio would contain $0.100V_t$ in cash, $0.648V_t$ in what are now two-year bonds, and $0.352V_t$ in three-year bonds.[8] Duration would now be 2.000 years; but, again,

---

[6] Fisher, Lawrence and James H. Lorie, 1977, *A Half Century of Returns on Stocks and Bonds*, Graduate School of Business, University of Chicago.

[7] Fisher, Lawrence and Roman L. Weil, 1971, "Coping with Risk of Interest Rate Fluctuations," *Journal of Business*, Vol. 44, No. 4 (October), 408-431. (Reprinted in *Pros & Cons of Immunization*, edited by Martin L. Leibowitz, Salomon Brothers Inc, 1980.)

[8] Hamburger, Michael, and Elliott N. Pratt, 1975, "The Expectations Hypothesis and the Efficiency of the Treasury Bill Market," *Review of Economics and Statistics*, Vol. 57, No. 2 (May), 190-199.

cash must be reinvested. An appropriate course is to follow the strategy suggested for a two-year holding-period. If the interest rate no longer equals 10%, total wealth will differ, but the strategy remains the same: adjust the portfolio so as to hold an appropriate mixture to two-and three-year bonds. Et cetera.

To summarize: Immunization with a particular time horizon t requires at least the following steps:

1. Select the initial portfolio.

2. Each time cash is received either as interest or as repayment of principal, reallocate the portfolio so that it will remain immunized.

The strategies just outlined meet Redington's [12] and the Fisher and Weil [4] definitions of immunization, i.e., the derivative of the current market value of the portfolio with respect to its yield is equal to the derivative of the present value of L, and the market value of the portfolio is equal to the present value of L.

In general, however, the present value of L cannot be defined until the immunization strategy has been found. We, therefore, propose an alternative definition of immunization.

Notation:

L_t = liability due at time t.

W_h = market value of portfolio at time h.

$TA_j(t)$ = amount of one (future value) accumulated over the period j through t under the anticipated behavior of interest rates and the strategy that are being considered.

Recall that the elasticity of a variable z with respect to a variable x is defined as

$$\left(\frac{dz}{dx}\right)\left(\frac{x}{z}\right) = \frac{d(\ln z)}{d(\ln x)}.$$

Then, at time t - j, a portfolio is immunized with respect to a lump-sum liability L_t due at time t if

1. The future value at time t of assets held at t - j, which is the product $[W_{t-j}][TA_j(t)]$, is equal to L_t

2. The sum of the elasticities of W_{t-j} and $TA_j(t)$ with respect to the hazard that is being immunized against is equal to zero.

These are first-order conditions. They imply that the derivative of the net future value with respect to the relevant hazard is equal to zero.

Second-order conditions for immunization would require that the net future value be minimized by applying the immunization strategy. Both Redington's [12] and the Fisher and Weil [4] analyses suggest that this second-derivative condition is met easily whenever the first-order conditions are met and the only liability is a single lump sum due at time t. However, the analysis becomes much more difficult when liabilities are due at a variety of dates.

As we shall see, under the fixed-yield definition of *anticipated* and a proportional shift in 1 + yield, condition 2 is met by setting Macaulay's duration of the portfolio equal to t - j.

Under both the Lutzian and rolling-yield-curve definitions of anticipations, however, realizing anticipations implies that yields on particular bonds *will* change. In such cases, Macaulay's durations must be calculated at "horizon yields," which are the yields anticipated for the date at which the next adjustment of the composition of the portfolio will be made—one year hence in the simple case treated here. Some circumstances, e.g., a substantial change in the level of interest rates or the opportunity to make an advantageous purchase or sale, may make more frequent reallocation desirable. However, such decisions will, in fact, have to take account of the transaction costs involved.

III. SOME COMPUTATIONAL FORMULAS

The problem of finding target returns for immunized portfolios is interesting only when the yield curve is not flat. In order to examine the implications of the alternative definitions of *anticipated*, we must be able to convert par-bond yield curves to forward-rate curves and vice versa. We must also be able to state the duration of any bond that might be included in the portfolio. Finally, we must find the returns for each year under each definition of *anticipated*.

The formulas we need are not readily available. Some are scattered through the literature. Others are brand new. Therefore, we present them here.

Yield Curves and Forward-Rate Curves

Many textbooks show the relationships between forward rates and "bond" prices for "bonds" that pay interest only on their maturity dates. If such bonds were readily available, immunization would not be a topic of much practical interest because liabilities could easily be matched by assets. However, until recently, such bonds have been available in the United States only for maturities of less than one year.

The general relationship between a yield curve and a forward-rate curve may be inferred from Lutz [8] or Fisher and Weil [4]. For the purposes of this paper, which are primarily expository, we make the following simplifying assumptions:

1. Marketable securities consist of coupon "bonds" as defined further below.

2. Bonds are traded only in a spot-cash market.

3. Time is measured in years and has only integer values, 0 (now), 1, 2,..., t,..., k,....

4. A bond that matures at time k pays interest at times 1, 2,..., k and also pays its par value at k.

5. At any time j there exist bonds maturing at each future time k that sell at par (100% or 1.00). These bonds have coupon rates $C_{j^*}(k)$.

6. Bonds that sell at other prices because their coupons differ from $C_{j^*}(k)$ may also exist.

7. There are no taxes, transaction costs, or risks of default.

8. Payments are made according to the original schedule, i.e., bonds may not be called for early redemption by either issuers or holders.

9. Forward interest rates and bond yields may be computed by assuming that the principle of value additivity holds, i.e., that the market value of a "portfolio" of future payments is equal to the sum of the market values of each payment.

We employ the following additional notation:

Let $P_j(C,k)$ = spot price at time j of a bond with a coupon rate of C which is due at time k,

$v_j(k)$ = present value (at time j) of $1 due at time k,

$s_j(k)$ = the spot interest rate or promised return as an annual rate, compounded annually, for a single payment of $1 due at time k, as of time j,

$r_j(k)$ = the forward rate applicable to the period k - 1 to k as of time j,

$a_j(k) = \displaystyle\sum_{i=j+1}^{k} v_j(i)$, the present value (as of time j) of an annuity of $1 per annum payable at time j + 1 through time k,

D = duration in years.

N.B. When the subscript j is equal to 0, it will usually be omitted, e.g.,

$$P(C,k) = P_0(C,k).$$

Inferring Forward-Rate Curves

Suppose that at time j a lump sum due at time k has the same present value as another lump sum due at time k - 1. Then by definition, the *forward interest rate* for the period k - 1 to k is

$$r_j(k) = \frac{\text{lump}(k) - \text{lump}(k-1)}{\text{lump}(k-1)} \qquad (2)$$

or

$$r_j(k) = \frac{\text{lump}(k)}{\text{lump}(k-1)} - 1. \qquad (3)$$

In a consistent system, this relationship can be defined in terms of present value:

$$\text{lump}(k) \, v_j(k) = \text{lump}(k-1) \, v_j(k-1). \qquad (4)$$

Rearranging terms and subtracting one from each side of equation (4)

$$\frac{\text{lump}(k)}{\text{lump}(k-1)} - 1 = \frac{v_j(k-1)}{v_j(k)} - 1. \qquad (5)$$

Substituting from equation (3),

$$r_j(k) = \frac{v_j(k-1)}{v_j(k)} - 1. \qquad (6)^9$$

To find the set of forward rates, r(1), r(2),..., r(t),...r(k), from the par-bond yield curve C*(1), C*(2),..., C*(t),..., C*(k), note that the price of any bond with annual coupon C and a face value of $1 is

$$P(C,k) = v(k) + C \, a(k). \qquad (7)$$

If the bond sells for par,

$$1.00 = v(k) + C^*(k) \, a(k), \qquad (8)$$

---

[9] Kessel, Reuben A., 1965, *The Cyclical Behavior of the Term Structure of Interest Rates* (NBER Occasional Paper Number 91), National Bureau of Economic Research, New York.

or since a(k) = a(k - 1) + v(k) and a(0) = 0,

$$1.00 = v(k) + C^*(k) \ [a(k - 1) + v(k)]. \tag{9}$$

Collecting terms,

$$v(k) \ [1 + C^*(k) = 1 - C^*(k) \ a(k - 1) \tag{10}$$

Thus we have the recursive formula

$$v(k) = \frac{1 - C^*(k) \ a(k-1)}{1 + C^*(k)}, \tag{11}$$

and r(k) may be found from equation (6).

Par-Bond Yield Curve

The par-bond yield for each maturity may be found by solving equation (8) for C*(k), i.e.,

$$C_{j*}(k) = \frac{1 - v_j(k)}{a_j(k)} \ . \tag{12}$$

In slightly different form, this relationship between the yield of a par bond and forward interest rates was first stated by Lutz [8, p. 37] as

$$C^*(k) = \frac{[1 + s(1)][1 + r(2)] \cdots [1 + r(k)] - 1}{\begin{array}{l}[1 + r(2)][1 + r(3)] \cdots [1 + r(k)] + \\ [1 + r(3)] \cdots [1 + r(k)] + \cdots + [1 + r(k)] + 1\end{array}} \tag{13}$$

Equation (12) may be found from equation (13) by multiplying the numerator and the denominator by v(k).

Duration

Frederick R. Macaulay [9, p. 48] actually presented two definitions of *duration*. His *verbal definition* implies that, for a bond whose current price is P and which matures at t,

$$D'(t) = \frac{tv(t) + C\sum_{k=1}^{t} kv(k)}{P} \; . \tag{14}$$

Let the promised yield on such a bond be y. Then, by Macaulay's *algebraic formula*,

$$D(t) = \frac{t(1+y)^{-t} + C\sum_{k=1}^{t} k(1+y)^{-k}}{P} \; . \tag{15}$$

Unless the spot rate s(1) and all forward rates for years 2 through t are exactly equal to y (i.e., unless the current yield curve is flat), equations (14) and (15) are not equivalent (cf. Fisher and Weil [4]). Hence D' and D will differ. However, for individual bonds, the differences are likely to be small. We may therefore use equation (15) as the definition because it is more convenient. From it we may derive either Macaulay's computational formulas or the following logically equivalent ones, which are more convenient than his.

$$D(t) = \frac{1+y}{y} - \frac{1+y+t(C-y)}{C(1+y)^t - (C-y)} \; . \tag{16}$$

Equation (16) holds if y > 0. If y = 0,

$$D(t) = t\left[1 - \left(\frac{1}{2}\right)\frac{t-1}{t+1/C}\right] . \tag{17}^{10}$$

For par bonds, C = y = C*(t). Then equation (16) becomes

$$D^*(t) = \frac{1+C^*(t)}{C^*(t)}\left\{1 - [1+C^*(t)]^{-t}\right\} \tag{18}$$

Bonds with Frequent Interest Payments. In actual markets, bonds generally pay interest more often than once a year. Let C and y now stand for the annual nominal rate and annual yield, each compounded as often as interest is actually paid. For example, most bonds issued in the United States pay interest semiannually. For such bonds

$$D = \frac{1}{y} + \frac{1}{2} - \frac{[1+y/2 + t(C-y)]}{[C(1+y/2)^{2t} - (C-y)]} \tag{19}$$

---

[10] Leibowitz, Martin L., 1979, *Total Return Management*, Salomon Brothers Inc, New York.

Figure 4: Duration of 10% Par Bonds with Annual Coupons

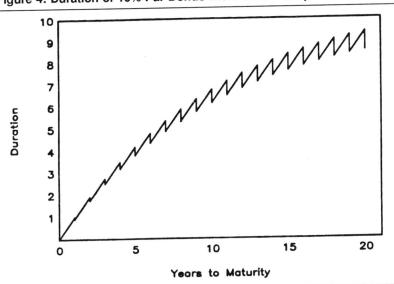

if 2t is an integer. More generally, if interest is paid m times a year,

$$D = \frac{1}{y} + \frac{1}{m} - \frac{1 + y/m + t(C - y)}{C(1 + y/m)^{mt} - (C - y)} \tag{20}$$

if mt is an integer. Note that as the making of payments approaches continuity, the limiting value of duration is

$$D^0 = \frac{1}{y} - \frac{1 + t(C - y)}{Ce^{yt} - (C - y)} . \tag{21}$$

In all of these cases y is a nominal yield. The effective yield is $(1 + y/m)^m - 1$, which approaches $e^y - 1$ as payment becomes nearly continuous.

　　Bonds Between Interest Payments. The above formulas for duration are correct only for bonds that have no interest accrued. Attempts to use them between interest-payment dates overstate duration. Figure 4 shows actual duration as a function of time to maturity for a 10% bond with annual coupons and a yield of 10.00%. If yield is constant, then day by day, as interest accrues, all present values increase at identical rates given by the yield as each payment comes closer. Hence, each day, duration falls by one day. However, when interest is finally paid at the end of each year, what had been the nearest payment drops out of the calculation and duration rises again.

Let f be the time (in years) until the next interest payment and N be the total number of payments to be made. Equation (20) may be generalized to

$$D = \frac{1}{y} + f - \frac{(1 + y/m) + (C - y)N/m}{C(1 + y/m)^N - (C - y)} \qquad (22)^{11}$$

Anticipated Returns for the Current Period

Maintaining an immunized portfolio requires reallocation among assets each time interest (or principal) is received. In Section IV we will sometimes find target holding-period returns from a series of single-period, anticipated returns. Therefore, we present the appropriate formulas here.

Let

$$RA\left(\begin{Bmatrix} L \\ R \\ F \end{Bmatrix}, h, k\right)$$

be the return anticipated during year h on a par bond that matures at k under the Lutzian (L), rolling-yield-curve (R), or fixed-yield (F) definition of *anticipated*.

Lutzian Returns. A well-known implication of the Lutzian definition of *anticipations* is that, in any period in which expectations are met, all securities, including par and nonpar bonds, have the same realized return. Hence, the Lutzian definition implies that the Lutzian anticipated return is

$$RA(L, h, k) = r(h). \qquad (23)$$

Note that $RA(L, h, k)$ is independent of the maturity date k.

Fixed-Yield Returns. Since the fixed-yield definition asserts that *anticipated* means no change in a security's yield to maturity, each year's anticipated return is the same as the yield to maturity at time 0. Such a definition implies that each security has its own anticipated return. Thus, the fixed-yield yearly return is

$$RA(F, h, k) = C_0^*(k) \qquad (24)$$

Note that $RA(F, h, k)$ is independent of h but does depend on the value of k.

---

[11] _____, 1980, "Bond Immunization: A Procedure for Realizing Target Levels of Return"; "Bond Immunization—Part II: Portfolio Rebalancing"; "Bond Immunization Part III: The Yield Curve Case." Reprinted in *Pros & Cons of Immunization*, edited by Martin L. Leibowitz, Salomon Brothers Inc.

Rolling-Yield-Curve Returns. The rolling-yield-curve definition of *anticipated* implies that as each security approaches maturity, it rolls along the yield curve—that its yield rolls down an upward-sloping yield curve or rolls up an "inverted" yield curve.

During any period, the realized return RR on a security that pays interest at the end of the period is equal to the sum of its "current yield" and the percentage change in its price, i.e.,

$$RR(h, k) = \frac{C + P_h(C, k) - P_{h-1}(C, k)}{P_{h-1}(C, k)} . \tag{25}$$

Under the Lutzian and fixed-yield definitions, for any given yield curve, the anticipated return is independent of a specific bond's coupon rate C. However, under the rolling-yield definition, the anticipated return for a period does depend on C, i.e., on what the interest rate was at the time the bond was acquired if it was bought at par. The effect is very small for reasonable differences between C(t) and C*(t). For simplicity we shall assume that at the beginning of a period only par bonds are held, i.e., we take

$$RA(R,x,k) = RA(R, 1, k - x + 1). \tag{26}$$

Then,

$$RA(R, 1, k) = C_0^*(k) + P_1(C_0^*, k) - 1. \tag{27}$$

In this case P_1 is an anticipated price, not an actual price. However, just as there are two definitions of Macaulay's duration for a coupon bond [equations (14) and (15)], there are two definitions of $P_1(C^*, k)$ under the rolling-yield-curve definition of *anticipated*.

First, one may assume that prices of all coupon bonds—par and nonpar—are consistent with the set of forward rates. From equation (7),

$$PA_j\,'(C^*, k) = v_j(k) + C^*(k)\, a_j(k). \tag{28}$$

The rolling-yield-curve definition of anticipated implies

$$v_1(k) = v_0(k - 1),$$
$$a_1(k) = a_0(k - 1),$$

and

$$C_1^*(k) = C_0^*(k - 1). \tag{29}$$

Hence, the first version of the anticipated price is

$$PA_1\,'(C_0^*, k) = v_0(k - 1) + C_0^*(k)a_0(k - 1). \tag{30}$$

Second, one may assume that all bonds with the same maturity date will have the same yield. Then the standard formula for the price of a bond applies:

$$P(C, k) = \frac{C}{y} + \left(1 - \frac{C}{y}\right)(1+y)^{-k}.$$ (31)

Under the rolling-yield-curve anticipations, if we substitute $C_0^*(k)$ for C in equation (31), according to equation (29), we must substitute $C_0^*(k - 1)$ for y in solving for $PA_1(C^*, k)$. Thus

$$PA_1(C_0^*, k) = \frac{C^*(k)}{C^*(k-1)} + \left[1 - \frac{C^*(k)}{C^*(k-1)}\right]$$

$$[1 + C^*(k-1)]^{-(k-1)}.$$ (32)

The first variant implies that

$$RA'(R, 1, k) = \frac{[1 - v(k)]^2}{a(k)} + v(k)r(k).$$ (33)[12]

If we substitute PA_1 from equation (32) in equation (27) and simplify, we find that the second variant implies that

$$RA(R, 1, k) = C^*(k)\left[1 + \frac{1}{C^*(k-1)}\right]$$

$$+ \left(1 - \frac{C^*(k)}{C^*(k-1)}\right)[1 + C^*(k-1)]^{-(k-1)} - 1.$$ (34)

For examples in this paper, the magnitude of the difference between RA′ and RA tends to increase with k. But the differences are very small. The maximum difference of about 2 basis points was associated with a difference of about 0.02 points between PA′ and PA. We shall use RA(R) rather than RA′(R) for simplicity just as we use duration D rather than duration D′.

Comparison of Lutzian and Rolling-Yield-Curve Year-by-Year Anticipated Returns. We have noted that under the Lutzian definition of anticipations, each year's return is also that year's forward rate. Hence the series of anticipated returns on any instrument is s(1), r(2), r(3), . . . , r(k). If the rolling-yield-curve definition applied to yields of zero coupon bonds instead of yields of par bonds (so that $s_1(k) = s_0(k - 1)$ rather than equation (29) supplied the working definition), the series of anticipated one-year returns would depend on k and would be reversed: r(k), r(k - 1), . . . , r(2), s(1). Finally, if the fixed-yield definition

---

[12]Lutz, Friedrich A., 1940, "The Structure of Interest Rates," *Quarterly Journal of Economics*, Vol. 55, No. 1 (November), 36-63.

applied to zero coupon bonds, the annual returns would be simply s(k), s(k), $\cdots$, s(k), s(k). In these series

$$s(k) = \sqrt[k]{[1 + s(1)][1 + r(2)]\cdots[1 + r(k)]} - 1 \; , \tag{35}$$

i.e., $1 + s(k)$ is the geometric mean of the applicable values of $1 + r(j)$.

When we deal with coupon bonds that now sell at par (and assume implicitly that bonds are traded for new, par coupon bonds with the same total market value each year), the sequence, as we have seen, is much more complicated. The value of $1 + C_0^*(k)$ may still be thought of as an average of $1 + r_0(j)$; but it is a weighted average, and the relative weights of the early years' forward rates rise with C^*. The sequence of $1 + RA(R, 1, j)$ is also a complicated set of averages of $1 + r_0(j)$.[13]

IV. CALCULATION OF TARGET HOLDING-PERIOD RETURNS FOR IMMUNIZED PORTFOLIOS

In this section we shall use the formulas presented in Section III to find target future values of one dollar (or, equivalently, target holding-period returns) in general and for each of the illustrative definitions of *anticipated*. In general, we will find that the target future value of one depends on both the investor's anticipations and on the strategy that he uses.

Let

$$TA_j\left(t, \begin{Bmatrix} L \\ R \\ F \end{Bmatrix}, \begin{Bmatrix} M \\ D \\ I \end{Bmatrix}\right)$$

refer to the target future value or target amount (TA) of one for a portfolio in which

- The investment is made at time j and held until time t.

- According to the Lutzian (L), rolling-yield-curve (R), or fixed-yield (F) definition of *anticipated*.

- Using a maturity (M), duration (D), or truly immunizing (I) strategy.

---

[13] Macaulay, Frederick R., 1938, *Some Theoretical Problems Suggested by the Movements of Interest Rates, Bond Yields and Stock Prices in the United States since 1856*. National Bureau of Economic Research, New York. (Partially reprinted in *Pros & Cons of Immunization*, edited by Martin L. Leibowitz, Salomon Brothers Inc, 1980.)

Under the "maturity" strategy, the portfolio consists entirely of the coupon bond that currently sells at par, pays interest at the end of each year, and matures at time t.

Thus, under the maturity strategy,

$$TA(t,x,M) = \prod_{k=1}^{t} [1 + RA(x,1,k)] .$$

That is,

$$TA(t,L,M) = \prod [1 + r(k)] = \frac{1}{v(t)} ,$$

$$TA(t,F,M) = [1 + C^* (t)]^{\,t} ,$$

$$TA(t,R,M) = \prod [1 + RA(R,1,k)] .$$

But note that, although the maturity strategy is far less risky than some strategies, such as always holding Treasury bills or always holding long-term bonds, it nevertheless has more risk than one would like to bear.

Under a duration strategy, the portfolio is chosen so that, at the schedule of yields that are anticipated for the next date that the portfolio will have to be rebalanced, the current value of Macaulay's duration for the portfolio is equal to the time until the liability is due.[14] Under the simplifying assumptions of this paper, portfolios need to be rebalanced only when interest is received at the end of each year. Typically, if it is possible to follow the duration strategy at all, there are a large number of portfolios that will qualify as immunized according to the duration strategy. For simplicity, in the examples we will use Bierwag's "bullet" portfolios. If there is a single security with the appropriate duration, it will constitute the entire portfolio. Otherwise, the portfolio will be divided between the security with the next shorter and next longer durations. If we were testing the duration strategy rather than merely illustrating it, we would also try a number of other methods for meeting the duration criterion.

Whether the duration strategy (or any other) actually immunizes the portfolio, in the sense that the target amount is sure to be achieved, depends on what anticipations of future interest rates the investor actually holds and whether the departures from anticipations are or are not of the form that is assumed implicitly by employing a particular strategy—just as type-A influenza vaccine is

---

[14]McCulloch, J. Huston, 1975, "An Estimate of the Liquidity Premium," *Journal of Political Economy*, Vol. 83, No. 1 (February), 95-119.

likely to work much better against type A virus than against type B virus, and vice versa.

For example, consider a liability due two years hence. We noted in Section II that such a liability would be immunized with a portfolio that initially held a mixture of two-year and three-year bonds. One year from now, the longer bonds will be sold, and the proceeds, along with the interest just received, will be used to buy what then will be one-year bonds. If, at that time, one-year and two-year interest rates are both higher than anticipated, the gain from higher-than-anticipated interest income in year 2 will be offset by the loss incurred in selling the two-year bonds at the end of year 1. If both interest rates fall, the loss of interest income will be offset by the capital gain. In either case, the target might be achieved. However, if the rates depart from anticipations in opposite directions, the gains or losses will be reinforcing. Unless the departures from anticipations of "long-term" and "short-term" interest rates are closely and appropriately associated, a duration strategy might be riskier than a maturity strategy.

Formal Definition of the Immunization Problem

We are now in a position to characterize the immunization problem in more formal terms. Suppose that at time j we had assets worth W_j and planned an investment strategy that had anticipated portfolio returns

$$PRA(h), \qquad h = j + 1, \ldots, t,$$

where

$$PRA(h) = \sum_k w(h,k)\, RA(x,h,k),$$

in which

$$w(h,k) = \text{fraction of } W_h \text{ invested in bonds}$$
$$\text{that mature at } k$$

and

$$\sum_k w(h,k) = 1.$$

Then the target would be

$$W_j TA_j(t) = W_j \prod_{h=j+1}^{t} [1 + PRA(h)] \, . \tag{36}$$

Suppose that, immediately after the portfolio has been purchased, there were an unanticipated shift in the term structure of interest rates. If the elasticity of W_j with respect to the unanticipated change were equal in magnitude but opposite in sign to the elasticity of $TA_j(t)$, then the logarithm of the product would not change and, therefore, the portfolio would be immunized—at least for small changes. Both the elasticity of W_j and of $[1 + PRA(h)]$ may depend on the composition of the portfolio as well as on the form of the departure from anticipations of the term structure of interest rates.

Since $PRA(h)$ is a weighted average of RA's and $TA_j(t)$ is a product, the elasticity of $TA_j(t)$ does depend on the specific securities to be held with the possible exception of the case where the shift is such that all $\ln(1 + RA)$ change by identical amounts. Then, we must see whether the elasticity of price of each security is given by its duration.

If both conditions are true, then it is fairly simple to find $TA_j(t)$. If not, then we have a problem that appears to be soluble only by numerical methods.

Special Cases

Let us examine the cases in which the duration strategy provides portfolios that are immunized against some particular hazard. First, note that all $\ln(1 + RA)$ change by identical amounts if all $(1 + RA)$ are multiplied by $1 + \Delta$. Hence, the first criterion will be met if there are proportional changes in $1 + RA$.

Lutzian. Under the Lutzian definition of *anticipated*,

$$RA_j(L,h,k) = r(h) \qquad \text{for all } k.$$

Therefore, a proportional shift in $1 + RA$ means a proportional shift in $1 + r$. From equation (35), we see that a proportional shift in $(1 + r)$, in turn, implies a proportional shift in $(1 + s)$; and from equation (1), that implies that changes in $\ln[1/v_0(k)]$ will be proportional to k.

Thus, it appears that a portfolio which has the proper duration according to equation (14) (D′) is immunized with respect to proportional changes in $1 + r$. This corresponds to the case proved for large as well as small changes by Fisher and Weil [4].

Fixed Yield. Under the fixed-yield definition,

$$RA_j(F,h,k) = C_j^*(k).$$

Hence, under the fixed-yield definition of *anticipated*, the duration strategy corresponds to immunization against a proportional shift in $1 + C^*$.

Rolling-Yield Curve. Under the rolling-yield-curve definition, $RA'(R,h,k)$ is a nonlinear function of the whole par-bond yield curve for maturities 1, 2, . . . , k - h + 1; and RA(R,h,k) depends on $C^*(k - h)$ and $C^*(k - h - 1)$. Hence we may define a proportional change only in terms of $1 + RA'(C,1,k)$ or $1 + RA(C,1,k)$ for $k \leq t$. Then, it seems to us on preliminary analysis that a portfolio with a duration (calculated on the basis of yields that are anticipated one year from now) that is equal to $t - j$ is immunized with respect to proportional changes in $1 + RA$.

As soon as we know that a particular strategy is appropriate, we may calculate the target amount of one (future value) $TA_j(t)$ by projecting the appropriate curve ($C^*,r,$ or RA) to $j = t - 1$ and setting $TA_{t-1}(t) = 1 + C^*_{t-1}(t)$. Then, stepping back to $j = t - 2$, we construct the appropriate portfolio for year t -1, find PRA(t - 1) under the definition of *anticipated* that we are using, and compute

$$TA_{t-2}(t) = [1 + PRA(t - 1)] \, TA_{t-1}(t).$$

We continue stepping back until we have found $TA_0(t)$ for the definition and strategy in question.

We have already examined TA's under maturity strategies. Moreover, we have noted, that since under Lutzian anticipations,

$$RA(L,h,k) = r(h)$$

and is, therefore, independent of the securities actually held. Hence, the Lutzian TA's are independent of the strategy that is planned. In the other cases, to apply a duration strategy, we must plan on what the composition of the portfolio for each period is to be if anticipations are correct. To do so, we must compute each security's duration at the subsequent period's anticipated yield and select the appropriate portfolio in the manner discussed in Section II. From the projected RA's of the securities to be held and the year-by-year planned composition of the portfolio, we may find TA in a straightforward manner.

While we assume that duration strategies under each definition of *anticipated* all lead to portfolio immunization, it is important to remember that

1. For each definition, portfolio returns are computed under a unique set of anticipated yields (recall Figure 1).

2. Each definition assumes a different *process* by which realizations depart from anticipations.

Hence, a portfolio that is immunized under a particular definition of *anticipated* and for a particular process of changes in interest rates is very unlikely to be immunized under another definition or another process of change. Changing the definition means moving from one set of anticipations to another, thereby altering TA. Changing processes alters the nature of the hazard against which the portfolio is immunized. In any case, portfolio composition will be altered. In all but the Lutzian case, TA will also change, To see why, we turn to a discussion of the general case.

General Case

Suppose we wanted simultaneously to select an immunized portfolio of coupon bonds and to estimate its target anticipated compound amount of one, $TA_j(t)$. For formal discussion we introduce the following notation.

For a portfolio held to meet a liability due at time t, let w(h,k,t) be the fraction of the planned portfolio at time h that will be invested in the security maturing at time k, e.g., w(1987, 1993, 1991) stands for the fraction of the portfolio for 1987 that will be invested in bonds that mature in 1993, given that the liability is due in 1991.

Then we must consider several elasticities, which are derivatives of logarithms of the following variables with respect to the logarithm of "$1 + \Delta$," the hazard being immunized against:

$1 + RA(x,h,k)$, $1 +$ anticipated security return [this elasticity will be denoted by $\alpha(x,h,k)$].

$1 + PRA(x,h,t)$, $1 +$ anticipated portfolio return;

$TA(j,t)$, anticipated future value, i.e., $1 +$ anticipated holding-period return.

$PA_{j+1}(k)$ as of time j, anticipated security price [this elasticity will be denoted by $\beta(j,k)$].

W_j using PA_{j+1}, anticipated value of portfolio.

As noted above, the portfolio is chosen according to the constraint

$$\sum_k w(h,k,t) = 1 . \tag{37}$$

Since portfolio returns are a weighted average of security returns,

$$\frac{d \ln[1 + PRA(x,h,t)]}{d \ln (1 + \Delta)} = \sum_k w(h,k)\alpha(x,h,k) . \tag{38}$$

Since TA is a product,

$$\frac{d \ln [TA(j,t)]}{d \ln (1 + \Delta)} = \frac{\sum_{h=j+1}^{t} d \ln [1 + PRA(x,h,t)]}{d \ln (1 + \Delta)} . \tag{39}$$

From the alternative definition of elasticity given in Section II, we note

$$\frac{1+\Delta}{W_j} \frac{dW_j}{d(1+\Delta)} = \sum_k w(j,k)\, \beta(j,k) .$$ (40)

With the sign reversed, the elasticity $\beta(j,k)$ may be considered a "horizon duration" of the security *for the particular hazard being immunized against.*

If $TA(j,t)$ is consistent with the planned strategy, then a portfolio is immunized with respect to anticipated returns and the hazard being immunized against if and only if weighted average horizon duration, equation (40), is equal to the elasticity of $TA(j,t)$ with respect to that hazard.

One could attempt to immunize against other hazards either in addition to or instead of proportional shifts in (1 + interest rate), as suggested in the papers by Brennan & Schwartz, Ingersoll, and Vanderhoff in this volume. In doing so, it is important to consider effects on both TA and W (or, as Vanderhoof has done, effects on the liability), not merely the effects on W. However, it may not be feasible to immunize against all hazards simultaneously.

Example. Recall that, under rolling-yield-curve anticipations, a duration strategy immunizes against proportional changes in 1 + RA. Suppose, however, we wish to change policy and immunize against proportional changes in 1 + C*. How should the portfolio and plans for future portfolios be changed?

Recall that the hazard is measured by a proportionality factor $1 + \Delta$ and that the elasticity of any arbitrary function is equal to

$$\frac{d \ln F}{d \ln (1+\Delta)}$$

or

$$\frac{dF/d \ln (1+\Delta)}{F}$$

and that, for small Δ,

$$n(1+\Delta) = \Delta .$$

Before the change in policy, each security's α was equal to 1.0 and each security's β was equal to the negative of its duration. For the new hazard, β's will still be equal to the negative of duration [which may change slightly because it will be appropriate to use equation (15) instead of (14)]. However, α's must change unless the yield curve is flat.[15] It may be shown that for a par bond maturing at time $k + 1$,

[15] Nelson, Charles R., 1972, "Estimation of Term Premiums From Average Yield Differentials in the Term Structure of Interest Rates," *Econometrica*, Vol. 40, No. 2 (March), 277-287.

$\alpha(R, 1, k+1) =$

$$= \frac{1 + C*(k+1) + [1 - C^*(k+1)/C^*(k)]\{1/C^*(k) + [k+1/C^*(k)][1+C^*(k)]^{-k}\}}{C^*(k+1)[1+1/C^*(k)] - [1 - C^*(k+1)/C^*(k)][1+C^*(k)]^{-k}}$$

The elasticity differs from unity by

(41)

$\alpha(R, 1, k+1) - 1 =$

$$\frac{[1 - C^*(k+1)/C^*(k)]\{1 + 1/C^*(k) + [1 + k + 1/C^*(k)][1 + C^*(k)]^{-k}\}}{C^*(k+1)[1+1/C^*(k)] - [1 - C^*(k+1)/C^*(k)][1+C^*(k)]^{-k}}$$

(42)

The formulas hold only for $C^* > 0$. The denominator of equations (41) and (42) is positive so long as RA > -100%. All elements in the braced expression in the numerator of equation (42) are positive. Hence, for a proportional shift in $1 + C^*$ and rolling-yield-curve anticipations, $\alpha(R,1,k)$, the elasticity of $1 + RA$, is less than one for yield curves that rise with increasing maturity and greater than one for falling yield curves. Thus, the change of hazard being immunized against requires that the duration of the portfolio be increased if the term structure falls with increasing maturity and requires reducing duration if the term structure is a rising one (a portion of the "change" comes about automatically through the change in the formula for calculating duration [equation (15) instead of (14)]). Changing the hazard may also result in changing the target return.

Similarly, one might hold Lutzian anticipations and decide to change the hazard being immunized against from forward rates to yields. Since the value of RA(L,h,k) depends only on r(h), we need to know the elasticity of $1 + r$ with respect to $1 + C^*$. An analytical computation is not tractable because r(h) is a function of $C^*(1),\ldots, C^*(h)$. However, our numeric results suggest that the relationship is elastic when yield curves rise with maturity and inelastic when yield curves fall. Moreover the departure of the elasticity from unity is several times larger for Lutzian anticipations than for rolling-yield-curve anticipations. It would appear that immunizing against proportional shifts in $1 + r$ is a rather different policy from immunizing against a proportional shift in $1 + C^*$ if one has Lutzian anticipations.

Calculations

To date, we have applied the computations described in this section only for the maturity and the duration strategies. Hence, even for the limited number of yield curves examined in this paper, our conclusions about the magnitude of the effect of the definition of *anticipated* on target values for holding-period returns are only tentative.

Results: Maturity Strategy. The results of applying our analysis under the maturity strategy to five different yield curves are shown in Table 1. For panel A, we used actual yields on U.S. Treasury bonds and notes that were quoted at or above par on December 31, 1980. The usual annual bond yields (compounded semiannually) were converted to effective rates (rates compounded annually), and the effective rates were used to estimate the other numbers in the table for holding periods of 1 through 10 years. The curve for the end of 1980 was a falling yield curve. Note that TA(10,L,M) = 3.3068, which is equivalent to an effective rate of 12.70%; but TA(10,R,M) = 3.3546, which is equivalent to 12.87%, a difference (from unrounded figures) of 16 basis points. Note also that r(2),. . ., r(10) are in narrow range from 12.42% to 12.67%.

For panel B, we smoothed the forward rates by setting them all to 12.50%. The effect on the estimated yield curve was negligible. Again, for horizons of two or more years, TA(t,R,M) exceeds TA(t,L,M). This time TA(10,R,M) exceeds TA(10,L,M) by the equivalent of 18 basis points. The difference in effective rates arises from the fact that, although both definitions of *anticipated* imply a return of 14.27% in one of the 10 years in the holding period, the returns for the other years would be 12.50% under the Lutzian anticipations but about 12.70% under the rolling-yield-curve anticipations. Panel C illustrates the reverse relationship that is implied by a rising yield curve. For this example, we kept the forward rates at 12.50%, but we set s(1) 177 basis points below r(2), viz., at 10.73%, instead of 177 basis points above it. The par-bond yield curve is the exact mirror image of the curve for panel B. Now, TA(10,L,M) is equivalent to an effective rate of 12.32% and TA(10,R,M) to 12.15%. The magnitude of the difference is about the same—17 basis points—but the sign has changed.

In these three examples, TA(t,F,M) lies between TA(t,R,M) and TA(t,L,M) and is generally closer to the former for t ≥ 2.

Panel D is for the moderately humped yield curve of March 17, 1981. Like other typical humped yield curves, its peak par bond yield was for a rather short maturity. In this case, the par bond yield falls substantially from C*(3) through C*(10). Consequently, TA(t,R,M) exceeds TA(t,L,M) for holding periods longer than about three years. In this case, however, the fixed-yield definition of *anticipated* produces the lowest target holding-period return for horizons in the neighborhood of the point where TA(t,R,M) and TA(t,L,M) cross. We must warn that these are not general results for humped yield curves. If the peak yield is at a longer horizon (as in November 1981) or if the yield declined less rapidly as the horizon lengthened, TA(t,L,M) might exceed TA(t,R,M) for all t > 1.

In panels A, B, and C, the forward rate curves level off at k = 2, and in panel D by about k = 3. Panel E is for the yield curve of August 17, 1981. Many of its implications were shown in Figures 1 to 3. Yields declined sharply from C*(1) to C*(2) and then nearly linearly through C*(10). Hence, r(k) was a declining function of k over the entire range examined.

Table 1: Anticipated Amounts of One Under Three Assumptions and the Maturity Strategy

Due Date t (1)	Par-Bond Yield C*(t) (2)	Forward Rate r(t) (3)	Rolling-Yield-Curve Anticipated Return RA' (R,I,t) (4)	Anticipated Amount of One		
				Lutzian TA(t,L,N) (5)	Rolling-Yield TA(t,R,M) (6)	Fixed-Yield TA(t,F,M) (7)

A. Actual Yield Curve, December 31, 1980

(In Percent)

1	14.27	14.27	14.27	1.1427	1.1427	1.1427
2	13.40	12.42	12.64	1.2846	1.2871	1.2860
3	13.18	12.65	12.82	1.4472	1.4521	1.4498
4	13.04	12.51	12.71	1.6282	1.6367	1.6328
5	12.94	12.40	12.64	1.8300	1.8436	1.8375
6	12.88	12.45	12.67	2.0578	2.0772	2.0687
7	12.84	12.47	12.68	2.3145	2.3406	2.3294
8	12.82	12.59	12.73	2.6058	2.6386	2.6248
9	12.81	12.67	12.76	2.9360	2.9753	2.9589
10	12.80	12.63	12.75	3.3068	3.3546	3.3350

B. Curve for December 31, 1980 with Forward Rates Smoothed

(In Percent)

1	14.27	14.27	14.27	1.1427	1.1427	1.1427
2	13.44	12.50	12.71	1.2855	1.2879	1.2868
3	13.16	12.50	12.70	1.4462	1.4515	1.4491
4	13.02	12.50	12.70	1.6270	1.6359	1.6318
5	12.94	12.50	12.70	1.8304	1.8437	1.8377
6	12.89	12.50	12.70	2.0592	2.0778	2.0696
7	12.85	12.50	12.70	2.3166	2.3417	2.3309
8	12.82	12.50	12.70	2.6062	2.6390	2.6252
9	12.80	12.50	12.70	2.9319	2.9741	2.9567
10	12.78	12.50	12.70	3.2984	3.3518	3.3303

C. Similar, Sharply Rising Forward Rate

(In Percent)

1	10.73	10.73	10.73	1.1073	1.1073	1.1073
2	11.56	12.50	12.32	1.2457	1.2437	1.2446
3	11.84	12.50	12.31	1.4014	1.3968	1.3989
4	11.98	12.50	12.31	1.5766	1.5687	1.5722
5	12.06	12.50	12.31	1.7737	1.7618	1.7669
6	12.11	12.50	12.31	1.9954	1.9786	1.9857
7	12.15	12.50	12.31	2.2448	2.2220	2.2315
8	12.18	12.50	12.31	2.5254	2.4955	2.5076
9	12.20	12.50	12.30	2.8411	2.8025	2.8178
10	12.22	12.50	12.30	3.1962	3.1474	3.1662

(continued)

Table 1: (Continued)

Due Date t (1)	Par-Bond Yield C*(t) (2)	Forward Rate r(t) (3)	Rolling-Yield-Curve Anticipated Return RA' (R,I,t) (4)	Anticipated Amount of One		
				Lutzian TA(t,L,N) (5)	Rolling-Yield TA(t,R,M) (6)	Fixed-Yield TA(t,F,M) (7)

D. Humped, March 17, 1981

(In Percent)

1	13.49	13.49	13.49	1.1349	1.1349	1.1349
2	13.59	13.70	13.68	1.2904	1.2901	1.2903
3	13.57	13.52	13.54	1.4649	1.4648	1.4648
4	13.52	13.33	13.40	1.6601	1.6611	1.6607
5	13.36	12.48	12.89	1.8673	1.8752	1.8720
6	13.26	12.53	12.91	2.1013	2.1173	2.1109
7	13.20	12.64	12.96	2.3669	2.3918	2.3819
8	13.14	12.44	12.88	2.6613	2.6998	2.6849
9	13.08	12.23	12.79	2.9868	3.0453	3.0232
10	13.04	12.36	12.84	3.3559	3.4362	3.4066

E. Actual, August 17, 1981

(In Percent)

1	17.33	17.33	17.33	1.1733	1.1733	1.1733
2	16.85	16.29	16.44	1.3645	1.3662	1.3654
3	16.61	16.01	16.23	1.5829	1.5879	1.5857
4	16.40	15.55	15.93	1.8290	1.8410	1.8357
5	16.20	15.04	15.65	2.1040	2.1290	2.1185
6	16.00	14.44	15.35	2.4078	2.4559	2.4364
7	15.81	13.91	15.12	2.7427	2.8271	2.7940
8	15.62	13.25	14.86	3.1060	3.2471	3.1935
9	15.43	12.55	14.61	3.4957	3.7213	3.6380
10	15.24	11.80	14.34	3.9084	4.2558	4.1308

In this case, both r(k) and RA(R, 1, k) also decline substantially for successive future dates. Qualitatively, the target amounts of one are like those of panels A and B, viz.,

$$TA(t, R, M) > TA(t, F, M) > TA(t, L, M) \tag{43}$$

for t > 1.

In addition to interpreting differences among TA's as differences in effective interest rates, we may also look at them relative to the "interest on interest" that the portfolio must earn to achieve its promised yield of $C_0^*(t)$ on the bond. Interest on interest is the difference between the holding-period returns accumulated at a given nominal rate under compound interest and under simple interest. Interest on interest is relevant because it represents the difference between the total return and the amount that the actual issuer of the bond has promised to pay. Its value is

$$\text{II}(t) = \text{TA}(t) - [1 + t\text{C}_0^*(t)] \ . \tag{44}$$

For example, in panel A, $\text{II}(10) = 1.055$. Since TA(10,R,M) -TA(10,L,M) = 0.0478, the difference is about 0.045 times II(10). Also in panel A, TA(5,R,M) - TA(5,L,M) = 0.0136, which is smaller than the difference for 10 years. However, II(5) is only 0.1905. Hence, the difference for 5 years is 0.071 times II(5).

It appears that $|\text{TA}(t,R,M) - \text{TA}(t,L,M)|$ increases as either t or the general level of interest rates increases. The same conclusion appears to follow when the difference is converted to a difference in effective rate of return. However, the ratio of the magnitude of the difference to II(t) seems to be affected in the opposite manner.

Results: Duration Strategy. Table 2 presents estimated values of TA for the duration strategy in those cases from which computations have been completed. Since TA is independent of strategy for Lutzian anticipations, TA(t,L,M) = TA(t,L,D).[16]

In panel E, since the yield curve falls, reducing risk by moving from the maturity strategy to the duration strategy has the effect of reducing TA for both rolling-yield-curve and fixed-yield anticipations. As a result, in panel E,

$$\text{TA}(t,L,D) \approx \text{TA}(t,R,D) \approx \text{TA}(t,F,D).$$

Now, we have a truly interesting result. *Sometimes*, the form on one's anticipations of future interest rates will affect the target holding-period return for a portfolio that is immunized by following the duration strategy, but, *other times*, it will not. And here *sometimes* refers to actual quoted yield curves from the recent past.

Results: Immunization Strategy. First recall that, with Lutzian anticipations, the choice of strategy does not affect TA. Hence,

$$\text{TA}(t,L,D) = \text{TA}(t,L,I). \tag{45}$$

Moreover, if the portfolio is immunized for the hazard of proportional changes in $1 + \text{C}^*$, the duration strategy is also the immunization strategy for fixed-yield anticipations. However, without performing the full-scale calculations, there is little that we can say about difference in target values for rolling-yield-curve anticipations.

---

[16]Redington, F.M., 1952, "Review of the Principles of Life-Office Valuations," *Journal of the Institute of Actuaries*, Vol. 78, No. 3, 286-340. (Reprinted in *Pros & Cons of Immunization*, edited by Martin L. Leibowitz, Salomon Brothers Inc, 1980.)

Table 2: Anticipated Amounts of One Under Three Assumptions and a Duration Strategy

Due Date t (1)	Par-Bond Yield C*(t) (2)	Anticipated Amount of One		Fixed-Yield TA (t,M,D) (5)
		LutzianTA (t,L,D) (3)	Rolling-Yield TA (t,R,D) (4)	

B. Curve for December 31, 1980 with Forward Rates Smoothed

Due Date t	Par-Bond Yield C*(t)	LutzianTA (t,L,D)	Rolling-Yield TA (t,R,D)	Fixed-Yield TA (t,M,D)
1	14.27%	1.1427	1.143	1.1427
2	13.44	1.2855	1.288[a]	—
3	13.16	1.4462	1.451[a]	—
4	13.02	1.6270	1.636[a]	—
5	12.94	1.8304	1.844[a]	—
6	12.89	2.0592	2.078[a]	—
7	12.85	2.3166	2.342[a]	—
8	12.82	2.6062	2.639[a]	—
9	12.80	2.9319	2.974[a]	—
10	12.78	3.2984	3.352[a]	—

E. Actual, August 17, 1981

Due Date t	Par-Bond Yield C*(t)	LutzianTA (t,L,D)	Rolling-Yield TA (t,R,D)	Fixed-Yield TA (t,M,D)
1	17.33%	1.1733	1.1733	1.1733
2	16.85	1.3645	1.3657	1.3648
3	16.61	1.5829	1.5848	1.5833
4	16.40	1.8290	1.8306	1.8282
5	16.20	2.1040	2.1033	2.1007
6	16.00	2.4078	[b]	[b]
7	15.81	2.7427	[b]	[b]
8	15.62	3.1060	[c]	[c]
9	15.43	3.4957	[c]	[c]
10	15.24	3.9084	[c]	[c]

Notes:

[a] Estimated from asymptotic yield (AC)
[b] Strategy requires holding bonds with more than 10 years to maturity
[c] Strategy is not feasible with nonnegative holdings of par bonds

V. CONCLUSIONS

In this paper, we have examined the problem of immunizing portfolios under a variety of assumptions about the nature of the future interest rates that may be anticipated on the basis of the current term structure of interest rates for par bonds. We have noted that Lutzian, rolling-yield-curve, and fixed-yield anticipations may provide very different "forecasts" of future interest rates.

The compound amount of one (and long-term holding-period return) may be inferred from the par-bond yield curve only under Lutzian assumptions unless the investor's strategy is specified in detail. As a result, we found it necessary to redefine *immunization*. In order to find a target amount of one (future value), both the definition of *anticipated* and the strategy (or, better, the hazard to be immunized against) must be specified. Then, immunization against a particular hazard will be attained if, for each year between now and the due date of the liability, the planned portfolio is such that the weighted average elasticity of security prices in the portfolio is equal to the sum of the elasticities of (one plus anticipated portfolio return) for that year and through the remaining years that the portfolio is to be held.

We noted that, under some conditions, a duration strategy is an immunization strategy. However, the hazard immunized against depends on the type of anticipations the investor holds; and immuniation against other hazards, which may have been considered equivalent in the past, may be very imperfect.

We have not found any simple relationship between the form of the yield curve and the differences in target values that are implied by various strategies or definitions of *anticipations*. We can only note that an examination of a limited number of yield curves that are based on recent price quotations shows that the differences can sometimes be substantial.[17]

To sum up, there are still many interesting problems connected with the idea of immunization of portfolios.

ACKNOWLEDGMENTS

The authors wish to thank George R. Morrison and Alfred Weinberger for their incisive comments on earlier drafts of this paper.

---

[17] Rich, C. D., 1952, "Review of the Principles of Life-Office Valuations, Abstract of the Discussion," *Journal of the Institute of Actuaries*, Vol. 78, No. 3, 319-320. (Reprinted in *Pros & Cons of Immunization*, edited by Martin L. Leibowitz, Salomon Brothers Inc, 1980.)

NOTES

1. Changes in yield are reflected by opposite changes in price. If "small" changes in short-term and long-term yields (compounded continuously) are equal, price changes will be proportional to Macaulay's duration. However, if short-term and long-term yields move in the same direction but short-term yields move more, price changes will tend to be less than proportional to duration. Moreover, the magnitude of the departure from proportionality will itself be an increasing function of duration. Hence, under the stated condition, immunized portfolios should have longer Macaulay's durations than those implied by the assumption of parallel shifts in yield curves.

2. However, the return under the rolling-yield-curve definition will be between the spot rate and the forward rate, while the return under the unmodified Lutzian definition will be at the current spot rate. (See also note 13.)

3. Nelson's theoretical result is the reason that we use the term *Lutzian anticipations* rather than the more common term *expectations hypothesis*. His result may be summarized as follows:

Let R(j) = actual interest rate on one-period loans during time j,

   r(j) = the Lutzian forward interest rate on such loans that is implied by the yield curve at time zero,

   u(j) = R(j) - r(j).

As usually stated, the expectations hypothesis is that u(j) is a random variable whose expectation is zero, i.e., that r(j) is an unbiased forecaster of R(j) for j ≥ 2 [R(1) is always equal to r(1)].

Let $\qquad\qquad P[R(t)] = [1 + R(1)] [1 + R(2)] \ldots [1 + R(t)],$

$\qquad\qquad\quad p[r(t)] = [1 + r(1)] [1 + r(2)] \ldots [1 + r(t)].$

Then the expectations hypothesis is that

$$E \{P[R(t)]\} = p[r(t)]. \qquad\qquad (1a)$$

However, Nelson showed that, for equation (1a) to hold under the assumption stated above, there is an additional necessary condition: the covariance of u(h) and u(j) must be zero for all h $\neq$ j, i.e., the errors of forward rates as forecasts of future spot rates must be uncorrelated. Empirically, both long-term and short-term interest rates tend to move in the same direction; and the whole term structure is likely to remain high or low for periods of several years or even longer. Hence, there appears to be positive correlation among the forecast errors. In that case,

$$E \{P[R(t)]\} > p[r(t)], \qquad t \geq 3. \tag{1b}$$

The exact relationship depends on the covariance of $u(j)$ and $u(k)$ for $j = 2, \ldots,$ $t - 1$; $k = j + 1, \ldots, t$, and also on $r(j)$ for $j = 2, \ldots, t$.

Equation (1) may hold even in the presence of positive covariance if the expectation of u is less than zero by an amount that just offsets the bias due to serial covariance. If r's, as forecasters of R's, have upward bias, one may say that there is a "liquidity premium." However, Nelson's analysis shows that such liquidity premiums do not imply liquidity preference on the part of investors.

Thus, even the assumptions that all investors have the same time horizon and are maximizers of expected terminal wealth do not imply Lutzian anticipations in the presence of correlated forecast errors.

Nelson went on to see whether actual liquidity premiums were equal to those implied by the covariance of forecast errors. However, he treated estimates of yields of long-term coupon bonds as if they were yields of zero coupon bonds, which is an invalid procedure. Whether there is liquidity preference in the bond market is still unknown.

4. The hazards that we discuss as examples in this paper are all in the form of proportional changes in a set of (1 + interest rate). Bierwag, Kaufman, and Toevs [1a] have recently proposed a hazard that may be easier to analyze and which appears to be consistent with market equilibrium. They propose the hypothesis that the unanticipated change in each single-payment bond is linear function of the realized hazard. If that hypothesis is correct, then it follows that the unanticipated price change of any default-free bond or portfolio of such bonds is also a linear function of the hazard. See also Fisher [2b].

5. Note, however, that when the term structure is not flat, *present value* may become an ill-defined concept.

6. Traditional immunization—by holding a variety of assets—will not be feasible if t is greater than the duration of longest-duration bond. However, immunization might still be achieved by increasing relatively short-term liabilities. One appropriate method would be short-term borrowing with the proceeds invested in long-duration bonds. Another method would be to buy long-term bonds in the futures market. Both methods introduce complexities that we will not deal with here.

If the assumption of parallel shifts of yield curves is dropped, the feasibility of immunization also depends on the correlation among changes in long-term and short-term rates.

7. The initial portfolio may be broken into interest and principal payments due at times 1, 2, and 3. Between 0 and 1, each time until payment—and hence duration—declines at the uniform rate of 1 day per diem, so long as interest rates remain the same. At time 1, interest is received in cash. Therefore, the duration of the first interest payment can no longer decline. Thus, unless the rest

of the portfolio is reallocated, portfolio duration will be more than 364 days at time 1 + 1/365.

8. The respective fractions of the portfolio are 0.0909, 0.5891, and 0.3200.

9. Note that equation 3.5 is far less awkward than the common textbook formula $r_j(k) = [1 + s_j(k)]^k / [1 + s_j(k-1)]^{k-1} - 1$. "Forward" rates are implied by value additivity. They carry no direct implications about expectations. See McCullogh [10]. However, value additivity may have its own empirically testable implications.

10. We have derived equation (16) directly from Macaulay [9, p. 48], directly from equation (15), and from the known alternative definition of duration as an elasticity (cf. Fisher [2a]). Equation (17) was derived algebraically and compared with Macaulay's formula.

A convenient formula restated from Macaulay [9, p. 49] for the duration of an annuity with rents due at times 1,. . ., t is

$$D_a = \frac{1+y}{y} - \frac{t}{(1+y)^t - 1} \, . \tag{17a}$$

11. Equation (22) was derived by noting that the difference between the duration at time 0 and time 1/m - f (with $0 \le f < 1/m$) is 1/m - f and that at time 0, N = mt.

12. From equations (27) and (28),

$$PA_1'(C^*, k) = C^*(k) a(k-1) + v(k-1),$$
$$RA'(R, 1, k) = C^*(k)[1 + a(k-1)] + v(k-1) - 1 \, .$$

But

$$a(k-1) = a(k) - v(k)$$

and

$$v(k-1) = v(k)[1 + r(k)].$$

Recalling equation (12),

$$C^*(k) = \frac{1 - v(k)}{a(k)}$$

and substituting into the second equation of this footnote,

$$RA'(R,1,k) = \frac{1 - v(k)}{a(k)} [1 - v(k) + a(k)] + v(k)[1 + r(a)] - 1$$

$$= \frac{[1 - v(k)]^2}{a(k)} + 1 - v(k) + v(k) + v(k) r(k) - 1.$$

Canceling offsetting terms yields equation (33).

13. Under some conditions we can simplify the calculations through use of an asymptotic yield which may be dubbed "the long-term interest rate." Suppose the series of $r_0(k)$'s leveled off so that for $k > z$, $r(k) = r(z)$. Then the series of $s(k)$'s, $C^*(k)$'s, and $RA(R,1,k)$'s would all approach limiting values asymptotically. It is well known that $s_0(j)$ approaches $r_0(z)$ as k increases without bound. However, $C^*(k)$ and $RA(R,1,k)$ approach a different asymptote, the long-term interest rate, which we find as follows: from equation (12),

$$C^*(k) = \frac{1 - v(k)}{a(k)} \ .$$

For $k \geq z$,

$$C^*(k) = \frac{1 - v(z)\,[1 + r(z)]^{-(k-z)}}{a(z) + v(z) \displaystyle\sum_{h=z+1}^{k} [1 + r(z)]^{-(h-z)}}$$

But, as k increases without bound,

$$[1 + r(z)]^{-(k-z)} \to 0.$$

and

$$\sum_{h=z+1}^{k} [1 + r(z)]^{-(h-z)} \to \frac{1}{r(z)}$$

Hence,

$$C^*(k) \to \frac{r_0(z)}{r_0(z)\,a_0(z) + v_0(z)} = AC \ , \tag{35a}$$

where AC is the asymptotic par-bond yield. Moreover, $RA(R,1,j)$ and $RA'(R,1,j)$ also approach AC because, if C^* approaches AC, $C^*(k-1) - C^*(k)$ approaches 0. Indeed, when the asymptotic conditions apply, $RA'(R,1,k)$ approaches AC even more rapidly than $C^*(k)$ does. The process is so rapid that the ratio in equation (35a) may be taken as a good estimate of $RA'(R,1,z)$ whether asymptotic conditions hold or not.

As we shall see, when the asymptotic conditions exist, this approximation can be of great convenience under Rolling-Yield-Curve anticipations. For portfolios that consist entirely of securities that mature at or after time z, the single-year anticipated return of the portfolio may be estimated with negligible error without knowing the portfolio's exact composition, thereby simplifying the estimation of the target holding-period return.

The accuracy of the approximation may be found for $k \geq z$ by subtracting equation (35a) from equation (33) and performing some algebraic manipulation. We find

$$RA'(R,1,k) - AC = \frac{v(k)}{a(k)} \left[\frac{1}{a(k)\, r(k) + v(r)} + a(k)\, r(k) + v(k) - 2 \right] \qquad (35b)$$

$$= \frac{v(k)}{a(k)} \left[\frac{AC}{r(k)} + \frac{r(k)}{AC} - 2 \right] \qquad (35c)$$

The bracketed term is likely to be small, and the ratio of $v(k)$ to $a(k)$ must be less than $1/k$ for positive interest rates.

When the asymptotic conditions do apply, AC may be called the *long-term interest rate*, because if it exists, AC is the yield on a perpetual annuity. We may also note that for "smoothly" rising yield curves, $r(z) > AC > C_0^*(z)$, and for smoothly falling curves, $r(z) < AC < C_0^*(z)$.

14. This is equivalent to setting the "horizon duration" of the assets equal to the horizon duration of the liability. See Leibowitz [7b].

15. For simplicity of notation, let

$$c = C^*(k + 1), \qquad y = C^*(k).$$

Note that

$$1 + RA = c + \frac{c}{y} + \left(1 - \frac{c}{y} \right)(1 + y)^{-k}$$

Then,

$$\frac{d(1 + RA)}{d(1 + \Delta)} = 1 + c + \frac{1}{y} - \frac{c}{y^2} + k\left(1 - \frac{c}{y} \right)(1 + y)^{-k} + \left(\frac{1}{y} + \frac{c}{y^2} \right)(1 + y)^{-k}$$

Collecting terms and substituting the formal notation for the derivative and for $(1 + RA)$ provide the numerator and denominator of equation (41).

16. Moreover, the form of the duration strategy that we use requires holding bonds that mature either at the due date of the liability (for $j = t - 1$) or no earlier than the due date (for $j < t - 1$). In panels B and C, RA(R,1,k) differs from AC by less than 2 basis points for $k \geq 2$. Therefore, in those panels, we may estimate TA(t,R,D) by TA(t,R,M).

Further, although TA(t,F,D) has not been calculated as yet, lengthening the maturity of the portfolio in order to apply the duration strategy under fixed-yield anticipations makes TA(t,F,D) < TA(t,F,M) for panel B and TA(t,F,D) > TA(t,F,M) for panel C (cf. panel E).

17. These observations suggest that the empirical findings in several of the papers in this volume, as well as in other articles, need further careful scrutiny. In addition, the attempts to immunize against two hazards simultaneously as in the papers by Brennan and Schwartz and by Ingersoll might be developed further via the methods suggested here.

Addendum

We are pleased to see that the *CRSP Government Bond File* is being used to test immunization strategies. Fisher compiled the file with that use as his original motivation. Leibowitz's firm supplied most of the quotations. However, we suspect that many of the tests reported in the papers in this conference have neglected an important point that must be kept in mind whenever one selects securities for a portfolio—real or hypothetical. That factor is *suitability*.

For much research on the stock market, this factor may be ignored because, if prices are in equilibrium and transaction costs may be ignored, many stocks that might tend to be excluded from a portfolio for tax reasons will still be included because of their contribution to diversification.

But, if bonds have low risk in nominal terms, inclusion of bonds that have the wrong tax position will tend to reduce after-tax return by far more than might be justified by their contribution to diversification.

There are two kinds of special tax status to worry about (besides things like "flower-bond" status, which affects both maturity date and taxes). The first is explicit tax exemption or partial tax exemption. All Treasury securities for which data appear in the *CRSP Government Bond File* and which were issued before 1940 were at least partially tax-exempt. Interest on bonds issued up to 1917 and on nearly all short-term and intermediate-term issues during the 1930s (1929-February 1941 for Treasury bills) was wholly tax-exempt. Such bonds had much appeal to investors who were in high tax brackets but very little attraction for tax-exempt pension funds, etc. Some of the tax-exempt bonds remained outstanding until the early 1960s.

Second, many nominally taxable securities also have partial exemption from Federal income taxes: all of those that sell for less than par and have at least a year to maturity (six months for most of the period covered by the CRSP file). The differential taxation of capital gains and "net interest" implies that tests which are conducted without explicit tax allowances should confine themselves to taxable instruments that are selling at or above par. We suspect that failure to make that restriction will do more harm than failing to exclude flower bonds and bonds that are callable within say 5-10 years. At times these restrictions may result in an empty set. That is a practical problem which should also be investigated.

We could make other comments, but they would be about relatively minor problems.

Chapter III D-13

Duration Targeting and the Management of Multiperiod Returns
[1990]

Modern portfolio management increasingly includes the use of targeted-duration strategies as a means of achieving a desired balance between risk and return. In such strategies, a constant duration is maintained through periodic rebalancing.

One of the most important characteristics of duration-targeting strategies is the "focusing" of the return distribution on a minimum-variance point. This point occurs when the duration is equal to about one-half the investment horizon. It is consequently possible to achieve "partial immunization" of a bond portfolio by simply maintaining its duration at one-half the length of the investment horizon.

Many performance benchmarks, including the Salomon Brothers BIG Index, exhibit an almost constant duration. It follows that, by tracking a bond index, one can obtain many of the results of a duration-targeting strategy.

Modern portfolio management is making increasingly use of targeted-duration strategies as a means of achieving a desired balance between risk and return. Immunization and pension fund surplus management clearly use targeted duration. Many other styles of fixed income management are tantamount to maintaining portfolio duration within a relatively narrow range. Many asset allocation studies, for example, assume that the bond component is characterized

Terence C. Langetieg, Martin L. Leibowitz, and Stanley Kogelman, "Duration Targeting and the Management of Multiperiod Returns," *Financial Analysts Journal*, September/October 1990. Reprinted with permission.

by some prescribed level of volatility. Inasmuch as bond return volatility is estimated by multiplying interest rate volatility by bond portfolio duration, setting
the volatility level is equivalent to setting the duration level.

A less obvious example of duration targeting is the use of a performance
benchmark or creation of an index-tracking portfolio. The durations of major
fixed income market indexes tend to be relatively stable, despite wide fluctuations in interest rates. Over the past six years, for example, the durations of the
Salomon Brothers Broad Investment-Grade (BIG) Bond Index^{SM} and the Salomon Brothers Large Pension Fund (LPF) Baseline Index^{SM} have ranged from 3.9
to 4.5 years and 5.3 to 6.0 years, respectively. During the same period, the yields
on these indexes have moved within a much wider, 600-basis-point band.

Duration-targeting strategies should be useful to a wide range of investors,
including

- the "asset allocator," who sets long-run targets for the stock/bond
  mix and for the duration of the bond portfolio;

- the "immunizer," who seeks a reasonable degree of risk control over
  a fixed investment horizon;

- the "indexer," whose goal is to meet or outperform the return on a
  benchmark portfolio; and

- the pension fund manager, who must develop a strategy for achieving high returns while controlling surplus risk.

A great amount of research has focused on duration-based strategies, but
there has been only limited analysis of the long-term investment characteristics
of duration targeting and its impact on overall fund policy decisions.[1] This article reviews those areas in which duration targeting is used, demonstrates some
of the basic characteristics and features of duration targeting and considers the
advantages and disadvantages of various types of targeted-duration strategies.

We find that one of the most interesting investment characteristics of duration-targeting strategies is the "focusing" of the return distribution on a minimum-variance point. This point occurs when the duration is equal to about
one-half the investment horizon. Although duration targeting does not achieve a
zero-return volatility, it controls investment risk reasonably well.

---

[1] For a comprehensive review of duration and immunization, see M.L. Leibowitz, ed,
"Pros and Cons of Immunization" (Salomon Brothers Inc, New York, 1982); G.G.
Kaufman, G.O. Bierwag and A. Toevs, *Innovations in Bond Portfolio Management:
Duration Analysis and Immunization* (Greenwich, CT: JAI Press, 1983); and G.O. Bierwag,
Duration Analysis: Managing Interest Rate Risk (Cambridge, MA: Ballinger Publishing,
1987).

GLOSSARY

Targeted-Duration Strategy: Strategy of maintaining a constant duration by periodically rebalancing the portfolio.

Bond Return Volatility: The annualized standard deviation of returns.

Macaulay Duration: The weighted-average maturity of a cash flow stream. The weights are the present values of the cash flow that occur at each point in time. With some slight modification, the duration can be used to estimate the sensitivity of a bond's price to instantaneous yield changes.

Incremental Bond Return: The percentage change in a bond's price resulting from an instantaneous yield change.

Buy-and-Hold Strategy: Strategy of buying a security and holding it until maturity. All cash flows will be either spent or reinvested at the prevailing market rate.

Immunization: A specialized technique for constructing and rebalancing a bond portfolio in order to achieve a target return over a specified investment horizon. The goal of this strategy is to meet or exceed the return target regardless of changes in interest rates over the investment period.

It is consequently possible to achieve some degree of immunization of a bond portfolio by simply maintaining the duration at one-half the length of the investment horizon. This process will lead to a significant reduction in return variablility at the end of the investment horizon. Because duration targeting does not achieve zero volatility, we can view it as a form of "partial immunization."

Compared with duration targeting, immunization clearly offers more in the way of risk reduction at the *end* of the investment horizon. This is *not* the case for *shorter* holding periods, however. Return volatility over the first year of immunization is double that of duration targeting. Duration targeting offers greatly reduced return volatility over most of the investment horizon, but only partial, rather than full, immunization.

Because many standard performance benchmarks exhibit an almost constant duration, it follows that one can obtain many of the beneficial results of a duration-targeting strategy by taking a position in a bond index. With duration of the BIG index currently at 4.2 years, partial immunization at 8.4 years can be obtained simply by maintaining a position in the BIG index. The LPF has a duration of 5.7 years, offering partial immunization at 11.4 years. For an immunization or planning horizon of 8.4 to 11.4 years, a portfolio combining the BIG and LPF indexes might be used. For longer or shorter immunization horizons, another index would be required to achieve partial immunization.[2]

Duration-targeting strategies can be applied to pension funds. In the case of a plan with retirees only and a liability duration of six years, investment returns nearly equivalent to the pension liability can be attained by targeting and maintaining a duration of six years. This is so even though the duration of the pension liability (averaging six years) fluctuated between 4.0 and 9.8 years at the six-year point. As long as the average durations of the duration-targeting strategy and the pension liability are the same, investment results will be nearly identical.

Duration targeting can be integrated with active management by incorporating sector, quality and other bond characteristics. In addition, by establishing a range about a target duration (for example, plus or minus two years), interest rate forecasts can be actively implemented by managing the duration within this range.[3]

DURATION AND BOND RETURNS

Conceptually (the Macaulay), duration can be thought of as the weighted-average maturity of the cash flow stream, where the weights are defined in a present value sense.[4] (Thus, for a zero-coupon bond, the duration is simply equal to the bond's maturity.) But it is its relation to interest rate changes and bond returns

---

[2] For a discussion of alternative ways to construct strategies to "beat" an index in the presence of mean reversion in interest rates, see M. R. Granito, "The Problem with Bond Index Funds," *Journal of Portfolio Management*, Summer 1987, and "The Secret of Duration Averaging," in F. Fabozzi and T. D. Garlicki, eds., *Advances in Bond Analysis & Portfolio Strategies* (Chicago: Probus, 1987).

[3] Several of these results are similar to characteristics that have been observed in solutions to other financial management problems. For example, in the design of optimal strategies for hedging floating-rate debt with Eurodollar futures, Salomon Brothers discovered that the duration that minimizes variance is equal to half the horizon and that constant-duration strategies have an advantage over immunization strategies when performance over the entire horizon is considered. See J. Showers, M. Koenigsberg and J. McClure, "Liability Management—A Developing Country Perspective" (The Salomon Brothers Asset and Liability Workshop for Monetary Authorities, May 1989).

[4] The Macaulay duration of a coupon-bearing bond with a current price or present value of P, a coupon of C, a maturity of M, a face value of F and a discount rate or yield to maturity of R is given by:

$$\text{Duration} = \frac{1}{P}\left\{ \sum_{t=1}^{M} \frac{tC}{(1+R)^t} + \frac{MF}{(1+R)^M} \right\}.$$

Figure A: Using Duration to Approximate Bond Prices

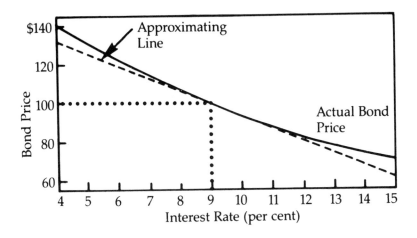

that makes duration an unusually useful investment management tool. A bond's incremental return, resulting from an immediate change in the yield, is approximated by the bond's duration times the change in the bind's yield.[5]

$$\text{Incremental Bond Return} = -\text{Duration} \times \frac{\text{Yield Change}}{1 + \text{Yield}} \quad (1)$$

Figure A shows the approximating price line that results from Equation (1) for a 10-year, 9% coupon bond. For interest rate changes of 100 basis points or less, the approximation line is very close to the actual bond price. For 200-basis-point change in rates, the approximating line errs by about 1% relative to the actual bond price. For interest rate changes of 500 basis points or more, approximation errors as large as 8% arise.

Approximation errors increase with increasing rate changes because actual bond price is related to bond yield in a nonlinear fashion; this is often referred

---

[5] Equation (1) is based on a first-order Taylor expansion about the current yield. More accurate approximations can be obtained by extending the Taylor expansion to second and third-order terms. See G.O. Bierwag, *Duration Analysis, op. cit.*, Appendix 5B.

to as the convexity effect. Over short investment horizons, interest rate changes are likely to be small; thus the approximate results from Equation (1) are extremely accurate. Over longer investment horizons, Equation (1) must be used with caution, because interest rate changes are likely to be larger and because duration itself changes with both time and interest rates.

BOND RETURNS OVER A MULTIYEAR HOLDING PERIOD

Another important investment property of duration emerges when we examine multiyear bond returns. Consider again a 10-year, 9% coupon bond that is held until maturity, with all coupons reinvested. (This is commonly known as a *buy-and-hold* strategy.) For simplicity, suppose that the current bond yield is 9% and that this yield changes once at the beginning of the 10-year investment horizon.

Figure B shows the bond's returns over four, seven and 10-year holding periods.[6] Falling interest rates produce a higher return over a four-year investment horizon but a lower return over a 10-year investment horizon. Observe that the bond's return variability is lowest at the seven-year holding period, which corresponds to the bond's seven-year duration. This observation has led to many important duration based strategies for immunization and risk-reduction.[7]

---

[6] The formula for the annualized holding-period return over H years for a coupon-bearing bond with a maturity of M years, a coupon of C, a face value of F and an initial price of P_o is:

$$HPR = \left[\frac{1}{P_0}\left\{\sum_{t=1}^{H} C(1+R_t)^{H-t} + \sum_{t=H+1}^{M} \frac{C}{(1+R_H)^{t-H}} + \frac{F}{(1+R_H)^{M-H}}\right\}\right]^{1/H} - 1 \ .$$

Here P_o, the present value with respect to the current interest rate R_o, is given by:

$$P_0 = \sum_{t=1}^{M} \frac{C}{(1+R_0)^t} + \frac{F}{(1+R_0)^M} \ .$$

The first summation is the reinvested coupon received on or before time H. The second summation plus the term involving F is the price at time H.

[7] For example, duration has proved to be a useful tool for immunization over a fixed investment horizon, immunization of pension liabilities, contingent immunization, immunization of futures positions and even immunization of a firm's net worth position. See footnote 1 for references in all these areas.

Figure B: Holding-Period Return for a Seven-Year Duration Bond

---

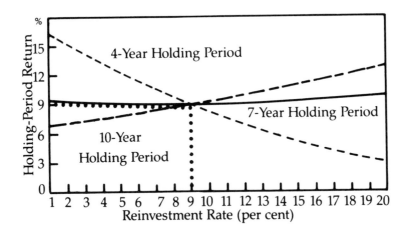

In analyzing bond returns over multiyear holding periods, the Babcock approximation formula is useful:[8]

$$\text{Holding-Period Return} \approx \text{Yield} + [1 - \text{Duration/Holding Period}]$$

$$\times \text{Change in Yield.} \qquad (2)$$

Equation (2) assumes that there is a single rate change at the beginning of the investment horizon and that all cash flows are reinvested at the new rate.

Table I illustrates the accuracy of the Babcock approximation. Over a seven-year holding period, the maximum difference between actual and approximated holding-period returns is only 19 basis points for interest rate changes of up to plus or minus 500 basis points. Over holding periods of four years (10 years), maximum errors of 50 basis points (10 basis points) result for interest rate

---

[8] See G.C. Babcock, "Duration as a Link Between Yield and Value," *Journal of Portfolio Management*, Summer 1984 and Fall 1984. A derivation of the formula can be found in the appendix to this article.

Table I: Approximation Error of the Babcock Formula

Reinvest-ment Rate	4-Year Holding Period			7-Year Holding Period			10-Year Holding Period		
	Actual Return	Approx. Return	Error	Actual Return	Approx. Return	Error	Actual Return	Approx. Return	Error
4%	13.23	12.74	0.495	9.18	9.00	0.186	7.60	7.49	0.104
6	11.42	11.24	0.175	9.06	9.00	0.067	8.13	8.09	0.037
8	9.76	9.74	0.019	9.01	9.00	0.007	8.70	8.70	0.004
9	9.00	9.00	0.000	9.00	9.00	0.000	9.00	9.00	0.000
10	8.27	8.25	0.019	9.01	9.00	0.007	9.30	9.30	0.004
12	6.91	6.75	0.165	9.06	9.00	0.065	9.93	9.90	0.038
14	5.70	5.25	0.449	9.18	9.00	0.180	10.60	10.50	0.104

changes of up to 500 basis points. The Babcock approximation is very accurate, at least for the assumed interest rate process.[9]

Equation (2) serves as a simple analytical model for the interest risk exposure of any bond portfolio over a multiyear investment horizon.[10] Immunization results when the bond's duration is set equal to the investment horizon. This is evident from Equation (2), where the factor that multiplies the yield change is zero for this level of duration.

Immunization might be regarded as a passive or a neutral strategy. Any departure from this "riskless strategy" entails some exposure to interest risk and should be regarded as an active portfolio decision. Equation (2) indicates that the magnitude of the risk exposure is approximately proportional to the absolute difference between the duration of the bond portfolio and the length of the holding period.

DURATION-TARGETING STRATEGIES

Many portfolio managers try to maintain their portfolios within a prescribed range of stock/bond mixes and durations. Rebalancing to maintain a target duration produces a portfolio with investment characteristics similar to those of an immunized portfolio. Maintaining a five-year target duration, for example, produces minimum return variability over a 10-year horizon. It is thus similar to a strategy of immunizing to a 10-year point. (The investment characteristics of the duration-targeting strategy and immunization are compared in the next section.)

In order to analyze bond returns from a duration-targeting strategy, we'll look at three cases—portfolios rebalanced periodically to maintain durations of one year, five years and 7.5 years. For simplicity, we assume that interest rates follow a random walk with a volatility of 150 basis points per year.

Each bar in Figure C represents the 80% confidence interval for the indicated holding period. With a starting bond yield of 9%, the average bond return

---

[9] For a different interest rate process, the error of the Babcock approximation may be substantially greater. For example, with annual rate changes, rather than a single change at the start of the investment period, we find a seven-year return volatility of more than 100 basis points, compared with zero basis points in the single-change model.

[10] The standard deviation of return is often used as a proxy for risk. The standard deviation for the holding-period return over H years can be estimated from Equation (3) in the text:

$$\sigma(HPR_H) = |1 - Duration/H| \, \sigma(R_H)$$

where $\sigma(R_H)$ is the estimated interest rate volatility over the next H years.

Figure C: Bond Returns with a Target Duration Maintained at One Year

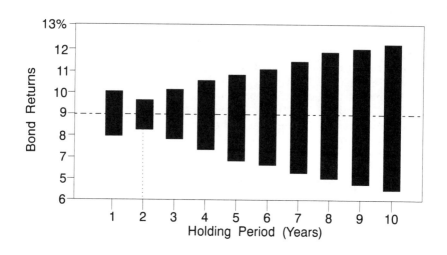

is also 9%, as indicated by the handlebars in Figure C (which, in this case, coincide with the 50th percentile bond return, or the median return).

Figure C, with duration maintained at one year, shows an ever-widening uncertainty about the bond's return. This uncertainty corresponds to the increasing interest rate uncertainty as the investment horizon lengthens.

In Figure D, duration is maintained at five years. We observe that return volatility is high in early years and decreases to a minimum volatility in about 10 years. Thereafter, bond return volatility increases. Figure E shows a duration target maintained at 7.5 years. In this case, volatility stars out very high and decreases steadily as the investment horizon lengthens to about 15 years, when return volatility widens again.

The results in Figures C, D and E are based entirely on a zero-coupon bond, or bullet. The duration of the bullet in Figure D, for example, was maintained at five years by periodic rebalancing to a five-year, zero-coupon bond. To ascertain whether these results are robust with respect to convexity, we examined an extreme barbell portfolio. The duration of this barbell portfolio was also maintained at five years through periodic rebalancing between at one-year, zero-coupon bond and a 30-year, zero-coupon bond.

Figure F presents the results for the bullet and barbell portfolios. The ranges of return for different holding periods and different portfolios are nearly the

Figure D: Bond Returns with a Target Duration Maintained at Five Years

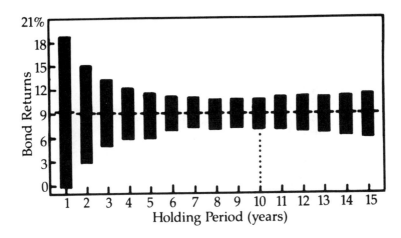

Figure E: Bond Returns with a Target Duration Maintained at 7.5 Years

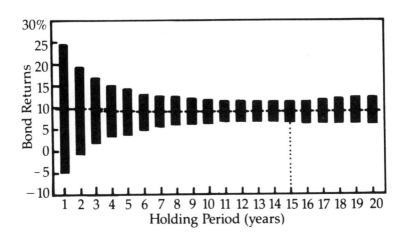

**Figure F: Barbell versus Bullet Portfolios with Target Durations
Maintained at Five Years**

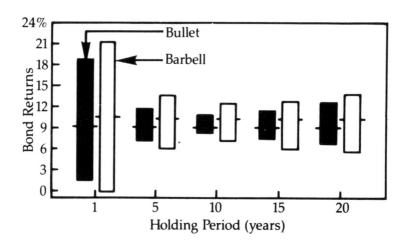

same. More importantly, the return volatilities of both barbell and bullet portfolios are minimized at about 10 years (when the duration is targeted at five years). The differences between the two portfolios can be attributed to "convexity effects," combined with a flat term structure.[11]

DURATION TARGETING VS. IMMUNIZATION

One of the most interesting aspects of duration-targeting strategies is the "focusing" of the return distribution. Our examples suggest a particularly simple rule for minimizing the return variability over any given investment horizon:[12]

$$\text{Target Duration} = 1/2 \times \text{Investment Horizon}. \tag{3}$$

---

[11] See J. Ingersoll, J. Skelton and R. Weil, "Duration Forty Years Later," *Journal of Financial and Quantitative Analysis*, November 1978, for a discussion of arbitrage opportunities that arise with a flat term structure.

[12] The appendix provides a full derivation of this rule for minimizing return volatility at the horizon.

Figure G: Bond Volatility versus Duration, 10-Year Investment Horizon

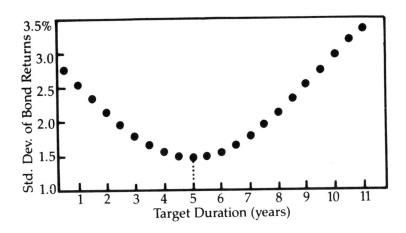

Figure G shows that the standard deviation of the return distribution is minimized over a 10-year investment horizon by maintaining a target duration of five years.

Below, we compare the return variability from duration targeting with the return variability from an immunization strategy. We note at the outset that immunization assumes a special interest in a particular investment horizon. A judgment as to whether one strategy is superior to another may depend on the investment horizon chosen.

For simplicity, we use an immunization strategy that consists of purchasing a single zero-coupon bond with a maturity equal to the investment horizon. This strategy leads to perfect immunization and is a rigorous benchmark indeed! The duration-targeting strategy consists of periodic rebalancing to maintain a target duration equal to one-half the investment horizon. Again, we assume a flat term structure at 9% and an interest rate volatility of 150 basis points per year.

Figure H illustrates the return distributions for the two strategies over holding periods ranging from one year to 10 years. By construction, the return variability for immunization is nil at the 10-year point. Duration targeting—while reaching its minimum variability point at about 10 years—never achieves zero variability. Duration targeting produces a "residual" return volatility, or standard deviation, of 1.4%.

Although this variability is significant and is clearly not immunization, for many portfolio managers it may be sufficiently close to the immunization result. Duration targeting might thus be regarded as a type of "partial immunization." Naturally, those investors who consider a return volatility of 1.4% excessive will not regard duration targeting as a viable alternative to immunization.

Immunization is clearly superior to duration targeting at the 10-year point. This is not the case, however, over the entire investment horizon. The return volatility over the first year of immunization, for example, is double that of duration targeting. In fact, immunization has a higher return volatility for all investment horizons shorter than eight years.

Many investment managers are concerned about performance at different points in time prior to their investment horizons. It is therefore reasonable to weigh the superior performance of the duration-targeting strategy in early years against the superior performance of immunization in later years. The advantage of duration targeting is a greatly reduced volatility over most of the investment period; the disadvantage is that only partial, rather than full, immunization is achieved over the entire period.

Figures I and J compare the two strategies over two different investment horizons. Figure I considers immunization over a five-year holding period; Figure J considers a holding period of 15 years. In Figure I, the target duration is maintained at 2.5 years; in Figure J, the target duration is maintained at 7.5 years.

Again, for the first year return volatility for the duration-targeting strategy is only half that of immunization. In Figure I, duration targeting has a lower volatility than immunization in years one through three, about the same volatility in year four and, of course, a higher volatility—about 1%—in year five. The 80% range in year five for duration targeting is 7.6% to 10.1%.

Figure J shows the results for the 15-year holding period. Again, the duration-targeting strategy demonstrates a significantly lower volatility in early years (one through 11), while immunization is clearly superior in later years (12 through 15). The volatility of the duration-targeting strategy at the 15-year point is nearly 2%, with an 80% confidence interval of 6.5% to 11%. This is a fairly wide range and clearly not immunization. But duration targeting does provide a significant reduction in risk starting in the first year and continuing for another 10 years.

Compared with immunization, a duration-targeting strategy has two advantages. First, it clearly has lower volatility in earlier years, with one-half the volatility in year one (because, by construction, the duration is one-half the duration of the immunization strategy). Second, duration targeting is more of a "perpetual strategy," while immunization is more an "end-game strategy."

Figure H: Immunization versus Target Duration Maintained at Five Years

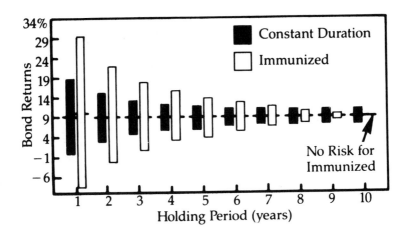

Figure I: Immunization versus Target Duration Maintained at 2.5 Years

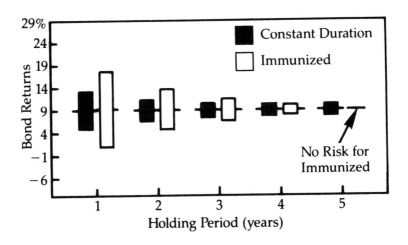

Figure J:
Immunization versus Target Duration Maintained at 7.5 Years

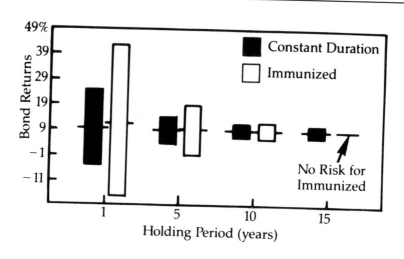

Immunization is clearly superior at the end of the investment horizon, because by construction its volatility is zero at this point. Duration targeting, by
contrast, has a return volatility ranging from 1% over a holding period of five
years to 2% over a holding period of 15 years (see Figures H through J). This
level of return volatility may be acceptable to many investment managers who
seek reasonable control over the variability of returns. Thus many portfolio
managers may regard duration targeting as a viable alternative to immunization.

DURATION TARGETING AND INDEXATION

As performance measurement has gained increasing attention, indexation has
become an important investment strategy. Below, we compare the investment
performance of indexation with the duration-targeting strategy. For simplicity,
we model the index portfolio as an eight-year coupon bond that sells initially at
par. The initial coupon rate and the discount rate are both 9% and, as the interest rate changes, the coupon rate gradually changes to bring the bond back to
par value.

Each year, the rate of return is calculated with respect to the start-of-year coupon rate. A new coupon is then calculated to bring the eight-year bond back to par value over four years, assuming that there are no further changes in interest rates.[13] Given an initial interest and coupon rate of 9%, we have an initial duration of six years. By the end of six years, the 80% range for the duration is from 5.6 years to 6.5 years. This 80% range of duration corresponds to a range for interest rates (and current coupon rates) of 2.4 to 12.7 years at the six-year point.

The duration-targeting strategy maintains a six-year duration by annually rebalancing the annuity part and the principal part of an eight-year coupon bond. The eight-year coupon bond serves as the basis for constructing both the index portfolio and the constant-duration portfolio. In the first year, the two portfolios have identical durations and coupon rates and, therefore, identical returns. At the end of the first year, the duration-targeting strategy requires rebalancing into an eight-year bond with a coupon level that maintains the duration at six years; the index requires rebalancing into an eight-year bond with a coupon that keeps the bond's price progressing toward par value.

We're interested in how well the duration-targeting strategy and the indexation strategy work for a pension plan. For simplicity, we focus on a pension plan with only retirees. Each year, new retirees are added to the plan so that the initial cash flow profile is preserved. When the discount rate is at 9%, the first year of the cash flow stream represents 15.5% of the total present value of the benefits to be paid to retirees over the next 20 years. The present value of the cash flows declines to less than 0.5% by the end of 20 years.[14]

Table II presents a variety of investment statistics for the duration-targeting strategy, the indexation strategy with a lagged movement to par and a pension liability (cash flow stream described above). The most surprising observation is that the bond returns are almost identical.

Over a six-year holding period, the average returns have a maximum difference across strategies of 17 basis points, and the standard deviations of return have a maximum difference of five basis points. This return difference is minor,

---

[13] The bond's coupon rate is adjusted at the end of each period as follows:

$$Coupon(t + 1) = Coupon(t) + 0.25[Coupon \text{ for New Par Bond}(t) - Coupon(t)].$$

In the absence of further changes in the interest rate, this adjustment process will bring the bond's coupon back to a current coupon level and the value back to par by the end of four years.

[14] See T.C. Langetieg, L.N. Bader, M.L. Leibowitz and A. Weinberger, "Measuring the Effective Duration of Pension Liabilities" (Salomon Brothers Inc, New York, November 1986) for a discussion of some of the more important aspects of pension liability duration.

Table II: Investment Statistics for Alternative Strategies

Statistic	Strategy	2-Year Holding Period		6-Year Holding Period	
		Average	Standard Deviation	Average	Standard Deviation
Bond	Duration Targeting	9.21%	5.20%	9.08%	1.98%
Returns	Index: Lagged Adjustment to Par	9.21	5.32	9.08	2.01
	Pension: Retirees	9.38	5.36	9.25	2.03
Duration	Duration Targeting	6.00 yrs.	0.00 yrs.	6.00 yrs.	0.00 yrs.
	Index: Lagged Adjustment to Par	6.03	0.22	6.04	0.50
	Pension: Retirees	6.09	0.93	6.12	1.12

considering that the difference in durations in some cases is as much as three years.[15]

To investigate this surprising result of nearly identical returns despite significant differences in durations across strategies, we examined the correlations between the returns of different strategies. Table III shows that the return correlations are almost perfect (that is, almost one). By contrast, the correlations of the durations of the different strategies are much lower. By construction, the correlation between the duration-targeting strategy and any other strategy is zero. The correlation between the duration of the index portfolio and the duration of the pension liability is 0.85 over the two-year horizon and 0.79 over the six-year horizon.

Table III: Correlations Between Returns

	6-Year Holding Period			
	Duration Targeting (D = 6)	Index (Avg. D = 6)	Pension Liability (Avg. D = 6)	Cumulative Rate Change
Duration Targeting (D = 6)	1.000	0.996	0.989	-0.822
Index (Avg. D = 6)		1.000	0.997	-0.819
Pension Liability (Avg. D = 6)			1.000	-0.818
Cumulative Rate Change				1.000

---

[15] The duration-targeting strategy is maintained at a constant six years. The duration of the indexation strategy ranges from 4.90 to 7.27 years at the six-year point, while the duration of the pension liability ranges from 3.96 to 9.78 years.

We can draw two conclusions from our investigations. First, it appears that as long as the average durations and yields of different strategies are the same, the return distributions will be nearly the same. This result is largely independent of the volatility of duration about its average value. In other words, as long as the *average* duration is the same across strategies, the return distribution will be the same, whether or not the duration is maintained at a constant value or is allowed to fluctuate about its average value. Second, an index portfolio may be viewed as a substitute for a duration-targeted portfolio, and both may be useful instruments in the management of pension liability risk.

DURATION TARGETING AND ACTIVE MANAGEMENT

Duration targeting can be integrated into active asset management in several ways. Because duration targeting does not preclude the selection of sector, quality and many other characteristics that affect bond returns, the manager can use many combinations of sector and quality to produce a desired duration target.

The manager can also actively implement interest rate forecasts while managing duration within a given target range (say, plus or minus two years). On average, the duration of the bond portfolio should equal the target duration. Any forecasting ability will show up as an enhanced return relative to the return on the targeted-duration portfolio.

Selection of investment horizon, a target duration and a performance benchmark should be regarded as critical elements in developing a successful investment management policy. The investment horizon should reflect the goals of the fund and the investment manager. In the case of multiple objectives, such as concern for both a liability and a performance index, a duration-targeting strategy may provide a good compromise solution. That is, the fund manager does not try to maximize either objective, but rather seeks a duration target that provides satisfactory performance relative to both objectives. Given such multiple goals, a duration-targeted portfolio may represent a better performance benchmark than a standard bond index.

Finally, and perhaps most importantly, duration targeting forces the investment manager to identify the most relevant investment horizon with respect to fund goals. A well defined performance benchmark can then be established for any investment strategy.

Appendix

Assume a flat term structure to random, infinitesimal shocks. The total return on a bond portfolio with duration D(S) over a holding period (0,H) is assumed to be closely approximated by:

$$\text{Bond Return Over } (0,H) = \exp\left[\int_0^H R(S)dS - \int_0^H D(S)dR(S)\right] - 1,$$

(A1)

where R(S) is the interest rate, dR(S) is the change in interest rate and D(S) is the duration of the bond portfolio, all at time S. Equation (A1) holds exactly for zero-coupon bonds but only approximately for coupon bonds and portfolios of zero-coupon bonds.

If interest rates follow a random walk without drift or reversion, the interest rate process is given by:

$$dR(S) = \sigma(S)dZ(S),$$

(A2)

where dZ(S) represents a Brownian motion with increments that are identically and independently distributed N(0,dS) over time S, and σ(S) is the instantaneous interest rate volatility at time S.

Integrating Equation (A2), it follows that:

$$R(S) = R(0) + \int_0^S \sigma(U)dZ(U).$$

(A3)

Substituting Equations (A2) and (A3) into Equation (A1) gives the following:

Bond Return Over (0,H)

$$= \exp\left[\int_0^H \left\{R(0) + \int_0^S \sigma(U)dZ(U)\right\}dS - \int_0^H D(S)\sigma(S)dZ(S)\right] - 1. \qquad (A4)$$

Note that:

$$\int_0^H \left[\int_0^S \sigma(U)dZ(U)\right]dS = \int_0^H (H-S)\sigma(S)dZ(S).$$

Using this fact in Equation (A4) and rearranging terms results in the following:

Bond Return Over (0,H) =

$$\exp\left[R(0)H + \int_0^H [(H-S)-D(S)]\sigma(S)dZ(S)\right] - 1. \qquad (A5)$$

Minimization of bond return volatility is equivalent to minimizing the variance of the second term in the exponent of Equation (A5). This variance is given by:

$$V\left[\int_0^H [(H-S)-D(S)]\sigma(S)dZ(s)\right] = \int_0^H [(H-S)-D(S)]^2\sigma(S)^2dS.$$

The first-order condition for minimization of volatility over the horizon H is thus:

$$\frac{\partial}{\partial D}\left\{\int_0^H [(H-S)-D]^2\sigma(S)^2dS\right\} = 0. \qquad (A6)$$

When duration and interest rate volatility are independent of S (that is, $D(S) \equiv D$ for all S and $\sigma(S) \equiv \sigma$ for all S), Equation (A6) reduces to the following condition:

$$D = \frac{H}{2}.$$

In words, the risk-minimizing duration for a given holding period of H years is equal to one-half the length of the holding period.[16]

DERIVATION OF THE BABCOCK FORMULA[17]

Suppose an N-year, annual-pay bond with coupon C is priced at yield R. The relation between the price P and the discount rate R is given by the following:

$$P = PV(R) = \sum_{k=1}^{N} C/(1+R)^k + 100/(1+R)^N.$$

In addition, we assume that the yield curve is flat, that there is an instantaneous shift to a new level R^*, and that rates then remain at this new level. All coupons are assumed to be reinvested at rate R^* until some horizon H prior to the maturity of the bond. Under the above conditions, the future value of the bond, including coupon and reinvestment income, will be $(1 + R^*)^H PV(R^*)$. The annualized holding-period return HPR over H years can then be determined from the equation:

$$(1 + HPR)^H PV(R) = (1 + R^*)^H PV(R^*). \tag{A7}$$

Our goal is to find an expression for the holding-period return in terms of R^*. The Taylor series for HPR is as follows:

$$HPR(R^*) = HPR(R) + \frac{dHPR}{dR^*}\bigg|_{R^*=R} (R^* - R) + \cdots \tag{A8}$$

If the reinvestment rate is the same as the yield (that is, $R^* = R$), the yield and holding-period return are identical; that is, $HPR(R) = R$. We can find $dHPR/dR^*$ by implicitly differentiating Equation (A7):

$$H(1+HPR)^{H-1}\frac{dHPR}{dR^*}PV(R) = H(1+R^*)^{H-1}PV(R^*) + (1+R^*)^H\frac{dPV}{dR^*}.$$

Evaluating this equation at $R^* = R$ and solving for $dHPR/dR^*$ results in the following equation:

---

[16] It should be noted that the volatility-minimizing holding period for a given duration can be shown to be $\sqrt{3D}$, which is somewhat shorter than 2D.

[17] See Babcock, "Duration as a Link," op. cit. for an intuitive derivation of the Babcock formula. See Bierwag, Duration Analysis, op. cit., for an alternative mathematical derivation.

$$\left.\frac{dHPR}{dR^*}\right|_{R^*=R} = 1 + \frac{(1+R)}{P}\frac{1}{H}\left.\frac{dPV}{dR^*}\right|_{R^*=R}.$$

But the Macaulay duration D is:

$$D = -\frac{(1+R)}{P}\left.\frac{dPV}{dR^*}\right|_{R^*=R}.$$

Thus:

$$\left.\frac{dHPR}{dR^*}\right|_{R^*=R} = 1 - D/H.$$

Equation (A8) then becomes:

$$HPR(R^*) \approx R + (1 - D/H)(R^* - R).$$

This is the Babcock formula. In words, it can be expressed as follows:

$$\text{Holding–Period Return} \approx \text{Yield} + \left[1 - \frac{\text{Duration}}{\text{Holding Period}}\right] \times \text{Change in Yield.}$$

Chapter III D-14

A Shortfall Approach to Duration Management

INTRODUCTION

Over the past decade, fixed-income portfolio managers have almost universally embraced "duration" as the preeminent predictor of portfolio performance. The popularity of the duration measure stems from its ability to provide an estimate of the price response of fixed-income investments to sudden changes in interest rates. Duration provides more insight into prospective portfolio performance than any other single number, and as a result, selecting a target duration is one of the portfolio manager's most important decisions.

In many investment situations, special committees representing the sponsoring organization establish the maximum risk exposure that is consistent with their investment objectives. For the individuals who are involved in this process, it may be more important to have an approximate risk yardstick whose implications are well understood than to have a more refined theoretical measure that lacks intuitive appeal. Thus, in this paper, we offer some intuitive solutions to portfolio risk management by providing a simple analytical model that offers a means of both quantifying downside risk and determining the maximum allowable duration within the established risk tolerance.

We will measure risk—not just by return volatility or duration, but also by the probability of shortfall over a predetermined horizon. The "shortfall probability" is a simple measure of downside risk that qualifies the likelihood that a given portfolio strategy will result in a performance "shortfall" relative to a spe-

Martin L. Leibowitz, Stanley Kogelman and Thomas E. Klaffky, "A Shortfall Approach to Duration Management," Salomon Brothers Inc, April 1990.

cific return threshold. By transforming this risk measure into a "shortfall constraint," the manager can determine which portfolios can satisfy the minimum return requirements with a given probability.[1]

The shortfall approach can be applied to general investment portfolios that consist of a combination of asset classes, for example, equities, bonds, international securities, and real estate. Moreover, this approach can be generalized to address risks associated with returns measured relative to a specified market benchmark or index. However, to provide a concrete example, we will focus the following discussion on setting the duration of a single-currency fixed-income portfolio.

To simplify the exposition, we first consider the case of a flat yield curve and one-year investment horizon. Later, we relax both of these assumptions. We show how the methodology can be applied to both a multiyear investment horizon and the case of a rising yield curve.

A SIMPLE MODEL FOR BOND RETURNS

Fixed-income portfolio managers typically are faced with a dilemma. From a long-term point of view, there may be many reasons to extend duration. In a liability context, volatility of surplus generally can be minimized by matching the duration of the assets to that of the liabilities. In addition, in a total return context, if the yield curve is fairly steep and positively sloped, the manager may hope to gain higher expected returns by extending maturity/duration. However, regardless of the long-term objective, portfolio performance still must be evaluated at regular intervals over the short term. Thus, we must always consider the short-term consequences of long-term duration targets. Because duration measures the sensitivity of price to changes in interest rates, long-duration instruments will react most violently to rate fluctuation. Sponsors and managers will be elated if the market rallies and their portfolio outperforms the market. However, they will be dismayed if their portfolio underperforms the market. This situation is complicated further by the desire to avoid negative returns, regardless of the market performance. Sponsors are unlikely to be pleased if the portfolio outperforms the market but still suffers a negative return. In a sense, when the market slumps, there is a natural tendency to compare the portfolio results—retroactively—to the risk-free rate.

To simplify our study of the impact of rate volatility, we make several assumptions. First, we begin with the assumption that the yield curve is flat, so that bonds of all durations offer precisely the same 8% yield. This yield curve is

---

[1] The concept of a shortfall constraint is discussed in greater detail in *Portfolio Optimization Under Shortfall Constraints*, Martin L. Leibowitz, Salomon Brothers Inc, August 1987.

Figure 1: The Flat Yield Curve

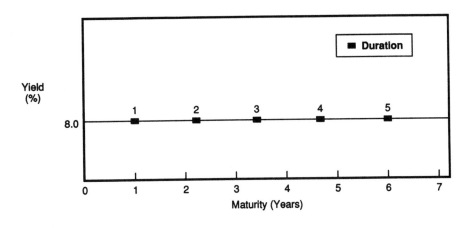

illustrated in Figure 1, where we also indicate the duration associated with various maturities.[2] Our second simplifying assumption is that the expected return over any horizon is equal to the yield. Finally, we avoid reinvestment effects over a one-year horizon by assuming that coupon payments are made annually.

As we move to the right along the yield curve, the expected return over a one-year horizon remains 8%, but the volatility inherent in that return increases. Naturally, over a one-year holding period, a one-year Treasury bill will provide an 8% return. That is, the return volatility is zero, because the security is being held to maturity and there is no price or reinvestment risk. As we move further to the right along the yield curve, the duration increases and the expected return is accompanied by greater volatility as a result of increased price variability over the one-year holding period. The impact of yield change on price is illustrated in Figure 2 for a four-year duration bond.

To obtain a more complete picture of return volatility, we must introduce a model of how interest rates change over a one-year horizon. To this end, we assume that interest rate *changes* follow a normal distribution with a zero mean

---

[2] In this paper, the "duration" generally should be assumed to be the Macaulay Duration. When actually computing the sensitivity of price to instantaneous changes in yields, we must use the modified duration. See, for example, *Understanding Duration and Volatility*, Salomon Brothers Inc, September 1985.

Figure 2: The Impact of Yield Changes (One-Year Horizon)

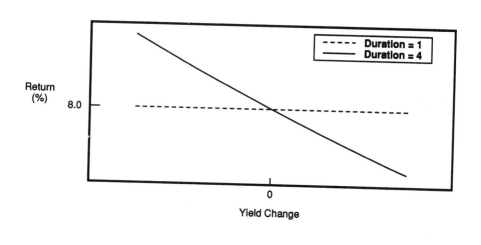

and a standard deviation of 150 basis points at all points along the yield curve. This distribution of interest rate changes is illustrated in Figure 3 and is generally consistent with the distribution of 12-month rate changes observed over the past ten years.

As a result of the assumption of a normal distribution, 68% of the rate changes is in the range of plus or minus 150 basis points (that is, within one standard deviation of the mean rate change of 0%). Thus, our normality assumption implies that there is an 84% probability that yields will remain above 6.5% (that is, the expected yield of 8% less 150 basis points).

The distribution of interest rate changes can be linked to the distribution of returns by means of a convenient approximate formula (see Appendix). For example, if the flat yield curve undergoes a 150-basis-point parallel shift over a one-year horizon, a four-year duration bond will experience return. In other words, if the yield volatility is 150 basis points, the return volatility will be about 450 basis points. The distribution of interest rate changes depicted in Figure 3 therefore leads to the distribution of returns in Figure 4.[3]

---

[3] For ease of exposition, we show a normal return distribution. In fact, a normal distribution of yield changes leads to a somewhat skewed return distribution, and this skewness increases with convexity. Thus, for example, in the case of an extreme barbell portfolio, there will be a significant departure from normality.

Figure 3: The Distribution of Interest Rate Changes (One-Year Horizon)

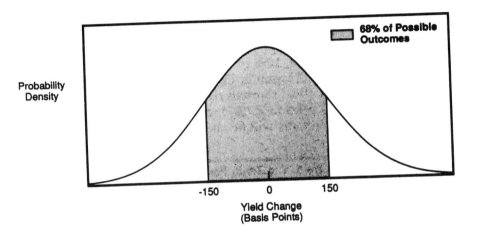

Figure 4: The Return Distribution for a Four-Year Duration Bond (One-Year Horizon)

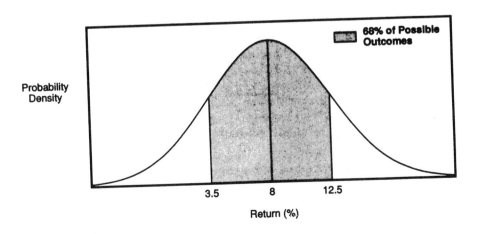

Figure 5: The Tenth Percentile Return (Four-Year Duration Bond)

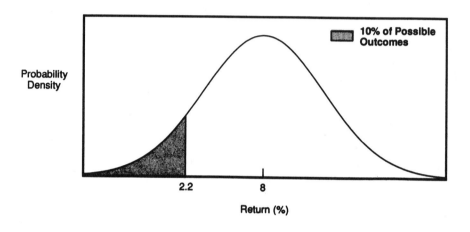

Return (%)

THE SHORTFALL RISK CONSTRAINT

Now, we reexamine our return distribution with an eye toward the likelihood of "unacceptable" returns. For example, for the distribution in Figure 4, 10% of the returns will be below 2.2%, as illustrated by the shaded region in Figure 5. We describe this situation by saying that there is a 10% "shortfall risk" that the return on the four-year duration bond will fall below a 2.2% threshold. Of course, there is also a 90% probability that the returns will be above 2.2%.

Shortfall risk addresses the "bad side" of risk. In this sense, it provides a more intuitive yardstick and is easier to communicate than the more traditional statistical risk measure, return volatility.[4] In addition, as we shall see, the shortfall risk affords a simple interpretation when viewed in terms of a return/risk diagram.

---

[4] The shortfall probability is an incomplete measure of risk, because it fails to provide any indication of how bad the shortfall will be in the event that one should occur. For a more fully developed theory of shortfall analysis that incorporates these "higher" considerations, see "Asset Pricing in a Generalized Mean-Lower Partial Moment Framework; Theory and Evidence," W.V. Harlow and R. Rao, in *Journal of Financial and Quantitative Analysis*, September 1989; and "Capital Market Equilibrium in a Mean, Lower Partial Moment Framework," V. Bawa and E.B. Lindenberg, in *Journal of Financial Economics*, November 1977.

We introduce the shortfall approach using an example. Suppose that the fund sponsor has specified the following "shortfall constraint":

It is required that there be at most a 10% probability that returns over a one-year horizon fall below a 3% threshold.[5]

Or, equivalently:

It is required that there be at least a 90% probability that returns over a one-year horizon lie above a 3% threshold.

We already have observed that there is a 10% probability that returns on our four-year duration bond will fall below 2.2% over a one-year horizon. Thus, this bond clearly fails to meet the shortfall constraint, because it will bear a greater than 10% probability that its return will fall below 3%. To fulfill the shortfall constraint, we must create a portfolio with a lower shortfall probability by either shortening duration or increasing expected return.

Because duration lengthens as we move to the right along the yield curve, it follows that the "riskiness" of returns also increases.[6] In Figure 6, we illustrate the relationship between expected return and risk by using duration as the risk measure. As indicated earlier, we assume that the expected return and yield are equal.

The impact of duration on shortfall risk is illustrated in Figure 7. In this case, we maintain an 8% expected return and superimpose the return distributions that correspond to durations of 3.6 and 4.0 years. The shorter duration leads to the diminished "spread" of the return distribution. As a result, a decreasing proportion of returns falls below the 3% threshold. In particular, a reduction in the duration from 4.0 to 3.6 years leads to a return distribution in which precisely 10% of the returns falls below the 3% threshold. Any further duration reduction would lead to an even smaller likelihood of returns below 3%. Thus, the maximum permissible duration for the given shortfall constraint is 3.6 years. All longer-duration portfolios will have a greater than 10% probability of returns falling below 3%.

THE SHORTFALL LINE

The impact of changes in expected return on shortfall risk is illustrated in Figure 8. We have superimposed the return distributions that correspond to expected returns of 8.0% and 8.8%, while maintaining a four-year duration. Because dura-

---

[5] There is no obvious "correct" choice of the appropriate minimum return threshold. Rather, it is likely to be arrived at after consideration of a variety of factors, such as the sponsor's objectives and risk tolerance.

[6] In general, return volatility depends on both duration and the level of interest rate volatility. Because we have assumed that interest rate volatility is the same at all points on the yield curve, only duration changes as we move along the yield curve.

Figure 6: Expected Return versus Risk (Duration) **in the Case of a Flat Yield Curve and One-Year Horizon**

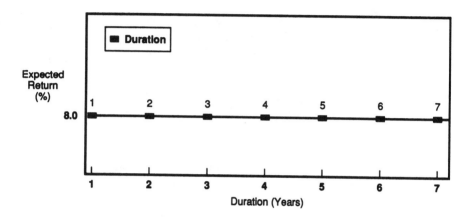

Figure 7: Probability of Returns Below 3%: Expected Return = 8%; Duration = 3.6 and 4.0 Years

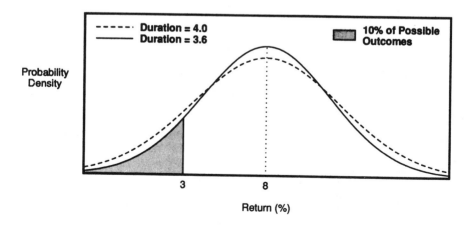

Figure 8: Probability of Returns Below 3%: Duration = 4.0 Years; Expected Return = 8.0% and 8.8%

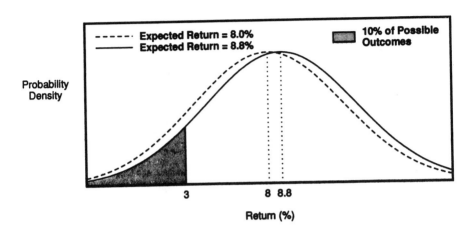

tion (and hence volatility) is held constant, the shape of the distribution is preserved, while the entire distribution shifts to the right as the expected return increases. Thus, higher expected returns decrease the proportion of returns that fall below the 3% threshold. In particular, when the expected return reaches the 8.8% level, only 10% of the returns falls below the 3% threshold, and the shortfall constraint is fulfilled.

Now we have two expected return/duration combinations that meet the shortfall constraint over a one-year horizon. These two combinations are illustrated as points in Figure 9. In addition, a one-year duration bond with an expected return of 3% would experience no volatility over a one-year holding period. This bond will achieve the 3% minimum return threshold and also is shown as a third point in Figure 9.

The fact that the three points just mentioned appear to fall on a straight line is not coincidental. Under fairly general conditions on the return distribution, a straight line will depict the relationship between a portfolio's duration and the expected return required to satisfy a shortfall constraint (see Appendix). This relationship is valid for all yield curves and is illustrated by the "shortfall line" in Figure 10.

The shortfall line intercepts the expected return axis at the minimum return threshold (which is 3% in our example). Its slope depends solely on the shortfall probability. All portfolios with return/duration combinations on or above the

Figure 9: Three Bonds That Meet the 10% Shortfall Constraint with a 3% Minimum Return Threshold

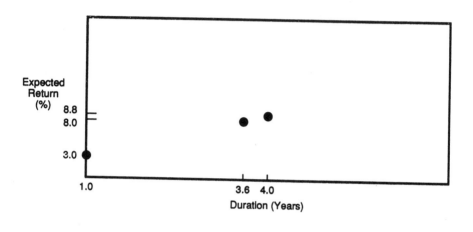

Figure 10: The 10% Shortfall Line with a 3% Minimum Return Threshold (One-Year Horizon)

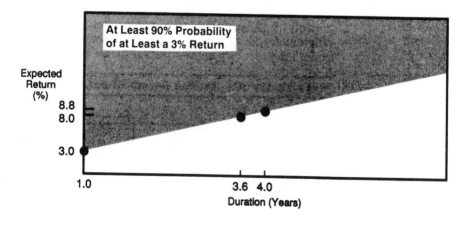

Figure 11: The 10% Shortfall Line with Corresponding Return Distributions

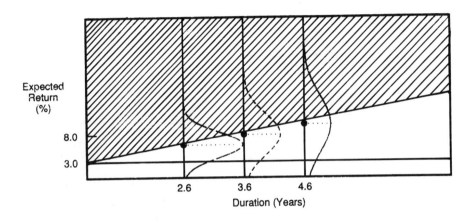

shortfall line will have at least a 90% probability of achieving a return greater than 3%; that is, they satisfy the shortfall constraint. All points below the line represent return/duration combinations that lead to more than a 10% chance of failing to achieve a 3% return over a one-year horizon; that is, they fail to satisfy the shortfall constraint. In Figure 11, we superimpose return distributions at several points along the shortfall line. As we already have seen, as duration lengthens, so does the spread of the distribution, and higher expected returns are required as an offset. Thus, the shortfall line divides the return/risk diagram into two regions: the upper region, where the shortfall constraint is satisfied; and the lower region, where it is not.

DURATION TARGETING WITH A SHORTFALL CONSTRAINT

The shortfall line now can be used to locate portfolios that can be expected to meet or exceed the shortfall constraint. To illustrate how this is done, we make the simplifying assumption that the yield curve represents all investment opportunities. In this case, Figure 6 can be interpreted as an "efficient frontier," with risk being measured by duration. In Figure 12, we superimpose the 10% shortfall line on this efficient frontier. Because all portfolios that fall on or above the

Figure 12: The 10% Shortfall Constraint and the Efficient Frontier

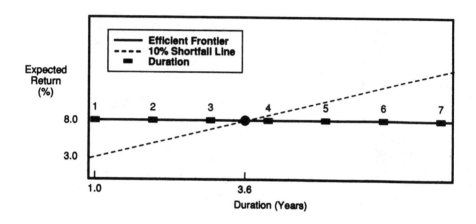

Duration (Years)

shortfall line fulfill the minimum return requirements, the part of the efficient frontier that falls above this line contains all admissible portfolios. Thus, the longest admissible duration portfolio will be found at the point where the shortfall line "cuts" the efficient frontier. This more general methodology, of course, leads to the same 3.6-year maximum duration as we found earlier.

VARIATIONS IN THE SHORTFALL SPECIFICATION

In this section, we consider the impact of changes in the shortfall probability and in the minimum return threshold on the longest admissible duration. For example, suppose our portfolio manager were willing to tolerate an increase from 10% to 15% in the probability of returns falling below the 3% threshold. This weaker 15% shortfall constraint is represented by a shortfall line that has a lower slope than for the 10% constraint. As a result, the point of intersection between the efficient frontier and the shortfall line moves to the right, and the maximum portfolio duration extends to about 4.2 years. By contrast, a 5% shortfall probability implies a steeper shortfall line that reduces the maximum allowable duration to 3.0 years. These results are illustrated in Figure 13.

Figure 13: The Shortfall Constraint with Varying Shortfall Probabilities

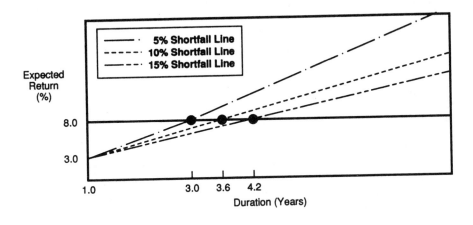

Figure 14: The Shortfall Constraint with Varying Threshold Returns

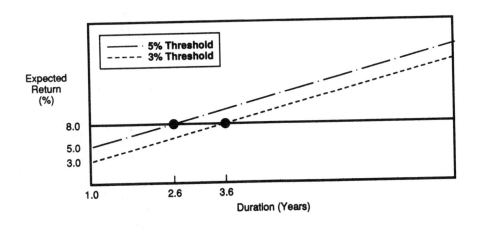

The implication of an increase in the minimum return threshold from 3% to 5% is illustrated in Figure 14, where the shortfall probability remains at our original 10% level. Because the shortfall probability does not change, the slope of the shortfall line is the same as for a 10% probability of the return falling below a 3% threshold. The only difference in the two shortfall lines is that the intercept with the return axis has been raised to 5%. This "lifting" of the shortfall line implies that less volatility (that is, less duration) can be tolerated. Thus, the maximum allowable duration now is reduced to about 2.6 years.

SHORTFALL CONSTRAINTS WITH VARYING INTEREST RATE VOLATILITY

To this point, we have assumed that the interest rate volatility is 150 basis points per year. Now we consider the impact of changes in the rate volatility assumption on our duration target. As rate volatility increases, so does the return volatility and, hence, this risk of shortfall. Thus, we should expect that in a high volatility environment, we will have to shorten duration to meet the shortfall constraint.

In our shortfall model, as illustrated in Figure 15, the slope of the shortfall line increases with greater rate volatility (see Appendix). As the slope increases, the point at which the shortfall line cuts the efficient frontier moves to the left, thereby reducing the maximum admissible duration. For example, if the rate volatility rises to 200 basis points per year, the new shortfall line intersects the efficient frontier at a duration of only 3.0 years, compared with 3.6 years for a rate volatility of 150 basis points per year. Similarly, if the rate volatility drops to 100 basis points per year, the maximum allowable duration increases to 4.9 years.

THE MULTIYEAR INVESTMENT HORIZON: FLAT YIELD CURVE

To this point, we have been considering a one-year investment horizon. To illustrate how the methodology of this paper can be extended to longer horizons, we now turn our attention to an analysis of a two-year investment horizon. In this case, the 10% shortfall constraint allows for considerably longer duration portfolios.

Over multiyear horizons, the relationship between risk, duration and interest rate volatility becomes more complicated (see Appendix for a more detailed discussion). Consequently, it is convenient to depart from the use of duration as our risk measure and return to the more traditional risk measure, the standard deviation of returns. In Figure 16, we illustrate the assumed relationship be-

Figure 15: The Impact of Rate Volatility on the Duration Target

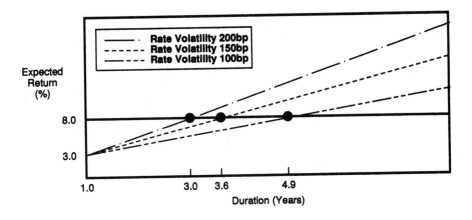

Figure 16: The One- and Two-Year "Efficient Frontier": Flat Yield Curve

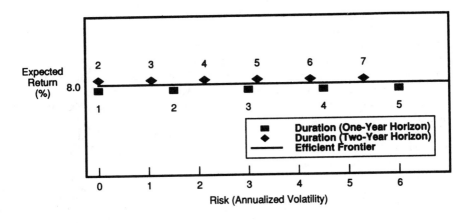

Figure 17: The Multiyear Shortfall Constraint: Flat Yield Curve

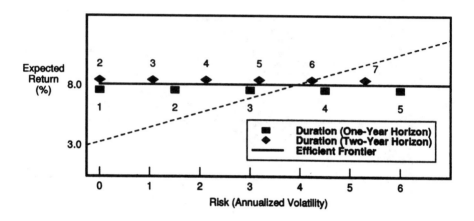

tween expected return and risk. On the upper side of the "efficient frontier," we indicate the durations that correspond to various risk levels over a two-year horizon. On the lower side of the "efficient frontier," we do the same for a one-year horizon.

Observe that, for a two-year horizon, at any duration there is a decrease in the volatility of the *annualized* expected return. For example, observe that the annualized return of a four-year duration bond is less volatile over a two-year horizon than over a one-year horizon. This volatility decreases as a result of two effects. First, price sensitivity declines as the horizon approaches the duration. Second, we implicitly assume that interest rates follow a random walk. Consequently, interest rate volatility increases fairly slowly as the holding period lengthens and the impact of this volatility on annualized returns actually decreases.

The 10% shortfall line with a 3% minimum return threshold now can be superimposed on the efficient frontier,[7] as illustrated in Figure 17. A single shortfall line can be used for both the one- and two-year horizons, because we

---

[7] The equation of the shortfall line must be recast in terms of the standard deviation of returns, which is our new risk measure. The result, which is derived in the Appendix, is as follows:
Required Expected Return = Risk Factor × Return Volatility + Threshold Return.

have used the *annualized* return and *annualized* return volatility as our expected return and risk measures. The admissible portfolios now have a maximum duration of about 5.7 years for a two-year horizon, compared with only 3.6 years over a one-year horizon.

The maximum duration that meets the two-year shortfall constraint will, as in the case of a one-year horizon, be sensitive to both the specified shortfall probability and minimum return threshold. Figure 18 exhibits the maximum duration under both a 10% and 20% shortfall constraint for a range of threshold returns.

Under similar shortfall constraints, a two-year horizon always leads to a considerably longer permissible duration than a one-year horizon. In addition, the sensitivity of the permissible duration to changes in the return threshold varies with both the shortfall probability and the investment horizon. For example, with a 10% shortfall probability and a one-year horizon, the duration decreases by about one-half year for each 100-basis-point increase in return threshold. By contrast, at a 20% shortfall probability (and a one-year horizon), when the return threshold increases by 100 basis points, the maximum permissible duration decreases by about three fourths of a year.

In addition, observe that as the horizon increases, so does the duration change. For example, at a 20% shortfall probability, a 100-basis-point increase in the threshold return leads to a decrease in duration of about 1.1 years over a two-year horizon and 1.4 years over a three-year horizon (not shown in Figure 18).

Figure 18: Maximum Permissible Duration for Varying Constraints
(Flat Yield Curve at 8%)

Threshold Return	10% Shortfall Probability Horizon		20% Shortfall Probability Horizon	
	1 Year	2 Years	1 Year	2 Years
0	5.2 Yrs.	7.9 Yrs.	7.3 Yrs.	11.0 Yrs.
1	4.6	7.1	6.5	9.8
2	4.1	6.4	5.7	8.7
3	3.6	5.7	*5.0*	7.6
4	3.1	4.9	4.2	6.5
5	2.6	4.2	3.4	5.4
6	2.0	*3.5*	2.6	4.2
7	1.5	2.7	1.8	3.1
8	1.0	2.0	1.0	2.0

As indicated earlier in this paper, portfolio managers often labor under different constraints for different investment horizons. For example, suppose that a portfolio manager is fairly risk tolerant over a one-year horizon and can accept a 20% probability of a one-year return less than 3%. This constraint implies a maximum duration of 5.0 years. However, suppose that over a two-year horizon, this same manager can tolerate only a 10% probability of an annualized return below 6%. This second constraint implies a maximum duration of 3.5 years—about 1 1/2 years shorter than the one-year maximum allowable duration. If we make the static assumption that a single portfolio is bought and held for the entire two-year period, the maximum acceptable duration that will enable *both* constraints to be fulfilled is 3.5 years.[8] This example illustrates how our analysis can be applied to determine the maximum duration that will fulfill a combination of multiyear constraints. Keep in mind, however, that the analysis is sensitive to the actual shape of the one- and two-year efficient frontiers.

THE RISING YIELD CURVE CASE

Although we have assumed a flat yield curve in the preceding development, the methodology of this paper can be applied to any yield curve. To illustrate how this is done, assume that the yield curve is positively sloped with a one-year bond yielding 8.0%.

As we move to the right along the yield curve, we again make the assumption that the expected return is equal to the yield. In Figure 19, we illustrate the "efficient frontier" for a one-year investment horizon. The risk measure is the standard deviation of returns, and the duration at various risk levels is indicated in the figure.

Now, in Figure 20, we superimpose the 10% shortfall line with a 3% return threshold on the "efficient frontier" in Figure 19. Because all portfolios that fall on or above the shortfall line fulfill the minimum return requirements, the part of the efficient frontier that falls above this line contains all admissible portfolios. Observe that the longest admissible duration is about 4.4 years, more than three fourths of a year longer than the 3.6-year duration limit in our example of a flat yield curve.

---

[8] For an in-depth discussion of the implication of targeted duration strategies where the portfolio is periodically rebalanced to maintain a constant duration, see *Duration Targeting: The Management of Multiperiod Returns*, Terence C. Langetieg, Martin L. Leibowitz and Stanley Kogelman, Salomon Brothers Inc, December 1989. See also *Liability Management—A Developing Country Perspective*, Janet L. Showers, Mark Koenigsberg and John McClure, presented at The Salomon Brothers Asset and Liability Workshop for Monetary Authorities, May 1989.

Figure 19: Expected Return versus Risk: Rising Yield Curve and One-Year Horizon

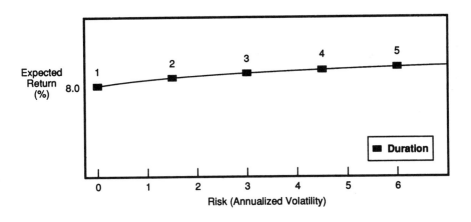

Figure 20: The Shortfall Constraint: Rising Yield Cruve

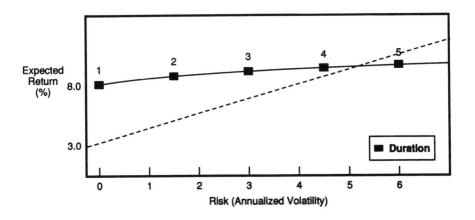

Figure 21: The Multiyear Shortfall Constraint: Rising Yield Curve

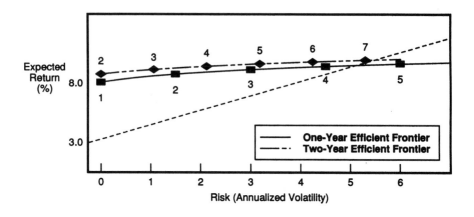

At this point, the extension of the shortfall methodology to arbitrary yield curve is straightforward. It simply requires superimposing the shortfall constraint on the appropriate efficient frontier and then locating the point of intersection with the shortfall line. The same is true for a two-year "efficient frontier" (see Figure 21). Observe that the longest admissible duration is about 7.2 years over a two-year holding period, almost three years longer than the duration limit for a one-year holding period.

SUMMARY AND CONCLUSION

In this paper, we first showed how a portfolio manager's need to achieve a certain minimum return even in the case of generally poor market performance could be expressed as a shortfall constraint. Then, we demonstrated how this shortfall constraint could be used to refine the portfolio duration targeting process over one-year and multiyear horizons. This process allowed for the longest duration consistent with the portfolio risk tolerance.

We also noted that, for a given shortfall constraint, the longest admissible duration is sensitive to the estimated volatility of interest rates. Thus, in a market in which the volatility estimate changes over time, one cannot focus solely on setting a fixed duration limit. In such a context, the shortfall approach provides a natural process for adjusting the duration limit required to meet a specified minimum return threshold.

The actual application of the methodology of this paper is straightforward once shortfall limits consisting of a minimum return threshold and a shortfall tolerance are set. Often, however, the portfolio manager does not explicitly think in these terms and may not have a well-defined return threshold or shortfall tolerance in mind. In such a case, our model can be used as a tool for testing the impact of various shortfall limits on the maximal permissible duration. In addition, given a duration target, we can back into the implied shortfall probability and gain new insight into the risk inherent in the portfolio's current duration level. Thus, the methodology of this paper can be helpful in finding a practical resolution to the conflicting objectives that often are encountered in the practice of portfolio management.

Appendix

THE BABCOCK FORMULA FOR ESTIMATING ANNUALIZED COMPOUND RETURN

If yields undergo an instantaneous parallel shift and remain at the new level until the horizon, the impact of the yield change on returns can be approximated by the following formula[9]:

Return Change $\approx$ (1 - Duration/Horizon) $\times$ Yield Change.

In this formula, the duration is the Macaulay Duration, and the return change is the difference between the annualized compound return and the yield to maturity (assuming that the bond under consideration pays annually). The real power of this formula becomes apparent when observing that it holds for horizons that may be *either* shorter *or* longer than the duration.

To illustrate the Babcock formula, assume that a four-year duration, annual-pay bond yields 8%. If yields undergo a 150-basis-point shift, the formula predicts that the resulting return change over a one-year horizon will be approximately 4.5%.[10]

THE SHORTFALL LINE

Suppose we wish to locate all portfolios whose return/risk characteristics are such that there is a probability k that the annualized compound return $\tilde{R}$ will

---

[9] The return approximation formula was developed by Babcock and is discussed at length in "Duration Analysis: Managing Interest Rate Risk," Gerald O. Bierwag, 1987, Chapter 5. A simplified derivation of this formula is provided in *Duration Targeting: The Management of Multiperiod Returns*, Terence C. Langetieg, Martin L. Leibowitz and Stanley Kogelman, Salomon Brothers Inc, December 1989.

[10] If yields move down by 150 basis points, the actual deviation from the yield to maturity is +4.63. If yields move up by 150 basis points, the actual return deviation is -4.37. The difference in the effects of upward and downward shifts reflects convexity effects that the first order Babcock formula does not take into account. The average absolute deviation is 4.5%, which is in agreement with our estimate.

exceed some minimum threshold R_{min}. This requirement can be expressed as follows:

$$P[\tilde{R} \geq R_{min}] = k.$$

This is equivalent to

$$P[(\tilde{R} - \bar{R})/\sigma \geq (R_{min} - \bar{R})/\sigma] = k,$$

where $\bar{R}$ is the mean return and σ is the standard deviation of returns. If the quantity to the left of the inequality is a standard normal variate, we can determine a positive value z_k (assuming $k > 0.5$) for the cumulative normal distribution such that

$$P[\tilde{R} \geq R_{min}] = k,$$

provided that

$$(R_{min} - \bar{R})/\sigma = -z_k$$

or

$$\bar{R} = z_k \, \sigma + R_{min}.$$

The above relationship is satisfied by all portfolios whose return/risk point lies above the "shortfall line" with the slope z_k emanating from the minimum return threshold point R_{min} on the return axis. For example, if $k = 0.90$, then $z_k = 1.282$.

The shortfall line can be related to interest rate volatility and duration by means of the Babcock formula. For example, if the horizon is one year, the Babcock formula predicts the return volatility σ as follows:

$$\sigma = (\text{Duration} - 1) \times \text{Interest Rate Volatility}.$$

Using this relationship, we can write the shortfall line as:

Required Expected Return = z_k × (Duration - 1) × Interest Rate Volatility
+ Threshold Return.

Over a two-year horizon, the interest rate volatility under the assumption that interest rates follow a random walk is $\sqrt{2}$ times the one-year interest rate volatility. In this case, by using the Babcock formula, we find the following equation for the shortfall line:

Required Expected Return = z_k × (Duration - 2) ($\sqrt{2}/2$) × One-Year
Interest Rate Volatility + Threshold Return.

PART III E

Corporate Bonds

Chapter III E-1

Sources of Return in Corporate Bond Portfolios

To fully understand the total return performance of a portfolio over any specified period of time, one must delve into the component sources of that return. This is particularly true in the bond market where the intents and outcomes of the portfolio manager can be readily identified with the resulting component return. By the same token, in developing a portfolio structure, the portfolio manager would be well-advised to "parse-out" the components of his expected return, both to ensure consistency with his market judgments as well as to evaluate the risk characteristics in his portfolio.

The preceding studies in this article provided a certain foundation for this process. However, the main focus was on the return derived from the yield curve and from anticipated changes in the yield curve. These factors are the main ingredients in the strategic decisions that determine a portfolio's maturity structure.

However, the *overall* return from a portfolio is an intricate blend of the portfolio's maturity structure and its sector structure. The nature of this blended return depends upon the interaction between sectors of the Corporate, Foreign, Agency, and Treasury markets. As a first step in trying to understand these

Martin L. Leibowitz, "Sources of Return in Corporate Bond Portfolios," Salomon Brothers Inc, August 1978. This paper was subsequently included in *Total Return Management*, Salomon Brothers Inc, 1979.

interactions, this study develops a general model of the behavior of sector yields and sector spreads in relation to the underlying yield curve.

By grafting this "sector model" onto the yield curve foundation, eight distinct components of bond return can be identified:

1) yield curve accumulation

2) sector spread accumulation

3) rolling yield effect

4) revaluation in sector spread

5) market shifts

6) yield curve reshaping

7) sector response to yield curve changes

8) specific issue spread action beyond that of the associated sector.

These eight components of return can be found in any marketable bond investment. More importantly, they can also be identified at the overall portfolio level. Thus, this classification scheme can help a manager to analyze market sectors as well as to evaluate the role of each sector in a balanced portfolio. With this analytic framework, the manager can integrate both strategic and tactical considerations into the development of a sector structure for his portfolio.

A MODEL OF SECTOR SPREADS

In the corporate bond market, a sector is usually defined to be a group of issues that are similar in maturity, industry type, quality, coupon, call protection, sinking fund characteristics, marketability, etc. These overt variables can be specified in terms of either very wide or very narrow limits, depending upon how refined a market structure is desired. In any case, from the viewpoint of the practitioner, the primary feature of a market sector is that all its issues can be treated as responding in an essentially similar fashion to changing market conditions. In other words, all issues in a common sector move together, or sufficiently closely in concert so as to be treated as a coherent group for the purposes of analysis.

The earlier articles in this series provided a technique for estimating the yield curve's return at a given maturity under a specified interest rate scenario. To build upon this foundation, we shall consider the behavior of sectors in terms of their yield spread relationship to the yield curve itself. In referring to the "sector spread," we mean the yield spread between some representative issue in the sector and the yield curve point corresponding to the maturity of that issue.

To estimate a sector's total return, we must specify how the sector spread behaves under changing market conditions. For our purposes, it will suffice to use a simple model which relates changes in the sector spread to two distinct types of market effects.

The first effect is the sector response to changing levels of the yield curve. This response is assumed to take the simple form of a given change in sector spread per b.p. (basis point) change in the yield curve at that maturity. For example, as depicted in Figure 1, a sector might have a "response factor" of +0.30. This means that every +100 basis point increase in the yield curve level at that maturity is expected to result in a +30 b.p. *increase* in the sector spread.

The second effect is an expected "Revaluation" in spread which is independent of any yield curve movement. In Figure 1, this second effect is expected to cause a Revaluation in the sector spread of -15 b.p. over the 1-year horizon.

Figure 1: The Sector Spread Model

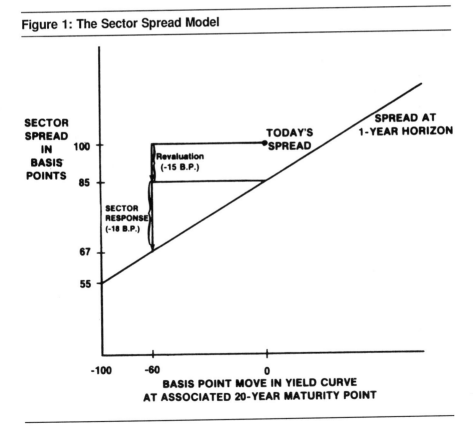

In this simple model, these two effects are assumed to be independent and their results are treated as additive. Thus, in Figure 1, if the yield curve value drops by 60 b.p., then the sector spread will narrow by

$$15 + (0.30 \times 60) = 15 + 18 = 33 \text{ b.p.}$$

It should be noted that this is the *change* in the sector spread. Thus, if the current spread is 100 basis points, then as the underlying yield curve point declines by 60 b.p., the sector spread will narrow—as shown above—by 33 b.p. to a final spread of:

$$100 - 33 = 67 \text{ b.p.}$$

COMPONENTS OF SECTOR RETURN

With this model for the behavior of sector spreads, one can create a component structure for the return derived from holding the sector over the horizon. These return components can be identified with the different kinds of market judgments made by a portfolio manager.

Over short-term horizons, there are two basic sources of return from any bond investment: 1) yield accumulation, and 2) price appreciation due to changes in yield.

In dealing with sectors, the yield accumulation can immediately be refined in terms of the sector spread and the yield at the associated yield curve point.

The Horizon Analysis approach, described in an earlier article, provides a technique for approximating the return contribution from price appreciation. This technique consists of multiplying the sector's overall yield change by a factor called the Horizon Volatility. The value of the Horizon Volatility can be computed in a relatively straightforward mathematical fashion from the sector's coupon, maturity, and yield. The sector's overall yield move can then be analyzed in terms of component yield moves that reflect different market forces.

These component yield moves are depicted in Figure 2. Our sector spread model identifies the sector spread change as consisting of a Revaluation effect together with a spread change resulting from movement in the yield curve. This yield curve movement can itself be usefully categorized in terms of three component yield moves:

1) *Roll-Down* - the drop in yield as the security "rolls down" the (positively) sloped yield curve. In essence, this reflects the process of "aging" over the horizon period. To provide a clear-cut specification, we shall define this Roll-Down in terms of a constant Treasury yield curve.

2) *Market Shift* - the change in the overall level of the yield curve. In actuality, the change in the yield curve will of course vary from maturity to

Figure 2: Component Yield Moves

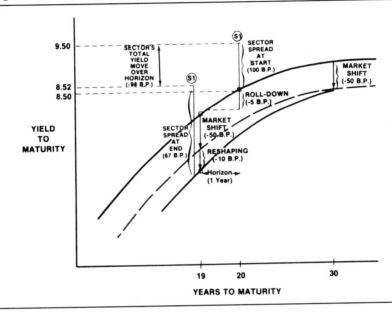

maturity. Hence, the definition of the Market Shift depends upon the maturity selected as the "benchmark" for market movements. In general, any convenient maturity can serve this benchmark role. However, in this study, it is convenient to use the 30-year point as the benchmark. In the ensuing discussion, the Market Shift over the horizon will be interpreted as the change in 30-year rates.

3) *Incremental Reshaping* - this is the remaining change at the yield curve point associated with the sector, after accounting for the Roll-Down and the Market Shift.

These three components, together with two effects associated with the changing sector spread, make for a total of five readily identifiable components comprising the sector's overall yield move. Adding the two components of the yield accumulation return, we arrive at the seven-part classification shown in Figure 3.

The eighth component of a bond's return is just the incremental return of an individual issue above and beyond the return from its sector. Because we wish to maintain our focus on the sector structure of portfolios rather than on individual issues, this eighth component will not be given further consideration in the subsequent discussion.

Figure 3: Sources of Return

MARKET SOURCE	COMPONENTS OF SECTOR RETURN MODEL	NUMERICAL EXAMPLE	MAJOR RISK CATEGORY
Yield Curve Accumulation			
Starting Yield Value at Associated Point on Yield Curve	Yield Curve	8.50%	
Sector Spread Accumulation			
Starting Sector Spread	+ Sector Spread		
Roll-Down			Rolling Yield 9.94%
Roll-Down the Yield Curve over the Horizon	+ (Horizon Volatility) × $\left(\begin{array}{c}\text{Roll–Down} \\ \text{in} \\ \text{Sector Spread}\end{array}\right)$	1.00	
Revaluation			
Expected Revaluation of Sector Leading to Change in Sector Spread Apart from Any Overall Market Movements	(Horizon Volatility) × $\left(\begin{array}{c}\text{Revaluation} \\ \text{in} \\ \text{Sector Spread}\end{array}\right)$	$8.75 \times 0.05 = 0.44$ $8.75 \times 0.15 = 1.31$	Revaluation 1.31%
Market Shift			
Overall Market Move	(Horizon Volatility) + (Market Shifts)	$8.75 \times 0.50 = 4.38$	
Reshaping			$\left(\begin{array}{c}\text{Total} \\ \text{Market} \\ \text{Volatility}\end{array}\right) \times \left(\begin{array}{c}\text{Market} \\ \text{Shifts}\end{array}\right)$
Yield Curve Reshaping Above and Beyond the Overall Market Move	$\left(\begin{array}{c}\text{Incremental} \\ \text{Reshaping} \\ \text{Volatility}\end{array}\right)$ × (Market Shifts)	$1.75 \times 0.50 = 0.87$	
Sector Response			13.65×0.50 6.83%
Incremental Change in Sector Spread in Response to Overall Market Movement and Yield Curve Reshaping	$\left(\begin{array}{c}\text{Incremental} \\ \text{Sector} \\ \text{Volatility}\end{array}\right)$ × (Market Shifts)	$3.15 \times 0.50 = 1.58$	

Total Return 18.08%

In the sector spread model, we have assumed that a relationship of simple proportionality exists between market-related changes in the sector spreads and movements at the underlying yield curve point. Now suppose that a similar "proportionality assumption" can be applied to the relationship between the yield curve reshaping and the Market Shift. With these assumptions, the last three components in Figure 3 become proportional to the magnitude of the Market Shift.

The second column in Figure 3 is a condensed statement of the mathematical model of sector return which can be derived from the preceding assumptions. A mathematical derivation of this model is presented in the Appendix.

This model can supply valuable insights regarding the nature of the market judgments *and* *risks* associated with an anticipated level of sector return.

A NUMERICAL EXAMPLE

The application of the sector return model is best illustrated through a numerical example. Consider a sector associated with the 20-year point on the yield curve. At the outset, the 20-year yield curve rate is 8.50% and the sector's yield is 9.50%, i.e., the sector spread is 100 b.p. To avoid the additional complexity of annualization, the investment horizon is 1 year in this and all subsequent examples. The sector's Horizon Volatility factor is 8.75. We shall assume that the sector response follows the pattern shown in Figure 1.

In this example, there is a sizable market improvement over the 1-year period. The overall effect of these movements is that the sector's yield moved from 9.50% to 8.52%, a decline of 98 b.p. This results from a Market Shift of 50 b.p. at the 30-year benchmark, plus an added 10 b.p. of reshaping at the 19-year point now associated with the "aged" sector, i.e., after the 1-year period. Meanwhile, the sector spread has changed through a 15 b.p. Revaluation on top of the 18 b.p. spread change in response to the 60 b.p. move in the underlying yield curve. A Roll-Down of 5 b.p. completes the tabulation of the total sector yield move of 98 b.p.

This market behavior leads to a total sector return of (approximately) 18.08%, composed of the component returns shown in Figure 3. (The detailed calculations are carried out in the Appendix.)

There are several points to note about the values in Figure 3. First of all, the sector contributed three components of return above and beyond that derived from the yield curve. These contributions add to

$$1.00\% + 1.31\% + 1.58\% = 3.89\%,$$

so that 3.89% out of the total 18.08% return was derived from holding this particular sector. The remaining 14.19% return would have been achieved by simply investing at the 20-year point on the yield curve.

Another way of analyzing these return components is in terms of the kind of risks they represent. Thus, the combination of the first three components is simply the sector's Rolling Yield, and their 9.94% return is fairly well assured for sectors whose quality is not in doubt. In contrast, the Revaluation Return of 1.31% reflects a spread judgment that the sector is undervalued. There may be considerable risk surrounding any such projected Revaluation.

The last three components of return all depend on the magnitude of the Market Shift and the resulting yield curve reshaping and sector spread response. Together, these components contribute a return of 6.83%, or about 38% of the sector's total return. As we would expect, the largest value, 4.38%, is derived from the Market Shift itself. However, the reshaping and the sector response each make incremental contributions at a significant level. In order to appreciate the overall sensitivity to Market Shifts, it is useful to combine all three volatility factors into a measure of the sector's "Total Market Volatility,"

$$8.75 + 1.75 + 3.15 = 13.65.$$

This Total Market Volatility of 13.65 reflects the vulnerability of the sector return to deviations in the Market Shift. Thus, if instead of improving, the market had deteriorated by 50 b.p., then the sector return would have been reduced to 9.94% + 1.31% - 6.83% = 4.42%.

This illustrates the great sensitivity of sector returns to unexpected changes in what is usually the most uncertain of all market variables, i.e., movements in the overall level of rates.

TOTAL MARKET VOLATILITY OF A SECTOR

The magnitude of this vulnerability to Market Shifts is illustrated in Figure 4.

At a Market Shift of 0 b.p., the sector return consists of the Rolling Yield plus the Revaluation return. As the Market Shift becomes significant in either direction, the three volatility factors combine to produce the return profile indicated by the broken line. The slope of this line represents the return change per b.p. of Market Shift, i.e., the slope corresponds to the sector's Total Market Volatility of 13.65.

The magnitude of this Total Market Volatility leads to some interesting interpretations. The Horizon Volatility of a 30-year 8.50% par bond is 10.78. Consequently, this sector's Total Market Volatility is almost 27% greater than that of the 30-year benchmark bond! This increased volatility is due to embedding the yield curve reshaping and the sector spread response in the Total Market Vola-

Figure 4: Sector Returns for a Range of Market Shifts

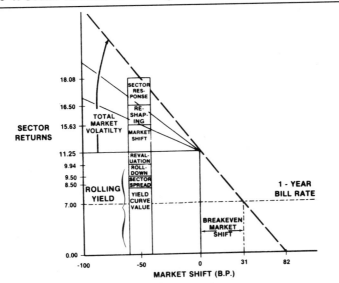

tility. Nevertheless, if the model assumptions are valid, then there has been a sizable increase in the vulnerability to Market Shifts as measured by movements at the benchmark maturity. (This is, of course, a two-way street. Other sectors with different sector response factors and/or different reshaping factors may lead to sizable reductions in the Total Market Volatility.)

The relative importance of the different return components is critically dependent upon the horizon period. As illustrated in Figure 5, the Rolling Yield over a 2-year horizon may be comparable to its value over a 1-year period. However, when return is expressed as an annualized figure, a longer horizon period is likely to result in a sizable reduction in the effects of Revaluation and Total Market Volatility.

INCORPORATING SECTORS INTO RETURN/RISK DIAGRAMS

In the preceding articles, it was shown how to transform the traditional yield-versus-maturity yield curve into a return-versus-risk framework. For each maturity point on the yield curve, the projected return was plotted against what essentially corresponded to the Total Market Volatility for that maturity point. Figure 6 shows an example of this return/risk diagram.

Figure 5: Risk Categorization and Multiple Horizons

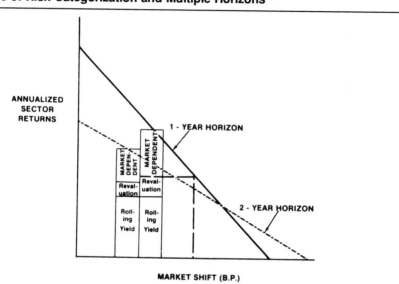

Suppose we now wish to introduce a sector investment into this return/risk diagram. Keeping to our earlier numerical example, this sector is "associated"—in terms of comparable maturity—with the 20-year point on the yield curve. However, the sector's projected return exceeds that of the 20-year yield curve point by 3.89%. Moreover, because of the incremental volatility derived from the sector response to Market Shifts, the sector's Total Market Volatility will exceed that of the 20-year curve point. Consequently, even though the sector is "associated" with the 20-year point, it would plot (as the point labeled S1) much further to the right and higher in Figure 6. This displacement reflects the sector's greater return and greater volatility.

Indeed, the sector S1 actually plots much further to the right than *any* part of the yield curve itself. As noted earlier, this is because the sector's Total Market Volatility is actually 27% greater than that of the 30-year benchmark bond. In fact, even if the yield curve was extended to include maturities beyond 30-years, it would still not be possible to reach the volatility of the sector S1. The reason is that the Horizon Volatility does not continue to increase with increasing maturity. For example, no matter how long its maturity, an 8.50% par bond will always have a Horizon Volatility of less than 12. This even holds true for perpetuals!

Figure 6: Incorporating Sectors into a Return/Risk Diagram

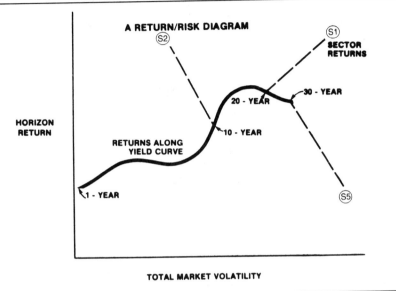

As illustrated by the plot of the different sectors in Figure 6, the inclusion of corporate sectors leads to a great enrichment of the return/risk characteristics available in the marketplace.

CORPORATE PORTFOLIOS

The classification techniques just described for an individual sector can also be applied to an entire corporate portfolio. The portfolio's investment in each sector is first analyzed into the seven basic components. Then, for each component of return, a weighted average is taken across all sectors in the portfolio. (The weighting factor is just the market value of the investment in each sector as a fraction of the portfolio's total market value. The computational procedure is described in the Appendix.)

This classification system can clarify the return/risk implications of the portfolio structure. It also makes explicit the magnitude and overall impact of the many different market judgments that the portfolio manager has embedded (perhaps implicitly) into his portfolio decisions. Figure 7 illustrates a number of

Figure 7: Hypothetical Portfolios and Their Projected Return Components

Return Component	P1	P2	P3	P4
Yield Curve Value	8.50%	8.50%	8.50%	8.25%
Sector Spread	1.00	2.00	1.50	1.40
Roll-Down	0.44	0.41	0.20	0.70
Yield Accumulation	9.94	10.91	10.20	10.35
Revaluation	1.31	-4.00	-1.00	5.93
Market Shift	4.38	4.10	4.90	2.97
Reshaping	0.87	0.82	0	0.89
Sector Response	1.58	2.46	-2.94	0
Market Dependent	6.83	7.38	1.96	3.86
Total Return	18.08%	14.29%	11.16%	20.14%
Total Market Volatility	13.65	14.76	3.92	7.72
Breakeven Market Shift	81B.P.	49B.P.	106B.P.	170B.P.

alternative portfolio structures with their returns analyzed in terms of the seven components.

The first portfolio, P1, consists solely of the sector S1 that we have used as an example throughout. It is included here only as a useful point of reference.

The portfolio P2 consists of a lower quality sector having maturities roughly comparable with P1. Compared with P1, the portfolio P2 has a wider sector spread, but the manager's primary motivation was to acquire the much greater sector response to improving markets. However, the manager believes that these sectors are overpriced, and he has projected a -4.00% Revaluation loss. Under the projected 50 b.p. Market Shift, the projected return for P2 is 14.29%, somewhat less than P1, and with considerably greater credit risk, more Revaluation risk, and a somewhat larger vulnerability to adverse Market Shifts.

The portfolio P3 includes a number of high-coupon cushion bond sectors. These bonds are selling at prices determined by imminent and/or future threats of call. The portfolio is characterized by a high yield, a negative Revaluation reflecting the yield-to-call effect over time, and a *negative* sector response factor, i.e., the cushion bond's *spread* over the yield curve is assumed to increase with decreasing market rates. On balance, this leaves portfolio P3 with a relatively modest 11.16% return, but with far lower vulnerability to adverse Market Shifts.

The portfolio P4 consists largely of certain intermediate maturity sectors which have recently been introduced into the U.S. marketplace. The manager anticipates a major positive Revaluation in these sectors as they become accepted. As the numerical results show, this leads to a sizable projected return. However, while his portfolio has a relatively low sensitivity to adverse Market Shifts, his return projection is of course highly dependent on the presumed Revaluation in the sector spreads.

BREAK-EVEN MARKET SHIFTS

The risk from adverse market movement can be quantified through use of a "break-even value." Given the Total Market Volatility of each portfolio, a reasonable question is how large an adverse Market Shift is required to reduce the return from each portfolio to some common level. A natural choice for this comparison level is the 1-year Bill rate, i.e., the risk-free rate for the 1-year horizon. In the example, the 1-year Bill rate is taken to be 7%. The nature of this calculation is depicted in Figure 4, and the procedure is described in the Appendix. The results are shown as the last line in Figure 7.

The Break-Even Market Shift reflects the adverse movement (measured from the projected 50 b.p. improvement) required to lower the portfolio return down to the 7% level of 1-year Bills.

Put another way, as long as any adverse Market Shift is less in magnitude than this Break-Even value, then the portfolio's return will still exceed the 7% risk-free rate. Thus, the portfolio P4 with its Break-Even of 170 b.p. is least vulnerable to Market Shifts (although it contains sizable Revaluation risk). In order of increasing vulnerability to Market Shifts, P4 is followed by P3, P1, and P2. In fact, the portfolio P2 was based upon obtaining the maximum response to the 50 b.p. market improvement. Without any market movement at all, P2 would only match the 7% risk-free rate.

These classification techniques have been developed to assist the investment manager in organizing and quantifying the many market judgments that are embedded in his portfolio structure. The classification process also highlights the nature of the different risks incurred, as well as the differences in their portfolio impact over varying investment horizons. By analyzing the marketplace in terms of this same classification system, the manager may be better able to construct a portfolio having a desired set of characteristics. The classification procedure could also prove helpful in sponsor/manager communications, e.g., by more precisely identifying the manager's motivation behind an intended departure from a goal-oriented Baseline Portfolio.

All of the preceding development has been oriented to applications of a prospective nature. However, the classification of return components also suggests an intriguing approach to the retrospective analysis of realized returns. By providing a method for factoring out the often overriding influence of Market Shifts, this classification procedure can help isolate the (perhaps more sustainable) contribution from other kinds of market judgments.

Appendix

THE SECTOR YIELD MOVE

The basic sector response model is

$$
\begin{pmatrix} \text{Sector} \\ \text{Spread} \\ \text{at} \\ \text{Horizon} \end{pmatrix} = \begin{pmatrix} \text{Sector} \\ \text{Spread} \\ \text{at} \\ \text{Outset} \end{pmatrix} + \begin{pmatrix} \text{Revalu-} \\ \text{ation} \end{pmatrix} + \begin{pmatrix} \text{Response} \\ \text{Factor} \end{pmatrix} \times \begin{pmatrix} \text{YieldCurve} \\ \text{Move} \end{pmatrix}
$$

or more simply,

$$
\begin{pmatrix} \text{Change in} \\ \text{Sector Spreads} \end{pmatrix} = \begin{pmatrix} \text{Revalu-} \\ \text{ation} \end{pmatrix} + \begin{pmatrix} \text{Response} \\ \text{Factor} \end{pmatrix} \times \begin{pmatrix} \text{Yield Curve} \\ \text{Move} \end{pmatrix}
$$

The (*Yield Curve Move*) refers to the movement in the underlying yield curve point associated with the sector at the end of the horizon. Thus, for a 20-year sector over a 1-year horizon, the (*Yield Curve Move*) would be the change in 19-year Treasury rates. (While the Response Factor is treated as a constant in this basic linear model, one may need to use more sophisticated relationships to describe certain sectors' response to changing markets.)

At any given point in time, the sector's yield level is

(Sector Yield) = (Yield Curve Level) + (Sector Spread),

so that the total sector yield move over the horizon becomes

$$
(\text{Sector Yield Move}) = \begin{pmatrix} \text{Change in Yield} \\ \text{Curve Level} \end{pmatrix} + \begin{pmatrix} \text{Change in} \\ \text{Sector Spread} \end{pmatrix}.
$$

The (*Change in the Yield Curve Level*) at a maturity can itself be analyzed in terms of two components,

(Roll-Down) + (Yield Curve Move).

Finally, the Yield Curve Move can be analyzed in terms of a Market Shift achieved at the designated benchmark maturity followed by an incremental re-shaping at the associated maturity,

(Yield Curve Move) = (Market Shift) + (Reshaping)

Putting all this together, one can define the sector's yield move in terms of five component yield moves,

(Sector Yield Move) = (Roll-Down)

+

(Yield Curve Move)

+

(Revaluation)

+

$$\left(\begin{array}{c}\text{Response}\\\text{Factor}\end{array}\right) \times \left(\begin{array}{c}\text{Yield Curve}\\\text{Move}\end{array}\right)$$

= (Roll-Down)

+

(Revaluation)

+

(Market Shift)

+

(Reshaping)

+

$$\left(\begin{array}{c}\text{Response}\\\text{Factor}\end{array}\right) \times \left[\begin{array}{c}\text{Market}\\\text{Shift}\end{array} + \text{Reshaping}\right]$$

where the last term represents the incremental sector response to the yield curve movement.

Under certain assumptions (i.e., the "proportionality assumption" described in Number 4 of this series), the Reshaping at each maturity can be related to the Market Shift by a simple factor,

(Reshaping) = (Reshaping Factor) × (Market Shift)

In this case, the equation for the Sector Yield Move can be written as

(Sector Yield Move) = (Roll-Down)

+

(Revaluation)

+

$$(\text{Market Shift})$$

$$+$$

$$(\text{Reshaping Factor}) \times (\text{Market Shift})$$

$$+$$

$$\begin{pmatrix} \text{Response} \\ \text{Factor} \end{pmatrix} \times \left[\begin{pmatrix} \text{Market} \\ \text{Shift} \end{pmatrix} + \begin{pmatrix} \text{Reshaping} \\ \text{Factor} \end{pmatrix} \times \begin{pmatrix} \text{Market} \\ \text{Shift} \end{pmatrix} \right].$$

SECTOR RETURNS

In the Horizon Analysis technique, a bond's total return is approximated by

$$(\text{Yield Accumulation}) + (\text{Horizon Volatility}) \times (\text{Yield Move}).$$

Yield Accumulation consists of return accruing under "constant markets," i.e., coupon income, price accretion at constant market rates, and interest-on-interest. When dealing with short-term horizons, the Yield Accumulation can be identified with the original yield and the interest-on-interest will be small. Thus, the sector's return can be approximated by

$$(\text{Sector Return}) = (\text{Sector Yield})$$

$$+$$

$$(\text{Horizon Volatility}) \times (\text{Sector Yield Move})$$

Inserting the preceding results for the Sector Yield Move, and using the symbol HV for the sector's Horizon Volatility, this becomes

$$(\text{Sector Return}) = (\text{Yield Curve Value})$$

$$+$$

$$(\text{Sector Spread})$$

$$+$$

$$\text{HV} \times (\text{Roll-Down})$$

$$+$$

$$\text{HV} \times (\text{Revaluation})$$

$$+$$

$$\text{HV} \times (\text{Market Shift})$$

$$+$$

$$HV \times (\text{Reshaping Factor}) \times (\text{Market Shift})$$

$$+$$

$$HV \times \left(\begin{array}{c}\text{Response}\\\text{Factor}\end{array}\right) \times \left[1 + \left(\begin{array}{c}\text{Reshaping}\\\text{Factor}\end{array}\right)\right] \times \left(\begin{array}{c}\text{Market}\\\text{Shift}\end{array}\right)$$

This is the classification system described in Figure 3, with two new factors defined as

$$\left(\begin{array}{c}\text{Incremental Reshaping}\\\text{Volatility}\end{array}\right) = HV \times \left(\begin{array}{c}\text{Reshaping}\\\text{Factor}\end{array}\right)$$

$$\left(\begin{array}{c}\text{Incremental Sector}\\\text{Volatility}\end{array}\right) = HV \times \left(\begin{array}{c}\text{Response}\\\text{Factor}\end{array}\right) \times \left[1 + \left(\begin{array}{c}\text{Reshaping}\\\text{Factor}\end{array}\right)\right].$$

AGGREGATION INTO MAJOR RISK CATEGORIES

In the context of yield curve analysis, the Yield Accumulation should include the Roll-Down return (since this would be received as a matter of course under constant market conditions). The sector's Rolling Yield can then be defined by

$$(\text{Rolling Yield}) = (\text{Yield Curve Value})$$

$$+$$

$$(\text{Sector Spread})$$

$$+$$

$$(HV \times \text{Roll-Down}).$$

The Revaluation is the return contribution from the anticipated change in sector spread apart from any market movements. Because of its total dependence on a spread judgment, it represents a major return (and risk) category by itself.

Finally, we see that the last three terms in the Sector Return equation all depend upon the Market Shift. Consequently, these three terms can all be grouped into a "Market-Dependent" risk category. Moreover, by defining the sector's

$$(\text{Total Market Volatility}) = HV$$

$$+$$

$$(\text{Incremental Reshaping Volatility})$$

$$+$$

$$(\text{Incremental Sector Volatility})$$

all three Market-Dependent terms can be combined in the expression,

(Total Market Volatility) × (Market Shift).

Thus, as shown in Figure 3, the Sector Return components can then be rearranged into three major risk components,

(Sector Return) = (Rolling Yield)

+

(Revaluation)

+

(Total Market Volatility) × (Market Shift).

NUMERICAL EXAMPLE

In the numerical example shown in Figure 3, we have the following values:

Yield Curve Value	=	8.50%
Sector Spread	=	1.00%
Roll-Down in Yield	=	-5 B.P
Revaluation in Yield	=	-15 B.P.
Market Shift	=	-50 B.P.

(Yield Change at Benchmark 30-year Treasury)

Reshaping in Yield   =   -10 B.P.
(Added Yield Change at 19-year point on yield curve)

Reshaping Factor   =   0.20
(Reshaping in Yield Per B.P. of Market Shift)

Response Factor   =   0.30
(B.P. Sector Spread Change Per B.P. Change in 19-year point on yield curve)

Horizon Volatility   =   8.75
(B.P. Change in Sector Return Per B.P. Change in Sector Yield Level)

With these values, the three newly defined volatilities become

$$\left(\begin{matrix} \text{Incremental Reshaping} \\ \text{Volatility} \end{matrix} \right) = HV \times \left(\begin{matrix} \text{Reshaping} \\ \text{Factor} \end{matrix} \right)$$

$$= 8.75 \times 0.2$$
$$= 1.75$$

$$\begin{pmatrix} \text{Incremental Sector} \\ \text{Volatility} \end{pmatrix} = \text{HV} \times \begin{pmatrix} \text{Response} \\ \text{Factor} \end{pmatrix} \times \left[1 + \begin{pmatrix} \text{Reshaping} \\ \text{Factor} \end{pmatrix} \right]$$

$$= 8.75 \times 0.3 \times [1 + 0.2]$$
$$= 8.75 \times 0.36$$
$$= 3.15,$$

and

$$\begin{pmatrix} \text{Total Market} \\ \text{Volatility} \end{pmatrix} = \text{HV} + \begin{pmatrix} \text{Incremental} \\ \text{Reshaping} \\ \text{Volatility} \end{pmatrix} + \begin{pmatrix} \text{Incremental} \\ \text{Sector} \\ \text{Volatility} \end{pmatrix}$$

$$= 8.75 + 1.75 + 3.15$$
$$= 13.65.$$

The return values are then computed as shown in Figure 3.

In all the preceding calculations, the problem of annualization has been sidestepped through the choice of a 1-year horizon. For horizon periods other than 1 year, appropriate annualization factors must be applied to obtain consistent results.

PORTFOLIO RETURN COMPONENTS

This classification scheme can be applied to a portfolio by simply computing weighted averages across each of the seven components. Thus, if M_i is the market value in the ith sector, then the weighting factor W_i is just the fraction that M_i represents of the overall portfolio,

$$W_i = \frac{M_i}{\sum_j M_j}$$

where $\sum_i$ means the "sum over all sectors." The portfolio's overall return will just be the weighted sum of all its sector returns,

$$(\text{Portfolio Return}) = \sum_i W_i \times (\text{Sector Return})_i.$$

This process can be carried through to each of the seven return components. Proceeding in this fashion, the projected return from an entire portfolio can be classified in the same fashion as shown in Figure 3 for a single sector.

BREAK-EVEN MARKET SHIFT

The return calculation in Figure 3 includes the results from a projected Market Shift. Since any such projection must be viewed as risky, it is important to evaluate the sensitivity of the projected return to adverse market movements. Specifically, the Break-Even Market Shift is the adverse movement (from the level of the projected Market Shift) required to reduce the sector or portfolio return to some specified level. While break-evens can be defined in terms of any specified return level, we shall interpret the Break-Even Market Shift as reducing all returns to the common level of the risk-free rate for the horizon. Thus, with this definition,

$$\text{(Projected Return) - (Total Market Volatility)} \times \text{(Break-Even Market Shift)}$$

$$= \text{(Risk-Free Rate)}$$

and we get that the

$$\text{(Break–Even Market Shift)} = \frac{\text{(Projected Return)–(Risk–Free Rate)}}{\text{(Total Market Volatility)}}$$

It is interesting to note that the Break-Even Market Shift has the form of a return/risk ratio. The higher this Break-Even value, the more the excess projected return is cushioned against the risk of adverse Market Shifts.

Chapter III E-2

Spread-Duration

The sensitivity of bond portfolio values to changing interest rates has been the subject of extensive research in recent years. For bonds with well-defined cash flows, such as most Treasury issues, the interest rate sensitivity is closely represented by the "modified duration," which describes how the price of the bond changes with small variations in its yield. For typical corporate bonds and mortgage-backed securities, which have embedded option features and, hence, cash flows that depend on the path of interest rates, we can still examine the price response to changes in the general level of rates. This sensitivity, usually called the "effective duration," provides portfolio managers with a method of controlling their interest rate exposure.

This duration measure is a valuable tool for estimating and controlling the volatility of fixed-income portfolios, as long as overall changes in interest rates represent the sole source of risk. However, a portfolio that includes corporate bonds generates returns that depend not only on changes in interest rates, but also on the changes in the spreads of the bonds that comprise the portfolio. A portfolio selection procedure that ignores this spread variability will be driven,

Martin L. Leibowitz, William S. Krasker and Ardavan Nozari, "Spread-Duration: A New Tool for Bond Portfolio Management," Salomon Brothers Inc, August 1988. (Later combined with "The Anaysis of Credit Barbells: An Application of the Spread-Duration Technique," Salomon Brothers Inc, August 1988, in *The Journal of Portfolio Management*, Spring 1990.)

for example, toward high-yield bonds, because it will understate their true risk. In this chapter we discuss the concept of "spread-duration," which represents the sensitivity of a portfolio to spread changes in the corporate bond market. (Although our discussion concentrates on the corporate market, the same ideas can be usefully applied to a variety of asset classes.)

For clarity, we begin the examining the effect of a spread change on a portfolio consisting of a single corporate bond. Subsequently, we will consider portfolios that combine a corporate bond with a Treasury bond. The spread-duration—the sensitivity of the portfolio value to the bond's spread change—depends on the product of the duration of the corporate bond and its weight in the portfolio.

Finally, we will consider spread-duration for general portfolios. For these, the key quantities are the empirically derived "sector spread betas," which describe how the spreads in subsectors of the corporate market tend to change, given a change in spread for the *corporate market as a whole*. The spread-duration of a general portfolio is defined as a weighted average of the durations of the various corporate sectors comprising the portfolio, in which the weight of each sector is the product of its sector spread beta and its market value percentage in the portfolio.

PRICE/YIELD RELATIONSHIPS WITHOUT SPREAD VARIABILITY

For simplicity, we focus on zero-coupon bonds. Exhibit 1 shows a hypothetical Treasury STRIPs curve. In this graph the vertical axis is the yield, and the horizontal axis is the bond's maturity. The 5-year Treasury zero-coupon bond with an 8.2% yield is highlighted on the curve. In addition, we include a corporate zero-coupon bond that has the same 5-year maturity, but trades at a higher yield.[1] The 150-basis-point spread is simply the vertical "yield distance" between the corporate bond and the Treasury bond.

First, consider the price response of these securities to changes in Treasury yields, assuming that the corporate bond maintains a constant spread. Exhibit 2 illustrates the prices of the two bonds as functions of the change in the Treasury yield. The Treasury bond has a slightly stepper curve, which implies a greater absolute price sensitivity to any particular yield change. However, the percentage price changes for the two securities—their returns—are nearly equal because

---

[1] For clarity of exposition, our example uses a hypothetical corporate zero-coupon bond. In more general cases, we would have to include consideration of coupon effects, optional calls and sinking fund features. This would require an extensive discussion of the role of interest rate volatility and its relationship to more sophisticated versions of the spread and duration concepts (such as the option-adjusted spread and the effective duration). However, this additional complexity is not required for our main purpose.

Exhibit 1: Yields and Maturities—The Case of Equal Durations

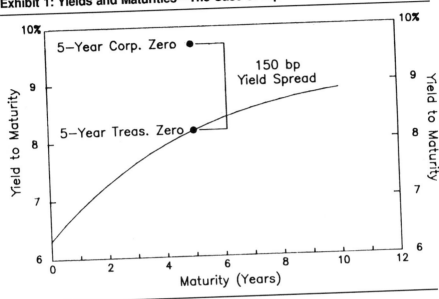

Exhibit 2: Bond Prices versus Yield Curve Shift

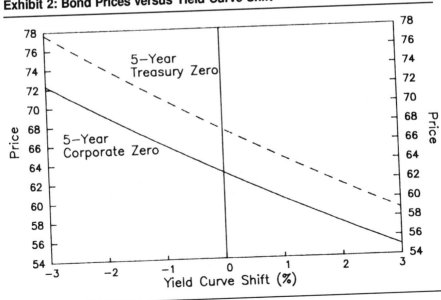

Exhibit 3: Effect of Spread Change

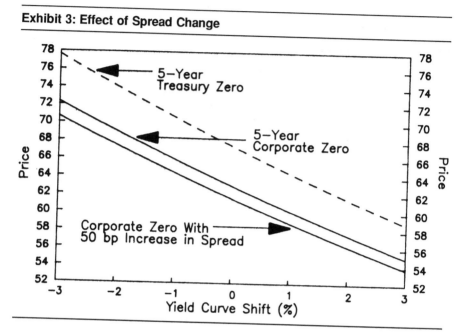

of their essentially equal durations. Thus, apart from credit risk, the securities have virtually identical risk characteristics.

THE EFFECT OF SPREAD CHANGES

Exhibit 3 contains a representation of the effect of a change in spreads. The upper two curves are the same as those in Exhibit 2, while the bottom curve shows the price of the corporate bond for different shifts in the yield curve, given a 50-basis-point increase in its spread relative to the Treasury curve. The magnitude of the drop in price—the vertical distance between the two solid curves—represents the sensitivity of the corporate bond to spread changes. The actual price change of the corporate bond, in a general setting in which both interest rates and spreads change, is represented in Exhibit 3 as a combination of two changes: (1) a spread change that determines the location of the bond's price curve in the figure; and (2) a change in interest rates that determines a particular point on the curve.

We can isolate the effect of a spread change on the bond's return by assuming that interest rates remain unchanged. This leads to Exhibit 4, in which the bond return is depicted as a function of its spread change. The return per unit

---

Exhibit 4: Corporate Bond Return versus Spread Change

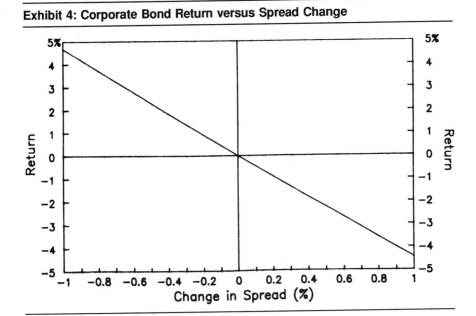

---

change in spread—the slope of the curve in the figure—can be regarded as the spread-duration relative to a benchmark portfolio consisting of just this bond. In this case, the spread duration of 4.77 years coincides with the corporate bond's modified duration, because a spread change has the same effect as a general change in yields.[2]

THE CASE OF UNEQUAL DURATIONS

Thus far, we have focused on the case of equal durations. Assume instead that the corporate bond has a 7-year maturity, as depicted in Exhibit 5. Exhibit 6 shows how the returns on the two securities vary as a function of the shift in the yield curve. The curve for the corporate bond is steeper, reflecting its greater sensitivity to yield changes. The slopes of the curves are simply the modified durations: 6.7 years for the corporate bond and 4.8 years for the Treasury bond.

---

[2] While the "Macaulay duration" for a zero-coupon bond of maturity N years is N, the proper measure of its instantaneous price sensitivity is called the "modified duration," which has the value $N/(1 + Y/200)$ for a bond with yield Y. Thus, the 5-year corporate zero at a yield of 9.7% has a modified duration of $5/(1 + 9.7/200)=4.77$ years.

Exhibit 5: Yields and Maturities—The Case of Unequal Durations

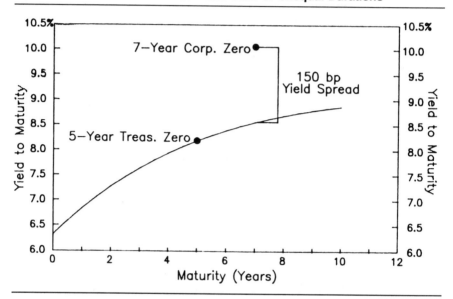

Exhibit 6: Bond Returns versus Yield Curve Shift with Unequal Durations

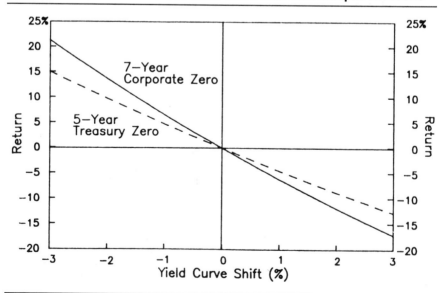

Exhibit 7: Difference in Returns versus Yield Curve Shift

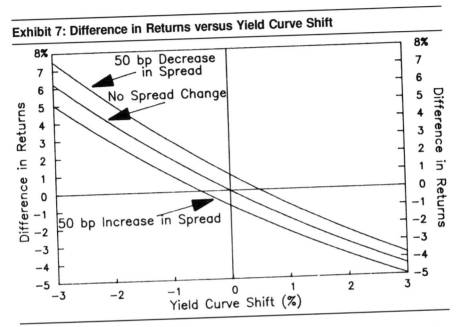

Exhibit 7 combines the effects of changes in interest rates and spreads on the returns of these two bonds. The middle curve in the exhibit shows the difference in the returns (corporate over Treasury) as a function of the shift in the yield curve, assuming that there is no change in the corporate bond's spread. Because of the corporate bond's longer duration, it will outperform or underperform the Treasury bond, depending on whether the yield curve shift is down or up. The top and bottom curves represent spread changes of - 50 basis points and + 50 points, respectively. Analogous to Exhibit 3, the difference in the returns has two components—the difference generated by the interest rate change, which reflects the duration gap, and the additional return to the corporate bond because of the spread change. In our representation, the second component determines the appropriate curve, while the first determines the location on that curve. The spread-duration is 6.7 years, which, once again, coincides with the modified duration of the 7-year corporate zero.

SPREAD-DURATION OF A SIMPLE PORTFOLIO

We now turn our attention to the portfolios. Consider a simple portfolio that consists of a 60%/40% mix of the 5-year Treasury bond and the 7-year corporate bond. As shown in Exhibit 8, the duration of this portfolio is the market-value-

Exhibit 8: Portfolio Yield and Duration

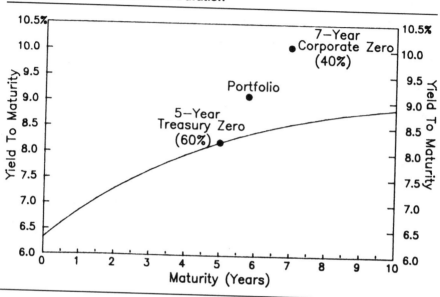

Exhibit 9: Portfolio Return versus Spread Change

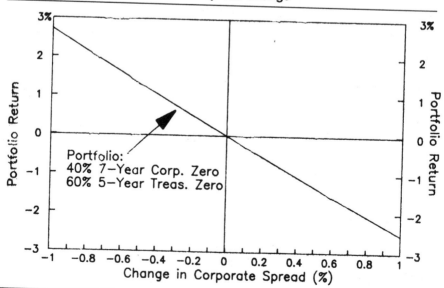

weighted average of the durations of the bonds that it comprises, and the portfolio yield (the internal rate of return) is approximately the weighted average of the individual yields, weighted by the product of the market value and duration. (Notice that, in general, the portfolio will not lie on the straight line between the two bonds in a yield curve diagram such as Exhibit 8.)

Exhibit 9 graphs the portfolio return as a function of the change in the corporate spread. The slope of the curve, 2.68, is the spread-duration, which, in this case, is the product of the duration of the corporate bond, 6.7, and its weight, 0.4, in the portfolio.

SPREAD-DURATION FOR GENERAL PORTFOLIOS

We can extend the concept of spread-duration to general portfolios by first defining a general benchmark "spread change" in the corporate market. We consider the market-weighted average change in spread of all the securities in the corporate component of the Salomon Brothers Broad Investment-Grade Bond Index^{SM} (the Broad Index) as such a benchmark. We then empirically estimate the sector "spread betas" for various subsectors of the corporate component of the Broad Index. These betas represent the amount by which the market-weighted average spread in each sector tends to change, given a change in the overall corporate spread. Finally, we define the portfolio spread-duration as a weighted average of the durations of the sectors comprising the portfolio, in which the weight of each sector is the product of its sector spread beta and its market value percentage in the portfolio.

For example, consider a portfolio consisting 65% of Treasury bonds with a 6-year duration and 35% of BBB-rated corporates with a 4-year duration. The sector spread beta is zero for Treasuries, and is approximately 1.3 for BBB securities. Thus, the portfolio spread-duration is 1.82 years, which is computed as follows:

65% Treasury	$0.65 \times 6 \times 0.0 =$	0
35% BBB Corporate	$0.35 \times 4 \times 1.3 =$	<u>1.82</u>

Portfolio Spread-Duration   1.82

We can illustrate the effectiveness of this approach by applying it to the corporate sector of the Broad Index itself. Exhibit 10 contains the scatterplot of the sequence of incremental monthly returns from the corporate sector of the Broad Index, net of the part of the return due to the shift in a Treasury benchmark, versus the overall corporate spread change over the corresponding month. The slope of the line drawn through the scatter plot is the average (1984-88) spread-duration for the Broad Index corporates. The tightness of the scatter

Exhibit 10: Incremental Broad Index Corporate Returns Adjusted by Yield Curve Moves versus Changes in Corporate Spread

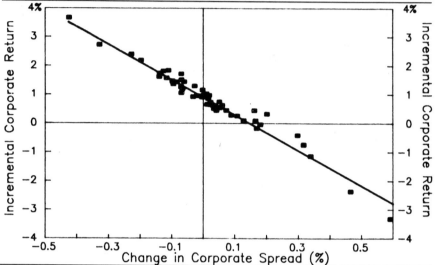

around this theoretical line suggests that the spread-duration can be a useful measure of the sensitivity of a portfolio to spread changes.

CONCLUSION

The power of the spread-duration is derived from its simplicity and corresponding ease of application. It provides a compact, one-dimensional measure of spread risk over short-term horizons. However, it should be pointed out that this simplicity entails certain costs. As with all duration measures, the spread-duration should be expected only to approximate incremental returns associated with modest changes in market spreads. To capture the effects of large market movements, we must turn to a broader set of more complex tools that can address other factors such a convexity, optional characteristics, various yield curve effects, etc. As with the basic modified Macaulay duration, the spread-duration concept has the virtue of being so simple and so intuitive that it can be readily incorporated into the day-to-day management of fixed-income portfolios.

Traditionally, a portfolio manager focuses on the percentage of corporate bonds in his or her portfolio, or perhaps the percentages within each credit sector, as a measure of the portfolio's credit risk. This approach may be appropriate for long-term horizons, where the risk consists of the possibility of actual defaults. However, with the increasing focus on short-term return as a measure of performance, portfolio managers need a correspondingly short-term gauge of credit risk. The spread-duration, by measuring the sensitivity of the portfolio return to spread changes over the short term, provides such a yardstick.

Spread-duration greatly facilitates the comparison of portfolios. For example, two portfolios, comprising very different securities, will nevertheless have similar risk characteristics if they have the same duration and spread-duration. This improved assessment of short-term spread risk can facilitate the comparison and control of overall portfolio risks, as well as help to construct portfolios that are actively oriented to exploit perceived market opportunities in specific sectors. Indeed, the very heart of duration-constrained active management is sector spread management. For these reasons, we believe that the spread-duration concept represents a fundamental new tool that should prove valuable for active management as well as for various structured strategies.

Chapter III E-3

The Analysis of Credit Barbells

In the previous chapter, we introduced the concept of credit spread-duration as a measure of the sensitivity of a portfolio's value to changes in corporate spreads. Spread-duration is defined as a weighted average of the durations of the various sectors comprising the portfolio. The weight of each sector is the product of its market value weight in the portfolio and a parameter, "beta," that describes how spreads in that sector respond to changes in overall corporate spreads. By setting the spread-duration at appropriate values, a portfolio manager can gain significant control over his portfolio's exposure to changing spreads.

In this chapter we focus on "credit barbells." A credit barbell is a portfolio that maintains a specified duration and spread-duration through a combination of two (or more) sectors having differing credit ratings and/or durations. Credit barbells often have advantages over single-sector portfolios with the same risk characteristics, such a higher yields, more desirable cash flow patterns, better

Martin L. Leibowitz, William S. Krasker and Ardavan Nozari, "The Analysis of Credit Barbells: An Application of the Spread-Duration Technique," Salomon Brothers Inc, August 1988. (Later combined with "Spread-Duration: A New Tool for Bond Portfolio Management," Salomon Brothers Inc, August 1988, in *The Journal of Portfolio Management*, Spring 1990.)

liquidity, etc. Using the spread-duration technique, a portfolio can be tailored to achieve these or other goals, while maintaining the same exposure to yield curve shifts and corporate spread changes.

SPREAD-DURATIONS FOR DIFFERENT CREDIT SECTORS

Exhibit 1 graphs the portfolio return as a function of an instantaneous change in the corporate spread, for several different spread-durations. (The overall level of interest rates is assumed to remain constant.) The larger the spread-duration, the steeper is the slope, reflecting the greater responsiveness of the portfolio value to changes in yields in the corporate sector as a whole. We refer to the corporate sector of the Salomon Brothers Broad Investment-Grade Bond Index[SM] (Broad Index) as a proxy for this corporate sector as a whole.

For a portfolio consisting entirely of bonds from a single homogeneous credit sector, the spread-duration will be proportional to the ordinary modified duration. The constant of proportionality, or "spread beta," will reflect the relative sensitivity of each subsector's yield spread to changes in the Broad Index corporate spread. In general, the spread betas for individual subsectors will tend to vary inversely with the quality level: Lower-grade credits will have a larger

Exhibit 1: The Spread-Duration Concept

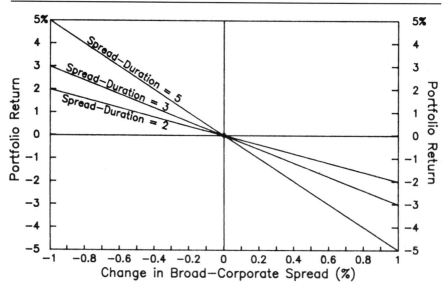

Exhibit 2: Spread-Duration for Various Credit Sectors

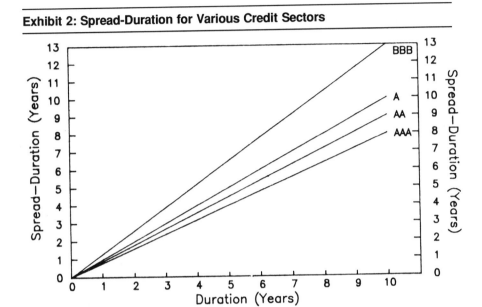

beta value. This relationship is depicted in Exhibit 2, in which we have taken beta values of 0.8, 0.9, 1.0, and 1.3, for AAA, AA, A, and BBB sectors, respectively. This implies, for example, that a portfolio consisting solely of AA-rated bonds with a modified duration of 5 years would have a spread-duration of 5.0 years × 0.9 = 4.5 years.

It is possible in principle (and desirable in application) to partition the corporate sector into smaller subsectors and then to determine the spread-duration of each subsector. However, for illustrative purposes, we will deal only with the above four aggregated rating classes.

From the duration and spread-duration, we can approximate the expected response of the portfolio to any combination of yield curve shifts and changes in the corporate spread. Assume, for example, that the yield curve shifts down by 100 basis points, while the corporate spread narrows by 20 basis points. For a portfolio with a duration of 5 years and a spread-duration of 5 years, the approximate return would be 6.00% as follows:

$$5 \times 1.0 = 5.00\%$$
$$5 \times 0.2 = \underline{1.00\%}$$

Approximate Return   6.00%.

Exhibit 3: Simple Portfolio of 100% A-Rated 5-Year Duration Bonds

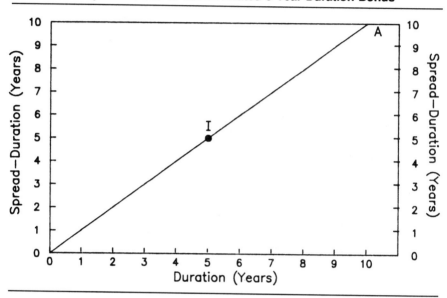

Exhibit 4: Credit Barbells Across Duration

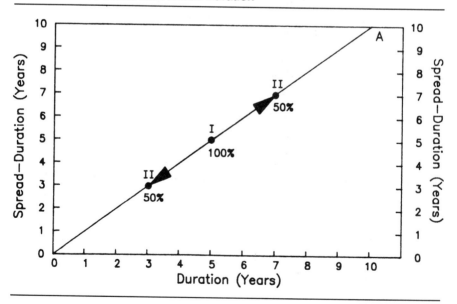

CREDIT BARBELLS ACROSS DURATION

A portfolio manager will often have specific targets for the sensitivity of the portfolio to changes in the level of interest rates and to changes in the corporate spread. These targets translate into values for the duration and spread-duration. However, there is usually a wide spectrum of vastly different portfolios that can satisfy any given duration and spread-duration target. For example, suppose a manager wants to maintain a 5-year duration and a 5-year spread-duration. Since the sector "beta" for A-rated corporates is taken to be 1.0, the portfolio manager could invest entirely in 5-year A-rated bonds. This would correspond to the homogeneous Portfolio I shown in Exhibit 3.

There are many other nonhomogeneous portfolios—credit barbells—that have the same risk characteristics (identical values for the duration and the spread-duration). The simplest example is a portfolio that combines low-duration and high-duration bonds within a single rating sector. In Exhibit 4, Portfolio II is equally weighted between 3-year duration and 7-year duration A-rated bonds. This barbell has the same 5-year duration and 5-year spread-duration as the initial homogeneous Portfolio I, and thus the same exposure to interest rate and spread changes (though not necessarily to other forms of credit risk, particularly default risk).

CREDIT BARBELLS ACROSS RATING CLASSES

Another example of credit barbell is one in which bonds of different rating levels, but identical durations, are combined in proportions that achieve the intended spread-duration. In Exhibit 5, Portfolio III has a mix of 25% BBB-rated bonds and 75% AA-rated bonds, all having a 5-year duration. The portfolio maintains the 5-year duration and also retains the spread-duration of 5 years:

25% BBB	$0.25 \times 5 \times 1.3 = 1.625$
75% AA	$0.75 \times 5 \times 0.9 = \underline{3.375}$
Portfolio Spread-Duration	5.000.

It is not necessary to restrict a credit barbell to securities of a single duration or rating sector. In Portfolio IV, longer-duration AA-rated bonds are combined with shorter-duration BBB-rated bonds to obtain a portfolio with the same duration and spread-duration as in Portfolio I.

Exhibit 5: Credit Barbells Across Rating Classes

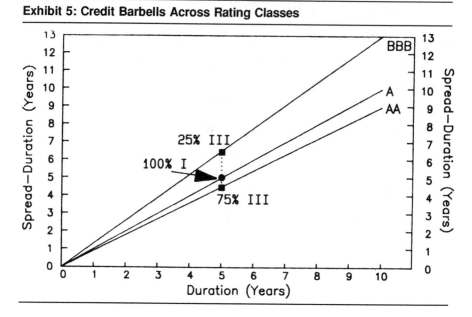

VARYING THE PROPORTION OF CORPORATE BONDS

Thus far we have examined portfolios that contain only corporate bonds. However, the same analysis applies to portfolios that combine corporate bonds with Treasury bonds. It should be evident that Treasuries have a spread-duration of zero. In Exhibit 7, Portfolio V has a duration of 5 years and a spread-duration of one year. The Treasury curve is depicted as a horizontal line corresponding to the Treasury's spread-duration of zero. The same duration/spread-duration levels as those of Portfolio V can be reached with Portfolio VI, comprised 80% of 5-year duration Treasury bonds and 20% of 5-year duration A-rated corporate bonds.

Exhibit 8 shows another alternative, Portfolio VII, which also achieves the same duration/spread-duration targets. This portfolio has 75% of its holdings in Treasury bonds with a duration of 5.33 years and 25% in A-rated bonds with a 4-year duration. This portfolio has a duration of 5 years.

75% Treasuries	$0.75 \times 5.33 = 4.00$
25% A-Rated Corporates	$0.25 \times 4.00 = \underline{1.00}$
Portfolio Duration	5.00,

and a spread-duration of 1 year,

Exhibit 6: Credit Barbells Across Rating and Duration

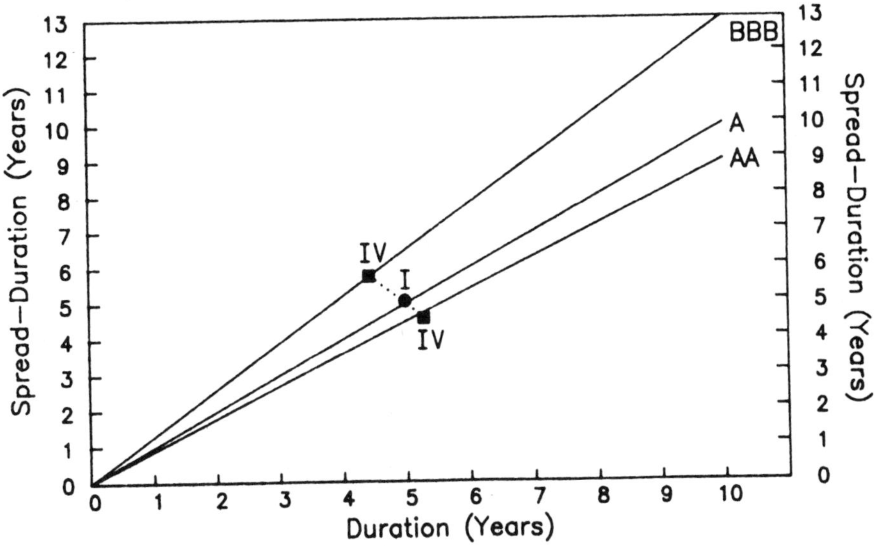

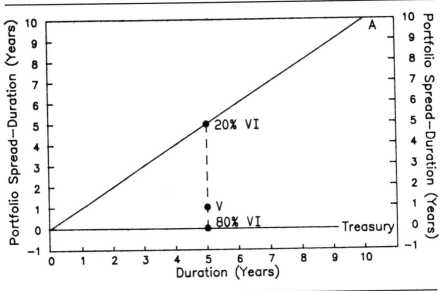

Exhibit 7: Combining Corporates and Treasuries with the Same Duration

Exhibit 8: Combining Corporates and Treasuries with Different Durations

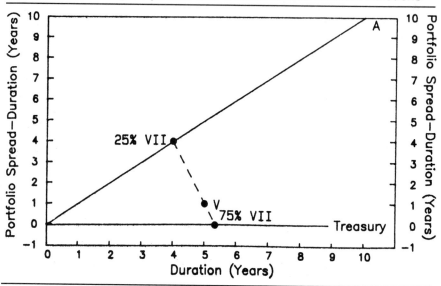

Exhibit 9: Alternative View of Varying Corporate Proportion

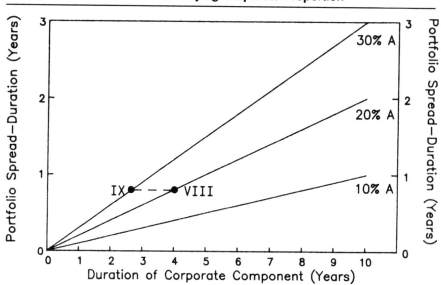

Exhibit 10: Varying Corporate Proportion and Credit Classes

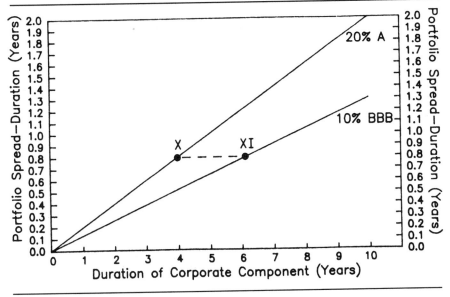

75% Treasuries	$0.75 \times 5.33 \times 0 = 0$
25% A-Rated Corporates	$0.25 \times 4.00 \times 1.0 = \underline{1.00}$

Portfolio Spread-Duration   1.00.

Exhibit 9 provides an alternative graphical representation of the effect of varying the proportion of corporate bonds. Portfolio VIII holds 20% in A-rated corporate bonds with a duration of 4 years and 80% in Treasury bonds with a 5-year duration, so that the portfolio duration is 4.8 years and the spread-duration is $(0.2 \times 4 \times 1.0) = 0.8$ years. By increasing the weighting of the corporate bonds to 30%, while decreasing their duration to 2.67 years, the spread-duration remains constant. If, at the same time, we increase the duration of the remaining Treasury bonds to 5.71 years, we obtain Portfolio IX, which maintains the overall duration at 4.8 years.

The portfolio manager can achieve further flexibility by altering the sector distribution within the overall corporate component. In Exhibit 10, the holdings of corporate bonds are changed from 20% A-rated with a duration of 4 years (Portfolio X) to 10% BBB-rated with a duration of 6.15 years (Portfolio XI). Under this change, the spread-duration remains constant at $0.1 \times 6.15 \times 1.3 = 0.8$

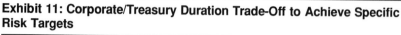

Exhibit 11: Corporate/Treasury Duration Trade-Off to Achieve Specific Risk Targets

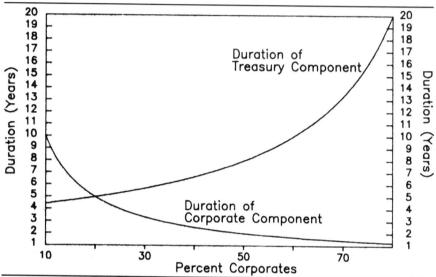

years. (To maintain the overall duration at 4.8 years, the duration of the Treasury component must then be decreased to 4.65 years.)

DURATION TRADE-OFFS

Exhibit 11 illustrates the trade-off between the durations of the corporate and Treasury components of the portfolio as the percentage of corporates increases, in order to hold both the duration and spread-duration constant at 5 years and 1 year, respectively. (For simplicity, the corporate sector is assumed, in this example, to have a spread beta of 1.0.) When the percentage of corporates is very small, the duration of the corporate component must be correspondingly large to achieve any desired spread-duration. At this point, the duration of the Treasury component will be nearly equal to the difference between the desired portfolio duration and the desired spread-duration. On the other hand, when the percentage of corporates is very large, the duration of the corporates itself approximates the spread-duration, and the duration of the Treasury component must swing widely in the appropriate direction to bring the overall duration into line.

CONCLUSION

In general, the preceding examples show how a portfolio manager can allocate assets over a wide range of rating sectors and durations, while maintaining constant levels of interest rate and credit-spread risk over the short term. This flexibility enables the manager to explore a spectrum of equal-risk portfolios in order to choose the one that best meets other objectives, such as yield maximization. In actual applications, a portfolio manager would also want to consider long-term credit fundamentals in addition to the short-term spread volatility. However, it should be evident that the analysis and construction of credit barbells (or more generally, of "optimal" fixed-income portfolios) can be greatly facilitated through application of the spread-duration approach.

Chapter III E-4

Leverageability of Corporate Assets [1990]

What is the debt capacity of a corporation? How much leverage should a corporation have?

The complexity of the leveraging decision reflects, to a great extent, the myriad interrelated factors managers and creditors must consider. One useful approach to the problem, however, may be to break down the leveraging decision into some of its basic elements. This article addresses the debt-capacity decision primarily from the creditor's point of view, specifically dealing with the narrow question of the adequacy of a firm's cash flows to support various levels of debt financing.

The goal in this case is to see how the level and riskiness of a firm's cash flows influence the amount of debt a creditor would be willing to supply. The specification of a minimum threshold return and maximum shortfall probability can be used to define the maximum amount of leverage the firm's cash flows will support.

What is the debt capacity of a corporation? How much leverage should a corporation have? These questions continue to intrigue (if not plague) corporate managers, corporate creditors, potential creditors and academics, despite voluminous research on the subject.

Martin L. Leibowitz, Stanley Kogelman, and Eric B. Lindenberg, "A Shortfall Approach to the Creditor's Decision: How Much Leverage Can a Firm Support," *Financial Analysts Journal*, May/June 1990.

There is at least some agreement on the major factors that should help creditors decide when and how much to lend. For example, creditors should be interested in the riskiness of the cash flows that are expected to service a company's debt. But they should also focus on the nature of the company's assets, in particular their potential value and liquidity in the event of bankruptcy. In addition, the company's prospects for improving its credit and its ability to sell off assets at opportune times should affect the value of its outstanding debt instruments. In some cases, the available supply of debt capital can expand greatly, even when short-term operating cash flow is uncertain.

The corporate manager, in determining a desirable level of leverage, should consider the extent to which interest payments can receive favorable tax treatment. The manager should also anticipate both the restrictions on operations that creditors may impose when debt levels are high and the signals about a company's prospects that adding leverage sends to the market.

Each of these factors is important. Even taking one factor at a time, it is difficult to model a specific leveraging decision. When we recognize that any practical decision must consider all these factors simultaneously, we conclude that there is no single modeling tool that can adequately capture the elements of the leveraging decision and give us an "optimal" level of leverage. Useful insights can nevertheless be obtained by breaking down the leveraging decision into some of its basic elements and applying basic theory to the problem.

This article addresses the debt capacity decision primarily from the creditor's point of view. Specifically, we discuss only the question of the adequacy of a firm's cash flow to support various levels of debt financing. Our intention is to see how the level and riskiness of those cash flows influence the amount of debt that a creditor would be willing to supply. We recognize that this focused analysis will not produce "the" answer for a creditor, but we hope that we can promote a useful way of thinking about the problem.

Creditors find healthy, stable cash flows attractive, because predictable cash flows offer a high probability that debt payment obligations will be met. In the ideal case of certain cash flows, creditors would know exactly the amount of cash available for debt-servicing requirements. They would thus know exactly how much debt could be supported. But cash flows are always subject to volatility, and this must be taken into account. Creditors will typically permit a firm to borrow only to the extent that there remains a high probability that sufficient cash will be available to meet payment obligations, even under relatively adverse circumstances.[1]

This article first shows how specification of a creditor's minimum acceptable return and maximum "shortfall" probability can be used to define the maximum amount of leverage the firm's cash flows can support under the assumption of a

---

[1] As noted, asset quality, liquidity and the potential for improving credit also influence the credit-granting decision.

fixed debt rate. The assumption of a fixed debt rate is then relaxed, and we show how the shortfall approach can be extended to the general case, in which the debt rate increases with leverage. The impact of leverageability on the returns to tax-free investors is also considered.

AFTER-TAX RETURNS FOR LEVERAGED AND UNLEVERAGED FIRMS

A firm's basic source of funds for reinvestment and for payment to creditors and stockholders is its net cash flow from operations. The amount of this cash flow fluctuates in response to changing market conditions, and these fluctuations directly affect the firm's return on equity.

In the theoretical case in which the firm has zero debt, its after-tax return on equity (ROE) is the same as the return on assets (ROA) on an after-tax basis. Thus the ROA of the unleveraged firm provides a convenient benchmark against which to measure the effect of leverage on ROE. (See the appendix for a more complete description.)

When considering a leveraged firm, we assume that cash raised through debt issuance is used to repurchase equity at book value. The total assets of the firm thus do not change, but its outstanding liabilities become increasingly weighted toward debt. If there is no growth, and depreciation is always offset by reinvestment, the same total amount of assets remains in place.

The benefits of leveraging will depend on both the fraction of assets leveraged, h, and the after-tax debt rate, i.[2] Figure A illustrates two cases—the unleveraged firm and the 25% leveraged firm. The fact that the ROE line for the leveraged firm rises more rapidly than the line for the unleveraged firm illustrates a well-known principle: The greater the leverage, the greater the sensitivity of ROE to changes in ROA.

Figure A incorporates several additional features of leveraging. The intersection of the two lines when ROA is the same as the after-tax debt rate, i, is not accidental. If ROA is greater than i, borrowing is advantageous (that is, it results in a higher ROE), because it allows higher returns. Conversely, when i exceeds ROA, increased leverage leads to a decrease in ROE. When ROA is exactly the same as i, there is no advantage (or disadvantage) to leverage. Consequently, when ROA equals i, the ROE of both leveraged and unleveraged firms equals i. Because this result is true for any degree of leverage, it follows that all ROE lines must intersect when ROA equals the after-tax debt rate, i.

---

[2] In general, the cost of debt will increase with leverage. At this point, we make the simplifying assumption that i is constant. We further assume a single-period model with all debt having a maturity coincident with the end of the period.

Figure A: ROE versus ROA for Unleveraged and 25% Leveraged Firms

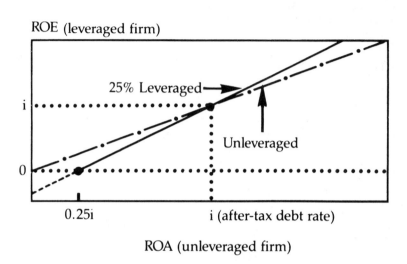

When ROA just equals the debt-service requirement, hi, there is no cash left to pay stockholders, and the ROE for the leveraged firm drops to zero.[3] Any further decrease in cash flow will result in a negative ROE, as indicated by the dashed portion of the leveraged ROE line in Figure A. In reality, the relationship in this region can become complicated once costs reach a level at which the firm is no longer taxable. At this point, however, we make the (somewhat unrealistic) assumption that tax losses can be utilized so that the net effective debt cost remains unchanged.[4]

THE IMPACT OF VOLATILITY ON RETURNS

So far, we have focused on the relation between the benchmark ROA and the ROE for the leveraged firm, assuming that those ratios can be measured with

---

[3] If A represents the firm's assets, the after-tax debt payment for the leveraged firm will be hiA. As a fraction of assets, this is just hi alone.

[4] In reality, when the firm earns negative ROEs (which becomes more likely with higher levels of leverage), it may be able partially to defer tax losses. In general, effective marginal tax rates begin to decline at high leverage limits.

certainty. Now we consider the implications of the fact that the basic ROA is volatile and uncertain.

In the absence of volatility, creditors would know whether there was sufficient cash to meet debt obligations, and stockholders would know their returns. In this case, the expected (average or mean) return and the realized return would always be identical. With volatility and uncertainty of returns, however, creditors need to assess not only the expected return, but also the likely minimal return.

As a simple representation of this uncertainty, suppose that ROA is normally distributed. The familiar bell-shaped curve, which describes the normal distribution, can be drawn knowing only the expected return, $\overline{ROA}$, and standard deviation (volatility) of returns, SD_A. The curve on the left in Figure B illustrates the ROA distribution for an unleveraged firm with an expected return of 14% and a standard deviation of 9%. The two vertical lines represent one standard deviation on either side of the expected 14% value. For the normal distribution, approximately 68% of the probability weight will be contained within these two lines.

How does this uncertainty affect the ROE of the leveraged firm? As we might suspect from the ROE-ROA relation depicted in Figure A, both the expected value and the shape of the ROE distribution change significantly. This is

---

Figure B: Return Distributions for Leveraged and Unleveraged Firms

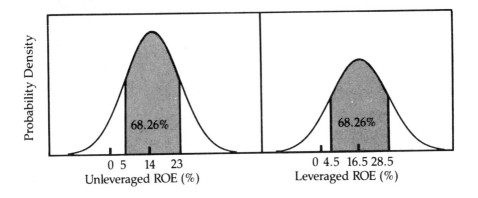

0 5 14   23
Unleveraged ROE (%)

0 4.5 16.5 28.5
Leveraged ROE (%)

illustrated by the right-hand curve in Figure B, which represents the ROE distribution for a firm that is 25% leveraged (h = 0.25).

The expected return and standard deviation for the leveraged firm are 16.50% and 12.0%, respectively.[5] Thus the return distribution for the leveraged firm is centered further to the right and is flatter and more spread out than the distribution for the unleveraged firm. The improvement in expected value (that is, the rightward shift) reflects the advantage of leverage when the expected value of ROA exceeds the after-tax debt costs. The greater volatility (that is, the widening of the distribution) is an intrinsic result of the steeper slope of the leveraged ROE line in Figure A. The leveraged firm offers both a greater likelihood of high returns and a greater probability of extreme values.

A SHORTFALL MODEL OF THE CREDITOR

Investors and creditors study the same return distributions from quite different perspectives. For the *investor*, the center of the distribution represents the return expected, while the distribution's dispersion serves as a gauge of the risks that must be tolerated. The procedure for finding an acceptable tradeoff between *investor* risk and return is well developed in the literature. The *creditor* has received less attention in financial theory. But with the increasing role that leverageability has played in determining the value (and, indeed, the very fate) of a firm in today's equity market, the creditor's role surely deserves more scrutiny.

Creditors are concerned with the timely payment of interest and principal. The promised debt rate is their maximum return.[6] Uncertainty, surprises and volatility in the firm's cash flows can only hurt them. Lower-than-anticipated cash flows can adversely affect the firm's ability to pay interest. Poorer-than-expected earnings can drain the liquidity base for principal repayments. And a bout of low returns can erode the valuation of the assets that support the firm's credit standing.

Thus creditors take a high negative view of volatility. More precisely, because the creditor does not benefit from positive surprises, he concentrates his

---

[5] We have assumed that the pretax debt rate is 10% and that the firm's marginal tax rate is 35%, so i = 0.65 × 10% = 6.50%.

[6] This assumes that creditors are, in essence, fixed income investors executing a buy-and-hold strategy. Secondary market trading can, of course, result in higher (or lower) returns than the promised debt rate.

attention on the left-hand side of the return distribution.[7] With a constant debt rate (which our basic model assumes at this point), the creditor's only decision is whether to lend. If the probability of adverse returns is too high, he will refuse to lend.

In this context, the key question becomes: What is the minimum return level (and the associated probability) at which a creditor will feel comfortable enough to lend? Choosing this cutoff criterion may be an involved process, and the answer may vary significantly from one corporate sector to another. We can, however, depict the structural *form* of the creditor's decision in terms of a basic "shortfall" model. This model assumes that a minimum ROE level can be determined, and that as long as there is an assurance that this ROE cutoff will be surpassed with some prescribed probability, the creditor will agree to make additional loans.

This simple model involves a "shortfall risk" constraint that has been used in many other investment situations.[8] Here, the shortfall constraint consists of a minimum ROE and the shortfall probability associated with a required level of assurance that the realized ROE will exceed this minimum.

We can express the creditor's criterion as the probability of exceeding a minimum ROE of zero. This return threshold is the point at which the company's operating profits just cover its annual interest costs. A cautious creditor would obviously require a very high probability that this condition be met. Thus, in our example, we set the probability of exceeding the minimum zero ROE at 90%; the probability of a shortfall is thus 10%.[9]

Using the return distributions given in Figure B, Figure C shows that, for the unleveraged firm, the probability of a shortfall below the zero ROE level is only 6%; equivalently, there is a 94% probability of achieving a positive ROE. This probability more than meets our assumed creditor's requirement; he would consequently be willing to lend to the unleveraged firm.

---

[7] From a broader perspective, we note that the upper tail could also be important to the creditor: Returns in this area, if they occur with sufficient frequency, can improve the firm's credit quality and enhance the value of its assets. The value of the creditor's position will improve in such a situation.

[8] See, for example, M.L. Leibowitz and W.S. Krasker, "The Persistence of Risk: Stocks versus Bonds over the Long Term," *Financial Analysts Journal*, November/December 1988; M.L. Leibowitz and T.C. Langetieg, "Shortfall Risks and the Asset Allocation Decision: A Simulation Analysis of Stock and Bond Profiles" (Salomon Brothers Inc, January 1989); and M.L. Leibowitz and R.D. Henriksson, "Portfolio Optimization with Shortfall Constraints: A Confidence-Limit Approach to Managing Downside Risk," *Financial Analysts Journal*, March/April 1989.

[9] The 0% ROE threshold facilitates the schematic development of the "shortfall" approach. However, more general criteria for the creditor's decision—such as achieving one or more debt coverage limits with a prescribed probability—can be analyzed readily within this shortfall context.

Figure C: Shortfall Probabilities for Leveraged and Unleveraged Firms

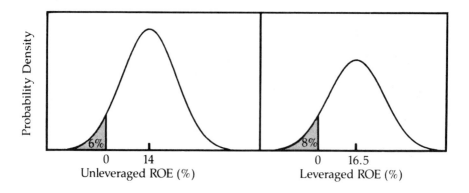

As the right-hand curve in Figure B showed, however, the act of borrowing itself affects the firm's return distribution in a fundamental way—it increases the spread of the distribution. In general, this wider spread will increase the probability of a return falling below the threshold return. The right-hand curve in Figure C shows that the shortfall probability grows to 8% for a 25% leveraged firm. Because this probability is still below the 10% limit, the creditor would presumably be willing to continue lending funds.

Lending would continue until leveraging and the consequent spreading of the ROE distribution result in a 10% probability of negative returns. At this point, the shortfall constraint has been reached, and the creditor would decide not to lend any more. For the firm, in this simple example, this is the point of maximum leverage.[10]

---

[10]See H. Hiller and C. Douglas Howard, "Floating-Rate Exposure: Fine-Tuning the Capital Structure" (Salomon Brothers Inc, June 1989) for an application of the use of a shortfall analysis in the determination of a level of floating-rate exposure that is consistent with a company's target leverage. The authors allude to the concept of shortfall risk from the corporate manager's perspective.

THE RISK-RETURN RELATIONSHIP FOR LEVERAGED FIRMS

The concept of a "firm line," in conjunction with a shortfall constraint, provides a straightforward analytical means for determining the maximum allowable leverage. This is done within the risk-return framework commonly used in the capital markets.

We have already seen that uncertain cash flows subject both leveraged and unleveraged firms to return variability or risk. This risk applies to both creditors and investors. We use the expected after-tax on equity, ROE, as our return measure and the standard deviation of those returns, SD_E, as our risk measure. In general, in efficient markets, higher returns cannot be achieved without accepting a higher level of risk. In particular, a leveraged firm will have both a higher risk and a higher expected return than it would if it were free of debt (see Figure D).

The general relationship between the points depicted in Figure D is close to what one would expect. However, it turns out that, with a constant debt rate, a single firm's risk-return trade-offs at all leveraged levels will plot along a *straight line*. (A derivation of this result is given in the appendix.) This result proves to be quite useful in determining maximum leverage.

Figure E shows the "firm line," which represents the risk-return relationships for the leveraged firm. The firm line always intersects the return axis at

Figure D: Return versus Risk for Unleveraged and Leveraged Firms

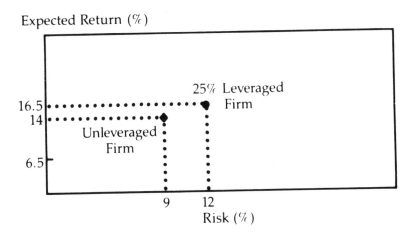

Figure E: The Firm Line: The Risk-Return Tradeoff for the Leveraged Firm*

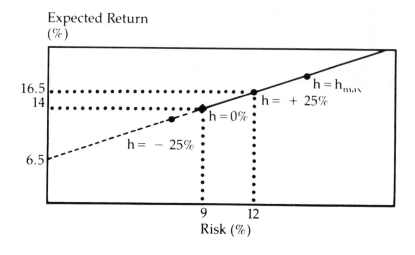

* h is leverage as a percentage of firm assets.

the level of the after-tax debt rate (in our example, 6.50%), and it always passes through the "unleveraged firm point," representing the risk and expected return of the unleveraged firm (9% and 14%, respectively, in our example). The firm line can thus be drawn without resorting to complicated technical details. Later, we will combine the firm line, which represents the range of risk-return possibilities available to the firm, with the shortfall concept to model the creditor's point of view.

Every possible risk-return combination attainable through leverage is represented by a point on the firm line. Because greater leverage leads to greater risk and higher expected return, more highly leveraged firms are found further out along the firm line. For example, the 25% leveraged firm (with a standard deviation of 12.0% and an expected return of 16.5%) lies above the unleveraged firm point.

The dashed portion of the firm line represents the unleveraged firm plus a cash investment with a yield that coincides with the debt rate. Here, leverage is considered negative, and the expected return on the firm's equity drops below that of the unleveraged firm. The ultimate state of negative leverage is the point at which *all* the firm's assets consists of cash investments. This corresponds to the after-tax debt rate (6.50%) on the vertical axis in Figure E. Negative leverage (or lending) may be particularly disadvantageous to tax-free investors, as noted below.

THE FIRM LINE AND TAX-FREE INVESTORS

Suppose that a tax-free investor has only two investment alternatives—to invest in the unleveraged firm or to invest at a pretax rate, i*, that corresponds to the firm's pretax debt rate. Such an investor can always do better by keeping part of his own assets in cash, rather than investing in the firm when it maintains a cash position, because the firm pays taxes on interest income, while the tax-free investor obviously does not. Thus the tax-free investor gains a tax benefit that is not available to the taxable firm.

In contrast, investment in the leveraged firm is more attractive to the tax-free investor than borrowing at rate i* and investing in the unleveraged firm. This is because the firm receives a tax benefit from leverage that is unavailable to the tax-free investor. Figure F compares the risk-return tradeoffs available to the investor with those available to the firm. This illustrates that leveraged firms are likely to be more attractive to tax-free investors than unleveraged firms with permanently large cash positions. The practical significance of this observation

Figure F: The Tax-Free Investor Line and the Firm Line

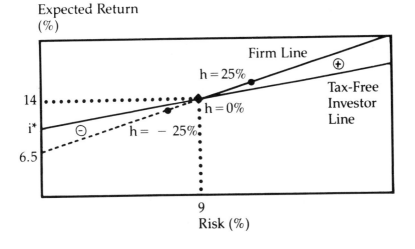

becomes increasingly important as certain sectors of the equity market become dominated by tax-free institutional investors.

THE SHORTFALL LINE

We can now locate a point of maximum leverage, using our example of a firm with an expected return of 14% and a standard deviation of 9%. We already know that the probability of negative returns is 6% when the firm is unleveraged and 8% when the firm is 25% leveraged. If lenders are willing to tolerate a shortfall probability that is higher than 8% (for example, up to 10%), the firm should be able to increase leverage beyond 25%. To see by how much leverage can be increased, we must study the shortfall constraint in more detail.

In a risk-return diagram, our hypothetical unleveraged firm will plot as the point shown in Figure G. The horizontal line drawn through this point intersects the vertical axis at 14%. In fact, all the points along this line correspond to hypothetical firms with an expected ROE of 14%, regardless of their volatility. As a result of the symmetry of the assumed normal distributions, *all* the hypothetical firms that lie on the horizontal line have one feature in common: The probability that they will provide a return below 14% is exactly 50%. We could say that all

---

Figure G: The 50% Shortfall Line

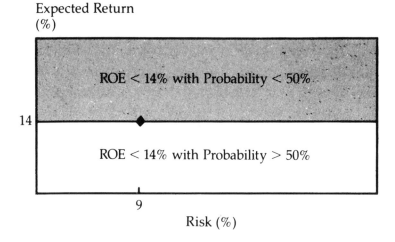

Expected Return
(%)

ROE < 14% with Probability < 50%

14

ROE < 14% with Probability > 50%

9

Risk (%)

firms along this horizontal line have a shortfall probability of exactly 50% relative to a 14% ROE threshold.

Now consider the hypothetical firms in the shaded region above the horizontal line. Each such firm has an expected ROE greater than 14%. Thus every firm that falls within this shaded region will, with *greater than 50%* probability, provide an ROE of *at least* 14%.

In other words, this horizontal line serves to divide the risk-return space into two regions. The area above the line contains firms that exceed the shortfall constraint at a 50% probability and 14% ROE limit. All firms below the line will not satisfy this constraint. We can refer to this dividing line as a "50% shortfall line."

Using the same procedure, we can locate all firms for which there is at least a 90% probability that returns will be positive. For normal distributions, we can show that all such firms will be found above a line with slope 1.282 emanating from the zero point of the risk and return axes.[11] Figure H illustrates this "shortfall line." All firms with risk-return combinations that fall above this line will have at least a 90% chance of achieving positive returns. All points below the line represent risk-return combinations that lead to a more than 10% chance of failing to achieve a positive return.

Recall that this shortfall constraint was designed to represent the creditor's decision criterion. As long as a firm provided a positive ROE with a probability of 90%, additional loans would be extended. Thus any firm plotting on or above the shortfall line is a viable candidate for further leverage.

Recall that the firm line represents all possible degrees of leverage for the given company, while the shortfall line represents risk-return combinations that meet the creditor's shortfall constraint. To locate the point of maximum leverage for the firm, we merely have to combine these two lines. The point of intersection of these two lines, as shown in Figure I, has exactly the characteristics we are seeking; it represents the firm with the maximum leverage that is consistent with the shortfall constraint.

---

[11] This requirement is equivalent to the following:

$$P[(\widetilde{ROE} - \overline{ROE})/SD_E > (0.0 - \overline{ROE})/SD_E] = 0.90,$$

where SD_E is the standard deviation of the return on equity. Because the return distribution is normal, this requirement will be fulfilled if $(0.0 - \overline{ROE})/SD_E = -1.282$; that is, $\overline{ROE} = 1.282 SD_E$.

Figure H: The 10% Shortfall Line

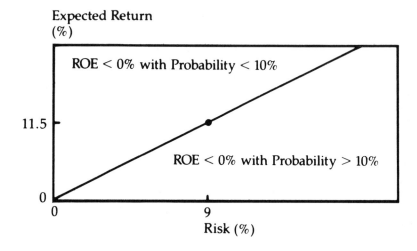

Figure I: Determination of Maximum Leverage

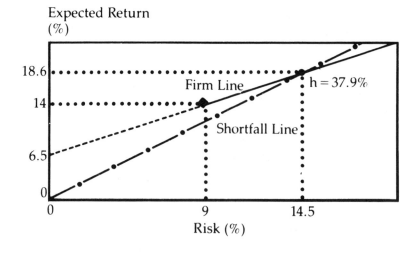

In our example, the maximum debt ratio is 37.9%, corresponding to a leveraged firm with an expected ROE of 18.6% and a volatility of 14.5%. These values are determined from the formulas that are derived in the appendix.[12]

MULTIPLE LAYERS OF DEBT

We have so far assumed that debt has only one form and that its rate and capacity are fixed. In practice, of course, the problem of debt capacity and optimal leverage is more complex. Debt takes on many forms, with varying maturities, seniorities and covenants. In general, the cost of additional debt will be an intricate function of the prior debt structure, as well as the form and magnitude of the added leverage. It is a formidable problem just to define an optimal debt structure within this broader (and more realistic) context.

As stated at the outset, this article does not attempt to address the overall debt structure problem. It may be useful, however, to provide an indication of how the shortfall approach can be extended to the case in which there are multiple layers of debt.

Suppose that the first debt layer consists of the highest-grade debt; the senior-creditor lends at a 10% pretax rate (6.5% after taxes) and will extend credit to the point of a 10% shortfall probability.[13] As we saw in the preceding example, this results in a maximum layer of senior debt amounting to 37.9% of the firm's assets. Now suppose that a more junior creditor is willing to extend additional loans at an 11% pretax rate (7.15% after taxes), as long as his shortfall probability remains below 15%.[14] It turns out that he would be willing to make additional loans amounting to a further 30.8% of the firm's assets. In this case, the firm's cumulative debt load would total 68.7%.

Figure J illustrates this hierarchy of debt. The first tranche of senior debt projects the risk-return profile to the point of intersection with the 90% shortfall line, exactly as shown in Figure I. The second tranche then projects this lever-

---

[12]The primary virtue of the shortfall approach is its simplicity. It does not, however, take advantage of richer theories of utility or partial moments. See, for example, W.V. Harlow and R. Rao, "Asset Pricing in a Generalized Mean-Lower Partial Moment Framework," *Journal of Financial and Quantitative Analysis*, September 1980, and V. Bawa and E.B. Lindenberg, "Capital Market Equilibrium in a Mean, Lower Partial Moment Framework," *Journal of Financial Economics*, November 1977. In addition, the shortfall approach is consistent with approaching the leverage decision within an option framework. See R.C. Merton, "On the Pricing of Corporate Debt: The Risk Structure of Interest Rates," *Journal of Finance*, May 1974.

[13]If senior debt is secured, the extent to which credit is extended may be more dependent on the collateral level than on the shortfall probability.

[14]There is a considerable body of literature on the precise nature of the debt rate function. See, for example, Merton, "On the Pricing of Corporate Debt," *op. cit.*

Figure J: Multiple Layers of Debt

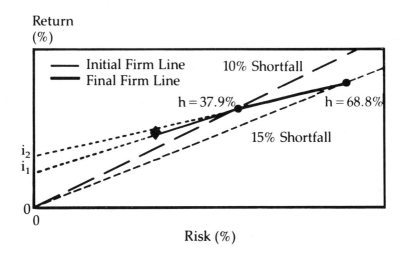

aged firm point along a ray that extends from the 7.15% debt rate on the vertical axis. The intersection of this ray with the line for a 15% shortfall constraint gives the risk-return position for the doubly leveraged firm.

The pattern traced by the firm's leveraging has several intersecting implications. First, it provides an indication of how the shortfall analysis might be expanded to include a fuller hierarchy of debt instruments. Second, it suggests a means of addressing the more realistic situation in which the cost of debt is not constant over incremental layers. By shrinking the size of the debt layers depicted in Figure J, we can see how a more analytical approach can be developed for the case in which the debt rate is a continuously increasing function of the debt level.

Finally, Figure K provides a schematic representation of the results of leveraging beyond the two debt layers described above. With ever-increasing debt costs, the slope of the new firm line becomes lower and lower. The process will eventually lead to a "firm curve." Such a curve has the property that, with each increment of increased leverage, the firm must accept an increasingly large increment of risk. Thus the theoretically "best" point of leverage could be found through various optimization criteria, and this optimal leverage point would fall significantly short of the firm's ultimate debt capacity.

Figure K: The "Leveraging Curve"

Return
(%)

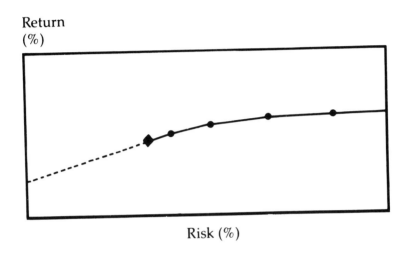

Risk (%)

CONCLUSION

We have presented a simple model, based on the concept of shortfall risk, to gain insight into a creditor's determination of how much debt to supply to corporate borrowers. At first, borrowing increases both the firm's return on equity and the volatility of that return. Consequently, the risk increases that the borrower will fail to cover required interest payments. When the probability of shortfall becomes unacceptable, the creditor either stops lending or increases the rate charged.

Our model enables us to calculate how much debt will be offered and provides a procedure for determining how that offered amount will change as a function of interest costs. We hope that this analytical model, with its intuitive orientation, will lead to a deeper appreciation of the creditor's perspective and its increasingly important role in today's financial markets.

Appendix

To model variable cash flows, we make the simplifying assumption that fluctuations are unpredictable and that the after-tax return on assets (RÕA) of an unleveraged firm is normally distributed with mean $\overline{ROA}$ and standard deviation SD_A. We then assume that the structure of the firm is changed through borrowing, but that the total assets of the firm do not change. In addition, we assume that there is no growth and that depreciation is always replaced by reinvestment, so that the same amount of capital remains in place.

We use the following variables:

A = total firm assets,

i^* = pretax debt rate,

t = marginal tax rate,

i = after-tax debt rate and

h = fraction of assets financed with debt.

We then have the following relationships:

$i = (1 - t)i^*$ and after-tax debt cost $= hiA$.

The after-tax return on equity, RÕE, is found by subtracting the after-tax debt cost from RÕA • A and dividing this difference by the equity portion of assets, $(1 - h)A$:

$$\tilde{ROE} = (\tilde{ROA} - hi)/(1 - h).$$

or

$$\tilde{ROE} = (\tilde{ROA} - i)/(1 - h) + i.$$

Note that, for the unleveraged firm ($h = 0$), $\tilde{ROE} = \tilde{ROA}$. In addition, if the $\tilde{ROA}$ is the same as the after-tax debt rate, i, so is the $\tilde{ROE}$, regardless of the degree of leverage.

The above equations enable us to write $\overline{ROE}$, the mean return on equity, in terms of $\overline{ROA}$:

$$\overline{ROE} = E[\tilde{ROE}] = E[(\tilde{ROA} - i)/(1 - h) + i],$$

$$\overline{ROE} = (\overline{ROA} - i)/(1 - h) + i. \tag{1}$$

Similarly, SD_E, the standard deviation of $\tilde{ROE}$, can be written in terms of SD_A. Because

$$SD_E^2 = E[(\tilde{ROE} - \overline{ROE})^2] = E[\tilde{ROA} - \overline{ROA})^2]/(1 - h)^2 ,$$

it follows that

$$SD_E = SD_A/(1 - h).$$

For example, if $h = 25\%$, $\overline{ROA} = 14\%$, $SD_A = 9\%$, $t = 35\%$ and $i^* = 10\%$, then $i = (1 - 0.35)10\% = 6.5\%$, $\overline{ROE} = 16.5\%$ and $SD_E = 12\%$.

We can now derive the relationship between $\overline{ROE}$ and SD_E by utilizing the fact that $SD_E/SD_A = 1/(1 - h)$. Thus Equation (1) can be rewritten as:

$$\overline{ROE} = mSD_E + i,$$

where

$$m = (\overline{ROA} - i)/SD_A.$$

If i is independent of h, the risk-return relationship can be graphed as a straight line emanating from the after-tax return point, i, on the return axis and passing through the unleveraged firm point $(SD_A, \overline{ROA})$. We call this line the "firm line."

THE SHORTFALL LINE

We wish to locate risk-return points that represent firms with returns that exceed some minimum return threshold, ROE_{min}, with probability k. This requirement can be expressed as follows:

$$P(\tilde{ROE} > ROE_{min}) = k.$$

This is equivalent to:

$$P[(\tilde{ROE} - \overline{ROE})/SD_E > (ROE_{min} - \overline{ROE})/SD_E] = k.$$

Because the quantity to the left of the inequality is a standard normal variate, we can determine a positive value Z_k (assuming $k > 50\%$) for the cumulative normal distribution such that

$$P(\tilde{ROE} > ROE_{min}) = k,$$

provided that

$$(ROE_{min} - \overline{ROE})/SD_E \le - Z_k,$$

or

$\overline{ROE} \geq ROE_{min} + Z_k SD_E$.

The above relationship is satisfied by all firms whose risk-return point lies above the "shortfall line," with slope Z_k emanating from the minimum return threshold point ROE_{min} on the return axis. For example, if $k = 90\%$, $Z_k = 1.282$.

DETERMINATION OF MAXIMUM LEVERAGE

The maximum leverage that can be achieved for a firm that satisfies a given shortfall constraint is determined from the intersection of the firm line and the shortfall line. To find h_{max} in terms of the required ROE_{min} and i, we must solve the following two equations for h:

$\overline{ROE} = (\overline{ROA} - i)/(1 - h) + i$ and

$\overline{ROE} = ROE_{min} + Z_k SD_A/(1 - h)$.

We obtain

$h_{max} = (\overline{ROA} - SD_A Z_k - ROE_{min}/(i - ROE_{min})$.

For example, for a 10% shortfall constraint ($k = 90\%$), $\overline{ROA} = 14\%$, $SD_A = 9\%$, $i = 6.5\%$ and $ROE_{min} = 0$, we find that $h_{max} = 37.9\%$.

PART III F

Financial Futures

Chapter III F-1

The Analysis of Value and Volatility in Financial Futures

1. INTRODUCTION: SOME CONCEPTS AND SEMANTIC DISTINCTIONS

The purpose of this study is to translate the language and concepts of financial futures into the portfolio and market context of the fixed-income manager. A generalized framework will be developed for viewing essentially *all forms* of financial futures contracts relating to interest-bearing securities. In striving for a high level of generality, we hope to gain a broader understanding of the potential role of financial futures in the portfolio management process.

For investors coming from the bond world into the realm of financial futures for the first time, there is often great confusion arising from the clash of terminology. In the futures world, the terminology has evolved from many years of experience with commodity futures. However, when dealing with interest-bearing securities that themselves have a specified maturity date, the opportunities for ambiguity and chaos become monumental. For example, the terms—"spread," "maturity," "basis," "carry," and even "cash"—all have important specific meanings in the commodity futures world. The problem is that they

Martin L. Leibowitz, "The Analysis of Value and Volatility in Financial Futures," New York University, Graduate School of Business Administration, Salomon Brothers Center for the Study of Financial Institutions, Monograph Series in Finance and Economics, Monograph 1981-1983.

also have very different meanings to the fixed-income investor. Even sophisticated investors in the financial futures market find themselves stumbling over the same terms because they are used in very different ways by different parties. Therefore, to develop a clear exposition of our generalized framework for financial futures, we have found it necessary to construct a more precise terminology. These new definitions are interwoven throughout the following sections.

A second source of confusion surrounding the subject of financial futures is the proliferation of multiple contracts, each with delivery terms that seem, at best, peculiar and, at worst, potentially ominous. Most studies attempting to explain futures delve ever more deeply into the nature, details, and special implications of each of these contract characteristics. This approach is akin to the close study of each tree within the proverbial forest. While necessary at some point in the learning process for newcomers to the forest, this approach often leads to overcomplication. In this study, we shall forgo discussion of the finer details associated with the different contract specifications and delivery mechanisms. When viewed in a generalized fashion, all financial futures can be seen as specific realizations of one basic concept.

This simple overview is, of course, a bit too simple. There are a number of complicating factors:

1. the initial and variation margin requirements for the financial futures;

2. the unavailability or even nonexistence of the deliverable security at a given point in time;

3. the fact that financial futures focus on specific Treasury securities at this point and hence, that a "basis risk" is involved in hedging against any other debt security;

4. multiple deliverable securities;

5. the potential issuance sometime hence of "better" delivery vehicles, etc.

While these real-life factors are intentionally set aside in this article, most of them can be incorporated into more sophisticated extensions of this study's basic approach.

To fully analyze futures contracts requires an interweaving of price effects with yield values. This problem is perhaps compounded by the natural tendency of participants in the futures markets to concentrate primarily on price effects and price spreads. While price is indeed the key yardstick by which contracts are bought and sold, and where the money is made or lost, it is *not* necessarily the driving force that determines activity in either the debt markets or the associated financial futures. In a sense, much of the development in this study represents an effort to embed financial futures into the context of the yield values and the yield curve associated with the underlying debt markets.

2. THE ANALYSIS OF VALUE IN FINANCIAL FUTURES

A key first step in our approach is to refine the traditional concept of the "basis" relationship between the cash security and the futures price. In the futures world, the "basis" is the price spread between the spot commodity and the futures contract. Our first step is to *split* this traditional price basis into two components: 1) a "carry-basis" reflecting the direct effect of debt market factors, and 2) a "value-basis" representing the theoretical advantage of the futures contract relative to the outright purchase of the underlying cash security. After having defined this *basis split* in terms of the conventional interpretation of the basis as a *price spread*, the second step is to translate this basis-splitting into the dimension of *yield spreads*. This analysis provides a natural way to embed the futures contract into the yield curve structure of the debt markets. A clearer picture then emerges of the behavior patterns of the futures contract in response to changing debt market conditions.

We shall proceed as follows below: As a first step we will separate conceptually (1) the acquisition of a futures contract for delivery of a given security from (2) the outright ownership of that security. To spell out the similarities and differences of these two approaches to acquiring assets (that is, to acquire the right to the cash flows generated by these assets), we shall compare directly the cash flows from the holding of futures and the cash flows from outright holding of securities. Included in these comparisons is the opportunity cost (or return) on the two different ways of holding assets.

The Delayed Delivery Situation

At the simplest level, a financial future is essentially a standardized contract providing for delayed delivery of a debt security. From this viewpoint, the financial future offers the portfolio manager a convenient way to buy (or sell) a debt security (or debt sector) without the necessity of having the cash in hand to accept immediate delivery.

As with the delayed delivery agreement, a futures contract allows an alternative method of purchasing a cash flow spanning a specified time period. To make the discussion more concrete, consider the numerical example posed in Figure 1. Suppose one wishes to make an investment over a 5-year period. In the bond market, the most natural response would be to consider a bond with a 5-year maturity. For purposes of the example, this "cash security" (in the terminology of the futures world) will be taken to be a 5-year 9% par bond. On the other hand, suppose that there exists a futures contract for the purchase of this same 9% bond, 2 years hence, at a price of 97. (It should be noted that this example consists of a strictly hypothetical futures contract, i.e., these simplistic contract terms do not correspond to any currently traded exchange contract.)

Figure 1: The Hypothetical Situation

Cash Security = 5-Year 9% Bond Priced at 100

Versus

Futures Contract:

1. Deliverable Security = 3-Year 9% Bond

2. Time to Delivery = 2 Years

3. Futures Price = 97

A. The Futures Contract

Figure 2 shows the cash flow associated with the direct purchase of the underlying instrument—the 5-year 9% par bond. In this case, the investor hands over his initial purchase funds at the outset, and then immediately begins to receive the full cash flow from the bond. On the other hand, the futures contract enables the same 9% coupon flow to be purchased, but on a 2-year delayed delivery basis. (In this example, it is assumed that the 3-year 9% bond is the unique deliverable security. This immediately avoids many of the complications in-

Figure 2: The Cash Security

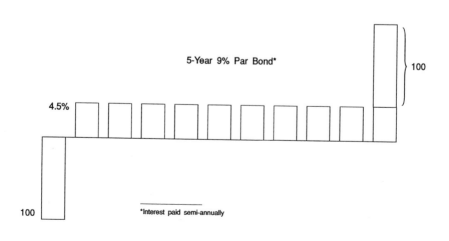

5-Year 9% Par Bond*

100

4.5%

100

*Interest paid semi-annually

Figure 3: The Futures Contract

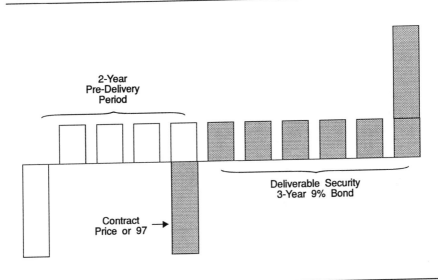

2-Year Pre-Delivery Period

Contract Price or 97 →

Deliverable Security 3-Year 9% Bond

volved in analyzing specific contracts.[1]) In Figure 3, the cash flow associated with this delayed delivery purchase is superimposed on the cash security's flow.

There are three key differences in the cash flow between the delayed delivery situation and the outright purchase: 1) the actual purchase price is different (i.e., 97 for the delayed delivery); 2) the purchase amount is not paid until the delayed delivery point; and 3) the 9% cash flow derived from the instrument is not received until after delivery.

One is tempted immediately to decide that the delayed delivery route provides the better value. After all, the investor saves 3 points in the purchase price and is spared the need to come up with the purchase money for a period of 2 years.

The Front-End Rate

However, because of structural differences in their respective cash flows, delayed delivery cannot be directly compared with outright purchase. In order to

---

[1] Moreover, this simplification is replicated in real-world futures trading of GNMA contracts where a multiplicity of rates is converted to a single 8% contract rate.

Figure 4: The Front-End Bond

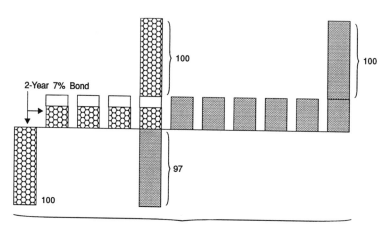

2-Year 7% Bond

100

97

100

100

Purchase of 5-Year Cash Flow Via The Front-Ended Future

achieve a comparable basis for evaluation, the delayed delivery cash flow must somehow be transformed into an equivalent cash flow that spans the same 5-year period as that associated with the outright purchase.

This comparison is achieved by presuming that the cash needed to fund the delayed delivery can be immediately put to work at some rate for the pre-delivery period. In other words, the investor is presumed to buy a bond with a maturity that precisely matches the delivery date. When this bond matures, the maturing proceeds will then be used to help fund the settlement of the delayed delivery agreement.

For our example, this "front-end bond" is assumed to consist of a 2-year 7% par bond. The combination of a 2-year "front-end bond" together with the delayed delivery leads to the combined cash flow shown schematically in Figure 4. The investor has, in essence, purchased a blended "2-stage" instrument having the same maturity as the original investment. Over the pre-delivery period, it provides the 7% "front-end" rate. At the point of delivery, the investor receives a 100-point payment of maturity proceeds from the front-end bond. This payment more than covers the 97 point takedown price for the delayed delivery contract. Following delivery, the 9% cash flow is identical to that of the underlying instrument. This blended 2-stage cash flow from the "front-end" futures contract can now be theoretically evaluated in terms which are directly comparable with that of the underlying instrument.

B. The Rate of Return

The Carry Spread

The futures/cash problem has thus been characterized in terms of two alternative routes to purchasing a cash flow over the same 5-year period. The comparison of these two alternative cash flows is facilitated by examining the "net flow" showing their period-by-period differences. In Figure 5, this net flow is shown in terms of the advantage of the front-ended futures contract over the cash security. In terms of the relative advantage for the futures route, this net cash flow consists of two distinct components: 1) a net interest "cost" of 2% per year over the 2-year pre-delivery period, and 2) a "revenue" gain of 3 points from the lower purchase price for the futures contract. These two components have specific names in the futures world. The first component reflects the extent to which the cash security's 9% interest rate exceeds the 7% front-end rate. In the classic "short-hedge" arbitrage situation, this difference corresponds to the net interest cost to "carry" the long cash position. For this reason, this net rate spread of 2% is often called the "carry spread."

The carry spread is said to be "positive" when the cash security yield exceeds the front-end rate (i.e., the financing rate in the "short-hedge" situation). At first, this terminology may be confusing since Figure 5 indicates that a *posi-*

Figure 5: Net Cash Flow for Long Futures Contract

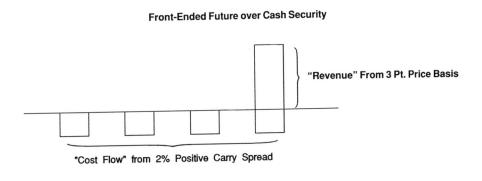

Front-Ended Future over Cash Security

"Revenue" From 3 Pt. Price Basis

"Cost Flow" from 2% Positive Carry Spread

tive carry spread would have a negative effect on the value of the futures contract. However, it must be remembered that this terminology is adopted from the "short-hedge" situation, a basic arbitrage in which a short position is established with respect to the futures contract. Thus, the positive carry which helps the short hedger becomes disadvantageous to the investor seeking to evaluate the futures contract in terms of a long position.

The Price Basis

The second component of net flow in Figure 5—the price difference of +3 points—is, of course, just the traditional "price basis" between the cash security and the futures contract. (To be precise, we define the price basis to be the extent by which the price of the cash security exceeds that of the futures contract.)

The relative advantage of the front-ended future then becomes the extent that the accumulated "cost" of the positive carry spread exceeds the "revenue" gained as a result of the price basis. This profit analysis is depicted in more detail in Figure 6. The positive carry spread of 2% for 2 years accumulates to 4 points (in the simple-interest procedure that we have adopted here for the sake of clarity). The only "revenue" to offset this cost is the raw price basis of 3 points.

Figure 6: Revenue and Costs from Front-Ended Future Relative to Cash Security

---

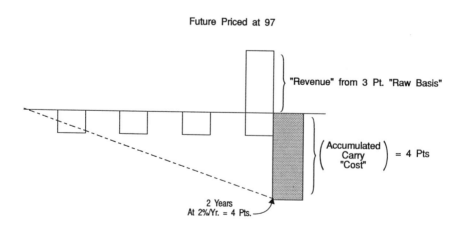

Future Priced at 97

"Revenue" from 3 Pt. "Raw Basis"

$\left(\begin{array}{c}\text{Accumulated} \\ \text{Carry} \\ \text{"Cost"}\end{array}\right) = 4\ \text{Pts}$

2 Years
At 2%/Yr. = 4 Pts.

Thus, in spite of its apparent appeal, the front-ended futures contract is inferior to the cash security as a 5-year investment. This means that the futures contract is overpriced at 97.

Relative Value and the Raw Basis

This example illustrates a common problem with financial futures. A financial future can often look cheap when it is not. This false impression results because one tends to grasp upon the price basis as being a pure advantage to the futures contract. As we have just seen, this advantage from a positive price basis should always be evaluated in the context of implied costs associated with the carry spread over the pre-delivery period. In other words, the relative value of any financial future must always be evaluated in the broader context of other debt market factors.

Example of a Cheaper Futures Contract

The preceding example raises the question: what price basis is needed for the futures contract to begin to be advantageous? From Figure 6, it should be clear that a break-even situation will exist when the revenue from the price basis covers the accumulated costs from the carry spread. Thus, in this example, a price basis of 4 points is needed for break-even. This result defines a futures break-even price of 96.

From this point forward, we wish to explore the situation where the futures contract enjoys a relative advantage over the cash security. We shall achieve this by changing our numerical example so that the futures contract is priced at 94. This revised example leads to the net cash flows depicted in Figure 7. Since the futures price was chosen to be 2 points below the break-even futures price of 96, it should be no surprise that the futures contract now has an advantage of 2 points.

3. COMPARING THE TWO MARKETS

Splitting the Price Basis

At this point, it becomes helpful to introduce the concept of "basis splitting." In the new example, the price basis is:

$$100 - 94 = +6 \text{ points.}$$

Figure 7: Carry-Basis as Price Spread

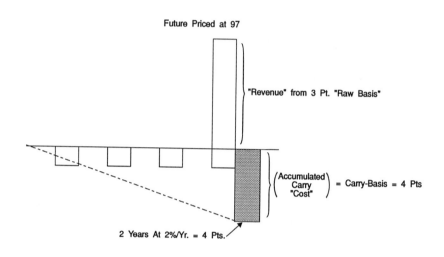

Future Priced at 97

"Revenue" from 3 Pt. "Raw Basis"

$\left(\begin{array}{c}\text{Accumulated}\\ \text{Carry}\\ \text{"Cost"}\end{array}\right)$ = Carry-Basis = 4 Pts

2 Years At 2%/Yr. = 4 Pts.

This "raw" price basis can now be viewed as consisting of two components. The first component—which we shall call the "carry-basis"—is the accumulated costs associated with the carry spread. In the example, this carry-basis amounts to +4 points.

The second component must then have a numerical value of +2 points. Moreover, it obviously represents the extent to which the revenues exceed the costs associated with pursuing the front-ended futures contract over the cash security. Thus, the second component of the raw price basis reflects the relative advantage of the futures contract. The larger this component, the better value represented by the futures contract. For this reason, we call this second component the "value-basis."

The value-basis is defined so that positive values reflect an increased incentive to go long futures relative to the cash security. A large positive value-basis means that the futures are cheap relative to the cash security. This basis split is further illustrated in Figure 8. It should be remembered that all the preceding examples have been developed using simple interest calculations for purposes of clarity. While this procedure simplifies the explanation of the key concepts, the precise calculations require appropriate time-valuing of the cash flows being compared.

Figure 8: Relative Value in Long Futures Contract

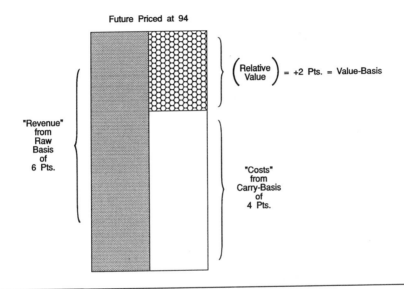

Future Priced at 94

$\left(\begin{array}{c}\text{Relative}\\\text{Value}\end{array}\right) = +2$ Pts. = Value-Basis

"Revenue" from Raw Basis of 6 Pts.

"Costs" from Carry-Basis of 4 Pts.

The Yield of the Futures Contract

As noted at the outset, most trading in the futures market is based upon direct price quotations. Nevertheless, one can define the yield value for futures contracts with an assumed deliverable instrument. The yield value can be very illuminating in tracing out the futures relationship to the debt market as a whole.

The yield of a financial future is simply the conventional bond yield-to-maturity for the cash flow derived from the deliverable instrument priced at the contract price. Thus, for the present numerical example, the futures yield would be the yield-to-maturity of a 3-year 9% bond priced at 94, i.e., the futures yield would be 11.42%

The ability to determine the futures yield opens the door to a new yield-related interpretation of the "basis" concept.

The Yield Basis

The basis as a yield spread will be defined as the futures yield over the yield of the cash security. Thus, in the example, the futures yield of 11.42% over the cash

Figure 9: Raw Basis as Yield Spread

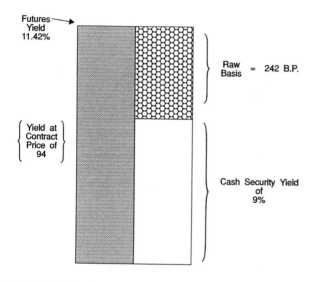

Futures Yield 11.42%

Raw Basis = 242 B.P.

Yield at Contract Price of 94

Cash Security Yield of 9%

security 9% yield results in a yield-basis of 242 basis points. This example is depicted schematically in Figure 9.

The break-even approach can then immediately be extended into the yield dimension. As noted earlier, a break-even situation results when the price basis matches the carry-basis, i.e., the accumulated costs of the carry spread. In the example at hand, this led to a break-even futures price of 96. One can then proceed to define a break-even futures yield as the yield corresponding to this price level. At this break-even price of 96, the break-even futures yield turns out to be 10.59%. Thus, the futures contract will precisely cover its carry costs when it yields 10.59% (Figure 10). At higher yields, the futures more than cover these carry costs and hence gain an advantage relative to a long position in the cash security.

It should be noted that the futures break-even yield is only one of three break-even computations that can be used in comparing the front-ended future with the cash security. There are three distinct debt instruments involved in the comparison: 1) the cash security; 2) the futures contract; and 3) the front-end rate. Any two of these elements can be used to determine a break-even level (price and/or yield) for the third element. The futures break-even yield is determined from the cash security yield and the front-end rate. Another break-even approach would be to develop the break-even front-end rate given the futures

Figure 10: Break-Even Futures Yield

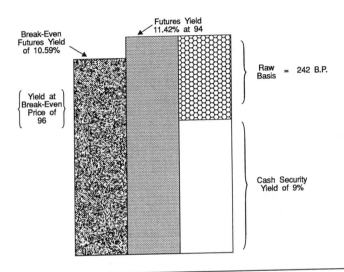

contract and the cash security. A third approach would result in a break-even value for the price/yield levels of the cash security. For the same set of values, all such break-even approaches naturally lead to the same conclusion with respect to the relative advantage of the front-ended futures. However, for our purposes in this study, we chose to work with the futures break-even value since it can be directly compared with the futures actual market level.[2]

Carry-Basis as a Yield Spread

A natural application of the break-even futures yield is to achieve a split of the yield-basis that is analogous to our earlier breakdown of the price basis. As illustrated in Figure 11, a break-even yield value of 10.59% means that the yield-basis must reach 159 basis points (i.e., 10.59% - 9.00%) just to break even. In other words, for any yield-basis less than 159 basis points, the futures contract will not offer a sufficient price advantage to cover carry costs and hence will not represent a positive value relative to the cash security. It is, therefore, a natural step to define the "carry-basis" component of the yield-basis to be this difference

---

[2] The break-even futures yield also has a number of interesting interpretations relating to the theory of implied "forward rates" as well as to the concept of the Rolling Yield.

between the futures break-even yield and the yield of the cash security. In a sense, the carry-basis serves to "calibrate" the yield-basis between the futures and the cash security.

Value-Basis as a Yield Spread

Thus, the structure of the yield-basis can be categorized in a fashion that is essentially identical to that of the price-basis. As depicted in Figure 11, the carry-basis of 159 basis points is needed just to achieve comparability with the cash security. The extent to which the total yield-basis exceeds the carry-basis then reflects the futures relative advantage. As before, this will be called the "value-basis." In the example in Figure 11, the value-basis is seen to be 83 basis points (i.e., 242-159). The value-basis can be said to express the futures relative advantage as a yield spread. Indeed, this was the motivation behind the choice of the expression "value-basis."

This ability to immediately "calibrate" the basis is a useful property. However, a perhaps even greater benefit to this approach is that it allows the futures yield to be embedded in the general yield curve context of the debt market.

Figure 11: The Carry-Basis and the Value-Basis as Yield Spreads

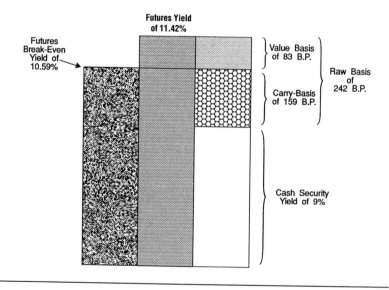

The Debt Market Context

This embedding process is illustrated in Figures 12 and 13. For simplicity, the cash security is assumed to plot directly on the yield curve. Similarly, the front-end rate available over the 2-year pre-delivery period is plotted at the 2-year point on the yield curve. (In a more general treatment, appropriate spreads off the yield curve could be used.) From these two plotted points, we can readily see that the carry spread depends on the shape of the yield curve.

The "basis-component" approach followed above provides for the financial futures yield to be directly compared with that of the cash security. For this and other reasons, it is most convenient to plot the futures yield at the same maturity point as that of the cash security (Figure 12).

The relevant yield spreads are then shown in Figure 13. In the preceding discussion, the carry-basis was determined to be 4 points (as a price spread) and 159 points as a yield spread. These values were derived from the *simple-interest* accumulation of the +2% carry spread over the 2-year pre-delivery period. This simple-interest approach was adopted at the outset for clarity of illustration. However, in order to achieve consistency, these calculations really should include compounding to reflect the time-value of money over the respective periods. Hence, from this point on, the examples will be amended so as to use compounded values for the carry-basis and the value-basis. In these revised

---

Figure 12: The Debt Market Context

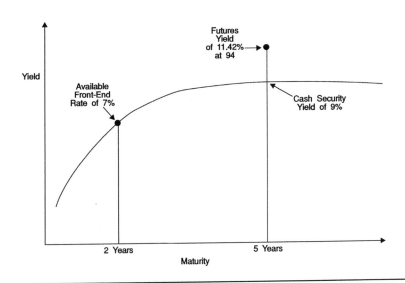

Figure 13: The Original Situation

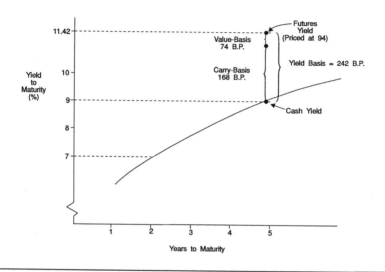

terms, the carry-basis has a price spread value of 4.21 points and a yield spread value of 168 points. The value-basis then becomes 1.79 points of price spread (i.e., = 6 - 4.21) and 74 basis points of yield spread (i.e., = 242 - 168).

Response Patterns of the Carry-Basis

For purposes of analysis, the carry-basis mirrors the *direct* effect of the other debt market factors on the futures price. Consequently, it will also mirror the effects of changes in underlying debt market factors. These relationships are outlined in Figure 14. Thus, a change in the shape of the yield curve will directly affect the carry spread. In turn, this will *directly* affect the carry-basis thereby influencing the futures yield and price. Parallel shifts in the yield curve will naturally shift the yield level of the cash security without affecting the carry spread. This can lead to *direct* changes in the futures yield. The passage of time shortens the pre-delivery time and this will directly lead to a reduced carry-basis. This leads to the "price convergence" effect that is well-known in all the futures markets. Actually, these statements provide a highly simplified view. As one takes into account the many complicating factors associated with both the futures contract and the debt market itself, the need for more refined analysis becomes quickly apparent.

Figure 14: Carry-Basis Response Patterns

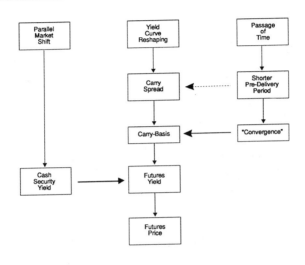

4. VOLATILITY CHARACTERISTICS OF THE FUTURES CONTRACT

The preceding sections showed how financial futures contracts on interest-bearing instruments could be embedded in the context of the traditional bond market yield curve. In essence, this was achieved by viewing financial futures as being related through a yield spread to the yield curve point for the underlying cash security. This section will explore how financial futures respond to changes in this yield curve context.

Yield curve movements can be analyzed in terms of two basic types of actions: (1) parallel market shifts, and (2) yield curve reshapings. This section demonstrates how these basic yield curve movements lead to two fundamentally different types of volatility behavior in the futures contract. It will then become evident that the volatility characteristics of the futures contract can be very different from that of the cash security. In particular, the futures contract can prove extremely sensitive to yield curve reshapings even when the cash security's yield remains unchanged. These results suggest that there is considerable danger in taking the futures contract as a simple surrogate for the volatility behavior of the cash security. (The futures contract closely approximates the cash security's volatility behavior only for the special case where the pre-delivery period is short compared with the post-delivery period—e.g., for near contracts on long Treasury bonds.)

A. The Parallel Market Shift

A parallel market shift is a movement in which every point on the yield curve immediately shifts by the same number of basis points. For example, Figure 15 illustrates the case where the yield curve shifts by +100 basis points at all maturities. In particular, this means that there will be a +100 basis point shift at the two maturity points that are relevant to the analysis of the financial futures—the delivery point at 2 years and the cash maturity at 5 years. If the cash security yield increases by +100 basis points under the parallel market shift, and if the yield-basis remains constant, *then* the futures yield will naturally increase by the same 100 basis points. This would lead to the simplest possible description of the futures behavior under market shifts.

However, one must ask whether the assumption of a constant yield basis is valid. The yield basis can be viewed in terms of its two components—the carry-basis and the value-basis. The carry-basis essentially reflects the added yield needed to compensate for positive carry spreads that could be attained through

Figure 15: Parallel Market Shift

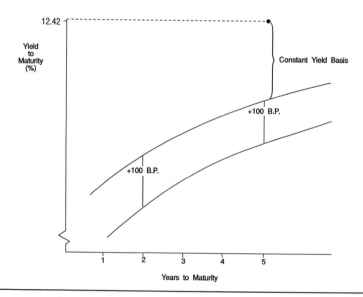

investment in the cash security over the pre-delivery period. For the simple case when both the cash security and front-end rate lie on the yield curve, the carry spread is determined by the shape of the yield curve. Since this shape remains unchanged (by definition) under parallel shifts, it follows that the carry spread will also remain constant under these moves. At first glance, this constancy in the carry spread would seem to provide a sufficient argument for expecting the carry-basis component of the yield basis also to remain constant. This argument is tempting and ultimately turns out to be a reasonable approximation of the facts. (However, a somewhat more complex analysis is needed to really prove this simple and intuitively appealing statement.)

Given that the carry-basis as a yield spread remains approximately constant under the parallel shift, one must then consider the situation with the value-basis component. The behavior of the carry-basis is fairly predictable by definition. By the same token, the value-basis was defined so as to capture all those effects which are *not* readily explained by the yield curve context alone. Hence, the dynamics of the value-basis are intrinsically more difficult to identify and characterize. Hence, for purposes of this article, we shall simply assume that the value-basis as a yield spread is not affected directly by any of the yield curve activity being discussed. In essence, this assumption enables us to focus on the more predictable patterns associated with the carry-basis.

Market Shift Volatility

With the carry-basis shown to be essentially constant and with the value-basis assumed to also remain unchanged, it immediately follows that the overall yield basis relationship between the futures and the cash security will remain stable during parallel shifts. This implies that every basis point of parallel market shift will induce an equal basis point change in the futures yield. In other words, a +100 basis point market shift leads to a +100 basis point change in the futures yield. This result enables the futures price to be directly related to the market shift as shown in Figure 16. In essence, the futures contract responds to market shifts in accordance with the price changes that would be associated with the deliverable instrument, i.e., a 3-year 9% bond.

It is interesting to note that the cash security will also respond to the market shift in a direct basis-point-for-basis-point fashion. In Figure 17, the price response associated with the cash security is superimposed upon that of the futures contract. Since the cash security responds in accordance with its 5-year maturity, there is naturally a greater price volatility associated with the cash security. This means that the *price basis* between the two securities must change under parallel market shifts, even when the *yield basis* between the futures and the cash remains constant. As shown in Figure 17, after a +100 basis point parallel shift, the price basis will shrink by approximately 1.5 points.

Figure 16: Futures Response to a +100 Basis Point Market Shift

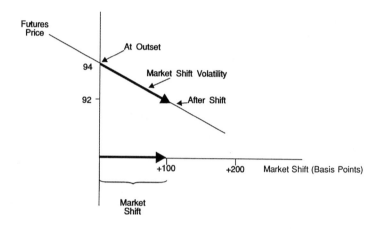

Figure 17: Changing Price Basis Under Market Shift

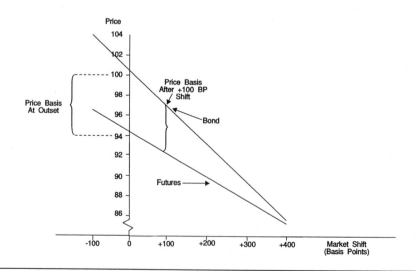

This differential in market shift volatility between the cash and the futures is an important consideration for potential investors in the futures market. To the extent that this differential exists, it represents a potential source of deviation in the price response between two instruments that may be superficially considered to be analogous investments. For investors who seek to match the volatility characteristics of the underlying cash instruments, it is important to consider the magnitude of this differential volatility and to try to compensate for it.

The magnitude of this volatility differential will diminish as the maturity of the deliverable instrument comes closer and closer to that of the underlying cash security. More precisely, whenever the maturity of the deliverable instrument is large relative to the pre-delivery period, the volatilities will start to closely approximate one another. Thus, on the one hand, near contracts in long Treasury bonds will exhibit very little differential volatility. On the other hand, 9-month contracts for 3-month Treasury bills will naturally exhibit large volatility differences relative to the corresponding 1-year cash security.

B. CHANGES AND YIELD STRUCTURE

Yield Curve Reshaping

Any changes in the *shape* of the yield curve will generally lead to changes in the carry spread. Since the carry-basis component of the futures/cash relationship is fundamentally determined by the carry spread, any change in the carry spread will have an important impact on the futures price behavior.

Figure 18 illustrates one of the simplest forms of yield curve reshaping—a snap-up affecting only the front-end interest rate. The yield curve here moves from a positive shape to a mildly inverted shape. The movement is anchored at the 5-year maturity, so that the yield of the cash security remains unchanged at 9%. The front-end rate, on the other hand, undergoes a snap-up of +250 basis points, moving from 7% to 9.50%.

This yield curve snap-up radically changes the prior relationship between the cash and the futures contract. In terms of a new investor evaluating his choice of alternatives for a 5-year investment, the futures route now offers a 9 1/2% front-end rate over the 2 years prior to delivery. This 9 1/2% rate exceeds by 50 basis points the 9% interest rate from a direct investment in the cash security. Thus, after the snap-up, a new investor finds himself with an initial *incentive* to pursue the futures route—as opposed to the *disincentive* in the prior situation when the yield curve was positively sloped. With the initial positive carry of +200 basis points, the futures contract had to be priced below the cash security in order to make it a relatively attractive alternative investment. However, when the yield curve is inverted, the negative carry spread becomes an

Figure 18: The Situation: 250 Basis Point Snap-Up

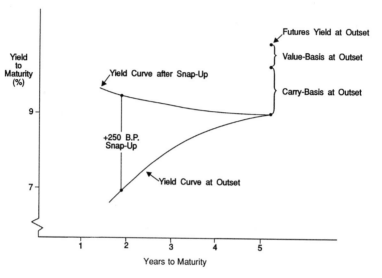

incentive and the futures contract could be priced somewhat above the cash security and still provide an attractive relative value.

Changing Carry Spreads

This situation is described more precisely through the sequence of net cash flows shown in Figure 19. Each of these cash flows represents the net advantage to an investor who decides to take the blended futures route over the direct purchase of cash security. The top figure recalls Figure 7. This figure represents the original situation of a +200 basis point carry spread, i.e., the futures route provides 200 basis points less yield than the cash security over the 2-year pre-delivery period. To overcome the accumulated "cost" of this lower yield, the futures must be priced below the cash security. This leads to the 4.21 point carry-basis in terms of price. The second cash flow shows the situation where the carry spread shrinks to +100 basis points per year. The shortfall in yield is now only +100 basis points over 2 years with the result that the carry-basis is reduced to 2.12 points. Similarly, when the carry spread is 0—corresponding to a flat yield curve—then the carry-basis will itself be 0. Finally, if the carry spread becomes a negative 50 basis points, then there will be a *benefit* to the futures

Figure 19: Changing Carry-Basis with Different Carry Spreads

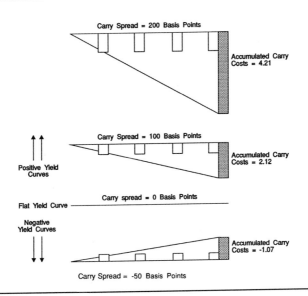

route over the 2-year pre-delivery period. The accumulated carry "cost" then becomes an accumulated carry "benefit." At a carry spread of -50 basis points, this accumulated benefit means that the futures can be priced 1.07 points over the cash security and still represent an equivalent value.

The sequence depicted in Figure 19 corresponds to the yield curve snap-up shown in Figure 18. The carry spread started out at +200 basis points. With the yield curve snap-up, the carry spread declined as the front-end rate moved through the 9% cash security yield to a final level of 9.50%. The 250 basis point *snap-up* in the yield curve thus leads to a 250 basis point *decline* in the carry spread. The net result is a carry spread of -50 basis points and an associated carry-basis of -1.07 points in price.

The effect of these changes in the carry spread is shown in Figure 20. At the original carry spread of +200 basis points, the carry-basis amounted to +4.21 points as a price spread (left-hand vertical axis). As the carry spread declines with the snap-up, the carry-basis also falls, eventually reaching zero points for a flat yield curve, and then continuing to drop until it reaches its final value of -1.07 points corresponding to the -50 basis point carry spread at the end of the snap-up. Since the carry-basis acts as a "cost" against the futures relative value, this *decrease* in the carry-basis leads to an *increase* in the futures price. In other words, the futures contract can be priced much higher and still represent a good

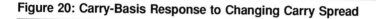

Figure 20: Carry-Basis Response to Changing Carry Spread

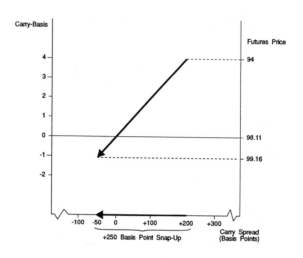

relative value when there is less of the adverse effects of a positive carry spread to be overcome. These corresponding price changes are shown on the right-hand vertical axis in Figure 20. (Since the value-basis is assumed to be constant as a *yield spread*, the futures price movement is also affected by small changes in the value-basis as a *price spread* at the different yield levels.)

The price responses of the futures contract and the cash security are directly compared in Figure 21. Since the price of the cash security remains constant at par, the price basis between the cash and the futures can be seen to be extremely vulnerable to changes in the carry spread.

Such radical changes in the price basis will also have a strong impact on the yield basis relationship. For this example of a snap-up to an inverted yield curve, the carry-basis as a yield spread flips from a positive 168 basis points down to a negative 41 basis points as shown in Figure 22.

5. CONCLUDING REMARKS: RELATIVE VALUES

The futures contract exhibits a form of volatility not evident in the cash security. A cash security is related to a particular maturity point in a yield curve and will be directly sensitive to changes at that particular point. However, the futures

Figure 21: Futures Price Response to a Change in Carry Spread

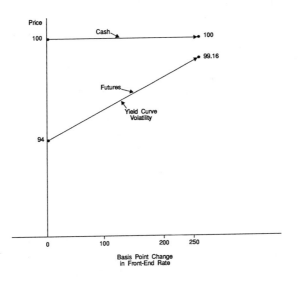

Figure 22: Futures Response to Yield Curve Reshaping

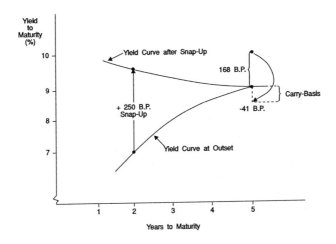

contract is seen to be vulnerable to yield curve changes that impact the carry spread, i.e., to any changes in the intermaturity spread between the front-end rate and the cash security. In reality, the carry spread is composed of a series of more complex relationships than just the maturity spread along the yield curve. However, even for the more general case where the carry spread is determined by considerations relating to the financing of the "driving arbitrages," the inter-maturity spread derived from the yield curve itself will clearly continue to play an important role. Thus, changes in the yield curve shape will lead to corre-sponding changes in the carry spread. For this reason, we shall refer to the slope of the price response curve shown in Figure 21 as the "yield curve volatility."

As noted earlier, the futures yield curve volatility contrasts strongly with the cash security's insensitivity to yield curve reshapings. This underscores the dan-ger in viewing the futures contract as being directly equivalent to an investment in the cash security.

General Yield Curve Movements

The financial futures has been shown to be characterized by two different di-mensions of price volatility. The first dimension is the response to parallel mar-ket shifts, while the second volatility dimension relates to yield curve reshapings. These volatilities differ in magnitude and, more importantly, in di-rection.

The market shift volatility responds in the fashion that is usually associated with fixed-income volatility: as yields move up, the market shift volatility leads to declining futures prices. However, the yield curve volatility operates quite differently. As the yield curve snaps up with higher rates in the early maturities, the financial futures actually improves in price. The conflicting effects of these two volatilities can lead to some surprising and counterintuitive results.

The character of these two volatilities and their interaction becomes particu-larly important because any yield curve movement can be shown to be a combi-nation of a parallel market shift and pure yield curve reshaping. For a specific financial future, this is achieved by simply defining the market shift to be the yield movement that takes place at the cash security's maturity point. The re-mainder of the general yield curve movement then becomes a yield curve re-shaping. Thus, with this definition, the cash security yield first changes as part of the market shift, and then remains constant throughout the "subsequent" yield curve reshaping. The movement in the front-end rate is then comprised of the market shift followed by the yield curve reshaping.

This is illustrated in Figure 23, which shows a rise in the yield curve to-gether with movement toward an inverted shape. This particular yield curve movement turns out to be a simple process of combining the +100 basis points parallel move that was used in the preceding example with the +250 basis point

PART III G

Tax Effects

Chapter III G-1

Integrating Tax Effects into Bond Portfolio Management

The conventional yield-to-maturity value, in both its pretax and after-tax forms, leaves much to be desired as a comprehensive tool for investment analysis. In *Inside the Yield Book*[1] the use of a total-return measure called realized compound yield was suggested for evaluating bond purchases and swaps. This subject has since been explored in some detail[2]; the conclusion[3] is that it is far from obvious how the realized compound yield approach could be properly extended into the complex world of the taxed portfolio. However, once two key concepts—*effective par rate* and *opportunity dollars*—are identified, this extension is not only possible, but indeed could prove a most valuable investment tool. In fact, in certain taxed environments, this extension proves more informative and provides more counterintuitive surprises than the comparable tax-free case.

This article describes how realized compound yield can be translated into a consistent, useful concept for taxed bond portfolios.

---

[1] Homer & Leibowitz, *Inside the Yield Book* (Prentice-Hall, Inc., 1972).

[2] Leibowitz, "New Tools in Bond Portfolio Management," Trusts and Estates (1973).

[3] Leibowitz, *Total After-Tax Bond Performance and Yield Measures* (1974).

Martin L. Leibowitz, "Integrating Tax Effects Into Bond Portfolio Management," *The Bankers Magazine*, Spring 1975. Reprinted with permission.

While this article explains ways of integrating different tax structures into an analytic investment framework, no corporation's specific tax situation is discussed. All examples presented are strictly for the purpose of illustrating the various analytic techniques and are not necessarily applicable to any given individual or corporate entity. Moreover, the author does not wish to represent himself as being qualified to provide advice relating to tax matters; and neither the author nor Salomon Brothers is in the business of providing such advice.

SOURCES OF RETURN IN TAXED PORTFOLIOS

The sources of bond return in taxed portfolios include the same three basic elements as in the tax-free case—coupons, capital gains or losses, and interest on interest. These elements must be adjusted, of course, for the effects of taxation.

The stream of after-tax coupons will have a time value that can be represented either figuratively or literally by reinvestment at some specified rate. *Interest on interest* is the dollar return arising from the reinvestment and compounding of a bond's after-tax coupon receipts. (However, depending on the nature of the reinvestment, its applicable tax rate may be quite different from the coupon income rate.)

In any case, a practical point of departure is to assume a fixed reinvestment rate and a fixed tax rate applicable to it. While it is usually a good idea to identify these two rates as constituting two distinct assumptions, the net effect is the determination of a single after-tax reinvestment rate.

Table 1: The Disproportionate Effect of Taxation

Assumed Tax Rates (%)	
Coupon	48
Reinvestment	48
Capital Gains	30

4%, 25-Year Discount Bond Priced at 50.594 for 9% Yield to Maturity

	Without Taxes	With Taxation	Change
Coupon income	$1,000	$ 520	-48%
Interest on interest at 6%	1,256	259	-79
Capital gains	494	346	-30
Total return per bond	$2,750	$1,125	-59%
Conventional yield to maturity	9.00%	5.43%	-40%

Tax rates have a surprisingly disproportionate impact upon different sources of return. For example, one might expect that applying an identical tax rate to both coupon and reinvestment income would reduce their return fairly equally. But, in fact, there would be a much more severe reduction in the interest-on-interest figure. For example, as shown in Table 1, given a pretax reinvestment rate of 6% over a twenty-five-year maturity period, the imposition of a 48% tax rate would slash the interest on interest by 79%! At higher pretax reinvestment rates, taxation would have an even more dramatic effect: At a 10% reinvestment rate, there would be an 84% reduction in the interest-on-interest return.

AFTER-TAX CAPITAL GAIN ON A PROPOSED PURCHASE

The tax liability on capital gains is assumed to be due and payable upon the bond's sale or maturity. (We will use the term *capital gain* for any return derived from principal appreciation realized upon a bond's sale or maturity. I make this point because commercial banks and thrift institutions technically classify all such returns as *"income* derived from security transactions.") There may be accounting tax reserves set aside yearly to match a bond's book accretion, but the actual tax liability is triggered by the act of selling. The portfolio manager selects the time of sale (or he elects to await maturity); consequently, he determines, to some degree, the timing of capital gains flow. This flexibility can prove a primary resource in the management of overall tax liabilities.

For the moment, let's discuss capital gains in the context of a bond being proposed for purchase. Such a bond will be called a P-bond, as distinguished from an H-bond which is already held in the portfolio. If the bond is held to maturity, the capital gain realized over the life of such a P-bond will be the difference between its current market price and its redemption value (par).

The special nature of capital gains taxation has some interesting implications for discount bonds. Because capital gains constitute a significant portion of the discount bond's return, a correspondingly lower percentage of the total return derives from coupon income and interest on interest. As interest on interest is the component most severely impacted by taxation, there is a disproportionately greater reduction in the total return of a par bond than of a discount bond. Thus, even when capital gains are taxed at the same rate as coupons, a discount bond has a greater after-tax return than a par bond with the same pretax yield. This is one of the many excellent points made by Dr. William M. Cox of The Lincoln National Life Insurance Company in a recent paper.[4]

---

[4] *Cox, After-Tax Compounded Yields for Corporate Bonds* (1973).

AFTER-TAX REALIZED COMPOUND YIELDS

Given the tax rates to be applied to coupon income, reinvestment, and capital gains, one can readily compute the after-tax cash flow and total return over the life of a given P-bond. Divide the total after-tax return by the cost; that gives the dollars of return per invested dollar. The compound interest tables then tell us what semiannually compounded interest rate would generate this same level of growth. The result is the after-tax realized compound yield.

Figure 1 illustrates this process for the sample case of a twenty-five-year, 4% P-bond priced at 50.594 to yield 9% and subject to "48%, 30%" taxation.

A NEW CONCEPT: THE EFFECTIVE PAR RATES

Especially in taxable portfolios, it is most helpful to be able to "benchmark" a given bond's after-tax realized compound yield against the net returns available in the comparable new-issue market. The *effective par rate* provides this measurement of a given bond's return against a scale of comparable par bonds. More precisely, the effective par rate is the coupon (or yield) rate of that noncallable par bond which would match the given bond's dollar return over a specified period.

The calculation of the effective par rate is simple. Take the 4% discount bond illustrated in Figure 1. The total after-tax return per dollar invested is $2.223, or a return of $2,223 for each matching par bond purchased. The assumed after-tax reinvestment rate is 3.12% (.52 × 6%). The compound interest tables tell us that for each dollar of a semiannual after-tax coupon payment, reinvested and compounded semiannually at this 3.12% (annual) rate, we would accumulate a total return of $74.896 by the end of the twenty-five-year period. Dividing $74.896 into the required return of $2,223, we see that each coupon payment must provide $29.68 of after-tax income. Since the tax rate assumed was 48%, this would require a pretax payment of $29.68 ÷ .52 = $57.08, or an annual payment of $114.16 (2 × $57.08) per $1,000 par bond. The effective par rate would thus have to be 11.42%. In other words, we have a twenty-five-year, 4% discount bond selling on the basis of a 9% conventional pretax yield, a 5.43% after-tax conventional yield, and a 4.74% after-tax realized compound yield. However, from its effective par rate, we now know that this discount bond will provide better long-term return than any bond in the new-issue market with offering rates below 11.42%.

This effective par rate provides major advantages in terms of a yardstick with an intuitively comfortable scale which can be readily benchmarked against the new-issue market.

Figure 1: Realized Compound Yield and Effective Par Rate in Taxable Environment

---

Assumed Tax Rates (%)

Coupon	48%
Reinvestment	48%
Capital Gains	30%

Realized Compound Yield
4%, 25-Year Discount P-Bond Priced @ 50.594 for 9% Yield to Maturity

$$\underbrace{\frac{\text{Cost}}{506} \frac{\text{Coupon}}{520}}_{} + \underbrace{\frac{\text{Interest on}}{\text{Interest @ 6\%}}}_{259} + \underbrace{\frac{\text{Capital Gain}}{346}}_{} \quad \underset{\text{(\$2.22 per \$1 Invested)}}{= 1,125}$$

After–Tax Return   Future Total Return

GROWTH RATE (AFTER–TAX REALIZED COMPOUND YEILD)
4.74%

Effective Par Rate
11.42%, 25-Year Par Bond Priced @ 100 for 11.42% Yield to Maturity

$$\underbrace{\frac{\text{Cost}}{1,000} \frac{\text{Coupon}}{1,484}}_{} + \underbrace{\frac{\text{Interest on}}{\text{Interest @ 6\%}}}_{739} + \underbrace{\frac{\text{Capital Gain}}{0}}_{} \quad \underset{\text{(\$2.22 per \$1 Invested)}}{= 2,223}$$

RETURN   Future Total Return

GROWTH RATE (AFTER–TAX REALIZED COMPOUND YEILD)
4.74%

Table 2 shows the effective par rates for the sample discount bond under a variety of reinvestment rates and tax structures.

In taxed portfolios, bonds are benchmarked not only against the new-issue market of fully taxable issues, but also against markets of bonds having various degrees of tax exemption. In particular, the fully tax-exempt municipal market almost always serves as an important reference point for taxed portfolios. The general concept of the effective par rate can be readily adapted to the tax charac-

Table 2: Effective Par Rates of Discount Bond in Various Tax Structures
4% 25-Year Discount Bond Priced @ 50.594 for 9% Yield to Maturity

Assumed Pre-Tax Reinvestment Rate	Tax Rates: Income Capital Gains					
	0%	48%	48% 30%	48% 0%	30% 30%	30% 0%
6%	9.64%	10.51%	11.42%	12.92%	10.15%	11.11%
7.50	9.29	10.25	11.06	12.41	9.84	10.67
9	9.00	10.00	10.73	11.94	9.56	10.27

teristics of the underlying standard par bond for the new-issue market in question.

THE CONCEPT OF OPPORTUNITY DOLLARS

A bond holding in a portfolio subject to taxation has a fundamentally different investment value from the exact same issue not held in the portfolio. This is because the bonds in the portfolio have their unique tax cost. The appreciation subject to capital gains taxation will always be measured using this tax cost as a basis; hence, this tax cost is an element in any rational investment decision.

When an H-bond is sold, the portfolio receives its market value in dollars and theoretically could use these dollar receipts to purchase other bonds. However, when such an H-bond sale also incurs a capital gains tax liability, then some of the immediate dollar receipts must, in effect, be put aside to pay the tax. This leaves the portfolio with fewer free dollars available for new investment: the proceeds from the H-bond's sale less the capital gains tax liability. We will use the term *opportunity dollars* for this figure.

The concept of opportunity dollars can be generalized to represent the dollars that *would* be freed up for new investment *if* a given H-bond with an "embedded" capital gain were to be sold at any given time. Thus, every such H-bond has an opportunity dollar value at every point in time.

As an example, suppose a portfolio had purchased our 25-year, 4% discount bond five years ago at a price of 40.594. Today, this H-bond would have an embedded capital gain of $100 per bond. If tax liability were triggered by a sale today, this liability would amount to $30 at a 30% effective capital gains tax rate.

Thus, the opportunity dollars per bond freed up today would be $505.94 -$30.00 = $475.94.

So far, we have discussed only the cheerful case of capital gains. What about selling bonds at capital losses? This loss may be usable as an offset to capital gains in current or future fiscal years. If this leads to a saving in the portfolio's capital tax liability, the loss will have a concrete positive value. This value (of each dollar of loss-offset) can be represented through an appropriate "capital loss tax rate." The actual value assignable to this rate depends on several factors relating to the portfolio's overall tax status.

Let us assume the portfolio already has an overwhelming surplus of capital gains in this fiscal year and that any contemplated capital losses may be fully usable as offsets against the existing tax liability. In such a case, the capital loss tax rate will coincide with the assumed capital gains tax rate. Again, take the 4% discount bond, but now assume that it had been purchased earlier at a price of 98. As shown in Table 3, a sale today at a price of 50.594 would create a capital loss of 47.406 points, or $474.06 per bond. At a capital loss rate of 30%, $142.22 of this loss would be usable as an offset against existing tax liabilities. Under the presumed conditions, this loss-offset would free $142.22 in additional opportunity dollars for investment.

This example provides the key to extending the concept of opportunity dollars to include H-bonds with embedded tax losses. The opportunity dollar value

---

Table 3: An H-Bond's Value in Opportunity Dollars

**4%, 25-Year Discount H-Bond Priced at 50.594 for
9% Yield to Maturity
But Purchased Earlier for a Tax Cost of 98**

30% Capital Gains Tax

Market proceeds if sold now		$ 505.94
Offset against capital gains tax liability		
Tax cost	$980.00	
Market proceeds	505.94	
Capital loss	$474.06	
Capital loss offset rate		
(capital gains rate)	× .30	
Amount of offset of		
prior tax liability	$142.22	+142.22
Opportunity dollars released if sold now		$ 648.16

of such an H-bond is its current market value *plus* the loss-offset figure. With this extension, every H-bond can now be viewed as always having a certain opportunity dollar value, determined by market forces and the portfolio's over-all tax status.

Up to this point, we have defined the opportunity dollars associated with an H-bond as funds that would be freed by its sale. However, every such sale can be considered as a decision between selling the bond and holding it. A decision for holding can, in turn, be viewed as a sort of purchase decision, i.e., the H-bond is "purchased" in exchange for the funds that would have been freed by its sale. This means that the opportunity dollars reflect the current "cost" of a decision to hold a given H-bond.

An H-bond's opportunity dollar value thus can be interpreted in several related ways: (1) as the net usable funds that would be freed up by its sale; (2) as the net usable funds that are tied up by its continued holding; and/or (3) as the "cost," in terms of post-tax exchangeable funds, if we decide to "purchase" its continued holding. Thus, the measure of the dollars "invested" in an H-bond is the bond's opportunity dollars. The concept of opportunity dollars also clari-fies the determination of an H-bond's "capital gain" over a future review period. As shown in Table 4, at the bond's maturity in 25 years the investor would receive his $1,000 redemption subject to a tax liability of $6—a future net pay-ment of $994 in fully usable opportunity dollars. However, the investment re-turn should include only the additional portion of the capital gain accrued over the next 25 years. Since the bond today has an opportunity dollar value of

---

Table 4: Net Gain in Opportunity Dollars if H-Bond Held

**4%, 25-Year Discount H-Bond Priced at 50.594 for
9% Yield to Maturity
But Purchased Earlier for a Tax Cost of 98**

Market proceeds at maturity		$1,000.00
Capital gains tax liability at maturity		
Market proceeds	$1,000	
Tax cost	980	
Capital gains	$ 20	
Capital gains tax rate	× .30	
Capital gains tax incurred	$ 6.00	- 6.00
Opportunity dollars released at maturity		$ 994.00
Opportunity dollars released if sold now		- 648.16
Net gain in opportunity dollars by holding to maturity		$ 345.84

$648.16, the net gain is $994.00 - $648.16 = $345.84. The net gain in opportunity dollars exactly coincides with the simple net capital gains figure of $346 for the P-bond (see Figure 1) because we have tacitly assumed that the future tax rate will be the same as today. In the more general case, where there are changes in capital gains tax rates or in tax status, these figures will differ, but the computation method (Table 4) will give the correct investment returns.

THE OPPORTUNITY YIELD

With the opportunity dollars as an investment base, we can now proceed to compute an after-tax return for both H-bonds and P-bonds.

Staying with the example of a 4% H-bond purchased at 98, we first determine the total dollars of return over the 25-year review period. As shown in Figure 2, the after-tax contributions from coupon income and interest on interest will be identical to the $520 and $259 given in Figure 1 for the 4% P-bond. Moreover, the H-bond's after-tax capital gain return, when properly allocated to the next 25 years, also coincides (in this instance) with the $346 associated with the P-bond. The H-bond's *total after-tax return* will therefore be $1,125 (in this case, the same value as for the comparable P-bond). However, using the H-bond's opportunity dollars as an investment base, the total after-tax return *per invested dollar* becomes $1,125 ÷ $648.16 = $1.735, in comparison with $2.22 for the comparable P-bond.

What fully compounded rate of interest provides this same level of return over 25 years of semiannual compounding? For a return per invested dollar of $1.735, the compound interest tables supply the rate of 2.035% per semiannual period, or 4.07% on an annual basis. For H-bonds, 4.07% is the analogue of the after-tax realized compound yield. However, it is useful to distinguish this realized compound yield value as reflecting an investment base measured in opportunity dollars; thus, we refer to it as "opportunity yield."

(Opportunity yield can be applied to both P-bonds and H-bonds. The H-bond with the embedded capital loss has a lower opportunity yield than the P-bond because the H-bond's return is earned on a larger investment base of opportunity dollars (because of the tax recovery inherent in the embedded capital loss). Hence, the H-bond is a less valuable hold than the P-bond, and the lower opportunity yield reflects this reduced value.

It should be reemphasized at this point that the opportunity yield is a completely consistent representation of the after-tax dollars return. Thus, under the same assumed tax and reinvestment conditions, an H-bond with an opportunity yield of 4.07% always provides a lower after-tax return per invested dollar than a P-bond with a greater opportunity yield, and vice versa. To see it another way, envision the sale of the H-bond and the reinvestment of all released opportunity dollars in a new P-bond. If the new bond has an opportunity yield exceeding the H-bond's 4.07%, the swap is a winner in dollars-and-cents return. Similarly, in comparing any two H-bonds with similar maturities, the one with the smaller opportunity yield is the better *sale*; the higher the opportunity yield, the better the *hold*.

Thus, the opportunity yield simply, compactly, and consistently integrates the effects of several different elements which affect a bond's investment value: the portfolio's explicit reinvestment rate assumption; its anticipated future tax rates on coupon income, reinvestment, and capital gains and losses; the portfolio's present capital gains tax status; the given bond's position as an H-bond or a P-bond; and, if an H-bond, its adjusted tax cost basis.

THE OPPORTUNITY PAR RATE

The opportunity yield will have the same problems of intuitive scaling and market benchmarking as the realized compound yield. We again turn to the hypothetical noncallable par bond which would match the bond's level of opportunity yield. This leads us to the effective par rate or—to stress the fact that the underlying rate of return is based upon an investment base of opportunity dollars—the "opportunity par rate."

Figure 2 illustrates the computation of the opportunity par rate of 8.9% for the 4% H-bond purchased at 98. This bond provides the same after-tax return par invested (opportunity) dollar as a twenty-five-year par bond with a fully taxable 8.91% coupon rate. Any swap into a twenty-five-year par bond with a coupon rate above 8.91% will provide a better long-term return. (A tax-exempt opportunity par rate could also be constructed for benchmarking against the tax-exempt market.)

The opportunity par rate is a remarkably compact and convenient tool. Suppose we compute the opportunity par rate for every bond in a given portfolio. Whenever the level of the comparable new-issue market exceeds the opportunity par rate of any H-bond, a swap into the new issue would work out profitably. Moreover, the best swap would, everything else being equal, entail the sale of that bond with the lowest opportunity par rate. (However, a word of caution: The new-issue par market, while a convenient point of comparison, may not represent the best possible P-bond sector for a given portfolio move.)

OPPORTUNITY YIELDS OVER THE SHORT TERM

The opportunity yield is readily adapted to periods shorter than maturity. The bond's pricing at the end of such a review period becomes the critical new assumption to be explicitly determined. This pricing assumption can reflect simple

---

Figure 2: Opportunity Yield and Opportunity Par Rate

Assumed Tax Rates (%)

Coupon	48%
Reinvestment	48%
Capital Gains	30%
Capital Loss Offset	30%

Opportunity Yield
4%, 25-Year Discount H-Bond Priced @ 50.594 for 9% Yield to Maturity
But Purchased Earlier for a Tax Cost of 98

Present Value in Opportunity $ 648	RETURN			Future Total Return in Opportunity $ 1,125 ($1.74 per Opportunity $)
	$\dfrac{\text{Coupon}}{520}$ +	$\dfrac{\text{Interest on Interest @ 6\%}}{259}$ +	$\dfrac{\text{Net Gain in Opportunity \$}}{346}$	

GROWTH RATE (OPPORTUNITY YIELD)
4.07%

Opportunity Par Rate
8.91%, 25-Year Par Bond @ 100 for 8.91% Yield to Maturity

Present Value in Opportunity $ 1,000	RETURN			Future Total Return in Opportunity $ 1,735 ($1.74 per Opportunity $)
	$\dfrac{\text{Coupon}}{1,158}$ +	$\dfrac{\text{Interest on Interest @ 6\%}}{577}$ +	$\dfrac{\text{Net Gain in Opportunity \$}}{0}$	

GROWTH RATE (OPPORTUNITY YIELD)
4.07%

---

amortization beliefs regarding future levels of interest rates, yield curve effects, estimates of future yield spread relationships, or the search for break-even future yields. In any case, once the pricing assumptions are made explicit, the increase in the bond's opportunity dollar value measures the after-tax capital gains return.

Apart from its specific role as a tool for evaluating potential portfolio actions, opportunity returns over short-term periods can provide some general insights into how different bond characteristics contribute to portfolio performance. For example, there is the large sensitivity of one-year returns to small changes in the market. (This should not surprise us for the tax-free case, since it corresponds to the findings in *Inside the Yield Book*.) However, it is interesting to observe how taxation leads to strong increases in this sensitivity. In the "48%, 30%" tax case, the one-year opportunity par rate of a twenty-five-year, 4% P-bond leaps by 197 basis points under a 10-basis-point yield decline. The magnitude of this effect is, of course, due to the fact that the capital gain is assumed to be taxed at 30%, while the coupons of any par bond would be subject to 48% taxation.

The "maturity effect" is another general result which can be quantified. If a bond's pricing is assumed to be based on constant yield amortization, then the one-year opportunity par rate can show the annual changes in after-tax contribution during the course of a given bond's life. For the example of the twenty-five-year, 4% P-bond in a "48%, 30%" tax environment, the opportunity par rate in the first year is 9.40%, compared with an opportunity par rate of 11.42% over the bond's remaining twenty-five-year life (see Figure 1). It may seem strange that this 9.40 return in the first year could build to an average of 11.42%, for the one-year returns would later have to grow to well above the 11.42 level. In fact, this is precisely what happens. By the last year of this bond's life, its one-year opportunity par rate will have grown to 12.52%! The primary explanation for this maturity effect lies in the changing mixture of income and capital gains generated by accretion at a constant yield.

Even this cursory use of the opportunity yield approach has uncovered a number of interesting items. Many are well-known, and our analytic approach has merely served to confirm them. (Some of the other points are considerably less well-known.) The opportunity yield over short-term review periods permits investment analysis tailored to natural portfolio horizons, permits easier comparisons among bonds of different maturities, forms a basis for investigating swap situations, and even provides a foundation for the development of after-tax performance measures.

TAX LOSSES AND TAX OFFSETS

Estimating the effective capital gains tax rate for a given portfolio is usually far more difficult than it first appears. The capital gains tax on a contemplated H-bond sale depends on the gain or loss status of the portfolio not just in the present fiscal year, but over future years as well.

For example, assume the portfolio carries unrealized losses of such huge proportions as to far outweigh any foreseeable capital gains, and further suppose that the portfolio is blessed with the flexibility to freely realize these losses as needed to offset capital gains. The effective capital gains tax rate will be 0%!

Every gain can be readily offset without depleting the portfolio's reservoir of losses. (By the same token, any particular capital loss realized during this period conveys no special benefit, i.e., it simply adds to an already more than abundant resource; hence, the capital loss tax rate would also correspond to 0%.) On the other hand, if the portfolio has a mountain of unrealized losses but is unable to take additional tax or book losses in the current fiscal year, then any further transactions in the current year should be taxed at the full capital gains rate. However, if capital losses become more freely realizable in future years, this rate might decline to 0%.

The management of capital gains and losses obviously can become intricate and lead to some thorny estimation problems. However, its difficulty should not lead to its neglect. The subject has many fascinating theoretical facets. Practically, it would seem that correct strategic decisions at this level might well have an enormous (and relatively risk-free) impact on the portfolio's total performance.

INDIRECT FACTORS INFLUENCING AFTER-TAX RETURN

The foregoing development of the opportunity yield approach was focused on the relatively *direct* tax factors affecting income, reinvestment, and capital gains or losses. However, many *indirect* factors can have a powerful influence on portfolio strategy. Some of these factors can be readily measured and incorporated into an opportunity yield. Others are more qualitative and defy efforts to introduce them into a formal analytic framework.

An important measurable factor is the "asset tax" which arises in connection with life insurance company portfolios. Through the complexities of their taxation structure, many such companies believe, they become subject to an implicit tax on their portfolio's asset value. (Estimates of this tax range up to 1.25%.) Such an asset tax could readily be incorporated into the opportunity yield measure and would have a major effect on portfolio strategy.

Many important but less measurable factors surround the whole issue of realizing book and/or tax losses. As we have seen, it often makes sense to take losses in terms of the direct dollars-and-cents effects. However, taking losses can have powerful effects not just on the portfolio but on the corporation's overall reporting and statutory status as well. Obviously, a corporate policy is needed which balances the very real benefits of portfolio loss realization against their possible adverse "reporting" effects. Unfortunately, many taxed portfolios labor under an unexamined and unmeasured dictum which arbitrarily restricts—or even prohibits—*any* form of loss realization.

OPPORTUNITY YIELDS AS SIMPLE MEASURES IN COMPLEX ENVIRONMENTS

The interaction of the effects of taxation, coupon reinvestment, realized and unrealized capital gains and losses, and market actions creates quite a decision-making environment for the manager of a bond portfolio subject to taxation. The opportunity yield is designed to integrate these factors into a relatively simple and intuitive yardstick which can be readily benchmarked against the marketplace. The validity of the resulting measurements, of course, still depends totally on the validity of the assumptions relating to the portfolio and market conditions. But at least the roles played by these conditions become clearer through making the assumptions explicit.

The opportunity yield concept permits a clear-cut quantitative approach to many general and specific investment problems. The following is a concise list of some general results. (A more detailed explanation, with examples, is provided in Footnote 3.)

1. Conventional pretax yields and yield spreads can be deceptive for taxed portfolios and can result in apparent yield pick-up swaps which actually turn out to be losers.

2. The conventional after-tax yields and yield spreads, when computed using the common approximation formula, can prove very unreliable.

3. The conventional after-tax yields and yield spreads (even when computed exactly) can either overstate or understate—or even reverse—the actual dollars-and-cents relationship between two bonds.

4. Unlike the conventional yields, the opportunity yield par rate provides investment measures which will be consistent with the dollars-and-cents return to be received under specified portfolio and market conditions.

5. Discount bonds have an intrinsic after-tax advantage over par bonds priced at the same conventional pretax yield—even when capital gains are taxed at the same rate as coupon income.

6. Short and intermediate discounts have a special advantage, all else being equal, in tax structures favoring capital gains.

7. In selecting potential sale candidates within the discount portion of a portfolio with a tax structure favoring capital gains, there is a strong incentive to focus on the longer-maturity bonds.

8. A portfolio with a large reservoir of unrealized losses relative to gains, and the freedom to realize these losses, can, up to a certain point, reduce its effective capital gains tax rate to zero by offsetting gains with losses.

While no portfolio willingly seeks losses, once they have occurred, they constitute a valuable resource for tax liability management.

9. For portfolios with large, usable loss reservoirs, discount bonds with their "locked-in" capital gain have an even greater structural advantage. (*As always, for any given portfolio, this structural advantage must be evaluated in the context of existing market levels, spreads, and prospects.*)

10. Taxation leads to a much greater erosion in dollars-and-cents return than is indicated by the tax rates or any of the after-tax yields.

11. Any tax structure on income greatly reduces the incremental dollars-and-cents return from pure yield pick-up swaps (no matter how accurately the yields are figured).

12. The effective volatility of a bond's return under changes in yields and/or yield spreads is greatly enhanced by any tax structure favorable to capital gains.

13. Income taxation renders yield pick-up swaps far more vulnerable to adverse market moves in yields and/or yield spreads.

14. Taxation increases the payoff from sector spread swaps and substitution swaps even when a yield give-up is involved.

15. In taxed portfolios, rate anticipation swaps entail both greater risks and more significant opportunities.

16. It can be argued that an appropriate form of active management is actually more valuable for portfolios subject to taxation than for tax-free portfolios. There are many reasons for such an argument: the tax erosion of pure yield accumulations; the magnification of market moves; the year-by-year change in a bond's portfolio contribution (i.e., the maturity effect); the overwhelming advantage of certain coupon and maturity sectors; and the need to manage both realized and unrealized gains and losses.

17. Bond portfolio planning and actions should integrate investment and tax considerations throughout the entire fiscal year. It is simply not possible to have a "pure investment swap" free of tax considerations in a portfolio subject to taxation. By the same token, investment opportunities are not likely to conveniently concentrate themselves at the end of the fiscal year. Moreover, "pure tax swaps" by themselves throw away the opportunity to make every portfolio action count fully toward portfolio improvement.

The opportunity yield approach can be extended, via computer, into the high-payoff areas of swap analysis, break-even yields, sector spread swaps, loss recovery times, and the more complex cash flows resulting from sinking-fund bonds and mortgage-like securities. The opportunities are unlimited.

Chapter III G-2

The Municipal Rolling Yield

In an earlier study[1] it was shown how investments along the Treasury yield curve could be analyzed in terms of the component sources of return. For the initial case of an unchanging yield curve, return is derived from three components:

- the initial coupon rate of the par bond

- the reinvestment of that coupon income

- the price appreciation achieved as the bond ages and "rolls down" the yield curve to lower yield levels.

Over short investment horizons, the first factor—the bond's yield rate—is, of course, the most significant of these three factors. For horizons measured in months or even stretching over a few years, the second factor—the reinvestment effect—will be comparatively minor. However, the third factor—the roll down

---

[1] *The Rolling Yield*, Salomon Brothers, April 21, 1977. (Reprinted in this book.)

Martin L. Leibowitz, "The Municipal Rolling Yield—A New Approach to the Analysis of Tax-Exempt Yield Curves," Salomon Brothers Inc, July 1980.

on the yield curve—often turns out to have a surprisingly strong impact on total return.

In these earlier studies, we were able to show many realistic instances where the process of rolling *down* a *positive* yield curve (or rolling *up* a *negative* yield curve) could result in significant price movements over relatively short horizons. This suggested that investors wishing to assess the attractiveness of a particular maturity sector—even under the assumption of a constant market—should look beyond the yield rate to the total return generated by this roll-down process. In other words, to evaluate the case where no specific movements in yield are anticipated, the investor should not look just at the traditional yield curve, but at the yield curve after adjustment for this roll-down effect, i.e., the Rolling Yield curve.

THE MUNICIPAL YIELD CURVE

In principle, this recommendation holds true for the tax-exempt market as well. In fact, the tax-exempt market generally provides a stronger roll-down effect. There are several reasons for this. First of all, the municipal yield curve almost always has a positive shape. (Inversions do occur, but they are rare.) Second, the yield spreads between maturities are generally considerably wider in the municipal market than in the Treasury market. In other words, not only is the municipal market more consistently characterized by a positive yield curve, but the slope of the tax-exempt curve is usually greater than in the Treasury market. This is evident, for example, in the 30-year to 1-year spreads charted in Figure 1. The magnitude of these maturity spreads is even greater when viewed in terms of percentages, as shown in Figure 2, rather than raw basis points. Finally, the lower yield level of the tax-exempt market leads to a considerably greater Duration[2] (i.e., price sensitivity to a given change in basis point yield) than is found in the higher-yielding Treasury and Corporate markets. This greater price sensitivity leads to an enhanced price "jump" resulting from a given number of basis points of roll-down.

For all these reasons, the roll-down effect is likely to be much larger in the municipal market than in the taxable area. Thus, for tax-exempt investors who either seek total return or would like to have the additional price protection that is implicitly derived from a greater total return, the traditional view of the yield curve should be supplemented by an evaluation of the "Rolling Yield curve" which incorporates this total return effect.

---

[2] *The Risk Dimension*, Martin L. Leibowitz, Salomon Brothers, October 5, 1977. (Reprinted in this book)

Figure 1: Yield Curve Spreads
(30-Year/1-Year Spreads Within Municipal and Treasury Markets)

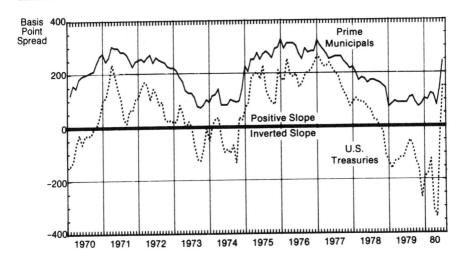

Figure 2: Yield Curve Spreads as Percentage
(30-Year/1-Year Spreads as Percentage of 1-Year Rate)

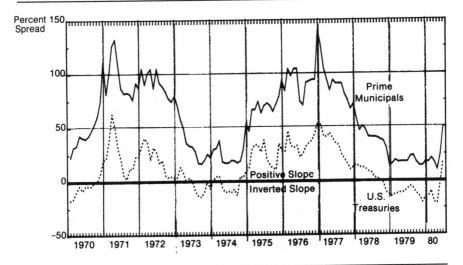

THE ROLLING YIELD COMPUTATION

To adapt the Rolling Yield concept to the municipal market, one must make certain adjustments to account for the specific tax environment of the investor. Figure 3 illustrates the computation of the Rolling Yield value for a 1-year investment in a 15-year par bond. The initial yield of 6.70% provides the basic coupon return over the 1-year horizon. However, the positive shape of the yield curve results in 14-year maturities being priced to yield 6.56%, i.e., 14 basis points less than the coupon rate on the bond purchased. If there is no change in the yield structure of the market, the investment will become a 14-year bond priced at 101.269 to yield 6.56%. (This makes an implicit assumption that the yield curve's par bond rate provides a reasonably close estimate for the yield of a premium bond.) The additional points of price gain constitute a source of total return over the 1-year horizon. If the investor is subject to capital gains taxation at the 28% rate, then approximately 0.914 points would be retained after-tax. The total 1-year return would then become the original 6.70 points of coupon income plus the 0.914 points of after-tax capital gain (plus a minor reinvestment effect) for a total return—or Rolling Yield—of 7.582% after taxes. Thus, the roll-down effect here produces an incremental after-tax return of 88 basis points. The incremental return from the roll-down process can clearly be a material factor in determining the most attractive maturity area along the yield curve.

Figure 4 shows a prime municipal yield curve for July 1, 1980. The Rolling Yield associated with each maturity point can be computed following the same procedure illustrated in Figure 3. The resulting series of Rolling Yield values can then be plotted against the corresponding maturity values. The resulting Rolling Yield curve is shown in Figure 5.

Figure 3: The Rolling Yield Computation (A 15-Year 6.70% Par Bond Rolling Down to a 14-Year Yield Curve Value of 6.56% over a 1-Year Horizon)

Coupon Income (As % of Par)	6.700%
Reinvestment Income (As % of Par)	.112

Market Appreciation

Nominal Price 1 Year Hence Based on Yield Curve Value of 6.56%	101.269	
Price Today	(100.000)	
Gross Price Appreciation	1.269	
Capital Gains Liability @ 28.0% Tax Rate	(.355)	
Net Price Appreciation	.914	.914
Total Return (Simple Annual)		7.726%
Total Return (Semiannual Basis)		7.582%

Figure 4: Prime Municipal Yield Curve (July 1, 1980)

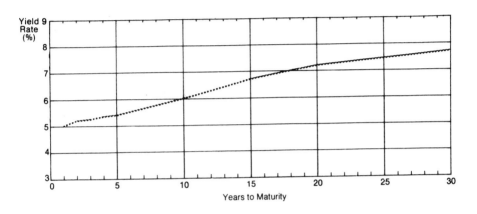

Figure 5: The Rolling Yield Curve (Rolling Yields Based on the Prime Municipal Yield Curve of July 1, 1980)

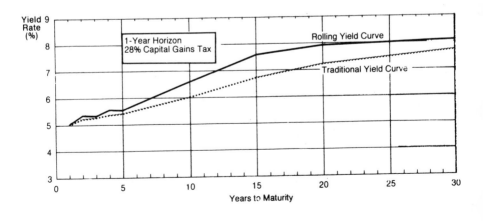

CHARACTERISTICS OF THE ROLLING YIELD CURVE

In the tax-exempt market, with its virtually assured positively shaped yield curve, all Rolling Yield curves will have certain common features. They will always lie above the actual yield curve. They will always coincide with the actual yield curve at the early maturity point that matches the investment horizon. They will tend to approach the underlying yield curve at the longer maturity where the curve tends to be flat and the roll-down effect is minimal.

All this suggests that the Rolling Yield curve will often have a maximum "hump" point somewhere in the intermediate maturity range. Within the narrow context of the "unchanging market" assumption that underlies this calculation, such a hump point can represent the most attractive total return along the curve.

For a more comprehensive evaluation, it becomes necessary to go beyond the static market assumption and to explore the effect of dynamic changes in the level and shape of the underlying yield curve.[3]

HORIZON AND TAX EFFECTS

The same yield curve may generate completely different types of Rolling Yield curves for various tax rates and/or investment horizons. For example, with a 3-year investment horizon, the July 1st prime municipal curve generates the Rolling Yield curve shape shown in Figure 6. Longer horizons tend to create somewhat flatter Rolling Yield curves, largely because the price changes must be amortized over longer periods of time. Another "flattening" factor is the reduced volatility of the investment vehicle at the end of the longer-aging period.

Tax rates will also affect both the shape as well as the level of the Rolling Yield curve. Because of the secular bear market over the past two decades, many institutional bond portfolios are saddled with a large reservoir of loss holdings. In many cases, these loss holdings can be realized selectively to offset any capital gains tax liabilities. An institution that can utilize this offset process will enjoy a marginal effective capital gains tax rate of 0%! The roll-down effect will then be unencumbered by capital gains taxes, and one would consequently expect to see higher Rolling Yields. This is evident in Figure 7, which shows the Rolling Yield curve for a completely tax-free environment.

---

[3] *The Rolling Yield and Changing Markets*, Salomon Brothers, June 13, 1977. (Reprinted in this book.)

Figure 6: The Impact of Longer Investment Horizons (3-Year Rolling Yields Based on the Prime Municipal Yield Curve of July 1, 1980)

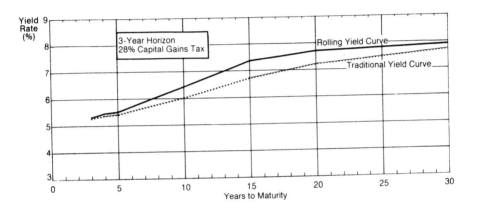

Figure 7: The Impact of Freedom from Capital Gains Taxation (Fully Tax-Free Yields Based on the Prime Municipal Yield Curve of July 1, 1980)

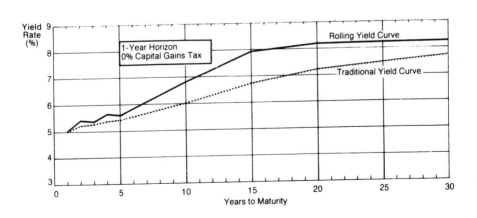

HISTORICAL ROLLING YIELD CURVES

Figures 8 and 9 show Rolling Yield curves for a 28% capital gain taxpayer, derived from the prime municipal curves that prevailed at the beginning of 1980 and 1976. The variation in level and shape is dramatic, but perhaps even more striking is how the Rolling Yield consistently has a significant impact on the tradeoff between return and maturity.

As noted earlier, interpretation of the shape of the Rolling Yield curve must be blended with a dynamic assessment of potential changes in the level and the shape of the yield curve. Nevertheless, it can already be seen how the process of transforming a traditional yield curve into a Rolling Yield curve tends to put a new and interesting slant (both literally as well as figuratively) on maturity selection within the tax-exempt market.

Figure 8: Rolling Yield Curves from the Past: January 1980 (Rolling Yields Based on the Prime Municipal Yield Curve for the Beginning of January 1980)

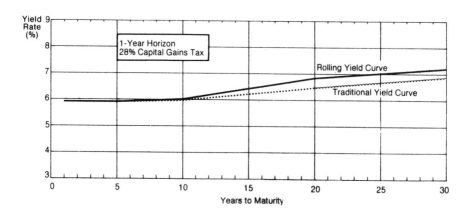

**Figure 9: Rolling Yield Curves from the Past: January 1976
(Rolling Yields Based on the Prime Municipal Yield Curve for the
Beginning of January 1976)**

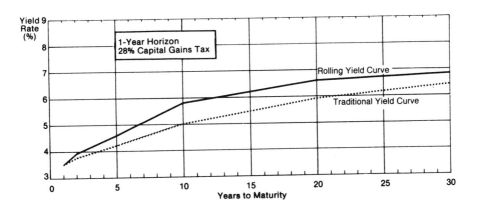

Chapter III G-3

Volatility in Tax-Exempt Bonds

The duration concept provides an estimate of what the price movement in a bond of a specific maturity, coupon and starting yield will be for each basis point of yield change. However, duration essentially relates a bond's price changes to changes in its gross yield. In many cases, a tax-exempt bond's gross yield will not correspond to its net yield. For instance, tax-exempt par bonds will be subject to capital gains taxes when they move into the discount range as a result of adverse yield moves.

The "net yield factor"—the ratio of a bond's gross yield movement to the corresponding movement in net yields—indicates how much a specific outstanding bond's gross yield must increase above the movement in market rates in order to give the purchaser an after-tax yield equal to the current market yield on tax-exempts. The net yield factor will exceed one when a tax-exempt bond sells at a discount. Tax-exempts selling at a premium will have a factor of one; i.e., their gross yields will equal their net yields.

The net yield factor for adverse yield moves significantly increases the effective volatility of tax-exempt bonds, although its significance declines with maturity, since the capital gain has little impact in a present value sense at the longer maturities. Combining the effects of the net yield factor and duration

Martin L. Leibowitz, "Volatility in Tax-Exempt Bonds: A Theoretical Model," *Financial Analysts Journal*, November/December 1981. (Received Graham & Dodd Scroll for 1981.) Reprinted with permission.

shows that price volatility will be greater for adverse yield moves than for positive yield moves, and that the discrepancy will be greatest in the intermediate and shorter maturities.

Finally, one can relate movements in tax-exempt yields to movements in taxable yields via the "ratio model," which states that tax-exempt yields at a given maturity represent some fraction of taxable (Treasury) yields—historically 75% and 54% for 30-year and one-year maturities, respectively. Integrating this ratio model with duration and the net yield factor results in a general volatility model that will approximate the percentage price change in a given tax-exempt bond per change in general interest rates as represented by the Treasury yield curve.

The general volatility model indicates that tax-exempt par bonds will exhibit two general volatility factors, depending on the direction of yield moves. In the case of favorable yield moves, tax-exempts will exhibit less upside price volatility than corresponding Treasury bonds, especially at shorter maturities. For adverse yield moves, however, tax-exempt bonds across all maturities will experience virtually the same price volatility as corresponding Treasuries.

Most estimates of bond volatility—the yield value of 1/32nd, duration, etc.—rely on the special relationship between a bond's price and its yield. This relationship occurs in accordance with the mathematical formula that determines the bond's price for a specified yield value. Using this formula, one can quickly find the price movement induced by any given change in the bond's yield.

This simple relationship does not, however, answer all the questions relating to bond volatility. It does not, for example, tell us how a bond's price movement relates to changes in the general level of interest rates. In other words, rather than the specific volatility of a given bond, how can we determine the relative riskiness of specific segments of the debt market?[1]

One problem that arises in dealing with questions of general volatility in tax-exempt bonds is the question of tax effects. In particular, the special capital gains tax implications of price movements in tax-exempt bonds have a major impact on price volatility. We incorporate these special tax effects through use of a simple net yield model. This model enables us to develop volatility and duration factors that relate a specific bond's price movement to yield movements at the appropriate maturity points along the tax-exempt yield curve.

This brings us to a second problem—that is, how to relate price movements in specific tax-exempt bonds to changes in "the general level of (taxable) interest rates." Since many market participants view the Treasury yield curve as the key factor determining the structure of rates in all facets of the U.S. debt market, our comprehensive volatility model uses (taxable) Treasury yields as a proxy for the

---

[1] See Martin L. Leibowitz, *The Risk Dimension*, Salomon Brothers, 1977. (Reprinted in this book.)

general level of interest rates. We then define the relationship between tax-exempt and taxable rates in terms of the familiar "ratio model."

By integrating three basic market factors—duration, net yield and the ratio of tax-exempt to taxable yields—we are able to construct a comprehensive general volatility model that relates the price volatility of a specific tax-exempt bond to movements in the general level of interest rates as represented by the Treasury yield curve.[2] A number of intriguing market implications emerge from this model:

1. Basis point for basis point, tax-exempt bonds are considerably more volatile than taxable bonds of comparable maturity.

2. Thirty and 40-year tax-exempts are only moderately more volatile than 20-year tax-exempts, especially under adverse yield movements.

3. Discount tax-exempts are much more volatile than premium bonds.

4. Adverse yield movements induce a larger price change in tax-exempt par bonds than favorable yield movements.

5. An intermediate tax-exempt can usually be replaced by a barbell combination of shorter and longer bonds that will have the same average maturity but less price volatility. (However, under the positive yield curves that typically prevail in the tax-exempt market, the barbell combination will tend to have a lower average yield-to-maturity than the intermediate.)

6. Tax-exempt par bonds have virtually the same volatility as comparable Treasury bonds under adverse yield movements.

7. The average maturity of a tax-exempt portfolio can be a very poor gauge of its volatility risk.

DURATION

For a given movement in its yield value, a bond will experience a price change that depends upon its maturity, coupon rate and starting yield. For a given coupon rate, price volatility increases (at least at the outset) with increasing maturity. Most practitioners are well aware of the fact that the price movement of a two-year bond is almost twice that of a one-year bond, but that volatility does

---

[2] The theoretical structure can readily accommodate more refined models for each of the basic market factors. The structure can also be extended to deal with other market factors not explicitly incorporated in this initial model—e.g., reshapings in the taxable yield curve and the generally greater volatility in the shorter maturities.

Figure A: Price Changes Across Maturity
(8% Par Bonds Under +100 Basis Point Yield Change)

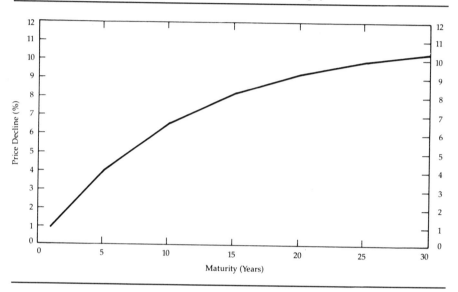

not continue to increase as rapidly with the longer maturities. Thus a 30-year, 8% bond is only 31% more volatile in price movement than a 15-year, 8% bond.

Figure A illustrates these maturity effects, assuming that bonds along an 8% flat yield curve are subjected to a 100 basis point increase in yield—i.e., a parallel shift in the flat yield curve. The curve shown in Figure A represents the plots of the resulting price declines. While price changes increase at a proportional pace in the early years, the incremental price volatility decreases with the longer maturities. (In fact, with very long maturity bonds, the curve in Figure A would have a discernible peak under certain conditions.)

Practitioners will also know that bond price movements are not symmetrical. In other words, the price decline associated with a 100 basis point increase in yield will not be of the same magnitude as the price appreciation associated with a 100 basis point decrease in yield. The price improvements will always exceed the corresponding price declines. Figure B shows the price moves for bonds along the 8% flat yield curve under both a +100 and -100 basis point movement.

The curves in Figure B can be interpreted as price volatilities—i.e., the price change per 100 basis point change in yield. It is possible to determine the ratio of price change to yield change for different magnitudes of yield movements. With smaller yield changes, the discrepancy between positive and negative re-

Figure B: Price Volatility and Duration (8% Par Bonds)

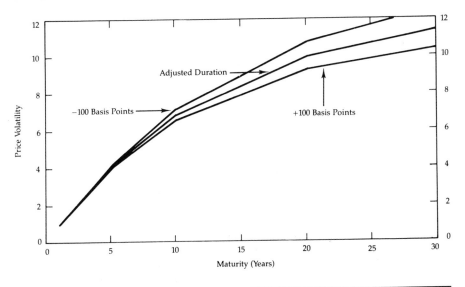

Maturity (Years)

sponses to yield movements will shrink. Thus the gap between the price volatilities associated with +25 and -25 basis point yield moves would be considerably smaller (on a per-basis-point basis) than the gap shown in Figure B.

The question arises whether sufficiently small yield moves will lead to a common volatility value that could provide a single standard value for a bond's price volatility. In other words, we would like to be able to find a value that—at least approximately—answers the following question: What is the price movement for each basis point of yield change? A relatively simple mathematical formula can indeed give us such a number, although, because of the asymmetry that exists in larger movements in yield, it must necessarily be a compromise between the values for upward yield moves and downward yield moves. However, it remains a useful approximation for small yield movements and, furthermore, proves to be extremely convenient for developing theoretical models of bond volatility.

The formula was first developed by Frederick Macaulay in 1938.[3] It is based upon a concept he called the *duration* of a bond. Macaulay was actually trying to

[3] Frederick R. Macaulay, *Some Theoretical Problems Suggested by the Movements of Interest Rates, Bond Yields and Stock Prices in the United States Since 1856* (New York: National Bureau of Economic Research, 1938), pp. 44-53.

find a better measure for a bond's average life. It was not until many years later that academics recognized that, with a slight adjustment, the duration concept could provide a valuable theoretical gauge for a bond's volatility. (In the meantime, the marketplace was functioning well with a similar concept—the yield value of 1/32nd.)

There is a precise value for the adjusted duration of any bond. Figure B plots the values for our 8% par bond. As one can see, the curve falls roughly midway between the price changes associated with +100 and -100 basis point yield movements.

DURATION VALUES IN THE TAX-EXEMPT MARKET

As we have noted, a bond's volatility also depends on its initial yield level. A given yield movement has one effect starting from an 8% yield and quite another effect starting from an 11% yield. One might well expect that a +100 basis point change would have a greater price effect on an 8% par bond than on an 11% par bond (if only for the reason that 100 basis points constitute a larger percentage yield move at the 8% level). This turns out to be the case.

Figure C shows the adjusted duration values for bonds of different maturities along an 8% flat yield curve and along an 11% flat yield curve. The securi-

Figure C: Price Volatility and Initial Yield (8% Tax-Exempt and 11% Taxable Par Bonds Both Subjected to Same Gross Yield Changes)

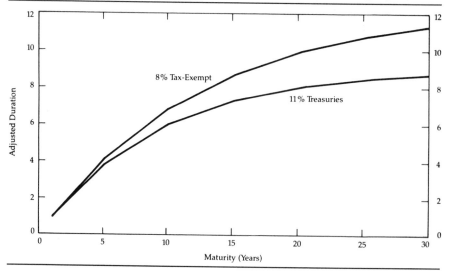

ties along the 8% curve are obviously considerably more volatile than the corresponding securities along the 11% yield curve.

This observation has immediate implications for the tax-exempt market: Since the tax-exempt yield curve will almost uniformly be at lower yield levels than the taxable yield curve, one can expect that tax-exempt bonds will display more price volatility than taxable bonds of the same maturity. In this relatively narrow sense, one might then conclude that tax-exempt bonds tend to be more volatile than comparable Treasury or corporate securities. However, there are several other factors that must be considered before we can interpret such a sweeping theoretical statement as a market fact.

THE CAPITAL GAINS EFFECT

The return from a tax-exempt security is not totally free from tax liability. The coupon income will, of course, be tax-exempt in the appropriate geographical regions. However, the gain or loss realized from a tax-exempt security is subject to capital gains tax treatment. In particular, this means that a tax-exempt bond purchased at discount will have an embedded capital gain at maturity, and that this capital gain will be subject to the appropriate tax liability. This "capital gains effect" has a major impact on the volatility characteristics of tax-exempt bonds.

To this point, our discussion of a bond's yield has implicitly assumed that no taxes of any kind were imposed upon the bond's cash flow; to be more precise, we should refer to this yield value as the bond's *gross yield*. The entire cash flow for a tax-exempt *par* bond will be fully tax-exempt, hence the bond's gross yield will correspond to its *after-tax yield*. However, for *discount* bonds (i.e., bonds selling below par), the gross yield fails to take into account the capital gains tax liability due at maturity. The after-tax yield, or *net yield*, of discount bonds will thus be lower than the gross yield. For example, a 10-year, 8% bond at a price of 91.96 will have a gross yield of 9.25%. Assuming that the capital gain at maturity of 8.04 points (100 - 91.96) is subject to a 46% tax rate, the bond's net yield becomes 9.00%—25 basis points below the bond's gross yield.[4]

This capital gains effect has a major impact on the volatility of tax-exempt bonds. As yields on new bonds rise, an outstanding bond essentially increases its yield by declining in price; the new purchaser thus obtains a greater capital gain as well as a higher current yield. However, for taxpaying investors, each new increment of capital gain is subject to tax liability. Consequently, the bond's price decline must create a sufficient capital gain to keep up with the increase in

---

[4] This article treats all discounts as if they had been originally issued as par bonds; i.e., there is no consideration of the special problems of "original issue discount" bonds.

general yield levels even after taking into account the additional tax liabilities created by the new capital gain.

Consider, for example, a 100 basis point increase in the level of the tax-exempt market, say from 8% to 9%. In order for a 10-year, 8% par bond to provide a 9% net yield to a taxpayer in the 46% bracket, the bond would have to decline to a price of 91.96. This price corresponds to a gross yield of 9.25% (as the example above illustrated). Thus a rise of 125 basis points in gross yield is needed to make this particular bond comparable to new issue rates under a 100 basis point increase in net yields.

Figure D illustrates the capital gains effect. The solid line represents the *traditional* price movements associated with changes in the gross yield of the 10-year, 8% tax-exempt bond. However, the concept of market movements is usually associated with a change in the yield level of the tax-exempt *par bond* market. In other words, the statement that "10-year rates have increased by 100 basis points" usually means that the rate for new 10-year *par* bonds has risen by 100 basis points. In order for an outstanding bond to maintain the same relationship to the par market on an after-tax basis, its net yield must increase by the same 100 basis points.

The broken line in Figure D depicts the fact that, as seen in the earlier example, a 100 basis point increase in the net yield leads to a more severe price decline than a 100 basis point increase in the gross yield. Thus a yield change of

Figure D: Price Changes from Movement in Gross Yields and Net Yields (10-Year, 8% Par Bond and 46% Capital Gains Tax)

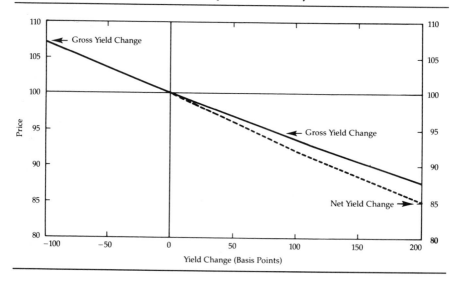

+100 basis points starting from the 8% level will lead to different prices depending on how it is interpreted. At a 9% net yield, the bond will be priced at 91.96 (the dotted line), or approximately 1 1/2 points lower than the price of 93.50 that would correspond to a 9% gross yield (the solid line). Similarly, for a +200 basis point movement, the resulting net yield of 10% would lead to a price of 84.92—roughly 2 1/2 points lower than the corresponding price for a gross yield of 10%.

When yields decline below the par rate—here 8%—the bond becomes a *premium*—i.e., it sells at prices above par. The new purchaser of a premium tax-exempt bond will lose principal, but the loss will be amortized against coupon income over the life of the bond. As a result of this amortization process, the new purchaser receives no capital loss over the course of the bond's life. Hence the bond's after-tax cash flow will coincide with its pretax cash flow, and its net yield will be exactly the same as its gross yield. Thus there is essentially no capital gains effect for premium bonds held to maturity. The bond's price change will be the same under a 100 basis point change in gross yield and a 100 basis point change in net yield.[5]

THE NET YIELD FACTOR

The capital gains effect can be viewed another way: The movement in net market yields can be directly related to the corresponding move in the gross yield of a specific security. Figure E shows this correspondence, assuming that a 46% capital gains tax rate prevails in the marketplace.

The horizontal axis in Figure E corresponds to the movement in net market yields—i.e., movements in the tax-exempt yield curve. The vertical axis, on the other hand, depicts the resulting change in the yields of a specific security—in this case, the outstanding 10-year, 8% bond. The solid line in the graph shows the net yield change for the security. In this model, a plus or minus 100 basis point change in the market's net yield corresponds to a plus or minus 100 basis point change in the security's net yield. However, the security's gross yield must undergo larger changes, as indicated by the dotted line. Thus, as we saw earlier, a 100 basis point increase in the market's net yield requires a 125 basis point increase in the gross yield of the specific 10-year, 8% bond. Similarly, a 200 basis point increase in tax-exempt market rates would require an approximately 250 basis point increase in the gross yield of this bond.

These two numerical examples indicate that the security's gross yield will undergo a movement that is approximately 1.25 times the movement in market

---

[5] It should be noted that, for simplicity, the important effects of the call features are purposely neglected in our treatment of premium bonds.

Figure E: Relationship of Gross to Net Yield Changes (10-Year, 8% Par Bond and 46% Capital Gains Tax)

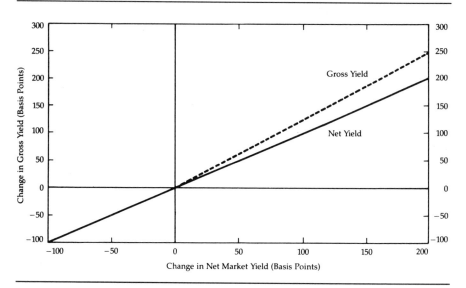

rates. This observation leads to a new concept, which we call the *net yield factor*. The net yield factor is the ratio of the gross yield movement to the corresponding movement in net yields. For the bond moves represented in Figure E, the net yield factor would be 1.25. For yield movements leading to lower rates, hence to premium bonds, the gross yield would coincide with the net yield. Thus, for premium bonds, the net yield factor will always be 1.00.

Figure F summarizes the general calculation procedure used to determine the net yield factor. (A precise mathematical formulation for the net yield factor is presented in the appendix.) Figure G shows how net yield factors vary for par bonds of different maturities and at different market yield levels. Of course, the net yield factors shown correspond to the movement of par bonds under adverse yield movements into the discount area; favorable yield movements would lead to premium bonds all having net yield factors equal to one.

These net yield factor curves imply that, for the longer maturities, where the capital gain has little impact in a present value sense, the net yield factor is relatively low, approaching a value of one. With shorter and shorter maturities, the impact of the capital gain becomes more important, and this leads to a growing value for the net yield factor. At a maturity of one year, the net yield factor is 1.75 (for the 8% bond yields). Thus the one-year tax-exempts have to move almost twice as much in gross yield to compensate for a given change in

Figure F: Net Yield Factor Calculation (10-Year, 8% Par Bond and 46% Capital Gains Tax)

	Change in Net Yield	
	Adverse +100BP	Favorable -100BP
New Net Yield	9.00%	7.00%
New Price	91.96	107.11
Capital Gain at Maturity	8.04	0
Gross Maturity Proceeds	100	100
Capital Gains Tax	3.70	0
Net Maturity Proceeds	96.30	100
Yield of Bond with These Net Maturity Proceeds (= Net Yield)	9.00%	7.00%
Yield of Bond without Capital Gain Tax (= Gross Yield)	9.25%	7.00%
Change in Gross Yield	+125BP	-100BP
Approximate Net Yield Factor	1.25	1.00

Figure G: Net Yield Factor and Maturity (46% Capital Gains Tax)

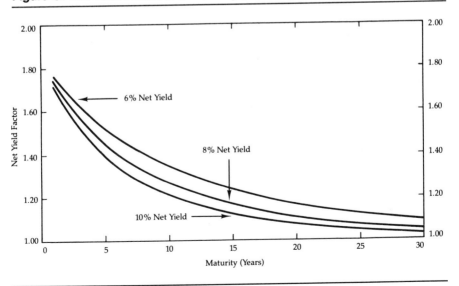

market yields. This extreme volatility in the short end of the market should come as no surprise to many investors.

On the one hand, net yield factors relate gross yield changes of a specific tax-exempt bond to movements in net market rates. On the other hand, the duration concept provides an approximation of the price change in a specific bond for a given change in gross yield. By combining net yield factors with the duration concept, we should thus be able to relate the price movements of a specific tax-exempt bond to changes in market yields. The three curves in Figure H illustrate the results.

The two lower curves are identical to the "basic duration" curves in Figure C for 8% par tax-exempts and 11% par Treasury bonds of various maturities. The top curve, however, represents the combined impact of the net yield factor and the duration on the price volatility of the 8% tax-exempt given an adverse movement in yields. The net yield factor for adverse yield moves significantly increases the effective volatility of tax-exempt securities. In particular, if one believes that it is adverse yield movements that constitute "risk" in the fixed-income markets, then the net yield factor greatly increases the "riskiness" of tax-exempt securities.

Figure H also shows how the net yield factor effect changes with maturity. At the longer maturities, price movement in the adverse direction is close to the positive movements. However, in the 10-year range there is a significantly greater price volatility for adverse yield moves than for positive yield moves. At

Figure H: Price Volatilities for Parallel Yield Moves

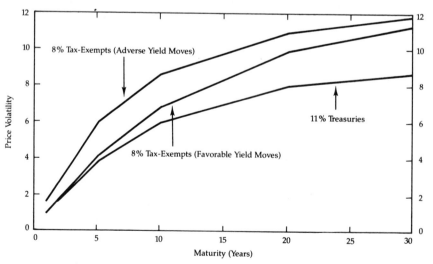

the shorter maturities, all volatilities decrease in magnitude, but the adverse volatility remains proportionally much greater than the positive volatility. The net yield factors in Figure G and the price volatilities in Figure H relate to the movement of par bonds lying on the indicated yield curve at the indicated maturity. Discount and premium bonds would naturally exhibit somewhat different patterns of price-yield behavior. One aspect of this difference derives from the "coupon spread" effect—i.e., different coupon levels trade at certain spread relationships relative to the par bond market. Putting aside this coupon spread effect, however, one still finds variations in duration and net yield factor depending on the coupon rate of a specific bond.

The formula for the net yield factor provided in the appendix can be applied to any coupon, maturity, tax rate and starting yield level. It turns out that the net yield factors are not highly sensitive to coupon level, provided the distinction is made between discount and premium bonds. Modest discount bonds will thus exhibit a pattern of price volatility similar to the uppermost curve in Figure H (the curve for adverse yield moves in par bonds). Since deep discount bonds have significantly longer durations, they will exhibit greater overall volatility. By the same token, premium bonds will generally follow the pattern described by the middle curve in Figure H (par bond price volatility under favorable yield curve movements). The main point is that discounts will generally be more volatile than premium bonds. Moreover, with appropriate adjustments, this price volatility concept can be extended to all coupon and maturity sectors.

THE RATIO MODEL

To this point, we have not explicitly discussed how movements in tax-exempt yields relate to movements in taxable yields. The volatilities represented in Figure H are comparable only under the assumption that each basis point move in the Treasury markets corresponds to a basis point move in the tax-exempt markets. In fact, such parallel movements correspond neither to the practitioners' view nor to historical experience.

A more reasonable description of the relation between tax-exempt and taxable yields is provided by the "ratio model." The ratio models states that tax-exempt yields at a given maturity represent—at least approximately—some fraction of the taxable yields at the corresponding maturity. This model is a far from perfect description of real markets. The top line in Figure I depicts the ratio of 30-year prime municipal yields to 30-year long-term Treasury yields on a monthly basis from January 1971 through December 1980. The average ratio over this 10-year period has been the 74% value represented by the horizontal line. It is very evident that historical ratios have varied widely around this average, ranging from a high of 85% in late 1971 to a low of 65% in early 1980. The

**Figure I: Ratio of Prime Municipal to U.S. Treasury Yields
(January 1971—December 1980)**

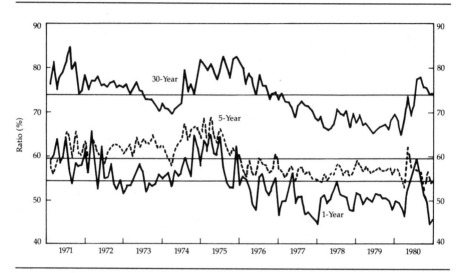

lower two curves in Figure I represent the monthly ratios for five- and one-year maturities.

Clearly the ratio model provides only a crude approximation of historical behavior. Nevertheless, it does demonstrate that the tax-exempt market displays a certain sensitivity to the level of taxable yields. (It should be noted that many factors could lead to potential changes in any relation between tax-exempts and taxables; the prospect of changes in the tax law in particular could create significant departures from historical ratios.) Furthermore, it is important to find some way to relate movements in the tax-exempt market to movements in the overall level of interest rates—i.e., the Treasury yield curve—if we are to proceed with the theoretical analysis of volatility models. We thus adopt the ratio model as a description of the relation between the two markets.[6]

The ratio model is subject to a number of different market interpretations. For example, if the after-tax spread advantage of tax-exempts remains a constant percentage of the taxable yield rate, then the ratio model would be expected to hold. The precise mathematical relationship is derived in the appendix.

---

[6] Our methodology can, of course, be applied to any more refined model of the relation between the taxable and tax-exempt markets.

Figure J: The Average Ratio Curve Based on Average Monthly Ratios over the Decade (January 1971—December 1980)

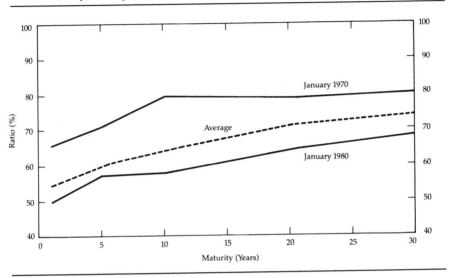

Assuming that the average historical values for the yield ratio for the 1970s represent the "correct" values, Figure J shows the "average ratio curve" for the decade. The assumed ratio value will range from 74% for 30-year maturities to 54% for one-year maturities. For comparative purposes, Figure J also displays the actual ratio curves that occurred in January 1970 and January 1980.

This average ratio curve could presumably be used to help explain the shape of the tax-exempt yield curve. Thus a positive Treasury yield curve would lead to an even more positive tax-exempt yield curve. A flat Treasury yield curve would still result, under the ratio model, in a positive tax-exempt curve. Indeed, for the tax-exempt yield curve to become flat, the Treasury yield curve would have to take on a historically extreme degree of inversion.

If the ratio model held precisely for yield levels, then it would be logical to assume that it also held precisely for changes in yield. Thus a +100 basis point change in 30-year Treasuries would lead to a +74 basis point change in 30-year tax-exempts. Similarly, a +100 basis point change in one-year Treasuries would result in a +54 basis point change in the tax-exempt curve at the one-year point. One can now see how the ratio model can be used to determine the yield changes along the tax-exempt yield curve that result from a specific set of yield changes in the Treasury yield curve.

THE GENERAL VOLATILITY MODEL

Using the ratio model to relate changes in tax-exempt market yields to changes in taxable rates, we can now proceed to relate the price volatility of a specific tax-exempt bond to changes in the general level of (taxable) interest rates. The percentage price change of a given tax-exempt security per change in the Treasury yield rate at the same maturity will be referred to as the bond's *general volatility factor*. (As with duration, the general volatility factor is only a rough approximation of the actual price move of the bond; however, like the duration concept or the yield value of 1/32nd, it is a very useful and compact way of viewing price volatility.)

The general volatility factor of a tax-exempt bond comprises three different component factors:

1. the ratio model that relates movements in the tax-exempt yield curve to movements in the Treasury yield curve;

2. the net yield factor that relates the gross yield move of a given tax-exempt security to the net yield move represented by changes in the tax-exempt yield curve;

3. the duration of the individual bond that relates its percentage price change to changes in its gross yield.

The general volatility factor turns out to be the product of these three component factors. The appendix provides a detailed derivation of this result; however, a simple numerical example can show how these factors blend together.

First, suppose the Treasury yield curve is perfectly flat at 11%. Then, in order to be consistent with the ratio model, we will assume that the shape of the tax-exempt yield curve is determined by the average ratio curve (Figure J). Thus the one-year tax-exempt rate is 5.94% (0.54 × 11%), the five-year rate is 6.60% (0.60 × 11%), the 10-year rate is 7.04% (0.64 × 11%), etc.

Now suppose the Treasury yield curve shifts downward by 50 basis points. This means that 10-year Treasury yields decline by 50 basis points. In accordance with the ratio model, this will lead to a 32 basis point decline at the 10-year point on the tax-exempt yield curve. (This results from using the average ratio of 64% for the 10-year point as shown in Figure J). This 32 basis point improvement, when multiplied by the duration of 7.09 (for a 10-year par bond with a 7.04% coupon rate), results in a price move of approximately 2.27 points (versus an actual change of 2.30 points). Since the bond in question is presumed to be a par bond, the downward movement in interest rates takes it into the premium range. Consequently, the net yield factor has a value of one. In other words, the 32 basis point change in the market's net yield rate leads to a 32 basis point change in the yield rate for this particular tax-exempt bond as well.

Now suppose that the Treasury yield shifts in an adverse direction—i.e., moves up by 50 basis points. From the ratio model, the net yield will again correspond to a movement of +32 basis points. However, the net yield factor for adverse movements (taking the par bond into a discount) is approximately 1.30 (for a 10-year, 7.04% par bond). This means that the bond's gross yield must move by 1.30 times the +32 basis point net yield move in order to generate sufficient capital gains to compensate for the capital gains tax liability incurred. The combination of the net yield factor of 1.30 and the +32 basis point movement in the tax-exempt yield curve leads to a +41.6 basis point movement in the gross yield for this bond. Multiplying this value by the duration of 7.09 results in an approximate price decline of 2.95 points (versus an actual price decline of 2.88 points for a +32 basis point change in net yield).

These results can be summarized in terms of general volatility factors. In the case of the favorable yield moves, the 10-year tax-exempt par bond can be said to have a general volatility factor of 4.54—that is, a 100 basis point decline in 10-year Treasury rates leads to an approximate +4.54 price advance in the tax-exempt bond. On the other hand, because of the different net yield factor, an adverse yield movement of the same magnitude leads to a general volatility factor of 5.90. In other words, a 100 basis point increase in 10-year Treasury rates leads to an approximately 5.90 point decline in the price of the tax-exempt bond.

Figure K: General Volatility Factors under the Ratio Model

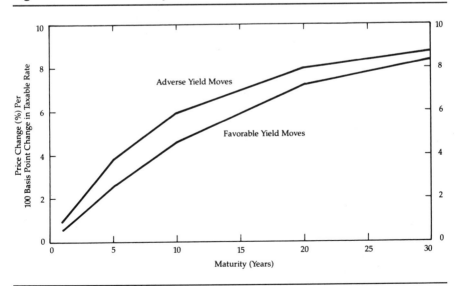

Thus tax-exempt par bonds will exhibit two different general volatility factors depending upon the direction of yield moves. These general volatility factors will, obviously, depend upon the maturity of the tax-exempt bond. Figure K plots these two general volatility factors across a range of maturities; it is apparent that the two general volatility factors display the greatest discrepancy in the intermediate range.

Figure K also shows that the general volatility of tax-exempt bonds displays even more of the "saturation effect" than occurs with simple price volatility. In other words, the increase in volatility decreases as one goes to longer and longer maturities. In particular, this suggests that 30-year tax-exempts are only 22% more volatile than 15-year tax-exempts and only 9% more volatile than 20-year tax-exempts (if one focuses on adverse yield moves as being the appropriate risk measure). Thus maturities of greater than 20 years may not have much more volatility risk than many tax-exempt securities in the 10- to 20-year range.

As Figure K shows, tax-exempt par bonds have asymmetric general volatility factors—i.e., different values apply for movements in different directions. In contrast, for discount or premium bonds, the general volatility factor will be symmetric—under the presumption of small yield moves that do not lead to prices crossing the par level. While there will be some difference depending upon the coupon level, the general volatility factors for discount tax-exempts will generally correspond to the "adverse yield move" curve in Figure K. By the same token, the general volatility factors for premium bonds will correspond to the lower curve in Figure K. This immediately suggests that one should be able to construct certain interesting combinations of premium and discount bonds that would have advantageous volatility characteristics. Using the formulas derived in the appendix, one can develop more refined general volatility curves for tax-exempt bonds having different coupons and corresponding to different starting yield levels.[7]

Theoretically, Figure K indicates that the traditional average life is a poor way to assess the volatility risk of a portfolio of tax-exempt bonds. This is true for several reasons. For example, consider a portfolio consisting of one 30-year bond and one one-year bond. The portfolio's average maturity would be 15 1/2 years. However, the general volatility factor of such a portfolio would be about 4.8—far less than the general volatility factor of 7.2 that would be associated with 15 1/2-year securities under adverse yield moves. This observation has immediate implications for the volatility characteristics of a barbell portfolio relative to a single-point maturity.

---

[7] These results focus entirely on *market* volatility. For a given portfolio, fluctuations in the after-tax value of a holding will depend on the bond's market volatility as well as on its specific gain/loss status. This leads into the subject of the holding's "opportunity value," which is discussed at length in Martin L. Leibowitz, "Integrating Tax Effects into Bond Portfolio Management," *The Bankers Magazine*, Spring 1975.

A far better approach to characterizing a portfolio's volatility would be to determine its average general volatility factor. This value will have direct significance in terms of the portfolio's overall price risk. Thus, for a portfolio having an average general volatility factor of 4.8, a +100 basis point movement in (taxable) rates would lead to an approximately 4.8% decline in price.

Those who prefer the more traditional characterization in terms of an equivalent maturity value can use the general volatility factors to develop the averages. The resulting average general volatility factor could then be related to an equivalent par bond maturity. Thus a portfolio with a general volatility factor of 4.8 could be described as having the "volatility equivalent" of a single seven-year par bond.

RELATIVE PRICE VOLATILITY

So far, we have focused on how the prices of tax-exempt bonds change with changes in the yield level of the taxable market. Under such conditions, of course, there will also be changes in the price levels of taxable bonds. We will now explore how price changes in taxable securities relate to the corresponding price changes in tax-exempt bonds.

Figure L: Relative Price Volatilities under Parallel Yield Moves

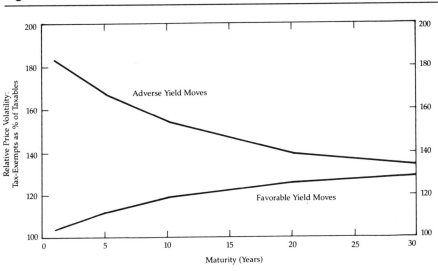

First, suppose that yields move by the same amount in both the Treasury and tax-exempt markets—i.e., a parallel movement in the two yield curves. We know that, for favorable yield movements, the higher duration of the tax-exempt bond (see Figure C) will lead to greater price movements. The lower curve in Figure L depicts the ratio of tax-exempt price volatility to the price volatility in Treasuries under declining rates. For example, at the 30-year maturity, the relative price volatility of tax-exempts is 128%.

The upper curve in Figure L depicts the higher levels of relative price volatility that prevail when rates move adversely to higher yield levels. In this case, the net yield factor comes into play. Under a +100 basis point move in both the taxable and tax-exempt markets, there will be 183% as much price decline in one-year tax exempts as in one-year Treasuries! For 30-year securities, the relative price volatility of tax-exempts is 134% that of Treasuries.

The relative price volatilities in Figure L are based on the highly tenuous assumption of parallel movements in the two yield curves. As discussed earlier, tax-exempt yields will not in general move basis point for basis point with Treasury yields. If we apply the ratio model for yield changes, then tax-exempt yields will experience reduced yield movements for a given change in Treasury rates. The relative price volatility of tax-exempts must consequently be reduced by the ratio value for each maturity. Figure M shows what happens when we superimpose the ratio curve on the two relative price volatility curves.

Figure M: Average Yield Ratio Curve and Relative Price Volatilities under Parallel Yield Moves

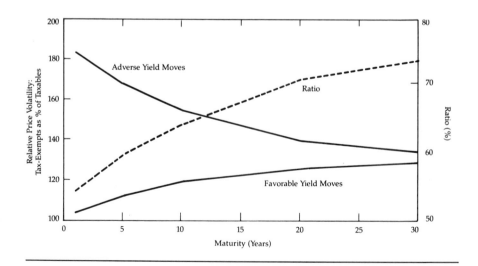

In the case of favorable yield movements, this will bring the relative volatility of tax-exempts well below the 100% mark; i.e., tax-exempts will exhibit less price volatility than the corresponding Treasury bonds. For example, the ratio of yield moves for 30-year bonds is 74%. Combining this with the relative price volatility (for favorable parallel movements) of 128% gives a relative price volatility of approximately 95%. Shorter maturity tax-exempts will exhibit even less relative price volatility, since both the ratio and the duration curve decrease with decreasing maturities.

On the other hand, in the case of adverse yield moves, the ratio curve decreases with shorter maturities, but the relative price volatility increases (as a result of the net yield factor). Because of these two opposing effects, it is not obvious just how the relative price volatilities will behave across maturities until one actually carries out the calculations. The results of these computations, at least for the numbers assumed in this study, are surprising.

Taking the 30-year maturity, the relative price volatility (under parallel moves) of 134% must be multiplied by the ratio value of 74%. This leads to a value of approximately 99% for a revised relative price volatility. In other words, under adverse yields, the tax-exempt bond should experience virtually the same decline in price as a 30-year Treasury bond. For the one-year maturity, the relative price volatility rises to 183%, while the ratio value declines to 54%. This results in a relative price volatility under the ratio model of 99%.

Figure N: Relative Price Volatilities under the Ratio Model

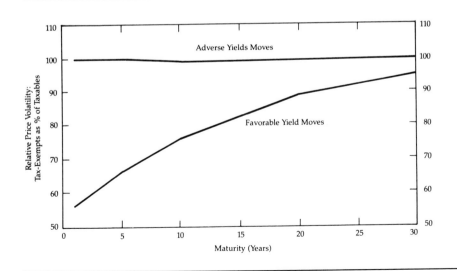

Carrying out these computations for the other maturities results in the top curve shown in Figure N. This curve is virtually a straight line at the 100% mark across all maturities! This surprising result implies—for the values used in this study—that the tax-exempt bond is subject to virtually the same price changes as the corresponding Treasury bond when rates move in an adverse direction. In other words, tax-exempt bonds are every bit as risky—in terms of adverse price volatility—as Treasury bonds.

CONCLUSION

Price volatility is only one of many variables that enter into the selection of a maturity target for an entire portfolio or for new cash investment. Other critical factors may include the yields available along the yield curve, the anticipated holding period and the corresponding horizon effects, the tax environment of the portfolio—both in terms of operational tax prospects as well as the embedded gain/loss positions in the portfolio itself—and the organization's sensitivity to various reserve ratios that are either actually (or potentially) based upon market valuation. At the same time, in addition to its direct effects, volatility behavior enters in some indirect way into virtually every dimension of the portfolio management problem. Given its importance in the decision process, one has to question the all too common—but erroneous—practice of using the average maturity as a simplistic yardstick for bond volatility. There would seem to be a considerable incentive to strive for a deeper understanding of the volatility characteristics of tax-exempt bonds, especially in terms of their effect on overall portfolio behavior.

Appendix

THE CONCEPT OF GENERAL VOLATILITY

The basic concept of the price volatility for a specific bond is represented by the following defining equation:

$$\begin{matrix} \% \text{ Price} \\ \text{Change} \end{matrix} = \begin{matrix} \text{Specific} \\ \text{Volatility} \\ \text{Factor} \end{matrix} \times \begin{matrix} \text{Change} \\ \text{in} \\ \text{Bond's Yield} \end{matrix} . \tag{1}$$

For small yield changes, a slight adjustment in Macaulay's duration can serve as a satisfactory approximation for the specific volatility factor, so that:

$$\begin{matrix} \% \text{ Price} \\ \text{Change} \end{matrix} = \begin{matrix} \text{Adjusted} \\ \text{Duration} \end{matrix} \times \begin{matrix} \text{Change} \\ \text{in} \\ \text{Bond's Yield} \end{matrix} . \tag{2}$$

These two equations deal with the relation between a bond's price and the gross yield to maturity of that same bond. However, we want to relate the price volatility of a tax-exempt bond to changes in the overall level of taxable (e.g., Treasury) rates. Thus we want to find a *general volatility factor* such that:

$$\begin{matrix} \% \text{ Price} \\ \text{Change} \end{matrix} = \begin{matrix} \text{General} \\ \text{Volatility} \\ \text{Factor} \end{matrix} \times \begin{matrix} \text{Change in} \\ \text{Overall} \\ \text{Interest Rates} \end{matrix} . \tag{3}$$

The analysis proceeds in three basic steps:

1. Find the price volatility of the tax-exempt bond to changes in its gross yield to maturity.

2. Find the change in the bond's *gross yield* produced by changes in the tax-exempt yield curve.

3. Relate changes in the tax-exempt yield curve to the changes in the Treasury yield curve.

Since the duration concept is based upon tax-free cash flows, the first step is immediately achieved by using the adjusted duration:

$$\frac{\text{\% Price}}{\text{Change}} = \frac{\text{Adjusted}}{\text{Duration}} \times \frac{\text{Change in Bond's}}{\text{Gross Yield .}} \tag{4}$$

We make the simplifying assumption that a change in the tax-exempt yield curve will lead to a parallel change in the *net yield* of outstanding bonds of the same maturity, so that:

$$\begin{array}{c}\text{Change in} \\ \text{Bond's} \\ \text{Net Yield}\end{array} = \begin{array}{c}\text{Change in} \\ \text{Tax–Exempt} \\ \text{Yield Curve .}\end{array} \tag{5}$$

We further assume that all market participants—or at least those setting prices—are subject to a common tax rate on capital gains. A change in the bond's net yield will then induce a price change and a corresponding change in the bond's gross yield. For small yield moves, this gross yield change can be related to the net yield change through a factor we call the *net yield factor*:

$$\begin{array}{c}\text{Change in} \\ \text{Gross Yield}\end{array} = \begin{array}{c}\text{Net} \\ \text{Yield} \\ \text{Factor}\end{array} \times \begin{array}{c}\text{Change} \\ \text{in} \\ \text{Net Yield .}\end{array} \tag{6}$$

One can derive a formula for the net yield factor for a bond with any maturity, coupon and starting yield level in any given tax environment. (This derivation is given later.) Using the net yield factor, one can combine Equations (4), (5) and (6) to obtain an expression that relates a bond's price volatility to changes in the tax-exempt yield curve:

$$\frac{\text{\% Price}}{\text{Change}} = \left[\frac{\text{Adjusted}}{\text{Duration}} \times \frac{\text{Net Yield}}{\text{Factor}}\right] \times \begin{array}{c}\text{Change in} \\ \text{Tax–Exempt} \\ \text{Yield Curve .}\end{array} \tag{7}$$

In order to forge a connection between the tax-exempt and the taxable markets, we make use of the well-known *ratio model*. The ratio model states that, for comparable maturities, tax-exempt yields trade as a certain fraction of taxable yields:

$$\begin{array}{c}\text{Tax–Exempt} \\ \text{Par} \\ \text{Yields}\end{array} = \begin{array}{c}\text{Ratio} \\ \text{Factor} \\ \text{for} \\ \text{Maturity}\end{array} \times \begin{array}{c}\text{Taxable} \\ \text{Par} \\ \text{Yields .}\end{array} \tag{8}$$

While often at variance with historical experience, the ratio model serves as a familiar and useful starting point for many explorations of the tax-exempt/taxable relationship. There are of course different ratio values for different maturities. When we refer to the "ratio curve," we mean a plot of ratio values across a range of maturity values.

If the ratio model is assumed to hold precisely, then one immediately finds that the same ratio model applies to *yield changes*, so that:

$$\begin{array}{c} \text{Change in} \\ \text{Tax–Exempt} \\ \text{Par} \\ \text{Yields} \end{array} = \begin{array}{c} \text{Change in} \\ \text{Net} \\ \text{Tax–Exempt} \\ \text{Yields} \end{array} ,$$

$$= \begin{array}{c} \text{Ratio Factor} \\ \text{for Maturity} \end{array} \times \begin{array}{c} \text{Change in} \\ \text{Taxable Par} \\ \text{Yields} . \end{array} \qquad (9)$$

This provides the link required for the third step in our procedure. By combining Equations (7) and (9), we can relate the price volatility of a tax-exempt bond to changes in the taxable yield curve:

$$\begin{array}{c} \% \text{ Price} \\ \text{Change} \end{array} = \begin{array}{c} \text{Adjusted} \\ \text{Duration} \end{array} \times \begin{array}{c} \text{Net} \\ \text{Yield} \\ \text{Factor} \end{array} \times \begin{array}{c} \text{Ratio} \\ \text{Factor} \\ \text{For} \\ \text{Maturity} \end{array} \times \begin{array}{c} \text{Change in} \\ \text{Taxable} \\ \text{Par Yields} . \end{array} \qquad (10)$$

We have thus derived an expression for a bond's *general volatility factor*:

$$\begin{array}{c} \text{General} \\ \text{Volatility} \\ \text{Factor} \end{array} = \begin{array}{c} \text{Adjusted} \\ \text{Duration} \end{array} \times \begin{array}{c} \text{Net} \\ \text{Yield} \\ \text{Factor} \end{array} \times \begin{array}{c} \text{Ratio Factor} \\ \text{for} \\ \text{Maturity} . \end{array} \qquad (11)$$

This achieves our primary goal of integrating the three key factors into a model of general volatility.

RELATIVE PRICE VOLATILITY

A related problem is to determine the relative price volatility between tax-exempt bonds and taxable bonds of comparable maturity, or:

$$\begin{array}{c} \text{Relative Price} \\ \text{Volatility} \end{array} = \dfrac{\begin{array}{c} \% \text{ Price Change} \\ \text{in} \\ \text{Tax–Exempts} \end{array}}{\begin{array}{c} \% \text{ Price Change} \\ \text{in} \\ \text{Taxables} . \end{array}} \qquad (12)$$

In essence, this expression is simply the ratio of the respective general volatilities, so that:

$$\frac{\text{Relative Price}}{\text{Volatility}} = \frac{\substack{\text{General Volatility Factor} \\ \text{for Tax–Exempts}}}{\substack{\text{General Volatility Factor} \\ \text{for Taxables}}} . \tag{13}$$

Of course, if "taxables" are taken to be par bonds along the taxable yield curve, then:

$$\substack{\text{General Volatility Factor} \\ \text{for Taxables}} = \substack{\text{Adjusted} \\ \text{Duration} \\ \text{for} \\ \text{Taxables}} . \tag{14}$$

The above result also assumes that the taxable par bond market has a net yield factor of 1.00—i.e., that price movements in par taxables are not affected by tax considerations.

Equation (14) leads to an expression for the relative price volatility:

$$\substack{\text{Relative} \\ \text{Price} \\ \text{Volatility}} = \frac{\substack{\text{General Volatility Factor} \\ \text{for Tax–Exempts}}}{\substack{\text{Adjusted} \\ \text{Duration} \\ \text{for} \\ \text{Taxables}}} , \tag{15}$$

$$= \frac{\substack{\text{Adjusted} \\ \text{Duration} \\ \text{for} \\ \text{Tax–Exempts}}}{\substack{\text{Adjusted} \\ \text{Duration} \\ \text{for} \\ \text{Taxables}}} \times \substack{\text{Net} \\ \text{Yield} \\ \text{Factor}} \times \substack{\text{Ratio} \\ \text{Factor} \\ \text{for} \\ \text{Maturity}} .$$

From this expression, it can be seen how—even with reduced yield movements (represented by ratio factors of less than 1.00)—tax-exempts, with their greater duration and their net yield factor, can have price volatilities that are comparable to those of taxables.

IMPLICATIONS OF THE RATIO MODEL

While the ratio model is a familiar concept, some of its implications are less well-known. In other words, what does the ratio model say about the behavior of intermarket participants? There are various interpretations. However, one of the most appealing is based upon the concept of a *net spread*—i.e., the basis point advantage of the tax-exempt rate over the after-tax rate available in the taxable market, or:

$$\text{Net Spread} \equiv \text{Tax-Exempt Rates} - \text{After-Tax Value of Taxable Rates .} \tag{16}$$

This can be simplified by defining a "pass-through rate" as the fraction of taxable income that is retained on an after-tax basis:

$$\text{Pass-Through} \equiv 1 - \text{Income Tax Rate .} \tag{17}$$

This enables us to rewrite Equation (16) as:

$$\text{Net Spread} = \text{Tax-Exempt Rates} - \text{Pass-Through} \times \text{Taxable Rates .} \tag{18}$$

Now, by combining Equations (8) and (18), we can derive the following result:

$$\text{Ratio Factor for Maturity} = \frac{\text{Tax-Exempt Rates}}{\text{Taxable Rates}} , \tag{19}$$

$$= \text{Pass-Through} + \frac{\text{Net Spread}}{\text{Taxable Rates}} .$$

This result states that the ratio factor is the sum of the tax pass-through rate and the net spread as a fraction of taxable rates. This has the appealing special case that when the net spread vanishes, the ratio value simply coincides with the tax pass-through rate. Moreover, if the net spread advantage is maintained at a stable level as a proportion of the level of taxable rates, then the ratio factor will also maintain a stable value (given a constant pass-through rate).

In essence, this suggests that the ratio model is equivalent to a statement that the net spread advantage of the tax-exempt market is stable as a given percentage of the level of taxable rates.

MATHEMATICAL FORMULA FOR THE NET YIELD FACTOR

Let $P_G(Y_G)$ be the basic price formula for a bond's price, P_G, as a function of its gross yield to maturity, Y_G (as a semiannual fraction), so that:

$$P_G(Y_G) = \frac{C}{Y_G} + \frac{1}{(1+Y_G)^M}\left[100 - \frac{C}{Y_G}\right], \tag{20}$$

where C is the coupon rate and M is the maturity (in terms of numbers of semiannual periods).

Now consider a tax-exempt bond priced at P. At maturity, there will be a capital gain, G, equal to:

$$G = 100 - P. \tag{21}$$

If CGT is the capital gains tax, then the after-tax proceeds at maturity will be:

$$(1 - CGT) \times G + P = 100 - CGT \times G. \tag{22}$$

By substituting Equation (22) for the maturity proceeds of 100 in Equation (20), we obtain an expression for the price function, P_N, associated with a net yield value, Y_N:

$$P_N[Y_N, G(Y_N)] = \frac{C}{Y_N} + \frac{1}{(1+Y_N)^M}\left[100 - CGT \times G(Y_N) - \frac{C}{Y_N}\right]. \tag{23}$$

It will be noted that the gain function, $G(Y_N)$, also depends on Y_N through the implicit function:

$$G(Y_N) = 100 - P_N[Y_N, G(Y_N)]. \tag{24}$$

The next step is to take the total derivative of Equation (23):

$$\begin{aligned}
\frac{dP_N}{dY_N} &= -\frac{C}{Y_N^2} + \frac{1}{(1+Y_N)^M}\left[-CGT \times \frac{dG}{dY_N} + \frac{C}{Y_N^2}\right] \\
&\quad - \frac{M}{(1+Y_N)^{M+1}}\left[100 - CGT \times G(Y_N) - \frac{C}{Y_N}\right] \\
&= \left\{-\frac{C}{Y_N^2}\left[1 - \frac{1}{(1+Y_N)^M}\right] - \frac{M}{(1+Y_N)^{M+1}}\left[100 - CGT \times G(Y_N) - \frac{C}{Y_N}\right]\right\}
\end{aligned} \tag{25}$$

$$-\frac{CGT}{(1+Y_N)^M}\frac{dG}{dY_N}$$

The expression within the brackets is the derivative that would result with a fixed capital gain, G—i.e., it corresponds to the partial derivative:

$$\frac{\partial P_N}{\partial Y_N}.$$

Thus:

$$\frac{dP_N}{dY_N}=\frac{\partial P_N}{\partial Y_N}-\frac{CGT}{(1+Y_N)^M}\frac{dG}{dY_N}. \qquad (26)$$

From Equation (24) we have:

$$\frac{dG}{dY_N}=\frac{dP_N}{dY_N}. \qquad (27)$$

Thus Equation (26) can be rearranged as follows:

$$\frac{dP_N}{dY_N}=\left(\frac{\partial P_N}{\partial Y_N}\right)-\frac{CGT}{(1+Y_N)^M}\left(-\frac{dP_N}{dY_N}\right),$$

$$\frac{dP_N}{dY_N}\left[1-\frac{CGT}{(1+Y_N)^M}\right]=\left(\frac{\partial P_N}{\partial Y_N}\right),$$

or, finally:

$$\frac{dP_N}{dY_N}=\frac{1}{\left[1-\dfrac{CGT}{(1+Y_N)^M}\right]}\left(\frac{\partial P_N}{\partial Y_N}\right). \qquad (28)$$

This result can be expressed in terms of "adjusted durations." The definition of the basic (pretax) adjusted duration is just the percentage price sensitivity to changes in the *gross yield*, or:

$$\begin{matrix}\text{Adjusted}\\ \text{Duration}\\ \text{Without}\\ \text{Taxes}\end{matrix}\equiv\frac{1}{P}\left(\frac{dP_G}{dY_G}\right). \qquad (29)$$

Similarly, we can define an after-tax adjusted duration as the percentage price sensitivity to changes in the *net yield*, or:

$$\begin{matrix} \text{Adjusted} \\ \text{Duration} \\ \text{After} \\ \text{Taxes} \end{matrix} = \frac{1}{P}\left(\frac{dP_N}{dY_N}\right). \tag{30}$$

Combining Equations (28) and (30), one finds that:

$$\begin{matrix} \text{Adjusted} \\ \text{Duration} \\ \text{After} \\ \text{Taxes} \end{matrix} = \frac{1}{\left[1 - \dfrac{CGT}{(1+Y_N)^M}\right]} \frac{1}{P}\left(\frac{\partial P_N}{\partial Y_N}\right). \tag{31}$$

Below, we show how the partial derivative in Equation (31) can be readily evaluated using an ordinary table of pretax durations. Thus the after-tax duration can be related through Equation (31) to pretax duration values.

By using Equation (28), we can derive an expression for the *net yield factor:*

$$\frac{dY_G}{dY_N} = \frac{\left(\dfrac{dP_N}{dY_N}\right)}{\left(\dfrac{dP_G}{dY_G}\right)}, \tag{32}$$

$$= \frac{1}{\left[1 - \dfrac{CGT}{(1+Y_N)^M}\right]} \frac{\left[\dfrac{\partial P_N(Y_N, G(Y_N))}{\partial Y_N}\right]}{\left(\dfrac{dP_G}{dY_G}\right)}.$$

This result can also be restated in terms of adjusted duration values:

$$\frac{dY_G}{dY_N} = \frac{1}{\left[1 - \dfrac{CGT}{(1+Y_N)^M}\right]} \times \frac{\begin{matrix}\text{Adjusted Duration}\\\text{of Bond}\\\text{With Fixed Capital Gain}\end{matrix}}{\begin{matrix}\text{Adjusted Duration}\\\text{Wihtout Taxes}\end{matrix}}. \tag{33}$$

The advantage of the formulation in Equation (33) is that we can reduce the calculation to a factor multiplied by a ratio of common duration values. This is accomplished by treating the "bond with fixed capital gains" as a totally tax-free bond that is redeemed through call. The hypothetical call price is simply the after-tax maturity proceeds of the original bond. A procedure described in *Inside the Yield Book* is then used to transform a called bond into an equivalent straight bond.[8] The duration of this equivalent bond can be used for the numerator of the ratio in Equation (33).

This means that, if one has a calculational procedure or tables for bond durations, Equation (33) can be used to determine quickly values for the net yield factors.

The preceding equations apply to tax-exempt bonds having any coupon rate. However, the full formula as set forth in Equation (33) is needed only for discount bonds. Considerable simplification is possible for premium and par bonds.

For a premium bond, because the loss is amortized year by year, there is no capital gain or loss at maturity. Hence G equals zero, Y_N equals Y_G, and:

$$\frac{\partial P_N[Y_N, G_N(Y_N)]}{\partial Y_N} = \frac{dP_G(Y_G)}{dY_G} .$$

(34)

Thus Equations (32) and (33) simplify to:

$$\frac{dY_G}{dY_N} = \frac{1}{\left[1 - \dfrac{CGT}{(1+Y_N)^M}\right]} .$$

(35)

Moreover, since the effective capital gains tax, CGT, equals zero for premium bonds, the net yield factor for premium bonds reduces to:

$$\frac{dY_G}{dY_N} = 1 .$$

(36)

For par bonds, the initial gain, G, is again zero, so that Equation (35) holds. However, for par bonds, the effective capital gains tax depends on the direction of the yield movement. For favorable movement—i.e., declines in yield—the bond moves to a premium with an effective capital gains tax, GCT, of zero. On the other hand, for adverse yield movements, the capital gains tax rate literally applies. Thus the net yield factor for par bonds must be represented as a split function:

$$\frac{dY_G}{dY_N} = \begin{cases} 1 & \Delta Y < 0 \\ \dfrac{1}{\left[1 - \dfrac{CGT}{(1+Y_N)^M}\right]} & \Delta Y > 0 \end{cases} .$$

(37)

---

[8] Sidney Homer and Martin L. Leibowitz, *Inside the Yield Book* (Englewood Cliffs, NJ: Prentice-Hall, Inc., 1972).

From the form of Equation (37) for adverse yield movements, we can now see why the net yield factors plotted in Figure G grow larger with shorter maturities and lower yields—i.e., with smaller values for M and Y_N.

Index